· 下卷 ·

学术论文

下卷目录
Table of Contents of Volume II

1. **图书馆建设与管理** ·· (647)
   Library Development and Management

   国际图书馆界最近的重要发展 ·· (647)
   Recent Important Developments in the Library World

   科技信息中心的管理：国际发展研究中心（IDRC）与中国科技信息研究所
   　（ISTIC）培训课程规划 ·· (650)
   Management of Scientific and Technical Information Centres: Aspects of Planning a
   Course Sponsored by the International Development Research Centre (IDRC) and
   the Institute of Scientific and Technical Information of China (ISTIC)

   美国图书馆现状及其发展动向 ·· (659)
   The Current Situation and Development Trends of Libraries in the U. S.

   图书馆服务的新观念与新技术 ·· (664)
   New Concepts and New Technology in Library Services

   中国医学图书馆学专业的最近发展 ·· (670)
   Medical Librarianship in China: Recent Developments

   募款成功的十个原则 ·· (674)
   The Ten Principles for Successful Fundraising

   巴布亚新几内亚发展高等院校图书馆 ··· (682)
   Developing Higher Education Libraries in Papua New Guinea

   中国教育院校图书馆与信息管理研修班 ·· (690)
   Workshops and Consultation on the Management of Libraries and Information for the
   Institutes of Education in China

   管理资讯技术——俄亥俄州大学图书馆之经验（中文） ······································ (698)
   Managing Information Technology—The Experience of Ohio Academic Libraries

   管理资讯技术——俄亥俄州大学图书馆之经验（英文） ······································ (707)
   Managing Information Technology—The Experience of Ohio Academic Libraries

全球信息获取：图书馆乃民众通向世界的大门 …………………………………（717）
Global Information Access：Libraries as Citizens' Gateway to the World

基本教育项目（CPR/91/420） ……………………………………………………（723）
Program CPR/91/420 Basic Education：Administration and Teachers Training

信息获取和资源共享的最大化：OhioLINK 的方法 ……………………………（731）
Maximizing Information Access and Resources Sharing：The OhioLINK Approach

俄亥俄大学图书馆 1998—1999 年度报告 ………………………………………（736）
Ohio University Libraries 1998 – 1999 Annual Report

知识管理与图书馆在新世纪的角色 ………………………………………………（762）
Knowledge Management and the Role of Libraries in the New Century

谁应该掌管知识管理，图书馆员，图书馆，还是其他人？ ……………………（778）
Who Should Be in Charge of Knowledge Management, Librarians/Libraries or Someone Else?

知识管理：图书馆的作用 …………………………………………………………（786）
Knowledge Management：The Role of Libraries

图书馆在知识管理中担当什么角色 ………………………………………………（793）
Does Library Have a Role in Knowledge Management?

实施知识管理　提供优质服务　促进知识创新 …………………………………（799）
Implementing Knowledge Management, Providing Quality Services, and Advancing Knowledge Renovation

图书馆在知识管理中的战略方向 …………………………………………………（805）
Strategic Direction of Libraries in Knowledge Management

快速变化中的图书馆：资讯管理对知识管理 ……………………………………（812）
Libraries in Rapid Transition：Information Management vs. Knowledge Management

大学图书馆实行知识管理的新理念 ………………………………………………（820）
Implementing the New Concept of Knowledge Management in University Libraries

衡量图书馆的服务品质 ……………………………………………………………（827）
Measuring Library Service Quality：The LibQUAL + Tool

关于图书馆服务效益评估的若干问题 ……………………………………………（833）
Issues Relating to the Evaluation of Cost Benefits of Library Services

实行知识管理的步骤 ………………………………………………………………（840）
Steps in Implementing Knowledge Management

2. 图书馆交流与合作 ……………………………………………………………（848）
Library Exchange and Cooperation

留美学生所面对的实际问题及其认识 ……………………………………………（848）
Real Problems and Realizations Facing Students Studying in the U. S.

泰国学校图书馆发展的伙伴 ………………………………………………………（854）
Partner for School Library Development in Thailand

泰国建立国际连续出版物数据系统地区中心的可能性 …………………………（856）
The Possibility of Establishing a Regional Centre for the International Serials Data System in Thailand

第三次东南亚图书馆员会议 ………………………………………………………（872）
The Third Conference of Southeast Asian Librarians

国际信息系统和国际技术信息系统项目的影响 …………………………………（874）
Impacts of International Information Systems and Programs on NATIS

国际教授对校园国际化教育的贡献 ………………………………………………（882）
Contributions of International Faculty to International Education on Campus

扩展俄亥俄与中国图书馆的联系 …………………………………………………（891）
Expanding Ties between Ohio and Chinese Libraries

非营利组织在电子期刊出版行销市场的合作模式：以 SPARC 与 OCLC 合作 BIO-ONE 为例 ……………………………………………………………………（894）
The Cooperation of Non-Profit Organizations Publish and Market Electronic Periodicals：The Case of BIO-ONE by SPARC and OCLC

美国对中国图书馆现代化发展的贡献：历史回顾 ………………………………（906）
American Contributions to Modern Library Development in China：A Historic Review

富布赖特资深专家项目：富布赖特故事 …………………………………………（916）
Fulbright Senior Specialist Program：Fulbright Story

注重信息与知识管理：重新制订清迈大学图书馆与资讯学研究生培养计划 ……（918）
Focusing on Information and Knowledge Management：Redesigning the Graduate Program of Library and Information Science at Chiang Mai University

图书馆合作和资源共享 ……………………………………………………………（934）
Library Cooperation and Resources Sharing

推进学术沟通的积极改变：SPARC 创始计划 ……………………………………（938）
Promoting Positive Changes in Scholarly Communications：The SPARC Initiative

全球思维与行动：中美图书馆员专业交流合作项目 ……………………… （941）
Think Globally, Act Globally: U.S.—China Librarian Collaboration Project

分享中文数字资源的契机与探讨 …………………………………………… （943）
Opportunities and Discussions on Sharing Chinese Digital Resources

3. 图书馆数字化与网络化 ………………………………………………… （952）
Library Digitization and Networking

关于亚洲理工学院建立地区科技信息中心的建议 ………………………… （952）
Proposal for a Regional Information Center for Science and Technology at the Asian Institute of Technology

亚洲理工学院的图书馆自动化 ……………………………………………… （962）
Library Mechanization at the Asian Institute of Technology

曼谷亚洲理工学院的图书馆自动化 ………………………………………… （974）
Library Automation at the Asian Institute of Technology – Bangkok

应用计算机和其他信息技术推广　东南亚地区图书馆和信息服务的可能性 …… （999）
Possibilities in Employing Computer and Other Information Technologies to Further Library and Information Services in Southeast Asia

关于在泰国建立国际连续出版物数据系统（ISDS）东南亚地区中心的建议 …… （1005）
Proposal for the Establishment of an ISDS Regional Center for Southeast Asia in Thailand

线上作业与图书馆 …………………………………………………………… （1010）
Online Revolution and Libraries

俄亥俄大学图书馆的图书馆自动化：过去、现在与未来 ………………… （1014）
Library Automation at Ohio University Library: Past, Present and Future

20 世纪 60 年代以来美国图书馆自动化的重要里程碑 …………………… （1026）
Major Milestones in American Library Automation Since the 1960s

图书馆自动化和网络化的新境界——俄亥俄走向 90 年代（中文） ……… （1031）
New Visions in Library Automation and Networking—Ohio's Approach to the 1990s

图书馆自动化和网络化的新境界——俄亥俄走向 90 年代（英文） ……… （1038）
New Visions in Library Automation and Networking—Ohio's Approach to the 1990s

俄亥俄州高等院校图书馆联网：技术与团队合作改变俄亥俄州图书馆 ……… （1049）
OhioLINK: Technology and Teamwork Transforming Ohio Libraries

未来从现在开始：俄亥俄州图书馆自动化、资讯服务与网络化 ………………（1054）
The Future Begins Now: Ohio's Library Automation, Information Services, and Networking

俄亥俄州学术图书馆准备迎接21世纪 ……………………………………（1055）
Ohio Academic Libraries Prepare for the twenty-first Century

领先信息技术——国家图书馆的作用 ………………………………………（1066）
Advancing Information Technologies: The Role of National Libraries

网络化、电子化的虚拟图书馆——20世纪90年代的图书馆（中文）………（1071）
Networked, Electronic and Virtual Library: Libraries of the 1990s

网络化、电子化的虚拟图书馆——20世纪90年代的图书馆（英文）………（1075）
Networked, Electronic and Virtual Library: Libraries of the 1990s

图书馆资源共享：OhioLINK 模式 ……………………………………………（1080）
Sharing of Library and Information Resources: The OhioLINK Model

OhioLINK 网络化资讯获取和资源共享的成就（中文）……………………（1081）
The Success of OhioLINK for Information Access and Resources Sharing in a Networked Environment

OhioLINK 网络化资讯获取和资源共享的成就（英文）……………………（1092）
The Success of OhioLINK for Information Access and Resources Sharing in a Networked Environment

网络时代的图书馆合作和资源共享 …………………………………………（1104）
Library Cooperation and Resource Sharing in a Networked Environment

21世纪数位化及网络化知识时代中的图书馆（中文）………………………（1109）
Libraries in the Digital and Networked Knowledge Age of the Twenty-first Century

21世纪数位化及网络化知识时代中的图书馆（英文）………………………（1123）
Libraries in the Digital and Networked Knowledge Age of the Twenty-first Century

亚洲图书馆：数位时代图书馆的新生 ………………………………………（1138）
Libraries in Asia: New life for Libraries in the Digital Age

陈钦智：华美图书馆与资讯学界的明星和典范 ……………………………（1141）
Ching-chih Chen: A Shining Star and Model of Chinese American Library and Information Science Professionals

美国图书馆自动化五十年的主要里程碑 ……………………………………（1149）
Main Milestone in American Library Automation in Past 50 Years

4. 亚洲研究与区域研究资源 ……………………………………………（1156）
Resources for Asian Study and Area Study

杜肯大学图书馆的非洲收藏 …………………………………………（1156）
Africana Collections at Duquesne University Library

中国近期的教育改革 ……………………………………………………（1158）
The Recent Educational Reform in China

第一百万册图书（节选）………………………………………………（1164）
The Millionth Volume（extract）

东南亚特藏在美国的成长：俄亥俄大学的经验 ……………………（1165）
Southeast Asia Collection Growth in the United States: Ohio University's Experience

俄亥俄大学邵友保博士海外华人文献和研究中心十周年（1993—2003）………（1173）
First Decade of the Dr. Shao You Bao Overseas Chinese Documentation and Research Center at Ohio University (1993 - 2003)

美国国会图书馆为区域研究、文化保存、全球共识和知识创新建立世界级的
　亚洲馆藏 ………………………………………………………………（1186）
Building a World-Class Asian Collection in the Library of Congress for Area Studies, Culture Preservation, Global Understanding, and Knowledge Creation

共享美国国会图书馆的亚洲文献宝库 …………………………………（1201）
Sharing the Treasures of the Asian Collection in the Library of Congress

海外华人与海外华人研究——兼介绍美国俄亥俄大学邵友保博士海外华人文献
　研究中心 ………………………………………………………………（1209）
Overseas Chinese and Overseas Chinese Studies—Dr. Shao You Bao Overseas Chinese Documentation and Research Center at Ohio University, U. S. A.

美国国会图书馆建立世界级亚洲馆藏 …………………………………（1228）
Building a World-Class Asian Collection in the Library of Congress

美国国会图书馆的汉学资源 ……………………………………………（1236）
Sinological Resources in the Library of Congress

美国国会图书馆有关郑和研究的中文收藏 ……………………………（1244）
Chinese Resources for Zheng He Studies in the Library of Congress

美国国会图书馆建立世界级的数位时代亚洲馆藏 ……………………（1253）
Building a World-class Asian Collection in the Digital Age at the Library of Congress

美国国会图书馆数字时代的亚洲馆藏 ·· (1264)
Asian Collections in the Digital Age at the Library of Congress

美国国会图书馆的亚洲馆藏：历史概览 ·· (1273)
Asian Collections in the Library of Congress：A Historical Overview

他山之石——向海外推广中文书的秘籍 ·· (1289)
Promotion of Chinese Books Outside China：Important Lessons

美国国会图书馆建立全美的亚太美裔特藏 ·· (1291)
Building a National Asian Pacific American Collection in the Library of Congress, USA

美国国会图书馆藏有关中国东北与日本的历史文献 ································ (1299)
Historical Resources on Northeast China and Japan in the Library of Congress

美国国会图书馆东亚收藏的历史：书目指南 ·· (1305)
A History of the East Asian Collections in the Library of Congress：A Bibliographic Guide

美国国会图书馆亚洲部进展报告 ··· (1311)
Progress Report of the Asian Division, Library of Congress

5. 序言与书评 ·· (1317)
Preface and Review

《图书馆新技术应用国际学术讨论会论文集》序 ································ (1317)
Preface of *The Proceedings of the International Symposium on New Techniques and Applications in Libraries*

《海外华人研究机构国际合作会议论文与摘要集》序 ···························· (1319)
Preface of *International Conference of Institutes and Libraries for Overseas Chinese Studies Papers and Abstracts*

《持守中正：易经的介绍》序 ··· (1321)
Foreword of *The Centered Life：An Introduction to I Ching—Book of Changes The Universal Principles of Living and Its Amazing Oracle*

《英汉图书馆情报学词汇》序 ··· (1323)
Preface for *An English-Chinese Dictionary of Library and Information Science*

《养生之道》序 ·· (1324)
Preface for *The Guide to a Healthy Life*

《图书馆与信息科学年鉴》书评 ……………………………………………（1325）
Book Reviews in *Library and Information Science Annual*

《美国参考书年鉴》书评 ………………………………………………（1327）
Book Reviews in *American Reference Books Annual*

附录1：李华伟著述系年 ………………………………………………（1336）
Appendix Ⅰ：A Chronicle of Hwa-Wei Lee's Writing

附录2：李华伟研究资料 ………………………………………………（1351）
Appendix Ⅱ：Research Materials about Hwa-Wei Lee

（1）书评 …………………………………………………………（1354）
　　　Book Reviews

（2）记述 …………………………………………………………（1364）
　　　Articles

（3）信函 …………………………………………………………（1553）
　　　Letters

后记 ……………………………………………………………程焕文（1561）
Epilogue by Cheng Huanwen

1. 图书馆建设与管理
Library Development and Management

国际图书馆界最近的重要发展[①]

Recent Important Developments in the Library World

国际图书馆事业的发展，主要是从"二次大战"后才慢慢发展，尤其在最近五六年中有重大的突破，造成此项突破的原因很多，一般说来，可归纳为以下四点：

1. 二次大战后世界各地出版物之量与种皆激增，图书馆界认识到以旧的方式来处理众多的资料，实嫌不足，必须借新的方法、新的方式、新的技术来处理，以谋改进。

2. 学术研究突破国家界限。

3. 国际机构的领导与影响；如联合国文教组织、国际文献联盟、国际档案联合会、国际图书馆协会联合会、国际科技团体联合会；等等，皆对图书馆事业的发展有很大贡献。

4. 其他诸如电脑、电信技术、复印、显微片等技术的快速发展，也促进了图书馆事业的发展。

"二次大战"后，国际图书馆的重大发展约可归纳如下：

一、世界科学资讯系统（UNISIST）建立与发展

UNISIST 的由来，开始于 1967 年。当时联合国文教组织与国际学术团体联合会认为有成立国际性科学资料系统的必要，于是组织了联合小组，研究如何成立的细节。至 1971 年，该小组乃提出可行性的研究报告。1971 年 9 月，联合国文教组织在巴黎召开了各国政府代表会议，决定由联合国文教组织下的一个有关科学的部门，负责推行世界科学资讯系统的活动，遂成立指导委员会，决定了数项目标（工作方针）：

1. 促进各国资讯系统间相互衔接的工具：欲使图书馆间能彼此交换资料，促进合作，首先应于目录系统中根据同一标准采取同一格式，此唯赖各工具以达相互衔接之目的（Tools for Systems Interconnection），故有 ISBN 等的发展。

2. 协助各国发展科学资讯系统——应帮助各国设立国内科学资料系统，联合国曾帮助若干国家设立科学资料中心，今后应加强这方面的工作。

3. 加强资讯专业人员的训练。

4. 鼓励各国政府迅速制定有利于科学发展的政策与法令，同时也要加强各国科资中心的联系。

5. 对于发展中国家应给予特别的援助：因发展中国家经费不足，进展较慢，故应予

[①] 本文由徐秀兰、张秀琴根据 1975 年 6 月 3 日在"中央图书馆"台湾分馆的演讲记录整理而成。

以特别援助。在东南亚国家方面,联合国文教组织做了几件值得注意的事情:

A. 自 1973 年起联合国文教组织派两名专家,在一年时间内,至泰、菲、新、印、越、寮、高①等国考察其图书馆及科资发展情形,提出改进的建议、期望,能加强图书馆资料中心的业务,并设立东南亚地区图书资料网。

B. 印度尼西亚因有一位国家资料中心的主管为 UNISIST 指导委员会委员之一,故于两三年来,得到联合国文教组织专家之协助,设立"全国图书资料系统"的发展计划,设立全国四大图书资料网,科学资料中心负责科学技术图书资料的业务,博物馆图书馆负责生物、农业、科学、医学方面的资料,另于"加卡拉"图书馆扩充改为社会、人文科学国家图书资料中心,并设专管农业、医学、物理的资料中心,此四中心,归于图书馆委员会指导之下,使业务能作协调,作有计划的发展,1974 年开始,印度尼西亚并与南加州大学合作,由南加州大学于印度尼西亚选择若干图书馆做实验,此等图书馆可以免费利用南加州大学计算机贮藏的资料。

C. 联合国亦有意于泰国设立"东南亚地区的期刊统一目录",以计算机作业,此工作正在进行,可望年底完成。

二、国际标准的厘订与推广:

1. 国际图书著录标准 [ISBD(M)]。

此标准之来源,可追溯到 1961 年图书馆协会联盟在巴黎召开的"国际编目原则会议"通过一项极为重要的"原则说明"(Statement of Principles)希望能达到各国编目的一致化,其后乃有"英美编目规则"的出版。1969 年召开"国际编目专家会议"决定了四点计划:

A. 各国应设立国家编目机构,负责该国出版图书的编目工作,不仅供国内图书馆之用,同时亦供给国外图书馆之用。

在著录上,各国应采取划一的格式。

C. 每一国家之编目机构,应设法将外国的图书编目资料供给国内图书馆。

D. 统一变电符号的使用:使计算机能自动识别著录的项目,1971 年此标准公布后,即获各国的支持与采用,于 1974 年正式出版,望我图书馆界能迅速将之译为中文。

2. 国际期刊著录标准 [ISBD(S)]。

此标准之目的、内容、要点、均与 ISBD(M) 相似,所不同的,是于版本著录上较为详尽。

3. 国际期刊资料系统指南(ISDS)。

1971 年在"建立世界科学资讯系统可行性的研究报告"提出的同时,联合国文教组织与国际科学团体联合会的一个著录工作小组亦提出"建立一个国际刊物资料系统可行性的报告"获 UNISIST 的通过,成为其主要活动之一,1972 年底在巴黎成立"刊物登录的国际中心"。总管刊物登录及编号事宜,根据该中心的指南(Guidelines for ISDS),世界各国或地区应分别设立各国或地区的 ISDS 中心,实际负责刊物登录及编号的工作,其编号为一种八位数字的号码,分成两组四位数字,中以一连字符号连接。各国家或地区的 ISDS 中心,先向巴黎的国际中心报备,取得各国或地区的已编过号的刊物名单,并由中心配给一批未用的号码作为编号之用。各国新设之中心,对此批号码应特别留意以免重复。

4. 国际图书标准号码(ISBN)。

---

① 寮——老挝;高——柬埔寨

此标准以英国最先实行,此后乃由各国相继效仿,其编号为十位数的号码,每一号码包括四部分:

A. 国家或地区的识别号码。
B. 出版商号码。
C. 图书号码。
D. 核对数字。

这些号码伸缩性颇大,可灵活运用变化无穷。

三、全球目录的控制(Universal Bibliographic Control)

U.B.C 亦由国际图书馆协会联盟推动,在英国设立全世界推广中心,其活动用意有四:

1. 希望每一国家设立目录中心,负责全国出版图书之编目。
2. 著录格式应根据国际标准。
3. 著录内容应印行,使国内外能采用。
4. 成立全球性的联合目录。

四、专门性国际资讯系统的建立与发展

1. 国际原子能资讯系统(INIS):由国际原子能总署发起,凡参加之国须成立中心,负责搜集全国有关原子能的书刊及报告,并作索引和摘要,将此等资料送交国际中心,以计算机作业,每月印出全球性原子能科学资料分送各国,此工作已进行若干年,颇具成效。

2. 世界粮农组织于1972年成立一筹备小组,欲成立世界农业资料系统(AGRIS),由世界粮农组织(FAO)负责,去年(1974年)年初开始,东南亚方面,菲律宾大学农学院设立东南亚农业资料系统中心,于1975年5月开设讲习班,讲习有关事宜。

3. 发展资讯系统(DEVIS):加拿大国际研究发展中心,为加拿大对外援助机构,对发展中国家给予经济援助,并欲成立全球性"发展资料系统",此中心有四项工作,其中之一为协助发展中国家图书馆及资料中心的业务,并搜集其有关本国发展的资料,由各国自由参加,程序如原子能资讯系统。

五、全国性咨询系统的建立(National Information System)

NAIS 由联合国文教组织提出,有两大发展:

1. 发展世界科学资料系统。
2. 发展各国图书馆资讯系统。

1974年9月,在巴黎召开"世界各国政府代表会议",计划于1978年,召开会议检讨各国进展,再联合各国建立全球性的资讯系统,此一工作极为重要,若各国并无全国性资讯系统,欲谈国际合作,何异空中楼阁,故建立全国性资讯系统实为首要之务。

(原载《中华图书馆协会会报》1975年第27期,第34–36页。)

科技信息中心的管理：国际发展研究中心（IDRC）
与中国科技信息研究所（ISTIC）培训课程规划

Management of Scientific and Technical Information Centres: Aspects of Planning a Course Sponsored by the International Development Research Centre (IDRC) and the Institute of Scientific and Technical Information of China (ISTIC)[①]

I Introduction

The People's Republic of China recognized, in the late 1970's, that modernization of its library and information service would be a vital factor for national economic development. ISTIC, with responsibility for the delivery of scientific and technical information for all of China, also recognized that it had a basic need to upgrade its information course in the management of scientific information centres and to training for senior Chinese administrators. To this end, an agreement was concluded between IDRC and ISTIC early in 1980, and the development of the program itself began.

The overall objective for the course was defined by ISTIC: strengthening of China's capacity to provide improved information services by instructing senior personnel in practical management methods. Specifically, IDRC was asked to:

– provide participants with enough fundamental knowledge of modern information procedures to improve their work and to pass the experience on to others;
  – increase the ability of participants to grasp the principles of scientific management;
  – improve decision making;
  – provide the basis for further training.

With the objectives established, it was left to ISTIC to determine the location or venue for the course and to choose the participants. IDRC assumed responsibility for selecting the lecturers, planning the curriculum and course content, developing support material, and identifying equipment that would be required for successful delivery of the program and which might not be available in China.

II Planning the course: IDRC/Canada

1. Selection of lecturers

It was felt that, ideally, the lecturers should speak Chinese, and efforts were made to meet this goal. However, with a roster of five identified as necessary for the delivery of the course as desired, only two people qualified to deliver lectures on information science in Chinese and who could be available for a trip to China sometime in 1982 were found. Dr. Hwa Wei Lee, Director of Ohio University Libraries, and Dr. T. C. Ting, Head of the Department of Computer Science at Worcester Polytechnic Institute, were both experienced lecturers in Chinese. They, with Kieran Broadbent, course director for IDRC who was also fluent in Chinese and team leader for the IDRC/ISTIC course, provided the Chinese component of the lecturing group. Supplementing them were Brian Wills, and Margaret Beckman, the Chief Librarian, University of Guelph, and it was hoped that the extensive experience of the latter in both lecturing and the management of scientific

---

① Co-authors: M. Beckman and Huang Jianyuan. Presented at the International Federation for Documentation (FID) Pre-Congress Workshop on *Curriculum Development in a Changing World*, The Hague, September 3–4, 1984.

information centres in libraries would compensate for their lack of fluency in Chinese.

One common characteristic was essential for this instructional group. With so many unknown factors, such as venue, level of understanding of the participants and availability of support equipment, flexibility in both approach and temperament was of supreme importance.

2. Curriculum planning

ISTIC had made an initial request for topics to be included in the course, and the curriculum followed this basic outline:
- Function, planning and management of information centres;
- Budgetary and fiscal control;
- Facility planning and administration;
- Improved bibliographic services;
- Systems analysis and design;
- Information technology;
- Planning for new technology;
- Sources of information;
- Personnel development and performance evaluation.

With these broad topics, the 12 day course (China works a six day week) was divided into time periods, and lecture headings identified. The lecturers met together in June 1981 and in February 1982, discussing various approaches, identifying individual strengths, refining the lectures' content and scheduling.

In addition to meeting the broad topic goals of the curriculum, an attempt was made to intersperse concrete or practical examples of different aspects of information technology with the more theoretical discussions. Audio-visual presentations—slide, tape, film—were considered important as was variety, and both of lecturers and method of lecturing.

Two other considerations shaped the final curriculum. The first was a request for a case study, based on a visit to a Chinese scientific information centre. The other was the need to allow time for formal opening and closing ceremonies and for course evaluation by the participants.

3. Lecture preparation

Each lecturer was asked to prepare his/her presentations, using the tentative curriculum and time schedule as a guide. These assignments were to be completed and, for the English lecturers at least, needed to be translated, three months in advance. This was a fairly heavy schedule, particularly for two lecturers, with more than ten lectures to be prepared. Illustrative material for individual presentations was also the responsibility of each lecturer. As a precautionary measure, a few auxiliary papers were also prepared as a contingency, in case the timing in the schedule had been under-estimated. Synopses or outlines of all lectures were routed by IDRC to ISTIC several months in advance of the course, to ensure ISTIC approval of the course directions.

A final overview, meeting on the course outline and content was held in Hong Kong, where the IDRC group assembled prior to flying on to Kunming (the site selected by ISTIC). Lectures were re-grouped into broad topics, with attention given to the work loads of individual lecturers. It was also agreed that we would meet daily as a group to adjust either schedules or lectures dependent on the experiences gained in the actual presentation.

4. Ancillary material and equipment

While the lecturers were busy writing their presentations and assembling slide sets, films or overheads, IDRC staff prepared as much background material as could be identified. A very valuable tool was a list of the acronyms which North American and European librarians or information scientists delight in using. MARC, ASCIB, L. C., AACR, and MINISIS were among the 300 terms translated into Chinese and provided to the participants. In addition, relevant reprints, bibliographies and notebooks were gathered, as were general audio-visual materials.

CISTI (Canada Institute for Scientific and Technical Information) was particularly helpful in providing resources which would be appreciated by its sister organization, ISTIC.

To guarantee delivery of the course, it was felt necessary to supply a variety of audio-visual and reprographic equipment. These were selected and sent to ISTIC in advance and donated to them at the end of the course. IDRC added two support members to the "China team", a secretary and a back-up lecturer with expertise in course preparations. Also, the IDRC secretary from the Singapore regional office, fluent in Chinese, joined the team in Hong Kong to provide essential liaison and logistical services.

III Kunming, December, 1982

1. Course location

ISTIC and IDRC had decided to hold the course away from the more populous areas of China and those most frequently visited by foreign visitors. Kunming, the capital of Yunnan Province, the most southerly and undeveloped part of China, was selected primarily for four reasons:

a) Since the course was to be held in December, a southerly location with a pleasant climate was thought desirable, particularly for North Americans not used to the lack of centralized heating.

b) A course held in Kunming would attract local attention and boost local morale and prestige, a result that would not be obtained in the larger centres such as Beijing or Shanghai.

c) Kunming had a reputation as a resort area, and a trip to this land of eternal spring was viewed as a reward for the participants and an unusual experience for the lecturers. Natural phenomena such as "the Stone Forest", a geological wonder, early Chinese temples, and large settlements of ethnic minorities provide elements of interest not experienced by most Chinese.

d) Beijing and Shanghai are the normal sites for scholarly conferences, particularly those involving foreigners. Exposure to the course and lecturers was considered a real opportunity for the information workers, librarians and documentatlists of Kunming: an opportunity that would not normally be available.

2. The participants

The IDRC China team learned about the course participants for the first time at the formal course ceremonies in Kunming on December 6. This was unfortunate since advance identification of the participants' backgrounds and course needs would have been useful in planning the curriculum. Since this information was not available, a general survey of the 65 participants was conducted to ascertain personal information, professional experience and individual needs. This established that most were senior managers of middle or mature years, frequently deputy directors of their respective institutions (e.g. provincial information centres). Most, also, were university graduates, and many had a fair to good understanding of English.

The participants indicated that the topics of greatest interest to them were:
- how to set priorities;
- how to plan and evaluate information services.

Although these interests did not exactly match the objectives for the course assigned to the IDRC team by ISTIC, the evaluation at the end of the course revealed that our original direction had been valid.

In addition to the official participants, each session was also attended by ISTIC staff members from Beijing or Kunming.

3. The Green Lake Hotel

The course was given in the Green Lake Hotel meeting room, a large pleasant space with lecturer's tables, screens, overhead projectors, and chairs for some 70 people. A logistical team of interpreters, secretaries and technicians had been supplied by ISTIC, and they, in addition to the IDRC group, were all housed in the same Green Lake Hotel, simplifying course logistics immensely. Typing and copying course changes, setting up audio-visual support, arranging for bus tours, telex messages and a myriad of other details were expatiated competently by the ISTIC/IDRC support staffs, leaving the lecturers and participants free to concentrate on the teaching/learning experience.

4. **Kunming course**, Day 1, December 6, 1982

Most of the first morning was spent in an exchange of formal greetings from ISTIC personnel, from Beijing, and from the representative of the provincial governor. As well, an opportunity was afforded to the participants themselves to get acquainted and learn of each others' background and experience. (The eight women in the course soon became a close, identifiable group.) Dr. Lee gave a course overview and distributed the initial survey questionnaire, and the film, "Goodbye Gutenberg" was shown to give the participants an introduction to North American libraries and technology.

The first formal lecture of the course was given that afternoon, by one of the English speaking members of the IDRC team, and so the first exposure to sequential translation occurred. It took much more time than anticipated as each Chinese sentence seemed twice as long as the English one which proceeded it.

An opportunity was also provided that afternoon for the participants to tell a bit about themselves and gets to know each other. ISTIC also announced the various entertainments and tours which would be worked into our schedule: three trips into the country-side to visit the Chinese temples, a commune and the Stone Forest as well as two evenings of acrobatics and operetta. The ISTIC course organizers also requested that at least two evenings be reserved for small group discussions, allowing the participants to choose topics which were of particular interest to them.

By the end of that first day's sessions, it was obvious that a restructuring would have to take place and a new schedule would have to be prepared.

5. Course Restructuring

The IDRC team met as planned to assess the first day's experiences and to re-arrange the lectures to accommodate the group sessions, the entertainment, and the complications of the translated sessions. This was not as difficult as it might seem as it already was clear that some topics could be compressed or merged with others. A new schedule was developed which met everyone's needs.

Translations posed a more serious problem, and it was not until after another day's experience that a solution was found. During the second day with several lectures being given by Dr. Lee and Dr. Ting, it was apparent that a more informal style, speaking to prepared outlines projected on the screen from overhead transparencies, allowed the participants to become more involved with the lecture. They felt more at ease, interrupting the lecturer with questions and asking to have different points explained in more detail. The formal prepared English texts, read and then translated sentence by sentence, did not permit this informality or encourage this valuable exchange of ideas.

It was therefore agreed at the IDRC group meeting, after the second day's lectures that Mrs. Beckman and Mr. Wills would attempt to rework their lectures to encourage a more informal approach. Accordingly, outlines of each lecture were developed on transparencies, using multi-coloured markers to highlight different headings. During the lecture itself, the transparency in English was projected onto the screen. Although Mrs. Beckman, for example, followed the English text of her prepared lecture in order not to confuse Mr. Zhao, her ISTIC translator who had his Chinese version before himself, both Mrs. Beckman and Mr. Zhao could speak to the transparency on the screen. With this visual representation before them, the participants seemed more at ease with the ideas being discussed and soon learned to break in and question Mr. Zhao, who frequently wrote an interpretation of the outline on the blackboard. In addition, Dr. Lee or

Dr. Ting, who fortunately made themselves available during all the lectures, also offered assistance as concepts of North American management or information technology proved too difficult for Mr. Zhao to explain. The English fluency of several of the participants was also used to advantage.

With a few days' experience, this method of instruction became a smooth operation, taking little more time than a lecture entirely in Chinese. Mrs. Beckman learned to sense when an idea had not been understood; Mr. Zhao learned when to question her himself, particularly about topics which he realized would be of special interest or concern to the participants and hence require more detailed explanation. The discussions after each lecture became enthusiastic exchanges, with Dr. Lee, Dr. Ting, Mrs. Beckman, Mr. Zhao and the participants all arguing in a mixture of Chinese and English which did not impede either their understanding or value. Lecturing in this manner, in spite of the handicap of the translation, became quite pleasurable, and, although not as worthwhile as they might have been if totally in Chinese, the English lectures in this modified style nonetheless were viewed as highly successful.

IV Evaluation

So the course continued for the rest of the two weeks, with both lecturers and participants gaining confidence and understanding. The informal outings and banquets also provided opportunities to share ideas and to learn from exposure to different philosophies and experiences.

Two activities concluded the course and gave further insight into the needs of information centres and information science education in China.

1. The Case Study: Institute of Scientific and Technical Information, Yunnan Province (ISTIY)

The Commission of Science and Technology for Yunnan Province, of which ISTIY is a division, had recently moved to a new building especially designed for it. A tour of the facilities therefore was viewed as a unique opportunity to learn of the resources and services of a modern scientific information centre. The visit did prove very useful, although not necessarily as intended.

The tour was organized with the total group divided into five teams, each assigned responsibilities for specific investigation: collections, services, technology, physical facilities, and staffs. After a presentation about the institute, the groups circulated around the building, speaking with staff and viewing the facilities and services.

After time for each group to coordinate responses to their particular assignment in the afternoon, the participants presented their views of what they had seen in a panel discussion. It was soon apparent that ISTIY had been viewed from two totally different perspectives.

The building itself, for example, was considered by the participants to be spacious, with a flexible interior layout, effective use of daylight, a generally pleasing ambience, and good potential for the use of modern materials and methods. Some faults were identified: high noise level emanating from a nearby market, poor location of the central reference card bibliographic area, lack of directional signs, and scattering of related subject materials. But overall, ISTIY was categorized as a success.

This view was not shared by the North Americans. Aside from the location, close to universities and scientific or technical industries, the Institute had features which contravened all standard library design concepts. The structural column spacing, for example, at four metres was too small to allow an efficient placement of stack ranges so that aisles were unnecessarily wide and stack ranges were too short. Ceiling lighting had been located with no relation to the stack ranges so that some aisles would be in total darkness after the natural lighting had disappeared. The dispersal of like functions, fixed (and hence inflexible and inefficient) walls, badly placed core areas which interrupted information functions, inadequate signage, and poor sound control were all identified as serious problems. Lack of identity as an information centre, with its purpose clearly recognized and accessible to the entering user, was also deemed a serious fault of the new building.

Collections, due to the recent and unfortunate experience of similar institutions, were out of date and had major gaps in all serial publications. Both technical and public services and the equipment, such as printers or copiers so necessary to facilitate them, were quite inadequate by North American standards.

In the general discussion which followed the participants' presentations, it was possible to use the trip to ISTIY to demonstrate concepts of service and building planning more dramatically than the more theoretical lectures had been able to provide. A slide presentation of the comparable Canada Institute of Scientific and Technical Information (CISTI), provided a concrete comparison and demonstrated the importance of building planning for scientific information centres.

2. Course evaluation

All participants were asked to submit detailed evaluations filling in forms developed by Hwa-Wei Lee and Kerry Broadbent during the course itself. As in the case study, everyone was assigned to one of five groups, and a team leader gave the group evaluation. Basically all group spokesmen reported similar feelings:

– a lot had been learned about information processing and technologies in other countries, particularly North America;
– the emphasis on services adjusted to meet user needs had not been understood previously and was much appreciated;
– the lectures and discussions on library facility planning had proven most enlightening;
– human resource management was also a new concept in China and its importance was now understood;
– practical discussions were preferred to the theoretical;
– resource sharing networks and cooperation, a concept not known in China, should be studied and emulated;
– modernization of information services could not be achieved without cost efficiency and effectiveness;
– particularly beneficial had been the opportunity which the course afforded to meet other Chinese information workers, to exchange ideas and to make friends.

Major criticisms of the course were also identified:
– the lectures should have been available, in translation, in advance;
– the participants' group was too diverse: there were teachers, managers and practitioners—all with different experiences and needs;
– the course was not long enough to cover the breadth of material included: for so many new ideas the experience was too intense;
– insufficient time had been scheduled for informal discussion periods.

On a personal note, the evaluators noted that the IDRC team had been very serious and hardworking, well prepared with slides, over-heads and films. It was considered unfortunate that the weather had been so cold, but appreciation was expressed for the fact that the lectures had carried on in spite of adverse conditions and illness. In summary, the final evaluator noted that the course was of vital importance at this time, and it provided a first opportunity for the participants to learn in depth about Western technology and methods. The level of awareness of information science had been raised, and it was felt that all participants could return to their own information centres with an enhanced ability to adopt new ideas, and to contribute to the modernization of China.

V Conclusions and Recommendations

What had been learned by IDRC about organizing and handling a course of this nature in China:

1. Subject Scope

There can be a temptation to attempt to provide an all encompassing course, more appropriate to a year's curriculum than a two or three week session. The course content should focus on practical issues and day to day organization of work. As well, the timetable should allow the students time for recreation, personal study and informal discussion.

2. The Lecturers

As noted previously, it would be ideal if all lecturers could speak Chinese or that a good proportion of the participants could speak English. Although the translation problems were overcome—it is believed—quite successfully, eliminating translation would have been preferable.

3. Participants

A key factor in the success of such a program is the ability to meet participants' needs. This cannot occur if there is too much diversity. Not everyone is able to understand and assimilate the lectures to the same degree. If possible, the participants should not only be a fairly homogenous group but they should also be identified in advance so that the lectures could be composed more specifically to match predetermined interests.

4. Advance Preparation

All lectures, whether in Chinese or in English and translated, should be delivered to the participants in advance trial for a successful course. In the instance of the Kunming course, most of the lectures had been completed and sent by IDRC to ISTIC several months in advance. They had not been translated or copied. The lack of truly adequate reprographic services in China would make it advisable to have the translations and copying done in Canada and taken to China with equipment identified below.

5. Course Logistics

Again because of facilities and equipment in China, it is advisable not only to send all needed support facilities—photocopier, slide, film and overhead projectors, typewriter—to China. In addition, support staff able to type, photocopy, act as liaison with Chinese officials, run errands, and attend to a myriad of details which surround a course of this nature are indispensable and must accompany the lecturing team. Although the host, in this case ISTIC, also provided logistical staff, they could not meet the many needs identified by the IDRC group.

6. Spirit

The esprit de corps developed by the IDRC team was an important part of whatever success the course achieved. Their flexible and friendly working relationships also extended to the ISTIC headquarters group, and the sociability which was extended by ISTIC, by the participants, and by the people of Kunming allowed a sense of accomplishment to prevail for all involved.

COURSE ON MANAGEMENT OF INFORMATION CENTRES DECEMBER 6–18, 1982, KUNMING, CHINA					
MONDAY, December 6	TUESDAY, December 7	WEDNESDAY, December 8	THURSDAY, December 9	FRIDAY, December 10	SATURDAY, December 11
8:00: Formal Opening Session 9:00: Group seats, get acquainted 10:30: BREAK 11:00: Course overview (by Chinese speaking lecturers) 12:00: LUNCH 13:00: Film—Introduction to modern information problems	8:30: Value of information as a resource (TING) 10:00: BREAK 10:30: Continuation of above with defined specifics (TING) 12:00: LUNCH 13:30: Discussion groups on morning work (ALL LECTURERS) Parallel session The online revolution (LEE) 15:00: BREAK 15:30–17:00: Parallel sessions (ALL LECTURERS) CODOC system (BECKMAN) AGRIS system (LENDVAY)	8:30: Information Systems development 10:00: BREAK 10:30: Application of new information technology (LEE) 12:00: LUNCH 13:30: Discussion groups & parallel session (ALL LECTURERS) Software for information services; MINISIS (BRDADRENT) 15:00: BREAK 15:30: Parallel session (ALL LECTURERS) CUSS system (BECKMAN)	8:30: Overview of the main types of informat centres (ALL LECTURERS) 1/2hr, presentation on national, regional & international centres Specialized Information Centres (BRDADRENT) Organization and management of special libraries; agriculture as an example (LENDVAY) AGE regional centre (LEE) Bell Canada (BECKMAN) 10:00: BREAK	8:30: Function, planning & information centres (RECKMAN) 10:00: BREAK 12:00: LUNCH 13:30: Coordination networking with examples Chinese case (LEE-BECKMAN-WILLS) Planning national Infrastructure for Library and information services with reference to China's situation (LEE) 15:00: BREAK 15:00–17:00: Institutional budgeting (LEE)	8:30: ISIIC/CISII presentation How to manage and link all components together (WILLS-RECKMAN) 10:00: BREAK 10:30: Cost effectiveness and recovery (LEE) 12:00: LUNCH 13:30: Facility planning and management (RECKMAN) 15:00: BREAK 15:30–17:00: Discussion on day's work International Cooperative Information systems; Agriculture as an example (BRDADBENT)
		Predecessors of modern computerized systems; manual and semi-mechanized information systems (LENDVAY)	10:30: IDRC's support for information services (BRDADBENT) 12:00: LUNCH 13:30: Information for small scale industry; slide presentation (BRDADBENT)		
			15:00: BREAK		
14:30: Introduction to Information Science, Past Present, Future (BECKMAN)			15:00–17:00: Discussion groups		
15:00: BREAK 16:00-17:00: Answer session—to identify individual situations & evaluate (ALL LECURERS)					

(续上表)

MONDAY, December 13	TUESDAY, December 14	WEDNESDAY, December 15	THURSDAY, December 16	FRIDAY, December 17	SATURDAY, December 18
8:30……. 10:00:BREAK 10:30:Improving bibliography control from the national perspective (LEE) 12:00:LUNCH 13:30:Quantitative methods(TIMG) 15:00:BREAK 15:30-17:00: Parallel session On-line circulation (BECKMAN) OCLC (LEE) Regional information services: slide presentation (AIBA) (BRDADBENT)	8:30:Systems analysis design (TING) 10:00:BREAK 10:30:Project management (TING) 12:00:LUNCH 13:30:Quantitative methods (TING) 15:00:BREAK 15:30–17:00: Continuation	8:30:Sources of information (BRDADBENT) 10:00:BREAK 10:30:Computer data bases-bibliography & non-bibliography (LEE) 12:00:LUNCH 13:30:Non-conventional information (WILLS) 15:00:BREAK 15:30–17:00: Non-conventional media, Non-print materials (TING-WILLS)	8:30:Case study presentation-ISIIC ISIIC case study discussion (BECKMAN) 10:00:BREAK 10:30:Discussion on case study (ALL LECTURERS) 12:00:LUNCH 13:30:Non-conventional Information (WILLS) 15:00:BREAK 15:30–17:00: Micrographics: overview and slide presentation (BRDADBENT)	8:30:Organizational structure of info. centres (BECKMAN) 10:00:BREAK 10:30:Performance evaluation (LEE) 12:00:LUNCH 13:30:Discussion on case study (ALL LECURERS) 15:00:BREAK 15:30–17:00: Need for group Evaluation (ALL LECTURERS)	8:30:Training of professional staff (BECKMAN) 10:00:BREAK 10:30:In-service training, internship, &continuing education (LEE) 12:00:LUNCH 13:30:Manpower development (BECKMAN) 15:00:BREAK 15:30-17:00: Group evaluation Closure

美国图书馆现状及其发展动向[①]

The Current Situation and Development Trends of Libraries in the U. S.

我这次承蒙福建省人才交流中心和福建协和大学校友会的邀请，回到老家讲学（李博士是福州人），很高兴有机会与大家作学术上的交流，我是带着学习的心情回来的，因为我知道国内图书馆界在物质条件欠缺的情况下，仍然做了很多工作，前几天我参观了省图书馆，对他们的工作成绩感到非常佩服。今天我讲的题目是：美国图书馆现状及其发展动向。各位都知道，在 20 世纪下半期，尤其是 60 年代以后，有几个重要的因素促使美国图书馆界发生了变动，这几个因素是：

（1）教育普及，知识和生活水平普遍提高，人民对图书馆的需求大为增加。

（2）社会结构的改变。美国在 20 世纪初是一个工业的社会，到了 60 年代以后逐渐由工业社会转变为情报社会。

（3）电子计算机及电信技术取得了飞速发展。

（4）图书刊物和各种资料的不断增加以及形式的改变。

由于上述 4 个主要因素的影响，20 世纪以来美国图书馆的发展非常迅速，这几年可说是后来居上，在世界处于领先地位。这表现在：

1. 美国图书馆真正地成为地方上教育与文化的中心

在美国，无论是大城市的图书馆，还是偏僻的乡村图书馆都担负着地方上教育与文化中心的任务。举一个很有趣的例子来说明美国公立图书馆当初是怎样产生的。1800 年左右，美国南北战争结束后，美国许多退役军人，由政府安顿在俄亥俄州的东南部。那时美国工会通过一个特别立案，要建立一所大学给这些退役军人提供受教育的机会。俄亥俄州立大学就是在这样情况下建立的。这与公共图书馆有什么关系呢？那时候在俄亥俄州的东南部，人口稀少，生活艰苦，而退役军人还不忘求学，不忘吸收新知识，他们和当地的百姓一起打猎，一起把获得的兽皮带到波士顿出卖。他们请当时哈佛大学的一位哲学教授替他们开个书单，拿这笔钱购买了 180 多本书，从而在亚典城建立了第一所公立图书馆。我们称之为"肯斯金"图书馆，意为浣熊皮的图书馆。这是美国公共图书馆发展历史上的真实故事，这是一个重要的发展，就是说美国图书馆从此已成为地方上教育与文化的中心。

2. 图书馆馆际间的合作和资源共享

（1）美国图书馆一向很重视图书馆馆际间的合作，馆际互借在 20 世纪初期就已经开始，早期的馆际互借多半是邻近图书馆之间的馆际互借，到了 60 年代间变为全国性的馆际互借。那时还没有自动化，主要是依靠美国国会图书馆编制的全国图书馆的图书目录来查寻图书，而后以馆际互借的方式由小的图书馆向大的图书馆借。实现自动化后，美国现在有"OCLC"（OCLC 是全国性的、联机作业的、联合编目的一个共同书目，这个资料库现在贮存的目录，有一千二百万种，现在每年增加一百多万种，是查阅图书非常有用的资料库）。我们可以随时查出任何一本书收藏在哪个图书馆，从中挑一所有合作关系的图书馆去借，这是馆际互借、馆际合作的一个很好的例子。

[①] 本文由晋阳根据演讲的录音整理而成，未经演讲人审阅。

（2）美国图书馆还有合作采购制度。面对当前这么多的图书、期刊及科学文献，即使条件很好的图书馆，也无法买全所有的图书资料，最多也只能侧重采购他们所需要的书。所以，在六十年代美国有好几项图书采购的全国性计划，其中最有名的叫"法明顿"计划。这个计划是1948年开始的，由美国一些大的图书馆联合起来，通过协商，指定某一个大学图书馆或研究图书馆负责购买某一个国家的出版物。计划实施后，世界上大多数国家出版的书刊，在美国至少有一个图书馆负责采购。1968年美国国会图书馆着手另一项称之为"国家采购和编目"的计划。五六十年代，美国政府通过援外的途径把粮食卖给发展中的国家，用这些国家购买粮食的本国货币，来买这些国家出版的书刊，同时，编好目录寄回国内，分给有合作关系的图书馆，美国国会图书馆在非洲、南美、亚洲等许多国家设立购买图书的中心。我们俄亥俄大学除一般藏书外，还有一个特藏，即：东南亚藏书。由于我馆是国会图书馆"国家采购和编目"计划中的一个图书馆，国会图书馆替我们收购东南亚国家的图书，所以收集的这方面图书十分丰富。

（3）还有一个合作组织，在美国是很有成绩的。这个组织的名称是"研究图书馆中心"，成立于1951年，由美国一些研究图书馆共同组成。对那些实用性不大，但却很有研究价值的图书，往往会碰到一个馆买不起，或许买得起不经常使用，而别的图书馆用起来又不方便的情况。于是，就采取各个图书馆出钱，由研究图书馆中心专门来购，统一保存的方法。这是研究图书馆中心的一个服务项目，另一个服务项目是有些研究图书馆的馆藏到了一定的限度，没有空间了，可以把一些不用的书或是较少用的书送到这个中心去保存。目前，这个中心收集了大量剔除的书，每种至少保留一本以供学术研究参考。

3. 大规模的图书馆自动化网络的建立

美国图书馆60年代开始应用计算机。有些图书馆自己买计算机做试验，设计本馆自动化系统。在俄亥俄州有个很特殊的例子，当时十二所州立大学联合起来向州政府申请了一笔经费，发展自动化系统，建立了俄亥俄大专学校图书馆中心，也叫"OCLC"。为了设计一个俄亥俄大专学校图书馆中心自动化系统，请了一个图书馆自动化的专家来为他们设计了一套联合图书编目的系统，并且购置了计算机，所有参加的图书馆都有终端机与这个计算机相联。"OCLC"购买了美国国会图书馆的编目资料磁带，而参加"OCLC"的图书馆要进行编目时，可以先检索一下这本书是否已经由国会图书馆编目好了，如果还没编好，就要自己进行编目，然后移入资料库里，那么其他图书馆就可以利用了，"OCLC"是1971年建立的，至1973年就有十几个州要求加入，而到了1975年，几乎美国五十个州都加入了这个系统，很快成了全国性的系统。1978年"OCLC"改名为"联机图书馆自动化中心"，这几个单词字首也是"OCLC"，只是意思不同罢了。现在不光美国五十多个州六千多个图书馆参加这个中心，甚至连欧洲、南美的许多图书馆都参加进来了，"OCLC"现在正在发展中、日、韩文系统，有了这个系统，这几种文字的图书编目就不需要目前这样用罗马拼音来做。这对中国图书馆界同样很有用处。

"OCLC"之所以能够取得成功的秘诀是什么呢？主要有三点：

（1）合作编目。各位都知道，过去用手工操作时，每本书都需要自己编目，现在"OCLC"采用合作编目的方式，所有参加"OCLC"的图书馆，估计有将近93%的新书不需自己编目，可以通过资料库找到资料。另一方面，过去编目最大的问题就是积压，自从有了联机编目系统，新书第二天就可以上架了。

（2）联合目录。经过合作编目以后，"OCLC"资料库，本身就成为一个联合的图书目录。目前有一千两百多万的资料贮存在资料库里；这个资料库每年增加的数量超过一百万，由此可见，联合目录包含的内容之广，用途之大。

（3）馆际互借系统。"OCLC"贮存的资料非常之多，读者只要在计算机上检索出哪些图书馆有这本书，然后从这些图书馆中挑出5个距离较近的有合作关系的图书馆，用终端机把借书信息送到第一个图书馆，若第一馆在二十四小时里无答复或回复它不能借或已借出，计算机就会自动把这个信息按顺序送到第二、第三个图书馆，从而减少了打字和邮寄的时间。若可以外借，计算机也会马上在终端机上回答你，并告诉你付邮时间，你就知道过多少天可以收到这本书。

以上是"OCLC"三个成功的原因。我之所以花这个时间介绍"OCLC"的情况，就是想启发各位如何在国内开展图书馆自动化合作。现在国外有很多资料库，要是能够设立省级或全国性的资料中心，把国外的资料库引进来，再加上国内图书馆的相互合作，就可以建立起具有中国特色的资料库。

4. 推广图书馆编目和机读格式标准化

美国实行大规模图书馆的自动化，一个先决条件就是编目和机读格式的标准化，为了实施这一计划，美国国会图书馆1965年就开始设计图书编目和机读的标准格式，称为"马克"，即"机器可以阅读的格式"。这个格式经过美国国会图书馆发展之后，被国际标准局接受，随即成为国际机读标准格式，一些国家可以通过机读目录直接交换他们的图书目录。比如，美国现在可以很容易地把从英国、加拿大买来的机读目录，放进"OCLC"中供美国的图书馆使用。这就是标准化的一个重要的贡献，美国称得上是"马克"标准化的创始国家。除此之外还有其他标准格式：①国际图书标准号码；②国际期刊标准号码；③国际图书著录标准，美国图书编目规则。据我所知，中国在编制《中国图书分类法》、《中国图书编目规则》时，原则上也尽其可能与国际标准相吻合，这样为国际合作创造很多方便条件。同时我也希望国内图书馆在自动化设计时也应考虑到国际标准的要求。

5. 索引、文摘编制的自动化

世界上最大的一个文摘就是化学文摘，现在化学文摘每年制作文摘五十万件，而这五十万件的文摘都是从一万两千多种化学期刊或同化学有关的期刊中挑选出来的，收集的范围包括一百多个国家，是一个收集非常广泛的文摘刊物库。60年代开始，文摘编制从手工作业方式改成自动化，建立了大规模的计算机资料库。有了资料库，进行联机检索就非常方便，化学文摘的资料库就贮存为时20年至30年的资料，如果我们要检索关于化学方面的情报和文献，都可以通过计算机或联机检索取得。美国目前有好几个大的资料库服务中心，为美国提供了很完整的资料库检索服务项目。

6. 计算机在图书馆中的广泛应用

前面讲过"OCLC"仅是计算机在图书馆应用的一部分，是馆际之间联合使用，另一部分是计算机在馆内业务部门的应用，如图书馆流通、采购、人事资料的管理、经费的管理，甚至有些馆内编目的工作，联机图书目录的检索；等等，这些最好由馆内自己来做，而后与全国性的资料库作联合编目，开展馆际互借。福建省图书馆目前也在做这方面的试验，福建师范大学也在用计算机做些馆内作业的试验。在美国，很多图书馆用小、中、大型计算机来做图书馆的业务工作，他们在做这些作业时有两个主要原则：①尽可能与全国性的资料网络联机合并，避免重复。②馆内系统设计时尽可能地设计成综合性系统，具备多种功能。美国最近在图书馆界除了广泛应用计算机外，还有两项较新的技术正在研究阶段，第一项是怎样用现代电子通信技术，把资料文献从一个图书馆传到另一个图书馆，现在这种复印传真的技术已经进入实用阶段。第二项是研究用光束或电射的磁片来做图书资料贮存工具。

7. 图书馆教育与专业人员的培训

美国非常重视图书馆教育。过去欧洲国家是在图书馆内培训专业人员，没有专门的图书馆学校。1876年，美国纽约州的州立图书馆与哥伦比亚大学合作建立了第一所图书馆大学，以后美国各大学陆续建立图书馆学系。开始，图书馆学系是属大学部的，就是说，招收高中毕业的学生，学制4年，这4年的教育包括一般的通才教育和专业教育。自三十年代至40年代，他们逐渐把大学部教育提升到研究所的程度。40年代至50年代，美国对图书馆员有了新的要求，即至少要有图书馆学士的学位。从60年代至70年代，自动化和情报服务等新的科目增加到图书馆里来。光是学士学位还不够，有很多图书馆，尤其是大学图书馆的图书馆员，除了学士学位之外，还要有一个专科的学士学位。这种学历我们称之为"高级文凭"。美国有五十多所被美国图书馆学会承认、立案的图书馆学院，在这五十多所学院中将近十七所设置了博士学位的课程。自从图书馆学院开设硕士学位的课程后，招收的学生都是大学毕业的学生，主要偏重图书馆专业方面的训练。现在图书馆专业课程的训练范围太狭窄了，所以有的图书馆学校就加上高级文凭，或把学士学位由一年制改为两年制，增加了一些别的课程。这些课程对于培养图书馆管理人才，领导人才非常有用，例如，关于人际关系、信息方面的课程，关于新的管理理论或实际管理应用方面的课程，关于市场学方面的课程以及社会公共关系、捐款方面的课程。

8. 新的管理学在图书馆的应用

过去，旧式的图书馆很注重馆长的权威，馆员多半没有什么发言权，现在这种情况改变了。馆长虽然是领导人员，可是在进行决策时仍要尽可能地让馆员有参与决策的机会。所以，现在美国在图书馆管理方面，较多地引进了科学管理和人际关系这一方面的新的观念；在配合行为科学新学说方面，他们不但着重经济因素，同时也着重个人的需求。很多图书馆把目标管理与参与式管理两种方式配合起来使用，建立了比较健全的人事制度。过去馆长有很大的用人权，而现在则不然，比如在招收专业人才的问题上，根据规定，大多数人员要在全国范围内公开征求最合适的人选，在征求过程中要经过选择委员会初步审定，而后再向馆长推荐，馆长这时才做最后的选择。这是比较民主化的管理方式。

9. 加强服务观念

刚才讲过，图书馆要真正成为社会教育和文化的中心，它在社会上无形当中就要起一种领导的作用。很多社会上的公众活动利用图书馆的场所举行，图书馆本身也想尽各种方法扩大服务对象。三四十年代美国的图书馆都是等读者上门，没有把服务做到外面去。现在美国的公立图书馆在这方面做了很多工作。老弱病残的人及接受福利补助的穷人，因为行动不方便或是住得太远、又没钱坐车，图书馆的人就把目录寄到这些人的家里，根据他们的需要，开展邮寄服务，图书馆还按照老弱病残者的名单，用流动车送书上门，由于图书馆关心老人们的生活，因而很多孤独的老人过世后，不把财产留给自己的儿女，而把财产捐给图书馆。每个公立图书馆的经费开支是由地方税收来维持的。我们俄亥俄州过去是用地方上买卖股票的税收来支持公立图书馆，这对于大城市的图书馆很有必要。因为，美国公立图书馆积极处理好与地方的关系，使得地方上的广大读者觉得图书馆对他们有利，从而取得地方上的支持。美国的各类型图书馆都愿意把收藏的资料提供给工商业界利用，公立图书馆则免费提供，这同样由于图书馆经费的大部分是由工商业缴税来提供的。此外图书馆往往都根据地方上的需要来收集资料，最大限度地满足需要。

以上我讲了九个问题，都是美国图书馆最近的一些重要发展情况，下面想向各位提出几点我个人对国内图书馆界的一些希望和意见。

1. 我觉得国内图书馆虽然物质条件较差，但图书馆工作人员的精神是很可贵的，做了很多工作

我希望分管图书馆的有关部门，向政府呼吁，多要些钱来支持图书馆的建设。因为图书馆的工作非常重要，尤其是省馆需要有一个现代化的新馆舍，以便向社会提供更多的服务。很多地方的图书馆都太破旧，结构不合理，必须增建图书馆大楼。图书馆有很多特藏，如果没有很好的保护环境，将会造成很大损失。

2. 希望有更多受过专业教育的人员来加入图书馆工作

我知道国内图书馆现在还不能做到所有工作人员都受过专业训练。很多图书馆自己创造专业训练的机会，这是一个很好的方法。我们要向社会宣传图书馆工作的伟大意义，让更多的人才充实到图书馆来。图书馆学会要经常举办各类训练班，除了图书专业教育外，还应多办一些其他专业教育的培训班，应为馆员创造机会去参加国际性的会议，以使把国外先进的经验、技术引进来，也可以把我国的经验介绍到国外。另外，很重要的一点就是我们的工作需要统筹规划，比如说图书馆学校的课程要有统筹规划。

3. 图书馆标准化的推广，馆际互借的开展

著录、编目、分类、主题词表等等工作，尽可能做到标准化，特别是计算机的应用要有全局观念。国内图书馆界要多做一些馆际互借的工作，国外在这方面就做得很好。这并不是说国外图书馆不存在本位主义，不同的是政府用了很好的办法来鼓励馆际互借，把各类型图书馆之间的资源联合起来。怎样的鼓励呢？就是一个图书馆每借一本给另一个图书馆，政府就奖励 5 美元，使得各图书馆都乐于开展馆际互借，这对他们有好处。图书采购也进行合作，用少数的经费起最大的效用。要建立一个全国性或全省的图书刊物书目资料库，这是馆际互借的一个重要条件，有了共同的目录，才能知道各个图书馆的馆藏。现在国外的期刊价格昂贵，大部分的图书馆都没有足够的资金来独立订购，因此我建议建立一个"中国期刊服务中心"，机构可以设在北京图书馆或在中国科技情报所，服务的对象是全国的图书馆。每一个图书馆都可以向他们借所需的文献，服务中心也可以从中收回一部分费用。这样全国各级图书馆在购买期刊上就可以节省大笔费用。另一个建议是设一个全省性的缩微片服务中心。国内图书馆有很多特藏，由于纸张老化，破损很厉害，而每一个图书馆都花钱添置设备来做缩微片，既费时费力，又浪费资金。

（原载《福建省图书馆学会通讯》1986 年第 1 期，第 34－38 页。）

图书馆服务的新观念与新技术[①]

New Concepts and New Technology in Library Services

一、前言

谢谢各位百忙中参加今天的座谈会。由于我对台湾中山大学一直非常向往——也非常敬佩李馆长这几年来在图书馆界的表现,尤其是前年陈秀薇主任到我们俄亥俄大学图书馆进修,从她的谈话中,让我一直觉得应该亲自来台湾中山大学图书馆看看。很高兴今天能来到中山大学,也很感谢李馆长安排这么好的机会让我和各位见面,交换一点我的工作经验。三十年来,我在图书馆服务可说是从最基本的工作做起:1957年留学美国俄亥俄大学学习教育,并在图书馆打工,后来又攻读图书馆学,并一直留在俄亥俄大学图书馆服务,这三十年来,我对图书馆工作一直有相当浓厚的兴趣,如果让我重新选择,我还是会选图书馆这个行业。以往我有很多机会向大家报告图书馆服务的新技术,因为这30年来新技术的发展对图书馆的服务和工作项目有很重大的影响;但是最近这几年我觉得光讲新技术是不够的,因为新技术只是图书馆服务的工具,要想把图书馆的工作做好,除了新技术外还要有新观念。所以,我今天想借这个机会和各位谈谈图书馆服务的新技术和新观念。首先我要讲的是图书馆在社会变迁过程中所遭遇的重大影响,然后报告图书馆服务的新技术,最后讲新观念。

二、图书馆在社会变迁过程中所遭遇的重大影响

图书馆的历史相当悠久,但过去的图书馆和现在的图书馆有很大的差别:过去的图书馆是静态的,类似藏书楼的性质,负有保存人类知识文化遗产的任务;现在图书馆的功能已有相当大的改变,这主要是受社会变迁的影响。

这三十年来的社会变迁有:

(1) 由于知识及生活水平的普遍提高,读者对图书馆的需求也大量增加,图书馆服务的对象不再像过去仅限于高阶层的知识分子,而是广及于一般社会大众。例如现在公共图书馆的服务对象包括儿童、青少年、老年人、残障人士,甚至属少数民族的国外移民等,并且随时针对所提供的服务项目作适当的调整。

(2) 十九世纪工业革命之前,美国从事农业的人口占就业人口的百分之五十到六十,工业革命之后慢慢减少,到60年代以后,已降到仅占百分之八。而在工业方面,60年代以前,美国从事制造业的就业人口比例曾高达百分之六十,现已降为百分之三十到四十之间。目前,从事"知识工业",如教育、新闻、图书出版事业等的人口已占百分之二十到三十,预估到2000年,从事"知识工业"的人口会提高到占就业人口的一半以上。我们国内目前也有这种趋势。这些社会转型的现象对图书馆的服务也有很重大的影响。

(3) 近三十年来的出版事业非常发达,根据联合国教科文组织的统计,日、美、苏三国每年出版的新书均有五万种以上,而祖国大陆每年也有二万种以上。出版事业的蓬勃发展造成图书馆收藏及目录控制的问题。即使像美国国会图书馆(Library of Congress)每年新编的图书有二十万种,也仅占新出版图书的小部分。OCLC每年新增的编目资料则有二百五十万

[①] 本文由台湾中山大学图书馆谢雪莺记录,1989年12月12日,台湾中山大学国际会议厅。

笔，较美国国会图书馆多出十倍以上，所以全世界每年出版的图书数量实在相当惊人。

（4）人类知识迅速累积。1850 年，全世界出版的期刊不到一千种；到 1980 年，全世界出版的期刊估计达数万种。世界最大的文摘社——化学文摘社（Chemical Abstract Service）于 1907 年成立于俄亥俄州的 Columbus，它第一年所搜集的化学文献只有二万五千种，而现在它每年搜集的文献则有五十万种之多。据统计，现在科技文献的出版率是每天七千五百篇，年增加率为百分之十三，也就是说科技文献每隔五年半就增加一倍。这些不断迅速累积的知识对图书馆在资料的搜集、处理及服务上都造成很大的影响。

三、图书馆服务的新技术

最近三十年来新技术的变动很大，影响所及，也使图书馆换了一个型态。这些新技术的发展主要是电脑、电脑的内储设施，以及通讯技术和设备。很凑巧地我们可以把每十年当作一个阶段，每个阶段均有很明显的改变，我现在将这三十年来新技术的发展分为三个阶段向各位报告：

（一）60 年代：60 年代在图书馆自动化的发展上是个相当重要的奠基阶段。电脑在 50 年代就开始使用，到 60 年代才较为普遍，当时的电脑体积庞大，速度也慢，然而，已有图书馆尝试用电脑来增进工作的效率。尽管因电脑的内储量很小而且没有通讯网络的配合，在图书馆的应用有限，60 年代仍然有几个重要的发展对图书馆自动化有很重大的影响，那就是：

（1）美国国家医学图书馆（National Library of Medicine）在 1963 年间开始将大量的医学资料储存于电脑，做成了"医学资料储存检索系统"（MEDLARS），这是图书馆将大规模的资料用电脑处理的开始。

（2）美国国会图书馆于 1965 年开始用电脑进行图书编目的工作，并将编目规格标准化，研制完成了 LC MARC Format（Library of Congress Machine-readable Cataloging Format），现已成为全世界公认的标准机读编目格式。MARC 的出台，可说是非常有远见，并且是必要的。美国国会图书馆亦将利用电脑做成的图书编目纪录转录于磁带上，提供给其他图书馆使用。遇到美国国会图书馆没有的书，就由各个图书馆作原始编目并将编目资料输入电脑，以充实国会图书馆的书目资料库，联合编目于是开始。OCLC 也于一九六七年正式成立，对后来的图书馆自动化造成很重大的影响。

（3）化学文摘社在 60 年代以前的作法是，将搜集的化学文献用手工处理、排版，非常浪费时间，而且出版速度相当慢，脱期现象非常严重，往往要在化学文献出版一、二年后才看得到文摘。60 年代起，改用电脑处理搜集来的化学文献，建立机读资料库，大大缩短了原始资料和文摘出版的间隔时间。到了 70 年代，这些机读资料库更进步到可以联机检索的阶段。

（二）70 年代：70 年代上半期，一方面 OCLC 愈做愈好，于是发展成全国性的网络，成为全美国图书馆联合编目、共享资源的中心，资料库的数量也愈来愈多。及至 70 年代中期，又有中型电脑（Minicomputer）的出现，它的某些性能比大型电脑还要好，价格却便宜很多，于是有很多图书馆开始用中型电脑来处理业务，造成了地区性网络（Local System）的出现。我可以用我们俄亥俄大学图书馆自动化系统——ALICE（艾丽斯系统）的发展作为典型的例子加以说明：

60 年代到 70 年代上半期，俄亥俄大学图书馆同其他大部分的美国图书馆一样，均用 OCLC 作联合编目及馆际互借。1979 年起，除一方面仍和 OCLC 作全国性的联合编目、馆际互借工作外,另一方面发展自己的地区性网络,并于 1983 年废除卡片目录,提供以终端机检索的联机公用目录,并可作流通、期刊控制、采访、图书馆的管理等本地的业务(附图一)。在硬件配备方面,我们的网络系统有五个 IBM 主机,构成本校整体性的校园网络。图书馆另有 HP3000/950 和全校计算器网络连接。所以,在全校每个角落,只要有终端机和全校网络联机,即可用电话线检索到图书馆的资料,甚至在图书馆闭馆时间,读者也可利用不同的线路及电话号码打进来查询并打印。对不熟悉系统的读者,我们有简易的查检系统(Novice User Search System),引导读者一步步地检索图书馆的资料(附图二)。

(三)80 年代:80 年代前半期,图书馆使用中型电脑进行自动化愈来愈普遍,卡片目录也渐渐被终端机所取代。中叶以后,微电脑(Microcomputer)出现,它的价钱非常便宜,内储容量又可扩充,很适合小型图书馆使用,就连大型图书馆也常利用微电脑作办公室自动化,如字处理、统计的工作。到了 80 年代后期,光盘设备的使用已相当普遍,电讯传真的技术也很发达,更加速了图书馆自动化的脚步。

(四)90 年代的新趋势:70 年代至 80 年代的图书馆自动化系统,多是各馆个别发展,例如俄亥俄州有十三所州立大学,几所独立的医学院及一些小学校,均用自己的系统(附图三),这样一来,读者利用馆外的终端机检索每个不同系统的资料,就须用不同的检索方式,非常不方便,于是才开始考虑如何将这些不同的系统连接起来。这几年来,光纤(Optical fibre)技术的发展慢慢取代了电话线。光纤的阻挠性小,传递错误少,不但电脑数字讯号可以传送,其他如声音、图片也可以传送,为图书馆自动化的发展提供另一个很好的方向,也因此图书馆间不同系统的网络化得以进行得更好。目前我所在的俄亥俄州正计划建立州图书馆系统,把州内不同图书馆的不同系统连接起来,让用户用同一种检索方式就可检索到同一州内不同系统的资料。在 90 年代里,我们更想进一步完成全国性网络联机,如此一来,每个教授或学生均可在学校里,利用图书馆提供的终端机或是他自己的工作站(Workstation)来检索本系统的编目资料、期刊索引、学校资讯及部分期刊论文的全文。如果本地没有所需资料,电脑会经由 OHIO WAN 自动转接到州图书馆系统——OLIS Network,去检索州的联合目录、期刊索引以及部分期刊论文全文。如果州图书馆系统仍不能满足读者的需求,就再经由 NATIONAL WAN 转接到全国性的网络(National Network)去检索 OCLC、BRS、DIALOG 以及其他大学的资料库(附图四)。在检索的过程中,读者不需要知道或指定他要检索哪一个系统,他只要操作一部终端机就可同时接触到很多的资料库,从中查检到他所需的资料。目前我们对俄亥俄州图书馆系统(OLIS)的建立已有详细的计划,并且也和一些厂商在合作发展软件中,预计 1991 年 6 月可以完成并启用。

四、图书馆服务的新观念

前面所提到的社会变迁和图书馆服务的新技术对图书馆造成很大的冲击,也对图书馆服务读者的作法和观念造成了非常深远的影响。这些新观念和新作法是:

(1)图书馆服务项目及服务范围不断增加和调整:由于社会的变迁,图书馆的服务项目不像过去那么单纯,有很多图书馆兼做很多其他的社会服务项目,例如提供工商资讯服务等。以俄亥俄大学图书馆为例:①在参考咨询服务方面,对立了对外服务部门,聘请专人负责,针对校外人士的需求搜集资料、重组资料、提供精华资料,这项服务是要收费的。②受其他图书馆委托担任全州十一县十三所公共图书馆的后援图书馆——由于现代读者需求的资料愈来愈专精,当一般公共图书馆无法提供服务时,可打电话到俄亥俄大学图书馆咨询服务部门，利用其大型资料库代为检索资料。而州的图书馆每年补助俄亥俄大学图书馆六至七万元以便聘请专人负责。

（2）评量图书馆方式的改变及馆际合作的加强：过去多以藏书数量的多寡评量一所图书馆的好坏，现在的新观念则认为应以图书馆是否可满足读者的需求及其搜集资料的能力来作为评量的依据。也就是说，一所好的图书馆应该有能力将全国甚至全世界图书馆的资源变成本身图书馆的资源。有了这种新的服务观念，所以现在图书馆界在研究制订图书馆标准时，多将藏书数量一项取消，数字观念愈来愈淡薄，代之而起的是读者对图书馆满意度的调查。

也正因为图书馆评量方式的改变，加强馆际合作就成为做好图书馆服务最重要的方式之一。美国图书馆一向重视合作，而且也做得最好，在本世纪初，美国就订有很好的馆际合作办法，而且各图书馆也非常遵守。不过，由于这几年来服务观念的改变，觉得需要更加强图书馆间的合作与协调。例如藏书的分工合作，过去多是讲讲，现在由于书刊费用愈来愈高，各馆想将所有资料搜集完整是不可能的，故有分工合作发展馆藏及联合图书采购等办法。像美国这几年来，非常重视其他国家资料的搜集，于是就采取分工合作的方式，像俄州总共设有六个东南亚资料中心，其中俄亥俄大学图书馆负责马来西亚、印度尼西亚两国资料的搜集。

（3）合作编目，建立联合目录：OCLC合作编目的方式非常成功，现已发展成为全国性、世界性的联合编目网络。利用 OCLC 作联合编目成功的例子很多，像：俄亥俄大学图书馆在 OCLC 开始设立之前，十五位编目人员一年可编二万五千册新书，现在则二年编四万五千册到五万册，而编目人员减为五位，也就是工作量增加一倍，而人员减少了三分之二。这都是由于联合编目带来的成果，因为有百分之九十三的新书均不需原始编目。所以合作编目大大增加了编目的速度，也缩短了上架的时间。我认为国内可考虑设立联合编目中心，减轻各馆编目工作的负担。

建立联合目录还有另一个好处，就是可利用来做馆际互借的工作。像参与 OCLC 的图书馆有九千四百所之多，所以用 OCLC 的终端机就可立刻查出图书所在并办理借书，而且 OCLC 的馆际互借系统可让读者挑出五个图书所在图书馆，并自己安排借书的顺序，系统会按顺序向各馆借书，并立刻显示借书的结果，非常方便。根据我的了解，现在国内各图书馆纷纷规划自己的自动化系统，为免重蹈美国各馆独立发展、后来才想到以联网来弥补的覆辙，应考虑联网的需要，不但所需费用可以大大减少，而且很快就可以完成。

（4）改善服务的态度，加强读者教育：新技术是为了提升图书馆的服务，但光有新技术是不够的，主要还是要有服务的观念。像有很多外国图书馆员到俄亥俄大学图书馆来做短期训练，他们最大的感触就是：美国图书馆员的服务态度真是好，总是笑容满面，全心全意的服务读者。这就是因为我们特别强调参考咨询服务，并安排受过图书馆专业训练及专门学科背景、具双学位的人担任参考服务的工作，以便提供较有深度、较专门的服务。美国相当重视图书馆员的职位和待遇，虽然待遇不算顶高，但其职位很受重视，尤其是自动化之后，更提升了图书馆员的地位。目前台湾图书馆员的待遇、地位都不很高，也许有人要问：我们是应该等到待遇和地位提高后，才把图书馆的服务做好呢？还是先把服务做好，再来要求我们应得的待遇和地位？我们还是应该先把服务工作做好，很自然地，社会大众就会对我们的努力加以肯定，从而重视我们的地位，提高我们的待遇。

另外，图书馆的资料类型愈来愈复杂，再加上新技术所需的很多新设备，以及服务项目的增加，都需要图书馆教导读者使用，所以，对读者教育也是非常要紧的；何况，多和读者接触，也有助于改善对读者的服务。

还有一点，现在的社会是一个开放的社会，光是把自己的工作做好是不够的，必须重视对外的宣传，以提高社会对图书馆的重视。

五、结语

今天的演讲，我要提出二点结论：

其一，图书馆的发展日新月异，图书馆从业人员绝不能满足现实。我们回想这二三十年来的改变，实在太大了，所以，我们必须时时刻刻不断地追求更美好、更充实的明天。其二，图书馆从业人员要具备敬业乐业的精神，任重道远的使命感，要勇于超越现状，开创我们自己的未来。

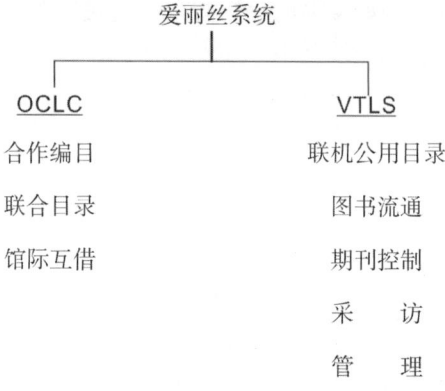

附图一　俄亥俄大学的艾丽斯系统（ALICE）

附图二　Dial Access to ALICE

University of Akron	Virginia Tech Library System
Ohio University	Virginia Tech Library System
Youngstown State	Virginia Tech Library System
Bowling Green	LS/2 (quasi-orphan) CincinnatiWashington Lib. Network (orphan)
Ohio State	LCS (locally developed)
Wright State Univ.	DRA (Digital Research)
Cleveland State	NOTIS (from Northwestern) Kent State Univ. NOTIS
Miami	No System (presently bidding)
Central State	No System
Medical College of Ohio	No System
NEOUCOM	No System
Shawnee State	No System
Toledo	No System

附图三　AUTOMATED LIBRARY SYSTEMS IN OHIO PUBLIC UNIVERSITIES

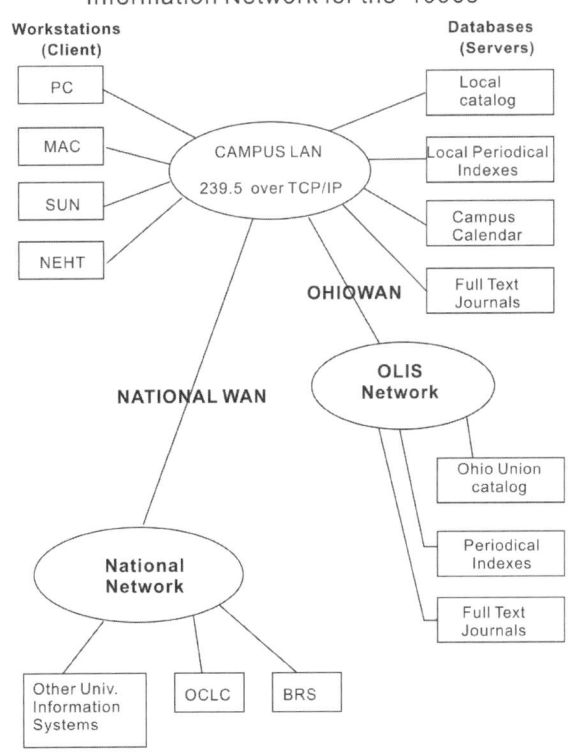

附图四　Information Network for the 1990s

（原载《图书馆学讲座专辑之十》，台湾中山大学图书馆，高雄，1989年）

中国医学图书馆学专业的最近发展

Medical Librarianship in China: Recent Developments

Introduction

From November 22 to December 13, 1990, the authors were invited by the Faculty of Medical Library and Information Science, Hunan Medical University, Changsha, China, to give a series of 15 lectures on modern library management, automation and technology, medical librarianship, collection development, resource sharing, user services, professional education, and related topics. The lectures were attended by third-, fourth-, and fifth-year students as well as many faculty members and librarians and information professionals from other libraries in Hunan Province. In addition to the lectures, which were two and a half hours each, the authors visited the Hunan Provincial Library and several university and college libraries. Of particular note were Jishou University in western Hunan, which is devoted to minority education in the region, and Changde Public Library, which was founded in 1903, and is the first library in China to use the word "library" in its name. (For thousands of years libraries were called "Chang-shu Lou", which means "The building where books are kept".)

Hunan

The program offered by the Faculty of Medical Library and Information Science at Hunan Medical University is relatively new. It is one of four such undergraduate programs founded between 1985 and 1987. The others are at Bethune Medical University in Changchun, Tongchi Medical University in Wuhan, and the Chinese Medical University in Shenyang, The Faculty in Hunan was founded in 1986 and offers a 5-year undergraduate program leading to a Bachelor's degree. About 40 students are admitted each year through a highly competitive national entrance examination. The 16 full-time teaching faculties include two professors, seven associate professors, and seven lecturers. Most have either medical or library science qualifications and a few have both.

Most of the lecturers are in their early thirties and the associate professors in their early forties. All are enthusiastic and dedicated.

Prior to the establishment of the programs in medical library and information science, there was no formal program for training medical librarians and medical information specialists in China.[2]

The staff in most medical libraries consisted of:

1) Those who had completed library education and training from a technical secondary school program, a 2-year college program, a 4-year university program, or a postgraduate program. Only a very small percentage of the medical library staff had such qualifications.

2) Those that had had formal education and training in medical or health sciences. Some may have had additional short-term training in library and information sciences. The percentage of staff with these qualifications was also low.

3) Those who had studied library and information science through in-service training or correspondence education, the Radio-Television University, or workshops offered by various

---

[1] Co-author: Anne S. Goss. This paper, which is based on a report for Chinese authorities, examines the establishment of medical librarianship as a specialized area of studies in China, particularly in Hunan Province.

[2] Zili Xiao. "Professional education in library and information science—current situation and developing trends" in *Education and Research in Library and Information Science in the Information Age: means of modern technology and management*. Proceedings of the IFLA/China society of Library Science Seminar, Beijing, September 1-5, 1986. Tess, M. H. ed. Munich: K. G. Saur, 1988; IFLA Publications 43, p. 31.

library organizations and societies at the provincial or municipal level. Most library staff had this type of qualification.

4) Those that have had no library training or medical education.

According to a report on the status and development of biomedical libraries in China, which was published in 1987,[①] 53% of the 2415 library staff in 88 medical college/university libraries was college graduates; 30% of which had studied medicine or pharmacology. Among medical library directors or deputy directors, 40% had medical or pharmacological specializations. The report gave no information on the percentage of library staff with training in library and information science.

To cope with the shortage of trained medical librarians and information professionals, it was reported[②] that in the early 1980s groups representing Chinese medical libraries were sent abroad to study medical library and network management in Australia, Canada, Japan, the United Kingdom, and the United States. A number of fellowships offered by the World Health Organization (WHO) also allowed some Chinese medical librarians and information specialists to receive library management training in the United States, West Germany, and at WHO headquarters. In the United States, the National Library of Medicine and several medical libraries participated in the WHO fellowship program.

Guidelines

According to the Guidelines on Professional Medical Education for the Nation's Institutions of Higher Education, which were promulgated by the State Commission of Education in August 1987,[③] the aim of professional education in medical library and information science is to train high-level specialists in medical library and information work. For graduates to perform capably in medical librarianship and use modern information techniques, they should have basic knowledge of medical science as well as basic knowledge and skills of library and information science. The Guidelines further stipulate that the knowledge and skills required are[④]

1) basic knowledge of medical science;

2) basic theories and methods for selecting, cataloging, and classifying medical literature;

3) basic theories and methods for processing, organizing, analyzing, researching, and forecasting medical science information;

4) basic knowledge of electronic information storage and retrieval;

5) being able to provide readers with the materials that they need in an efficient fashion.

To meet the above, the following courses are suggested:
- introduction to general medical science
- introduction to clinical medicine
- introduction to preventive medicine
- introduction to traditional Chinese medicine
- introduction to pharmacology
- basic knowledge of library science
- information retrieval language
- search of documents in medical science and technology
- analysis and research of medical information
- organization of journals and other materials

---

① Daxun He, Fenian Cai, Zijun Wu. "The status and development of biomedical libraries in China." *INSPEL*. V. 21, No. 1 (1987): p. 6.

② Huang, K. "A leap forward in medical librarianship: a glimpse of the Biomedical Information Center and Network, People's Republic of China." *Bulletin of the Medical Library Association*. V. 71, No. 3 (July 1983): p. 299.

③ Ping Feng, Xiao-chun Liu. "China's medical librarianship and information science education." *Journal of Library and Information Science*. V. 15, No. 2 (October 1989): p. 199. [In Chinese]

④ *Ibid*., p. 201.

Certificate program

At Hunan Medical University, prior to 1986, at the request of the National Working Committee of Libraries of Institutions of Higher Education, a 1-year certificate program for medical librarians and medical information specialists was offered over a 4-year period. The program was designed for medical college graduates wishing to become medical librarians or medical information specialists. Since its establishment in 1986, the Faculty of Medical Library and Information Science has emphasized the integration of both medical science and library and information science into a unified curriculum. Students take general medical courses, library and information science courses, computer technology, foreign languages, and courses in the social sciences, humanities, and natural sciences. To graduate, a student must take a total of 60 courses, 40 of which are compulsory and 20 are electives. The student must also complete a one semester library practicum and a thesis. The 60 courses are grouped in the following five clusters:
1) basic medical science;
2) library and information sciences;
3) general studies;
4) computer technology and its applications;
5) foreign languages.

These requirements are far more specialized and comprehensive than those for medical librarianship in the West. Because of the urgent need for more qualified medical librarians and information specialists, the Faculty of Library and Information Science at Hunan Medical University continues the 1-year certificate program for medical graduates who plan to work in medical libraries.

There are, however, two basic dangers in the Chinese model of education for medical librarianship. First, too much emphasis may be placed on learning medical subjects at the expense of library and information sciences. For example, according to Feng and Lius, some of the programs in China, with the exception of Hunan's, have devoted the first 3 years to the study of medical subjects with the last 2 years divided between the practice of clinical medicine and the study of library and information science. The time allowed for the latter is about one semester, which is far from adequate. Second, because Chinese medical education begins at the undergraduate level, as is the case with all majors and specialized subjects, high school graduates do not have very broad knowledge. The addition of courses in the social sciences, humanities, natural sciences, and foreign languages at Hunan Medical University compensates for this weakness.

Although the first class of students at Hunan will not graduate until June 1991, many are concerned already about future employment. Based on the "Survey of the Profession of Medical Librarians and Information Scientists" undertaken in May to July, 1986—commissioned by the State Commission of Education,[①] there should have been a serious shortage of trained medical librarians and information workers in China. A sampling of 44 medical libraries showed that about half of the staff had reached retirement age. The report estimated that, among the nation's 129 university level medical school libraries, 515 junior college level medical school libraries, 323 medical research institute libraries, 11,497 hospital libraries above the county level, and 730 other special hospital libraries, about 15,000 trained library and information professionals, both new and replacement, are needed. This figure did not include the need for teaching faculty in medical librarianship. For the four existing medical library schools, the annual number of graduates is only 160—far short of the need.

In reality, the authors were told, many of the library positions are filled by unqualified personnel assigned to the libraries by higher authorities. Many openings are filled from within,

---

① *Report of a Survey of the Profession of Medical Librarians and Information Scientists.* Beijing: State Commission of Education, 1988. [In Chinese]

with little concern for professional competence or credentials needed for the particular position. It remains to be seen if the first group of graduates—armed with high-level professional knowledge and skills—can be placed satisfactorily.

Contrary to countries in the West, where there is a premium on medical education and high rewards for doctors, in China doctors do not enjoy a higher social status than professionals in other fields and many do not seem to mind changing to medical library and information science. The authors were impressed with the caliber of the students that they met. Selection is highly competitive and those who qualify are the cream of the crop.

Recommendations

At the end of the lecture series, the authors offered three recommendations to the Hunan Medical University and, through it, to the Ministry of Public Health and the State Commission of Education.

(1) The program at Hunan Medical University should be upgraded to the Master's degree level by extending the length of studies from 5 to 6 years. This would enable the inclusion of more theory and research. It would also encourage even more highly qualified students to enter the field of medical librarianship and to be better placed after graduation.

(2) To implement the above, faculty development is of the greatest importance. Qualified foreign faculty should be invited regularly to teach at Hunan—preferably for one semester or longer—while younger teachers from the Faculty should be sent abroad for further studies. (The authors were very pleased to learn that three faculty members were sent abroad as visiting scholars and one has returned after one year of study at Indiana University. The Head of the Faculty will soon come to Ohio University as a visiting scholar for 6 months. Another young lecturer, after the completion of her medical education, was given the opportunity to study information science at Wuhan University for 2 years. More of such continuing education is needed.)

(3) To assure the success of the education program in the four universities and that new graduates have an opportunity to use their knowledge and skills to benefit the medical and health science professions; both the Ministry of Public Health and the State Commission of Education should assist in the placement of the 160 or so graduates a year in strategic positions in major medical libraries. A method of monitoring their work and progress as a way to evaluate the effectiveness of the program should also be developed.

(Published in *Asian Libraries*. V. 1, No. 1 (March 1991): pp. 80 – 84.)

募款成功的十个原则

The Ten Principles for Successful Fundraising①

The topic of private fundraising has generated considerable interest among academic librarians in recent years, and there are reasons to believe that the climate of the next decade will enhance this trend. Colleges and universities expect tight budgets through most of the nineties. There are remarkably few conventional sources of support for higher education: tax revenues, student tuition, and externally funded research. All are coming under increasing pressure. For those of us in the state-support sector, state and local taxes are the most important revenue source. But many states are in fiscal crisis. In 1991, for the first time in thirty years, the amount allocated by states to higher education actually decreased from the previous year: a drop of $80 million nationally. Measured as a percentage of state budgets, higher education support has been shrinking since 1982.②

In response, tuition has been going up, by thirteen percent on average, at the four-year institutions in 1991. But legislatures are feeling the pressure from students and parents to limit tuition increases. In Ohio, for example, tuition hikes by public universities were capped at seven percent last year. Private schools legally are free to set their own tuition, but they must contend with the discipline of the marketplace, where higher tuition drives potential students to seek lower cost alternatives. Contracted research is a significant source of income at many larger universities. But the last few years have been troubled by scandals over indirect cost recovery and inappropriate expenditures at some of our leading research institutions such as Stanford University. Many schools are facing federal audits and much tighter financial controls on government grants. The net impact of the Clinton administration's budget priorities on federally-sponsored research remains unclear at this point.

For many colleges and universities, private fundraising is seen as one way to close the gap between conventional revenues and expenditure demands. More and more university capital campaigns are being launched, with dollar goals that would have seemed astonishing just a few years ago. [See Table 1] Nor is fundraising confined to private colleges and universities. A recent survey by the Council for Higher Education reveals that by 1986, for the first time, corporate donors split their contributions equally between private and public universities. By 1988, the state-assisted schools actually had moved ahead of private ones in securing corporate support.③

How are academic libraries doing in the fundraising game? Good comparative data on library fundraising is in short supply, but there is plenty of anecdotal evidence to suggest that all too often libraries do not fare well in university capital campaigns. Often there is no established dollar goal at all for the library. In other cases the library goal is much too small. In still other cases, the campus-wide campaign succeeds brilliantly, while the library is left far short of achieving its own goal.

Unfortunately, library administrators enter the fundraising arena with some distinct disadvantages or **strategic liabilities.** With more and more institutions playing the fundraising game, the competition for funds is getting fierce. Academic libraries must compete against not only other philanthropic organizations outside the university but with other units on their own campuses

---

① Co-author: Gary A. Hunt. Presented at the ACRL Chapters Council meeting, held at the ALA Midwinter Conference in Denver, Colorado, on January 25, 1993.

② Anthony DePalma. "Bad times force universities to re-think what they are." *New York Times*. February 3, 1992: Section A, 1.

③ Maria Newman. "As states cut aid, public colleges work harder for private money." *New York Times*. March 29, 1993: Section A.

for attention by the development office, assistance by the president, and access to donors. In this competition, **libraries are at a disadvantage because they have no alumni base of their own.**

Unlike the colleges, schools, and teaching departments on campus, the library does not grant degrees. The intellectual, professional, and human bonds that exist between former students and their teachers are simply not present. In the language of politics, support for the library tends to be "broad but shallow". Everyone has warm feelings about the library, but few are passionately devoted to us. We have a "fuzzy image", both with donors and with development office staff. The negatives are low, but the positives are weak. People don't know us very well, so they easily can be drawn to other candidates with a clearer message and a more direct appeal for their philanthropic support. Finally, librarians must combat the "Bottomless Pit Syndrome", the perception that no amount of money is ever enough to purchase all the books, all the periodicals, all the media resources, and all the databases we claim to need. Donors, like chief academic officers, want to know what their dollars will accomplish in concrete, human terms.

To overcome these strategic liabilities and enjoy success in the fundraising game, library administrators must be prepared to follow certain proven techniques that have worked for others. We have summarized our own experience and that of other successful library fundraisers into what we call the **ten principles for successful fundraising.** If you follow the concepts embodied here, you will be in an excellent position to raise money for your library.

ONE: Develop a positive image

The very first question to ask before launching a fundraising program is whether your library has a strong positive image and a clear plan for the future. If the answer is "no," you should address this issue **before** trying to raise funds. There are many libraries that should not even attempt fundraising until they have addressed more basic problems.

Table 1 Some Recent Capital Campaigns

Princeton University	$410 million
Stanford University	$1.1 billion
Univ. of Pennsylvania	$1 billion
Columbia University	$1 billion
Cornell University	$1.25 billion
Yale University	$1.5 billion
Harvard University	$2 billion

Source: *The Chronicle of Higher Education*, **13 May 1992: A32**

Assuming that your reputation is solid, you still must take steps to communicate the library's accomplishments to the public in order to prepare the way for successful fundraising. Jerry Campbell of Duke University Library has a rule-of-thumb that he wants to see at least one good story about the library each month in the local papers, the student paper, the alumni newsletter, or the national press. You might want to conduct a year-long publicity campaign, building and sharpening the library's public image, before launching a major fundraising effort of any kind. If you are in doubt about your image, develop your annual giving program, both as a means of testing the waters and as a way to promote the library's reputation and identify future donors.

TWO: Find your market niche

Even if your image generally is good, people won't give just because they feel warmly toward you. They need to know who you are and what you are doing. Your image must be both positive and clear. You need to achieve product definition and discover your market niche within the philanthropic community. Always remember that there are many good causes to support, ranging from AIDS research, to homelessness, to disaster relief, to church and synagogue, to the local symphony, to the Girl Scouts. Why should a donor want to support you?

It is critical to begin with a careful self-examination of your library's unique contributions to society. Discover what it is that you do especially well. Identify the **specific accomplishments** that make you stand out from other libraries, as well as from other units on campus. How does your library promote such things as student learning, faculty teaching, research discovery and creative activity, or cultural enrichment of the community? Is there anything unusual or unique about your service mission? Do you meet certain information needs outside the campus community that set you apart? Libraries sometimes have a way of emphasizing their resources: how many volumes they have, what treasures they own in special collections, how many periodical subscriptions they carry. Donors rarely are interested in these things. They want to hear about what you are doing to help people.

Always remember that in the mind of a typical donor, libraries do not have needs. People have needs that libraries can satisfy. **The trick is to find out how you are satisfying important human needs and then dramatize those accomplishments in ways that donors can appreciate.**

After you have done some soul-searching to clarify your mission, identify what you perceive to be your strengths and weaknesses. It can be very helpful to conduct a market survey as a kind of reality check to find out what people on the outside think about you. Sometimes these are called "campaign feasibility studies", because the results can tell you whether it is possible to conduct the campaign in the first place. They also can help determine where to set the dollar goal for a campaign, and what specific themes you should emphasize to reach your philanthropic market.

In general, the purpose of a feasibility study is to get organized feedback from important external constituents as to how they perceive the library. Usually this information is gathered from a combination of written questionnaires, followed up either by focus group discussions or one-on-one interviews. The selection of people to be interviewed is crucial. They should include a cross-section of faculty, staff, alumni, friends, community leaders, friend's board members, and other constituents who may be potential donors. What you are trying to discover in the process is: what are their overall feelings about the library? What do they most like and dislike? How do their feelings about the library compare to the way they feel about possible competing charities that may hold a claim on their support? Under what circumstances might they be persuaded to give to the library? Would they be willing to take on a leadership role in the campaign by urging others to give? What are their specific motivators: that is, what projects or programs or initiatives in the library would really turn them on and make them want to get involved in the campaign? What do they think would excite others to do the same?

Normally, interviews of between fifty and seventy well-chosen individuals will provide fairly accurate information. Generally you want to have the interviews conducted by an outside consultant, or at least by someone who is not directly connected with the library, so that the subjects feel free to respond honestly to the questions. You need to make it clear that this is not a fundraising visit, but only an information-gathering exercise. And, of course, you need to thank everyone who participates.

The findings of the market survey should be used to set the dollar goal for the campaign and shape its major themes. You may find, for example, that building a collection endowment provokes little interest outside the institution, but that new information technologies have a strong appeal and are in some ways better understood by local business leaders than by your own faculty. This may not mean that you should give up trying to endow the collections, but it certainly will influence the way you market your campaign.

THREE: Pick the best leadership

Fundraising is necessarily a team undertaking. In addition to the key library administrators and development officers, a large number of **volunteers** are needed. They must work together to ensure the success of any fundraising program. Volunteers must be recruited early. They can be recruited from previous donors, library friends and supporters, community and civic leaders. In a university setting, they also may come from boards of trustees, loyal alumni, university administrators, faculty, staff, and students. The quality of the volunteer leadership often can make or break a fundraising campaign. Strong leaders make their own commitments first and then convince others to follow suit. They must enjoy the respect of their peers. It will pay big dividends later on if, at the outset, you **recruit leaders who have either "influence" or "affluence", preferably both.**

One example which was experienced by the co-authors was a gentleman who was a former member of the Ohio University Board of Trustees and once served as its chair. Because of his previous interest in the Library, he was recruited to be a member of the Library's major gift committee. To set an example, he made a pledge of a $40,000 cash gift to be paid in five annual installments. Since his wife was a former City Councilwoman in Cincinnati, and both remain active in civic affairs, we discussed with them the possibility of launching a "mini-campaign" in Cincinnati to match their gift with an equal amount, for a total of $80,000. With their introduction, we met and recruited a foundation executive in Cincinnati to help us plan the campaign. Within a period of six months we raised the matching amount in honor of the couple.

Although there may be many forms of campaign organization, volunteers are needed for leadership gifts (each $500,000 and up), major gifts (each between $100,000 and $500,000), special gifts (each between $10,000 to $100,000), and general gifts (any amount under $10,000). When setting the realistic dollar goal of a campaign, the number of gifts in each category as well as the number of volunteers who can be relied on should be estimated carefully. Interviews with key donors and volunteers should be a part of the external audit mentioned earlier.

FOUR: Target prospects carefully

When targeting donor prospects, one must keep in mind the fact that a high percentage of gifts in a fundraising campaign comes from individual donors. Using the current $100 million capital campaign of Ohio University as an example, about sixty-five percent of the dollars raised have come from individual donors, thirty percent from foundations and corporations, and five percent from government and other organizations.

Based on your feasibility study, you should construct a **gift table** for your campaign. [See Table 2] Note that the top few gifts in the leadership and major categories account for two-thirds of the total package. This lopsided ratio is commonly observed in fundraising. A rule of thumb is that eighty percent of the funds will come from just twenty percent of the donors. Other fundraising experts refer to the so-called "Rule of Thirds": about one-third of the dollars raised come from the top 10 to 15 donors; the second one-third come from the next 100 to 125 donors; and the last one-third come from all other donors combined.

Table 2 THE OHIO UNIVERSITY THIRD CENTURY CAMPAIGN GIFT TABLE
$6 Million Goal University Library

	Number of Gifts	Gift Level	Total Required	Cumulative Total	%
Leadership Gifts	1	1,000,000	1,000,000	1,000,000	
	2	500,000	1,000,000	2,000,000	33.3
Major Gifts	4	250,000	1,000,000	3,000,000	
	10	100,000	1,000,000	4,000,000	66.6
Special Gifts	20	50,000	1,000,000	5,000,000	
	50	10,000	500,000	5,500,000	91.6
General Gifts, Annual Support & all other gifts	all others	up to 10,000	500,000	6,000,000	100.0

Because of these characteristics common to capital campaigns, it is very important to organize your time to emphasize the leadership donors. Remember that a capital campaign can be defined as an intensive, time-limited project to raise a large amount of money. To have any hope of achieving the goal, one must target prospects carefully and then focus "like a laser beam" on the most promising in the group. Most fundraising campaigns develop a ranked list and begin their efforts at the top. ①

FIVE: Face the costs honestly

The success of any fundraising effort requires a total institutional commitment involving both time and money. The time required by the library director, development officers, assigned staff, and volunteers to conduct a successful capital campaign will be considerable. Even with the help of others, it is easy for a director to spend up to twenty percent of her or his time on fundraising activities.

In terms of dollar costs, one must recognize that there is substantial truth in the old adage that "it takes money to raise money". Depending on the type of fundraising involved, it will cost anywhere between three to thirty-seven percent of each dollar raised. Annual giving programs are the most expensive (from 11 to 37 percent); major gifts, 5 to 11 percent; corporate gifts, 3 to 11 percent; deferred gifts, 0.6 to 3 percent; while foundation gifts, a mere 0.5 to 2 percent. The overall fundraising cost, for all types combined, is about twelve percent, or twelve cents for each dollar rose. ②

SIX: Concentrate on relationships

Creating and maintaining a good relationship with potential donors is of critical importance in fundraising. It is relationships that raise money, especially when it comes to major gifts. This is where most of the time of the library director and the development staff is spent. They must spend enough time with volunteer leaders and highly ranked prospects to cultivate a good relationship based on mutual respect and trust. Such a relationship may lead to a lasting friendship. At times, the use of well-placed connections will be very useful in making the initial contact. This can be done through the introduction of a highly respected volunteer or someone serving on the board of a corporation or foundation. By careful research, one often can find such connections.

In fundraising, the process of developing a relationship is referred to as "cultivation." Before the actual cultivation, a plan for cultivation and solicitation should be devised. In the case of prospects with which you do not already enjoy a strong relationship, a minimum of four contacts is recommended before the actual solicitation is made. These contacts can be made by development staff, volunteers, the library director, and possibly others. The visits may be carried out by a team of two. After each visit, a brief contact report should be completed in order to record the activity type (phone, personal visit, alumni event, campus visit, other) and status (identification, cultivation, solicitation, pending, stewardship, etc.). The contact report also should state the next step and set a date for follow-up.

SEVEN: Make the ask

After a donor prospect has been properly cultivated, the next step, using fundraising terminology, is the "solicitation". In actual practice, fundraisers prefer to ask for an investment in the library for the benefit of the society. **Making them ask is the most difficult but also the most challenging step in fundraising.** Normally, at this stage, a donor prospect is ready to be asked and may already expect that this is coming. Some donors may make a donation of a small amount even before being asked. But this sort of "preemptive gift" should not preclude you from asking again for a larger gift, based on the giving capacity rating.

---

① There are several methods which can be used to identify your top prospects and establish priority rankings. These include the "Weighted Method for Giving Capacity", the "Weighted Method for Interest Level", and the "Income/Asset Gift Rating Formula". For details, see pp. 75 – 6 in our book, *Fund Raising for the 90s*.

② Thomas E. Broce. *Fund Raising: The Guide to Raising Money from Private Sources*. Norman, OK: University of Oklahoma Press, 1979: 188.

When making them ask, one must state the amount asked, the purpose and use of the gift, the method of recognition, and the benefits and impacts of the gift to the institution and the society. In the case of large solicitations, you well may wish to summarize the gift request in the form of a written proposal; but it should always be presented orally in a face-to-face meeting. It may take more than one session to secure the contribution and to have a gift agreement form signed.

EIGHT: Listen and be patient

If you have done your homework, rating the donor at the proper level and taking time to cultivate him or her, you should seldom get a flat-out refusal. But you may get evasions and equivocations. Don't get discouraged. An experienced development person is one who knows when to give up and when to persist. Listen carefully for the reasons behind the prospect's reluctance, and be prepared to suggest alternatives. Is it lack of motivation? Then find ways to get the donor more involved in your program. Is it a perceived lack of funds? Try to explore alternative ways of making the gift in the amount you are seeking. There's an old saying that donors are supposed to "give until it hurts". But a clever fundraiser knows how to administer the novocaine so it doesn't hurt at all. And **planned giving** is one way to lessen the pain.

Listed below are some of the popular deferred giving plans:
- Bequest in will.
- Life insurance policy.
- Gift of stock or security.
- Gift annuity.
- Charitable remainder annuity trust.
- Charitable remainder unitrust.
- Life income contract.
- Life estate contract.
- Short term charitable trust.

There are many ways that one can make an investment. Each donor prospect may find an acceptable way to give. Even though an outright cash gift is always preferred, it may be possible to secure a much larger gift in the form of a multi-year pledge, a term life insurance policy made out to your institution, a trust agreement of some kind, or a bequest. Some gifts may be in the form of gifts-in-kind, especially in the case of libraries. Based on the experience of Ohio University's Third Century Campaign, of the $105 million raised so far, outright cash gifts account for 42 percent, bequests 27.5 percent, pledges 14 percent, gifts-in-kind 9 percent, life insurance 4 percent, and trust agreements 3.5 percent.

Professional development staff should be able to suggest various planned giving options to prospective donors and explain their advantages and disadvantages based on the donor's particular circumstances. Often, tax considerations are of paramount importance in this area, so it is wise to have an expert available to conduct the final negotiations.

NINE: Support the cause yourself

Often a donor will ask what you have done yourself to support the library's fundraising effort. In fact there are two aspects to this question: what have you done personally, and what has the library staff done collectively? Your own personal commitment to the campaign should be made early. The same applies to staff, especially those who work directly with prospects. Most people understand that librarians do not have a lot of money. What counts is not the dollar amount, but the number of people on your staff who are participating. During our own campaign at Ohio University Library, we were very proud to have had one of the highest participation rates of any area on campus: over seventy-five percent. We advertised this fact to potential donors as a way of demonstrating the high morale in the library and the enthusiasm we all felt for what we were trying to accomplish.

TEN: Never forget a donor

Have you ever met someone who makes a great first impression, then disappoints you later on with his aloofness and lack of concern? We all have had that experience in personal relationships, and donors experience it as well. From their point of view, charities come on like gangbusters until the gift is made, then one of two things happen: either they fade away or else they keep pestering them incessantly for more money before the ink has had a chance to dry on their last check.

Neither of these behaviors is conducive to building a good relationship. Both strike the donor as selfish. What you want to provide your donors is a sense of **community and shared purpose**. You want them to feel like participants in the enterprise, and you want them to understand that their gifts are really making a difference to the library.

Most capital campaigns draw the library director and development staff into an intense whirl of fundraising activity, meeting people of wealth and influence from the community, the region, and across the nation. From these contacts you will assemble a major gifts committee. As the gifts begin to materialize, you will involve these new friends in your stewardship program, recognizing their support in appropriate ways and inducting them into gift societies. You will correspond with them on a regular basis, at least annually, to keep them informed of how their funds are being used and how the library is doing.

Donors want to be kept informed about the library, and they want to know in specific terms how their support has made a difference. We call this "return on investment", and in our book we talk at some length about how to create this feeling for donors. In fact, one of the advantages libraries have over other organizations is the great variety of ways to establish personal connections with donors. Books are very concrete things, and attaching your name to one with a bookplate still holds a lot of appeal. Libraries have many departments, reading areas, computer laboratories, and collections. They are filled with different kinds of equipment. All of these things provide excellent naming opportunities for donors at all levels, from a thousand dollars to a million dollars or more.

But actually these gift recognition programs are only one aspect of **donor stewardship**. They are only one way to provide return on investment. The heart of good stewardship is a sound campaign communications strategy designed to keep your various publics regularly informed about the progress of the campaign and to support particular objectives. Campaign publications can take the form of printed materials (newsletters, promotional brochures, press releases) as well as multi-media productions (slide shows or video). Special events also are a form of stewardship. Gala events often are held to launch a campaign, as well as to celebrate its successful conclusion. In the period between, it is common to bring together the volunteer leadership with the campaign staff at regular intervals for events that combine a little business, a little education or consciousness rising about the institution, a little companionship, and a little entertainment. Effective stewardship must rely on good gift accounting systems so that donors can be assured that their gifts are being promptly acknowledged and put to their proper uses. The management of funds, especially endowments, trusts, and planned giving arrangements, must be conducted in ways that inspire the confidence of the donor.

Finally, a truly successful campaign always should lay the groundwork for future fundraising. A good way to do this is to create a **constituent society** for the library similar to those that are being developed for academic colleges and schools on many university campuses. At many larger universities, academic colleges and departments are organizing national "boards of visitors," consisting of prominent alumni who are brought back to campus on a regular basis to be updated on the direction of the program and consult with the dean. These same individuals are available to transition to a fundraising mode when planning starts for the next capital campaign.

As you carry out the activities of your campaign, always try to work as a network builder. Find ways to draw your supporters together to meet one another. Convey a sense that you value their participation in library affairs beyond just giving money. When the campaign is over, it will be a simple matter to convert your major gifts committee into a "board of visitors" or a "national advisory council". Then you will have created the nucleus of a local, regional, or national support network both to increase annual giving levels during the post-campaign years and to lay the groundwork for the next big capital campaign.

We regard the expanding role of private fundraising in higher education, especially in the context of the major capital campaign, as an exciting opportunity for academic libraries. Armed with these ten principles for successful fundraising, you should be able to sally forth and do battle in the fundraising arena. Best of luck in your own fundraising efforts!

(Published in *The Bottom Line*, V. 6, No. 3/4, Winter 1992/Spring 1993: pp. 27 – 33. Also Published in *Sponsoring fur Bibliotheken*, edited by Rolf Busch. Berlin: Deutsches Bibliotheksinstiut, 1997: pp. 130 – 141.)

巴布亚新几内亚发展高等院校图书馆

Developing Higher Education Libraries in Papua New Guinea[①]

INTRODUCTION

A recent article in *Information Development* outlined the main recommendations of a library development plan for Papua New Guinea, prepared as an outcome of a consultancy by Dr. D. E. K. Wijasuriya.[②] That plan was very much concerned with the improvement of the nation's public library services, with particular emphasis on the rural areas. As a result of this emphasis, certain other sectors within the library field were not widely commented on. The recommendations of the plan had been discussed and accepted by May 1991. Fortunately, slightly later in 1991, it was possible to have a further study undertaken on another important library sector—that of libraries within higher education institutions. The higher education libraries study and its main recommendations are outlined in the present paper as a natural supplement to the previous article.

Within Papua New Guinea a draft National Library and Information Services Policy has been prepared as a consequence of the Wijasuriya report by a Working Party of the Library Council. Another interesting development that is anticipated is the passing of a Library and Archives Act—a very comprehensive piece of legislation.

The higher education libraries sector is of great importance given the very limited resources of the present public library services.[③] The major information resources of Papua New Guinea are to be found in the country's higher education institutions. Within these there are collection strengths and centres of excellence, but these are often not widely used or known outside the institutional user community. In addition to strengths there are also deficiencies in resources and some overlap and duplication that need to be corrected through appropriate planning measures to enhance the value of the information resources for the national benefit.

BACKGROUND

Papua New Guinea counts as a large country amongst the South Pacific island states. However, compared to countries in other regions, the population is small, at a 1990 Census estimate of 3,529,538 persons. Despite this, the higher education sector in Papua New Guinea is characterized by a large number of small and generally inefficient institutions—an outcome of its colonial past which it has not yet been possible to rationalize. There has been much concern shown over the system and reports and recommendations for its improvement have been made-but little has been achieved in the way of results. The latest investigation has been the work behind the 1990 National Higher Education Plan produced by the Commission for Higher Education of the Papua New Guinea government.[④] There are sixty-two institutions within the higher education sector, comprising:

· pre-service tertiary education to develop human and personal skills directly related to productive activities (technical and primary industry colleges)

· pre-service technical education to develop skilled personnel to work in primary health and general education (paramedical and teaching colleges)

[①] Co-author: John Evans.

[②] Wijasuriya, D. E. K. and Evans, J. "Public library development in Papua New Guinea." *Information Development*. V. 8, No. 1, January 1992: 16-21.

[③] Evans, J. "Public library service in Papua New Guinea-the poor get poorer." *Libraries Alone*. V. 2, No. 1, 1990: 21-28.

[④] Papua New Guinea. "Commission for Higher Education." *National Higher Education Plan*. Waigani, 1990.

· pre-service tertiary academic and professional education that serves as the basis for the scientific, artistic, teaching, legal, health, technological and other professions (universities)

While the National Higher Education Plan was in draft form it was widely circulated for comment amongst institutions within the country. It was during this phase that the University of Papua New Guinea expressed disquiet at the lack of any coverage of the role of libraries and their resources within the Higher Education Plan. Here it should be noted that there are very few reports on the higher education libraries in Papua New Guinea—except for occasional reports on the two universities and their libraries.

The only comprehensive sectoral report available is that by Miles Jackson on teachers' college libraries,① which dates from 1981. The effect of this report has been reviewed by Calvert.② Concern about their library resources remains an issue amongst the teachers' training colleges in Papua New Guinea.

The views of the University as to the library element of the Higher Education Plan were made known to the Commission for Higher Education, but libraries are still not mentioned in the published plan. However, in correspondence, Dr. Naomi Martin, the Chairperson of the Commission, indicated in late 1990 that the Commission wished this omission to be rectified by the provision of a separate detailed report and recommendations on library resources in institutions of higher education. The second author of this paper was initially asked to produce such a report. However, it was maintained from the outset that an external review would be preferable. This would allow for recent developments in networks and computerization achieved elsewhere to be more readily taken into account and helps to open up the rather closed Papua New Guinea library system, which, because of the isolation of the country, sees few visitors and is isolated from new ideas.

In accordance with this idea attempts were made by the Commission for Higher Education to obtain the services of an external reviewer who could visit the country and provide such a new outlook. Fortunately, it was possible to find a consultant who was both interested in the assignment and able to make the visit at relatively short notice. The Asia Foundation, through its Suva office, generously provided a grant for the work on this project.

Aims, scope and benefits of the planning exercise

The agreed aim of the consultancy was: to undertake a survey of higher education information resources in Papua New Guinea. The survey was to identify strengths and centres of excellence, suggest norms for the upgrading of resources, and develop guidelines for more effective resource sharing through the phased introduction of automation and networking and the creation of a database of information resources.

The eventual creation of a centralized database of information resources will be of considerable benefit to the higher education institutions and also to private and public sector agencies and will assist them in contributing to the development process. Higher education information resources which are coordinated, further upgraded and conveniently accessible can provide effective support for key development sectors in Papua New Guinea as well as more effectively serve teaching and research requirements.

The major anticipated benefits of the project are:
· strengthened support for quality academic programmes
· identification of resources and highlighting of collection strengths and deficiencies
· development of relevant norms for progressive and systematic improvement of resources
· creation of a database of national information resources

---

① Jackson, M. M. *Teachers college libraries in Papua New Guinea*. Honolulu, 1981.
② Calvert, P. "Teachers college libraries in Papua New Guinea." *Australasian College Libraries*. V. 2, No. 4, November 1984: 151 – 156.

Project activities

The consultancy visit took place from 11 August to 6 September 1991 and the consultant was responsible for the project to the Commission for Higher Education—although, as in the case of the Wijasuriya report, the Library Council of Papua New Guinea also played a role. Despite the limited time available, it was possible to arrange visits to twenty-six of the sixty-two institutions of higher education defined in the Commission's Higher Education Plan. In addition to this a further fifteen non-academic libraries were visited in order to complete the picture. Further information was also collected by means of a questionnaire and through the literature. While many libraries are in the capital of Port Moresby, it is in the provinces that the real difficulties are found and there are many institutions in the provinces. The consultant also visited the provincial capitals of Rabaul, Lee, Madang, Wewak, Goroka and Mount Hagen to take account of the provincial situation.

The preliminary report was produced by 20 September 1991. Entitled "Library development, resource sharing, and networking education institutions in Papua New Guinea" it makes forty recommendations which are detailed below. The preliminary report was faxed to Papua New Guinea allowing early widespread dissemination for responses and comments. This process was completed by mid-December 1991 and twelve written comments were received. The final report[①] was available in Papua New Guinea in early 1992 and is to be published by the Commission for Higher Education. In the final report the number of recommendations has been slightly reduced, to thirty-seven.

Overall findings

The study was able to identify six major library resources within the country, which were suggested as the major building blocks of a potential library and information network. In addition, a small number of special libraries with reasonably good collections were identified. These librarians were within:
- The Department of Agriculture and Livestock
- The Forest Research Institute
- The Institute of Medical Research
- The Port Moresby In-Service College

As to the remaining libraries, the situation could only be described as very sad. The libraries in the teachers' colleges for community school teachers were considered slightly better than those in the agricultural, fisheries or forestry colleges, while the libraries in the nursing and technical colleges were even worse. It was noticeable that the high school libraries were generally better than the libraries of many of the post-secondary institutions. The collections in most of the sub-standard institutions have become outdated owing to a lack of recent relevant purchases, as stocks have been mainly been built up from gifts. Few libraries were able to subscribe to journals and few had audiovisual materials or equipment. Library premises were small and in need of repair and, with the exception of the teachers' colleges, many colleges did not have a full-time trained librarian to run the library. Most libraries evidenced serious signs of neglect by the college administration. However, discussions at the various institutions did indicate a strong desire to improve the current situation-a situation that was noticeable among most sub-sectors.

General explanations for the current desolate situation were given as being:
- decreasing government funding
- lack of economies of scale with too few students and programmes in each college
- absence of trained librarians

---

① Hwa-Wei Lee. "Library development, resource sharing, and networking among higher education institutions in Papua New Guinea: final report and recommendations." Athens, Ohio, December 1991.

· low pay and low status of library positions causing frequent turn-over amongst the staff in post

· lack of support by college administration and inadequate concern for library issues by teaching staff, resulting in a cycle of deprivation

· outdated methods of instruction and learning in the institutions

The net result of this inadequate situation is a poor quality of education received by the students at these institutions—one which could not live up to the name of higher education.

Despite the unfortunate situation encountered, there were also brighter spots that kindled the idea of a possible Papua New Guinea Library and Information Network and a belief that an improvement in higher education library resources could, in fact, take place. These brighter signs were:

· the emphasis on quality higher education as emphasized in the National Higher Education plan

· the existence of centres of excellence within the libraries with little overlap and great complementary strength

· the possibility of a unified national bibliographic database

· a good national telecommunications system

· a spirit of cooperation amongst libraries to share resources

RECOMMENDATIONS OF THE SURVEY REPORT
National approaches to improvement (recommendations 1—6)

Appointment of a Library Services Coordinator within the Commission for Higher Education (recommendations 1-3)

A senior position should be created within the Commission for Higher Education Secretariat for a Library Services Coordinator to plan and coordinate the development of library and information resources in institutions of higher education in Papua New Guinea. This coordinator would be advised by the Library Council and would work with the Department of Education, the National Library and the Office of Libraries and Archives and other related agencies to achieve the desired improvements in library and information resources in the sector. The coordinator would draw up a national development plan for university and college libraries taking into account the recommendations of the report.

National Library role (recommendations 4-5)

The National Library should play a key role in the development of libraries in government agencies and community and high schools, and of public libraries in the capital and the provinces which complement and support the development of libraries in higher education institutions. The Basic standards for college libraries' developed by the National Library need to be re-examined and revised to upgrade the minimum requirements for space, collections, services, staff and funding as well as to add certain performance measurements.

Funding (recommendation 6)

A formula for funding libraries should be developed to ensure that, even in difficult economic times, they will not be stripped of minimum funding. The suggested criterion is that a minimum of 5 percent of the institution's operating budget should be spent for library resources (books, journals, audiovisual materials, etc.). To correct the long-time neglect of the many college libraries in recent years, special funding from the Government should be specifically designated for library improvement.

Development of a Papua New Guinea Library and Information Network (PNGLINET) (recommendations 7-18)

Network structure (recommendations 7-8)

Certain libraries which were identified as having major collections should be recognized as centres of excellence. Adequate funding should be provided for these libraries, each of which has strengths in certain subject areas. Together with the National Library and the Administrative College, these libraries should be considered as major building blocks of a proposed Papua New Guinea Library and Information Network. The proposed network is illustrated in Figure 1. These libraries have little duplication of information resources and could each in their turn serve as the national resource centre for other libraries in the same field of specialization, as illustrated in Figure 1.

Proposed Papua New Guinea Library and Information Network

Government and Public Library and Information Network

| • Government depts. & agencies
• Public libraries
• School libraries
• Continuing education | Comprehensive collection
Bibliographies (online & CD)
PNG Collection
Government publications
A-V materials
Children & YA literature
Archives & Public Records | National Library & National Archives and Public Records |

Research Library and Information Network

| University of PNG Main Library | Comprehensive collection
Reference collection
Bibliographies (online & CD)
Humanities
Law
PNG Collection
Sciences
Social Sciences | • All libraries & researchers
• Law offices & courts
• The Pacific Legal Information Network |

Engineering and Technology Library and Information Network

| • Agricultural colleges
• Fisheries colleges
• Forestry colleges
• Technical colleges
• Research institutes
• Business & industries | Science reference
Agriculture/Forestry/Fisheries
Business
Engineering
Tchnology
Engineering & technology indexes (online & CD) | PNG University of Technology Library |

Medical and Health Library and Information Network

| University of PNG Medical Library | Medical science
Health & allied sciences
Medical/clinical A-V materials
PNG Medical Collection
Medline (online & CD) | • Dept. of Health
• Hospitals
• Nursing schools
• Medical personnel
• Medical research institutes |

Management Library and Information Network

| • Government depts & agencies
• Management firms | Management
Public policy and administration
Development information
Office automation | Administrative College Library |

Education Library and Information Network

| University of PNG Goroka Teachers College Library | Education
Behavioral science
Model school library collection
A-V materials
Curriculum materials
ERIC database(CD) | • Dept. of Education
• Teachers colleges
• Teachers & educators |

National Union Catalog and Databases

International Databases

Figure 1.

Buildings and storage facilities (recommendations 9 – 10)

To house the growing collections of the key libraries, adequate and functional library buildings with sufficient space for growth will need to be provided. These buildings will require temperature and humidity controls for the benefits of collections and users and should be designed to accommodate the proposed computerization plans. Ample seating is also to be planned for. This recommendation springs from the fact that all of the key libraries visited were in urgent need of additional space. However, for the economical storage and preservation of less-used research materials which must be retained, a central storage facility with high-density compact shelving is suggested to be built for the use of all libraries. The contents of the collection in this facility should be recorded both in the local catalogue and in the online union catalogue, for easy search and retrieval when needed.

A well developed library systems software capable of networking for the key libraries should be selected and installed. Selection of the package would be undertaken by a committee of all participating libraries with the advice of an experienced and unbiased consultant. The needs and requirements for the system should be communicated through a planning document and a "request for proposal" prepared by the committee.

To implement this recommendation, capital funding of USD 900,000 for a period of three years, and an annual operating budget of USD 100,000 (adjusted for inflation each year) should be provided, to maintain the collection and make it accessible by computer from remote locations. In addition, for the development of information resources and services there is a need to create a position of systems librarian in each of the six resource libraries.

There should be a national database of the resources within the Papua New Guinea Library and Information Network using the MARC format—which should be developed by the National Library in close adherence to major international standards. The online national union catalogue should contain all resources, including books, serial titles and holdings information, audiovisual materials, indexed journal articles, archival materials, local databases, etc. of the key libraries. The network will serve as the gateway to library and information services outside the country. PACESAT and other advanced telecommunication technologies should be used to access worldwide databases including OCLC, Medline, Dialog, etc.

At an appropriate stage in the development of PNGLINET, a governing structure should be put in place to ensure the full participation of all major resource libraries. The exact form of governing structure and its composition should be decided by the Commission for Higher Education in consultation with other related government agencies. The Library Services Coordinator may serve as Executive Director of PNGLINET for day-to-day operations with adequate operating budget and staffing.

When PNGLINET is operational, it will be necessary to make provision to extend access to other libraries. Procedures will need to be developed and opportunities provided, with central funding, for libraries wishing to join PNGLINET as full participants.

College and other academic libraries (recommendations 19—29)

Remedies for past neglect (recommendations 19-22; 26-29)

The library and information resources in most of the colleges are generally inadequate and major augmentation is necessary to bring each a minimum acceptable standard. As a particular instance, the transition of the community—school teacher's colleges from a two-year to a three-year programme requires that the libraries of these colleges be greatly improved. Major remedial infusions of funding for additional staff and information resources should be considered a priority for a period of five years. Minimum quantitative standards and performance measures should be established and enforced, for example on the basis of the recommendations made at the 1990 Library Workshop.①

As the libraries in the nursing schools, technical colleges, and other special colleges in general show signs of long-standing neglect and impoverishment, major efforts and actions are urgently needed to improve them. Here it is suggested that the Library Services Coordinator of the Commission for Higher Education, working with the appropriate government departments, develop guidelines and minimum standards for these libraries and seek annual funding for them. However, to realize economies of scale, many of the small colleges with inferior programmes and library resources should be merged into larger units or incorporated with the universities or better-established institutions.

Other than this, it is recommended that for each teachers' college library a minimum of 300 new books and twenty audiovisual kits of relevance to the curriculum should be added to the collection each year and at least fifty journal subscriptions be maintained. For each nursing, technical and special library, the minimum requirement should be 150 books, fifteen kits and twenty-five journal subscriptions. These materials are to be specially selected—rather than being happenstance gifts as is often the case at present—to support the curriculum, and should be

---

① Library Workshop, 18-24 March 1990. *Report.* Port Moresby, 1990.

catalogued for easy access. Since some 90 percent of the collections of most of the libraries were outdated, major attention needs to be paid to acquisitions and cataloguing. Effective use of shared acquisitions and cataloguing could afford savings in manpower and costs. Vendors and the National Library could provide such services.

Further recommendations relate to the provision of an audiovisual room and equipment and to the adequacy of college library buildings, equipment and furniture. A survey of the situation is called for.

Staffing and training (recommendations 23 – 25)

A minimum of one full-time qualified librarian and two trained assistants is required for every teachers' college library, and a minimum of one full-time qualified librarian and one trained assistant for each of the technical, nursing and special colleges. This goal is suggested for achievement by 1997. The position classifications and salary scales of library staff should be uniform and comparable to those of teaching staff with equal educational requirements and qualifications. There needs to a clear career path for the promotion and movement of both professional and support library staff. The staff classification and fringe benefits should be made equitable with university libraries.

Opportunities for in-service training and continuing education should be made available to college librarians to help them acquire new knowledge and skills suitable for modern library and information services. The existing programmes in the Department of Library and Information Studies, University of Papua New Guinea should be expanded to meet such needs.

Other issues (recommendations 30—40)

Statistics (recommendations 30 – 31)

The Library Services Coordinator should develop a system for the collection of annual statistics and other relevant information to be stored in a computer and used for management purposes. A directory of library and information resources in higher education institutions should be published annually. Similar data and directories for all government, public, special and school libraries should be collected and kept by the National Library.

Incentive for resource sharing (recommendation 32)

Those libraries with net interlibrary lending should receive a subsidy of 5 kina (approx USD 5.00) per item from a special fund established by the Government.

Development of publications (recommendation 33)

The National Library and the Department of Education should promote indigenous publications in all subjects, especially for children and young adult audiences.

Library literacy and model collections (recommendations 34 – 36)

Instruction in library and learning skills should be a part of the regular college curriculum and available to all students. This is considered especially important for those college students who will be transmitting these skills to future generations. It is recommended that the Department of Education and the Commission for Higher Education develop necessary guidelines and implementation plans for such library instruction.

There should also be assistance from the Department of Education and the National Library in the development of model collections for school libraries as future teachers need to be familiar with such collections. Such model collections should also be placed in every community (or primary) school library in the country and updated annually. At the High School Level the Department of Education, the National Library and the Goroka Teachers' College should develop a model collection for all the high school libraries. Such a collection to be placed in each high school library and updated annually.

University Extension Centres (recommendation 37)

As the University of Papua New Guinea has a network of University Extension Centres which it is intended will cover all provinces eventually, it was thought advisable to make some recommendations within the higher education libraries plan as to the future of library development for these centres. The application of this recommendation will vary according to the circumstances of the individual province, but it is suggested that the library in some centres should be ideally be established as a cultural centre combining the public library, the vocational centre library, and the University Centre library in one joint facility. Since the funding of all these is borne by the provincial government such a shared facility will eliminate unnecessary duplication and be more cost-effective. Both the National Library and University of Papua New Guinea Library should assist in the design and establishment of these cultural centres.

CONCLUSION

Within the higher education library sector, as in the public library sector, dramatic efforts are needed to compensate for past deficiencies and to lay the foundations of networking and resource sharing. It is hoped that the recommendations outlined will, if carefully considered, lead to such efforts being made and to the very necessary plans being laid for a phased introduction of library networking, to allow for effective sharing of resources and much improved library services. Discussions on these issues will result from the formal publication of the report. Improvements will have to be undertaken in the face of the very real economic and financial difficulties facing the country. Improvement in the library infrastructure is essential to meet the vision of the National Higher Education Plan, as the quality of education in the institutions is largely dependent on the strengths of their respective library and information resources. Only thus will the appropriate and much needed quality human resources become available for Papua New Guinea's further economic and social development.

(Published in *Information Development*. V. 8, No. 2, November 1992: pp. 221 – 227.)

中国教育院校图书馆与信息管理研修班

Workshops and Consultation on the Management of Libraries and Information for the Institutes of Education in China[①]

I. Introduction and Objectives

Both lecturers/consultants, Angela Lew of California State University at Northridge and Hwa-Wei Lee of Ohio University, were pleased for the opportunity to offer the workshop and consultation assignments in China under the joint sponsorship of the China Institute of the California State University at Northridge (CSUN), which served as our primary contact in the United States, and the State Education Commission of the People's Republic of China. The assignment was a part of the Teacher Training Project funded by a World Bank loan.

The assignment included a two-week workshop in Tianjin, on the **Management of Libraries and Information**, designed for senior librarians from various institutes of education in many parts of China and two one-week workshops, one each in Beijing and Shanghai, designed for the library staff of institutes of education at both the city and district levels of the two largest cities. In all three places, extensive consultation on library automation, building planning, collection management, user services, staff development, identification of special area of strength, fund-raising, etc. were also given to the libraries of each host institute.

An outline of the course contents (see Appendix 1) and the lecture notes (see Appendix 5) were prepared in advance and were sent to the Tianjin Institute of Education about two months prior to our arrival. The course outline was used by all three host institutions (Tianjin Institute of Education, Beijing Institute of Education, and Shanghai Institute of Education) to prepare the respective workshop schedules (see Appendix 2).

It is to be noted that there are 216 institutes of education (IOE) in China—many at the provincial and district levels. Our three host IOEs are leaders and serve as models for others. Their libraries have been designated as national clearinghouses for libraries in other IOEs.

According to the original project document (Project NO.: 1908-CHA), the aim and objectives of the assignment for the lecturers/consultants were:

Two experts will be invited and assigned by the State Education Commission to Beijing Institute of Education—two weeks for consultancy and two weeks for a seminar. The aim of consultancy is to improve theoretical level and working method and to help Beijing Institute of Education build inquiry system of books and reference materials. The objectives of the seminar are to introduce significance, scope and method of work in the field of educational information system and [to] do training work about information collection, data processing and data transferring etc.

The document further specifies the main functions of the two experts as follows:
1) help Beijing Institute of Education build a modern information center of education;
2) analyze and instruct the library management of the institute;
3) supply high-quality materials about modern techniques to the library of the institute;
4) help [the] institute to build library inquiry system by theoretic consultation and technical support; [and]
5) instruct information staff to carry on all kinds of practice in the field of management of

---

[①] Co-author: Angela Lew. The workshops were held in Tianjin, Beijing, and Shanghai, July 11 to August 8, 1993. It is Part of A World Bank Funded Teacher Training Project.

books and reference materials.

During subsequent contacts with CSUN and China, the project was expanded to include Tianjin and Shanghai, and the number of workshops and consultation was tripled. The total time for the assignment remained four weeks. These changes were welcomed by the lecturers/consultants and were seen as a better way to reach out to more IOEs in China which could benefit from the workshops and consultancy. As a direct result of these changes, the schedules for the lecturers/consultants became very full throughout the four-week period.

II. Description of the Workshops and Consultation

During the planning stage, the lecturers/consultants were informed about the changes in the original plan. Below is a brief report of the actual project activities.

1. Dates and Locations

The dates and locations of the three workshops and consultation were:
1) July 12 - 24, 1993, at Tianjin IOE;
2) July 26 - 31, 1993, at Beijing IOE;
3) August 2 - 7, 1993, at Shanghai IOE.

2. Participants

(1) In Tianjin, the workshop was attended by senior librarians and information specialists from many parts of China. Appendix 3.1 lists 48 registered participants, including a large number from remote regions of China such as Hunan, Qinghai, Sichuan, Xinjiang, Yunnan, and elsewhere. At least 10 more non-registered participants came from other academic and special libraries in Tianjin.

(2) In Beijing, the workshop participants were mainly from the Beijing IOE and the Beijing Institute of Educational Administration. These two institutes are to be merged in 1994. Appendix 3.2 lists the names of 25 participants.

(3) In Shanghai, the workshop participants included 10 library staff from the Shanghai IOE and an estimated 40 other librarians and information specialists from 25 other district level IOEs in Shanghai City. Appendix 3.3 lists only the names of those from the Shanghai IOE.

3. Scheduling and Logistical Support

In all three locations, the schedules were well constructed and able to accommodate the various local needs. (see Appendix 2). For workshops, in general, each morning was designated for lectures by the two lecturers and each afternoon, for presentation of videotapes and slides followed by discussions.

Despite the best of efforts of the Tianjin host, the lecture room at Tianjin IOE was far from satisfactory. It had no air conditioning and no curtains to darken the room for A-V presentations. Noise from construction work outside the building was quite disruptive at times. Dust caused by the construction was everywhere. In Beijing and Shanghai, the conditions were much better. The rooms used for the workshops were air conditioned and were equipped for A-V presentations.

Equipment for showing transparencies, slides, and videotapes was readily available in all three places. All also provided a microphone system for use by the lecturers. Unfortunately, electric power outrages occurred at least once at each place—adding an obstacle to the effective use of A/V materials.

Other than the physical conditions, logistical support by all three hosts was excellent. Library directors and key staff of the host institutes went out their way to make certain that we had the best support possible to carry out our assignments.

4. Brief Description of the Workshop Contents

At the workshop in Tianjin, lectures covered the following ten topics:

1) The development of modern libraries and future trends;
2) The management functions of libraries;
3) The management techniques of libraries;
4) Collection development in libraries;
5) Users services and education;
6) Technical services;
7) Library automation and methods;
8) Library cooperation and networking;
9) Library construction and facility planning;
10) Current status of higher education libraries in Taiwan and the Asian-Pacific region.

Attempts were made by the lecturers to balance the theories and practices of modern librarianship with special attention given to the needs and conditions of libraries in IOEs in China.

Through the arrangement of Tianjin IOE, the workshop also included three excellent presentations by leading librarians from other university libraries in Tianjin. These presentations were:

1) Collection development in Chinese university libraries and statistical comparison (By Mr. Cao Huan Xu, Deputy Director, Nankai University Library);
2) User services in Chinese university Libraries (By Ms. Ma Zhi Qing, Deputy Director, Tianjin University Library);
3) Comparison of university libraries between China and U. S. (By Professor Feng Cheng Bo, Director of Nankai University Library);

Complementing these presentations were visits to the libraries of Nankai and Tianjin Universities, the two best in Tianjin. Through these visits, participants were able to connect the lectures and actual library practices in two well established libraries in China.

At the workshop in Beijing, a somewhat modified and condensed schedule was adopted to include the following eight topics:

1) Current status of academic libraries (including colleges of education);
2) Introduction to technical services;
3) The management functions of academic libraries;
4) Introduction to user services;
5) The management techniques of academic libraries;
6) Organization of instructional materials of primary and secondary schools, development of information resources to support teaching, etc. ;
7) Library construction and facility planning;
8) The education and training of school librarians and media specialists in the U. S.

Mr. Du Fang Cang, Deputy Director of the Library and Information Center, Beijing Institute of Education, also gave a detailed presentation on the current status and future direction of the libraries and information centers in the institutes of education in China.

At the Shanghai workshop, the following seven topics were covered:

1) Status of academic libraries in the U. S. ;
2) Technical services in American academic libraries;
3) Management functions and techniques in academic libraries;
4) User services and the influence of automation upon information services;
5) Library building and facility planning;
6) Current status of libraries in Taiwan and the Asian and Pacific region;
7) Current status of libraries or learning resources centers in American primary and secondary schools.

5. Living Conditions, Communications and Transportation

For the lecturers/consultants, the living conditions in all three places were adequate and satisfactory. In Tianjin, we stayed at the Guest House of Nankai University. In Beijing, we stayed at the Guest House of Peking University. Both campuses are most beautiful and located not far from the workshop site. In Shanghai, we stayed at the Guest House of Shanghai IOE which was quite convenient and well located.

We noticed, however, that the living condition for the participants in Tianjin was poor. The most serious problem was mosquitoes. Many participants complained of lack of sleep and requested mosquito netting. The problem was not solved until near the end of the workshop. The heavy dust and noise caused by construction work on the campus was also quite annoying.

Communications with our host IOEs, both prior to and during our workshops and consultation, were prompt and effective. We were highly impressed by the responsiveness of our hosts despite the limited telephone and telefacsimile facilities in China.

In all three locations, our hosts met us upon our arrival either by train or by plane and saw us off at our departure. In Tianjin, we were picked up from and returned to our housing by car each day. In Beijing, we used taxies most of the time and found these quite convenient.

6. The Impact of Our Workshops and Consultation

From all indications, we are confident that all three workshops and consultation were successful and well received. Some of the important indicators are:

1) High and sustained attendance throughout each workshop despite the uncomfortable weather in July and August in Tianjin, Beijing, and Shanghai;

2) Enthusiastic participation by most of the participants in both the lecture and discussion sessions as well as the quality of questions and contributions of participants;

3) Positive feedbacks from all host institutes and participants during and after each workshop and consultation.

At the Tianjin workshop, many of the participants came from remote regions of China. We were told by some that we were the first foreign experts they have met and the workshop was an unique experience for them.

In all three places, we were met by the president of each host institute. Our consultation with other officials, library directors and staff were extensive and highly constructive. The wide range of topics covered in the consultation included the following:

1) Preparation for library automation, including the selection of a software package and the creation of cataloging and circulation databases;

2) Planning of library building and facilities;

3) Development of information resources and services with particular interest in those areas where income can be generated;

4) Identifying areas of strength to create specialties which may be of national significance;

5) Importance of library cooperation and resources sharing;

6) Effective ways for staff development and retention;

7) Measures to increase the library usage;

8) Possibilities for fund-raising.

Although all three host institutes face serious financial difficulties at present, the situation at Tianjin IOE was much the worst. We tried our best to persuade the president to restore funding for the library and to encourage the library director and staff to continue their best efforts.

For our evaluation of the three host IOEs, please see Appendix 4.

III. Observations and Recommendations

During our brief stay in China, the lecturers/consultants closely observed libraries and information centers of the key institutes of education in Tianjin, Beijing and Shanghai and learned from participants about others in different regions of China. Following are our observations and recommendations.

1. Observations

(1) Most IOEs in China were established between 1954 and 1966 to provide short-term and/or in-service training for school administrators and teachers who were urgently needed in China. Since the ten years of interruption by the Cultural Revolution, many IOEs have been re-established after 1978. Because of the disruption, most of the libraries in IOEs have gone through a period of rebuilding, often beginning from scratch.

(2) The library collections of the three host IOEs range from 150,000 volumes in Tianjin to 360,000 volumes each in Beijing and Shanghai. Staff sizes range from 22 in Beijing to 26 in Tianjin and to 45 in Shanghai. The annual acquisition budget is 60,000 Yuan in Tianjin, 100,000 Yuan in Beijing, and to 300,000 Yuan in Shanghai. The variation in collections, staffing, and funding is an indication of the lack of standards for library support and the different levels of funding for IOEs.

(3) In all three host IOEs, we sensed strong pressure for libraries to generate additional funds. This is very difficult for the library directors and staff since library services and products are not of the directed toward money-making. Fee-based library services can further impact the low-use rate already experienced by many IOE libraries.

(4) Despite the very difficult financial conditions most IOE libraries have faced, we were greatly moved by the high morale and dedication of the library directors and staff in all three host IOEs. They all work very hard to under adverse conditions and do their best to survive in the hope that things will get better soon.

(5) It is our impression that the funding for IOEs is far from adequate and has a negative affect on the funding for the libraries. This situation must be corrected to avoid further deterioration of library collections and services and loss of talented young librarians and information specialists who cannot afford to stay in library and information work for lack of opportunities.

(6) The World Bank loan has benefited the IOE libraries by providing much needed funds for microcomputers, library acquisitions, and some A-V equipment. The latest models of computers require software packages and trained staff to make them work. Furthermore, they require continuing funding for operations and maintenance. Staff training in the use of computers is an urgent need.

(7) We were happy to see that all three IOE libraries are working hard to develop their own unique specializations in addition to common library and information services. These efforts are supported by their respective president.

(8) The concept of inter-library cooperation for coordinated collection development and resource sharing is understood by most librarians and information specialists. There is a need to put the concept into action.

2. Recommendations

(1) The lecturers/consultants strongly recommend that the funding for IOEs be substantially increased to enable them adequately carrying out their important functions.

(2) The State Education Commission should develop a minimum standard for the IOE libraries and information centers and ensure that adequate funding and support are provided to meet and exceed the minimum standard.

(3) All IOE libraries and information centers should be encouraged to increase their usage rate rather than pressured to divert their energies in generating funds.

(4) All IOE libraries and information centers should be encouraged to work together in selecting the most suitable computer software for library automation and to develop unified standards for cataloging and bibliographic control. Using the same software package and bibliographic standards will facilitate library cooperation, shared cataloging, and resource sharing.

(5) Staff development and in-service training for IOE library staff should be a high priority to improve the quality of library and information services to meet changing needs.

(6) Each of the three host IOE libraries and information centers should be encouraged to further develop their unique specializations and become the national centers for these specialties.

IV. Acknowledgements

Before ending the report, the lecturers/consultants wish to express their sincere gratitude to the following individuals for their assistance and support which have been critical for the successful completion of the project assignments.

At CSUN:
Dr. Tung-Po Lin, Professor of Mathematics and Co-Director of the Teacher Training Project
Dr. Paul Chow, Professor of Physics and Co-Director of the Teacher Training Project
At Tianjin:
Professor Shen Fu Lin, President of Tianjin IOE
Mr. Shou Shao Lu, Vice President of Tianjin IOE
Mr. Dong Songwen, Dean of Studies, Tianjin IOE
Mr. Li Xianghe, Library Director, Tianjin IOE
Mr. Min Fanlin, Deputy Library Director, Jianjin IOE
Ms. Bao Man, Head, Library Administrative Office, Jianjin IOE
At Beijing:
Mr. Liu Xiaochu, State Education Commission
Mr. Zhang Jing, State Education Commission
Mr. Zhang Wei Shan, Vice President, Beijing IOE
Mr. An Bang-xun, Head, Department of Educational Technology, Beijing IOE
Ms. Wang Guo-lan, Deputy Director, President's Office, Beijing IOE
Prof. Jiang Xi-ze, Library Director, Beijing IOE
Mr. Du Fang Cang, Deputy Library Director, Beijing IOE
AT Shanghai:
Mr. Zhang Min Sheng, President of Shanghai IOE
Mr. Bao Siu De, Vice President of Shanghai IOE
Prof. Wang Yun Wu, Vice President of Shanghai IOE
Mr. Qian You-li, Deputy Library Director, Shanghai IOE
Ms. Xu Li-hua, Deputy Library Director, Shanghai IOE
Mr. She Guang-he, Librarian, Shanghai IOE

APPENDIX 1: Course Outline

"图书馆及教学资料管理" 讲习班——课程表

日期	单元	讲题	讲员
7/13/93	一	变迁中的图书馆与图书馆的任务	李华伟
7/14/93	二	图书馆管理的职能	李华伟
7/15/93	三	图书馆管理的方法与技巧	李华伟
7/16/93		〈国内专家讲学〉	
7/17/93	四	馆藏发展	左四藏
7/18/93		〈参观访问〉	
7/19/93	五	读者服务	左四藏
7/20/93	六	技术服务	左四藏
7/21/93	七	图书馆建筑设备与器材	李华伟
7/22/93	八	图书馆自动化与资料管理新科技	左四藏
7/23/93	九	图书馆合作与网络	左四藏
7/24/93	十	台湾及其他亚太地区高教图书馆现状	李华伟

＊＊上列日期仅供参考，请照贵校方便安排日程

"图书馆及教学资料管理" 讲习班——宗旨

> ——介绍高教图书馆管理的理论与实践
> ——交换中外的经验与心得
> ——介绍高教图书馆自动化的现况
> ——注重如何能在国内实施
> ——介绍新的服务观念
> ——以加强国内高教图书馆的功能

APPENDIX 2：Schedules of Workshops & Consultation 2.1 Tianjin

"图书馆及教学数据管理讲习班"课程安排（天津）

日期	星期	活动内容			
		上午	主讲人	下午	主讲人
7月13日	二	开学典礼（1小时）现代化图书馆的发展	李华伟	咨询	外专
7月14日	三	图书馆管理功能	李华伟	咨询	外专
7月15日	四	图书馆管理技术	李华伟	咨询	外专
7月16日	五	图书馆馆藏发展	左四藏	大学图书馆藏书与藏书统计	曹焕旭
7月17日	六	参观天津大学图书馆	读者服务	左四藏	
7月18日	日	技术服务	左四藏	高校图书馆读者服务工作	马志清
7月19日	一	参观南开大学图书馆		大连税专图书馆系统软件演示	王小平
7月20日	二	图书馆自动化及其技术	左四藏	咨询外	专
7月21日	三	图书馆合作与网络化	左四藏	咨询	外专
7月22日	四	图书馆建筑设备与器材	李华伟	咨询	外专
7月23日	五	中、美大学图书馆比较	冯承柏	台湾及其他亚太地区高校图书馆现状	李华伟
7月24日		旅游		旅游	
作息时间		早餐：7：30 上午上课：8：30－11：30		中餐：12：00 晚餐：17：15 下午上课：14：00－17：00	

APPENDIX 3：Schedules of Workshops & Consultation 2.2 Beijing

"图书馆及教学资料管理"班美国专家来京咨询讲学活动的日程安排（北京）

日　期	上午（8：30－11：30）9：50－10：10	下午（2：30－4：30）
7月26日（星期一）	座谈会，拟定计划	准备
7月27日（星期二）	①大学图书馆（包括教育学院图书馆）之概况（李华伟）放映录像。②技术服务介绍（左四藏）	咨询，讨论

（续上表）

日　期	上午（8：30－11：30）9：50－10：10	下午（2：30－4：30）
7月28日（星期三）	①大学图书馆管理功能（李华伟） 　放幻灯片。 ②读者服务介绍（左四藏）	教育学院院校系统图书馆事业建设与发展（杜坤仑）
7月29日（星期四）	①大学图书馆管理技术（李华伟） ②中小学教学资料管理，文献资源开发及为教学服务的措施（左四藏）	咨询，讨论
7月30日（星期五）	①图书馆的建筑与设备（李华伟） ②美国中小学图书馆及专业人员培训现况（左四藏） 　放映录像。	咨询，讨论
7月31日（星期六）	讨论，总结	

APPENDIX 4：Schedules of Workshops & Consultation 2.3 Shanghai

美国专家有关"图书馆及教学资料管理"咨询讲学活动日程安排（上海）

日　期	上午（8：30－11：30）	下午（1：30－3：30）
8月2日（星期一）	座谈会，拟定计划	准备
8月3日（星期二）	①美国大学图书馆之概况（李华伟） ②美国大学（包括教育学院）图书馆之技术服务（左四藏）	咨询、讨论
8月4日（星期三）	①大学图书馆管理功能与技术（李华伟） ②读者服务及自动化对信息服务的影响（左四藏）	准备
8月5日（星期四）	①图书馆的建筑与设备；台湾与亚太地区图书馆现状（李华伟） ②中小学图书及教学资料中心现状（左四藏）	咨询、讨论
8月6日（星期五）	参观上海教育学院图书资料中心	对上海教育学院图书资料中心工作进行咨询
8月7日（星期六）	工作总结	

上海教育学院外资办公室
上海教育学院图书资料中心
1993.8.2

管理资讯技术
——俄亥俄州大学图书馆之经验

Managing Information Technology
——The Experience of Ohio Academic Libraries

一、资讯技术的近期发展

最近三十年资讯技术的快速变革,对许多国家的图书馆及资讯服务产生莫大冲击,尤以美国为然,因其深入而普遍的应用资讯技术。传统观念对于馆藏"财产所有权"(ownership)的认定,也已由"检索取得"(access)所取代,目前常听到的名词——"虚拟图书馆"(Virtual Library)——各馆用户运用资讯检索技术所取得的资源,远大于任何图书馆实质馆藏。

资讯技术的重要发展及影响如下:

1. 电脑硬件及图书馆应用软件的精进,改变了图书馆的运作及服务方式。
2. 电信及电子传输技术的改良将图书馆网路及资源共享赋予新义,"电子的"(electronic)宛若"出版"(publishing)的形容词。
3. 磁盘贮存技术的革新,光学/磁学的进步,将以往安置于机房的磁盘设备,缩小至可放在桌面或膝旁,对于资讯的贮存及检索起了革命性的变化。
4. 超媒体及多媒体(hyper-and multi-media)技术的互动运用,扩大资讯的本质及结构。

上述及相关的发展是令人振奋的,图书馆界无论其形态、规模或国家现况,均要密切注意技术的发展,以应用革新产品来改善图书馆及资讯服务。

在美国,图书馆的进步历历可证,从60年代的"纸本图书馆"到70年代及80年代前期的"自动化图书馆",从80年代后期的"网路图书馆"到90年代的"电子图书馆"。10年前Michael Buckland也曾说:"后阶段的发展未必会取代前者,相反的,二者可并存,图书馆运作及服务技术的革新是循既有的基础逐步扩充。"①

二、俄亥俄州大学图书馆经验

自60年代以来,在许多方面,俄亥俄州大学图书馆于有效的开发资讯技术上已居领导地位,本文将作经验的回顾与分析。

1. OCLC 的成立及成长

俄亥俄州大学图书馆其合作及创新由来已久,这可追溯至60年代中期,当OCLC创立之初,命名为"俄亥俄州大学图书馆中心"(Ohio College Library Center)——反映其最初成员为俄亥俄州的大学图书馆,加入OCLC后可利用美国国会图书馆所提供的机读编目磁带编目,进而合作编目,并建立电脑化的联合目录。于1971年上线成功后,就像干草燎原般,迅速席卷全国②,不管任何规模及形态的图书馆均成为OCLC的用户。OCLC俨然成为国家性组织,于是1977年更名为OCLC,Inc.,1981年又更名为线上电脑图书馆中心

---

① Michael Keeble Buckland. Redesigning Library Services A Manifesto. Chicago:American Library Association,1982:pp.5-6.

② 1971年8月26日,Ohio大学图书馆首先将第一笔编目数据在线送至OCLC电脑系统。

(OCLC Online Computer Library Center)①。

由于书目资料库快速的递增,运用其强而有力的线上联合目录,将 OCLC 的功能由合作编目扩充至馆际互借。线上馆际互借系统于 1979 年正式推出,这又是另一成功的例证。

1992 年 6 月 30 日,OCLC 已有 24,837,459 笔书目记录,平均一年大约增加 200 万笔新纪录,大部分是由散布美国及其他 47 个国家 15,362 个合作馆所键入的。仅 1991—1992 年,就有 2,260 多万笔图书及其他资料是利用 OCLC 的编目系统完成编目,同时线上亦处理了 610 万笔的馆际互借②。

为充实及多样化服务,OCLC 增加了许多新功能:

A. 推出使用者取向的"FirstSearch"线上参考服务
B. 扩充馆员取向的"EPIC"线上资料库
C. 出版第一份同侪评论电子医学期刊"The Online Journal of Current Clinical Trials"
D. 筹备新到期刊目次表资料库——"ArticleFirst"和"ContentFirst"
E. 计划提供文件传输
F. 研究全文贮存及检索

2. 区域系统(Local System)发展

当 1970 年代 OCLC 致力于全国性的需求,而忽略了俄亥俄州图书馆其他自动化功能的需求,诸如采访、线上公用目录、期刊控制。因此俄亥俄州的许多图书馆不得不另谋选择,以满足本身的需求。Ohio State 大学图书馆首先利用大型主机发展本馆系统③。自 1970 年代迷你电脑推出后,其实质的运算能力及可担负的价格,诱使许多图书馆自行开发系统,因此商业软件包及自行开发的系统一时如雨后春笋。1980 年 Ohio 大学图书馆购买由弗吉尼亚工学院发展之弗吉尼亚工业图书馆系统(Virginia Tech Library System,以下简称 VTLS)。

在当时这套系统因许多优点而入选,例如:

* 它是整体自动化系统,补全了 OCLC 除编目及馆际合作的不足
* 它有功能完整的流通及线上公用目录,容易使用
* 软件的发展持续进行,硬件维护费用直接而合理
* 有网路功能
* 拥有较高的自主权

1988 年,一份对象为俄亥俄州政府补助的 13 所大学的调查报告显示:只有 Ohio State 大学使用自行开发的系统;有 8 所大学分别购买了 5 个不同的系统,其中 Akron 大学、Youngstown State 大学、Ohio 大学采用 VTLS;其余 4 所大学正在计划或评选中。一般皆可用拨接方式查询各校的资料库,但是必须学习各系统不同的检索方式④。

不兼容区域系统的剧增,使线上目录联结受挫,不同的系统其架构、软硬件、资料库结构、命令语言、检索策略皆异。因此尽管 13 所州立大学在馆际互借、影印、邮寄及稍后的传真等馆际合作彼此有长期的协议,但区域系统的各自为政阻碍了彼此的资源共享。

---

① Hwa-Wei Lee. "Trends in Automation in American Academic libraries: Ohio University's Experiences" in Librarianship in World Perspective·Selected Writings, *1963 – 1989*, by Hwa-Wei Lee. (Taipei: Student Book, 1991), pp. 225 – 239.
② OCLC Annual Report 1991 – 1992 (Dublin, Ohio: OCLC Online Computer Library Center, 1992)
③ Ohio State 大学图书馆自行开发的这套系统之更新版,目前为伊利诺伊州图书馆系统所采用。
④ Hwa-Wei Lee. "Ohio Academic Libraries Prepare for the Twenty-First Century" presented at the International Symposium and Exhibition on the Latest Development in Technologies for Library Service, September 6 – 10, 1992, Beijing, China.

3. 网络系统的演进

许多区域系统有网络功能，而网络亦有各式联结，如校园网络、地域性系统或合作图书馆网等，迄今仍持续不断的发展中，以达成更宽广的联结。近年来，借由持续扩展及不断升级的电信系统联结了美国境内及世界各地许多电脑，大大的便利资讯的传输。目前许多大学皆可免费使用Internet（虽然有时有限额），对于研究人员、学者、图书馆、资讯专业人员及其他人员线上沟通有莫大裨益。由俄亥俄州政府资助的超级电脑中心（Super Computer Center）所发展的网络主干——OARnet（Ohio Academic Resources Network）提供了高速多频的联结功能，串联本州的主要电脑中心。

步入电子图书馆的纪元，为达成有效合作及资源共享，本州的十七所大学图书馆及一所州立图书馆又跨出了另一划时代的脚步——建立图书馆网络——亦即OhioLINK。

OhioLINK成员，如下：

（1）13所州立大学
University of Arkron
Bowling Green State University
Central State University
University of Cincinnati
Kent State University
Miami University
Ohio State University
Ohio University
Shawnee State University
University of Toledo
Wright State University
Youngstown State University

（2）2所大型私立大学
Case-Western Reserve University
University of Dayton

（3）2所州立医学院
The Medical College of Ohio
Northeast Ohio University College of Medicine

（4）1所州立图书馆
State Library of Ohio

三、OhioLINK

1986年，图书馆研究委员会（Library Study Committee）在俄亥俄州州立大学董事会（Ohio Broad of Regents，以下简称OBOR）的委任下，历时一年，于1987年发表研究报告："Academic Libraries in Ohio: Progress Through Collaboration, Storage and Technology"[①]。报告中建议筹划俄亥俄州图书馆资讯网路（Ohio Library and Information Network，取其头字

---

① Ohio Board of Regents, Library Study Committee. Academic Libraries in Ohio: Progress Through Collaboration, Storage, and Technology. Report of the Library Study Committee (Columbus, Ohio: Ohio Board of Regents, 1987). OBOR为俄亥俄州督导高等教育的专责机构。

语 OhioLINK），OhioLINK 计划自此展开；1988 年 1 月起，筹划的过程经馆员、电脑及系统管理者、大学教职员、OBOR 成员及其他等逾百人的积极参与，热烈讨论，产生许多相关文件均纳入实际的规划中，于同年 11 月出版"计划报告"（Planning Paper）[①]；1989 年 8 月完成了经长时间详尽研拟的"系统规格需求书"（Request for Proposal）；1989 年 12 月出版 OhioLINK 纲要"Connecting People, Libraries and Information for Ohio's Future"[②]；1990 年 7 月决定购买 Innovative Interfaces, Inc.（以下简称"III"）的软件；预备 1988—1990 年及 1990—1992 年会计年度的成本预算、1989—1991 年会计年度的运作费用预算，正式成立管理组织，聘任执行长（Executive Director）；1991 年 2 月与"III"订约，1991 年 7 月展开第一阶段安装工程。

四、主要服务目的及益处

1. 服务目的

主要服务目的在 1989 年 12 月发表的纲要中已阐明，摘要如下：

＊联结 18 所合作馆，各馆读者宛如使用单一大馆资源。

＊进步的软硬件技术，对于用户有效使用图书馆及资讯资源，提供更宽广便利的指引。

＊检索网路图书馆资源，会员读者（user initiated）可线上借书，而索借的资料，不管是原件借出或是影印服务，可利用特约递送服务，或是电子方式（通常为传真），快速的送至。

＊为开启世界资讯的转接站。

＊合作采购以发挥现有资源的最大效益，在全州基础上做协商，达成软件维护及硬件支持的整体效益。

2. 益处

＊提高俄亥俄州高等教育团体面对快速的出版脚步（包括传统出版品及电子出版品）时，能平衡其馆藏资源，这绝非单独一馆的采访、编目、典藏能力所能达到。

＊检索及传输能力的提升，将州政府对于图书馆的投资做最大利用。

＊促使读者借由资讯检索方式掌握日新月异、各式各样的出版资讯。

＊提供快速检索。

五、安装

"III"系统计划分二阶段安装：第一阶段自 1991 年 7 月 1 日至 1992 年 6 月 30 日，首先装置 6 个图书馆及中心；第二阶段自 1992 年 7 月 1 日 1994 年 12 月，对象为其余 12 馆。

第一阶段安装的 6 馆为 Bowling Green, Case-Western Reserve, Central State, Cincinnati, Miami, Wright State, 及位于 Wright State 大学的中心。第一阶段直到 1992 年 12 月才完成；第二阶段安装延至 1993 年，延迟主要是为了等州议会的立法拨款，意即实际上第二阶段安装始于 1993 年 5 月，较预定时程晚了 9 个月。安装状况详见图 I。

[①] OLAS steering Committee. Ohio Library Access System Planning Paper, November 2, 1988 (Columbus, Ohio: Ohio Board of Regents, 1988). 最初 OhioLINK 命名为 the Ohio Library Access System（OLAS），后来更名为 Ohio Library and Information System（OLIS）最后定名为 Ohio Library and Information Network（取其头字语为 OhioLINK）。

[②] Ohio Library & Information System, OLIS. Connecting People, Libraries, & Information for Ohio's Future (Colum-bus, Ohio: Ohio Board of Regents, 1989).

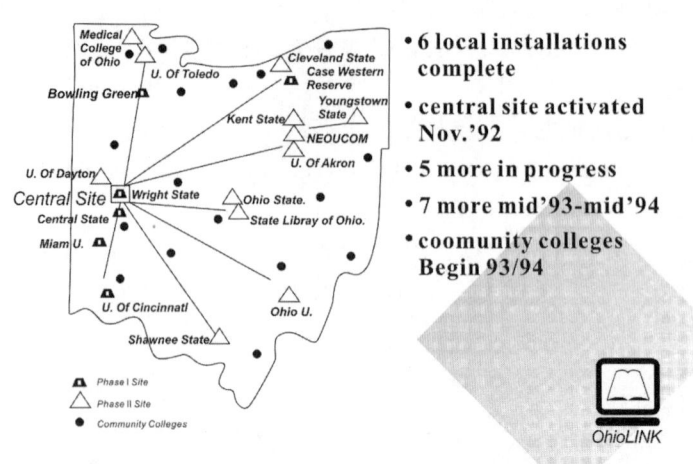

图 I 系统安装状况

一旦 18 个馆的 "III" 系统安装完毕，OBOR 计划再加入本州 17 所小区学院（二年制）图书馆；Ohio LINK 亦希望能扩大纳入大型公共图书馆、更多的私立大学图书馆及其他馆，而经费需由这些馆自行负担，或寻求其他补助。（因为 ORBR 不包括公共图书馆）

六、OhioLINK 计划的特点

在选择软件系统时，已认知没有任何一个系统会完全符合"系统规格需求书"中的每一点，基于共识，选择了最能满足大多数需求的系统加入 OhioLINK，以体现现有特色，并开发新功能：

OhioLINK 计划要件：

* 功能完整的区域系统

* 中心编目主档——能及时快速更新

* 可顺畅检索——由区域目录至中心目录

* 会员读者/非间接的馆际流通服务

* 报纸/期刊文献资料库可连接馆藏记录及流通功能

* Internet "gopher" [①]

图 II 为 OhioLINK 的硬件配置。以 Ohio 大学为例，其 III 系统主机采用 2 台 DEC5900 迷你电脑。

OhioLINK 计划扩充的服务如下：

目前正在测试中：

* 经由 OCLC FirstSearch 共享资料库

* 透过 Internet 的传真 (fax)，高质量的文献"影像"传输。

* 线上全文影像传送

研发中：

* 以 ASCII 贮存的期刊全文资料库

* 期刊目次表——完全整合

---

① 部分数据是由 OhioLINK 副执行长 Tom Sanvile 所提供，如图 I：系统安装状况、图 II：OhioLINK 硬件配置。

* 图书目次表——完全整合
* 全州健康科学文献资料库
* 电子文件传输工作站
* 工作站软件

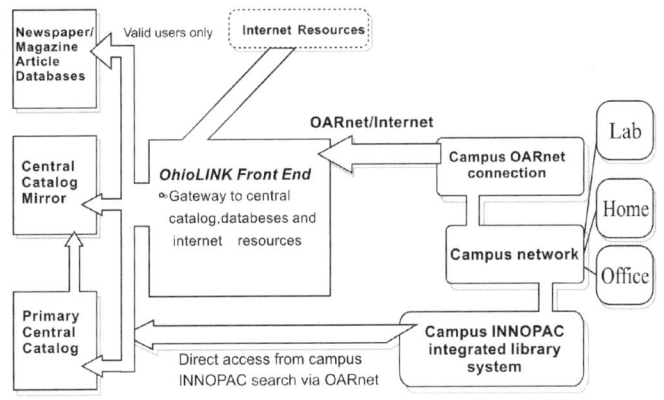

图 II　OhioLink 硬件配置

为了 OhioLINK 能成功的安装及运作，参与的合作单位必须改善本身电信系统。Ohio 大学采纳专家的建议及在电算中心电信网路服务的援助下，展开分三阶段进行的电信网路计划，校本部经费为 106,027 美元，分部为 35,789 美元。第一、二阶段已大致完成，第三阶目前正在进行中。（三阶段皆完成后的整体配置，详见图 III）

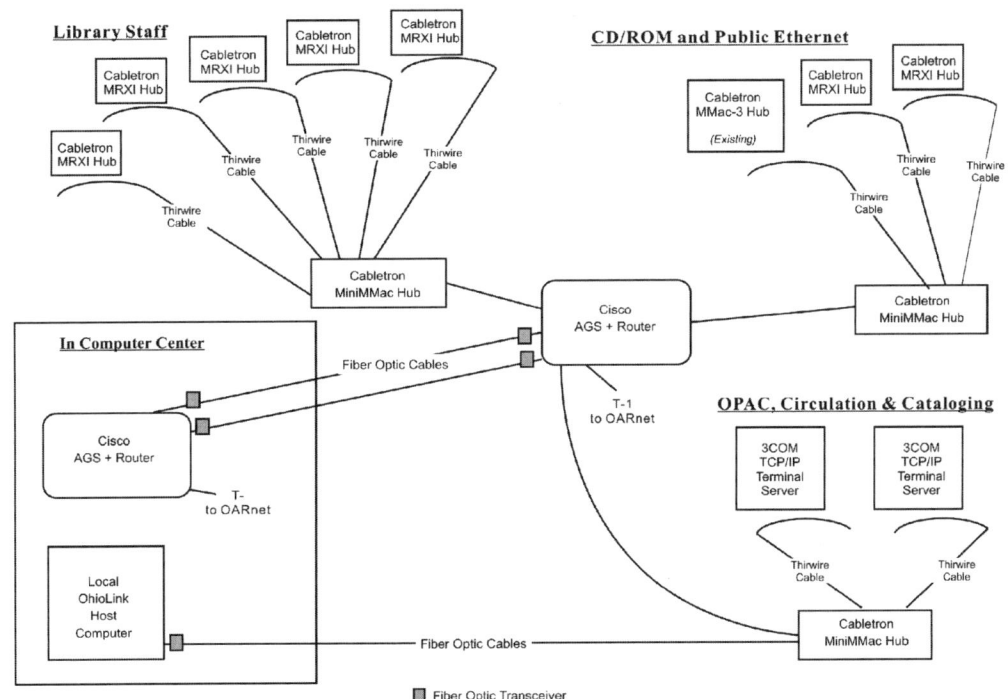

图 III　Alden Library Networking Project

七、管理

OhioLINK 的成功大部分应归功于州立大学董事会（OBOR）的有力领导及支持，其对于图书馆在提升高质量教育及促进研究上所扮演的角色给予相当肯定。在计划之初，OBOR 就指定 OhioLINK 为董事会选定的杰出创制之一，给予经费支持以落实计划。

在管理组织上，OBOR 希望 OhioLINK 得到其应有的关注，目前组织包括：

管理委员会（Governing Board），执行长（Executive Director），政策顾问委员会（Policy Advisory Council），及图书馆顾问委员会（Library Advisory Council）。在图书馆委员会下再设若干常设委员会。图 IV 为管理组织结构。

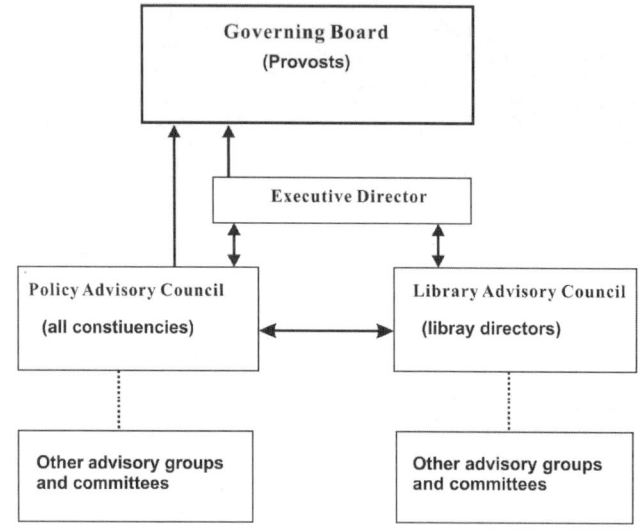

图 IV　管理架构

1. 管理委员会

由 OhioLINK17 所大学中选出 9 名教务长担任委员，具投票权，任期三年；OBOR 首长、OhioLINK 执行长、政策顾问会议主席及副主席为当然委员；两年制学院派一位代表担任观察员。委员会应选主席一名，会期一年三次或应需要召开，主要任务为核准预算或审阅重要政策提案。核准的预算要送至 OBOR 并入欲提交州长的总提案，以纳入州预算。

2. 政策顾问委员会

由 17 名具有投票权的委员所组成，任期三年。州立大学代表、OARnet 首长为当然委员、两年制大学有代表一名。委员中至少包含 3 位教授、4 位馆长、3 位电算中心主任、3 位学院院长及 2 位系统馆员，成员系大学推荐及管理委员会所指定。每 2 个月开一次会或应需要召开，主要为建议政策性或预算事宜，选举主席一名，由图书馆顾问委员会主席担任本会副主席。

3. 图书馆顾问委员会

包含所有 OhioLINK 合作馆馆长，两年制学院代表一名；请本州法律图书馆协会派一名代表担任观察员。本会又分设许多常设委员会，目前的委员会及任务如下：

＊合作资讯资源的管理
—协调合作馆藏之管理及发展
—综合馆藏、检索资讯及各项政策
—选择电子资讯资源
＊资料库的管理及标准
—INNOPAC 采访及期刊控制（INNOPAC 即 III 系统软件名称）
—书目、权威及馆藏的标准及实务
—回溯资料的转换
—资料库的准备、维护及管理
＊馆际服务
—馆际流通及资料传输
＊使用者服务
—馆员及读者的资讯及教育资料
—安装电子资讯资源
—用户接口的设计、内容及标准

同时亦有由各馆系统主要负责人所组成的 Lead implementors Group（Ohio 大学是由系统馆员及电算中心人员代表），每月会同 OhioLINK 系统总召集人开会一次，商讨安装细节。

目前正在评估更新政策顾问委员会组织，任何的变动均会涵盖至整体管理。

八、财政

图书馆已投入了大量经费来转换 III 系统，主要经费来自州政府。对于经费需求的认同，OBOR 先前已核拨了设备费、行政部门及中心的运作费、资料传输及设于中心的参考资料库费用。各馆负责维护费、未来软硬件的扩充、区域电信设备的升级（包括连接各分馆及其他远距离联线）。

1. 中央经费：来自州政府

设备费
—1990/1992 $ 9,200,000
—1992/1994   10,800,000

运作费
—1989/1991 $ 400,000
—1991/1993   1,700,000
—1993/1995   4,600,000

2. 地方经费：各馆支出

Ohio 大学费用：设备费及维护费（包含校本部及 5 个分部）。详见下表：

Summary of Projected OhioLINK Costs				
	Athens Campus		University Centers	
	Initial One-time Athens Campus Costs	Annual Athens Campus Costs	Initial One-time University Center Costs	Annual University Center Costs
III Software	$ 49,950	$ 52,281	$ 23,800	$ 14,571
DEC II Hardware*	$ 17,585	$ 11,296	$ 19,321	$ 4,188
Networking—CNS**	$ 106,027	$ 16,714	$ 35,789	$ 5,337
Retrospective Con-version***	$ 15,110	NA	$ 10,560	NA
Total	$ 188,672	$ 80,291	$ 89,470	$ 24,096

* Hardware costs are based on the best estimate of Library and Computing and Technology Services staff.

** Networking costs were detailed in a February 27, 1992, memo from Tom Reid and sent to the Provost.

*** This cost to convert older records will be covered about 80% by OBOR/Ohio LINK, the figures here reflect the remaining share to be covered by Ohio University. On July 16, 1992, We were advised that OhioLINK likely will contribute less to the cost of Retrospective Conversion than previously projected—meaning that Athens and University Center shares will increase.

九、未来发展

自60年代以来，俄亥俄州图书馆已成图书馆界自动化及革新的先锋。OCLC的建立，划下了图书馆合作编目、联合目录、馆际合作及网络连作的新纪元；Chemical Abstracts Service、CompuServe、Mead Data、Battle连同OCLC，使俄亥俄州成为世界资讯中心。90年代OhioLINK的发展，提供了新的视野，冀望OhioLINK的重要性能与OCLC并列，成功的联结人、资讯和图书馆。

随着OhioLINK渐次实践，为求有效的运作，所以持续不断的研发、测试及实行新的方法、政策、程序。预期将运用新颖的软件纳入许多新功能如全文资料库、电子文件传输、多任务工作站等。

虽然许多图书馆对于换装III系统未必全然满意，但大家深信过渡期的不便只是暂时的，而使用同一系统，联成虚拟图书馆，将带来长远的效益。由于添加许多新的特色功能，OhioLINK大幅提高了联合资源的检索率与取得率。高速电信传输能力提供了进入电子资讯世界的入口。利用OhioLINK合作及协调采访、馆藏发展及管理、典藏、资源共享、学术交流，获益匪浅。当III安装完毕，OhioLINK其跨越全州之图书馆资讯网络效应将是无与伦比的。

（原载《政大图资通讯》1993年11月第7期，第1-11页。）

管理资讯技术
——俄亥俄州大学图书馆之经验

Managing Information Technology
—The Experience of Ohio Academic Libraries[1]

RECENT DEVELOPMENT OF INFORMATION TECHNOLOGIES

The accelerated pace of innovation in information technologies during the last thirty years have profoundly impacted library and information services in many countries. This is especially evident in the United States where, because of the extensive and widespread application of information technologies, the traditional concept of "ownership" of library collections has been replaced by "access". The frequently heard phrase today, "Virtual Library", means that library users can now access information resources, using information technologies, far greater than those actually owned by any single library.

The most important of these developments in information technologies and their impacts include:

1) advancements in computer technologies and sophistication of library applications software have transformed libraries' operations and services;

2) improvements in telecommunications and electronic delivery technologies have given new meaning to library networking and resource-sharing as well as adding "electronic" as an adjective to "publishing";

3) innovations in disk storage technologies, optical and magnetic, which place on a desk-top or your lap what earlier required a dedicated computer room, have revolutionized information storage and retrieval, and

4) the growing use of interactive hyper- and multi-media technologies is expanding the nature and organization of information.

These and other developments are exciting and require that all libraries, regardless of type, size, or stage of development of the nation, must be more involved in monitoring technological change and more proactive in adopting appropriate information technologies to improve library and information services.

In the United States, we have seen the progressive changes of libraries from the "Paper Library" up into the 1960s, to the "Automated Library" in the 1970s and the early half of the 1980s, to the "Networked Library" in the latter half of the 1980s, and now on to the "Electronic Library" of the 1990s and beyond. A decade ago, in Redesigning Library Services, Michael Buckland observed that the later stages have not necessarily replaced the previous ones; instead, each coexists with and expands on the technological bases of library operations and services of its predecessors.[2]

THE EXPERIENCE OF OHIO ACADEMIC LIBRARIES

Academic libraries in Ohio, in many respects, have been leaders in the effective exploitation of information technologies since the 1960s. In this paper, the experience of academic libraries in Ohio will be reviewed and analyzed.

---

[1] Presented to the IX Congress of Southeast Asian Librarians (CONSAL) in Bangkok, May 2 – 7, 1993, and the Seminar on National Academic Library Networking, May 12 – 14, 1993, Chiang Mai, Thailand.

[2] Michael Keeble Buckland. *Redesigning Library Services: A Manifesto*. Chicago: American Library Association, 1982: pp. 5 – 6.

1. The Formation and Growth of OCLC

Academic libraries in Ohio have a long tradition of cooperation and innovation. This can be traced to the formation of OCLC in the mid-1960s. When OCLC was founded, it was named the Ohio College Library Center, reflecting its initial membership—academic libraries in Ohio, which had joined to take advantage of the MARC cataloging records on magnetic tapes provided by the Library of Congress and to use them for cooperative cataloging and the creation of a computerized union catalog. The success of OCLC after it came online in 1971, like dry grass, caught fire and soon spread across the country.① Libraries of every type and size became OCLC users. Its emergence as a national organization led OCLC to change its name to OCLC, Inc. in 1977 and then to OCLC Online Computer Library Center in 1981.②

The rapid numerical growth of OCLC's bibliographic database and its powerful information on library holdings in the online union catalog have expanded OCLC's usefulness from cooperative cataloging to interlibrary loan. The introduction of OCLC's online interlibrary loan system in 1979 was another instant success.

As of June 30, 1992, 24,837,459 bibliographic records were stored in OCLC's database. Annually, some two million new records are added, mostly by the 15,362 participating libraries throughout the United States and in 47 other countries. In 1991—1992 alone, 22.6 million books and other materials were cataloged through the OCLC cataloging system and 6.1 million interlibrary loans were transacted online.③

To expand and diversify its services and products, OCLC has entered into a number of new areas recently:

A. Introducing "FirstSearch" online reference service for end-users;

B. Expanding the databases in the "EPIC" online reference service for libraries;

C. Publishing the first peer-reviewed Electronic medical journal, The Online Journal of Current Clinical Trials;

D. Preparing new serials table-of-contents databases— "ArticleFirst" and "ContentsFirst";

E. Planning to offer a document delivery service;

F. Researching full-text storage and retrieval.

2. The Development of Local Systems

While OCLC concentrated on national needs in the 1970s, it neglected those of Ohio libraries for automation of other library functions, such as: acquisitions, circulation, online public access catalogs, and serials control. Consequently, many libraries in Ohio sought alternatives to meet their automation needs. Ohio State University Library was the first to develop its own local library system using a mainframe computer.④ During the 1970s, the introduction of minicomputers with substantial computing power at an affordable price enticed other libraries to explore library systems. A growing number of commercially developed library systems and home-developed systems based on minicomputers were appearing on the market. In 1980, Ohio University Library purchased the Virginia Tech Library System (VTLS) developed by the Virginia Polytechnic Institute and State University. The system was selected for its many superior features at that time, such as:

* Its design as an integrated library system offering a variety of library functions complemented the OCLC cataloging and interlibrary loan subsystems.

* Its circulation and online public access catalog (OPAC) modules were well developed and

---

① On August 26, 1971, Ohio University Library was the first library in the world to catalog online and interactively enter a record into the OCLC computer system.

② Hwa-Wei Lee. "Trends in Automation in American Academic Libraries: Ohio University's Experiences" in *Librarianship in World Perspective: Selected Writings, 1963 – 1989*, by Hwa-Wei Lee. Taipei: Student Book, 1991: pp. 225 – 239.

③ *OCLC Annual Report 1991 – 1992* (Dublin, Ohio: OCLC Online Computer Library Center, 1992).

④ A improved version of the Ohio State University's system is now used in Illinois as the statewide library system.

easy to use.

* It could directly download OCLC's MARC records to create a local database.
* Its software development was ongoing and maintenance charges were reasonable and straightforward.
* It was capable of networking among libraries.
* It allowed a high degree of local control and flexibility.

A 1988 survey of the thirteen state-supported universities in Ohio revealed that. Ohio State University was alone in using a locally developed system, while eight others had acquired local systems from five different vendors. VTLS was used by the University of Akron and Youngstown State University as well as Ohio University. Four institutions without a system were in the process of either selecting or planning one. It was possible to dial into the online public access catalogs on other campuses but users had to learn the different search methods of each local systems. ①

The proliferation of incompatible local systems frustrated desires to interconnect the online catalogs because of different system designs, hardware, software, database structures, command languages, and search engines. As a result, local advances in automation failed to support inter-institutional resource sharing despite long-standing agreements among the libraries at the thirteen universities to give priority to reciprocal borrowing and provide free photocopying, mailing, and (later) faxing for interlibrary loans.

3. The Evolution of Networked Libraries

Even though many of the local systems support networking, and a variety networks may be in place within a campus, a university system, a region, or among a group of cooperating libraries, continued development is needed in the 1990s to achieve greater interconnectivity. In recent years, the expansion and upgrading of telecommunication systems to interconnect computers across the United States and many parts of the world have greatly facilitated transmission of a very large amount of information electronically. The availability of the Internet at most universities with no cost to individual users (although sometimes rationed) has had a dramatic effect on electronic communication among researchers, scholars, library and information professionals, and others. In Ohio, this was facilitated by the establishment of the state-funded Super Computer Center with a communications backbone—OARnet (Ohio Academic Resources Network) —which provides high speed, broadband telecommunication linkage of all major computer centers in the state.

As we enter the era of the electronic library, seventeen academic libraries in Ohio, in alliance with the State Library of Ohio, have decided to take yet another giant step by creating a sophisticated library network for effective cooperation and resource sharing. The seventeen include:

13 state supported universities:
* University of Akron
* Bowling Green State University
* Central State University
* University of Cincinnati
* Cleveland State University
* Kent State University
* Miami University
* Ohio State University
* Ohio University
* Shawnee State University
* University of Toledo
* Wright State University

---

① Hwa-Wei Lee. "Ohio Academic Libraries Prepare for the Twenty-First Century" presented at the International Symposium and Exhibition on the Latest Development in Technologies for Library Service, September 6 – 10, 1992, Beijing, China.

* Youngstown State University

2 large private universities:
* Case-Western Reserve University
* University of Dayton

2 state-supported medical schools:
* The Medical College of Ohio
* Northeast Ohio University College of Medicine

These comprise the most recent manifestation of networked libraries, the Ohio Library and Information Network—OhioLINK.

THE BEGINNING OF OHIOLINK

Following a year-long study by a Library Study Committee appointed by the Ohio Board of Regents (OBOR) in 1986 and the recommendations in the Committee report, Academic Libraries in Ohio: Progress Through Collaboration, Storage, and Technology, issued in September 1987[1], the planning for an Ohio Library and Information Network, with the acronym OhioLINK, was begun soon thereafter. Since January 1988, through a broadly based process of planning including the active participation of over one hundred librarians, computer and systems managers, university faculty and administrators, OBOR staff, and others, considerable documentation of broad interest has been produced in addition to the actual planning. Important outputs from the process include a Planning Paper issued in November 1988[2], a lengthy, comprehensive, and detailed Request for Proposal completed in August 1989, an overview of the OhioLINK, Connecting People, Libraries and Information for Ohio's Future, published in December 1989[3], selection of Innovative Interfaces, Inc. (III) as the software system vendor in July 1990, preparation of biennial capital budgets for 1988 – 1990 and 1990 – 1992 and the biennial operating budget for 1989 – 1991, formalization of the governance structure and hiring an Executive Director, signing of the contract with III in February 1991, and beginning Phase I implementation in July 1991.

MAJOR SERVICE GOALS AND BENEFITS

1. Service Goals

The major service goals of OhioLINK as stated in the December 1989 overview can be summarized:

* Linking the 18 participating libraries so that they appear as a single resource to library users.

* Using advanced software and hardware technology to provide library users with a comprehensive and intelligent guide to the effective use of library and information resources.

* Enabling library users' easy and effective access to the networked library and information resources through user-initiated online borrowing. Requested materials, either original or photocopy, will be delivered expeditiously by a specially contracted delivery service or by electronic means (predominantly fax at this stage).

* Serving as a gateway to the rapidly expanding world of information stored in electronic formats.

---

[1] Ohio Board of Regents, Library Study Committee. *Academic Libraries in Ohio: Progress Through Collaboration, Storage, and Technology. Report of the Library Study Committee* (Columbus, Ohio: Ohio Board of Regents, 1987). OBOR is the state agency charged with coordinating and overseeing the development of public higher education in Ohio.

[2] OLAS Steering Committee. *Ohio Library Access System Planning Paper*, November 2, 1988 (Columbus, Ohio: Ohio Board of Regents, 1988). Initially, OhioLINK was called the Ohio Library Access System (OLAS), then was changed—to avoid trademark infringements or challenges, to Ohio Library and Information System (OLIS) and, finally, to Ohio Library and Information Network, with the acronym OhioLINK.

[3] Ohio Library & Information System, OLIS. *Connecting People, Libraries, & Information for Ohio's Future* (Columbus, Ohio: Ohio Board of Regents, 1989).

* Providing for more cost-effective use of existing resources by cooperatively managing the purchase of new books and journals, by negotiating for information services on a statewide basis, and by bringing economies of scale to software maintenance agreements and the support of library computer systems.

2. Benefits

The major benefits that OhioLINK is to yield for the State of Ohio include:

* Enhancing the Ohio higher education community's ability to leverage it: resources to respond to the accelerating pace of newly-published materials both traditional and electronic, that is outstripping the ability of any single library to acquire, catalog, and store.

* Maximizing the utility of the State's major investment in library resource; through improved access and delivery mechanisms.

* Improving Ohio information user's ability to keep up with the ever-increasing volume of information published in more diverse formats.

* Providing rapid access to material the users need.

IMPLEMENTATION

In a two-phase implementation plan, III system will be installed in six libraries and the central site during the Phase I period from July 1, 1991, to June 30, 1992, and the remaining 12 libraries will come in during the Phase II period from July 1, 1992 to December 1994.

During the Phase I implementation, III system were installed at Bowling Green, Case-Western Reserve, Central State, Cincinnati, Miami, and Wright State, as well as the central site physically located on Wright State campus. Phase I was not completed until December 1992, and Phase II was delayed into 1993 due to delays in appropriations by the state legislature. This has meant that the actual implementation of Phase II commenced in March 1993, a delay of nine months. Diagram I on the following page shows the status of installations.

Once the III system has been installed at all eighteen institutions, the OBOR plans to add the seventeen community (two year) college libraries in the state. Eventually, OhioLINK may be extended to large public libraries, more private university libraries, and others; however, funding for these likely will come from the individual institutions or other state agencies (since public libraries are not covered by OBOR).

SPECIAL FEATURES OF THE OHIOLINK PROJECT

In selecting a software system, it was recognized that no system was perfect nor could meet all of the high expectations described in the Request for Proposal. With this understanding, the collective desire was to select the system that had the most wanted features provided by a vendor willing to be a partner with OhioLINK in continuing refinement of existing features and in development of new features. Among the initial components of the OhioLINK project were:

* Fully functional local systems.
* Master record central catalog—updated continuously in real time.
* Seamless searching from local to central catalog
* Interlibrary patron-initiated/non-mediated circulation.
* Centrally-mounted additional databases through the same interface.
* Newspaper/journal article databases linked to holdings and circulation.
* Internet "gopher". [1]

---

[1] A part of the information in this section, including Diagrams I and II were provided by Tom Sanville, Executive Director of OhioLINK.

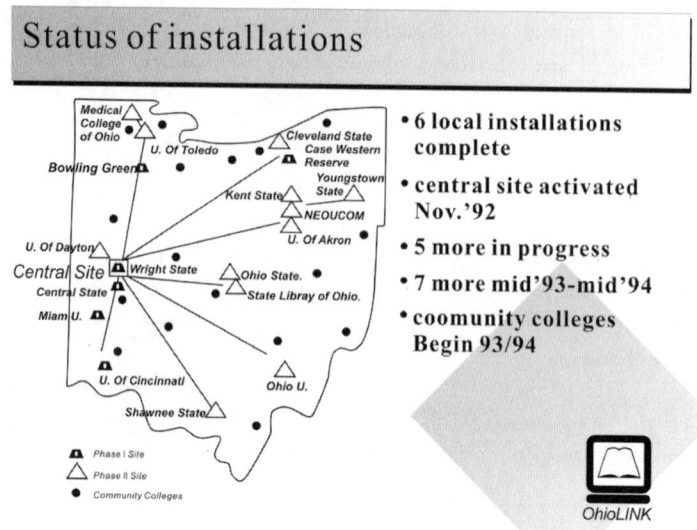

DIAGRAM I Status of installations

Diagram II on the next page shows the configuration of OhioLINK's initial components. At Ohio University, the III system will run on 2 DEC System 5900 minicomputers.

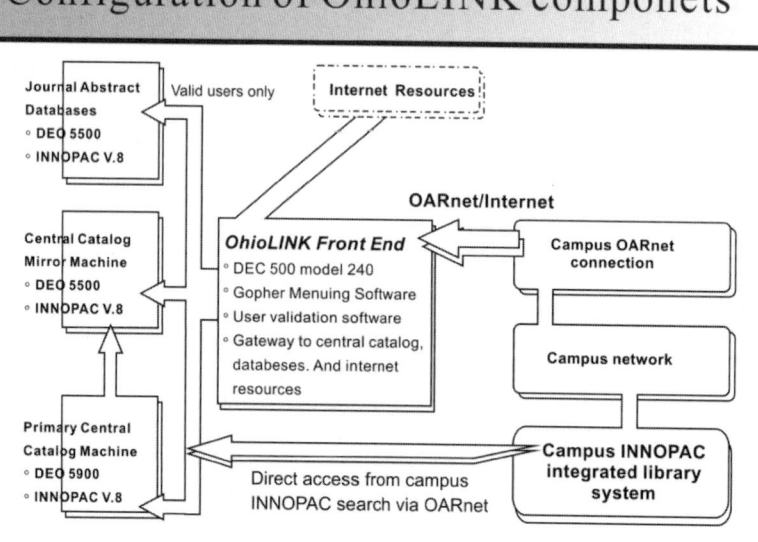

DIAGRAM II Configuration of OhioLINK components

Additional components under active consideration by OhioLINK are:
Currently testing:
  * Additional databases via **OCLC FirstSearch**.
  * High-quality article "image" delivery, by fax through the Internet.
  * Full-text article image delivery online.
Investigating:
  * Journal article database with ASCII full text.

* Serials table of contents—fully integrated.
* Monograph table of contents—fully integrated.
* Statewide health sciences databases.
* Electronic document delivery workstations.
* Workstation software.

For successful implementation and operation of OhioLINK, each participating institution has had to upgrade its telecommunications infrastructure. At Ohio University a three-phase communication networking plan has been adopted with the expert advice and assistance of the Communication Network Services of the University's Computing and Technology Services. The one-time cost of the upgrading for the main campus is $106,027 and for the regional campuses is $35,789. The first and second phases largely have been completed and, the third phase is currently underway. Diagram III shows the configuration after Phase III is completed.

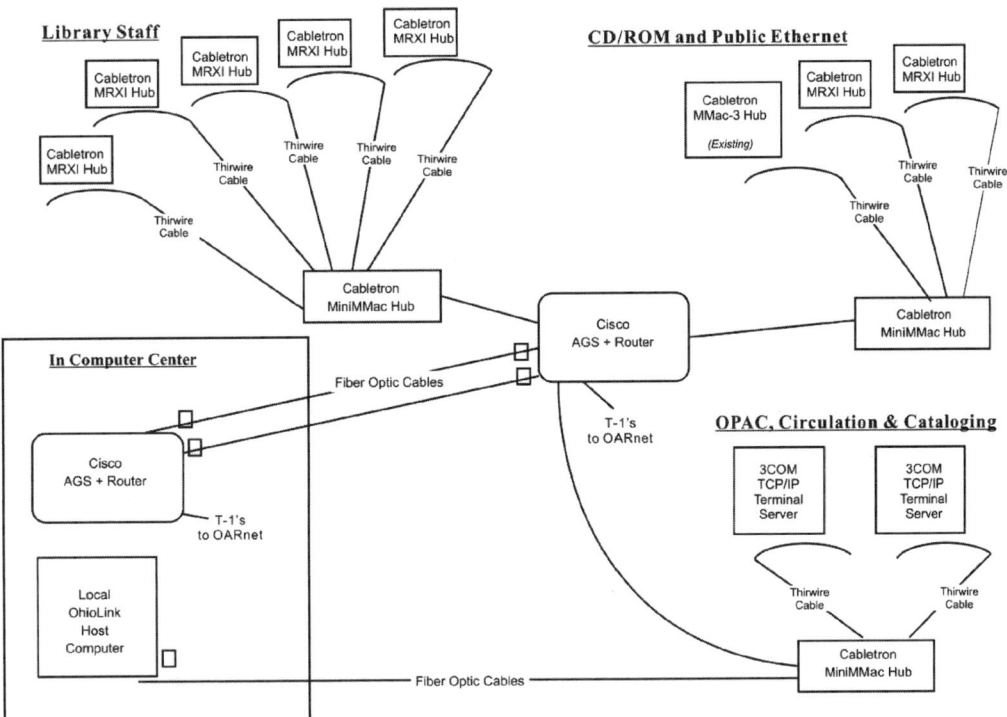

DIAGRAM III   Alden Library Networking Project

GOVERNANCE

To a great extent, the success of OhioLINK thus far is due to the strong leadership and support of the Ohio Board of Regents which has recognized the critical role of libraries in promoting high-quality education and productivity in research. OBOR, at the beginning of the project, designated OhioLINK as one of the Regents' Selective Excellence Initiatives and has provided the necessary funding for its realization.

In the governance structure, OBOR wanted to make certain that OhioLINK received the attention and visibility it needed and deserved. The current structure includes a **Governing Board**, an **Executive Director**, a **Policy Advisory Council**, and a **Library Advisory Council**. Under the Library Advisory Council there are a number of standing committees. Diagram IV shows the governance structure which has been in existence since the inception of OhioLINK.

The GOVERNING BOARD consists of nine university provosts (principal academic officer) selected from among the seventeen OhioLINK institutions. These nine voting members serve staggered, three-year rotating terms. The Chancellor of OBOR, the OhioLINK Executive Director, and chair and vice-chair of the Policy Advisory Council serve ex-officio. A representative of two-year colleges is to be added as an observer. The Governing Board elects its own chair and meets three times a year or as needed to approve budgets and review major policy recommendations. Biennial budget recommendations will be approved and forwarded to OBOR for incorporation into its request to the Governor of Ohio for inclusion in the state budget.

The POLICY ADVISORY COUNCIL consists of seventeen voting members serving staggered three-year terms. It includes representatives of all of the OhioLINK universities plus the Director of OARnet ex-officio, and a representative of two-year colleges. Members include at least three faculty members, four library directors, three computer center directors, three academic deans, and two systems librarians. These are recommended by the universities and appointed by the Governing Board. The Council meets every other month or as needed to advise the Executive Director on policy and budget matters. It elects its own chair. The Chair of the Library Advisory Council serves as Vice-Chair. The Executive Director serves ex-officio.

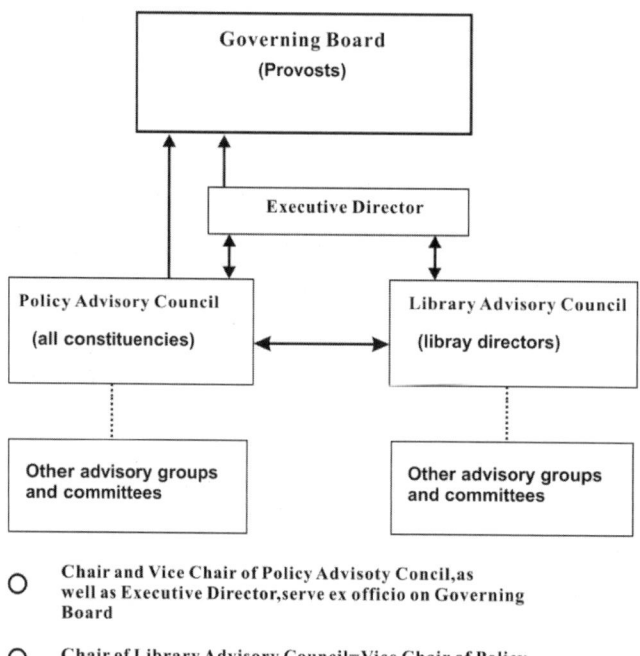

DIAGRAM IV   OhioLINK GOVERNING STRUCTURE

The LIBRARY ADVISORY COUNCIL includes all OhioLINK member library deans/directors and one representative of two-year colleges. The state-wide association of law libraries is invited to send a representative as an observer. The Council also has a number of standing committees. The recently re-structured committees and responsibilities are:
* Cooperative Information Resources Management
    – Coordinating cooperative collection management and development
    – Composite collection and access information and policies
    – Electronic information resource selection
* Database Management and Standards
    – Acquisition and serials control modules of the INNOPAC software

- Bibliographic, authority, and holdings standards and practices
- Retrospective conversion
- Database preparation, maintenance and quality control
* Inter-Library Services:
  - Inter-library circulation and document delivery
* User Services:
  - Informational and educational materials for users and staff
  - Electronic information resource implementation
  - User interface design, content and standards

There is also a **Lead implementers Group** which consisting of the key person(s) at each institution directing the system (for Ohio University, the systems librarian and a computer center staff member). The group meets with the Director of Library Systems of OhioLINK once a month to work on implementation details.

A recent review is underway to re-structure the Policy Advisory Council. Any change may have implications for other components of the governance.

FINANCE

For libraries which have already invested a large amount of funds for local systems to switch to the III system, central funding from the State is critically important and necessary. In recognition of this need, OBOR early committed to funding initial start-up costs, the operational expenses of both the office of the Executive Director and the central site, and the costs for document delivery and selected external databases to be made available through the central site. Each of the participating libraries is responsible for maintenance costs, future incremental expansion of both hardware and software, and upgrading local telecommunications (including connecting branch libraries and remote sites).

1. **Central Funding**:

   State funding for OhioLINK is from two sources:
   * Capital funding:
   - 1990/92 biennium $ 9.2 million
   - 1992/94 biennium   10.8 million
   * Operating budget:
   - 1989/91 biennium   0.4 million
   - 1991/93 biennium   1.7 million
   - 1993/95 biennium[①]4.6 million

2. **Local Funding**:

   The estimated expenditures for Ohio University, both the initial costs and ongoing maintenance costs, for the main campus and 5 university centers are summarized in Table 1.

THE ROAD AHEAD

Ohio libraries have been in the forefront in library automation and innovation since the 1960s. The creation of OCLC drastically changed the world of library cataloging, union catalogs, interlibrary loans, and networking. The growth and development within Ohio of the Chemical Abstracts Service, CompuServe, Mead Data, Battelle, and others as well as OCLC have made Ohio a world information center. The design and implementation of OhioLINK in the 1990s provides a new vision for the future. It is hoped that OhioLINK will equal the importance of OCLC and set the pace for connecting people, libraries, and information.

---

① This has been requested but is still in the legislative process.

As OhioLINK increasingly becomes a reality, new methods, policies and procedures will be developed, tested and adopted for effective operations. Many new features such as full-text databases, electronic document delivery, multi-tasking workstations equipped with powerful intelligent software will be added.

Table 1 Summary of Projected OhioLINK Costs

	Athens Campus		University Centers	
	Initial One-time Athens Campus Costs	Annual Athens Campus Costs	Initial One-time University Center Costs	Annual University Center Costs
III Software	$ 49,950	$ 52,281	$ 23,800	$ 14,571
DEC II Hardware*	$ 17,585	$ 11,296	$ 19,321	$ 4,188
Networking—CNS**	$ 106,027	$ 16,714	$ 35,789	$ 5,337
Retrospective Con-version***	$ 15,110	NA	$ 10,560	NA
Total	$ 188,672	$ 80,291	$ 89,470	$ 24,096

* Hardware costs are based on the best estimate of Library and Computing and Technology Services staff.

** Networking costs were detailed in a February 27, 1992, memo from Tom Reid and sent to the Provost.

*** This cost to convert older records will be covered about 80% by OBOR/Ohio LINK, the figures here reflect the remaining share to be covered by Ohio University. On July 16, 1992, we were advised that OhioLINK likely will contribute less to the cost of Retrospective Conversion than previously projected—meaning that Athens and University Center shares will increase.

Although the changeover to III likely will be difficult for libraries satisfied with their current systems, everyone is convinced that the long-term benefits from a single system and a virtual library will outweigh temporary inconveniences during the transition. Armed with many new and powerful features, OhioLINK will greatly enhance the availability and accessibility of pooled information resources. High-speed telecommunication capability will provide a gateway to the ever-growing world of information stored in electronic formats around the world. It is well recognized that much can be gained in cooperative and coordinated acquisitions, collection development and management, preservation, resource sharing, and scholarly communications through OhioLINK. When fully implemented, OhioLINK will be the most powerful statewide library and information network in the nation with unparalleled sophistication and efficiency.

(Published in *CONSAL IX Papers: Future Dimensions and Library Development*. Bangkok: CONSAL IX Secretariat, 1993: pp. B45 – B62. And *Chiang Mai University Library Journal*. V. 4, 1994: pp. 20 – 43.)

全球信息获取：图书馆乃民众通向世界的大门

Global Information Access: Libraries as Citizens' Gateway to the World[①]

The Historical Role of Libraries

While libraries are often thought of in association with books and reading for information and scholarly pursuit, historically it would be more accurate to think of them as institutions for the collection, organization, preservation, and dissemination of knowledge. In reflecting on the origin and nature of libraries, I do not wish to depreciate the close and vital relationship among libraries, paper, and printing during the past millennium. But, in looking at libraries today and tomorrow, I need emphasize that knowledge and libraries have not been confined to a single medium. As an observer three decades ago observed:

Today's American library is dedicated, as it never was before, to promoting enlightened citizenship and enriching personal life. The things that are important to contemporary society are important to the library. People, rather than books, come first in modern library thinking.[②]

In approaching my theme today, I wish to reassert this overriding concern with helping people to become better informed and more enlightened citizens continues to characterize the library profession. One of joys that a library dean or director experiences comes from the disposition of citizens to share with a librarian such as myself their early experiences with libraries—memories of how they discovered that the world was far more immense in time and space than they had imagined.

As I, in this paper, look at the extent to which modern information technology is at our doorsteps, I do not wish to undervalue or under-appreciate that libraries have been performing similar functions for hundreds of years—as reading books and magazines has enabled millions of children and adults to travel to far-off lands and times in their imaginations. To use a little computer jargon, today they can make these mind-broadening trips, life-enriching trips in "real time".

Libraries in Transition

During the past thirty years, prompted by developments in information technology, libraries have increasingly incorporated electronic resources into materials available to users and have employed such technologies as computers, telecommunications, electronic storage, and multimedia to cope with great increases in the amount of information. The impacts of these technological advances can be summarized as follows:

1) Advancements in computer technologies and sophistication of library applications software have transformed libraries' operations and services.

2) Improvements in telecommunications and electronic delivery technologies have given new meaning to library networking and resource-sharing.

3) Innovations in storage technologies have revolutionized information storage and retrieval.

4) Growing use of interactive multimedia technologies has expanded the nature and organization of information.

As a result of these developments, libraries have gone through several stages of changes which

---

[①] 本文为日本中部大学开学 30 周年纪念的生涯学习研究会上的发言，日本春日井市，中部大学，1995 年。
[②] Edith Patterson Meyer. *Meet the Future: People and Ideas in the Libraries of Today and Tomorrow*. Boston: Little, Brown and Co., 1964: p. 34.

can be characterized as:
   1) the "paper library" before the 1960s,
   2) to the "automated library" from the 1970s,
   3) to the "networked library" emerged in the 1980s, and
   4) to the "electronic library" of the 1990s. ①

All these parallel and complementary developments lead the libraries of the future to a new type of "virtual library" which means that library users will be able to access information resources far greater than those actually owned by any single library, in all formats, and without regard to geographical locations or distance.

I should emphasize that the evolution of information technology has not been a straight and narrow road. There has been any number of detours and false trails. For example, even the most successful—OCLC, the Online Computer Library Center located in Columbus, Ohio—was created to solve most of the problems of Ohio academic libraries back in 1967. It solved some of these (such as the soaring personnel costs required to extract the intellectual content of library resources—a process we call cataloging) and resource sharing. But it became so caught up with its successes, it was unable to address a multitude of other (then largely local) needs for library automation. ②

Another example would be online searching. Back in the 1970s when I first came to Ohio University, this was a grand innovation—one that would put the world of knowledge at a scholar's fingertips. Through online searching, one could access hundreds of different bibliographic databases (provided through an online vendor such as Dialog or BRS). But it had two major shortcomings. The first was the cost. The online vendors charged for each title looked at with a further charge for any title printed out or downloaded. Additionally, a user also had to pay phone charges. In Ohio University's case, this included a long-distance call to Columbus, Ohio, where we connected to a time-share network which entailed additional connect-time charges. In all, a simple search might cost $10 to $15 and a complex search or a search in an expensive database could run $50 to $75.

Because of these charges, we had to require those who used the service to share the costs. We did work out a system under which the library would pay one-half of the cost, but a search could still be expensive for a user and for the library. Additionally, to control costs at even those levels, it was necessary that a librarian undertake the search. An unskilled searcher could easily run up a bill of $100 or more. Because of these barriers, with the library and librarians as gatekeepers, the number of searches conducted was limited. In the peak year, 1986 – 1987, 1,535 online searches were conducted. At about that same time, the Ohio University Libraries introduced CD-ROM searching.

The contrast between online searching and CD-ROM searching is staggering. For a single cost or an annual subscription fee, an unlimited number of searches can be performed on a CD-ROM database. Two years later, we placed the more popular CD-ROM databases on a network which also meant that search stations (microcomputers with Ethernet connections) could be spread throughout the library. In 1993 – 1994, more than one hundred times as many database searches were conducted (177,000) as the peak for online searches. The immediate availability of a variety of databases, the absence of charges, and the ability of students or faculty members to

---

① This theme is more fully developed in a paper which I will present in China, "Networked, Electronic and Virtual Library—Libraries of the 1990s" to be presented at the International Seminar on Information Technologies and Information Services, October 20 – 24, 1994, Shanghai, China.

② Founded in 1967 by a group of academic libraries in Ohio for cooperative cataloging, computer union catalog, and interlibrary loan using a central computer, OCLC soon expanded to become a national and international online computer library network encompassing 17,000 libraries in the United States and 51 other countries and territories. Annually, member libraries contributed more than two million cataloging records to the union catalog which in June 1993 consisted of over 27 million cataloging records with 483 million holding and location information. Some 6.5 million interlibrary loan requests were transacted through OCLC between July 1992 – June 1993. See OCLC Annual Report 1992/93 (Dublin, Ohio: OCLC, 1993).

conduct the searches themselves contributed to this popularity.

Despite fears of some that electronic resources would eliminate the need for librarians, we have found to the contrary. But now the role of the librarian is no longer to control the search behavior of the user or serve as a stand-in for the user. Rather, the librarians have encountered an enormous demand to teach users to make CD-ROM searches effectively. And I would add that, despite the growth in the workload, the librarians have been much more comfortable with the role of facilitator than of gate keeper. Indeed, one of the commitments of our profession today is to empower the library users so that they can effectively and efficiently utilize the exploding array of information resources.

The Coming of OhioLINK

To further utilize the latest information technologies available, Ohio University is currently participating in a statewide network and resource sharing initiative that will open all major collections around the state to students, faculty members, researchers, and other users. After three years of intensive planning, the new initiative, OhioLINK (Ohio Academic Library and Information Network), is being installed now in 17 large university and research libraries, plus the State Library of Ohio, and 23 community and technical college libraries. OhioLINK will enable registered library users in any of the participating libraries to search the library holdings of other OhioLINK libraries and request the needed items online by themselves. If an article is desired, it may be faxed, or if a book, it is sent by a courier service. Thus, library users should receive requested materials in two or three days, at the most. ①

One of the immediate characteristics of OhioLINK is that it goes well beyond traditional automated library systems. In addition to allowing students, faculty, and others to identify what resources are available in the member libraries, it includes many bibliographic databases covering other materials. These include indexes or abstracts of newspaper and periodical articles, many medical databases, and other databases covering most academic disciplines—some including full texts. A library user will be able to look at a single computer and search for information both locally and throughout the state and then through journals, newspapers, dissertations, and special reports.

Many of the databases offered by OhioLINK are currently offered by member libraries (including Ohio University) on CD-ROM. Under OhioLINK, these will be mounted on tapes on large computers and be shared among members. A major advantage is that the user can use a single computer (without needing to go to a CD-ROM-networked workstation). Eventually, all of these information sources will be searchable with a single entry. A student at Ohio University can look for information on Japanese education and search through the resources at Ohio University. The student can then request that the same subject be searched in all of the major academic libraries in Ohio. And if he or she identifies information at another library, they can type in the request for this information without leaving the computer. The request will be transmitted to the library that owns the material and the material will be shipped by courier to Ohio University within a day or two.

The Gateway for Global Information Access

Through OhioLINK, the user is also connected to a variety of databases and resources around the world, through the Internet. This worldwide connectivity, which Vice President Gore of the United States has referred to as the "information superhighway", overpowers the notion of gateway. ② Traditionally, a gateway was not only a place of entrance and exit but also a means of

---

① This author has written several papers on OhioLINK. The latest one, "Networked, Electronic and Virtual Library—Libraries of the 1990s" is cited fully in footnote 2.

② See, for example among his many interviews and speeches on the subject, Albert Gore. "The Information Superhighways of Tomorrow." *Academic Computing*. V. IV (Nov. 1989): pp. 30 – 31.

controlling the flow of people, animals or things. Today, librarians are not concerned about controlling the flow but about opening the gate as wide as possible to let students, faculty, and citizens freely and ably seek and retrieve the information which they need, from anywhere in the world.

The reference to a gateway recalls an earlier, slower era. Today, the information superhighway might more aptly be likened to a bullet train. And we are eager to pack as much information and as many users as possible into the system. But even that analogy breaks down because this is a bullet train that spans oceans and joins continents and islands as easily as cities.

Another characteristic of OhioLINK and the Internet is the sense of "virtual library", a conceptual entity with no visible physical boundaries. While libraries as buildings, collections, and people will continue to exist and function as a place for housing printed and multimedia materials, for processing and preservation, for learning and consultation, for information dissemination, for information literacy training, and for face-to-face interaction among users and librarians, it is also a place where the services of the library are unconstrained by walls or physical facilities. In fact, the resources of OhioLINK and the Internet are available to faculty and students from their homes, offices, and dormitory rooms. Most still come to the library, we think because it is a pleasant and productive environment in which to engage in intellectual activity. And helpful librarians are readily at hand. In reality, it is a location unbounded by geography but one in which one find assistance in synthesizing information into knowledge.

But this does point to the changing nature of our world. Information tends to know no national or institutional boundaries. Some would say that "information wants to be free", but my experience with library budgets convinces me that this has never been the case and is unlikely ever to be the case. What is important is that access to information needs to be available to all citizenry, at modest cost. This is another role of the library as the open gateway.

There has recently been considerable debate over the size of the Internet, whether it currently has 16 million or 32 million or more or fewer computers connected. [1] Even the detractors, however, are aware that the Internet is a growing and increasingly pervasive presence in most areas of our life, such as education, research, work, communications, and business. This is even more the case where individuals or businesses are engaged in planning, developing, or using high-technology. It is also a symptom of what has been called the "information age". In the past, finding the information that one sought often required travel to distant depositories of information or participation in an "invisible college" where information was shared among an inner circle.

Internationally, according to a recent statistics released by the Internet Society, the amount of global Internet data traffic exceeds 10 terabytes every month, the figure is an equivalent of the entire contents of the U. S. Library of Congress!

Today, the problem is no longer a scarcity of information but a need to winnow the information needed from environments saturated in information, to remove the rice from the chaff. This is a skill that is central to librarianship (and information science). We have long amassed resources well beyond the ability of most of our clientele to use, simply so we would have information that a user needed when that information was needed. Our training and experience have been directed at finding the best information from among millions of pages (and now electrons). As everyone is bombarded with more information (and entertainment) than they could ever want or deal with, this is an important skill.

Education for Information-seeking Literacy

The value of this skill has been recognized at Ohio University. A report prepared by distinguished citizens and faculty and administrators at Ohio University undertook to assess what the University should be doing as it neared its 300th birthday in 2004, *Toward the Third Century*:

---

[1] See, for example, Bob Metcalfe, "From the Ether: Counting Users isn't easy on the Incredible (Shrinking?!) Internet." *Info World*. V. 16, Issue 34 (August 22, 1994): p. 46.

Issues and Choices for Ohio University, emphasized:

In the era of computers a base for continued learning also requires developing what has been labeled as "information-seeking literacy". No one can carry away from the campus experience an adequate knowledge or information base. **What university education can and should provide is a developed capacity to search for what is needed, an ability to find, interpret, and evaluate information. The Ohio University libraries have a key and expanding role in providing... access to and training in the processes of information seeking so essential to contemporary life.** [1] (emphasis added)

Learning information-seeking skills is therefore a most important part of university education for every student. All of them must be adequately equipped with such skills to continue their learning throughout their life.

The library and librarian are no longer the gateway which controls access but rather are the experts at building gateways so faculty and students are able to screen out superfluous information and concentrate their attention on their work. Library research seldom any longer consists of pouring over indexes for hours to find what has been researched or written in a particular area. Now a computer-mediated search of CD-ROMs or online sources (such as offered by OhioLINK) can produce hundreds or thousands of references in minutes. And the printing is done automatically—no more hand-copying of notes about sources. But thousands of references on a subject are little more useful than a handful of relevant ones. It becomes necessary for researchers to consider and carefully define the subjects of their interests. They then can use various information tools, such as Boolean search techniques, to refine their searches to return just the 25 articles and books most directly relevant to their interests.

This is a new skill which even the best scholars have only begun to develop. Yet it is essential, not only for a successful academic career, but for professional growth and development throughout one's life. The teaching role of the librarian is ever more central. We have long recognized that the library was the heart of the university but today we are also aware that the skills of librarianship are at the heart of the educational mission of the university.

The Power of Internet

While describing the virtues (and vices) of the marriage of libraries and computers, I am happy to advise you as current or future users of Internet that the marriage is also yielding increasingly powerful and relatively easy-to-use tools for information seeking on the Internet. Yet I would also caution that much of the Internet remains esoteric both in what is needed to use it and what it contains. This is less true today than last year and hopefully less true than next year.

Among the second generation of tools is Gopher. This menu-driven search system basically automates the rudimentary Internet tools of Telnet and FTP. [2] Telnet is a way of interacting with a remote computer, and FTP is a means for transferring files between your local computer and a remote computer. Gopher gets its name from the mascot of the state of Minnesota and its university (the Golden Gophers) where the software was developed as well as a play on the pejorative an administrative assistant, "go-fer", who goes for things at his/her bosses direction. This latter is essentially what Gopher does, but you—the information seeker—is the boss. Gopher's abilities have been greatly enhanced by a more recent development, VERONICA, a software program that periodically surveys all of the Gopher servers around the world and indexes the materials which they contain.

An intermediate step to gain some intellectual access to the mushrooming resources has been identified as Wide Area Information Servers (WAIS), which indexes data or information files

---

[1] *Toward the Third Century: Issues and Choices for Ohio University.* A Report to the University by the Colloquium on the Third Century (Athens, Ohio: Ohio University, 1988).

[2] Telnet and FTP (File Transfer Protocol) are a part of the pervasive TCP/IP (Transmission Control Protocol/Internet Protocol) system which has become the dominant environment on the Internet.

available on machines around the world. Its counterpart, ARCHIE, has done much the same for program files.

While these efforts to improve access to an exploding universe of information are less than comprehensive, they have made use of Internet less demanding in technical expertise. While I comment on the weaknesses of these efforts, I should also note their versatility. For example, after considerable trial and error, OhioLINK has selected a Gopher to link its various resources and many OhioLINK libraries are making their library systems begin with a Gopher. This enables a user to look at the local system, to bypass it and go to OhioLINK Central, or simply to jump into the Internet.

A far more aesthetically pleasing approach has been the browser for the World Wide Web (WWW) called Mosaic. No longer focused simply on text, Mosaic adds pictures (moving as well as photos and illustrations) to the previously text-oriented tools. ①

Global Information Access

The upshot is that librarians are finding bigger and more important roles in helping members of university communities and the citizenry at large to cope with the information explosion. They are best prepared to help users traverse the gateway to the world that libraries have become and to translate the chaotic universe of information into knowledge.

With the wide spread of Internet to every corner of the world, not only has global information access become a reality, but an effective means for the delivery and support of distance education also has been made available and affordable. Through the Internet, libraries the world over can play an essential role in the enhancement of distance education and in making lifelong learning an easy and attractive part of every adult life. ②

(Published in *the Proceedings of the Chubu University-Ohio University Conference on Lifelong Learning for the 21st Century: Local and Global Dimensions*, October 4 – 6, 1994.)

---

① With a graphical interface, software such as Mosaic for the WWW is much more adept at handling non-Roman script languages than the other software based on ASCII text. Good examples are the Japan Virtual Library from Stanford University (URL: http://fuji.stanford.edu/VL/WWW-VL-Japan.html) and the NTT home page (URL: http://www.ntt.jp/). URL is Universal Resource Locator and provides address and directory information for connections on the WWW. Particularly noteworthy is the manner in which a number of Japanese universities and organizations provide an on-screen "pushbutton" for choosing between Japanese and English versions of display.

② In one encouraging recent development, some institutions offering distance education have recognized that remote programs tend to place a burden on libraries in the area where the students reside, whether as gateways or for resources. Some have negotiated agreements with the local public or academic library for the services which that library provides to students from the institution providing remote instruction and degree programs.

基本教育项目（CPR/91/420）

Program CPR/91/420 Basic Education: Administration and Teachers Training[①]

1. Project Description

The Consultant was engaged by UNESCO, within the framework of Program CPR/91/420—Basic Education: Administration and Teachers Training, to undertake a mission to the People's Republic of China from 8 May 1995 to 7 June 1995 for the following assignments:

1.1　Prepare a detailed work and teaching plan prior to the mission.

1.2　Investigate the two information and resource centers in Hubei and Zhengzhou and provide constructive suggestions for the development of these centers.

1.3　Draw up guidelines in terms of library management for both Hubei and Zhengzhou institutes with respect to the whole systematic management of normal secondary school libraries throughout China.

1.4　Participate in the seminar titled "Modern Library Information Management and Services" and give lectures on the following subjects:
- Modern library information management and services;
- Management functions and management techniques of modern libraries;
- Purchasing policies of library stock, shared resources, co-operative acquisitions;
- Readers' services;
- Library buildings, equipment, installation of automation and applied techniques;
- Library cooperation and library networks.

1.5　Submit a report after the mission on the lectures given, investigation undertaken and work accomplished during the mission.

2. Work Undertaken

2.1　Based on the contract, I worked closely with my Chinese counterpart, Prof. Wang You-Mei, Department of Information Technology and Management, Beijing Normal University, during most of March and April of 1995 to plan mission details and course outlines. Prof. Wang was appointed by the State Education Commission of PRC to be the native expert. With his help, we drafted our travel plan and the course schedule prior to my departure from U.S.A. to China. For the two-week seminar on "Modern Library Information Management and Services", I prepared a 79-page document, Lecture Notes, together with 15 selected articles for supplementary reading. These materials were air-mailed to Prof. Wang on March 30, 1995. Likewise, Prof. Wang prepared his part of the lecture notes and supplementary materials.

2.2　After arriving Beijing on May 7, I met with Prof. Wang to review our plans and schedule for needed revisions. We had separate meetings with officials of the State Education Commission (SEC) and officers of the UNESCO Office in Beijing on May 8. At the request of the State Education Commission, a number of visits to normal schools in Beijing, Wuhan, Shayang, and Loyang were added to our schedule in addition to the Hubei Provincial College of Education in Wuhan and Zhengzhou Normal School in Zhengzhou which was the primary focuses of our mission.

2.3　The names and titles of officials with whom we met at the State Education Commission were:

[①] Submitted to United Nations Educational, Scientific and Cultural Organization, June 30, 1995: p.13. (SECTOR/BUREAU REF: CPR/91/420 - 11 - 303; ROC REF: 864.675.5)

Ms. Zhang Linyi, Chief, Division of Primary School Teachers Training, Department of Teachers Education, SEC.

Mr. Sang Changyong, Deputy Chief, Division of Primary School Teachers Training, Department of Teachers Education, SEC.

Mr. Bao Tongzeng, Assistant Director, Department of Teachers Education, SEC.

Prof. Li Zhibao, Senior Technical Advisor on International Cooperation, SEC.

Mr. Wang Fu, Vice Director, Department of Technology and Equipment. SEC.

Mr. Dong Zheqian, Chief, Division of Library and Information, Department of Technology and Equipment, SEC.

2.4 The names and titles of those officers whom we met at the Enesco Office in Beijing were:

Mr. Shikon Takei, UNESCO Representative to China, Mongolia and DPR Korea.

Dr. John Elfick, UNESCO Education Advisor to China, Mongolia and DPR Korea. Ms. Tania Nelson, Programme Officer.

2.5 Both Prof. Wang and I were very pleased with these instructive meetings and are grateful for the much useful information and many suggestions. We owe the success of our mission assignment to those whose names are listed in 2.3 and 2.4.

2.6 All together, we visited eight schools. These were:

In Beijing
Beijing No. 3 Normal School
Beijing City Child Pedagogical School
In Wuhan
Hubei Provincial College of Education
Wuhan No. 2 Normal School
In Shayang
Shayang Normal School
In Zhengzhou
Zhengzhou Normal School
In Loyang
Loyang No. 1 Normal School

In addition to these eight schools, we also visited the officials of the Jinzhou City Education Commission and had a discussion about the general condition of school libraries in Jinzhou.

In Wuhan, we were privileged to meet Mr. Jia Bao Chen, Chief, Teachers Training Division, Hubei Provincial Education Commission, who accompanied us in our visits to Shayang and Jinzhou. During these two days of field trip, we learned a great deal about teacher training and primary education in Hubei from Mr. Jia.

2.7 The key assignment of my consultancy in Wuhan was to participate in the two-week seminar on "Modern Library Information Management and Services" and to give lectures on the following topics:

– Development of modern library and information services;
– The functions of modern library management;
– The techniques of modern library management;
– Management of library and information resources;
– Reader services and instruction on library use;
– Technical Services;
– Library cooperation, networking, and resource sharing.

In addition, Prof. Wang gave the following lectures:
– Teachers education and the library;
– Information services of normal school libraries;
– Information services and research for education;
– Qualification and education of library personnel;

— Planning for new library buildings and additions;
— Comparison of Chinese and foreign libraries.

Another guest lecturer, Mr. Shi Shuwen, Chief of the Automation Development Department, Beijing Normal University Library, was invited to give a series of lectures on library automation and computerization.

All these lectures, together with discussions, hands-on practice, and library visits were scheduled seven days a week, including Saturday and Sunday, throughout the two-week period. It was very intensive for the participants as well as the lecturers. After the first three days of lectures, I began to lose my voice and required treatment by Chinese herbal medicines.

2.8 Throughout the seminar, participants demonstrated high levels of enthusiasm and eagerness to learn. Among the 55 participants in the seminar, 29 were from Hubei Province and 26 from 19 other provinces, autonomous regions, and capital cities. (Please see Appendix I for a list of the participants.)

2.9 We were told by many participants that the announcement of the seminar did not reach a large number of normal school librarians. Some of those who came to the seminar learned about it from second-hand sources. As a result of the lateness of receiving the information, two participants from Guangdong Province did not get to Wuhan until the second week of the seminar.

2.10 Despite the problems in notification, for which we don't know whom to blame, those participants did arrive and were happy to come and very pleased with the results. The participant from Sichuan Province, Mr. He Changping, was representing the normal school libraries of the entire province. Another participant, Mr. Tien Yongqi of Shenyang Normal School, will report on his experience to other normal school librarians in his province.

2.11 By their own initiative, participants from colleges of education and from normal schools met separately several times after dinner during the seminar to exchange information and experiences among themselves. At their meetings, participants from normal school libraries proposed to establish a national organization for the promotion, research, and development of normal school libraries since this is the only library group that does not have its own national organization as yet. They drafted bylaws, elected officers, and planned the first national meeting to be held in Beijing in August 1996, coinciding with the 1996 IFLA Beijing Conference.

Prof. Wang and I were asked to serve as honorary chairs of the Board in the newly formed national organization which will be headquartered at Zhengzhou Normal School.

2.12 At the Hubei Provincial College of Education and Zhengzhou Normal School, the two schools which have been chosen as demonstration centers for library and information resources for their respective type of teachers education and training, and are receiving UNDP grants, Prof. Wang and I spent a great deal of time visiting the facilities, reviewing the plans, talking to officials, meeting with the library staffs, and offering our suggestions.

For the Hubei Provincial College of Education, we held three rather lengthy meetings with the college officials, including President Huang Yuan Qi, Vice President Xiong Yunji, Project Coordinator Wang Xianliang, Library Director Chen Xian Rong, etc. In addition, at our request, we met with the entire library staff to hear their views and concerns.

At the Zhengzhou Normal School, we also spent considerable time talking with the school officials. A day-long seminar on information center management and services was given to all the administrators and staff who are involved in the work of the information and resources center for teacher education and training.

3. General Observation

3.1 Despite the overall success of the seminar at the Hubei Provincial College of Education which was made possible by the support of college officials as well as by the hard work of the library staff under the leadership of Mr. Chen Xian Rong, the Library Director, we encountered a few problems.

3.1.1 Even though the seminar was nearly free to the participants, many provinces and autonomous regions did not take the opportunity to send the allowable two librarians for each province or region. Many of these provinces and regions such as Inter Mongolia, Xinjiang Uygur, Tibet, Qinghai, Heilongjiang, Hainan, Shaanxi, Zhejiang, and Fujian could have been benefited from the participation.

3.1.2 It was regrettable also that none of the library staff and others involved in the Teachers Education Information Resources Center at the Hubei College of Education was asked by the College to attend the seminar. We were told by the library staff that they were required to maintain the library service during the Seminar and, hence, were unable to attend. This was the main reason that we asked to meet with the library staff for one afternoon after the seminar so that we could talk to them.

3.1.3 There was clear evidence that the College Library was not given the appropriate role in the operation of the Teachers Education Information Resource Center despite the fact, as stated in the planning document of the College, that the Library is also the core of the Center. (Please see Appendix II for the plan.)

3.1.4 Much of the equipment provided by UNDP funding was either still in storage or has been given to other college units. Lacking the necessary equipment, such as computers, printers, and copying machines, the Library's work as the Information Resources Center has been hampered. For example, because a new copying machine was still in the packing box, our lecture notes and supplementary reading materials could not be reproduced in time for use. Operating the old copying machine took a great deal of staff time and prevented them from attending the seminar. Without the new computers, Mr. Shi could not offer hands-on practice vital to his lecture on computer applications. The Information Resources Department of the Library has no computer at all to properly perform its work.

3.1.5 The College's Teachers Training Center which was built for purpose of education and training was also used for commercial activities. As a result, we could use the well-equipped lecture room in the Center only half of the time. Many of the participants could not stay at the Center because some of rooms were rented out to tourist groups.

3.2 It was noted by Prof. Wang that, in the progress report provided to us on May 29—the last day of our stay in Wuhan, there were few changes from what he had seen in an earlier visit in September of 1994. The College put the blame on the following:

3.2.1 The publication of a journal was delayed for three reasons: (1) Still waiting for government approval; (2) editorial team is inexperienced, and (3) distribution channel is yet to be established.

3.2.2 Computerized database has not attained the set quota. The reasons are twofold: (1) UNDP equipment arrived late, and (2) lack of technical training for the staff.

3.2.3 The acquisition of books and journals are below the required number. The reason is that the allocation of acquisition funds from the UNDP project is for the second half year of 1995.

3.2.4 The production of audio-visual materials is behind schedule. This is due to the late arrival of UNDP funded equipment. (Please see Appendix III for the progress report.)

3.3 In our observations, however, the general lack of progress is due largely to the following factors:

3.3.1 The organization of the Teachers Education Information Resources Center places the Library as one of five units. These units are: Teaching and Research Information, Teacher Training Information, Information Resources Development (i.e., Library), Theoretical Research, and Production of Audio-Visual Materials. Instead of having the Library as the lead unit of the Center as stated in the original planning document issued by the College on June 15, 1994 (Appendix II), the Library—to the contrary—has little or no voice in the overall planning and management of the Center. The five units are placed under the coordination of Mr. Wang Xianliang, Vice Director of the College's International Cooperation Office of Middle School Teachers Training Center, who reports directly to the College President. Both Mr. Wang and President Huang have low regard for the ability of the library staff—which they expressed whenever we brought up the issue of the library being the leading force in the organization.

3.3.2 Furthermore, both President Huang and Mr. Wang are very busy people with a variety of other responsibilities. They just do not have time to oversee day-to-day operations. This loosely linked organization, with little or no interactions among the five administratively separated units, needs strong leadership and effective coordination other than President Huang and Mr. Wang.

3.3.3 In our meeting with the library staff, we observed a strong desire to play a larger role in the operation of the Information Resources Center, but, regrettably, these very important staff resources and energy have not been adequately recognized and deployed.

In our opinion, unless some drastic changes are made in the organization of the Center with more responsibility—and corresponding authority—assigned to the Library, Hubei Provincial College of Education will be unable to carry out its mission as the national model for teachers education information resources center. This change in organization should be accompanied by a change in the perception of the Library's new role by the top administration of the College.

3.4 To our surprise, our visit to Shayang Normal School was an unexpected discovery. Of all the schools we visited, Shayang greatly impressed us with its new vision of teacher's education, outstanding leadership, and exemplary program. The campus is well designed with modern buildings and facilities. Unlike other schools, Shayang Normal School has an excellent program of building maintenance and campus beautification. With no financial aid from any foreign sources, the School is able to utilize its limited financial resources wisely to acquire a good number of new computers and other modern equipment and, more importantly, has put them to good use. Managed by six staff members, its library has installed an integrated computer system which is connected to the campus-wide computer network, a rare occurrence in China, especially among secondary schools and colleges at present! Its collection of 11,000 books and 600 current journals, though small, is well used by teachers and students in open stacks. The Library is open 10 hours a day and daily attendance averages 750 persons, about 60 percent of the student population. This review led us to wonder how appropriate it would have been if Shayang were chosen as the national model for teachers education information resources center instead of Hubei Provincial College of Education? (Please see Appendices IV and V for descriptions of the School and its library.)

3.5 Although Zhengzhou Normal School is also no comparison to Shayang Normal School, we saw many encouraging developments. Among these were the new leadership of the school (the new principal, Mr. Li Chunchao, has assumed the position about one year ago) and the importance placed on the UNDP project to establish a model information resources center for teacher education and training at the primary education level. Included in the School's plan is a new library building to be constructed within the next two or three years. According to Mr. Feng Yirong, the Coordinator of the Center who is also the Assistant to the Principal, the School will do its utmost to carry out the Center's plan. However, because of the late start and rather inadequate resources, it may take longer to achieve the Center's goal. (Please see Appendix VI for the Center's plan.)

3.6 At the other normal schools visited, we observed a general inadequacy in their libraries. Some of the common characteristics were:

3.6.1 Most libraries are in poor quarters with small collections, largely book-oriented. Funding for library acquisitions is irregular and inadequate.

3.6.2 Library hours are short, no formal library instruction is offered, and they are not used much by students or teachers.

3.6.3 There is little teacher involvement, and library use is not part of the curriculum.

3.6.4 Library staff members vary in qualifications, many have much lower status than teachers. There is little opportunity for staff training and development.

3.6.5 School administrators do not recognize the importance of the library in the education and learning process. The one exception we saw is the Shayang Normal School. The different effects are quite obvious.

4. Recommendations

Based on the work undertaken and the observations made, both Prof. Wang and I have had numerous discussions on our joint recommendations below:

4.1 In regard to the Seminar:

4.1.1 There is a need for more seminars on various topics. Computer applications and networking, information retrieval and services, management, and others are all important. But a special seminar on the importance of library and information center is especially needed for college and school administrators. It is our feeling that, unless these top administrators know the significant role of their libraries in teacher's education and training and is very supportive of them, these libraries will not be able to discharge their proper educational functions.

4.1.2 Future seminars should be held in those institutions whose libraries are more advanced, whose administrators are supportive of their libraries, and where the facility for holding seminars are adequate.

4.1.3 Participants expressed their appreciation to the Division of Primary School Teachers Training, Department of Teachers Education, SEC, for organizing this seminar. They felt that having the seminar is an important indication of the government's emphasis of the library's role in education. They further suggested that SEC would issue special guidelines for normal school libraries with the following directives:

(1) The library should be placed directly under the school principal or a vice principal.

(2) Professional librarians should be classified as teachers with comparable ranks and salaries. This should be done by SEC instead of the Ministry of Culture.

(3) Library budgets should be set as a fixed percentage of the school's budget (e.g., 5 percent or better).

(4) There should be minimum standards for library organization, staffing, and services.

(5) Library instruction such as information retrieval and use should be included in the curriculum.

(6) Teachers should be encouraged to work with librarians on lesson plans and should bring students to the library to learn.

(7) There should be basic requirements for library buildings, equipment, and furniture.

During inspections performed by various levels of the education commission, it is suggested that library should always be included. This will force school administrators to pay more attention to the library.

4.2 In regard to Hubei Provincial College of Education:

4.2.1 We have suggested to President Huang that the Library Director be appointed as the Co-coordinator for the Information Resources Center so that the Library will have more direct interaction with other units.

4.2.2 More support is needed from the college administration, including operating funds and the turnover of UNDP funded equipment intended for the Library, in order for the Library to carry out its key role in the Information Resources Center.

4.2.3 UNDP money for library acquisitions should be released as soon as possible for the Library to acquire the needed materials.

4.2.4 The Library should expand its collections of information resources in other formats including multimedia and electronic materials. Computer equipment for the use of these new formats should be planned for acquisition.

4.2.5 There is a need for a mid-to-long-range plan beyond the current two-year plan for the full implementation of the Information Resources Center.

4.2.6 It is suggested that SEC and UNESCO Beijing Office would closely monitor the implementation and to make sure that the College is in compliance with the 1994 plan.

4.3 In regard to the Zhengzhou Normal School:

4.3.1　If possible, we recommend the extension of current support by UNDP for three additional years so that the School can achieve its goal as the model Information Resources Center for Teachers Education and Training at the primary school level. The School should be asked to submit a proposal describing its needs and projects. Some of these projects may include a Multimedia Demonstration Laboratory, an integrated computer system and necessary networking, on-going staff training, support of the newly established National Association of Normal School Libraries which will be headquartered at Zhengzhou Normal School, a model school library which will provide book reviews, ordering and cataloging services, and other services to school libraries in the country.

4.3.2　It is our feeling that unless more funding can be made available either from UNDP or from SEC, the School's efforts alone will not be enough to achieve the intended goals. In conjunction with the funding proposal to be developed by Zhengzhou Normal School, the School should first map out a mid-to long-range plan acceptable by the City, Province, and State education authorities.

4.4　In regard to Shayang Normal School:

4.4.1　As a way of encouragement for schools which, by their own initiatives and efforts, have created outstanding programs, we would strongly recommend that UNESCO, the UNDP, and/or the SEC provide a one-time grant to Shayang Normal School. Such a grant should be large enough to enable the School to do even more as the nation's model school truly worthy of the name.

4.4.2　During our visit to Shayang Normal School, we were told that the School's reputation has already spread to many parts of the country. Since last November, more than 1,000 visitors from all over China have come to see the School. This averages nearly 200 visitors per month. School officials expressed mixed feelings about the suddenly gained fame. On the one hand, they are very pleased with the recognition, but, on the other hand, they are burdened by the influx of visitors which interrupt the School's normal operations. The special grant will help to defray the costs of the growing number of visitors.

4.5　One other school caught our attention:

4.5.1　During our visit to Loyang No. 1 Normal School we found the School in a situation very different from others, that is, seven of the nine counties served by the School is classified nationally as poverty-stricken counties. These counties are located in a mountainous region, very difficult to access, and severely short of water. Nearly 75% of the School's students are from these poverty-stricken counties. They will return to teach after graduation. Even though the School doesn't charge these student any tuition and fees, each student needs at least 50 Yuan more per month for living expenses. The Principal of the School, Mr. Li Chengben, made a strong plea for financial assistance from UNDP or other sources.

5. Acknowledgements

5.1　Firstly, I would like to express my sincere gratitude to UNESCO Beijing Office for engaging me as the foreign consultant for this worthy project funded by UNDP. The advice and assistance of the Beijing Office staff were most helpful for the successful completion of my mission assignments.

5.2　Secondly, I want to extend my profound thank to Ms. Zhang Linyi and her staff in the Division of Primary School Teachers Training, Department of Teachers Education, State Education Commission. Without the guidance and support of Ms. Zhang and her able staff, particularly Mr. Sang Changyong, the mission would not have gone so smoothly with the multiple assignments and the severe time constraints.

5.3　Finally, I must not forget the kindness and thoughtfulness of my counterpart, Prof. Wang You-Mei, who worked very hard to take care of me in addition to his own work. The team work with Prof. Wang, and joined in part by Mr. Shi Shuwen, has made the challenging task both enjoyable and rewarding. I am most grateful to Prof. Wang for his full cooperation and, more importantly, his friendship.

6. Appendices

6.1　Appendix I: List of Participants in the Seminar on Modern Library Information Management and Services. (May 1995)

6.2　Appendix II: Plan for the Establishment of the Information Resources Center of Hubei Provincial College of Education. (Issued June 15, 1994)

6.3　Appendix III: Progress Report on the Development of the Information Resources Center of Hubei Provincial College of Education. (May 1995)

6.4　Appendix IV: A Brief Introduction to Hubei Shayang Teacher School. (1994)

6.5　Appendix V: Brief Introduction of the Hubei Shayang Teacher School Library. (May 27, 1995)

6.6　Appendix VI: Some Thoughts on Establishing the Information Resources Center for the Education and Training of Primary School Teachers, Zhengzhou Normal School. (January 12, 1995)

信息获取和资源共享的最大化：OhioLInk 的方法

Maximizing Information Access and Resources Sharing: The OhioLINK Approach

Introduction

Since the 1960s, many changes have taken place in libraries of all types throughout the world. In the U.S., the most significant forces accelerating the pace of change in libraries have been the revolutions in computer, information, and telecommunications technologies. In the 1960s, the development of several major applications of computer technology in libraries provided the foundation for subsequent development, including the MARC (Machine-Readable Cataloging) format by the Library of Congress, the Medical Literature Analysis and Retrieval System (MEDLARS) by the National Library of Medicine, the Ohio College Library Center (OCLC—now renamed the Online Computer Library Center) for online shared cataloging and resource sharing, and large computerized databases by major indexing and abstracting publishers (e.g., the Chemical Abstracts Services). Building on these, the following technological advances have stimulated drastic changes every five to ten years:

- faster and more powerful computers,
- sophistication and integration of software packages for library applications telecommunications and networking,
- information storage and retrieval techniques, including CD-ROMs,
- interactive hyper- and multi-media,
- electronic publishing, and
- the Internet and World Wide Web.

The combined effects of these changes, coupled with the information explosion, have transformed libraries from paper-based libraries prior to 1960, to computer-based libraries from the 1970s, to networked libraries from the l980s, and to electronic, digital and virtual libraries in the 1990s. It is clear that the direction of libraries in the 21st century will be a further merger of the various technologies in a networked environment.

Challenges to Libraries

In addition to the rapid transformation in computer, information, and telecommunication technologies, libraries everywhere are also faced with the following challenges:
- exploding information resources,
- skyrocketing costs of library materials,
- growing diversity in information formats,
- shrinking library funding,
- high costs of library automation,
- increasing demand for library staff skilled in information technologies,
- changing nature of library collections, and
- expanding user demands and expectations.

Faced with these multiple challenges, libraries in the U.S. responded proactively to seize the opportunities available to them. In many ways, they have played a leading role in the deployment of new and emerging technologies that broaden their resources and expand their services.

The traditional concept of ownership in collection development is gradually being replaced by access to information and knowledge without regard to location and format. True resource sharing among libraries through networking has become the common desire and growing practice.

The OhioLINK Approach

The formation of OhioLINK (Ohio Library and Information Network) among academic libraries in Ohio, beginning in 1990, for cost-effective networking and resource sharing has proved to be a successful approach. This paper will address the following topics:
- A serendipitous beginning
- The OhioLINK vision
- Where OhioLINK stands today
- How OhioLINK works
- What's next for OhioLINK?

A Serendipitous Beginning

The formation of OhioLINK was a direct result of a year-long study by a blue-ribbon panel appointed in 1986 by the Ohio Board of Regents (the governing body for post-secondary education in Ohio) to study library needs of state universities. In its report[①], the panel made several recommendations. The most important was to implement "as expeditiously as possible a statewide electronic catalog system". Collateral recommendations included retrospective conversion of remaining paper cataloging records to MARC format, development and implementation of a statewide delivery system for library materials, and a plan for a cooperative preservation program.

To plan and implement these recommendations, a Steering Committee was established by the Regents with a number of task forces and subcommittees composed of librarians, systems staff, and faculty members from the initial 13 state-supported universities, two large private universities, two independent state-supported medical universities, and the State Library of Ohio.

Through the investment of thousands of person-hours in hundreds of meetings, several planning documents were completed. Most important of these were a request for information (RFI) issued in August 1988[②], a planning paper issued in November 1988[③], a request for proposal (RFP) issued in August 1989[④], and an overview, Connecting People, Libraries & Information for Ohio's Future, issued in 1989[⑤]. Based on the responses to the RFP, a commercially developed library system by Innovative Interface, Inc. was selected in 1990 and installations began in 1991.

After the system was installed in all 18 initial participating libraries in 1994, OhioLINK expanded to cover all 23 state-supported two-year colleges and many private colleges and universities in Ohio. As of this writing, fifty-six academic libraries in Ohio have joined OhioLINK, providing access to more than 4500 simultaneous users at 104 locations serving more than 500000 students, faculty and staff. An overall description of OhioLINK can be found at http://www.ohiolink.edu/about/what-is-ol.html.

The OhioLINK Vision

At its inception, a basic concept of OhioLINK was to use the existing statewide telecommunication infrastructure built by the Ohio Academic and Research Network (OARnet) to link the library systems in all the participating libraries-each with a common computer hardware

---

① Ohio Board of Regents. Library Study Committee. Academic Libraries in Ohio: Progress Through Collaboration, Storage, and Technology. Report of the Library Study Committee. (Columbus, OH: Ohio Board of Regents, 1987)

② Request for Information for the Ohio Library & Information System (OLIS) on Behalf of the Ohio Board of Regents and Ohio Library & Information System. (Columbus, OH: OLIS, August, 1988)

③ OLAS Steering Committee. Ohio Library Access System Planning Paper, November 2, 1988. (Columbus, OH: Ohio Board of Regents, 1988)

④ Request for Proposal for the Ohio Library & Information System (OLIS) on Behalf of the Ohio Board of Regents and Ohio Library & Information System. (Columbus, OH: OLIS, 1989)

⑤ Ohio Library & Information System. Connecting People, Libraries, & Information for Ohio's Future. (Columbus, OH: Ohio Board of Regents, 1989)

(from Digital Equipment Corporation-DEC) and software (provided by Innovative Interfaces Inc.) platform. By means of this linkage and a central union catalog with location information and access to real-time circulation records from local systems, users of all participating libraries can access both online local and central catalogs and can initiate borrowing requests for items not available locally. Through a 48-hour-maximum courier service, all interlibrary borrowing can be completed within two or three days in most cases.

The shared vision of OhioLINK can be summarized as:
- link all major academic libraries in Ohio in an electronic network environment,
- pool all library resources for easy access and effective sharing,
- tap existing computer and telecommunication infrastructure[1],
- deliver materials quickly by various means,
- cooperate in collection development,
- acquire large and expensive electronic resources cost-effectively through consortia purchasing power, and
- become a model for interlibrary cooperation.

Where OhioLINK Stands Today

Even though OhioLINK is still developing and expanding its capacities in resources and services, some concrete results have already been achieved. These are:
- The demonstrated benefits and economies of scale have enabled OhioLINK to seek more State funding in support of its central operations, delivery services, acquisition of major bibliographic, reference, and full-text databases, and undertaking other new initiatives.
- More than 20 million volumes represented by seven million individual titles held by 56 libraries are now available to approximately 460000 students and 40000 faculty and staff. Of these seven million unique titles, about 57% of them are held at only one library, 15% are at two libraries, 7% are at three libraries, 5% are at four libraries, 3% are in five libraries, and 14% are held by more than five libraries.
- In 1993, the OhioLINK central catalog was searched about 450000 times. This number has grown to more than 2.5 million times in 1997.
- In 1994, patrons placed 75000 online borrowing requests with other OhioLINK libraries. This rose to 534000 requests in 1997. The fill rate was 85%. This in effect has reduced the cost of an interlibrary loan from $15 ~ $30 per item by traditional methods to $8.00 per item through OhioLINK patron online borrowing.
- For the statewide access to electronic information: In December of 1992, there were only two databases, but in October 1997, there were 65 databases. The annual searches of all OhioLINK reference databases have gone up from 500000 in 1993 to 9600000 in 1997. The cost per search has been reduced from $3.80 per search in 1993 to less than $0.30 per search in 1997.
- For the access to full-text journal articles: In 1993, nothing was available, but in 1997, a total of 22000 full-text journal articles or 560000 pages were printed online by users. The average cost per article was $0.90.
- Using consortia purchasing power, OhioLINK's reference database licensing costs are 30% to 80% less than would be charged to individual libraries.
- OhioLINK has successfully negotiated license fees for electronic journals at 5% to 10% more than existing print subscriptions but has gained access to five to ten times more titles.

---

[1] As it has developed, OhioLINK has become a major stimulant to upgrading telecommunications bandwidth among campuses and computing resources on campus. When it began, many campuses were linked with 57 Kb lines, today T-1 (1.5 Mb) lines are considered the minium acceptable. "OhioLINK/OARnet White Paper: Strategic Directions for Providing Networked Information Services in Ohio." (Columbus, OH: OhioLINK and OARnet, Dec. 1997)

How OhioLINK Works

1. Systems architecture

The OhioLINK systems consist of 56 individual campus systems and a central site in a distributed system. Each local system has its own CPU, OPAC, acquisitions and serial control module, user data file and circulation system. The central site system (which was moved from Dayton to Columbus in August 1997 and is now located in the Ohio Supercomputer Center) includes the central bibliographic catalog (derived from local records) with locations, citation and full-text databases (including electronic journals), and massive multimedia databases. While different databases utilize different search engines (and user interfaces), these are increasingly being consolidated into two common search engines adapted for OhioLINK's needs.

2. Governance

OhioLINK's Governing Board is composed of representative provosts (chief academic officers), the chair and vice chair of the Library Advisory Council, and the liaison staff from the Ohio Board of Regents. It reports directly to the Regents. The Governing Board hires the Executive Director and oversees the financial and administrative operations of the Headquarters.

At the policy-making and planning level, the Library Advisory Council consists of library directors from the 18 initial libraries and representatives from the two-year colleges, private universities and colleges, law libraries, and medical libraries. The Chair, Vice Chair, and the immediate Past Chair constitute the Coordinating Committee.

At the operational level, there are the Lead Implementers and four standing committees. The Lead Implementers is made up of the systems librarian or other designated staff member of the participating libraries. The four standing committees whose members are nominated by library directors and appointed by the Executive Director are:
- Cooperative Information Resources Management;
- Database Management and Standards;
- Inter-campus Services;
- User Services.

3. Funding

Funding for OhioLINK has come from a state appropriation to the Ohio Board of Regents and is in two forms: an Operating Budget and a Capital Budget. The Operating Budget pays for personnel, office facilities, administration, recurrent software and database licenses, and other operations. The Capital Budget pays for computer hardware and software at the central site, the initial local systems, the purchase of reference databases (where owned rather than licensed), database conversion, infrastructure support of the Ohio Academic and Research Network, etc. In 1998, the Operating Budget is $5157000 and the Capital Budget is $2500000.

With the exception of the initial local system and some partial subsidies for group licensing of electronic journals that have been paid by central funds, all the other expenses for the maintenance and upgrading of local systems and operations as well as ongoing electronic subscription costs (including access to some databases, such as Lexis-Nexis) are the responsibility of each library.

What's Next for OhioLINK?

Because of the initial success of OhioLINK, many have viewed OhioLINK as the model for effective information access and resource sharing in an electronic network environment. However, from our vantage point, we see opportunities to do more as we enter the fast lane of the information superhighway of the 21st century. Several strategic priorities have been identified for action in the immediate future.

• Expanding current databases—especially content (such as full-text, maps, numeric, and image) -oriented rather than citation-oriented.
• Promoting more effective means for cooperative collection development.
• Adding new capacities such as the delivery of all services to the desktop via integrated WWW based platforms and the electronic transmission of articles.
• Making available a more uniform and user-friendly interface.
• Encouraging and coordinating digitization projects.
• Supporting alternative methods and strategies in electronic publishing to lower costs and prevent commercial publishers monopolizing the intellectual property right of authors.
• Seeking alliances with other state, national and global networks.

It is clear from viewing the list of strategic priorities, OhioLINK has a full and exciting agenda ahead.

(Published in its *Proceedings of the International Conference on New Missions of Academic Libraries in the 21st Century*. Beijing: Peking University Press, 1998: pp. 283 – 287.)

俄亥俄大学图书馆 1998—1999 年度报告

Ohio University Libraries 1998 – 1999 Annual Report[1]

PREFACE
Julia Zimmerman

In the past few months, as I have become acquainted with Ohio University and its Libraries, I have been privileged to share in the celebration of several important milestones. These include the thirtieth anniversary of the Alden Library and the dedication of the Hwa-Wei Lee Library Annex.

The impending retirement of Dean Hwa-Wei Lee, culminating two decades of dedicated leadership of the Ohio University Libraries, is another significant milestone. Dr. Lee's recent accomplishments are chronicled in this report, but his contributions are too widespread and numerous to detail fully. The Libraries' excellent service record, dedicated staff, effective use of technology, and rich and varied collections are testimony to Dr. Lee's vision and hard work throughout the past twenty years.

As successor to Dr. Lee, I look forward to working with the students, staff and faculty at Ohio University to continue this tradition of excellence. I congratulate him and the staff of the Ohio University Libraries on their many achievements.

OVERVIEW
Hwa-Wei Lee, Ph. D.

After my announcement of retirement eighteen months ago, a national search was conducted to find a new Dean. I am very pleased that the university-wide search committee, chaired by Dean Leslie Fleming of the College of Arts and Sciences, successfully completed its task. Ms. Julia Zimmerman, from the Georgia Institute of Technology Libraries, will assume the deanship on August 26, 1999. At Georgia Tech, "Ms. Zimmerman has an outstanding record of accomplishment," said Provost Brehm, and "is well informed and savvy about technology, dedicated to customer service, and is a skillful administrator who can build teamwork within the library as well as collaborations across campus, state, and nation. She will be a superb dean of libraries."

As my retirement date of August 31, 1999 is fast approaching, I submit my final annual report to the Ohio University Community as an expression of my sincere appreciation for all of the guidance and support that I have received over the past twenty-one years.

I am especially grateful that, through a resolution by the Board of Trustees, the Library Annex has been named Hwa-Wei Lee Library Annex and the first floor of the Alden Library will be named the Hwa-Wei Lee Center for International Collections: This latter will occur after the Fail-Quarter completion of renovation, made possible by a very generous gift from Dr. Vernon R. Alden, the fifteenth president of Ohio University, 1961 – 1969—for whom the main university library building is named.

Even through 1998 – 1999 was my last year as dean of libraries, I am pleased that with the shared vision, team work, tireless efforts, and unshaken courage of all my library colleagues, the Libraries have accomplished a great deal despite a very tight budget, serious staff shortages, and new technological demands.

---

[1] Athens, Ohio: Ohio University Libraries, 1999: p. 13.

In addition to expressing my heartfelt thanks to all my library colleagues for their cooperation, guidance, and support, I want to single out Dr. Gary Hunt, Associate Dean, for special recognition. Gary has been an unsung hero during the many years that he has worked very closely with me. In the following section I will highlight some of the notable accomplishment which we have achieved this year under very difficult and trying circumstances.

For Ms. Julia Zimmerman, our new Dean, I will list some of the opportunities and challenges ahead. I am confident that under the leadership of Zimmerman the Ohio University Libraries will continue to shine and to reach new heights.

NOTABLE ACCOMPLISHMENTS

Continuing growth of library collections

Even with a very tight library acquisition budget, we managed to continue the growth of library collections in all formats. Appendix IV shows that during 1998 – 1999 we added a total of 58,791 volumes of new monographs, documents, and bound journals; 145,597 units of microform materials; 48,041 pieces of non-print materials, and 3,006 new journals (more than one-half in electronic format and few representing new subscriptions). As of June 30, 1999, our total library resources of all campuses consist of 2,233,465 volumes of printed collections, 2,968,584 microform units, 386,826 non-print materials, and 19,351 journal titles.

These additions included some of the major gift and area studies collections received as well as a number of research collections purchased through the 1804 Special Library Endowment and the Arts and Humanities Junior Faculty Endowment funds.

In October 1998, Ohio University became a participant in the Statewide Collection Building initiative with Yankee Book Peddler, the vendor we had been using for an approval plan. Under this initiative, we are able to increase our discounts by 18% on new purchases and by 25% on standing orders/continuations, as well as, for the first time, gain a discount on British publications, and eliminate shipping costs on returned titles. Lower prices yielded added purchasing power of more than $20,000 for monographs and continuations. Additionally, the statewide plan provides information about the availability of other copies of a book in the state, at the time purchasing decisions are being made. This enables bibliographers to not purchase a book that may be readily available through OhioLINK from other institutions, but to purchase another title that would otherwise be unavailable to scholars locally and statewide.

Expanding electronic information resources

By combining local and OhioLINK efforts, the number of electronic reference databases and journals continue to expand by leaps and bounds. Forty-eight new databases became available to users in 1998 – 1999: seven OhioLINK databases, Twenty-three of our own Web subscriptions, five CD-ROM files on the IAN, and thirteen standalone CD-ROMs. A total of 251,840 accesses of Web-based databases, both local and OhioLINK resources, were recorded from the Libraries' Web pages. This represents a 175% increase over last year's recorded usage.

Available e-journals also are growing dramatically. In June 1999, we introduced access to about 75 titles previously available only in print from Oxford and Cambridge University Presses. In conjunction with OhioLINK, all titles from Kluwer, Springer Verlag, and the American Physical Society are being loaded and will be available in the fall, with the Royal Chemical Society and Institute of Physics titles also likely in the fall. For the humanities and social sciences, our subscription to the publications of Johns Hopkins University Press through Project Muse was transferred to OhioLINK. Project Muse has just announced that it will offer titles from other university presses, bringing available titles in the year 2000 to more than 100. Comparably, JSTOR—which offers complete backruns—is now completing its initial commitment of 100 + titles and defining a new phase for additional titles.

Improving access to electronic information resources

To improve the access to the Libraries' electronic information resources, two important steps have been taken this year.

1. New "smart" search engine introduced

OhioLINK successfully introduced a new web-based user interface and search engine, "Dataware", this year for the 16 databases provided through OhioLINK. Complementing Dataware is a refinement to the OhioLINK Electronic Journal Center (EJC) that utilizes "push" technology, which allows users to save their searches and have the search automatically executed at user-selected intervals (daily, weekly, or monthly) against journals in the EJC. The results are then e-mailed to the requestor.

2. Global access provided for remote users

In spring, we also implemented a new remote-user authentication protocol that allows Ohio University students, faculty members, and employees to have access to licensed databases mounted at OhioLINK from their homes or anywhere in the world through the Internet. In the past, authentication was based on machine-generated IP addresses. Now authentication is individualized by name and social security number. We continue to work with OhioLINK to establish similar access to databases at providers' web sites (such as the Encyclopedia Britannica).

Acquiring significant collections

The Libraries' Archives and Special Collections has recently acquired several highly valued special collections:

(1) The George V. Voinovich Political Papers and Archives. Personal papers of the current senator, past-governor, and former mayor of Cleveland.

(2) The Alwin Nikolais/Murray Louis Collections on Modern Dance. The archive (including costumes, props, scores, photographs, posters, and audio and videotapes) of world-renowned choreographer and dancer Murray Louis is a leading collection on modern dance.

(3) The Bob DeMott Collection of Dave Smith Memorabilia. Complementing an existing collection on scholar-poet Dave Smith (an early graduate of Ohio University's creative writing program), this collection includes manuscripts, galleys, offprints, letters, and other materials dealing with Smith.

(4) The John Haines Manuscripts. Personal papers of a leading American poet and nature essayist who earlier served as a visiting poet at Ohio University.

(5) The Farfel Collection of Manuscript and Incunabula Leaves. Dr. Gilbert and Ursala Farfel donated a collection of more than five hundred rare pages from manuscripts and books dating as far back as the 8th century.

(6) The late former president John C. Baker's Diaries and Personal Papers. Dr. Baker was 14th president of Ohio University (1945 – 1961).

(7) The late Distinguished Professor of Education Ed Stevens' Papers. Dr. Stevens was a respected scholar of 19th century literacy and training and a campaigner for the promotion of literature.

For the Alwin Nikolais/Murray Louis Collection, we applied for and received a two-year grant of $125,466 from NIPAD (National Initiative to Preserve America's Dance) to reformat the collection for preservation and easy access.

We continued to receive from Dr. Fred Harris, an American architect and interior designer in Japan, selections from his outstanding fine arts book collection. Fred and his wife, Kazuko, have finalized a planned gift of $500,000 to endow the Fine Arts Collection.

Implementing major digitization project

With private gift funds from the Scripps family, the library has begun digitizing the correspondence and papers of journalism pioneer E. W. Scripps, In addition, we have been designated as a participating partner in OhioLINK's new Digital Media Center (DMC). The DMC will mount the Scripps archive on its server, opening up access to this rich manuscript collection to scholars worldwide. It will constitute by far the largest, most complex contributed collection at the DMC.

IMTS is responsible for installing and maintaining multimedia equipment in classrooms

At the end of June 1999, ninety of the approximately 140 commonly-scheduled classrooms across the campus have been equipped with various levels of multimedia equipment for instructional use. This represents a 125% increase over a year ago. While Instructional Media and Technology Services is doing their best to maintain these facilities, it is desperately in need of additional high-level technical support staff.

Winning national recognition for cost efficiencies and high productivity

Resource sharing is an inherently cost-effective approach to satisfying the information needs of library users. Through participation in OhioLINK's interlibrary borrowing and lending, we have become a national leader in resource sharing. According to the 1998 ARL statistics, Ohio University Libraries borrowed 52,136 items from other libraries for use by our faculty and students, placing us sixth highest among the 111 academic ARL libraries in the U.S. and Canada. Equally impressive, our transaction cost for interlibrary borrowing was only $5.07 per item—less than one-third of the ARL mean of $18.35 per item. In addition, in 1998 – 1999, we loaned 65,705 items to others—making us a net lender by 13,569, a reflection of the strength of our collections and our willingness to share.

Based on generally accepted measures of library workload, it is clear that our staff is among the most productive of any academic research library in the Association of Research Library. Using indicators of "imputed demand" for library services and resources (such as the number of students and faculty to librarians ratios), for example, the average ARL library has one staff member for every 6.3 faculty members and every 90 students on campus. In contrast, we are serving 7.3 faculty and 165 students for each library staff member, placing us near the bottom of the ARL in both ratios. Measuring "actual utilization" of library services and resources as a function of staffing levels, the efficiency of our operation becomes even more apparent. For instance, the average ARL library circulates about 2,700 items a year per staff member. We circulate more than 5,000. The average ARL library conducts 129 interlibrary loans and 77 interlibrary borrows per staff member. Our numbers are four times greater in both categories. The average ARL library answer 784 reference questions per staff member. We answer almost 2.000 per staff member, while also teaching more than twice as many classes.

Succeeding in library fund-raising

Fund-raising for a library is complicated by the lack of its own constituency or source of donor prospects, especially when colleges are going all out to contact their respective donor prospect pools. However, with the effective assistance of the Libraries' National Advisory Council and the hard work of Assistant Dean Salinda Arthur, we have achieved a high level of success. This year, we continued our effort to honor Dr. Vernon R. Alden by contacting his friends and colleagues for a library endowment fund to be established in the name of Dr. and Mrs. Vernon R. Alden made another major gift to the Libraries—to renovate the first floor of Alden Library as a Center for International Collections. The remainder of their gift will create an endowment for international collections.

Through the joint efforts of Mr. Robert Fallon and Dr. Fred Harris, the Libraries submitted a successful proposal to the Japan Foundation which permits donations made in honor of Dr. Alden by his friends in Japan to be channeled through the Japan Foundation. Having been granted permission now by the Japan Foundation, Mr. Fallon and Dr. Harris are presently contacting our Japanese donor prospects.

In January of this year, Mr. Sanford Elsass, Chair of the Library's Major Campaign

Committee, made a planned gift of $500,000 to set up a Samuel and Susan Crowl Library Endowment for the Humanities Collection. This Endowment, honoring Distinguished Professor of English, Samuel Crowl and Professor of English, Susan Crowl, will be administered jointly by the Ping Institute for Teaching of Humanities and the Libraries.

In honoring my retirement, the Friends of Hwa-Wei Lee Committee, chaired by Ms. Charlotte Coleman-Eufinger, also launched a special campaign to raise funds for the library. Dr. Daniel Shao, Mrs. Beth Stocker, Dr. You Bao Shao, Mr. and Mrs. Robert Hill, Mr. And Mrs. John and Charlotte Eufinger, Dr. and Mrs. Robert Glidden, Dr. Jeanette Grasselli Brown, Dr. Jing Chen, and Mrs. Su-Chen Chang are among the key donors. A full list of 1998—1999 library donors is included in the section, Recognizing Contributions (p. 28).

Culminating regional library cooperation

For the past 24 years, the Libraries have been contracted by Ohio Valley Area Libraries (OVAL) to serve as the resource library for the public libraries in ten southeastern Ohio counties. Under the contract, we were reimbursed by federal funds ($45,000 in 1998-1999) to provide reference, interlibrary loan, and staff training for our neighboring public libraries. Through the outstanding efforts of Ms. Karen Williams, our OVAL Librarian of the past 24 years, our services have been rated most satisfactory by librarians at all OVAL libraries. As library funding for public libraries in the region has greatly improved in recent years and almost all of these libraries are now staffed by professional librarians, the need to continue our services decreased to the point that our mission was successfully completed. At the OVAL'S annual banquet held in May, both Ms. Williams and I were invited to attend and each was presented with a special plaque of appreciation. Regional services in the future will be handled internally or by the Cincinnati Public Library under a State Library of Ohio contract.

OPPORTUNITIES & CHALLENGES AHEAD

Welcoming new library dean

The entire library staff and university community eagerly await the arrival of Ms. Julia Zimmerman, our new Dean of University Libraries. Ohio University Libraries are well positioned for the new digital age of the twenty-first century. The new vision and leadership of Dean Zimmerman will usher the Libraries into a new era.

Urgently needed additional funds

Regrettably, the library budget for 1999-2000 may be the worst in many years. With the exception of a 4% increase in the acquisitions budget (about one-half the increase needed to keep pace with inflation in costs of books and journals), we did not receive any additional funds for staffing, student wages and operations. Even the acquisitions increase compares unfavorably with the 6.8%-8% increase at other ARL libraries in Ohio. Worse still, through the newly implemented "tax" system, the Libraries lost one half percent of its operating funds (acquisitions was excluded) —a reduction of $30,000 from last year's base.

In the Libraries' well-documented budget requests for 1999-2000, we stated our three areas of most urgent need.

Our first priority is to improve service quality through an increase in staffing. The three new staff positions we requested are for technical support, circulation, and classroom media maintenance. In the earlier section of this report, we have demonstrated the serious staff shortage with facts. We feel the request is totally justified.

Our, second priority is to increase the student employment budget. Because our staffing levels are so low, we have become highly dependent on student help to operate the library system. Unfortunately the number of hours worked by student assistants has been declining primarily as a result of cutbacks in the federal work-study program. This factor alone has reduced staffing levels in the library by the equivalent of six full-time employees over the past four years.

Our third and final priority is to seek an increase in funding to meet the non-personnel costs associated with technology support. With a deployed infrastructure of 300 workstations, eight servers, and numerous peripheral devices, our operating budget for technology has become woefully inadequate to support even ongoing maintenance and replacement costs let alone to develop innovative new applications of information technology.

It is my sincere hope that some new funds can be made available to address these urgent needs after Dean Zimmernan's arrival. Otherwise, the Libraries ability to maintain the current levels of collections and services will be seriously hampered and cutbacks in some services may be necessary.

Responding to emerging user needs

For many years we have used written survey instruments to assess user satisfaction with the library. We also participate in university assessment efforts, such as the freshman treatment study which attempts to evaluate freshman perceptions of a whole range of service providers on campus, including the library, health services, the registrar's office, and academic advising. To gain a more in-depth view of how freshmen are using the library and what we can do to make their experience more positive, we conducted seven focus group sessions in March with about fifty randomly selected freshmen. In some ways the results were surprising. Virtually every one of these first year students had already used the library's web page from outside the building, logging into our databases from their dorm rooms or from home. But they were overwhelmed and confused by the sheer number of database choices to clarify what is available and criteria for selecting specific resources (especially for users outside the Libraries-in dorms or home,) we are spending the summer redesigning and simplifying our web pages to help off-site users identify the best resources for their research.

In response to other themes that emerged from the focus groups, we are working to improve signs, library aesthetics, service patterns, and instruction. Based on the useful feedback from the freshmen groups, plans are underway to host similar focus composed of upper-class and graduate students and faculty.

Launching OhioLEARN project

OhioLEARN (Ohio Libraries Education, Access, and Resource Network) which will become operational in September of 1999 is a new initiative to address library education and training needs in a coordinated fashion across the entire state. It is based on a partnership involving the Kent State University School of Library and Information Science, OhioLINK, Bowling Green State University, the University of Cincinnati Libraries, and Ohio University Libraries. Through a grant awarded by the State Library of Ohio under the Library Services and Technology Act (LSTA), an electronic videoconferencing network has been installed connecting the four participating universities with OhioLINK. Education and training programs to be delivered through the network will include OhioLINK-sponsored training, a specialized version of the KSU Master of Library Science degree program, and a variety of continuing education opportunities. The network will also be available for education and training experiences hosted by membership organizations such as the Academic Library Association of Ohio. The network will expand opportunities for collaborative in-service training programs developed for library staff at all levels. Participants at each site will benefit from innovative approaches to technology-enhanced learning.

Achieving the Libraries' goals in the 2004 Campaign

After the successful completion of the Third Century Campaign three years ago, the University—under the new leadership of Vice President Leonard Raley has launched another major campaign. To address the variety of needs identified, the Libraries' new goal for the 2004 Campaign is $11,250,000. To the right is the breakdown of our new goal in ranked priority order.

We regret very much that Ms. Salinda Arthur, our most able Assistant Dean for Development, left us for Iowa State University in May. Her departure at the time of my retirement dealt a double blow to our fund-raising efforts. Luckily, before Salinda's parting, she helped to form a very powerful Library Campaign Cabinet with Dr. Vernon R. Alden as the Chair. Dr. Alden will be assisted by Mr. Robert Fallon, Dr. Fred Harris, Mr. Sanford Elssas, and many others from the Libraries National Advisory Council.

Technology advancement	$ 1750000
Collection excellence	$ 3500000
Library general endowment	$ 2000000
Educating for the Information Age	$ 1250000
Facility renovations	$ 1750000
Expanding Global Linkages	$ 1000000
Campaign Total	$ 11250000

The need for a new Sciences, Medicine and Engineering Library

To provide faculty and students in engineering, health sciences, medicine, and natural sciences with state-of-the-art access to information resources and library services in an era of rapid change in information gathering, organizing, access, delivery, and service, we propose construction of a Sciences, Medicine and Engineering Library located in the lower campus area, in close proximity to the Russ College of Engineering and Technology, the College of Osteopathic Medicine, the College of Health and Human Services, and science departments in the College of Arts and Sciences. Planning for this project should be carried out in close consultation with deans, department heads, faculty and students in those disciplines. The architectural design, staffing and organization of the new library must incorporate the most advanced concepts in information technology, knowledge management, and global communications—emphasizing close collaboration between librarians, students and faculty—while allowing for more efficient use of space than would be possible in conventional library construction. If this goal is realized within the next decade, Alden Library can be renovated to better serve the other components of the university community while continuing to function as the main library on the Athens campus. Early this year, we prepared a concept paper on this proposal with the hope that more discussion on the merits of this proposal could be carried out next year.

CONCLUSIONS & ACKNOWLEDGEMENTS

It is indeed a great pleasure to conclude my final annual report just a few days prior to my retirement after twenty-one challenging yet rewarding years at Ohio University. Words are inadequate to fully convey my appreciation to so many people who have had confidence in me and who have given me their utmost support and guidance. I am especially grateful to all my library colleagues for their cooperation, hard work, trust, and comradeship—without these we would not be able to accomplish so much with barely minimum resources. To President Glidden and all of the senior administrative staff, I thank them most sincerely for their strong support and recognition of the importance of a library in a highly ranked and outstanding university. I also am indebted to all members of the Libraries' National Advisory Council, the University Library Committee, the Board of the Friends of the Libraries, Faculty Representatives from all academic disciplines, others who have served on library-related committees, and concerned faculty and staff members for their advice, suggestions, and contributions.

Inadequate state funding for public universities in Ohio has negatively impacted library development. Fortunately, through the joint efforts of state university libraries to form the OhioLINK consortium (with the full support of the Ohio Board of Regents) to stimulate library cooperation in resource development and sharing, we have been able to expand our collective resources and deploy new technologies for better services. We owe many of our recent accomplishments to private support that we have received through fund-raising, partially offsetting inadequate library funding. As of June 30, 1999, our library endowments have reached an all time high of $9,086,811 in market value. (See Appendix VII). On behalf of the library staff and the university community who have benefitted from private gifts, I want to thank all of the library donors (most of whom are identified in the Recognizing Contributions section) for their generosity.

When one's debts are so great, it is difficult to acknowledge all of the contributions made by so many. I beg forgiveness for unintentional omissions.

Finally, I want to conclude by reemphasizing my welcome to Dean Julia Zimmerman to Ohio University. I urge the University community to continue to support her vigorous new leadership guiding the Libraries into the new century.

APPENDICES

I. Organizational Chart
II. Statistics of Library Collections, All Campuses
III. Summary of Funds for Library Acquisitions (Athens Campus)
IV. Analysis of Athens Campus Collections as of 6/30/99
V. Changes in Funds for Library Acquisitions (Athens Campus)
VI. Summary of Total Library Expenditures (All Campuses)
VII. Market Value of Established Library Endowments as of 6/30/99
VIII. Statistics of Library Staffing from 1978–79 to 1998–99

RECOGNIZING CONTRIBUTIONS

National Advisory Council
University Library Committee
Library Committees
Faculty Library Representatives and Subject Bibliographers
1998–99 Donors

APPENDIX I

Ohio University Libraries' Organization Chart
August 30, 1999

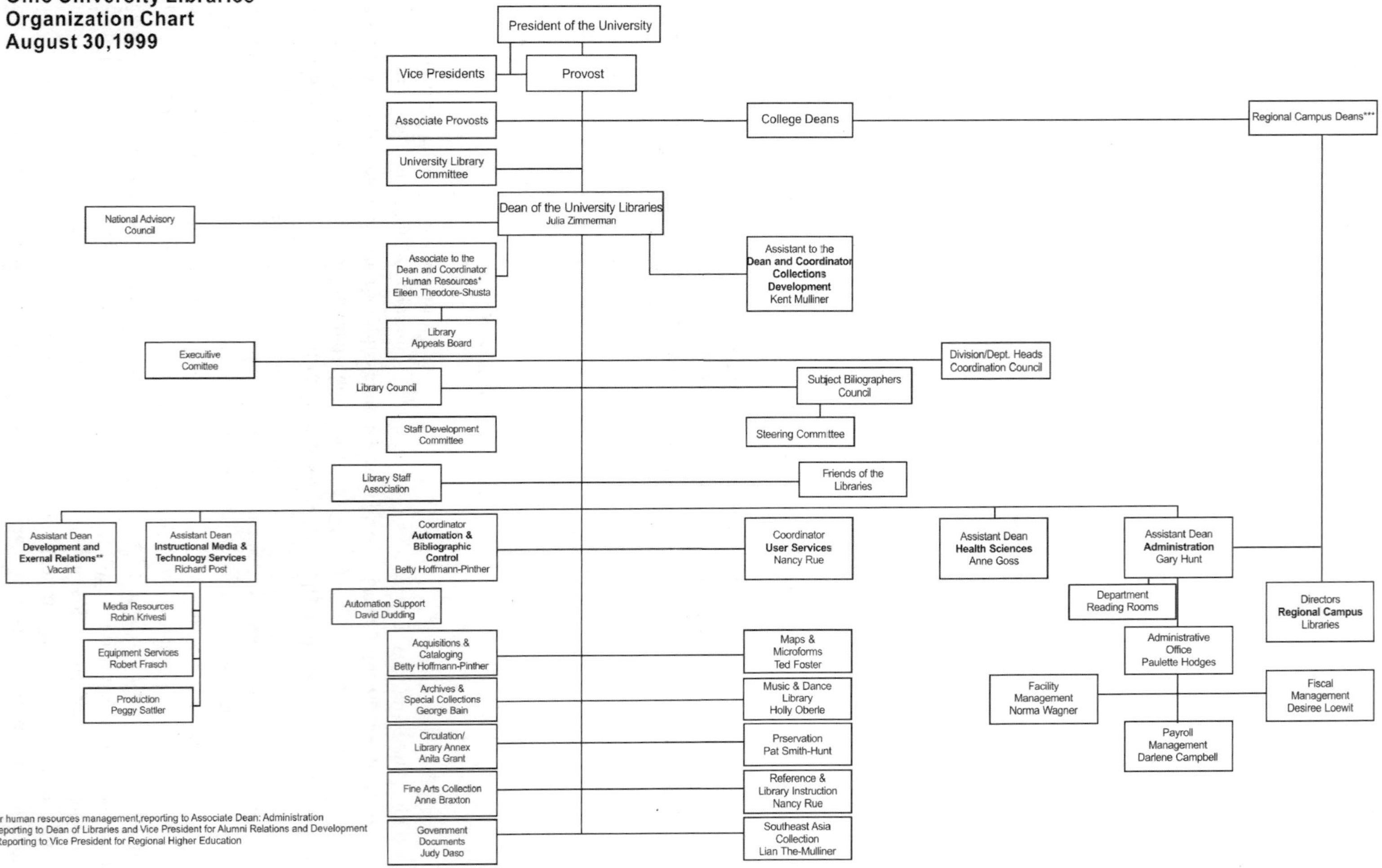

*For human resources management,reporting to Associate Dean, Administration
**Reporting to Dean of Libraries and Vice President for Alumni Relations and Development
***Reporting to Vice President for Regional Higher Education

APPENDIX II Statistics of Library Collections, All Campuses, 1978-79 to 1998-99

Fiscal Year	Books&Bound Serials (Volumes)	Government Documents (Volumes)	All Printed Material (Volumes)	Total Volumes	Microforms (Units)	Microforms (Units)	Total Microforms
	Athens	Athens	Regional*		Athens	Regional*	
1978-79	743,360	306,780		1,050,140	640,663		640,663
1979-80	769,732	337,945		1,107,677	679,877		679,877
1980-81	813,314	361,485		1,174,799	754,768		754,768
1981-82	876,794	375,648		1,252,442	820,622		820,622
1982-83	912,884	230,4612		1,143,345	1,062,283		1,062,283
1983-84	952,263	239,052		1,191,315	1,137,833		1,137,833
1984-85	985,227	249,471		1,234,698	1,233,129		1,233,129
1985-86	1,029,869	254,261		1,284,130	1,319,107		1,319,107
1986-87	1,074,050	260,862		1,334,912	1,411,636		1,411,636
1987-88	1,119,744	264,239		1,383,983	1,478,872		1,478,872
1988-89	1,161,186	269,753		1,430,939	1,626,815		1,626,815
1989-90	1,203,215	274,456		1,477,671	1,738,726		1,738,726
1990-91	1,254,832	279,394	241,263	1,775,489	1,823,172	36,650	1,859,822
1991-92	1,308,676	284,125	242,007	1,834,808	1,956,851	44,397	2,001,248
1992-93	1,354,885	288,067	248,932	1,891,884	2,067,207	46,552	2,113,759
1993-94	1,398,433	292,089	256,356	1,946,878	2,179,780	50,604	2,230,384
1994-95	1,434,755	295,550	261,761	1,992,066	2,266,695	54,476	2,321,171
1995-96	1,486,646	299,362	257,832	2,043,840	2,352,147	60,720	2,412,867
1996-97	1,541,460	302,836	266,298	2,110,594	2,427,031	64,709	2,491,740
1997-98	1,597,932	306,125	270,617	2,174,674	2,500,542	322,445	2,822,987
1998-99	1,650,463	308,998	273,444	2,232,905	2,580,239	388,3455	2,968,584

(续上表)

Fiscal Year	Other① (Pieces)	Other (Pieces)	Total Other	Current Periodicals③ (Titles)	Periodicals (Titles)	Total Periodicals
	Athens	Regional*		Athens	Regional*	
1978－79	265,539		265,539	5,542		5,542
1979－80	272,507		272,507	5,754		5,754
1980－81	272,973		272,973	6,022		6,022
1981－82	276,620		276,620	6,004		6,004
1982－83	309,303		309,303	8,003		8,003
1983－84	327,087		327,087	8,857		8,857
1984－85	334,578		334,578	9,426		9,426
1985－86	346,538		346,538	9,705		9,705
1986－87	353,324		353,324	9,968		9,968
1987－88	364,084		364,084	10,261		10,261
1988－89	370,927		370,927	10,326		10,326
1989－90	244,332		244,332	10,705		10,705
1990－91	250,482	51,480	301,962	10,938	2,082	13,020
1991－92	300.247④	53,400	353,647	11,083	2,063	13,146
1992－93	307,290	55,120	362,410	11,217	2,051	13,268
1993－94	311,218	40,093	351,311	11,414	2,064	13,478
1994－95	315,900	36,071	351,971	11,600	2,081	13,681
1995－96	320,945	42,233	363,178	12,122	1,914	14,036
1996－97	327,765	68,636	396,401	13,053	1,979	15,032
1997－98	333,327	55,418	388,745	14,445	1,900	16,345
1998－99	339,560	47,266	386,826	17,150	2,201	19,351

* Regional Campuses

①Others includes maps, discs, tapes, cassettes, photographs, films, exhibition catalogs, drymounts, posters, scores, and multi-media kits. Excluded from these are OU archives, manuscripts, and local government records.

②The volume count of government documents was revised based on a complete inventory and weeding. Because many titles are bound in one volume, the count by volumes is less than the count by title.

③The Slides Collection was transferred to the College of Fine Arts, 132,143 slides; therefore the number of "Others" was reduced.

④The Slides Collection was transferred to the College of Fine Arts, 132,143 slides; therefore the number of "Others" was reduced.

⑤The large increase is due to the acquisition of ERIC by the Lancaster campus library.

APPENDIX III   Summary of Funds for Library Acquisitions (Athens Campus) 1998-99

Source of Funds	$ Allocation	Carryover① 1997-98	$ Available	$ Spent	$ Encumbered	$ Balance
General Appropriation						
Library Acquisitions	3,432,310	274,792	3,707,102	3,435,193	305,693	-33,784
College of Medicine	277,423	1,000	278,423	234,968	4,005	39,450
Replacements	0	16,443	16,443	4,166	800	11,477
Binding	36,448	0	36,448	34,445	0	2,003
Subtotal	3,746,181	292,235	4,038,416	3,708,772	310,498	19,146

Endowment Funds						
1804 Special Library Endowment	56,322	11,602	67,924	43,462	159	24,303
Contemporary History Endowment	49,532	4,659	54,191	38,491	14,198	1,502
Southeast Asian Collection Endowment	31,307	1,947	32,984	23,853	400	8,731
Marion Alden S. E. A. Endowment	9,410	1,026	10,436	8,990	652	794
Junior Faculty Endowment②	36,519	28,498	65,017	35,645	20,325	9,048
Phillip Zenner Book Fund	1,750	659	2,409	212	86	2,111
LaTourrette-Hatcher HPER Endowment	3,145	1,257	4,402	4,340	0	62
Earl C. Shively Memorial Fund	876	737	1,613	1,042	0	571
Fleeman Memorial Fund	1,119	295	1,414	213	1,333	-132
Fieler Book Fund	1,218	231	1,449	1,357	50	42
Joseph Wayland & Helen Bosart						
Morgan Endowment	610	205	815	749	0	66
B. A. Renkenberger Memorial Fund	2,562	3,667	6,229	2,074	1,706	2,449
Class of 1892 Super Memorial Fund	170	141	311	311	0	0
You-Bao Shao Endowment	10,000	7,865	17,865	5,683	872	11,310
Feng Chia University Endowment	806	513	1,319	1,237	0	82
Donald & Marian Spencer Endowment	3,869	1,635	5,503	2,971	171	2,361
Edward & Claudette Stevens Endowment	302	457	759	0	0	759
Stocker Engineering Endowment	4,000	0	4,000	3,807	59	134
Stocker Electrical Engineering Endowment	3,000	0	3,000	407	0	2,593
Sun-Chen Chang Endowment	784	0	784	395	133	256
Tun Razak Chair Endowment	10,000	0	10,000	9,657	343	0
Subtotal	227,030	65,394	292,424	184,896	40,487	67,042

(续上表)

Grants/Gifts/Contracts						
SEA-Luce Foundation	0	2,523	2,523	0	40	2,483
O. U. Foundation						
Friends of the Library	0	9	9	0	0	9
Library Enrichment Specified	0	17,604	17,604	2,779	259	14,566
Miscellaneous Gifts	0	20,940	20,940	4,775	1,636	14,529
OVAL	0	143	143	0	0	143
Special Funds③	10,000	23	10,023	5,261	5,072	−310
Subtotal	10,000	41,242	51,242	12,815	7,007	31.420
TOTAL	3,983,211	398,871	4,382,082	3,906,483	357,992	117,607

① Does not include encumbrances
② Includes outstanding awards
③ Includes African Studies grant and Special Gift funds

APPENDIX IV   Analysis of Athens Campus Collections as of 6/30/99

	Total 6/30/98	Additions	Withdrawals	Net Additions	Total 6/30/99
Non-Book (Units) cont'd					
Photographs	60,811	0	0	0	60,811
Films	1,578	1	0	1	1,579
Filmstrips	29	0	0	0	29
Exhibition Catalogs	750	0	0	0	750
Drymounts	9,365	0	0	0	9,365
Posters	1,455	605	0	605	7,301
Scores	6,696	1,146	0	1,146	5,913
Kits (Mixed Media)	394	3	0	3	397
TOTAL	333,327	6,366	133	6,233	339,560
Archives (feet)					
O. U. Archives	5,952	69	0	69	5,994
Manuscripts	2,319	1,915	0	1,915	4,234
Local Govt. Records	1,400	60	0	60	1,460
Periodicals/Serials (Titles)					
Active Periodicals	13,195	2,718	37	2,681	15,876
Documents-US	1,091	11	0	11	1,102
-OH	159	13	0	13	172

(续上表)

Subtotal	14,445	2,742	37	2,705	17,150
Active Serials	10,515	638	0	638	11,153
Documents-US	1,230	14	0	14	1,244
-OH	124	2	0	2	126
Subtotal	12,315	655	0	655	12,970
Active Newspapers	405	79	17	62	467
TOTAL Active Titles	27,165	3,476	54	3,422	30,587
Inactive Periodicals	9,744	0	0	0	9,744
Documents-US	331	5	0	5	336
-OH	124	2	0	2	126
Subtotal	10,199	7	0	7	10,206
Inactive Serials	15,627	428	0	428	16,055
Documents-US	1,416	56	0	56	1,472
-OH	353	0	0	0	353
Subtotal	17,396	484	0	484	17,880
Inactive Newspapers	1,352	0	0	0	1,352
TOTAL Inactive Titles	28,947	491	0	491	29,438
Gifts Processed					
Books & Other Materials		13,215	10,327	2,888	2,888
Periodical issues		4,045	3,542	503	503
Periodical replacements		259	0	259	259
Books & Bound Periodicals/Serials					
(Volume Count)					
Cataloged	1,541,222	53,063	1,338	51,725	1,592,947
Documents-US	285.846	2,541	0	2,541	288,387
-OH	15,121	332	0	332	15,453
-UN	5,158	0	0	0	5,158
Uncataloged	56,710	1,711	905	806	57,516
TOTAL	1,904,057	57,647	2,243	55,404	1,959,461

(续上表)

(Title Count)					
Cataloged	1,113,825	40,552	983	39.569	1,153,394
Documents-US	750,820	1,815	0	1,815	752,635
-OH	8,838	258	0	258	9,096
-UN	2,774	0	0	0	2,774
TOTAL	1,876,257	42,625	983	41,642	1,917,899
Microforms					
(Unit Count)					
Cards	46,501	0	0	0	46,501
Fiche	2,012,132	73,034	0	73,034	2,085,166
Film (reels)	129,501	6,663	0	6,663	136,164
Prints	312,408	0	0	0	312,408
TOTAL	2,500,542	79,697	0	79,697	2,580,239
(Title Count)					
No. of books titles	451,057	14,096	0	14,096	465,153
No. of period, titles	7,084	5	0	5	7,089
TOTAL	458,141	14,101	0	14,101	472,242
Non-Book (Units)					
Maps	169,309	1,773	133	1,640	170,949
Discs-phono	11,006	104	0	104	11,110
-CD Music	1,412	253	0	253	1,665
-Video	64	241	0	241	305
-Opitical	3,050	951	0	951	4,001
Disks	2,369	195	0	195	2,564
Tapes-Audio	2,889	0	0	0	2,889
-Video	684	0	0	0	684
-Data	5	0	0	0	5
Cassettes-Audio	25,467	748	0	748	26,215
-Video	11,273	1,438	0	1,438	12,711
DVDs	0	46	0	46	46
Slides	24,721	0	0	0	24,721

APPENDIX V
Changes in Funds for Library Acquisitions (Athens Campus), 1978-79 to 1998-99

Fiscal Year	University Regular Budget	% of Change	College of Osteo. Medicine	% of Change	Others①	Total	% of Change	Carryover②	Total Available	Spent	Encumbered	Balance
1978-79	$469,691	—	$85,000	—	$67,053	$621,744	—	$38,692	$660,436	$639,671	$70,367	$-49,602
1979-80	527,351	12.28	67,000	-21.18	60,489	654,840	5.32	47,580	702,420	611,194	66,293	24,933
1980-81	597,351	13.27	95,000	41.79	114,577	806,928	23.23	61,517	868,445	801,470	92,723	-25,748
1981-82	627,351	5.02	85,500	-10.00	239,090	951,941	17.97	61,308	1,013,249	911,955	85,563	15,731
1982-83	847,351	35.07	106,618	24.70	206,197	1,160,166	21.87	101,598	1,261,764	978,789	203,588	79,387
1983-84	915,000	7.98	121,700	14.15	143,529	1,180,229	1.73	286,027	1,466,256	1,237,042	229,368	-154
1984-85	937,300	2.44	138,913	14.14	89,906	1,166,119	-1.20	235,179	1,401,298	1,282,242	149,026	-29,970
1985-86	1,048,119	11.82	151,600	9.13	172,080	1,371,799	17.64	122,644	1,494,443	1,331,738	162,004	701
1985-87	1,254,715	19.71	166,304	9.70	154,552	1,575,571	14.85	148,943	1,724,514	1,574,060	164,144	-13,690
1987-88	1,499,523	19.51	195,453	17.53	147,334	1,842,310	16.93	157,727	2,000,037	1,828,363	246,875	-75,201
1988-89	1,858,460	23.94	197,245	.92	137,889	2,193,594	19.07	176,116	2,369,710	2,062,016	188,244	119,450
1989-90	2,047,029	10.15	202,658	2.74	131,118	2,380,805	8.53	305,779	2,686,584	2,073,240	269,700	343,644
1990-91	2,193,870	7.17	232,216	14.59	142,677	2,568,763	7.89	570,979	3,139,742	2,652,476	364,764	122,502
1991-92	2,213,796	.91	211,459	-8.94	155,214	2,580,469	.46	503,928	3,084,397	2,869,090	296,577	-81,270
1992-93	2,134,640	-3.58	209,381	-.98	184,512	2,528,533	-2.01	196,150	2,724,683	2,665,935	215,116	-156,368
1993-94	2,335,509	9.41	211,769	1.14	210,704	2,757,982	9.07	79,564	2,837,546	2,514,550	272,569	50,427
1994-95	2,532,580	8.44	221,769	4.72	227,135	2,981,484	8.10	264,101	3,245,B85	2,755,782	320,519	169,284
1995-96	2,808,943	10.91	255,049	15.01	211,437	3,275,429	9.86	337,172	3,612,601	3,286,487	396,495	-70,381
1996-97	3,082,972	9.76	263,771	3.42	187,272	3,534,015	7.89	334,028	3,868,043	3,457,395	353,317	57,331
1997-98	3,468,758	6.33	270,199	2.44	203,448	3,751,619	6.16	450,725	4,202,344	3,787,939	294,935	119,470
1998-99	3,468,758	B.82	277,423	2.67	237,030	3,983,211	6.17	398,871	4,382,082	3,906,483	357,992	117,607

Figures are rounded to the nearest dollar.
①Includes gifts, endowment income, grants, contracts, replacements and binding
②Includes adjustments

APPENDIX VI
Summary of Total Library Expenditures (All Campuses), 1998 – 99

Object Code	Descriptor	Operating	Rotaries	Grants	Endowments	Gifts	Grand Totals
1110 – 1190	Contract salaries	$2,298,205	$40,608	$23,471	$10,749	$57,250	$2,430,283
1700	Classified salaries	$1,964,320	$12,334	$82,582	$11,918	$12,255	$2,086,409
1520	Student wages	$347,440	$29,926	$36,645	$2,471	$1,096	$417,578
2000's	Benefits	$1,642,914	$11,414	$48,052	$5,400	$0	$1,707,780
Total:	Salaries, Wages, Benefits	$6,252,879	$94,282	$190,750	$30,538	$73,601	$6,642,050
3000's – 9000's	Supplies, Travel, Communication, Service Contracts, Equipment	$969,413	$153,204	$169,683	$49,853	$183,365	$1,525,518
Total:	Supplies, Travel, Communication, Service Contracts, Equipment	$969,413	$153,204	$169,683	$49,853	$183,365	$1,525,518
5101	Electronic Journal Subscriptions	$27,214	$0	$0	$0	$0	$27,214
510B	Document Delivery Services	$1,631	$0	$0	$0	$0	$1,631
5201	Database Access Fees	$189,720	$0	$0	$0	$0	$189,720
5202	Consortia Memberships (CRL)	$67,594	$0	$0	$0	$0	$67,594
6460	Film & Video Rental Fees (IMTS) Serials	$3,126	$0	$0	$0	$0	$3,126
9530	Microfilms	$337,161	$0	$5,485	$2,092	$0	$344,738
9531	Audiovisual Materials	$165,452	$0	$85	$30,997	$0	$196,534
9532	Computer CD's	$84,126	$0	$4,423	$10,033	$161	$98,743
9533	Periodicals	$130,813	$0	$0	$7,656	$407	$138,876
9550 – 9560	Binding	$1,793,834	$0	$232,467	$2,698	$0	$2,028,999
9570	Books	$93,045	$0	$18,000	$0	$0	$111,045
9580 – 0590	Acquisitions/Access	$1,071,200	$0	$20,913	$122,399	$11,876	$1,226,388
Total:		$3,957,620	$0	$263,373	$175,875	$12,444	$4,434,608
Grand totals:		$11,179,912	$247,486	$623,806	$256,266	$269,410	$12,576,880

APPENDIX VII
Market Value of Established Library Endowments as of June 30, 1999

Name	Market Value of Principal
1804 Special Library Endowment	$1,280,180
Library Preservation Endowment	1,328,761
Contemporary History Endowment	1,170,791
You-Bao Shao Overseas Chinese Documentation and Research Center	960,553
The Arts and Humanities Junior Faculty Library Endowment	859,058
The Ohio University Libraries General Endowment	852,735
The Southeast Asian Collection Endowment	766,309
The Vernon & Marion Alden Library Endowment	479,469
The Daniel K. C. Shao Endowment Curator of the You Bao Shao Overseas Chinese Documentation & Research Center Endowment	286,960
The Marion Alden Endowment Fund for the Southeast Asian Library Collection	223,966
Constance Sands/Candus Martzolff Endowment for Archives & Special Collections	125,569
C. L. and Candus Martzolff Memorial Fund	16,423
Lynn Shostack Endowment for the Physically Challenged	107,235
Donald & Marian Spencer Endowment	99,708
B. A. Renkenberger Memorial Endowment	59,990
LaTourrette-Hater HPER Endowed Library Fund	58,035
Dr. Phillip Zenner Book Fund	52,254
The Frank B. Fieler Book Fund	29,526
The James Carl Fleeman Memorial Fund	27,052
Earl C. Shively Memorial Scholarship	26,143
Su-Chen Chang Endowment/Chinese Collection	20,340
Feng Chia University Endowment/Chinese Collection	19,019
The Joseph Wayland Morgan and Helen Bosart Morgan Endowment	15,274
Class of 1892 Super Memorial Fund	13,052
Edward & Claudette Stevens Library Endowment	10,736
Friends of the Library Scholarship Fund	15,907
The Hwa-Wei Lee Center for International Collections Endowment	93,433
Total of Library Endowments	$9,086,811

Note: This list includes only those endowments directly controlled by the Library. It does not include endowments controlled by academic units which designate some of the earnings for the Library, such as the Stocker Engineering and the Tun Abdul Razak Chair Endowments.

APPENDIX VIII
Statistics of Library Staffing from 1978 – 79 to 1998 – 99

	Staff Full-time Equivalent (FTE)					Part-Time Student Assistant Hours					Grand Total
	Contract		Classified		All					All	Staff/ Student
Fiscal Year	Operating Fund	Non-Operating	Operating Fund	Non-Operating	Staff (FTE)	Operating Fund	Non-Operating	Work Study	Total Hours	Student (FTE)	(FTE)
1978 – 79	24.11	0.50	53.00	0.00	77.61	33,977	n/a	41,120	75,097	36.11	113.72
1979 – 80	24.11	1.17	53.00	0.57	78.85	35,356	n/a	44,156	79,512	38.23	117.08
1980 – 81	25.11	2.08	53.00	4.39	84.58	28,713	n/a	50,961	79,674	38.30	122.88
1981 – 82	25.44	3.92	53.00	6.11	88.47	25,742	11,052	49,734	86,528	41.60	130.07
1982 – 83	26.28	5.45	53.00	6.72	91.45	31,220	10,597	50,265	92,082	44.27	135.72
1983 – 84	26.94	3.17	52.50	4.13	86.74	37,009	9,908	58,456	105,373	50.66	137.40
1984 – 85	29.28	1.25	48.00	0.63	79.16	36,748	8,611	56,965	102,324	49.19	128.35
1985 – 86	29.28	1.75	48.00	3.51	82.54	40,586	11,469	59,365	111,420	53.57	136.11
1986 – 87	30.28	2.00	48.00	1.90	82.18	49,087	15,981	54,583	119,651	57.52	139.70
1987 – 88	28.77	1.57	52.00	3.40	85.74	44,494	11,583	56,640	112,717	54.19	139.93
1988 – 89	30.20	2.65	53.50	3.15	89.50	50,060	9,553	53,111	112,724	54.19	143.69
1989 – 90	30.90	3.52	54.00	3.89	92.31	48,694	9,494	53,108	111,296	53.51	145.82
1990 – 91	32.60	3.98	52.50	4.45	93.53	51,824	15,542	43,343	110,709	53.22	146.75
1991 – 92	37.46	3.45	57.50	7.50	105.91	56,385	15,924	55,839	128,148	61.61	167.52
1992 – 93	39.66	5.25	56.50	5.60	107.01	51,812	25,631	60,270	137,713	66.21	173.22
1993 – 94 *	52.25	6.92	70.40	2.10	131.67	90,983	15,989	65,700	172,672	83.01	214.68
1994 – 95 *	54.50	5.52	69.50	3.50	133.02	67,197	17,175	69,196	153,568	73.83	206.85
1995 – 96 *	53.75	6.67	72.83	4.00	137.25	70,441	21,176	57,731	149,348	71.80	209.05
1996 – 97 *	53.25	1.52	73.21	4.00	131.98	73,375	38,754	50,890	163,019	78.37	210.35
1997 – 98 *	53.25	4.75	72.79	3.50	134.29	71,762	15,061	53,503	140,325	67.46	201.76
1998 – 99 *	55.25	4.38	73.75	4.50	137.88	68,274	20,304	51,871	140,449	67.52	205.40

* includes regional campuses

Breakdown of 1998 – 99 Library Staffing

ATHENS	39.50	1.50	55.50	4.50	101.00	51,449	16,625	45,700	113,775	54.70	155.70
ATHENS-IMTS	6.75		4.00		10.75	5,787			5,787	2.78	13.53
ATHENS-INTERNS		2.88			2.88				0	0.00	2.88
ATHENS-TEMPS					0.00				0	0.00	0.00
CHI lli COTHE	2.00		2.00		4.00	3,072		1,637	4,709	2.26	6.26
IRONTON	1.00		4.00		5.00	2,194		2,726	4,920	2.37	7.37
LANCASTER	2.00		2.90		4.90	5,025			5,025	2.42	7.32
EASTERN	2.00		1.85		3.85	747		45	792	0.38	4.23
ZANESVILLE	2.00		3.50		5.50		3,678	1,763	5,441	2.62	8.12
Total	55.25	4.38	73.75	4.50	137.88	68,274	20,304	51,871	140,449	67.52	205.40

RECOGNIZING CONTRIBUTIONS

National Advisory Council / Advancement Committee

Honorary Members
Dr. Vernon Alden*
President Emeritus
Ohio University
Boston, MA

Dr. You-Bao Shao
Owner
Van Yu Trading Co. Ltd.
Hong Kong

Ms. Beth K. Stocker
Stocker Foundation
Oberlin, OH

Chairs

Mr. Donald A. Spencer*
NAC Chair
Retired Real Estate Broker
Cincinnati, OH

Mr. Joseph Marsalka*
AC Chair
Chair/President
StarTec, Inc.
Dublin, OH

Members

Dr. Jeanette G. Grasselli
Brown
Former Director
Corp. Research for BP America

Mem. of Ohio Board of
Regents
Chagrin Falls, OH

Mr. Sydney E. Buck*
Vice President
The Koll Company
Corona del Mar, CA

Mr. Sanford D. Elsass*
Chairman & CEO
The Arbor Acquisition Corp.
Boston, MA

Atty. Charlotte Coleman
Eufinger*
Coleman & Eufinger
Executive Director
Marysviile, OH

Ms. Rene Ghdden
First Lady
Ohio University

Ms. Ann B. Harris*
Former Exotic Flower Infl. Exp.
Guatemala

Mrs. Susan Hostetler
Director of Hostetler Gallery
Nantucket, MA

Mr. Danel Shao*
Executive Director
Van Yu Trading:Co:, Ltd.,
Hong Kong

Mr George Spina*
President
Pillsbuny & Company
Washington, DC

Mr. Lou Vlasho*
Owner
Water Professionals
Fort Myers, FL

* Advancement Committee Members

Committee to Honor Vernon Alden

Interim Chair
T. Michael Long, Partner
Brown Brothers Harriman & Co.
New York, NY

Chair
Sanford D. Elsass
Milton, MA

International Chair
Robert Fallon
Chase Manhattan Bank
New York, NY

Members
William L. Haines
The Bromley Companies
New York, NY

Frederick Harris
The Design Studio
Tokyo, Japan

Davis llingworth
Irvine, CA

Jon Rotenberg
Brookline, MA

Lynn Shostack
Chairman of the Board
Joyce International New York, NY

University Library Committee
Douglas Baxter, Ph.D., Chair

Dean of Libraries,
Ex-Officio

Library Appeals Board
Eileen Theodore-Shusta, Chair
Faculty:
Sharran Parkinson, Ph.D,
Letty Workman
Students:
Kimberly Amicon
Lesley Collett

Faculty representatives:
Anne Cooper-Chen, Ph.D.
Edward A. Leach, Ph.D.
Yolande Helm, Ph.D.
William Miller, Ph.D.
Janusz Starzyk, Ph.D.
Bruce Steiner, Ph.D.
James Yanok, Ph.D.

30th Anniversary Committee
Safinda Arthur, Chair
Gloria Devol
Betty Hoffmsri-Pinther
Gary Hunt
Edie Luce
Doag McCabe
Peggy Sattler
Eileen Theodore-Shusta

Library Council
Salinda Arthur
Darlene Campbell
Cheryl Ewing
Ted Foster
Jeff Fulk
Anne Goss
Gary Hunt

Student representatives:
Candace Stewart
Courtney Desman
Maggie Hajduk

Libraries Special Endowment Funds, Advisory Committee
Kent Mulliner, Chair
Members:
Joseph Bernt, Ph.O.
William Condee, Ph.D.
John Faulkner, Ph.D.
David Hendricker, Ph.D.
Steven Miner, Ph.D.
Jack Matthews, Ph.D.
Ben Stuart, Ph.D.
Morgan Vis-Chiassori, Ph.D.
Margaret Thomas

Library Council (cont'd)
Hwa-Wei Lee
Richard Post
Peggy Sattler
Steve Steward
Eileen Theodore-Shusta
Wanda Weinberg
Teresa Winning

Administration:
Hwa-Wei Lee, Ph.D.
Brad Cecil
Mark Smith

Friends of Ohio University Libraries
Margaret Thomas, Chair
Betty Hollow, Vice-President, President Elect
Howard Dewaid, Ph.D.
George Klare, Ph.D.
William Owens, Ph.D.
Rich Purdy
John Ray
Frank Robinson
Carolyn tice, DSW

Allocation Formula Review Committee
Robert Houdek, Chair
University Library Committee:
Douglas Baxter, Ph.D.
Howard Dewald, Ph.D.
Library Staff:
Anne Braxton
Betty Hoffmann-Pinther
Kent Mulliner
Dan Olson
Wanda Weinberg

Staff Development Committee
Judy Daso
RoseAnne Douglas
Susie Rohrbough
Sandy Seetey
Susie Sorden
Teresa Winning
Eileen Theodore-Shusta

Bibliographer's Council Steering Committee
Kent Mulliner, Chair
Members:

George Bain, Ph.D.,
Executive Secretary
Salinda Arthur, Executive Administrator
Hwa-Wei Lee, Ph.D,

Ted Foster
Michael Farmer
Anita Grant
Betty Hoffmann-Pinther
Robert Houdek
Laura Hudson
Dan Olson
Patricia Smith-Hunt
Laura Windsor

Technology Advisory Group
Betty Hoffmann-Pinther, Chair
Members:
Janet Carleton
David Dudding
Anita Grant
Robert Houdek

Gary Hunt
Kent Mulliner
Richard Post
Nancy Rue
Tim Smith

Faculty Representatives and Bibliographers

College	School/Department	Faculty Representative	Bibliographer	Asst. Bibliographer
Arts & Sciences	African American	Robert Rhodes	Pat Smith-Hunt	
	Biological Sciences	Anthony Brown	Anne Goss	
	Chemistry	David Hendricker	Robert Houdek	B. Hoffmann-Pinther
	Classical Language	William Owens	Timothy Smith	
	Economics	David Klingaman	Robert Politylo	
	English Language & Literature	Janis Holm	Sharon Huge	
	Envir. & Plant Biology	Brian McCarthy	Robert Houdek	
	Geography	Nancy Bain	Ted Foster	
	Geological Sciences	Greg Nadon	Michael Farmer	
	History/Cont History	Katherine Jelfison	Dan Olson	Doug McCabe
	Linguistics	Hiro. Oshita	Laura Windsor	
	Mathematics	Paul Jan Steptycki	Michael Farmer	

Faculty Representatives and Bibliographers continued...

College	School/Department	Faculty Representative	Bibliographer	Asst. Biblio
	Modern Languages			
	– French	Ruth Nybakken	Barry Scott	
	– German	Carl Carrier	Barry Scott	
	– Italian	Bartolomeo Martello	Barry Scott	
	– Russian	Karen Evans-Romaine	Barry Scott	
	– Spanish	Betsy Partyka	Barry Scott	
	Philosophy	Albert Mosley	Bill Rhinehart	
	Physics & Astronomy	David Drabold	B. Hoffmann-Pinther	
	Political Science	Delysa Burnier	E. Theodore-Shusta	Judy Connick
	Psychology	Francis Bellezza	Anne Goss	Janet Carleton
	Social Work	Carolyn Tice	Anita Grant	
	Sociology & Anthropology	Marty Schwartz/ Anne Freter-Abrams	Jeffrey Ferrier Robert Politylo	
Business				
Communication	Communication Mgmt.	Philip Campbell	Sheppard Black	Laura Hudson
	Interpersonal Comm.	Anita James	Sheppard Black	Laura Husdon
	Journalism	Joseph Bernt	Sheppard Black	Laura Hudson
	Telecommunications	William Miller	Sheppard Black	Laura Hudson
	Visual Communication	Gary Kirksey	Anne Braxton	
Education	All of Education	James Williams	Wanda Weinborg	
Engineering &	Chemical	Darin Ridgway	Robert Houdek	B. Hoffmann-Pinther

Technology	Civil	B. Stuart	Robert Houdek	Laura Windsor
	Electrical	Hollis Chen	Robert Houdek	Laura Windsor
	Industrial & Systems	H. T. Zwahlen	Robert Houdek	Laura Windsor
	Industrial Tech	Patrick McCuistion	Robert Houdek	Laura Windsor
	Mechanical	L. Urieli	Robert Houdek	Laura Windsor
Fine Arts	Art	Charles McWenny	Anne Braxton	
	Dance	Susan Van Pelt	Holly Oberle	
	Music	Richard Wetzel	Holly Oberle	
	Theatre	William Condee	Anne Braxton	
	Comp. Arts	Charles Buchanan	Anne Braxton	
	Film	Jenny Kwok Lau	Anne Braxton	
Health & Human Services	Health Sciences	Michele Morrone	Cheryl Ewing	
	Recreation & Sports Sciences	Beth VanDerMeer	Susie Rohrbough	
	Hearing & Speech. Sci	Travis Milliken	Cheryl Ewing	
	Human & Consumer Sci.	Marjorie Hagerman	Karen Williams	
	Nursing	Sharon Deneham	Cheryl Ewing	
	Physical Therapy	Averall Overby	Anne Goss	
Osteopathic Medicine	Osteo. Medicine	John C. Wolfe	Anne Goss	
Interdisciplinary	African/Asian Languages	Hiro Yuki Oshita	Laura Windsor	
	African Studies	Stephen Howard	Ted Foster	
	Condensed Matter	David Drabold		
	Developmental	William Romoser	Lian The-Mulliner	
	East Asian Studies	Ruth Nybakken	Wei Yan	Liren Zheng
	Latin American Studies	Tom Walker	Eric Alstrom	Laura Hudson
	Condensed Matter	David Ingram	B. Hoffmann-Pinther	
	East Asian Studies	Ruth Nybakken	Wei Yan/Liren Zheng	Swee-Lan Quah
	Environmental Studies	Geoffrey Smith	Laura Windsor	
	Women' Studies	Aileen Hall	Judy Daso	
Library	Children's Literature		Wanda Weinberg	
	Documents		Judy Daso	
	General		Kent Mulliner	
	– Bestsellers & Award Books		Kent Mulliner	
	– Electronic Resources		Laura Hudson	
	– Library Science		H-W. Lee	
	– Newspapers		Kent Mulliner	
	Leisure Reading		Sharon Huge	
	Maps		Ted Foster	
	Microform Subscriptions		Kent Mulliner	
	Reference		Nancy Rue	
	Replacements		Kent Mulliner	
	Special Collections		George Bain	

Donors

$500,000 or more
Sanford D. Elsass

$100,000 to $499,999
Murray Louis
Daniel K. C. Shao

$50,000 to $99,999
Beth K. Stocker

$10,000 to $49,999
William L. Haines
Robert L. and Joan Hill
Jon F. Rotenberg
You-Bao Shao

$5,000 to $9,999
John M. and Charlotte C. Eufinger
Helen Claire Sagstetter Trust

$1,000 to $4,999
Michael C. and Victoria Bida
Glenn and Jeanette Grasselli Brown
Lurene C. Brown
Su-Chen Chang
Jing Chen
Daniel J. Edelman Inc.
Robert and Rene Glidden
Martha Daniel Hansgen
Gary A. Hunt
Edward R. Kruse Jr.
Charles and Ruth Overby
Eileen A. Pickenpaugh
Richard R. Edith Post
Vivian & Lionel Spiro Fund
Julia G. Shulman
Claudette C. Stevens
Margaret & Robert Walter Fund
Westinghouse Foundation
James M. and Marie White

$500 to $999
George W. and Nancy R. Bain
Thomas W. and Janet E. Bolland
James R. and Phyllis A. Burkhard
David D. and Elaine Dabelko
Ruth Anna Duff
Friends of Hwa-Wei Lee

$500 to $999 continued...
Diane Gibbs
Patricia Grean
Peter and Elizabeth Hoffmann-Pinther
Louise Luckinbill
Arthur J. and Kathleen A. Marinelli

$100 to $499 continued...
OU Emeriti Association
OU Women's Club, Youngstown
Kathy K. Oliver
William M. Owens and Kay Tousley

James S. McDonald
Nancy Miller
Lian H. The-and Kent Mulliner
D. Scott Peters
Joan Galbreath Phillips
Charles J. and Claire O. Ping
Mr. and Mrs. David W. Russell
Sven and Rosamond Vaule Fund
Jia Xiang and Ling Jin Zhang

$100 to $499
Jocelyn B. Alexander
Steven D. Arnold
Athens Rotary Club
Shirley Baxter Bemdsen
Mary O. Black
Blackwell's Book Services
Judith A. Bleses
Michael Allen Bodkin
Lester A. Lawana Bowers
Ernst Breitenberger
Jeffery Alan Brier
Paul A. and Kay Jeannine Briner
John L. Brown Jr.
Tracy C. Browning
Karen G. Burch
Carl E. Carrier
Su-Jung Chang
Ching-Chih and Sow-Hsi Chen
Vivian Chen
Li-Min Cheng
Mei-Chu Cheng
Anthony G. and Helen Chila
Francine C. Childs
Yu-Lan Margaret Chou
Thomas L. and Pamela H. Cornn
Mark A. Cottrill
Christopher Cunningham
Donna M. Daniel
John Charles and Ruth Marian Day
Robert J. and Andrea B. DeMott
David Descutner and DeLysa Burnier
Francine C. DiFilippo
Mary C. Donovan

$100 to $499 continued...
Gifford B. and Mary C. Doxsee
Richard R. Duncan
Ningping Fan and May M. Hu

Lorie B. Owens-Robb
Jerry P. and Sue E. Peppers
Stanley and Margaret Planton
Pro Care Vision Center
Procter & Gamble

Jean Fair Fieler
Marvin E. and Hilary M. Fletcher
Friends of the Library
Leonard Frieling
Robert L. and Barbara Gale
Kathleen Garland-Rike
Alan H. and Sandra L. Geiger
Timothy A. Gooden
Anne S. Goss
Walter S. and Marsha L. Greaves
William S. and Jayne Guthrie
J A. Hake
Alonzo L. and Joyce L. Hamby
David G. and Sara A. Hendricker
Nancy E. Hibbert
Mrs. Jeanne A. Horton
Hong-Chu Huang
Ruth T. Ingham
Ernest H. Johansson and Linda Carter
Annette Fox Johnson
Richard E. and Patricia M. Jones
Linda Ann Kennedy
R. Kenneth and Teri Kerr
Yong Won Kim
Earl A. Elizabeth R. Knies
John F. and Alma L. Kuffner
Elinor M. Lee
Elizabeth P. Lee
Hwa-Wei and Mary F. Lee
Lucy Te-Chu Lee
Yueh-Mei Lee
Tze-Chung and In-Lan W. Li
Wei-Ming Lin
Don Lindley
Frederick C. Littmann
Elona K. Lucas
Luna T. Lung
Daniel and Natalie A. Luskevich
D. H. and Mary M. Malcolm
Ralph E. and Marilyn Martin
David A. and Barbara J. Miller
Sue Ellen Miller
Melissa S. Montag
Dan Moyer and Merry J. Speece
William J. Muthig
NCR Foundation
Nationwide Insurance Enterprise Fdn.
Judith A. Nouzak
Ruth E. Nybakken

REM Systems, Inc.
Gerald E. Radcliffe
John C. and Jeannette Ray
Richard E. ReedAlan E. and Ruby T. Riedel

Kenneth L. Rhoads	Teri G. Sherman	Kelly Lynn Vickers
Donald E. and Jane V. Riggs	Lee C. and Margaret Soltow	Gert P. and Ching Y. Volpp
Wanda Sue Rohrbough	Margaret E. Stevens	Chen-Ku Wang
James I. Ross	Lynn E. Stratey	Karen T. Wickliff
Marta Ann Roth	David E. and Carolyn C. Sutherland	Kirsten H. Williams
Robert W. and Lelia Russell	Holley Marker Thompson	David W. and Tracy L. Wineland
Karl L. Schaab	Zhiyong and Yi Li Tian	William A. and AnneT. Withington
Martin D. Schwartz	Kenneth B. and Eleanor Unterbrink	Lin Xie
Don H. and Martha G. Shamblin	Paul and Barbara Van der Veur	Tsing and Pat L. Yuan

Credits
Hwa-Wei Lee, Dean Emeritus of University Libraries
Julia Zimmerman, Dean of Libraries
Gary Hunt, Assoc. Dean for Administration
Richard Innis, Media Artist, Layout, Design, and Production

Contributors to content:
George Bain, Archives and Special Collections Head
Anne Braxton, Fine Arts Collection Head
Judy Daso, Government Documents Head
Ted Foster, Map Collection and Microforms Head
Anne Goss, Asst. Dean and Director of Health Sciences
Anita Grant, Circulation Head
Paulette Hodges, Office Manager
Karen Jones, Senior Secretary
Betty Hoffmann-Pinther, Automation and Bibliographic Control Coordinator
Kent Mulliner, Asst. to the Dean and Collection Development Coordinator
Richard Post, Asst. Dean and Director of Instructional Media & Technology Services
Nancy Rue, User Services Coordinator
Holly Oberle, Music/Dance Head
Pat Smith-Hunt, Preservation Head
Lian The-Mulliner, Southeast Asia Collections Head
Eileen Theodore-Shusta, Asst. to the Dean and Human Resources Coordinator

Photography:
Lars Lutton, Photographer
A. F. Sidlo

Proofreading:
Peggy Sattter, Graphic Design Mgr.
Karen Jones, Senior Sec.
Joann McKibben, Office Mgr.

Library Staff, June 1999

Kevin Angel	Darlene Campbell	RoseAnne Douglas
Theresa Bailey	John Canter	David Dudding
George Bain	Frank Carano	Cheryl Ewing
Anita Baird	Janet Carleton	Mike Farrner.
Tom Baker	Geotge Cheripko	Jeff Ferrier
Sheppard Black	Susan Chesser	Connie Flores
Jeremy Blazier	Lucy Conn	Ted Foster
Pat Born	Judy Connick	Robert Frasch
Anne Braxton	Lois Coutant	Jeff Fulk
Kin Brooks	Martha Crabtree	Gary Ginther
Teresa Brown	Judy DaSo	Anne Goss
Lyn Brown	Gloria Devol	Anita Grant
Wanda Brunk	Marine Dillon	Florence Grueser
Laura Burns	Shirley Dorman	Nancy Haddox

Ralph Harvey
Doreen Hockenberry
Paulette Hodges
Betty Hoffmann-Pinther
Robert Houdek
Laura Hudson
Sharon Huge
Gary Hunt Richard Innis
Karen Jones
William Kimok
Robm Krivestf
Sharon Lamb
Wendy Langdon
Dawn LaPorte
Linda Leyer-Furumoto
Hwa-Wei Lee
Desiree Loewit
Rita Lonas
Edie Luce
Lars Lutton
Doug McCabe
Janice Mcknight
Graig Mehr
Davb Miller
Suzanne Mingus
Steve Moyvrey
Kent Mulliner
Kate Nally
Holly Oberle

Melyn Odenttial
Dan Olson
Darla Perry
Gary Poling
Robert Politylo
Richard Post
David Prince
Swee-Lari Quah
Bill Rhinehart
Judy Rich
Susie Rohrbough
Shirley Ross
Nancy Rue
Sherri Saines
Peggy Rattler
Esther Sclianzenbach
Barry Scott
Sandy Seeley
Christa Sigman
Greg Sigman
Catby Sitko
Kay Six
Tim Smith
Pat Smith Hunt
Susie Sorden
Steve Steward
Elizabeth Story
Andrew Stuart Annette Talbert
Lian The-Mulliner

Eileen Theodore-Shusta
Karen Thompson
Zhiyong Tian
Norma Wagner
Wanda Weinberg
Karen Williams
Laura Windsor
Teresa Winning
Wei Yan
Liren Zheng

Custodial Staff
Kim Bolin.
Steve Cooper
Sharon Darnell
John. Dewey
Rufus Dillon
Floyd Flowers
Naomi Goins
Roger Imboden
Barbara Lyons
Bill Mingus
Roger Riley
Lori Russell
Connie Seme Isberger
Gary Zeigler

Zone Maintenance
Rocky Exline

知识管理与图书馆在新世纪的角色

Knowledge Management and the Role of Libraries in the New Century

Introduction

"Knowledge Management" has become a popular term in the business world during the last decade of the 20th century. It is the business world that recognizes at first the importance of knowledge in the "global economy" of the "knowledge age". In the new knowledge economy, knowledge is power especially if it is shared and put to creative use. The possession of relevant and strategic knowledge and its unceasing renewal enables businesses to gain competitive advantage.

The management of information and knowledge has long been regarded as the domain of libraries. Librarians and information professionals are trained to be experts in information and knowledge searching, selecting, acquiring, organizing, preserving, repackaging, disseminating, and serving. It is necessary for libraries to reassess their strengths and weaknesses in knowledge and information management and to provide leadership in the advancement and implementation of knowledge management. An important step for libraries in the 21st century is to play a key role in fostering, furthering and facilitating knowledge identification, capture, organization for use, renewal, innovation, and creation of new knowledge in the broadest sense to benefit mankind.

Knowledge management is much more than information and data management. It is also much broader in scope than information technology. Knowledge management has a goal to identify useful and relevant knowledge, to organize, merge, and synthesize knowledge, and to stimulate the creative use of knowledge. Information technology provides the technical tool to achieve this goal. Since knowledge is processed, used, renewed, expanded, and often resides in the minds of people, and is the creation of human wisdom, the human element is the most important part of knowledge management.

This paper will describe the characteristics of the knowledge age, trace the rise of knowledge management, its definition, perspectives, and processes, examine the emerging trends in knowledge management, review the changes in the library and information profession at a time of rapid advancement in information technology, look at the many challenges faced by libraries as well as the new role of libraries, and discuss the relationship between libraries and knowledge management.

The Coming of the Knowledge Age

In the second half of the twentieth century, the rate of technological change has greatly accelerated, accompanied by exponential growth in human knowledge—the information explosion! It is safe to predict that the rapid rate of change will continue into the twenty-first century and our lives and societies will be increasingly knowledge-based. Although many of the changes have resulted from the technological revolution, especially in the area of computer, telecommunication, and network technologies—which are truly phenomenal to say the least, we must clearly understand that all of these technological breakthroughs have been the result of human knowledge, ingenuity, creativity, and wisdom. We are the driving force of technological change. In fact, we can and will make certain that technological advances benefit mankind and usher us into the digital and networked "knowledge age" of the twenty-first century.

What is the "knowledge age" and what are its common characteristics? These questions need to be defined and answered.

Daniel Bell defines knowledge as "a set of organized statements of facts or ideas presenting a reasoned judgment or an experimental result, which is transmitted to others through some communication medium in some systematic form"①. As for information, Marc Porat states, "Information is data that have been organized and communicated."②

Stephen Abram sees the process for knowledge creation and use as a continuum where data transforms into information, information transforms into knowledge and knowledge drives and underpins behavior and decision-making. Below are his definitions on data, information, and knowledge:③

Data are raw facts that have no context or meaning on their own. The key success factors in data management are implementing standards and quality control procedures to allow the data to be used effectively and confidently. It rarely has value to end-users except in the context of turning it into information.

Information is a tangible representation of data or knowledge within a specific context— usually in some end-user oriented product like a book, magazine article, or study. The key success factor is the effectiveness of the representation in communicating the information. The same data can be represented many ways in order to meet the needs of different types of users. It only has value to the end-user if it meets their specific needs at the time they need it.

Knowledge is information in context of an individual's role, learning behavior, and experiences. The key success factors include the congruity between the information and the individual's perspective. It only has value in the context of the situations where it is applied. The major steps that occur in the transforming of information into knowledge are learning, knowing, filtering, evaluating, and balancing.

In the "knowledge age" we will see the accumulation of human knowledge at an unprecedented rate which affects every aspect of our life and society. It is through human ingenuity, creativity, and wisdom that our world of information and knowledge is compounded in the passing of every second, minute, and hour. It was estimated that about 850,000 publications of scholarly interest are published annually throughout the world, and this number is increasing by about 2.5 percent per year. Serials publications have grown from 70,000 titles in 1972 to 118,500 in 1997. Every two minutes, a scientific article is completed around the world. This fast rate of accumulation of explicit human knowledge is only the visible part of an iceberg of a much larger body of tacit knowledge, which resides in human minds and experiences. This is the basic characteristic of the "knowledge age". The term of "knowledge age" emphasizes the role that knowledge, both explicit and tacit, will play in the new millennium.

A major reason for the expansion of knowledge has been advances in computer, telecommunication, and network technologies in recent times. The faster we can communicate information and knowledge, the more knowledge will flourish. The invention of printing in China in the late seventh century and in Europe in the fifteenth century greatly facilitated the preservation and dissemination of human knowledge. But only with the invention of the telegraph by Samuel Morse in 1844, just 156 years ago, could information travel faster than a horse or a man could run. Now, with the coming of the Internet and its World Wide Web, we are in a true sense a global village where digitized information and knowledge can be disseminated at the speed of light regardless of distance or other constraints.④

---

① Bell, Daniel. *The Coming of Post-industrial Society: A Venture in Social Forecasting.* New York: Basic Books, 1973: p. 175.

② Porat, Marc. *The Information Economy: Definition and Measurement.* Washington, D. C.: U. S. Department of Commerce, Office of Telecommunications, 1977 (Publication 77 – 12): p. 1.

③ Abram, Stephen. "Post Information Age Positioning for Special Librarians: Is Knowledge Management the Answer?" *Information Outlook.* June 1997. pp. 20 – 21.

④ Lee, Hwa-Wei. "Libraries in the Digital and Networked Knowledge Age of the Twenty first Century" published in *Proceedings of 21st Century Public Libraries—Vision and Reality.* Taichung, Taiwan: National Taichung Library, 2000: pp. 1 – 44 – 1 – 45.

The Rise of Knowledge Management

As early as 1965, Peter Drucker already pointed out that "knowledge" would replace land, labor, capital, machines, etc. to become the chief source of production. His foresight did not get much attention back then. It was not until 1991 when Ikujiro Nonaka raised the concept of "tacit" knowledge and "explicit" knowledge as well as the theory of "spiral of knowledge" in the Harvard Business Review, that the time of "knowledge-based competition" finally came. In 1993, when Drucker stated the dominance of knowledge workers in his book, *Post-Capitalist Society*[①], the importance of knowledge became a worldwide topic for discussion. Since then "knowledge management"[②] has gained prominence. Many more articles and books dedicated to the advancement of knowledge management have appeared. Bill Gates in his book, Digital Nerve System, published in 1999, further pointed out that knowledge and network would become the basis of all future enterprises. In his latest book, *Building Organizational Intelligence: A Knowledge Management Primer*[③], Jay Liebowitz stated:

"In today's movement towards knowledge management, organization are trying to best leverage their knowledge internally in the organization and externally to their customers aim stakeholders. They are trying to capitalize on their organizational intelligence to maintain their competitive edge."

"The thrust of knowledge management is to create o process of valuing the organization's intangible assets in order to best leverage knowledge internally and externally. Knowledge management, therefore, deals with creating, securing, capturing, coordinating, combining, retrieving, and distributing knowledge. The idea is to create a knowledge sharing environment whereby sharing knowledge is power as opposed to the old adage that, simply, knowledge is power."

Some Definitions of Knowledge Management

Because knowledge management is still a relatively new concept and viewed differently by different writers from different focuses, its definitions vary. In her article, "What is knowledge management?" Jennifer Rowley offers her definition below:

"Knowledge management is concerned with the exploitation and development of the knowledge assets of an organization with a view to furthering the organization's objectives. The knowledge to be managed includes both explicit, documented knowledge, and tacit, subjective knowledge. Management entails all of those processes associated with the identification, sharing and creation of knowledge. This requires systems for the creation and maintenance of knowledge repositories, and to cultivate and facilitate the sharing of knowledge and organizational learning. Organizations that succeed in knowledge management are likely to view knowledge as an asset and to develop organizational norms and values, which support the creation and sharing of knowledge."[④]

Rowley's definition was based on the four different types of perspectives on knowledge management identified by Thomas H. Davenport et al in their study of a number of knowledge management projects. From the analysis of the projects' objectives, Davenport et al were able to categorize them into four broad types of perspectives:[⑤]

---

① Drucker, Peter Ferdinand. *Post-Capitalist Society*. New York: HarperBusiness, 1993.

② Arthur Anderson Business Consulting. *The First Book on Knowledge Management*, translated into Chinese by Liu Jin-Wei. Taipei: San Chou Publisher, 2000; p. vi-vii. (In Chinese)

③ Liebowitz, Jay. *Building Organizational Intelligence: A Knowledge Management Primer*. Boca Raton, FL: CRC Press, 2000; p. 1.

④ Rowley, Jennifer. "What is Knowledge Management?" *Library Management*. V. 20, No. 8 (1999): pp. 416-419.

⑤ Davenport, Thomas H., DeLong, D. W., and Beers, M. C. "Successful Knowledge Management Projects." *Sloan Management Review*. V. 39, No. 2 (1998): pp. 43-57.

1. To create knowledge repositories, which store both knowledge and information, often in documentary form. These repositories can fall into three categories:
- Those which include external knowledge, such as competitive intelligence.
- Those that include structured internal knowledge, such as research reports, and product oriented marketing materials as techniques and methods.
- Those that embrace informal, internal or tacit knowledge, such as discussion databases that store "know how".

2. To improve knowledge access and transfer. Here the emphasis is on connectivity, access and transfer.
- Technologies such as video conferencing systems, document scanning and sharing tools and telecommunications networks are central.

3. To enhance the knowledge environment, so that the environment is conductive to more effective knowledge creation, transfer and use. This involves tackling organizational norms and values as they relate to knowledge.
- Increase awareness on sharing knowledge embedded in client relationship and engagements.
- Provide awards for contributions to the organization's structured knowledge base.
- Implement decision audit programs in order to assess whether and how employees were applying knowledge in key decisions.
- Recognize that successful knowledge management is dependent upon structures and cultures.

4. To manage knowledge as an asset, and to recognize the value of knowledge to an organization.

Others, however, sought to take a process view to define knowledge management. For example, Jan Duffy defines it as "a process that drives innovation by capitalizing on organizational intellect and experience."[1] Gartner Group defines it as "a discipline that promotes an integrated and collaborative approach to the process of information asset creation, capture, organization, access and use"[2].

Below is a set of knowledge management processes proposed by P. Galagan:[3]
- Generating new knowledge.
- Accessing knowledge from external sources.
- Representing knowledge in documents, databases, software and so forth.
- Embedding knowledge in processes, products, or services.
- Transferring existing knowledge around an organization.
- Using accessible knowledge in decision-making.
- Facilitating knowledge growth through culture and incentives.
- Measuring the value of knowledge assets and the impact of knowledge management.

From both the project perspectives and the operational processes described above we can gain a general understanding of the current scope and contents of knowledge management.

Emerging Trends in Knowledge Management

Funded by the U. K. Library and Information Commission, an interim report on Investigation of Underpinning Skills for Knowledge Management: Training Implications published in January

---

[1] Duffy, Jan. *Harvesting Experience: Reaping the Benefits of Knowledge.* Prairie Village, KS: ARMA International, 1999. Also from her article, "Knowledge Management: To Be or Not to Be?" *Information Management Journal.* V. 34, No. 1 (Jan. 2000): pp. 64 – 67.

[2] Bair, Jim. "Knowledge Management is About Cooperation and Context." *Gartner Advisory Services Research Note.* May 14, 1999.

[3] Galagan, P. "Smart Companies (Knowledge Management)." *Training and Development.* V. 51, No. 12 (1997): pp. 20 – 25.

1999 revealed several emerging trends in knowledge management. [1]

First, most organizations talk about the need to identify achievable knowledge management activities that will have an impact on the business and to concentrate on those.

Second, knowledge management is no longer confined to very large commercial corporations. Both public and private organizations are now considering ways of benefiting from some of the knowledge management concepts.

Third, there is no blueprint for knowledge management. Knowledge management is a homegrown activity, which has to reflect the organization, its unique place in the market, and its culture.

Fourth, the importance of commitment from the very top of the organization is essential for knowledge management to have a fighting chance.

Fifth, the role of the CKO (Chief Knowledge Officer) is becoming more dearly defined as a leadership role, generally time limited, to provide the necessary focus and drive to steer a change management through the crucial stages.

Sixth, knowledge management labeled roles are more likely to emerge as a realignment of an existing role, become an additional role for an existing post, or if identified as a new role, to be filled by existing staff. However, there are a number of new roles being coined such as knowledge analysts, knowledge architects, knowledge manager, knowledge brokers, knowledge auditors, knowledge navigators, knowledge guardians, and the like[2]—many of these roles are held by former librarians and information specialists.

Changes in the Library and Information Profession

While the business world is changing in the new knowledge economy and digital age, libraries of all types are undergoing drastic changes also. Since the 1960s, a noticeable change in the library and information profession has taken place every five to ten years. Prior to the 1960s, majority of libraries were paper- or print-based. The pace of development was slow and uneventful. During the 1960s, however, we saw the beginning of library automation, the standardization of a machine-readable cataloging format, and the establishment of a library cooperative—OCLC. During the 1970s we saw the introduction of online information search and retrieval and the beginning of CD-ROM. In the 1980s, library networking became the norm, so were the integrated library automation systems. In the 1990s, electronic publishing, multimedia, Internet, and digitalization gained dominance. As we enter the 21st century, libraries are moving in the direction of a hybrid, virtual, and digital world greatly influenced by Internet, World Wide Web and the knowledge age. Metadata, Dublin Core, the Cooperative Online Resources Catalog (CORC), and knowledge management have received wide attention both in and outside the library and information profession.

Major Challenges Faced by Libraries

During the periods of rapid changes, the library and information profession faced many challenges. They are:[3]
- Exponential growth in human knowledge as a result of interaction with the advancement of science and technology.
- Abundant information resources, good or bad, available through the Internet.
- Growth in library size, functions, resources, services, and complexity.
- Development of education at all levels, growth of the world economy, rise in culture and standards of living, and booming publishing, telecommunications, and mass media.

---

[1] Abell, A. and Oxbrow, N. *Investigation of Underpinning Skill for Knowledge Management: Training Implications, Interim Report.* London: TFPL, Inc. 1999.

[2] Liebowitz, Jay (2000). p. 58.

[3] Lee, Hwa-Wei (2000). pp. 1 -52 -1 -53.

- Addition of new curricula, fields of study, and research interests in universities.
- Changes in the pattern of scholarly communication and publishing caused by the rapid growth, popularity, and globalization of Internet.
- Skyrocketing costs of library materials, especially journal publications in the fields of science, technology, and medicine, which are increasingly concentrated among a few powerful, highly-profit-motivated international commercial publishing conglomerates.
- Negative impacts on libraries by increasing restrictions on "fair use" in copyright laws and intellectual property rights protection.
- Growing diversity in information formats.
- Internationalization of library collections and services.
- Changing nature of library collections from "ownership" to "access".
- Shrinking, or lacking adequate increase, in library funding.
- High costs of acquiring, maintaining, and upgrading library systems. Rapid technological advancement has also resulted in seemingly instant obsolescence of computer and network systems. Periodic replacement costs have not been factored into library budgets.
- Public demand for greater management accountability.
- Need for libraries to make further efforts in automation, interlibrary cooperation, resources sharing, staff development, reader education, modern management, and quality services.
- Increasing demands for library staff skilled in information technologies and knowledge management.
- Expanding user demands and expectations and decreasing ability of libraries to meet these demands.
- Increasingly vital role of information literacy and lifelong learning.
- Growing pressure from the accelerated rate of change.
- Inadequate recognition by governments and society at large of the importance of libraries.
- Threat of the demise of libraries and uncertainty of the future.

Of all these 21 challenges, many can be considered universal problems faced by libraries in any part of the world. Some may be more serious than others and may be more relevant in some countries than in others.

Fueled by the information explosion and by the expansion of Internet and WWW, our society is faced with additional problems. One of these is that while drowned by the flood of information we are starving for relevant knowledge. Another is the widening gap between the information "haves" and the "have-nots", which divides the "information rich" and the "information poor" individuals and nations. These challenges are serious for libraries which are concerned with the quality of information and the equality of knowledge access.

The Role of Libraries in the New Century

In order to cope with these challenges libraries must take appropriate actions to overcome them. Some of these actions require libraries to work together in cooperative and concerted efforts. Below are recommended actions:[1]

- Libraries should form local, regional, national, international, and specialty library networks or consortia to improve library cooperation, services, and resource sharing in order to meet a variety of needs of their users. Two of the most successful models, OCLC and OhioLINK, will be described later.
- Based on its special missions, goals, and needs, each library should develop a unique plan for resources development, taking into consideration the wide array of information formats available and the existing strength of library resources in other cooperating libraries.

---

[1] Ibid., pp. 1-53-1-55.

- Strive to fully realize the potentials of computer, information, telecommunication, and network technologies to improve library services, resources, and management through computerization and networking.
- Strongly support the development of Internet 2 and the Next-generation Internet for faster and more effective information resource development, gathering, archiving, and dissemination, as well as for scholarly communication.
- Library staff should regularly and systematically surf for useful information resources on the Internet and make them available to users.
- Libraries should use consortia power to obtain better prices for the purchase of books and other library materials as well as to negotiate better licensing agreements for the access to electronic databases, journals, and other digital resources.
- Libraries should join forces to develop or seek new alternatives in scholarly communications and to free themselves from the unreasonable price dominance and use restriction imposed by some commercial publishers. One good example of this is the founding of the SPARC initiative (Scholarly Publishing and Academic Resources Coalition) by members of the Association of Research Libraries—a membership organization of 122 major research and university libraries in the U.S.A. and Canada.
- Libraries should participate in collaborative or coordinated projects to digitize selected collections, which have no copyright restriction or have the permission of copyright holders. Such digitized collections will contribute to the realization of the digital library of the 21st century and bring the library to distant readers in a way not possible before.
- Libraries should give high priority to the continuing education and training of staff and to build organizational intelligence.
- Libraries should develop effective programs to recruit new staff skilled in information technology and its application in user services.
- Libraries should give further attention to user education in order to equip their users with the information-seeking skills necessary for living in the knowledge age.
- Libraries should further strengthen their function as the place for lifelong learning. Public libraries especially are situated to serve as community centers for continuing adult education.
- Libraries should adopt new management theories and practices, including, especially, knowledge management.
- Libraries should periodically reassess their mission, goals, and strategic directions and review their organizational structure for renewal and rejuvenation.
- Libraries must prove their value and usefulness by instituting a continuing process of improvement in information gathering, organization, and services to their users. Only in this way, can they gain the respect of their users and win the support of their government and society.
- Libraries should strive to become a learning organization.
- Libraries should develop appropriate programs to serve the under-served population in their communities, including the poor, uneducated, ethnic minorities, new immigrants, physically disabled, etc.
- To live in an interdependent world of the 21st century, libraries must internationalize their collections, programs, and services.
- Libraries should adopt the concept of knowledge management and take concrete steps to implement it.
- Whenever possible, libraries should conduct research and development projects to advance the knowledge and practice of library and information science.

The new role of libraries in the 21st century needs to be a learning and knowledge center for their users as well as the intellectual commons for their respective communities where, to borrow the phrase from the Keystone Principles, "people and ideas interact in both the real and virtual environments to expand learning and facilitate the creation of new knowledge"[1].

OCLC Online Computer Library Center

The original OCLC, the Ohio College Library Center, was established by a group of academic libraries in Ohio in 1967. The primary purpose at that time was to develop a computer system which would enable participating libraries to do online, shared cataloging, to create an online union catalog, and to share library resources through online interlibrary loan. Prior to OCLC, most libraries had to perform original cataloging on every item of library materials acquired. It was a time-consuming, labor-intensive, and costly operation. By participating in online shared cataloging, libraries can reduce duplication in original cataloging and, at the same time, create an online union catalog of library holdings—all in a very efficient and cost-effective way. During the late 1960s and early 1970s, few libraries could afford the cost of a mainframe computer, nor had they the staff to operate it. Computer software especially written for library operations was also non-existent. The creation of OCLC was a revolutionary step taken by Ohio academic libraries to meet the challenge of that time. The instant success of OCLC after its online cataloging went into operation in 1971 attracted libraries in other states to want to join. In a few years, OCLC's participating libraries had spread to the entire country, causing it to change its governance structure and its name to OCLC, Inc. in 1977, and to the OCLC Online Computer Library Center in 1981. The change in governance structure enabled libraries outside Ohio to become OCLC members, to have a representation in the Users Council, and to participate in the election of the Board of Trustees.

According to recent information released by OCLC, as of June 30, 1999, more than 34,700 libraries in 67 countries and territories were users of a variety of OCLC services. Among them 8,650 libraries were full OCLC members. These member libraries do all their cataloging with OCLC either online or via batch load. They use records in OCLC'S WorldCat to catalog materials and to input original cataloging records when there are no corresponding records in the database.

The online catalog of OCLC, which is called WorldCat, is by far the largest bibliographic database in the world, which consisted 39,697,399 bibliographic records as of June 30, 1999. About 2.2 million new records added each year by OCLC member libraries at a rate of 15 seconds a record. These records contain over 720 million location listings, in 400 languages, and over a span of 4,000 years of recorded knowledge.[2]

OCLC is organized for the public purpose of furthering access to the world's knowledge and reducing library costs. As a nonprofit corporation, OCLC:

- Is entirely self-supporting and does not rely on outside funding agencies.
- Charges libraries based on use of and contribution to OCLC services.
- Reviews its pricing with the OCLC membership through the Users Council and Advisory committees.
- Seeks to reduce the rate of rise of per unit costs in libraries.
- Provides libraries with credits for their original cataloging and resource sharing activities.
- Supports research, scholarship and education.
- Seeks to increase access to and use of the ever-expanding body of information worldwide.

In addition to the variety of cataloging services, OCLC also offers some very useful online reference services. The most important of these is the OCLC FirstSearch Service, which provides easy access to more than 2,200 electronic journal titles and 85 databases. More than 5.5 million

---

[1] On September 24-25, 1999, eighty academic library leaders met during a two-day Strategic Issues Forum of Academic Library Directors held in Keystone, Colorado, organized jointly by the Association of Research Libraries and OCLC. Three basic principles were declared as the expanded vision for libraries in the digital knowledge age of the 21st century. The three principles are called the Keystone Principles.

[2] OCLC *Annual Report 1998/99. A Great Time for Libraries*! Dublin, Ohio: OCLC Online Computer Library Center, 1999: pp. 1, 4-5, 32.

full-text articles are available online through FirstSearch. Users can also place interlibrary loan requests from this growing number of databases that include library holdings information. Since the inception of the OCLC Interlibrary Loan Service in 1979, it has processed over 94 million loans. ①

Established in 1978, the OCLC Office of Research is one of the world's leading centers devoted exclusively to confronting the problems and challenges of libraries in the knowledge age. During the past 10 years, OCLC has invested more than $100 million to research and develop new services.

The latest new service launched by OCLC since 1997 has been the establishment of the OCLC Institute to provide library professionals with opportunities for advanced education and knowledge exchange in the emerging global, digital environment of the 21st century. Some of the more popular courses offered by the Institute are:
 · Continuity and Innovation in Resource Sharing
 · Knowledge Access Management
 · Knowledge Management: Methods and Systems
 · Technology Planning in a Time of Rapid Change
 · Using Metadata for Knowledge Management

In 1999 alone, a total of 52 advanced seminars were conducted both at the OCLC Headquarters in Columbus, Ohio and in other parts of the USA and several regions of the world. Currently OCLC Institute is recruiting new adjunct faculty members with the intent to develop and expand new course offerings. A major focus for the year 2000 has been to extend the educational and training programs to Asia.

Entering the 21st Century, OCLC is scheduled to launch another new service on July 1, 2000, the "Cooperative Online Resource Catalog" (CORC). In January 2000, more than 200 libraries of all types, including about 30 non-U.S. libraries, have already participated in the development and testing of the project, which will provide a tool to cooperative libraries for creating descriptions of electronic resources using newly developed international standards such as Metadata and Dublin Core.

OhioLINK (Ohio Library and Information Network)

Academic libraries in Ohio have been known for their innovative and cooperative spirit. The establishment of OCLC in 1967 was a giant step. Even with the tremendous success of OCLC to greatly improve the development of and access to the bibliographic records of the world's knowledge, academic libraries in Ohio still felt a need to form a statewide academic library consortium for a closer cooperation in many other areas of library and information services within the State. After a year-long study by a blue-ribbon panel appointed in 1986 by the Ohio Board of Regents ②, a report entitled "Academic Libraries in Ohio: Progress Through Collaboration, Storage, and Technology" was issued. ③ Among the recommendations of the report were:
 · to implement as expeditiously as possible a statewide electronic catalog system which will include retrospective conversion of remaining paper cataloging records to the MARC (Machine-readable catalog) format,
 · to develop and implement a statewide delivery system of library materials among participating libraries, and
 · to plan for a cooperative preservation program.

---

① *An Overview of OCLC Services: Look What You're Doing Now ... With OCLC.* Dublin, Ohio: OCLC Online Computer Library Center, 1999: p. 3.

② The Ohio Board of Regents is a state coordinating agency reporting to the Governor with the responsibility of planning and overseeing the general policies and funding of all state-supported institutions of higher education.

③ Ohio Board of Regents. Library Study Committee. *Academic Libraries in Ohio: Progress Through Collaboration, Storage, and Technology. Report of the Library Study Committee.* Columbus, Ohio: Ohio Board of Regents, 1987.

From this initial report and a series of actions undertaken by a Steering Committee established by the Regents, OhioLINK—with ambitious plans and programs—was formed in 1989. The 18 participants in the initial group of libraries included the 13 comprehensive state universities, two large private universities, two state medical universities, and the State Library of Ohio. By November 1999, this number had expanded to 79, including all of the two-year state community and technical colleges and virtually all of the private colleges and universities.

Building on an existing statewide telecommunication infrastructure, OARnet (Ohio Academic and Research Network), OhioLINK is a distributed library network with a central computer system, which is linked to the computer systems at each or combinations of participating campuses. By design, both the central and local sites are equipped with common computer hardware and a software platform to enable maximum connectivity and compatibility. At the central site, an online union catalog is constructed with real-time circulation and location status of each library item. One of the unique features of OhioLINK is allowing library users in any one of the libraries to check the library holdings of all other libraries and to initiate borrowing requests for items not owned or available in the borrower's library. This user-initiated borrowing can be done from offices, labs, and home via campus networks or the Internet. The requested materials are then collected and sent by the lending library to the requestor's library by the specially arranged delivery service which aims at a 48-hour delivery time. This means that most interlibrary borrowing can be completed within two to three days. It is a great convenience and at no cost to the users. Currently, OhioLINK's central online union catalog consists of more than seven million individual titles representing 20 million volumes. 56% of the seven million titles are held by one library only. It serves an estimated 460,000 students and about 50,000 faculty and staff statewide. In 1998, the number of searches made in the central catalog reached 2,800,000 times and there were 550,000 interlibrary borrowing requests.

Within the past few years, in addition to the very popular and heavily used interlibrary borrowing service, OhioLINK has also launched other cooperative activities to expand shared electronic resources and to initiate other services. Most important of these are:
- The acquisition of many much-in-demand electronic databases from bibliographic to full text.
- Expanding the number of full-text databases, especially electronic journals.
- Employing consortium-purchasing power to obtain large discounts and/or more favorable licensing agreements from publishers.
- Adopting a statewide approval plan for library materials to avoid unnecessary duplication.
- Expanding online interlibrary borrowing from books to other types of library materials, which can be lent, such as microforms, videos, and CDs.
- Developing a more sophisticated search engine to ease the search of multiple databases.
- Establishing an Electronic Journal Center to manage the increasing number of electronic journals.
- Establishing a Digital Media Center with a much expanded storage space available at the Ohio Supercomputer Center for digital collections created by members, other non-profit institutions, or commercial firms.
- Improving off-campus access to OhioLINK resources from a distance.

Thus far, OhioLINK member libraries have accomplished the following goals that were among their shared visions:
- Tapping the existing computer and telecommunication infrastructure.
- Linking all major academic libraries in Ohio in an electronic networked environment.
- Pooling all library resources for easy access and effective sharing.
- Delivering materials quickly by various means.
- Expanding commonly needed electronic reference databases some of which cannot be afforded by individual or small libraries.
- Cooperating and coordinating in a statewide collection development to broaden collections

and reduce unnecessary duplication.
- Acquiring large and expensive electronic resources in a cost-effective way through consortia purchasing power.
- Getting much better deals in licensing agreements.
- Reducing the unit costs in information access and delivery.

Because of the demonstrated benefits and economies of scale, OhioLINK has been able to obtain adequate funding annually from the State with strong endorsement and support from the Ohio Board of Regents. Much of the state funding supports the central operation, delivery services, acquisition of major bibliographic, reference, and full-text databases, continuing software development, new initiatives, and others. Beginning in 1999, member libraries also voted to create a central fund for acquisitions through annual assessment from each library's acquisition budget.

For the implementation of a cooperative preservation program, five large regional storage centers have been built and are in operation. These centers are strategically located in the central, northeastern, northwestern, southeastern, and southwestern parts of Ohio for the purpose of storing lesser-used library collections of all the state universities and colleges. These high-density, low-cost storage facilities provide much needed relief for the congested shelving space in the main or branch library buildings on most of the campuses and allow these libraries to better serve their users. All stored library materials can be retrieved and returned to the library for use on the same day or the next day after a request, or dispatched to other OhioLINK libraries. Stored materials also are available for use on site.

Relationship Between Libraries and Knowledge Management

As a learning organization, libraries should provide a strong leadership in knowledge management. Unlike those business organizations whose goal for knowledge management is for competitive advantage, libraries, with the exception of company libraries (which may be known or called corporate libraries, special libraries, or knowledge centers), most public, academic, and research libraries have a different orientation and value. Instead of competition, internal use only, and little sharing of knowledge with others outside, the most important mission of public, academic, and research libraries is to expand the access of knowledge for their users. Charged by this mission, libraries should aim their knowledge management goal high. Below are examples of what libraries can do to improve their knowledge management in all the key areas of management and services.

Knowledge Resources Management

Because the exponential growth in human knowledge in a variety of formats libraries need to develop their resources access strategies from printed to electronic and digital resources in concert with their mission and charges. Restricted by limited funding, staff, and space, libraries must carefully analyze the needs of their users and seek to develop cooperative acquisition plans to meet these needs.

The changing concept from "ownership" to "access" and from "just in case" to "just in time" should be the goal of a sound resources development strategy.

An integrated online public access catalog (OPAC) with both internal and external resources as well as printed and other formats of knowledge should be developed and maintained. Many thousands of useful websites and knowledge sources should be included in OPACs by hard links. A system of regular inspection and updating should be installed.

Going beyond explicit knowledge, libraries should also develop means to capture all that tacit knowledge that is of importance to users and to the internal operation of libraries. The web sites of libraries should serve as portals for all sources of selective and relevant knowledge and information whether explicit or tacit, whether on site or remote, and in all formats. [1]

As a part of its knowledge management activities, Arthur Anderson Business Consulting has developed a highly useful web site: KnowledgeSpace. Three types of knowledge are provided by KnowledgeSpace. They are:
- News—important company news and hot topics of interest to all staff members worldwide.
- Resources—contains "Global Best Practices", "Ask Network", and "Community Resources".
- Connections—for active interactions and discussion by special interest. groups across organizational structure and departmental lines.

All information in the KnowledgeSpace is updated frequently and user feedbacks are encouraged. [2]

Libraries can develop their own types of KnowledgeSpace. Through each library's intranet, strategic planning documents, annual reports, team and department reports, council and committee minutes, statistical analyses, grant proposals, policies and procedures, operational manuals, "best practices", "lessons learned", internal announcements, library news of major events, personnel actions, training and staff development opportunities, etc. can be made available to all staff members.

Human Resources Management

A great amount of expert knowledge is possessed by library staff and users, both in and outside the libraries. In university and research communities such expertise is abundant and should be inventoried, indexed, and updated regularly and be made searchable and accessible through electronic databases created and maintained by libraries.

The knowledge and accumulated experiences of library staff members form the intellectual assets of any library and should be valued and shared. An organizational culture for sharing of knowledge and expertise should be established with appropriate rewards and incentives. An organizational culture which emphasize cooperation, sharing, and innovation can only be established by a strong leadership and commitment from the library director and a shared vision by the library staff.

As a learning organization, libraries should allocate annual funding to provide continuing education and staff training to all staff members. Knowledge must be renewed and expanded to prevent it from becoming stagnant.

Libraries should also encourage the transfer of knowledge and experience from experienced staff to new staff members. A mentoring system should be in place to help newcomers to learn from experienced library staff. Informal seminars and brownbag sessions where staff can interact and exchange "lessons learned", "best practices", and other specific experience and knowledge should be scheduled at regular intervals and at convenient times. Through intranet special interest groups and chat rooms can be created.

As an integral part of annual performance evaluation, those staff members who share their tacit knowledge and experiences through writing, publishing, lecturing, or mentoring, should be appropriately recognized and rewarded.

Since many valuable experiences have been accumulated over time, libraries should pay attention to favorable working conditions and environment, which will contribute to better staff retention.

---

[1] Duffy (1999) defines tacit knowledge as "personal, undocumented knowledge; context-sensitive, dynamically-created and derived, internalized, and experience-based; often resides in the human mind, behavior, and perception" and explicit knowledge as "knowledge that is documented and public; structured, fixed-content, externalized, and conscious".

[2] Arthur Anderson Business Consulting (2000). p. 225 – 229.

Resources Sharing and Networking

Libraries have had a long tradition for resources sharing and networking. These have been greatly expanded by the rapid development of computer, telecommunication, networking, and digital technologies since the 1960s. It is very common for libraries to be a member in several consortia at the same time for various types of cooperative work and resources sharing. The best examples of these are the OCLC Online Computer Library Center and OhioLINK (Ohio Library and Information Network).

The CORC project of OCLC should be especially useful for libraries to cooperatively capture digital resources of all types, describe them in a standard format, and make them easily searchable by users.

Information Technology Development

To facilitate the implementation of knowledge management, a well-designed and operational knowledge management system should be in place. Latest information technology should be used as an enabler.

In a networked environment, libraries participating in the same consortium may want to coordinate the selection of a common system enabling the maximum connectivity and compatibility among cooperating libraries.

Intranet technology should be used to support knowledge management efforts via shared documents/products and the gathering and publication of lessons learned and best practices.

Internet functions should also be used for knowledge exchange with users, resource persons (faculty, researchers, and subjects specialists, etc.), publishers, government agencies, businesses and industries, and other organizations.

User Services

Know your users should come first. This information can be gathered from statistical analysis of user registration databases, circulation and interlibrary loan records, most frequently asked reference questions, telephone and email services, use of electronic journals and digital resources, etc. These should be done without invading the privacy of individual library users.

All user services should be tailored to suit individual needs. New publications alert and selective dissemination of information should be matched with users interest profiles. User satisfaction and needs should be collected through periodic users survey. The findings should be used for the planning and redesign of library services.

A file of "Best Practices" should be maintained, analyzed, and shared.

Conclusion

Although knowledge management has become one of the latest management buzzwords, whether it will fade away or not, just as some of the other buzzwords before it, will depend on how we make it work. In the business world, knowledge management has been regarded as strategically important for organizations to gain a competitive advantage over their competitors, to add value to their products, and to win greater satisfaction of their customers.

In the library world, there is a lesson to learn from the business world. Knowledge management is as important for libraries as for the businesses minus the competitive, proprietary, and moneymaking concerns. In fact, libraries have a long and rich experience in the management of explicit knowledge. Now we need to extend our know-how to the management of tacit knowledge as well. This is necessary not only for meeting the needs of library users but also for the betterment of libraries per se. For any libraries to succeed in implementing knowledge management will require a strong leadership and vision from the top administration, which can influence the organization's knowledge sharing efforts in a positive way. As libraries enter the knowledge age of the 21st century, we should not take a back seat in the development of knowledge management. Instead, armed by our professional knowledge and experiences, we should be in the driver's seat.

Among the newly created positions such as "Chief Knowledge Officer" (CKO), "Knowledge Management Specialist", "Knowledge Manager", etc. in business organizations, CKO is often in the senior executive's position of a company—a position higher than "Chief Information Officer" (CIO), In the past two decades, many of the CIO positions have gone to people with training in information technology rather than in library and information science for the reason that CIO is more technology-based. Now, with the coming of knowledge management and CKO positions, library and information professionals with vision, leadership, and know-how should be most suitable for the CKO positions, unless we try to shy away from knowledge management which will be the new role of libraries in the 21st century.

In the implementation of knowledge management, libraries of all types, including academic and research libraries, special libraries, government libraries, information centers, knowledge centers, etc., should work with "library schools", in whatever their current names, to design new curriculum, to undertake new studies and researches, to develop new theories and practices, and to better prepare the present and future knowledge professionals for the challenges and opportunities of a much broader job market ahead.

Finally, knowledge management should never be viewed as a way to control the process of knowledge creation. In his book, Enabling Knowledge Creation, Georg Von Krogh et al made a strong argument for supporting knowledge creation rather than control it. In the process of knowledge creation, every library should strive to be an enabler and facilitator by mobilizing all its efforts and resources. [1]

References

Abell, A. and Oxbrow, N. *Investigation of Underpinning Skill for Knowledge Management: Training Implications, Interim Report.* London: TFPL, Inc. 1999.

Abram, Stephen. "Post Information Age Positioning for Special Librarians: Is Knowledge Management the Answer?" *Information Outlook.* June 1997, pp. 18 – 25.

Allee, Verna. *The Knowledge Evolution: Expanding Organizational Intelligence.* Boston, Butterworth-Heinemann, 1997.

Arthur Anderson Business Consulting. *The First Book on Knowledge Management*, translated into Chinese by Liu Jin-Wei. Taipei: San Chou Publisher, 2000. (In Chinese)

Bair, Jim. "Knowledge Management is About Cooperation and Context." *Gartner Advisory Services Research Note.* May 14, 1999.

Bell, Daniel. *The Coming of Post-Industrial Society: A Venture in Social Forecasting.* New York: Basic Books, 1973.

Boisot, Max H. *Knowledge Assets: Securing Competitive Advantage in the Information Economy.* New York: Oxford University Press, 1998.

Borghoff, Uwe M. and Pareschi, Remo. (eds.) *Information Technology for Knowledge Management.* Berlin: Springer, 1998.

Brendan, Loughridge. "Knowledge Management, Librarians and Information Managers: Fad or Future." *New Library World.* V. 100, No. 6 (1999), pp. 245 – 253.

Carbeurim, Alberto. "How Does Knowledge Management Influence Innovation and Competitiveness?" *Journal of Knowledge Management.* V. 4, No. 2 (2000), pp. 87 – 98.

Davenport, Thomas H., DeLong, D. W., and Beers, M. C. "Successful Knowledge Management Projects." *Sloan Management Review.* V. 39, No. 2 (1998), pp. 43 – 57.

---

[1] Von Krogh, Georg, Ichijo, Kazuo, and Nonaka, Ikujiro. *Enabling Knowledge Creation: How to Unlock the Mystery of tacit Knowledge and Release the Power of Innovation.* New York: Oxford University Press, 2000.

De Jager, Martha. "The KM AT Benchmarking Knowledge Management." *Library Management.* V. 20, No. 7 (1999): pp. 367 – 372.

Devlin, Keith J. *Infosense: Turning Information Into Knowledge.* New York: W. H. Freeman, 1999.

DiMattia, Susan and Oder Norman. "Knowledge Management: Hope, Hype, or Harbinger?" *Library Journal.* Sept. 15, 1997: pp. 33 – 35.

Drucker, Peter Ferdinand. Post-*Capitalist Society.* New York: HarperBusiness, 1993.

Duffy, Jan. *Harvesting Experience: Reaping the Benefits of Knowledge.* Prairie Village, KS: ARMA International, 1999.

– – –. "Knowledge Management: To Be or Not to Be?" *Information Management Journal.* V. 34, No, 1 (Jan. 2000): pp. 64 – 67.

Galagan, P, "Smart Companies (Knowledge Management)." *Training and Development.* V. 51, No. 12 (1997): pp. 20 – 25.

Gumbley, Helen. "Knowledge Management." *Work Study.* V. 47, No. 5 (1999): pp. 175 – 177.

Huseman, Richard C. and Goodman, Jon P. *Leading with Knowledge: The Nature of Competition in the 21st Century.* Thousand Oaks, CA: Sage Publications, 1999.

Ishikawa, Akira. "Knowledge Management, Autopoiesis and Apoptosis." *Kybernetes.* V. 28, No. 6/7 (1999): pp. 821 – 825.

Lee, Hwa-Wei. "Libraries in the Digital and Networked Knowledge Age of the Twenty-first Century." *Proceedings of 21st Century Public Libraries—Vision and Reality.* Taichung, Taiwan: National Taichung Library, 2000: pp. 1 – 43 – 1 – 67.

Liebowitz, Jay. *Building Organizational Intelligence: A Knowledge Management Primer.* Boca Raton, FL: CRC Press, 2000.

O'Dell, Carla and Grayson, C. Jackson, Jr. *If Only We Knew What We Know: The Transfer of Internal Knowledge and Best Practice.* New York: The Free Press, 1998.

OCLC Annual Report 1998/99. *A Great Time for Libraries*! Dublin, Ohio: OCLC Online Computer Library Center, 1999.

Ohio Board of Regents. Library Study Committee. *Academic Libraries in Ohio: Progress Through Collaboration, Storage, and Technology. Report of the Library Study Committee.* Columbus, Ohio: Ohio Board of Regents, 1987.

An Overview of OCLC Services: Look What You're Doing Now... With OCLC. Dublin, OH: OCLC Online Computer Library Center, 1999.

Pfeffer, Jeffrey and Sutton, Robert I. *The Knowing-Doing Gap: How Smart Companies Turn Knowledge Into Action.* Boston, MA: Harvard Business School Press, 2000.

Porat, Marc. *The Information Economy: Definition and Measurement.* Washington, DC: U. S. Department of Commerce, Office of Telecommunications, 1977. (Publication 77 – 12)

Rowley, Jennifer. "What is Knowledge Management?" *Library Management.* V. 20, No. 8 (1999): pp. 416 – 419.

Srikantaiah, T. Kanti and Koenig, Michael E. D. (eds.) *Knowledge Management for the Information Professional.* Medford, NJ: American Society for Information Science, 2000. (ASIS Monograph Series)

Teece, David J. *Managing Intellectual Capital: Organizational, Strategic, and Policy Dimensions.* New York: Oxford University Press, 2000.

Tissen, Rene, Andriessen, Daniel, and Deprez, Frank Lekanne. *Value-Based Knowledge Management.* Amsterdam: Addison Wesley Longman, 1998.

Von Krogh, Georg, Ichijo, Kazuo, and Nonaka, Ikujiro. *Enabling Knowledge Creation: How to Unlock the Mystery of tacit Knowledge and Release the Power of Innovation.* New York: Oxford University Press, 2000.

Wiig, Karl M. "Knowledge Management: An Introduction and Perspective." *Journal of Knowledge Management.* V. 1, No. 1 (Sept. 1997): pp. 6 – 14

---"Knowledge Management: Where Did It Come From and Where Will It Go?" *Expert Systems With Applications.* V. 13, No. 1 (1997): pp. 1 – 14.

(Published in ***Prospects of the 21st Century***, Taichung, Taiwan: Feng Chia University and Liao Ying-Ming Cultural and Educational Foundation, 2000: pp. 397 – 436.)

谁应该掌管知识管理，图书馆员，图书馆，还是其他人？

Who Should Be in Charge of Knowledge Management, Librarians/Libraries or Someone Else?[①]

1. Introduction

The concept and name— "Knowledge Management"—was started and popularized in the business world during the last decade of the 20th century. It was the business world that first recognizes the importance of knowledge in the "global economy" of the "knowledge age". In the new knowledge economy, the possession of relevant and strategic knowledge and its unceasing renewal enables businesses to gain competitive advantage. The applications of knowledge management have now spread to other organizations including government agencies, research and development departments, universities, and others.

The management of information has long been regarded as the domain of librarians and libraries. Librarians and information professionals are trained to be experts in information searching, selecting, acquiring, organizing, preserving, repackaging, disseminating, and serving. However, professionals in information technology and systems have also regarded information management as their domain because of the recent advances in information technology and systems which drive and underpin information management. One of the clearest evidences of this is that the positions of "Chief Information Officer" (CIO) in many organizations are generally held by information technologists instead of librarians. In fact, most of the work of CIOs has to do with developing and managing the IT infrastructure and systems, not the managing of information per se.

With the growing interest in knowledge management, many questions have been raised in the minds of librarians regarding: the difference between information and knowledge, between information management and knowledge management; who should be in charge of information and knowledge management; would librarians and information professionals with appropriate education and training in library and information science be most suitable for the position of "Chief Knowledge Officer" (CKO) in their organizations; and what libraries can do in implementing knowledge management.

This paper attempts to answer these critical and pressing questions from the librarians' perspective.

2. Is there a difference between information and knowledge?

Daniel Bell defines knowledge as "a set of organized statements of facts or ideas, presenting a reasoned judgment or an experimental result, which is transmitted to others through some communication medium in some systematic form"[②]. As for information, Marc Porat states, "Information is data that has been organized and communicated."[③]

Stephen Abram sees the process for knowledge creation and use as a continuum where data transforms into information, information transforms into knowledge and knowledge drives and

---

[①] Presented in the International Seminar on Digital Library Age: Current Situation and Development Trend ("数字图书馆时代：现状与发展趋势"国际学术研讨会), Beijing, China, October 23 – 25, 2002.

[②] Bell, Daniel. *The Coming of Post-industrial Society: A Venture in Social Forecasting.* New York: Basic Books, 1973: p. 175.

[③] Porat, Marc. *The Information Economy: Definition and Measurement.* Washington, D.C.: U.S. Department of Commerce, Office of Telecommunications, 1977 (Publication 77 – 12): p. 1.

*underpins behavior and decision-making.*① Below are simple definitions of Data, Information, Knowledge, and Wisdom—all of them are available within every organization:

Data: Scattered, unrelated facts, writings, numbers, or symbols.

Information: Selected, organized and analyzed data.

Knowledge: Information combined with user's ability and experience that is used to solve a problem or to create new knowledge.

Wisdom: Forward looking and thinking based on one's values and commitment.

The differences between information and knowledge can be summarized as:

Information is visible, independent from action and decision, different in format after processing, physical product, independent from existing environment, easily transferable, and duplicable.

Knowledge is invisible, closely related to action and decision, different in thought after processing, spiritual product, identified with existing environment, transferable through learning, and not duplicable.

In the business world, two types of knowledge have been noted. They are explicit knowledge and tacit knowledge. Jan Duffy defines explicit knowledge as "knowledge that is documented and public; structured, fixed-content, externalized, and conscious" and tacit knowledge as "personal, undocumented knowledge; context-sensitive, dynamically-created and derived, internalized, and experience-based; often resides in the human mind, behavior, and perception."② This set of definitions can be applied to all other human endeavors and intellectual activities.

3. The rise of knowledge management

As early as 1965, Peter Drucker already pointed out that "knowledge" would replace land, labor, capital, machines, etc. to become the chief source of production.③ His foresight did not get much attention back then. It was not until 1991 when Ikujiro Nonaka raised the concept of "tacit" knowledge and "explicit" knowledge as well as the theory of "spiral of knowledge" in the Harvard Business Review that the time of "knowledge-based competition" finally came.④ In his latest book, *Building Organizational Intelligence? A Knowledge Management Primer?* Jay Liebowitz stated:⑤

"In today's movement towards knowledge management, organizations are trying to best leverage their knowledge internally in the organization and externally to their customers and stakeholders. They are trying to capitalize on their organizational intelligence to maintain their competitive edge."

"The thrust of knowledge management is to create a process of valuing the organization's intangible assets in order to best leverage knowledge internally and externally. Knowledge management, therefore, deals with creating, securing, capturing, coordinating, combining, retrieving, and distributing knowledge. The idea is to create a knowledge sharing environment whereby sharing knowledge is power as opposed to the old adage that, simply, knowledge is power."

---

① Abram, Stephen. "Post Information Age Positioning for Special Librarians: Is Knowledge Management the Answer?" *Information Outlook*. June 1997: pp. 20 – 21.

② Duffy, Jan. "Knowledge Mnagement: To Be or Not to Be?" *Information Management Journal*. V. 34, No. 1 (Jan. 2000): pp. 64 – 67.

③ Drucker, Peter. *Post-capitalism Society*. Oxford, Great Britain: Butterworth-Heinemann, 1993

④ Nonaka, Ikujiro. "The Knowledge-Creating Company." *Harvard Business Review*. (Nov. -Dec. 1991) pp. 96 – 99. Also, Nonaka, Ikujiro and Hirotaka Takeuchi. *The Knowledge-creating Company: How Japanese Companies Create the Dynamics of Innovation*. New York: Oxford University Press, 1995.

⑤ Liebowitz, Jay. *Building Organizational Intelligence: A Knowledge Management Primer*. Boca Raton, FL: CRC Press, 2000: p. 1.

4. Some definitions of knowledge management

Because knowledge management is still a relatively new concept and viewed differently by different writers from different focuses, its definitions vary. In her article, "What is knowledge management?" Jennifer Rowley offers her definition below:

"Knowledge management is concerned with the exploitation and development of the knowledge assets of an organization with a view to furthering the organization's objectives. The knowledge to be managed includes both explicit, documented knowledge, and tacit, subjective knowledge. Management entails all of those processes associated with the identification, sharing and creation of knowledge. This requires systems for the creation and maintenance of knowledge repositories, and to cultivate and facilitate the sharing of knowledge and organizational learning. Organizations that succeed in knowledge management are likely to view knowledge as an asset and to develop organizational norms and values, which support the creation and sharing of knowledge." [1]

Rowley's definition was based on the four different types of perspectives on knowledge management identified by Thomas H. Davenport et al in their study of a number of knowledge management projects. From the analysis of the projects' objectives, Davenport et al were able to categorize them into four broad types of perspectives: [2]

(1) To create knowledge repositories, which store both knowledge and information, often in documentary form? These repositories can fall into three categories:

Those which include external knowledge, such as competitive intelligence.

Those that include structured internal knowledge, such as research reports and product oriented marketing materials, such as techniques and methods.

Those that embrace informal, internal or tacit knowledge, such as discussion databases that store "know how".

(2) To improve knowledge access and transfer. Here the emphasis is on connectivity, access and transfer.

Technologies such as video conferencing systems, document scanning and sharing tools and telecommunications networks are central.

(3) To enhance the knowledge environment so that the environment is conductive to more effective knowledge creation, transfer and use. This involves tackling organizational norms and values as they relate to knowledge.

Increase awareness on sharing knowledge embedded in client relationship and engagements.

Provide awards for contributions to the organization's structured knowledge base.

Implement decision audit programs in order to assess whether and how employees were applying knowledge in key decisions.

Recognize that successful knowledge management is dependent upon structures and cultures.

(4) To manage knowledge as an asset and to recognize the value of knowledge to an organization.

Others, however, sought to take a process view to define knowledge management.

For example, Jan Duffy defines it as "a process that drives innovation by capitalizing on organizational intellect and experience"[3]. Gartner Group defines it as "a discipline that promotes an integrated and collaborative approach to the process of information asset creation, capture,

---

[1] Rowley, Jennifer. "What is Knowledge Management?" *Library Management*. V. 20, No. 8 (1999), pp. 416–419.

[2] Davenport, Thomas H., DeLong, D. W., and Beers, M. C. "Successful Knowledge Management Projects." *Sloan Management Review*. V. 39, No. 2 (1998): pp. 43–57.

[3] Duffy, Jan. *Harvesting Experience: Reaping the Benefits of Knowledge*. Prairie Village, KS: ARMA International, 1999. Also from her article, "Knowledge Management: To Be or Not to Be?" *Information Management Journal*. V. 34, No. 1 (Jan. 2000): pp. 64–67.

organization, access and use"①.

Below is a set of knowledge management processes proposed by P. Galagan:②
  Generating new knowledge.
  Accessing knowledge from external sources.
  Representing knowledge in documents, databases, software and so forth.
  Embedding knowledge in processes, products, or services.
  Transferring existing knowledge around an organization.
  Using accessible knowledge in decision-making.
  Facilitating knowledge growth through culture and incentives.
  Measuring the value of knowledge assets and the impact of knowledge management.

From both the project perspectives and the operational processes described above we can gain a general understanding of the current scope and contents of knowledge management.

5. Knowledge management in libraries

While the business world is changing in the new knowledge economy and digital age, libraries of all types are undergoing drastic changes also. The new role of libraries in the 21st century needs to be as a learning and knowledge center for their users as well as the intellectual commons for their respective communities where, to borrow the phrase from the Keystone Principles, "people and ideas interact in both the real and virtual environments to expand learning and facilitate the creation of new knowledge."③

As a learning organization, libraries should provide a strong leadership in knowledge management. Unlike those business organizations whose goal for knowledge management is for competitive advantage, most public, academic, and research libraries, with the exception of company libraries (which may be known or called corporate libraries, special libraries, or knowledge centers), have a different orientation and value. Instead of competition, internal use only, and little sharing of knowledge with others outside, the most important mission of public, academic, and research libraries is to expand the access of knowledge for their users. Charged by this mission, libraries should aim their knowledge management goal high. Below are examples of what libraries can do to improve their knowledge management in all of the key areas of library services.

5.1 Knowledge resources management

Because of the exponential growth in human knowledge in a variety of formats, libraries need to develop their resources access and sharing strategies from printed to electronic and digital resources in concert with their mission and charges. Restricted by limited funding, technology, staff, and space, libraries must carefully analyze the needs of their users and seek to develop cooperative acquisition plans to meet these needs. The changing concept from "ownership" to "access" and from "just in case" to "just in time" should be the goal of a sound resources development strategy.

An integrated online public access catalog (OPAC) with both internal and external resources as well as printed and other formats of knowledge should be developed and maintained. Useful websites and knowledge sources should be regularly searched and selected from the Internet and included in OPACs by hard links. A system for the reviewing and updating of these resources should be performed.

---

① Bair, Jim. "Knowledge Management is About Cooperation and Context." *Gartner Advisory Services Research Note.* May 14, 1999.

② Galagan, P. "Smart Companies (Knowledge Management)." *Training and Development.* V. 51, No. 12 (1997): pp. 20 -25.

③ On September 24 - 25, 1999, eighty academic library leaders met during a two-day Strategic Issues Forum of Academic Library Directors held in Keystone, Colorado, organized jointly by the Association of Research Libraries and OCLC. Three basic principles were declared as the expanded vision for libraries in the digital knowledge age of the 21st century. The three principles are called the Keystone Principles.

Going beyond explicit knowledge, libraries should also develop means to capture all that tacit knowledge that is of importance to their users, their organizations, and to the internal operation of libraries. The web site of each library should serve as a portal for all sources of selective and relevant knowledge and information whether explicit or tacit, whether on site or remote, and in all formats.

The term "portal" has been defined by Michael Looney and Peter Lyman as "a means of gathering a variety of useful information resources into a single, one-stop Web page, helping the user to avoid being overwhelmed by info-glut or feeling lost on the Web"[1].

In the current digital and networked knowledge age, the size of information resources on the Web is growing exponentially. No one really knows exactly how many Web pages are on the Internet because new Web pages are added every second. The latest statistics of Internet hosts numbered close to two billion and is growing fast at the speed of 25% from 1/2001 to 1/2002.[2] Most of the frequently used Internet search engines have also expanded their index sizes. For examples, Google reported to have indexed 1.5 billion Web pages according to the December 18, 2001 issue of the *Search Engine Report*. Other search engines such as FAST, AltaVista, Inktomi, and Northern Light indexed from a high of 625 million pages to a low of 390 million pages.[3] In a 1999 study by Lawrence and Giles, each search engine may cover only 15% of the Web resources at any given time. Combined coverage of search engines is estimated at 42 percent of the relevant resources.[4] It is also very frustrating that many of the results found—in the tens of thousands of hits—are irrelevant. One has to comb the large number of findings in order to find the few relevant pieces of information. Still, information on the Web can be very useful if only we can employ advanced artificial intelligent tools to surf the Internet and to select, find, arrange, classify, and automatically deliver the needed information to each user based on his/her special interests and needs. Many such new knowledge management systems are under development and testing and hold promise for greatly enriched knowledge resources, improved user services, and the more efficient use of knowledge for creation and decision-making.

Universities and research organizations are themselves knowledge reservoirs. These highly valued intellectual assets, regardless of whether they are explicit or tacit, should be inventoried, archived, indexed, frequently updated, and made accessible in digital form.

In addition, the traditional, time-honored methods of cataloging and classification are barely adequate to handle the finite number of books, journals, and documents, but are inadequate to deal with the almost infinite amount of digital information in large electronic databases and on the Internet. Using the Dublin Core metadata and the Cooperative Online Resources Catalog (CORC) has been a new approach to capture Web information by cooperative efforts. Other new methods such as data mining, text mining, content management, search engines, spidering programs, natural language searching, linguistic analysis, semantic networks, knowledge extraction, concept yellow pages, and such techniques in information visualization as two-dimensional or three-dimensional knowledge mapping, etc. have been a part of recent developments in knowledge management systems.

5.2 Resources sharing and networking

Libraries have had a long tradition of resources sharing and networking. These have been greatly expanded by the rapid development of computer, telecommunication, networking, and digital technologies since the 1960s. In the U.S. it is very common for libraries to be a member of several consortia at the same time for various types of cooperative work and resources sharing. The

---

[1] Looney, Michael and Peter Lyman, "Portals in Higher Education: What are They, and What is Their Potential?" *EDUCAUSE Review*. V.35, No.4 (July/August 2000): p.30. http://www.educause.edu/pub/er/erm00/article004/looney.pdf

[2] http://www.isc.org/ds/www-200201/hosts.gif

[3] http://searchenginewatch.com/reports/sizes.htlm

[4] Lawrence, S. and C. L. Giles. "Accessibility of Information on the Web." *Nature*. No. 400 (July 1999): pp. 107 – 109.

best examples of these are the OCLC Online Computer Library Center and OhioLINK (Ohio Library and Information Network). In China, the recent developments in cooperative library networking such as CALIS (Chinese Academic Library and Information System), the National Science and Technology Library, and the National Engineering Technology Library, etc. also provide excellent models that are especially tailored to the Chinese situation and needs.

The CORC project of OCLC should be especially useful for libraries to cooperatively capture digital resources of all types, describe them in a standard format, and make them easily searchable by users.

The successes of most of these examples in resources sharing and networking are largely the result of the full cooperation and participation of all member libraries without selfishness. Large and major libraries must take the lead in such an endeavor. Supports in policies and funding from the government or parent organizations are also critically important. Experiences indicate that all libraries, regardless of size and specialties, have been benefited by library cooperation and resources sharing.

5.3 Information technology development

To facilitate the implementation of knowledge management, a well-designed and operational knowledge management system should be in place. Latest information technology should be used as an enabler. In this regard, the library director should consider him/her self as the chief knowledge officer of the entire organization and should work together with the CIO, heads of the planning department, the computer and information technology center, the human resources management department, the finance department, etc. to design and develop such a system. Such a knowledge management system should be built on existing computer and information technology infrastructures, including upgraded intranet, extranet, and Internet, and available software programs to facilitate the capture, analysis, organization, storage, and sharing of internal and external information resources for effective knowledge exchange among users, resource persons (faculty, researchers, and subjects specialists, etc.), publishers, government agencies, businesses and industries, and other organizations via multiple channels and layers.

In recent years, many of the newly developed information technologies for database and information/document management can be utilized in knowledge management; such as, data warehousing, data mining, text mining, content management, knowledge extraction, knowledge mapping, groupware, and information visualization, etc. It was observed by Hsinchun Chen that "since the mid 1990s, the popularity of search engines and advances in web spidering, indexing, and link analysis have transformed IR systems into newer and more powerful search tools for content on the Internet."[①]

5.4 User services

The utmost goal of knowledge management is to provide users with a variety of quality services in order to improve the communication, use and creation of knowledge. As much as possible these services should be tailored to the interest and needs of each user. Information about each user can be obtained by analyzing the records of user registration, surveys, circulation and interlibrary loans, frequently asked reference questions, and the use of e-journal and digital resources, etc. User satisfaction and needs should be collected through periodic users' surveys. The findings should be used for the planning and redesign of library services. It is very important, however, that user's privacy should always be protected.

Some of the manual services such as "new publication alert" and "selective dissemination of information", which libraries have been providing, can now be done automatically by employing the "push technology" with great efficiency and convenience. Each library user can also set up his/her virtual "MyLibrary" enabled by library systems and networks for collecting and organizing

---

① Chen, Hsinchun. *Knowledge Management Systems: A Text Mining Perspective*. Tucson, Arizona: University of Arizona, 2001: p. 18.

resources for personal use and to stay informed of new resources provided by the library. ①

The Library and Information Technology Association (LITA) has defined MyLibrary-like services as the number one trend "worth keeping an eye on". It further stated that "Library users who are Web users, a growing group, expect customization, interactivity, and customer support. Approaches that are library-focused instead of user-focused will be increasingly irrelevant."②

5.5 Human resources management

A great amount of expert knowledge is possessed by library staff and users, both in and outside the libraries. In university and research communities such expertise is abundant and should be inventoried, indexed, and updated regularly and be made searchable and accessible through electronic databases created and maintained by libraries.

The knowledge and accumulated experiences of library staff members form the intellectual assets of any library and should be valued and shared. An organizational culture for sharing of knowledge and expertise should be established with appropriate rewards and incentives. Those staff members who share their tacit knowledge and experiences through writing, publishing, lecturing, tutoring, or mentoring should be appropriately recognized and rewarded. An organizational culture which emphasizes cooperation, sharing, and innovation can only be established by strong leadership and commitment from the library director and a shared vision by the library staff.

As a learning organization, libraries should allocate annual funding to provide continuing education and staff training to all staff members. Knowledge must be renewed and expanded to prevent it from becoming stagnant.

Libraries should also encourage the transfer of knowledge and experience from experienced staff to new staff members. A mentoring system should be in place to help newcomers to learn from experienced library staff. Informal seminars and brownbag sessions where staff can interact and exchange "lessons learned", "best practices" and other specific experience and knowledge should be scheduled at regular intervals and at convenient times. Special interest groups and chat rooms can be created through intranet.

Since many valuable experiences have been accumulated over time, libraries should pay attention to favorable working conditions and environment, which will contribute to better staff retention.

6. Conclusion

In the business world, knowledge management has been regarded as strategically important for organizations to gain a competitive advantage over their competitors, to add value to their products, and to win greater satisfaction from their customers. In the library world, there is a lesson to be learned from the business world. Knowledge management is as important for libraries as for the businesses minus the competitive, proprietary, and moneymaking concerns. In fact, libraries have had a long and rich experience in the management of information. Many of such knowledge and skills of librarianship can be applied to knowledge management.

For any library to succeed in implementing knowledge management will require a strong leadership and vision from the top administration, which can influence the organization's knowledge sharing efforts in a positive way. As libraries enter the knowledge age of the 21st century, we should not take a back seat in the development of knowledge management. Instead, armed with our professional knowledge and experiences, we should be in the driver's seat.

Information technology and systems can provide effective support in implementing knowledge management. Librarians should work together with IT professionals and others to develop the appropriate knowledge management systems.

---

① Cohen, Suzanne and others. "Personalized Electronic Services in the Cornell University Libraries." *D-Lib Magazine*, V. 6, No. 4 (April 2000): pp. 1 – 2. http://www.dlib.org/dlib/april00/mistlebauer/04mistlebauer.html

② "Technology and Library Users: LITA Experts Identify Trends to Watch." *Chicago: LITA*, 1999. http://www.lita.org/committe/toptech/trendsmw99.htm

Furthermore, knowledge management should never be viewed as a way to control the process of knowledge creation. In his book *Enabling Knowledge Creation?* Georg Von Krogh et al made a strong argument for supporting knowledge creation rather than controlling it. In the process of knowledge creation, every library should strive to be an enabler and facilitator by mobilizing all its efforts and resources.[①]

The best knowledge creators are academics. Knowledge creation is best performed by universities. As a learning and knowledge organization, universities should empower their libraries to develop campus-wide knowledge management systems. It is now time for libraries to reposition themselves in the central stage of and as a leading player in knowledge management.

(Published in Journal of Academic Libraries, supplement issue, 2002, pp. 79 – 84)

[①] Von Krogh, Georg, Ichijo, Kazuo, and Nonaka, Ikujiro. *Enabling Knowledge Creation: How to Unlock the Mystery of Tacit Knowledge and Release the Power of Innovation.* New York: Oxford University Press, 2000.

知识管理：图书馆的作用①

Knowledge Management: The Role of Libraries

1. 引言

"知识管理"的概念和名称于 20 世纪 90 年代起在商界兴起并流行，商业领域首先意识到知识在"知识时代"的"全球经济"中的重要性。在新知识经济中，对相关的战略性知识的拥有及其持续更新有助于企业获得竞争优势。如今，对知识管理的应用已经普及到了其他类型的组织中，如政府机构、研发部门和大学等。

长期以来，信息管理被视为图书馆员和图书馆的专有领域。图书馆员和信息专业人员经过培训，成为信息检索、信息筛选、信息获取、信息组织、信息保存、信息重组、信息传播和信息服务等方面的专家。但是，由于近来信息技术和信息系统的进步推动和支持了信息管理的发展，信息技术和信息系统的专业人员也将信息管理视为其领域。一个很显著的例子就是，许多组织中的"首席信息官"的职位通常由信息技术专家而非图书馆员担任。事实上，首席信息官的大多数工作涉及开发和管理信息技术基础设施和信息系统，而并非信息管理本身。

随着人们对知识管理兴趣的日增，图书馆员不禁会问这样的问题：信息和知识有什么区别？知识管理和信息管理又有什么区别？谁应当承担起信息管理和知识管理的职责？受过图书馆学信息学教育和培训的图书馆员和信息专业人员会成为组织中"首席知识官"的最佳人选吗？对于实现知识管理，图书馆员究竟能做些什么？

本文将试从图书馆员的角度回答以上亟待解决的关键问题。

2. 信息和知识有区别吗

丹尼尔·贝尔将知识定义为"一组有组织的、有关事实和概念的陈述，是经过论证的判断或实验结果。它以某种系统的形式、通过某种传播媒介传递给他人"②。对于信息的定义，Marc Porat 认为，"信息是经过组织和传播的数据"③。

Stephen Abram 认为知识创造和使用的过程是一个连续的统一体。在这个连续统一体中，数据转化为信息，信息转化为知识，知识推动并支持行为和决策④。以下是数据、信息、知识和智慧的简单定义，它们适用于任何组织。

（1）数据：分散、无关联的事实、文字、数字或符号。
（2）信息：选择、组织和分析过的数据。
（3）知识：与用户的能力和经验相结合的信息，用来解决问题或创造新知识。
（4）智慧：一个人基于价值观和信念的前瞻和思想。

信息和知识的区别可以概括为：

---

① 崇敬译。
② Daniel Bell. *The Coming of Post-industrial Society: A Venture in Social Forecating* (New York: Basic Books, 1973): 175.
③ Marc Porat, *The Information Economy: Definition and Measurement* (Washington, D.C. : U.S Department of Commerce, Office of Telecommunications, 1977, Publication 77-12): 1.
④ Stephen Abram, "Post Information Age Positioning for Special Librarians: Is Knowledge Management the Answer?" *Information Outlook* (June 1997): 20-21.

· 信息是可见的，独立于行为和决策之外，经过加工处理后在形式上有所改变，是物理产品，不依赖于周围环境，易于传递且可复制。

· 知识是不可见的，和行为与决策密切相关，经过加工处理后在思想内容上有所改变，是精神产品，与周围环境保持一致，经过学习后可传递，但不能复制。

在商业领域存在两种知识：显性知识和隐性知识。Jan Duffy 将显性知识定义为"经文献记录下来的、公共的、结构化的、内容固定的、外在化的和有意识的知识"，将隐性知识定义为"个人的、未经文献记录的知识，对语境敏感，是动态创造和获取的，是内在化的和基于经验的，常存在于人的思想、行为和感知中"[1]。这两个定义适用于其他所有人类有目的的行为和智力活动。

3. 知识管理的兴起

早在 1965 年，Peter Drucker 就已指出，"知识"将取代土地、劳动力、资本和机器等，成为生产力的主要源泉[2]，但他的预见在当时并没有引起人们的注意。直到 1991 年，当 Ikujiro Nonaka 在《哈佛商业周刊》中提出"隐性"知识和"显性"知识的概念以及"知识螺旋结构"理论时，"知识竞争"的时代才最终到来[3]。在 Jay Liebowitz 的最新著作《建立组织智慧：知识管理入门》中，他说：

"如今，在向知识管理前进的过程中，组织正试图在其内部和相关客户及利益群体的关系中最大程度地利用知识，并使其组织智能资本化，从而保持其竞争优势。

倡导知识管理的目的在于建立一种珍重组织无形资产的途径，以最大限度地利用内外部知识。因此，知识管理就是对知识的创造、保护、获取、调整、组合、检索以及分配。知识管理的中心思想是创造一个知识共享环境，在这里，知识共享就是力量，而非仅仅是如以往人们所推崇的那样，知识就是力量。"[4]

4. 知识管理的一些定义

因为知识管理仍是一个较新的概念，并且不同的作者从不同的侧重点得出不同的观点，所以它没有固定的定义。在 Jeninifer Rowley 的《什么是知识管理》一文中，她提出如下定义：

"知识管理是指对组织知识资产的开发和发展，目的在于强化组织目标。被管理的知识包括显性的、记录的知识和隐性的、主观的知识，管理包括对知识的鉴别、共享、创造以及与此有关的所有过程。这需要设计用来创建和维护知识库的系统，以培养并促进知识共享和组织学习。成功运作知识管理的组织都将知识视为财富，并注重对组织规范和组织价值的开发，因为它们是知识创造和共享的基础。"[5]

Rowley 的定义的基础是 Thomas H. Davenport 等人通过研究若干知识管理项目所确定的四种不同的知识管理观点。通过对这些项目目标的分析，Davenport 等人将知识管理的

---

[1] Jan Duffy. "Knowledge Management: To Be or Not to Be?" *Information Management Journal*. V. 34, No. 1 (Jan. 2000): 64 – 67.

[2] Peter Drucker. *Port-capitalism Society* (Oxford, Great Britain: But-terworth-Heinemann, 1993).

[3] Ikujiro Nonaka. "The Knowledge—Creating Company." *Harvard Business Review* (Nov. -Dec. 1991): 96 – 99. Also Ikujiro Nonaka and Hirotaka Takeuchi. *The Knowledge—creating Company: How Japanese Companies Create the Dynamics of Innovation* (New York: Oxford University Press, 1995).

[4] Jay Liebowitz. *Building Organizational Intelligence: A Knowledge Management Primer* (Boca Raton, FL: CRC Press, 2000): 1.

[5] Jennifer Rowley. "What is Knowledge Management?" *Library Management*. V. 20, No. 8 (1999): 416 – 419.

观点划分为四种宽泛的类型①：

（1）创建知识库，用来存储知识和信息，这些知识和信息通常以文献形式存在。知识库又可分为三类：

· 存储外部知识的知识库，例如竞争情报。

· 存储结构化的内部知识的知识库，例如研究报告和产品导向型营销材料，如技巧和方法。

· 存储非正式的、内部的或隐性的知识，例如那些存储"诀窍型知识"的讨论型数据库。

（2）改进知识存取和传递。关键在于可连通性、存取和传递。

· 核心技术是电视会议系统、文档扫描和共享工具以及远程传输网络。

（3）加强知识环境。使环境有助于更有效地创造、传递和使用知识。这就涉及与知识相关的组织规范和价值观念等。

· 增加对基于客户关系和客户参与的知识共享的认识。

· 奖励对组织的结构化知识基础所做的贡献。

· 贯彻决策审核制度，评估员工在进行关键性决策时是否和如何应用知识。

· 肯定成功的知识管理有赖于组织结构和组织文化。

（4）将知识作为资产来管理，肯定知识对于一个组织的价值。

也有人寻求从过程的角度定义知识管理。例如，Jan Duffy 将其定义为"通过将组织的智慧和经验资本化以促进创新的过程"②。Garter Group 则定义为"促进一体化、协作性的信息资产的创造、获取、组织、存取和使用的领域"③。

以下是 P. Galagan 提出的知识管理过程④：

· 产生新知识

· 从外部来源获取知识

· 以文献、数据库和软件等形式表达知识

· 在过程、产品或服务中运用知识

· 在组织内传播现有知识

· 在决策中使用可获取的知识

· 通过组织文化和组织激励推动知识增长

· 评定知识资产的价值和知识管理的作用

通过以上对项目视角和操作过程视角的叙述，我们可以对目前知识管理的外延和内涵有一个大体的了解。

5. 图书馆中的知识管理

当商业领域在新知识经济和数字时代发生变革之际，各类图书馆也在经历着巨大的变化。21世纪的图书馆应该承担起用户的学习和知识中心这个新角色，以及成为它们各自

---

① Thomas H. Davenport, DeLong, D. W., and Beers, M. C. " Successful Knowledge Management Projects." *Sloan Management Review*. V. 39, No. 2 (1998): 43 – 57.

② Jan Dufiy. *Harvesting Experience*: *Reaping the Benefits of Knowledge* (Prairie Village, KS: ARM A International, 1999). Also from her article, "Knowledge Management: To Be or Not to Be?" Information Management Journal. V. 34, No. 1 (Jan. 2000): 64 – 67.

③ Jim Bair. "Knowledge Management is About Cooperation and Context." *Gartner Advisory Services Research Note* (May 14, 1999).

④ P. Galagan. "Smart Companies (Knowledge Management)." *Training and Development*. V. 51, No. 12 (1997): 20 – 25.

所在社区的智力场所。借用 Keystone 原则的一句话，在这样的公共场所里，"人们和思想在现实和虚拟的两个环境中交互作用，从而扩展了学习过程，促进了新知识的产生"[①]。作为一个学习性组织，图书馆应当在知识管理中起到强有力的带头作用。和那些旨在利用知识管理获得竞争优势的商业组织相比，除公司图书馆（又称为企业图书馆、专业图书馆或知识中心）外，大多数公共的、学院的和研究型的图书馆有不同的方向和价值观念。公共的、学院的和研究型的图书馆最重要的使命是拓展用户获取知识的途径，而非仅仅服务于机构竞争和内部使用，很少和外界进行知识共享。在这种使命的感召下，图书馆应该将知识管理的目标定在更高的层次上。以下将具体说明图书馆在其各关键的服务领域内能怎样改善知识管理的水平。

（1）知识资源管理

由于各种形式的人类知识呈指数增长，为了与其使命和职责相一致，图书馆需要将其资源存取和共享的战略从印刷型转向电子型、数字型资源。受资金、技术、人员和空间所限，图书馆必须认真分析用户需求，寻求开发合作性获取机制以满足需求。合理的资源发展战略的目标应该是使观念从"拥有"向"存取"转变，从"长期"向"即时"转变。

应开发和维护一种能涵盖内部和外部、印刷型及其他形式知识资源的一体化在线公共存取目录（OPAC），要定期从因特网中搜索和筛选有用的网站和知识资源并在 OPAC 中建立实链接，还要建立审查和更新这些资源的系统。

除了显性知识，图书馆还应该开发获取对用户、组织和内部运作具有重要意义的隐性知识的途径，图书馆的网站要成为所有经过选择的重要知识和信息的入口（portal），无论它们是显性还是隐性的、站内还是远程的。

Michael Looney 和 Peter Lyman 将"入口"定义为"一种集各种有用信息资源于一个网页的手段，可帮助用户避免受信息超载的困扰或在网络上感到无所适从"[②]。

在当今数字化和网络化的知识时代，网络信息资源的规模正在以指数速度增长。没人确切知道因特网上究竟有多少网页，新的网页每秒都在增加。最新数据表明，因特网主机数量已经接近 20 亿，并且在 2001 年 1 月至 2002 年 1 月这一年以 25% 的速度飞速增长。[③] 大多数常用的网络搜索引擎也增加了索引的数量，例如，根据 2001 年 12 月 18 日第一期的《搜索引擎》所载，Google 称其已经为 15 亿个网页建立了索引。其他搜索引擎如 FAST，AltaVista，Inktomi 和 Northern Light 标引的网页数量多则达 6.25 亿，少则也有 3.9 亿[④]。Lawrence 和 Giles 于 1999 年的研究表明，在任一指定时刻，每一搜索引擎只可能覆盖所有网络资源的 15%，所有搜索引擎总共也才覆盖相关资源的约 42%。[⑤] 更加不尽如人意的是，成千上万的检索结果都是不相关的，不得不从大量的检索结果中进一步寻找那些为数不多的相关信息。尽管如此，如果能够利用先进的人工智能工具在网上冲浪，去选择、寻找、组织、分类信息，并自动按用户的特殊兴趣和需要将其所需传递给他们，那么网上信息还是非常有用的。许多这样的新型知识管理系统正处于开发和测试阶段，它们有

---

① On September 24 – 25, 1999, eight academic library leaders met during a two-day strategic Issues Forum of Academic Library Directors held in Keystone, Colorado, organized jointly by the Association of Research Libraries and OCLC. Three basic principles were declared as the expanded vision for libraries in the digital knowledge age of the 21st century. The three principles are called the Keystone Principles.

② Michael Looney and Peter Lyman. "Portals in Higher Education: What are They, and What is Their Potential?" *EDUCAUSE Review*. V. 35, No 4 (July/August 2000): p. 30. Available online from http://www.educause.edu/pub/er/erm00/article004/looney.pdf

③ http://www.isc.orp/ds/www-200201/hosts.gif

④ http://searchenginewatch.com/reports/sizes.html

⑤ S. Lawrence and C. L. Giles. "Accessibility of Information on the Web." *Nature*. 400 (July 1999): 107 – 109.

希望极大地丰富知识资源，改善用户服务，并有利于更有效地利用知识来进行创造和决策。

大学和研究型组织本身就是知识库。这些具有很高价值的智力财富，无论是显性知识还是隐性知识，都应该对其进行编目、存档、索引、及时更新，并将它们转换为数字化形式。

另外，那种传统的、历史悠久的编目和分类方法对于处理数量有限的书籍、期刊杂志和文档还勉强应付，但是对于处理大型电子数据库和因特网上的无限数字信息却是远远不够的。使用 Dublin Core 元数据和联合在线资源目录（CORC）已成为一种以合作方式获取网络信息的新途径。其他新方法还包括数据挖掘、文本挖掘、内容管理、搜索引擎、监视程序、自然语言检索、语言分析、语义网络、知识提取、概念黄页以及像二维或三维知识绘图这样的信息可视化技术等，它们是知识管理系统近期发展成果的一部分。

（2）资源共享和联网

图书馆有着资源共享和资源联网的悠久传统。自20世纪60年代以来，在计算机、远程通讯网络和数字技术快速发展的推动下，图书馆的资源共享和联网得到了极大拓展。在美国，图书馆在各类合作性工作和资源共享领域同时作为几个图书馆联盟的成员是非常普遍的现象，其中典型的例子就是 OCLC 联机计算机图书馆中心和俄亥俄 LINK（俄亥俄图书馆和信息网络）。

OCLC 和 CORC 项目对于图书馆之间合作获取数字资源、开展标准化格式描述和简化用户检索都很有帮助。

这些在资源共享和资源网络方面成功的例子在很大程度上取决于所有成员馆无私的通力合作和参与，大型图书馆必须在其中起到领头羊的作用，同时政府和上级组织在政策和资金上的支持也至关重要。实践表明，无论是何种规模和专长的图书馆都能从图书馆合作和资源共享中受益匪浅。

（3）信息技术的发展

为了推动实施知识管理，应该建立一个经过精心设计的操作型知识管理系统，使用最新的信息技术作为辅助工具。在这方面，图书馆馆长要视自己为整个组织的首席知识官与首席信息官（CIO），与规划部门、计算机和信息技术中心、人力资源管理部门、财务部门等的负责人合作设计和开发这样的系统。这样的知识管理系统应该建立在现有计算机和信息技术基础设施的基础上，包括升级过的内网、外网、因特网，以及能够辅助获取、分析、组织、存储和共享内外信息资源的软件程序，它们有助于通过多种渠道和层次实现用户、资源人员（教员、研究者和学科专家等）、出版者、政府机构、商业、企业和其他组织间有效的知识交流。

近年来，很多新开发的、用于数据库和信息/文档管理的信息技术也能应用在知识管理上，如数据仓库、数据挖掘、文本挖掘、内容管理、知识提取、知识绘图、组件和信息可视化等。据 Hsinchim Chen 的观察分析，"20世纪90年代以来，搜索引擎的普及和网络监视、索引与链分析技术的进步已经使情报检索（IR）系统转变为更新、更强大的因特网内容检索工具"[①]。

（4）用户服务

知识管理的最终目标是为用户提供各种高质量的服务，以改善知识的传播、利用和创

---

① Hsinchun Chen. *Knowledge Management Systems: A Text Mining Perspective*（Tucson, Arizona: University of Arizona, 2001）: 18.

造，这些服务应尽可能地满足每个用户的兴趣和需求。关于用户的信息可通过分析用户注册、用户调查、流通和馆际互借记录、咨询问题记录、电子期刊杂志和数字资源的使用记录获得，用户满意度和用户需求应在定期的用户调查中收集，调查分析的结果可被用来规划和重新设计图书馆服务。但与此同时，对用户隐私的保护也始终不容忽视。

一些图书馆以往所提供的如"新书预告"和"精选信息公告"这样的手工服务，如今通过利用"推送技术"可以高效便利地自动完成。每个图书馆用户还可以借助于图书馆系统和网络建立个性化的、虚拟的"我的图书馆"，收集和组织供个人使用的资源，并随时了解图书馆提供的最新资源状况①。

图书馆和信息技术协会（LITA）认为，类似于"我的图书馆"这样的服务是最"值得关注"的趋势。它还进一步说，"图书馆用户是正在成长的网络用户群体，他们期待着个性化、交互性和客户支持服务，以图书馆、而非用户为中心的方法和手段将越来越无关紧要"②。

（5）人力资源管理

无论在馆内还是馆外，图书馆员工和用户都拥有大量的专业知识。在大学和研究性团体中，这种专业知识大量存在，因此有必要对其进行编目、索引和定期更新，使其在由图书馆建立和维护的电子数据库中能够被检索和获取到。

图书馆员工的知识和经验构成了图书馆的智力财富，应该受到珍重和共享。要建立鼓励共享知识和专业技能的组织文化，并配以适当的奖赏和激励机制。那些通过写作、出版、演说、指导或顾问的形式与他人分享其隐性知识和经验的员工应得到恰当的认可和奖赏。一个强调合作、共享和创新的组织文化只有通过图书馆馆长强有力的领导以及全体员工的共同努力才能够建立起来。

作为学习性组织，图书馆应当利用每年经费的一部分为所有员工提供继续教育和培训的机会，知识必须经过更新和扩展才能防止老化。

图书馆还应当鼓励经验丰富的员工向新员工传授知识和经验，并建立一种指导系统来帮助新员工向老员工学习。应定期在员工方便的时间安排非正式的研讨会和自由交谈会议，以便员工相互交往，交流"心得"、"最佳行为"以及其他具体的经验与知识。在图书馆内部的局域网上还可创建特殊兴趣小组和聊天室。

既然许多有价值的经验需经长期积累才能形成，图书馆应该注意为员工创造有利的工作条件和环境，以期留住人才。

6. 结论

在商界，知识管理对于组织从竞争对手那里获得竞争优势、增加产品价值和赢得更高的客户满意度等方面具有重要的战略意义，图书馆有向商界同仁学习的必要。除去在竞争性、所有权和赢利等方面的考虑，知识管理对于图书馆和对于商业企业来说一样重要。其实，图书馆在信息管理上有着长期丰富的经验，许多这样的知识和技能同样可以应用到知识管理当中。

任何一个图书馆如果想成功地实施知识管理，最高管理层必须要有坚强的领导能力和远见卓识，这样才能积极推动组织内部的知识共享。随着图书馆进入 21 世纪的知识时代，

---

① Suzanne Cohen and others. "Personalized Electronic Services in the Cornell University Libraries." *D-Lib Magazine* V. 6, No. 4 (April 2000)：1 - 2. Available online from：http：//www. dlib. org/dlib/aprill00/mistlebauer/04mistlebauer. html
② "Technology and Library Users：LITA Experts Identify Trends to Watch." (Chicago：LITA, 1999) Available online from http：//www. lita. rfi/committe/toptech/trendsmw99. htm

我们不能在知识管理中退居次席,而要用专业知识和经验来武装自己,坐在领航者的位置上。

信息技术和信息系统为实施知识管理提供了有效的支持,图书馆员应与信息技术(IT)专业人员和其他人合作开发适用的知识管理系统。

此外,绝不可把知识管理看作控制知识创造过程的手段。在《推动知识创新》一书中,George Von Krogh 等人坚决认为知识管理要支持知识创新,而非对其进行控制,任何图书馆都应竭尽全力,调动一切资源,推动和促进知识创新的进程[①]。

最佳的知识创新者就是学术机构,知识创新在大学可以得到最好的实施。作为学习型和知识型组织,大学应当赋予其图书馆开发校园知识管理系统的权力,现在已经是图书馆作为知识管理中央舞台的领舞者对自身进行重新定位的时候了。

(原载《津图学刊》(*Tianjin Library Journal*), 2003 年第 1 期,第 1-5 页。)

[①] George Von Krogh, Kazuo Ichijo, and Ikujiro Nonaka. Enabling *Knowledge Creation*: *How to Unlock the Mystery of Tacit Knowledge and Release the Power of Innovation* (New York: Oxford University Press, 2000).

图书馆在知识管理中担当什么角色

Does Library Have a Role in Knowledge Management?[①]

1. INTRODUCTION

"Knowledge Management" has become a popular term in the business world during the last decade of the 20th century. It was the business world that recognizes at first the importance of knowledge in the "global economy" of the "knowledge age". In the new knowledge economy, knowledge is power, especially if it is shared and put to creative use. The possession of relevant and strategic knowledge and its unceasing renewal enables businesses to gain competitive advantage.

The management of information and knowledge has long been regarded as the domain of libraries. Librarians and information professionals are trained to be experts in information and knowledge searching, selecting, acquiring, organizing, preserving, repackaging, disseminating, and serving. However, it is necessary now for libraries to reassess their strengths and weaknesses in knowledge and information management and to provide leadership in the advancement and implementation of knowledge management.

Knowledge management is much more than information and data management. It is also much broader in scope than information technology. Knowledge management has a goal to identify useful and relevant knowledge, to organize, merge, and synthesize knowledge, and to stimulate the creative use of knowledge. Information technology provides the technical tools to achieve this goal. Since knowledge is processed, used, renewed, expanded, and often resides in the minds of people, and is the creation of human wisdom, the human element is the most important part of knowledge management.

2. IS THERE A DIFFERENCE BETWEEN INFORMATION AND KNOWLEDGE?

Daniel Bell (1973) defines knowledge as "a set of organized statements of facts or ideas, presenting a reasoned judgment or an experimental result, which is transmitted to others through some communication medium in some systematic form". As for information, Marc Porat (1977) states, "Information is data that has been organized and communicated."

Stephen Abram (1997) sees the process for knowledge creation and use as a continuum where data transforms into information, information transforms into knowledge and knowledge drives and underpins behavior and decision-making. Below are simple definitions of Data, Information, Knowledge, and Wisdom:

- ● ***Data***: Scattered, unrelated facts, writings, numbers, or symbols.
- ● ***Information***: Selected, organized and analyzed data.
- ● ***Knowledge***: Information combined with user's ability and experience and is used to solve a problem or to create new knowledge.
- ● ***Wisdom***: Forward looking and thinking based on one's values and commitment.

The differences between ***information*** and ***knowledge*** can be summarized as:
- ● ***Information*** is visible, independent from action and decision, different in format after

---

[①] Presented at the 12th International Conference on New Information Technology, May 29 – 31, 2001, Beijing, China. It is modified and updated from the author's earlier paper, "Knowledge management and the role of libraries in the new century" in *Outlook of the 21st Century: a Collection of Essays*. Taichung: Liao Ying-Ming Cultural and Education Foundation, 2001. (In Chinese and English)

processing, physical product, independent from existing environment, easily transferable, and duplicable.
- ***Knowledge*** is invisible, closely related to action and decision, different in thought after processing, spiritual product, identified with existing environment, transferable through learning, and duplicable.

In the knowledge age we will see the accumulation of human knowledge at an unprecedented rate that affects every aspect of our life and society. It is through human ingenuity, creativity, and wisdom that our world of information and knowledge is compounded in the passing of every second, minute, and hour. The term of knowledge age emphasizes the role that knowledge, both explicit and tacit, will play in the new millennium.

In the business world, two types of knowledge have been noted. Jan Duffy (2000) defines explicit knowledge as "knowledge that is documented and public: structured, fixed-content, externalized, and conscious" and tacit knowledge as "personal, undocumented knowledge; context-sensitive, dynamically-created and derived, internalized, and experience-based; often resides in the human mind, behavior, and perception".

3. THE RISE OF KNOWLEDGE MANAGEMENT

As early as 1965, Peter Drucker already pointed out that "knowledge" would replace land, labor, capital, machines, etc. to become the chief source of production. His foresight did not get much attention back then. It was not until 1991 when Ikujiro Nonaka raised the concept of "tacit" knowledge and "explicit" knowledge as well as the theory of "spiral of knowledge" in the *Harvard Business Review* that the time of "knowledge-based competition" finally came. In his latest book, *Building Organizational Intelligence: A Knowledge Management Primer*, Jay Liebowitz (2000) stated:

> "In today's movement towards knowledge management, organizations are trying to best leverage their knowledge internally in the organization and externally to their customers and stakeholders. They are trying to capitalize on their organizational intelligence to maintain their competitive edge."

> "The thrust of knowledge management is to create a process of valuing the organization's intangible assets in order to best leverage knowledge internally and externally. Knowledge management, therefore, deals with creating, securing, capturing, coordinating, combining, retrieving, and distributing knowledge. The idea is to create a knowledge sharing environment whereby sharing knowledge is power as opposed to the old adage that, simply, knowledge is power."

4. SOME DEFINITIONS OF KNOWLEDGE MANAGEMENT

Because knowledge management is still a relatively new concept and viewed differently by different writers from different focuses, its definitions vary. In her article, "What is knowledge management?" Jennifer Rowley (1999) offers her definition below:

> "Knowledge management is concerned with the exploitation and development of the knowledge assets of an organization with a view to furthering the organization's objectives. The knowledge to be managed includes both explicit, documented knowledge, and tacit, subjective knowledge. Management entails all of those processes associated with the identification, sharing and creation of knowledge. This requires systems for the creation and maintenance of knowledge repositories, and to cultivate and facilitate the sharing of knowledge and organizational learning. Organizations that succeed in knowledge management are likely to view knowledge as an asset and to develop organizational norms and values, which support the creation and sharing of knowledge."

Rowley's definition was based on the four different types of perspectives on knowledge management identified by Thomas H. Davenport et al in their study of a number of knowledge management projects. From the analysis of the projects' objectives, Davenport et al. (1998) were able to categorize them into-four broad types of perspectives:

1) ***To create knowledge repositories***, which store both knowledge and information, often in documentary form? These repositories can fall into three categories:
- Those which include external knowledge, such as competitive intelligence.
- Those that include structured internal knowledge, such as research reports, and product oriented marketing materials as techniques and methods.
- Those that embrace informal, internal or tacit knowledge, such as discussion databases that store "know how".

2) ***To improve knowledge access and transfer.*** Here the emphasis is on connectivity, access and transfer.

Technologies such as video conferencing systems, document scanning and sharing tools and telecommunications networks are central.

3) ***To enhance the knowledge environment***, so that the environment is conductive to more effective knowledge creation, transfer and use. This involves tackling organizational norms and values as they relate to knowledge.
- Increase awareness on sharing knowledge embedded in client relationship and engagements.
- Provide awards for contributions to the organization's structured knowledge base.
- Implement decision audit programs in order to assess whether and how employees were applying knowledge in key decisions.
- Recognize that successful knowledge management is dependent upon structures and cultures.

4) ***To manage knowledge as an asset***, and to recognize the value of knowledge to an organization.

Others, however, sought to take a process view to define knowledge management. For example, Jan Duffy (1999) defines it as "a process that drives innovation by capitalizing on organizational intellect and experience". Gartner Group defines it as "a discipline that promotes an integrated and collaborative approach to the process of information asset creation, capture, organization, access and use" (Bait, 1999).

P. Galagan (1997) proposed the following set of knowledge management processes:
- Generating new knowledge.
- Accessing knowledge from external sources.
- Representing knowledge in documents, databases, software and so forth.
- Embedding knowledge in processes, products, or services.
- Transferring existing knowledge around an organization.
- Using accessible knowledge in decision-making.
- Facilitating knowledge growth through Culture and incentives.
- Measuring the value of knowledge assets and the impact of knowledge management.

From both the project perspectives and the operational processes described above we can gain a general understanding of the current scope and contents of knowledge management.

5. KNOWLEDGE MANAGEMENT IN LIBRARIES

While the business world is changing in the new knowledge economy and digital age, libraries of all types are undergoing drastic changes also. The new role of libraries in the 21st century needs to be as a learning and knowledge center for their users as well as the intellectual commons for their respective communities where, to borrow the phrase from the Keystone Principles, "people and ideas interact in both the real and virtual environments to expand learning and facilitate the creation of new knowledge?" ①

As a learning organization, libraries should provide a strong leadership in knowledge management. Unlike those business organizations whose goal for knowledge management is for competitive advantage, libraries, with the exception of company libraries (which may be known or called corporate libraries, special libraries, or knowledge centers), most public, academic, and research libraries have a different orientation and value. Instead of competition, internal use only, and little sharing of knowledge with others outside, the most important mission of public, academic, and research libraries is to expand the access of knowledge for their users: Charged by this mission, libraries should aim their knowledge management goal high. Below are examples of what libraries can do to improve their knowledge management in all the key areas of library services.

5.1 Knowledge Resources Management

Because of the exponential growth in human knowledge in a variety of formats libraries need to develop their resources access and sharing strategies from printed to electronic and digital resources in concert with their mission and charges. Restricted by limited funding, staff, and space, libraries must carefully analyze the needs of their users and seek to develop cooperative acquisition plans to meet these needs. The changing concept from "ownership" to "access" and from "just in case" to "just in time" should be the goal of a sound resources development strategy.

An integrated online public access catalog (OPAC) with both internal and external resources as well as printed and other formats of knowledge should be developed and maintained. Useful websites and knowledge sources should be regularly searched and selected from Internet and included in OPACs by hard links. A system of reviewing and updating of these resources should be performed.

Going beyond explicit knowledge, libraries should also develop means to capture all that tacit knowledge that is of importance to users and to the internal operation of libraries. Each of the web sites of libraries should serve as portals for all sources of selective and relevant knowledge and information whether explicit or tacit, whether on site or remote, and in all formats.

As a part of its knowledge management activities, Arthur Anderson Business Consulting (2000) has developed a highly useful web site: KnowledgeSpace. Three types of knowledge are provided by KnowledgeSpace. They are:

- News—important company news and hot topics of interest to all staff members worldwide.
- Resources—contains "Global Best Practices", "Ask Network", and "Community Resources".
- Connections—for active interactions and discussion by special interest groups across organizational structure and departmental lines.

All information in the KnowledgeSpace is updated frequently and user feedbacks are encouraged. Libraries can develop their own types of KnowledgeSpace. Through each library's intranet, strategic planning documents, annual reports, team and department reports, council and committee minutes, statistical analyses, grant proposals, policies and procedures, operational manuals, "best practices", "lessons learned", internal announcements, library news of major events, personnel actions, training and staff development opportunities, etc. can be made available to all staff members.

5.2 Human Resources Management

Library staff and users, both in and outside the libraries, possess a great amount of expert knowledge. In university and research communities such expertise is abundant and should be

---

① On September 24 – 25, 1999, eighty academic library leaders met during a two-day *Strategic Issues Forum of Academic Library Directors* held in Keystone, Colorado, organized jointly by the Association of Research Library and OCLC. Three basic principles were declared as the expanded vision for libraries in the digital knowledge age of the 21st century. The three principles are called the Keystone Principles.

inventoried, indexed, and updated regularly and be made searchable and accessible through electronic databases created and maintained by libraries.

The knowledge and accumulated experiences of library staff members form the intellectual assets of any library and should be valued and shared. An organizational culture for sharing of knowledge and expertise should be established with appropriate rewards and incentives. Those staff members who share their tacit knowledge and experiences through writing, publishing, lecturing, or mentoring should be appropriately recognized and rewarded. An organizational culture which emphasizes cooperation, sharing, and innovation can only be established by a strong leadership and commitment from the library director and a shared vision by the library staff.

As a learning organization, libraries should allocate annual funding to provide continuing education and staff training to all staff members. Knowledge must be renewed and expanded to prevent it from becoming stagnant.

Libraries should also encourage the transfer of knowledge and experience from experienced staff to new staff members. A mentoring system should be in place to help newcomers to learn from experienced library staff. Informal seminars and brownbag sessions where staff can interact and exchange "lessons learned", "best practices" and other specific experience and knowledge should be scheduled at regular intervals and at convenient times. Special interest groups and chat rooms can be created through intranet.

Since many valuable experiences have been accumulated over time, libraries should pay attention to favorable working conditions and environment, which will contribute to better staff retention.

5.3 Resources Sharing and Networking

Libraries have had a long tradition for resources sharing and networking. These have been greatly expanded by the rapid development of computer, telecommunication, networking, and digital technologies since the 1960s. It is very common for libraries to be a member in several consortia at the same time for various types of cooperative work and resources sharing. The best examples of these are the OCLC Online Computer Library Center and OhioLINK (Ohio Library and Information Network).

The CORC project of OCLC should be especially useful for libraries to cooperatively capture digital resources of all types, describe them in a standard format, and make them easily searchable by users.

5.4 Information Technology Development

To facilitate the implementation of knowledge management, a well-designed and operational knowledge management system should be in place. Latest information technology should be used as an enabler.

Intranet technology should be used to support knowledge management efforts via shared documents/products and the gathering and publication of lessons learned and best practices. Internet functions should also be used for knowledge exchange with users, resource persons (faculty, researchers, and subjects specialists, etc.), publishers, government agencies, businesses and industries, and other organizations.

5.5 User Services

Knowing your users should come first. This information can be gathered from statistical analysis of user registration databases, circulation and interlibrary loan records, most frequently asked reference questions, telephone and email services, use of electronic journals and digital resources, etc. These should be done without invading the privacy of individual library users.

Libraries have collected a great amount of user information and statistics for reporting purpose but have seldom used them to improve user services. Now, by means of the "push" technology, libraries can provide a variety of tailored-made services to suit individual needs. User satisfaction and needs should be collected through periodic user surveys. The findings should be used for the planning and redesign of library services.

6. CONCLUSION

Although knowledge management has become one of the latest management buzzwords, whether it will fade away or not, just as some of the other buzzwords before it, will depend on how we make it work. In the business world, knowledge management has been regarded as strategically important for organizations to gain a competitive advantage over their competitors, to add value to their products, and to win greater satisfaction of their customers. In the library world, there is a lesson to be learned from the business world. Knowledge management is as important for libraries as for the business minus the competitive, proprietary, and moneymaking concerns. In fact, libraries have a long and rich experience in the management of explicit knowledge. Now we need to extend our know-how to the management of tacit knowledge as well. For any libraries to succeed in implementing knowledge management will require a strong leadership and vision from the top administration, which can influence the organization's knowledge sharing efforts in a positive way. As libraries enter the knowledge age of the 21st century, we should not take a back seat in the development of knowledge management. Instead, armed by our professional knowledge and experiences, we should be in the driver's seat.

Furthermore, knowledge management should never be viewed as a way to control the process of knowledge creation. In his book, *Enabling Knowledge Creation*, Georg Von Krogh et al (2000) made a strong argument for supporting knowledge creation rather than controlling it. In the process of knowledge creation, every library should strive to be an enabler and facilitator by mobilizing all its efforts and resources.

REFERENCES

Abram, Stephen. (1997, June) "Post information age positioning for special librarians: Is knowledge management the answer?" *Information Outlook*. pp. 20 – 21.

Arthur Anderson Business Consulting. (2000) *The First Book on Knowledge Management*, translated into Chinese by Liu Jin-Wei. Taipei: San Chou Publisher. pp. vi – vii. (In Chinese)

Bair, Jim. (1999, May 14) "Knowledge management is about cooperation and context." *Gartner Advisory Services Research Note*.

Bell, Daniel. (1973) *The Coming of Post-industrial Society: A Venture in social Forecasting*. New York: Basic Books.

Davenport, Thomas H., D. W. DeLong, and M. C. Beers. (1998) "Successful knowledge management projects." *Sloan Management Review*. 39 (2): 43 – 57.

Duffy, Jan. (1999) *Harvesting Experience: Reaping the Benefits of Knowledge*. Prairie Village, KS: ARMA International.

Duffy, Jan. (2000) "Knowledge management: To be or not to be?" *Information Management Journal*. 34 (1): 64 – 67.

Galagan, P. (1997) "Smart companies (knowledge management)." *Training and Development*. 51 (12): 20 – 25.

Liebowitz, Jay. (2000) "Building Organizational Intelligence." *A Knowledge Management Primer*. Boca Raton, FL: CRC Press.

Porat, Marc. (1977) *The Information Economy: Definition and Measurement*. Washington, D. C.: U. S. Department of Commerce, Office of Telecommunications. Publication 77 – 12.

Rowley, Jennifer. (1999) "What is knowledge management?" *Library Management*, 20 (8) 416 – 419.

Von Krogh, Georg, Kazuo Ichijo, and Ikujiro Nonaka. (2000) *Enabling Knowledge Creation: How to Unlock the Mystery of Tacit Knowledge and Release the Power of Innovation*. New York: Oxford University Press.

(Published in *Global Digital Library Development in the New Millennium*, edited by Ching-Chih Chen, Beijing: Tsinghua University Press. 2001: pp. 145 – 152.)

实施知识管理　提供优质服务　促进知识创新[①]

Implementing Knowledge Management, Providing Quality Services, and Advancing Knowledge Renovation

前言

中科院从实行知识创新工程试点以来，已有四年的经验及成效，对加强中科院的科技研究及人才培养，已奠定了良好的基础。作为科技研究、知识创新及人才培养的后盾及动力的文献信息服务——中科院文献情报中心也为此做出了积极的努力与显著的贡献。

为了面对21世纪知识时代的需求及配合全院推行知识创新工程的努力，中科院文献情报中心应考虑到自身的优势及弱点，掌握外在环境及整个科技信息工作发展的趋势，重新定位，并配合当前世界潮流，吸取"知识管理"的优点，在文献信息工作中特别强调知识管理、信息资源开发、优质服务及人才培养，以完成知识时代所赋予的使命。

知识管理的重要性

20世纪末，知识管理已变成在企业界一个时髦的术语。企业界首先意识到知识创新在知识时代"全球经济"中的重要性。在新知识经济中，特别是当人们能共享及创造性地使用知识时，知识就是力量，拥有并不断地更新相关及策略性的知识会使企业在竞争上获得优势。

信息的管理长久以来被当作图书馆和文献信息中心的首要职责，图书馆员和信息专业人员被训练成为信息查询、选择、获取、组织、储存、再包装、传播和服务的专家。当我们进入21世纪的知识时代，图书馆员和信息专业人员有必要重新评估他们在信息管理方面的优势和不足，为图书馆重新定位。

史蒂芬·亚伯伦（Stephen Abram）把知识的创造及使用过程看作为从数据转变为信息，信息转变为知识，及知识驱动与支持人类的行为和决策的一个连续的流程。[②]

图书馆和文献信息中心在21世纪的一个重要使命是要以丰富的信息资源，优质的读者服务来支持、促进和推动知识的更新，改革和更广泛地创新知识以造福人类。因此，在重新定位时，图书馆和文献信息中心应该从信息管理的基础上提升到知识管理的层次，以起到知识交流、使用和创新的中介作用；强化图书馆和文献信息中心的效能。

江泽民主席曾经说过："创新是一个民族的灵魂，是一个国家兴旺发达的不竭动力……"[③] 知识的创新则是一切创新的源泉。只有实行知识管理才能加速及深化可持续性的知识创新。

知识管理不仅仅是信息和数据的管理，也不仅仅是指信息技术的开发和使用。知识管理的一个目标是识别有用的、相关的、策略性的知识；去组织、吸收、综合知识；促进创造性的使用知识。信息技术为实现这一目标提供了有效的技术工具。因为知识是通过人们

[①] 本文为作者在中国科学院文献情报中心新馆开馆庆典"知识管理：图书馆的机遇与挑战"学术研讨会上的主旨演讲，中国北京，2002年5月19日－22日。

[②] Abram, Stephen. "Post Information Age Postioning for Special Librarians; Is Librarians: Is Knowledge Management the answer?" *Information Outlook* (June 1997): pp20－21.

[③] 李瑞环在全国政协九届五次会议闭幕会上的讲话，人民日报海外版，2002年3月14日，第二页。

的大脑来加工、使用、更新、扩展的,是人类智慧的产物;所以人是知识管理的最重要部分。

利博维茨(Jay Liebowitz)在他发表的《建立组织智能:知识管理导论》一书中指出:"在走向现代知识管理的行动中,很多机构正设法平衡其组织内部的知识和其顾客及股东或利益有关者(stakeholders)之间外部知识的关系。他们设法扩大其组织自身的智能来保证其竞争能力。

知识管理的结果是为更好地平衡内部知识和外部知识而创造一个重视机构无形知识财产的程序。因此,知识管理指的是知识的创造、保护、获取、协调、统合、查寻以及传播。其目的是建立一个知识共享环境;在这个环境中知识共享是力量,而不像格言说的那样知识是力量。"①

知识管理的定义

由于知识管理仍然是一个比较新的概念,不同的作者从不同的角度给予不同的定义。对于"什么是知识管理?"简妮佛·罗利(Jennifer Rowley)所给的定义为:

"知识管理是对一个有志于扩展其目标的组织在知识财产方面的开发和发展。需要管理的知识包括显性的、记录的知识和隐性的、主观的知识。管理是一个所有与知识的识别、共享和创造有关的过程。这需要知识库的创立和维护系统,以及对知识共享和组织学习的培养和促进。那些成功的知识管理组织通常把知识当作一种资产来发展该组织的模式和价值,这些模式和价值又反过来帮助知识的创造和共享。"②

图书馆和信息专业的变化

当企业界在新知识经济和数字化时代中发生变化的时候,各种类型的图书馆和文献信息中心也在经历着剧烈的改变。从 20 世纪 60 年代起,每五年到十年,图书馆和信息专业就会发生一次显著的变化。60 年代以前,大多数图书馆的收藏是以纸张或者印刷式资料为主,包括缩微卷片。大部分的操作仍然是手工的,发展的步伐缓慢,而且平淡。然而,到了 60 年代,我们就看到了图书馆自动化的开始、机读目录格式的标准化、使用计算机处理的大型数据库的出现(比如美国的化学文摘社和国家医学图书馆等),以及图书馆自动化合作机构的建立(OCLC 的前身——俄亥俄州学院图书馆中心——Ohio College Library Center)。在 70 年代,开始出现联机信息查寻和检索,CD-ROM 也开始使用。80 年代,图书馆网络开始普及,图书馆的集成自动化系统趋于成熟,图书馆之间的联网组织也成为一时的风尚。经由馆际联网组织,各种类型的图书馆和文献信息中心可以进行有效的馆际合作及资源共享。90 年代,电子出版、多媒体、因特网、万维网、数字化文献、检索引擎、专家系统、网页、电子信件等等得到普遍重视及广泛使用。当我们进入 21 世纪时,图书馆和文献信息中心正向着综合的、虚拟的、数字化方向迈进。数字化的世界深受因特网(Internet)、万维网(World Wide Web)、信息管理系统和人工智能型检索工具的影响。元数据或诠释资料(Metadata)、都柏林核心集(Dublin Core)、网上资源合作编目(Cooperative Online Resources Catalog)以及知识管理等都受到图书馆和信息专业的广泛关注。

---

① Liebowitz, Jay. *Building Organizational intelligence*: *A Knowledge Management Primer*. Boca Raton, FL: CRC Press, 2000: 1.
② Rowley, Jennifer. " What is Knowledge Management?" *Library management*. V. 20, No. 8 (1999): 416-419.

图书馆及文献信息中心与知识管理的关系

作为一个知识交流、使用和创新的中介机构及学习型组织（Learning Organization），图书馆及文献信息中心应该在知识管理中起带头作用。下面是图书馆及文献信息中心该怎样在所有关键的管理和服务领域中来改善其知识管理。

知识资源的管理

由于人类知识增长的速度越来越快，对于图书馆及文献信息中心的信息资源发展是一严峻的挑战。因为受到有限的资金、技术、人员、和空间的限制，图书馆及文献信息中心必须要仔细地分析其使用者的需求及本身的目标，拟定一个合适于国情及本身信息需求的资源发展策略和计划。

从"拥有"（Ownership）到"获取"（Access），从"万一"（Just in Case）到"及时"（Just in Time）这种概念的改变应该是一个健全的信息资源发展策略目标。

应该发展和维护一个集成的网上公共获取目录（OPAC——Online Public Access Catalog），该目录应包含本馆或中心内部和外部的相关知识，以及印刷的和其他形式的知识。OPAC 要包含众多的、有用的网站和知识资源，还应该设计一个定期检查和更新这种资源的系统。

除了显性知识，要想办法发掘、获取、转化和贮存所有对读者和图书馆有用的隐性知识。图书馆的网站应该作为筛选所有知识的窗口，不论是显性的或隐性的，还是现场的或远距离的，以及各种形式的资源。

在目前的数字及网络的知识时代，网上信息资源数量庞大，运用最新的人工智能型检索工具去查询有用的信息，加以筛选、整理及分类；并能按照个别研究人员的兴趣和需要，自动提供。这样将会大大地丰富知识的资源，优化对用户的服务，促进知识的使用和创新。

作为国家级的科研机构，中科院内部各研究所的专家们拥有大量的专业知识。这些宝贵的知识资产，不论是有形的或无形的，都应该尽可能地收集及保存，并编入目录和索引，使其可以在文献信息中心所创建并维护的电子数据库中检索到。

另外，图书馆传统式的分类及编目手段，对于数量有限的显形书刊文献尚可应付，但是对大量数字化的信息则有力不从心之感。利用人工智能型检索工具去检索大型电子数据库及上亿的网上信息资源，也是知识管理所必需采取的措施。

资源共享和联网合作

图书馆和文献信息中心具有悠久的资源共享和联网合作的历史。以美国为例，用手工处理的馆际互借，在 20 世纪初即已开始。20 世纪 60 年代以来，计算机、电讯、网络、数字化等技术的迅速发展加快了这方面的进展。图书馆和文献信息中心通常会因为各种合作项目以及资源共享而同时成为几个合作网的成员单位。其中最好的例子是美国的 OCLC（图书馆计算机联网中心——Online Computer Library Center）和 OhioLINK（俄亥俄学术图书馆信息网——Ohio Academic Library and Information Network）。在中国，高等院校图书馆的文献保障系统（CALIS, Chinese Academic Library and Information System），及最近刚成立的国家科技图书文献中心和国家工程技术图书馆等，也是效果显著，适合中国国情的合作模式。

在网络环境中,参加同一联盟的图书馆和文献信息中心要协调选择一个通用的系统,使各合作馆或中心之间能够最大限度地联通及兼容。

根据国内外的经验,成功的资源共享和联网合作有赖于每一个参与的图书馆和信息中心充分而无私地合作。大的图书馆尤其要起带头作用。上级的主管机构也要在政策和经费上大力支持这种极有效益的活动。

信息技术的发展和使用

想要推动知识管理,使其有效地执行,就必须有一个计划周详,使用最新信息技术的"知识管理系统"。在这一方面,图书馆长或中心主任应该当仁不让地担负起整个机构"知识管理执行长"(Chief Knowledge Management Officer)的角色来和机构内的计算机、信息技术、人事、财务等部门主管进行密切合作和协调,以设计及开发一个合适的系统。这个系统应该设立在现有的内外部互联网络的 基础上,使机构里所有的员工都能方便地使用各种检索引擎去查询各种内部储存的 及外部因特网上的信息资源——不管是数据的,全文的,或是多媒体的——并充分地进行多渠道,多层次的知识交流。

近二十年来,许多新开发的数据及文献信息管理系统和技术都可以使用到知识管理上;像数据储存库(Data warehousing)、数据挖掘技术(Data mining)、全文挖掘技术(Text mining)、知识提取技术(Knowledge extraction)、知识地图绘制(Knowledge mapping)、群组软件(Groupware)、及信息视觉化(Information visualization)等。①

互联网络的各种功能也应该用来为用户(包括上级领导)、知识者(教授、研究员和专家等)、出版商、政府机构、商业和工业,以及其他组织之间作为知识导航和交流之用。

加强对用户的服务

知识管理的最终目的是要对用户提供优质的服务,以促进知识的流通、使用和创新。对用户的服务项目很多,应该尽可能的个人化以符合各人的兴趣和需要。用户信息可以从用户的注册和调查记录、流通和馆际借阅记录、最常问的参考咨询问题、电话和电子信件服务、电子刊物和数字化资源的使用等的统计和分析中得来。但是,要注意不能侵犯用户的隐私权。图书馆和文献信息中心也可以通过定期的用户调查来收集用户的满意程度和要求。调查结果可以用来计划,调整及重 新设计对用户的服务。

过去用手工方式提供的新出版物的通知(new publications alert)及信息选择性分析(selective dissemination of information)现在可以由计算机及"推出"技术(Push technology)来自动处理,十分快捷、方便。同时,每位用户还可以在图书馆的网络上建立虚拟的"我的图书馆"(My Library)来专门收藏自己感兴趣及所需的文献信息——也包括图书馆所自动提供的。

美国的图书及信息学会(The Library and Information Technology Association)认为类似"我的图书馆"这样的服务是目前最值得注意的一个发展趋势。该会的专家们公认"越来越多的那些惯于使用万维网的图书馆用户会期望图书馆加强个别设计(Customization)、交互作用(Interactivity)、及对用户的支持(Customer support)。以图书馆为焦点而不以用户

---

① Chen, Hsinchun. ***Knowledge Management Systems: A Text Mining Perspective***. Tucson, Arizona: University of Arizona, 2001.

为焦点的服务方式将会越来越不适用。"①

人力资源管理

文献信息中心员工的知识以及所积累的经验构成了中心的智慧资产,应该受到重视和共享,使其成为一种共享知识和专业技术的组织文化,并实施恰当的奖励和鼓励。一个强调合作、共享和革新的组织文化环境只有在中心主任的有力领导下,及在员工达成共识的前提下,才能建立起来。

作为一个学习的组织,文献信息中心应该拨出一些年度经费来为全体员工提供继续教育和在职培训。知识和经验必须要不断地更新和扩充以防止其老化或停滞不前。为了革新,有时也要有破釜沉舟的决心,进行机构的重整(Reengineering)。

文献信息中心还应该鼓励资深员工把丰富的知识和经验传授给新的员工,建立一个辅导(Mentoring)制度来帮助新的员工向有经验的员工学习。在方便的时候,定期安排非正式的研讨会和茶叙,让大家可以在那里交流"成功的经验",吸取"失败的教训",相互学习特殊的经验和知识。还可以在文献信息中心内部的网站上建立特别兴趣组群和讨论小组。很多这些类似的措施就是有意地要把隐性的知识转变为显性的知识。

作为年终考核的一部分,那些通过写作、出版、讲座,或以辅导的方式来与他人共享自己的隐性知识和经验的员工应受到适当的表扬和奖励。

因为资深的员工已经积累了许多宝贵的经验,文献信息中心应该注重创造一个良好的工作条件和环境,使这些有经验的员工能够愿意留任。

这些针对中心内部的措施也可以扩展到整个中科院。由中心的主任担任全院的"知识管理执行长"来推行全院的知识管理。

对中科院文献情报中心进行知识管理的建议

在21世纪网络技术及数字信息迅速发展的大环境下,中科院文献情报中心应该跨越传统式文献情报工作的范围和局限,大步地迈向知识管理的新方向,把文献情报中心定位为全院知识管理和知识资源开发和服务的主导部门——将中科院内部及外部的有用知识,包括各种显性及隐性的知识、书本及数字化的知识、成功的研究成果及最佳的服务经验等——进行有系统地筛选、整理、组织、加工、储存,以供院内外的科研人员使用,以促进和加快知识的创新。知识管理的精神是在于充分发掘和利用中科院本身所积累的知识财富,加入外部的相关知识,采用适当的技术,透过一个能够共享知识的组织文化,使有用的知识能够不断地升值和更新,促成知识的新陈代谢,扩大知识创新工程的成效。

以下是对知识管理的一些建议,以供中科院决策者的参考及采用:

➢ 将中科院文献情报中心定位为中科院的知识管理中心。
➢ 知识管理中心的主任职位应视为中科院的"知识管理执行长"(Chief Knowledge Management Officer)。
➢ 拟定中科院知识管理的使命、目标、策略、规划和行动方案。
➢ 设立全院的知识管理协调小组,由院长担任组长,中心主任担任副组长。
➢ 使用最新的信息和电讯技术来加强中科院内部的网络建设及与院外各系统的联网,以加强信息和知识的交流。

---

① "Technology and Library Users: LITA Experts Identify Trends to Watch." 1999. 可在下列网页上查到 http://www.lita.org/committe/toptech/trendsmw99.htm.

- 参与和支持国家科技图书文献中心的工作，面向全国开展服务。
- 设计一个多功能并具有吸引力的网站来指导用户直接使用各种有用的网上资源。
- 改变资源管理策略，从"拥有"到"获取"，从"万一"到"及时"，以提高馆藏的使用率以发挥最大的经济效益。
- 扩大对于电子及数字信息的发掘、整理、组织及使用，并加强网上信息的开发。
- 加强与用户的沟通和联系，了解用户的需要和专长，提供优质的、多层次的及个人化的服务。重视院内外相关的隐性知识和经验，经由网络系统转化为显性的知识，鼓励分享。
- 对于那些通过写作、出版、讲座或以辅导方式来与他人共享自己隐性知识和经验的科研人员要实施有效地奖赏与鼓励，以形成一种共享知识和专业技术的组织文化。
- 加强员工的在职培训及继续教育，以保证专业知识的更新和扩充，防止其老化或停滞不前。
- 收集及分析用户对各种信息使用的情况，以了解用户所需及满意程度，作为改进知识管理的参考。
- 把有用的知识传遍整个组织，为个别用户提供个人化的服务，全力促成知识的创新。
- 21世纪的图书馆将是以知识创新为目标；结合信息、技术、用户、馆员为一体；是充满生机和活力的有机组织。

（原载《知识管理：图书馆的机遇与挑战学术研讨会录》，中国科学院于2002年出版，第90－94页。又载于《图书情报工作动态》（*Newsletter of Library and Information Service*）2002年第4期，第2－6页。）

图书馆在知识管理中的战略方向

Strategic Direction of Libraries in Knowledge Management[①]

1. Introduction

"Knowledge Management" has become a popular term in the business world during the last decade of the 20th century. It was the business world that recognizes at first the importance of knowledge in the "global economy" of the "knowledge age". In the new knowledge economy, knowledge is power, especially if it is shared and put to creative use. The possession of relevant and strategic knowledge and its unceasing renewal enables businesses to gain competitive advantage.

The management of information and knowledge has long been regarded as the domain of libraries. Librarians and information professionals are trained to be experts in information and knowledge searching, selecting, acquiring, organizing, preserving, repackaging, disseminating and serving. However, it is necessary now for libraries to reassess their strengths and weaknesses in knowledge and information management and to provide leadership in the advancement and implementation of knowledge management.

Knowledge management is much more than information and data management. It is also much broader in scope than information technology. Knowledge management has a goal to identify useful and relevant knowledge, to organize, merge, and synthesize knowledge, and to stimulate the creative use of knowledge. Information technology provides the technical tools to achieve this goal. Since knowledge is processed, used, renewed, expanded, and often resides in the minds of people, and is the creation of human wisdom, the human element is the most important part of knowledge management.

For libraries to play a key role in knowledge management it is necessary for libraries to reposition themselves in the new digital and networked environment. This new role is the strategic direction for libraries that want to upgrade themselves from focusing on information management to focusing on knowledge management. Table 1 below shows the subtle differences between information management and knowledge management.

Table 1 Differences Between Information Management and Knowledge Management

Information Management	Knowledge Management
—Focus on information organization	—Focus on knowledge renewal and creation
—Prefer static objects	—Action oriented
—Document-and information-centered	—People-and customer-centered
—Emphasis on processing and preserving	—Emphasis on utilization and sharing
—External orderliness	—Add value to knowledge resources

2. Is there a difference between information and knowledge?

Daniel Bell defines knowledge as "a set of organized statements of facts or ideas, presenting a

---

① This article was presented at the 2001 International Seminar on the Standard of the Development of Digital Information Resource and Knowledge Repository (2001年数字化信息资源与知识仓库建设标准国际研讨会).

reasoned judgment or an experimental result, which is transmitted to others through some communication medium in some systematic form"[1]. As for information, Marc Porat states, "Information is data that has been organized and communicated."[2]

Stephen Abram sees the process for knowledge creation and use as a continuum where data transforms into information, information transforms into knowledge and knowledge drives and underpins behavior and decision-making.[3] Below are simple definitions of Data, Information, Knowledge, and Wisdom:

> Data: Scattered, unrelated facts, writings, numbers, or symbols.
> Information: Selected, organized and analyzed data.
> Knowledge: Information combined with user's ability and experience and is used to solve a problem or to create new knowledge.
> Wisdom: Forward looking and thinking based on one's values and commitment.

The differences between information and knowledge can be summarized as:

> Information is visible, independent from action and decision, different in format after processing, physical product, independent from existing environment, easily transferable, and duplicable.
> Knowledge is invisible, closely related to action and decision, different in thought after processing, spiritual product, identified with existing environment, transferable through learning, and duplicable.

In the knowledge age we will see the accumulation of human knowledge at an unprecedented rate which affects every aspect of our life and society. It is through human ingenuity, creativity, and wisdom that our world of information and knowledge is compounded in the passing of every second, minute, and hour. The term of knowledge age emphasizes the role that knowledge, both explicit and tacit, will play in the new millennium.

In the business world, two types of knowledge have been noted. Jan Dully defines explicit knowledge as "knowledge that is documented and public; structured, fixed-content, externalized, and conscious" and tacit knowledge as "personal, undocumented knowledge; context-sensitive, dynamically-created and derived, internalized, and experience-based; often resides in the human mind, behavior, and perception"[4].

3. The rise of knowledge management

As early as 1965, Peter Drucker already pointed out that "knowledge" would replace land, labor, capital, machines, etc. to become the chief source of production. His foresight did not get much attention back then. It was not until 1991 when Ikujiro Nonaka raised the concept of "tacit" knowledge and "explicit" knowledge as well as the theory of "spiral of knowledge" in the Harvard Business Review that the time of "knowledge-based competition" finally came. In his latest book, Building Organizational Intelligence: A Knowledge Management Primer, Jay Liebowitz stated:[5]

"In today's movement towards knowledge management, organizations are trying to best leverage their knowledge internally in the organization and externally to their customers and stakeholders. They are trying to capitalize on their organizational intelligence to maintain their competitive edge."

---

[1] Bell, Daniel. *The Coming of Post – industrial Society: A Venture in Social Forecasting.* New York: Basic Books, 1973: p. 175.

[2] Porat, Marc. The Information Economy: Definition and Measurement. Washington, D. C. : U. S. Department of Commerce, *Office of Telecommunications*, 1977 (Publication 77 – 12): p. 1.

[3] Abram, Stephen. "Post Information Age Positioning for Special Librarians: Is Knowledge Management the Answer?" *Information Outlook* (June 1997): pp. 20 – 21.

[4] Duffy, Jan. "Knowledge Management: To Be or Not to Be?" *Information Management Journal.* V. 34, No. 1 (Jan. 2000): pp. 64 – 67.

[5] Liebowitz, Jay. *Building Organizational Intelligence : A Knowledge Management Primer.* Boca Raton, FL: CRC Press, 2000: p. 1.

"The thrust of knowledge management is to create a process of valuing the organization's intangible assets in order to best leverage knowledge internally and externally. Knowledge management, therefore, deals with creating, securing, capturing, coordinating, combining, retrieving, and distributing knowledge. The idea is to create a knowledge sharing environment whereby sharing knowledge is power as opposed to the old adage that, simply, knowledge is power."

4. Some definitions of knowledge management

Because knowledge management is still a relatively new concept and viewed differently by different writers from different focuses, its definitions vary. In her article, "What is knowledge management?" Jennifer Rowley offers her definition below:

"Knowledge management is concerned with the exploitation and development of the knowledge assets of an organization with a view to furthering the organization's objectives. The knowledge to be managed includes both explicit, documented knowledge, and tacit, subjective knowledge. Management entails all of those processes associated with the identification, sharing and creation of knowledge. This requires systems for the creation and maintenance of knowledge repositories, and to cultivate and facilitate the sharing of knowledge and organizational learning. Organizations that succeed in knowledge management are likely to view knowledge as an asset and to develop organizational norms and values, which support the creation and sharing of knowledge." ①

Rowley's definition was based on the four different types of perspectives on knowledge management identified by Thomas H. Davenport et al in their study of a number of knowledge management projects. From the analysis of the projects' objectives, Davenport et al were able to categorize them into four broad types of perspectives:②

(1) To create knowledge repositories, which store both knowledge and information, often in documentary form? These repositories can fall into three categories:
- Those that include external knowledge, such as competitive intelligence.
- Those that include structured internal knowledge, such as research reports, and product oriented marketing materials as techniques and methods.
- Those that embrace informal, internal or tacit knowledge, such as discussion databases that store "know how".

(2) To improve knowledge access and transfer. Here the emphasis is on connectivity, access and transfer.
- Technologies such as video conferencing systems, document scanning end sharing tools and telecommunications networks are central.

(3) To enhance the knowledge environment, so that the environment is conductive to more effective knowledge creation, transfer and use. This involves tackling organizational norms and values as they relate to knowledge.
- Increase awareness on sharing knowledge embedded in client relationship and engagements.
- Provide awards for contributions to the organization's structured knowledge base.
- Implement decision audit programs in order to assess whether and how employees were applying knowledge in key decisions.
- Recognize that successful knowledge management is dependent upon structures and cultures.

(4) To manage knowledge as an asset, and to recognize the value of knowledge to an organization.

---

① Rowley, Jennifer. "What is Knowledge Management?" *Library Management*. V. 20, No. 8 (1999): pp. 416 – 419.
② Davenport, Thomas H., DeLong, D. W., and Beers, M. C. "Successful Knowledge Management Projects." *Sloan Management Review*. V. 39, No. 2 (1998): pp. 43 – 57.

Others, however, sought to take a process view to define knowledge management. For example, Jan Duffy defines it as "a process that drives innovation by capitalizing on organizational intellect and experience"[①]. Gartner Group defines it as "a discipline that promotes an integrated and collaborative approach to the process of information asset creation, capture, organization, access and use"[②].

Below is a set of knowledge management processes proposed by P. Galagan:[③]
- Generating new knowledge.
- Accessing knowledge from external sources.
- Representing knowledge in documents, databases, software and so forth.
- Embedding knowledge in processes, products, or services.
- Transferring existing knowledge around an organization.
- Using accessible knowledge in decision-making.
- Facilitating knowledge growth through culture and incentive.
- Measuring the value of knowledge assets and the impact of knowledge management.

From both the project perspectives and the operational processes described above we can gain a general understanding of the current scope and contents of knowledge management.

5. Knowledge management in libraries

While the business world is changing in the new knowledge economy and digital age, libraries of all types are undergoing drastic changes also. The new role of libraries in the 21st century needs to be as a learning and knowledge center for their users as well as the intellectual commons for their respective communities where, to borrow the phrase from the Keystone Principles, "people and ideas interact in both the real and virtual environments to expand learning and facilitate the creation of new knowledge."[④] As a learning organization, libraries should provide a strong leadership in knowledge management. Unlike those business organizations whose goal for knowledge management is for competitive advantage, libraries, with the exception of company libraries (which may be known or called corporate libraries, special libraries, or knowledge centers), most public, academic, and research libraries have a different orientation and value. Instead of competition, internal use only, and little sharing of knowledge with others outside, the most important mission of public, academic, and research libraries is to expand the access of knowledge for their users. Charged by this mission, libraries should aim their knowledge management goal high. Below are examples of what libraries can do to improve their knowledge management in all the key areas of library services.

5.1 Knowledge resources management

Because of the exponential growth in human knowledge in a variety of formats libraries need to develop their resources access and sharing strategies from printed to electronic and digital resources in concert with their mission and charges. Restricted by limited funding, staff, and space, libraries must carefully analyze the needs of their users and seek to develop cooperative acquisition plans to meet these needs. The changing concept from "ownership" to "access" and from "just in case" to "just in time" should be the goal of a sound resources development

---

① Dully, Jan. *Harvesting Experience: Reaping the Benefits of Knowledge.* Prairie Village, KS: ARMA International, 1999. Also from her article, "Knowledge Management: To be or not to be?" *Information Management Journal.* V. 34, No. 1 (Jan. 2000): pp. 64 – 67.

② Bair, Jim. "Knowledge Management is About Cooperation and Context." *Gartner Advisory Services Research Note.* May 14, 1999.

③ Galagan, P. "Smart Companies (Knowledge Management)." *Training and Development.* V. 51, No. 12 (1997): pp. 20 – 25.

④ On September 24 – 25, 1999, eighty academic library leaders met during a two-day Strategic Issues Forum of Academic Library Directors held in Keystone, Colorado, organized jointly by the Association of Research Libraries and OCLC. Three basic principles were declared as the expanded vision for libraries in the digital knowledge age of the 21sr century. The three principles are called the Keystone Principles.

strategy.

An integrated online public access catalog (OPAC) with both internal and external resources as well as printed and other formats of knowledge should be developed and maintained. Useful websites and knowledge sources should be regularly searched and selected from Internet and included in OPACs by hard links. A system of reviewing and updating of these resources should be performed.

Going beyond explicit knowledge, libraries should also develop means to capture all that tacit knowledge that is of importance to users and to the internal operation of libraries. Each of the web sites of libraries should serve as portals for all sources of selective and relevant knowledge and information whether explicit or tacit, whether on site or remote, and in all formats.

As a part of its knowledge management activities, Arthur Anderson Business Consulting has developed a highly useful web site: KnowledgeSpace. Three types of knowledge are provided by KnowledgeSpace. They are:[1]

> News—important company news and hot topics of interest to all staff members worldwide.
> Resources—contains "Global Best Practices", "Ask Network", and "Community Resources".
> Connections—for active interactions and discussion by special interest groups across organizational structure and departmental lines.

All information in the KnowledgeSpace is updated frequently and user feedbacks are encouraged. Libraries can develop their own types of KnowledgeSpace. Through each library's intranet, strategic planning documents, annual reports, team and department reports, council and committee minutes, statistical analyses, grant proposals, policies and procedures, operational manuals, "best practices", "lessons learned", internal announcements, library news of major events, personnel actions, training and staff development opportunities, etc. can be made available to all staff members.

5.2 Human resources management

A great amount of expert knowledge is possessed by library staff and users, both in and outside the libraries. In university and research communities such expertise is abundant and should be inventoried, indexed, and updated regularly and be made searchable and accessible through electronic databases created and maintained by libraries.

The knowledge and accumulated experiences of library staff members form the intellectual assets of any library and should be valued and shared. An organizational culture for sharing of knowledge and expertise should be established with appropriate rewards and incentives. Those staff members who share their tacit knowledge and experiences through writing, publishing, lecturing, or mentoring should be appropriately recognized and rewarded. An organizational culture which emphasizes cooperation, sharing, and innovation can only be established by a strong leadership and commitment from the library director and a shared vision by the library staff.

As a learning organization, libraries should allocate annual funding to provide continuing education and staff training to all staff members. Knowledge must be renewed and expanded to prevent it from becoming stagnant.

Libraries should also encourage the transfer of knowledge and experience from experienced staff to new staff members. A mentoring system should be in place to help newcomers to learn from experienced library staff. Informal seminars and brownbag sessions where staff can interact and exchange "lessons learned", "best practices" and other specific experience and knowledge should be scheduled at regular intervals and at convenient times. Special interest groups and chat rooms can be created through intranet.

Since many valuable experiences have been accumulated over time, libraries should pay attention to favorable working conditions and environment, which will contribute to better staff

---

[1] *Arthur Anderson Business Consulting*. The First Book on Knowledge Management, translated into Chinese by Liu Jin-Wei. Taipei: San Chou Publisher, 2000: p. vi – vii. (In Chinese)

retention.

5.3 Resources sharing and networking

Libraries have had a long tradition for resources sharing and networking. These have been greatly expanded by the rapid development of computer, telecommunication, networking, and digital technologies since the 1960s. It is very common for libraries to be a member in several consortia at the same time for various types of cooperative work and resources sharing. The best examples of these are the OCLC Online Computer Library Center and OhioLINK (Ohio Library and Information Network).

The CORC (Cooperative Online Resource Catalog) project based on the Dublin Core Metadata of OCLC should be especially useful for libraries to cooperatively capture digital resources of all types, describe them in a standard format, and make them easily searchable by users.

5.4 Information technology development

To facilitate the implementation of knowledge management, a well-designed and operational knowledge management system should be in place. Latest information technology should be used as an enabler.

Intranet technology should be used to support knowledge management efforts via shared documents/products and the gathering and publication of lessons learned and best practices. Internet functions should also be used for knowledge exchange with users, resource persons (faculty, researchers, and subjects specialists, etc.), publishers, government agencies, businesses and industries, and other organizations.

5.5 User services

Knowing your users should come first. This information can be gathered from statistical analysis of user registration databases, circulation and interlibrary loan records, most frequently asked reference questions, telephone and email services, use of electronic journals and digital resources, etc. These should be done without invading the privacy of individual library users.

Libraries have collected a great amount of user information and statistics for reporting purpose but have seldom used them to improve user services. Now, by means of the "push" technology, libraries can provide a variety of tailored-made services to suit individual needs. Many of the personalized services already offered by e-commerce should be a good model for libraries. User satisfaction and needs should be collected through periodic user's surveys. The findings should be used for the planning and redesign of library services.

6. Conclusion

Although knowledge management has become one of the latest management buzzwords, whether it will fade away, or not, just as some of the other buzzwords before it, will depend on how we make it work. In the business world, knowledge management has been regarded as strategically important for organizations to gain a competitive advantage over their competitors, to add value to their products, and to win greater satisfaction of their customers. In the library world, there is a lesson to be learned from the business world. Knowledge management is as important for libraries as for the businesses minus the competitive, proprietary, and moneymaking concerns. In fact, libraries have a long and rich experience in the management of explicit knowledge. Now we need to extend our know—how to the management of tacit knowledge as well. For any libraries to succeed in implementing knowledge management will require a strong leadership and vision from the top administration, which can influence the organization's knowledge sharing efforts in a positive way. As libraries enter the knowledge age of the 21st century, we should not take a back seat in the development of knowledge management. Instead, armed by our professional knowledge and experiences, we should be in the driver's seat.

Furthermore, knowledge management should never be viewed as a way to control the process of knowledge creation. In his book, Enabling Knowledge Creation, Georg Von Krogh et al made a strong argument for supporting knowledge creation rather than controlling it. In the process of knowledge creation, every library should strive to be an enabler and facilitator by mobilizing all its efforts and resources.①

In the effort to support, strengthen, and advance the intellectual and cultural foundation of our society, the strategic direction of libraries should be twofold: to actively and aggressively support and encourage access to and the creative use of all forms of knowledge; and to serve both as catalysts and participants in the intellectual process that transforms data into information, information into knowledge, and knowledge into wisdom.

[Published in *New Technology of Library and Information Service* (《现代图书情报技术》), S1, 2002: 13-17.]

---

① Von Krogh, Georg, Ichijo, Kazuo, and Nonaka, Ikujiro. *Enabling Knowledge Creation: How to Unlock the Mystery of Tacit Knowledge and Release the Power of Innovation*. New York: Oxford University Press, 2000.

快速变化中的图书馆：资讯管理对知识管理

Libraries in Rapid Transition:
Information Management vs. Knowledge Management[①]

Libraries in Rapid Transition
> "Change is the normal rather than the exception."
> However, the speed of change has been accelerated at an unprecedented rate in recent decades.
> This has happened in libraries too.

We get sucked into the patterns of behavior that have produced success for us in the past, not realizing that it may no longer be appropriate for us in the fast-moving present and future.

New directions for the Libraries
> Actively and aggressively support and encourage access to and the creative use of recorded knowledge in all formats.
> Serve both as catalyst and participant in the intellectual process that transform information into knowledge and knowledge into wisdom.
> Support, strengthen, and advance the intellectual and cultural foundation of our society.
Adapted from Dr. James Billington, The Librarian of the Library of Congress

The digital and knowledge age of the 21st century
> Today we live in a highly competitive world, everything is knowledge-based.
> Peter Drucker said: "More and more, the productivity of knowledge is going to become, for a country, an industry, or a company, the determining competitiveness factor."
(Peter Drucker. *Post-capitalism Society*. Oxford: Butterworth-Heinemann, 1993.)

Where are libraries in this new age?
> Capturing, organizing, and preserving the knowledge asset and its creative use are critically important for every organization, enterprise, as well as library.
> The rapid expansion of Internet and Web and their widespread use have moved libraries into the digital and knowledge age.

Great Advantages of Internet
> Its global reach has six key advantages:
1. A cost-effective global network backbone.
2. Anytime, anywhere.
3. Distributed connectivity.
4. Robust global data path.
5. Easy access to the world of information.
6. Ability to handle a variety of formats and is platform independent.

---

① This PPT was presented at the *International Conference on Challenges and Opportunities for Libraries and Information Professionals in Knowledge Management and the Digital Age*, 20 – 22 March 2003, Chiang Mai, Thailand. Organized by Department of Library Science, Faculty of Humanities, Chiang Mai University, Chiang Mai, Thailand, 2003.

Do you know how many Internet hosts there are?
> 8/1981   213
> 1/1991   376,000
> 1/1996   9,472,000
> 1/2001   109,574,429
> 1/2003   171,638,297
> 1/2005   317,646,084
> 1/2007   433,193,199

Source: http://www.isc.org/ds/host-count-history.html

What is the digital world like?
> E-books, e-journals, and e-publishing
> E-commerce, e-banking, e-finance, and e-trade
> E-communication and e-mails
> E-education and e-learning
> E-entertainment and e-games
> E-government, e-citizen, and e-society
> E-news and e-information
> E-libraries
> E-everything...

The traditional role of libraries
> The management of information has long been regarded as the domain of librarians and libraries.
> Librarians and information professionals are trained to be experts in information searching, selecting, acquiring, organizing, preserving, making them available to users.

The role has now been challenged
> Because of the recent advances in information technology and systems which drive and underpin information management, professionals in the IT & IS fields have also regarded information management as their domain.
> Most of the "Chief Information Officer" positions are now held by information technologists instead of librarians.

Key questions faced by librarians
> In the light of growing interest in knowledge management, many questions have surfaced:
✓ Difference between information and knowledge.
✓ Difference between information management and knowledge management.
✓ Who should be the "Chief Knowledge Officer" of an organization?
✓ Should libraries reposition themselves from information management to knowledge management?

What is Information?
Information is data that has been organized and communicated.
(Marc Porat. *The Information Economy: Definition and Measurement.* Washington, D.C.: U.S. Department of Commerce, Office of Telecommunication, 1977.)

The Information Explosion
John Naisbitt put it—
"We are drowning in a sea of information and starving for knowledge."

What is Knowledge?

Knowledge is a set of organized statements of facts or ideas, presenting a reasoned judgment or an experimental result, which is transmitted to others through some communication medium in some systematic form.

(Daniel Bell. *The Coming of Post-industrial Society: A Venture in Social Forecasting.* New York: Basic Books, 1973.)

Another Description of Knowledge

> Knowledge is a fluid mix of framed experience, values, contextual information, and expert insight that provides a framework for evaluating and incorporating new experiences and information.

> It originates and is applied in the minds of knower.

> In organizations, it often becomes embedded not only in documents or repositories but also in organizational routines, processes, practices, and norms.

(Thomas H. Davenport & Laurence Prusak. *Working Knowledge.* Boston: Harvard Business School Press, 1998: p. 5.)

The process of knowledge creation

It is "a continuum where data transforms into information, information transforms into knowledge and knowledge drives and underpins behavior and decision-making".

(Stephen Abram. "Post information age positioning for special librarians: Is knowledge management the answer?" *Information Outlook* (June 1997): 20-21.)

Data, information, knowledge, and wisdom

> Data: A set of discrete, objective facts about events.

> Information: Selected, organized and analyzed data with relevance and purpose.

> Knowledge: Information combined with user's ability and experience and is used to solve a problem or to create new knowledge.

> Wisdom: Forward looking and thinking based on one's values and commitment.

Difference between Information & Knowledge

> Information	> Knowledge
Visible	Invisible
Independent from action and decision	Closely related to action and decision
Format changes after processing	Thought changes after processing
Physical product	Spiritual product
Independent from existing environment	Identified with existing environment
Easily transferable	Transfer through learning
Can be duplicated	Can't be duplicated

What is knowledge management?

> It may begin with data and information management but goes beyond the two.

> It is also much broader in scope than information technology and systems.

> It is the process in which relevant and useful knowledge is identified, organized, merged, synthesized, and used creatively.

A simple definition of knowledge management

Gartner Group defines it as——A discipline that promotes an integrated approach to identifying, capturing, evaluating, retrieving and sharing all of an enterprise's information assets.

(Jim Bair. "Knowledge management is about cooperation and context." *Gartner Advisory Services Research Note*. May 14, 1999.)

Another definition

Library science is—A discipline that promotes an integrated approach to identifying, capturing, evaluating, retrieving and sharing all of **a society's knowledge and** information assets.

Why is knowledge management needed now?

> Exponential growth in human knowledge.

> The fast expansion of Internet and World Wide Web enabling the dissemination and access of a growing body of digital information and knowledge.

> The recognition of the importance of both **explicit** and **tacit** knowledge to an organization.

> In the knowledge age organizations, especially those in the business sector, are trying to capitalize on their organizational intelligence to maintain their competitive edge.

> Changing concept from **knowledge is power** to **knowledge sharing is power**

> Librarians, armed with our professional knowledge and experiences, should not take a back seat in the movement toward KM. Instead, we should be in the driver's seat.

What are the differences between explicit and tacit knowledge?

> Explicit knowledge—
Is documented and public.
Is structured, fixed-content, externalized, and conscious.

> Tacit knowledge—
are personal, undocumented, context-sensitive, dynamically-created and derived, internalized, and experience-based.
often resides in the human mind, behavior, and perception.

(Jan Duffy. "Knowledge management: to be or not to be?" *Information Management Journal*. V. 34 No. 1 (Jan. 2000): 64 - 67.)

"All knowledge exists on a continuum between tacit knowledge and explicit knowledge."

Tacit Knowledge Transfer

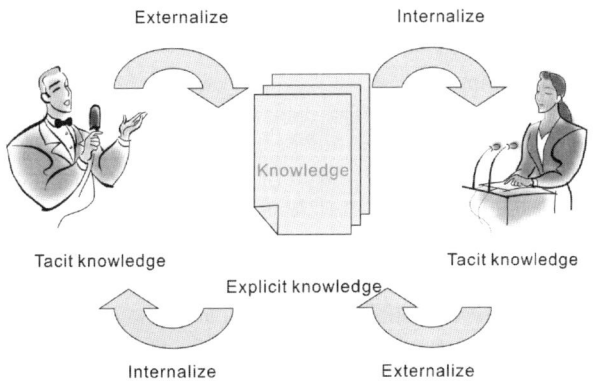

Knowledge interaction flow

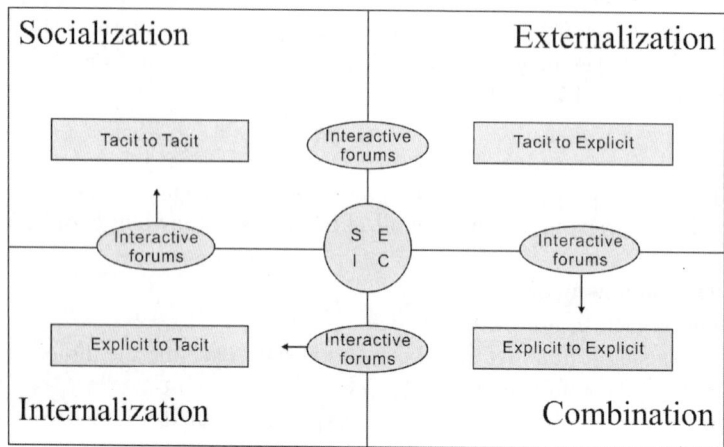

Relationship between libraries and knowledge management
> As a learning organization, libraries should provide a strong leadership in KM.
> Unlike those business organizations whose goal of KM is for competitive advantage, most public, academic and research libraries have a different orientation and value.
> The most important mission of public, academic and research libraries is to expand the access of knowledge for their users.

Similarities between KM and IM
> Selection and filtering
> Search and retrieval
> Archiving and indexing
> Cataloging and Classification *
> Ordering and integration
> Use and sharing
> Analysis and evaluation
(* IT people call this taxonomy, knowledge map, ontology, or categorization.)

Differences between KM and IM

> Knowledge management	> Information management
Focus on knowledge renewal and creation	Focus on information organization
Action oriented	Prefer static objects
People-and customer-centered	Document-and information centered
Emphasis on utilization and sharing	Emphasis on processing and preserving
Add value to knowledge resource	External orderliness

What are the achievable KM activities in libraries?
> We will look at each of the following areas:
✓ Library organization and leadership
✓ Knowledge resources management
✓ Resources sharing and networking

✓ Information technology development
  ✓ User services
  ✓ Human resources management

Library Organization and Leadership
  > Library administrators should take the **leadership** role in implementing KM both-
  ✓ Within the library, and
  ✓ extending to the parent organization.
  > Establish a **planning team** to design, plan, and implement KM within the library.
  > Work with senior executives of the parent organization to design, plan, and implement an **organization-wide** KM.
  > Establish **vision, strategies** and goals for implementing KM.
  > **Align** the KM vision and strategies to the organization's mission and management.
  > Build an **organizational culture** that will encourage knowledge sharing and team work.
  > Take **incremental steps** to implement KM.

Knowledge resources management
  > **Inventory** the existing information and knowledge depositories within the library and the parent organization.
  > Survey and analyze the **needs of users**.
  > Develop resources access strategies from printed to electronic and digital resources in concert with a library's mission and charges.
  > Change from **ownership** to *access* and from **just in case** to **just in time**.
  > Go beyond **explicit** knowledge.
  > Develop means to capture **tacit** knowledge.
  > Use the library web site to serve as a **portal** for all sources of selective and relevant knowledge and information whether explicit or tacit, whether on site or remote, and in all formats.
  > Universities and research organizations are themselves knowledge sources and reservoirs. A great amount of expert knowledge is possessed by people inside and outside of each library.
  > This knowledge should be inventoried, indexed, and updated regularly and be made searchable and accessible through electronic databases created and maintained by each library.
  > The traditional, time-honored methods of cataloging and classification are barely adequate to handle the finite number of books, journals, and documents, but are inadequate to deal with the almost infinite amount of digital information in large electronic databases and on the Internet.
  > Using the Dublin Core metadata for cooperative cataloging of online resources has been a new approach to capture Web information by cooperative efforts.
  > Other new methods have been a part of recent developments in knowledge management systems:
  ✓ Data mining, text mining, content management, linguistic analysis, etc.
  ✓ Search engines, natural language searching, knowledge extraction, etc.
  ✓ Information visualization such as the two-dimensional or three-dimensional knowledge mapping, etc.
  (Hsinchun Chen. *Knowledge Management Systems: A Text Mining Perspective*. Tucson, AZ: Univ. of Arizona, 2001.)

Resource sharing and networking
  > Libraries have had a long tradition of resource sharing and networking.
  > These have been greatly expanded by the rapid advances in computer, telecommunication, networking, and digital technologies.
  > Best examples on resource sharing and networking by libraries are:
  ✓ OCLC Online Computer Library Center

✓ OhioLINK (Ohio Library and Information Network)
> Important factors for success:
✓ The full commitment to cooperation by participating libraries.
✓ Demonstrated leadership from large and major libraries.
✓ Strong support in policies and funding from the government or parent organizations. Good executive director.

Information technology development

> The latest information technology should be used as an enabler to create well-designed and operational knowledge management systems.

> In a networked environment, maximum connectivity, compatibility and interoperability should be considered among cooperating libraries.

> Library director should play the role of CKO (Chief Knowledge Officer) of the entire organization.

> Providing leadership in coordinating with others: CIO, the heads of the planning, computer and IT, human resources management, and finance departments, etc.

> **Intranet** technology should be used to support KM efforts for sharing internal knowledge such as the best practices, lessons learned, and other news and communication.

> **Internet** functions should be used for knowledge exchange with users and others.

KM Architecture and Design

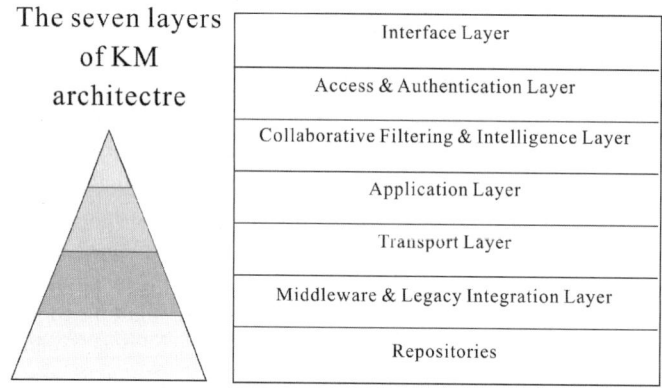

The seven layers of KM architectre

- Interface Layer
- Access & Authentication Layer
- Collaborative Filtering & Intelligence Layer
- Application Layer
- Transport Layer
- Middleware & Legacy Integration Layer
- Repositories

User services

> The utmost goal of KM is to provide users with a variety of quality services in order to improve the communication, use, and creation of knowledge.

> These services should be tailored to the interest and needs of each user.

> Information about users can be gathered from:
✓ Analysis of the registration and survey data of users.
✓ Circulation and interlibrary loan records.
✓ Most frequently asked reference questions.
✓ Telephone and e-mail services.
✓ Use of electronic journals and digital resources.

> Users can also set up their own virtual "MyLibrary" for collecting and organizing resources for personal use and to stay informed of new resources provided by the library.

> MyLibrary can empower each user to either search for content (the pull approach) or subscribe to content (the push approach).

Human resources management

> A great amount of expert knowledge is possessed by library staff and users, both in and outside of the library.

> In universities and research communities such expertise is abundant and should be made searchable and accessible through the library's KM system.

> The knowledge and experiences of library staff are the intellectual assets of any library and should be valued and shared.

> An organizational culture for sharing of knowledge and expertise should be cultivated with appropriate rewards and incentives.

> Such an organizational culture can only be established by a strong leadership and commitment from the library director and a shared vision of the library staff.

> As a learning organization, opportunities for continuing education and training should be provided for all staff members.

> Knowledge must be renewed and expanded to prevent it from becoming stagnant.

> Libraries should also encourage the transfer of knowledge and experience from experienced staff to new staff members.

✓ Mentoring system for new staff.
✓ Informal seminars and brownbag sessions.
✓ Sharing *lessons learned*, *best practices*, etc.
✓ Intranet special interest groups and chat rooms.

> Using annual performance evaluation and other methods to recognize and reward that staffs who shares their tacit knowledge and experience through writing, publishing, lecturing, mentoring, or in team work.

Basic requirements for successful implementation of KM

> **Leadership**: "knowledge evangelists" should be created in the organization.

> **Communication**: It is important to keep KM in front of the employees.

> **Reward and Recognition**: A frequently overlooked aspect, it is an important motivator.

> **Infrastructure**: No KM system will work without an in-house infrastructure to store and transfer information.

> **Education/Learning**: Training is essential to build a KM culture in an organization.

(Todd Kulik. *Knowledge Management: Becoming an E-Learning Organization*. New York: The Conference Board, 2000: p. 5.)

Conclusion

> To stay **competitive** and **innovative** in the knowledge age, all organizations including libraries must effectively and efficiently create, locate, capture, share their **organizational knowledge**, and bring that knowledge to bear on new problems and opportunities in a timely manner.

> The best knowledge creators are academics. Knowledge creation is best performed by universities.

> As a learning and knowledge organization, universities should empower their libraries to develop campus-wide knowledge management systems.

Questions and Discussion

Thank you!

大学图书馆实行知识管理的新理念

Implementing the New Concept of Knowledge Management in University Libraries

什么是管理？
What is management?
管理是与他人合作或通过他人来具体实现组织及其成员目标的活动。
» It is working with and through other people to accomplish the goals and objectives of both the organization and its members.

管理的五项职能
Five Management Functions
» 计划。
» 组织。
» 人力资源和财力资源的管理。
» 领导，协调和实施。
» 评估与改进。

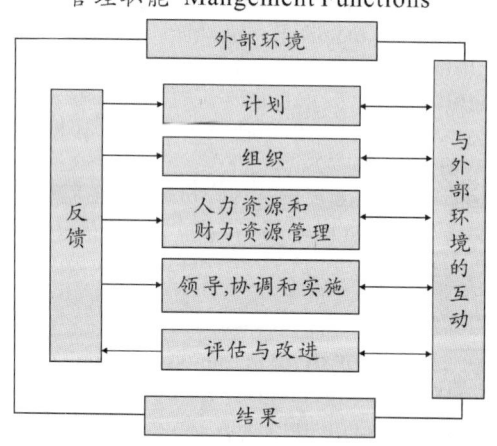

管理职能 Mangement Functions

有效的管理工具
Effective management practices
» 目标管理（MBO）—战略规划
» 参与式管理（PM）
» 全质量管理（TQM）
» 知识管理（KM）

---

① 本文系作者于 2010 年 6 月 1-3 日在上海"全球化视野·大学图书馆馆长论坛"上的讲演文稿。

知识管理
Knowledge management

如今，我们生活在一个高度竞争的世界，一切都以知识为基础。

彼得·德鲁克说："知识生产力将日益成为一个国家、产业或公司竞争力的决定性因素。"

——彼得·德鲁克（Peter Drucker）．后资本主义社会（*Post-capitalism Society*）．牛津（Oxford）：Butterworth-Heinemann 出版公司，1993．

新时期图书馆的定位
Where are libraries in this new age?

》获取、组织、保存知识资产并对其进行创造性的使用，对于每个组织、企业都至关重要，对图书馆也是如此。

》因特网和网络的迅速发展及其广泛应用把图书馆推进到数字和知识时代。

图书馆的传统角色
The traditional role of libraries

》信息管理长期以来被视为图书馆员和图书馆的领域。

》图书馆员和信息专业人员被训练为信息搜集、选择、获取、组织、保存并使其能够成为用户使用的专家。

图书馆的传统角色受到了挑战
The role has now been challenged

》信息技术和信息系统既是信息管理的基础，也是推动信息管理进步和发展的动力。由于信息技术和信息系统近年来的发展，信息技术和信息系统领域的专家也将信息管理视为自己的研究领域。

》目前，"信息主管"的职位大都由信息技术专家担任，而不是由图书馆专家担任。

图书馆员面临的主要问题
Key questions faced by librarians

随着人们对知识管理的日益关注，许多问题已经浮出水面：

》信息与知识的区别

》信息管理与知识管理的区别

》谁应该是组织的"知识主管"？

》图书馆是否应该为自己重新定位，从信息管理转向知识管理？

知识的创造过程
The process of knowledge creation

知识的创造是一个"由数据转变为信息，信息转变为知识，知识驱动和支持人的行为和决策的连续不断的过程。"

——斯蒂芬·艾布拉姆（Sthphen Abram）．"后信息时代为专业图书馆员定位：知识管理就是答案吗？"（"Post information age positioning for special librarians: Is knowledge management the answer?"). 信息展望(*Information Outlook*),（1997年6月）(June, 1997), 20 – 21.

数据、信息、知识、智慧
Data, information, knowledge and wisdom
- 数据：是一组不连续的关于事件的客观事实。
- 信息：是经过选择、组织和分析的具有相关性和目的性的数据。
- 知识：是信息与个人的能力和经验结合起来，用于解决问题或创造新的知识。
- 智慧：是建立在个人特定价值观和责任感基础上的前瞻性的思想。

信息与知识的区别
Difference between information and knowledge

信 息	知 识
» 有形的	» 无形的
» 独立于行动和决策	» 与行动和决策紧密联系
» 经过处理后形态发生改变	» 经过处理后思想发生改变
» 物质产品	» 精神产品
» 独立于现实环境	» 与现实环境相统一
» 易传递	» 须经过学习才能传递
» 可复制	» 不可复制

什么是知识管理？
What is knowledge management?
- 知识管理虽可始于数据管理和信息管理，但超越数据管理和信息管理。
- 知识管理在范围上也比信息技术和信息系统要宽泛得多。
- 知识管理是一个对相关有用知识进行识别、组织、融合、综合和创造使用的过程。

知识管理的简单定义
A simple definition of KM

Gartner 集团对知识管理的定义：

知识管理是一门学问。它使用一个整合统一的处理过程，促成个别企业内所有信息资产的识别、获取、评价、检索与共享。

——吉姆·拜尔（Jim Bair）. 知识管理是合作与文件（"Knowledge management is about cooperation and context,"）. Garter 集团咨询服务研究笔记（*Gartner Advisory Services Research Note*）. 1999. 5. 14.（May 14, 1999）

图书馆对知识管理的定义
Definition of KM by library

图书馆对知识管理的定义：

知识管理是一门学问。它使用一个整合统一的处理过程，促成全社会所有信息资产的识别、获取、评价、检索与共享。

现在为什么需要知识管理？（1）
Why is knowledge management needed now?
» 人类知识以指数速度爆炸性增长。
» 因特网和万维网的迅速发展使人类能够对不断增长的数字化信息和知识进行传播和存取。
» 显性知识和隐形知识对组织的重要性得到社会的公认。

显性知识与隐形知识的区别
Difference between explicit and tacit knowledge
显性知识
» 是公开的，记录的知识。
» 是结构性的、内容固定的、具体化的及有意识的。
隐形知识
» 是个人的、非记录的、内在的、基于自身体验的知识。
» 常常存在于人的意识、行为和感觉之中。
——简·达菲（Jan Duffy）. 知识管理：存在还是不存在？（"Knowledge management：to be or not to be？"）. 信息管理杂志，2000，1（34）：64－67. [*Information Management Journal*. V.34, No.1 (Jan. 2000): 64－67]

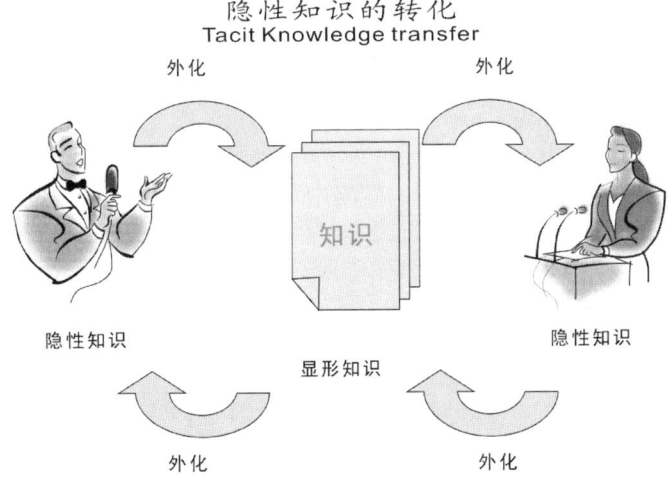

现在为什么需要知识管理（2）
Why is knowledge management needed now?
» 在知识时代，组织，尤其是商业组织，都力图利用组织的智力来保持自己的竞争优势。
» "知识就是力量"这一观念正在转变为"知识共享就是力量"。
» 图书馆员拥有我们图书馆学专业知识和专业经验的优势，在走向知识管理的过程中，我们不应该走在后面，而应该成为知识管理的先行者。

知识管理与信息管理的相同点
Similarities between KM and IM

- 选择与过滤
- 搜集与检索
- 存档与标引
- 编目与分类*
- 整序与整合
- 利用与共享
- 分析与评价

＊IT（信息技术）界人士称之为 taxonomy（分类学），knowledge map（知识地图），ontology（本体论，机会模型）或 categorization（归类）。

信息管理与知识管理的区别
Differences between IM and KM

信息管理	知识管理
» 关注信息组织	» 关注知识更新与创新
» 倾向于静态对象	» 面向行动
» 以文献和信息为中心	» 以人与用户为中心
» 强调加工和保存	» 强调利用和共享
» 外部形态的整合	» 知识资源的增值

图书馆的组织与领导（1）
Library organization and leadership

- 图书馆的管理者应该在知识管理的实施中承担起领导者的角色：
  - ✓ 不但在图书馆内部实施知识管理，
  - ✓ 还应将知识管理延伸到上级组织之中。
- 组建规划小组，负责馆内知识管理的设计、规划及实施。
- 会同上级组织行政主管设计、规划和实施在整个组织范围内的知识管理。

图书馆的组织与领导（2）
Library organization and leadership

- 为知识管理的实施建立愿景、战略和目标。
- 使知识管理愿景和战略，与组织的任务和组织的管理相一致。
- 塑造鼓励知识共享和团队合作的组织文化。
- 采取渐进措施实施知识管理。

知识资源管理（1）
Knowledge resources management

- 大学和研究机构本身就是知识资源和知识库。大学和研究机构图书馆的馆员和读者拥有大量的专业知识。
>> 大学和研究机构的这些知识资源需要定期地进行调查、整理、编目、标引和更新，使其能够通过各图书馆建立和维护的电子数据库进行检索和存取。
>> 根据用户需求主动向用户提供知识。

知识资源管理（2）
Knowledge resources management
图书馆传统的分类和编目方法久享盛誉，但其仅适用于处理有限的图书、期刊和档案，而对大型电子数据库和因特网上几乎是无限的数字信息的处理则难以应付。

知识资源管理（3）
Knowledge resources management
下面这些新的信息处理手段是近年来在知识管理系统中开发的：
>> 数据挖掘、文本挖掘、内容管理、语义分析等。
>> 搜索引擎、自然语言搜索、知识提取等。
>> 信息可视化处理，如二维或三维知识地图的绘制等。
——陈与春（Hsinchun Chen 的音译）. 知识管理系统：一个文本挖掘的视角（*Knowledge Management Systems：A Text Mining Perspective*）. 亚利桑那州图来市（Tucson AZ）：亚利桑那大学（Univ. of Arizona），2001.

信息技术的发展（1）
Development of information technology
>> 最新的信息技术应该应用于创建设计优良、便于操作的知识管理系统。
>> 在网络环境下，具有业务合作关系的图书馆之间，业务运作应考虑最大的连通性、兼容性和协同操作能力这些问题。

信息技术的发展（2）
Development of information technology
>> 内部网技术应该用于对致力于内部知识共享的知识管理的支持。内部知识包括经验、教训、其他消息和需要相互沟通的内容等。
>> 互联网的功能应该用于同用户以及其他人员或机构的知识交流。

图书馆网站的发展
Developing Library Website
>> 建立联机原始资料和知识库
>> 提供在线参考咨询服务：
✓ 图书馆网站上电子邮件
✓ 询问图书馆员
✓ 使用 QuestionPoint
>> 使用"同时发送信息"服务 RSS（Really Simple Syndication）feeds：Webcasts 视频，Podcasts 播客，Blog 博客，and YouTube 等。

关于知识管理的结论
Conclusion

在知识经济时代，为了保持竞争力和创新活力，包括图书馆在内的一切组织都必须有效且高效率地组织、整理、获取和共享其组织知识，及时运用这些知识解决新的问题，把握新的机遇。

（原载《全球化视野·大学图书馆馆长论坛2010会务手册》，上海财经大学图书馆，2010年）

衡量图书馆的服务品质

Measuring Library Service Quality: The LibQUAL + Tool[①]

In recent year, I think that there has been real interest in finding a good tool to measure or assess a library's performance. This also increases pressure for libraries to move toward Outcome-based assessment instead of relying merely on input/output or resources metrics. For many years the association of research libraries in the United States. Publishes every year a rate order of research libraries in the United States. The one tool of research libraries in the United States receive many criticisms because what they measure as the ability of the library is based on the member of volumes the size of your collection, the annual budget of the library, the number of staff you have, the number in the addition of new books, and the number of periodicals you prescribe to.

These are the so-called input dismetrics to determine the ranking of major research libraries in the United States and include Canada. So the research library association members for several years were thinking to try to find something more commensurate in determining the rank of research libraries. So what I am talking about today, is the LibQUAL + Tool is one of the tools which have been developed to be used to measure library service quality. Earlier I mentioned the common methods of assessment. Many way and methods have been used for assessing library performance. The most common one is compiling and comparing library statistic, and inputs/outputs, the resources. Many libraries also undertake user surveys at regular intervals such as every three or five years. My library, Ohio University, has done a user survey every four years in order to get some feedback from the user in regard to our performance. But the one short coming of this is that we don't have enough sense to compare with other peer institutions.

We do a user survey. It's just for our library, so we can only use the results of this year to compare with the results of last year to get a comparison but we cannot compare our performance with other libraries of similar size. Another method being used for assessment is organizing focus group meetings. Many libraries have done this by convening a group of faculty, graduate students as undergraduate students to meet for lunch or a pizza party to get their feedback about their perceived performance of the library. Also we have been analyzing feedback from the suggestion box as are found in many libraries for users to put in complaints on suggestions into the box, so we can find out if we need to do something to improve or correct our services.

And also, because Americans universities go through periodic accreditation revues every ten years, or if you are a new program you may have to be revues every three years till you get a ten year approval so you don't have to do it every 3 – 4 years—you do it every 10 years, but prior to doing this accreditation revue, normally the university will spend a whole year doing a self-study in great detail and then submit the results of the self-study to the agencies doing the accreditation, and then they will send a team to come to spend several days in your university to look at everything you have done in terms of your self-study, which they consider an important component in the type of revue. Also the university, itself, has conducted surveys of both current students and others who had left the university in the past. We do a follow-up with these former students every 5 or 10 years to see how the students perceive the education they received from the university. Normally this will include a number of questions, library related, so we can get feedback from this kind of university conducted surveys.

[①] Present at the International Conference *on Challenges and Opportunities for Libraries and Information Professionals in Knowledge Management and the Digital Age*, 20 – 22 March 2003, Chiang Mai, Thailand. Organized by Department of Library Science, Faculty of Humanities, Chiang Mai University, Chiang Mai, Thailand, 2003: pp. 122 – 128.

What to measure—input. That is what we get and mentioned earlier; the annual budget, the number of books purchased, the number of journals subscribed to.

Next is process—how we process, how many books we cull out in comparison to how many we acquired. Output—what kind of outcome have we received from the input and the process. These are basic system models many libraries have used for years to measure their performance. Now we are interested in measuring the outcomes and the impact. What kind I impact we have been able to get through the performance. The American Institute that we see on the server, this is a government agency and to oversee the general policies and trends of library and museum service in the United States. The Institute defines all kinds of benefits or changes for individuals or populations during or after participation in program activities including new knowledge, increased skills, changed attitudes or values, modified behaviors, improved conditions or altered status. It defines all kinds of changes taking place after you have participated in the program activities.

American research libraries, social research libraries. Several years ago they decided to study different methods of self-evaluation, so there are several projects, including higher education all kinds of research revue investigation of course drivers like technical service calls studies, assessing inter-library loans, document delivery services and also e-metrics including measures for electronic resources. In addition to these 4 projects, one project has received most attention—is the LibQUAL and project. This is one of the key projects of the association for research libraries and responds to the need for measuring all kinds of performance, either input or output.

The LibQUAL + survey instruments pertains to major user perceptions of library service quality, and to identify gaps between desired, perceived and minimum expectations of service. This is an interesting concept. To measure library service quality, who is the last one to do such things? The customers, the users of the library services should be the best ones to make judgements about the quality of a libraries service, so they decided to use a tool which was developed in business and industry back in the 1970's called the SERVQUAL and then modify it according to a library's need to become a library tool LibQUAL. The LibQUAL tried to base on users perception of the desired level of service desired and what is the minimum level of service acceptable, and then between the two, or even above or below these, what is the current status of the perceived expectation.

Later I will explain how to measure the gaps between these 3 different types of perceptions in order to arrive at the quality service measurements of the library service.

Before I mentioned some measurements call LibQUAL which is grounded in the gap theory of service quality demanded by three marketing professors of business in schools back in the 70's and have been used very widely in the business and community.

Judgement by customers—I think that these 3 professors felt that only customers judge quality. All other judgements are essentially irrelevant. Only the customer / user are able to give the best judgement in terms of quality of performance. The concept of service quality was advances by marketing experts in the 70's. And then in the 80's this method was applied to total quality management GPM, but Peter Hernon and Ellen Altman were the two to first introduce the service quality measurement into the library in the 1990's.

What is quality? This was defined: there are 4 elements of quality. The first one is excellence; the second one is value; the third one is conformance to specifications; the fourth is meeting or exceeding expectations.

There are the 4 dimensions of quality which we try to measure. What is service quality? For libraries, service quality applies to 4 general areas. The first one I think we all probably agree is access to information; the second is the affect of service; the third is the library as a place; the fourth one is personal control—the user control of their knowledge needs.

Each of these consists of a number of variables which encompass 10 elements of service quality. Let's take a look at these 10 elements. The first one is reliability; the second one is responsiveness; third is the competence; fourth is access; fifth is courtesy; the sixth is communication; the seventh is credibility; eight is security; ninth is understanding; tenth is tangible. So these are the major elements by which we measure service quality. From the library point of view, we can see that for the affect of service which included empathy, responsiveness, assurance, reliability. For the information access estimation including performance kindness, physical location, comprehensive collections. For personal control includes ease of navigation, convenience, modern equipment. In terms of measure of library as place—we look at utilitarian space, space which is available and spacious. Symbols of the internet, lethargy where we can go just go to reflect and to do quiet study. All of these elements should be included in the development of tools to measure library service quality.

In terms of the affect of service—this emerged as the key element, the dominant factor. Everybody felt that the affect of service was very important. This also absorbed several of the SERVQUAL questions measuring responsiveness, assurance and empathy. In the 2002 analysis added reliability into this dimension of measurement. All in all the human dimension of service quality talks about the human dimension of the service quality. In terms of access to information, and we have several considerations here. In terms of the library as a place, in the idea of the library as a campus center for intellectual activities. Also, as long as physical facilities are adequate, the library as a place may not be an issue. If you have good new facilities, this may not be an important concern in the quality of service.

Personal control—how user interacted with the modern library. Personal control of the information universe in general and web navigation in particular.

The basic design of LibQUAL intends to measure library users' perception of service quality (I mentioned about trying to measure that gaps between desired, perceived, and minimal expectations of service). This diagram shows you—we tried to let users indicate his perception of level of desired services—his or her perception of minimal level of service expected. And then the users' perception of the level of service being offered by the library.

Between these 3 levels of perception we measure the gaps, using the gaps to determine the quality of library service. Texas A&M University's libraries was the first one to make use of SERVQUAL instrument to measure library service quality for several years and with the cooperation of Texas A&M University and the associations of research libraries, modified from the SERVQUAL instrument to suit the library needs.

The goal of LibQUAL plus, first was to establish a library service quality assessment program at ARL (Assoc. of Research Libraries) develop web-based tools for assessing library service quality, developing mechanisms and protocols for evaluating libraries and identification of best practice in providing library service. I want to explain a little about these few points. In the past when libraries do a survey of this kind, they do it manually, so we had to select samples-we sent out by mail or we delivered to faculty or students and users, for whom we select as samples to fill in the form, the questionnaire and send it back to the library and then the library will spend many man-hours to tabulate, to key into the computer and then tabulate them and then compile all the statistical analysis that resulted. But the LibQUAL, which is now available on the internet, so the design of the LibQUAL to reduce the human manual intervention as much as possible, so we use computers to reach the address of every student and faculty member. We select a sufficient number of samples. We send them the questionnaire by E-mail to the samples.

The sample person that receives the questionnaire would fill in (reply) the questionnaire electronically and then send back, not to the library but to a processing center established by Texas A&M. The processing center will use a computer program to analyze all the returns and then mechanically analyze, to produce the statistical data and then inform every participating library about their results. So all these are done automatically without much human intervention, so it makes this kind of survey much easier to administer and so you can do it every year. We used to have to wait 3, 4, or 5 years in order to conduct such a big scale survey.

Benefits of LibQUAL. Each participation library can identify where its service needs improvement from the eyes of the users. It can also compare the service quality with other participating libraries through the different benchmarks I mentioned earlier when I talked about measuring or evaluating the results of KM systems. We mentioned 2 companies employed method wide bench marks. Another one is Biding score card. The LibQUAL actually takes into consideration some of the key advantages of the 2 methods included in the LibQUAL measurement instrument. Here the bench marking is an important part. By increasing the number of participating libraries, in 2002 these were 162 libraries in the United States and Canada participating in this library service quality survey, so they came up with a national norm of 132 participating libraries, they also break down into subsets such as ARLs or all the 4 year universities. There are also some 2 year college libraries, plus some specialized libraries such as law libraries, medical libraries. So you get a subset of known, which can be compared by libraries within the group. The LibQUAL measures can show how well a library serves its users. It may also demonstrate the efficiency and effectiveness of the operation. This notion about the methods of conducting the surveys which we do mostly by machine, so that we don't have to spend much manpower to do this survey.

In the year 2002, the survey form consisted of 25 questions divided into 4 dimensions—for the access to information there are 5 questions; for the affect of service, 9 questions; for the library as a place, 5 questions; for personal control, 6 questions. This number of questions was much reduced from the survey done in 2001. The 2001 survey had more than 40 questions. Some people thought that was too many, so we reduced the number of questions to 25, and statistically proved these 25 questions are good, valid questions for the intended measurement.

Let us look at the 5 questions under the access to information. 1) A complete runs of journal titles where the library has the complete run of the issues; 2) Times documents delivered on interlibrary loan; 3) Interdisciplinary library needs being addressed (this is a sequence number from the list of 25 questions); 4) Convenience of business hours the library has committed to users; 5) Comprehensive print collection. These are the 5 questions under the access to information section.

The 9 questions under the affect of service: 1) willingness to help users; 2) employees who are consistently courteous; 3) dependability of being able to service users' problems; 4) giving users individual attention; 5) employees who deal with users in a caring fashion; 6) employees who have the knowledge to answer users' questions; 7) readiness to respond to users' questions; 8) employees who instill confidence on the part of users; 9) employees who understand the needs of the users. Instead of using the term librarians, we use employees in recognition of conditions in a university library situation, when at times we use non-professional staff or in the evening we use a great deal of student assistants to provide some non-essential, not high level type of reference services. So we have a lot of non-librarians working in the library, dealing with the users. So we want to use employees rather than just librarians.

In terms of the library as a place, these are 5 questions: 1) space that facilitates quiet study; 2) a haven for quiet and solitude; 3) place for reflection and creativity; 4) a comfortable and inviting location; 5) a contemplative environment.

In terms of personal control there are 6 questions: 1) making electronic resources accessible from my home or office; 2) modern equipment that makes it possible to easily access the information that I need; 3) a library website enabling me to locate information on my own; 4) easy to use access tools that allow me to find things on my own; 5) making information easily accessible for independent use; 6) convenience in access to library collections. These are 6 questions under personal control.

In addition to the 25 questions, there is other demographic information such as the age group of the person answering the survey, sex, what field (engineering, business, teaching), user categories, graduate on under-graduate or faculty or non-university outside users.

Like a usage pattern, our library premises all use electronic library service remotely. Then we have, for higher links, like the web, there are an additional 5 questions added by the Ohio link specific to needs of the Ohio link are: 1) comprehensive collection of full text articles online; 2) convenience of borrowing books from other colleges (because our system has a unique library loan service); 3) ease of using library's online article index; 4) availability of online help when using my library's electronic resources; 5) informing me of useful library services. This is sort of push technology. For each of 25 questions there are 3 sets of numbers to indicate their choice: 1) my minimum service level: the best will be 9 and the poorest will be one; 2) my desired service level, also 1 – 9 to be selected by the respondent; 3) perceived service performance, also 1 – 9 for the respondents to indicate.

The results of the 2002 survey. I'd like to show you comparisons of responses to questions, different a non Ohio universities, Ohio link, 4 year colleges and ARL (the major research libraries in the United States).

Ohio University's Participation, During spring quarters of 2001 and again 2002, Ohio University Libraries administered the LibQUAL + survey on the Athens campus. In 2002 we mailed a random select group of 3000 undergraduate students, 1500 graduate students and 600 faculty members on the Athens and the main campus.

The institutional Norm scores of the 162 libraries—the mean score for access to information 52 remember 9 is the highest and 1 is the lowest, so 52 is about 60% of the points. Affect of service was 65, which is a little better than accessing information, the library as a place 63, personal control, surprisingly the highest score 83 out of 90. These are the average score for the 162 participating libraries.

This is a diagram. You can see the comparison, I'll just use access to information Ohio University is this blue color, Ohio link 4 year universities is this purple color, national 4 year universities is the yellow color, and ARL in this green color. For the first one, completeness of journal titles, Ohio university is doing very poorly—we have a minus point one five (– 15) in scores while others are doing better, but the national 4 year universities and ARL are also on the minus side.

The reason for Ohio University doing poorly in this score is because in the early 70s these was a period of 5 years when funds were drastically cut in the state of Ohio, so we cancelled many journals during those years and never had a chance to go back to pick that up, so the faculty members especially, were not happy that the library didn't get all the serial gaps filled they gave us a very low score in terms of completeness of journal titles. But for other type dimensions, we got very high scores. Timely document delivery in interlibrary loan. Ohio University was higher than Ohio link libraries, higher than national 4 year colleges and higher than ARL libraries. In terms of inter disciplinary library needs being addressed—again Ohio University was higher than the others and in terms of community visit library hours, also Ohio University is doing very well in terms of perception on the part of the users. Comprehensive print collection (the last item) —even though we didn't do well in journals but the overall print collection we did very well compared with the others. If we look at personal control, in all categories of making electronic accessible, modern equipment, library website, easy to use access, making information easily accessible for independent use, community access to library collections Ohio University scored much higher than Ohio link. Ohio link get higher than ARL, so that made us feel very good, that we got a good response back from our users. So this is the way to measure how effective, how efficient in terms of your own operation is when you compare with other peer institution, where you stand in this scale.

The other way we talk about is the undergraduates. When we look at graduate students, again you can see the different measurements. But in terms of faculty. In the category of making electronic service available they rated us lower than the ARL libraries. So from different groups you can get different results.

In terms of people using the library on the library premises or using the library electronic resources remotely, on a daily or weekly basis, ARL library-undergraduates about 53%. Ohio about 54%, graduate students used more (74%) compared to the ARL library loan and faculty members and 47% of ARL and Ohio University 44%. For libraries that serve users remotely, Ohio University does better compare with ARL in all categories. So this is the kind of information that is very useful for us to plan, refine or improve our library services.

Basic contributions of LibQUAL: shifts the focus of assessment from expenditure driven metrics to user centered measures of quality; re-around gap theory for the library sector, especially academic libraries; grounded the questions yield data of sufficient granularity to be of value at the local level. So these are some of the basic contributions I won't deal with some additional ones.

If you are interested in learning more about LibQUAL, I have 3 website here, so please feel free to visit these website for more information.

Recently I learned that UK's equivalent of ARL has decided to join and use LibQUAL in the year 2003 survey so that in the future we will have the results for the UK for comparison. In Australia, the university libraries are also interested in joining this service so eventually this will become internationally accepted method for the measuring the quality of library service.

I had intended to give you each a copy of the questionnaire, but couldn't manage it through the internet, so we won't do that.

Thank you very much.

关于图书馆服务效益评估的若干问题[①]

Issues Relating to the Evaluation of Cost Benefits of Library Services

1. 图书馆服务效益简析

（1）图书馆服务创造的价值表现为社会效益与经济效益

图书馆服务效益是指图书馆为读者工作产生的效果和利益。一般说来，图书馆文献信息得到充分的开发和利用，其服务效益就高，反之则服务效益低。

图书馆的价值体现在社会公众对图书馆的利用，社会公众对图书馆服务的需求是图书馆存在的条件和发展的动力。图书馆服务创造的价值表现为社会效益与经济效益。

（2）图书馆服务以社会效益为最高宗旨

图书馆服务的社会效益主要体现在图书馆通过多元化的服务体系，传播和弘扬先进的文化思想，指导人们的社会实践，对推动社会进步产生的积极作用和影响。

图书馆服务的社会效益主要是由公益性服务产生的。由于图书馆主要经费来源是国家和地方政府拨款，所以图书馆的服务应主要是公益性服务，即社会公众有权利免费使用图书馆。图书馆服务的社会效益是图书馆存在的主要价值体现。图书馆的性质决定了图书馆服务必须以社会效益为最高宗旨。

（3）直接和间接经济效益

经济效益有直接和间接之分。直接经济效益来自有偿服务即收费服务，图书馆向其服务的受益者适度收取一定的服务费用，使服务的成本得到一定程度的补偿，增强了图书馆自我发展的活力，也激励了图书馆员的服务热情。有偿服务是公益性服务的延伸，如课题查新服务、情报检索服务、定题跟踪服务等等，往往满足了更高层次的社会需求。

间接经济效益是指读者和用户通过图书馆的服务，利用图书馆提供的情报和信息进行科学研究、发明创造、技术推广、产品开发等活动而创造的效益。

（4）社会效益和经济效益的统一

从某种意义上讲，社会效益可以转化为经济效益，经济效益也会带来社会效益。图书馆服务追求社会效益的同时，间接地给社会带来巨大的经济效益。有偿服务的成果虽直接表现为经济效益，但它始终以社会效益为前提，与社会效益相伴而生。在获得经济效益的同时，间接地产生社会效益。

图书馆服务产生何种效益及效益的大小，取决于图书馆的服务管理模式、运作方式和服务类型，以及服务质量、服务深度和广度。社会效益和经济效益的统一是图书馆在市场经济中生存和发展的需要。图书馆要谋求高质量生存和快速持续发展，必须追求社会效益和经济效益的统一。

2. 图书馆服务效益评估的目的

在兰卡斯特（F. W. Lancaster）所著的《假如你要评估你的图书馆》一书中，他认为

[①] 与楼宏青合著。

评价至少有以下几个目的①：

（1）要找出现行服务的水平点和标志，以作为日后评估的比较。

（2）要与其他图书馆比较彼此的成果。

（3）要证明图书馆存在的价值及其成本效益。

（4）要诊断图书馆作业的缺点，以便采取改善的措施。

这几点自然适用于作为图书馆评估工作一部分的服务效益评估。但笔者认为最重要的是第四点，就是以评促建。评估工作不但是为了证明和总结，更是为了改进和提高。通过评估对现行的工作进行检查，找出好的部分，继续保持提高；发现存在的问题，开出"治疗"处方，以"治病强身"，谋求发展。

服务效益评估的过程是收集有用的资料数据说明和解决实际问题、为决策服务的活动。建立科学的服务效益评估指标体系，对图书馆的读者服务进行定量、定性客观评价，可以为图书馆各级领导制定建设规划、调整宏观政策、控制运行过程提供依据，使图书馆建设工作不但注意投入，更要注意产出的结果和效益。

3. 制定图书馆服务效益评估指标原则

（1）导向性和信息性

评估指标的导向性应十分明确，要引导各馆进行科学化、规范化、标准化管理，引导各馆合理地配置图书馆设备资源，使其得到充分的利用，产生最大的服务效益。

英国学者莱恩（M. B. Line）1990年（时任英国图书馆协会主席）在《图书馆好坏的概念：用户与图书馆对质量和价值的知觉》一文中指出，不便于使用，不提供所需的个别帮助（高水平的），不提供有效的联机服务和馆际利用服务的大学图书馆，就不能认为是好的图书馆②。如在传统观念中，图书馆的服务效益是由其拥有的纸本资源规模和这些资源被利用的情况来体现；而在网络环境下，突破单一馆的馆藏限制，综合利用本馆馆藏、外馆馆藏以及其他网上资源已经成为图书馆用户的必然选择，衡量图书馆服务效益的标准也由衡量其独立向用户提供服务的能力转变为组织社会已有信息、为读者提供服务并产生效益的能力。

（2）客观性和实效性

图书馆服务效益评估指标应切合实际，反映图书馆在新形势下改革、发展、提高的情况。注意对图书馆恰如其分地提出当前评估的尺度，并充分认识到各地各类型的图书馆之间发展的不平衡性，事实上不同类型图书馆的服务性质、服务对象不尽相同；就目前图书馆读者服务的现状与效益来看，规模、进展、水平往往存在很大差距。因此评估工作必须从实际出发，在指标的制定上既要有统一的标准，又要考虑针对不同地区、不同类型图书馆制定不同指标和评分标准。可针对某一类型图书馆提出专用指标和评分标准。

（3）可比性和可操作性

图书馆服务效益评估指标不能只适用于某一图书馆，应适用于某一类型的多个图书馆。评估指标的制定应注意具体化和具有可操作性，使图书馆可以客观地进行横向或纵向比较，从而发现自己的优势和弱势，谋求自身的发展。

图书馆的许多服务工作的社会效益难以定量，宜采用定量与定性相结合的评价方式。定性评估可以用标准化的问卷形式来评估读者对各项服务的觉察及感知，并用问卷分析来

---

① 李华伟. 现代化图书馆管理. 台北：三民书局股份有限公司, 1985：210.
② 初景利. 西方图书馆评价理论评介. 中国图书馆学报, 1999（3）：53－60.

测量。定量评估是运用数学或统计学的方法来进行评估的方法，可建立一定的数学模型来进行评估。

定性评估的优点是方便、易于掌握，但易受评估者观念、水平的影响。应注意问卷对象的代表性并尽可能增加答卷人数，以增加评估的客观性。定量评估的优点是使一些含糊的概念精确化，减弱主观性和随意性，具有较高的可信度；缺点是比较复杂、麻烦，且量化指标的制定未必能恰当准确地反映评估对象的水平。量化数据的采集也有一定的难度，评估者可采用随机抽样的方法，从不多的用户样本中获取可靠的数据，使评估工作更经济高效。

定量与定性是辩证的统一，量化是可操作性的主要标志。应努力增加量化指标的比率，对那些能量化的指标应尽量量化，以增加评估结果的说服力。

4. 图书馆服务效益评估指标的设计

中国图书馆界于 20 世纪 80 年代开始研究和引进图书馆评估管理，并制定了各系统的评估指标体系。例如，国家教委 1991 年下发的《关于开展普通高等学校图书馆评估工作的意见》和附件《普通高等学校图书馆评估指标体系大纲》，教育部高等学校图书情报工作指导委员会于 2002 年 6 月下发的"关于征求《普通高等学校图书馆评估指标》（初稿）意见的通知"和附件"关于《普通高等学校图书馆评估指标》及评估办法的说明（征求意见稿）"。文化部依据公共图书馆行政级别而统一制定了各级图书馆评估标准，如《省级图书馆评估标准》、《县级图书馆评估标准》（1998，2002）。国家图书馆于 2001 年开始着手建立《国家图书馆绩效评估指标体系》。这些指标的制定对全国各种类型图书馆的评估工作有重要的指导意义和规范作用。

笔者参考上述几个指标体系特别是关于读者服务的内容，结合当代图书馆建设的实际情况，提出如表 1 所示的图书馆服务效益评估指标。由于水平有限及缺少相关参考资料，定有不合理、不完善之处，希望能起到抛砖引玉的作用。现将图书馆服务效益评估指标（见表1）的设计思路和评估方法作以下说明：

（1）随着数字化时代的到来，人类对信息储存、传递、获取的能力和条件得到了极大的提高和改善，作为信息中心的图书馆得到了空前的发展。近年来中国在数字图书馆的研究和实践方面也取得了很大成绩，图书馆自动化、网络化、数字化程度不断提高[1]。数字化资源在图书馆越来越显示出不可估量的作用。进行资源共建、共享，形成分工合作、互通有无，实现高效低耗地提供服务显得尤其重要。因此图书馆服务效益评估指标的设计应比较突出网络服务与资源共建、共享的内容。

（2）由于地区之间、各类图书馆之间存在发展的不平衡，难以用完全一致的标准去衡量，评估时，各地可对各级指标的指标值和权重系数自行确定或调整，也可以对各级指标中的说明进行增项或减项。

（3）由于图书馆界对图书馆服务直接经济效益的范围界定、得失利弊等问题意见不一，各图书馆的领导部门对图书馆的相关政策有所不同。故本指标不考虑直接经济效益问题。

（4）指标内容有基本服务、网上服务、信息咨询服务、信息素质教育、特殊服务六大项目，前五项适用于高校及其他类型图书馆，第六项仅适用于公共图书馆。

（5）评估指标设四级，指标代码中含一位数字的是一级指标，含二位数字的是二级指

---

[1] 楼宏青. 中美两国数字图书馆的发展状况及比较分析. 图书馆论坛，2002（5）：61-65.

标，依此类推。参加前五项一级指标评估的图书馆总分满分（即各一级指标值之和）为1000分，（参加一至六项一级指标评估的公共图书馆总分满分为1200分）。一级、二级、三级和四级设权重。一级指标值是1000分乘以该指标权重系数所得，二级指标值是一级指标值乘以该指标权重系数所得，一级指标的实得分值是二级指标实得分值（取其一级指标值为满分）乘以权重系数所得分值相加之和①，依次类推。

（6）进行图书馆评估，很难全部以定量来计分，但是评估指标又必须量化，才能测出一个分数来进行比较。因此，对定性指标可以采用分两步走的办法，即：第一步先给一个模糊量化的等级概念；第二步从这个模糊量化界定的数量范围内（如A等界定为180－200分；B等界定为160－179分），给出一个相对恰当的分数②。

表1 图书馆服务效益评估指标

指标代码（一级指标值）	指标内容	一级指标权重	二级指标权重	三级指标权重	四级指标权重	说明
1（200）	基本服务	0.2				
1.1	开馆时间		0.3			读者可获得图书馆服务的时间
1.2	读者情况		0.3			
1.2.1	办证人次			0.3		馆内及馆外办理各种证卡的人次
1.2.2	接待读者人次			0.7		年接待读者人次
1.2.2.1	流通读者				0.4	年借书读者人次
1.2.2.2	阅览读者				0.3	年进书库读者人次
1.2.2.3	电子阅览室及视听、声像阅览室读者				0.3	年进电子阅览室及视听、声像阅览室读者人次
1.3	纸本文献流通		0.4			
1.3.1	开架率			0.2		开架服务的书刊文献占全部馆藏文献的比例
1.3.2	人均外借量			0.35		年读者借书量（册）
1.3.4	文献复制量			0.15		年图书馆为读者复制各种文献的数量（页或次）
1.3.5	纸本馆际互借、文献传递及联合采购			0.3		年馆际互借和文献传递量（次或页），需求满足率。进行联合采购、分工保刊的情况。
2（300）	电子文献资源服务	0.3				
2.1	图书馆集成管理系统		0.35			图书馆集成管理系统的运行情况

---

① 教育部高等学校图书情报工作指导委员会. 普通高校图书馆评估指标（初稿），2002.6.
② 教育部高等学校图书情报工作指导委员会. 普通高校图书馆评估指标（初稿），2002.6.

（续上表）

指标代码 （一级指标值）	指标内容	一级指标权重	二级指标权重	三级指标权重	四级指标权重	说　明
2.1.1	馆藏数据库			0.7		已建馆藏图书、期刊目录数据库数据占馆藏种数的比例
2.1.2	读者数据库			0.3		已建读者数据库数据占持证读者总数的比例
2.2	电子文献数据库建设		0.45			
2.2.2	自建数据库			0.3		自建专业数据库或专题数据库的数量、水平和使用情况，参加共建共享情况
2.2.3	引进数据库			0.7		引进专业数据库或专题数据库的数量、水平和使用情况，参加集团采购情况
2.3	电子文献信息传递流通		0.2			
2.3.1	网上点击量			0.3		年图书馆主页点击量（次）
2.3.2	生均下载量			0.35		年读者下载电子刊量（篇次）
2.3.3	电子文献馆际互借			0.1		年电子文献馆际互借和文献传递量（次或页），需求满足率
2.3.4	上网信息			0.25		新书预告书目数，外国教材评价（篇次）及其他
3（200）	信息咨询服务	0.2				
3.1	信息咨询		0.3			面对面及在线交互式信息咨询等服务情况
3.2	专题、定题服务		0.25			年专题、定题服务量（个）
3.3	信息编译报道		0.2			年编译篇数或次数
3.4	科技查新项目		0.25			年科技查新项目（个）
4（150）	信息素质教育	0.15				
4.1	读者教育		0.25			年接受教育读者数及年接待参观人次
4.2	宣传资料		0.25			编印资料种类、数量及散发面
4.3	文检课教育		0.25			年开课课时数，听课人数，通过考试人数
4.4	校园文化建设		0.25			年办展览数、讲座数，宣传栏数
5（150）	读者评价	0.15				

（续上表）

指标代码 （一级指标值）	指标内容	一级指标权重	二级指标权重	三级指标权重	四级指标权重	说　明
5.1	读者调查		0.3			年读者问卷、座谈会、实物意见箱收集意见数，电子意见箱或其他方式收集意见数，年调查次数
5.2	读者满意率		0.7			对读者抽样，采用口头或书面方式调查读者对特定部门服务的满意程度
6（200）	特殊服务项目	0.2				适用于公共图书馆
6.1	为弱势人群服务		0.1			指为老年人、残疾人等服务
6.1.1	有残疾人通道			0.2		
6.1.2	设立盲文阅览室			0.3		
6.1.3	有专门服务措施			0.5		
6.2	为地方服务		0.1			
6.2.1	送书上门、送书下乡服务			0.2		
6.2.2	基层服务			0.3		开展基层辅导工作协助基层图书馆建设情况
6.2.3	地方文献服务			0.5		地方出版物入藏及服务情况

5. 图书馆服务效益评估对图书馆员的素质提出更高要求

19 世纪 80 年代，帕拉休拉曼（A. Parasuraman）等人提出了评价图书馆服务质量的 SERVQUAL 模式，即五个层面理论。

服务质量的五个层面的定义如下[①]：

可靠性：可靠而准确地开展承诺的服务的能力。

反应性：帮助用户并提供快捷服务的意愿。

保证性：工作人员的知识和礼貌及其传达信用和信心的能力。

移情性：对用户寄予关切和个别的关注。

可感知性：物质设施、设备、人员和通讯资料的外在形式。

该理论以此作为用户评价服务质量的核心标准，作为管理者制订战略规划、改进服务质量的指南。从这五个层面的定义不难看出对图书馆员服务态度、服务能力、服务水平的要求。

21 世纪是信息时代，以网络环境为基础的信息服务已成为图书馆服务的大趋势。要适应升格的读者服务工作的需要，信息的组织者和服务者——图书馆人是非常重要的因素，必须形成一支思想过硬、高素质的图书馆员队伍。要不断加强对馆员的职业道德教育，提高馆员的事业心和敬业精神，增强其工作责任感，树立全心全意为读者服务的工作

---

① 初景利. 西方图书馆评价理论评介. 中国图书馆学报，1999（3）：53-60.

作风。

图书馆开展现代化服务的一项重要任务是培养一批既懂专业又具备计算机操作技术的图书馆馆员。如果一个图书馆拥有较多的高素质、高学历的图书馆人才，这个馆就必然有较强的现代化服务功能。就国内大多数图书馆而言，图书馆员本科生以上学历的比例逐年上升，这些新鲜血液的注入无疑给图书馆带来了活力。在引进人才的同时也要注意对在职人员结合岗位进行业务培训和计算机知识技能培训。

图书馆应努力培养"研究型馆员"，建设能为读者提供高水平优质服务的精良队伍，从而使图书馆由纯传递服务型向传递服务加科研型转化。鼓励图书馆员钻研业务，开展研究工作，撰写研究报告，发表论文，使一批图书馆员真正掌握图书馆学、情报学及相关专业知识并开展专业服务，不断深化图书馆的服务工作，提高图书馆的服务效益。

总之，服务效益评估指标的制定和实施将对现阶段图书馆服务工作起到推动和促进作用。服务效益指标体系应是动态发展的评估系统，在一段时期应保持相对稳定，但应随着时间推移和工作发展有所调整和变化，以期不断接近实际情况。

参考文献

1. 李华伟. 现代化图书馆管理. 台北：三民书局股份有限公司，1985：210.
2. 初景利. 西方图书馆评价理论评介. 中国图书馆学报，1999（3）：53-60.
3. 楼宏青. 中美两国数字图书馆的发展状况及比较分析. 图书馆论坛，2002（5）：61-65.
4. 教育部高等学校图书情报工作指导委员会. 普通高校图书馆评估指标（初稿），2002.6.
5. 李晓明，马涛. 国家图书馆读者服务工作绩效评估指标体系的制定. 国家图书馆学刊，2002（3）：15-20.
6. 安邦建. 高校图书馆自动化应用评估方案的探讨——兼论单项评估的优势. 大学图书馆学报，1997，15（5）：9-11.
7. 国家文化部. 省图书馆评估标准，2002.12.
8. 富平. 确立绩效评估体系，进一步完善国家图书馆科学管理. 国家图书馆学刊，2002（2）：6-12.
9. 林雯. 医院图书馆评估刍议. 中华医学图书情报杂志，2002，11（2）：22-23.
10. 李文萍. 图书馆服务效益浅析. 河南图书馆学刊，2001，26（3）：46-48.
11. 任学宾. 试论高校图书馆服务评估的几个问题. 广西教育学院学报，2000（2）：126-131.
12. 王姗姗. 高校图书馆自动化评估指标刍议. 山东图书馆季刊，2001（2）：63-65.
13. Colleen Cook and Bruce. Thompson. "Reliability and validity of servqual scores used to evaluate perceptions of library service quality." *The Journal of Academic Librarianship*. 2000，26（4）：248-258.

（原载《大学图书馆学报》2003年第5期，第18-22页。）

实行知识管理的步骤

Steps in Implementing Knowledge Management[①]

This morning I will continue with what I did yesterday. Yesterday I dealt with the importance of knowledge management and the role libraries should play in implementing knowledge management in our institutions and universities. Today I would like to talk about the steps in implementing KM because, after we have stated the importance, we must go ahead to implement so we need to know how to implement, what are the necessary considerations and steps that need to be token in order to implement knowledge management.

Yesterday we spoke about the need for KM, so I am going to skip that. In order to get the good ideas out of the book by Dr. Amrit Tiwana. He wrote a book called *Knowledge Management ToolKit* published in 2000. I have consulted his book and have made a good number of adaptations in order to change his toolkit material for business organizations. I made the changes to make them more suitable for application in the library environment. In this book, he remarks 10 steps knowledge management road map and for implementation. He grouped the 10 steps into 4 phases.

The first one is infrastructural evaluation to find out what we already have in terms of the IT infrastructure. The second phase is knowledge management system analysis, design and development. So we are going into the design phase of the knowledge management system. The third phase is system deployment. Now we have a system to implement and deploy the system. The fourth phase is evaluation. We need to evaluate whether we do the right things or not and if there is a need to make adjustments, revisions, refinements in the knowledge management system.

Now we will talk about the first phase—the infrastructural evaluation. This is done in two steps. The first is to analyze the existing infrastructure. The second step is to align knowledge management and organize strategy in other words, the knowledge management system has to be aligned with the organization's goals, objectives and action plans.

Phase 2 is the analysis, design and development phase. This phase includes 5 steps (5 of the 10 steps called for in the book). The first is to design the knowledge management infrastructure and integrate the existing infrastructure; in other words, we try to develop something that can be used in the existent infrastructure. The second is to audit and analyze existing knowledge assets and systems. To find out what we already have in terms of knowledge database within the organization. The third is to design the knowledge management team. In order to plan and implement a good knowledge management system, we need a good team to work toward this goal. The next one is to create the Knowledge management blueprints to develop a plan—how the knowledge management is like, looks like. The fifth step is to develop the knowledge management system. Now we go ahead to build the system, to put it into action.

The third phase—deployment—includes 2 steps. The first one is to deploy, using the result driven incremental methodology. I will explain this is more detail later on. Now will try to do it slowly, step by step, so we call this a result driven, incremental mythology. The next step is manage change, design culture and reward structure and to decide on the position of the chief knowledge officer. Yesterday, I mentioned that the head, the IT people are the most suitable for the position of chief information operator. Today I would like to advocate that I feel that the professional library information professional are the most suitable to be the chief knowledge officer of the organization.

[①] Presented at the International Conference on *Challenges and Opportunities for Libraries and Information Professionals in Knowledge Management and the Digital Age*, 20 – 22 March 2003, Chiang Mai, Thailand. Organized by Department of Library Science, Faculty of Humanities, Chiang Mai University, Chiang Mai, Thailand, 2003.

The last phase is evaluation. This is the last step (10) of the real map. This step will evaluate the performance, measure its costs and benefits, and incrementally refine the knowledge management system. In this last phase we try to fine tune the system, to find out where the system is in relation to what we want the system to do and to initiate improvement which we discover during the process of deployment.

Now I will try to look at each of the ten steps with some details, because of time limits I don't dare say we will look at every step for greater details. I will just add a few more details I the 10 steps.

The first phase we mentioned earlier includes the analysis of the existing infrastructure. We need to understand the role of existing, networks, intranet, extranet of knowledge management. The purpose of that is to broaden the reach and enhance the speed of knowledge transfer. knowledge management's key concept is to transfer to facilitate to promote—to make it easier for the knowledge to be transferred. So this is one of the things we need to do.

The second one—to integrate the island of information and knowledge that dot the organizations landscape. If you look carefully at your own organizations, such as Chiang Mai University, you will find that there are many information items that exist in the organization, in the departments, in the faculty in the varying interests within the group of researchers. Or we do the library—you have many separate knowledge depositories in there, but each one is an isolated island of knowledge. They are not interconnected or linked, they are not networked. Therefore, they don't really enhance our knowledge resources.

Link your existing networks intranet and extranet to your knowledge management strategy. I mentioned that first we look at what we already have in terms of knowledge management infrastructure. Next is to link these, some of you have already done some of this. I'm sure that every library has had some knowledge management infrastructure already avoidable, such as the internet connections and you have inter system discussions from these other things. And we need to think how we can link all of these together for the good of knowledge management.

Consider the use of knowledge server for organization wide integration. We need to provide knowledge servers in order to integrate the knowledge repository in the organization. Integrate is taking over internet and extranet and group ware into the knowledge management system. Learn the limitations of implemented tools. There are many tools available—we have many experts here—a lot of knowledge management, but they learn much more the tools available. We need to learn what tools are most suitable—their advantages and disadvantages, their limits, so we need to understand this before we can make use of the tools to the best benefit of all of the system. Identify existing gaps in the current technology infrastructure. By analyzing what we already have, we can identify the gaps and then we can close the gaps and make some improvements. Leverage and build upon existing infrastructure. We try to build on what we already have and so we don't have to waste resources that are already available.

The golden rule for building a good knowledge management system is to build systems around people instead of molding people to work with system. For example we build a system and then we bring people to use the system. So people have to make adjustments in order to use a system. But this knowledge management system is built around people. People are what are most important. They are the ones making this work. We should build the systems around people and make it easy for people to use the systems.

Step two is to align knowledge management and organization strategy. An effective knowledge management strategy is not simply a technology strategy. Technology is very useful, but technology is not the only solution to all needs. So we need a well balanced mix of technology, cultural change, new reward systems and organizational focus that is perfectly in step with the organizations strategy. A high level organizational strategy can be translated into pragmatic, do able goals that can drive knowledge management strategy. In other words, we need to have our own strategy which is compatible or in line with organization mission and goals and objectives.

Knowledge drives strategy. Strategy drives knowledge management. You can see the steps in implementing knowledge management. We begin with knowledge. Knowledge will drive strategic vision and strategic vision will drive strategic thinking and strategic thinking will drive strategic planning and then to strategic programming and then knowledge management. With knowledge management we discover new knowledge and then we start the cycles over again. That's the way knowledge management works the best.

Perform a knowledge based SWOT which means strengths, weaknesses, opportunities and threats. In order to do strategic planning we normally would look to see what are our strong points what are our weaknesses and look onward to see the opportunities and threats. We need to create a knowledge map for our organization, just to find out what is the knowledge that this organization creates, what is the knowledge most useful to this organization. Are there gaps that need to be closed. We must think of all of these before we design a management system.

Raise knowledge management system designed to the level of organization and library strategies and pull them down to the level of system design. We need to look up to the overall goals of our organization and then come back to the level of the system design. To identify the gaps in terms of what the organization must know—that's our goal. What we must know to be an effective organization, and then we look at what the organization knows—what we know how and what we need to know at a higher level. That is the gap we need to discover. And our goal in the knowledge management system is to model the gap. Another one, from a strategic point of view, we need to know what the organization must do and what the organization can do and we find the strategic gap and this needs to be noted too, so we could decide on a design a good knowledge management system. We need to look into gaps and then try to narrow them. In a business organization we often see the 3 levels of knowledge—the core knowledge, the advanced knowledge, the innovative knowledge. Core knowledge is just the basic knowledge needed to play the game, just to stay alive in the business.

The next level, called advanced knowledge is what makes your organization competitively viable. We are likely to compete with other businesses or organization. If I know more than you, for the rest to know I'll be better than you so this is advanced knowledge.

Third, higher level, is innovative knowledge. This knowledge allows the organization to lead others. The organization to lead others to an extent that clearly differentiates it from the competition. Make sure you are far superior to all your competitors. That is innovative knowledge. That's in the business world. Perhaps from a knowledge point of view we may not see knowledge in the same way. Analyze knowledge gaps and identify how knowledge management can fill those gaps, I mentioned earlier in the diagram. There is a cost benefit analysis to prioritize filling such gaps. We cannot do everything with limited resources, so we need to set priorities and the priorities should be set in such a way as to know which are the most cost effective. We will do that one first before we do others. Codification versus personalization focus. Our experience is in the next line, and then thirdly strategy knowledge management into knowledge management systems design characteristics.

Let us now look at the next line for the codification versus personalization focus. Codification strategy is too hard to organize the knowledge. It is more focused on technology that enables storage, indexing, retrieval and reuse. How to codify, organize the knowledge using technology. The personalization strategy is more focused on connecting knowledge workers through networks for better access to tacit knowledge and expertise. Codification deals with explicit knowledge, the knowledge is already in created form and expressed forms, but the personalization focuses on people. The knowledge of the knowledge workers. That's the way we try to bring tacit knowledge into play. Both approaches are useful and should be balanced.

Mobilize initiatives to help sell the knowledge management project internally. We need to sell this in order to get the system accepted by the organization internally to let people know the benefits. We need to mobilize initiative rather than to try to sell the system. Diagnosis invalidates the strategic knowledge management link and uses this to drive the rest of the design process peaceful for the design of the knowledge management system.

Step three talks about architecture and design of knowledge management system. The two primary enablers for knowledge management systems was the storage and retrieval, another was the communication. We need to consider cost versus value as technology. Some technology we must have so we call them the "must have to". The others we may or may not need. It's good to have, but if it costs too much it is not cost effective so this may be done if we have money available. There are 2 types of tools. One is the web. The web itself is a knowledge management tool and it is free. There are also commercial tools called LOTUS Notes. It is just one of many tools available. It has a cost, but it is more structured and has more power for improving knowledge management. The 7 layers of KM architecture. Yesterday I mentioned these seven layers. I'm going to expand each layer, in slightly more detail because to handle every management system, you need to consider all 7 of the layers.

The first layer we call interface layer. This layer is between the user and the system, called user interface layer, where the user by means of a portal they will come into the system to make use of the knowledge within the system.

The second layer is access and certification layer. When we have a KM system, we don't want to open wide to everyone. So there should be some limitations, restrictions, who should be allowed to have access to the system. So we need to have a certification, we need to have regulation to be able to recognize every person when they come into the use of this system. Security concerns, fire walls to separate the internet the intranet, etc. so this is a security layer.

The third layer is a collaborative intelligence filtering layer. This layer really makes the system work wonders because we have many technologies available, intelligence aiding tools so called content personalization, search, indexing matatagging, etc. (We will talk about this in the next 3 slides)

Application layer. We have a multi-management system. We have to have some usable, useful applications. So knowledge includes many things. So another fault that usually interfaces with systems to discover the significant elite. We need to know who are the experts in the organization with the expertise on certain areas. So we need the skill directory of people with expertise in different fields, just like the telephone yellow pages. We can create electronic yellow pages within our KM system. We can develop work tools for collaboration, such as video conferencing, digital white board (now called a digital black board where people can share information with each other, electronic forms, rational capture tools, I was told there were device for when we have a conference—everyone has something like notebook things so, when you are having a discussion, you can write down what you think or to take notes and the system will capture all that you wrote into the device. They analyze it and provide you a summarized minutes of the meeting electronically so you don't have to do it manually and they will give you all kinds of analysis of some of the things you haven't even written down or you just draw a picture there and they'll try to interpret it, based on the discussion and try to make sense out of the things you wrote or drew. So there are many technologies that can be used in the KM system.

The 5th layer is the transport layer. This layer is the networking internet connections based on some agreed on protocol so we can share, transfer knowledge over the internet, over the network system. There are many protocols which support such operation.

Number 6 layer is middleware and legacy integration layers. Example—computer technology has gone through very rapid change over the last 20 – 30 years. So some of the first generation of computer. 20 – 30 years ago we created database, stored in those older machines. Now with the change to newer generations machines. The older files we call legacy files. The newer machines may not be able regularize or to read these things, so we need this layer with the appropriate software that can read the messages stored on the old computer system and they integrate them with the newer files, created with newer computers. So this is called the middle ware and legacy integration layer in the KM system.

The last layer is the repositories. That is called the knowledge resize including legacy, data warehouse, discussion forums, document database and others.

Let's look at the pictures. They make more sense than words sometimes. Any good KM system will normally consist of these 7 layers. There may be others, but I believe these are the most important ones we need to take into consideration in designing a KM system.

Steps four with a knowledge audit also the analysis of knowledge available. We need to do this in order to know the knowledge assets of all of our organization in order to do a good job in planning for the system. These steps provide special knowledge of the direction in which KM strategy must be focused. We need to sample a preliminary knowledge audit team. We need a team, different from the one I mentioned about designing the KM system. This is a field to see what we already know. We need to select an inter-disciplinary from the representative groups of people. The members should include senior management planners and evangelists, people who are very excited, people who are true believers in KM system. Budgetary officers, human resource managers, public and technical service librarians, IT experts, knowledge manager, CKO, or knowledge analyst. These are the who need to be included in the team to do the knowledge audit. Audit and analyze your organization existent knowledge which we need to do audit for defines the specific goals and focuses. Learn about your organization and its mission, mainly the financial and time constraints determine the ideal state, since we want to accomplish in our KM system. Select appropriate audit methods. Perform the knowledge audit, documents knowledge assets. That is very important the object the purpose is to document, to write down, record what we have in terms of knowledge depositories. Track knowledge growth over time. We need to be able to track over a period of time, what kind of growth we can expert in terms of knowledge accumulation. Determine your library's strategic position.

The fifth step. We need a team to set up the design. We should decide whether the team will be a long term or short term one. How can the teams position themselves in the organizationally strategically and technologically? Where does the team fit in the organizational hierarchy. Should they report directly to the president of the university or to the director of the library or to someone else. We need the organization which is best. My suggestion is the higher the better. Who are the key stakeholder's management, IT parent, key of the organization end users vendors, consultants. These are all we group as stakeholders. We should identify them. These are the people who will work with us with the key to design the KM system. How to manage their diverse expectations, bringing people from all different backgrounds. Since they all have different expectations, how are we going to manage this diversity of expectation—that is very important. Who should be the team leader? He must have a sufficient level of authority and resources capability; it must be a visionary and true believer in KM must be credible and knowledgeable about KM, must know how to resolve conflicts, must take charge of the conventional project management, scheduling and coordinative duties. We need a visionary person as leader the design team, must have a direct reporting capability to upper management, and must manage the life cycle of the team, not just do a shorter, the person must be responsible from the beginning to the end, must encouraged structured decision making—the person should be able to build consensus, to make decision Balancing counteraction requirements of the team people, between the risks and payoff—the short term and the long term impact between the bottom line and strategic impacts, between managerial expertise and technical expertise. These are counteracting requirements of the team members. We need to build a balance between these counteracting requirements. Maintain the link between the user and the KM system at all times and identify critical points of failure in terms of unmet requirements, control management buy-in and end users buy in. Do not let support suddenly evaporate. When you start something you get a lot of support, but over a period of time, if you don't come up with some results, that support may disappear quickly. So we need to keep the support thee, and we need to do something to show the results, the benefits of doing this, so later on there is gradual implementation on the methodology.

In step sixth we need to create the KM system blueprint that will be a large plan for the KM system. Basic understanding of the caring architecture includes the following: information technology is a great enabler for sharing applications, validation and distribution of knowledge, especially for explicit knowledge. However, the weakness of IT becomes apparent when the organization tries to use the same techniques and system to leverage tacit knowledge. So we need a new way to deal with tacit knowledge. One should try to strike the right balance between which knowledge should be made explicit and which is best left tacit. Those are the kinds of items we need to keep in mind. When we create the KM system blueprint, there are several components which need to be included—knowledge repositories, collaborative platforms, networks and culture. These are the 4 main components in a successful KM system.

We talk about knowledge repositories. A knowledge platform may consist of several repositories; in other words when we develop this kind of platform, normally they can take care, enter everything, number of reports to it. Each repository may hold, explicit formal and informal knowledge and each with a structure that is appropriate for the particular type of knowledge or content that it stored. Such repository may be logically linked to form a cohesive, consolidated repository. I think this calls for particular technology and I do not have much expertise on it, but I felt that at least we should share this. To enter a good integrated repositories do not require the user to know in which repository the knowledge resides. There should be signs, transparent, so the user does not a lot of technical details. They are interested in how to "get the things I want". That is what a good management knowledge system should try to develop, this kind of capability another thing that is very important—managed content in the repositories should not be limited to just any users in the repositories. We need to think about slowing up, weed out all old and dated content. Otherwise the content becomes unmanageable, so we need to think about how to add things, how to replace things no longer needed or outdated. The part left after the weeding must be defragmented to eliminate redundancies, combine similar files, etc. We need to use open systems to ensure that the user can access the repository from the same place, at any time, and there are many industrial standards such as HTML, XML. These are many retrieval tools which should be selected. We mentioned many of the tools that are available and I am sure that many experts have more knowledge about relevant tools that in the KM system. I mentioned yesterday about the application of the pull technology and the push technology. Any good KM system enables the users to use both the pull and the push approach. We need to balance push and pull based mechanisms for knowledge delivery. The push approach sends relevant, actionable information to the user. A pull approach requires that the recipient pull out the needed information from the repositories. But these are the 2 things we need to be able to perform. We need to do 2 things—integrate ability and interactive ability. I will skip this because you can read it.

We talked yesterday about how knowledge interaction flows that knowledge is the true socialization process that takes this knowledge is the true socialization process that takes this knowledge to move to explicit knowledge, to externalization and then to combinations to internet. This is the way the transfer between tacit knowledge and explicit—the information flow, the cycle. The overall system architecture can be seen from this diagram. We have functional architecture, hardware architecture a software architecture and then we have a repository architecture. In the hardware architecture you can see we have network architecture we have a middleware architecture, we have a server architecture. And in the network architecture we have a remote exit from the architecture. Under the software architecture we have middleware architecture an operating system architecture. Under application architecture we have KM applications which include integrated and interactive kinds of applications.

Because the technology changes are fast, we design a system to take into consideration future proof. This means we look ahead to see what kind of change may take place in the near future so that our system will not run out of gas before it is put into application, so we need to be able to look into the next wave of fancy technology to take into consideration in designing our system.

Step seventh, relating to these 7 layers again. We need to talk more about develop the 1st layer, the interface layer. This layer connects people in the KM system to create, explicate, use, retrieve and share knowledge. This layer moves information in and out of the KM system.

Since this information is available, timely and actionable it represents knowledge. It must also provide a channel tacit as well as explicit knowledge to flow, so that is the interface layer. We saw yesterday this information was available through external portals becomes explicit knowledge and in this internalized process we can test the knowledge and continue to make the circle. Step 7 has more capabilities in the interface layer. It should be platform independent, should be able to leverage the internet, should enable universal authorship, should optimize the content, including videos, audio streaming. These are some of the uses which can be done in the KM system.

The second layer, the access and authentification layer we talked about earlier. The purpose is to restrict access for the other layers to be able to maintain necessary security. There are many ways to develop authentification layer including access privilege, including a firewall, including back-ups. We can use the NPN (visual private networks) technology to ensure web security while we are receiving we can use holistic technology to ensure the security. There are many things, technological details, but I myself am still in the learning cycle, so I won't go any further here. The purpose of mentioning it here is that there are many tools our technical people can advise us on and keep us to make use of these tools for us to design a good KM system.

The 3rd layer, the collaborative layer, the filtering and intelligence layer. This layer constitutes intelligence within the knowledge management system of aiding tags and making tags to knowledge elements through automated mechanisms or manual procedures starts at this level.

The next layer, the application layer mentioned earlier, the transport layer is to take advantage of existing networks already available in places such as the already mentioned technologies.

The next layer the number 6 the middleware and legacy integration layers we have already talked about some.

The last one is the repository layer, including operational data base, discussion data base, reference archives, legacy data, digitized documents archive, object repository.

Now we go to step 8 which is pilot testing and deployment. In previous steps we talked about design and to follow a blueprint for the KM system. Now we are going to implement it, we are going the system into tests. Before implementing. I think one of the best things to do is a pilot test, try a "to scale" testing to see how things work before we make it fully operable. The pilot test can uncover design flaws and will lead new insights experience, feedback, and refinement. We need to select a right, non-trivial, visible, representative and manageable pilot test, not too big. Select something workable that can demonstrate the results, the benefits set tangible deadlines and metrics for success, involve the users throughout the pilot test. Use the result driven incremental technique to deploy the system. The result driven incremental. The project should be broken up into a series of short, fast paced development cycles. These cycles are coupled with intensive implementation cycles. Each of these cycles delivers a measurable benefit. Benefits are realized as each discrete stage is complete.

Let's look at a picture, a diagram to show how this can be described in a picture form. Here is a diagram. We can break a project up into Target One, Target Two, Target Three. We can implement them in stages and each would have the target able to show some benefits. So if we implement target able show some benefits. So if we implement target one, we will have some benefits. And then we go on to target two. We use the greater benefits. We go on to target three and we can get even greater benefits. So finally we can see good return in the investment in the design of a good KM system. So this is called the result driven incremental technique to deploy the system.

Create cross functional synergy is very important because synergy refers to the ability of the system to produce that is greater than the sum of individual components. So a successful KM system should bring in synergy between knowledge workers in different functional areas and departments. We are looking at the result that is not centrally, mathematically $1+1=2$. We need the synergies with $1+1=3$ or 4. That's the way we try to create the kind of synergy for the implementation of KM. You have to bring all the different people into the team. They should create much more results than they would individually they can achieve by adding together. Coping with functional complexities. There are many complexities that we need to address. So there are the complexities we need to address.

In number nine, we talk about the chief Knowledge management officer for structure, technology, change management. This step, from a personal point of view, I think is very important. This is a step we want to change the organizational culture. For sharing that we talked about earlier, knowledge is power, but actually knowledge sharing would yield even greater power. We all as individuals, as humans, sometimes we like to keep things to ourselves—we don't want to share. If I know more, I'm better than you, but that is human nature, so if we want, in the organization, to implement a successful KM system, we need to change that kind of culture. Instead of keeping our knowledge to ourselves, we need to build in a reward system to encourage people to share. That is perhaps the most difficult to do. We need the candidates that campaign to succeed. The chief knowledge officer comes with many gifts and with many titles. Some are called chief knowledge officer, some called knowledge manager, some called knowledge specialists, but they are interested in getting things done appropriately. This leader should know of the KM. Successful chief knowledge officer needs to have the following abilities—be very knowledgeable about the organization, knowledgeable of current state and future possibilities of information technology, knowledgeable about library and information services, KM evangelize, Entrepreneurial spirit, effective manger people skills. We are looking for a thinker, leader, doer. The person has to be able to lead but also be able to do—a doer. This summarizes a statement I made earlier—technology consists of only 30% of the KM system. The other 70% is not technology. It's people, it's the culture of the organization, it's the leadership of the people, leading the effort in the KM. Successful KM takes more than technology, it takes culture change, and a change in the reward system.

Number Ten—the last step. We talk of the measured result of KM. Einstein would say, "what can be measured is not always important, and what is important cannot always be measured." How true. Sometimes we try to measure things, but we don't really get a good hold to measure things we feel are important. So I would like to share with you a couple of things about measuring the success, the performance of the KM system. Either one of these would take more than an hour to explain in detail. However, in my next 2 lectures I will be talking about LibQUAL—how to measure service quality. This like a plug includes the best part of both benchmarking measurement and a balanced score card in these. So I'm going to leave the explanation of these things to the next presentation about measuring service quality of the library service.

2. 图书馆交流与合作
Library Exchange and Cooperation

留美学生所面对的实际问题及其认识[①]

Real Problems and Realizations Facing Students Studying in the U. S.

近年来，由于留美台湾学生人数逐年递增，美国各大学主管外国学生事务顾问及入学资格审查人员最近将连续举办了两次讨会论（workshop），其目的主要在于磋商、研究以及交换有关处理台湾留美学生入学申请以及英文能力鉴定、经济来源与移民法规等各项问题之经验，进而探求统一的步调、共同的对策和相互协调的态度，冀期改善目前各校各自为政、步骤纷乱及尺度宽严不一的弊端。

第一次研讨会历时两周（自去年 11 月 29 日至 12 月 10 日），由美国外国学生事务协会（National Association for Foreign Student Affairs）[②] 主办，在夏威夷大学的东西文化中心举行。研讨地区除台湾外，尚包括日本、印度和菲律宾等亚洲国家。第二次研讨会历时两日，（本年元月 10 日和 11 日），由美国国际教育社（Institute of International Education），会同美国大学注册暨入学资格审查人员协会（American Association of Collegiate Registrars and Admission officers），大学入学考试联合会（College Entrance Examination Board）及美国外国学生事务协会等三单位联合举办。会议地点在明尼苏达州的明尼亚波利斯城（Minneapolis，Minnesota）与会者约八十人，皆为美国中西部地区各大学外国学生顾问及注册人员。笔者与一位美国驻香港外交官员罗勃·尼可斯先生（Mr. Robert Nichols）应邀分别讲演台湾及香港地区教育制度及高等教育发展之现况，同时解答有关之若干问题。中国学人列席会议者，有教育部董彭年君和一位在南伊州大学国际学生中心服务的朱君（Joseph Chu——中文大名不详），董、朱两君在讨论时，均曾数度发表精辟见解，贡献良多。

此次会议主题原则上虽仅限于中国台湾、香港两地区来美留学生的入学申请问题，但讨论范围牵涉甚广，而各项研讨结果和决议将印成专集分送各大学有关之工作人员，藉供参酌。因此，对今后各大学在处理中国台湾地区留学生的政策和步骤上，必有深远的影

[①] 本文为作者出席美国中西部各大学中国台湾地区留学生申请入学审查研讨会的纪要。原文发表时在正文前附有信函文字如下：敬启者：本人最近曾应邀出席美国中西部各大学处理中国台湾地区留学生申请入学工作研讨会，并演讲台湾教育制度及高教发展概况。该项会议系由四机构联合举办，与会者多为美国中西部各大学注册主任及外国学生顾问。会议历时两日，除听取各有关专题演讲及个别报告外，并讨论处理中国台湾地区留学生入学申请、英文能力审定，以及经济来源与移民法规等实际问题。其中若干重要之意见和决议，可提供台湾一般有志留学之莘莘学子及教育当局斟酌参考之用，并进而了解美国各大学当前对台湾地区留学生所采取之基本态度。兹就会议经过，作成短文，投寄贵刊发表。文笔欠妥之处，尚祈惠予指正。谨附上会议议程表及本人简历各一份，藉供参阅。专此即颂撰安，此致《中国一周》编辑委员会，李华伟敬上，一九六六年三月二十日于美国。

[②] 美国外国学生事务协会系由各大学外国学生顾问（Foreign Student advisors）及有关人员组成。

响。笔者不吝识浅，特将两日内个人所见所闻及一些杂感，简略报道于后，希望有助于台湾相关部门及有志留美之一般青年作为参考。

一、会议议程

为使读者对整个研讨会有一概括的了解，谨先将两日议程内容简介如下：

第一日议程——开始后，先由笔者讲演"当前台湾的教育制度"，次由尼可斯君讲演"当前香港的教育制度"，继之以三小时之问题与解答，与会者发问极为踊跃，关于台湾地区教育方面，举凡留学制度政策、中学课程内容、大专入学考试、专上教育之分科与年限、设备与教学、新设立专上学校的设施与师资、研究所的科系及容量、转学问题、军训问题、人力资源之供求、留学考试、办理出国手续及学成归来辅导服务等问题，都加以广泛地讨论，当场由董、朱两君和笔者分别予以答复。

在此一般性的教育制度演讲与讨论后，会议即进入专题研究。三个专题报告逐一由一位具有经验的专家提出：第一个专题报告为"处理外国留学生申请入学的一般步骤"（Foreign Student Admission Procedures and Practices）。

主讲人为印第安纳大学的入学资格审查主任（Director of Admission, Indiana University）威廉·施健君（Mr. William Strain）。第二个专题报告为"英语测验——（English Language testing：Diagnostic and remedial）诊断及补救"，主讲人黎斯理·潘玛君（Mr. Leslie Palmer）为教育测验服务社（Educational Testing Service）主持测验"英语为外国语"（Testing English as a foreign Language）的专家。第三个专题报告为"经济来源与移民法规"（Financial resources and immigration regulations），主讲人为伊利诺大学外国学生顾问（Director, office of Foreign Student Affairs, University of Illinois）罗勃·施盖德曼君（Mr. Robort Schuiteman）。每一报告完毕后，继之以半小时的讨论。

第二日会议议程——包括分组个案研究，全体与会人员分十组，每组讨论一项预先选定的个案资料。十份个案资料中，台湾与香港各占二分之一，讨论结果由各小组作成结论，然后，在下午的全体会议中提出报告，再由全体与会人员决议其是否适当。

此次会议高潮产生于第二日中午的餐后演说；主讲人为奥克兰大学（Oakland University）政治学教授亚波顿博士（Dr. Sheldon Appleton），讲题为"台湾政治经济情况对于教育的影响"（Social and Political conditions in Taiwan：Their impact on education）。亚波顿博士于1958年访问过台湾，逗留时间极短，返美后，著书讨论中国、美国与联合国的问题[①]；对台湾的实际情况所知有限，但偏见颇深。其演说内容妄谬错误之处甚多，当场由董彭年君起立予以驳斥，董君义正词严，对亚波顿见解偏差之点逐一提出有力的反驳，使之狼狈不堪。

二、中心课题

此次会议结果，值得向台湾报道的约有下列三项：

（一）今后美国各大学对申请入学之审查将趋向严格。

关于此一趋向的成因，根据笔者个人的观察，大致可归结为以下三点说明：

（1）近年来，台湾留美学生申请人数剧增。

（2）大多数台湾留学生学成不归。

---

① Appleton, Sheldon, Eternal riangle "Communist China", the U. S. and the United Nations. Ann Arber, Michigan State University Press, 1961.

（3）美国国内大学生人数比例激增，学校容量不敷。

其中关于最后一点，最属重要，因为，既使以美国学生本身而论，欲入著名大学求学并非易事，其中学毕业时学业成绩在中等者，仅可进入二三流之大学就读，而能入第一流学府者，多属智力及学业成绩超群者。

在会议中，很多与会者主张在审查学历证件时，应极谨慎从事，以宁缺毋滥为原则，举凡申请学生的在学成绩、名次、推荐信、经历及留学动机等，均应列入被考虑之条件。一般说来，平均成绩低于八十分；名次不在百分之十以内者，今后申请美国大学、研究所的入学许可将较为困难，尤其是被一些具有声誉的第一流学府获准的可能性更小。除此之外，申请学生原就读院校的教育水平也将并入考虑之列。若干新近设立的大专院校，除少数已具备优良师资和教学设施外，其余的将遭遇严格的审查。三年制专科毕业生，依照大多数与会者的意见，最多只能承认其两年的学分，两年制专科毕业生只能承认其一年的学分。

许多与会者还提出对推荐信不能过分信赖的意见，他们察觉有很多所谓的"推荐信"，实际上乃由学生自己执笔；或委托他人代为捉刀。在个案资料中，即有此一显著例子，如某生的三封推荐信，其语气，措词一看即知是出于同一人之手笔。此类情形对于申请人不仅无益，反而有害。

今后美国各大学对英语能力的要求更高。

从专题报告和一般发言看来，今后美国大学在考虑是否给予入学许可前，将要求非英语语系国家的申请学生参加一项英语能力测验，其英语程度必须达到相当水准始可发给入学许可证。此项性质的测验，目前已有数种正在通用中；其中最新颖的一种称为："英语为外国语的测验"（Test of English as a Foreign Language，简称为TOEFL）已被普遍采用，大有后来居上之势。

兹将目前通用的数种测验简介如下：

（1）美国大学语言中心所编制的测验（American University, Language Center，或简称AULC test）。美国大使馆签证前的英语考试和美国新闻处所举办的英语考试皆采用此一测验。此种测验内容包含四部分：

英语应用测验（AULC test of English usage）

听懂能力测验（Test of aural comprehension）

阅读能力测验（Test of reading comprehension）

口试（AULC oral interview）

其中，第二三部分系分别借用密歇根大学及教育测验服务社所编制的测验。此一测验的缺点，根据与会专家们的意见认为不能保密，因无备用试题可资更换使用，故试题易于外泄，考试结果未必完全可靠。

（2）密歇根大学英语能力测验（Michigan Test of English Proficiency）。此一测验包括三部分，系由密歇根大学英语研究所（English Language Institute, University of Michigan）编制。

文法（Grammar）

字汇（Vocabulary）

阅读能力（Reading comprehension）

但除此以外，尚有作文（Composition）及口试（Oral rating）两种测验一并举行。主试者根据全部测验结果加以总评（Examiner's comments）。

此一测验的缺点，不仅也不够保密，同时，与会专家们更认为"口试"一项，缺乏客观的给分标准，似欠公允。

（3）英语为外国语的测验（Test of English as Foreign Language，或简称：TOEFL）

前述两种测验，除了不易保密和不够客观外，其最大缺陷在于测验本身不是专为非英语语系国家学生而设计，因之，在试题选择及编制方面有很多不符理想与不合需要之处。为了弥补此一缺点，早在1962年5月，美国的若干有关团体即开始筹备编制一套新的测验，1963年1月，一个专负其责的新机构——英语为外国语测验委员会（National Council on The Testing of English as a Foreign Language）——正式宣告成立，历时两年，积许多专家的精力，耗费了25万美元（由福特基金会资助），此一新测验终于编制完成，并于1965年2月初正式采用。此一测验现由教育测验服务社主持，每年定期举行三次，测验地区遍及世界各地，台湾方面，包括台北和台中两地。测验内容共分五部分，总共需三个半小时，试题全部是新法考试的选择题（四个答案中选一个），兹将其分类罗列如下：

A. 听懂能力（Listening Comprehension）

测验学生对一般英语会话听懂的能力（会话是预先录好在唱片上）。

B. 英文结构（English Structure）

测验学生对文法的了解程度，问题偏重于外国学生常犯的错误。

C. 字汇（Vocabulary）

此一部分包括许多艰难而罕见的生字，以测验学生阅读的效率。

D. 阅读的了解力（Reading Comprehension）

测验学生阅读短文的了解力，短文的选择依据一般大学生的程度。

E. 写作能力（Writing Ability）

测验学生英文写作的格式与文体，以及对措辞，用字的能力。

为了保持高度的可靠性，每一次测验皆采用不同的试题，以防泄密。根据与会专家们的报告，目前美国大使馆已规定凡申请"学生护照"签证的学生，必须先通过此一考试。由于这个缘故，最近一次在台湾举行的考试（元月十日在台北举行），参加者极为踊跃，据说超过一千人以上。关于此一测验的详细情形，教育测验服务社印有专集说明函，索要即寄。①

（二）今后美国各大学对于经济来源的规定将从严执行。

按照美国移民局的规定：凡前往美国的留学生，除少数获有奖学金外，其余的一律需筹足全年的各项费用，其数额则依据所拟就读学校的学杂费用，以及当地的生活程度而定。由于台湾内生活程度较低，人民所得有限，因此，大多数自费留学生不得不千方百计筹足一笔为数颇巨的保证金，以符合美使馆签证时之规定，而于来美后，即将借款清还。至于入学后的生活开支，则有赖于课余兼工收入以维生计，此种艰苦奋斗的精神，在我们过来人看来是很自然的，是值得同情和钦佩的。因为，绝大多数能够"自费"来美留学的青年是属于清寒子弟，他（她）们除了半工半读，自力更生，别无他途。但是，站在移民局及外国学生顾问的立场看来，则又不同，他们认为这种行为是不容许的，而且更与留学

---

① 教育测验服务社印有小册两种：一为一般说明，函索即寄；一为学生手册，凡办妥申请考试者，皆奉送一本，内容详细说明考试步骤及须知，并附该社地址为：
Test of English as a Foreign Language
Educational Testing Service
Princeton, New Jersey 08540
U. S. A.

的初旨相抵触。有几位与会人员甚至批评很多台湾留学生一来到美国就积极进行工作，似乎找工作的兴趣还在留学读书之上。殊不知这种情形实有不得已的苦衷，并非人人愿意如此。当然，也有些"留学生"借留学之名，而来此"淘金"，这一类的"留学生"究竟还是少数。

外国学生初来美国的第一年，照章是不准工作的，第一学年修毕后，若成绩优异可依法申请半工全读（即每周工作不得超过二十小时，而每学期至少须选修十二个学分），很多与会人员认为，大多数新来的留学生有人地生疏、语言隔阂之感，再加上繁重的课业，所有的时间应付功课尚嫌不足，实不宜再兼顾工作。因此，依照他们的意见，认为要真正帮助台湾学生达成留学之目的，经济上的保证应特别加以强调，务使留学生在美的第一年内，无经济上匮乏之虑。

以上三点——入学资格之审查，英文能力之鉴定和经济来源之保证，实为本次研讨会的中心课题。但在讨论与问题之解答过程中，很多其他问题也会涉及，因限于篇幅，不克一一详列，仅就其中重要者，参以笔者个人之管见，陈述如下：

三、感想与建议

（一）学成不归问题：

根据笔者之了解，大多数台湾留学生于学业完成后，希望暂时留在美国，此种情形非独中国留学生如此，其他国家，包括欧洲国家留学生亦然。其中原因诚然多而复杂，然而，最显明者不外乎因美国有理想的研究和工作环境，以及待遇优厚，生活水平较高等因素。不过，笔者愿意在此特别强调，"暂时"两字，毫无讳言的，事实上，大多数中国留学生皆非有心在国外久留，落叶归根，回台湾之心，人人有之，只要台湾真正需要，而回台湾后能学以致用，深信大多数留学生都会应召返台服务的。此次研讨会也会谈及此一问题，认为治本的方法应从两方面着手：一为严格考察申请学生的动机与留学目的，对于视留学为达成移民的手段者，将严予拒绝。美国大使馆对于申请签证者若发觉其有此企图，亦将拒予签证。同时，申请签证者，若已有兄弟姐妹等久滞美国，学成不归，其获得签证将较为困难。二则希望台湾能采取更积极地步骤，以充实岛内学术研究的设备和改善工作与生活的环境，从而吸引更多学成留学生返国服务。

关于第二点，笔者曾在会中提出报告，列举台湾地区近年来，在这一方面所作的努力和成就。但这种改善并非一蹴可及。我们试从近年来返台留学生人数逐年增加的趋势看来，只要客观环境能够继续改善，相信今后必有更多学成的留学生源源不断地返台服务。

（二）种族中心（Ethnocentric）的问题：

一般言之，在美国大学里台湾留学生人数较多的地方，往往有一种不好的现象，就是台湾留学生自己形成一个小圈子，很少与美国学生或其他国家的学生交往。此种情形几乎是与会人员的一致同感，他们认为，这种情形不仅影响台湾留学生学习英语的进度，同时，也有悖于了文化交流的基本宗旨。在美国大学的教育观点看来，他们期望台湾留学生能与美国学生真正地打成一片，无论在学业上，抑或生活上能相互砥砺，共同磋磨，以促进文化的交流和彼此的了解，这种看法是非常正确而切要的。凭心而论，笔者多年来亦深具同感，倒不是笔者反对台湾留学生自己保持密切联系与来往。事实上基于种族、国籍、语言以及生活习惯等因素，台湾留学生自成一群、互助合作，是一件很自然的事，尤其是大家身处异邦，理应彼此照应，但这种情形不宜太过分。留学生的使命除了追求高深的学问，取人之长，补己之短外，还要兼负文化交流与"国民外交"的双重责任。因此，我们一方面互助合作，团结一致，另一方面，对于美国师生和其举办的有意义的活动，应主动地参加，以发挥文化交流与国民外交的作用。

(三) 加强报道台湾文教发展的动态

最近若干年来，由于台湾文教界人士不懈地努力和奋斗，一般教育与文化的进展颇为可观，遗憾的是，这种成就缺少作有系统的宣传和报道。据笔者所知，很多美国人民对台湾的进步实况，所知相当有限，而报章杂志上常见的文章对台湾有利的报道极少，诬蔑诽谤的论调却比比皆是，这种情形的演变，可能导致别人的误解和偏见。

关于台湾文教，军事，经济发展和社会福利等各方面的进步情形，笔者认为值得广泛报道与介绍的地方很多，希望台湾学人能群策群力，透过岛外的书刊、杂志以及大众传播工具，作正确而深入的报道。

(原载《中国一周》1966年4月18日第834期，第12-15页。)

泰国学校图书馆发展的伙伴

Partner for School Library Development in Thailand

Bangkok is the capital city of Thailand. It is also the regional capital of Southeast Asia, the home of many regional and international organization. Because of this, a large number of international librarians are happily congregated in Bangkok.

About five years ago, an informal organization of the international librarians in Bangkok was founded under the table leadership of Dr. Maria Lao-Sunthara, formerly the Programme and Documentation Specialist of the UNESCO Regional Office for Education in Asia. The purpose of the organization is very simple. It intends to provide a forum for the international librarians to meet, to exchange information on each other's librarian, to promote inter-library cooperation, and more importantly, to encourage the participation of international librarians in library development activities of Thailand.

It was largely through Dr. Maria Lao-Sunthara's personal effort and enthusiasm, the group has met almost uninterruptedly once every two or three months ever since it was founded. At present, its membership consists of approximately 60 libraries, both Thai and "farang", representing 25 international and foreign libraries in Bangkok. The open membership provides an excellent opportunity for international librarians and Thai librarians to interact together for better understanding and friendship between them. This partnership has been demonstrated in many joint projects aimed at improving library services in Thailand.

The latest project of the International Librarians is to establish a special annual award to be presented each year to a school library for the purpose of encouraging school libraries in Thailand to formulate their own programs for improving library services. In 1974 the amount of the special award is 5,000 baht. The money was raised by means of special sales and auctions held during each of the meetings and by voluntary donations of the members.

For the previous years, similar amounts of money were raised each year and were presented annually to the Thai Library Association in support of their activities or projects. One such projects were the "Books for the Hill Tribes" under the patronage of Their Majesties. Starting in 1974, the members decided to undertake the school library improvement project and to make it through the form of an annual award. In order to work out the details of the special award, a committee was founded which consists of Mrs. Lynn Herrick of the U.S. Special Service Library, Miss Ann Martin of the AUA Library, Mr. Betty Van Duyn of the International School Library, Dr. Maria LaoSunthara of UNESCO until her departure in January 1974, and Dr. Hwa-Wei Lee of the Asian Institute of Technology Library. Two officials of the Supervisory Unit, Department of General Education, Ministry of Education were also invited to serve in the committee as consultants. They are Mrs. Nitaya Chudhamataya and Miss Karnmanee Suckcharoen. The details for the award finalized by the committee are given below.

The Special Award of the International Librarians In Bangkok

The International Librarians In Bangkok is offering an award of 5,000 baht in the interests of improving library service to elementary school pupils. The award will be made to the school library which submits the best proposal for the utilization of these funds in a stated project related to the improvement of library services to its students.

To be eligible, the school library must meet the following criteria:
1. The school must be a prathom level (1~4 or 1~7) school.
2. The school must be located in the metropolitan Bangkok area.
3. Only schools under Ministry of Education or municipal sponsorship are eligible.

4. The school must have a designated librarian who does not need to be fulltime, however.

5. The school librarian and principal must complete and submit the attached application form to the Supervisory Unit, Department of General Education, Ministry of Education, by March 15, 1974.

The application form will serve as the proposal statement for the library's planned project. It should be filled out completely by the school principal, giving as many details as possible regarding the implementations of the plan. Care should be taken not to exceed the $5,000 limit, although it is hoped that the initial project will encourage the school or the community to provide additional assistance to the school.

Projects, as outlined in the attached application forms, will be judged by the Special Award Committee on the basis of:

1. Originality—Has thought been given to developing a new approach or technique?

2. Practically—Can this project be complete within the budgetary and time limitations? Will it improve existing services and facilities?

3. Economy—Dose this project get the greatest possible return for the amount invested?

4. Resources used—Does this project make use of staff skills, local materials, and the interest and financial support of the local community?

5. Adaptability—Can other schools use the ideas employed in this project?

The deadline for the submission of application forms is March 15, 1974. The award will be publically announced in April and the award will be presented at the Ministry of Education. The school should be prepared to carry out its project beginning with the new school term in May. A preliminary progress report must be submitted to the Supervisory Unit not better than August 1, 1974. The project must be completed and a final evaluation report submitted not later than November 1, 1974. The Committee will present its report on the award and its results at the next Thai Library Association's annual meetings.

The Special Award Committee International Librarians in Bangkok

At this writing, the above announcement for the special award has received the official approval of Dr. Kaw Swadipanich, Director General of the Department of General Education whose office will assist in the distribution of the announcement and the application form to all the government prathom schools in the metropolitan Bangkok area. As attached, both the announcement and the application form are in Thailand. It is hoped that these school libraries will give this project their most enthusiastic support. Furthermore, it is hoped that the special award for school libraries will not only serve to stimulate an interest in the development of school libraries but also attract a wider support for the development of all library services in Thailand.

(Publish in *Asian Institute of Technology*. Bangkok, Thailand, January 1971: p. 13.)

泰国建立国际连续出版物数据系统地区中心的可能性

The Possibility of Establishing a Regional Centre for the International Serials Data System in Thailand

The Mission Report

An exploratory mission was undertaken by the consultant to examine the possibility of establishing a Regional Centre for the International Serials Data System (ISDS) in Thailand. The mission was successfully carried out between 16 November and 13 December 1975. The result of the mission is presented in two main parts:
Part I: The Mission Report
Part II: The Programme Proposal

I. Background

In his letter to all member states dated 6 November 1972, the Director General of UNESCO declared the establishment of the International Centre of the International Serials Data System (ISDS) in Paris pursuant to resolution 2.141 (C) adopted by the General Conference at its sixteenth session. To enable the system to function effectively through the early establishment of an operational network, the Director General, in the same letter, invited the Government of each member state to either designate a national ISDS centre or participate in forming regional ISDS centres.

In response to this invitation, the Royal Thai Government, after having an encouraging discussion with UNESCO, submitted in 1974 a formal request to UNESCO for the necessary support in establishing an ISDS Regional Centre for Southeast Asia in Thailand conceived as one of the pilot projects of UNESCO within the framework of the UNJSIST programme.

Resulting from this request, this consultant was engaged by UNESCO in November 1975 to undertake a four-week expiratory mission to examine, with appropriate officials in selected Southeast Asian countries, the possibility of establishing such a Regional Centre in Thailand. The countries selected for the exploratory mission were Indonesia, Malaysia, the Philippines, and Singapore, in addition to Thailand.

The mission which was carried out between 16 November and 13 December 1975 was based on the following basic scheme and understanding:

1. It is proposed that the Regional Centre for ISDS be established in Thailand under the auspices of its National Library.

2. The countries interested in participating in the Regional Centre may do so on a voluntary basis.

3. Each participating country should designate a national agency to act as the national representative for the Regional Centre. (The national agency should be the one which has a general responsibility in the handling of serial publications of the country, such an the national library or the national documentation centre.)

4. The designated national agency in each country should agree to supply to the Regional Centre information on serial publications of its country on the standardized worksheet adopted by the International Centre for ISDS.

5. The Regional Centre will check the correctness of each worksheet and will assign an ISSN to each serial publication.

6. The Regional Centre will arrange to keypunch the information from the worksheet for the computerized regional serials data base and to send a magnetic tape to the International Centre at

regular intervals.

The main tasks of the consultant as was charged by UNESCO were:

1. To visit the different countries interested in the establishment of the Regional Centre and negotiate the possibility of their participation;

2. To give advice on the creation of such a Regional Centre.

To prepare for the mission, a travel plan was drawn up in consultation with UNESCO.

II. Travel Plan

The mission to Southeast Asia was to have the following seven objectives:

1. To assess the present situation of serial publications in these countries;

2. To evaluate the current status of bibliographical control for serial publications in these countries;

3. To identify the national body and, possibly, the individual person(s) responsible for the bibliographical control of serial publications in each of these countries;

4. To negotiate with appropriate authorities in each of these countries for their participation in the proposed Regional Centre;

5. To solicit inputs from various sources for the establishment of the Centre;

6. To hold an open discussion on the preliminary plan of the Centre at the Third Conference of Southeast Asian Librarians held in Jakarta from 1 – 5 December 1975;

7. To prepare a mission report and a programme proposal for UNESCO at the end of the mission.

To provide a base for the open discussion at the Third Conference of Southeast Asian Librarians a position paper on "Regional Cooperation for ISDS" was written by the consultant. (See Appendix I)

In addition to this paper, a survey form consisting of 14 questions was designed which enabled the consultant to collect necessary information concerning serial publications and activities in bibliographical control for serials in each of the countries visited. (See Appendix II) The information thus collected is presented in Appendices III, IV and V.

The itinerary of the four-week mission is given below:

16 November 1975	Leaving Fort Collins, Colorado for Washington, D. C.
17 – 18	– Visiting the National Serial Data Program (NSDP) in the Library of Congress.
18 – 19	Traveling from Washington, D. C. to Paris
19 – 20	– Briefing at both the UNESCO Headquarters and the International Centre of ISDS.
21 – 22	Traveling from Paris to Bangkok
23 – 25	– Consulting with the Director of the National Library of Thailand in the drafting of a preliminary plan for the Regional Centre.
26	Traveling from Bangkok to Kuala Lumpur
27	– Discussing the draft plan with the Deputy Director of the National Library of Malaysia and with his staff on related matters.
28	Traveling from Kuala Lumpur to Singapore
	– Discussing the draft plan with the Director of the National Library of Singapore and with her staff on related matters.
29	Traveling from Singapore to Jakarta
30 – 5 December	– Discussing the draft plan with the Director of the Indonesian National Scientific Documentation Centre and with her staff on related matters.
	– Presenting the position paper at the Third Conference of Southeast Asian Librarians.
	– Meeting with Dr. James F. McDivitt of UNESCO Regional Office for Science and Technology for Southeast Asia and Mr. H. Arthur Vespry of the International Development research Centre (Canada) to brief them of the proposed research Centre.
6	Traveling from Jakarta to Manila

7 – 8	– Discussing the draft plan with the Project Director of the Scientific Library and Documentation Center, National Science Development Board.
9	Traveling from Manila to Bangkok
10 – 11	– Meeting with the Director of the National Library of Thailand to review the findings of the exploratory mission and to discuss the contents of the programme proposal to be prepared by the consultant for submission to UNESCO.
11 – 12	Traveling from Bangkok to Paris
12	– Reporting the major findings to Dr. Wolfgang Lohner at UNESCO.
13	Returning from Paris to Fort Collins
14 – 20	– Writing the mission report and the programme proposal

A list of the key persons visited is given in Appendix VI.

III. Summary of Findings

The four-week mission which included 9 stops in 7 cities (Washington, D. C., Paris, Bangkok, Kuala Lumpur, Singapore, Jakarta and Manila) and covered approximately 30,000 tiles was a great success owing to the excellent planning arid support provided by Dr. Wolfgang Lohner of UNESCO. The visit to the National Serial Data Program of the U. S. A. was a very useful one in that the consultant was able to observe the smooth functioning of the first and, also, the largest national centre for ISDS in operation. The briefings at both UNESCO and the International Centre for ISDS helped to acquaint this consultant with the details of his mission.

The general findings of the mission are summarized below:

1. Although three of the five Southeast Asian countries have responded to the 6 November 1972 letter of the Director General by designating a national centre of ISDS (Indonesia, the Philippines and Thailand), none is in operation as yet.

2. Despite the expression by some at CONSAL III in favor of national centres based on nationalistic or other considerations, all responsible officials in countries visited gave their support to the proposal of establishing a Regional Centre for ISDS in Thailand. Their support was based on the following reasons:

1) Economically, because the number of current serial publications in most of the Southeast Asian countries is relatively small, it will not pay for each country to develop and maintain a computer based serial data bank separately. The Regional Centre is economically feasible particularly if the use of a computer is considered.

2) In terms of funding, the Regional Centre will have far more leverage than a national centre in seeking financial supports.

3) The Regional Centre also provides an answer to the scarcity of trained manpower in the Region. In addition, the proposed Regional Centre can provide training opportunities for serial librarians in the Southeast Asian countries. The experience of designing and. developing a computerized serials data system can be shared by all participating countries through training programmes and workshops.

4) The establishment of a Regional Centre will help those countries that may otherwise not be able to participate in ISDS for some time to come.

5) With a computer based serial data system, a variety of services can be provided as a by-product to the participating countries. e. g., the printing of new serial titles, both regional and national, at desired intervals.

6) The computer based serials data system can be easily duplicated to provide each participating country with a ready-made serial record in machine-readable form whenever needed.

7) The regional centre could serve as a catalyst for further cooperation in the Region.

3. To serve as the host country for the Regional Centre, the National Library of Thailand has pledged its contribution by providing both office space and 6taff required for the Regional Centre at the National Library. This pledge of substantial support by Thailand is very generous indeed. It

will help to reduce the operating cost of the Regional Centre by half.

4. The National Library of Thailand plays a leading role in the ongoing project for a computerized union list of serials in major Thai libraries which has been in progress since September 1974. It plans to start a new project in 1976 for an automated union catalog of books in large libraries in Thailand. The experience gained from these two projects will be very useful for the computerization of the Regional Centre's data base.

5. To participate in the Regional Centre, each participating country agrees to designate a national agency responsible for preparing worksheets of defined serials published in the country in accordance with the ISDS Guidelines and sending these worksheets to the Regional Centre at regular intervals. The cost for such operations will be borne by the national agency of each participating country. The national agencies which have been officially designated or in effect acting as one are:

Indonesia: Indonesian National Scientific Documentation Centre.

Malaysia: National Library.

Philippines: The Scientific Library and Documentation Center, National Science Development Board.

Singapore: National Library.

Thailand: National Library.

6. For the initial five years the Regional Centre will require financial support from UNESCO and other funding sources for the following purposes:

1) The necessary equipment such as typewriter, keypunch or terminal, etc.

2) The cost of computer time and programming.

3) The cost of annual meeting of the Advisory Board.

4) The cost of conducting workshops and training programmes.

7. UNESCO is interested in supporting the Regional Centre by providing the initial funds needed to hold the first organizing meeting and workshop in Bangkok scheduled for March 1976.

8. Requests for additional funds as delineated in the Programme Proposal will be submitted to UNESCO and, through it, to other funding agencies for support of the Regional Centre during the first five years of operation.

9. It was generally accepted that if the Regional Centre proves to be valuable during the initial three years, the Advisory Board may work out a cost sharing formula to further extend the operations of the Regional Centre on a long term basis.

10. A resolution in support of the proposed Regional Centre for ISDS in Southeast Asia was adopted at the Third Conference of Southeast Asian Librarians. A major session of the Conference was devoted to the presentation and discussion of the paper, "Regional Cooperation for ISDS" prepared by this consultant.

11. As a result of discussions with all concerned officials and individuals during the exploratory mission a programme proposal was drawn up by this consultant as Part II of the mission document. It contains the basic scheme of the Regional Centre, its financial requirements, and the drafts of both the Charter and the agreement to be approved and signed by each of the national representatives at the organizing meeting.

12. It is hoped that the Advisory Board of the Regional Centre can be founded at the organizing meeting so that the work of the Regional Centre can commence immediately following the March 1976 meeting.

IV. Acknowledgement

I am very grateful and honored to have been chosen for this mission and am greatly indebted to Dr. Wolfgang Lohner of UNESCO and Mrs. Maenmas Chavalit of the National Library of Thailand for their joint invitation to serve as the consultant for this worthwhile project.

The warm receptions given by those persons met during the mission, whose names are listed in Appendix VI, are also deeply appreciated. Their support for regional cooperation in general and for the proposed Regional Centre for ISDS in Southeast Asia in particular helped to make the mission a very pleasant and rewarding one.

The assistance provided by the UNDP Offices in Kuala Lumpur and Manila is also gratefully acknowledged.

Appendix I
THIRD CONFERENCE OF SOUTHEAST ASIAN LIBRARIANS
DECEMBER 1 – 5, 1975 JAKARTA – INDONESIA

REGIONAL COOPERATION FOR ISDS①

Appendix II
GENERAL QUESTIONS CONCERNING THE UNESCO PROJECT OF ESTABLISHING AN ISDS REGIONAL CENTRE

1. What is the number of known serial titles published in the Country under each of the following categories?
   1) Periodicals and regular serials
   2) Monographic series
   3) Document series
   4) Newspapers
   5) _____ Others (please specify _____)
2. How many of these titles are current?
   1) Periodicals and regular serials
   2) Monographic series
   3) Document series
   4) Newspapers
   5) Others (Please specify _____)
3. What is the estimated number of new serial titles published in 1974?
   1) Periodicals and regular serials
   2) Monographic series
   3) Document series
   4) Newspapers
   5) Others (please specify _____)
4. Which organization in the Country is responsible for collecting and maintaining a largest file of serial titles published in the Country?
5. Who is the key person in the organization who is responsible for such operations?
6. How effective is the depository law or any other laws concerning deposits in the Country?
7. Are there published national lists or catalogs for serial titles published in the Country? What are they?
8. Are there indexing and abstracting services for serial titles published in the Country? What are they?
9. Is there any plan for computerization?
10. How many languages are in use in the Country? What are they?
11. Is a standardized or generally acceptable transliteration system available?
12. Has an ISDS national centre been declared? When? Where? and in what stage of operation?
13. Will the Country give tentative support to the proposed Regional Centre at this stage?
14. Do you have any comments or suggestions?

Appendix III
CURRENT STATUS OF SERIAL PUBLICATIONS IN THE FIVE PARTICIPATING COUNTRIES

	Indonesia	Malaysia	Philippines*	Singapore	Thailand
1. Number of serial publications known:					
1) Periodicals and regular serials	2,269	3,115		N. A.	894
2) Monographic series	N. A.	N. A.		N. A.	N. A.
3) Document series	N. A.	N. A.		N. A.	N. A.
4) Newspapers	1,397	78			98
5) Others (school magazines)	—	556		—	—

---

① See *Regional Cooperation for ISDS*, in Section III International Cooperation of *Librarianship In World Perspective*, Volume I

(续上表)

2. Number of current serial publications：				
1）Periodicals and regular serials	280	1,855	41 3	466
2）Monographic series	N. A.	97	N. A.	N. A.
3）Document series	N. A.	N. A.	N. A.	N. A.
4）Newspapers	66	44	12	16
5）Others（school magazines）	—	476	—	—
3. Number of new serials appearing in 1974				
1）Periodicals and regular serials	36	247	171	91
2）Monographic series	N. A.	N. A.	N. A.	22
3）Document series	N. A.	N. A.	N.	N. A.
4）Newspapers	N. A.	3	0	3
5）Others（school magazines）	—	3	—	—

* The information for the Philippines was not received in time for inclusion.

Appendix IV
LIST OF LANGUAGES USED IN SERIAL PUBLICATIONS

Indonesia	Malaysia	Philippines	Singapore	Thailand
Indonesian	English	Pilipino（Tagalog）	English	Thai
English	Malay	English	Malay	English
	Chinese	Spanish	Chinese	Chinese
	Tamil	Chinese	Tamil	
	Arabic			
	Punjabi			
	Tehign			
	Malayalam			
	Iban*			
	Murut*			
	Kayan*			
	Kenyah*			
	Saban*			
	Kadazan*			
	Dayah*			
	Biclayuh*			
	Bisayah*			
	Biatak*			

* East Malaysian languages

Appendix V
SELECTED BIBLIOGRAPHIES FOR SERIAL PUBLICATIONS

Indonesia：
A. Lists：
1. Indonesia. Lembaga Perpustakaan. <u>Daftar Malalah Dan Surat Indonesia</u>（Directory of Indonesian Periodicals and Newspapers）. Jakarta, 1972.
2. Indonesia. Pusat Dokumentasi Ilmiah Nasional. <u>Preliminary List of Scientific Journals in South East Asia</u>; Survey of Scientific Journals In South East Asia by UNESCO Field Science Office. Jakarta, 1971.
3. "List of Serials" in <u>Index of Indonesian Learned Periodicals.</u>
4. U. S. Library of Congress. Field Office. <u>Accessions List</u>：Indonesia, Malaysia. Singapore and Brunel, 1964 - Jakarta, 1964 -

B. Indexes：
1. <u>Index of Indonesian Learned Periodicals</u>（Indeks Majalah Iimiah）, 1960 - Jakarta, Indonesian National Scientific Documentation Centre, 1961 -

2. Indonesian Abstracts. 1958 – Jakarta, Indonesian Institute of Sciences, 1958 –

Malaysia:

A. Lists:

1. Bibliografi Negara Malaysia/Malaysian National Bibliography, 1973 – Kuala Lumpur, Perpustakaan Negara Malaysia, 1974 –

2. Current Malaysian Serials: Government (Majalah Kini Malaysia: Kerajaan), Kuala Lumpur, Perpustakaan Negara Malaysia, 1974.

3. Current Malaysian Serials: Non-government. Kuala Lumpur, Perpustakaan Negara Malaysia, (in preparation).

4. Lim, Patricia Pui Huen. Newspapers Published in the Malaysian Area; With a Union List of Holdings. Singapore, Institute of Southeast Asian Studies, 1970. (Institute of Southeast Asian Studies. Occasional Paper, No . 2).

B. Indexes:

1. Indeks Majalah Malaysia (Malaysian Periodicals Index), 1973 – Kuala Lumpur, Perpustakaan Negara Malaysia, 1974 –

2. Index to Current Malaysian. Singapore and Brunei Periodicals, 1967 – 68. Singapore, Joint Standing Committee on Library Cooperation and Bibliographical Services, Persatuan Perpustakaan Singapura and Persatuan Perpustakaan Malaysia, 1971.

Philippine:

A. Lists:

1. Morales, Cecilia T. (comp.). A Checklist of Periodical Titles Published in the Philippines During the Period July1966 to October 15, 1969. Quezon City, 1970. (Typescript)

2. Philippine Bibliography. 1963/4 – Quezon City, University of the Philippines Library, 1973 –

3. Philippines. National Library. Catalog of Copyright Entries, 1964 – 1968. V. 1 Manila, 1972. (TNL Research Guide Series, 5). (Sequel to the 1958 – 1963 Catalog of Copyright Entries)

4. Philippines. National Library. Philippines Serials on Microfilm. Manila, 1973. (TNL Research Guide Series, 8)

B. Indexes:

1. Index to Philippine Periodicals, v. 1-March 1956-Manila, Inter-Departmental Reference Service, Institute of Public Administration, University of the Philippines, 1956 –

2. Philippine Abstracts, 1960-Manila, National Institute of Science and Technology, 1960 –

3. Philippine Science Index. 1963-Manila, National Institute of Science and Technology, 1963 –

4. Philippines. University. Library. Index to Philippines Periodical Literature. 1946 – 1967. Quezon City, 1972. 5 v. (Research Guide Series, 10)

Singapore:

A. Lists:

1. Lim, Patricia Pui Huen. Newspapers Published in the Malaysian Area; With a Union List of Holdings.

2. Singapore. National Library. Checklist of Southeast Asian Serials. Singapore, 1973.

3. Singapore National Bibliography. 1967-Singapore, National Library, 1969 –

4. University of Singapore. Library. Cataloguing Department. Catalogue of the Singapore/Malaysia Collection. Boston, Mass. , G. K. Hall, 1968.

5. _____. Catalogue of the Singapore/Malaysia Collection of the University of Singapore Library. Supplement, 1968 – 1972. Singapore, Singapore University Press, 1974.

B. Indexes:

1. Index to Current Malaysian, Singapore and Brunei Periodicals, 1967 – 68.

2. Singapore Periodicals Index. 1969/70-Singapore, National Library, 1974 –

Thailand:

A. Lists:

1. Thailand. National Library. Periodicals and Newspapers Priced in Thailand Between 1844 – 1934. 1935 – 1971, 1972 – 1973. Bangkok, 1972, 1972, 1974.

2. Thailand. Royal Institute. List of Periodicals Published in Siam. Bangkok, B. E. 2471 (1928).

B. Indexes:

1. Index to Thai Newspapers. B. E. 2507 (1964), B. E. 2508 (1965). Bangkok. , National institute of Development Administration, B. E. 2511 (1968), B. E. 2512 (1969).

2. Index to Thai Periodical Literature, B. E. 2502 – 2504 (1959 – 1961). Bangkok, Ministry of Education, B. E. 2508 (1965).

3. Index to Thai Periodical Literature. Bangkok, Department of Teacher Training, Ministry of Education, B. E . 2505 – 2511 (1962 – 1968). 5 v. v. 1 B. E. 2503 (1962), v. 2 B. E. 2508 (1965), v. 3 B. E.

2509 (1966), v. 4 B. E. 2510 (1967), v. 5 B. E. 2511 (1968).
   4. Index to Thai Periodical Literature, B. E. 2503 - 2506 (1960 - 63), B. E. 2507 - 2510 (1964 - 1967). Bangkok, National Institute of Development Administration, B. E. 2507 (1964), B. E. 2510 (1967).
   5. Thai Abstracts, 1974-Bangkok, Thai National Documentation Centre, 1974 –

Appendix VI
LIST OF KEY PERSONS VISITED

U. S. A
Mr. Joseph W. Price
Chief, Serial Record Division
Processing Department
Library of Congress
Washington, D. C. 20540

Mr. Robert D. Desmond
Assistant Chief (Management)
Serial Record Division

Ms. Mary Sauer
Head
National Serial Data Program
Serial Record Division

Mr. Joseph H. Howard
Assistant Director (Cataloging)
Processing Department

France
Mme. M. Rosenbaum
Director
International Centre for the
Registration of Serial
Publications
Paris

Thailand
Mrs. Maenmas Chavalit
Director
National Library
Tawasukree, Samsen Road
Bangkok 3

Ms. Nilawan Indageha
Executive Secretary
Thai Library Association
241 Prasumain Road
Bangkok

Dr. Tongchat Hongladaromp
Director
Computer Center
Asian Institute of Technology
P. 0. Box 2754
Bangkok

Mr. Abdul Kadir
Serials Librarian

Indonesian National Scientific
Documentation Centre

Mr. Achir S. Nasution
Head
Centre for Library Development
Ministry of Education and Culture
Merdeka Selatan 11
Jakarta

Mr. John P. Rompas
Secretary General
Ikatan Pustakawan Indonesia
Merdeka Selatan 11
Jakarta

Dr. James F. McDivitt
Director
UNESCO Regional Office for Science
and Technology for Southeast Asia
DJ. Thamrin 14
Tromolpos 273/JKT
Jakarta

Philippines
Miss Delia E. Torrijos
Project Director
Scientific Library & Documentation
Center
National Science Development Board
Bicutan, Tagig, Rizal
Manila

Miss Marina G. Dayrit
University Librarian
University of the Philippines
Diliman, Quezon City

Dr. Serafin D. Quiason
Director
National Library
Manila

Mrs. Adoracion M. Bolos
Chief
Filipiniana Division
National Library

Malaysia
Mr. D. E. K. Wijasuriya

Deputy Director
National Library
Kuala Lumpur

Miss Philomene Ng Soo Ching
Assistant Director
National Library

Miss Ch'ng Kim See
Head, Cataloguing Department
National Library

Mr. J. S. Soosai
Librarian
Rubber Research Institute of Malaysia
Jalan Ampang
Kuala Lumpur

Singapore
Mrs. Hedwig Anuar
Director
National Library
Stamford Road

Singapore 6

Miss Quah Swee Lan
Higher Library Officer
National Library

Mr. H. Arthur Vespry
International Development Research Centre (Canada)
RELC International House 30 Orange Grove Road
Singapore 10

Indonesia
Miss Luwarsih Pringgoadisurjo
Director
Indonesian National Scientific Documentation Centre
Jl. Gatot Subroto
P. O. Box 3065/JKT
Jakarta

Mr. Zultanawar
Assistant Director
Indonesian National Scientific Documentation Centre

The Programme Proposal

Based on the findings reported in Part I, a programme of action for the establishment of an ISDS Regional Centre for Southeast Asia is proposed here as Part II, It is hoped that this programme proposal will be favorably considered and approved by UNESCO for implementation in 1976.

I. Major Recommendations

In view of the favorable responses received from the countries visited and the generous offers made by the National Library of Thailand to host the proposed ISDS Regional Centre for Southeast Asia (ISDS-SEA), it is recommended that:

1. The programme proposal detailed in Part II is approved by the executive office of UNISIST and by UNESCO for immediate implementation.

2. The National Library of Thailand should take steps to convene an organizing meeting and workshop in Bangkok which is tentatively scheduled in March 1976. A request for financial support of the organizing meeting and workshop should be submitted to UNESCO in January 1976. Both Dr. Wolfgang Lohner of UNESCO and Mme. M. Rosenbaum of the International Centre should be invited to attend as advisors.

3. An official letter from the National Library of Thailand together with a copy of the approved programme proposal should be sent to the appropriate national agencies in Indonesia, Malaysia, the Philippines, and Singapore, with copies to their respective national commission for UNESCO, inviting each national agency to nominate one national representative to attend the organizing meeting, and one serials librarian who will be responsible for the preparation of worksheets, to attend the first workshop.

4. The organizing meeting should have the following major tasks:
1) To review, revise and ratify the draft Charter of the Regional Centre.
2) To review, revise and sign the draft Agreement Between the National Agency of a Participating Country and the Regional Centre.
3) To officially establish the Regional Centre in accordance with the Charter.

4) To convene the first meeting of the Advisory Board.

5. The Advisory Board should have on its agenda the following items for consideration:

1) The scope of serial publications to be included in the Regional serials data base.

2) The selection of optional and additional ISDS data elements for the Regional serials data base which are not required by the International Centre but may be desirable for regional or national uses.

3) Other operational details.

6. The National Library of Thailand should consult with UNESCO in regard to financial support for the operation of the Regional Centre as specified in page 13 of the programme proposal. It is recommended that for the first five years, the operational costs other than those to be contributed by the Thai Government as well as by the participating countries should be sought from UNESCO and other funding agencies.

7. The International Development Research Centre (Canada) is recommended as one of the major funding sources for the Regional Centre.

8. The Regional Centre should begin its operation as soon as the required financial support is assured.

9. A greater and more prompt technical support for newly established national or regional centres from the International Centre is urged as such support has been considered very inadequate in the past.

II. Rationale of the Proposal

This proposal to establish an ISDS Regional Centre for Southeast Asia is necessary for the early implementation of the International Serials Data System.

Most of the countries in Southeast Asia are still in the developing stage, many lack the required skills and funds to operate national centres. The proposal to establish a Regional Centre has many advantages:

1. Economically, because the number of current serial publications in most of the Southeast Asian countries is relatively small, it will not pay for each country to develop and maintain a computer based serial data bank separately. The Regional Centre is economically feasible particularly if the use of a computer is considered.

2. In terms of funding, the Regional Centre will have far more leverage than a national centre in seeking financial supports.

3. The Regional Centre also provides an answer to the scarcity of trained manpower in the Region. In addition, the proposed Regional Centre can provide training opportunities for serial librarians in the Southeast Asian countries. The experience of designing and developing a computerized serials data system can be shared by all participating countries through training programmes and workshops.

4. The establishment of Regional Centre will help those countries that may otherwise not be able to participate in ISDS for some time to come.

5. With a computer based serial data system, a variety of services can be provided by a by-product to the participating countries, e.g., the printing of new serial titles, both regional and national, at desired intervals.

6. The computer based serials data system can be easily duplicated to provide each participating country with a ready-made serial record in machine-readable form whenever needed.

7. The Regional Centre could serve as a catalyst for further cooperation in the Region.

In addition to these advantages, the success of the Regional Centre as a pilot project of UNESCO under the framework of the UNISIST programme could provide a model for developing countries in other regions of the world in their participation of the International Serials Data System.

During the initial period of five years, the Regional Centre will be funded by many sources including the participating countries themselves and the substantial contribution pledged by the

Thai Government. External support is necessary during the initial years to supplement the local efforts. A cost sharing scheme should be developed by the participating countries once the Regional Centre is on a sound operational basis as this will place the Regional Centre on a more permanent footing.

III. The Proposed Charter of the Regional Centre

To provide a base for discussion at the organizing meeting, a draft Charter of the ISDS Regional Centre for Southeast Asia is proposed below. Included in the draft Charter are preamble, objectives, membership, organization, Advisory Board, and amendments.

THE CHARTER OF THE ISDS REGIONAL CENTRE FOR SOUTHEAST ASIA

1. Preamble

1) The name of the Centre should be the ISDS Regional Centre for Southeast Asia (ISDS-SEA).

2) The term of Southeast Asia should be broadly defined so that all countries within the geographical area can participate in ISDS-SEA.

3) The Centre should be located in Bangkok, Thailand under the auspices of the National Library of Thailand.

2. Objectives

1) To establish a computer based regional serials data bank for serials published in each of the participating countries and to assign ISSN (International Standard Serial Number) to these serials.

2) To serve as a regional node of the ISDS International Centre by putting the local data into the data bank of the International Centre and by acting as a liaison between the International Centre and the national agencies of participating countries in the Region.

3) To improve the bibliographical control of serial publications in each participating country.

4) To facilitate the information transfer on serial publications both within and beyond the Region.

5) To foster a spirit of cooperation among participating countries.

3. Membership

There should be two categories of membership, namely the Charter Members and the Regular Members:

1) The Charter Members are those countries that participate in the initial formation of the Centre including the ratification of this Charter.

2) The Regular Members are those countries that join the Centre after its establishment.

3) Each of the Charter Members is entitled to nominate one national representative to participate in the organizing meeting of ISDS-SEA and subsequently serve as a member of the Advisory Board.

4) Before a membership can be accorded, the participating country must take the following steps:

a. Designate a national agency.

b. Inform ISDS-SEA of its intention to participate.

c. Sign the Agreement Between the National Agency of a Participating Country and the Regional Centre

5) As provided in the Agreement, any member can withdraw its membership from ISDS-SEA by submitting a written notification which is to take effect after 30 days.

4. Organization

1) ISDS-SEA should be established within the National Library of Thailand which provides the Centre with both quarters and staff. The Director of the National Library should serve also as the Director of ISDS-SEA.

2) Each member country should designate a national agency to interact with ISDS-SEA. The National Agency should normally be the one which has a general responsibility in the handling of

serial publications of the country.

3) Each national agency of the Charter Member should nominate a national representative to serve in the Advisory Board.

4) Each national agency, irrespective of whether it is a Charter Member or a Regular Member, should appoint a person from its staff who is responsible for the preparation of worksheets to serve as the Liaison Officer between the National Agency and ISDS-SEA.

5) National agencies should notify ISDS-SEA of any change in their national representatives (for Charter Members only) or liaison officers.

6) A full-time Executive Secretary should be appointed by the Director to take charge of day-to-day operations.

7) ISDS-SEA should have an adequate number of staff to handle the flow of work.

8) Initially, ISDS-SEA should have two divisions under the Executive Secretary, namely Serials Registration and Data Processing. Additional divisions may be added as needed.

9) An organization chart of the Centre is given below:

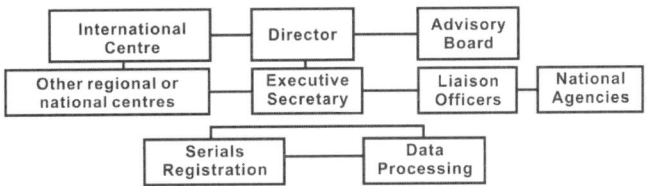

5. Advisory Board

1) The advisory Board, a policy making body, should consist of 5 to 10 members with one national representative nominated by each Charter Member and 1 to 3 technical experts appointed by the Director.

2) The Board should meet once a year to consider policy, procedure and budget of the Centre.

3) The Director of ISDS-SEA should serve as the chairperson of the Advisory Board. An annual report should be prepared by the Director and be distributed to Board Members at least two weeks in advance of Board meetings together with the agenda of the meeting.

4) Should there be recommendations which require a vote, only the national representatives are empowered to vote.

6. Amendments

1) Amendments to the Charter can be proposed by any national representative serving on the Advisory Board.

2) Proposals for amendments to the Charter shall be submitted in writing to the Chairperson of the Advisory Board at least one month before a Board meeting. The text of the proposed amendment shall then be circulated to all Board Members.

3) Such amendments shall become effective on receiving the approval of a two-thirds majority of those empowered to vote at the Board meeting.

Ratified by the following national representatives on _____

Date

_____ (   )
(Signed)   (Country)

_____ (   )
(Signed)   (Country)

_____ (   )
(Signed)   (Country)

_____ (   )
(Signed)   (Country)

_____ (   )
(Signed)   (Country)

IV. The Draft Agreement Between the National Agency of a Participating Country and the Regional Centre

This draft document, intended also for discussion at the organizing meeting, sets down the operational agreement between each national agency and the Regional Centre. The responsibilities of both parties are outlined to ensure the successful operation of the regional project.

DRAFT AGREEMENT BETWEEN

_____

AND THE

ISDS REGIONAL CENTRE FOR SOUTHEAST ASIA

1. The _____ ① has been designated by its Government to act as the national agency for the ISDS Regional Centre for Southeast Asia.

2. (For the Charter Members only) The national agency may nominate one of its senior officers to serve on the Advisory Board of the Regional Centre.

3. The national agency agrees to supply the Regional Centre with the complete information on all serial publications as defined by the Advisory Board on the standard worksheet provided by the International Centre together with one photocopy of the cover and/or title pages of each serial publication reported.

4. The national agency agrees to complete each of the worksheets in accordance with both the Guidelines for ISDS set up by the International Centre and the supplementary guidelines which may be established by the Advisory Board of the Regional Centre. The worksheets shall be sent to the Regional Centre no less than six times a year.

5. The national agency agrees to update the records in the Regional Centre by sending a new worksheet for each addition, correction or deletion of the serial publications previously reported.

6. Once an ISSN is assigned to a serial publication, the national agency is responsible for informing the publisher of the number assigned and for promoting its use.

7. The national agency shall appoint a person from its staff who is responsible for the preparation of worksheets to serve as the liaison officer between the national agency and the Regional Centre. This liaison officer may be different from the one nominated for the Advisory Board in the case of a Charter Member.

8. The costs for the preparation of worksheets, photocopies of the cover and/or title pages, mailing, and in-country promotion are to be borne by the national agency.

9. The Regional Centre is established in Bangkok, Thailand under the auspices of the Thai National Library which agrees to provide office quarters and personnel for the Regional Centre.

10. The Regional Centre agrees to assume the responsibility for the registration of all serial publications reported by the national agencies and for the assignment of ISSN.

11. The Regional Centre agrees to develop and maintain a computerized Regional serials data base should funds for such activities be provided by UNESCO or by other funding sources.

12. The Regional Centre agrees to supply the national agency with a list of those serial publications of the Country to which ISSN have been assigned by other agencies prior to the establishment of the Regional Centre.

13. The Regional Centre agrees to supply each national agency with a periodic list, or a computer printout, of all records reported by the national agency.

14. The Regional Centre agrees to provide each national agency with a magnetic tape of complete records reported by the national agency should this be requested in lieu of a printed list.

15. The Regional Centre agrees to publish a complete list of serial records reported by all national agencies at least once a year. A number of free copies will be made available to the national agency.

---

① The name of the organization which is designated as the national agency.

16. Depending on the availability of funds, the Regional Centre agrees to conduct workshops for the training of liaison officers in the preparation of worksheets and other related matters.

17. The Regional Centre agrees to keep the national agency informed of all matter of concern to ISDS.

18. Both the Regional Centre and the national agency agree to comply with the following conventions established by the International Centre in their operations, transactions or publications:

1) The publications and computer readable services disseminated by ISDS Centres must not be used to generate subset publications or services that violate copyright held by organizations that originally provided these subsets to ISDS for file building purposes.

2) No organization or individual cam copyright any ISSN nor any ISSN and key title combination, nor will royalties be required for the use of ISSN, even though they may appear in copyrighted publications.

3) Publications and computer readable services produced by ISDS must not be used to generate publications or services that violate copyrights held by the IC or a NC or RC.

4) Not withstanding anything contained in the foregoing national centres and regional centres shall not be precluded from compiling and distributing within their territories catalogues and list containing records from the International file.

19. This agreement constitutes the entire understanding of the parties hereto. Any changes or modifications to, or intent to cancel, this agreement shall be made only by mutual written agreement of the parties hereto. Notification of such action shall be submitted in writing by one party to the other at a minimum of thirty (30) days prior to the intended date of such action.

On behalf of the ISDS
Regional Centre for
Southeast Asia
Maenmas Chavalit

On behalf of
_____
_____

_____
Date

_____
Date

V. The Proposed Five-Year Budget

In order the Centre can achieve its objectives stated in its Charter, it is necessary to have an adequate budget for its operations. The five-year budget as given in the tables below is based on the following assumptions:

1. The national agencies of each participating country, including Thailand, will underwrite the costs for collecting the relevant data on all serials published in one's country according to the scope as defined by the Advisory Hoard, preparing the worksheets, photocopying the cover and/or title pages, mailing them to the Regional Centre, and promoting the use of ISSN.

2. As the host Country, the National Library of Thailand will provide office quarters and staff needed for the Regional Centre.

3. As a pilot project within the framework of the UNISIST programme, the UNESCO will provide funds to convene the organizing meeting and the first workshop in Bangkok. In addition, a small annual subsidy will be made to meet a part of the operating expenses.

4. The expenses for computer operations, equipment, office supplies, Board meetings, and training programmes sire to be sought from another funding source, preferably the International Development Research Centre (Canada).

Table I Contribution by Each Funding Source

Source	1st Year	2nd Year	3rd Year	4th Year	5th Year
The Four Participating Countries	$3,600	$4,000	$2,200	$2,400	$2,600
National Library of Thailand	17,500	19,260	20,636	22,695	24,956
UNESCO	8,400	3,300	3,630	3,993	4,392
IDRC or others	16,800	14,100	15,510	17,064	18,771
Total	$46,300	$40,660	$41,976	$46,152	$50,719

Table II The Proposed Five-Year Budget

Item	1st Year	2nd Year	3rd Year	4th Year	5th Year	Source
1. The organizing meeting:						
1) Travel expenses for four national representatives*	$1,600					UNESCO
2) Daily subsistence for five persons, 3 days each	600					UNESCO
3) Meeting expenses*	500					UNESCO
2. The workshop:						
1) Travel expenses for four liaison officers*	1,600					UNESCO
2) Daily subsistence for five persons, 3 days each	600					UNESCO
3) Workshop expenses	500					UNESCO
	$5,400					UNESCO
3. Operating costs:						
1) Director's salary and fringe benefits (1/10 of $6,000)	600	660	726	799	879	Thailand
2) Executive secretary's salary and fringe benefits ($4,800 annually)	4,800	5,280	5,808	6,389	7,028	Thailand
3) Keypunch operator's salary and fringe benefits ($5,000 annually)	3,000	3,300	3,630	3,995	4,395	Thailand
4) Clerk/typist's salary and fringe benefits (1/2 of $1,200)	1,200	1,320	1,452	1,597	1,757	Thailand
5) Office and furniture	6,000	6,600	7,260	7,986	8,785	Thailand
6) Overhead	1,000	1,100	1,210	1,331	1,464	Thailand
	$16,600	$18,260	$20,086	$22,095	$24,306	Thailand
7) Computer time and programming costs	4,800	2,400	2,640	2,904	3,195	IDRC
8) Equipment (Remote terminal, etc.)	10,000	4,000	4,400	4,840	5,324	IDRC
9) Office supplies	2,000	2,200	2,420	2,662	2,928	IDRC

（续上表）

Item	1st Year	2nd Year	3rd Year	4th Year	5th Year	Source
10) Annual meeting of the Advisory Board:						
a. Travel expenses for 4 members		31,760	$1,936	$2,130	$2,343	IDRC
b. Daily subsistence for 5 persons, 2 days each		440	484	533	586	IDRC
c. Meeting expenses		550	603	666	733	IDRC
11) Annual workshop:						
a. Travel expenses for 4 participants		1,760	1,936	2,130	2,345	IDRC
b. Daily subsistence for 5 persons, 2 days each		440	484	533	586	IDRC
c. Workshop expenses		550	605	666	733	IDRC
	$16,800	$14,100	$15,510	$17,064	$18,771	IDRC
12) Postage, telex, cable, etc.	1,000	1,100	1,210	1,331	1,464	UNESCO
13) Printing and publication costs	2,000	2,200	2,420	2,662	2,928	UNESCO
	$3,000	$3,300	$3,630	53,993	$4,392	UNESCO
4. Worksheet preparation:	900	1,000	550	600	650	Each Country
(Based on the estimate of $90 per worksheet for the first year and $.10 more per year thereafter. Costs for photocopying and mailing are included.)	$900	$1,000	$550	$600	$650	

An alternative to the proposed budget is to reduce the scheduled Board meetings and workshops from annual to biennial after the first one, making them alternate as below:

1976	1977	1978	1979	1980
Board Meeting		Board Meeting		Board Meeting
Workshop	Workshop		Workshop	

If this alternative is accepted, a saving of 12,766 from the proposed budget can be achieved. Furthermore, additional savings can be made if some of the Board meetings and workshops can be scheduled in such a way as to coincide with other regional conferences such as CONSAL IV (1977) so that both the Board meeting and an enlarged workshop can be held with a minimum of expense.

(Published by UNESCO, SC-76/WS/7, 1975: p. 42.)

第三次东南亚图书馆员会议

The Third Conference of Southeast Asian Librarians

About 150 librarians from Malaysia, the Philippines, Singapore, Thailand, Australia, Canada, Papua-New Guinea, U. K., U. S. A., and the host country of Indonesia attended the Third Conference of Southeast Asian Librarians (CONSAL III) held on December 15, 1975 in Jakarta. The theme of CONSAL III was "Integrated Library and Documentation Services within the Framework of NATIS", featuring the latest international program of UNESCO to promote the establishment of the National Information System (NATIS) in every country of the world.

The compilation of a Regional Masterlist of Southeast Asian Microforms was proposed by the Southeast Asian Regional Branch, International Council on Archives (SARBICA) in 1973, and was endorsed by CONSAL II in the same year. The project is intended to establish a comprehensive file of all Southeast Asian microforms held by archives, libraries and other institutions in the Region. A two year grant awarded by the International Development Research Centre (Canada) enabled the project to commence in the beginning of 1975. A progress report on the project was made by Miss Winarti Partaningrat (Indonesia), the Editor of the project.

The second day of CONSAL III was devoted both to country reports from Malaysia, the Philippines, Singapore, Thailand, and Indonesia and to the discussion of the paper "Bibliographic and Documentation Service" presented by Mrs. Rosemary Yeap. This paper described some of the recent developments and progress in bibliographic control and documentation services in Singapore, and Malaysia. The titles of the country reports are as follows:

"A Malaysian National Information System (**MANIS**)" by D. E. K. Wijasuriya (Malaysia).

"The Decree on Legal and Cultural Deposit under the New Society: A Country Report" by Dr. Serafin D. Quiason (Philippines).

"National Policies of Library, Documentation and Information Services in Singapore: A Country Report" by Miss Wee Joo Gim (Singapore).

"National Library, Documentation and Information Services in Thailand: A Country Report" by Mrs. Maenmas Chavalit (Thailand).

"Country Report on Library Development in Indonesia" by Mr. A. S. Nasution (Indonesia).

On the third day, two major papers were presented and discussed. "A System of Secondary Services for Southeast Asia" by Mr. Zultanawar described the various secondary services available in the countries of the Region. "Regional Cooperation for International Serials Data System ISDS" by Dr. Hwa-Wei Lee was the one paper presented from outside the Region. The proposal to establish an ISDS Regional Center for Southeast Asia as a pilot project within the framework of UNISIST and its International Serials Data System received considerable interest and support from the participants.

The draft of the new Constitution changed the name of the group from "Conference of Southeast Asian Librarians" to "Congress of Southeast Asian Librarians". The acronym CONSAL remained unchanged. The participants also passed seven resolutions, one of which was in support of NATIS and its implementation in the Region.

A set of papers presented at CONSAL III is available for interlibrary loan from Hwa-Wei Lee, Associate Director of Libraries, Colorado State University, Fort Collins, Colorado 80-523.

Besides learning much from the programs of the Conference, there was an informal aspect which is worth the consideration and perhaps some action by IRRT or IRC: that was the desire expressed by many Southeast Asian libraries to send some of their professional staff to the U. S. for either practical training in a selected library for a period of 3 – 6 months or continuing education on some special subjects in a library school. The majority of these candidates, many of whom are in senior positions, were either trained outside the U. S. or in the U. S. a long time ago. The opportunity for them to receive practical training or take refresher courses will be very useful to expedite library development and modernization in their countries. Furthermore, it can strengthen the tie between American libraries and libraries in the Southeast Asian countries, some of which have thus far followed European practices. Those libraries wanting to cooperate with the U. S. libraries are: the National Library of Thailand, the Scientific Library and Documentation Division, National Science Development Board of the Philippines and the Indonesia National Scientific Documentation Center, to name just a few.

(Published in *Leads*, V. 18, No. 1, March 1976: pp. 3 – 4.)

国际信息系统和国际技术信息系统项目的影响

Impacts of International Information Systems and Programs on NATIS[①]

I. Introduction

The last decade has been an important period in the development of library and information services at the national, regional and international levels. The increasing sophistication of information technologies in reprography, micrography, telecommunications and electronic data processing, coupled with a growing need for information transfer and sharing on a global basis have been the main causes, but it has been the establishment of the UNISIST program and concept[②] and the active promotion of the NATIS program by UNESCO with the support of its Member States in collaboration with several international and intergovernmental organizations that has provided the necessary climate and stimulants for such a development.

To set a stage for discussion and projection of current and future directions, this paper will trace the development of major international information systems and programs in recent years including INIS, AGRIS, DEVSIS, ISDS, UBC, etc.; the restructure of UNESCO just completed to provide a single, unified administrative unit to be responsible for all library and information programs and activities; and the effects of such developments on building national information systems and infrastructures.

II. The Development of International Information Systems and Programs

Perhaps the single most significant development of all international information systems and programs in recent years has been the development of the UNISIST program stemming from a feasibility study undertaken jointly by the United Nations Educational, Scientific and Cultural Organization (UNESCO) and the International Council of Scientific Unions (ICSU) from 1967 to 1971[③]. The implementation of the UNISIST program by UNESCO is in direct "response" to the increasing demand of scientific and technical communities for an international mechanism playing a coordinating and catalytic role in the development of national and international information services"[④] with the ultimate goal of creating "a loosely connected world network of existing and future national and international information systems and services, based on their voluntary cooperation."[⑤] Although, initially, UNISIST concerned itself mainly with scientific and technological information, its definition of "scientific information" has considerably broadened and will eventually be extended to embrace social sciences and humanities.

UNISIST, in a way, is not a system, rather, it should be regarded as a program "designed to provide a conceptual framework for the establishment of national and international scientific and technological information systems and services to facilitate access to the world information resources

---

[①] This is an UNESCO program for the development of national documentation, libraries and archives infrastructures. Presented at the 4th Congress of Southeast Asian Librarians on Regional Co-operation for the Development of National Information Services, June 5–9, 1978, Bangkok, Thailand.

[②] UNISIST is an intergovernmental program of UNESCO for cooperation in the field of scientific and technological information.

[③] Unesco and the International Council of Scientific Unions, *UNISIST STUDY REPORT ON THE FEASIBILITY OF A WORLD SCIENCE INFORMATION SYSTEM*. Paris: UNESCO, 1971: p. 161.

[④] Adam Wysocki. "UNISIST Programme: General Characteristics." *INTERNATIONAL FORUM ON INFORMATION AND DOCUMENTATION*. V. 2 No. 2 (April 1977): p. 5.

[⑤] *Ibid.*

and to create the necessary conditions for systems' interconnection and compatibility"①.

The five main objectives of the UNISIST programs as approved at the Seventeenth Session of the UNESCO General Conference in 1972 are:

Improvement of tools of systems' interconnection.

Improvement of institutional components of the information transfer chain.

Development of specialized information manpower.

Promotion of scientific and technical information policies and improvement of national information networks.

Special assistance to developing countries in strengthening their information infrastructure.

In order to achieve these objectives, particularly in the formative period of the UNISIST program, its activities were divided into three broad categories:

Conceptual: Preparing guidelines, manuals, and other documents of a methodological nature.

Normative: Developing draft standards and normative documents for possible transformation into international standards.

Operational: Providing a wide range of assistance to countries in the implementation of their national information infrastructures upon request.

Among the major international information systems established within the framework of the UNISIST program are the International Nuclear Information System (INIS) and the International Information System for the Agricultural Sciences and Technology (AGRIS). A brief description of these two operational systems is given below.

INIS

In fulfilling its statutory requirement to foster the exchange of nuclear information for peaceful uses among its members, the International Atomic Energy Agency (IAEA) began its planning for a cooperative international information system know as the International Nuclear Information System (INIS) as early as 1965. From its inception, INIS has been conceived as "one that would serve the information requirements of countries of varying levels of development and with different backgrounds and traditions in the methods and techniques of information handling"②.

The system which was approved by the IAEA Board of Governors in 1969 and began its operation a year later is based on the following principles:

It is a mission-oriented, international information system coordinated by an intergovernmental agency with the cooperation of its member countries whose participation in the system is completely voluntary.

Although all information is processed and merged centrally in the international office, the tasks of identifying and recording relevant literature produced in each country (or territory), and, subsequently providing information services in the country based on the various output furnished by the international office, are the responsibility of each participating country.

To facilitate the merging of bibliographic information by the international office, all bibliographic records either reported on manually prepared worksheets or in one of the machine-readable forms must conform with accepted standards and format.

For non-conventional literature such as scientific and technical reports, patent documents, non-commercially published materials, and standards, the participating countries are requested to submit a copy of the text to the international office for microfilming, so that they can be available to users outside the original countries. All output products of the international office can be purchased in the currency of the purchaser's country at low cost.

---

① *THE ESTABLISHMENT OF A NETWORK FOR THE EXCHANGE OF TECHNOLOGICAL INFORMATION*; Report of the Secretary General, U. N. Economic and Social Council. (61st Session, Agenda Item 14, Doc. E/5839. 14 June 1976)

② *INIS TODAY: AN INTRODUCTION TO THE INTERNATIONAL NUCLEAR INFORMATION SYSTEM.* Vienna: International Atomic Energy Agency, 1977: p. 5.

The international office maintains close contact with the national authority and its designated liaison officer in each participating country on both policy and operating matters.

The principle of having each participating country responsible in the preparation of bibliographic input and the dissemination of combined output is advantageous in that it will:

ensure the best coverage of relevant literature in a particular country or territory with little chance for duplication;

enable each participating country to have access to the complete information pool, not merely its own;

spread the cost of data gathering and reporting equitably among large and small producers of literature;

provide the most effective method of handling information in different languages;

assist in improving the national information infrastructures; and

permit each participating country to give better service to its users.

Currently, the available output products from INIS include:

The INIS magnetic tape service—a semi-monthly service provided to all participating countries. The tapes contain all records submitted to the system and can be manipulated by national centers to provide a variety of bibliographical services.

INIS Atomindex—a semi-monthly abstracting journal available to the public on subscription.

The INIS non-conventional literature on microfiche—These fiches are available to the public through either standing or individual orders.

In 1977, 49 countries and 12 international and intergovernmental organizations participated in INIS. The number of bibliographic references published by INIS has grown from 4,053 in 1970 to 60,479 in 1976. The significant contributions of INIS toward the realization of UNISIST objectives include:①

It has improved the tools of systems interconnection through its adoption of existing standards and the development of new ones.

It has stimulated the development of national information systems and improved the institutional components of the information transfer chain through its reliance on decentralized input and output.

It has assisted in the development of specialized information manpower through its training program.

It has paid special attention to the information needs of developing countries.

AGRIS

Using basically the same model developed and tested by INIS, the international Information System for the Agricultural Sciences and Technology (AGRIS), after four years of planning by the Food and Agriculture Organization of the U. N. (FAO), began its operation in 1975 with a two-level design.

Level I —to create a single rapid current awareness system aiming at comprehensive coverage of all newly available literature within the scope of FAO's field of interest and responsibility.

Level II —to develop cooperative networks of specialized centers and services, both existing and future, with responsibility for well-defined subject fields across national borders and language barriers, providing informative abstracts and reviews with detailed indexing.

The operation of AGRIS Level I does not differ much from the operation of INIS. In fact, the bibliographic entries submitted by AGRIS input centers are currently merged and sorted in Vienna, through the computer facilities of INIS, to generate a monthly data base from which both the monthly AGRINDEX and the output magnetic tape are produced for distribution.

Within the short time of its existence, AGRIS has made significant progress in the Level I

---

① *INIS TONDAY*, op. cit., p. 11.

activities. The number of AGRIS participating centers has grown from 59 at the beginning of 1975 to 103 at the end of 1977. The number of input received also has increased from 55,670 in 1975 to 98,581 in 1977. The following table summarizes the inputs by different types of input methods.[①]

Number of Citations Received

Year	Input Sheets		OCR Sheets		Paper Tapes		Magnetic Tapes		Total
1975	12,886	23.1%	0	0%	1,220	2.2%	41,564	74.7%	55,670
1976	16,052	21.8%	2,841	3.9%	1,611	2.2%	52,979	72.1%	73,483
1977	7,992	8.1%	5,969	6.0%	3,500	2.8%	81,120	82.3%	98,581
Total	36,930	16.2%	8,810	3.9%	6,331	2.8%	175,663	77.1%	227,734

From the above table, the use of the manual input method has decreased greatly in the three-year period while the trend towards using machine input has increased noticeably.

According to the Report on the Independent Appraisal of AGRIS[②] completed in April 1977 in pursuance of a request made by the 17th Session of the FAO Conference in 1973, the following benefits of AGRIS were singled out in the findings by the UNESCO study team:

It has contributed to the development of national capabilities for the transfer and management of agricultural information, more particularly in countries without fully developed systems devoted to this end, by facilitating the development or creation of units or cooperative systems for collecting and processing agricultural documents, by training input personnel and by making national agricultural literature more generally available than was previously the case.

It has also operated to create a climate of opinion within which such developments in information activities, particularly within a framework of international cooperation, are possible.

The majority of countries submitting input to AGRIS Level I consider that the benefits of involvement in AGRIS outweigh the cost.

It is recognized to be potentially of great importance in the transfer of agricultural technology between developed and developing countries.

Continuing the development of AGRIS at the present pace will aid the developing countries' access to information of a practical nature which is of immediate utility to them.

The above findings of the UNESCO Study Team are largely confirmed by the recent report of the Agricultural Information Bank for Asia (AIBA), one of the four multinational (or regional) centers of AGRIS[③].

Organizationally, AIBA is a program of the Southeast Asian Regional Center for Graduate Study and Research in Agriculture (SEARCA), one of the regional centers founded under the auspices of the Southeast Asian Ministers of Education Organization (SEAMEO). With financial support from the International Development Research Centre (IDRC) of Canada, 11 national centers in eight countries, three of which are non-SEAMEO counties, participate in AIBA[④].

In addition to converting regional input to OCR (optical character recognition) sheets for submission to the AGRIS Input Unit in Vienna, AIBA also publishes a AGRIASIA which includes additional literature designed to serve regional users. Planning is under way to produce national

---

① FAO, PROGRESS REPORT ON AGRIS, 1975-77. Rome: February 1978 (GIL: AGRIS/TC/1/3): p.1&7.
② REPORT ON THE INDEPENDENT APPRAISAL OF AGRIS: INTERNATIONAL INFORMATION SYSTEM FOR THE AGRICULTURAL SCIENCES&TECHNOLOGY. SUMMARY. Rome: FAO, 1977 (FAO Conf. 17th Session): p.4-5.
③ Ella T. Ricaforte. REGIONAL REPORT ON THE AGRICULTURAL INFORMATION BANK FOR ASIA (AIBA), SEARCA, PHILIPPINES. (GIL: AGRIS/TC/1/INF. 1) p.13.
④ The five SEAMEO countries are: Indonesia, Malaysia, the Philippines, Singapore, and Thailand. The three non-SEAMEO countries are: Bangladesh, Hong Kong, and Sri Lanka.

bibliographies as well as to offer other bibliographic services using the AGRIS magnetic tapes and to establish a program for the collecting and disseminating of non-conventional literature on microfiche. Another area of activity in which AIBA is heavily engaged and having successful results is the training of staff and information users.

Other International Information Systems

Encouraged by the initial success of INIS and AGRIS and prompted by the need for international information systems in other specialized fields a number of new information systems have been proposed and the plans for their implementation are in various stages of development. One of the widely known ones is the International Information System for the Development Sciences (DEVSIS). A detailed design of the system has been made available by the DEVSIS Study Team co-sponsored by IDRC, ILO, OECD, U. N. Department of Economic and Social Affairs, UNDP and UNESCO[1].

Space does not allow separate discussion of DEVSIS or other international information systems under development. These include:

ARKISYST	—Architecture
ASFIS	—Aquatic Sciences and Fisheries
CARIS	—Current Agricultural Research
INFOTERM	—Terminology
ISONET	—Standards
ISORID	—Research in Documentation
POPINS	—Population and Demography
SPINES	—Science and Technology Policies
UNTIS	—Industrial Technology
WISI	—Informatics

Because there is a regional center of the International Serials Data System (ISDS) in operation now in Bangkok for the Southeast. Asia Region, it is appropriate to devote a section of this paper to ISDS.

ISDS

The International Serials Data System (ISDS), an important component of the UNISIST program, was established in 1972 after its original proposal which was contained in the "Report on the Feasibility of an International Serials Data System, and Preliminary System Design"[2] was approved by the UNISIST Central Committee, and recommended to UNSCO for implementation. The system as outlined in the report envisions a two-tier organizational structure consisting of an International Center and a network of national and regional centers jointly responsible for the creation and maintenance of computer based data banks, which hold essential information for the identification of serials. Unlike INIS and AGRIS which are mission-oriented, ISDS is concerned exclusively with a particular medium of publication that is serials, irrespective of their subject.

According to the first issue of the *ISDS BULLETIN* published in 1974, "The aim of ISDS is to provide a reliable registry of world serial publications covering the full range of recorded knowledge. It is responsible for assigning to each serial published under a given title, a unique and unambiguous numeric code identifier, the International Standard Serial Number (ISSN)."

Through an agreement between UNESCO and the French Government, the International Centre for the Registration of Serial Publications was established in Paris with funds provided by the two founding bodies. National and regional centers were established in or by UNESCO Member

---

[1] *DEVSIS Study Team. DEVSIS: THE PRELIMINARY DESIGN OF AN INTERNATIONAL INFORMATION SYSTEM FOR THE DEVELOPMENT SCIENCES.* Ottawa, Canada: IDRC, 1976; p. 247 (IDRC—065e).

[2] M. D. Martin&C. I. Barnes. *REPORT ON THE FEASIBILITY OF AN INTERNATIONAL SERIALS DATA SYSTEM*; prepared for UNISIST/ICSU-AB Working Group on Bibliographic Descriptions. London: INSPEC, 1970 (DM/CB/284).

States pursuant to a request made by the Director General of UNESCO in November 1972.

The operation policy of the ISDS network is based on a set of common rules and standards which cover the ISSN, rules for ISSN assignment, the content of ISDS data files on international, national and regional levels, the use of standard data element specifications, tagging schemes, character sets and magnetic tape formats for interchange and integration purposes. Detailed descriptions of the structure, policies, procedures and specifications of ISDS are given in the *GUIDELINES FOR ISDS*① and its updates.

It was reported recently that the ISDS international file consists of approximately 50,000 records and grows by an average of 20,000 records per year. Through the reporting mechanism of the 39 operational national and regional centers in the ISDS network, nearly 80% of the estimated world serials are covered.

The Regional Center for Southeast Asia (ISDS-SEA) which at present consists of Indonesia, Malaysia, the Philippines, Singapore, and Thailand was established in Bangkok in March 1976. There is now a computerized data base of serial publications published in the ISDS-SEA countries. Two training workshops have been conducted and a detailed regional operational manual has been compiled to supplement the *ISDS GUIDELINES*.

UBC

Before leaving the subject of international information systems and programs, it is difficult not to mention the Universal Bibliographic Control (UBC), a program currently been undertaken by the International Federation of Library Associations and Institutions (IFLA) with the support and collaboration of UNESCO and many countries of the world. The establishment of IFLA International Office for UBC has provided a central coordinating body for the national and international activities of the long-term program.

UBC has been envisaged as a world-wide system for the control and exchange of bibliographical information. The purpose of the system, according to a UNESCO document, "is to make universally and promptly available, in a form which is internationally acceptable, basic bibliographic data on all publications issued in all countries"②.

The procedure proposed by UBC shares some of the common features of the UNISIST model:

"The comprehensive bibliographic record of each publication be made once only in the country of its origin by a national bibliographic agency in conformity with international standards which are applicable to both manual and mechanized systems.

"This record is then made available very promptly in physical forms which are internationally acceptable.

"There would be a network made up of component units, each of which would cover its own publishing activities, all integrated at international level to form the total system."③

In order to achieve UBC, the adoption of acceptable international standards for bibliographic description and identification are essential. In the area of standardization of bibliographic descriptions, IFLA has played a leading role in recent years. This has resulted in the publication of International Standard Bibliographic Descriptions (ISBDs) which have already been accepted by many countries. Other internationally accepted standards for facilitating the identification, ordering and processing of the national book and serial production are the International Standard Book Numbering (ISBN) and, as mentioned earlier, the International Standard Serial Numbering (ISSN).

The further development of the UBC program has led to another program increasingly being

---

① International Centre for the Registration of Serial Publications. *GUIDELINES FOR ISDS: UNISIST, INTERNATIONAL SERIALS DATA SYSTEM (ISDS)* Paris: UNESCO, 1973: p. 58 (SC/WS/538).

② Dorothy Anderson. *UNIVERSAL BIBLIOGRAPHIC CONTROL.* Paris. UNESCO, 1974 (COM. 74/NATIS/Ref. 3): p. 5.

③ NATIS. *OBJECTIVES FOR NATIONAL AND INTERNATIONAL ACTION.* Paris: UNESCO, 1975 (COM. 74/NATIS/3 Rev.): p. 23.

voiced, the Universal Availability of Publications (UAP), which according to its promoters, is regarded as a necessary complement to UBC. ①

UAP is a very wide-ranging concept, affecting legal deposit and other methods of acquisition, the coordination of libraries by such means as union catalogs, the organization of library systems to offer ready availability, inter-library lending and photocopying, the exchange of publications, and the role of national libraries or national centers. Most of these may already be available and implemented either in full or in part within many countries but not necessarily between them to improve access to publications. The ultimate aim of UAP is to ensure that any individual throughout the world should be able to obtain for personal use any publication, wherever or whenever published, either in original or copy.

III. The Recent Restructure of UNESCO and General Information Program

UNESCO, according to its constitution, has a definite mandate within the United Nations system, to deal with matters bearing on the dissemination of knowledge, and the exchange of information and documentation.

For many years the planning and programming of scientific and technical documentation and information activities and the activities on documentation, libraries, and archives were handled by two separate divisions each in a separate sector of UNESCO.

The Division of Scientific and Technological Documentation and Information which was a unit of the Science Sector of UNESCO was responsible for the execution of the UNISIST program while the Division of Documentation Libraries and Archives which was a unit of the Culture and Communications Sector of UNESCO was in charge of implementing the NATIS program. Because of the unavoidable overlap of UNISIST and NATIS in some respects, there were clashes and duplication of efforts between the two divisions resulting in an unhealthy competition and waste of resources.

In order to solve this problem the 18th General Conference of UNESCO held in 1974 adopted a resolution (Resolution 7.21) requesting the Director-General to take steps to coordinate the two existing programs and to propose steps for eventual integration of the two divisions. Based on proposals developed by the Director-General, the 19th General Conference, held in Nairobi in November 1976, decided (Resolution 5.1) on the establishment of a single UNESCO General Information program, to become effective in 1977. The resolution resulted in the creation of a new Division of the General Information Program placed under the authority of the Director of the Bureau of Studies and Programming within the Secretariat and is therefore inter-sect oral in nature. The combined General Information Program is now guided by an Intergovernmental Council of thirty Member States and has as its overall objectives the following goals expanded from original UNISIST objectives.

Promote the formulation of policies and plans at the national, regional and global level.

Further the establishment and application of methods and norms and their dissemination.

Contribute to the development of information infrastructures and specialized international information systems.

Promote the training and education of information specialists and information users.

The restructure of UNESCO's two divisions has in effect integrated the NATIS program within the UNISIST program and made NATIS a component of UNISIST.

IV. Effects on NATIS

During the early stages of development of international information systems and programs there was considerable skepticism at the national level, particularly from the developing countries, about

---

① Maurice B. Line. "Universal Availability of Publications." *UNESCO BULLETIN FOR LIBRARIES*. V. 31, No. 3 (May-June 1977): p. 142.

the adverse effects of these giant systems and programs on the development of national information systems and infrastructures within the countries. Some feared that the proliferation of international information systems would prevent the developing countries from developing their own national information systems. Others feared that the developing countries would become totally dependent on the international information systems and fall victim to information colonialism. There were still others who saw the danger of having the international information systems controlled by the larger, developed countries with little or no interest in the needs of the developing countries. Suspicion also existed about the durability of international information systems and their ability to survive political, financial, and other obstacles.

Much of the skepticism and fear has gradually subsided in recent years because of the success of many of the existing international information systems and programs and the actual benefits many of them have brought about for the developing countries. It is hoped that the NATIS program formerly initiated by UNESCO's Division of Documentation, Libraries and Archives now merged with the General Information Program be continued as an integral, but important component of the UNISIST program.

(Published in *the Proceedings of Regional Cooperation for the Development of National Information Services*. Bangkok: Thai Library Association, 1981: pp. 133 – 146.)

国际教授对校园国际化教育的贡献

Contributions of International Faculty to International Education on Campus[①]

ABSTRACT

International faculty and staff represent a too-often unrecognized and underutilized asset on college and university campuses in efforts to encourage international education and to internationalize the curriculum. This paper examines the size of this resource, ways in which international faculty can contribute to international efforts, and the benefits to the campus and the individual resulting from participation in international programs. The conclusion is that international faculty members can broaden their participation in campus life, serve as vital role-models for students from abroad and those of recent foreign ancestry resident in America, and discover new career and professional opportunity by participating in international education.

INTRODUCTION

When I undertook to prepare this paper, I anticipated a relatively easy task: review the literature, analyze it, add my own experiences, and, voila, the paper would be ready. To my shock and dismay, I quickly learned that the task was much more daunting than I had imagined. There was very little literature on the subject to review, and most of what there was came at the subject only tangentially.

Most of the studies of faculty have treated ethnicity rather than origin as variable.[②] The one blatant exception has been the concern over foreign-born scientists and engineers, which I will address shortly.

What is international education?

In *International Education: What is it?* Stephen Arum begins by noting that "the concept 'international education' means different things to different people."[③] Against this background, he suggests the following definition:

all educational activities of any kind (i. e., teaching studying, doing research or providing technical assistance) involving people of two or more nations[④].

I appreciate the breadth of the definition for, while I may stretch it further in the following remarks, it hints at the variety of activities which deserve to be covered under the rubric of international education. My preferred definition, by Maurice Harari, incorporates everything cited by Arum but extends it much further:

International education must encompass not only the curriculum, international exchanges of scholars and students, cooperative programs with the community (local and international), training, research, and supporting administrative and other services **BUT also must incorporate**

[①] Presented at the 1992 Ohio Chinese Academic and Professional Association, Columbus, Ohio, April 1992.

[②] For example, the National Center for Education Statistics Survey report, *Faculty in Higher Education Institutions*, 1988: 1988 *National Survey of Post-secondary Faculty* (NSOPF – 88) by Susan H. Russell et. al.; NCES 90 – 365 (Washington D. C.: U. S. Department of Education, Office of Educational Research and Improvement, 1990) treats only ethnicity, i. e., American Indian, Asian, Black, Hispanic, and White. No attention is given to place of birth, whether "person of color" born with American citizenship or a transnational citizen or resident. According to the data, Asian account for 4% of faculty, Blacks for 3%, and Hispanics for 2%; however, it is likely that most of the latter two categories were born with American citizenship.

[③] Stephen Arum. *International Education: What Is It? A Taxonomy of International Education of U. S. Universities*, Occasional Papers on International Education Exchange No. 23, Forum Series (New York: Council on International Educational Exchange, 1987).

[④] Ibid., p. 8.

distinct commitments, attitudes, global awareness, an orientation, and a dimension which transcends the entire institution and shapes its ethos."①②

* **Why international education**?

Today, no scholar or academic discipline can afford to be parochial. With research and scholarship underway in virtually every nation in the world, no single nation or region enjoys a monopoly on knowledge. The American Association of State Colleges and Universities has emphasized that the object of improving and enhancing the international dimension on campuses "is to improve the general quality of education. In the modern world, quality is measured by the degree to which colleges, in their organization, instruction, research, and external relations, provide students with the knowledge, skills, and attitudes necessary for living in an interdependent world"③.

At Ohio University (pardon the parochial reference for a larger purpose), our President has identified three steps for achieving internationalization: "clear and repeated articulation of the goal of internationalization in institutional rhetoric, the translation of this rhetoric in the practice of decision-making, and the assessment of the results of these decisions"④.

While those words were intended for those at the highest reaches of universities, I believe that they also provide guidance through which we, as international faculty, can provide leadership in having our institutions adopt this strategy and in effectively implementing it.

* **Who are the international faculty**?

In discussing international faculty, I am concentrating on those members of a faculty who were born abroad as citizens of nations other than the U.S. and primarily who have permanent residence or citizenship in the U.S. In focusing on this group, I am in no way slighting the contributions of natural born U.S. citizens involved in international activities nor of faculty from abroad who teach in the U.S. temporarily.

I initially had hoped to identify that portion faculty to whom I am alluding; however, I have been unable to locate adequate data. As an alternative, I have looked at my own institution, Ohio University. In 1990, a survey was made of faculty and staff engaged in international activities.⑤ It was determined that about one-third of the faculty and staff had some involvement with international activities (occasionally the definition was severely stretched). In looking through the individuals listed in the directory, I was able to ascertain that approximately one-third of these were foreign-born, i.e., met my definition of international faculty. Extrapolating from this admittedly rough and limited data, I believe that a working estimate of 10 to 15 percent of faculty is "international faculty" offers a useful beginning point until more accurate data are available.

While I am concerned with all faculty, I have been able to check my estimate against more complete data for scientists and engineers. Information for 1982 reveals that, for this more specialized group, 18 percent of the scientists and engineers employed by four-year colleges and universities were foreign citizens (6 percent) or naturalized U.S. citizens (12 percent).⑥ The same source reports a lower percentage (11 percent) for those employed by junior colleges or

---

① Maurice Harari. *Internationalization of Higher Education: Effecting Institutional Change in the Curriculum and Campus Ethos*; Occasional Report Series on the Internationalization of Higher Education, Report #1 (Long Beach, CA: Center for International Education, California State University, Long Beach, 1989), p. 2.

② Emphasis added

③ American Association of State Colleges and Universities, *Guidelines: Incorporating and International Dimension in Colleges and Universities* (Washington, D. C.: AASCU, 1985; also available through ERIC as ED 256 213), p. 1.

④ Charles J. Ping. "Strategies and Leadership Options for Effective Internationalization" presented at a national conference for university presidents and other senior administrators, "Internationalizing U. S. Universities: A Time for Leadership" at Washington State University, Spokane, June 5-7, 1990: p. 1-2.

⑤ Reported in Ohio University, *Directory of International Activities*, 1991 [Athens: n. p. (Ohio University Center for International Studies), 1991].

⑥ *Foreign National Scientists and Engineer in the U. S. Labor Force, 1972-1982* (Oak Ridge Associated Universities, 1985) as reported in *Foreign Citizens in U. S. Science and Engineering: History, Status, and Outlook*. Surveys of Science Resources Series Special Report NSF-86-305 (Washington, D. G.: National Science Foundation, 1986), p. 111. Also available as ERIC ED 284 762.

technical institutes and a higher percentage (20 percent) for medical schools. Of all scientists and engineers engaged in teaching and training in 1982, 15 percent were foreign citizens or naturalized U. S. citizens. ①

Data indicate that, in 1985, non-citizens accounted for 39.5 percent of all post-doctorate fellows in all fields but for 67.4 percent in engineering and 55.4 percent in physical sciences compared to 10.8 percent in psychology, 34.5 percent in social sciences and 30.5 percent in the health sciences. ② It is reasonable to hypothesize that, with the possible exception of foreign language departments, the physical sciences and engineering departments are likely to contain the highest percentages of "international faculty".

In working with crude statistics, I should caution that there is likely to be substantial variation among institutions in percentages of "international faculty" and among departments as well. Even with this caveat, it should be evident that there is more "international faculty" on campuses than is generally recognized—even by "international faculty".

Failure to recognize their numbers coupled with a hesitancy about calling attention to one's foreign ancestry (a carry-over from the prevalent "melting-pot" image of past decades) and a sense of being a "stranger in a strange land" are some explanations for the neglect of a valuable international resource on many campuses.

Rather than suggesting sinister motives or attempting to provide definitive explanations for this combination of quiescence and benign neglect, I will focus—in the remainder of this paper—on how and why "international faculty" need to become more assertive in the widespread campaigns to internationalize campuses and why campuses can ill-afford to continue to ignore this valuable human resource, even while looking abroad to seek assistance in internationalizing intellectual life.

* **What roles can they play in international education**?

Having identified, in broad strokes, the numbers of international faculty, I would like to indicate some of the roles that they might be especially prepared to perform. I specifically will omit the case of those in teaching positions dealing specifically with their nation, region, and culture of origin, e. g., the large number of native speakers in foreign language departments or Chinese historians or political scientists focusing on China. My omission in no way slights these individuals, rather it recognizes that I will be saying would be preaching to the converted. In their daily academic life, they are hired to discuss their international heritage. Indeed, these scholars and teachers are the only segment of the international faculty who are likely to be recognized as resources in the internationalization process.

For this reason, I choose to address my remarks to the rest of us—those international faculty who have little occasion to draw on our cultural and linguistic roots and experience in the day-to-day exercise of our professions, our research, or our teaching.

– **Network Nodes.** I fear that this metaphor is sufficiently broad that it may encompass the other roles which I wish to discuss yet so abstract that it obscures very real associations which we have built through our lives. In using the term network, I am primarily referring to the series of acquaintances, associates, friends, and colleagues with whom we have interacted through our careers. I believe that it is safe to say that, for most of us at least, this will include people, faculty, and officials in the U. S. and abroad. We are likely to be familiar with at least some of the people working in our field in our country or region of origin and often in other countries as well as within the United States.

Even if not so inclined, we are likely to be asked by colleagues here to help establish contacts with counterparts there. For example, I am currently trying to help a colleague in philosophy who would like to teach in Taiwan for a year. I confess to being far removed from the realm of philosophical inquiry in Taiwan and generally better acquainted with faculty and administrators in more technical areas, but I am happy to draw on my contacts to draw on their contacts to see if

---

① *Ibid.*, p. 112.
② Data from the National Science Foundation reported in *Ibid.*, p. 35.

something can be arranged. I can assure you that it works the other way as well, as scholars and librarians from China seek my assistance in making contacts to spend a few months or a year in the United States.

But this is only one dimension. As faculty members, we come in contact with hundred and even thousands of students over the years. Some, of course, become closer than others. These especially will seek assistance when completing their education and commencing careers. It is expected that we will advise and guide them, as well as offering recommendations to appropriate companies, institutions, and individuals. With luck, these become a further mutually supportive network.

We each have had individual experiences, yet it is my observation that, as "international faculty" and perhaps before that as international students, we are likely to have broader international associations than Americans born in this country. For example, at the mid-point in my career, I was fortunate to be seconded by the United States Agency for International Development to direct the library and subsequent information centers of the Asian Institute of Technology in Bangkok. In seven years in that position, I was able not only to interact with Thai librarians and scholars but also meet with others in my profession from throughout the region and even around the world.

In citing these obvious examples, I simply want to reinforce that we are network nodes, whether we care to recognize it or not; therefore, we should be conscious of it and aware of how this consciousness can benefit our institutions as well as ourselves.

As a node, I find that I am frequently contacted by individuals and organizations seeking linkages with one of the areas with which I am familiar. I am only too happy, within the limits of my time and abilities, to oblige for this is how networks grow. As I noted, this may be as simple as extending the network, seeking a gateway, to assist a fellow faculty member in gaining international experience. It may also be scheduling appointments for our University President, deans, or other officials when they will be visiting Asia. Conversely, in conjunction with cooperation and exchange programs that I have been able to nurture, I will provide the same services to institutional presidents and officials from institutions in Asia.

While this activity may have air of the now much decried "old boy network", I can assure you that it is far more dynamic than anything referred to by that term and that, particularly in my profession, it is far from restricted to "boys". Indeed, it is the dynamism that is so important. I am continually meeting new people, from more nations, and adding them to my network. I then am able to help them when they seek information which my network can provide and they are able to others whom I know with whom they are unacquainted.

I see two important dimensions in this. There are a number of countries and areas of specialization within which I can offer crucial assistance to my institution as it seeks to internationalize. However, I am fortunate to have been encouraged by my institution to cultivate these activities. This occurred because I recognized that those offices normally responsible for international endeavors might not be aware of my personal background nor might they recognize the key role of library and information institutions in today's world. It has been my responsibility to make them aware of what I could contribute personally and professionally to their goals and then to work cooperatively with them to produce results. We as "international faculty" cannot "hide our lights under bushel baskets". Just as we may resent it when someone assumes that because we are of foreign birth that we somehow lesser equipped or equipped only in special areas, we must be assertive enough to make those responsible aware of our unique capabilities to contribute to this endeavor.

– **Culture brokers: multi-national and multi-cultural.** With the often heated discussion of multi-culturalism on university campuses, it is frequently overlooked or ignored that international faculty are vital elements of multi-cultural institution. This point was emphasized by Ohio University President, Charles J. Ping. He emphasized that one of the true meanings of multiculturalism is "meaning to live with differences"①. The editorial essay was a reaction to Arthur M. Schlesinger, Jr., who in *The Disuniting of America*,② "argues that the 'ethnic upsurge'—a strong and long overdue reinforcement of consciousness of the achievements of women, black Americans, Indians, Hispanics, and Asians-represents a clear but also potentially a dangerous turn in American society."③

Ping counters that, despite Schlesinger's assertion that "on the crest of that wave ④ we moved beyond the simple melting pot interpretation of the American ideal of E Pluribus Unum to a multicultural society. But I [Ping] suggest that the ideal remains and that, in seeming paradox, internationalizing the campus can serve that ideal. Out of many different groups the American ideal has created a society that accepts the many and the one. What we hold as most precious continues to be the individual, complete with the ethnic, racial and other differences that help define that individuality."⑤

It is in this regard that international faculty becomes key individuals. We are best prepared to interpret between the individualistic orientation of American society and the group orientation of Asian society. We can best interpret for our students and colleagues, whether American or foreign, that the beliefs and ideas of others should be respected. Ping offers a prescription for all educators but one for which we are probably best able to appreciate and best able to carry out:

We must be clear... that willful abuse of others will not be tolerated in the university; that the needed correctives of affirmative action will be imposed; that the embracing of differences will be encouraged; in short, that we are many and we are one. ⑥ [emphasis added]

– Role models. In emphasizing Affirmative Action in hiring and promotion and multiculturalism on campuses, considerable attention has been given to the importance of role models and mentoring. Less fortunately, such discussions have tended to be restricted to American minorities and then to emphasize African-American or Hispanic-American students and faculty. I will not pretend that Asian-Americans need additional initiatives to increase their university enrollments; however, I think that the potential value of international faculty as role models for students from abroad is generally overlooked. ⑦ Like many of the topics which I am addressing, this omission could be the subject of an important research effort.

Colleges and universities have increasingly recruited and admitted students from abroad. This is evident in Graph A. ⑧ While this table indicates that the rate of increase in foreign student enrollments has slowed, Graph B [*Ibid.*, p. 15.] demonstrates that this is from far the case for students from Asia. While overall foreign student enrollments increased 5.3 percent between 1989/90 and 1990/91, enrollments for students from Asia increased 10.4 percent and accounted for well over half of the foreign student population.

Most universities have a special office to handle the collective special needs of foreign students but few are equipped or prepared to provide culturally knowledgeable counseling, academic role models, or mentoring. Here international faculty plays a significant role, willingly or not. I believe that international faculty should be aware of this intrinsic role and strive to make it as positive as possible. Certainly this is a matter of temperament but international faculty who are aloof or withdrawn from foreign students probably have as much impact on foreign students as

---

① Charles J. Ping. "Campus Internationalization and Multiculturalism in American Life." *International Educator*. V.1, No.2 (Fall 1991): p.44.
② Athur M. Schlesinger, Jr., *The Disuniting of America* (New York: W. W. Norton & Co., 1992).
③ Ping. "Campus Internationalization...." p.44.
④ a "cult of ethnicity"
⑤ *Ibid.*
⑥ *Ibid.*
⑦ In preparing this paper, I attempted to locate information in the largest database on educational issues, ERIC (Educational Research Information Center). In a computer analysis (using Boolean operators), I found no papers, articles or reports dealing with "role models" and "foreign students" for the period 1981 – 1992.
⑧ Institute of International Education. *Open Doors, 1990/91: Report on International Educational Exchange* (New York: I. I. E., 1991): p.14.

those who choose to accept and accentuate their function as role models.

I prefer the latter approach. As a naturalized Asian-American, I am aware that associates and those with whom I have casual contact will interpret my behavior as representative of my ethnic heritage as well as my own preference. For Asian-American students and for foreign students, I am regularly reminded that my accomplishments and success speak well for American society in general and for its openness. I have chosen to carry this experience further by serving as faculty advisor to various foreign student groups, especially the Chinese Student Association and the Thai Student Association (this latter based on a seven-year assignment as a library director in Bangkok).

For foreign students, especially, the role is mixed: one represents the possibilities in America yet also recognizes how much the students' home countries may need their training and experience. "Brain drain" as a collective phenomenon needs to be discouraged, but it would be hypocritical to simply tell all of the students that they should return to their home countries. Need I add that this dilemma is especially pronounced in associating with students from the People's Republic of China. In such cases, one must be especially careful to warn them of the problems and pitfalls of life in America, dispelling any illusions about "streets paved with gold".

I should add that this same problem exists for any faculty working with foreign students; however, I believe that international faculty is better equipped to address the subject sensitively. We each have gone through an introspective struggle in seeking to identify what was best for ourselves, our families, and our careers. We, better than other faculty, can appreciate the dilemmas facing international students and empathize with their inner struggles. While this sensitivity can be demanding, and even heart-breaking, we represent a resource not otherwise available to the students.

— Catalysts. I deliberately use the plural because I believe that international faculty can serve as a catalyst in a variety of areas relating to internationalization. Depending on the institution, we can be innovators in pushing the campus toward internationalization, we can be supporters and boosters when the impetus to internationalization has begun with others or is well underway, we can be doers (translating the rhetoric in to action and programs) and we can be monitors (engaged observers). As mentioned above, some of us will be better suited to one situation and other to another. This we have to respect. Internationalizing a campus requires efforts of many types and in many quarters. It is important that we respect and support each other—that we recognize the strengths in the diversity of personalities and approaches to challenges. Some may be best in broad public arenas while others will work best with a small group of colleagues. Some may be the advocates of developing, expanding, and refining new international programs while others will implement these. Some will lead in introducing international content into existing courses while others will enrich colleagues and the institutions by developing ties abroad. In emphasizing the unity in our diverse undertakings, I seek to minimize jealousies and conflicts. There are enough arenas with enough varieties to allow each of us to pursue his or her strengths. It is only important to remember that we are working for a common purpose and not to lose sight of the contribution that each of us is making.

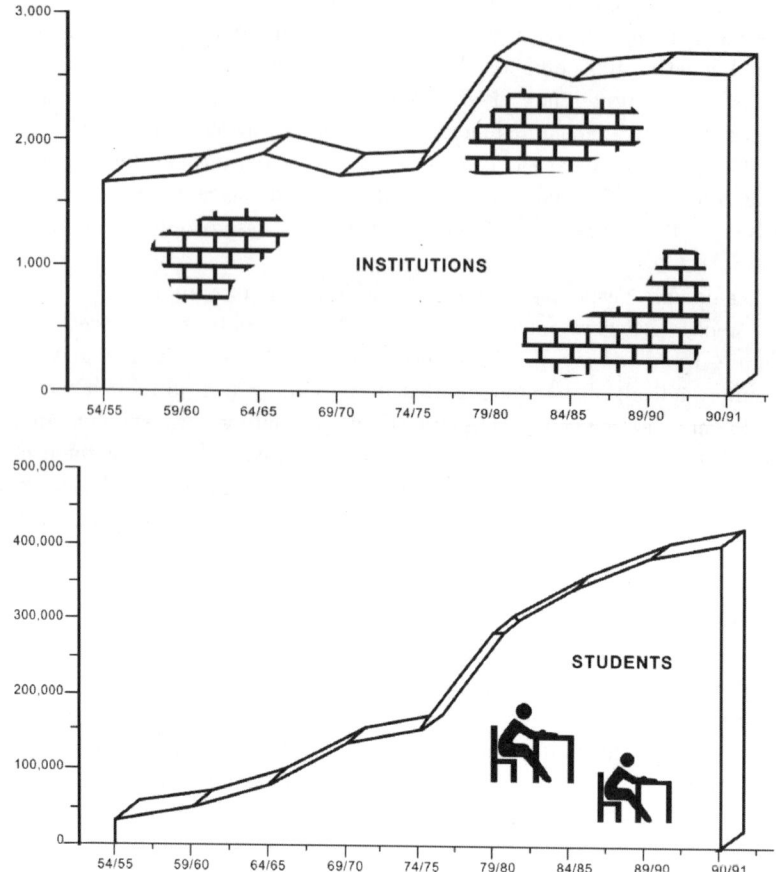

Graph A Foreign Student Enrollment and Institutions Reporting Foreign Students, 1954/55 – 1990/91

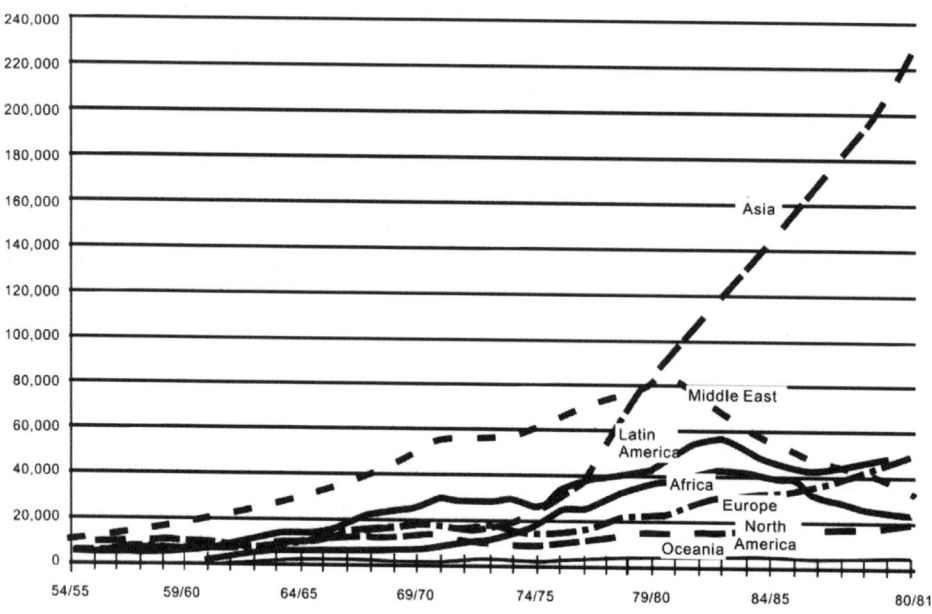

Graph B Foreign Students by World Region of Origin, 1954/55 – 1990/91

* **What are the benefits**?
  – **Enrichment of curriculum and of campus and community life.** International faculty can contribute to the curriculum and the cosmopolitanization of the campus and community even though their specific disciplines may not be amenable to incorporation of international dimensions as usually perceived. I can think of a good example in a colleague at Ohio University. Although he teaches in a technical engineering area, his range of interests and hobbies include such things as Tai Chi and Chinese artistic performance. Each year, he is invited to share these "hobbies", with alumni and citizenry in a program called Elder Hostel. In talking with past participants in this program, he has exerted a charismatic influence in stimulating interest in and appreciation of things Chinese.

Similarly, Ohio University offers a series of classes without credit, called Communiversity, in which international faculty, administrators, and students (as well as others) are able to teach students and community members about their interests and experiences. As an example, although most supermarkets in the Athens area now carry Asian foods such as Tofu and bean sprouts, only fifteen years ago these were available only at Asian groceries in Columbus. To enlighten Americans about the virtues of these traditional foods, an administrator of Chinese ancestry and her mother offered workshops through the Communiversity to teach people about how good these foods taste and how easy they were to make at home. While the present availability from commercial sources is unrelated, the example does indicate that there may be much greater interest in things which we may take for granted than we may be aware of. In some introductory classes on foreign cultures, offered through our International Studies Center, it has not been unusual to supplement formal classroom instruction with sensory experiences in cooking (and eating) foods of the region being studied. Faculty in a variety of disciplines (and their spouses) has often served as "instructor" for these "lab" experiences. I doubt that few of us would think that one could have a real appreciation of Chinese culture without some understanding of the important values manifest in our food and its consumption.

In a less publicly visible fashion, I am regularly asked to provide advice on Chinese culture and traditions (such as the Chinese animal calendar) to help faculty and administrators better understand unfamiliar belief systems and to incorporate this understanding into their interactions with students and community members.

  – **Internationalization of education.** As internationalization depends on people with meaningful international experience, international faculty obviously is among those best prepared to contribute. Moreover, because of their experience and contacts, they frequently can play an important role in facilitating international experiences for colleagues.

  – **Better international understanding.** Students from abroad are an important component on nearly every campus. And, as I mentioned in discussing role models, we international faculty have special responsibilities and capabilities to assure that the presence of these individuals, often drawn from among the best and brightest of their nation, are not looked on as curiosities but rather are seen as stores of talents and experiences which can add new dimensions to teaching and learning.

As I discussed under "Role Models" above, international faculty can be important in assuring that a campus is open to international students and that international students feel free to contribute to the campus experience. Certainly, it is tragic to have students come half-way around the world, only to have primary associations with those with whom they share a common language, ethnicity, and belief system, the ghettoization of foreign students. As a result, they are shortchanged in their education, receiving only a half- or two-thirds-education, dealing predominantly with their technical subject but neglecting to open them to a world of varying behavior patterns, mores, and traditions. Except possibly for the quality of their technical education, they may as well have attended universities in their home countries.

And this is a dual tragedy. Universities increasingly embrace the concept of internationalization but often neglect the richest resources for the process, the dozens of international faculty and staff and hundreds of international students. As a librarian, I would be the last person to degrade what can be learned from reading; however, reading can be no substitute for direct interpersonal experience. If we are to have true international understanding, it will be led by people who are comfortable living with, playing with, and arguing with those of different nationalities, religions, colors, and ideologies.

Most universities have an office, an international or foreign student office, responsible for meeting the special needs of students from abroad. They do an excellent job for the most part; however, we cannot expect them to carry this load. In fact, all faculty should share the commitment to encouraging international interactions and understanding. Nonetheless, we international faculty are especially prepared to meet this challenge. It would be wrong to define it as an arena in which we have special responsibilities, a denial of the collective responsibility of the institution's faculty and staff, but it is certainly an arena in which we should be prepared to lead by deed and example.

– **Appreciation of the importance of international faculty.** We international faculty owe our positions and our careers to our years of education, accomplishments, and performance in our individual roles. Virtually without exception, we were not hired because we were international faculty and, usually, have had to demonstrate that we were far more qualified in our professional area than any American national to earn our positions. Yet, viewed in the light of my foregoing remarks, our institutions have a "two-fer" —that is, they have an outstanding scholar in his or her field of expertise, and they also have someone pre-qualified to contribute to the internationalization most campuses are seeking.

I recognize my particular fortune at Ohio University where most of the campus, led by the university president (see his remarks in footnote 5) is committed to making internationalization a reality, but I am not so naive as to believe that this is the case on all campuses. In the latter case, one will have cultivated a number of allies in various departments and offices on campus who are also engaged actively in the internationalization effort. These can provide supporting documentation of one's activities if needed, and, collectively, you represent a potentially potent force for making internationalization from rhetoric to reality.

– **Recognition and rewards.** This actually continues my remarks in the previous section. While I believe that engagement in internationalization should be fulfilling to you as an individual, it should not be an altruistic endeavor. Most promotion, tenure, and merit raise committees with which I have been familiar consider service on the campus and in the community as vital to the faculty role. This is no time to be reticent in documenting your activities (in fact, this is part of the process of educating colleagues and deans). Again, your allies across the campus can be very helpful in this regard.

Having emphasized the need to assure that your activities are recognized and rewarded, I would prefer to conclude by focusing on what those rewards may be. I have mentioned the most important—the inner satisfaction with having materially contributed to international understanding- and the most material, recognition of your efforts outside your particular discipline as benefitting the campus and community in the form of promotions and salary increases. This, however, does not begin to exhaust the rewards. The more active one is, the more opportunities for further international activities will arise. This is part of the process of networking alluded to earlier and also simply becoming better known in international fields. The forms of rewards in this area are likely to vary greatly from individual to individual, among disciplines, and among geographic areas. It can be manifest in opportunities to present papers, lectures, and workshops abroad or even extended teaching opportunities. It may result in opportunities with international development projects or agencies. It most certainly will result in the development of dynamic new networks which may threaten to overwhelm you with requests for your services or assistance. And it will bring previously inconceivable opportunities to pursue your professional interests in a variety of arenas and to make many friendships which you will treasure for life.

扩展俄亥俄与中国图书馆的联系

Expanding Ties between Ohio and Chinese Libraries

INTRODUCTION

Since the early 1980s, libraries in China have been rebuilding from the devastation of the 1966–1975 "Cultural Revolution". To compensate for years of neglect and destruction, they have looked to the West for help, especially in the areas of new concepts in library and information services, modern library management, applications of information technologies, and education and training.

OHIO AND HUBEI PROVINCE

This has prompted an increasing number of contacts and visits between libraries in Ohio and China. This was enhanced when the Province of Hubei in China became a sister state of Ohio in the mid-1980s. A formal agreement for library cooperation and staff exchange between the Wuhan Library of the Chinese Academy of Sciences in Hubei Province and Ohio University Library was signed in 1985. Under this agreement, a librarian from each library has visited the other for a duration of one to three months each year.

EXPANDING TIES

Expanding from the experience of one-to-one cooperation, Ohio University has become a favored contact point for librarians from all over China. Most that come to Ohio have been attracted also by the world-renowned OCLC and the Chemical Abstracts Service. An increasing number of librarians from China have participated in Ohio University's International Library Internship program which has been in existence since 1979 and has provided training for more than one hundred librarians from developing countries. In September 1988, Ohio University and Xi'an Jiao tong University, one of the leading universities in China, jointly organized the International Symposium on New Techniques and Applications in Libraries in Xi'an, China, and published a 576-page proceedings. Among the 200 participants, sixty were from countries outside China including a large contingent from the U. S. (including Ms. Anne Goss and myself from Ohio University, Ms. Daphne C. Hsueh from Ohio State University, and then OCLC President Rowland Brown).

In recent years, a growing number of Ohio libraries and librarians have developed ties with libraries and librarians in China. Particularly noteworthy were the visit to China in October 1991 by Stephen Wood, then president of Ohio Library Association, at the invitation of the Wuhan Science and Technology Exchange Centre with Foreign Countries and the exchange of visits in 1991 by a group of library directors from four key institutions of higher education in Tianjin, China, led by the Director of Tianjin Higher Education Bureau, and the library deans/directors of Bowling Green State, Cleveland State, Miami, and Ohio Universities. There have been many other visits and contacts by Ohio librarians. For example, Dean Rosemary Du Mont of Kent State School of Library and Information Sciences has lectured in China and has maintained regular contacts with several Chinese libraries and information centers. Kent's library school also has enrolled many Chinese librarians.

LIBRARY PROGRESS IN CHINA

During frequent visits to China for lectures and consultancies over more than a decade, I have witnessed the rebuilding process in libraries throughout China, especially in the cities. Libraries in China have a long history, dating back two thousand years. Wars and political turmoil in the past have destroyed many great libraries, but a tradition of preserving the intellectual heritage and respect for recorded human knowledge have endured. Since the Cultural Revolution, China has experienced rapid recovery. Between 1980 and 1990, the number of public libraries at the county level and above grew by 46%, from 1,732 to 2,527. In 1990, nearly 80% of all counties had a county public library. Below the county level, 53,000 cultural centers and stations (which provide library functions) can be found in urban districts and rural villages. Since 1985, 128 bookmobiles have been added to serve remote areas in 24 provinces, municipalities, and autonomous regions. There are more than fifty separate children libraries. In addition to public libraries, there are 1,075 college and university libraries, 4,500 scientific and special libraries, some of which are called documentation or information centers, 16,246 secondary school libraries, and 246,901 various labor union libraries. Despite the financial difficulties faced by most libraries, many new library buildings have been constructed. Some new university libraries have been built with funds donated by rich business leaders in Hong Kong.

During the early years of the People's Republic of China, Chinese libraries followed closely the model of the Soviet Union. In recent years, however, American influence has grown. A large number of small reading rooms often organized by subject, type of materials, or type of user are now being consolidated. Closed stacks are increasingly giving way to open stacks. Old rules and practices are being updated. New library buildings are constructed using modular design concepts instead of the traditional fixed-function approach. Since 1985, more and more libraries have attempted to use computers for various library operations. A number of locally developed library system software has been in use with varying degrees of success. Before 1978, there were only two undergraduate library schools in the whole of China. By 1992, this had grown to more than fifty library and information science schools, with programs ranging from certificates, associate degrees, and baccalaureates, to masters, and doctoral degrees in many specialties. To counter the serious shortage of trained library staff and librarians, in-service training and correspondence education have been offered by the Central Radio and Television University to a large number of library practitioners. As a result, more professionally trained librarians are employed in senior positions.

GENERAL OBSERVATIONS

Despite significant progress, libraries and information centers in China still face serious challenges. The most critical of these is the lack of adequate funding. Government policies have switched from full to partial funding of universities, government agencies, and other parent organizations of libraries. The result has been to require libraries to generate up to one-half of needed funds. Instead of charging for library and information services, which would not generate sufficient income while discouraging use, libraries are pressured to generate money by other means such as renting space for business and entertainment, operating photocopying, printing, and data processing services, nurseries, bookstores, and other services. Some libraries even run taxis, restaurants, and dance halls to earn sufficient money to pay staff salaries and benefits. Additionally, the low salaries for government employees, including librarians and support staff, have prompted some younger staff to seek employment in the private sector where wages are higher.

Even though, books and journals published in China are still very cheap, prices have risen steadily in recent years. This situation has affected libraries' ability to develop their collections. Buying foreign publications is increasingly beyond the financial ability of most libraries, except the few with access to foreign exchange from special government funds, grants, or World Bank loans.

Early retirement, at age 55 for women and age 60 for men, has caused the loss of many experienced librarians. In universities in particular, respected academic professors with no knowledge of modern librarianship or library management often are made library directors. Just as they begin to become familiar with library operations, they reach retirement age and the process is repeated.

Especially in universities, library services often are decentralized. Even in a central library, collections and services are divided into numerous reading rooms either by broad subjects, by type of materials, or by readers. Faculty and graduate students have collections and reading rooms distinct from undergraduates. Until recently, most library buildings were highly compartmentalized, resulting in poor space and staff utilization as well as poor service for the readers. Some newer buildings have been constructed with modular design and with the concept of open stacks in mind. Building maintenance, even for the new facilities, is generally inadequate. Few have temperature and humidity control.

Although, library cooperation and resource sharing among different type of libraries has improved in recent years, the process has only begun. Better and more effective coordination of library and information services at the local, provincial, and national levels, needs to be a higher priority for appropriate government agencies.

In my contacts with Chinese librarians and information professionals, I have been quite impressed by their dedication and strong desire to do better, despite the many problems. With their hard work and determination to overcome the odds, the future of libraries in China is bright. Modern libraries are the cornerstone for democracy and an open society. Increased contacts with the outside world through cooperative programs, exchanges of visits, conferences, seminars, correspondence, and other means have helped Chinese librarians to learn modern theories and practices of librarianship. The expanding ties between Ohio and Chinese libraries have helped to speed up this process and, at the same time, helped librarians in Ohio to better understand China. In our world of growing interdependence, librarians have a key role in building bridges for mutual cooperation, respect, and appreciation.

(Published in *Ohio Libraries*. V. 6, No. 4, Fall 1993: pp. 22 – 23.)

非营利组织在电子期刊出版行销市场的合作模式：
以 SPARC 与 OCLC 合作 BIO-ONE 为例[①]

The Cooperation of Non-Profit Organizations Publish and Market Electronic Periodicals: The Case of BIO-ONE by SPARC and OCLC

前言

据美国 1998 年统计，正式登记的非营利组织（NPO：Non-Profit Organization）已高达七十五万家，非营利组织已成为美国社会中最大的雇主[②]。而非营利组织的种类繁多，从大学到医院到文教基金会到专业团体，已随着时代的变迁，亦趋多样化，而非营利组织的兴起基础在社会的价值多元化后，许多团体意识到该团体的社会需要，尤其在面临合作及跨领域议题。无法经由政府机构或是企业体系来达成。因为愈是民主国家，政府的流程从选举反映到民意代表，再从民意机构反映到行政部门，再由行政部门设立专责单位，该流程可能造成的行政流程冗长，因而缺乏效率，因此有志之士，乃组成团体，解决一些社会及专业社群的问题，以达成本身的理想。但往往非营利组织的发起社群，是以理念出发居多，或多或少有所谓的"反商情结"，故在经营组织上，忽略掉"开放系统"。"交换资源"是一组织得以生存并服务人民或专业社群的基本要素，此开放系统是指非营利组织与政府、国内国际组织、个人或专业人士之间，存在着互相依存及既合作又竞争的特质。交换资源是经由募集、捐赠、政府预算、组织的行销经营的途径，获得有效的资源。此有效资源在形式上就比私人企业来的丰富多了。因为私人企业的有效资源重点在金钱，再以金钱去换取其他形式的资源，然非营利组织的有效资源其形式可能是金钱，亦可能是人才、物力、一些专业计划、学术作品、甚而是一个观念。所以，一个非营利组织必须也有它的市场经营及行销策略，而其与私人企业不同者，在获利后的资源途径走向不同，私人企业走向企业主或特定投资该公司的股东，而非营利组织的获利资源走向为社会、人民或特定的社群。在图书馆专业社群中，除了学会、协会等非营利组织外，国际间著名的图书馆中的图书馆 OCLC 线上电脑图书馆中心，可说是一具有三十多年悠久历史的代表，另外，SPARC 学术出版及学术资源联盟，则是新兴的、具有三年多经验的此类组织，本文以下针对此两个图书馆界重要的非营利组织，作一介绍。

SPARC（Scholarly Publishing and Academia Resources Coalition）
学术出版及学术资源联盟

一、SPARC 产生的背景

近年来如何令学术出版转型的议题引起了广泛的讨论，然而对于学术刊物成本过高的问题，却一直提不出一个具体的解决之道。在 1986 至 1997 年间，期刊订购的价格上涨了 169%，虽然图书馆每年编列约增加 7% 的期刊费用上涨的百分比，但仍旧赶不上期刊平

[①] 与刘淑德合著。
[②] Lester M. Salamon. "Nonprofit Organization: America's Invisible Sector." *Democracy*. USIA Electronic Journal 3: 1 (Jan. 1998): pp. 10–15.

均近12%的上涨率,1999年对电子期刊的采购,曾被认为是控制期刊价格的一个契机,但事实证明电子期刊的费用比纸本期刊还不可预期。学者发现,最根本的原因,要溯及源头,出版体系的变革,才是解决之道。1989年,经济顾问服务公司(Economic Consulting Services Inc.)就曾经建议图书馆界,图书馆应该鼓励更多的新型态出版团体进入期刊市场,来刺激市场竞争,因而可使图书馆从中得以主导期刊定价的地位。1994年,美国大学协会(AAU:American Association of Universities)负责科技资讯的工作小组,建议大学以更具竞争性的定价鼓励营利及非营利团体致力于电子出版科学研究的成果。1998年,Pew Higher 的美国教育圆桌报告(Education Roundtable(U.S.)report),提出"To Publish and Perish",呼吁图书馆慎选、购买期刊,注重品质,以支持好的出版社[1]。

另一个让期刊上涨之因素,是近年来,美国各大企业并购之风气也吹向出版界,其并购的基本因素来自降低成本,但出版界在并购后,发现文化企业不同于一般消费产品的企业,会因为企业的合并造成大众消费的蒙利,出版界的合并会因为缺乏竞争,更助长了价格的上涨。美国亚利桑纳大学(University of Arizona)的生态学教授 Michael L. Rosenzweig 叙述他个人在学术出版的一个经验,1984年,Rosenzweig 教授与 Chapman & Hull 合办了一个生物学术期刊,该刊一年的订费为100美元,个人订费为35美元。三年后的1987年,ITC(International Thomson Co.)并购了 Chapman & Hull,ITC 将该期刊价格提高了275%。更严重的是,1999年 Wolters Kluwer 又并购了 ITC 旗下部分公司,使该期刊价格又上涨100%。当 Rosenzweig 教授发现,唯有自救才能救学术界,因此请辞了该期刊的主编,另行出版了 Evolutionary Ecology Research。这是一个因为企业并购造成图书馆更大负担的一个实例[2]。

这些因素,也就是 SPARC(学术出版及学术资源联盟)成立的背景之一。SPARC 是一个结合200所美国及加拿大的国家、研究及大学图书馆,在研究图书馆学会(ARL:Association of Research Libraries)的领导下,于1998年6月成立了新联盟。其目的在开创与另外的一些出版机构的"伙伴(Partner)"关系,发展高品质低价格的学术出版品。

二、SPARC 的目标

SPARC 的目标是非常具体的,只要集合会员的力量,持续支持,从每年图书馆的订购费中,即可将 SPARC 的各项目标达成,其总目标为三大项:

(一)创造一个更具竞争力的市场,使期刊的采购与使用费用降低,并奖励对客户的需求,予以合理回应的出版机构。

(二)在加强保护财产权与作者权益时,仍能确保公平使用电子资源的原则。

(三)应用科技改善学术交流的过程,并降低制作与销售权利。

三、SPARC 三项主要的合作出版计划[3]:

(一)SPARC 替代计划(SPARC Alternatives Program)

支援能直接与高价位的科学、技术或医学期刊竞争的低价位替代品。此出版品必须提供 SPARC 会员较低的资料获得成本,整体而言,SPARC 的合作伙伴必需给图书馆一个减

---

[1] Richard K. Johnson. "Competition:A Unifying Ideology for Change in Scholarly Communications." http://www.arl.org/sparc
[2] Michael L. Rosenzweig "Reclaiming What We Own:Expanding Competition in Scholarly Publishing." http://www.arl.org/newsltr/205/reclaiming.html (14 May 2001)
[3] SAPRC. "Information for potential publisher partners." http://www.arl.org/sparc/ (16, Oct. 2000)

少高价位期刊订购数量的机会，以便施行一个更均衡的收集期刊计划。此外，SPARC 协助图书馆从专业角度来判断使用者的需求，并用此依据作为该取舍哪一种期刊的标准。这类馆藏计划也希望提供编辑和作者另一个选择，使它们不用对在某些领域中垄断市场的大出版商过分依赖。

（二）SPARC 前端计划（SPARC Leading Edge Program）

支援使用新技术和有竞争力的商业模式，来满足新兴或快速发展的新科学、技术医学领域对资讯的需求。另外更具挑战的是，以学术界的力量来革新商业模式，特别是能以机构联合订购方式帮助减少出版成本的方法。这类计划可以是全新的或刚起步的，最重要的是能够提供学者一个发表论文和研究成果的新管道，以及能让研究者更轻松地掌握最新资讯。

（三）SPARC 支持科学社群计划（SPARC Scientific Communities Program）

支持发展各学科非营利的学术同侪审核出版品（Peer Reviewed Research），以集合同侪评估过的研究结果及其他内容来满足个别学科社群的需要。并且赞助对科学团体之研究和资料收集有所助益的非营利网站。SPARC 在成立一个以大学为基础的资讯团体来服务科技和医疗领域中的使用者。

因此，SPARC 也鼓励大学间的合作和联盟，以期能累积更多资讯。符合资格的计划必须是非营利性质且在学术领域中的，除此之外，这类计划也需包括以下几点，以期更能回应使用者及图书馆员的需求：

1. 整合使用者所需的内容和联结，以供使用者做进一步查询。
2. 能够处理大专院校中研究工作和奖学金的检定、传播、索引和记录。
3. 让使用者能够更有效率地在网上找到特定学科所需的资料，并希望能在未来满足可以跨学科的整合需要。
4. 培养一个更开放的竞争市场，让使用者能将研究报告的学术资料传播更广。

四、SPARC 的伙伴策略

SPARC 关键在专业伙伴（Partner）的合作，伙伴在此的定义是学术及专业团体的出版单位、大学社团及大学出版部、公家机关、其他非营利出版商和一些独立的出版商。我们可从 SAPRC 的伙伴策略中，了解到 SPARC 的发展与未来计划。

SPARC 的伙伴审核策略中，标准条件如下：

1. 能扩展市场影响力并能对科技和医疗研究的传播有帮助。
2. 具国际观。
3. 能使用电子媒体或其他技术来降低成本或获得竞争优势。
4. 具有清楚的目标。
5. 伙伴的声誉以及出版商的经营方式和图书馆的利益是否相容。
6. 伙伴保证促进智慧财产权和使用权的维护。
7. 确保内容的品质和数量，以吸引有知名度的编辑和作家。
8. 具有稳定及可靠的财务能力。
9. 具有管理计划的能力。

SPARC 对伙伴的有效、具体的助益

由于 SPARC 伙伴能获得最大的利益就是 SPARC 会员的购买承诺。这些会员都是出版合伙人争取订购的购买源。除此之外，SPARC 会努力透过以下方式，确定市场对合伙刊物

的接受度:
1. 协助伙伴评估市场大小、帮助确认出版资源及做市场调查、帮助制订吸引市场的策略（如定价、媒体选择、作家费用、资料档案保管计划等。）
2. 行销公关至广大消费市场包括:
（1）在图书馆、学术界及大众传播媒体做最初的公开发表。
（2）提供 SPARC 的企业标识，用来标明此产品为 SPARC 所推荐。
（3）SPARC 安排在学术界的会议、研讨会、学术活动中，介绍伙伴们的产品。
（4）在图书馆中做广告。
（5）在 SPARC 和 ARL 的网站上持续宣传。
（6）SPARC 在伙伴的产品主题的专业期刊上，发表文章介绍 SPARC 与该伙伴之讯息。

若伙伴候选人能符合 SPARC 的条件，且初步协商也顺利的话，SPARC 会草拟一份协议备忘录作为合作的依据。在合作之初，均是以三年为一期的合约。2001 年 3 月，SPARC 与全球图书馆领域中最大的非营利组织 OCLC 正式成立伙伴关系，然本次合作中，重点在 SPARC 联盟 OCLC 的三万多个使用 OCLC 服务的图书馆，建立学术组织的渠道，帮助 SPARC 推广并发展来自学术界的理念。

五、SPARC 的未来展望

（一）增加会员人数：
开放 ARL 以外的机构加入会员，扩增会员组织。
（二）国际化的扩展：
目前 SPARC 有 13 个会员来自加拿大。但更进一步，期待欧洲及亚太地区的图书馆加入，并开始建立国际的伙伴合作。
（三）突破窠臼，开发市场：
SPARC 寻找每个可能的机会赞助学术研究传播的革新模式，并希望此新模式能保留让同侪检阅的价值，能透过优良的资讯系统，让该领域的大多数学者阅读到。SPARC 希望结合会员制的知名专业学会及图书馆，和一个有电子出版能力的非营利出版商。创造学术出版新契机的雏形已成，目前更要找出一个完善的振兴市场方案，希望终能发展出一套更开放且更多人能共用的学术传播方式。

OCLC：Online Computer Library Center
线上电脑图书馆中心

一、OCLC 会员及共建的 WorldCat 书目资料库[①]

1967 年，俄亥俄学院图书馆成立 Ohio College Library Center，发展出一套电脑系统，使参与的图书馆做线上合作编目，建立线上联合目录，透过馆际互借，以分享图书馆资源。经过三十多年的发展，根据 2000 年初的统计，全球使用并参与 OCLC 服务的团体共计 34,775 家图书馆，正式参与 OCLC 组织成为会员的图书馆计 8,859 家（表一）。2001 年，全球使用并参与 OCLC 服务的图书馆已超越 35,000 家

OCLC 的线上目录 WorldCat，是目前全球最大的书目资料库，根据 2000 年 6 月 30 日

---

① 表一至表四，OCLC Annual Report 1999/2000

的记录为 42,476,614 笔，其各类型书目记录统计，如表二。

其所收录的记录跨越 21 个世纪，其收录书目的年代统计，如表三。

而其所收录的全世界语言的书目，更可证明 OCLC 不仅是一个美国组织，更是一个国际组织。如表四。

表一　OCLC 正式会员图书馆类型统计

会员种类	统计家数	比率
图书馆与资讯科学系所	80	0.9%
大学及学院图书馆	2,964	33.5%
学校图书馆	521	5.9%
公共图书馆	1,410	15.9%
专职技院图书馆	750	8.5%
学会及基金会	372	4.2%
州政府图书馆	376	4.2%
联邦政府图书馆	822	9.3%
公司企业图书馆	1,087	12.3%
郡镇图书馆	110	1.2%
其 他	367	4.1%

表二　OCLC 收录各类型书目记录统计

资料类型	国会图书馆记录笔数	会员图书馆记录笔数	国会图书馆的记录，经由会员图书馆修改的笔数	总笔数
图 书	4,935,467	28,185,522	2,449,644	35,570,633
连续性出版品	209,082	1,882,726	54,079	2,145,887
视听资料	104,973	1,155,137	27,425	1,287,535
地 图	202,713	368,737	6,925	578,375
混合资料	240	297,115	442	297,797
录音资料	156,700	1,237,501	51,768	1,445,969
乐谱	57,360	890,639	54,786	1,002,785
电脑档	4,578	142,583	472	147,633
合计	5,671,113	34,159,960	2,645,541	42,476,614

表三　OCLC 收录书目的年代统计

年代	书目记录笔数	年代	书目记录笔数
2000B. C. – 1B. C.	1,054	1920 – 1929	1,151,878
1A. D. – 1449	2,865	1930 – 1939	1,364,721
1450 – 1499	13,283	1940 – 1949	1,346,511
1500 – 1599	118,742	1950 – 1959	2,037,882
1600 – 1699	276,781	1960 – 1969	3,691,766
1700 – 1799	606,066	1970 – 1979	6,162,341
1800 – 1899	3,347,839	1980 – 1989	7,962,795
1900 – 1909	908,254	1990 – 1999	8,328,826
1910 – 1919	957,093	2000 – 2010	

表四　OCLC 收录的全世界语言的书目记录统计

语言	书目记录笔数	语言	书目记录笔数	语言	书目记录笔数
英文	26,869,669	韩文	168,234	芬兰文	50,251
法文	2,625,495	瑞典文	161,453	越南文	47,760
德文	2,532,416	丹麦文	110,618	意第绪文	39,034
西班牙文	1,799,910	印尼文	104,552	西班牙文	37,848
日文	861,906	匈牙利文	95,902	古斯拉夫文	34,989
俄文	845,905	现代希腊文	79,997	晤鲁都文	34,058
中文	834,847	挪威文	74,122	孟加拉文	31.054
意大利文	786,309	土耳其文	73,559	威尔斯文	25,268
拉丁文	351,227	波斯文	63,369	斯洛伐克文	24,128
葡萄牙文	395,782	古罗马文	60,496	坦米尔文	23,777
捷克文	311,850	北印度文	58,797	安曼文	20,762
荷兰文	246,602	夏威夷文	55,245	立陶宛文	18,363
阿拉伯文	239,641	保加利亚文	53,658	拉脱维亚文	18,327
希伯来文	232,916	泰文	52,375	古及拉特文	18,141
波兰文	217,628	罗马尼亚文	50,896		

（2001 年之最新统计资料显示，WorldCat 已拥有近 45,000,000 笔书目资料）

OCLC 为因应网络资源的庞大，于 2000 年，邀请了约 26 个国家约 500 个图书馆，共同合作线上资源目录服务（CORC：Cooperative Online Resource Catalog），收集并编目约 469,744 笔网络资源（至 2001 年 5 月止）。

二、OCLC 线上参考服务（FirstSear-ch）及线上电子期刊馆藏服务（ECO：Electronic Collections Online）

除了各会员的联合编目服务外，OCLC 自 1991 年起，开启了 FirstSearch 线上服务，目前已提供 85 种资料库，进而，在电子期刊开始盛行的 2000 年，OCLC 亦推出了 ECO 线上电子期刊馆藏服务，至 2001 年，ECO 已提供约 3,400 种电子期刊，计约 7,800,000 篇全文的文献服务，OCLC FirstSearch 及 ECO，透过其建立的全球代理商、经销商，向全世界的图书馆推广并建立会员图书馆之间的期刊全文馆际互借的文献传送服务。各图书馆使用者利用 FirstSearch 及 ECO 进行约超过 800,000,000 次检索。OCLC 的 ECO 特色是在全文电子期刊的策略中，保障图书馆的馆藏权益。因为 OCLC 为全球图书馆的图书馆，任何与他签约的出版商伙伴，是将电子期刊全文放置在 OCLC 的主伺服器上，透过全球网络集中服务全球图书馆。所以，当面临电子期刊来源商的合并、倒闭、政策改变 等不可预期的变数，导致图书馆及读者权益受损时，OCLC 不会面临此恶梦，保障了图书馆及读者的使用权。

三、OCLC Institute 学院

OCLC 于 1997 年，推出一个为图书馆提供高级教育与知识交换的机会，提供课程有，资源共用的持续与创新（Continuity and Innovation in Resource Sharing）；知识检索管理（Knowledge Access Management）；知识管理的方法与系统；诠释资料（Metadata）在知识管理上的应用，目前该学院已扩展到亚洲地区，2001 年在亚洲就已有约 10 场的教育课程的规划。

四、OCLC 研究部：OCLC Office of Research

1978 年 OCLC 成立了研究中心，是世界上研究图书馆学实务的主要研究中心之一，致力于带领图书馆勇敢地面对知识时代所面临的问题与挑战，加以研究并寻求对策。OCLC 在 20 世纪末的 10 年，已投资超过一亿美金来研究及发展新的服务，甚至带动图书馆界面临网路环境的角色转变，拟定行动计划，领导并创造出图书馆能在此网路环境中蓬勃发展，而不致于被资讯专业所淹没。例如：CORC、Dublin Core、Metadata、Extended WorldCat……等具体的成果。

五、OCLC 未来三年的具体计划

（一）Extended WorldCat 策略概述①：

OCLC 于 2000 年 10 月，针对图书馆与网路未来的发展，特订立了三年的计划策略，此计划策略暂拟称之 Extended WorldCat。此策略具体包括四大专案。

1. 诠释资料专案（Metadata Program）。提供诠释资料（Metadata）的制作和管理的服务给图书馆、图书馆使用者及伙伴同业。

2. 知识内容管理专案（Content Management Program）。提供保存及将研究资源数位化

---

① Extending the OCLC Cooperative: A Three-Year Strategy (23, Oct. 2000)

的服务。

3. 创新智慧型导航检索引擎专案（Discovery and Navigation Program）。提供适合搜寻 Extended WorldCat 所用、有效率的使用者检索，超链接及浏览的界面。

4. 完成客户要求专案（Fulfillment Program）。运用最新的科技并结合电子商务，快速地传递资讯发送服务。

（二）Extended WorldCat 的服务范例

我们以一个例子，带出 Extended WorldCat 的具体化。Babam 是一个对女性研究有兴趣的图书馆员，她在研究关于一位 16 世纪女性 Katharina von Bora 的史料。通过她的图书馆，她能利用 Extended WorldCat 来搜寻并取得想要的资料。先透过 Extended WorldCat 的创新智慧型导航检索引擎专案（Discovery and Navigation Program）发展的超强检索引擎，她找到超过 100 个关于此主题的记录，Bamm 发现这些记录很多都包含目录、评论、超链接及相关的主题，她检阅这些记录以及借 Extended WorldCat 的知识内容管理专案（Content Management Program），找到可获得到的电子内容，除此之外，她还运用 Extended WorldCat 的"完成客户要求专案"（Fulfillment Program），到其他图书馆或是某一处获得所需的原件。Babam 同时可也透过线上书商，买到了一本新出版有关研究 Katharina 的书。甚至，在网路搜寻的过程中，与一些研究 Katharina 学者，在网络上交换意见，甚至还可"虚拟旅行"，到与 Katharine's 一生有关的城镇，最后，Babara 使用 WorldCat 的"诠释资料专案"（Metadata Program）的技术，将以上一切整理并加上她个人的评论和意见，发表在图书馆资源网站上。

（三）Extended WorldCat 的资源

Extended WorldCat 将是一个以全世界为据点，来传送资料、元资料和链接等的资源。它同时将得到一系列知识组织工具的帮助。主要的元资料叙述将被连接到其他资讯，如评论、目录、图片和其他可取得的资料（如从图书馆及合作伙伴等处）。Extended WorldCat 将提供资料储存、索引、搜寻、取得和发送等功能。除此之外，它也会包含用来监控及维持 Extended WorldCat 合作品质的工具和资料。

（四）Extended WorldCat 遵循的标准

Extended WorldCat 将继续应用传统的图书馆标准，如 AACR2、MARC 和 Z39.50 等，但它也会创造并应用新开发的标准，如 RDF、XML、Dublin Core、OpenURL、ISO-13250 等。

（五）Extended WorldCat 的特色

1. 包涵范围更加广泛：使用者能找到由各种格式和媒介储存的记录，且大部分都能取得全文。能自世界各国取得全球资讯。由叙述性质的基本记录，链接到内容大纲、评论文章、相关照片、音效及幻灯片剪接和其他，如正在撰写的书籍首章的预告。

2. 更多元的使用方式：使用者将能以不同形式、不同管道使用 Extended WorldCat，通过各图书馆、Extended WorldCat 合作伙伴和 OCLC 本身的网站入口和当地图书馆连接；通过提供资讯的伙伴，如资料库整合人员、网络搜寻引擎和网络入口，获得多元化的丰富资源。

3. 增加与使用者互动的机制：使用者能在使用 Extended WorldCat 时，加上自己的注解和评论。

4. 强化个人化：使用者能选择适合他们需求的 Extended WorldCat 搜寻范围和检视模式。

5. 浏览功能：使用者能用相似的"寻得资料模式搜寻"Extended WorldCat，并寻得和搜寻目标相关的资料。

（六）OCLC 发展

在与图书馆合作团体共同创造 Extended WorldCat 的过程中，OCLC 达到：

1. 将全球网络化的参考书目工具、图书馆组织、国家图书馆等联合起来，建立一套全球共享的参考书目之诠释资料资源。

2. 创立一套架构，将不同来源的资讯组织起来，连接至 Extended WorldCat。

3. 和出版商、学术机构、独立作家和其他对 Extended WorldCat 有贡献并使用 Extended WorldCat 的人建立合伙工作关系。

4. 了解全球数目渐增的资讯搜寻者，对正确、可信度高的资讯的需求。

5. 维护 Extended WorldCat 的内容和品质，以满足使用者的需求。

6. 当必要时，采取行动来补全所提供之搜寻范围和服务的不全之处。

由以上对 OCLC 的介绍，当可了解，其与各资料来源者的合作，是多么重要。

2001 年 3 月，OCLC 完成与 SPARC 签约，正式将 SPARC 的 BIO-ONE 以 OCLC 的服务型态，推广到各生物科技及医学图书馆去。

六、BioOne 非营利组织

（一）BioOne 的组织

BioOne 是一个结合数十种小型学会，于 1999 年 6 月所发行的生物科学期刊的非营利组织，其董事均来自学术机构、图书馆联盟、学会。

例如美国生物科学学会（AIBS：American Institute of Biological Sciences）、学术出版及学术资源联盟（SPARC：Scholarly Publishing and Academia Resources Coalition）、BIG 12 PLUS 图书馆联盟组织、堪萨斯大学（University of Kansas）及 Allen Press 出版商。BioOne 的成立归功于各非营利机构的资源分享，亦是本文在前言所述，一个非营利组织的成功，必须建立在"开放系统"及"交换有效资源"，而所谓有效资源，其形式可能是金钱，亦可能是人才、物力、一些专业计划、学术作品，甚而是一个观念。BioOne 是一个典型的例子，SPARC 及 BIG 12 PLUS 图书馆联盟组织提供 BioOne 发展基金，BioOne 亦提供这些联盟图书馆五年期的免费使用 BioOne 电子馆藏。堪萨斯大学提供网路及硬体设备，Allen Press 建构资料及系统程式设计。2001 年 3 月，BioOne 与 OCLC 两大非营利组织订立伙伴关系，推出 BioOne 电子期刊馆藏服务。在 OCLC 的 ECO 中，可直接订阅 BioOne 的 40 种期刊，亦可从 OCLC 的 FirstSearch 的 85 种资料库中，链接到 BioOne 的电子全文中。本合作即将在 2001 年 7 月正式向使用 OCLC 服务的全球 35,000 个图书馆推广。

（二）BioOne 的内容[①]

目前 BioOne 的内容，共计 40 种电子期刊（表五），BioOne 的特色之一体现在固定的年订费中，陆续增加的电子期刊不再收费或涨价，其订购费是采取"年套装"模式，不但增加了读者的权益，也方便图书馆的预算控制。

---

① http://www2.oclc.org/oclc/fseco/publisher.asp?publisher=BioOne（June 2001）

表五 BioOne 收录电子期刊一览表（资料截至 2001 年 6 月）

电子期刊名称	ISSN	年代	目前发刊	刊期	格式
Ambio	0044-7447	2000	Available	8	PDF
AmericanBiology Teacher	0002-7685	2000	Available	9	PDF
AmericanMidlandNaturalist	0003-0031	2000	Available	2	PDF
AmericanZoologist	0003-1569	2000	Available	6	PDF
AMNHNovitates	0003-0082	2000	Available	1	PDF
AnnalsoftheEntomologicalSocietyofAmerica	0013-8746	2000	Available	6	PDF
TheAuk	0004-8038	2000	Available	4	PDF
Bioscience	0006-3568	2000	Available	12	PDF
TheBryologist	0007-2745	2000	Available	4	PDF
BulletinoftheAmericanMuseumofNaturalHistory	0003-0090	2000	Available	1	PDF
CellStress&Chaperones	1355-8145	2000	Available	4	PDF
TheColeopteristsBulletin	0010-065X	2000	Available	4	PDF
TheCondor	0010-5422	2000	Available	4	PDF
ConservationEcology	1195-5449	TBD	TBD	2	PDF
COPEIA	0045-8511	2000	TBD	4	PDF
EnvironmentalEntomology	0046-225X	2000	Available	6	PDF
Evolution	0014-3820	2000	Available	6	PDF
InVitroCellular&DevelopmentBiology – Animal	1071-2690	2000	Available	12	PDF
InVitroCellular&DevelopmentBiology – Plant	1054-5476	2000	TBD	4	PDF
JournalofAvianMedicineandSurgery	1082-6742	2000	Available	4	PDF
JournalofEconomicEntomology	0022-0493	2000	Available	6	PDF
TheJournalofEukaryoticMicrobiology	1066-5234	2000	Available	6	PDF
JournalofMammalogy	0022-2372	2000	Available	4	PDF
JournalofMedicalEntomology	0022-2585	2000	Available	6	PDF
JournalofPaleontology	0022-3360	2000	Available	6	PDF
JournalofParasitology	0022-3395	2000	Available	6	PDF
JournalofVertebratePaleontology	0272-4634	2000	Available	4	PDF
JournalofZooandWildlifeMedicine	1042-7260	2000	Available	4	PDF
MammalianSpecies	0076-3519	2000	Available	25	PDF

（续上表）

电子期刊名称	ISSN	年代	目前发刊	刊期	格式
MountainResearchandDevelopment	0276－4741	2000	Available	4	PDF
NortheasternNaluralist	1092－6194	2000	Available	4	PDF
Paleobiology	0094－8373	2000	Available	4	PDF
Photochemistry andPhotobiology	0031－8655	2000	Available	12	PDF
RadiationResearch	0033－7587	2000	Available	12	PDF
SWSBulletin	0732－9393	2000	Available	4	PDF
SystematicBotany	0363－6445	2000	Available	4	PDF
WeedScience	0043－1745	2000	Available	6	PDF
WeedTechnology	0890－037X	2000	Available	4	PDF
Wetlands	0277－5212	2000	Available	4	PDF
WilsonBulletin	0043－5643	2000	Available	4	PDF

七、结论

由以上 SPARC、OCLC、BioOne 三大美国与图书馆相关的非营利组织的发展与未来计划的叙述，得知彼此共同合作，运用个别的优势来建立新合作的资源，是 21 世纪跨领域跨组织典范之一。当我们观察国外他人成功的个案时，给予我们一个参考，限于台湾地区外在环境及文化之相异，有一些议题是可以再研究、再讨论的，也期待能有所突破。

（一）合作的权利义务议题：

从非营利组织的跨领域跨组织合作来看，我们如用一般习惯性"买卖"观念来看权利与义务，就会面临困难，当然也就无法享受到非营利组织具体成果时"大爱"的感觉回馈。如果我们用一般"公平"的价值来衡量彼此的权利义务，就会面临合作情绪管理问题，当然也就无法享受到因眼前的吃亏，而获得深耕后的大利。参与非营利组织的经营者与会员，都是需要将层次拉高、眼界拉广。

就 OCLC 在台湾的经验来看，台湾图书馆限于行政流程与观念，多数参与 OCLC 的合作，在购买 OCLC 的服务与产品，或研究 OCLC 的 Metadata、Dublin Core、Knowledge management 来作为自己未来书目的发展。以奉献之心来参与的，只有台湾大学图书馆与政治大学图书馆曾经参与 CORC 共同建置计划。但在其他参与 WorldCat 书目贡献中，台湾的图书馆仍还未起步。此影响力虽然目前看不出来，但十年后，会看到国际组织中，台湾的文化足迹已被吞噬。我们一定有过经验，当我们旅行至北欧国家时，与当地老百姓聊天，他们都不知道台湾，所以，如果我们再不加紧脚步，加入国际的图书馆相关组织，数年后，全世界的图书馆专业体系中，绝不知道在太平洋一角的台湾小岛，有如此高密集的高级图书馆学人才。以本次 OCLC 选举会员理事为例，列在候选名单的图书馆，是根据与 OCLC 互动最多、最频繁的标准来看，前言有提，非营利组织的有效资源不是局限于"金钱"单项思考，而是多项角度的资源，可能是人才、物力、计划，甚而是观念、参与的心等。所以 OCLC 的互动定义在于奉献多少书目在 WorldCat 中，每年使用 WorldCat 占馆藏的百分比。台湾在亚洲购买 OCLC 的服务或产品，不是最少的。但当候选名单出现时，澳洲有三个图书馆，祖国大陆有七家图书馆，新加坡有二个图书馆，香港有三家图书馆，日本有五十四家图书馆，台湾一家图书馆都没有在候选名单中，该候选名单于 2001 年 6 月宣布，香港浸会大学图书馆馆长梁王以荧女士当选本届 2001—2004 年 OCLC 会员理事，候补两位为上海图书馆的吴建中博士及清华大学的刘桂林教授。当选 OCLC 的会员理事的优点是在图书馆学专业的社群中，国际专业的发展讨论到标准或共同规范时，可为台湾的专业社群发挥一些力量，而不至于使台湾的专业发展与国际脱轨。今天，台湾是有实力，但我们不应该因为政策与观念的异质性，因而忽略了这个重要性。当然，我们参与国际组织也不是只有弱势的配合，当我们觉得彼此权利义务相距太大时，我们当一致地表达真正的想法，才能产生互动的机会，进而为自己创造出谈判的空间，从而带领台湾图书馆走向国际。

（二）市场行销观念的议题：

台湾的图书馆相关的非营利组织人士，均为学者及贤达人才，谈到经营必须有行销是被接受的，但要具体实施时，读书人是会有排斥心理的。再碰到产品促销或造势活动，这在台湾的图书馆专业中，是相当困难的。这些唯有在组织中，规划出市场行销部门，开发产品，建立专业品牌，重视市场与行销研究，建立专业社群的志工资源与服务导向，才会让一专业社群的非营利组织蓬勃发展，带来的利润与力量，才能再回馈专业的社群，进而推广全民参与图书馆事业。

Reference

一、中文部分

司徒达贤，非营利组织的经营管理。天下远见出版，2001 年。李华伟撰、赖丽香译，"21 世纪数位化及网路化知识时代中的图书馆"公共图书馆发展 实务研讨会论文集，台中图书馆，2000 年，第 69 – 85 页。

二、英文部分

May M. Case. "ARL promotes competition through SPARC: the Scholarly & Academia Resources Coalition," *Journal of Library Administration.* 29: 3/4, (2000), pp. 227 – 235.

Laverna Saunders, "Research libraries initiate scholarly publishing collaboration" *Computers in Libraries.* 18: 8 (Sept. 1998), pp. 20 – 21.

（原载《中国图书馆学会会报》2002 年 6 月第 68 期，第 14 – 25 页。）

美国对中国图书馆现代化发展的贡献：历史回顾

American Contributions to Modern Library Development in China: A Historic Review[①]

1. Introduction

The origin of libraries in China can be traced back to the time of Confucius (late 6th century BC) or even earlier (c. 1554 – 1045 BC) to the Shang Dynasty.[②] However, before the 20th Century, most of these libraries were imperial libraries, in academies, or private collections. The primary purposes were collection and preservation rather than access and use. The development of the modern libraries did not start until the beginning of the 20th Century. To counter the defeats and humiliation at the hands of foreign colonial powers during the second half of the 19th Century, the imperial government of the Qing Dynasty (AD 1644 – 1911) adopted a series of reforms focusing on modern education and Westernization. Under these reforms, American concepts of libraries found their way into China through the efforts of Miss Mary Elizabeth Wood and the dedication of many American-educated Chinese librarians. As a result, more and more of the new-type libraries were established. After the founding of the Republic of China in 1911, library laws were promulgated; courses on library economy were first offered by Nanjing University in 1913; the first library school, the Wenhua (Boone) Library School, was established in 1920; the Library Association of China (LAC) was founded in 1925, and modified American classification schemes were widely used. All of these developments revealed a strong American influence.[③]

Following the rapid development of libraries in China from 1911 to 1937, such efforts were severely curtailed during the Japanese invasion from 1937 to 1945. The subsequent Civil War in China from 1947 to 1949 delayed the recovery process.

In 1949, the "Nationalist Government" withdrew to Taiwan and, after a period of readjustment, libraries in Taiwan began to develop rapidly with considerable interaction with American librarians and libraries.

Between 1949, the founding of the People's Republic of China, and 1966, the beginning of the "Cultural Revolution", libraries flourished in 10 Journal of Information, Communication and Library Science 4: 4 (Summer, 1998) China, strongly influenced by the Soviet Union. American influence was virtually absent. However, the ten-year "Cultural Revolution" not only halted the progress made during the post – 1949 period but seriously retarded library development. Most libraries were closed, and collections were lost or destroyed.

When the "Cultural Revolution" ended in 1976 and the new Modernization Movement was launched, interaction with American libraries resumed with great speed.

This paper provides a historic review of major American contributions through these interactions, divided into the following six periods:

(1) **Pre-Republican China (Prior to 1911).**
(2) **Rapid Modernization Movement (1911 – 1937).**
(3) **Sino-Japanese War and Civil War (1937 – 1949).**
(4) **Founding of PRC to End of the Cultural Revolution (1949 – 1976).**

[①] An earlier version of this paper was presented at the *China – U. S. Conference on Global Information Access: Challenges and Opportunities*, held in Beijing on August 21 – 23, 1996.

[②] Lai Xinxia. *Zhong Guo Gu Dai Tu Shu Shi Ye Shi* (*The Ancient History of Books and Libraries in China*). Shanghai: Shanghai Jenmin Publishing, 1990: 21 – 23; and Wang Youmei. *Zhong Guo Tu Shu Guan Fa Zhan Shi* (*The History of Library Development in China*). Jilin: Jilin Education Publishing, 1991: 4 – 9.

[③] Chih-Chun Tien Au. "American Impact on Modern Chinese Library Development." (Master's thesis, The Graduate Library School, University of Chicago, 1964)

(5) Developments in Taiwan (1949 to the present).
(6) New Era of Library Development (1976 to present).

2. Pre-Republican China (Prior to 1911)

Following the defeat by British forces during the so-called Opium War and the signing of the humiliating Treaty of Nanjing in 1842, China suffered a series of other setbacks at the hands of foreign colonial powers. In response to pressures from the populace, the imperial government of the Qing Dynasty launched a series of reforms. By the end of the 19th Century, many enlightened government officials and intellectuals realized that in order for China to become strong again, five major areas of pursuit needed to be emphasized. These were:

(1) **development of a new education system**,
(2) **publication of newspapers**,
(3) **establishment of libraries**,
(4) **translation of Western books**, and
(5) **organization of study societies**.

A number of proposals were submitted to the government emphasizing the importance of having modern libraries open to the public. One of these, by Li Dan Fen on May 2, 1896, stated:

Many libraries have been established by western countries. The best libraries have collections numbering in the millions. Citizens can go and read in the libraries and that is the reason why there are so many talents in the West. [1]

Many articles were published during this period emphasizing the importance of new types of libraries developed in the West.[2] Some singled out the American style of librarianship as most desirable for China. One particular article published in October 1898 in the New Knowledge Newspaper (Zhi Xin Bao) described the establishment of a library school in the U.S. by Melvil Dewey to prepare professional librarians.[3]

In the "School Regulations" promulgated by Emperor Guangxu in 1903, detailed requirements for libraries in elementary schools, secondary schools, and colleges were defined. In 1904, the first two government-operated public libraries were established: the Hunan Library in Changsha and the Hubei Library in Wuchang.[4] These were the first to use "library" (tu shu guan) instead of the traditional "book depository" (cang shu lou). "Library Regulations for the Capital (Jingshi) and Provincial Libraries" were promulgated in 1909, and the Capital Library (the forerunner of the National Beijing Library), many provincial libraries, and a military library were established shortly after that.

Perhaps the most significant American contribution to modern library development in China during this period was made by Miss Mary Elizabeth Wood (1862 – 1931). Wood, a librarian of the Richmond Library in Batavia, New York, went to China to visit her missionary brother in Wuchang in 1899. Because of a shortage of teachers, Wood was hired as an English teacher by the mission-operated Wenhua (Boone) College. Recognizing the inadequacy of its library, Wood campaigned hard for improvement. She returned to the U.S. to study library science at Pratt Institute and Simmons College and came back to China to set up the "Public Use Library" (Kung Shu Lin) in the College in 1903. In 1910, she opened it to the public in a new library building with money she had raised in the United States. The Library was the first in China to display books and journals in open stacks and to open its collection to the public not affiliated with the school. Albeit a small library, it became the first library in China modeled after the American style of

---

[1] Wen Cheng Huan. "The Impact of American Librarianship on Chinese Librarianship in Modern Time (1840 – 1949)." Libraries and Culture. 26: 2 (Spring 1991): 374.
[2] Ibid., 373 – 374.
[3] Yen Wen-yu. Zong Guo Tu Shu Guan Fa Zhan Shi (History of the Development of Chinese Libraries). Taipei: Library Association of China, 1983: 14.
[4] Wen. Impact of American Librarianship, 374 & 386.

public library.①

In addition, Wood established a number of branch libraries in neighboring cities. From these, traveling collections were dispatched to faraway places along the Yangtze River. A few went to north China, and one journeyed as far as Beijing.②

Wood's zeal for library development can best be described in her own words, "I feel that I have a call to do this work and that it is part of God's plan for China."③ By combining her dedication to missionary work and her conviction of the importance of modern library development, she tirelessly devoted the next thirty-one years of her life to this noble cause, until her death from a heart attack in 1931.

The first known publications exchange between the U. S. and China began in 1868 when the U. S. Government, represented by the Smithsonian Institution, presented China with books and plant seeds along with a proposal to exchange publications between the two countries. Specifically, the U. S. Government wanted to obtain publications relating to the census and revenue of China.④ In response, the Chinese Government in 1869 presented the U. S. Government with 947 volumes comprised of the census records and other publications. These books were deposited in the Library of Congress and constituted the beginning of L. C. 's Chinese collection.⑤ Further exchanges of documents, books, and maps were undertaken in 1908 and 1909.⑥

3. Rapid Modernization Movement (1911 – 1937)

When the Qing Dynasty was overthrown in 1911 and replaced by the Republic of China, library development continued despite the chaotic political situation. By 1914, provincial libraries had been established in nearly all provinces except a few remote regions. Popular libraries, reading rooms, and mobile libraries flourished everywhere at amazing speed.⑦ In 1915, the Government of the new Republic promulgated two new regulations, one for all libraries and one for popular libraries.

To extend her ideas of American-type of library services, Wood felt the need to have a number of American-trained Chinese librarians. Through her efforts, she raised enough money to send two graduates of Wenhua College to the U. S. for library education—Mr. Shen Zhu Rong (Samuel T. Y. Seng) went in 1914 and Mr. Hu Qing Sheng (Thomas C. S. Hu) went in 1917. Both attended the New York State Library School in Albany. After Shen graduated and returned to China in 1917, Wood asked him and another Wenhua graduate, Mr. Yu Ri Zhang (David Yu), to go on a lecture tour around the country to promote modern librarianship in the American fashion.

When Hu returned from America in 1919, he joined Wood and Shen in their effort to establish the Wenhua Library School in 1920, with Shen as the director. This first library school in China adopted the model of the New York State Library School which required students to complete two years of university education before being admitted. The library school also used the American credit-hour system. Because of the success of the School, it was granted college status by the Ministry of Education in 1930 and most of its graduates became recognized library leaders.

In addition to Shen and Hu, many other Wenhua graduates and others received their library educations in America. They completed library science programs at library schools such as New

---

① Yen, Zong Guo, 26.
② Chiu, A. Kaiming. "Wood, Mary Elizabeth" in *Notable American Women, 1907 – 1950: A Biographical Dictionary* (Cambridge: Belknap Press of Harvard University Press, 1971), 3: 647 – 648.
③ Cheryl Boettcher. "Samuel T. Y. Seng and the Boone Library School." *Libraries and Culture*. 24: 3 (Summer 1989): 270.
④ Yang Chung-sen. "Sino-American Book Exchange: Exchanges Between the National Central Library and U. S. Institutions." *Journal of Library & Information Science*. 16: 3 (October 1990): 2.
⑤ Hu Shu-chao. "The Development of the Chinese Collection in the Library of Congress" (Doctoral dissertation at Florida State University, Tallahassee, Florida, 1977), 261. Also published with same title by Westview Press, 1979.
⑥ Yang, Sino-American, 2 – 3.
⑦ Wen, Impact, 376.

York State, Columbia, Illinois, and Wisconsin. Through their efforts, many summer lectures or short courses were held at Beijing Normal University in 1920, in Guangzhou in 1922, and at Nanjing Southeastern University in 1923—to name just a few. In 1925, the second library school, The Department of Library Science, was established at the National Shanghai University. It is worth mentioning that a number of those who studied in the U. S. and remained there, afterward, played key roles in developing major Chinese collections in several leading American libraries. [1]

With more librarians and more libraries being established, the need for a professional association became apparent. When the Chinese National Association for the Advancement of Education was founded in 1922, it set up a division on Library Education. At the second annual meeting of the Association in 1923, five resolutions were adopted by the Library Education Division. The fourth resolution called for the establishment of library associations in various parts of China. Because of this resolution, local library associations were formed in Beijing, Tianjin, Shanghai, Nanjing, Kaifeng, Nanyang, and Guangzhou in 1924.

About the same time, at the suggestion of Dr. David Yu, a graduate of Wenhua College and Secretary General of the Chinese Y. M. C. A., Wood went back to the U. S. with a petition signed by over 150 Chinese leaders. The petition asked the American Government to designate a portion of the remission of the indemnity imposed after the Boxer Rebellion of 1899 – 1900 to be used for public library development in China. In a tireless effort, Wood visited almost all the Senators and Congressmen in 1924 and successfully persuaded them to pass a bill with the provision that the money be used for "educational and other cultural activities in China"[2]. The administration of the fund, totaling $12,000,000, was entrusted to the China Foundation for the Promotion of Education and Culture. The board of the Foundation consisted of representatives from both countries. Among the many projects funded by the Foundation were the establishment of the National Library of Beijing and annual grants to the Wenhua Library School.

During her trip in the U. S. A., Wood also represented the Chinese National Association for the Advancement of Education in inviting the American Library Association to send its former president, Dr. Arthur E. Bostwick, Director of the St. Louis Public Library, to visit China in 1925. The visit of Bostwick coincided with the formal establishment of the Library Association of China (LAC) in Beijing on June 2, 1925.

In addition to attending the inaugural conference of LAC in Beijing, Bostwick also visited some 50 libraries in ten provinces and 14 large cities in China. He gave many lectures on American librarianship and strongly promoted open access. Under his influence, the China Foundation, at its first meeting in June 1925, decided to use part of the remission from the 1900 indemnity to support library development.

Under a provision of the LAC Constitution, ten other leading American librarians were invited to become honorary members of LAC. They were Melvil Dewey, Herbert Putnam, Ernest C. Richardson, Clement W. Andrews, James I. Myer, John C. Dana, Charles F. D. Belden, William W. Bishop, Carl H. Milan, and Ed wan H. Anderson. In accepting the honor, Dewey's reply was especially heart-warming. He recalled the humble beginning of the American Library Association 49 years earlier with only 50 members and no money. By 1925, its membership had grown to 10,000. Dewey offered his best wishes to LAC to advance popular education through libraries. [3]

At its 50th anniversary conference in Philadelphia in 1926, ALA extended an invitation to LAC. In response, a five-member delegation was sent. In recognition of the contributions made by LAC to promote popular education in China, ALA presented LAC a special award at the conference.

Besides the close cooperation between ALA and LAC, many cooperative projects were carried

---

[1] Ibid., 378 – 379.
[2] Chiu, Wood, Mary Elizabeth, 647 – 648.
[3] Yen, Zong Guo, 229 – 234.

out between individual libraries of the two countries. An example was the agreement for exchange of librarians between the Beijing Library and Columbia University Library signed in 1930. During the first six years, three Chinese librarians went to Columbia University for education and library work.

Just prior to the Sino-Japanese War of 1937 – 1945, library development reached an all time high in China. Government statistics show that the total number of libraries had grown from 502 in 1925 to 5,812 in 1935. ①

4. Sino-Japanese War and Civil War (1937 – 1949)

The Japanese invasion of China in 1937 dealt serious blows to library development. Indiscriminate bombing, burning, and looting by Japanese military forces reduced many libraries to ashes. According to an official estimate, at least 10 million books were lost or stolen, including numerous treasured collections. ②

Fortunately, some 30,000 volumes of rare books and manuscripts, including many Sung and Ming editions, from the National Beijing Library were rescued and shipped to the Library of Congress for safekeeping in 1937. In 1944, with the permission of the Chinese Government, this collection was microfilmed with copies given to the National Beijing Library, the National Central Library, and the Academia Sinica Library. These books were returned to the National Central Library in 1966 when it was re-established in Taiwan. ③

During the early years of the war, in order to replace the losses and to acquire needed books and journals, the government established a Committee on Wartime Library Acquisitions in Sichuan in 1938 and sent out a call for help from other countries. The Library Society of China also wrote to ALA asking for donations of books. In response to the call, ALA at its 1938 Annual Conference held in Kansas City launched a "Books for China" project and collected more than 25,000 books and journals. When the Second World War broke out in the Pacific in 1939, this project was interrupted due to shipping difficulties. To remedy this situation, an International Committee for the Supply of Academic Materials was established jointly by the U. S. Government, the China Foundation for the Promotion of Education and Culture, National Beijing Library, Academia Sinica, the Chinese Ministry of Education, and other agencies to collect scholarly materials on microfilm and airmail them to China. The microfilming was done by the Library of Congress. Some 60 scientific and technical journals were selected and microfilmed regularly. A number of microfilm readers were donated as well④

After the Second World War in 1945, several American librarians visited China to resume contacts with the Chinese library community. Dr. Charles Shaw, Librarian of Swarthmore University and representative of the United Board of Christian Higher Education in China, visited several church-related universities in Nanjing, Beijing, Wuhan, Chengdu, Guangzhou, and Fuzhou in October 1947. Based on his recommendation, six librarians from these universities were sent to the U. S. for further education.

In January 1948, Dr. Charles Brown, Chair of the Far East and Southwest Pacific Subcommittee of ALA and Library Director of Iowa State University, and Mr. Verner Clapp, Deputy Librarian of the Library of Congress, visited China to discuss library cooperation between China and the U. S. After his return, Brown drafted the "Tentative Plan for Library Development in Regard to Sino-American Cultural Relationship" which was submitted to ALA and the U. S. Government. Among the recommendations were:

(1) **Improve the coordination of various organizations interested in helping China to**

---

① *Ibid.*, 110 – 114.
② *Ibid.*, 140 – 141.
③ Wang Chen-Ku. "National Central Library of the Republic of China" in *Comparative and International Librarianship*. ed. P. S. Kawatra (New York: Envoy Press, 1987), 19.
④ Yen, Zong Guo, 145 – 146.

develop a unified action plan.

(2) Develop a cooperative acquisition plan to acquire Chinese publications with the help of the Library Association of China (LAC).

(3) Help Chinese libraries to rebuild their collections through a variety of ways.

(4) Establish an American Library in China.

(5) Encourage the study and understanding of China.

(6) Provide education and training for Chinese librarians.

(7) Establish a joint committee for Sino-American library relations between ALA and LAC.[①]

It was regrettable that this fine plan was shelved due to the unstable political situation in China and the expanding civil war.

5. From the Founding of the PRC to the End of the Cultural Revolution (1949 – 1976)

After the founding of the People's Republic of China, relations between China and the U.S. were cut off. With China's "leaning to one side" policy, Soviet influence replaced the previous American influence. According to one description, Soviet experts "flocked to China in droves" and Lenin's views of libraries as a means of mass education and indoctrination became the guiding principle. Therefore, the purpose of the library was "to serve politics, production, workers, peasants, soldiers, and scientific studies"[②].

From 1949 to 1965, Soviet-style libraries expanded rapidly. In addition to the common types of public, academic, school, and special libraries, a large number of rural libraries (reading rooms) and labor-union libraries sprang up. These latter were operated by labor unions in factories, mines and industries, intended primarily to propagate Marxism-Leninism-Maoism, to raise workers' political awareness, and to increase their knowledge of technology and production[③]

However, beginning in 1956, the relationship between China and the Soviet Union began to sour which led to the withdrawal of Soviet experts in 1957. The "Anti-rightist Movement" intended to defeat the counter-revolutionary "Revisionism" quickly evolved into the disastrous and destructive "Great Proletarian Cultural Revolution" which erupted in 1965.

During the 11 years of "Cultural Revolution", the majority of libraries were closed, and librarians were sent to the countryside to be rehabilitated through manual labor. Many books which were considered problematic were burned and card catalogs destroyed. Led by Mao's wife, Chiang Ching, and those self-styled radicals (the "Red Guards") who despised knowledge and the intellectuals, China was turned upside down in a fanatic turmoil unprecedented in its history.

After the death of Mao and the arrest of the "Gang of Four", including Chiang Ching, in 1976, the Cultural Revolution finally ended. Since, China has launched a new modernization effort to rebuild the country and to make up for lost time. Contacts with the U.S. were resumed.

6. Developments in Taiwan (1949 to the Present)

In Taiwan, the situation was quite different. After the "Nationalist Government" moved to Taiwan, there was a short period of chaos, then—through a series of economic and political reforms—things began improving. Libraries began to recover and move forward. The Library Association of China (LAC) was revived in 1953, the National Central Library re-opened its doors in 1954, and five library science programs have been established in colleges and universities since 1955. To meet manpower needs, the LAC began to offer an annual in-service training program.

---

① *Ibid.*, 237 – 40 & 260 – 269.

② Lee-hsia Hsu Ting. "Chinese Libraries and Library Education, 1949 – 1980: Truth and Myth in the People's Republic of China" (paper presented at the 100th Annual Conference of the American Library Association, San Francisco, CA, June 29, 1981; also ERIC ED 214 516), 2.

③ *Ibid.*, 4.

With the rapid economic development since 1960, a plan for cultural development was initiated by the "government" in 1977 with library development as a key component. The first National Conference on Libraries was held in 1989 under the joint sponsorship of the "National Central Library" and the Library Association of China. Based on one of its recommendations, the "Ministry of Education" established a "Committee on Library Development" to coordinate library planning and development in Taiwan. The Committee drafted a comprehensive Library Law and submitted it for formal adoption by the "government" through the legislative process. Currently, library development has been included as one of the components in the Six-year Plan for "National Building" for 1993 – 1998. ①

Through this entire period, relations between Taiwan and U. S. libraries were close and mutually beneficial. American influence in library development continues strong as the majority of library leaders in Taiwan received their professional education in the U. S. Many American librarians have been invited to Taiwan as consultants and lecturers. Some also have attended library conferences held in Taiwan. For example, Dr. David Kaser of Indiana University has been in Taiwan many times and was the highly respected building consultant for many newly constructed library buildings, including the "National Central Library"②. Dr. Tze-chung Li, the first Chinese American to serve as a library school dean in the U. S., was appointed director of the National Central Library during his tenure at Rosary College③

In 1968, during the Centennial of the First U. S. – China Book Exchange, books and journals on many subjects were donated to the "National Central Library" in Taiwan by American libraries with strong Chinese collections④. They were:

The "Library of Congress"	Physics
University of California, Los Angeles	Biology & Medicine
University of Chicago	Chemistry
Columbia University	General Sciences
Harvard University	Astronomy
University of Illinois	Physics
University of Kansas	General Sciences
University of Michigan	Engineering
University of Minnesota	Mathematics & Biology
University of Pittsburgh	Philosophy
Princeton University	Engineering & Mathematics
Stanford University	General Sciences
Yale University	Biology & Geology

In 1970 – 71, some 28,616 volumes of books and journals were donated to the "National Central Library" by the U. S. Information Services and Rotary International for distribution to other libraries in Taiwan. ⑤ From 1986 to 1990, the Asia Foundation also donated a total of 19,149 volumes to various libraries in Taiwan. ⑥

In reciprocity, the "National Central Library" also sent a large number of publications to the "Library of Congress" and to other American libraries. According to "NCL" statistics, between 1977 and 1989, some 50,627 volumes were sent to the "Library of Congress" by "NCL". ⑦ In

---

① Wang Chen-ku. "Recent Development of Library and Information Services in Taiwan." *Bulletin of the Library Association of China*. 49 (Dec. 1992): 1 – 6.
② Margaret Fung. "David Kaser and Sino-American Librarianship" in *Academic Librarianship Past, Present, and Future*. (eds.) John Richardson & Jinnie Y. David (Englewood, CO: Libraries Unlimited, 1989): 115 – 128.
③ James K. K. Ho. "Ardent, Trustworthy, and Erudite Dr. Tze-Chung Li." *Journal of Information, Communication, and Library Science*. 2: 3 (Spring 1996): 97 – 107.
④ Yang, Sino-American, 5.
⑤ Ibid., 6.
⑥ Ibid., 9.
⑦ Ibid., 7 – 8.

addition, "NCL" has participated in exhibits at the ALA Annual Conference since 1957 and has donated the exhibited books to various American libraries. One of the innovative examples of these was the cooperative program between "NCL" and Ohio University under which Ohio University provided internship training for "NCL" librarians and in return received several of the exhibited collections.①

Through the Fulbright Exchange Program and the USIA/ALA Book Fellows Program, a number of American librarians have gone to Taiwan for lectures and consulting work while a number of library professionals from Taiwan have come to the U.S. for education and scholarly research.

In the area of technical cooperation, Taiwan libraries were the first in Asia to participate in OCLC. "NCL" has also cooperated with OCLC and RLG to create MARC records for Chinese collections.

7. New Era of Library Development (1976 to the Present)

Following the Cultural Revolution, China launched a major effort to rebuild its libraries as an important part of the "Four Modernizations" movement (science and technology, industry, agriculture, and defense). Contacts with the American library community were resumed. In September, 1979, at the invitation of Beijing Library, a delegation of 12 American librarians headed by William Welsh, Deputy Librarian of the Library of Congress spent three weeks in China. In March/April of 1980 Seminars on Library Operation were conducted in Beijing and Shanghai under the joint sponsorship of the China Society of Library Science (CSLS) and USIA. Over 300 librarians from all parts of China participated. In June of 1980, the U.S. Department of Education and the U.S. National Committee for Sino-American Relations invited a delegation of 10 university librarians to visit American university and research libraries. In June of 1981, at the invitation of ALA the China Society of Library Science sent a delegation to attend the 100th Annual Conference of ALA in San Francisco.

Since China rejoined IFLA in 1981, exchange visits and cooperative agreements between libraries of China and the U.S. have increased. In May of 1982, The Chinese Academy of Medical Science and the Rockefeller Foundation organized a seminar on the Management of Medical Libraries in Beijing. In August, at the invitation of Seton Hall University Library, a delegation of librarians and information specialists from the Chinese Academy of Sciences visited many libraries on the East Coast and signed an agreement for staff exchange with Seton Hall University. In December of the same year, under the joint sponsorship of the Institute of Scientific and Technical Information of China and the International Development Research Centre (Canada), this author and three others from the U.S. and Canada were invited to conduct a two-week workshop on Management of Information Centres in China in Kunming.②

From 1982 to 1989, the frequency and variety of library contacts between China and the U.S. grew rapidly. They are too numerous to list. The spirit of cooperation was very high by any measure. Using Ohio University as an example, an agreement for mutual cooperation and staff exchange was signed between Ohio University Libraries and the Wuhan Library of the Chinese Academy of Sciences in June, 1986. Under that agreement, each year, Ohio will send a staff to Wuhan for one month and Wuhan will send a staff to Ohio for three months. In addition, over 70 Chinese librarians have participated in Ohio's International Librarians Internship program since 1984 for periods ranging from one month to one year. On September 8 – 11, 1988, an International Symposium on New Techniques and Applications in Libraries was jointly sponsored by

---

① *Ibid.*, 10.
② K. P. Broadbent. *Management of Information Centres in China: Results of a Course.* Held in Kunming, Yunnan Province, People's Republic of China, 6 – 18 December 1982 (Ottawa, Canada: IDRC, 1984).

Ohio and Xian Jiao tong University in Xian.①

The suppression of the pro-democracy movement of Chinese students in June of 1989 caused the suspension of some cooperative programs between China and other countries. Fortunately, this temporary setback did not last long. Again, China has continued its modernization reform and pragmatic approach for economic development.

Despite serious funding problems, libraries of all types continue to make great strides. Not only have the number of libraries expanded, so have collections, facilities, and services. More and more libraries have adopted the open-stack approach. American library practices are increasingly being adapted to Chinese needs. The Chinese Library Classification Scheme, the Chinese Subject Headings, the Bibliography of Chinese Rare Books, the National Bibliography, the Chinese Standard for Bibliographic Description, Cataloging in Publication practice, the National Center for Microfilming, the development of many standards for library and documentation work, and others have all been put into practice. From 1987 to 1990, a nationwide survey of library and information resources was conducted and results were analyzed for cooperative collection development. Library automation and networking have spread rapidly during the last decade. Since 1994, with the support of the State Education Commission and the State Planning Commission, the development of the China Education and Research Network (CERNET) has been undertaken by Tsinghua University. An agreement with OCLC was signed this year to make the OCLC's FirstSearch available to Chinese users via CERNET. Cooperation with OCLC to make existing and new Chinese databases accessible online will be the next step.

In the area of professional education and training, China is making substantial progress toward meeting its urgent manpower needs. Before 1978 there were only two undergraduate library science programs (Peking and Wuhan Universities). There are now more than 50 library and information science programs offering a wide range of degree programs: associate's, bachelor's, master's, to doctoral degrees. To prepare library support staff, high-school-level programs have also been established. For in-service training, the Bureau of Library Administration of the Ministry of Culture works with the Central Broadcasting and Television University in offering an associate degree program in Library and Information Science since 1985. By 1988, 10,769 students had graduated.②

8. Conclusion

This paper briefly has reviewed modern library development in China from the late 19th Century to the present time with a special focus on the relationship between libraries of China and the U.S. From what has been highlighted in this paper, it is clear that the relationship between the two countries has been close and mutually beneficial. American contributions to the development of modern librarianship in China were of particular significance in the first half of the 20th Century. Following the lead of Mary Elizabeth Wood, whose contributions were far reaching, many American-educated Chinese library leaders have made major improvements. For a young country, the U.S., too, has gone through rapid changes in librarian-ship in the 20th century. It is admirable that the U.S. has shared its progress in modern librarianship with China throughout most of these one hundred years. Both countries have much to gain from continuing and expanding these relationships to build more open and enlightened societies with better informed citizens. Libraries and information centers are the foundation for mass education, cultural enrichment, economic development, and social progress. They are also the base for global understanding and peace. The recent surge of more sophisticated information technologies will enable us to further develop our libraries and information services to meet our present and future information needs.

---

① *International Symposium on New Techniques and Applications in Libraries.* Xi'an, P. R. C. Sept. 8–11, 1988 (Xian, China: Xian Jiaotong University Press, 1988).

② Wu Wei-tse. "New Development of Librarianship in Mainland China During the Past Decade." *Bulletin of the Library Association of China.* 49 (December 1992): 29–43.

This China-U. S. Conference on Global Information Access: Challenges and Opportunities are held at this very important juncture as the two countries seek to reaffirm our mutually beneficial relationship in modern librarianship for the 21st Century.

(Published in *Journal of Information, Communication and Library Science.* V. 4, No. 4, Summer 1998: pp. 10 – 20.)

富布赖特资深专家项目：富布赖特故事

Fulbright Senior Specialist Program: Fulbright Story[①]

Even though I have many friends who participated in various Fulbright programs and had myself served once as a member of the Discipline Advisory Committee for Fulbright Scholar Awards in Library Science, I had never been a Fulbrighter until taking up my recent assignment in Thailand as a Fulbright Senior Specialist.

I was first approached by Associate Professor Ratana Na Lamphun, Head of the Department of Library Science, Chiang Mai University, Chiang Mai, Thailand, asking if I may be available to spend six weeks at her Department to assist in the redesign of the graduate program in Library and Information Science. She thought that the Fulbright Program might be able to support my trip. She was right! The formalities required were relatively easy to comply with and within three months I was in Chiang Mai ready to undertake the challenging assignment.

Chiang Mai, founded in 1296, is a major metropolitan city in Northern Thailand and is rich in the history and culture of the Northern Lan Na Thai. Its population is diversified with a variety of ethnic minorities living together in harmony. The climate is very comfortable with breezes and coolness at night.

Chiang Mai University is a key regional university established in 1964 to serve the needs of Northern Thailand. Its comprehensive academic and research programs have grown rapidly in recent years to include 17 faculties (colleges), a graduate school, and 6 research institutes. The main campus is located at the foot of the famous Doi (Mountain) Suthep and near the Doi Suthep-Pui National Park.

My first day after arrival was shadowed, however, by the tragic event of September 11. I was sitting in front of the television in my hotel room watching BBC reports all night. In the next few days, all the people I met, including my hosts, tried to comfort me by expressing their sympathy and condemnation of the brutal and senseless terrorist attacks on innocent people.

During the six weeks of my Fulbright assignment, I worked closely with Professor Ratana and a Planning Committee for Curriculum Redesign. We reviewed the existing curriculum, did an environment scan, interviewed a number students and graduates, discussed with all the faculty members in the department, consulted with the Dean of the Faculty of Humanities and other key administrators in the University, and visited all key libraries in the Chiang Mai area. Throughout our intensive interactions, a consensus for a new graduate program was easily reached. I worked very hard, but fruitfully, in drafting a report with a set of findings and recommendations, which was unanimously approved by the Planning Committee.

A two-day seminar was held just before the conclusion of my assignment. The seminar was attended by library educators and administrators from most of the other universities in Thailand. It was officially opened by Dr. Nipon Tuwanon, President of Chiang Mai University, and by Professor Em-On Chittasobhon, Dean of the Faculty of Humanities. I was very pleased and honored that Dr. Pimon Ruetrakul, Executive Director, Thailand-U. S. Educational Foundation, also came from Bangkok to take part in the seminar.

At the seminar, Professor Ratana and I presented our report and recommendations, including the proposed new graduate program in Information and Knowledge Management, which will replace the existing program in Library and Information Science. In addition to the final report, I also gave

---

[①] This article was presented at Department of Library Science, Faculty of Humanities, Chiang Mai University, Chiang Mai, Thailand, September 9, 2001 – October 20, 2001.

lectures on the Strategic Direction of Libraries in Knowledge Management and an Introduction to Dublin Core Metadata as a Tool for the Description of Digital Resources. Dr. Kanchit Malaivongs, Vice President and CIO, National Science and Technology Development Agency of Thailand, was invited to give a lecture on the Latest Development in Information Technology and Infrastructure in Thailand. Mr. Andrew Wang, Executive Director, OCLC Asia Pacific Services, was invited to give a presentation on global library cooperation and resource sharing. His assistant, Ms. Shu-En Tsai assisted in providing an online demonstration.

Despite the fact that I had to work very hard most of the time, including evenings and weekends, in order to complete my assignment, I still managed to take some time out for sightseeing in Northern Thailand. I visited the charming city of Lamphun-the hometown of Professor Ratana's husband; some of the Buddhist temples in Chiang Mai and Lamphun; the notorious Golden Triangle which borders Laos and Myanmar; and the Hmong and Yao ethnic minority villages. It was regrettable that due to work demands I had to cancel a trip to visit the long necked Karen tribe in Mae Hong Son.

Although my Fulbright assignment officially ended on October 20, 2001, undoubtedly my connection with Chiang Mai University will continue. I hope to develop an institutional tie between Ohio University and Chiang Mai University in academic cooperation and exchange. Furthermore, I will continue to help the Department of Library and Information Science in its effort to implement the proposed new graduate program. This will include faculty development, course preparation, writing the first book on Knowledge Management in Thai, and expanding the funding sources.

It is gratifying that the Fulbright program has given me the opportunity of doing something that is significant and useful during my retirement.

My new office at Chiang Mai University (From left to right: Faculty members Saithong Manomai-Udom, Tasana Saladyanant, Hwa-Wei Lee, Darunee Na Lampang, and Ratana Na Lamphun).

(Published at the website of The Fulbright Scholar Program. http://www.cies.org/specialists/stories/ss_hlee.htm)

注重信息与知识管理：
重新制订清迈大学图书馆与资讯学研究生培养计划

Focusing on Information and Knowledge Management: Redesigning the Graduate Program of Library and Information Science at Chiang Mai University[①]

IMPETUS FOR CURRICULUM REDESIGN

Library science education in Thailand began in 1951 at Chulalongkorn University. In 1955, the Department of Library Science was established at the same university to offer an undergraduate program. The first graduate program in library science in Thailand was added in 1964. As of now, there are more than eighteen universities and institutions that offer both undergraduate and graduate programs in library and information science.

The Department of Library Science in the Faculty of Humanities, Chiang Mai University was established in 1968, offering a BA degree in Library Science. Its initial curriculum was revised three times, in 1973, 1987 and 1994. As a result of the 1987 revision, the first course on "Information Science" was offered that year. Since 1994 more courses in information science were added, included among them was a course on "Information Technology". Planning for a graduate program was begun as early as 1977. Final approval by the Ministry of University Affairs was received in March 1995 and the first class of graduate students for a Master of Arts degree in Library and Information Science was admitted in 1997.[②] An interdisciplinary graduate program offering a Master of Science degree in Information Technology and Management by the Graduate School of Chiang Mai University began in 1999.

Even though the graduate program in Library and Information Science at Chiang Mai University is still relatively new, there are some obvious problems that require a thorough review. Some of these problems that have been identified are:

1. The program has failed to attract a sufficient number of applicants.

Ever since its inception in 1995 the number of applicants for admission each year was less than twenty-two which was its highest in 1998 and the number of them who passed the entrance examination (both written and oral) were nine at its highest, also in 1998. What are the reasons or causes for this low number of applicants? What are the remedies that are needed to correct this situation?

2. There are many questions about the curriculum and its focus in the changing profession.

As the profession is undergoing rapid and profound changes in recent years both in Thailand and abroad, what should be the appropriate changes in the graduate curriculum for library and information science at Chiang Mai University? What should be the new philosophy, objectives, and focus of the Chiang Mai program? Should the program be amended here and there as needed or should it be totally redesigned and refocused?

[①] Co-author: Ratana Na-Lamphun.

[②] Na-Lamphun, Ratana. "Information science at Chiengmai University." In *Library and Information Science Education: Essays in Honor of Professor Suthilak Ambhanwong*. Bangkok, Department of Library Science, Faculty of Arts, Chulalongkorn University, 1997: pp. 112–122.

3. There is a need for faculty development, but how?

All faculty members are very much aware of the need for faculty development and have sought every opportunity that is available, including the participation in conferences, short courses, certificate programs, and even further studies. How should the department develop a systematic approach and secure outside funding for continuing support of such a needs? What should be the priority areas for faculty development in the light of curriculum changes?

THE PLANNING PROCESS

To plan for the review and redesign of the graduate program, the head of the department, Associate Professor Ratana Na-Lamphun, appointed a Curriculum Redesign Committee which consisted of five faculty members and five external consultants. The five faculty members were:
- Assistant Professor Darunee Na Lampang
- Lecturer Pranee Wongchamras (secretary)
- Associate Professor Ratana Na-Lamphun (Chair)
- Lecturer Saithong Manomai-Udom
- Associate Professor Tasana Saladyanant.

The five external consultants were:
- Dr. Kanchit Malaivongs, Vice President and CIO, National Science and Technology Development Agency (NSTDA), Ministry of Science, Technology and Environment
- Dr. Kulthida Tuamsuk, Associate Dean for Foreign Relations and Information, Graduate School, Khon Kaen University
- Mr. Nopasit Chakpitak, Department of Computer Engineering, Chiang Mai University, and NSTDA Coordinator, Chiang Mai Software and Technology Park Co., Ltd.
- Dr. Pensri Kuaysuuan, Regional Manager, International Federation of Library Associations and Institutions.
- Dr. Samerkae Somhom, Department of Computer Science, Chiang Mai University.

In addition, in April 2001, the department head also approached the Thailand-US Educational Foundation for a Fulbright Senior Specialist to advise the review and redesign. This led to the selection of Dr. Hwa-Wei Lee, Dean Emeritus of Ohio University Libraries and Visiting Distinguished Scholar of OCLC Online Computer Library Center, for a six-week assignment from September 9 to October 20, 2001 in Chiang Mai, Thailand. After the arrival of the Fulbright specialist, the committee met weekly during the six weeks and carried out most of the committee work on a daily basis.

ENVIRONMENTAL SCAN

In order to provide a sound base for the redesign of the existing graduate program, a thorough review of the current strengths and weaknesses as well as the challenges and opportunities within the Department, the University, the Country, and the profession at large was conducted by the Curriculum Redesign Committee under the coordination of the Fulbright specialist. Below are the findings:

Within the Department

Being a relatively young department and with the graduate program only six years old, the Department, under the table leadership of two successive heads—Associate Professor Angsana Thongchai (1996-2000) and Associate Professor Ratana Na-Lamphun (2000 to the present) — and with the team efforts of all the faculty members, has made impressive progress. Four areas of the program were examined as below:

1. Faculty

In terms of faculty background and strength, nine of the ten faculty members in the Department have master's degrees either in library science, information science, or in computer science/technology. Four of them have also received advanced certificates in information science. The one without a master's degree is now working on a Master of Science in Computer Science degree and is expected to complete it this academic year. All faculty members are extremely competent and committed library and information professionals. However, due to the fact that the field of library and information science has been changing so rapidly in the past two decades and that so much new knowledge has been added, especially in the computer, telecommunication, network, Internet, WWW, digitization, and other related technologies, continuing and expanded faculty development has become critically important.

The need for a continuing and intensified program in faculty development was addressed under the advice of Dr. Jacques Vails, the former director of the Library and Regional Documentation Center, Asian Institute of Technology, who was invited to serve as an academic consultant for the Department in 1988. In collaboration with Khon Kaen University and the Prince of Songkla University, the three departments of library science outside Bangkok received an award for curriculum revision and staff development from the International Development Research Centre of Canada (IDRC) in 1988. A second award from IDRC was made in 1991 to further upgrade the information science education in the three Thai regional universities. These two awards made the following important impacts:

• A number of workshops on various topics in information science and technology were organized for the library science faculty members of the three universities.

• A microcomputer laboratory, the first one in a library science department in Thailand, was established at the Department of Library Science, Chiang Mai University.

• Internships were offered for faculty members at institutions where computers were used more extensively.

• Supports for attending national, regional and international seminars, meetings, etc. were provided.

• Supports for training abroad up to the diploma and MS in information studies levels were provided. [1]

In the area of faculty research, Ms. Ratana has appointed a Research Committee chaired by Associate Professor Tasana Saladyanant. Other committee members are Assistant Professor Darunee Na Lampang and Associate Professor Angsana Thongchai. Currently, two research projects funded by the University and the National Council of Research are undertaken. One is on the design of a management information system for the department. Another is a survey and analysis of the websites created and maintained by various agencies and departments of the Royal Thai Government. The University is promoting more research and publication by faculty members. Funding in the form of small grants is available for such a purpose. In the past five years, faculty members of the department published five research papers: four in Thai and one in English, all were published in Thai journals and publications.

Because of the cutting back in government funding to public universities in Thailand, the number of teaching faculty in the department has decreased from fifteen four years ago to ten at present as a result of retirement and the government's policy and encouragement for early retirement. No replacement is permitted, however, for the retired faculty members. The latest retirement by an experienced faculty member, Ms Saithong Manomai-Udom, will further reduce the number of faculty in the department to nine. It is felt that the reduced staff size and the increased teaching and workloads will create a serious hindrance for more faculty research.

---

[1] *Ibid.*

2. Curriculum

Presently the Department of Library Science offers two programs: a program for the degree of Bachelor of Arts in Information Studies and a program for the degree of Master of Arts in Library and Information Science.

The general requirements for admission to the graduate program in library and information science are:
- A bachelor degree in information studies, library and information science, or a related field.
- Acceptable scores in the entrance examination.
- One year of working experience in a library or in an information-related field.
- A personal interview.

The degree requirements are:
- The program of a two-year full-time study consisting of a total of thirty-six graduate credits; eighteen of these credits are for required core courses.
- Students may choose either the thesis option or the independent study option. For the thesis option, twelve credits will be allowed. For the independent study option, six credits will be allowed. If a student wants to change from the independent study option to the thesis option during the first year of graduate studies, she/he must have achieved a 3.75 grade point average in the first two semesters of graduate studies.
- The remaining credits required may be earned, according to the two chosen options, by taking either two or four elective courses.
- Students in the thesis option must present a thesis of acceptable quality and pass an oral examination on the subject of the thesis.
- A student who has fulfilled the degree requirements of the program with a grade point average not lower than 3.00 and within a period of study not less than four regular semesters will be awarded the Degree of Master of Arts in Library and Information Science.
- The maximum length for completing the MA degree is five years.

The total number of thirty-six graduate credits required for the MA degree is far less than the forty-eight graduate credits required by the same departments at Chulalongkorn University and Ramkhamhaeng University. It is also lower than the forty-two graduate credits required by Thammasat University and Khon Kaen University.

Because the number of credits for the thesis option (twelve) and for the independent-study option (six) are set by the Ministry of University Affairs, students at Chiang, Mai University can only take two to four elective courses (six to twelve credits) under the current requirement of thirty-six graduate credits total.

In comparison with Chulalongkorn and Khon Kaen, it seems that graduate students at Chiang Mai have a lower study load—only nine credits or three graduate courses per semester.

It was also felt by committee members that the contents of some courses overlap with each other, such as Information Technology for Libraries and Information Centers, Data Processing for Library and Information Centers, Information Storage and Retrieval, Application of Software Packages for Libraries and Information Centers, Information Systems Analysis for Libraries and Information Centers, and Library and Information Networks. More work is needed to redefine and consolidate some of these existing courses and to add new courses such as courses on Comparative and International Librarianship, Knowledge Management, and Research Design and Methodology.

A question was also raised about the purpose and need of requiring one year of library or information related working experience before applying for admission. None of the other graduate programs in LIS at other Thai universities has such a requirement. This and other concerns identified above should be considered in the discussion on curriculum revision and redesign.

3. Students

Because of the high standards imposed in the entrance examination for graduate students by the Department, the quality of current students is excellent but the quantity, or the number of students admitted, is far less than desired. For example, for the first year of the graduate program in 1995, there were fifteen applicants but none were admitted. In 1996, there were ten applicants; again, no one was admitted. (No applicant who took the entrance examination was able to score half of the total points.) In 1997, out of the eighteen applicants, five were admitted. In 1998, there were twenty-two applicants and nine were admitted. In 1999, there were eighteen applicants and six were admitted. In anticipation of the review and curriculum revision, no new students were admitted in 2000 and 2001.

By looking at these numbers, several questions surfaced.
- Has there been adequate publicity or promotion about the program?
- What are some of the causes for not attracting more applicants?
- Are the standards for the entrance examination set too high?
- Is it a discouraging factor to require a one-year experience in the library or information-related work?
- Do we miscalculate the market demands?
- Do we compete with other programs with similar or overlapping coverage in content but with more attractive program names? (One of these is the interdisciplinary graduate program; "Information Technology and Management" offered by the Graduate School, which is also chaired by Ms. Ratana Na-Lamphun and has a much larger enrolment.)
- Why couldn't that many students complete their studies in two years?
- Do we fail to take into consideration the need of part-time students in designing the program and in the scheduling of classes?

A study on the jobs held by the seven graduates shows that six of them actually returned to their original jobs in libraries and one found a job in the library after graduation. The Fulbright Specialist had the pleasure of interviewing Mr. Pattanin Sukaroj who had a BA degree in mass communication and worked for five years as a marketing specialist in the Cement Thai Company before entering the graduate program in Library and Information Science. After graduation, he found a position as an academic officer in the Women's Studies Center, Faculty of Social Sciences, Chiang Mai University, where he is now in charge of a variety of information related work including overseeing the information resources and services for the Center. Mr. Pattanin has high praise for the graduate program but wishes that it had more depth in some of the courses. He was very grateful that his faculty advisor, Ms. Ratana, and other faculty members gave him extra assignments and tutored him in many of the library science courses that he did not have in his undergraduate studies. His future plan is to prepare himself to become a faculty member in library and information science eventually.

For those who are still completing their independent studies for the degree, five are currently working in libraries and four are working in information science related work in other organizations. The Fulbright Specialist visited one of them, Ms. Vimolrudee Kasarak and her excellent library at the Chiang Mai Campus of Mahachulalongkornrajavidyalaya University, which specializes in the study of Buddhism.

Even though most of the graduates of the undergraduate program in information studies at Chiang Mai could find jobs easily, the few of them who want to enter a graduate program had to go to other universities that do not require the one year of experience. This may result in the loss of four to five potential graduate students each year.

4. Administration

The head of the Department, Ms. Ratana Na-Lamphun, has been appointed to the position in 2000. Ms. Ratana is an able and experienced department head in that she served the same leadership position twice before (1986 – 1990 and 1992 – 1995). In accordance with the central missions of the University in teaching, research, academic services to the community, and promotion of Thai art and culture, Ms. Ratana has established a number of committees to deal with each of these missions in addition to the planning committee for the revision and strengthening of the graduate program.

The Department is one of ten departments in the Faculty of Humanities and has a very good working relationship with the Dean, Associate Professor Em-On Chittasobhon, and other university officials. Ms. Ratana and her faculty members are also maintaining a good working relationship with faculty members in other departments in the university, including the Central Library, which hired many of the LIS graduates.

Within the University

Being the first regional university in Thailand outside the capitol city of Bangkok, Chiang Mai University was established in 1964 aimed at extending higher education into the northern part of the country and with a special attention to the priorities and needs of the North. The University has seventeen faculties and a graduate school providing a total of eighty-four undergraduate programs, ninety-nine programs leading to master's degrees, seventeen programs leading to doctoral degrees, and twenty-six programs leading to the graduate diploma programs.

The seventeen faculties which comprise the comprehensive university are: Agriculture, Agro-Industry, Associated Medical Sciences, Business Administration, Architecture, Dentistry, Economics, Education, Engineering, Fine Arts, Humanities, Medicine, Nursing, Pharmacy, Science, Social Sciences, and Veterinary Medicine.

The University owns a total of 3,489 acres on its main and branch campuses. The main campus is only four kilometers away from the center of the city and is very beautiful, modern, and spacious.

In recent years, the key emphasis of the University has been on research in order to raise the academic and scholarly standing among the world's leading universities. Library and computing facilities are fairly adequate. Global linkages for academic cooperation are expanding. In addition to the seventeen faculties and the graduate school, there are also a good number of research institutes such as Public Health Research, Social Research, Science and Technology Research and Development, Women's Studies; Promotion of Arts and Culture, Multiple Cropping, etc. Research grants are also available to support faculty researches.

However, due to the current economic situation in Thailand and relatively tight government funding, the University is in the process of belt tightening and trimming its staff size and operating expenditures. Alternative sources of funding have become a necessity for the coming years.

Within the Country

As one of the major countries in Asia, especially in Southeast Asia and among the ASEAN countries, Thailand has played a key role in regional economic development, social reform, and political stability.

In coping with the rapid transformation from an agricultural based economy to an industrial based economy that took place in the last half of the 20th century, and now to an information and knowledge-based economy of the 21st century, the Government of Thailand, through its eight successive National Economic and Social Development Plans, has placed an increasing emphasis on human resource development, equalization of urban and rural development, fair distribution of wealth and prosperity, upgrading the quality of life, environment, and natural resource management, improving the national information infrastructure, and maintaining economic growth at an appropriate level to ensure sustainability. Under all these endeavors, the creation of a nation of learning that is information and knowledge based is ever more important if Thailand is to maintain its competitiveness in the new global and knowledge economy. The ninth five-year National Economic and Social Development Plan, which began on October 1, 2001, places special emphases on the development of IT industry and a knowledge-based economy (KBE).

In the development of human resources, education, both formal and informal, plays a vital role. Libraries of all types should transform themselves to become a major educational institution supporting both formal education and lifelong learning. In addition, the new knowledge-based society requires a new breed of library and information professionals who possess the broad knowledge and technical skills necessary for the new type of library and information services. In a recent survey conducted by Malivan Praditteera on "Planning of Computer Technology Personnel in Academic Libraries" it was found that forty-five academic libraries in Thailand needed a total of 831 staff who is technologically competent.① It is to be noted, however, this number did not include the same type of library and information professionals who are needed in other organizations such as government agencies, international organizations, universities, research institutes, business enterprises, and corporations, etc.

Since the establishment of the first library science department at Chulalongkorn University in 1955, there are now more than eighteen universities and institutions of higher learning in Thailand offering both undergraduate and graduate programs in library and information science. A variety of training courses and seminars have also been offered, many of these are on the topics of computer applications and information technology for libraries. There is a clear trend in library and information science education that more attention is being given to information science and technology in the changing curriculum of library and information science education. In a 1998 survey conducted by Ratana Na-Lamphun, Fongnuan Sakkaravej and Songkram Chawsilpa, it was found that most of the library science departments in Thailand have changed their names to "department of library and information science" with the exception of Chiang Mai University which is still using the name of "department of library science".②

Under the UNESCO guidelines, the National Information System of Thailand (Thai-NATIS) was established in 1986 with the following objectives:③

1. Providing information resources and services to serve government agencies, public and private organizations for the benefit of personal development as well as national development.

2. Organizing information systems and providing information services according to international standards.

3. Eliminating duplication of efforts in developing information resources.

4. Providing information resources of all disciplines for national development.

5. Providing means for cooperation, coordination and exchange of information at national, regional, and international levels.

The Government in 1987, with the Deputy Prime Minister as chairperson, established a National Committee for Direction and Coordination of Thai NATIS. By the mandate of the Seventh National Economic and Social Development Plan, the effort to build up a national information infrastructure was intensified. The establishments of the National Electronics and Computer Technology Center (NECTEC) in 1988 and the Thai Social/Scientific, Academic and Research Network (Thaisarn) in 1992 were all a part of this effort. In 1995, IT 2000 (The National Information Technology Policy for the 21st Century) was drafted by a committee under the auspices of NECTEC.④ On December 9, 1997, the Thai Government Information Law became effective. Prior to this law, all government documents were considered confidential. Now, however, all government documents are open to the public unless there is a strong reason to keep some of them confidential.⑤ In lieu of the 1997 Constitution and the, 1999 Education. Act, the Government is

---

① Praditteera, Malivan. *Planning of Computer Technology Personnel in Academic Libraries*. (Master's thesis) Bangkok, Chulalongkorn University, 1995. (In Thai) As described by Premsmit, Pimrumpai, in her paper on "Thailand's Transition to an Information Society: Status for Future Strategies." *Library and Information Science in Thailand: Essays in Honor of Professor Suthilak Ambhanwong*. Bangkok, Department of Library Science, Faculty of Arts, Chulalongkorn University, 1997: p. 91.

② Na-Lamphun, Ratana; Sakkaravej, Fongnuan; and Chawsilpa, Songkram. *An Analysis of Library Science, Information Science or Related Curricula of Academic Institutions, Ministry of the University Affairs*. Chiang Mai: Chiang Mai University, 1998. (In Thai)

③ Premsmit, Pimrumpai. 1997: pp. 96 – 97. (See ref. 3.)

④ *IT2000* (3rd Draft). Bangkok, National Electronics and Computer Technology Center, 1995. (In Thai)

⑤ Malaivongs, Kanchit. *Information Resource Management in Thailand*. October 12, 2000. PowerPoint presentation.

determined to launch educational reforms with the aim of developing Thailand into a knowledge-based society, which is a pre-requisite for becoming a knowledge-based economy. ①

Currently, for the promotion, application, and development of information technology in Thailand, a National Information Technology Committee (NITC) has been established and is chaired by the Deputy Prime Minister. NITC has several subcommittees and NECTEC is the office of the NITC secretariat.② A new national plan called IT 2010 was announced on October 3, 2001 aimed at building a knowledge-based economy in Thailand. ③

Besides the national efforts, university library networks were also established as a means for cooperative library automation, resource sharing and document delivery. The Provincial University Library Network (PULINET) was established in 1986 and consisted of twelve members. The Thai Academic Library Network (Metropolitan) -THALINET (M) was initiated in 1993 for university libraries in the Bangkok Metropolis.④ At present, both PULINET and THALINET (M) have joined to form the ThaiLis.⑤ In 2000, a new project-Network of Digital Library of Theses and Dissertations (NDLTD) was proposed jointly by the Technical Information Access Center of the National Science and Technology Development Agency (Ministry of Science, Technology and Environment) and the Asian Institute of Technology. The project will require students to submit their completed theses and dissertations in standardized digital format, including metadata using the XML scheme, for storage and easy retrieval. ⑥

The promotion of the effective use of information technology by the government has created a major impact in the academic, government, and business institutions throughout Thailand. To prepare for the growing demand for trained library and information professionals in libraries as well as in other organizations where library and information services are also needed, most of the departments of library and information science in Thai universities have gone through continuing review and revision of their curriculum at both the undergraduate and graduate levels by expanding the traditional library science programs to library and information science programs, and by adding new courses in information science and technology.

In The World Beyond

What has been done in Thailand is also happening in other parts of the world. Changes both in library and information services and education in the United States of America in recent years provide good examples for comparison. The transformation of library and information services since the 1960s can be categorized as outlined below.

In the 1960s, libraries began to change from manual operations to computerized operations. The Library of Congress was the first one to use computers for cataloging operations and, by doing so, created the MARC (Machine-Readable Catalog) format. OCLC Online Computer Library Center (formerly the Ohio College Library Center) was the first to initiate online shared cataloging and to create the online union catalog. The Medical Literature Analysis and Retrieval System (MEDLARS) of the National Library of Medicine was the first information storage and retrieval system developed by a national library. Many of the large abstracting and indexing services such as the Chemical Abstracts Service, Engineering Index, etc. also began to use computers for database creation and maintenance.

In the 1970s, the availability of mini-computers had enabled libraries to experiment with computerization and to create in-house automation systems. Online search of remote bibliographic databases was made available to libraries by companies such as Dialog and BRS. OCLC's online

---

① see <http://www.thaigov.go.th>
② Malaivongs, Kanchit. 2000. op. cit.
③ See <http://www.thaigov.go.th>
④ *The Thai Academic Library Network (Metropolitan) Project. Fiscal Year 1995 – 1997.* Bangkok, n. d. (In Thai)
⑤ See <http://www.mua.go.th>
⑥ Malaivongs, Kanchit. 2000. op. cit.

interlibrary loan system was initiated. In Thailand, the Library and Information Center of the Asian Institute of Technology was the first one in Asia to engage in library automation in 1969 and the Department of Library Science, Chulalongkorn University, was the first one to offer a course on "Library Mechanization" in 1970. ①

In the 1980s, integrated library systems, library networks, electronic full texts, CD-ROMs, etc. became common applications in libraries.

In the 1990s, Internet, WWW, digital publications, digitization, etc. extended the traditional libraries beyond their walls. The concepts of "virtual" and "digital" libraries became the buzzwords in the library and information profession.

In the world of library science education, first was the growth in the number of library schools and their enrolments in the 1960s; second was the expansion of their curriculum to include computer applications in the 1970s; third was the wave of library school closings due largely to cost-cutting measures taken by their universities in the 1980s; then was the change of names and curriculum by most of the library schools to reflect the changing or broadening mission of their schools in the library and information profession in the 1990s. This latest change was prompted by the realization that there is a greater market demand in jobs outside the traditional libraries for the new breed of library school graduates who possess the knowledge and skills in library system design and management, web design and management, Internet and web resource management, digital library management, information and knowledge management, etc.

In the recently completed KALIPER Report on *Educating Library and Information Science Professionals for a New Century*—a landmark study undertaken between 1998 and 2000 by a team of twenty scholars from thirteen library and information science schools in the US, Canada, and England-six trends that are shaping curricula changes in library and information science (LIS) programs were identified. ②

KALIPER is the abbreviation of the "Kellogg-ALISE Information Professions and Education Renewal Project". ALISE is the abbreviation of the "Association for Library and Information Science Education". The purpose of the KALIPER project was to analyze the nature and extent of major curricular changes in LIS education. Multiple methods were used to collect data, including surveys, case studies, content analysis, and interviews. Below are the six trends:

1. In addition to libraries as institutions and library-specific operations, LIS curricula are addressing broad-based information environments and information problems.

2. While LIS curriculum continues to incorporate perspectives from other disciplines, a distinct core has taken shape that is predominantly user-centered.

3. LIS schools and programs are increasing the investment and infusion of information technology into their curricula.

4. LIS programs are experimenting with the structure of specialization within the curriculum.

5. LIS schools and programs are offering instruction in different formats to provide students with more flexibility.

6. LIS schools and programs are expanding their curricula by offering related degrees at the undergraduate, master's and doctoral levels.

The project team also sought to identify, the forces that motivate curricula change and affect its direction. It was found that the factors that promote change might, in some situations, be the same ones that inhibit it. Some of these factors are:

1. Demands of students, employers, graduates, and professional associations for graduate competencies;

2. Growth and expense of supporting emerging technology;

---

① Hwa-Wei Lee, then the Director of Library and Information Center, Asian Institute of Technology, was invited by Professor Suthilak Ambhanwong, Chair of the Department of Library Science, Chulalongkorn University, to teach this new course.

② *Educating Library and Information Science Professionals for a New Century*: The KALIPER *Report. Executive Summary, July 2000.* Reston, VA, KALIPER Advisory Committee, Association for Library and Information Science Education, 2000.

3. Internal campus relationships and positioning;
4. Availability and/or presence of faculty with new subject expertise;
5. Competition from other LIS programs; and
6. Availability of financial support for innovation.

Looking ahead into the future, the report has found the LIS field to be vibrant, dynamic and changing and LIS schools are undertaking an array of initiatives to face the changes.

Aside from the report, one other change that has become apparent in LIS education is the growing realization that the whole LIS field should reposition itself from information management to knowledge management. In traditional librarianship, library and information science has been the core of studies. In fact, a wealth of knowledge and skills has been accumulated by the LIS profession and been taught in the LIS schools. This body of knowledge such as identification, selection, acquisition, organization, analysis, preservation, dissemination, and use of information has founded the basis of modern librarianship. However, if we compare the differences between information and knowledge as well as the differences between information management and knowledge management we would find that the LIS profession has positioned itself in the lower end of the continuum in the chain of knowledge creation—that is, from data to information, from information to knowledge, and from knowledge to wisdom. The two tables below show the differences between information and knowledge, and between information management and knowledge management.

Table 1 Differences between information and knowledge

Information	Knowledge
Visible	Invisible
Independent from action and decision	Closely related to action and decision
Format changes after processing	Thought changes after processing
Physical product	Spiritual product
Independent from existing environment	Identified with existing environment
Easily transferable	Transfer through learning
Can be duplicated	Can't be duplicated

Table 2 Differences between information management and knowledge management

Information management	Knowledge management
Focus on information organization	Focus on knowledge renewal and creation
Prefer static objects	Action oriented
Document- and information-centered	People- and customer-centered
Emphasis on processing and preserving	Emphasis on utilization and sharing
External orderliness	Add value or knowledge resources

As of now, nearly all LIS schools have focused their programs on one or more of the following: information science, information studies, information technology, information management, or information resources management, but the world outside is paying more and more, attention to knowledge management. Do we miss something here by not positioning our LIS program at a higher level on the knowledge creation chain? Do we leave ourselves out of the new challenges and opportunities of the knowledge age?

The term "knowledge management" has become a popular buzzword in the business world in the 1990s. It was the business world that recognized first the importance of knowledge in the "global economy" of the "knowledge age". The possession of relevant and strategic knowledge and its unceasing renewal enables business to gain competitive advantage. This same principle is also true for other organizations, as well as applicable to other countries in the world, including Thailand.

Knowledge management is much more than information and data management. It is also much broader in scope than information technology. Knowledge management has as a goal to identify useful and relevant knowledge, to organize, merge, and synthesize knowledge, to transform tacit knowledge into explicit knowledge, and to stimulate the creative use of knowledge. Information technology provides the technical tools to achieve this goal. Since some of the knowledge resides in the minds of people and is the creation of human wisdom, the human element is the most important part of knowledge management.

For LIS schools to play a key role in the education of a new breed of LIS professionals for a variety of job opportunities in and outside libraries and information centers, it is necessary to redesign their curricula and to prepare their students as leaders in information and knowledge management.

A NEW PHILOSOPHY AND OBJECTIVES

To prepare for the curriculum redesign a statement of the "Philosophy and Objectives" for the graduate program in library and information science at Chiang Mai University was drafted by the Curriculum Redesign Committee. It was carefully reviewed, revised and adopted.

Philosophy

Information and knowledge are significant factors in the new knowledge age of the 21st century and will play an important role in the development of the education, economy, society, and culture of the country, which is in the process of rapid transformation from an agricultural/industrial society to an information society, and is heading toward a knowledge-based society.

The revised MA in LIS program aims at producing a new breed of information and knowledge professionals for the knowledge-based society. Graduates of the program should be able to undertake a managerial and leadership role in a variety of information-and knowledge-based organizations such as libraries, archives, government agencies, international organizations, universities, research institutes, business enterprises, and corporations.

Objectives

1. To educate and produce graduates with an emphasis on an integrated knowledge of the core and related areas in the information and knowledge profession in order to have the capability of managing all relevant information and knowledge resources in a variety of organizational settings.

2. To educate and produce graduates who have the necessary knowledge and skills in the use of appropriate computer, network, Internet, web, telecommunication, and other information technologies for the effective performance of professional tasks and services.

3. To educate and produce graduates who are capable of evaluating, designing, and establishing the appropriate information systems necessary for the searching, analyzing, selecting, organizing, synthesizing, communicating, and archiving information and knowledge resources in all formats.

4. To educate and produce graduates who have a strong professional ethics and commitment for quality and excellence in services.

5. To educate and produce graduates who are dedicated to further the knowledge and mission of the information and knowledge profession.

Guided by the Philosophy and Objectives, the Curriculum Redesign Committee was able to move swiftly into the curriculum redesign and other considerations.

RECOMMENDED ACTIONS

Based on findings from the environmental scan as well as discussions among committee members the following actions were recommended by the Curriculum Redesign Committee:

• Adopt the new statement of Philosophy and Objectives for the graduate program.

• Change the name of the department from Department of Library Science to Department of Library and Information Science. Change the name of the graduate program from Library and Information Science to Information and Knowledge Management.

• Revise the curriculum to reflect the changing focus on Information and Knowledge Management.

• Increase the number of graduate credits required from thirty-six to forty-two.

• Actively recruit new graduate students with a goal of admitting at least ten qualified new students each year.

• Provide opportunities for part-time degree and non-degree graduate students and for continuing education by scheduling some of the courses in the evenings and on Saturdays.

• Consider the possibility of establishing a Knowledge Management Institute (or Center) to provide consulting services on knowledge management and in-service training in the form of short courses, workshops, etc.

• Work with other academic programs to develop interdisciplinary programs that meet the job demands and societal needs. One of the good examples is the graduate-program in Information Technology and Management.

• Increase the minimum number of full-time faculty in the Department to ten and adding a number of adjunct faculty members on an as needed basis.

• Seek funding supports for faculty development, especially for attending international conferences, seminars, and short courses; allowing study leaves for advanced degrees; and undertaking research projects. Some of the possible funding sources to be explored were identified.

• Develop cooperative relationship with LIS schools in other countries to facilitate faculty exchange; joint research, and information sharing. One or two such schools should be selected and contacted.

• Inviting specialists with expertise in knowledge management to conduct workshops for faculty members in the Department. Several of such specialists have been identified.

• Mr. Nopasit is a member of the Curriculum Redesign Committee and has agreed to conduct a series of workshops on KM for the Department faculty and has scheduled a day-long workshop on "Strategy in the Development of KM for Library – and Information Science Professionals" as the first of the series.

• Ms. Ratana Na-Lamphun, Mr. Nopasit Chakpitak, and Ms. Tasana Saladyanant are encouraged to coauthor a first Thai book on KM focusing on the particular situation and need of Thailand. Whenever the first opportunity for study abroad occurs, Ms. Ratana should be encouraged to go.

• Establish co-op projects with libraries, information centers, government agencies, business enterprises, etc. for student internships as this will enable students to gain valuable working experience and enhance employment opportunities. Dr. Kanchit and Mr. Nopasit may be able to help in making such arrangements.

• A case study of organizations in Thailand that have already practiced knowledge management should be conducted in order to obtain information on current status of knowledge management in Thailand and on the potential job market for graduates in IKM.

• Consider the possibility of fund-raising to create student scholarships, to fund faculty development, and to periodically update IT systems and equipment for teaching and research.

In order to share the findings and recommendations of the committee, a two-day seminar was conducted in Chiang Mai on October 17 – 18, 2001 with invitation extended to all the key library and information science educators and professionals in Thailand. The seminar on "Strategic Direction for Information Studies and the Profession" covered a detailed report by the committee and the Fulbright Specialist; a panel discussion by external consultants on the recommendations; and three lectures on knowledge management, the Dublin Core Metadata, and global library cooperation in information resource access and sharing by the Fulbright Specialist and OCLC representatives. An excellent presentation on the latest development in national information infrastructure in Thailand was given by Dr. Kanchit Malaivongs.

Another two-day seminar on "Transforming the Library: Topics in Modern Librarianship" to be conducted by the OCLC Institute has been planned for November 7 – 9, 2002. At that time a follow-up review on the recommended actions and other progress will also be taken.

PROPOSED NEW GRADUATE PROGRAM IN INFORMATION AND KNOWLEDGE ANAGEMENT

Name of the degree:
Master of Arts (Information and Knowledge Management)

Admission and degree requirements: The general requirements for admission are:
1. A bachelor degree in library and information science or in a related field such as business, communication, computer science, engineering, information technology, management, telecommunication, etc.
2. Acceptable scores in the entrance examination.
3. A personal interview.
Both full- and part-time students will be admitted.

The degree requirements:
1. The program consists of a total of forty-two graduate credits.
2. Eighteen of these credits are for required core courses.
3. Students may choose either the thesis option or the independent study option. For the thesis option, twelve credits will be allowed. For the independent study option, six credits will be allowed.
4. If a student wants to change from the independent study option to the thesis option during the first year of graduate studies, she/he must have achieved a 3.75 grade point average in the first two semesters of graduate studies.
5. The remaining credits required may be earned, according to the selected option, by taking four to six elective courses.
6. Students in the thesis option must present a thesis of acceptable quality and pass an oral examination on the subject of the thesis.
7. A student who has fulfilled the degree requirements of the program with a grade point average not lower than 3.00 and within a period of study not less than four regular semesters will be awarded the Degree of Master of Arts in Information and Knowledge Management.
8. The maximum length for completing the MA degree is five years.

Core courses:
There are five core courses that are required for all of the first-year graduate students. Each course is for three credits:
1. Information and knowledge management: theory and practice (New)
2. Information and knowledge architecture and organization (708 modified)
3. Information technologies and systems for information and knowledge management (706 modified)
4. Information and knowledge access and services (707 modified)

5. Research design and methodology for information and knowledge management (New).
Another core course that will be required for all the second-year graduate students is:
6. Seminar in information and knowledge management (791 modified).

Elective courses:
- Management of libraries and information or knowledge centers (705 modified)
- Management of government publications and records (715)
- Information and knowledge resources for Northern Thai studies and research (723)
- Database management for libraries and information or knowledge centers (709 modified)
- Information storage and retrieval (731)
- Software packages for libraries and information or knowledge centers (733)
- Information systems for libraries and information or knowledge centers (734, 735, and 736 combined)
- Selected topics in information and knowledge management (789 modified)
- Issues and trends in the development of digital libraries (new)
- Intellectual property protection and copyright (new)
- Comparative and international librarianship (new)
- Design and management of websites (new)
- Users training and education (new)
- Case studies in knowledge management (new)

With the permission of the IKM Program advisors, students may also take some of the following elective courses from other faculties or departments.

From the Graduate School (Information Technology and Management):
- Data communication and information infrastructure (906701)
- Information system development (906703)
- Database management and design (906721)
- Information knowledge-based system (906722)
- Strategic information systems (906761)
- Social impacts of information technology (906763)
- Information resources management (906765)

From the Faculty of Business Administration (Business Administration):
- Business organization and management (703733)
- Management information system (703741)
- Human resource management (703735)

Table 3 Summary of the graduate credits

Degree options	Required core-course credits	Elective course credits	Credits for independent study	Credits for thesis	Total credits
Independent	18	18	6		42
Thesis	18	12		12	42

From the Faculty of Education (Educational Technology):
- Instructional system design and development (059733)
- Advanced media production in education (059744)

From the Faculty of Humanities (Industrial and Organizational Psychology):
- Managerial psychology and leadership (033761)

- Organizational analysis and development (033762)

From the Faculty of Science (Computer Science):
- Information retrieval (204722)
- Analysis and design of information system (204723)
- Decision support system (204724)
- Design of management information system (204725)
- Design and management of database system (204726)

From the Faculty of Social Sciences (Public Administration)
- Organization and management (158710).

Independent study or thesis:
- Independent study (798, required for those graduate students who are enrolled in the independent-study option)
- Thesis (799, required for those graduate students who are enrolled in the thesis option)

A study plan for each student should be developed toward the end of the first semester between each student and her/his faculty advisor. Based on the background and career goal of each student the study plan should include those elective courses to be taken and the decision on taking either the independent-study option or the thesis option.

The research design and methodology course should help each student to develop her/his research focus and topic.

CONTINUING EFFORTS

It is obvious that the six-week assignment of a Fulbright Senior Specialist to advise on the review and redesign of the graduate program is too short a time to complete all the necessary tasks. Much is yet left to be done in the coming months. Continuing work between the Fulbright specialist and the department faculty will be needed and is ongoing.

Through the joint effort of Ms. Ratana and Dr. Nopasit, the establishing of a Knowledge Management Research Center has been approved by Chiang Mai University and ten computers and a server have been donated to the new center from a private source. The center is now in the process of planning its training programs to be offered in 2002.

For the promotion of knowledge exchange on KM, a demonstration website—Thailand Knowledge Management has been created by Dr. Nopasit as one of MSN communities. ①

Table 4 Study plan for the thesis option

First semester (12 credits)	Second semester (12 credits)
1. Information & knowledge management 2. Information & knowledge architecture & organization 3. Information technology and system for IKM 4. Information & knowledge access & services	1. Research design and methodology for IKM 2. Elective 3. Elective 4. Elective
Third semester (9 – 12 credits)	Fourth semester (6 – 9 credits)
1. Seminar in information & knowledge management 2. Elective 3. Thesis (3 – 6 credits)	1. Thesis (6 – 9 credits)

---

① The URL is: http://communities.msn.com/Thailarid-KnowledgeManagement

Table 5 Study plan for the independent-study option

First semester (12 credits)	Second semester (12 credits)
2. Information & knowledge management 3. Information & knowledge architecture & organization 4. Information technology and system for IKM 5. Information & knowledge access & services	1. Research design and methodology for IKM 2. Elective 3. Elective 4. Elective
Third semester (12 credits)	Fourth semester (6 credits)
1. Seminar in information & knowledge management 2. Elective 3. Elective 4. Elective	1. Independent study (6 credits)

As the first step in writing a KM book in Thai, a recently completed manuscript on *Knowledge Management: Theory and Practice*, written in Chinese and authored jointly by Dr. Dong Xiaoying, Dr. Zuo Meiyun, and the Fulbright specialist, to be published in Beijing this month, will be translated into Thai from its English version.

The prospect for linking the department with an American library school under the Fulbright Educational Partnership Program is also been pursued and an application will likely be submitted in January 2002 by the American library school.

All members of the department at Chiang Mai University are extremely excited with the new direction of their graduate program in Information and Knowledge Management and are committed to making it work as the first of its kind in the world of library and information science education.

(Published in ***Information Development***. V. 18, No. 1, March 2002: pp. 47 - 58.)

图书馆合作和资源共享

Library Cooperation and Resources Sharing[①]

I am here again. (Greetings) When I talk about library cooperation and resources sharing. I always get so excited because that is the way our library professional has been doing very well and we believe in cooperation, we believe in sharing. But now with the advances in technology making possible for us to do cooperation, networking and sharing much more effective, much better in result. I know there many, many successful models, but I personally am very familiar with two. So I would like to share with you briefly about these two successful models in library cooperation and resource sharing. The first one is the OCLC (On-line Computer Library Centre). The second one is Ohio-Link (Ohio Library and information Network).

In talking about OCLC, Mr. Andrew Wang (I always call him Mr. OCLC) covered this topic in much more detail. So I just very quickly pass very soon to a few slides. OCLC was started 1967, 35 years ago to be exact, and at that time was called Ohio College Library Center. It was organized by a group of college, university libraries wanting to work together to share resources. Because the model was so successful, in the next few years it became an internet library network. As of January 2002, according to my up-to-date information, there were 41,000 libraries of all types and sizes in 82 countries being OCLC users. Among these 41,000 thousand libraries, 9,200 are full members. OCLC has been most successful in term of cooperative cataloguing. Before OCLC was formed, every library purchased books, subscribed to journals, and every library catalogued every book it purchased and every journal it subscribed to. There was a lot of duplication and work. With OCLC, the libraries are doing cooperative cataloguing.

They catalogue cooperatively. In other words, every library does not have to catalogue every item acquired. They share the cataloguing information among themselves to reduce the time taken to catalogue book and also to create an on-line. So people can find out the things available in all catalogue other 41,000 (or 9,000) libraries and do interlibrary loans. As of last year, there are 45 million unique cataloguing records available in the world catalogue. The rate of growth annually is about 2.6 million new records a year. No single libraries can do this alone. This is a joint, cooperative effort. In terms of scope of world catalogue, this record of about 45 million contains over 800 million location listings in 400 languages in over a span of 4,000 years recorded knowledge. Within one year, from July 2000 to June 2001, 77.9 million (almost 78 million) searches were made on the worldCat and 8.7 interlibrary loans were performed successfully during that one year's time. So you can see that resource sharing can be done very effectively through cooperative networking and consortiums. This is the breakdown of OCLC's 45000 records. They include books, serials, visual materials, maps, mixed or multimedia materials, sound recordings, scores and computer fides.

In terms of languages (I mentioned about 400 language in the OCLC'S worldCat database), the top ten are England, German, French, Spain, China, Japan, Russia, Italy, Latin, Portuguese. Thai? I do not know. I think Thai is about 15th place or may be pretty good, in the top 25 I think we do have a lot of Thai materials in the OCLC WorldCat. This is the OCLC Headquarters in Dublin, Ohio-near Columbus. I'll skip the rest because Mr. Andrew Wang and Miss Tsai will talk about this afternoon. So I don't want to overlap their presentations.

I'm going to jump over to OHIO-Link. OHIO-Link received two awards for the access of their

---

[①] Presented at the International Conference on *Challenges and Opportunities for Libraries and Information Professionals in Knowledge Management and the Digital Age*, 20 – 22 March 2003, Chiang Mai, Thailand. Organized by Department of Library Science, Faculty of Humanities, Chiang Mai University, Chiang Mai, Thailand, 2003.

work: one from Council of State Governments and the other one from American Council of Education. OHIO-L is a library consortium estate in 1989 by libraries of higher education institutions in Ohio for library co-operation and resource sharing. You may ask why we have OCLC in the state of Ohio and now we still need to have another one called Ohio-Link. The reason is very simple: because OCLC has become a world-wide library consortium. So some of the things we need locally for interlibrary co-operation which can be done more effectively by mean of a state-wide library network. That was the reason that in 1989 Ohio-Link was formed. It currently consists of 81 colleges and universities and the State Library of Ohio. The combined collection has exceeded 30 million items and 8 millions of them are unique titles. In other words, of 81 college and university libraries in Ohio, about 8 million items of the total 30 million items are unique. Only one library possesses them. So this makes sense for resource sharing and library co-operation.

The vision of Ohio-Link originally was better access to and coordination in purchasing of our shared collection. In other words, we have a co-operation acquisition, so we don't want to buy unnecessary duplications—so we want to buy more items with the limited funding resource available. The second one is "expanded access to electronic information resources". There are so many electronic journal, electronic books. We try to use state-wide purchasing power to negotiate the best possible price with publics. So that we can provide them with lower cost to all the participating libraries. Thirdly it is "improved access to information infrastructure". We've developed based on the backbone of the state-wide supercomputer system for the use of Ohio-Link's, the network collections. Then it is 'the promotion of improved scholarly communications'. We try to create many databases including the so called knowledge depositories for works and researches done by universities or colleges within the Ohio-Link system. Lastly it is "improved and advantageous economics in the purchase and use of electronic-information resources". As you can see this is the map of Ohio. The 81 libraries are really distributed throughout the State of Ohio.

Why as a consortium? Most libraries did not, do not and will not have all the information resources their patrons need. The use of information is highly elastic based on ease of access. Sometimes if you don't make things easily accessible, the people will say, "Forget it. I don't have time, I don't want to waste my time. To look for this thing." So sometimes the use is created by easy access. If you make it easier for the patrons to have an access to resources, you'll find the use of library resources will be quickly increased. Current and future electronic information systems greatly ease access. Because of information technology, now access has become easily available.

This is Ohio-Link's objective economically sustainable, increased students and faculty access to and use of library, provided information to support and improve instruction and research as a consortium.

These are some of the programmer's philosophies.
– User empowerment rather than medication
– Abundant rather than rationed access
– Universal rather than selective access
– Immediate rather than delayed access
– Integrated rather than segregated access
– Leveraged spending rather than reduced or less efficient spending
– Progressive, vested interest co-operation rather than parochial orientation

(In other word we try to really expand co-operation of all the libraries participating in the Ohio-Link.)

As you can see of the 81 libraries (all the number of records in the central catalogue), 72% is by university libraries, 22% by independent colleges, 3.4% by 2-year colleges, and 2.3% by CRL (Centres for Research Libraries—a libraries consortium in Chicago serving the need of research libraries in terms of the materials less use but important to have for scholarly research). So the CRL's database is also part of Ohio-Link's central catalogue.

And this one is an interesting slide. I always like to use it. When we talk about library co-operation, the big libraries are always a little hesitant because they feel they have more to lose and little to gain. This is because a small library wants to use a big library's resources, and the big library has nothing to gain. In terms of participating in a library consortium, there are many small libraries. But this statistic shows the big libraries making about as many requests (70.2%) as the received number of requests. In fact they made more requests than the requests they received (69.8%). While they make requests to others, it is over 70%. The independent colleges, universities made 22% of requests and received 23.4% of requests. The two-year colleges made 7.7% of requests and received 6.8% of requests. So in other words, the number of requests is in proportion with the number of requests received in terms of size of their collections. So it is a very fair kind of co-operation relationship. This graph shows that 56% of the records are held at only one library. So this means this much material can be shared by all the participating libraries.

All participating libraries use the same type of hardware and software systems for maximum connectivity and interoperability, and to establish a union catalog, including real-time circulation transaction. In other words, of the 81 libraries, the circulation records are real-time. In other words, if we have a book borrowed by a patron, that will be shown immediately in the union catalogue, so the 2nd person trying to find or to locate the same material would know where the book or the item has been circulated.

I'll jump over because of time.

I want to show some statistics of resource development and use in 2001 by the participating libraries of Ohio-Link. About 550,000 items were successfully borrowed by the uses through inter-library lending among the Ohio-Link libraries. So 550,000 items were lent within the Ohio-Link within 1 year. 95 databases were purchased centrally. The number of searches in these 95 databases was 12,700,000 items. These 95 databases were searched over 12 million times by the users. The number documents downloaded in that year was over 65 million centrally subscribed e-journals are of 4,000 titles. The number of uses and downloads of these 4,000 e-journals was over 2 million articles within the year. The e-books purchased centrally were of 17,000 titles. The number of times of use and download of these 17,000 titles were 12,000.

You can see that by co-operation consortium, you can acquire more materials and the materials can be used more by the users. So the cost per use is much reduced. If you do it just by 1 library, the cost per use may be quite high, but by working together, the cost per use is much lower.

This is Ohio-Link's filled patron borrowing requests. I mentioned about 500,000 items in 2001 compared to when Ohio-Link started with about just 50,000 items borrowed among the libraries in the Ohio-Link.

The graduated students are among largest number of users. This shows faculty members, grad students and under grad students about equal percentage. That is an annual search of Ohio-Link's reference Database about 11.5 million in year 2000.

General/business journals searches are here and this is scholarly/research journals searches. I am going to jump over.

Ohio-Link's governance. There is the governing board and Executive. Director. The library directors Advisory Council. There are many committees. One is the Lead Implementers' Committee. And there are other standing committees: Cooperation Information Resources Management Committee, Database Management and Standards Committee, Inter-campus Service Committee and User Services Committee.

That is the organizational structure. That is Ohio-Link office, the Headquarter staff.

I want to talk about funding. 1994 the year Ohio-Link started will be used as the base year. The budget has gone up a little bit, but not much. But you can see that book borrowing has gone up a lot. So has the search of Database. The e-journal article uses and the number of data base and the number of central catalogue records all have gone up much more than the increase in funding for Ohio-Link. So this has become a much more effective operation over the years.

This is about the budget for Ohio-Link. This year, 2002, the total budget is about 12 million

US., which is provided by the state government of Ohio Staff and administrations are kept very low under 2 million US. The majority of expenditure was to acquire contents and for content delivery. Technical infras. In the initial years was high and then subsequently the cost has gone down. So this is the expenditure of Ohio-Link.

I think I am going to skip Ohio-Link's accomplishments such as to lower unit cost of Information access and delivery and et cetera.

Ohio-Link's Initiatives include:
— add interactive online reference service. This is something new that has been added as part of OCLC's question point word-wide reference services.
— Broaden the scope of online inter-library lending to include video, CD, (not just books and articles but also other multimedia materials)
— Speed up digital resources of Digital Management Media Centre (DMC)
— Expand the collection of e-books and e-theses/dissertations
— Survey user's need for and understanding of library services

I think we still have a few minutes for questions. Thank you so much.

推进学术沟通的积极改变：SPARC 创始计划

Promoting Positive Changes in Scholarly Communications: The SPARC Initiative[①]

I know we are very close to the time for lunch, and I don't want to cut short your lunch time, so I will try to shorten my presentation to 10 – 15minute. You have the notes, so we will do it as quickly as we can.

Actually we do have a problem in scholarly communication and we need to take some actions to change the situation so that we can alleviate the problems we have increasingly felt in the library, and also in the academic community. This effort has been undertaken by SARC which stands for Scholarly Publishing and Academic Resource Coalition. This is an organization established by the Association of Research Libraries in 1998. The reason for doing this is because we do have a serious problem with scholarly publication and also with scholarly communication. The scholarly communication crisis is recipe low. One is the price for scholarly journals in science, technology, and medicine fields are out of control. All of us working in the library notice that we pay more and more each year for scholarly journals. Either we subscribe less and less or for fewer titles. This is a situation that can no longer keep up.

Commercial publisher have increasingly taken over the situation. What they do, because we in the academic community we all know very well—faculty members, in order to meet requirement for commercial material, have to submit their scholarly research that results in wanting and hopefully to be published in scholarly journal. In the last 20 – 30 years the scholarly publications have been taken over by commercial publishers. I know that in the 40s and 50s the publication of scholarly work was done by scholarly societies. However, after the 1940s, the commercial publishers went to the learning societies.

Scattered the opposition and said "let us publish a journal for you, so you don't have to worry about the publication." That's the way many scholarly publications were taken over by the commercial publishers. In fact the publications became more and more expensive and the end result is that the annual rate of growth in the cost of scholarly journals is always more than 10% per year, sometimes as much as 15% per year, while the library budget increase for subscription to journals may be only 3% to 4% a year, so the libraries are falling behind each year in terms of their ability to maintain the subscription of scholarly journals.

The scholarly loss (and this is a resource user.) Statistical diagram compiled by library, you can see the annual cost has gone up by 215% from 1986 to the year 2000. However, there is a drop in the year 2001 because the libraries stood up to fight back, saying we could not accept the situation. That was part of SPARCs activities to force the publishers to reduce the cost increase in publications, because the increase was in serial expenditure for libraries increased 210%, the cost has gone up 215%. The medical and monographic publications unit costs went up by 68% where the consumer price index went up 62%. Therefore the purchasing power the library has for purchasing for books and other printed publications has gone up about 66%. As the result of this, the serial purchase actually reduced by 5% from 1986 to 2000 and the monographics purchased was reduced by 9% in the same period of time.

The scholar has lost control as well. The scholars are aware that this creates a concern for scholarly information. The scholars add the true value to the scholarly communications. However,

---

[①] Presented at the International Conference on *Challenges and Opportunities for Libraries and Information Professionals in Knowledge Management and the Digital Age*, 20 – 22 March 2003, Chiang Mai, Thailand. Organized by Department of Library Science, Faculty of Humanities, Chiang Mai University, Chiang Mai, Thailand, 2003.

because publishers are only interested in the profit, so the scholars lost control of their own work.

The year 1986 to 2001 the number of serials published worldwide increased 100%. North American research libraries this includes the libraries in the United States and Canada. The distribution fever actually reduced by 5% while the total output of scholarly journals actually doubled in the same period of time, but production in the world increased by 50%. North American research libraries' possession of monographs reduced by 9. For the eleven most expensive science, medical, technology journals the average price per year is expressed in US dollar. There is a crisis of values between scholars, societies, and libraries against commercial publishers. The commercial publishers see information as a commodity from which they can make money. But the scholar community sees information as a public good that should be free, it should have easy access to scholars. The scholars' interest in this scholarship and commercial publishers maximize the profit as their main motive. Scholars are interested in broad distribution of their research. The publishers' interest in control of this in pricing. Scholars are interested in copyright protection of the authors and creators. The commercial publishers are interested in copyright instructions restrict access rather than to protect their process. Among the action taken by SPARC to create the scholarly publishing identity resource consortium in correlation with this organization. These was some success by this action were central in some of the editorial board scholarly journals, especially this one Evolutionary Ecology from the publisher Kluwer published a separate journal called An Evolutional Ecology Research. They reduced the price from 777 per year to under 300. Because of this action, the publisher of the original journal by 40%. This is just one examples. One of the reasons for SPARC is to try to create a more competitive market place, try to encourage other for publishing to reduce the cost and also try to protect the library and the library to provide our service under the copyright protection under the fair use of electronic resource. Currently the membership of SPARC includes more than 240 institutions in North America, Europe, Asia and Australia. A SPARC Europe has also been organized to promote the same purpose. Japan has also a similar initiative. SPARC is funded by the membership. The libraries believe they cannot stand still, we have to fight back, so everybody contributes funding for SPARC to take care of some of these initiatives. There are 3 major initiations. One is Alternatives for programs, low-cost competitive alternatives, encourage other ways of publishing scholarly work. It is just a little journal, with lower cost, with easy decisions. SPARC will guarantee its publication 600 at least subscriptions from year one. SPARC also encourage college age program. Our country is laid out such as a community of scholars tries to use electronic publication to make the cost of publication much less and to deposit their publication free of charge and for scholarly use. There are also efforts to set up scientific communities in our later.

One of the leading edge program is there are 10 campuses of the University of California. They have joined so that BioMed Central can help publish peer journals at a very low cost and encourage their free access to many articles published in those journals. California University Press also established something called the UCIAS (California International and Area Studies) digital collection. This is a larger way to create a knowledge depository for this type of publications by scholars interested in international and area studies made essentially free for scholars. But they also goes through a peer review process to there can be qualified for faculty members wanting their work to be considered for promotion material. You might want to take a look at this website. The creation of e-journals, Bio-One these are 50 about 50 full-case bio-science journals being published now by the learning society. OCLC has been designated as a distributor for this Bio-One e-journals publications outside the United States.

There is a so-called Tempe Principles costs which is adopted by the research library association in the United States. I would like to share with you very quickly, these Tempe Principles. The first one is that the creation, dissemination and application of new knowledge are fundamental to the development of our society. The member one principle of the nine, the cost to academic of published of research should be contained. That is, we should develop ways to contain the cost in the publication of scholarly research.

The second principle—electronic capabilities should be used among other things. The achieving and preserving of scholarly publications in all media is critical to any credible system of scholarly publication.

The fourth principle—the system of scholarly publication must continue to include process for evaluating the quality of scholarly work.

The fifth principle—the concept of copyright and fair use should be encouraged.

The sixth principle—In negotiating publishing agreements, faculties should not give away their rights.

The seventh—the lag of time between submission and publication should be shortened as much as possible.

Number eight—the evaluation of faculty should place a greater emphasis on quality of publication and a reduced emphasis on quantity.

Number nine—the digital environment—scholars and students should be assured privacy with regard to their use of materials.

These are the nine principles proposed by the association of research libraries.

These are another thing that is promoted by SPARC. The open-archives, metadata harvesting protocol. They try to make this an open file, so that the scholars can deposit their publications indifferent knowledge depositories making available easily for others to sue.

Authors would deposit records and all copies of the published version of the article in such servers. Readers worldwide would be able to access these articles without paying subscription access to the source electronic journals. This would speed up some keyers of research and access to the new knowledge.

Several universities are doing this and the key the library of the Massachusetts Institute of Technology has been spear heading this effort to promote the cooperating open archives initiatives. This method used together in harvesting social urgings and other core interest technologies will provide a stimulated way for attracting contents from dispute networked information service and knowledge repositories.

There are many examples of these I met when I visited different websites of these scientists, in field of computer science, physics, mathematics, and the field of chemistry. They work together to create this kind of common knowledge depositories, with the goal to make them as easily accessible as possible and also free of charge. Caltec and many key libraries are among the key lead players in these efforts.

I encourage you to look at the website of these places, because there are many uses for scholarly work and am available, easily accessible, free of charge.

The conclusion of this, the growing impact of SPARC. Competitive mark forces must be unleashed if the status quo is to be challenged. Mr. Johnson, Director of SPARC. The success of SPARC will benefit libraries as well as researchers, authors, publisher partner. We talk about the publishers—they support SPARC's efforts, whereas the commercial ones try to make a lot of money out of authors and scholarly community. In the knowledge world we already saw the price reduction of serials in 2001.

全球思维与行动：中美图书馆员专业交流合作项目[①]

Think Globally, Act Globally:
U. S. – China Librarian Collaboration Project

  各位好，谢谢谭教授的介绍，很高兴再次回到图书馆来，跟各位做一些交流，我今天发言的题目是促进中美文化交流的中美图书馆员交流合作项目，这个项目是一个新的项目，已经做了一年多，我很荣幸担任这个项目的评审员，下面就把这个项目给大家报告一下。

  2007年，美国总统秘书及人文委员会和中国的文化部首先进行了一次官方的相互的访问，那时候我还在国会图书馆工作，我记得我们的馆长也是这个艺术委员会的委员之一，他就随着美方团到中国来，当时他的演讲稿还是我替他草拟的。美国的政府博物馆和图书馆服务所也就直接参与这个项目的执行，这是为期两年的项目，由美国政府提供50万美金，中国文化部也提供对等的经费支持，在美国国会图书馆签约。中国国家图书馆的馆长和文化部的部长都到美国参与了这个签约的活动。

  这个项目的主办单位在美国是美国的博物馆、图书馆服务所，在中国就是文化部。执行单位在美国是伊利诺伊大学厄本那香槟校区，还有伊利诺伊大学的国际活动合作中心负责，中国图书馆学会代表中国执行这个项目。今天中国图书馆学会的汤秘书长也在场，她对这个项目可以说尽了很大的心力，对这个合作项目来讲，她是非常大的贡献者。这个合作机构除了刚才讲的执行机构以外，还有华美图书馆协会，在座的李志钟教授是华美的创办者。这个组委会的成员有伊利诺伊大学图书馆的蒋树勇、陈同美，伊利诺伊州大学莫藤森中心。我个人也很荣幸被邀请担任这个项目的评审员。

  这个项目的活动包括了下面几项，第一个是在中国的不同地区办6至10个为期3天的高级研修班。现在我们在北京、南京、兰州、西安办了4个，最近刚刚在广西南宁又办了一个。另外在美国方面，伊利诺伊大学也专门为中国的图书馆馆长办一个为期3个月的培训，这个项目已经做完了。这个项目除了馆员培训之外，另外一个项目就是跟中国的合作机构共同发展一个依靠互联网可以分享及推广中国学研究及中国文化的数据资源门户，还要在美国举办一次研讨会介绍这个数据库和资源门户，准备在明年做。

  这个照片中的场景是今年5月份在北京中国项目的启动仪式。当时主管单位文化部跟美方的代表正式在国家图书馆签约中国培训的计划。在北京这个启动仪式的时候，我们每个专家同时做几个报告，这个报告当时就现场传播到天津的泰达图书馆、东莞图书馆、吉林省图书馆、四川省图书馆、山东省图书馆、江苏苏州的独树湖图书馆等，我们每次办这种活动，都希望更多的图书馆参与。这个图片是现场的情况，我们在北京举办的时候有6个远距离场所同时参与了这个项目。这是美方的第一批代表，有4位华裔，两位美籍的，我也参与了。这是第一批美方专家成员，张沙丽、刘梦雄、张文雯、赵力沙等几位。这是在南京办的第一个讲习班，各位可以看到参加的图书馆员都非常专注、积极地参与。这次美方做报告的专家都是经过公开的挑选，在40多位申请者中挑出的6位，根据中国政府提供的6个题目，有这些题目专长的专家，我们选出来到中国做报告。

  南京研习班的6个讲题由中方提出来的，第一个是想了解美国图书馆行政的情况；第

[①] 本文根据作者于2009年11月16日在深圳举行的"公共图书馆研究院"成立大会上的发言内容整理而成。

二个是美国有关图书馆的法规;第三个是美国的公共图书馆服务;第四个是美国图书馆评估及专业馆员的资格;第五个是美国公关和社区活动;第六个是美国图书馆的专业组织,还有国际图联的专业介绍。

这个项目在东北师范大学设立,筹划建立中国的第一个关于历史文化数据库资源的门户网站,由东北师大在筹建。在美国办了一个高级研修班,这是在今年的6月底、7月份办的,中国的文化部选派了10位省馆的副馆长和馆长参加研修班,他们分别来自重庆、广东、河北、河南、吉林、辽宁、四川、西藏、云南和浙江,他们平均的年龄是44.2岁,他们的活动首先是在伊利诺伊大学进行9天的培训,由伊利诺伊大学的教授给他们开课,同时参观伊利诺伊州的州图书馆、县市图书馆,还有其他地方图书馆,然后到芝加哥参加美国图书馆学会年会。他们10个人分成5个组,每个组的人到不同的地方参观图书馆和公共图书馆。这是他们到美国去的时候,伊利诺伊州大学欢迎他们的镜头。这是他们在伊利诺伊州大学受训完成以后欢送的晚宴镜头。

第二批美方的专家在9月8日到了北京,他们先参加国家图书馆100周年的馆庆,然后到兰州和西安去为甘肃省和陕西省两省的图书馆员进行培训,这是第二批美方的专家,本来有7位,包括我在内,可是有两位美籍的专家,有一位在动身之前他的母亲去世了,就没法去,第二位是到了上海之后发现他的签证过期了,所以又马上返回,所以他们两个人报告就由其他人承担。第二批专家有蒋树勇、张鸿运等等,这是我们参加国家图书馆100周年馆庆晚宴,我觉得很荣幸,不仅是参加了国家图书馆的100周年馆庆,还参加了几个省馆的馆庆。在国家图书馆馆庆的同时,国家图书馆举办了一个促进知识全球共享国际研讨会的论坛。然后我们又到兰州办了一个为期3天的培训班,这个是开幕式的照片,还有上课的情况。兰州和西安预计的人数是150位左右,可是报名的时候非常踊跃,超过了200名,所以参加研习班的会场有时候都容不下,可以看出他们的兴趣都非常高。这是我们在西安参加陕西图书馆建馆100周年的庆典,还有西安研修班的开班典礼,这个典礼开幕的时候人很多,由于很多人没有座位,还自己搬凳子坐在旁边。

中国图书馆学会对这个项目的评价,我可以采用詹福瑞说的话,他说:这个项目与学会以往的国际交流的活动有所不同,它在交流规模、交流频次、交流目标和评估办法等方面均创新高,在学会历史上尚属首次。詹馆长给我们的评价很高,也给我们一个鼓励,我们一定要把这个事情做得更好。

我们到每个地方都做一些评估,在兰州也发了一些问卷,让学员给我们的讲课一个集体的评价。他们评价说,第一报告内容充实、专家讲解精彩;第二个是学员听、思认真,交流互动热烈;第三个是答疑求证彻底,研讨效果显著;第四个是深入拓展应用,促进共同发展。我们收到这些的评价,感到很受鼓舞,我们每次办这个班都做了很多准备,就希望能够回来对国内的图书馆做一点贡献,尤其是现在文化部主导这个项目,他们就希望这个项目的重点放在公共图书馆方面,可是实际上在每个地方办培训班的时候,参加的大概有一半左右的是公共图书馆员,另外一半是大学跟学院的图书馆员,所以说参加的图书馆员的面是非常广的,不仅是公共图书馆。

各位如果对这个项目有兴趣的话,有两个相关的网站,各位可以去看一下,一个是中国图书馆学会的网站,我的PPT上已经列出来了;第二个是美国伊利诺伊州大学的图书馆网站,你们都可以去看看。

谢谢大家!

(原载《公共图书馆》2009年第4期,第57-58页。)

分享中文数字资源的契机与探讨[①]

Opportunities and Discussions on Sharing Chinese Digital Resources

报告要点
Key Points of My Speech

这篇报告主要是探讨最近所召开的第五届中国和北美图书馆合作会议的主要论题和结论。

The speech is based largely on the major topics and conclusions of the recently held Fifth China-North America Library Conference.

第五届中国和北美图书馆合作会议
The 5th China-US Library Conference

这个会议是在今年 9 月 9 – 11 日在北京召开。是由中国国家图书馆和美国国会图书馆联合主办。美方参加者包括加拿大的数位图书馆专家们。

This conference was held in Beijing on September 9 – 11, 2010 organized jointly by the National Library of China and the U.S. Library of Congress. American participants included a number of digital library specialists from Canada.

会议宗旨
Mission of the Conference

本次大会旨在促进业界对数位资源的共享进行更广泛和深入的研究与探讨；加强中国和北美图书馆界在此领域的交流与合作。

This conference aims to promote the profound research and exploration in digital resources sharing, and to further mutual exchanges and cooperation between China and North America.

开幕式致辞
Opening Remarks by Deanna Marcum, Associate Librarian of the Library of Congress

在今天全球的、多样文化的及多元的世界里，对哪里所发生的快速变化和了解，必须从多种的观点来观察。因此，图书馆及图书馆员对于数位资源分享所包含的潜力和复杂性必须有所了解。

Today's world is global, multi-cultural, and multi-polar, where rapid changes occur and where understanding is only achieved when viewed from multiple perspectives. In response..., libraries and librarians need to understand both the potential and complexity involved with sharing digital resources.

---

① 这是作者于 2010 年 11 月在台北"第八次中文文献资源共建共享合作会议"上的演讲文稿。

第五届中美图书馆合作会议的主要议题
Main Discussion Points of the Conference

（1）资源共享政策与趋势
Resource sharing policies and perspectives
（2）数位资源的基础架构与藏储技术
Digital infrastructure and repository technology
（3）研究数据的共享
Research Data Sharing
（4）共享数位保存方法
Sharing digital preservation methods
（5）数位资源的访问、检索及利用
Shared digital access, retrieval and use

詹福瑞副馆长开幕式致辞
Opening Remarks by Zhan Furui, Deputy Director of NL China

中国国家图书馆的数字资源共享战略与实践：近年来，中国国家图书馆以"同一个中国，同一个数字图书馆"为愿景，积极拓展数位资源的共建共享业务。

In recent years, on the basis of the vision "The whole of China will share and benefit from one digital library", the National Library of China actively promoted the joint construction and sharing of digital resources.

数位资源共享战略与实践
Strategic Planning & Practices for Digital Resources Sharing

1. 国家图书馆的战略规划

The strategic plan of the National Library：

1）建设国家数字图书馆工程
Implement the national digital library project
2）促进全国公共图书馆的协调发展
Promote a coordinated development of the nation's public libraries
3）开展深度和广泛的资源共享
Develop an in-depth and broad-based resource sharing
4）实现数字图书馆的价值融合和增值服务
Realize the combined value and value-added service of digital libraries

2. 国家图书馆的探索与实践

Search and implement by the National Library：

1）通过各类网络平台，服务互联网用户
By means of a variety of network platforms to serve Internet users
2）建设国家数字图书馆地方分馆，服务基层读者
Establish local branches of the national digital library to serve local readers
3）实施"县级数字图书馆推广计划"，服务基层图书馆

Implement the "County Digital Library Plan" to serve local libraries

4）搭建立法决策服务平台，为中央国家机关服务

Construct service platform for legislative decision-making

5）开通残疾人数位图书馆，服务弱势群体

Establish digital libraries for handicapped users to better serve the disadvantaged

6）建设儿童数位图书馆，引导儿童阅读学习

Establish children libraries to cultivate reading habit at an earlier age

7）拓展新媒体服务，创新阅读新经验

Expand new media service to create new reading experience

8）继往开来，规划"国家数字图书馆推广工程"

Learn from the past and develop the future, in the planning of the "Extended National Digital Library Project"

论文宣读与讨论
Presentation and Discussion

在两天的会议里，双方的专家们围绕着5个主题宣读了19篇精彩及高水平的论文，并进行了热烈的讨论。

During the two-day conference, based on the five sub-themes, a total of 19 excellent papers were presented by experts from China and North America, followed by active discussions.

以下为主要论文的讨论要点：

Below are key discussion points in the major papers：

1. 资源共享政策与趋势
Resource sharing policies and perspectives

多伦多大学图书馆馆长提出六个政策：

Carole Moore, The Library Dean of University of Toronto, Carole Moore, proposed six policies：

1）让不受版权限制的资料能公开及自由的使用。

Keep materials already in the public domain openly and freely accessible.

2）把馆藏的复件存放在不同的档案中心以保证长期的保存和使用。

Ensure long-term preservation and accessibility by keeping copies of collections in multiple archives.

3）建立合作式的开放文档以便于无限制的文档主权的交换。

Build open content collaboration in which there is no requirement for the transfer of content ownership or rights.

4）鼓励个别作者注明任意使用的限制和引用的条件。

Encourage individual contributors to indicate any restrictions on use and conditions for appropriate attribution.

5）按照国际标准提供可以查寻各种文献的元数据。

Ensure accessibility of metadata at the collection and item level according to appropriate international standards depending on format.

6）鼓励发展能够经由开放式标准促进文献使用的工具。
Encourage the development of tools that enhance the usability of materials through open service standards.

美国国家科学院讨论知识产权法规和数位资源共享的模式，指出两个新的发展
Paul Uhlir of the NAS discussed intellectual property laws and models of digital resource sharing and pointed out two new developments：
1）推动"创造公共园地"和"科学公共园地"的新发展
The advent of the "*Creative Commons*" and "*Science Commons*" initiatives
2）"开放式获取"的运动
The "*Open-access*" movement

中国文化部全国文化信息资源建设管理中心张彦博主任提出"消弭数位鸿沟，共享文化资源——全国文化信息资源共享工程建设与实践"的建议。
Zhang Yanbo, Director of the National Cultural Information Resources Sharing Management Center spoke on "Narrow the Digital Divide and Share the Cultural Resources—The Construction of the National Information Resources Sharing Project".

北京大学图书馆馆长朱强教授提出了"关于我国资源共享政策的若干建议"：
Zhu Qiang, Professor and Director, Peking University Library, spoke on "Suggestions to Resource Sharing Policies in China"：
朱强关于资源共享政策的若干建议：
Suggestions on Resource Sharing Policies in China：
1）要推进和加速与图书馆相关的立法工作
Push and Expedite legislative work on library related laws
2）要坚持并完善数位图书馆联席会议机制
Continue and improve the work of Joint Council of Digital Libraries
3）要加强有关标准制定工作
Strengthen the work on adopting related standards
4）要促进开放获取运动的开展
Promoting the development of Open Access movement
5）要从更高层级统筹协调资源共享
Should coordinate resource sharing from higher levels

2. 数位资源的基础架构与藏储技术
Digital infrastructure and repository technology

Johns Hopkins 大学主管图书馆数字项目副馆长，赛义·乔杜里，关于"数据保存：基础框架的全球视野"的演讲。
Sayeed Chounhury, Associate Dean of Library Digital Programs, Johns Hopkins University spoke on "Data Conservancy：A Global Perspective on Infrastructure".

科学已经国际化了。数据保存基础框架的发展必须按照能强调共同的科学问题和要求

的新的协作模式。

Science has become an international endeavor so Data Conservancy infrastructure development must account for new modes of collaboration that emphasize common scientific questions or requirements.

美国国会图书馆亚洲部主任关于数字资源共享有关的要求的报告。

Peter Young, Chief of the Asian Division, Library of Congress, reported on "Requirements for Transfer, Archival Storage, Administration, Access, and Management of Shared Digital Resources"

他的报告主要是针对数字资源的传送、文献藏储、行政、获取和管理各种要求。提出促成数位资源共享所要求的基础架构与藏储技术。

His paper addresses requirements for transfer, archival storage, administration, access, and management of shared digital resources. The paper identifies infrastructure requirements and repository technology needed to facilitate digital resource sharing.

3. 研究数据的共享
Research Data Sharing

美国洛杉矶加州大学资讯研究所教授关于"研究数据:何者共享,与谁,何时,及为什么?"的报告。

Christine Borgman, Professor of Information Studies, UCLA spoke on "Research Data: Who will share what, with whom, when, and why?"

她分析了四个争论点:

Four arguments are examined:

1) 要把用公款研究的数据成果公开

to make the results of publicly-funded research data available to the public

2) 要让他人对数据提出新问题

to enable others to ask new questions of extant data

3) 要促进科学的现状

to advance the state of science

4) 要能复制研究的结果

to reproduce research

武汉大学图书馆学系肖希明主任关于"构建我国信息资源共享政策保障体系"的六项建议:

Professor Xiao Ximing, Head of the Library Science Department, Wuhan University, spoke on the policy assurance for information resource sharing in China and made six recommendations:

1) 信息资源整体布局政策

Integrated development plan for information resources

2) 信息资源协调采集政策

Coordinated acquisition of information resources

3) 书目信息资源共建共享政策

Cooperative building and sharing bibliographic information resources

4) 文献传递补贴和收费政策

Subsidy and fees for document delivery

5) 文献传递中知识产权问题的解决

Solutions for intellectual property right issues in document delivery

6) 信息资源公共获取政策

Public access of information resources

中国社会科学院图书馆蒋颖副馆长关于该院"人文社会科学学术资源开放获取现状分析"的报告：

Ms. Jiang Ying, Deputy Director of Chinese Academy of Social Science Library reported on the current status for open access of scholarly resources in the humanities and social sciences：

1) 根据她的调查，中国人文社科领域对数字信息资源开放获取远远落后于自然科学领域。

According to her survey, open access to information resources in humanities and social sciences is far behind those in natural sciences in China.

2) 在数据资源的保存和共享方面，大学和研究机构的数据基本上是分散保存和内部使用，不对外提供。

In regard to data resources, they are scattered in different places and are only for internal use.

3) 值得一提的是国家统计局网站已将《中国统计年鉴》的数据在网站上免费开放

However, it is worthy of note that the database of the *China Statistical Yearbook* provided by the Chinese National Bureau of Statistics is now available from its website and is free of charge.

4. 数位资源保存方法
Sharing digital preservation methods

中国国家图书馆张志清副馆长关于"中华古籍特藏资源库构建"报告的三个要点：

The report on "The Digitization of Chinese Rare Books and Special Collections" by Zhang Zhiqing, Deputy Director of the NL of China：

1) 国家图书馆古籍特藏数字化

Digitization of Chinese rare books and special collections at the National Library

2) 中华古籍保护计划

The Chinese Ancient Books Conservation and Preservation Project

3) 中华古籍特藏资源库——包括中华古籍目录检索平台及分布式古籍影像资源库等

Resource database of Chinese ancient books and special collections

美国 Emory 大学图书馆馆长对数字资源保存所提出的设想与合作方案

Richard Luce, Library Director of Emory University spoke on "Digital Preservation：Proposing Scenarios and Collaborative Projects".

他认为中美之间对数字资源保存的合作可从以下三点着手：

Three possible approaches for cooperation：

1) 保存数字化后的收藏和原始的数字化档案
Preserving digitized collection & born digital archives
2) 保存网站上的存档
Preserving web site archiving
3) 保存数据、数据集及应用工具
Preserving data, datasets & application tools

浙江图书馆刘晓清副馆长关于浙江网络图书馆数字资源的报告要点：
Key points in the Report on digital resources in Zhejiang Network Library by Liu Xiaoqing, Deputy Director of Zhejiang Library：
1) 数字资源利用的策略
Strategies for the use of digital resources
2) 数位资源的整合
Integration of digital resources
3) 读者资源的共享
Sharing digital resources with users
4) 数位资源利用的方法
Methods for the use of digital resources

美国 Smithsonian Institution 图书馆副馆长关于"生物多样性遗产图书馆：保留一门知识生态学"的报告。
Thomas Garnett, Associate Director of U. S. Smithsonian Institution Libraries reported on "The Biodiversity Heritage Library：Preserving a Knowledge Ecology."

中国科学院也是这个国际合作项目的参与机构之一。
The Chinese Academy of Sciences is also one of the participants of this international cooperative project.

以下是一些共同的原则：
Below are the general principles of BHL：
1) 保证数位化数据库长期及连续地获取
Ensure long-term continued access to digital files
2) 责任分布及资源结合
Distribute responsibilities and pool resources
3) 建立有责任的所有权
Create responsible ownership
4) 将复制的数位化数据库分布在不同的地点
Replicate the content in different locations
5) 用不同的系统结构和管理方式
With different system architectures and management

5. 数位资源的访问、检索及利用
Shared digital access, retrieval and use

美国 ITHAKA 公司总裁 Kevin Guthrie 的报告:"网络演变的三个趋势:推进数字资源共享的实用指南"。这三个趋势是:

The speech by Kevin Guthrie, President of ITHAKA on "Three Trends in the Evolution of the Web: A Practical Guide to Promote Shared Use of Digital Resources". The three trends are:

1) 链接

Linking

2) 搜索引擎

Search engines

3) 社会化网络

Social networking

北京市档案局副局长李立军关于"北京市国家综合档案馆馆藏信息资源共享机制建设研究"的报告。

The report "On Mechanism of Resources Sharing of the Beijing Municipal National Comprehensive Archives" by Li Lijun, Deputy Director of Beijing Municipal Archives.

依据国家信息化建设"统筹规划、国家主导、统一标准、联合建设、互联互通、资源共享"的战略原则进行。

Actions guided by the strategic principles of national informationization: "Coordinated planning, government leadership, unified standards, cooperative construction, networked and linked, and resources sharing".

中国国家博物馆信息网络部主任肖飞关于"资源共享:数位社会中的博物馆"的报告。

Report on "Resource Sharing: Museums in the Digital Society" by Xiao Fei, Director of the Information Network Department of the National Museum of China.

她认为博物馆的资源共享不应该是简单的信息发布。博物馆不仅要提供藏品的直观信息,而且要还原、说明藏品作为社会生活物化载体的立体信息。

She believes that as a museum, not only the basic information of a collection item should be open to the public, but also the cultural and the realistic information about the item.

一些总结
Some Conclusions

第五届中美图书馆合作会议被扩大为中国及北美图书馆员的会议。

The 5th China-U.S. Library Conference was expanded to include library professionals from Canada.

按照第四届会议的模式也邀请了档案界和博物馆界的专家一同参加。

It continued the trend of the 4th conference by inviting professionals from archives and museums to join.

这个会议有深度及广泛地回顾和探讨了有关数字资源共享的各种重要问题。

It reviewed and discussed extensively and in greater depth the wide range of important issues relating to sharing digital resources.

双方都希望能在这个会议后达成一些具体的合作项目。

Both sides showed strong desires to develop cooperative projects as a follow up of the conference.

很高兴能看到很多经由国际合作的数位资源共享项目在快速发展中，并且试图克服一些不合理的限制。

It was exciting to see the many expedited developments in a worldwide effort to share digital resources and to overcome unreasonable restrictions.

像台湾地区一样，中国内地也在大力的计划和推行各种信息资源数位化项目。

Like what has happened in Taiwan, Mainland China has placed great effort on planning and implementing digitization projects for information resources of various types.

近年来，信息和网络技术的快速发展也促进了信息资源数位化的进展。

The rapid advancement in information and network technologies in recent years have also facilitated this movement.

目前，在信息资源共建共享方面有更多可供国际合作的机会。这是采取行动的好时机。

Opportunities for greater international cooperation in building and sharing digital resources are ever more present. It is time to act!

对正在进行中的中文古籍数位化合作项目，美国国会图书馆要向台湾的"中央图书馆"在过去五年的大力赞助表示感谢。

The Library of Congress is deeply grateful to the "Central Library" in Taiwan for the on-going cooperative digitization of the rare Chinese materials in the Library of Congress.

第五届中美图书馆合作会议 The 5th China-US Library Cooperation Conference http：//www.nlc.gov.cn/yjfw/zm/index.html

第五届中美图书馆合作会议在京隆重召开 The opening of the 5th China-US Library Cooperation Conference in Beijing http：//www.nlc.gov.cn/syzt/2010/0909/article_565.htm

中国国家图书馆－中国国家数字图书馆 National Library of China-National Digital Library of China http：//www.nlc.gov.cn

全国文化信息资源共享工程 National Cultural Information Resources Sharing Project http：//www.ndcnc.gov.cn

3. 图书馆数字化与网络化
Library Digitization and Networking

关于亚洲理工学院建立地区科技信息中心的建议

Proposal for a Regional Information Center for Science and Technology at the Asian Institute of Technology[①]

PART I: BACKGROUND

Introduction

Several diverse factors have provided the opportunity of bringing into being a Southeast Asian regional information network. They are:

(1) the need for international information transfer;
(2) increased demands on academic libraries;
(3) recent developments in hardware;
(4) recent developments in software;
(5) the creation of a favorable political and emotional environment for the implementation of such a system, accomplished through the efforts of various international organizations; and
(6) plans by the Asian Institute of Technology in Bangkok to build a new campus featuring a computerized library and regional information center in accordance with its function as a post-graduate university for Southeast Asia.

Need for International Transfer of Information

It is possible that nothing contribute more to better understanding between nations leading ultimately to permanent peace, than an effective international system of information transfer. Upon such a system could be built educational progress, economic and social development, and scientific and technological advancement.

Information is one of the most important and powerful resources existing in the world today. It is one of the chief reasons for the great disparity in technological, economic, social, and educational development between the developed and developing countries. A strong information base and the ability to use it can contribute importantly to the well-being of a nation. Information is seen as a means by which a developing nation can narrow the gap between the have and the have-not nations of the world and, as such, it should flow freely across national boundaries to the mutual benefit of all.

The idea of the transfer of information across geographic distance is as old as civilization. The creation of the United Nations in 1945, and subsequently of UNESCO with the objective of bringing about a freer flow of information among nations, has given particular encouragement to the concept of international exchange and transfer.

---

① Submitted to Asian Institute of Technology, Bangkok, Thailand, January 1971.

Many of the problems and limitations of international transfer are the same ones faced in the past. Some of these are: the lack of a central responsibility and of an adequately supported mechanism in many countries, publication in insufficient quantity for international distribution, delays in transmitting materials, limitations in staff, space, and funds to acquire and distribute on the one hand and receive, and make available on the other. In order to prevent the development of permanent barriers between disciplines, languages, differing computer technologies, and even to some extent nations, a start must be made now to provide the effective means of interchange among existing and planned systems.

Demands on Academic Libraries

Academic libraries must play an important role in achieving the international transfer of information in addition to their historic and conventional role.

The library has traditionally been regarded as the heart of the university, serving the students in their educational needs and the faculty and research staff in their teaching and research needs. Most of the tools and concepts currently in use in academic libraries including the card catalogue, subject headings, and classification systems, were developed and introduced in the second half of the nineteenth century. Since then many great libraries have been doubling in size every twenty years, and the only response that has been possible to increasing growth and workloads has been to add manpower and to build more space to house the books, staff, and catalogues.

Using traditional methods, libraries apparently cannot respond to the demands of modern scholarship unless they continue to grow according to a geometric progression. The "information explosion", painfully apparent to engineers, is demonstrated by such statistics as two-million technical articles published last year. It is not surprising that there is so much information available, considering that 90 percent of all engineers who have ever lived are still alive today. It is obvious that new techniques and concepts are needed, especially in the emerging countries where the lack of information is the greatest single obstacle to development.

Recent Developments in Hardware

A period of innovation in libraries was started in the past decade with the development of new technology in (1) reprography, (2) computer-based systems, and (3) communications.

Reprography refers to the class of processes whose purpose is to replicate by optical or photomechanical means previously created graphic or coded messages. It embraces all the methods, materials, and equipment of reproduction. New developments have led to new systems for compact storage, the direct access to stored files of film, expanded use of microfilm reader-printers in support of academic activities such as research, and an increase in the volume and rate of microform material into and out of a library.

Third generation computers are now commonplace and they are faster, smaller, cheaper, easier to maintain, better capable of performing several operations at once, and easier to interface with communications equipment. Pertinent applications for a university library include: (1) business type data processing such as serial records, acquisitions, ordering circulation control, and book catalog preparation; (2) storage and retrieval through remote communications of very active files of specialized information; (3) computer assisted learning; (4) computer-aided design; and (5) the use of the computer for administration management.

A vastly superior world communication system is emerging. Conventional systems are adding more coaxial cable and more microwave relay stations to their existing facilities. Considerable progress has been achieved in creating a global communications satellite system. Specifically, several new satellites have been positioned successfully in synchronous orbit and placed in operational service, extending full time service to the Pacific region, and highly reliable wideband service capable of carrying voice, data, and video is now available between America, Europe and Asia extending along a perimeter of Japan, Thailand, and Australia. A new computerized library can therefore look forward to active use of audio, video, and graphic media. Examples are: (1) provision of service through direct-access systems from audio files via the touch-tone telephone, (2) facilities for the frame-by-frame slow scan transmission of hard copy or microfilm material with or without sound to student carrels, faculty offices, and even between terminals located in different countries, and (3) facsimile transmission as a replacement for inter-library loan.

Recent Developments in Software

Interest in mechanized information handling has risen rapidly in the last few years due to the realization that new and more advanced hardware will result in improvements in services. The potential impact of the computer, for example, on the interaction of men and ideas is enormous, the only effective limitation apparently being the inability of man to express, in the detail required by the computer, what man himself is able to do. Present and future information handling systems can, and will, perform a range of operations constrained less by the size and speed of the memory and supporting processing equipment (hardware), than by the ingenuity of the memory organization-designer (software).

Within the span of the past human generation, we are entering what might be called the third generation in man-machine communications, by analogy with the third generation of computers themselves. We have passed from the first generation where the computer had to be addressed in its own language (machine language) through the second generation or stage where English-like languages (FORTRAN, ALGOL, etc.) could be used to address the computer. Still it was a case of man-machine communication on the machine's term. Now, man is entering into a dialog with the computer on his own terms using "problem-oriented" languages. The name for the computer software that promises third generation benefits is "generalized" or "task-oriented" programs. Our interest in these systems is for use as retrieval packages for the mechanized data and information that are to constitute the data bases of computerized libraries and information networks of the future.

In summary, there are increasingly large numbers in the form of machine readable files, many of them available at nominal charge, being created. These include the Library of congress MARC (Machine Readable Cataloging), MEDLARS (Medical Literature Analysis and Retrieval), and the HRIS system (Highway Research Information Service) —to name a few. In addition a respectable number of interactive retrieval systems are now operational, and are commercially available as packaged software systems.

Efforts of International Governmental organizations

There has been a growing concern for improved international transfer of information over the past few years by various international governmental organizations such as UNESGO and ICSU (the International Council of Scientific Unions); international non-governmental organizations such as FID (the International Federation for Documentation); national governmental agencies including the U. S. Department of Agriculture, Department of Defense, Library of Congress, and many others; quasi-public organizations such as INTELSAT (the International Telecommunications Satellite Consortium); and various professional associations such as the American Chemical Society. The efforts of UNESCO appear to be most significant and most pertinent to the problem as it is seen in Southeast Asia.

UNESCO has committed itself the following goals: a much more liberal attitude toward reciprocity, particularly for the developing countries, and as wide a geographical extension of exchange as possible; the addition of summaries in foreign languages at the end of every scientific work published in a less well-known language; publication within a region of lists of material for exchange between nations; and speedier circulation of exchange material. The last step could best be accomplished by the elimination of bulk transport where possible and the direct forwarding of exchange material by electronic transmission.

The Conference on the Application of Science and Technology to the Development of Asia (CASTASIA), which was held in August 1968, recommended as one of the priority areas for action— "the development of information and documentation facilities through strengthening existing centers, establishing new centers and links between national centers, rationalizing existing systems and making maximum use of modern techniques of reproduction, abstracting and data processing, considering the establishment or one or more regional information clearinghouses." As an initial response to the CASTASIA recommendations, UNESCO is investigating the possibility of the setting up of a regional scientific and technological center in Asia.

The stand taken by UNESCO and other international and national organizations dramatizes the need for a regional information center in Asia and has accomplished much in the creation of a favorable political and emotional environment for the implementation of such a system. However, the establishment of such a center from the ground up completes with buildings, reference materials, and hardware will cost millions of dollars. Fortunately, the basic facilities for such a center exist in the proposed library and information center of the Asian Institute of Technology (AIT). Although much of the initial planning of the AIT facilities was based on its own specific requirements in its function as a regional post-graduate university, this present proposal is to give additional emphasis to the outward dimension of the proposed center and to increase its capacity to act as a clearing-house for the region.

New AIT Campus and Development Program

A library is concerned fundamentally with the goals of the organization of which it is a part.

The Asian Institute of Technology located centrally in Bangkok, is a regional graduate school of engineering. It has an international faculty and its students come from 18 countries in Asia to study in the diploma, master's and doctoral programs and to do research. Its graduates stay in Asia to apply their newly gained knowledge to the development of this vast region—only 2% has left Asia to work in the west.

The AIT is uniquely chartered as a private non-profit regional institution and is recognized as an "international organization" in every respect.

Since its inception in 1959 AIT has grown steadily and its sphere of activities in Asia has widened greatly—both geographically and in services and programs offered. Its objectives are to provide:

1. Educational opportunities at the master's and doctorate levels.
2. Through post-graduate diploma courses and short-term institutes, opportunities for practicing engineers in the region to keep abreast of technological developments and their application to the needs of the region.
3. Stimuli for the development of research oriented specifically to the needs of the region by the establishment of a major research center within AIT.
4. Opportunities for faculty members from other educational institutions to study and conduct research at AIT.
5. A focus for the development of engineering education to meet the unique needs of the region.
6. Mechanisms for the introduction into the region of the latest developments in technology and for the development of their application to its needs.
7. A center for the development of equipment for research and instructional laboratories.
8. An outstanding library to serve the needs of both AIT and the region.
9. A major computing center, designed and operated to serve AIT and other institutions in the region.
10. A regional focal point and catalyst for the development of professional activities, including conferences and seminars, and a center for the publication of technical information for the region.

Pursuant to the objectives, a ten-year capital development program featuring a new 400-acre residential campus eventually supporting a 96-member faculty and 700 students in civil, mechanical, and electrical engineering and supporting fields by 1978 was approved by AIT's international Board of Trustees in July 1968. Plans are near completion and construction is underway. The basic facilities will be completed in 1972 with the entire campus to be completed in 1978. The library and computer center, the functional foundations upon which the proposed regional information center will be built, are scheduled for completion in 1974.

PART II: REGIONAL INFORMATION CENTER

Motivation

The lack of national bibliographies, indexing and abstracting services, and effective means for the preservation and dissemination of published and processed information in many of the countries in the region, coupled with the language differences, have prevented information from being readily accessible to engineers, researchers, and specialists. Much valuable time and energy is often wasted in the Southeast Asian region on projects of economic and technological development because of the lack of effective bibliographical control and dissemination of available engineering and technical information. This situation has contributed to the frustration of many engineers and research workers who could otherwise be more productive in their work.

In order to remedy the situation, it is proposed that a regional library and information center for Southeast Asia be established at the Asian Institute of Technology. Since the AIT Library has already developed one of the best engineering collections in the region, its resources can be easily expanded to serve as a regional information center in science and technology. The establishment of the regional engineering information center for Southeast Asia will greatly facilitate the flow and exchange of technical information among the countries within the region as well as between the region and the rest of the world. It is a necessary step toward the realization of a world science information system advocated by UNESCO, discussed earlier in this Proposal.

Official Designation

The center is to be called the Regional Information Center for Science and Technology. It will be located at the Asian Institute of Technology and be designated AIT/RICSAT.

Goals and Objectives

The Center would provide resources and guidance to national centers, thereby assisting them to keep abreast of current development. It would provide a stock of materials within the region which would be available for ready reference. Perhaps most important, it would provide a base for the integration of information systems in the participating countries, advising national centers during this period of evolution on appropriate standards and procedures so that materials will be handled uniformly and consistently, thereby facilitating the transfer of scientific and technical information in the region. Finally, it would provide access to world information networks as they develop.

Within this context, the Center would embrace the following broad objectives:
(1) To assure close cooperation between all documentation centers in the region.
(2) To process scientific and engineering information by modern methods.
(3) To facilitate dissemination by publishing information in the officially adopted languages.
(4) To organize symposia and conferences and to publish their proceedings.
(5) To publish at regular intervals materials devoted to summaries of periodicals.
(6) To carry out bibliographical work for engineering and scientific organizations.
(7) To organize research services for unifying and improving documentation methods in the region.

(8) To promote relations between all engineers, scientists, and managers in the region.

Anticipated Services

The specific services to be provided by the Center toward fulfillment of these goals and objectives will be planned under the guidance of an advisory board consisting of library and information system specialists, representatives of engineering societies, and experts from participating countries. Dr. John A. Hrones, Provost of Science and Technology at Case Western Reserve University and member of the Executive Committee of the AIT Board of Trustees, is currently making contacts with individuals who may be invited to serve on the advisory board.

The Center will use the very latest developments in computer implemented information systems. While the Center builds its own data base, it will also seek to participate in such data banks as the Library of Congress MARC program (Machine Readable Cataloging), the MIT's INTREX project (Information Transfer Experiment), the MEDLARS file (Medical Literature Analysis and Retrieval System) the HRIS system (Highway Research Information Service), the DDC system (U.S. Defense Documentation Center), the NASA Scientific and Technical Information Collection, the National Agricultural Library's CAIN data tapes, as well as the Engineering Index and Chemical Abstracts which are on magnetic tapes.

With these data banks available, in addition to the library's own expanded collection processed for storage and retrieval, the following functions and services will be possible:

(1) To acquire, collect, index, catalog, abstract, translate, and disseminate publications, journals, documents, published and unpublished technical reports, and other material relevant to the scientific and technological development of the region.

(2) To develop and experiment with an effective and feasible system for the storage and retrieval of scientific and technical information utilizing the latest technological developments in computers, microforms, and telecommunications.

(3) To publish at regular intervals abstracting journals, subject bibliographies, book catalogs, union list of scientific and technical serials, and state-of-the-art studies.

(4) To render literature searching, photocopy, microfilming, selective dissemination of information in the officially adopted languages, and other reference services for engineering and scientific institutions, laboratories, the offices of various industries, and the ministries of governments in the region.

(5) To act as a clearinghouse for information concerning scientific and engineering projects and research in progress by conducting surveys, making reports, and publishing directories.

(6) To collaborate with national documentation centers and other major library and information centers within the region in the formation of a science information network.

(7) To cooperate with major information centers and data banks of the world in the exchange of machine-readable bibliographic information on a broad international basis.

(8) To organize, consistent with its role as a branch of AIT, symposia and conferences on problems related to all the branches of science and engineering, and to publish their proceedings.

(9) To provide educational programs and training facilities, both regular and short-term, for the training and upgrading of library and information scientists to meet the needs of the region. Eventually, this could be expanded into a new concept in regional education being investigated by AIT called AITOPS (Asian Institute of Technology Overseas Programs) in which selected courses would be videotaped and transmitted to classrooms in local centers in the RICSAT network.

Information Coverage

The literature to be covered will, initially, include all fields of engineering research and applications that are related to the region. Selected information in the interdisciplinary and related subject areas will be added until all the relevant fields of science and technology are represented.

Although AIT/RICSAT implies that its primary responsibility is for South east Asia, the term

"Southeast Asia" is broadly interpreted so that as many countries as possible may be benefitted by inclusion. A tentative listing of countries and territory to be included is given as follows:

Bhutan
Burma
Cambodia
Ceylon
China (Taiwan)
Hong Kong
India
Indonesia
Korea
Laos
Malaysia
Nepal
Pakistan
Philippines
Singapore
Thailand
Vietnam

It is planned that a communication network employing the newest communication media available such as the Intelsat III Satellite will be established enabling the direct transmission of the most recent information from the several major data banks in the United States and other countries to Bangkok and then transference to the affiliated network stations in each of the Southeast Asian countries. The countries where a network station would be established are to be decided on a voluntary and cooperative basis.

To be of maximum usefulness, publications of all languages are to be included although the primary emphasis will still be given to those written in English. It is planned that in staffing the center, a number of linguists with proficiency in Asian languages will be employed so that transliterated author names end translated titles of publications in any one of the Asian languages may be provided along with an abstract of the content in English for bibliographic input and retrieval. Service for translation of full text will be provided subject to the availability of staff capability and time. Whenever possible, outside translation services will be contracted to perform the service for the client.

Approaches

Two basic approaches appear to be open to AIT. First, there is the "wait and see" approach which can be supported on the grounds that computer-based library systems must still be considered to be in the developmental stage and that their cost-effectiveness has never been established. Secondly, there is the direct approach of designing a total or integrated system to fulfill the needs of South and Southeast Asia from the start. Here the premise is that, because of the interrelated and interconnected characteristics of a libraries operation, the logical procedure is to design a total system from the start to include all machinable operations in order to make efficient and economical use of whatever computer is available.

The first consideration would leave automation to others and would be unworthy of the most outstanding technical library in Southeast Asia. However, AIT rejects this conservative approach on other grounds—the opportunity is here now. Anticipating its move to its new campus, AIT cannot wait for the developmental stage of computerized libraries to shake-down and stabilize. Moreover, to build a conventional library to fulfill the Center's objectives would probably be impossible.

Asia, unlike America and Europe, does not have a large investment in conventional information and communication systems. Therefore, it is probable that new highly sophisticated information systems are economically more justifiable in developing regions than they are in the developed parts of the world. AIT believes that the opportunity for Southeast Asia to bridge the information gap has manifested itself, and that it lies in the immediate application of the most advanced technologies. Thus, AIT is planning to build a library to contain the Center using the very latest developments in computer implemented information systems. Its design and operation will be of such flexibility as to insure the timely inclusion of new techniques in the rapidly

Preliminary discussions held with the following agencies tend to support this approach:

◇ Comsat Corporation concerning use of satellite link to the United States.

◇ Library of Congress regarding participation in the MARC program which would provide the AIT library with magnetic tape catalogue information on current English monographs (not limited to engineering or science).
◇ MIT Intrex program relative to the use of the system being developed to machine access a 50,000 volume experimental library.
◇ National Library of Medicine regarding participation in its automated medical library program.
◇ National Agricultural Library concerning its agricultural sciences information network.
◇ UNESCO relative to the development of a regional communication system linking the AIT Library to other focal points in Southeast Asia.

Development Plan

At the point in time, AIT sees the realization of RICSAT, a regional information center for science and technology in Southeast Asia ultimately forming part of a global information network, as being accomplished in two broad phases. Essentially what will be achieved in the first phase, Phase A, which will commence in July 1971, is the forming of an advisory committee composed of world renowned experts in the library, information, computer, and communication fields to advise in the detailed planning of the information center; the securing of initial funds to support both the planning activities and the design and construction of the buildings for the library and the computer center at the new campus at AIT where the information center will be operated; the recruiting and training of staff; the system designing; the selection and installation of adequate computer equipment; etc. The acquisition of available data bases and development of computer programs should begin at the earliest possible date during the Phase A period paralleling the planning activities. Additional funds will be sought according to the planned program and the needs so determined. During Phase B, the Center will become imbedded in, and integrated with, communications systems in an ever-increasing interconnecting network eventually reaching worldwide proportions.

The development of the computerized library and information center described in Phase A involves the following rather well-defined activities:

(1) Planning Study—The purpose of the system, the broad outlines of its technical organizations, the cost factors and sources of income and support, and the schedule for future development of it are all determined in sufficient detail to provide a set of guidelines and preliminary specifications.

(2) Design and Construction of Library and Computer Center—The Library will require an estimated 60,000 square feet of space to house 300,000 volumes of books and bound journals, 5000 scientific and technical journal titles, 100,000 documents, and a large stock of microtexts. It will also provide reading space for 500 readers and office and working area for approximately 60 staff members. The computer center will require an estimated 19,500 square feet of space to accommodate the large computer system, eleven staff offices, two classrooms, one conference room, and adequate space for computer operations. The funds required for construction are to be sought from the contributions of the U.S. Government under the capital development program of AIT.

Work on the planning of these two buildings is described in Proposed Library Building Program,[①] a document that will serve as a guide for the architect in the design of the library and the computer center.

(3) Detailed System Design—The organization of the system, its workload, its hardware, its software, its operating procedures, and its administrative organization are all defined in great detail, sufficient for inclusion as terms of reference in contracts for delivery and installation of

---

① Asian Institute of Technology, Proposed Library Building Program, Prepared by Hwa-Wei Lee, Head Librarian (Bangkok: 1969).

equipment and for programming.

(4) Hardware Ordered—Based on findings in (3).

(5) Software Acquisition and Implementation—The equipment is installed, the systems designs for software and procedures are translated into proven computer programs and manuals of operation, personnel are trained in the operation of the system, and the entire Center becomes a reality.

(6) Acquisition of Library Material and the Building up of a Data Bank—The building up of a data bank including both the accumulation of locally prepared input data and the data bases acquired from existing sources such as the MARC, MEDLARS, INTREX, HRIS, DOD, NASA, CAIN, Engineering Index, Chemical Abstracts, etc.

The Phase A period is planned to extend from July 1971 to June 1975. The scheduling of activities in Phase A is summarized in the accompanying figure, "Development Timetable for Phase A". The second phase, Phase B, will begin immediately after this period if not sooner. It is anticipated that by then, most of the computer/communication interface problems will be solved and the modes (participants) and the links (channels and media) will be evident. Specifically then, this phase will include the following:

(1) A plan for linking the Center via communication links to other centers of activity in Southeast Asia would be developed and means for implementation established.

(2) On line communication with the U.S. via satellite for certain activities would be initiated.

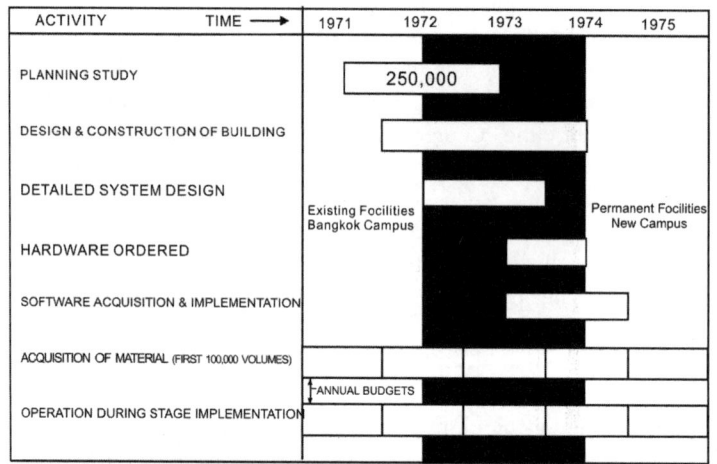

DEVELOPMENT TIMETABLE FOR PHASE A

In conclusion, the extent to which RICSAT is operable from a series of remote consoles in Asia is limited only by the state-of-the-art and economic realities of communications in the region and in the world.

Planning Study

This aspect of Phase A of the Development Plan is essentially a feasibility study. The first step in the study is to demonstrate the need for a regional information center in this part of the world which has been presumed to be valid based on the arguments expanded in Part I of this Proposal. The next step is to explore the design problem engendered by the need and to identify its elements. Finally, the potentially useful solutions will be sorted out of the plausible set on the basis of physical realizability, economic worthwhileness, and financial feasibility.

The study must address itself to a projection of the role that mechanization will play in the Center and the pace at which it should develop. Several problems will be faced by the ATT library in extending its scope of operation to acquire the many machine-readable data bases that are available, processing them, and providing "information services" based on them.

Some of the issues relate to content: What kinds of material should the Center acquire? Some of them concern library processes: How should magnetic tape materials be utilized? Some of the problems are technological: How do we provide man-machine communication? Some of them are fiscal: How can the Center be made financially viable? Some are administrative: How do we relate the library to the computing facility and each to the Center and to the University?

The approach will be to both recruit a staff to work in residence at AIT while also forming an advisory committee composed of world renowned experts in the pertinent disciplines as consultants and advisors. Such modest attempts at mechanization as the conversion of the AIT library catalog to machine readable form, the acquisition of inexpensive data bases, and the development of computer programs to implement them will be undertaken to provide inputs for the feasibility study.

The proposed budget for the first year of the Planning Study to begin in July 1971 is as follows:

Residence Professional Staff	50,000
Advisors and Consultants	25,000
Travel and Per Diem to Meetings	15,000
Regional Conferences of heads of national documentation centers	10,000
Acquiring the available data bases	10,000
Communications	2,000
Publication and Reproduction Expenses	3,000
Computer Time	10,000
Total	125,000

亚洲理工学院的图书馆自动化

Library Mechanization at the Asian Institute of Technology

BACKGROUND

Strategically located in the centre of Southeast Asia, the Asian Institute of Technology is a unique regional postgraduate institution for advanced study and research in engineering and related subjects in Asia. Although founded in Bangkok, Thailand, it is chartered as a private non-profit regional organization governed by an international board of trustees presently consisting of Australia, France, Indonesia, Malaysia, Pakistan, Philippines, Thailand, United Kingdom, United States of America, and Vietnam. New board members from Canada, China, Hong Kong, Japan, Netherlands, New Zealand, and other countries and regions are in the process of being added. The student body, now totaling 200, comes from 17 Asian countries and regions: Afghanistan, Taiwan, Hong Kong, India, Indonesia, Iran, Japan, Korea, Laos, Malaysia, Nepal, Pakistan, Philippines, Singapore, Thailand, Turkey, and Vietnam. These students, all holding a bachelor's degree, are enrolled in three types of programme of studies, namely, one-year postgraduate diploma programme, 21-month Master's degree programme, or a doctoral programme. By mid-1972 the Institute will be moved from its present site, which is temporarily situated on the campus of Chulalongkorn University, to its 400-acre new campus in the outskirts of Bangkok where, according to the development plan, the enrollment will grow to 1000 in 1980.

Since the objectives of AIT are closely identified with the economic and technological development of the region, the library has been charged, as stated in one of the objectives of the Institute, to provide "An outstanding library to serve the needs of both AIT and the region". To be in line with this objective, ever since its inception, the Institute has given special emphasis and support to the development of a strong library with a regional outlook and perspective. As a long-range development goal, the library plans to expand its collection from 30,000 volumes of books at the present to 300,000 volumes in the 1980s. During the same period, it expects to increase the journal titles from 1000 to 6000. Besides being an outstanding library, plans have been undertaken to expand the library's role so that it may also serve as a regional information centre for science and technology in Southeast Asia to expedite the process of economic and technological development in the region by making available the technical knowledge which has thus far helped to widen rather than to narrow the gap between the so called developed countries and the developing countries.

In order that the library can rapidly expand its resource and services to meet the needs within the shortest span of time and with the least financial encumbrances, the library has been planning for computer applications since October 1968. It is envisioned that through total system planning and design there will be a gradual implementation from simple mechanized library routines to a more complex system of storage, retrieval and dissemination in successive stages.

The availability of an IBM 1130 computer system at AIT enables the library to begin initial experimentation in the house-keeping operations such as journal listing and control and acquisitions and accounting. The successful implementation of these operations by computer in the last two years at the AIT library has demonstrated that small or medium size libraries which have access to small computers can also make the computers work for them without incurring high costs. This paper intends to describe the two computer-aided operations in some detail for the benefit of other libraries that may want to begin computer applications in a gradual and practical way.

PLANNING AND DESIGN ELEMENTS

The first step taken in the planning was to conduct a thorough self study to determine the areas of library work for which computer application is both feasible and needed. This was followed by an extensive review of available literature on successful computer applications in other libraries. As a result, several libraries with similar conditions and requirements were chosen as models. Correspondences with the librarians and the technical staff of these libraries followed and much useful information was received and studied.① Since no two libraries are identical in their operations, the system developed in one library does not always fit another without some modification and alteration. With this in mind, we adopted many excellent features of the several operating systems and incorporated them into our own design.

There were several basic requirements underlying our design.

(1) The systems had to be able to be run at the IBM 1130 computer on an off line, batch process mode. These systems also had to be sufficiently flexible and expandable so that they could be adapted to a larger computer system whenever it becomes available at AIT.

(2) The system designed had to be considered as subsystems of a total system which is to be developed as we go along. Therefore, each of the subsystems has to be compatible and be an integral part of the whole.

(3) Even within each subsystem, there should be sub-subsystems to facilitate staged implementation in sequence.

With the expert assistance and enthusiastic support of Mr. Kanchit Malaivongs, the head of AIT's computer laboratory, who also serves as our programmer, the initial design for both the journal listing and control system and the acquisitions and accounting system were completed in December 1968. During the following two months, computer programmes for the two systems were written and tested. In preparation for their implementation, newly designed forms were either ordered or printed and the detailed procedural manuals were prepared.

For the journal listing and control system, the work on the conversion of journal records from the existing kardex file to the IBM cards was completed for computer manipulation in May 1969 and the first computer printout of the complete list of journal holdings in the AIT library was issued in June 1969 together with several other by-products. Since September 1970, this system has been expanded to include the estimated 3000 serial publications in the AIT library. A complete list of serial holdings will begin to be issued as soon as the work on the conversion is accomplished.

For the acquisitions and accounting system, due to the delay in getting the four-part multiple library order form made from the United States, the system did not actually get started until September 1, 1970. It is now fully operational and the initial result has been quite satisfactory.

THE COMPUTER-AIDED JOURNAL LISTING AND CONTROL SYSTEM

This system is designed to provide a broad data base for both the current and non-current journals in the collection. The data to be recorded in the *Periodical Input Data Card* (see Fig. 1) falls into four categories: (1) title information—including title, location, cross reference if any, publisher, and address; (2) holding information—including the exact holdings, binding decision, and if not retained for permanent collection; (3) subscription information—including the order number, cost, the year the subscription was first placed, source of subscription, frequency, publication pattern, area of interest, language, and country of publication; (4) historical information—including the following types of instance such as: Formerly..., Translation of..., Title changed to..., Merged with... to form..., and Ceased publication with....

---

① The following literature was consulted. The authors correspondences and their generosity in sharing their experiences is much appreciated.

C. Dunlap (1967). Automated acquisitions procedures at the University of Michigan Library. Libr. Resour. tech. Servs 11, 192 – 202.

Fig. 1 Periodical input data card. Several new additions and changes have been made in the past two years of operation. First, new sources have been added; the 7 is for standing order, and the 8 is for exchange. Second, four new subject areas have been added. Third, for catalogued serial publications, call numbers are included.

The information, some are coded, contained in each of the input data cards is then keypunched onto a set of IBM cards with fixed fields (see Fig. 2). Since the holding information for a current periodical is indicated by a hyphen (-) after both the volume number and the corresponding date, no frequent updating of the holding information is necessary. When updating, only the card that contains the particular information needed to be added or replaced, other cards remain unaltered. A new deck of IBM cards is to be keypunched only when a new periodical is added the first time. These sets of cards can be read into computer to generate the following outputs as needed: (1) to print out journal renewal lists by Source; (2) to print out a master journal list by title withholding information, location, sources and historical information (see Fig. 3); to print out other lists as may be desired such as list of abstracting and indexing journals in the library, lists of journal holding in the library by academic area, by language, or by country of publication, list of journals with volumes now completed that should be collected for binding.

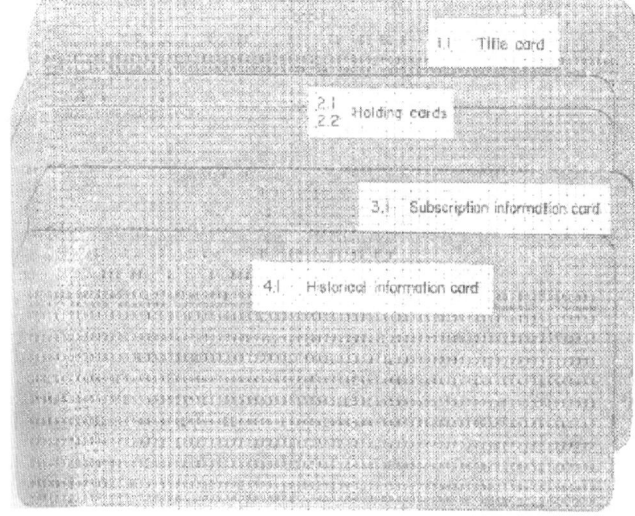

Fig. 2 The keypunched periodical data card set. This consists of four types of card. Each card type, except card 3, could have more than one card if necessary.

This system is intended to be very flexible. It may be expanded to include automatic check-in and other difficult operations in the future when an on-line, real-time system becomes available. Until then, the kardex file will be maintained manually to check in new arrivals, to claim for missing issues, and to prepare bindings.

An expansion of this system to include the catalogued serial publications which are not listed in the kardex file is now underway. When this is accomplished, the library will have at its disposal an all inclusive master serials file in machine-readable form capable of performing a variety of services.

```
                                                                    PAGE 8
AM SOC OF CIVIL ENGINEERS. TRANSACTIONS  PERIODICAL STACK
V. 35 -        (1896 -    )                         SUBSCRIPTION (FAXON)
INDEX  v. 1 - 82 (1867 - 1920)   V. 83 - 99 (1921 - 34)   V. 100 - 113 (1935 - 48)
AM SOC OF MECHANICAL ENGINEERS. TRANSACTIONS         PERIODICAL STACK
V. 34 - 50 (1912 - 28)    *FILM V. 72 - 80 (1950 - 58)  *
TITLE CHANGEO TO AM SOC OF MECHANICAL ENGINEERS. TRANS. J OF
AM SOC OF MECHANICAL ENGINEERS. TRANS. J OF APPLIED MECHANICS (SER. E)
                                                    CURRENT/JOURNAL STACK
 *FILM  V. 26 - 30   (1959 - 63)*   V. 31 -   (1964 -  )   SUBSCRIPTION (FAXON)
FORMERLY JOURNAL OF APPLIED MECHANICS.
AM SOC OF MECHANICAL ENGINEERS. TRANS. J OF BASIC ENGG (SER. D)
                                                    CURRENT/JOURNAL STACK
 *FILM  V. 81 - 85   (1959 - 63)*   V. 86 -   (1964 -  )   SUBSCRIPTION (FAXON)
AM SOC OF MECHANICAL ENGINEERS. TRANS. J OF ENGG FOR INDUSTRY (SER. B)
                                                    CURRENT/JOURNAL STACK
 *FILM  V. 81 - 85   (1959 - 63)*   V. 86 -   (1964 -  )   SUBSCRIPTION (FAXON)
AM SOC OF MECHANICAL ENGINEERS. TRANS. J OF ENGG FOR POWER (SER. A)
                                                    CURRENT/JOURNAL STACK
 *FILM  V. 81 - 85   (1959 - 63)*   V. 86 -   (1964 -  )   SUBSCRIPTION (FAXON)
AM SOC OF MECHANICAL ENGINEERS. TRANS. J OF HEAT TRANSFER (SER. C)
                                                    CURRENT/JOURNAL STACK
 *FILM  V. 81 - 85   (1959 - 63)*   V. 86 -   (1964 -  )   SUBSCRIPTION (FAXON)
AMERICAN STATISTICAL ASSOCIATION. JOURNAL           CURRENT/JOURNAL STACK
V. 65 N. 329 -                       (MARCH 1970 -  ) SUBSCRIPTION (DIRECT)
AMERICAN STATISTICIAN                               CURRENT/JOURNAL STACK
V. 24 -           (1970 -  )                         SUBSCRIPTION (DIRECT)
AMERICAN WATER RESOURCES ASSOC. JOURNAL SEE
     WATER RESOURCES BULLETIN
AMERICAN WATER WORKS ASSOCIATION. JOURNAL           CURRENT/JOURNAL STACK
V. 1 -           (1914 -  )                          SUBSCRIPTION (FAXON)
INDEX    1881 - 1939
FORMERLY. AM WATER WORK ASSOC. PROCEEDINGS.
AMERICAN WATER WORKS ASSOCIATION. PROCEEDINGS       PERIODICAL STACK
1903      1905 - 13/.
CONTINUED BY AMERICAN WATER WORKS ASSOCIATION. JOURNAL.
AMRITA BAZAR PATRIKA (NEWSPAPER)                    STUDENT READING
CURRENT VOLUME ONLY.                                 GIFT (EMBASSIES)
```

Fig. 3 Sample page of the *List of Journals in the AIT Library.*

In order to keep an actual and up-to-date account of the expenditures on journal subscriptions and renewals paid and the period each of the subscriptions covered, a fifth card is added to record the following information: status (whether it is a new subscription, a renewal, or an additional charge); date payment processed; length of subscription or renewal (one, two or three years); starting month and year; expiring month and year; or if only a particular volume or year is concerned, number of copies, cost, etc. This card is punched each time when a payment is made for a new subscription, a renewal, or an additional charge. At the end of each month, the cards for that month will be batch processed to record the total expenditures of the month and the accumulation from previous months of the fiscal year. This expenditure combined with expenditures for acquisitions and bindings are stored in the computer to the monthly report of library expenditures.

THE COMPUTER-AIDED ACQUISITIONS AND ACCOUNTING SYSTEM

This system is somewhat more complex than the journal listing and control system. It intends to consolidate the many time consuming manual operations into one streamlined operation assisted by a computer. The essence of the computer-aided acquisitions system is to generate one set of cards of each bibliographic record at the beginning of the ordering process after the request has been searched and verified (see Figs. 4 and 5). Presently there are four basic cards, one each for the author, title, publishing information, and series, if any. Two updating cards are also keypunched at the same time to provide for the additional inputs which are to be added later. This set of cards is machine-readable and can perform a multiple of tasks required. For example, using this set of cards as an input, it can do the following jobs automatically:

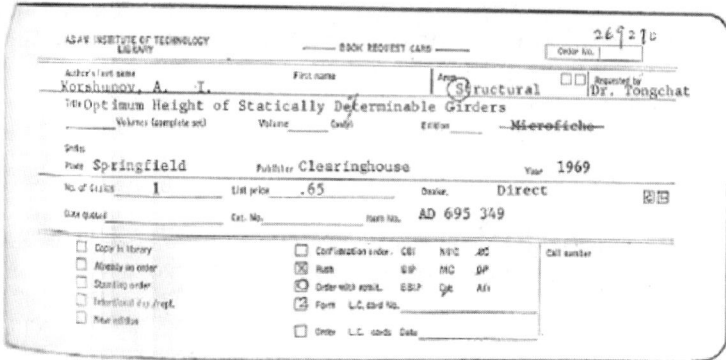

Fig. 4 The book request card. This card is designed to be used for the following purposes:

(1) as a library book order request to be filled in or typed on by a requester;
(2) as a work slip in the search and verification routine;
(3) as a source document for keypunch after it is coded;
(4) as a notification to the requester that a requested item has been catalogued or that for the specified reason a requested item is unobtainable.

Form code: 1, microfilm; 2, microfiche; 3, microcard; 4, map; 5, film; 6, card; 7, slide; 8, photocopy. Type of orders code: A, added copy; N, new addition; R, replacement; S, serial publication.

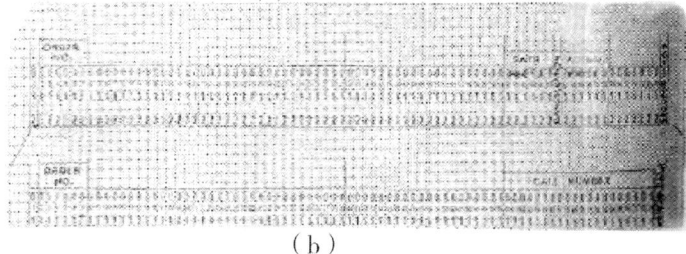

(b)

Fig. 5 The keypunched order card set. (a) Four basic cards. (b) Two updating cards. A two-digit subject code by academic areas is added preceding the call number to provide for correct subject grouping of titles in the new titles list.

(1) print out the multiple order form (MOF) which consists of a purchase order, a vendor report, an accounts slip, and a control slip (see Fig. 6).

(2) print out a *Book-on-Order List* as frequently as desirable including all outstanding orders and in process material.

(3) keep a detailed and up-to-date account of encumbrances and expenditures (see Fig. 7).

(4) print out a monthly *New Titles List* after the books are catalogued (see Fig. 8).

(5) print out a list of orders which are to be claimed when the order has exceeded the length of time predetermined. A new multiple order form can be printed for use as the first and second claims.

(6) keep statistics of the library accessions.

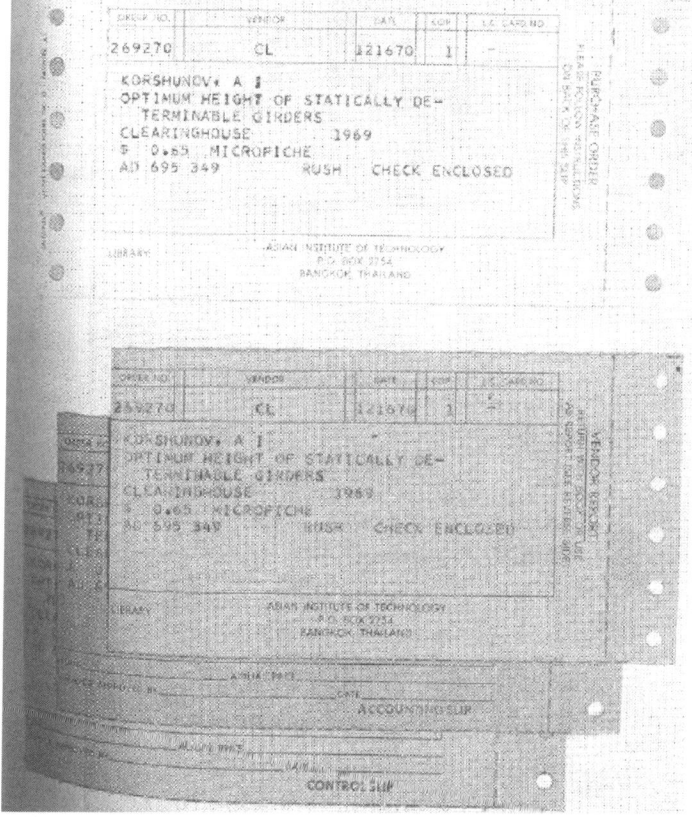

Fig. 6 The multiple order form (MOF).

ALLOCATION		ORDERS PLACED THIS MONTH NO. ORDERS	AMOUNT	ACC. SINCE JULY IST NO. ORDERS	AMOUNT	BALANCE	AMOUNT PAID	BALANCE AMOUNT PAID
BOOK MATERIALS	$30000.00							
DIVISION/FUND								
ENVIRONMENTAL		79	$613.37	328	$2171.69		$665.70	
GEOTECHNICAL		37	$309.32	89	$ 772.78		$588.58	
STRUCTURAL		35	$300.76	92	$ 750.22		$234.12	
TRANSPORTATION		80	$304.06	309	$1273.20		$778.84	
WATER SCIENCE		39	$253.81	172	$1143.73		$723.98	
LIBRARY/GENERAL		28	$165.39	72	$ 585.44		$1318.17	
MATH&COMPUTERS		27	$199.54	152	$1226.85		$ 997.92	
SYSTEM		12	$ 70.89	26	$128.23		$138.25	
ENGLISH		0	$ 0.00	19	$101.60		$ 82.27	
SPECIAL		79	$2138.56	86	$2217.50		$ 0.00	
SUB-TOTAL		416	$4355.77	1345	$10371.31	$19628.69	$5527.87	$24472.12
JOURNALS	$14000.00							
NEW SUBSCRIPTIONS		6	$156.00	36	$ 920.81		$967.65	
RENEWALS		30	$976.95	100	$5071.22		$5042.02	
SUB-TOTAL		36	$1132.95	136	$5992.03	$8007.97	$6009.66	$7990.33
BINDINGS	$1000.00							
JOURNALS		142	$150.20	392	$			
BOOKS		2	$ 2.16	7	$			
SUB-TOTAL		144	$152.36	399	$420.46	$579.54	$420.46	$579.54
TOTAL	$45000.00		$5641.08		$16783.80	$28216.19	$11958.00	$33041.99

Fig. 7 Report of library expenditure (as of 30 November 1970).

BELLMAN, RICHARD ERNEST
ALGORITHMS, GRAPHS, & COMPUTERS
ACADEMIC PRESS 1970
MATHEMATICS IN SCIENCE & ENGG
V.62
157.83 B4

BILLINGSLEY, PATRICK
ERGODIC THEORY & INFORMATION
JOHN WILEY 1965
WILEY SER IN PROBABILITY & MATHE
MATICAL STATISTICS
QA268 B5

BLACKWELL, DAVID
THEORY OF GAMES & STATISTICAL
DECISIONS
JOHN WILEY 1966 2 ED.
QA269 B6

BROWN, L M
SOLVING PROBLEMS IN DIFFERENTIAL
CALCULUS
OLIVER & BOYD 1968
SOLVING PROBLEMS IN MATHEMATICS,
NO.1 & 6
QA304 B87

BULL, GORDON
COMPUTATIONAL METHODS AND ALGOL
GEORGE G HARROP & C 1966
ENGINEERING SCIENCE MONOGRAPHS,
NO.8
QA297 B83

CARROLL, ROBERT WAYNE
ABSTRACT METHODS IN PARTIAL DIF-
FERENTIAL EQUATIONS
HARPER & ROW 1969
HARPER'S SER IN MODERN MATHEMA-
TICS
QA377 C33

COHEN, JACOB WILLEM
SINGLE SERVER QUEUE
NORTH HOLLAND PUB. 1969
NORTH-HOLLAND SER IN APPLIED
MATHEMATICS & MECHANICS, V.8
QA273 C723

DAVID, FLORENCE NIGHTINGALE
RESEARCH PAPERS IN STATISTICS
FESTSCHRIFT FOR J NEYMAN
JOHN WILEY & SON 1966
QA276 D33

DAVID, HERBERR ARON
METHOD OF PAIRED COMPARISONS
CHARLES GRIFFIN & 1969
GRIFFIN'S STATISTICAL MONOGRAPHS
& COURSES, NO.12
QA273 D31

DEPREE, JOHN D
ELEMENTS OF COMPLEX ANALYSIS
ADDISON-WESLEY PUB 1969
QA255 D4

DEVINATZ, ALLEN
ADVANCED CALCULUS
HOLT 1968
QA303 D48

DEWAN, EDMOND M
NONLINEAR CROSS-SPECTRAL ANALY-
SIS AND PATTERN RECOGNITION
U.S. AIR FORCE 1969
PHYSICAL AND MATHEMATICAL SCIENC
ES RES. PAPERS, NO.367
QA3 U58 NO.367

FENYO, ISTVAN
MODERN MATHEMATICAL METHODS IN
TECHNOLOGY
NORTH HOLLAND PUB 1969
NORTH-HOLLAND SER IN APPLIED
MATHEMATICS & MECHANICS, V.9
QA37 F51

FETTIS, HENRY E
TABLE OF THE COMPLETE ELLIPTIC
INTEGRAL OF THE FIRST KIND F
U.S. AEROSPACE RES 1970
ARL TECHNICAL REPORT NO.70-0081
QA3 U51 NO.70-0081

FRYER, HOLLY CLAIRE
CONCEPTS & METHODS OF EXPERIMEN-
TAL STATISTICS
ALLYN & BACON, INC 1966
QA276 F8

Fig. 8 A sample page of the monthly new titles list.

A complete flowchart for the acquisitions and accounting system is shown in Fig. 9.

When an ordered item arrives, a first updating card with receiving date and actual cost is keypunched to update the previously stored information. If for some reasons the order is cancelled, the updating card can also delete the previous record in the file and adjust the account. Once the book is catalogued, a second updating card with the call number is keypunched to update the record in storage. A monthly new titles list with full bibliographic information will be printed out for distribution.

When a larger computer system becomes available in the future, the sets of IBM cards including the updating cards will be read into magnetic tape or disk to form the data base for storage and retrieval of bibliographic information, and for publication of book catalogues and subject bibliographies.

An extension of the present system to print out labels for use in the book card, book pocket, as well as the span of the book will be planned soon to simplify the processing work.

ADVANTAGES GAINED FROM THE COMPUTER APPLICATIONS

Despite the simple nature of these two computer applications and in spite of the fact that they are still to be improved and refined, several positive results have been accomplished: (1) they enable the library to streamline its work flow, standardize its work procedure, and thereby not only greatly speed up its operation but also increase the accuracy of the work performed; (2) they help to reduce the repeating, drudgery and time-consuming operations in typing, record keeping, and accounting thereby enabling the effective utilization of staff time; (3) they enable the library to make its collection of journals and books more readily available through the frequent issuance of journal holding lists, new titles lists, book catalogues, etc. in various formats and arrangements to meet the varying needs of the users; (4) the data-manipulation characteristics of the computer enables the automatic accumulation of management data (statistics) previously ignored because of the labour required to accumulate them; (5) they provide the best training opportunity to the library staff in learning about computer applications and data processing techniques and help them to gain confident in the use of the computer in library work.

As far as the cost of using a computer as in our case is concerned, since both the computer time and programming staff are made available to the library without extra cost to the Institute, the two systems implemented have not resulted in an increase in operating costs to the library. The expenses incurred for the printing of special forms do not differ much from the previous expenditure for such items when forms were also required for manual operations.

FUTURE PLANS IN COMPUTER APPLICATIONS

Future plans for computer applications at the AIT library will be in the higher order. Investigation will soon begin to study the possibility of obtaining the MARC (Machine-Readable Cataloguing) magnetic tapes of the Library Congress for use in book selection, acquisition, cataloguing, SDI (Selective Dissemination of Information) service, etc. This computer application, if it can be implemented, will be made available to other libraries in Thailand as well as the national documentation centres in the countries of Southeast Asia on a cost sharing basis to reduce the unit cost of such operation to a minimum.

Because of the critical high cost in indexing and abstracting of scientific and technical journals, proceedings, and other publications, the library intends to utilize the existing indexing and abstracting services available in machine-readable form as the major input of its data base and to supplement it by its own selected bibliographic data catalogued and indexed from its own collections. Following are the several widely known bibliographic data sources now available in magnetic tapes which can be obtained either by subscription or by special arrangement.

(1) *Chemical Abstracts Condensates* (consists of 375,000 items since 1968; current growth rate is at 5000 items per month).

(2) *Engineering Index Compendex* (6000 items each month beginning with January 1970).

(3) The HRIS (Highway Research Information Service) data file (with over 25,000 items on tapes and with the addition of 10,000 new items annually).

(4) The MEDLARS (Medical Literature Analysis and Retrieval System) data file (contained about 1,300,000 items published since 1963; current growth rate is at 200,000 items annually).

(5) *Metals Abstracts* (120,000 items since 1966; current growth rate is 1900 per month).

(6) National Agricultural Library's CAIN (Cataloguing and Indexing) data tapes (10,000 records each month beginning with January 1970).

(7) The NASA (National Aeronautics and Space Administration) Scientific and Technical Information Collection (600,000 items since 1962; current growth rate at 6000 items per month).

With these data sources available plus others which may be developed later and supplemented by the AIT Library's own input, a variety of information and bibliographic services may be made possible to the region. Having access to such a pool of massive data bases at AIT is a necessity if the AIT library is truly to function as a regional information centre for science and technology in Southeast Asia. By means of modern telecommunication facilities now generally available in the region, coupled with the recent advancement in the information-processing technology, effective and rapid information transfer is now possible to facilitate the free flow of scientific and technical knowledge among the countries in this region. In co-operation with national documentation centres in various countries, a regional information network could be established, a concept which has been given particular encouragement by UNESCO and by other international organization such as the International Council of Scientific Union (ICSU) and the International Federation for Documentation (FID). ①

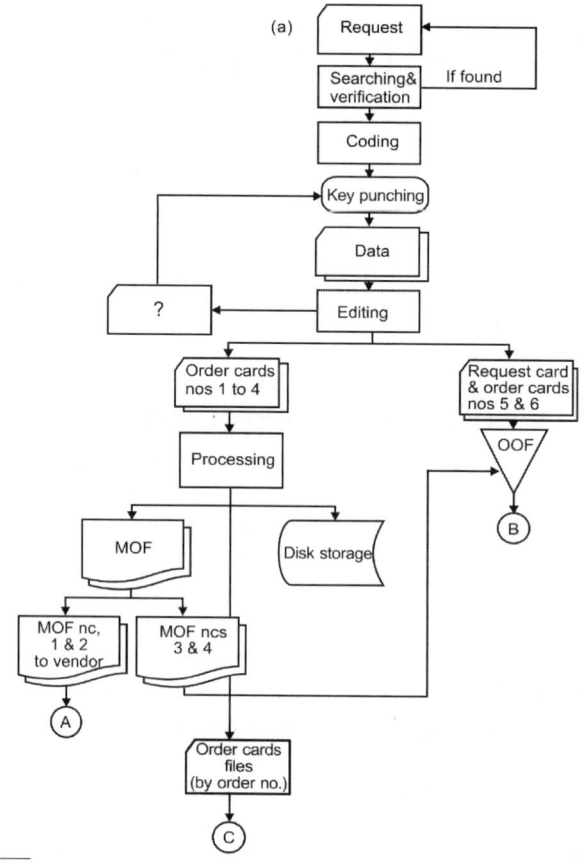

① Conference on the Application of Science and Technology to the Development of Asia New Delhi, 9 – 20 August 1968 (1969). *Final Report*. Part I: Conclusions and Recommendations. Paris: UNESCO.

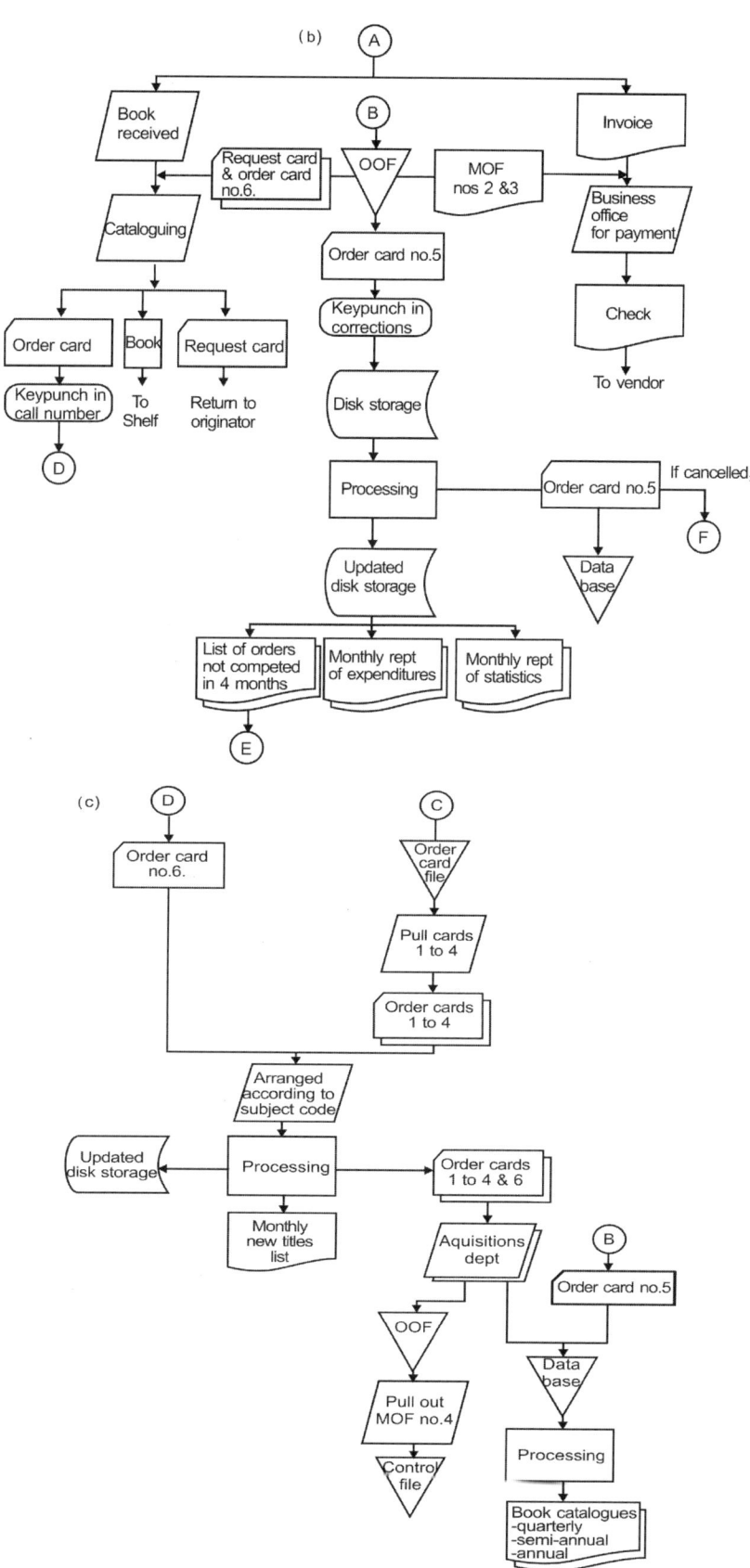

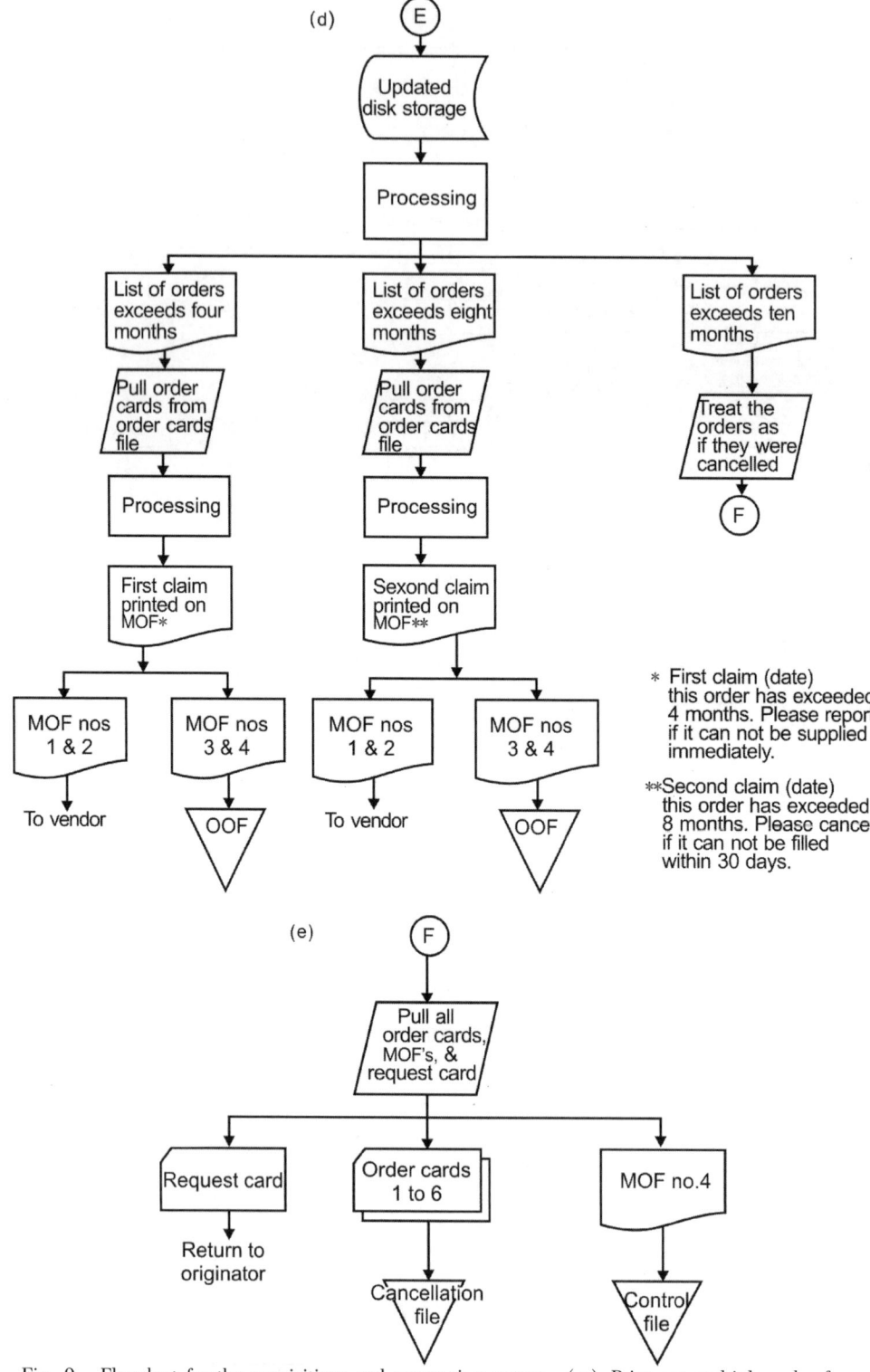

Fig. 9 Flowchart for the acquisitions and accounting system. (a) Print out multiple order forms. Disk storage includes the following information: order number, vendor, fund, date ordered, volumes in a set, type of orders, listed price, number of copies, form. OOF stands for Order Outstanding File (by titles). (b) Receiving procedures. (c) Print out monthly new titles list and book catalogues. (d) Claims for unfilled orders. (e) Cancellation.

Reference

1. C. Dunlap. (1967) Automated acquisitions procedures at the University of Michigan Library. Libr. Resour. tech. Servs 11, 192-202.

2. I. H. Pizer, D. R. Franz, and Brodman. (1963) Mechanization of library procedures in the medium-sized medical library: I. The serial record. Bull. med. Libr. Ass. 51, 313-338.

3. F. W. Roper. (1968) A computer-based serials control system for a large biomedical library. Am. Docum. 19, 151-157.

(Published in *International Library Review.* V. 3, No. 3, July 1971: pp. 257-270.)

曼谷亚洲理工学院的图书馆自动化

Library Automation at the Asian Institute of Technology – Bangkok[①]

FOREWORD

The opportunity to report on library automation activities at the Asian Institute of Tech especially welcome in view of current developments. The system that has been operational years is being reviewed for implementation on a new machine and the AIT Library and Info Center is ready to develop its systems with local and regional co-operation in mind.

The present housekeeping systems have been reported in brief[②]; this Report gives a full description of the systems as they have been modified over the years and as they are now operating. Further sections deal with projects in co-operation amongst libraries in Thailand, the use of the ISDS and MARC data bases in particular and a first venture into computerized information retrieval. State of work in these projects is as of writing and progress will have been made by publication date so the interested readers are invited to write in for further information.

Acknowledgement is made to Mr. Kanchit Malaiwongs of the Computer Center at AIT for his work in programming and advice at all stages of library mechanization. Thanks are due Miss Aim-Orn Purpipanyawong for her help as typist in preparing this Report.

INTRODUCTION

BACKGROUND

The Asian Institute of Technology is a regional postgraduate institution for advanced study and research in civil engineering and related subjects in Asia. Established in Bangkok, Thailand, it is chartered as a non-profit regional organization governed by an international Board of Trustees drawn from many countries within and outside Asia. The student body now totaling 350 comes from 22 Asian countries. Students all holding a Bachelor's degree enroll in three types of programmes namely: one-year diploma courses, 21-month Master's degree courses, and Doctoral studies. Enrollment is intended to reach 900 by 1980. Faculty come from America, Europe, Australasia and Asia and teach in the major divisions of Environmental, Structural, Geotechnical, Systems Management and Hydrological Engineering; Industrial Development and Human Settlements studies are new areas and social and urban contexts of technological developments will be increasingly covered. There are centers for English Language Teaching and Mathematics and Computer Science. English is the medium of instruction.

The Institute which was founded in 1959 and moved to a new 400-acre campus in 1973 plays a major role in education and development in Southeast Asia. The objectives of the AIT are closely attentive to the economic and technological needs of the region and a prime objective has been the building up of an outstanding library to serve the informational needs of both the Institute and the region. This regional outlook involves a long-range library development goal of expanding the present collection of 50,000 volumes to 300,000 by the 1980's and to increase the member of serials subscriptions from 1700 to 6000 over the same period. In addition, the Library interprets its role in the wider sense of information centre so that it may participate in the dissemination of

---

① Co-author: Stephen W. Massil.
② Lee, Hwa-Wei. "Library Mechanization at the Asian Institute of Technology." *International library review*. V. 3 No. 3, June 1971: pp. 257–270.

scientific and technical information throughout Southeast Asia. Its Asian Information Center for Geotechnical Engineering (AGE see section 3.3) is intended to be the first of several specialized information centres handling technical information and servicing needs of users throughout Asia.

AUTOMATED SYSTEMS

The mechanized systems described in the first part of this report were developed on an IBM 1130 computer starting in 1968 when the size of the library was quite small and the urgency for automated housekeeping was slight. Design of automated systems was undertaken relatively early in order to gain experience and to introduce the use of computers into the planning of library development. The developments undertaken were for a computer-aided journal listing and control system and a (book) acquisitions and accounting system. The objectives of these systems were as follows:

- to simplify and standardize acquisition and serials procedures;
- to facilitate fast and more efficient handling of an increasing flow of acquisition work anticipated in the years ahead;
- to render better services to faculty and students;
- to train library staff in new library techniques;
- to provide a model in library automation for libraries in Southeast Asia;
- to plan for an overall system to cover eventually other phases of library work.

It was envisaged that there would be a gradual implementation from simple mechanized routines through to a more complex system of storage, retrieval and dissemination in successive stages.

The constraints of relying on an 1130 without storage capacity necessarily limited the initial design and it is only with the installation of a CDC 3600 at the beginning of 1974 that development has been contemplated; present systems have been transferred to this machine; immediate redesign may not be taken very far as it is expected that the Institute will acquire an IBM 370 series machine within the next two years. The larger and faster machines open the opportunity for planning the more complex systems envisaged at the outset and for encouraging co-operative ventures as well so that instead of providing a model for other libraries to implement on their own, new systems under development will have the perspective of network implementation, centralization of processing systems and interaction of information systems, as prime objectives. Hitherto, the successful implementation of small scale housekeeping operations in the AIT Library has demonstrated that smaller libraries with access to small computers can introduce mechanization without incurring high costs.

SYSTEMS DESIGN AND IMPLEMENTATION

Initial design of the systems to be described followed intensive analysis and literature review. Detailed correspondence was made with several libraries in America that had adopted computer applications and whose circumstances were similar to those of AIT. Design was joint activity of the AIT Library and Computer Center, with the Director of the Library taking the initiative and programming being undertaken in the computer center. Programs were written in Basic FORTRAN to run on an IBM 1130 with 8 K and one 2315 disk; input is on cards, processing is off-line of course, in batch mode.

The CDC 3600 has 64K, 2 disk drives, 5 tape units, programs will be in FORTRAN 4.

To undertake new systems design and supervise proposed developments the Library has appointed as Associate Director an experienced library systems analyst. Continued full cooperation with the Computer Center staff is anticipated. Costs of the system are in-house; expenditure on input forms and punch cards is no greater than on the previous stationery requirements of the manual systems.

1. COMPUTER-BASED ACQUISTIONS AND ACCOUNTING SYSTEM
SUMMARY

The system is intended to consolidate many time-consuming manual operations. Its basis is the generation of a set of cards for each bibliographic record, their input to produce a multi-part order record and their retention to serve as an eventual new title listing. In the process detailed accounting records to cover commitments and expenditure are derived and claims records can be generated at designated periods. The limitations of the system are that without disk storage (envisaged in the overall plan but not available) cards require to be re-input each month for the financial tabulations to be derived; and all sorting remains a manual operation both to print orders and the new title listing.

1. Block diagram (See Fig. 1)
2. Input devices.
(1) Book request card (Fig. 2)

This card is designed to be used for the following purposes:
- A. as a library book order request to be filled in or typed on by a requester,
- B. as a work slip in the search and verification routine,
- C. as a source document for keypunch after it is coded, and
- D. ultimately, as a notification to the requester that a requested item had been catalogued or that for the specified reason a requested item is unobtainable.

Two types of source information are included:
- A. Text identification: (To be provided by the requester as fully as possible)
  - a. author
  - b. title
  - c. volumes (complete set or a particular volume or volumes)
  - d. edition
  - e. series
  - f. place of publication
  - g. publisher
  - h. year of publication
  - i. number of copies desired
  - j. price
  - k. special identification, if any (such as an item number) e. g., for U. S. government documents—the Superintendent of Documents Number, for publications distributed by the U. S. NTIS, NASA, etc. —the assigned item number.

As required, these numbers must appear on our purchase order.
- B. Control information:
  - a. order number
  - b. area and fund (code)
  - c. requested by
  - d. source where the order will be placed (code)
  - e. searcher's checks (CC, OF, etc.)
  - f. verification notes (CBI, BIP, BBIP, LC, MC, CAT., AD., etc.)
  - g. call number, if has one
  - h. L. C. card number, if available
  - i. whether this is a confirming order
  - j. whether this is a standing order
  - k. whether this is an intentional duplication or replacement
  - l. whether this is to be a rush order
  - m. what is the form, if not a book? (e. g., film, map, microfilm, etc.) (Code)
  - n. whether OWR (order with remittance) is required
    A-Additional copy, N-New edition, R-Replacement copy, S-Serial.

(2) IBM order-card deck (Fig. 3)

The IBM order-card deck consists of 6 cards. Each decklet of cards is for one title. The information on the BOOK REQUEST CARD is now keypunched into the appropriate fields of the first four cards in the deck. From these four original keypunchings, two abbreviated IBM cards, referred to as UPDATING CARDS, are produced automatically.

CARD 1 contains the following fields of information:

Column 1 (1) Sequence number—This is the number of the card in a deck.

Column 2 – 7 (6) Order number—This is repeated in all six cards. The first four numerals of the order number is to be assigned from 0001 to 9999 according to numerical order. The last two numerals of the order number represents the fiscal year, e. g., 032173 means this is the 321st order placed during the 1973 – 74 fiscal year.

Column 8 – 75 (68) Author—This field is divided into two sub-fields: col. 8 – 42 (35) and col. 43 – 75 (33). If the author's name is short enough, only col. 8 – 42 is used. When col. 43 – 75 must be used, its information in the printout will form the second line with two indentions back from the first line.

 e. g., SOUTHEASTERN WISCONSIN REGIONAL   (35)
    PLANNING COMMISSION

Column 76 (1) Fund—A one-letter code is adopted as follows:
 EEnvironmental Engineering
 GGeotechnical Engineering
 IIndustrial Development and Management
 LLibrary/General
 MMathematics and Computer Science
 SStructural Engineering
 TTransportation Systems
 WWater Resources Engineering
 XSpecial
 YSystems Engineering and Management
 PPeriodicals
 ZLanguage and Media

Columns 77 (1) Confirmation, 78 (1) Standing order, 79 (1) Rush, 80 (1) Form.

CARD 2 contains the following fields of information:

Column 8 – 75 (68) Title—Similar to the author field, this field is also divided into two sub-fields. The second field is reserved for long title only.

 e. g., COMPUTER SIMULATION OF A DEMAND –   (35)
   SCHEDULED – BUS SYSTEM OFFERING...

This title is unusually long and has to be shortened by stopping at the end of word "OFFERING."

Column 76 – 77 (2) Set—Indicates the number of volumes in a set when the entire set is to be purchased, e. g., if the number is 3, the printout should read 3 volumes.

Column 78 – 80 (3) Volume—Indicates that that particular volume of a set is to be purchased, e. g., if the number is 013, the printout should read Vol. 13 only.

CARD 3 contains the following fields of information:

Column 8 – 19 (12) Place of publication—This is necessary only when the publisher is less known. Abbreviation of a place name may be used whenever possible.

Column 20 – 38 (19) Publisher—May be abbreviated or shortened as long as it is recognizable. If the publisher is the same as the author, as frequently found in institutional publications, the publisher may be stated simply as "the author".

 e. g., AUTHOR: WASHINGTON UNIV. GRADUATE SCHOOL OF BUS. ADM. PUBLISHER: THE AUTHOR

Column 39 – 42 (4) Year of publication—The following exceptions may require special attention.

e. g. , In a multi-volume set the year of publication between the first volume and the last volume might be quite apart. In such a case, only the year for the latest volume is punched in.

The year of the latest printing or edition should be used if the latest edition is to be desired.

Column 43 – 44 (2) Edition—To be stated if only it is other than the first edition.

e. g. , Second edition 02
Fifth edition 05
Revised edition 02

Column 45 – 46 (2) Vendor—A two digit numerical code is adopted as follows:

e. g. ,
BW = Blackwells
MX = Maxwell

Column 47 – 52 (6) Order date.

Column 53 (1) Number of copies.

Column 54 – 62 (9) L. C. Card number—To be punched if known.

Column 63 – 80 (18) Item number—Some publications bear a special identification number.

e. g. , U. S. Government document nos. which it is important to register when ordering.

CARD 4 contains the following fields of information:

Column 8 – 72 (65) Series name—Also similar to the author field, it is divided into two sub-fields. The second field is reserved for a long series name. But, when it is not used, the second field might be used for any additional order information which is not covered in the existing fields;

e. g. , Set—If the set is more than 9 volumes.

Such as: Eleven volume set

Volume—If in a multi-volume set more than one volume is to be ordered. Such as: Volumes 1, 3, and 6

Column 73 – 78 (6) List price—All to be converted into U. S. dollars; the last two digits are for cents.

Column 79 (1) Order with remittance-To be designated when advance payment is required. Letter O signifies.

Column 80 (1) Type—A: Additional copy, N: New, R: Replacement, S: Serial

CARD 5 and CARD 6 serve as "UPDATING CARDS" and are produced automatically by the computer from the input data of the first 4 cards. Both CARD 5 and 6 contain an author and a short title field. The remainder is reserved for updating information to be added later.

CARD 5 (the first updating card) contains the following fields for use in updating:

Column 53 (1) Fund—Same as col. 76 on card 1.

Column 54 – 59 (6) List price—Same as col. 73 – 78 on card 4.

Column 60 – 65 (6) Date received.

Column 66 (1) Cancellation.

Column 67 – 72 (6) Actual price.

Upon receiving and item, the acquisition librarian notes with pencil the date received and the actual cost. This information is then keypunched into the appropriate fields. The card will be processed through the computer to record receipt of the item and to adjust the corresponding account if there is a discrepancy between the list price and the actual price.

If the item is reported unavailable, A "C" standing for cancellation is noted on the same card and subsequently keypunched into col. 66.

CARD 6 (the second updating card) contains the following fields for use in the printing monthly "New Titles" list.

 Column 51 – 54 (4) Country code
 Column 55 – 56 (2) Subject code
 Column 57 (1) Blank
 Column 58 – 59 (2) Classification code
 Column 60 – 79 (20) Call number or the classification number

  The second updating card is used only when the item is received in the library and accompany the newly acquired item to the cataloguing librarian. When the item catalogued, the call number is written on the second updating card for keypunch This card will then be fed into the computer and a list of new acquisitions will be print monthly.

3. Forms of output:

From the set of 6 IBM-cards, a number of outputs can be generated through computer.

a) Four-part multiple order form (Fig. 4)

This printout is produced on the 3 × 6-inch, four-part, continues order forms designed especially for AIT library.

 PART 1: The Purchase Order—To be sent to the vendor or to the publisher in the case of a direct order.

 PART 2: The Vendor Report—Also goes to the vendor or the publisher. But it is to be returned with the item ordered or is to be used as a report by the vendor when an item cannot be supplied.

 PART 3: The Account Slip—This slip along with the part 2 and the invoice after being approved by the acquisitions librarian is sent to the Business Office for payment.

 PART 4: The Control Copy—After an item is received the control copy will then be filed by order number in the library's control file for possible future reference.

The acquisitions librarian maintains an "Order-Outstanding File" which consists the following cards in a set:

A. The Book Request Card,
B. The 2 Updating EBM Cards, and
C. The Part 3 and Part 4 of the Four-part Multiple Order Form. These sets are arranged alphabetically by main entries to await receipt of items ordered.

b) Monthly financial report (Fig. 5)

The computer also prints out a monthly statement of library expenditures by area (or fund). Credits are given to appropriate funds for items cancelled.

The amount actually paid is entered in a separate column since it might include items ordered in the previous fiscal year but which have just been received and billed and is to be paid from the current budget.

c) Monthly "New Titles" list (Fig. 6)

After an item is catalogued, the call number is key-punched onto the second updating card. At the end of each month, these cards are fed into the computer and a list of current acquisitions is printed out

d) Monthly statistics and other outputs may be generated as required.

Besides the financial statement, the computer can also provide the following statistical information such as:

 A. The total number of orders placed each month
  —number of titles
  —number of volumes
  —number of non-book items by type

Standing order is counted only when it is entered the first time. After this, only the

confirming order will be counted.
    B. The total number of items catalogued each month
        —number of titles
        —number of volumes
        —number of added copies
        —number of continuations
        —total number of new volumes added (the sum of above)
        —number of non-book items catalogued by type
  e) Other printouts.

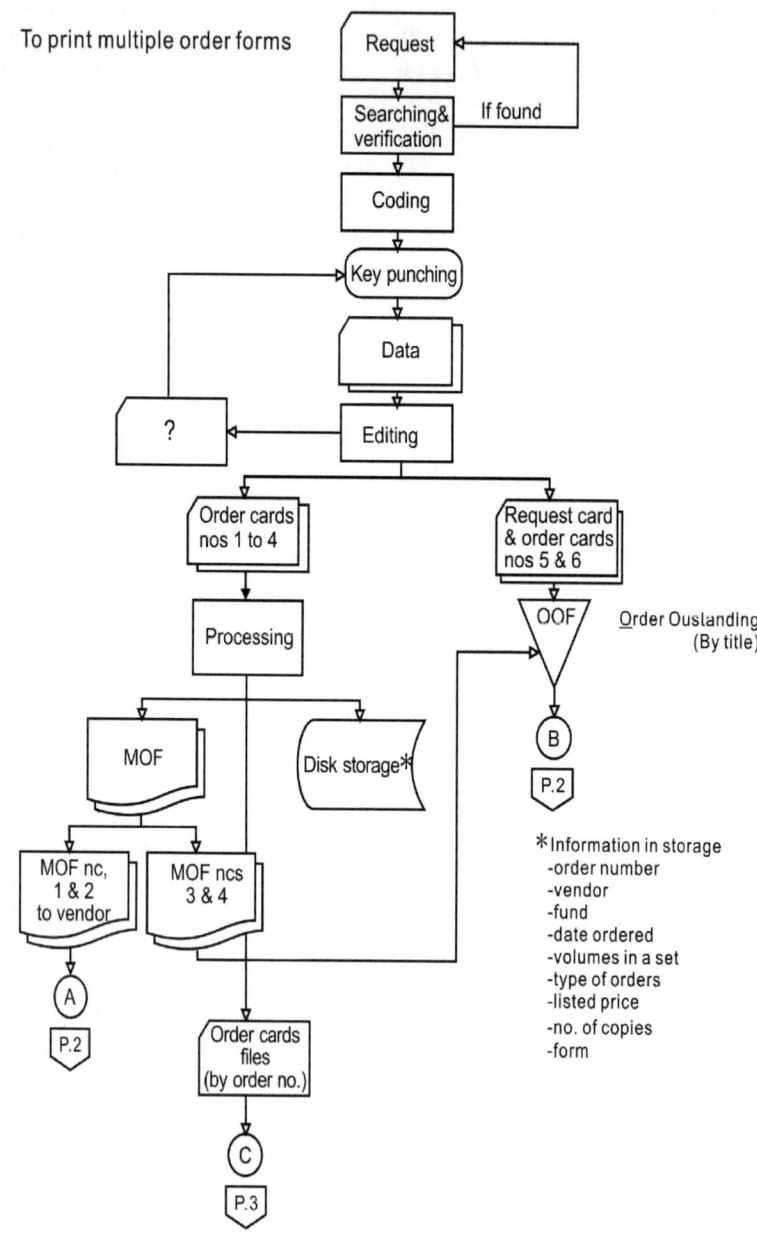

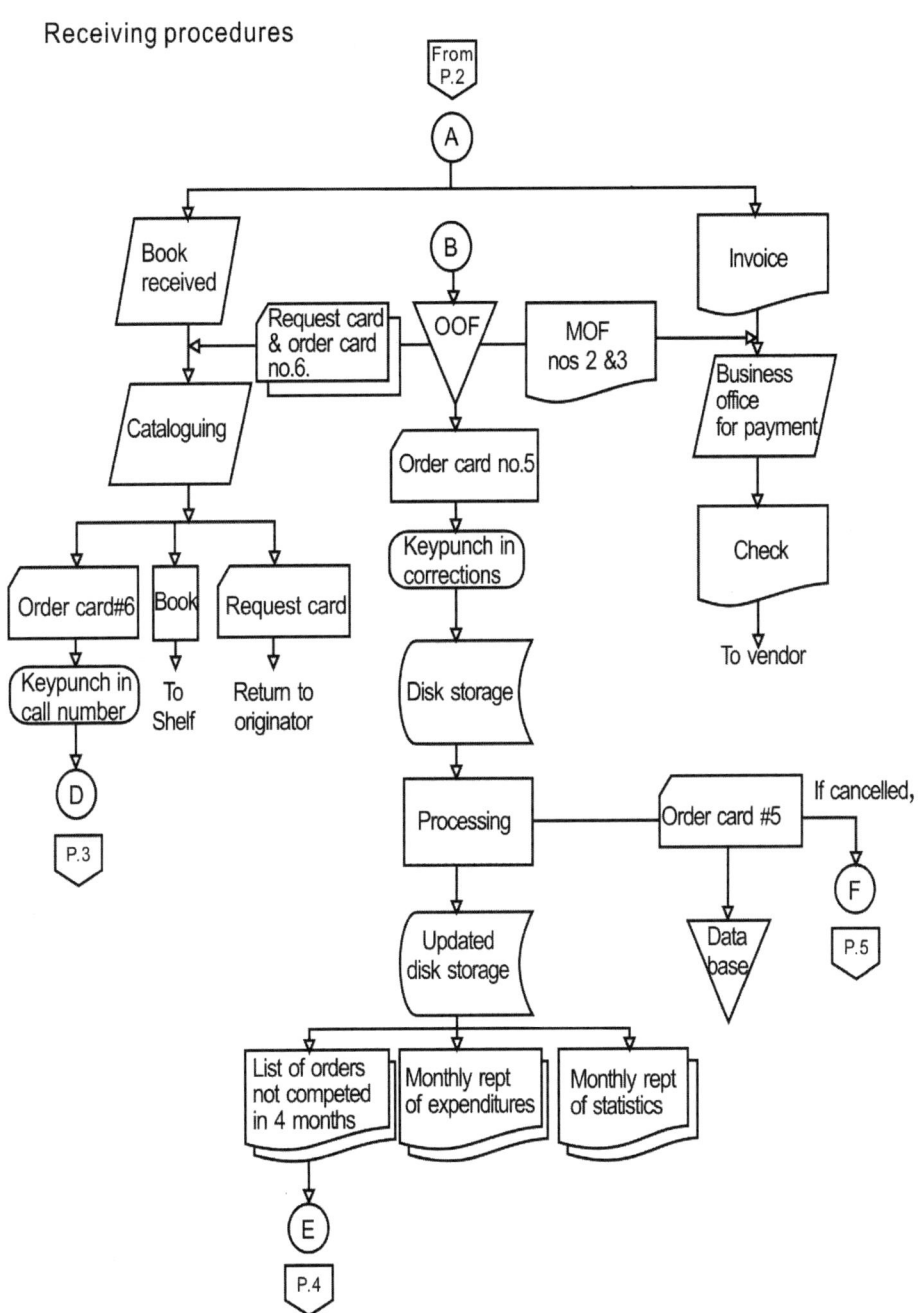

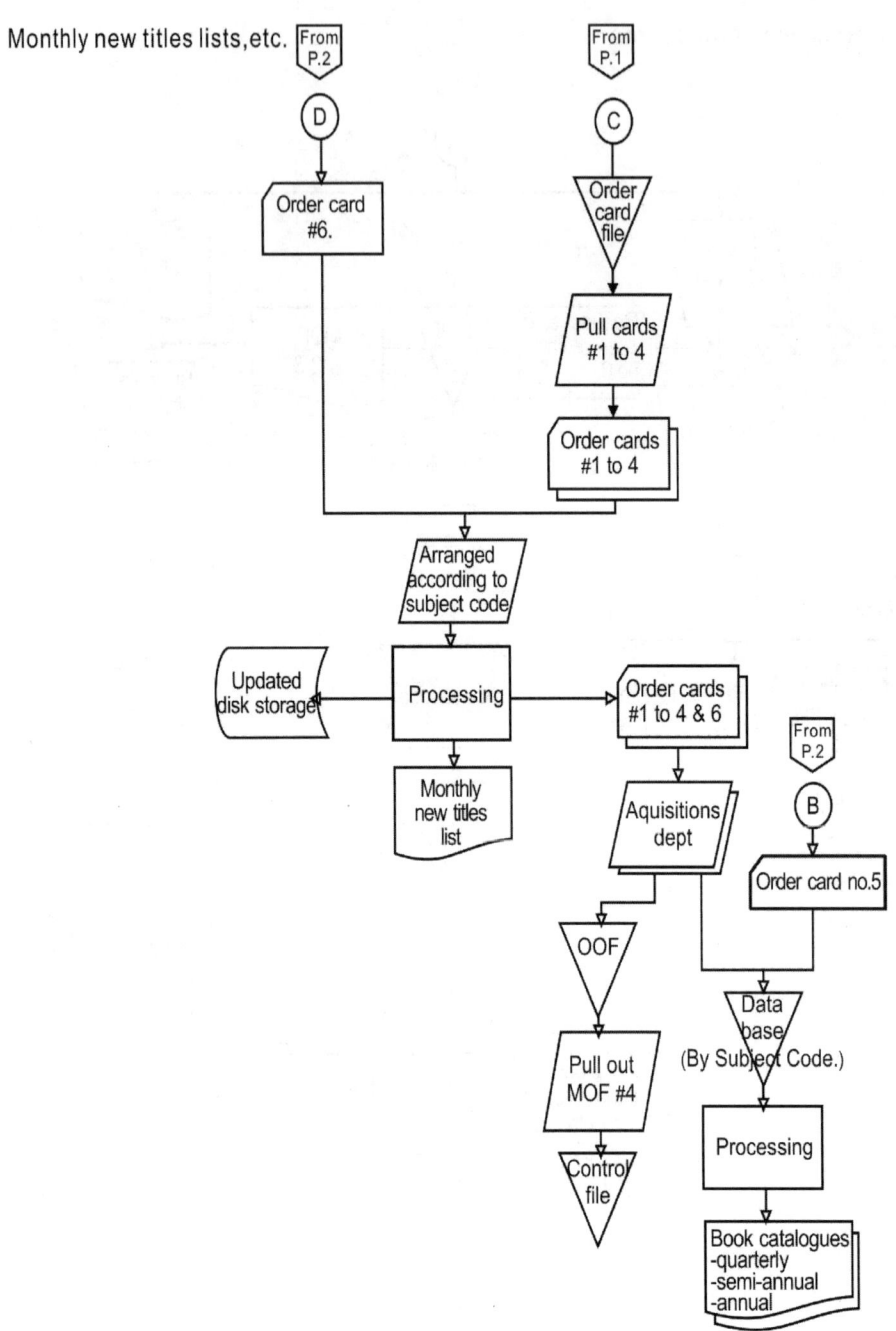

曼谷亚洲理工学院的图书馆自动化   983

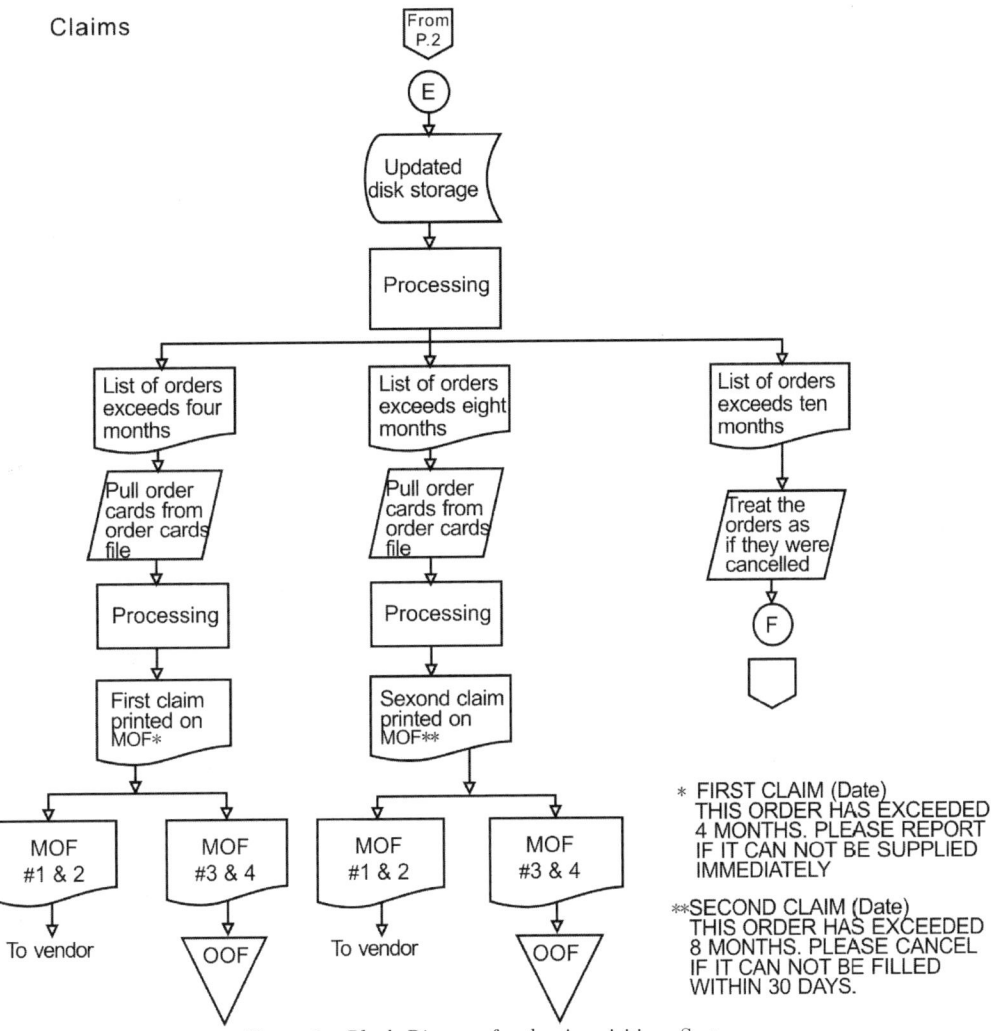

Figure 1   Block Diagram for the Acquisitions System

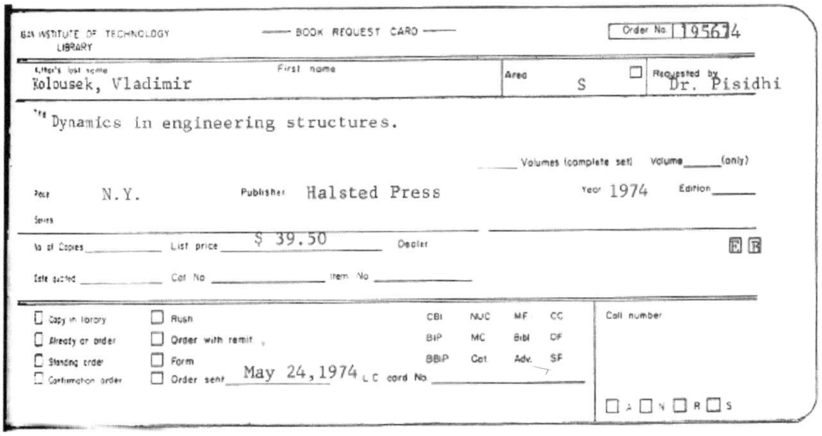

Figure 2   Book Request Card

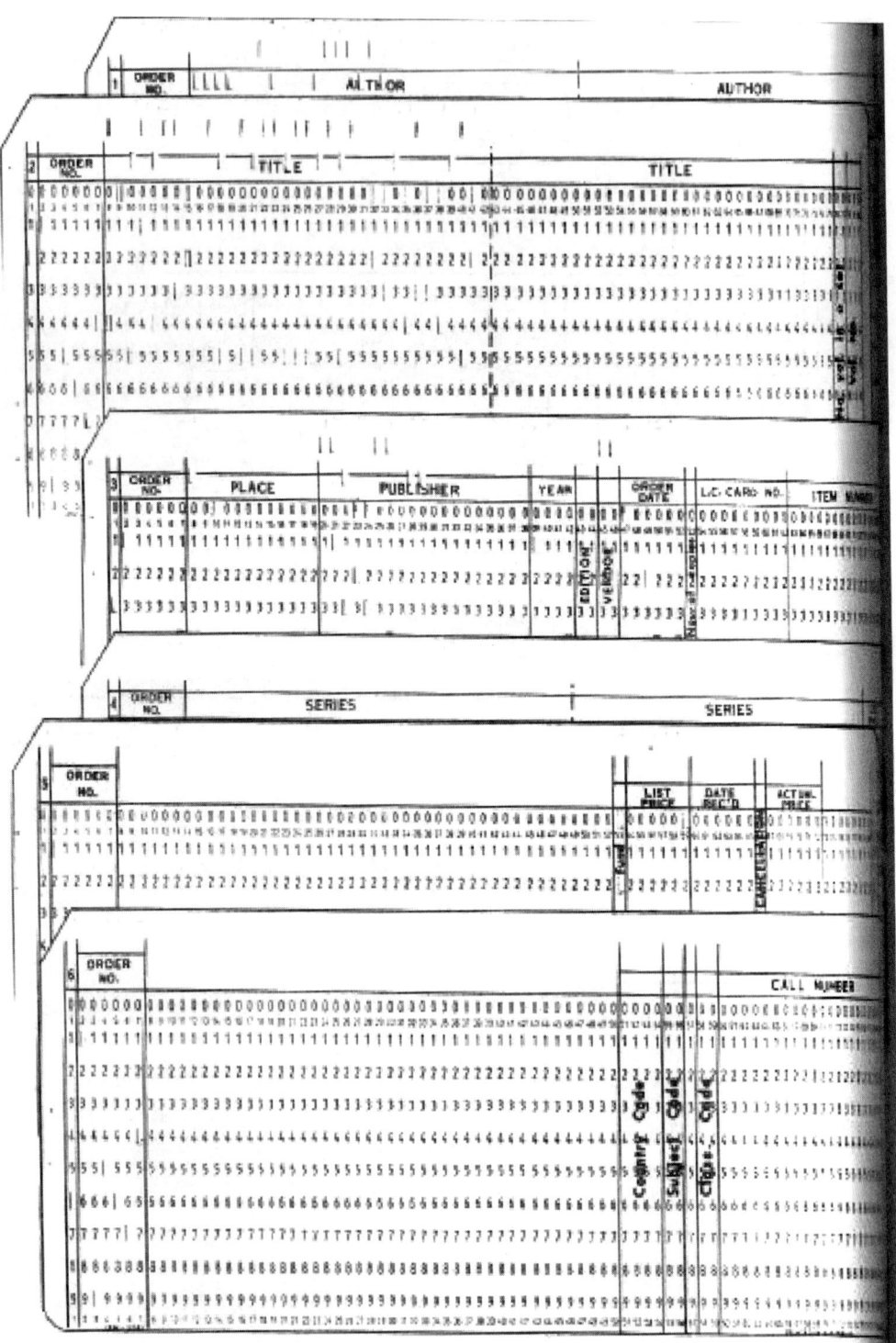

Figure 3　IBM Order-Card Deck

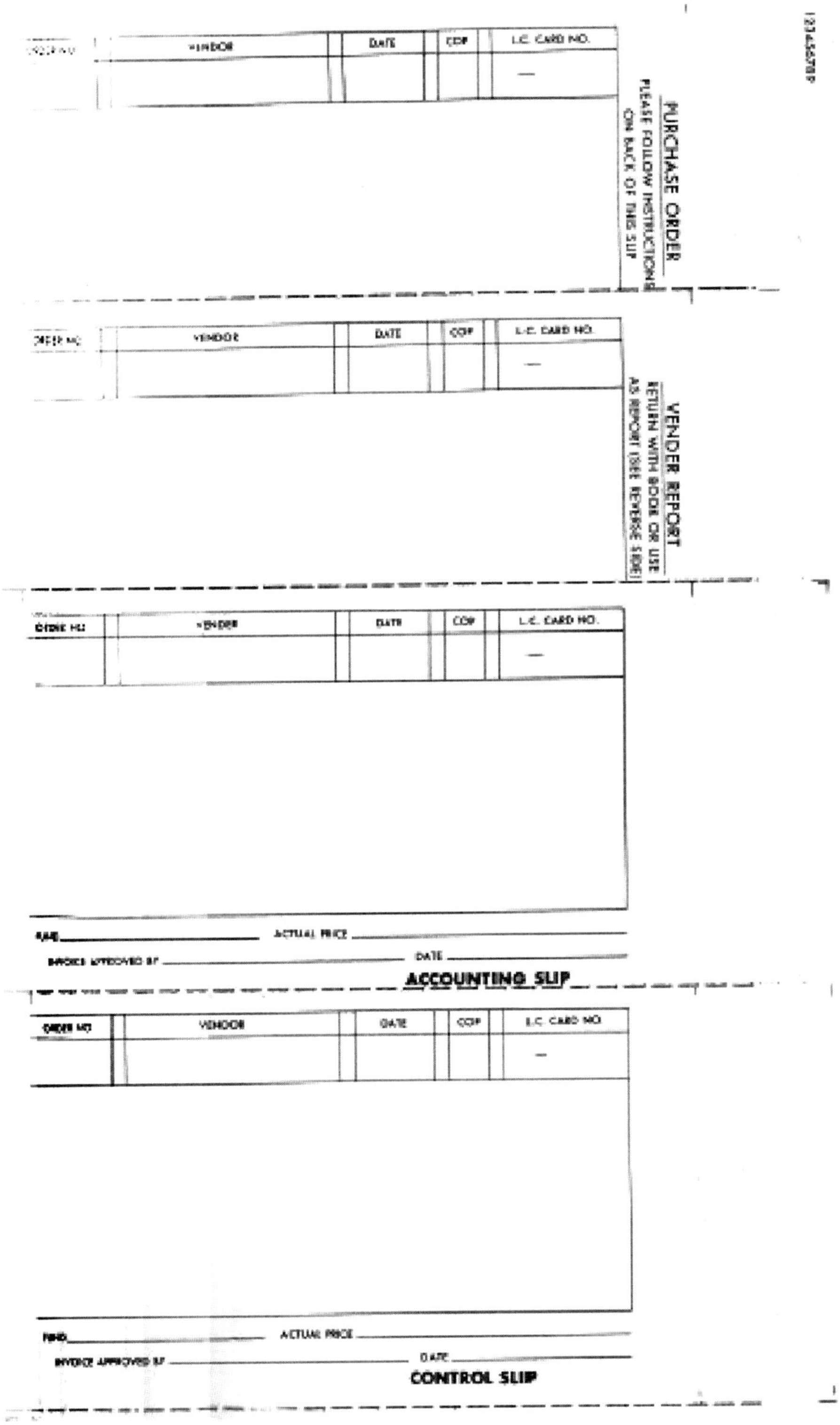

ORDER NO.	VENDOR	DATE	COP	L.C. CARD NO.
				—

PURCHASE ORDER
PLEASE FOLLOW INSTRUCTIONS ON BACK OF THIS SLIP

ORDER NO.	VENDOR	DATE	COP	L.C. CARD NO.
				—

VENDER REPORT
RETURN WITH BOOK OR USE AS REPORT (SEE REVERSE SIDE)

ORDER NO.	VENDOR	DATE	COP	L.C. CARD NO.
				—

FUND ______ ACTUAL PRICE ______
INVOICE APPROVED BY ______ DATE ______
ACCOUNTING SLIP

ORDER NO.	VENDOR	DATE	COP	L.C. CARD NO.
				—

FUND ______ ACTUAL PRICE ______
INVOICE APPROVED BY ______ DATE ______
CONTROL SLIP

Figure 4 Multiple Order Form

Figure 5 Monthly Financial Report

REPORT OF LIBRARY EXPENDITURE (AS OF DECEMBER 31, 1973)

ALLOCATION		ORDERS PLACED THIS MONTH		ACC. SINCE JULY 1ST, 1973				BALANCE
		NO. ORDERS	AMOUNT	NO. ORDERS	AMOUNT	BALANCE	AMOUNT PAID	AMOUNT PAI
BOOK MATERIALS	$ 22900.00							
DIVISION/FUND								
ENVIRONMENTAL		3	$ 44.45	391	$ 4518.98		$ 4950.77	
GEOTECHNICAL		10	$ 115.25	235	$ 2332.83		$ 1238.25	
INDUSTRIAL DEVEL		5	$ 10.00	41	$ 165.60		$ 39.11	
STRUCTURAL		7	$ 102.10	134	$ 1554.23		$ 1280.42	
WATER RESOURCES		6	$ 159.75	129	$ 1096.02		$ 416.06	
LIBRARY/GENERAL		15	$ 143.20	145	$ 1475.56		$ 1730.90	
MATH & COMPUTERS		18	$ 258.80	280	$ 3397.19		$ 4358.81	
SYSTEMS		30	$ 300.00	510	$ 4139.97		$ 3508.95	
LANGUAGE & MEDIA		3	$ 41.55	44	$ 321.75		$ 320.09	
SPECIAL		0	$ 0.00	84	$ 581.02		$ 1250.17	
SUB-TOTAL		97	$ 1175.09	1993	$19583.14	$ 3316.85	$ 19093.92	$ 3806.47
JOURNALS	$ 25000.00							
NEW SUBSCRIPTION		0	$ 0.00	27	$ 389.79		$ 389.79	
RENEWALS		36	$ 653.15	264	$11617.97		$ 11577.97	
SUB-TOTAL		36	$ 653.15	291	$12007.75	$ 12992.24	$ 11967.75	$ 13032.24
BINDINGS	$ 2000.00							
JOURNALS		123	$ 171.60	886	$ 1135.70		$ 1135.70	
BOOKS		26	$ 32.10	105	$ 130.68		$ 130.68	
SUB-TOTAL		149	$ 203.69	991	$ 1266.38	$ 733.62	$ 1266.38	$ 733.62
L.C. CARDS	$ 100.00		$ 6.47		$ 15.22	$ 84.78	$ 15.22	$ 84.78
TOTAL	$ 50000.00		$ 2038.41		$32873.50	$ 17127.50	$ 32342.88	$ 17657.12

Figure 5 Monthly Financial Report

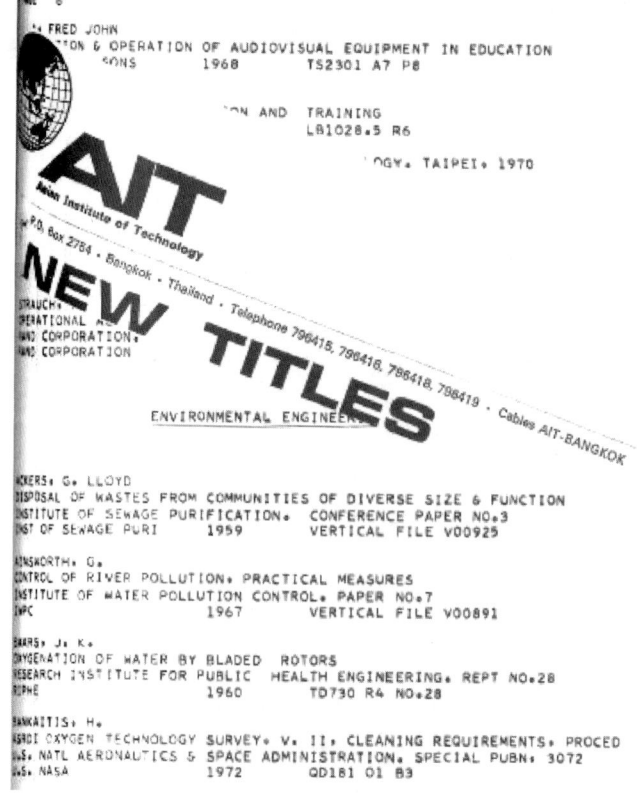

Figure 6 Monthly New Titles List

2. COMPUTER-BASED JOURNAL LISTING AND CONTROL SYSTEM.

Summary

This system is more simple than the acquisitions system. It comprises the input of bibliographic and holding information and certain acquisitions control data and the main product is an annual listing together with a subject index. Scope to extend the accounting and acquisition modules is available. Various title listings as by-products have been generated.

1. Block diagram (Fig. 8)

2. Input devices:

Placing new subscriptions and ordering of back runs are to be treated in the same manner as for books. After they have been searched and verified by the Serials Librarian, the request cards are to be passed on to the Acquisitions Department. The following special instructions in keypunching are to be observed:

A. New subscription:

a) Keypunch the title in the title card followed by beginning volume and year and a dash signifying it is an open entry, e. g.,

   American Meteorological Society. Bulletin. V. 49 – 1958 –

b) Keypunch the following caption in the series card; e. g.,

   PERIODICAL-NEW SUBSCRIPTION

c) Also note the difference in <u>order number</u>-periodical order number is proceeded by a prefix "S". e. g.,

   S – 0329

B. Back runs:

a) Keypunch the title in the title card followed by the inclusive volumes and years desired, e. g.,

   American Meteorological Society. Bulletin. V. 20 – 48, 1940 – 1957.

b) Keypunch the following caption in the <u>series card</u>, e. g.,

   PERIODICAL-BACK RUN

c) For ordering of back run of a periodical, the order number is the same as for a book.

After the multiple order form is printed, the Acquisitions department is to retain the 4 IBM-cards, the accounting and control slips in the Order Outstanding File. The request card, the purchase order, the vendor report, and the two updating IBM cards are to be turned over to the Serials Department.

The Serials Librarian will mail out the purchase order and the vendor report to the vendor and file all others in the Periodical Order Outstanding File to await the arrival of first issue or the back volumes, in the case of a back run order, and invoice.

When the expected issue or the back volumes arrive, the first Updating Card is to be used to record the receiving date and actual cost. The first Updating Card will then be returned to the Acquisitions Department for use in updating the account and the weekly Book On Order list.

a) Periodical Input Data Card.

While the acquisition phase is in progress the Serial Librarian should also prepare a "5 × 8" "Periodical Input Data Card" for the purpose of setting up the computer based periodical system. Figure 9 shows the Periodical Input Data Card.

The Periodical Input Data Card is designed to gather all essential input information in a sequence corresponding to the fields on the IBM Periodical Data Cards.

The Periodical Input Data Card could be used on two occasions:

A. When a new title is added.

B. When updating previous information.

In either case, the appropriate box is to be checked. All data of a periodical is to be recorded on the Periodical Input Data Card in accordance with the following instructions:

1.1 Title:

Enter full title according to standard library practice:

—enter under the <u>title</u> if it is distinctive, e. g. ,
JOURNAL OF GEOPHYSICAL RESEARCH

—enter under the name of the responsible institution, society, or other corporate body if the title is not distinctive, e. g. ,
SEISMOLOGICAL SOCIETY OF AMERICA. BULLETIN
(Not BULLETIN OF....)

—when entry is made under title, the title is followed by the name in parenthesis of the responsible body, if any. e. g. ,
JOURNAL OF GEOPHYSICAL RESEARCH (AMERICAN GEOPHYSICAL UNION)

—when entry is made under an acronym, the title is followed by the full name in parenthesis, e. g. ,
AIAA JOURNAL (AMERICAN INSTITUTE OF AERONAUTICS &
AIAA JOURNAL (AMERICAN INSTITUTE OF AERONAUTICS & ASTONAUTICS)

—when there is a question as to how a title should be entered, check the NST or other standard periodical listings for authority.

—the following common abbreviations can be used when a title is longer than the 70-column space provided:

ABS	ABSTRACTS	TRANS	TRANSACTIONS
AM	AMERICAN	U. S.	UNITED STATES
APPL	APPLIED	UNIV	UNIVERSITY
BIBL	BIBLIOGRAPHY	LIB	LIBRARY
BRIT	BRITISH	&	AND
ASSN	ASSOCIATION	REPT	REPORT
BULL	BULLETIN	TR	TRANSLATION
INST	INSTITUTE	DEPT	DEPARTMENT
INSTN	INSTITUTION	NATL	NATIONAL
J	JOURNAL	SEC	SECTION
PROC	PROCEEDINGS	DIV	DIVISION
PUBN	PUBLICATIONS	CONF	CONFERENCE
Q	QUARTERLY	GT. BRIT.	GREAT BRITAIN
REV	REVIEW	ED	EDUCATION
SOC	SOCIETY		

—If a "see" reference is needed, either "SEE" or "SEE ITS TR." (see its translation) is added three indentions after the end of the title. The title to which it referred is then entered in the second line (1.2). e. g. ,

1.1 SOVIET FLUID DYNAMICS SEE
1.2 FLUID DYNAMICS
1.1 AKEDEMIIA NAUK SSSR. IZVESTIIA. MEKHANIKA
                 ZHIDKOSTI I GAZA SEE ITS TR.
1.2 FLUID DYNAMICS

—Location symbol: the following location symbols are to be indicated in the box provided after the title:

 AI Abstracts & Index Area
 AR Archival Collection
 CG Catalogued in general collection
 CR Catalogued in reference collection
 CS Current display shelf then periodical stack
 FD Free distribution shelf
 MB M. E. Bender collection

MC　　Microcard & microfiche cabinets
MF　　Microfilm cabinets
NR　　Newspaper rack
OF　　Office
PS　　Goes to the periodical stack upon receipt
SR　　Student Reading Room

——The information about the publisher and its full address is to be entered next to the title. If a publisher is already a part of the title, it can simply be indicated "the Assn.", "the Inst.", or "the Society" and followed by the address.

2.1　Holding：

V.	volume	V.1
N.	number	V.1 N.2
Ser.	series	Ser. A V.1
NS	new series	NS V.1
;	(volumes or independently numbered issues are separated by semi-colons)	V.2(1950);4(1952)
,	(numbers within a volume are separated by commas)	V.4 N.1,3,5,(1951)
-	(when used in between two holding information it means the library's holding extends from the volume or number before the hyphen, that following the hyphen, and all in between) (when used after a holding information it means that the library has all volumes from thereon and is receiving the periodical currently)	V.1-10(1929-1939) V.2 N.1-4,6-7,9(1967) V.15(1965-)
Suppl.	Supplement	
/	(for publications which have appeared in more than one series of numbers, this symbol indicates the end of a series. In the example below, series ended with vol.10; the next vol. published was series 2, vol.1) e.g.,	Ser.1 V.1-10(1880-1899)/ Ser.2 V.1(1911-)
/.	(if a journal has ceased publication; the last issue listed was the last which appeared, "/." means that there are no further issues published) e.g., (for the corresponding year or years) (Holding listed in quotation marks are incomplete) e.g.,	V.1-3 N.3(1950-1952)/.
( )	(for the corresponding year or years)	
"	(Holding listed in quotation marks are incomplete) e.g.,	"V.10-11"(1950-1951);12-(1952-)
card	(if a journal is not in the physical form, its other forms are to be indicated by a **symbol) e.g., (This means that V.1-5 is in the form of cards and V.6 is in the physical form)	*card V.1-5(1950-1959)* V.6-(1960-)
fische		
film		

——Binding symbol: the following binding symbols are to be indicated in the box provided after the holding information:

　　　　BD　denotes that all complete volumes of the title are bound.
　　　　RB　denotes that the periodical is kept in a ring binder upon receipt.
　　　　UB　denotes that the periodical is not bound.

——For those periodicals not retained, no holding information is recorded. Instead, the appropriate boxes are checked, e.g.,

　　　　　V____ Current __issueV ____ volume only

——In order to include new subscriptions in the print out even before the first issue arrives, the

holding of this title is to be recorded as:
                    To begin in Jan. 1974 -
This holding card will be corrected when the first issue is received, e. g.,
          V. 1 -   (1974 -   )
3.1 Subscription information:
To be recorded as completely as possible.
– Order Number: the hyphen between "S" and the numerals is omitted,
          e. g., S-0339 | S | 0 | 3 | 3 | 9 |
– Cost:
          e. g., $17.50 | 1 | 7 | 5 | 0 |
– Year   Subscription   First   Placed:
– Source: Check the appropriate box coded as follows

1.   Subscription (Faxon)   5.   Gift (Others)
2.   Subscription (Direct)   6.   Membership
3.   Gift (Direct)   7.   Standing order
4.   Gift (Embassies)   8.   Exchange

—Frequency: The following frequency table is to be used:

Code	Frequency	Code	Frequency
00	Irregular (unscheduled)	13	12 issues plus an annual vol./year
01	Annual (1 issue/year)	24	Semimonthly
		26	Bi-weekly
02	Semiannual (2 issues/year)	52	Weekly
		20	Biennial (1 issue per 3 year)
03	3 issues/year	30	Triennial (1 issue per 3 year)
04	Quarterly (4 issues/year)	40	Quadrennial (1 issue per 4 year)
05	5 issues/year		
06	Bimonthly	50	Daily
07	7 issues/year		
08	8 issues/year		
09	9 issues/year		
10	10 issues/year		
11	11 issues/year		
12	Monthly (12 issues/year)		

—Publication pattern: First indicate the number of volumes per year in the given box. Second indicate the month of the first issue and the month of the last issue.

   e. g., If it is one volume per year, write 1 in the box and then indicate the months when the 1st and the last issues of a volume appear.

     |1| Jan. to Dec.   or |1| Sept. to June

If it is more than one volume per year, write the number of volumes per year in the box and then indicate only the month of the first issue of the first volume and the month of the last issue of the last volume in the space provided.

     |4| Jan. to Dec.

—Areas: The following area code is to be used. If a journal is of interest to several areas, all these areas are to be checked. The maximum number of areas that may be checked is five.
          EN   Environmental Engineering
          GE   Geotechnical Engineering

    IN   Industrial Development
    ST   Structural Engineering
    TR   Transportation Systems
    MC   Mathematics/Computer Science
    LA   Language and Media
    LI   Library
    GE   General (Engineering and Science)
    GN   General (Non-technical)
    WA   Water Resources Engineering

—Language: If a periodical is published in languages other than English, it is indicated by the first two letters of each of the languages. e. g. ,

    CH   Chinese   KO   Korean
    DU   Dutch   NO   Norwegian
    FR   French   RU   Russian
    GE   German   SP   Spanish
    IT   Italian   TH   Thai
    JA   Japanese   AF   Afrikaans

As many as three languages other than English may be indicated for each title.

—Country: This is to record the country where a journal is published.

4.1 <u>Historical Information</u>:

Check the appropriate box and write in the lines provided the changes made, if any.

b) IBM Periodical-Card Deck:

The IBM Periodical-Card Deck generally consists of 4 cards. (See Fig. 10)

1.1 Title Card
2.1 Holding Card
3.1 Subscription Information Card
4.1 Historical Information Card

A second title card may be added if a <u>cross reference</u> is to be made: e. g. ,

    1.1 SOVIET FLUID DYNAMICS   SEE
    1.2 FLUID DYNAMICS

As many second <u>holding</u> cards may be added as needed if the holding information is complicated, e. g. ,

    2.1 SER. A. V. 1 – 15 (1929 – 1944)/
    2.1 SER. B. V. l111 (1945 – 1956); 13 (1958); 15 (1960)/
    2.3 SER. C. V. 1 – (1961 –)

(As a rule, each series is listed in one holding card)

All cards contain the following two identical fields:

—Card Code – 2 columns (column 1 – 2)

    1.1   1.2   1.3   ……
    2.1   2.2   2.3   ……
    3.1
    4.1   4.2   4.3   ……

—Periodical Number – 5 columns (column 3 – 7)

A 5 digit number is assigned to each title and is repeated in all cards in a deck. This number imposes alphabetical order in the printed list.

<u>Card 1</u> (1.1)

Column 8 – 9 (2) Location—Use the two-letter location symbols as previously stated.

Column 10 (1) Blank

Column 11 – 80 (70) Title

Card 2 (2.1)

Column 8 – 9 (2) Binding—Use the two-letter binding symbols as previously stated.

Column 10 (1) Blank

Column 11 – 80 (70) Holding information

Card 3 (3.1)

Column 8 – 12 (5) Order number—Use "S" preceding a 4-digit number, e.g.,

S – 0458 | S | 0 | 4 | 5 | 8 |

Column 13 – 18 (6) Cost—All to be converted into U.S. dollars and cents. The last two digits are for cents, e.g.,

$325.15 | 0 | 3 | 2 | 5 | 1 | 5 |

Column 19 – 22 (4) The year subscription first placed.

Column 23 (1) Source—Entered the code number as checked in the Periodical Input Data Card.

Column 24 – 25 (2) Frequency—Enter the total number of issues published per year.

Column 26 (1) Number of volumes per year.

Column 27 – 28 (2) Month of the first issue.

Column 29 – 30 (2) Month of the last issue. For a volume published from September to June, no issue is published during the months of July and August:

The number of volume per year is | 1 |

The month of the first issue is | 9 |

The month of the last issue is | 6 |

Column 31 – 32 (2)
       33 – 34 (2)
       35 – 36 (2) Areas—As many as five areas may be indicated. A two digit
       37 – 38 (2) letter code as previously stated is used.
       39 – 40 (2)

Column 41 – 42 (2)
       43 – 44 (2) Languages—As many as three languages other than English
       45 – 46 (2) may be indicated. A two-digit letter code as previously stated is used.

Column 47 – 58 (12) Country

Column 59 – 80 (22) Blank

Card 4 (4.1)

Column 810 (3) Blank

Column 11 – 80 (70) Historical information

3. Forms of output: From the set of IBM cards the following lists can be generated through the computer.

1) Complete List of Periodical Holdings in the Library (Fig. 11)

(Title) _____   _____ (Location) _____
(Holding) _____
(Title) SEE _____
(See reference) _____
(Title) _____   _____ (Location) _____
(Holding) _____
(Historical information) _____
(Title) _____   _____ (Location) _____
(Holding) _____

2) Periodical Renewal List by Source

(Source)

(Title)   (Subscription Date)

3) Periodical Titles in the Abstracts and Indexes Area
(Title)

4) List of Periodicals by Area
(Area)
(Title)

5) List of Periodicals by Language, and by Country of Origin

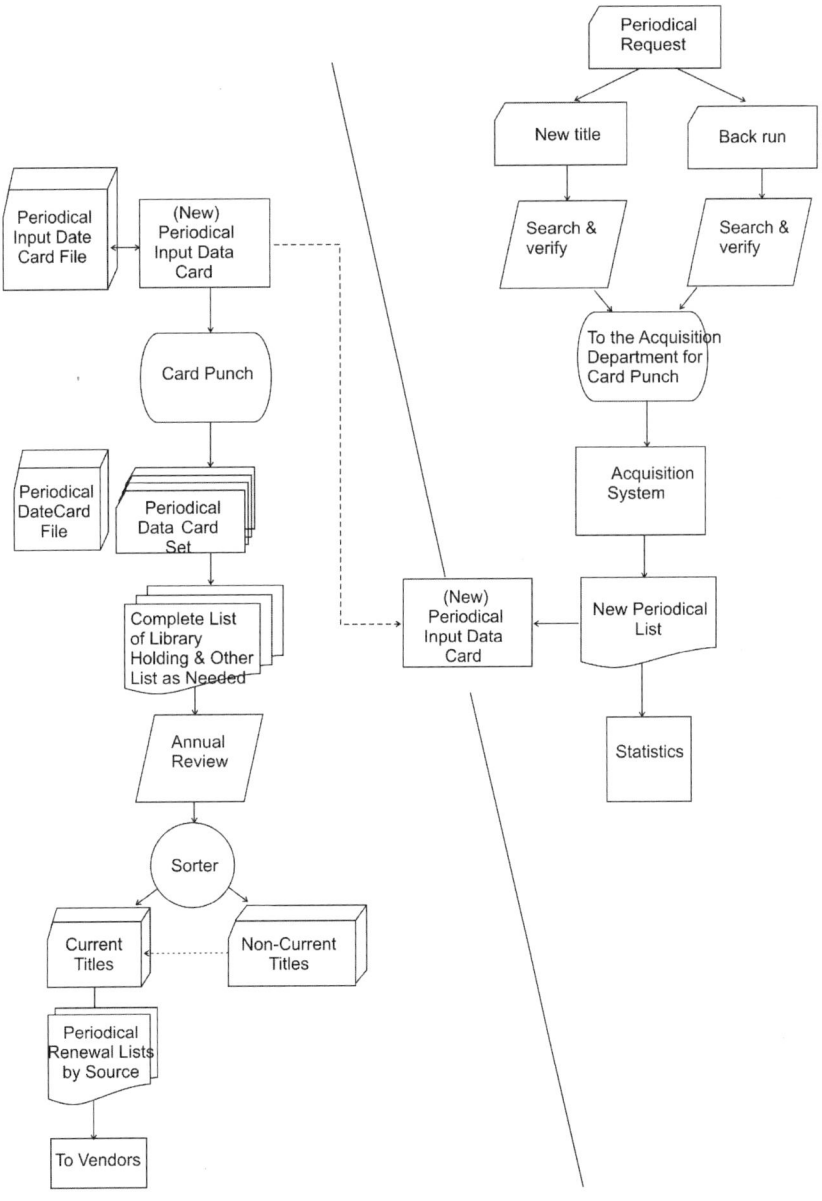

Figure 8 Block Diagram: Periodical Control Subsystem

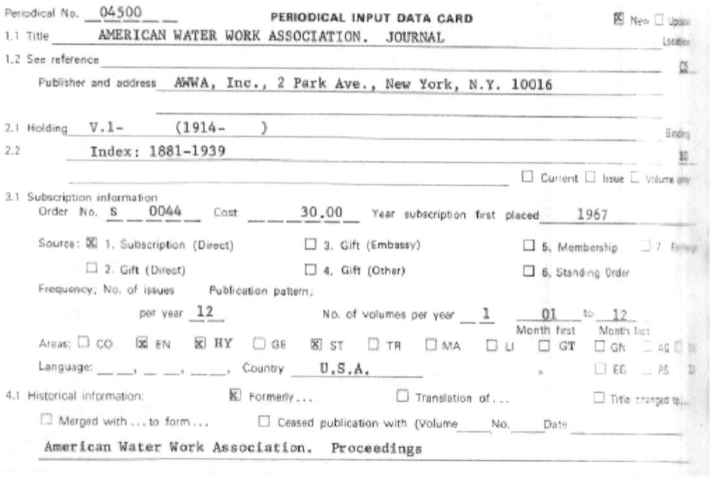
Periodical No. 04500 PERIODICAL INPUT DATA CARD ☒ New ☐ Update

1.1 Title AMERICAN WATER WORK ASSOCIATION. JOURNAL Location

1.2 See reference CS

Publisher and address AWWA, Inc., 2 Park Ave., New York, N.Y. 10016

2.1 Holding V.1- (1914-) Binding

2.2 Index: 1881-1939 SD

☐ Current ☐ Issue ☐ Volume only

3.1 Subscription information

Order No. S 0044 Cost 30.00 Year subscription first placed 1967

Source: ☒ 1. Subscription (Direct) ☐ 3. Gift (Embassy) ☐ 5. Membership ☐ 7.

☐ 2. Gift (Direct) ☐ 4. Gift (Other) ☐ 6. Standing Order

Frequency: No. of issues Publication pattern:

per year 12 No. of volumes per year 1 01 to 12

Month first Month last

Areas: ☐ CO ☒ EN ☒ HY ☐ GE ☒ ST ☐ TR ☐ MA ☐ LI ☐ GT ☐ GN ☐ AG

Language: ___, ___, ___, Country U.S.A. ☐ EG ☐ PS

4.1 Historical information: ☒ Formerly . . . ☐ Translation of . . . ☐ Title changed to . . .

☐ Merged with . . . to form . . . ☐ Ceased publication with (Volume No. Date

American Water Work Association. Proceedings

Figure 9 Periodical Input Data Card

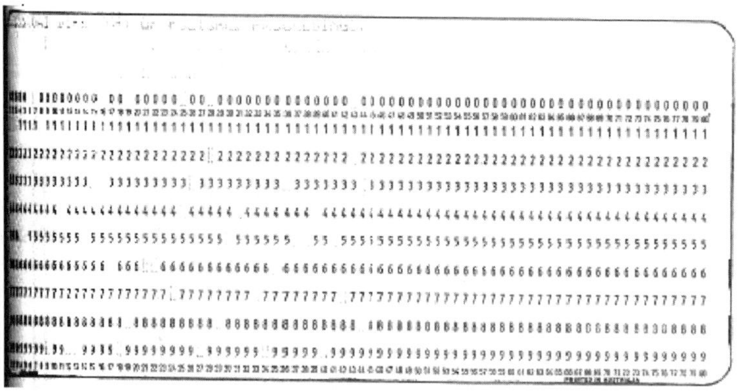

10. 1 Title Card

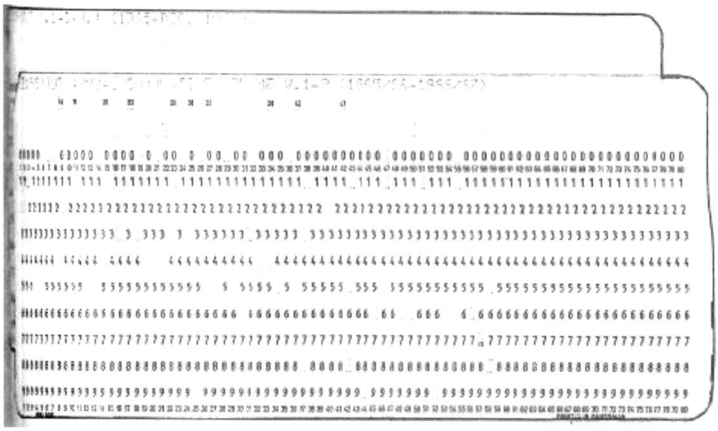

10. 2 Holding Cards

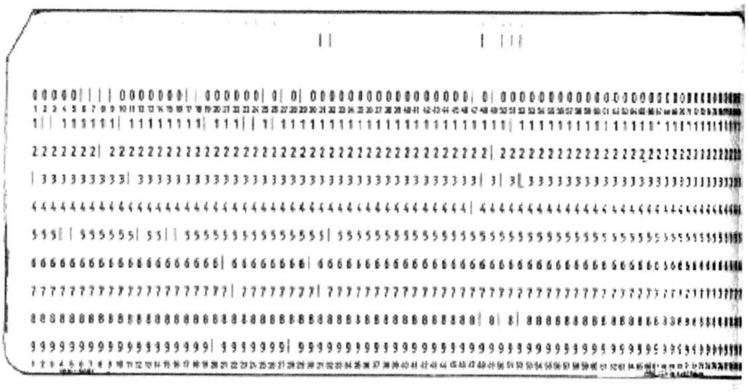

10.3 Subscription Information Card

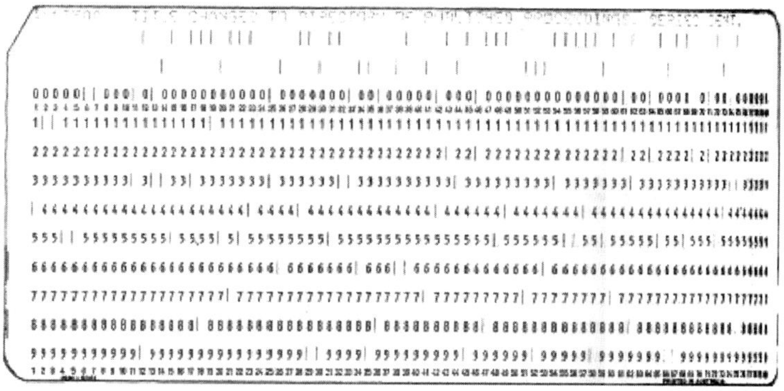

10.4 Historical Information Card

```
SOUTHEAST ASIAN REGIONAL CENTER FOR GRADUATE STUDY AND RESEARCH IN
    AGRICULTURE. ANNUAL REPORT                          CATALOGED (GENERAL)
    1968/69-                                            GIFT (DIRECT)
SOUTHEAST ASIAN SOCIETY OF SOIL ENGINEERING. JOURNAL    PERIODICAL STACK
    V.1 (1970)/.
    TITLE CHANGED TO GEOTECHNICAL ENGINEERING (SOUTHEAST ASIAN SOCIETY OF
    SOIL ENGINEERING)
SOVIET APPLIED MECHANICS                                CURRENT/JOURNAL STACK
    V.2-     (1966-                                     SUBSCRIPTION (DIRECT)
    TRANSLATION OF PRIKLADNAIA MEKHANIKA.
SOVIET CYBERNETICS REVIEW                               CURRENT/JOURNAL STACK
    V.3 N.11-      (NOV 1969-         )                 MEMBERSHIP
    FORMERLY SOVIET CYBERNETICS. RECENT NEWS ITEMS V.1-3 N.5
    (1967-MAY 1969)
SOVIET FLUID MECHANICS    SEE
    FLUID DYNAMICS
SOVIET HYDROLOGY    SELECTED PAPERS                     CURRENT/JOURNAL STACK
    1962-                                               SUBSCRIPTION (DIRECT)
SOVIET SOILS SCIENCE                                    CURRENT/JOURNAL STACK
    1965-                                               SUBSCRIPTION (DIRECT)
    TRANSLATION OF POCHVOVEDENIE.
SPANISH CULTURAL INDEX                                  ABSTRACTS & INDEX
    V.24-    (1969-    )                                GIFT (EMBASSIES)
SPECIAL LIBRARIES                                       OFFICE
    V.60-    (1969-    )                                SUBSCRIPTION (DIRECT)
SPECIAL LIBRARIES ASSOC GEOGRAPHY & MAP DIV. BULL       OFFICE
    N.67-    (1967-    )                                SUBSCRIPTION (DIRECT)
SPERRY RAND ENGINEERING REVIEW                          PERIODICAL STACK
    V.22 N.4-         (1969-     )                      GIFT (DIRECT)
STAHLBAU                                                CURRENT/JOURNAL STACK
    V.38-    (1969-    )                                SUBSCRIPTION (DIRECT)
    SUPPLEMENT TO BAUTECHNIK.
```

Figure 10   Periodical-Card Deck

3. PROPOSED DEVELOPMENTS

1. Co-operative use of MARC

A very high percentage of the library's intake is of English language publications. Certainly a proportion of these emanate from Asia or are of a specialist reports literature nature. Those that have to be ordered from Britain and America often take many ways to arrive and overall the likelihood of benefits from using MARC records is good. Reliance on a MARC tape subscription with the Library of Congress and the British National Bibliography would however, be excessive for a technology-based library considering that less than a half of the contents of a tape cover the relevant subjects.

Reliance on current NUC copy, LC catalogue cards and cards from Abel, Blackwell's and other suppliers is tantamount to use of MARC by libraries but this is a hidden factor with no possible further exploitation. Few libraries in the region have probably so high an English language intake as the AIT but overall the development of a MARC system would seem to be worthwhile, especially at a time when libraries are beginning to contemplate automated systems. The need to co-operate in the use of MARC tapes has been well established in Britain if not in America as well. The inexperience of libraries in Southeast Asia in computerized systems and the desirability of establishing standards in these from the outset make it imperative to adopt a co-operative approach if MARC tapes are to be introduced into library processing here. The AIT Library is prepared to co-ordinate the use of MARC in this way.

A proposal is now being discussed by the AIT, the National Library of Australian and the Australian Development Assistance Agency for the support of a project to utilize the NLA MARC service at the AIT in a regional system. Of the national MARC systems now issuing MARC tapes the NLA is the only one offering a search service based on its own data base with a tape of required entries only being generated. The AIT proposed to use in a system whereby LC and ISBN search numbers submitted by individual libraries are fed to the NLA on a regular basis. The AIT will receive and store a union tape of the required entries. Details of what follows have yet to be worked through in specific cases. Service can be of different degrees of involvement: some libraries may not be in a position to use machine produced records and prefer to maintain present arrangements for receiving card copy (from LC and other agencies) but at a later date will require to extract their own holdings from the MARC data base at AIT. Some libraries may require a regular tape of their records from the data base to develop their own systems immediately; others may utilize hard copy from the system and generate their own cards. It may be that AIT will consider setting up a proper card service too. The data base will serve in all ways and can be presented selectively or as a whole for union catalogue outputs, it may be that COM will be introduced for this purpose.

AIT's use of MARC in this way will be to derive records for an order system as well as cataloguing purposes and our systems will be available to other contemplating developments in automation beginning as participants in the minimal way outlined above. The proposal suggests a preliminary project for three years' introduction and assessment of the use of MARC to be followed by fuller involvement as appropriate. The crucial problem is the integration of local cataloguing for non-MARC materials, in particular for materials which the national libraries of the region are committed to recording. Local creation of MARC records for these and other items is to be encouraged and an attempt will be made in the first stages of the proposed project to review the problems and initiate local input so that the data base can assume also the function of a mode in the MARC network.

2. Union list of serials in Bangkok

Work has been going on since the beginning of 1974 towards the planning and implementation of a union serials data base to be maintained at AIT for libraries in Bangkok. The intention of this project is to draw upon ISDS and MARC serials files to build a bibliographic data base and to add local holding and other administrative information to ensure both a union catalogue capability and all the requirements to satisfy individual library purposes. Until access to the international files becomes feasible creation of bibliographic records is proceeding locally, in accordance with ISDS requirements. Such questions as the scope of the data base, the detail of the format, outputs required and arrangements for input of information about Thai titles in Thai and in transliterated form have been discussed and investigated by a group of libraries in Bangkok including representatives of the U. N. agency libraries, and of the University of Chieng Mai. An instruction manual has been prepared.① The conversion of the existing AIT file is being undertaken by computer so far as is feasible, and manually, and a strategy for conversion of other libraries' holdings has been devised. The basis of this is to eliminate duplicate input of bibliographic information. ISSNs are being inserted into the records where available but a present AIT control numbers and others of a similar neutral form are being relied upon to begin with. There seem to be between 7,000 and 9,000 titles amongst the libraries, mainly in European languages. It is intended that the first products of the system will be a union list of Abstract and Index journals and a listing of the Thai titles. Programs are being written at AIT and key punching will be centralized there.

Support for this project is still being sought. Interest of UNESCO has been expressed and a committee to be chaired by the Director of the National Library is being set up with a view to coordinating these activities within the terms of UNESCO requirements for setting up national centres of the ISDS. It will be seen that for this project as with the previous one the intention is to devise systems on a co-operative basis with a view to extension into the region and to consolidation of two way participation in the international network for bibliographic control.

3. Information retrieval system.

The Asian Information Center for Geotechnical Information (AGE) was set up in January 1973 at the AIT under the joint sponsorship of the Institute's Division of Geotechnical Engineering and the Library and Information Center. For the initial period of three years AGE is being funded largely by a grant awarded by the International Development Research Centre of Canada. AGE serves as a depository for technical documents and as a clearing house in the Asian region for information on soil mechanics, foundation engineering, rock mechanics, engineering geology, earthquake engineering and related fields. It attempts to collect information on all phases of geotechnical engineering research and projects either published or unpublished which are of relevance to Asia. It provided both current awareness and SDI services through publication of abstracts of articles and reports and of subject bibliographies. It offers reference, referral and reprographic services. ② The AGE now has subscribers in 17 countries most of whom are in Asia.

Data being collected has hitherto been handled manually. The intention is to devise mechanized systems for string, manipulating and retrieving information in a system that will provide more flexible references services and ensure a more creative use of the data that is being collected. The system is so designed will serve as a prototype to be used for information retrieval in other fields such as structural engineering projects and environmental engineering that AIT is

---

① Serials Project manual: input instructions for union serials cataloguing (English text). Bangkok, 1974.

② The full list of publications envisaged is as follows:

AGE Conference Proceedings List: An annual list of conference proceedings on various subjects of geotechnical engineering in AGE's collections.

AGE Current Awareness Service: A quarterly publication informing readers of recent geotechnical engineering publications and contents of selected geotechnical engineering journals received at AGE.

AGE Journal Holdings List: A list revised annually of geotechnical engineering journals held at AGE.

Asian Geotechnical Engineering Abstracts: A quarterly publication consisting of abstracts of available publications and reports on geotechnical engineering in or about Asia.

Asian Geotechnical Engineering Directory: A bi-annual publication to consist o information on various organizations and individuals who are doing geotechnical engineering work in Asia or work relevant to Asia.

Asian Geotechnical Engineering in Progress: A semi-annual publication to consist of information on current design, construction and research projects in geotechnical engineering being undertaken in Asia.

In addition to the regular publications listed above, AGE intends to bring out a bibliography series which will include subject bibliographies prepared on request or on those topics having recurrent interest.

interested in. Systems capability may entail limited hybrid systems to begin with (minimum input, and output restricted to references back to the published abstract service issued in parallel). Consideration is being extended to subscription to European and American data bases either in full or selectively and an experiment in communication by satellite to the KASC data bases in Pittsburgh is being devised.

(Published in *The Larc Reports*. V. 7, No. 3. Peoria, Illinois: The Larc Press, 1974.)

应用计算机和其他信息技术推广
东南亚地区图书馆和信息服务的可能性

Possibilities in Employing Computer and Other Information Technologies to Further Library and Information Services in Southeast Asia[①]

1. INTRODUCTION

One of the most pressing problems facing the developing nations in Asia today is the inability of their libraries and information centers to respond effectively and expediently to the wide range of information needs which are required for national development.

It has been observed that there exist two types of "information gap" in Asia. One is the lack of immediate access to the growing body of knowledge accumulated because of the rapid advancement in science and technology. Another is the lack of an effective mechanism to uncover useful indigenous information, to collect it from widely scattered sources, to index it for easy retrieval, and to publicize it for and to disseminate it to the potential users. It is an unfortunate fact that even among the Asian countries themselves, there is very little cooperation and interchange of useful information between the libraries and information centers.

A great deal of human and financial resources have been wasted in Asia as a direct result of these two types of "information gap". The perpetuation of this situation has rendered the works of Asian scientists, research workers, and technical specialists both ineffective and inefficient.

Recognizing such a serious problem, most of the Southeast Asian nations already have taken steps to correct it. This is shown in the findings of a recent UN-ESCO report.[②] It said:

> In each country visited there is active interest in the development of scientific and technical information, and plans for improvement of the present system. In Indonesia a Ford Foundation mission recently advised on the establishment of a national network of science information centres to be co-ordinated by the National Scientific Documentation Centre, and the Government has requested UNDP consultant services to assist in the actual planning. In Malaysia a mission was carried out in late 1971 under British Council sponsorship to advise on "Scientific and Technical Library and Information Services in Malaysia". In Singapore there has been no direct follow-up on the 1969 UNESCO sponsored "Proposals for the setting-up of a Scientific and Technical Information Centre", but there is active interest in revising this study to bring it in line with the changing situation in Singapore. In the Philippines the NSDB is setting up a new National Science Information Centre which will serve as the national co-ordinating body and as the linkage to regional and international networks or systems. The Government has requested UNDP advisory services in planning the Centre. In Hong Kong the Committee for Scientific Co-ordination has set up a Sub-Committee on Scientific and Technical Information to consider the establishment of a "Centralized Technical Information Service". In Thailand the Thai National Documentation Centre (TNDC) which is already well established is planning further services, and the Asian Institute of Technology has advanced plans for development of a complete information service on a regional level. In all

---

[①] This article is based on a paper by the author presented at the Regional Seminar on Information Storage, Retrieval and Dissemination organized by Asian Mass Communication Research and Information Centre in cooperation with National Research Council of Thailand, Bangkok, March 26 – 30, 1973.

[②] *Report of UNESCO Fact-Finding Mission on the Regional Information Network for Science and Technology in Southeast Asia.* 1972: p. 20(SCP/425/2 – 25).

countries the value of regional linkages was recognized and the concept of a regional information network in science and technology was strongly supported. ①

In the field of social sciences, a comparable study was made by Mr. Erwin Kristoffersen, former regional representative of the Friedrich-Ebert-Stiftung which resulted in a well documented proposal to establish a Clearing House for Social Development in Asia as an effective measure to meet the information needs in the Social Sciences. ② The study pointed out the serious deficiencies existing in the exchange and dissemination of indigenous information in the social sciences much of which is vital for developmental planning.

In the light of these two studies and the important groundwork they have laid, I would like to direct attention to the possible tools made available by recent advancements in information technology which can be applied to improve library-information services in the region.

2. THE INFORMATION TECHNOLOGY

Information technology is a term referring to those technologies which can be applied to library-information work. There are many such technologies available now. They generally come under the labels of 1) Reprography, 2) Computers, or 3) Telecommunications.

Each of these three actually represents a variety of applications and different degrees of sophistication. They may also work independently or together in a complex information system. Just as with other tools, not all the technologies are suitable for all situations and at all times. It is necessary that we give our attention to those technologies which are considered relevant to our particular situation and requirement at the present time.

3. REPROGRAPHY

Despite the fact that "Reprography" is a relatively new term, this technology is already under widespread use by many libraries and information centers in this region. Unlike the newness of the name, reprography consists of many not-too-new techniques such as microfilming and various methods of copying and duplicating.

The techniques of reprography are very important for the developing countries in that

1) they enable a wider dissemination of information some of which might not be available or accessible otherwise;

2) they have made it possible for libraries and information centers to interchange reproduced information;

3) various microforms are by far the most economic means for information storage and for dissemination to distant places by mail; and

4) the computer-output-microforms (COM) reduces the problem of storage and dissemination for the large amount of computer generated data.

4. COMPUTERS

Although the use of computers in library-information work has found wide acceptance throughout the world, it has just begun in our region. The computer is a very promising tool in that it has the power and versatility to process data with high speed and precision. The main obstacles standing in the way of wider application by libraries and information centers, in Asia are the factors of high cost, especially in the initial stage, and the lack of trained staff. These two obstacles can be overcome by setting up either national data processing centers within each country or multi-national (or regional) data processing centers within a number of cooperating countries. The former can be affiliated with either the national library, the national documentation center, an

---

① *Ibid.*, p. 4.

② Erwin Kristoffersen. *Clearing House for Social Development in Asia*; *Project Proposals and Report on the Findings of a Feasibility Study.* Bangkok, Friedrich-Ebert-Stiftung, Bangkok Office, 1972; p. 35.

institutional library or a special information center, whichever has the computer capability. The latter can be attached to a regional or international organization that is so equipped.

The essence of this setup is to share the costs of both owning or sharing a computer system and developing the software necessary for its support, and pooling together the trained personnel. By means of this arrangement, even small libraries and information centers can have the benefit of sharing a computer with large libraries and information centers. The work which can be best handled by such data processing centers would be:

1) Establish and maintain a national (or regional) data bank on indigenous publications. A by-product of this data bank is the publication of national (or regional) bibliographies.

2) Establish and maintain a national (or regional) data bank on major library collections in the country (or region). A by-product of this data bank is the publication of a national (or regional) union catalog and separate book catalogs for each participating library or information center.

3) Establish and maintain a national (or regional) data bank on periodicals and serial publications held by major libraries and information centers in the country (or the region). A by-product of this data bank is the publication of a union list of periodicals and serials and separate lists of holdings for each participating library or information center.

4) Establish and maintain a national (or regional) data bank for scientific and technical literature of relevance to the country (or the region). A by-product of this data bank is the publication at regular intervals of abstracting journals. A score of other services such as SDI service, current awareness service, and retrospective search of the data file can also be initiated.

5) Establish and maintain a national (or regional) data bank on such vital information as census data, demographic data, land use data, hydrological and meteorological data, inventories of communications and transportation, industrial and housing facilities, geological and natural resources, etc., and relevant economic and sociological data.

6) Act as a national (or regional) processing center for the acquisitions, cataloging, and processing of books, journals and other materials for the libraries and information centers that want to participate in such labor- and cost-saving operations. There are a wide range of activities that can be channeled through such a central processing service.

7) The center may also consider the possibility of acquiring the MARC (Machine-Readable Cataloging) tapes of both the U.S. Library of Congress and the British National Bibliography for local storage and manipulation. Arrangements may also be made to have either direct or indirect access to some of the major data bases in the developed countries by means of modern telecommunications.

8) Develop a library of computer programs for various library-information work including programs for automatic indexing, photocomposition, etc.

9) Provide consulting services to other libraries or information centers that are interested in establishing their own computer operations.

10) Provide various computer services to individual or special library-information projects.

11) Conduct short courses, seminars and workshops for the training and up-grading of librarians and information scientists in the use of computer and other information technology for library-information work.

5. TELECOMMUNICATIONS

Telecommunications is an important part of the new information technology which holds great promise for improving library-information services in Asia.

An effort has been made by the United Nations Economic Commission for Asia and the Far East (ECAFE) to make the countries of Asia into an "Asian Telecommunity". The program intends to develop in every Asian country a telecommunication network and to link the various national networks from Iran to Indonesia by a system of modern communication services provided at the most economical rates. It when fully realized will undoubtedly accelerate the interchange of information amongst the libraries and information centers in the region by making possible information transmission and facsimile reproduction at high speed and at low cost. It will also facilitate the development of national library-information systems and regional library-information networks similar to those systems and networks already in operation in many parts of the world. One such example is the ESRO system which was reported in a recent article by Isotta. ①

ESRO system is the information system for the Space Documentation Service of the European Space Research Organization located in Darmstadt, Germany. The ESRO system was designed on the concept of a centralized file maintenance and software responsibility, coupled with decentralized searching of the files by remote terminals sited in the member states. The total configuration consists of the central computer facility in Darmstadt, together with its own local terminal; a single leased line to Paris where two terminals are installed; a party-line connection from Paris to St. Mary Cray in Kent where a terminal is installed at the Technology Reports Centre; a party-line connection from Paris to Bretigny, where a terminal is installed at the Centre Nationale D'Etudes Spatiale; a terminal in the ESRO establishment in Noordwijk, Holland; and another terminal in the ESRO establishment in Frascati near Rome. ②

This type of system can be adopted in Asia if the "Asian Telecommunity" becomes a reality and the cost of telecommunications is substantially reduced.

Another important recent development in telecommunications which has an encouraging implication for Asia is the ability to transmit information among widely dispersed points of the world via satellites. The capability of communication satellites to transmit voice, teletype and facsimile signals to a distant place at the speed of light has a distinct advantage over other communication media for inter-continental communications. An inter-connection of computers, telephones, teletypes and communication satellites can provide a most effective network of national, regional and world information systems.

A highly sophisticated network system which saw the interfacing of all these was demonstrated recently at the 35th annual meeting of the American Society for Information Science held in Washington, D. C. on October 23 – 26, 1972. The system demonstrated was called "International Information Retrieval Network". Through the several on-line terminals located on the conference grounds, participants of the annual meeting were able to query not just the many data bases on computers located several hundred miles away in different parts of the U. S. A. but also the data files of the ESRO in Darmstadt, Germany via the INTELSAT IV communication satellite. The demonstration featured several recent innovations:

1) International communications via satellite.
2) Remote video and printing terminals.
3) On-line, interactive retrieval systems using both natural-text and index-based techniques.
4) Networking.
5) Access to multiple data bases.

The demonstration showed that international networks are technologically feasible, economically conceivable, and usable with minimal instruction③.

Another less sophisticated but operating system using only teletype machines and the INTELSAT IV F – 2 satellite is the satellite linkage between John Crerar Library (JCL) in Chicago, U. S. A. and Consejo Nacional de Investigaciones Cientificasy Tecnicas (C. N. I. C. T.) in Buenos Aires, Argentina. The basis of the system consists of some fourteen technical libraries in Argentina which are linked by Telex to each other and to C. N. I. C. T. in Buenos Aires. When an institution cannot fill its needs from its own collection, a message is sent to C. N. I. C. T. which then attempts to locate the needed item in one of the other libraries by use of the Union Lists and

---

① N. E. C. Isotta. "International Information Networks:1. The ESRO System ." *Aslib Proceedings*. V. 24 No. 1 (January 1972): pp. 31 – 37.

② *Ibid.* ,p. 33.

③ From "A World of Information", the program of the 35th annual meeting of ASIS. p. 8.

catalogs. If this is unsuccessful, the request is then transmitted to JCL and the latter provides a microfilm copy by return airmail. The costs of photocopies and the relay messages are borne by the National Academy of Sciences in the U. S. [①]

The JCL/C. N. I. C. T. system is a good example of what the developing countries can do to obtain the needed information from developed countries. Financial assistance of this kind is probably available from many international or foreign aid organizations.

6. AIT'S PLANS

As a regional institution for advanced engineering education and research, the Asian Institute of Technology (AIT) is deeply involved in the technical development of the Asian region and it is this involvement which has led AIT to an awareness of the urgent needs of Asian engineers for relevant information. To meet this need, AIT has devoted a large portion of its resources to develop an outstanding library and information center within the Institute. Steps have been taken to expand this facility into a regional library and information center for engineering and related fields, embracing the collection, organization and dissemination of useful technical information. The recently founded Asian Information Center for Geotechnical Engineering, under the joint sponsorship of the AIT Division Geotechnical Engineering and the Library, is an example of one such endeavor.

To improve library-information service in the region, especially in the application of the latest information technology, AIT is in a very unique position. We are now in the process of undertaking three major steps which, if successful, will undoubtedly have a far reaching effect on the development of a regional library-information network. These steps are (1) expanding computerized library-information service with a regional outlook, (2) establishing the Asian Information Center for Geotechnical Engineering, and (3) planning for an information transfer experiment via satellite between AIT and the Knowledge Availability Systems Center (KASC) of the University of Pittsburgh.

1) Expanding computerized library-information service:

With the installation in January 1974 of a large computer system (CDC 3600) at AIT to replace the currently overloaded IBM 1130, the Library plans to greatly expand its existing computerized systems in acquisitions, accounting, serials listing, etc. while converting them from IBM 1130 to CDC 3600. As a part of this plan, a library systems analyst from the U. K. has been employed to undertake the designing and implementing of the expanded operations. This specialist, Mr. Stephen W. Massil, from the University of Birmingham joined AIT Library as the Associate Director in September 1973. Mr. Massil has been actively working with the Birmingham Libraries' Cooperative Mechanization Project which utilizes MARC records in three libraries (Aston and Birmingham Universities, and the Birmingham Public Libraries) on a cooperative basis. Work of the Project has been reported regularly in *Program*. [②] It is hoped that with the background of this specialist on library cooperative mechanization, many of our new programs will have a broader perspective and regional outlook and will tie in with the regional library-information network development.

2) Establishing the Asian Information Center for Geotechnical Engineering (AGE):

To experiment with the setting up of a regional library-information service, we have selected a very important but highly specialized field—Geotechnical Engineering, as our pilot project. The idea of establishing AGE was conceived at the meeting of representatives of national societies of soil mechanics and foundation engineering in the Asian region which convened in Bangkok in July

---

[①] From the letter of William S. Budington, Executive Director and Librarian of the John Grerar Library dated August 30, 1971.

[②] Most recent report of the Project is: E. H. C. Driver, D. G. R. Buckle, S. W. Massil, D. J. Wilkins & A. R. Hall. "The Birmingham Libraries' Cooperative Mechanisation Project: Progress Report, June 1970 – January 1972." *Program*: *News of Computers in Libraries*. V. 6 No. 2 (April 1972): pp. 120 – 6.

1971. Through one of the resolutions of the meeting, AIT was requested to undertake the task of establishing and operating AGE for the benefit of engineers in Asia. The importance of this undertaking was recognized through a grant awarded by the International Development Research Centre of Canada to partially support the activities of the Center for the initial three-year period. Because of this support, AGE was formally established in January 1973.

Serving as a clearing house in Asia for information on all phases of Geotechnical Engineering such as soil mechanics, foundation engineering, engineering geology, rock mechanics, earthquake engineering and other related fields, the Center will undertake the responsibility to collect all relevant information and data useful to the region, to design a computer-based information storage and retrieval system, to disseminate such information through its publications and photocopying and microfilming services, and to provide the three-R services (Reference, Referral and Reproduction).

The detailed information concerning the data files, the publications, and the services of the Center are contained in an introductory brochure published by the Center. [①]

3) Planning for an information transfer experiment via satellite between AIT and the Knowledge Availability Systems Center of the University of Pittsburgh:

This experiment which is now being planned is patterned after both the ESRO system and the JCL/C. N. I. C. T. system already described. The Knowledge Availability Systems Center (KASC) is one of the six NASA Regional Dissemination Centers in the U. S. Under the directorship of Professor Allen Kent who is also the Chairman of the Department of Information Science at the University of Pittsburgh, KASC has not only the expertise in information/ computer/ communications areas but also the immediate access to almost every important computerized data base in science and engineering. The linkage to KASC via satellite will be a great advantage for both the AIT and the region in that we will have remote, immediate access to the many computerized data bases which are vital to our information requirement and yet, too expensive for us to own. It is our plan that subsequent arrangements will be made with all parties concerned to supply information drawn from KASC through AIT to other libraries and information centers in the region. This sounds so much like a dream, but it is not far from reality.

These above mentioned recent developments will have an important effect on the overall improvement of library-information service in the region. The advancement of information technology has definitely offered excellent possibilities for rapid improvement. It is of prime importance that the libraries and information centers in Asia will take full advantage of this development to close the "information gap" existing between the developed world and the developing world and to become a true partner in national and regional development.

(Published in *Network*. V. 1, No. 3, March 1974: pp. 10 – 12 & 24 – 28. Also published in *Library automation: the Orient and South Pacific.* edited by Jack D. Key, The LARC Association, Inc., 1975: pp. 61 – 67.)

[①] *Introducing Asian Information Center for Geotechnical Engineering.* Bangkok, Asian Institute of Technology, 1973: p. 9.

关于在泰国建立国际连续出版物数据系统（ISDS）东南亚地区中心的建议

Proposal for the Establishment of an ISDS Regional Center for Southeast Asia in Thailand

The United Nations Educational, Scientific and Cultural Organization (UNESCO) has been in recent years actively promoting the idea of a World Science Information System (Acronym UNISIST) which was officially launched in 1972 and has become a major program of UNESCO administered by its Division of Scientific and Technological Information and Documentation. While the long-range goal of the UNISIST program is to develop international networks of information services in various sectors of sciences, it has the following five intermediate objectives:

· To undertake activities for improvement of the tools of systems interconnection.

· To provide assistance for strengthening the functions and improving the performance of the institutional components of the information transfer chain.

· To help in the development of the specialized manpower essential for the planning and operation of information networks, especially in the developing countries.

· To encourage the development of scientific information policies and national networks.

· To assist member states, especially the developing countries, in the creation and development of their infrastructure in the field of scientific and technical information.

Under these five broad objectives, a variety of programs have been planned. One such program is the establishment of the International Serials Data System (ISDS) within the framework of UNISIST.

The main purpose of ISDS is to provide a reliable registry of world serial publications in all subjects and to assign to each of them, under a given title, a unique and unambiguous numeric code identifier—the International Standard Serial Number (SSN). In order to do this, a two-tier organizational structure has been envisaged which consists of an international center surrounded by a satellite system of regional or national centers established throughout the world.

In 1973, the French Government offered and made financial contributions to establish the International Centre for the Registration of Serial Publications in Paris as the international center of ISDS. Since then, more than 10 national centers and one regional center have been established to register serial publications in each of the countries and to assign ISSNS. Among the first of such centers is the National Serial Date Program of the U.S. established within the Library of Congress.

With the encouragement of UNESCO, the National Library of Thailand submitted in 1974, to UNESCO a request for the service of a consultant to undertake a feasibility study for the establishment of an ISDS regional center for Southeast Asia in Thailand. The consultant's assignments were:

· To assess the present situation of serial publications in Indonesia, Malaysia, the Philippines, Singapore and Thailand.

· To evaluate the current status of bibliographical control for serials in these countries.

· To identify the national body and, possibly, the individual person(s) responsible for the bibliographical control of serial publications in each of these countries.

· To negotiate with appropriate authorities in each of these countries for their participation in the proposed regional center.

· To solicit inputs from various sources for the establishment of the center.

· To hold an open discussion on the preliminary plan of the center at the Third Conference of Southeast Asian Librarians held in Jakarta from December 1–5, 1975.

· To prepare a mission report and a program proposal for UNESCO at the end of the mission.

Resulting from this request, this reporter was invited by UNESCO to serve as the consultant for the exploratory mission which took place between November 17 and December 20, 1975. Because of the positive responses made by library officials in the five Southeast Asian countries combined with the favorable conditions for regional cooperation prevailing in the Region, a recommendation to establish an ISDS Regional Center for Southeast Asia in Bangkok under the auspices of the National Library of Thailand was submitted to UNESCO as a part of the *Mission Report and Programme Proposal* prepared by this reporter at the end of his mission. [1]

The Mission Report consists of 4 sections and 6 appendixes. Important among these are the Summary of Findings, Current Status of Serial Publications, and Selected Bibliographies for Serials Publications. The *Programme Proposal* contains 5 sections, namely, Major Recommendations, Rationale for the Proposal, the Proposed Charter of the Regional Center, the Draft Agreement Between the National Agency of a Participating Country and the Regional Center, and the Proposed Five-Year Budget.

At the time of this reporting, the first recommendation, to hold an organizing meeting and a workshop in Bangkok, has been approved and funded by UNESCO and is scheduled on March 15 – 17 and March 22 – 24 respectively. It looks hopeful that the ISDS Regional Center for Southeast Asia can be established at the organizing meeting to provide a better bibliographic control for serial publications in the five Southeast Asian nations through regional and international cooperation. The success of this undertaking may very well provide a model for developing countries in other regions of the world.

I. Introduction:

The Center was officially established by the Asian Institute of Technology (AIT) on January 1, 1973 within AIT's Library under the joint sponsorship of AIT's Division of <u>Geotechnical Engineering</u> and the Library.

The Asian Institute of Technology is an independent, non-profit making, regional graduate school of engineering. It offers programs of advanced study and research to students from all parts of Asia. Since its inception in 1959, the Institute has grown steadily and its sphere of activities in Asia has widened greatly both geographically and in the services and programs offered.

The Division of Geotechnical Engineering at AIT under the chairmanship of Professor Za-Chieh Moh has been a major center for geotechnical engineering education and research in the region. It is the founder of the Southeast Asian Society of Soil Engineering and the publisher of the society's journal, Geotechnical Engineering. It has sponsored several regional conferences including the First Southeast Asian Conference on Soil Engineering, April 24 to 30, 1967 and the Fourth Asian Regional Conference on Soil Mechanics and Foundation Engineering, July 26 – August 1, 1971. The proceedings of these conferences which were also published by AIT have been highly regarded throughout the world.

It was at the meeting of representatives of national societies of soil mechanics and foundation engineering in the Asian region which convened in Bangkok in July 1971, the idea of establishing AGE was conceived. Through one of its resolutions, AIT was requested to undertake such a task.

During the initial period of three years, the Center is partially supported by a grant of 53, 630 Canadian dollars awarded to AIT by the International Development Research Centre of Canada (IDRC). The grant has been instrumental in the birth of AGE and its subsequent development. In addition to IDRC's grant, AIT has given generously both personnel and material supports to AGE since its inception. Several of the library staffs have spent a great deal of their time to AGE's operations. The acquisitions of the AIT Library on geotechnical engineering publications have been greatly expanded.

In preparation for the establishment of the Center, a policy and procedure statement was

---

[1] Copies of the *Mission Report and Programme Proposal* (SC-76/WS/7) are available from Dr. Wolfgang Löhner, STD/STID, UNESCO, place de Fontenoy, 75700 Paris.

drafted and issued on November 28, 1972 after its approval by the President of AIT. The Policy and Procedure Statement (LY-2) defines the aims and functions of the AGE and sets forth the administrative and organizational structure of AGE. (See Appendix I[①])

II Organization:

According to the Policy and Procedure Statement, AGE is guided by two committees:

The Policy Advisory Committee: As of June 30, 1973, 16 members have accepted invitations to serve on the committee which will be consulted on major policy matters.

The Technical Committee: At present, this committee consists of the 9 members who meet approximately once every two months to advise the Director of the Center on all important technical and operational matters.

In addition to the two committees mentioned, the Technical Committee recommended the appointment of liaison officers, at least one person in each country within the Asian region. As of June 30, 1973, 17 liaison officers from 13 countries have been appointed. Appendix II is a complete list of the members of the two AGE committees and liaison officers.

The main duties of liaison officers are as follows:

· To provide AGE with lists of government departments or offices and non-governmental agencies which are responsible for projects in and relevant to geotechnical engineering in one's country.

· To keep AGE informed of important projects in geotechnical engineering being undertaken and whether or not there are reports available.

· To help AGE in the collection of project reports and other publications which are not available otherwise and to forward them to AGE.

· To help AGE in the collection of other relevant information such as those indicated in the three survey forms and to forward them to AGE.

· To serve as a link between AGE and its clients in one's country whenever needed.

· To serve as a point of contact for AGE in one's country.

The staffs of AGE as of June 30, 1973 consists of four full-time staffs and five part-time staffs. Another part-time staff who will be responsible for systems development will be coming from the U. K. on October 1, 1973.

In addition, AGE also employs six graduate students from the Division of Geotechnical Engineering on a part-time basis to conduct literature search and indexing. The names of the staff members and part-time student assistants are given in Appendix III.

III. Data Bank:

One of the major and most urgent tasks of AGE is to collect various data and publications on Geotechnical Engineering which is relevant to Asia and to design and develop an effective information storage and retrieval system for their keeping. The AGE data bank as now being built consists of the following:

1. An index card file consisting of complete bibliographical information on all publications and reports on Geotechnical Engineering in or about Asia. Each index card has the following standard elements:

Control number
International Geotechnical Classification Number(s)
Call number
Year of publication
Total number of pages
Physical Form Code

[①] Appendixes are not attached (原文未附任何附录).

Language(s)
Geographical Code
Personal Author(s)
Corporate Author(s)
Title
Source/Series
Abstract

Key words (Using the Soil Mechanics Thesaurus prepared by the committee on Information Retrieval of the Soil Mechanics and Foundations Division, ASCE)

Index in...

At present, over 500 such index cards have been completed and filed. Approximately 200 cards are to be typed from work sheets. The monthly rate of growth in the number of index cards prepared will be greatly accelerated as the several new staff members become better trained and are more familiar with the literature search.

2. Separate data files for the following three types of information collected by specially designed questionnaires:

Survey of Organizations in Asia Concerned with Geotechnical Engineering.

Survey of Geotechnical Engineering Specialists in Asia.

Survey of Geotechnical Engineering Projects Completed or In Progress.

The initial responses toward the questionnaires have been very good. Over 100 such forms have been received and filed.

3. A separate catalog-card file of all publications on Geotechnical Engineering in the AIT Library. It is estimated that over 5,000 publications may be included in the catalog card file.

4. Lists of journals, selected serials and conference proceedings on Geotechnical Engineering at the AIT Library. The AGE Journal Holdings List just released lists 119 journal titles now held at AGE.

As soon as the CDC 3600 computer system is installed at AIT in October 1973 and Mr. Stephen W. Massil, the Library Systems Analyst arrives at about the same time, the abovementioned data files will be converted to a machine-readable form for computer storage and manipulation.

These data files together with the existing information services to which AGE subscribes including Geotechnical Abstracts, The Geodex Soil Mechanics Information Service and the Geodex Retrieval System for Geotechnical Abstracts, enable AGE to provide a wide range of information services.

IV. Publications:

In order to make AGE's collection of technical publications and reports as well as its data bank widely known to its potential users, the following regular publications have been planned, the first issues of four of the planned publications (A, B, C, D) are scheduled to appear at the end of July and early August:

A. AGE Current Awareness Service: A quarterly publication to inform readers of recent geotechnical engineering publications and contents of selected geotechnical engineering journals received at AGE.

B. AGE Conference Proceedings List: An annual list of conference proceedings on various subjects of geotechnical engineering held at AGE.

C. AGE Journal Holdings List: An annual list of geotechnical engineering journals held at AGE.

D. Asian Geotechnical Engineering Abstracts: A quarterly publication to consist of abstracts of available publications on geotechnical engineering in or about Asia.

E. Asian Geotechnical Engineering In Progress: A semi-annual publication to consist of information on current design, construction and research projects in geotechnical engineering being undertaken in Asia.

F. Asian Geotechnical Engineering Directory: A bi-annual publication to consist of information on various organizations and individuals who are doing geotechnical engineering work in Asia or relevant to Asia.

In addition to the regular publications listed above, AGE intends to bring out a bibliography series which will include subject bibliographies prepared on request or on those topics having recurrent interest.

To make AGE known, especially its functions and services, a special brochure entitled Introducing Asian Information Center for Geotechnical Engineering was published in February 1973. Over one thousand copies of this brochure were sent to all interested persons or organizations along with AGE's questionnaires and subscription forms. Publicity about AGE has begun to appear in many engineering journals.

V. Membership:

AGE is a non-profit making, regional information center. For an initial period of three years, AGE is financially supported in part by the International Development Research Centre of Canada, thus keeping the subscription fees and annual membership fees to a minimum enabling more interested individuals and organizations to become subscribing members.

Because of the many privileges accorded to members, all at a very low cost, the membership application drive has been reasonably successful. It is anticipated that once the AGE regular publications begin to appear, membership will increase. At this time of reporting, 22 individual members and 9 institutional members have already paid their respective dues.

VI. Acknowledgement:

AGE is very grateful for the encouragement and warm support it has received during the first six months of its formation. Without such encouragement and support AGE could not have been established. Although AGE owes its existence to both the Asian Institute of Technology and the International Development Research Centre of Canada for their supports; it also owes its existence to the advice and assistance of many individuals among whom are: Mr. John E. Woolston, Director of IDRC's Information Sciences Division and members of AGE's two committees and liaison officers.

It is regrettable that due to financial restraint, it will not be possible, at least in the foreseeable future, for AGE to convene a meeting in Bangkok for the members of the Policy Advisory Committee as well as for the liaison officers in order to discuss vital matters concerning AGE's operations and services. It is hoped, however, that the forthcoming Eighth International Conference on Soil Mechanics and Foundation Engineering to be held in Moscow this August will provide an opportunity for those members of the two committees and liaison officers attending this Conference to meet and discuss the present and future development of AGE. For those not attending this Conference, your written communications with AGE will be most welcome and appreciated.

(Published in *Leads*. V. 18, No. 2, July 1976: pp. 4 – 5.)

线上作业与图书馆

Online Revolution and Libraries

电子计算机的线上作业是最近二十多年才有的,但应用在图书馆编目、目录索引的编制,以及目录及资料的检索上,还是最近十年左右的事。时间虽短,但发展神速,在欧洲、美洲许多国家的图书馆,已被普遍采用。我在回台湾之前,曾见九月二十五日《中央日报》上所登的一则新闻,标题是:透过国际通信电话,可知百科资料。副题是:由美国两大资料网瞬间提供包括最新医学、农业、工程、军事知识。我们由这则新闻,可以知道台湾和美国线上作业与资料库的直接联系,在最近就可以实现了。所以我觉得今天这个题目,在时间配合得很好。

线上作业并不是很新的东西,岛内专家对这方面也已经很有研究。这里举出两篇著作,各位有时间可以看看,同时也可以作为今天讲题的补充参考资料。第一篇是张馆长鼎钟写的《图书馆与资讯》一书中的《资料库与资讯的利用》,对各资料库的内容及如何有效的使用,有非常详尽的说明。另外一篇是李德竹教授所写的《资料库与线上检索服务》,这篇文章是刊在最近一期(第五卷第一期)的《图书馆与资讯科学》(上),对线上作业与资料库近几年的发展,做了很详尽的报道。

由于电脑技术的发展与普遍化,以及无线电信的发展与资料网的建立,使得线上作业得以顺利实施。线上作业的功能是使图书馆人员能协助台湾各业的研究人员,经由可直接拨号的终端机(terminal),通过一般的电话或其他电信线路,直接与资料库的电子计算机对接,以检索储存在电子计算机中的有关目录或所需的资料。使用简便,也很快速。过去由于目录控制不安全,有很多科学家花了很多时间、金钱,等做完研究之后,才发现别人早已做过相同的题目。如何有效的控制图书、期刊的目录,使研究人员在研究之初,即可预先检索,查知是否曾有人做过此类的研究,以节省人力、时间、金钱,就是今日资讯界所努力的目标之一。

一般来讲现有的资料库,大约有三类:

第一种是美国国会所制作的 MARC Record 机器可阅读的目录。美国国会图书馆有鉴于过去未有电子计算机处理编目,既费时,对于出版目录的时间,也要拖得相当久,乃改用此法,将所有书目输入电子计算机中编目,如此不但在输入上做得更快、更好,而且也更普遍化。

第二种是俄亥俄大学图书馆中心所建的联合编目及目录库。

以上两种都是属于书刊方面的,第三种则是现有的一百零八种期刊文献的索引及摘要。六月一日的统计,MARC Records 有九十多万件,OCLC Shared Cataloging Network 有三百五十多万件,而一百零八种索引及摘要的资料库也非常丰富,如生物学的摘要,有二百二十万件,化学摘要有二百八十万件,INSPEC 英国电机工程师学会所出之索引摘要约有一百三十万件,MEDLINE 有二百七十多万,New York Times Information Bank 有一百三十多万,Science Citation Index 有二百万件,World Patents Index 也有一百三十多万件的资料。

下面我再把刚才所说的三种类型的资料库,分别解释如下:

国会图书馆所做的 MARC 是从 1965 年开始的,最初三年是实验阶段,叫做 MARC

Pilot Project，国会图书馆选择了十几所大学及专门图书馆，由国会图书馆统一编目，然后将资料输入电子计算机中，再制成磁带，分送给各合作的图书馆来使用，并根据使用结果，提出改进的意见。三年后，国会图书馆根据收集的各馆意见，将原来的格式加以改进，现在已成为全世界国际性的电子计算机处理图书馆目录的标准格式。

第二是 OCLC Shared Cataloging Network 这一计划是从一九六七年开始，最初是由俄亥俄各大学及学院图书馆合作，设立一个全州图书馆编目服务中心，由中心替图书馆提供图书编目的服务、印制卡片。最初构想是用电脑处理来建立一个联合资料库，从一九六八年至一九七一年间，是用分批处理 Batch Process，即由每一个参加的图书馆将编目所需用的资料，填入表格中的每一项，然后再送到中心，输入电脑；经由电脑的处理，印成编目卡，再送回各图书馆。从 1971 年开始线上作业，每一个图书馆可以经由终端机与中心电脑直接连接，查寻编目资料，包括作者、书名、国会图书馆卡片号码，以及国际图书标准号码等。如果图书馆所收到的新书已经由中心编目了，各图书馆可由终端机将该馆的简名输入电脑中的联合资料库，过几天便可收到编好的卡片目录。根据统计资料，有百分之九十的新购图书资料，都能在中心资料库中找到，节省许多人力，对图书馆专业编目人员的精简也有很大的效果。因为绩效很好，一九七三年起，许多外州的图书馆也纷纷要求加入，到一九七七年，OCLC 已经变成全国性的有四十六个州、两千多图书馆参与的资料网。这一年 OCLC 改组为 OCLC Incorporate，而在俄亥俄州另成立一个 OHIONET，代表俄亥俄州与中心联络。

早期 OCLC 所做的工作一是图书编目，另一是建立一个联合图书目录的资料库。1977 年后，又增加了许多服务项目，一九八七年建立了一个期刊的 Sub-system，可以把期刊及所藏之卷数输入电脑中，不但可以检索本馆的学术期刊，同时也可检索其他图书馆期刊的收藏记录。今年三月又加了馆际互借的 Sub-system，以电子计算机处理馆际互借的各种手续，方便、省时、效率很高，只要三至五日即可收到回音，最近又要增加两个服务：在年底要加入采购系统，即在采购书时即将资料输入系统中，如此不但可以查出某书已经为某馆所购，且可查出某书现在正在某馆的采购单上，减少复本书，解决各馆重复购书的情形。明年三月要推出纳服务，读者可由终端机中得知每一本书入藏所在，及是否已被借出的记录，还可办理保留预约借书的手续，节省读者许多时间。终端机也不只是设在图书馆中，各院系办公室及宿舍都可安装，使用起来非常方便。

OCLC 在美国已成为非常成功与有效的系统，在张馆长的书中，也有一篇专论这一系统的译文。OCLC 早年有许多缺点，经过这几年的研究、改进，缺点已渐减少，检索的速度也加快，使它不但成为美国全国性的图书服务中心，同时也逐渐向世界各地扩展。

兹举 OCLC 在一九七八年 7 月 9 日到十五日作业情形：在这一周内，OCLC 一共有一千四百多个图书馆经由二千一百八十九各线上终端机与其连接，（但在我回台湾前，已经增加到二千多个，参加的图书馆书目不断在增加中）国会图书馆提供了三千多 MARC Records，但 OCLC 各图书馆自己所编之书目有一万七千七百万多种，较国会 MARC 所编的多了六倍；各馆所编图书总数目是二十八万多，印出卡片张数有二百多万张，连前所存之图书目录总数有四百多万册及二千多万个位置记录，平均每本图书有五个图书馆收藏。

OCLC 虽然是美国最大的图书馆合作系统，现在又有另外两个新的图书馆服务系统：一是 BALLOTS，是由史丹福大学图书馆开始使用，专为其图书馆本身电子计算机作业而设计的，后来慢慢扩充到加州整个大学图书馆系统，如今几个东部大学如耶鲁、哥伦比亚、及密西根大学等也都加入了。另一个则是在美国西北部的 Washington Library Network。

这两个系统规模虽较小,但在设计上却较 OCLC 有后来居上之势,OCLC 原先是编目中心,所有图书馆的资料都可输入,没有品质控制,因此资料完整程度不一,此外 OCLC 不能做 Subject 科目检索。而前述两个系统吸收了 OCLC 的经验,能作科目检索,效用也较大。然 OCLC 正积极往这方面发展,希望在一九八一年可以提供此种检索,如果成功,将给编目带来更大的改革。

上面所说的资料库,多半是处理图书方面的,至于期刊文章、学术研究报及其他资料的资料库情形:根据美国资讯科学会会报一九七八年八月期的一篇调查资料显示,一共有一百零八个资料库,所含之资料有三千一百多万。该篇调查对所有资料库的情形报道甚详,各位可以参考。

美国对资料库的使用情形是由代理上买下来,或租下各个资料库,再向使用的顾客收取使用费的。目前大的代理商有三个,另外像纽约时报的资料库,是不卖给代理商的,如果需要,必须与纽约时报资料库另订合同。三个代理商中最大的是在加州的 Lockheed,一九六五年只有一个资料库,储存资料是二十万件,到了一九七八年,已增至六十个资料库,共有一千八百万件的资料;使用率以一九七〇年为基准一百来算,到一九七三年,增加了二十倍,一九七五年则比一九七〇年增加了一百五十倍,但费用却从一九七〇年的百分之一百降低至百分之二十。

资料库的种类,大致说来有五种:

(1) 书目资料的资料库,如 Air Pollution Abstracts 它是包括图书、期刊及研究报告的目录。

(2) 新闻报道,如纽约时报的资料库,专收各种新闻资料。

(3) 是法院判案的实例及法令。这种资料对美国法律界是非常需要的。

(4) 是数据资料,如统计数字,美国联邦人口调查等等。这种资料库,近年发展的非常快速,而以后要查有关数据的资料,也将会越来越容易。

(5) 是图案、图书,如各种建筑图样、化学方程式等。

至于线上作业的优点,则是:

第一,它的准确性及包涵的范围很广,读者可以从小题目扩大或从小范围缩小,各种途径去找寻资料。

第二,使用者与电子计算机直接接触,使得在检索时,使用者可以伸缩所要查询的资料,或给予某些限制以得到最佳的效果。

第三,是检索查询的结果是立即的,普通检索所花的时间,大约是在五至十分钟左右。

第四,经济效益。目前每一检索所花之代价是美金十至二十五元,但在国外来说,这种价格实在还算便宜。因为如果根据索引摘要所印出来的资料,用人工来检索,所费之时间、金钱实在几倍于此。我建议国内使用者也该考虑到这些因素,因为印好的摘要索引非常贵,而且还需要再买合订本。国内较小的研究机构,如果没有此类摘要的收藏,使用次数也不高的话,利用线上检索,算起来依然便宜。

第五,线上作业可以做多种检索,可以检索过去或现在的资料,同时也有 SDI 的服务。

线上作业对图书馆的影响,目前较显著的有下列几点:

(1) 使图书馆图书编目的速度加快,而费用却相对降低。

(2) 促进图书馆目录格式的标准化。

（3）提供图书馆使用者更完整、更有效的图书目录。
（4）增进馆际图书互借及合作。
（5）扩大图书馆的资源，使图书馆的藏书，不仅限于本身所藏有的。
（6）促成图书资料网的建立。
（7）目前图书馆所用的编目卡片有被线上目录所取代的趋势。

（原载《图书馆规划与媒体技术：图书馆实务研讨会会议记录》，台湾师范大学图书馆编，1980年，第14—17页。）

俄亥俄大学图书馆的图书馆自动化：过去、现在与未来

Library Automation at Ohio University Library: Past, Present and Future[①]

DEDICATION

This paper, a shorter form of which was written for the First Pacific Conference on New Information Technology for Library and Information Professionals held in Bangkok, Thailand on June 16 – 18, 1987, is dedicated respectfully to Dr. Chiang Fu-Tsung, Director Emeritus of the National Palace Museum and former Director of the National Central Library, in honor of his ninetieth birthday, and to join with others, in recognition of his profound leadership and contributions to library development over a span of sixty years.

I. Introduction

Historically American libraries have been in the forefront in applying information technologies: from the origins of the Hollerith punched card tabulating system in the latter part of the 19th century; through the growing use of micrographics in the 1930s; photocopying and data processing equipment in the 1950s; the wide-spread application of succeeding generations of computers and the accompanying developments in telecommunications in the 1960s and 1970s; to the mass storage as exemplified in optical discs in the 1980s. The pace of innovation accelerates as each new technology is adopted and refined.[②]

A comprehensive state university of 23,000 students founded in 1804, Ohio University has a main campus in Athens, Ohio, and five regional campuses in surrounding Southeastern Ohio. Just as in many American academic libraries, Ohio University Library has been in the main stream of information technology applications and library automation. Since the beginning of OCLC under its former name, Ohio College Library Center, back in 1967, the Ohio University Library has been an active participant and supporter. The case history of Ohio University Library in the applications of information technology and in library automation can be seen as fairly representative of many other academic libraries in North America. For the past three decades, despite differences in strategy, approach, and timing among academic libraries, the general trend has been largely parallel with that which I will describe for Ohio University.

II. Significant Developments in the 1960s

In the 1960s, computers were too expensive for most libraries and library applications software was generally unavailable, yet several major developments with far-reaching impact on library automation were initiated. These included the MEDLARS (Medical Literature Analysis and Retrieval System) project of the National Library of Medicine, the INTREX (Information Transfer Experiment) project by the Massachusetts Institute of Technology, the design and implementation of the MARC (Machine Readable Cataloging) format by the Library of Congress, and the establishment of the Ohio College Library Center (OCLC) by a group of academic libraries in Ohio, including Ohio University. At about the same time, Stanford University initiated its BALLOTS (Bibliographic Automation of Large Library Operations Using A Time Sharing System)

---

① This paper is a shorter form of which was written for the First Pacific Conference on New Information Technology for Library and Information Professionals held in Bangkok, Thailand on June 16 – 18, 1987.

② Stephen R. Salmon. "Library Automation." In *Encyclopedia of Library and Information Science* (New York: Marcel Dekker, 1975), V. 14, pp. 338 – 445.

project which evolved into the Research Libraries Information Network (RLIN). Another important trend in the 1960s was the beginning by many abstracting and indexing services to use computers in photo composition and typesetting of printed publications. This made possible machine searchable databases.

The MEDLARS Project and subsequent medical information network developed by the National Library of Medicine has benefited immeasurably medical and health sciences libraries and the professionals whom they serve. The INTREX project, from 1965 to 1973, reaffirmed the design concept that large libraries could become information transfer systems. But, as we assess the importance of the major developments in the 1960s, the most significant and far-reaching were probably the design in 1965 of a MARC format for bibliographic data (which is machine-readable, largely interchangeable, and internationally acceptable) and the establishment in 1967 of OCLC. The beginning distribution on magnetic tapes of MARC-formatted cataloging records by the Library of Congress undoubtedly affected the design of OCLC and its first computer-based shared cataloging and union catalog system. Other than these major applications, library automation in the 1960s tended to replicate manual processes including the use of computers for the production of catalog cards, accession lists, serial holdings, and the like.

III. The Mushrooming of OCLC in the 1970s

The founding of OCLC in 1967 by a small number of academic library members of the Ohio College Association and the Inter-University Library Council, which consisted of library directors of state universities in Ohio, followed sixteen years of study and deliberation and also involved the Ohio Library Association. [1] It was only after the successful implementation of the MARC project in November 1966 that cooperative, shared cataloging on a centralized computer system became practical. Through the foresight of the Ohio academic librarians and the effective leadership of Mr. Frederic G. Kilgour, Executive Director of OCLC from its inception in 1967 to his retirement in 1980, OCLC grew by leaps and bounds from a small organization of two staff members, with an initial budget of $67,000 and 54 participating libraries in Ohio to a complex organization of over 800 staff members, with a budget of $46 million in 1986 and a growing membership of 6,000 libraries of all types in the U.S. and 14 other countries. (Diagram 1) Initially OCLC provided a computer-based cataloging system in batch process mode. This was upgraded to an online, interactive mode in 1971. On August 26, 1971, Ohio University Library entered the first member-produced cataloging record online. Although the system immediately crashed, Ohio University Library ended that day with 147 titles cataloged. During the first two days an average of ten titles per terminal hour were entered. The instant success of the OCLC shared cataloging system attracted other Ohio libraries and, soon, libraries in other states. Reflecting broader library membership and geographical distribution, OCLC in 1977 changed its name to OCLC, Inc. In 1981, with the adoption of a new governance structure, the legal name became the OCLC Online Computer Library Center, Incorporated. [2]

Most significant in OCLC's growth was the expansion of its cataloging database. From its 1971 beginning, the database reached its one millionth record in September 1974, a period of over three years. The second million records took 18 months to accumulate. As the number of members increased so did the rate of growth in the records. The most recent million records, to 15 million, in December 1986 took only four months! This has made OCLC the largest and fastest growing bibliographic database in the world [3]. According to OCLC, of the 15 million bibliographic records, 80 percent were contributed by OCLC members. The remaining 20 percent were provided

---

[1] Lewis C. Branscomb and A. Robert Rogers. "The Conception and Birth Pangs of OCLC-An Account of the Struggles of the Formative Years." *College and Research Libraries*. V. 42, No. 4 (July 1981): pp. 303–307.

[2] Kathleen L. Maciuszko. OCLC, *A Decade of Development, 1967–1977* (Littleton, Colorado: Libraries Unlimited, 1984): p. 376.

[3] Diagram II

by the Library of Congress, the National Library of Medicine, the National Agricultural Library, the National Library of Canada, the U.S. Government Printing Office, and, recently, the British Library. Benefitting from the size and currency of the database, OCLC users can locate cataloging records from OCLC for 94 percent of the items they catalog and thus need to perform original cataloging for only 6 percent of their materials. This is a considerable saving in terms of time and cost in cataloging by member libraries. ①

Adding to OCLC's success is its online interlibrary loan system introduced in 1979. The system is built on the shared database which includes 243 million member-location symbols. OCLC reports that in 1986 more than 3,100 libraries used the system to enter an average of 55,000 borrowing requests per week. Better than 90 percent of the requests can be verified online and 87 percent are filled. Facilitated by electronic library-to-library communication through the OCLC telecommunications system, interlibrary loan items are shipped by mail or UPS to borrowers within an average of four days. ②

Although in recent years OCLC's services have extended to many other areas including serials control, acquisitions and a decentralized, minicomputer-based local system—US/2000, Ohio University has chosen to participate only in OCLC's online union catalog, shared cataloging, and interlibrary loan components. These, in our judgment, represent the services best offered centrally to facilitate resource sharing and take advantage of economies of scale. Other OCLC services are either less competitive or were offered too late.

While OCLC was concentrating on improving services at the national level in the late 1970s and early 1980s, many libraries were looking for local systems for local library functions. The trend in the late 1970s was to develop or purchase a local system for circulation, online public access catalog, etc., which could interface (often through tape loading) with the OCLC online union catalog and shared cataloging service. Such a system enables a library to participate in OCLC for shared cataloging and interlibrary loans while downloading the OCLC-created MARC catalog records into local computer storage to support local activities in such areas as circulation, acquisitions, fund accounting, serials check-in, and online public access catalog. The availability of the online public access catalog to replace the century-old card catalog and the COM (Computer-Output-Microform) catalog of the 1960s and 1970s is widespread in the 1980s. The OCLC online union catalog is, and will continue to be, the single most important cataloging and interlibrary loan tool, but its lack of subject access and cryptic search keys have made it unattractive as an online public access catalog, although this may be overcome with the refinements scheduled now for 1988. The declining cost and expanding power of minicomputers and microcomputers as well as the availability of software packages for library functions have lured many libraries to seek local alternatives either individually or in clusters.

IV. The Development of the Local Alice System in the 1980s③

In 1978, Ohio University opted to explore locally integrated library systems capable of interfacing with OCLC but operated independently on a dedicated minicomputer. The result has been the successful implementation of the ALICE system which became operational in July 1983.

In September 1978, a task force to explore local library systems was formed to investigate possibilities and approaches. Consisting of library and computer center staff, faculty, and students, the task force sought an integrated system which would use OCLC for shared cataloging and interlibrary loan but would support, in modular form, circulation, an online public access

---

① *OCLC Services for Libraries: Questions and Answers* (Dublin, Ohio: OCLC, Winter 1986/87), p. 3.
② *Ibid.*, pp. 3-4.
③ Hwa-Wei Lee, K. Mulliner, E. Hoffmann-Pinther, and H. McCauley. "Alice at One: Candid reflections on the adoption, installation, and use of the Virginia Tech Library System (VTLS) at Ohio University." In Second National Conference on Integrated Online library Systems. *Proceedings.* September 13 and 14, 1984. Atlanta, Georgia. Ed. by David C. Genaway. Canfield, Ohio: Genaway and Associates, Inc., 1984: pp. 228-242.

catalog, acquisitions, and other library functions. The system should be based on a central database created from the OCLC MARC records with added holdings and location information as well as the barcode number. The task force considered circulation and online catalog among the first priorities. Throughout 1980 and 1981, the task force studied nearly all available systems. On-site visits and presentations by vendors to the staff were arranged. In December 1981 the Virginia Tech Library System (VTLS), designed and developed by Virginia Polytechnic Institute and State University in Blacksburg, Virginia, was selected for the following reasons:

1. Provision for an integrated library system with an online linkage to OCLC's cataloging and the utilization of MARC records to create the local database.

2. Immediate availability of an automated circulation system and online public access catalog, with planned expansion to include serials control, acquisitions, and management information. All of which complement the OCLC cataloging and interlibrary loan subsystems.

3. Ease of use of the system by both staff and patrons. Searches can be by author, title, subject, keyword, call number, and others.

4. Reasonable cost of the software package and the annual maintenance fee compared with other available systems. (When Ohio University contracted for the software in 1982, the cost was $20,000 plus an annual maintenance fee of $3,000. The annual maintenance entitles the library to all enhancements released during the year.)

5. The quality and vision of the personnel on the VTLS team (including a common experience in an academic environment).

6. The degree of local control and flexibility allowed by the system, including local networking and short-form cataloging.

Recognizing that an automated library system requires a database of machine-readable cataloging records, the library, in 1979, began a massive effort to convert pre-1971 cataloging records to machine-readable MARC format with grants and gifts totaling $400,000. As the first library to participate in OCLC, the Ohio University was fortunate to own a large machine-readable database for materials cataloged online since 1971. With the pre-1971 cataloging records converted after 1979, when the VTLS System was installed in August 1982, nearly 400,000 catalog records, representing nearly one million volumes, were ready to be loaded from archival tapes. These comprised about 80 percent of the Library's monographs, excluding titles in governmental documents and a large portion of the microform, maps, and non-print collections which were indexed or cataloged manually. Typical of designated depositories of the U. S. government documents, the library maintains a separate collection arranged by the Superintendent of Documents classification number (based on issuing body rather than subject content) that relies on the printed Monthly Catalog of the United States Government Publications (and annual commutations) for access. At the same time that Ohio University was celebrating its centennial as a designated depository in 1986, we purchased the cataloging retrospective records on MARC tapes from the Government and have loaded these into the local database as an integral part of the online public access catalog. A similar effort was made to purchase cataloging records on MARC tapes for major microform sets which are becoming available through OCLC as a result of its (and RLIN's) Major Microforms Project.

With the signing of a contract with VTLS and the ordering and installation of a Hewlett Packard minicomputer (HP 3000/40) hardware and other peripheral equipment in the early part of 1982, a search for a name for the local system resulted in selecting ALICE, with a credit to Lewis Carroll's Alice in Wonderland and suggesting the wonderland which the system would open for library users. Clinching the argument, was the song, "White Rabbit", in which the Jefferson Airplane advised, "Go ask Alice, I think she'll know" —exactly the attitude we hoped to cultivate toward the new system. (Diagram III)

With the strong support of the University's Computing and Learning Services, where the Library's HP 3000 system is housed, installation and tape loading went well. The barcoding of a large portion of the library collection was time consuming, involving a majority of the library staff in 1982 and 1983. The completion of the tape loading in July 1983 enabled the library to formally inaugurate the online public access catalog and close its card catalog on July 15, 1983. Because creation of a patron file required additional preparation, the circulation function was implemented in September that year. By linking the library computer to the university-wide computer network from the beginning, the online catalog is accessible not only by library terminals located on every floor and in every service area of the main library building and the detached Music and Dance Library in the Music Building but also by terminals connected to the University network throughout the Athens campus. Dial access by microcomputers or terminals equipped with modems is also available regardless of location or distance. (Diagram IV) This is a special feature only an online system can provide. Almost immediately, the libraries on the five regional campuses took advantage of this capability.

Because VTLS included networking in its design, the Regional Campuses located 50 to 125 miles from Athens, have been able to network with the main library in the full use of VTLS for their library automation in a shared environment. The Lancaster campus was the first to become a secondary account of VTLS, and by 1985, had every feature that is available in Athens. By sharing the central computer but maintaining a separate database, O. U. -Lancaster has its own database and holdings for its users yet, by a simple command, they can switch to our much larger database and holdings. Conversely, users in Athens can also view the Lancaster database. At the present time, we are in the process of replicating this with other campuses, some by dedicated telephone lines and others by microwave telecommunications. (Diagram V)

Of course, every expansion of the local system requires the upgrading of the computer and peripheral equipment. Since the installation of an HP 3000/40 in 1982, we have upgraded to an HP 3000/64 in 1983, HP 3000/68 in 1984 and, most recently, to an HP 3000/70 in 1987. The expansion of the CPU was accompanied by adding more and more storage capacities [from three 404 megabyte (MB) disc drives (totaling 1,212 MB) in 1982 to seven 404 MB and two 570 MB drives (totaling 3,968 MB) in 1987]. The total value of the central hardware in 1987 approaches $400,000. (Appendix I)

As the only major library in Southeastern Ohio, the Ohio University Library serves as the back-up resource library for public libraries in ten surrounding counties grouped under the Ohio Valley Area Libraries (OVAL). Through State Library . funding, Ohio University Library provides reference and interlibrary loan services to OVAL libraries which amounted to 13,727 requests in 1986. There have been discussions of a computer network with the OVAL libraries based at Ohio University.① At the same time, the library of Hocking Technical College, located 15 miles north of Athens and whose students and faculty use the Ohio University Library heavily, is planning to join in a network similar to the one established for the Lancaster campus. The opportunities for resource sharing in the region will be greatly enhanced when these networks are completed. (See Diagram V for location of OVAL libraries and other community and technical colleges in the region.)

V. The Growth of Online Database Searching

Paralleling the development of library automation since the 1960s has been the development of computerized databases by indexing and abstracting firms. Ohio University Library began online database search service in its Health Sciences Library first in 1978. This was followed by a library-wide Computerized Information Retrieval Service (CIRS) inaugurated in 1979. Currently, we have online access to more than 300 databases in a variety of subject areas. In addition to those available in DIALOG and BRS, we also have direct access to MEDLARS, Wilsonline, LEXIS/NEXIS, OhioPi (Ohio Public Information), etc. The number of searches made has increased from 319 in 1980 to 1,600 in 1986, a fivefold increase in six years. To moderate the costs, users

---

① Jose-Marie Griffiths and Carolyn J. Goshen. *A Systems Analysis for the Ohio Valley Area Libraries (OVAL). Final Report.* Rockville, Maryland: King Research, Inc., 1985: p. 129.

without external funding are subsidized for one-half the cost by the Library. In 1986, 780 student searches received a subsidy, at a cost to the Library of $4,777.

Our original hardware, the Texas Instruments terminal, with its lack of memory and 300 baud transmission speed, was surpassed in efficiency by developments in personal computer technology. In 1983, the Library acquired an IBM-PC, equipped with a 1200 baud modem. We chose Smartcom II as the communication software. This system permitted downloading of data and printing at a faster speed, and increased the cost effectiveness of searching, thus lowering patron costs. Additional hardware purchases, from 1984 to the present, have upgraded our system to an IBM-XT with 20 megabytes of hard disk storage and 2400 baud modem. In 1986, the average cost per search in Health Sciences was $5.48 compared to $19.02 in other areas. The variation is due to the low cost of the government supported MEDLARS system used heavily and exclusively in Health Sciences. Further, as a means of providing fast and better reference service, guidelines were established on the use of CIRS for reference service at the discretion of the reference staff, free of charge. Thus the library absorbs the cost of "ready reference".

VI. Experimenting with New and Emerging Information Technologies

In coping with the ever growing new and emerging information technologies which have flooded the market place, Ohio University library has taken a number of steps to prepare itself for the inevitable. The future prospects are not only exciting but challenging. Among the steps taken are:

1. Expanding non-print collections include many new formats.

Beginning in the 1960s the Library deliberately expanded its Microform Collection as more scholarly and research materials became available on that format. In the 1970s and 1980s, the federal government has also published and distributed more and more of its publications in microfiche. To save space, money, and material, the library also decided early in 1979 to subscribe to both a paper copy and a microform copy of a number of selected journals and to discard the paper copy after the peak-use period. For the first time, in 1986 the library collection on microforms exceeded that in printed volumes (1,319,107 microform vs 1,284,130 printed volumes). It is typical that in 1986 the library added 85,978 new microform units compared to 49,432 new printed volumes.

Not only has the Library expanded it microform collections but it also has added a multitude of other new formats including audio and video cassettes, disks, optical discs, videodiscs, etc. To adequately service these newer formats, the Library has acquired a range of new equipment including digitizing/scanning equipment for image preservation and desk-top publishing.

2. Experimenting with the use of CD-ROM based information.

The coming of age for CD-ROM laser disc technology demands new knowledge, skills and methods of handling this Read-Only-Memory compact disc. To develop these, the Library has acquired reference tools on CD-ROM with required IBM PCs and disc players: *ERIC Index*, *Books-in-Print Plus*, *Ulrich's Guide to Periodicals*, *the MEDLINE file*, *psych INFO*, *Dissertation Abstracts*, and the *Academic American Encyclopedia* by Grolier. By use of this CD-ROM based information, the library hopes to develop methods and procedures for the handling of such technology to the best advantage. It is anticipated that end-user searching on CD-ROM will ease the demand for online searching (CIRS) while serving increasing numbers of users without the cost of online searching.

3. Experimenting with the use of a telefacsimile machine (fax) for document delivery and reference service.

Commencing in June 1986 the Health Sciences Library of Ohio University was chosen by the State Library of Ohio to operate an experimental telefacsimile network for the transmission of biomedical information in a multitype library environment. Seventeen Ohio libraries of various types are participating in the experiments. The focus of the one-year project is to study need, reliability, and speed in using telefacsimile equipment as a document delivery device for health related and biomedical interlibrary loan requests. The Fax equipment installed at all 17 sites is the Pitney Bowes 8150 costing $2,300 each.

While the state funded project was underway, the Vice Provost responsible for regional campuses also purchased and placed Fax equipment in the library of each regional campus. Although the Fax equipment on the regional campuses was, primarily for use in information transmission by the deans of these campuses and the Vice Provost, the libraries also use it for document delivery.

4. Providing 35 computer terminals and 50 stand-alone microcomputers for students and faculty in the library.

This has been done since 1982 in cooperation with the University's Computing and Learning Services (UCLS) with the library providing space necessary for the computer lab and UCLS providing both hardware and software. The laboratory was the first of many of its kind established on the Athens campus which are staffed and maintained by UCLS. The centrally linked computer terminals in these labs provide additional means to access the ALICE online catalog.

5. Providing microcomputers to every library department for use by the library staff.

To facilitate office automation, about 20 microcomputers (including 4 OCLC M-300 workstations that double as microcomputers) have been installed in library departments over the last three years. This is about one PC for every four regular staff. Microcomputers have been in use since 1982, but with an initial emphasis on sharing. Staff members have been encouraged to learn the use of microcomputer for data and word processing. One local area network (LAN) is in use and the Library has access to the University's wide area network (WAN). Many courses and workshops in the applications of microcomputer have been offered by UCLS and the Library. Several staff have since become experienced in microcomputers and have shared their expertise with others. Applications include calculation of the Library's acquisitions formula using Super Calc 4, specialized departmental databases, a variety of special bibliographies, a remote bulletin Board (RBBS) for Health Science faculty, and, most recently, desk-top publishing.

VII. Summary and Conclusion

In reviewing library automation at Ohio University during the last three decades with particular regard to the use of computers, the picture matches nearly exactly that described by Richard DeGennaro in 1983:

"We are well into our third decade of library automation. The first decade, the 1960s, was dominated by primitive local systems. The second decade, the 1970s, was dominated by large multitype and multipurpose library networks. The current and third decade, the 1980s, will be dominated by a return to local systems. But this time they will be sophisticated multifunction turnkey systems on mini- and micro-computers; and they will have lines to a variety of library and commercial networks on large mainframes." [1]

The general trend of moving from centralization in the 1970s to the decentralization in the 1980s and beyond, according to his reasoning, has been "shaped and driven by the cost and capabilities of the computer and telecommunications technologies..." of that time period. [2]

Such has been our experience. Ohio University Will seek to further refine its local ALICE system and to fully implement all functions making it a completely integrated system. The

---

[1] Richard De Gennaro. "library Automation and Networking Perspectives on Three Decades." *Library Journal*. Vol. 108, No. 7 (April 1, 1983): p.629.

[2] *Ibid*.

exploration of the potentials and impacts of CD-ROM and other new information technologies will continue. As the cost for computers further decreases and their capacity expands, it may be desirable that ALICE networking among regional campuses and other cooperating libraries be changed toward a distributed configuration. Appropriate employment of new information technologies for library services is necessary to harness the changing information environment and demands in the years ahead.

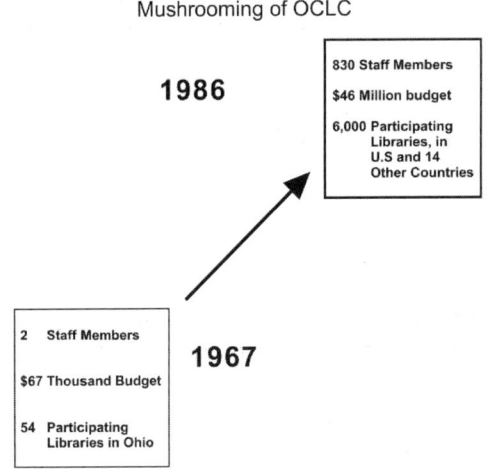

DIAGRAM I Mushrooming of OCLC

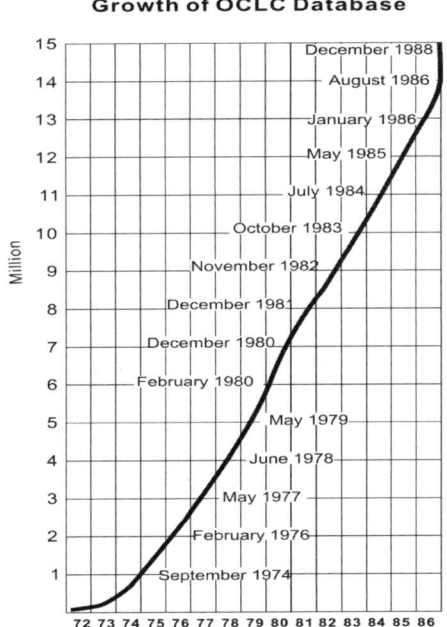

DIAGRAM II Growth of OCLC Database

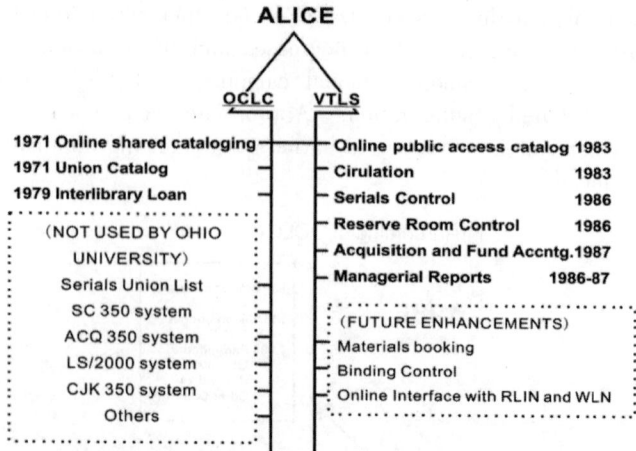

DIAGRAM III The Development of Local ALICE System in the 1980's

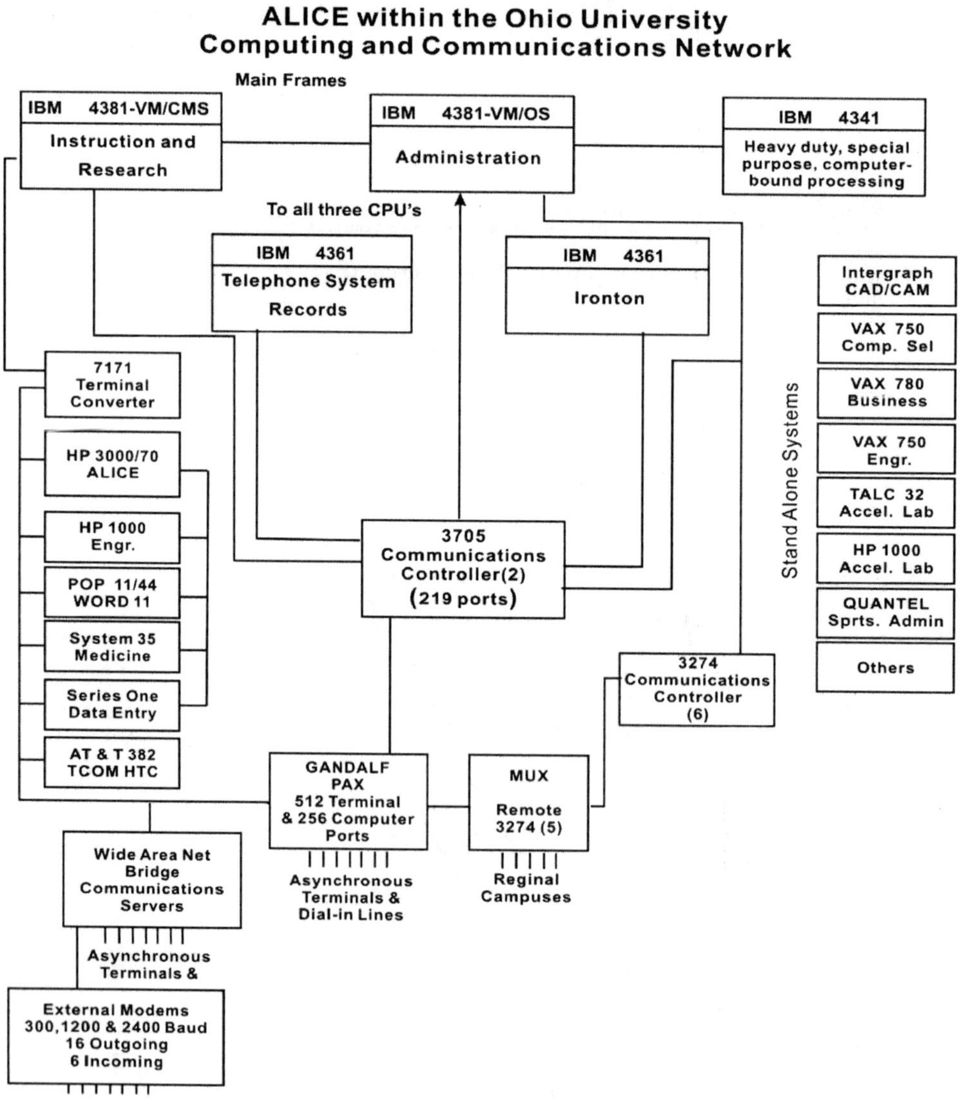

DIAGRAM IV within the Ohio University Computing and Communications Network

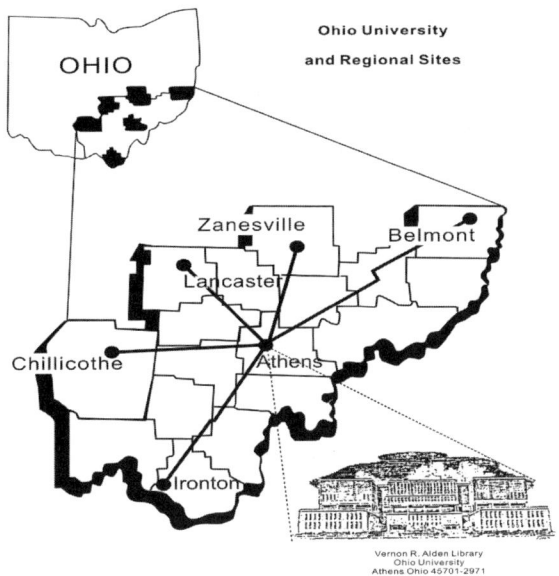

DIAGRAM V Ohio University and Regional Sites

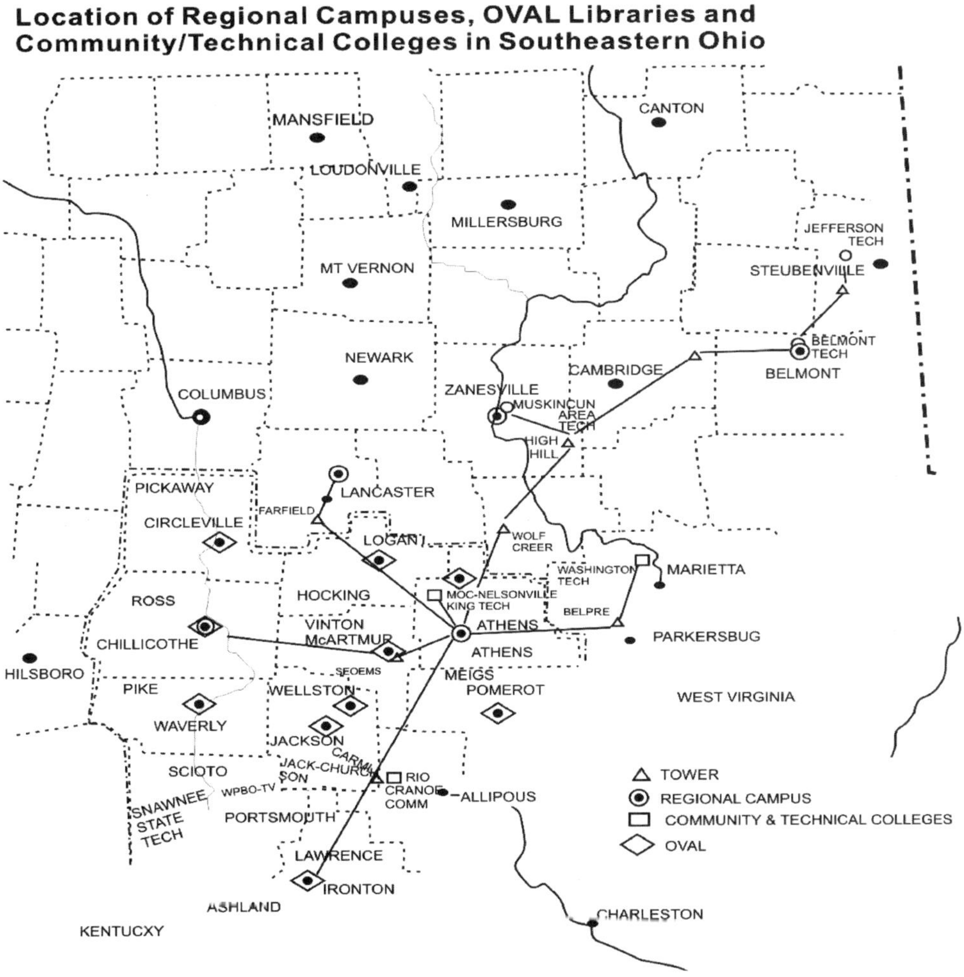

DIAGRAM VI Location of Regional Campuses, OVAL Libraries and Community/Technical Colleges in Southeastern Ohio

APPENDIX I
ALICE-OCLC/VTLS EQUIPMENT

Located at Haning Hall (University Computing and Learning Services)
1—HP3000/70, 7MB computer (with Disc Caching and Turbo Image), UB-MIT Delta II operating system, 336 ports available, 87 ports in use
7—404 MB disc drives
2—571 MB disc drives
2—Dual density tape drive: 6,250 BPI
1—Standard HP console
5—General interface controller for disc drives
1—HP 37212 A intelligent modem
1— HP 2563 printer
59—Micom modems

Located in Southeast Asia Collection and Microform, Map and Non-Print Collections (1st Floor, Alden Library)
1—M300 terminal
1—Facit printer
2—ADM-5 terminals
2—MICOM modems
1—Paradyne modem

Located in Fine Arts Collection (2nd Floor, Alden Library)
2—ADM-5 terminals
2—MICOM modems

Located in Reserve Reading Room (3rd Floor, Alden Library)
1—ADM-5 terminal
4—QUME terminals
1—Facit 4511 serial matrix printer
3—Barcode readers
5— MICOM modems

Located in Health Sciences Library (3rd Floor, Alden library)
2—ADM-5 terminal
2—MICOM modem

Located in Circulation Department (4th Floor, Alden Library)
1—HP 150 microcomputer with 2 disk drives (system backup) and barcode reader
1—HP inkjet printer (connected to microcomputer)
4—ADM-5 terminals with barcode readers
1—Intermec barcode printer—Code 39
1—HP2631B printer
5—MICOM modems

Located in Acquisitions Department (4th Floor, Alden Library)
1—OCLC terminal (M300 work station)
1—ADM-5 terminal
1—Interface unit (VTLS) with T-Bar
1—MICOM modems
1—Facit 4511 serial matrix printer

1—Short form line extender

Located in Cataloging Department (4th Floor, Alden Library)
2—OCLC/100 terminals
2—OCLC/105 terminals
3—M300 terminals
6—ADM-5 terminals
4—Concept 108 (ALA character set) terminals
3—Interface units (VTLS) with 3 T-bars
10—MICOM modems
4—INTERMEC barcode readers
2—Estern Union printers
2—Facit 4511 serial matrix printers
1—Paradyne modem (OCLC use)

Located in Reference Department (4th Floor, Alden Library)
1—OCLC 105 terminal
5—ADM-5 terminals
5—MICOM modems

Located in Interlibrary Loan (4th Floor, Alden Library)
1—ADM-5 terminal w/bar code reader
1—MICOM modem

Located in Archives & Special Collections (5th Floor, Alden Library)
1—ADM-5 terminal
1—MICOM modem

Located in Government Documents Dept (5th Floor, Alden Library)
2—ADM-5 terminals
2—MICOM modems

Located in Music and Dance Library (5th Floor, Music Building)
2—ADM-5 terminals for public use
1—ADM-5 terminal with barcode reader for circulation
4—MICOM modems
1—HP 150 microcomputer with 2 disk drives (system backup)

Terminals in public areas
12—ADM-5 (standing) plus 1 with Okidata printer attached, public catalog area, 4th floor entry
3—ADM-5 (seated), public catalog area, 4th floor entry
4—ADM-5 (seated), 2 each on 6th and 7th floor, main stack area
3—Ports for dial access or through intra-university computer network
19—MICOM modems

(Published in *Collection of Essays Honoring Chiang Wei-Tang on His Ninetieth Birthday*. Taipei, Taiwan, Library Association of China, 1987.)

20世纪60年代以来美国图书馆自动化的重要里程碑[①]

Major Milestones in American Library Automation Since the 1960s

60年代

美国图书馆自动化虽然起步较早,但真正讲自动化应该算是60年代才开始,当时因为大型电脑在大学及一般社会逐渐被普遍使用,替图书馆自动化的发展奠定了一个非常好的基础。60年代美国图书馆自动化的重要发展包括下列几项:

(1) 美国国家医学图书馆的MEDLARS(医学文献分析和检索系统)。
(2) 麻省理工学院的INTREX(资讯传递实验)。
(3) 美国国会图书馆的MARC(机读编目格式)。
(4) 俄亥俄州的OCLC(俄亥俄州学术图书馆中心)。
(5) 史丹福大学的BALLOTS(大型目录自动化的分时系统)。
(6) 大型文摘及索引机构开始使用电脑。

其中MEDLARS(Medical Literature Analysis and Retrieval System)是首次美国大型图书馆用电脑将其医学文献输入资料库中作为分析检索之用的系统。INTREX(Information Transfer Experiment)则系由麻省理工学院发展出来的,台湾大学李德竹教授曾参与这个计划。BALLOTS(Bibliography Automation of Large Library Operations Using a Time-Sharing System)是由史丹福大学发展出来,BALLOTS是目前与OCLC竞争比较激烈的RLIN(Research Library Information Network)系统的前身;此外,还有一项对70年代连机检索发展具有重要影响的,即是大型文摘及索引机构开始使用电脑,例如,化学文摘(Chemical Abstract)它是一个很大的资料库,每一年用人力整理出来的资料约五十多万篇,根据估计,一篇化学方面的文章从刊登在期刊上到收入化学文摘再被印出供读者查阅,通常需要一年到一年半左右的时间。因此为争取时效性,以电脑代替人力确是十分重要的。用人工检索到印成索引约需3个月,但如用电脑来做,则今天输进去,立刻就能印出来,将时间上的差距减至最低。

以上是60年代几项重要发展,同时在当时的图书馆界还有几个共同的现象:①较具规模的图书馆使用大型电脑来进行自动化业务,发展较大的系统。②自动化的情形不够普遍,因当时的电脑不但体积大、容量小、速度慢,而且有关图书馆自动化的软体系统多半尚未发展出来,故很多图书馆虽然想做自动化,但必须投入许多时间及人力去研究软体,因此自动化的情形并不普遍。

70年代至80年代初期

到了70年代,由于OCLC的急速成长为图书馆带来极大的方便,使整个情况又有了变化;创立于1967年,迄今不过二十余年,但其发展速度确实十分惊人,从以下统计数字即可明显看出(见下表):

[①] 本文由台湾"中央图书馆"陈冬兰小姐根据作者1989年6月2日在该馆的演讲记录整理而成。

	1967	1988
工作人员	2	885
经费	$67,000	$95,700,000
参与图书馆	54	9,400
包括地区	俄亥俄州	全美 50 州及 26 个其他国家
资料库	0	19,000,000

另外，在"OCLC1987/88"的工作报告中亦指出，OCLC 现有 8,481 个工作站，利用 OCLC 联合编目的次数已达二千一百余万次，各图书馆向 OCLC 购买卡片的量约在一亿一千五百万笔左右，OCLC 虽是非营利机构，但去年一年即净赚一千万美金。在资料库增长率方面，头一个百万笔资料的累积花了 4 年的时间（1971—1974 年），而现在每 100 万笔资料增加只需要 4~5 个月的时间，到 1988 年，卡片纪录累积已将近两千万笔，成长率不可谓不惊人。

前面提过，OCLC 创立于 1967 年，初名 Ohio College Library Center，到了 1977 年，OCLC 成为全国性自动化网路中心，故改名为 OCLC Inc.，自 1981 年起开始向全世界的图书馆进军，而不再以 Ohio 为代表，遂改全名为 Online Computer Library Center，仍简称 OCLC。OCLC 为图书馆带来最大的好处是它替图书馆省下了一大笔在编目方面的花费。以俄亥俄大学图书馆为例，1967 年参加之前，该馆编目部门有 15 名专业馆员，一年约编 25,000 册新书；而现在每年编新书约 50,000 册左右，专业编目馆员只有 5 位，工作人员比当初少了三分之二，但是工作成果却是原来的两倍。不仅人事费用减少，编目工作本身亦然，过去以人工编目，一般图书馆估计一本书约要花 10~15 美元，现由 OCLC 来统一编目，各图书馆利用 OCLC 的书目资料库编一本书付给 OCLC1.15 美元，再加上人工费用还不到 5 美元，如果图书馆欲编之书不在资料库中，则由该馆自行编目，编好后由 OCLC 付给 0.5 美元作为赔偿，因此 OCLC 对图书馆的编目具有相当大的贡献。

OCLC 另外一项很成功的业务则是 OCLC 的馆际互借（Library Loan），因为 OCLC 的资料库相当大（收录了九千多所图书馆约二千万笔书目资料），如果读者想借某书而该馆没有，则可利用 OCLC 连线目录，查出哪些图书馆收藏该书，再挑出其中 5 所图书馆，排定先后顺序，输入连线电脑里，第一所图书馆在接到讯息后的 24 小时内如无法提供该书，则会将此讯息自动转到第二个图书馆，依序类推之，就"馆际互借"来说，OCLC 的确扮演了相当重要的角色。

尽管 OCLC 对图书馆的业务提供相当大的帮助，但难免仍有些缺点存在。第一，OCLC 的书目资料库可以用 author，title，LC card No. 来检索，但却无法以 subject 来检索，因此仍不能完全取代卡片目录。第二，通信费用太高，因为 OCLC 网络是由 OCLC 位于中心，所有九千多所图书馆直接跟 OCLC 连线，检索时每一分每一秒都要算钱，是故通信费用相当高；正因为无法用 subject 检索加上 通信费用太高，因此 OCLC 没有发展采访（Acquisition）、流通（Circulation）、读者公共检索目录（OPAC）等系统。当各图书馆意识到不能再等 OCLC 提供这些系统，逐渐开始自行发展其他各项业务的自动化。除了上述原因外，70 年代中型电脑的普遍化使其价格日低而功能却愈来愈强，促使更多图书馆有能力发展自动化，因此 70 年代对图书馆发展自动化而言，可谓是"水到渠成"的时代。

以下介绍俄亥俄大学图书馆利用中型电脑发展出来的网路系统，这在 70 年代是很普遍的现象。俄亥俄大学创立于 1804 年，现设有 10 个学院、5 所分校，全校学生共约 24,000 人。该校的图书馆自动化系统称为 ALICE（爱丽丝系统），其结构大致如下：

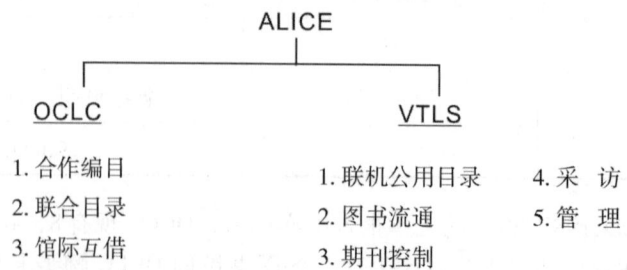

ALICE 系统除沿用原 OCLC 提供之合作编目、联合目录、馆际互借三项业务，另加上新发展出的系统进行联合公用目录、图书流通、期刊控制、采访、管理等作业。图书馆的电脑跟学校的主机是相连的，因此不论校内或校外，只要有一台微电脑（Microcomputer）及适当的调变器（MODEM）每位教授及学生都可直接检索学校图书馆里的资料，而不需亲自到图书馆去。甚至可在家中编制论文的书目资料档或可将图书馆的资料转入自己的电脑建立个人的资料库。而俄亥俄大学的各分校亦可透过地区网路分享校本部的自动化系统。因为学校的电脑主机是全天性 24 小时开放，故即使夜间图书馆关门后，教授或学生仍可自家中电脑检索图书馆的资料。

70 年代除了由各大学发展自动化软体系统外，还有不少商业机构投入这个市场。根据今年 3 月份 *Library Journal* 里一篇自动化市场现况报告中指出，目前美国国内约有 50 个厂商研究发展不同的地区性系统。而 VTLS 就是其中之一，它具有下列优点：

（1）VTLS 是一个一体化的集体系统（Integrated system），它可以与 OCLC 衔接，并直接使用 OCLC 的 MARC。

（2）VTLS 可以提供 OCLC 所缺乏的各种功能。

（3）它是为方便图书馆使用者而设计的，易于检索及使用。

（4）它的价钱较公道。

（5）它仍在继续发展及不断的改进中。

（6）它起初是专为大学图书馆之用而设计的，现已扩及其他类型的图书馆如农业图书馆、法律图书馆等，连马来西亚国家图书馆也采用它。

（7）它较有弹性，能配合各图书馆的个别需要，而且可以建立地区网路。

以上所述为 70 年代后期、80 年代初期美国图书馆自动化的发展，由于中型电脑的普遍使用，价格的下跌加上功能日益增强，使图书馆界多致力于各地区性系统的发展。

80 年代后期

80 年代后期有两项特色：

1. 微电脑的普遍使用

由于微电脑的普及，促成许多小的图书馆也开始建立自己的自动化系统，但当资料超过 50 万到 100 万笔时，微电脑的检索效果、速度及储存量都会发生问题。除了图书馆外，微电脑对办公室自动化有相当大的帮助，目前俄亥俄大学图书馆平均每二名馆员就拥有一部微电脑做办公室自动化的工作。

2. 光学储存的技术

光学储存主要可分三种 Card，Disk，Tape，其中以 Disk（光碟）的发展最快（见下图）：

```
                    Optical Storage Technnology
                              │
              ┌───────────────┼───────────────┐
            Card             Disk            Tape
                              │
                   ┌──────────┴──────────┐
               Read-only             Read/Write
                   │                      │
             ┌─────┴─────┐          ┌─────┴─────┐
           Video      Compact   Write-once   Erasible
             │           │          │           │
         ┌───┴───┐   ┌───┴───┐  ┌───┴───┐   
       Analog Digital Analog Digital
                        │
                   ┌────┴────┐
                 CD-DA     CD-ROM
                        │
                      CD-1
```

使用光碟的好处包括：①储存量大，像 Academic General Encyclopedia 共 20 多万页资料，可全部储存在一片光碟中。②不受通信费用的限制，过去做联线检索，每一分每一秒都要算钱，时间的掌握非常重要，用光碟则不用考虑这些。③使用配备并不复杂，一般光碟使用只需一部微电脑、一部光碟驱动器（CD drive）、再加印表机，即可利用光碟资料。至于光碟的缺点有二：一是缺乏统一的标准，因此不同公司生产的光碟有时不能用同一机器来检索。二是一个光碟驱动器只能同时检索一片光碟。虽然最近已发展出可同时连接好几个驱动器检索好几片光碟资料的技术，但因此系新产品，尚未普遍应用。

图书馆自动化的未来趋势

80 年代的特色是地区性图书馆个别系统的发展，但稍后又发现如各馆分别开发各自的系统，并不是解决图书馆合作问题的最好方式，故现在又回头准备将这些个别系统予以网路化。最近二三年，美国有些州如加州、北卡罗莱纳州、佛罗里达州、伊利诺伊州等已着手进行全州性图书馆网路的规划，希望能将州内不同的图书馆系统予以连接，使州内各图书馆能共用现有图书资源。俄亥俄州最近也开始进行这种系统的设计，以下将介绍这套系统，藉以反映未来图书馆自动化的趋向。俄亥俄州图书馆资讯系统（Ohio Library Information System，OLIS）系由全州 13 所州立大学及 2 所私立大学的图书馆共同连线而建立的。

OLIS 包括下列功能：

(1) 联合目录：编制 15 所参与图书馆的联合目录。

(2) 图书互借：此一图书互借不同于 Interlibrary Loan 之处，在于读者可直接向加入 OLIS 的各图书馆借书，而毋须由图书馆代替读者向他馆借书，省掉一道手续上的麻烦。

(3) 图书文献快速传递：为了配合前述特殊的图书互借方式，OLIS 必须有一套快速传递资料的方法以争取时效，现在利用的方式有电信传真、特殊邮件传递等。

(4) 期刊索引及部分全文：OLIS 还将建立期刊索引及部分全文的检索。

(5) 转换至其他资料库或资讯服务系统。

俄大学生可利用 PC Workstation，Mackintosh 等先检索学校图书馆的书目资料、期刊索引、全文期刊等，如查不到，再透过网路在 OLIS 系统里检索，如果再找不到，OLIS 还提供一个 gateway 使能检索到全国性的资讯系统如 OCLC。而 OLIS 系统在规划之前仍有些问题存在，目前俄亥俄 13 所州立大学及 2 所私立大学分别使用不同的资料库像 NOTIS、LCS、Database、Data Research Associate 等，如何予以连线？解决的方式可分三种：①保持现有各系统，另发展一软件系统使读者用同一种方法即可检索到不同的资料库。②就现有的系统中选择一种大家都满意的系统取代，建立一中心系统。③买一共同系统供大家使用，但没有中心系统，用分散式的方式使各系统仍保有主权，需要他馆资料仍可透过网路来检索，看起来像是同一个系统，实际上仍是个别的系统。以上三种方法以第一种方法最便宜但有时检索效率并不是很好，第二种方法最容易、最方便，但花费最高，因可能有些图书馆必须放弃旧有系统而购买统一的新系统，第三种方法所需费用则介于前二者之间。

目前对于 OLIS 系统有下列基本需求：

(1) OLIS 必须是一分散型的系统，所有的地区性系统都可连接中心系统，但仍以地区性系统为主。

(2) OLIS 是为方便读者使用而设计的，故不论检索那一种地区性系统，其解说方式须予统一标准。

(3) 检索时先查 Local Online Catalogue，如无再到全州性的系统中查询。

(4) OLIS 必须具有全州性图书流通系统，供 15 所大学师生查询之用。

(5) OLIS 必须提供各种不同的检索方式包括 OCLC 所没有的主题字及布林逻辑检索。

(6) OLIS 的流通系统是全系统性的，即将 15 所图书馆看成一个大馆，各馆的师生可直接向他馆借书。

(7) OLIS 要求具有高效率的图书文件传递方式。

(8) OLIS 不仅包括图书及期刊目录，还包括期刊中的每篇文章及图书的目次表内容。

(9) OLIS 须具备馆藏分析、合作发展及图书维护保管功能。

(10) OLIS 必须是及时的（real-time），即读者输入需求后，马上可完成，不需等待太久。

(11) 在选择厂商（vender）时，必须考虑其未来发展的潜能。

(12) OLIS 系统的实施过程须分成若干阶段，发展的时间、速度要根据实际情形而定。

(13) OLIS 系统需要 15 个图书馆共同来参与，以决定如何发展。

（原载台湾《"中央图书馆"馆讯》1989 年第 11 卷第 4 期，第 4-7 页。）

图书馆自动化和网络化的新境界
——俄亥俄走向90年代[①]

New Visions in Library Automation and Networking
—Ohio's Approach to the 1990s

历史背景

在20世纪的整个60年代,美国在图书馆自动化方面的一些成就对全世界的图书馆和情报服务机构有较深的影响。其中最为重要的有国家医学图书馆的医学文献分析和查询系统(MEDLARS),包含图书馆的机读目录格式标准化(MARC),出版商的大型文摘和索引数据库以及由俄亥俄州高校图书馆建立的俄亥俄高校图书馆中心(OCLC)。

1967年形成的OCLC系统,对图书馆文献作了很好的记录,它现在已经发展成由各种类型和规模的11000多个图书馆所组成的世界范围的网络,到1991年1月,它的联机书目数据库已经有2200万条书目记录供资源共享。早在1971年8月26日,俄亥俄大学图书馆就是世界上第一个与OCLC系统联机实行分担编目的图书馆。这种历史性的事件在1990年12月又一次重演,为了纪念俄亥俄大学图书馆对OCLC系统联机联合编目第一条记录的输入,OCLC邀请俄亥俄大学图书馆在新的OCLC PRISM(为管理用的可靠性信息系统)中输入了第一条记录。

OCLC的成功与失误

70年代和80年代,OCLC通过联机联合编目而实现的分担编目网络和帮助图书馆在控制经费、加速编目和馆际互借子系统上取得了空前的成功。OCLC的经验为图书馆的合作和网络工作提供了一个模式,但是OCLC对于其他的子系统,主要是地方操作系统,如联机公共检索目录(OPAC)、流通、期刊管理和采购等等的开发,不是迟于预定计划就是遭到了失败。这种情况使得许多图书馆在OCLC之外寻找可用的子系统来实现图书馆的自动化功能,容量大且价格合理的小型机的出现,正好满足了人们的要求。当大多数图书馆还在日益增多的操作系统中选取所需时,一些图书馆开发了自己的地方系统。

不同的地方系统要使用不同的查询方法,对于一般用户来讲,学会和使用许多不同的系统不是件容易的事。将不同的系统连接成一个互相联系的网络至多也只是一个临时的办法,因为它只能以系统的最弱功能作为整个系统的标准。

俄亥俄网的起源

1986年俄亥俄州负责调整和监督公共高等教育发展的州立机关——俄亥俄高校董事会受州立法机构的委托,任命一个由17位成员组成的图书馆研究委员会去考察各州立大学图书馆提出的扩大馆舍的经费需求,并探索解决的办法。主席由负责高校和特别计划的伊恩·海尔斯顿博士担任,委员会成员包括一位大学校长、一位教务长、两位副校长、两位系主任、两位图书馆馆长、一位教授、一位OCLC研究员、一位出版商和四位董事会的高级职员。

[①] 本文由鲍平、张晓艳译,经作者本人校订。

经过长达一年的研究，委员会于 1987 年 9 月发表了题目为《俄亥俄高校图书馆：通过合作，存储和技术得到发展》的报告，报告指出："较宽的视野是必要的，因为今日高校图书馆有三个作用，它是信息的储存库；是检索其他地方信息的基地；是情报教育中心。"

报告中最重要的一点建议是"尽快地完成州内电子目录系统"。其他建议包括将现有的图书馆卡片目录转换成机读目录形式，开发并完成州内图书馆资料传递系统以及制定一项合作保护方案，至此，对俄亥俄图书馆检索系统的设计已经开始。在开发过程中，俄亥俄图书馆检索系统改为俄亥俄图书馆和情报系统，后来名称又改为俄亥俄图书馆和情报网络，其缩略形式为俄亥俄网络（Ohio Link）。

俄亥俄网的规划

为了监督州内电子图书馆系统的设定，俄亥俄高校董事会成立了指导委员会，下设三个特别工作小组（分别代表图书馆员、系统管理者和用户的观点——但每个小组也有另外两种观点的代表），在代表图书馆员的观点的特别工作小组下有四个分委员会（目录的建立和维护；联机公共检索目录；流通、馆际互借和文献传递；采访、期刊、馆藏和发展），加上在俄亥俄网中起重要作用的 17 位高校图书馆馆长和俄亥俄州立图书馆馆长，参加这项计划的人数超过了 100 位。

俄亥俄图书馆和情报网络包括 13 所州立大学和 2 所独立的医学院。所有两年制的州立学院图书馆对俄亥俄网只有检索权而没有使用权。事实上，这种对图书馆系统部分的检索权（不包括借阅权力）也向全州的公民提供，对非图书馆数据库的检索，以后将由特定的协议确定。系统的设计者们还决定今后将在系统组织中增加不同层次的新成员。

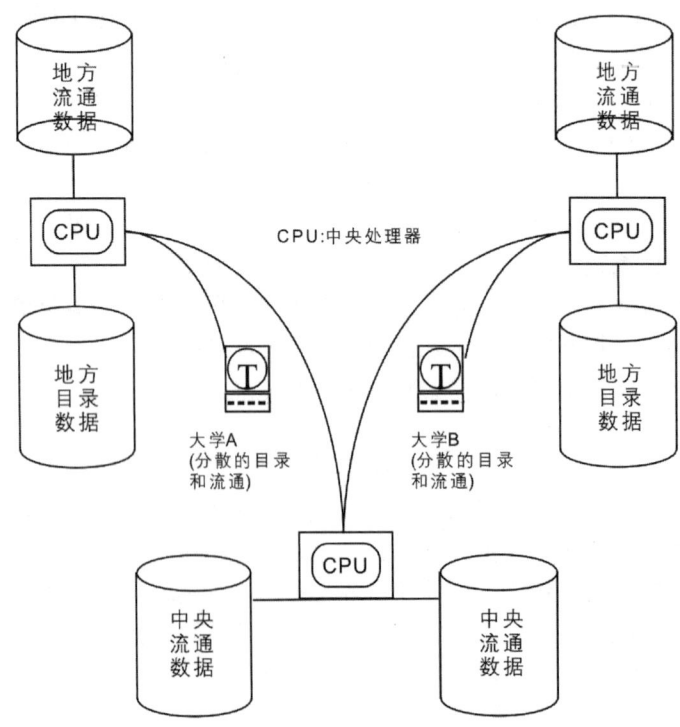

图 1　俄亥俄网概念的系统结构
中央系统通过高速网络来联接地方目录和流通数据库。

俄亥俄网的一般概念

为了系统的最好运行和使用方便,指导委员会决定为17所大学和中央地点(在地处代顿的州立赖特大学内)配置一个硬件系统(可以适应不同的藏书量和各大学的特殊情况)和一个软件系统。尽管这种基本的一致保证了兼容性,但选择的模式本质上是一个分布式系统,对中央和地方各有不同的作用。

中央系统包括目录和权威记录,一个拥有所有目录记录的联合目录,地方系统间转换查询的程序,附加数据库和利用俄亥俄网之外系统的衔接指导。系统应大小适中,并且要有足够强大的软件"查找机",以便对存储在全国和世界范围的大量的情报进行组织、排序和检索,它将通过俄亥俄的高速巨型计算机网络被连接到各个大学的远程网络(WAN)中。俄亥俄学术资源网络(OAR net)也已经安装,虽然某些地方要求升级至T-1。有极大潜在利用能力并以合理的费用来租借的主要电子数据库(目录的、原文或影像的)可以从中央地点购买,也可用更为经济的办法通过校园联机系统来检索。

各个地方校园系统将支持该大学的图书馆目录、流通、其他数据库和其他图书馆功能(包括分馆和分校)。凡是参加俄亥俄网的学校中的教员和学生都可以联机检索本校和网络中其他学校的资料,通过俄亥俄网的内部流通网络,他们不需要图书馆员的帮助,便能向其他学校索借所需资料而代替了传统意义上的馆际互借。大多数印刷型资料将根据传递服务约定来传递,文章和短文将由高清晰度传真机来传递(每时400个点或更高),电子形式的资料由电子方式传递。

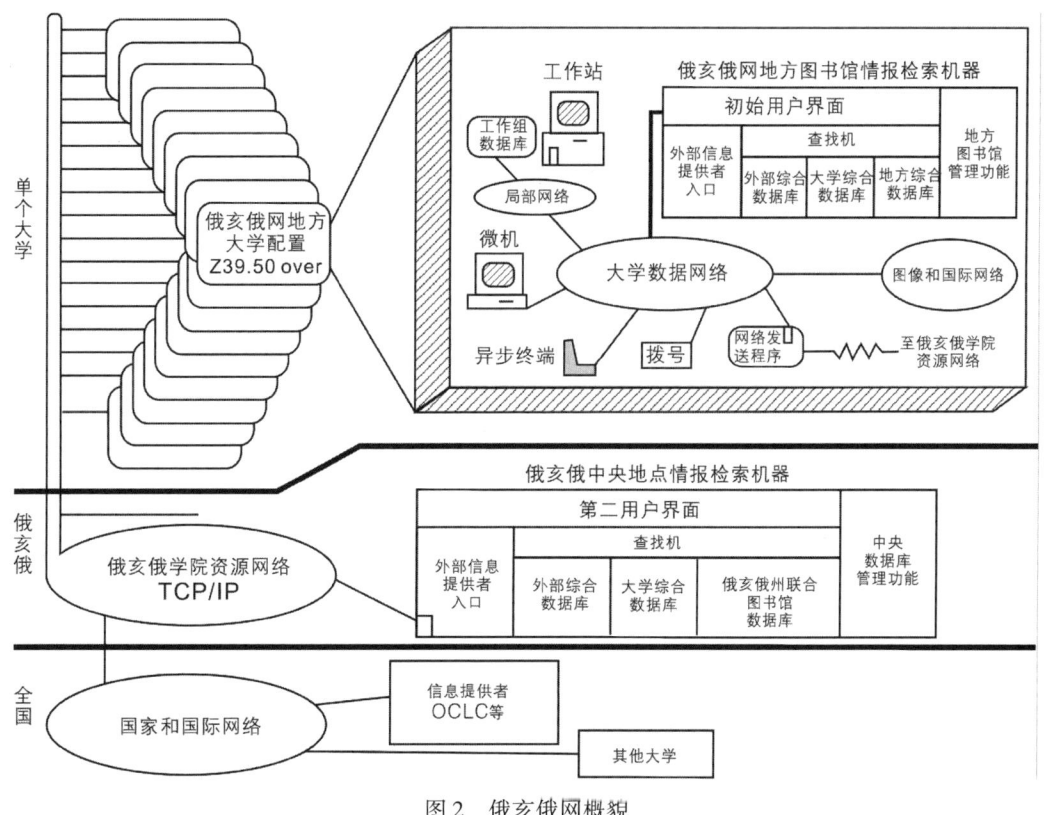

图2 俄亥俄网概貌

到1989年7月1日,根据"建议要求"提供的统计数字,17所高校的印刷型资料总和已经超过了 1900 万卷，每年增加近 550,000 卷。1977 年至 1988 年共订有杂志 146,000 种。在这期间，这些图书馆的图书流通总量为 610 万卷，通过馆际互借系统借进图书馆 119,143 册，借出图书馆 239,176 册，俄亥俄网将有效地开发这些资源，使其得到最大限度地利用。

系统和网络概念

系统和网络配置如框图 II 所示，设想一个三级网络，范围从单个大学到俄亥俄网中心并扩展到全国和国际网络。地方大学系统并入俄亥俄网后将支持他们自己的目录、数据库和图书馆应有的其它功能。通过联网，地方用户可以检索外界提供的情报。通过俄亥俄高校资源网络，用户可以查询其他地区或国内和国际范围的数据库，查询如果不成功，允许读者在其他系统中查询（通过中央系统）或到其他数据库中去查询，而不需要重新键入查询操作。框图 III 显示了在俄亥俄网中心查询的实例，用户从地方学校系统开始查询，然后到中央系统和其他的地方系统查询。

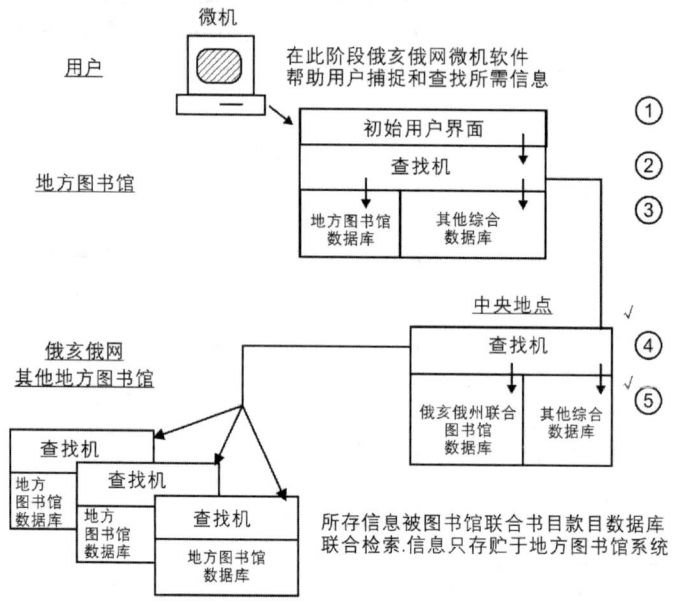

① 用户登录至地方系统。
② 用户初始查找项目。
③ 查找机在地方图书馆数据库查找合格条目，还在其他综合数据库中查找。
④ 如果地方查找不成功，用户可通过某些查找准则到中央系统查找。
⑤ 查找机在联合图书馆数据库中查找所需条目，也在中央综合数据库中查找。

图 3　俄亥俄网查询实例

系统的选择

选择一个系统不是件容易的事，应当承认没有一个完美的系统可以满足俄亥俄网的模式或《俄亥俄图书馆和信息系统建议要求》中共 242 页详细规定的技术指标。人们所期望的最好结果是在现有的较好系统中选择一个能满足大部分要求的，并且要软件系统公司做出承诺，即在俄亥俄网的技术环境、信息和需求发生变化时能与俄亥俄网一起对系统作进一步的开发。

1989年8月，选择系统所需要的参阅文件"建议要求"被送给了40多家软件系统公司。这是一个关键性的文件，它共有10章5000项技术要求，11个表格，文章的内容分别是总的要求、系统规范、目录的建议和维护、联机检索、流通、馆际互借、采访、期刊、馆藏的管理及发展等。

1989年10月，有8个软件系统公司提出了书面建议，1990年2月，公司开始介绍和演示，在1990年3月，"III"公司（Innovative Interfaces Inc.）被选中并随后开始进行了一系列谈判，1991年1月，合同草案产生，1991年3月，正式签订合同。

实施计划和时间表

按照合同草案的条款，俄亥俄网系统的全部运行是按阶段进行的。

1991年初开始的第一阶段（合同签订及俄亥俄州发放基金以后），III的软件和硬件将被安装在网络中的6所大学以及中央地点。这6所大学是：州立博林格林大学、凯恩斯西部保留地大学、州立中部大学、迈阿密大学、辛辛那提大学和州立赖特大学。

安装前，各个学校要选好地点和俄亥俄学术资源网络的远程通讯连接准备。在中央地点安装"III"软件和硬件的时间是1991年7-8月间，10月进行实验，并将第一个参加俄亥俄网的图书馆的机读目录记录输入到联合目录中，精选的期刊引文数据库也开始输入到系统中储存。与此同时，在各个学校安装包括流通、联机公共检索目录、采访、期刊等内容的地方系统。期刊引文数据库和III的地方期刊控制系统将于1992年3月合为一体。当检索到某一期刊引文的时候，系统将列出俄亥俄网中收藏这份期刊的图书馆名单及下列细节：

（1）这份期刊在各个图书馆的具体位置及索书号。
（2）各馆关于这份期刊的馆藏说明。
（3）各馆藏的最新一期。

第一阶段的大部分安装和运行工作将在1992年中期完成，对系统的其他改进将于1992年7月完成。其中包括变成批处理为快速处理的要求，不需要重新输入信息，就可以在其他学校或其他数据库中继续进行查找的能力，以及应读者的要求直接从其他学校传递所需资料的能力。

第二阶段将于1992年7月开始，此阶段将为俄亥俄网的另外11所院校安装软件和硬件，并将各个图书馆的记录输入到中央联合目录。在这个阶段还将设计联合目录的一些新的功能，例如在1992年初，俄亥俄网将与"III"谈判关于资料的电子影像传送。

管理机构的职责分配

俄亥俄网的成功在很大程度上依赖于州政府提供的足够的资金，不管是在工作的开始还是在进行之中。俄亥俄高校董事会的领导和支持也是非常重要，这一点从这项工作一开始就被证明了。更为重要的是董事会认识到俄亥俄网是一个对本州的经济发展能作出贡献的重要项目，认识到图书馆和情报服务对教育事业和经济发展有所贡献，这项工作反映了图书馆极强的生命力和它日益增大的作用。

经过与指导委员会和大学图书馆馆长会议的磋商，董事会成立了俄亥俄网管理机构，这一机构由管理委员会、执行主任、政策咨询委员会和图书馆咨询委员会组成。在系统的硬件和软件选择完成之后才开始讨论管理的问题，各个委员会将根据需要筹建顾问小组和分委员会，框图IV为管理机构。

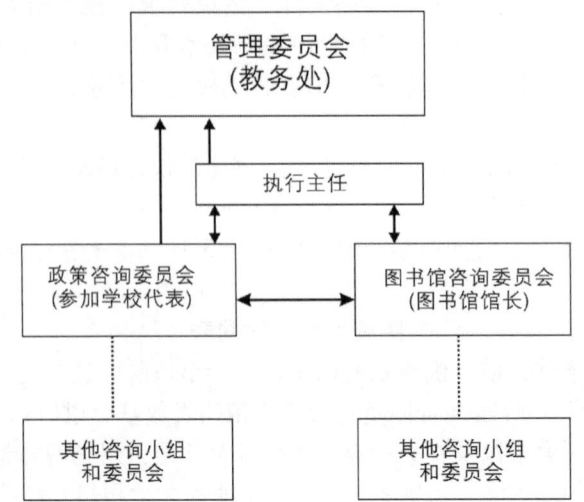

● 政策咨询委员会的主席和副主席也是执行主席，是管理委员会成员。
● 图书馆咨询委员会主席＝政策咨询委员会副主席。

图 4 俄亥俄网管理结构

　　从俄亥俄网 17 所大学中选举出来的 9 位大学教务长组成了管理委员会，任期 3 年，俄亥俄高校董事会主席、俄亥俄网执行主任及政策咨询委员会正副主席的任职期限依其职位而定，两年制学院的代表作为观察员进入管理委员会。委员会自己选举主席，每年开三次会，也可以根据需要随时召开会议以便批准预算，研究主要的政策建议、聘用执行主任、批准两年一度的预算并提交俄亥俄高校董事会以便得到立法部门的批准。

　　政策咨询委员会由俄亥俄网中 17 所大学的代表、俄亥俄学术资源网络主任和一位两年制学院代表组成，任期 3 年。成员中至少包括了校级领导、图书馆馆长、计算中心主任、系主任和系统图书馆员。他们都是由大学推荐，由管理委员会任命的。政策咨询委员会每 2 个月开会一次，也可以根据需要随时开会，会议内容主要是向执行主任提供政策和预算方面的建议。

　　图书馆咨询委员会的成员由俄亥俄网 17 所大学的图书馆馆长和一名两年制学院的代表组成，州法律图书馆学会也被邀请派一名观察员参加。

　　现在，一些咨询小组、分委员会和工作小组已经或正在建立，它们是：
（1）俄亥俄网联接工作小组
（2）目录建立和管理委员会
（3）流通、馆际互借和文献传递委员会
（4）采访和连续出版物委员会
（5）馆藏管理和发展委员会
（6）联机公共检索目录委员会
（7）教导和信息交流委员会

　　俄亥俄学术资源网络工作小组将要考虑到俄亥俄网的容量，看其在俄亥俄网流通量加大时能否满足巨大的需求，这项工作在 1991 年 3 月完成。除了教导和信息交流委员会以外，其他委员会属图书馆咨询委员会领导。人们期望这些委员会能够协助图书馆咨询委员会解决问题并向其提供有关系统范围内决策方面的建议。他们将协调各个学校的自主和系统需要一致这二者之间的关系。教导和信息交流委员会隶属于政策咨询委员会，其工作重点是开发介绍俄亥俄网的资料，加强教职员对俄亥俄网能力的认识，保证提供有关使用本系统的统一教材。

虽然人们对管理机构有各种各样的看法，但其工作效率和成果还有待事实的证明，人们希望这个模式将是灵活的、动态的，可以满足俄亥俄网在其形成过程中不断变化的需要。

如同常有的情形那样，有时无意中编制的图表比正式制定的图表更为重要。比如在 1990 年末，临时执行主任通过 BITNET（是一个全球性的计算机通讯网络，通过这个网络，目前世界上有 4000 多所大学计算中心的使用者可以很方便地进行电子通讯）编排了一个俄亥俄网通讯表以方便交流，从那时起，这个通讯表为及时交流思想和信息提供了机会。当大多图书馆员还不了解 BITNET 的时候，这个表的作用是帮助人们了解并积极参与 BITNET，除此之外，表的另一个作用是超越正式委员会的方式来探讨有关的问题。

前面的路

俄亥俄州的图书馆在图书馆自动化和革新方面自 1960 年以来就遥遥领先。俄亥俄高校图书馆中心的建立在世界范围内给图书馆目录、联合目录、馆际互借和网络化带来了极大变化，俄亥俄州内的化学文摘服务、计算机服务等机构的建立和发展使俄亥俄成为情报工业的中心。90 年代俄亥俄网的规划又给未来提供了一个新的模式。人们希望它能与俄亥俄高校图书馆中心一样，在连接人、图书馆和信息的工作中起到较为重要的作用。

随着俄亥俄网的继续发展，一些新的功能如电子文献传递、学者工作站等也将陆续增加。学者工作站被认为是在俄亥俄网之外的一项也很有影响的工程，它是一个研究和开发工程，目前进展很顺利。工作站将处在一个多重工作环境，就是能够提供简单的语言（从人工智能元素中提炼），从较广泛的情报源和网络中进行检索。它将了解读者经常寻找的信息类型、向读者提供全部最新情报、使读者得到最快和最满意的服务，不管是文字形式还是图表形式的信息都能以最快的速度和读者见面。除此之外，它允许读者使用自己所喜欢的运行方式而无需太多的计算机知识和繁琐的操作就能打印文件。把计算机转变成一种工具（如汽车），这种目标将使学者和研究人员更集中于自己的专业领域而不需要熟记过多的使用计算机的方法——如同汽车驾驶员不必是机械师，但是这种计算机的价格应能为人们所接受。

虽然全部转换成"III"的软件目前将会给一些图书馆带来一定的困难，但这种转换会长久受益，因为俄亥俄网是为下一个世纪设计的系统。可以毫不夸张地说，电脑软件商们还没有提供 21 世纪的系统。因此，以不定型、可变和预测为原则，俄亥俄大学正在计划放弃现存系统，因为它被证明功能是有限的。不管结果如何，这种大胆的工作对全世界图书馆界和学术界将会有指导意义。

（原载《大学图书馆学报》1992 年第 1 期，第 38 - 45 页。）

图书馆自动化和网络化的新境界
——俄亥俄走向 90 年代

New Visions in Library Automation and Networking
—Ohio's Approach to the 1990s[①]

HISTORICAL BACKGROUND

Several developments in library automation in the United States during the decade of the 1960s had far-reaching effects on the provision of library and information services throughout the world. Most important of these were the development of the Medical Literature Analysis and Retrieval System (MEDLARS) by the National Library of Medicine, the standardization of the Machine-Readable Catalog (MARC) format by the Library of Congress, the computerization of large indexing and abstracting databases by publishers, and the establishment of the Ohio College Library Center (OCLC) by academic libraries in Ohio.

The formation of OCLC in 1967 and its subsequent growth into a world-wide network of over 11,000 libraries of all types and sizes, sharing an ever expanding online bibliographic database of 22 million cataloging records in January 1991, has been well recorded in library literature. Back on August 26, 1971, Ohio University was the first library in the world to catalog online in the OCLC's system of shared cataloging. This historic event was recreated on November 12, 1990. Honoring Ohio University for its contribution of the first online record into the OCLC online union catalog, OCLC invited Ohio University to be the first library to input a record into the new OCLC PRISM system.

OCLC'S SUCCESS AND FAILURE

During the 1970s and 1980s, OCLC enjoyed unprecedented success with its online network of shared cataloging through its online union catalog, and interlibrary loan subsystem—which help contain the costs of library operations and speed up cataloging and interlibrary loan processes. The OCLC experience provided a model for library cooperation and networking; however, its efforts to develop other subsystems, mostly for local operations, such as an online public access catalog (OPAC), circulation, serials control, and acquisitions either lagged behind schedule or failed. This caused many libraries to seek other alternatives to automate the library functions not covered by OCLC. The advent of minicomputers with their large and expandable capacity as well as relative affordability in cost came just in time to meet the needs. Some libraries developed their own local systems, while the majority chose from among a growing number of turnkey systems.[②] Most of these systems did not offer a full range of library functions. Many were modular, offering various functions separately. The concept of an integrated library system was popular but seldom fully realized throughout the 1980s.

A 1988 survey of thirteen state-supported universities and two medical colleges in Ohio found that all were members of OCLC, one had a locally developed system, eight had acquired local systems from five different vendors, and the remainder were either in the process of selecting or planning for a local system.

Since the creation of OCLC, there has been a strong tradition of cooperation among all

---

[①] Presented at the International Conference on New Frontiers in Library Information Services, May 8-12, 1991.

[②] I have described my experiences in this area in "Applications of Information Technology in an American Library ~ The Case of Ohio University Libraries," *Proceedings of the First Pacific Conference on New Information Technology for Library and Information Professionals*. June 16-18, 1987, Bangkok, edited by Ching-Chih Chen and David I. Raitt (West Newton, MA: MicroUse Information, 1987), pp. 155-164.

libraries in Ohio. State-supported university libraries, for example, have long-standing agreements for reciprocal borrowing and free photocopying and mailing for interlibrary loans. When telefacsimile became common in these libraries in the late 1980s, it also was free for delivery of urgently needed documents. Dial access to each others' online public access catalogs also was offered. Further cooperation, however, was hampered by the different search methods required for each of the different local systems. It is not easy for the average user to learn and use the many different systems. Linking the different systems into an interconnected network was seen as, at best, a band-aid solution, making the functionality of the weakest system the norm for all.

THE BEGINNING OF OhioLINK

In 1986, the Ohio Board of Regents—a state agency which coordinates and oversees the development of public higher education in Ohio—responded to a mandate from the State Legislature by appointing a seventeen-member Library Study Committee to assess the growing need for additional space by state-supported university libraries and to explore possible alternatives. Chaired by Dr. Elaine Hairston, the then Vice Chancellor for Academic and Special Programs (now the Chancellor) of the Regents, the Committee members included a university president, a provost, two vice presidents, two deans, two library directors, a professor, an OCLC researcher, a publisher, and four senior staff of the Regents. Early in its deliberations, the Committee decided to broaden its original charges to include an assessment of "the role of the academic library... in its broadest contemporary sense" and "consider such opportunities for improving the quality of libraries as might appear in the context of its consideration"①.

According to its report, *ACADEMIC LIBRARIES IN OHIO: PROGRESS THROUGH COLLABORATION, STORAGE, AND TECHNOLOGY*, of a year-long study published in September 1987, the Committee felt that:

"This wider perspective is necessary because the academic libraries of today have a threefold purpose, serving not only as a storehouse of information, but also as a gateway to information held elsewhere, and as a center for instruction about information."②

Among the Committee's recommendations on collaboration, storage, and technology, the principal one for collaboration was to implement "as expeditiously as possible a statewide electronic catalog system". Collateral recommendations included retrospective conversion of remaining paper cataloging records to MARC format, the development and implementation of a statewide delivery system for library materials, and a plan for a cooperative preservation program.③ From the main and collateral recommendations, the planning for an Ohio Library Access System (OLAS) began almost immediately. During the course of development, the name of Ohio Library Access System was changed to Ohio Library and Information System (OLIS) and, again, to Ohio Library and Information Network. The acronym OLIS was changed to OhioLINK.

PLANNING FOR OhioLINK④

To oversee planning for a statewide electronic library system, the Ohio Board of Regents established a Steering Committee, supported by three task forces (one each to represent the views of librarians, systems managers, and users-but with representatives of the other two on each), and four subcommittees under the Librarian's View Task Force (Catalog Creation and Maintenance;

---

① Ohio Board of Regents. Library Study Committee. *Academic Libraries in Ohio: Progress Through Collaboration, Storage, and Technology*. Report of the Library Study Committee (Columbus, Ohio: Ohio Board of Regents, 1987), p. vii.
② *Ibid*.
③ *Ibid*.
④ The planning process was more fully described in my "Planning Process and Considerations for a State-wide Academic Libraries Information System in Ohio," in *Proceedings of the Second Conference on New Information Technology for Library and Information Professionals and Educational Media Specialists and Technologists*. May 29 – 31, 1989, Singapore, edited by Ching-chih Chen and David I. Raitt (West Newton, MA: MicroUse Information, 1989), pp. 203 – 210.

Online Public Access Catalog; Circulation, Interlibrary Loan, and Document Delivery; and Acquisitions, Serials, and Collection Management and Development). Adding the seventeen library directors of the Inter-University Library Council and the State Librarian of Ohio, all of whom play key roles in OhioLINK, well over one hundred people were involved in the planning.

Early in the planning process, the Board of Regents also commissioned two studies, one by RMG Consultants to carry out a feasibility study on linking state university automated library systems[1] and another by Hurley Consulting Corporation to evaluate centralized vs. distributed approaches to the statewide system. [2]

The cooperative efforts of all the participating institutions and individuals have resulted in the following accomplishments from January 1988 to the time of this writing in February 1991.

1. Issued a <u>PLANNING PAPER</u>[3].
2. Prepared following detailed documents:
   – <u>Request for Information</u> (RFI), August 1988
   – <u>Request for Proposal</u> (RFP), August 1989
   – <u>RFI for the OLIS Workstation</u>, October 1989
   – <u>RFP for Interlibrary Image Transfer (IIT) System</u>, completed December 1990—awaiting public release.
3. Published an introduction of the Ohio Library & Information System (OLIS): CONNECTING PEOPLE, LIBRARIES & INFORMATION FOR OHIO'S FUTURE[4].
4. Sponsored three state-wide workshops on the state-of-the-art in networked library systems, the OhioLINK model, and a scholars workstation.
5. Obtained funding from the capital budgets for 1988 – 1990 and 1990 – 1992 and the operating budget for 1989 – 1991.
6. Studied the responses to RFP from eight vendors (including two-day demonstrations by each—attended by a number of staff from each participating library), further investigated the four ranked highest, and selected the final one.
7. Conducted detailed contract negotiation with the selected vendor.
8. Developed and adopted a governance structure and conducted a nationwide search for an Executive Director.
9. Appointed Dr. Len Simutis as the Interim Executive Director.
10. Selected Wright State University (in Dayton, Ohio) as the OhioLINK central site.
11. Established the implementation schedule with Phase I to begin in March 1991.

PARTICIPATING LIBRARIES

Initially Ohio Library and Information Network was to include the thirteen state-supported universities and two independent state-supported medical colleges:

University of Akron
Bowling Green State University
Central State University
University of Cincinnati
Cleveland State University
Kent State University
Miami University

---

[1] RMG Consultants. *Alternative Approaches to Linking State University Automated Library Systems for the Ohio Board of Regents* (Chicago: RMG Consultants, 1988).

[2] Bernard Hurley. *Centralization vs. Decentralization for Large Library System in a Changing Technological Environment: A Position Paper for the Ohio Board of Regents* (Berkeley, California: Hurley Consulting Corp., 1988).

[3] OLAS Steering Committee. *Ohio Library Access System Planning Paper, November 2, 1988* (Columbus, Ohio: Ohio Board of Regents, 1988).

[4] Ohio Library & Information System, OLIS. *Connecting People, Libraries, & Information for Ohio's Future* (Columbus, Ohio: Ohio Board of Regents, 1989).

Ohio State University
Ohio University
Shawnee State University
University of Toledo
Wright State University
Youngstown State University
The Medical College of Ohio
Northeast Ohio University College of Medicine

However, early in the planning, it was decided that two large private universities also would be included:

Case-Western Reserve University
University of Dayton

The right of "access" but not "use" should be granted, at least initially, to all two-year state-supported college libraries.① Indeed, such access to library portions of the system (not including borrowing privileges) will be available to the entire citizenry of the state. Access to non-library databases will be determined later by licensing agreements. The system architecture, as envisioned by the planners, should be able to add new members at various levels of participation at later stages.

GENERAL CONCEPT OF OhioLINK

During early deliberations, after a careful analysis of responses to the RFI, the Steering Committee decided that for best system performance and easy use, there should be one hardware platform (adjusted for immense variations in the size of collections and constituencies) and one software system for all seventeen institutions, and the central site. Despite this basic uniformity to assure compatibility, the model selected is essentially a distributed system,② with distinct functions for the central and local sites. Diagram I presents the conceptual configuration of the system.

The central-site system will contain cataloging and authority records, a union list for each bibliographic record, a routing capacity to transfer a search request from one local system to another, additional databases, and gateways to systems outside of OhioLINK. The system should be adequate in size and have a sufficiently powerful software "search engine" to organize, sort, and retrieve vast quantities of information stored within the state and around the world. It will be linked to each institution's wide-area Network (WAN) through Ohio's high-speed supercomputer network, OARnet (Ohio Academic Resources Network), already in place (although requiring upgrading to T-1 for some sites). Major electronic databases (bibliographic, textual, or image) which have the greatest potential use and can be leased at reasonable cost will be made available in the central site and be accessible online to the campus systems for the benefit of economies of scale.

Each local campus system will support the institution's library catalog, circulation, other databases, and other library functions (including those for any branch libraries or campuses). Faculty and students from all OhioLINK universities will have online access to materials held in their own local libraries plus all participating libraries. They can request materials at other campuses online through the OhioLINK intra-circulation network (instead of interlibrary loan in the traditional sense) without library staff mediation. Most printed materials will be delivered by a

---

① The difference between "Access" and "Use" has been clearly delineated. "Access" to the OhioLINK union catalog will be available to all Ohioans through campus computer workstations and terminals and through dial-in access from personal computers equipped with standardized OhioLINK software. Implicitly, this includes any interested two-year or private colleges. Comprehensive "Use" of OhioLINK—including borrowing, document delivery, and non library databases—will initially be available to students, faculty, and staff of the seventeen participating university libraries.

② The model was reinvigorated by the report by Hurley, *Centralization vs. Decentralization*, and through Hurley's participation in a workshop attended by representatives of all participating institutions at Kent State University.

contracted delivery service; articles and smaller documents will be sent by telefacsimile with high-definition replication (400 dots per inch or higher); and materials in electronic formats will be transmitted electronically.

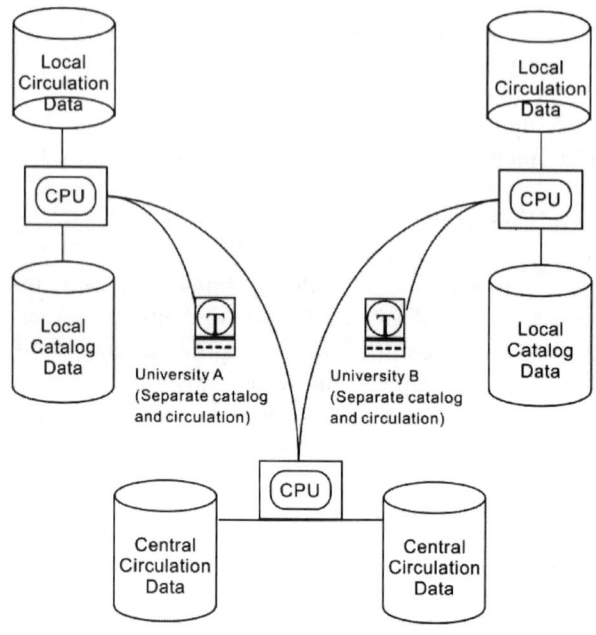

Central System Linked via LSP or Internal Protocols to Local Catalog and Circulation

DIAGRAM I   OhioLINK Conceptual System Configuration

As of July 1, 1989, according to the statistics provided in the RFP[①], the combined resources of the seventeen universities libraries exceeded 19 million volumes of printed materials. Nearly 550,000 volumes are added annually and 146,000 journals were subscribed to in 1987 – 1988. During the same year, these libraries circulated a total of 6.1 million volumes and, through interlibrary loan operations, borrowed 119,143 items and loaned 239,176 items. OhioLINK will effectively open these resources together and greatly expand the accessibility and usage of them.

THE SYSTEM AND NETWORK OVERVIEW

The conceptual system and network configuration, as shown in Diagram II, envisions a three-tier network ranging from the individual campuses to OhioLINK Central and extending into national and international networks. The local campus systems integrated into OhioLINK support their own catalogs, databases, and all desirable library functions. Through gateways, local users can access external information providers. Through OARnet, users can search the databases at other local sites or national and international networks. An unsuccessful search will offer the user an option of having the search continued at other sites (via the central site) or in other databases without need to re-enter the search. An example of user search of the local campus system and from there to the central system and other local campus systems in OhioLINK is shown in Diagram III.[②]

---

① "Request for Proposal for the Ohio Library & Information System (OLIS) on behalf of the Ohio Board of Regents and Ohio Library & Information System" (Columbus, Ohio: OLIS, August 4, 1989), pp. 203 – 208.

② *Ibid.*, pp. 8 – 9.

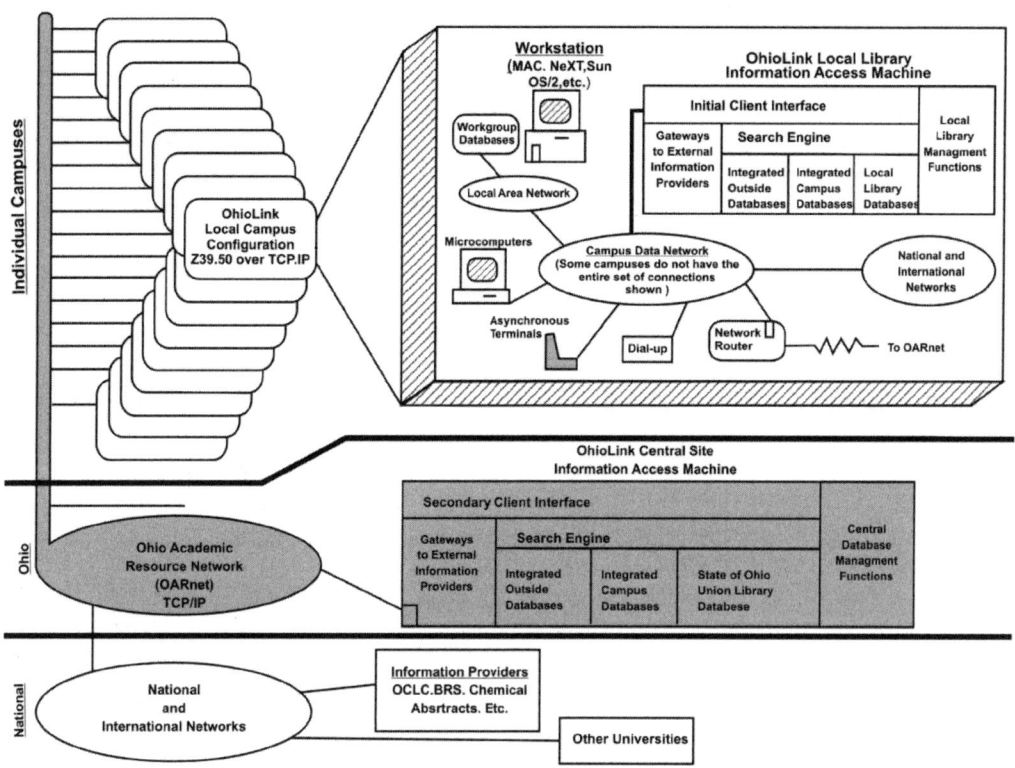

DIAGRAM II   OhioLINK NETWORKING OVERVIEW

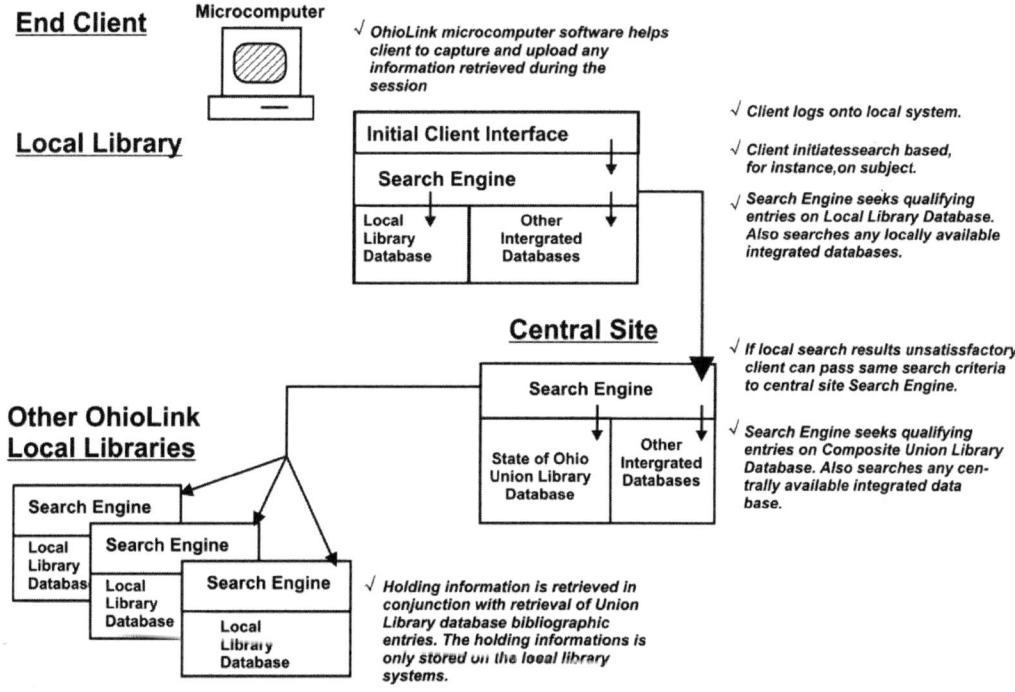

DIAGRAM III   OhioLINK USER SEARCH EXAMPLE

THE SELECTION OF A SYSTEM

The selection of a system was by no means an easy task. It was conceded that there is no one "perfect" system which met the OhioLINK model or the specifications detailed in the 242 - page RFP, REQUEST FOR PROPOSAL FOR THE OHIO LIBRARY & INFORMATION SYSTEM (OLIS). The best result that one could hope for would be to choose among the best available systems that met most of the requirements and gain a commitment from the vendor to work with OhioLINK for further development in an ever changing environment of technologies, information, and needs. In fact, from early stages, OhioLINK was seen as a practical effort to address immediate needs and a research and development effort to better serve information seekers. In the spirit of cooperation, all participating institutions agreed early that once a system is selected, everyone would give up its local system and switch to the one system within a reasonable time schedule (a change made more palatable by the commitment of the Board of Regents to cover the capital costs of the new system).

The RFP, which was the key document used in the selection of the system, was sent to more than 40 vendors on August 9, 1989. It was prepared by the Steering Committee with the help of more than one hundred people who participated in various task forces and subcommittees of OhioLINK and then was reviewed and commented on at each institution by hundreds more. It contains more than 5,000 specifications in 10 chapters, 11 tables, 2 glossary lists, and 11 appendices. Separate chapters treat General Requirements, System Specifications, Catalog Creation and Maintenance, Online Public Access Catalog, Circulation, Interlibrary Loan, and Document Delivery, Acquisitions and Serials, and Collection Management and Development

The vendors were given an opportunity to attend a vendor conference scheduled on August 28, 1989, and had until October 20, 1989, to respond in writing. Eight vendors submitted proposals:

Ameritech Information Systems, Inc. (with OCLC as a subcontractor)
CARL Systems Inc. (CARL)
Data Research Associates, Inc. (DRA)
Geac Computer Corp. (GEAC)
Innovative Interfaces, Inc. (III)
NOTIS Systems Inc. (NOTIS)
UNISYS
VTLS, Inc. (VTLS)

After the proposals were received, copies of the thousands of pages submitted by the vendors (including boiler plate, manuals, and specific responses to the RFP) were distributed to each of the participating institutions. Open hearings were held on some campuses as well as three state-wide hearings to solicit maximal input from all sectors of the academic community in Ohio.

During February 1990, each week two vendors were invited to make two-day presentations and demonstrations which were attended by all task forces, subcommittees, the Steering Committee, and anyone else that a participating institution might wish to send. In April 1990, based on evaluations submitted following the February sessions, the four vendors ranked highest were targeted for a series of site visits by an investigation team appointed by the Steering Committee. The four finalists were CARL, DRA, III, and VTLS. As a user of VTLS, Ohio University was visited by the Team on May 7 - 8, 1990. Following the site visits, Innovative Interfaces, Inc. (III) was recommended in July as the top choice for OhioLINK. Intensive negotiations with III began immediately after the selection and a contract was drafted for review in January 1991. The signing of the contract is expected in March 1991.

IMPLEMENTATION PLAN AND TIMETABLE

As outlined in the final draft of the Contract Agreement,[1] the full operation and implementation of OhioLINK will occur in phases. Phase I is set forth in the Implementation Schedule attached to the Agreement as Appendix C which states that "It is the firm plan of OhioLINK to install library automation systems at each of the 17 Affiliated Institutions and at the OhioLINK central site." (*Ibid.*)

In Phase I, which is to begin in early 1991 (following signing of the contract and release of funds by the State of Ohio), III software and hardware will be installed at six Affiliated Institutions and the central site. The six Phase I sites are:

Bowling Green State University
Case Western Reserve University
Central State University
Miami University
University of Cincinnati
Wright State University

In advance of installation, site preparation and OARnet telecommunications should be ready for each of these locations. After the installation of III software and hardware at the central site in July and August of 1991, followed by testing, loading of MARC catalog records from the initial participating libraries into the Union Catalog will commence in October 1991. Selected journal citation databases will also be loaded.

At the local sites, parallel installations will take place to create local systems which include circulation, OPAC, acquisitions, serials, etc. Demonstration of integration between journal citation databases and III's local serials control systems is scheduled in March 1992. When a journal citation is retrieved, the system will display a list of OhioLINK libraries that are using III serials check-in that have the journal, and the following detail:

* location and call number of the journal in each library's collection,
* summary holding statement of each library's holdings of that journal,
* most recent issue of that journal that has been received by each library.

It is anticipated that most of the Phase I installations and implementation will be accomplished by mid-1992. Other innovations to be included in the system by July 1992 include a requirement that most transactions take place in "real time" rather than in a batch process later, ability to continue searches at other campuses and in other databases without re-keying information (a failed search will offer this as an immediate option), and the ability of a user to directly request delivery of an item from another campus.

In Phase II, which begins in July 1992, III software and hardware will be installed at the 11 remaining Affiliated Institution libraries and their records loaded into the central union list. Other new features for the union catalog (e. g. , delivery of electronic images of documents—which will be negotiated by OhioLINK and III during early 1992) are planned for this phase as well.

THE GOVERNANCE AND DIVISION OF RESPONSIBILITIES

Because the success of OhioLINK, to a great extent, depends on sufficient funding—both initially and continuing—from the state government, the leadership and support of the Ohio Board of Regents are crucial but have been the evident from the beginning. It was especially important that the Regents recognized OhioLINK as one of the Regents' Selective Excellence Initiatives which are especially funded by the state to encourage outstanding programs and which contribute to the economic development of the state. This recognition of the contributions of library and information

---

[1] Agreement for an Automated Library System between Innovative Interfaces. Inc. and the Ohio Board of Regents on Behalf of the Ohio Library and Information Network.... Columbus, Ohio: OhioLINK, February 6, 1991.

services to the educational mission and economic health of the state reflects a greater awareness of the vital and expanding roles of libraries.

The Board of Regents, in consultation with the Steering Committee and the Inter-University Library Council, developed a governance structure for OhioLINK which consists of a Governing Board, an Executive Director, a Policy Advisory Council, and a Library Advisory Council. Early in the planning, the Board and the Steering Committee consciously deferred discussions of the governance until the selection of the system hardware and software were completed. They now believe that postponing the political questions kept the planning focused on the immediate tasks at hand. Each of the Councils may, as dictated by need, establish advisory groups and committees. Diagram IV illustrates the governance structure.

The GOVERNING BOARD consists of nine university provosts (principal academic officer) selected from the seventeen OhioLINK institutions, one of whom should be from a private university. These nine voting members serve staggered, three-year rotating terms. The Chancellor of the Ohio Board of Regents, OhioLINK Executive Director and Chair and Vice-Chair of the Policy Advisory Council serve ex-officio. A representative of two-year colleges is to be added as an observer. The Governing Board selects its own chair and meets three times a year or as needed to approve budgets, review major policy recommendations, and hire the Executive Director. Biennial budget recommendations will be approved and forwarded to the Ohio Board of Regents for incorporation into its requests to the State Legislature.

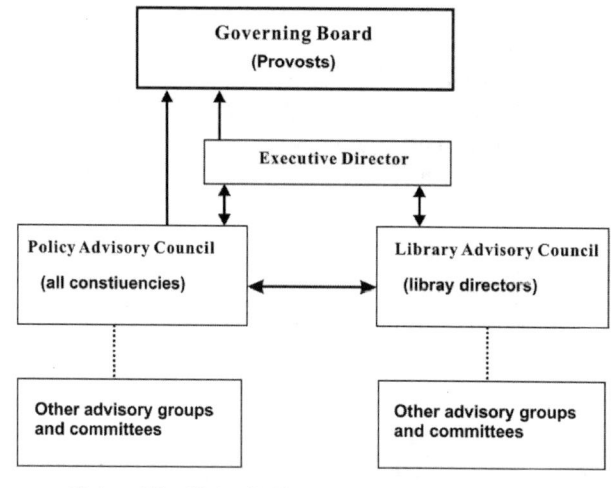

DIAGRAM IV OhioLINK GOVERNING STRUCTURE

The POLICY ADVISORY COUNCIL consists of seventeen voting members serving staggered three-year terms. All OhioLINK universities are represented plus the Director of OARnet ex-officio and a representative of two-year colleges. Members include at least three faculty members, four library directors, three computer center directors, three academic deans, and two systems librarians. They are recommended by the universities and appointed by the Governing Board. The Council meets every other month or as needed to advise the Executive Director on policy and budget matters. It selects its own chair. The Chair of the Library Advisory Council serves as Vice-Chair (although, at the first meeting of both bodies, the Chair of the Library Advisory Council was selected to Chair the Policy Advisory Council as well). The Executive Director serves ex-officio.

The **LIBRARY ADVISORY COUNCIL** includes all OhioLINK member library directors and one representative of two-year colleges. The state-wide association of law libraries has been invited to send an observer.

As of this writing, a number of advisory groups, committees, and task forces have been or are being formed, including:
* OhioLINK Network Connections Task Force
* Catalog Creation & Management Committee
* Circulation, Interlibrary Loan and Document Delivery Committee
* Acquisitions and Serials Committee
* Collection Management & Development Committee
* OPAC Committee
* Instruction and Communications Committee

Of these, the OhioLINK OARnet Task Force is to identify the considerations and capacities which OARnet will need to meet the explosion in demand anticipated by the addition of OhioLINK traffic. This Task Force is to complete its work by the end of March 1991. All of the remaining committees, except instruction and communications, are under the Library Advisory Committee. It is anticipated that these committees will devote their attention to implementation questions, bringing recommendations for system-wide policies to the Library Advisory Committee. They will attempt to balance institutional concerns for campus autonomy and system requirements for uniformity. The Instruction and Communications Committee is projected to be under the Policy Advisory Committee and to focus on developing promotional materials on OhioLINK, increasing faculty awareness of OhioLINK capabilities, and assuring the availability of uniform instructional materials throughout the system.

Although there are various views on the governing structure, both pro and con, its effectiveness and results are still to be seen. It is hoped that the model (which is based on the Board of Regents Supercomputer Center) will be flexible yet dynamic enough to meet the changing needs during the formative years of OhioLINK.

As is frequently the case, sometimes unplanned structures are more important than formal organizational charts. Exemplifying this, in late 1990, the Interim Executive Director arranged for an OhioLINK list on BITNET to facilitate communications. Since that time, the list has provided a forum for rapid exchange of ideas, concerns, and information. While relatively few librarians are particularly active on BITNET, the vitality of this list (and other library lists) is likely to serve as an impetus for more persons to become aware and involved and is likely to serve as a means of bypassing the formal committee structure to assure that issues are addressed.

THE ROAD AHEAD

Ohio libraries have been in the forefront in library automation and innovation since the 1960s. The creation of OCLC drastically changed the world of library cataloging, union catalog, interlibrary loan, and networking. The growth and development within Ohio of the Chemical Abstract Service, CompuServe, Mead Data, etc. have made Ohio a major center for the information industry. The planning of OhioLINK for the 1990s provides a new vision into the future. It is hoped that it will equal the importance of OCLC to set the pace for connecting people, libraries, and information. As one respected observer noted, after only reading the RFP:

Long-time library automation specialists may already be wondering whether (OhioLINK) is a reincarnation of the original Ohio College Library Center (the now-renamed Online Computer Library Center, aka OCLC). Apparently Ohio colleges and universities are still trying to "get it the way they want it." According to spokesmen, " (OhioLINK) will connect people, libraries, and information in a network of unparalleled sophistication and efficiency."

If they find a system that meets even half of their requirements, they will have a good chance to do that. But what will happen to the system once it succeeds? Will the libraries of the nation come banging on (OhioLINK's) door just like they banged on OCLC's 20 years ago? This author believes they will. ①

In the coming months, after the signing of a contract agreement with Innovative Interfaces, Inc. in March, installation of III software and DEC computers will begin on six campuses and the central site during the first phase. In addition to the catalog records, databases of journal citations will be loaded. The integration of serial records and journal citations will enhance the content and value of online catalog. The implementation of an intra-circulation system among all participating libraries, with user-inaugurated direct requests, will change the traditional interlibrary loan operations.

As OhioLINK continues to expand, electronic document delivery, scholar's workstations, and other new features will be augmented. The scholar's workstation is one project virtually assured to have impact well-beyond the OhioLINK system. It is clearly a research and development (R & D) project, well in advance of anything available today. According to the October 1989 RFI (the RFP likely will be released in the next few months), the workstation will be a multi-tasking environment, capable of providing plain language (refined by an artificial intelligence component) access to a wide range of information sources and networks. It will learn the types of information usually sought by a user, provide downloaded updates to such information without further mediation by periodically contacting likely sources of the information, and build on this knowledge core to provide serendipity comparable to browsing shelves. Such information, whether textual or graphic, will be presented in the form needed by the user—ready for immediate incorporation into reports and publications. Moreover, it should enable the user to use his/her preferred method of operations (menus, commands, or object oriented) and to do so without requiring computer expertise or tedious referral to printed documents (i. e., a short learning curve augmented by an intelligent "help" capability). The goal is to return the computer environment to the status of a tool which, like an automobile, will enable scholars and researchers to concentrate on their areas of expertise rather than protocols—to be drivers rather than mechanics—at an affordable price.

Although the changeover to III likely will be difficult for libraries satisfied with their current systems, the long-term benefits from a single system are expected to outweigh temporary inconveniences during the transition. OhioLINK was envisioned as a system for the next century. Not surprisingly, vendors are not yet offering twenty-first century systems. Thus, it is with a mixture of uncertainty, trepidation, and anticipation that universities in Ohio are planning to abandon proven but limited existing systems. Whatever the outcome, the audacity of the undertaking should prove instructive for the worlds of libraries and of learning.

(Published in *Proceedings of International Conference on New Frontiers in Library Information Services*. 2 vols. Taipei, Taiwan: Central Library, 1992.)

---

① Nancy Mellin Nelson, in her regular column, "Library Technology," "Ohio College Library Center: A Phoenix," *Information Today*, Vol. 6, No. 9 (October 1989), p. 17.

俄亥俄州高等院校图书馆联网：
技术与团队合作改变俄亥俄州图书馆

OhioLINK: Technology and Teamwork Transforming Ohio Libraries[①]

The state of Ohio has initiated a major library automation project that will link thirteen state-assisted university libraries, two large private university libraries, two medical college libraries, and the State Library of Ohio in a statewide network. Each participating library will maintain its own database and will also contribute its holdings to a central database of library holdings totaling nineteen million volumes. This network will provide a foundation for innovative new library services and improved resource management. Currently in its beginning stages, OhioLINK has already had a profound impact on Ohio libraries. This overview will discuss the development of the OhioLINK project and its effect on one participating library, Miami University.

Automation at Miami

Although sometimes confused with the University of Miami in Florida, Miami University is a state-assisted university located thirty-five miles north of Cincinnati in Oxford, Ohio. It presently serves over 20,000 students, faculty, and staff at its main campus and two regional campuses. Miami University Libraries includes a main library and three branch libraries on the Oxford campus, as well as two regional campus libraries. Its holdings total more than 1.4 million cataloged volumes.

Miami University Libraries made an early start in library automation by becoming a charter member of OCLC in 1971. For the next fifteen years, however, funding constraints and a conservative approach to automation slowed infusion of new technologies; outside of the cataloging department, most units operated manually. In 1986, the libraries were jump-started into the electronic age. The library director position was elevated to that of dean and university librarian, and a new dean was appointed. The libraries began to receive increased support and funding from the administration, and implementing new technologies was targeted as a high priority. As a result, the libraries embarked on a vigorous campaign to find an integrated library automation system to meet the university's needs.

At the time Miami was evaluating automated library systems, a proposal originating in the Ohio state government promised to revolutionize Ohio libraries. In 1987, the Ohio Board of Regents recommended the development of a statewide electronic library system that would provide the basis for new information services, resource sharing, and resource management. As a result of this recommendation, a steering committee and three task forces made up of librarians, library users, and systems managers worked closely to guide research and development efforts of the evolving project.

This development changed the focus of Miami's search for an automated system. The Miami libraries and the campus administration were keenly interested in participating in OhioLINK. However, the time line for OhioLINK implementation was stated in terms of years, and Miami hoped to implement its long-awaited system quickly. In addition, consultants hired by OhioLINK recommended that participating libraries operate on a uniform hardware platform and use the same library automation software. Therefore, Miami's choice of automated system became dependent on the state's choice of hardware and software vendor. Finally, the OhioLINK plan was in its early

---

[①] Co-authors: Judith Sessios & Stacey Kimmel.

stages and funding had not been secured. There was uncertainty as to whether the ambitious project would come to fruition.

Given all of these factors, Miami had a difficult choice to make. The libraries could defer selection of an automated system until OhioLINK plans took shape. This would delay implementation for two or more years but would ensure that the library system implemented was the same system supported by OhioLINK. Alternatively, the libraries could adhere to their original plans and select a system without knowing what system OhioLINK would support. Although the former option was less risky, the time line for the OhioLINK project would have greatly delayed Miami's automation implementation. On the Miami campus the automation of the libraries had become a mandate, and delays would have seriously affected the libraries' standing in the university community.

Because of a special arrangement made with the Ohio Board of Regents, the Miami administration chose the latter option. Under this agreement, Miami would select a system based on its "best guess" of which system OhioLINK would support. Based on both the Miami and OhioLINK system evaluations, Miami University took a calculated risk in selecting Innovative Interfaces Inc. (III) for its library automation system. In March 1991, when the OhioLINK contract with III was finally signed, Miami University had been using its system for almost a year.

Setting up OhioLINK

Planning for OhioLINK began as a result of an extensive study of the space and storage issues facing Ohio university libraries. In 1986, the state legislature of Ohio asked the Ohio Board of Regents (the state agency charged with overseeing development of public higher education in Ohio) to "conduct a study of the need for, and alternatives to, a significant expansion of space for state college and university libraries". The committee decided early in its deliberations to broaden the original charges to include an assessment of the "role of the academic library... in its broadest contemporary sense" and the examination of "such opportunities for improving the quality of libraries as might appear in the context of its consideration"①. The board recommended a solution that addressed a wide range of concerns: to implement "as expeditiously as possible a statewide electronic catalog system". Other components of the board's study included retrospective conversion of remaining paper cataloging records to MARC format, development and implementation of a statewide delivery system for library materials, and a plan for cooperative preservation. With these recommendations, planning for the Ohio Library Access System (OLAS) began almost immediately. During the planning process, this name was first changed to OLIS, and again to Ohio Library Information Network (OhioLINK).

The Board of Regents, in consultation with the steering committee and the Inter-University Library Council, developed a governance structure for OhioLINK that includes a governing board (a nine-member board of university provosts), an executive director (temporarily filled by Dr. Leonard Simutis, formerly dean of the Graduate School at Miami University), a policy advisory council (a mix of library directors, computer center directors, faculty members, academic deans, and systems librarians), and a library advisory council (all OhioLINK member library deans and directors).

One particularly effective means of written communication has been the use of an OhioLINK list on BITNET, arranged by the interim executive director. All committee minutes, timetables, and agendas are distributed via electronic mail.

Currently, OhioLINK has these mandates:

1. To establish high-speed telecommunications links among Ohio's university libraries that will support user searching of both the central site and other institutions' databases.

2. To develop a central database that contains the holdings of all Ohio academic libraries.

---

① Ohio Board of Regents, Library Study Committee. *Academic Libraries in Ohio: Progress through Collaboration, Storage, and Technology*. Columbus, OH: Ohio Board of Regents, 1987: vii.

This database will serve as a "central hub" for a wide range of library services and information, including circulation, interlibrary loan, user searching, cataloging, collection management, and other features. This database will be updated in real time, as records are added to local-site databases.

  3. To provide gateway access to a wide range of information stored in electronic formats, including databases purchased or leased by OhioLINK for member libraries, Internet resources, and commercial databases and services not specifically funded by OhioLINK

  4. To provide up-to-date circulation information to patrons and to allow patrons to initiate interlibrary loan and circulation transactions without library staff assistance.

  5. To offer document delivery service to participating sites, including telefacsimile, electronic image and document transfer, and traditional document delivery. A delivery turnaround time of forty-eight hours is targeted.

  6. To provide for retrospective conversion of those materials held by participating institutions whose records are not currently in electronic format.

  7. To provide collection management information for improved use and development of state resources.

  8. To develop a workstation that enhances user and staff interactions with OhioLINK services and databases. Included in this concept are capabilities for search-strategy formulation and iteration, data and image editing and capture, and post-search processing.

The OhioLINK structure

  Each local library system will support the OPAC, catalog maintenance, circulation, acquisitions, serials, and other library functions. Patrons will be able to search the local OPAC, other OhioLINK OPACs, and the central database from the same terminal. A menu choice will allow patrons to transfer a search strategy via the Oar-Net (Ohio Academic Research Network) and have it executed automatically. Patrons from OhioLINK institutions will be able to initiate a loan for materials held in their local libraries or in other OhioLINK member libraries. Patrons can conduct the transaction themselves at the terminal without staff mediation. Most printed materials from other sites will be delivered by a contracted delivery service; articles and smaller documents will be sent by telefacsimile with high-definition replication, and materials in electronic formats will be transmitted electronically.

  The individual library systems will be implemented in two phases. Sites in Phase I have begun to install hardware and software, prepare the database, and establish links to the statewide supercomputer network, OarNet. These Phase I sites will participate in testing of the central-site database capabilities and other software enhancements developed by Innovative Interfaces. Libraries in Phase II are tentatively scheduled for implementation during the 1992 – 1993 fiscal year.

  The central-site system will contain bibliographic and authority records, with each site's holdings, circulation, and order information linked to the bibliographic record. Major electronic databases, such as commercial journal citation databases, will be leased and made available on the central-site hardware for the campus systems. The central site will also serve as a gateway to systems outside OhioLINK The central-site resources will be linked to each institution's wide-area network through the OarNet.

  During early deliberations, OhioLINK planners decided to select a single hardware and software platform and one software system for all cooperating institutions and the central site. This uniformity offers many of the benefits of centralization, such as increased compatibility. However, the model selected is essentially a distributed system, with distinct functions for the central and local sites. Innovative Interfaces Inc. software was selected by OhioLINK and will reside on systems at all local sites and at the central site. All sites will run on state-of-the-art DEC RISC processor machines.

View from a Phase I site

Miami is participating in the first phase of implementation and will be among the first libraries to contribute their holdings to the central site. Participation in OhioLINK has had a profound impact on the goals and day-to-day functions of the local site libraries, including Miami.

Miami has enjoyed excellent representation on most OhioLINK committees. Staff from all areas of the library attend these meetings and participate in decision making. Each committee meets on the average of once or twice a month in Columbus for an entire day, although during times of intense work, two-day stints in Columbus are sometimes necessary. These committees make decisions of great importance, including database profiling and indexing, database preparation, circulation policies, and OPAC screen design. For this reason, participation and input from all participating libraries is crucial.

The amount of staff time and travel money Miami University Libraries has devoted to OhioLINK has been considerable. However, this intense committee work has given committee members an opportunity to work closely with other Ohio library staff on common problems. The strong support for OhioLINK among the member libraries can be attributed in part to the high level of involvement and influence this committee structure offers.

The OhioLINK project calls for a reasonable level of uniformity among the eighteen institutions' catalogs and the central-site catalog. It is generally agreed that designing the individual library and central-site systems to look the same and respond identically will make it easier for patrons to negotiate the OhioLINK network. Discrepancies in indexing, circulation and interlibrary loan policies, and screen design can confuse users. However, among the eighteen sites factors such as size, student body makeup, and faculty needs vary greatly. The diversity of the libraries participating in OhioLINK makes complete agreement among all cooperating sites unlikely. At Miami University the Innovative Interfaces system was up and running before OhioLINK officially selected it. Profiling, indexing, and other decisions were already made and would be difficult and/or expensive to reverse had OhioLINK departed significantly from Miami's decisions. For Miami, complete uniformity with other OhioLINK sites was unrealistic from the outset.

OhioLINK libraries have begun to plan for the creation of the central database. Many institutions have developed local cataloging practices that are unique to that institution and may be confusing when records are merged into the database at the central site. These anomalies are discussed in planning committees to assess their impact on the central site.

The OhioLINK project is based on the assumption that libraries have reliable access to the OarNet and the OhioLINK central database. The campus network at Miami University is in the early stages of formation, and the OhioLINK project has provided the impetus for upgrading both the library and the campus networks. The increased connectivity mandated by OhioLINK has elevated the status of the libraries in the campus community. OhioLINK has also driven the development of the statewide network. Connectivity between campuses, provided by OarNet, has been upgraded with new equipment and increased bandwidth. OhioLINK has fostered coordination between OarNet and the local sites to secure equipment and network upgrades, determine network paths and redundancy, and resolve network failures.

The OhioLINK project will provide funding to support retrospective conversion for participating libraries. The current level of funding is probably insufficient to completely convert all state paper cataloging records to electronic format. Currently only one-third of the records for the Miami University collection are in electronic format, so this part of the project is of utmost importance. In fact, most local retrospective-conversion efforts will be dependent on OhioLINK. Without OhioLINK funding, this process could take Miami as long as twenty years to complete.

Preparing Ohio libraries for the future

　　While still in its early stages, the OhioLINK project shows great promise. Currently, slippage in the implementation time line due to extended contract negotiations has presented the greatest challenge in the project's development. The cooperation among the eighteen sites has been extremely high, the state has demonstrated strong support for OhioLINK, and the Innovative Interfaces/OhioLINK partnership has made a promising start. New OhioLINK staff have been appointed, the central database load has begun, and external database loading is scheduled to begin in the next few months. Two of the six local sites have live databases, and the central database is scheduled to be "introduced" to OhioLINK libraries during the summer of 1992. The evolution of this project will be watched closely as OhioLINK introduces its vision of information technology for the twenty-first century.

　　　　(Published in *Wilson Library Bulletin*. V. 66, No. 10, June 1992: pp. 43 – 45.)

未来从现在开始：
俄亥俄州图书馆自动化、资讯服务与网络化

The Future Begins Now:
Ohio's Library Automation, Information Services, and Networking[①]

  Academic libraries in the state of Ohio pioneered cooperative library automation. They established OCLC in the 1970's and 1980's, libraries in Ohio introduced local systems, primarily by purchasing available turnkey systems for online public access catalogs, circulation, serials control, and acquisitions—ranging from separate modules to integrated systems. As institutions individually acquired systems, they found communications between systems nearly impossible. As a result, local advances in automation failed to support inter-institutional resource sharing.

  Looking toward the year 2000 and recognizing the necessity and desirability of a state-wide library network to link all major academic libraries (the original OCLC vision resurrected), a new, unified library system has been planned and is presently in the first stage of implementation. This paper describes the planning process for this new system supported by state and private university libraries which began three years ago and discusses its general concept, governance, and the future. Libraries working together for automation and networking offers the best approach to using advanced information technology to better serve library users and to cope with the information explosion.

  (Published in *The Proceedings*, edited by Chen Yu, published by Shanghai Scientific & Technical Publishers, 1992: pp. 59 – 60.)

[①] This is an abstract of the paper presented at "the International Seminar on Collection Development and Resource Sharing in Modern Library" (现代图书馆藏书建设与资源共享国际研讨会), May 17 – 20, 1992, Xi'an, China.

俄亥俄州学术图书馆准备迎接 21 世纪

Ohio Academic Libraries Prepare for the Twenty-first Century[①]

HISTORICAL BACKGROUND

Complementary developments in library automation and information handling in the United States during the decade of the 1960s laid the groundwork for the revolution in library and information services throughout the world. Noteworthy among these were the development of the Medical Literature Analysis and Retrieval System (MEDLARS) by the National Library of Medicine, the standardization of the Machine-Readable Catalog (MARC) format by the Library of Congress, the computerization of large indexing and abstracting databases by publishers, and more importantly, the establishment of the Ohio College Library Center (OCLC) by academic libraries in Ohio.

The formation of OCLC in 1967 and its subsequent growth into a world-wide network of 14,322 libraries of all types and sizes, sharing an ever expanding online bibliographic database of 25.3 million cataloging records in February 1992,[②] has been well recorded in library literature. Back on August 26, 1971, Ohio University was the first library in the world to catalog online into OCLC's online union catalog and shared cataloging system. This historic event was remembered and recreated on November 12, 1990. Honoring Ohio University for its contribution of the first online record into the OCLC online union catalog, OCLC invited Ohio University to be the first library to input a record into the new OCLC PRISM system.

OCLC'S SUCCESS AND SHORTCOMINGS

During the 1970s and 1980s, OCLC (by then renamed the Online Computer Library Center-reflecting its expansion far beyond the bounds of Ohio) enjoyed unprecedented success with its online network of shared cataloging through its online union catalog and interlibrary loan subsystems—which help contain the costs of library operations and speed cataloging and interlibrary loan processes. The OCLC experience provided a model for library cooperation and networking; however, its efforts to develop other subsystems, mostly for local operations—such as an online public access catalog (OPAC), circulation, serials control, and acquisitions, either lagged behind schedule or failed. This caused many libraries to seek other alternatives to automate the library functions not covered by OCLC. The availability of minicomputers with large and expandable capacities as well as relative affordability in cost (compared to mainframe computers) provided the instrument to meet these needs. Some libraries developed their own local systems, but the majority chose from among many turnkey systems.[③] Most of these systems did not offer a full range of library functions. Many were modular, offering various functions separately. The idea of an integrated library system was popular but seldom fully realized throughout the 1980s.

A 1988 survey of thirteen state-supported universities and two medical colleges in Ohio found that all were members of OCLC, one had a locally developed system, eight had acquired local

---

[①] Presented at the International Symposium and Exhibition on the Latest Development in Technologies for Library Service, September 6-10, 1992, Beijing, China, under the sponsorship of the National Library of China.
  "Speech Prepared for Library in the 90's International Symposium on the Latest Development in Technologies of Library Service."
[②] Statistics are from *OCLC Newsletter*, No. 195 (Jan./Feb. 1992), p. 11.
[③] I have described my experiences in this area in "Applications of Information Technology in an American Library—The Case of Ohio University Libraries," *Proceedings of the First Pacific Conference on New Information Technology for Library and Information Professionals*, June 16-18, 1987, Bangkok, edited by Ching-Chih Chen and David I. Raitt (West Newton, MA: MicroUse Information, 1987), pp. 155-164.

systems from five different vendors, and the remainder were in the process of either selecting or planning for a local system.

Since the creation of OCLC, there has been a strong tradition of cooperation among all libraries in Ohio. State-supported university libraries, for example, have long-standing agreements for reciprocal borrowing and free photocopying and mailing for interlibrary loans. When telefacsimile became common in these libraries in the late 1980s, it also was free for delivery of urgently needed documents. Dial access to each others' online public access catalogs also was available; however, the different search methods required by the different local systems proved a formidable barrier. It is not easy for the average user to learn and use many different systems. Linking the different systems into an interconnected network was seen as, at best, a band-aid solution, in which the functionality of the weakest system became the norm for all.

A SERENDIPITOUS BEGINNING

In 1986, the State Legislature of Ohio asked the Ohio Board of Regents (OBOR) —the state agency charged with coordinating and overseeing the development of public higher education in Ohio-to "conduct a study of the need for, and the alternatives to, a significant expansion of space for state college and university libraries". The Legislature had been increasingly asked to invest millions and hundreds of millions of dollars to build new libraries for state-supported universities. In response, the OBOR appointed a seventeen-member Library Study Committee to assess the growing need for additional space by state-supported university libraries and to explore possible alternatives. Chaired by Dr. Elaine Hairston, the then Vice Chancellor for Academic and Special Programs (she has since become Chancellor) of the Regents, the Committee decided early in its deliberations to broaden its original charges to include an assessment of "the role of the academic library ... in its broadest contemporary sense" and "consider such opportunities for improving the quality of libraries as might appear in the context of its consideration"[1].

According to the Committee's report, *Academic Libraries in Ohio: Progress Through Collaboration, Storage, and Technology*, of a year-long study published in September 1987, the Committee felt that:

"This wider perspective is necessary because the academic libraries of today have a threefold purpose, serving not only as a storehouse of information, but also as a gateway to information held elsewhere, and as a center for instruction about information."[2]

Among the Committee's recommendations on "collaboration, storage, and technology". the principal one for collaboration was to implement " as expeditiously as possible a statewide electronic catalog system". Collateral recommendations included retrospective conversion of remaining paper cataloging records to MARC format, the development and implementation of a statewide delivery system for library materials, and a plan for a cooperative preservation program.[3] From the main and collateral recommendations, the planning for an Ohio Library Access System (OLAS) began almost immediately. During the planning process, the name, Ohio Library Access System (OLAS), was changed to Ohio Library and Information System (OLIS) and, again, to Ohio Library and Information Network, with the acronym OhioLINK.

---

[1] Ohio Board of Regents. Library Study Committee. *Academic Libraries in Ohio: Progress Through Collaboration, Storage, and Technology*. Report of the Library Study Committee (Columbus, Ohio: Ohio Board of Regents, 1987), p. vii.
[2] *Ibid.*
[3] *Ibid.*

PARTICIPATORY PLANNING[1]

To oversee planning for a statewide electronic library system, the Ohio Board of Regents established a Steering Committee, supported by three taskforces (one each to represent the views of librarians, systems managers, and users-but with representatives of the other two on each), and four subcommittees under the Librarian's View Task Force (Catalog Creation and Maintenance; Online Public Access Catalog; Circulation, Interlibrary Loan, and Document Delivery; and Acquisitions, Serials, and Collection Management and Development). Adding the seventeen library directors of the Inter-University Library Council and the State Librarian of Ohio, all of which play key roles in OhioLINK, the number of people directly involved in the planning well exceeded one hundred and, with special working conferences to present interim findings and discuss alternatives, the total number was three or four times that high.

Early in the planning process, the Board of Regents commissioned two studies, one by RMG Consultants to carry out a feasibility study on linking state university automated library systems[2] and, later, another by Hurley Consulting Corporation to evaluate centralized vs. distributed approaches to the statewide system.[3]

The cooperative efforts of the participating institutions and individuals have resulted in the following demonstrable accomplishments from January 1988 to the time of this writing, March 1992. These have been the results of hundreds of meetings and thousands of person-hours.

1. Issued a PLANNING PAPER, November 1988.[4]
2. Prepared following detailed documents.
   - Request for Information (RFI), August 1988.
   - Request for Proposal (RFP), August 1989.
   - RFI for the OLIS Workstation, October 1989.
   - RFP for Interlibrary Image Transfer (IIT) System (draft), December 1990.
   - OhioLINK Networking Task Force-Phase I Report, March 1991.
   - RFP for Database Preparation, April 1991.
   - RFP for Retrospective Conversion, January 1992.
3. Published an overview of the Ohio Library & Information System (OLIS): *Connecting People, Libraries & Information for Ohio's Future*.[5]
4. Sponsored three state-wide workshops on the state-of-the-art in networked library systems, the OhioLINK model, and a scholar's workstation.
5. Obtained funding from the State of Ohio capital budgets for 1988-1990 and 1990-1992 and the operating budget for 1989-1991.
6. Studied the responses to RFP from eight vendors (including two-day demonstrations by each-attended by selected staff from each participating library), further investigated the four ranked highest, and selected the final one.
7. Conducted detailed contract negotiations with the selected vendor, culminating in a signed agreement, providing for installing systems after July 1, 1991.
8. Developed and adopted a governance structure and conducted a nationwide search for an

---

[1] The planning process was more fully described in my "Planning Process and Considerations for a State-wide Academic Libraries Information System in Ohio," in *Proceedings of the Second Conference on New Information Technology for Library and Information Professionals and Educational Media Specialists and Technologists*, May 29-31, 1989, Singapore, edited by Ching-chih Chen and David I. Raitt (West Newton, MA: MicroUse Information, 1989), pp. 203-210.

[2] RMG Consultants. *Alternative Approaches to Linking State University Automated Library Systems for the Ohio Board of Regents* (Chicago: RMG Consultants, 1988).

[3] Bernard Hurley. *Centralization vs. Decentralization for Large Library System in a Changing Technological Environment: A Position Paper for the Ohio Board of Regents* (Berkeley, California: Hurley Consulting Corp., 1988).

[4] OLAS Steering Committee. *Ohio Library Access System Planning Paper, November 2, 1988* (Columbus, Ohio: Ohio Board of Regents, 1988).

[5] Ohio Library & Information System, OLIS. *Connecting People, Libraries, & Information for Ohio's Future* (Columbus, Ohio: Ohio Board of Regents, 1989).

Executive Director and a Director of Library Systems.
9. Appointed Dr. Len Simutis as the Executive Director.
10. Selected Wright State University (in Dayton, Ohio) as the OhioLINK central site.
11. Established an implementation schedule with Phase I to begin in 1991.
12. Negotiated for databases to be loaded at the central site and available to all participants.

PARTICIPATING LIBRARIES

Initially Ohio Library and Information Network was to include the thirteen state-supported universities and two independent state-supported medical colleges:

University of Akron
Bowling Green State University
Central State University
University of Cincinnati
Cleveland State University
Kent State University
Miami University
Ohio State University
Ohio University
Shawnee State University
University of Toledo
Wright State University
Youngstown State University
The Medical College of Ohio
Northeast Ohio University College of Medicine

However, early in the planning, two large private universities were added:

Case-Western Reserve University
University of Dayton

The State Library of Ohio, which has cataloged its materials into the Ohio State University's LCS system also became a participant.

The right of "access" but not "use", at least initially, will be granted to all two-year state-supported college libraries.[1] Indeed, such access to library portions of the system (not including borrowing privileges) will be available to the entire citizenry of the state. Access to non-library databases will be determined later by licensing agreements. The system architecture, as envisioned by the planners, should be capable of adding new members at various levels of participation at later stages. OhioLINK. The system should be adequate in size and have a sufficiently powerful software "search engine" to organize, sort, and retrieve vast quantities of information stored within the state and around the world. It will be linked to each institution's wide-area Network (WAN) through Ohio's high-speed supercomputer network, OARnet (Ohio Academic Resources Network), already in place (although requiring upgrading to T-1 for some sites). Major electronic databases (bibliographic, textual, or image) that have the greatest potential use and can be leased at reasonable cost will be made available on the central site and be accessible online to the campus systems for the benefit of economies of scale.

---

[1] The difference between "Access" and "Use" has been clearly delineated. "Access" to the OhioLINK union catalog will be available to all Ohioans through campus computer workstations and terminals and through dial-in access from personal computers equipped with standardized OhioLINK software. Implicitly, this includes any interested two-year or private colleges. Comprehensive "Use" of OhioLINK—including borrowing, document delivery, and non-library databases-will initially be available to students, faculty, and staff of the seventeen participating university libraries.

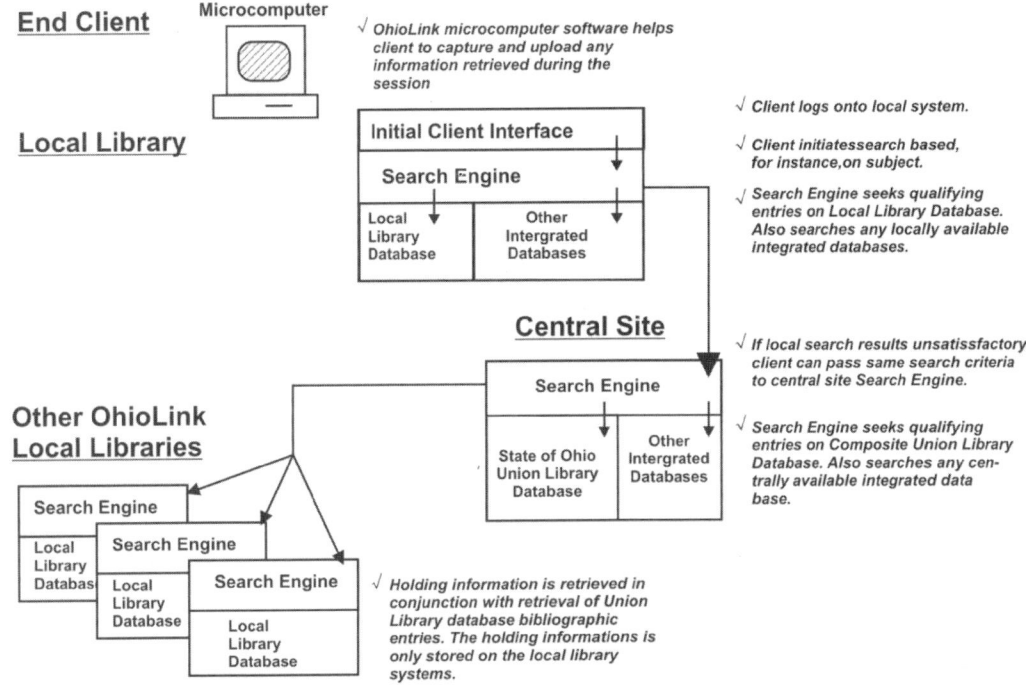

DIAGRAM I   OhioLINK USER SEARCH EXAMPLE

Each local campus system will support the institution's library catalog, circulation, other databases, and other library functions (including those for any branch libraries or campuses). Faculty and students from all OhioLINK universities will have online access to materials held in their local libraries plus all participating libraries. They can request materials at other campuses online through the OhioLINK intra-circulation network (instead of interlibrary loan in the traditional sense) without library staff mediation. Most printed materials will be delivered by a contracted delivery service; articles and smaller documents will be sent by telefacsimile with high-definition replication (400 dots per inch or higher); and materials in electronic formats will be transmitted electronically.

As of July 1, 1989, according to the statistics provided in the RFP[①], the combined resources of the seventeen universities libraries exceeded 19 million volumes of printed materials. Nearly 550,000 volumes are added annually and 146,000 journals were subscribed to in 1987 – 1988. During the same year, these libraries circulated a total of 6.1 millions volumes and, through interlibrary loan operations, borrowed 119,143 items and loaned 239,176 items. OhioLINK will effectively open these resources together and greatly expand the accessibility and usage of them.

THE SYSTEM AND NETWORK OVERVIEW

The conceptual system and network configuration, as shown in Diagram II, envisions a three-tier network ranging from the individual campuses to OhioLINK Central and extending into national

---

① "Request for Proposal for the Ohio Library & Information System (OLIS) on behalf of the Ohio Board of Regents and Ohio Library & Information System" (Columbus, Ohio: OLIS, August 4, 1989), pp. 203 – 208.

and international networks. The local campus systems integrated into OhioLINK support their own catalogs, local databases and CD-ROM networks, and all desirable library functions. Through gateways, local users can access external information providers. Through OARnet, users can search the cumulative central database or national and international networks. An unsuccessful search will offer the user an option of having the search continued at the central site or in other databases without need to re-enter the search. An example of a user search of the local campus system and from there to the central system and other local campus systems in OhioLINK is shown in DIAGRAM III[①].

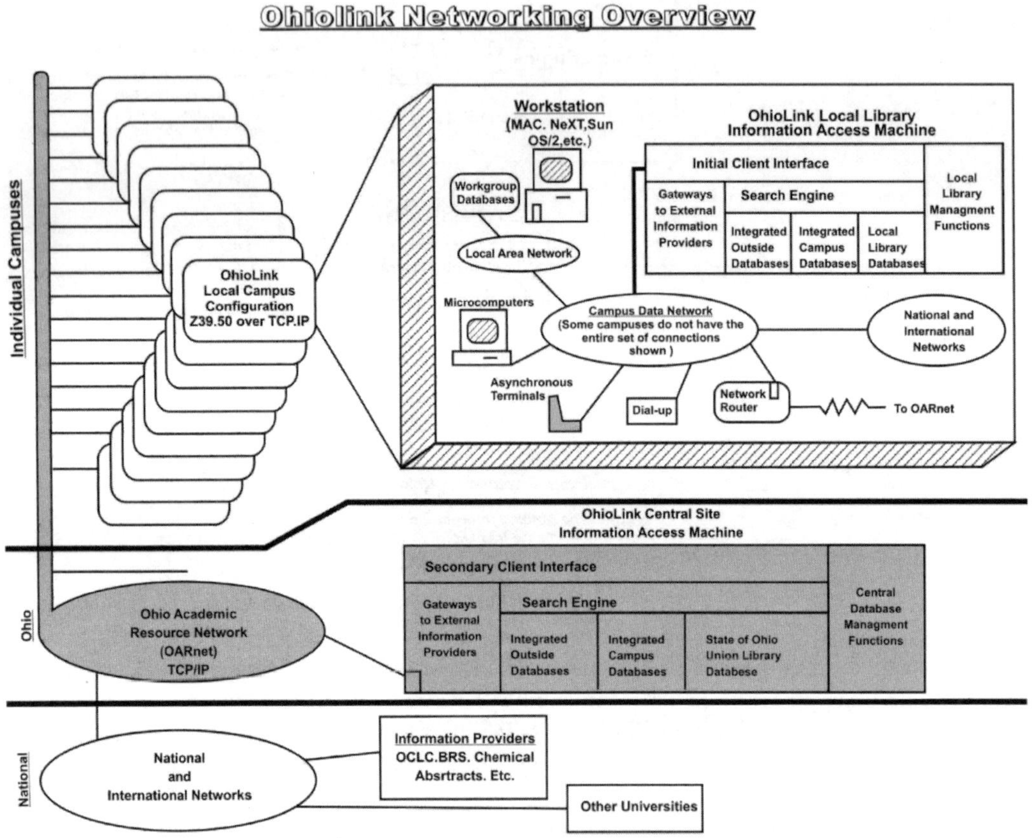

DIAGRAM II OhioLINK NETWORKING OVERVIEW

FROM MANY, ONE—THE OhioLINK VISION

During early deliberations, after a careful analysis of responses to the RFI, the Steering Committee decided that for best system performance and ease of use, there should be a single hardware platform (adjusted for quantum variations in sizes of collections and constituencies) and one software system for all seventeen institutions and the central site. Despite this basic uniformity to assure compatibility, the model selected is essentially a distributed system,[②] with distinct functions for the central and local sites. Diagram I presents the conceptual configuration of the system.

---

① *Ibid.*, pp. 8–9

② The model was reinvigorated by the report by Hurley, *Centralization vs. Decentralization*, and through Hurley's participation in a workshop attended by representatives of all participating institutions at Kent State University.

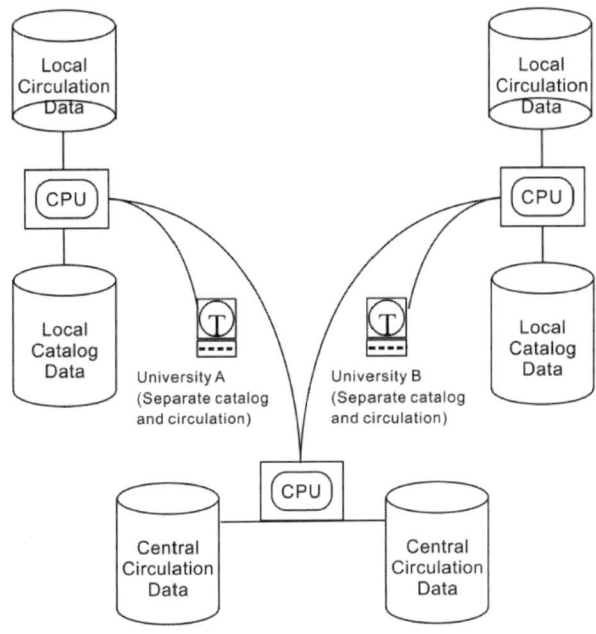

DIAGRAM III OhioLINK CONCEPTUAL SYSTEM CONFIGURATION

The central-site system will contain cataloging and authority records, a union list for each bibliographic record, a routing capacity to transfer a search request from one local system to another, additional databases, and gateways to systems outside.

SELECTION OF A SYSTEM

The selection of a system was no easy task. It was conceded that there was no one "perfect" system that met the OhioLINK model or the specifications detailed in the 242-page RFP, REQUEST FOR PROPOSAL FOR THE OHIO LIBRARY & INFORMATION SYSTEM (OLIS). The optimal result that one could hope for would be to select among the best available systems that met most of the requirements and to gain a commitment from the vendor to work with OhioLINK for further development in an ever changing environment of technologies, information, and needs. In fact, from early stages, OhioLINK was seen as a practical effort to address immediate needs and a research and development effort to better serve information seekers. In the spirit of cooperation, all participating institutions agreed early that once a system was selected, every institution would give up its local system and switch to the one system within a reasonable time schedule (a change made more palatable by the commitment of the Board of Regents to cover the capital costs of the new system).

The RFP—the key document in the selection of the system—was sent to more than 40 vendors on August 9, 1989. It contained more than 5,000 specifications in 10 chapters, 11 tables, 2 glossary lists, and 11 appendices. Separate chapters treat General Requirements, System Specifications, Catalog Creation and Maintenance, Online Public Access Catalog, Circulation, Interlibrary Loan, and Document Delivery, Acquisitions and Serials, and Collection Management and Development. By the October 20, 1989, deadline, eight vendors had submitted proposals:

Ameritech Information Systems, Inc. (With OCLC as a subcontractor)
CARL Systems Inc. (CARL) Data Research Associates, Inc. (DRA)
Geac Computer Corp. (GEAC)

Innovative Interfaces, Inc. (III)
NOTIS Systems Inc. (NOTIS)
UNISYS
VTLS, Inc. (VTLS)

After the proposals were received, copies of the thousands of pages submitted by the vendors (including stock phrases about the company and the system, manuals, and specific responses to the RFP) were distributed to each participating institution. Open hearings were held on some campuses as well as three state-wide hearings to solicit maximal input from all sectors of the academic community in Ohio.

During February 1990, two vendors each week were invited to make two-day presentations and demonstrations that were attended by all task forces, subcommittees, the Steering Committee, and anyone else that a participating institution might wish to send. In April 1990, based on evaluations submitted following the February sessions, the four vendors ranked highest were targeted for a series of site visits by

an investigation team appointed by the Steering Committee. The four finalists are CARL, DRA, III, and VTLS. As a user of VTLS, Ohio University was visited by the Team on May 7 – 8, 1990. At the end of the visits, Innovative Interfaces, Inc. (III) was recommended as the top choice for OhioLINK in July 1990. Intensive negotiations with III began immediately after the selection and a contract was drafted for review in January 1991. The contract was signed later in 1991.

IMPLEMENTATION PLAN AND TIMETABLE

As outlined in the final draft of the Contract Agreement.[①] the full operation and implementation of OhioLINK will occur in phases. Phase I is set forth in the Implementation Schedule attached to the Agreement as Appendix C which states that "It is the firm plan of OhioLINK to install library automation systems at each of the 17 Affiliated Institutions and at the OhioLINK central site."[②]

In Phase I, which began in mid-1991 (following signing of the contract and release of funds by the State of Ohio), III software and hardware has begun to be installed at six affiliated Institutions and the central site. The six Phase I sites are:

Bowling Green State University
Case Western Reserve University
Central State University
Miami University of Cincinnati
Wright State University

In advance of installation, site preparation and OARnet telecommunications should be ready for each of these locations. Because of delays in database preparation, the projected implementation schedule is slipping; however, it is anticipated (as of November 1991) that most of the Phase I installations and implementation will be accomplished by mid-1992. Other innovations to be included in the system by July 1992 include a requirement that most transactions take place in "real time" rather than in a batch process later, ability to continue searches at other campuses and in other databases without re-keying information (a failed search will offer this as an immediate option), and the ability of a user to directly request delivery of an item from another campus.

Integral to Phase I, an RFP was released in April 1991 for Database Conversion. An Ohio contractor in conjunction with AMIGOS and Blackwell North America was awarded the contract.

In Phase II, which begins in July 1992, III software and hardware will be installed at the 11

---

① Agreement for an Automated Library System between Innovative Interfaces. Inc. and the Ohio Board of Regents on Behalf of the Ohio Library and Information Network.... Columbus, Ohio: OhioLINK, February 6, 1991.
② *Ibid.*

remaining Affiliated Institution libraries and their records loaded into the central union list. Other new features for the union catalog (e.g., delivery of electronic images of documents) are planned for this phase as well.

THE GOVERNANCE AND DIVISION OF RESPONSIBILITIES

Because the success of OhioLINK largely depends on sufficient funding—both initially and continuing—from the state government, the leadership and support of the Ohio Board of Regents have been crucial from the beginning. It was especially important that the Regents recognized OhioLINK as one of the Regents' Selective Excellence Initiatives that are funded by the state to encourage outstanding programs which contribute to the economic development of the state. This recognition of the contributions of library and information services to the educational mission and economic health of the state reflects a greater awareness of the vital and expanding roles of libraries.

The Board of Regents, in consultation with the Steering Committee and the Inter-University Library Council, has developed a governance structure for OhioLINK that has a Governing Board, an Executive Director, a Policy Advisory Council, and a Library Advisory Council. Early in the planning, the Board and the Steering Committee consciously deferred discussions of the governance until the selection of the system hardware and software was completed. They believe that postponing the political questions kept the planning focused on the immediate tasks. Each Council may, as dictated by need, establish advisory groups and committees. Diagram IV shows the governance structure.

The GOVERNING BOARD consists of nine university provosts (principal academic officer) selected from the seventeen OhioLINK institutions and one private university provost. These nine voting members serve staggered, three-year rotating terms. The Chancellor of the Ohio Board of Regents, OhioLINK Executive Director and Chair and Vice-Chair of the Policy Advisory Council serve ex-officio. A representative of two-year colleges is to be added as an observer. The Governing Board selects its own chair and meets three times a year or as needed to approve budgets, review major policy recommendations, and hire the Executive Director. Biennial budget recommendations will be approved and forwarded to the Ohio Board of Regents for incorporation into its requests to the State Legislature.

The POLICY ADVISORY COUNCIL consists of seventeen voting members serving staggered three-year terms. All OhioLINK universities are represented plus the Director of OARnet ex-officio and a representative of two-year colleges. Members include at least three faculty members, four library directors, three computer center directors, three academic deans, and two systems librarians. They are recommended by the universities and appointed by the Governing Board. The Council meets every other month or as needed to advise the Executive Director on policy and budget matters. It selects its own chair. The Chair of the Library Advisory Council serves as Vice-Chair. The Executive Director serves ex-officio.

The LIBRARY ADVISORY COUNCIL includes all OhioLINK member library directors and one representative of two-year colleges. The state-wide association of law libraries has been invited to send an observer. As of this writing, a number of advisory committees have been formed, especially to address implementation issues, including:
* Database Preparation Committee
* Retrospective Conversion Committee
* Circulation, Interlibrary Loan and Document Delivery Committee
* Acquisitions and Serials Committee
* Collection Management & Development Committee
* OPAC Committee
* External Databases Committee
* Education and Training Committee

Although there are various views on the governing structure, both pro and con, its effectiveness and results are still to be seen. It is hoped that the model (which is based on the Board of Regents Supercomputer Center) will be flexible yet dynamic enough to meet the changing needs during the formative years of OhioLINK.

As happens, sometimes unplanned structures are more important than formal organizational charts. Exemplifying this, in late 1990, the Interim Executive Director arranged for an OhioLINK list on BITNET to facilitate communications. Since that time, the list has provided a forum for rapid exchange of ideas, concerns, and information. While relatively few librarians are particularly active on BITNET, the vitality of this list (and other library lists) is likely to serve as an impetus for more persons to become aware and involved and is likely to serve as a means of bypassing the formal committee structure to assure that issues are addressed. It has also provided rapid, systemwide distribution of committee minutes.

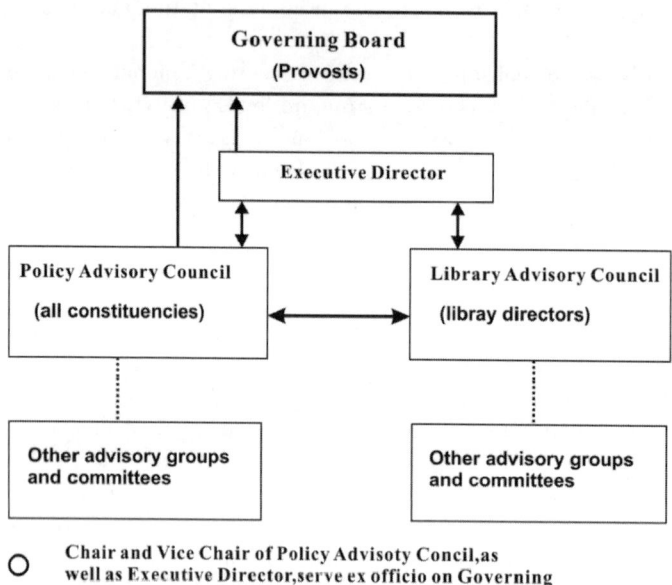

DIAGRAM IV   OhioLINK GOVERNING STRUCTURE

THE ROAD AHEAD

Ohio libraries have been in the forefront in library automation and innovation since the 1960s. The creation of OCLC drastically changed the world of library cataloging, union catalog, interlibrary loan, and networking. The growth and development within Ohio of the Chemical Abstract Service, CompuServe, Mead Data, etc. have made Ohio, a major center for the information industry. The planning of OhioLINK for the 1990s provides a new vision into the future. It is hoped that it will equal the importance of OCLC to set the pace for connecting people, libraries, and information.

As OhioLINK continues to expand, electronic document delivery, scholar's workstations, and other new features will be augmented. The scholar's workstation is one project virtually assured to have impact well-beyond the OhioLINK system. It is clearly a research and development (R & D) project, well in advance anything available today. The workstation will be a multi-tasking environment, capable of providing plain language (refined by an artificial intelligence component) access to a wide range of information sources and networks, of learning the types of information usually sought by a user and providing downloaded updates to such information without further mediation by periodically contacting likely sources of the information, building on this knowledge core to provide serendipity comparable to browsing shelves, and presenting the information in the form needed by the user-ready for immediate incorporation into reports and publications. Moreover, it should enable the user to use his/her preferred method of operations (menus, commands, or object oriented) and to do so without requiring computer expertise or tedious referral to printed documents (i. e., a short learning curve augmented by an intelligent "help" capability). The goal is to return the computer environment to the status of a tool which, like an automobile, will enable scholars and researchers to concentrate on the areas of expertise rather than protocols, at an affordable price.

Although the changeover to III likely will be difficult for libraries satisfied with their current systems, everyone is convinced that the long-term benefits from a single system will outweigh temporary inconveniences during the transition. Networking will greatly enhance the availability and accessibility of pooled resources. The high-speed telecommunications capability will provide a gateway to the ever-growing world of information stored in electronic formats around the world. Much can be gained in cooperative and coordinated acquisitions, collection development and management, preservation, resource sharing, and scholarly communication through OhioLINK. When fully implemented, OhioLINK will be the most powerful statewide library and information network in the nation with unparalleled sophistication and efficiency.

(Published in *Library in the 90's, Selected Papers of the International Symposium on the Latest Development in Technologies of Library Service*, September 6 – 10, 1992, Beijing, China. Edited by Sun Chengjian and Jiang Bingxin. Beijing: International Academic Publishers, 1993: pp. 292 – 308.)

领先信息技术——国家图书馆的作用

Advancing Information Technologies: The Role of National Libraries[①]

1. Recent development of information technologies:

During the last three or four decades, the pace of development in information technologies has accelerated greatly, inducing revolutionary changes in library and information services. The frequently heard phrase today is "Virtual Library", whereby users can access information resources far greater than those actually present in any single library. The advancement of computer technology and the sophistication of software packages for library applications have transformed the ways that libraries operate. Improvements in telecommunications and electronic delivery technologies have affected library networking, resource sharing, and electronic publishing. Optical disk storage technologies have transformed information storage and retrieval. And the growing use of interactive hyper- and multi-media technologies are expanding the nature and organization of information. These and many other developments are exciting and require that national libraries, regardless of the different stages of development in their respective countries, be more involved in the monitoring technological changes and be more proactive in the adoption of appropriate information technologies for improving library and information services.

For the past thirty years, we have seen the progressive changes of libraries from the "Paper Library", to the "Automated Library", to the "Networked Library", and now on to the "Electronic Library" of the 1990s. In a recent book, *Redesigning Library Services*, Michael Buckland observed that each of the later changes do not necessarily replace the others; instead, each coexists with and expands on the technological bases of library operations and materials of the earlier ones.[②]

Even though national libraries in various nations differ in their structures, charges, authorities, and responsibilities, each has a leadership role in the development and improvement of library and information services in the country. As a national library, it also represents the country in international arena where standards and cooperative arrangements, many with technological implications, are discussed and determined. This means that national libraries must be well informed and knowledgeable about technological development and are able to promote those appropriate to their respective countries.

Traditionally, each national libraries often has the responsibility to establish and maintain the national bibliography and union catalog of the country. It also provides cataloging information to libraries by way of **Cataloging in Publication** and by some forms of published catalogs and/or cards. All of these and more can be done effectively now by computers and telecommunications in an online, real-time, interactive, and networked mode.

Even with the greatest possible funding and the aid of information technologies, no national library can acquire all of the published information resources of the world and catalog them for access by users. However, through cooperation with the nation's libraries and by adoption of appropriate information technologies, national libraries can develop effective and implementable programs for cooperative acquisitions, cataloging, resource sharing, and preservation among major libraries in their respective countries. Providing leadership in the development of national library and information systems which are capable of achieving the above goal has become the major role

---

① Presented in International Conference on National Libraries: Toward the 21st Century, Taiwan, April 20 – 24, 1993.
② Michael Keeble Buckland. *Redesigning Library Service: a Manifesto*. Chicago: American Library Association, 1992: pp. 5 – 6.

of every national library.

Since the application of appropriate information technologies has become inevitable in developing countries, cooperative and coordinated efforts for the adoption and use of modern information technologies may become cost-effective. Using cataloging as an example, even where there may be relatively cheap labor costs and a huge labor force, trained professional catalogers are in short supply. Cooperative and shared cataloging can be facilitated by employment of information technologies to reduce duplication of effort, speed up cataloging operations, to save costs in the long run, to make library collections more rapidly available, and, through computerized union catalogs and networks, to improve accessibility of pooled resources. With a networked online union catalog, both interlibrary-loan operations and collaboration in collection development among the nation's libraries become possible. National libraries are often in the best strategic position to lead these efforts. These information technologies are now available and affordable if carefully planned and executed at the national level.

In the United States, even though the Library of Congress has long assumed the role of the national library, has established and maintained the National Union Catalog, and has provided cataloging records to libraries, the largest bibliographic databases are developed and operated by large bibliographic utilities such as OCLC Online Computer Library Center and RLIN. This situation in the U. S., even though it has worked well in some respects, does not necessarily mean that other countries should follow the American model. It indicates, however, that—if a national library does not take the action promptly and effectively when technology is ready and the timing is right—others may do it.

2. Maximizing the application of information technologies:

To maximize benefits from the application of information technologies, each country must take into consideration its own conditions, environment and needs. National libraries, therefore, must take the lead in monitoring the development of information technologies, adopting and adapting those most appropriate, and planning for their applications, to advise the government on the desirability, feasibility, and funding needs, to seek necessary legislation and government supports, to assist in building an information infrastructure, to promote national plans and to implement them. Most important in all these efforts is a clear vision of the future direction in the application of information technologies to enhance and expand library and information services.

In reviewing the recent efforts of the National Central Library in the people's Republic of China in the application, promotion, and implementation of appropriate information technologies, it is clear that the National Central Library has done an excellent job and has established a model for other countries which are contemplating in the application of information technologies.

Since 1980, in collaboration with the Library Association of China (Taiwan), the National Central Library has played a major role in the undertaking of the "*Chinese Library Automation Planning Project*". This included the compilation of the "*Chinese Character Code for Information Interchange*" (CCCII), development of the "*Chinese MARC Format*", complete revision of the "*Chinese Cataloging Rules*", and establishment of the **Chinese National Bibliography** and other computerized databases.[①] The success of this project has enabled the National Central Library to launch other automation projects, including the introduction of "*International Standard Book Numbers*" in Taiwan, "*Cataloging in Publication*," and others.[②] In 1987, with the approval of the plan to establish the "*National Bibliographic Information Network*" by Executive Yuan, the National Central Library launched another major effort to plan and implement a nationwide system for cooperative cataloging and an online union catalog of participating libraries. After four years of intensive work, close consultation with

---

① Hwa-Wei Lee. "Recent Breakthroughs in Library Automation in Taiwan" in *Librarianship in World Perspective* by Hwa-Wei Lee (Taipei: Student Book, 1991), pp. 199–209.

② *National Central Library* (Taipei: National Central Library, 1989), p. 10.

participating libraries, selection and acquisition of hardware and software, installation, preparation, training, and testing, the network was formally inaugurated on October 5, 1991. ①

In reviewing the first four issues of the National Bibliographic Information Network Newsletter published quarterly by the National Central Library, it is evident that the establishment of the Network was not without difficulties. ② This resembles the experiences of other such networks in the United States during their formative periods. ③

The development of the National Bibliographic Information Network in Taiwan, through careful planning and the wise adoption of the appropriate information technologies, is an excellent model of what a national library can to take advantage of the new opportunities. Economically, Taiwan is fast becoming an industrialized province with many of the necessary components for library automation and networking. These include:

* Well developed library systems: academic, public, research, and special.
* A large number of well educated and dedicated library and information professionals.
* A strong library association, active and committed.
* General availability of computers in many libraries.
* An up-to-date telecommunication system.
* A high degree of government awareness of the importance of libraries for national development.
* Available government funding.
* The leadership and vision of the National Central Library.

Even though OCLC was attracting favorable reactions with its online library network launched in the early 1970s, serious and organized discussions on nationwide library networking were not held until the formation of the Library of Congress Network Advisory Committee in 1976. ④ Under the table leadership of Henriette D. Avram (who retired from the Library of Congress in 1992), the Committee met twice a year and had most of its proceedings published by the LC's Network Development and MARC Standards Office in the "Network Planning Paper". Although the regular gatherings and discussions of the Committee have been constructive and useful, de facto realization of a national network came from the reorganization and expansion of OCLC.

3. The role of national libraries in the application:

Since the focus of this brief paper is on the role of national libraries in advancing information technologies, this section examines some of these roles from the viewpoint of an academic librarian. As a strong proponent for the application of appropriate information technologies in libraries, this author has witnessed the vital roles of national libraries to expedite applications and to maximize the benefits. National libraries are in a strategic position to assume these roles by acting as a catalyst, a consultant, a planner, a policy-maker, a demonstrator and trainer, a promoter, a coordinator, an implementer, a funding source, and, lastly, a research-and-development agent.

A. Catalyst

Being a catalyst means that national libraries should be the national agent to induce and expedite the process of change in the adoption and application of appropriate information technologies in their respective countries. In addition, to be a catalyst, national libraries should

---

① Hsiu-Ying Chiang. "Major events of the National Bibliographic Information Network." *National Bibliographic Information Network Newsletter.* V. 1, No. 1 (Oct. 1991): pp. 11 – 12.

② *National Bibliographic Information Network Newsletter.* V. 1, Nos. 2, 3, and 4 (Jan., April, and July 1932).

③ See the 22 reports of the *Network Planning Paper* series published by the Network Development and MARC Standards Office of the Library of Congress from 1978 to 1982. The latest report, for example, is on The Role of the National Libraries in the Evolving National Networking; *Proceedings of the Library of Congress Network Advisory Committee Meeting.* December 9 – 11, 1991 (Washington, D. C.: the Library of Congress, 1992; Network Planning Paper, No. 22): 80 p.

④ Lenore S. Maruyama. *The Library of Congress Network Advisory Committee: Its First Decade.* Washington, D. C.: The Library of Congress, 1985: p. 48.

provide strong leadership in technological development and be visionary and forward-looking.

B. Consultant

National libraries should serve as a consultant both to the government departments and to libraries on matters concerning library and information services. One of these is the application of information technologies. National libraries must develop the necessary knowledge and expertise to provide such advice in a timely manner.

C. Planner

National libraries must lead in the development of national library and information systems and networks. To do this, they must be a good planning agency and able to commend the respect and support of other government departments and the nation's libraries. When planning for the application of information technologies, all relevant factors (including financial resources, information infrastructure, library conditions, and varying needs) need to be taken into consideration. Rather than trying to be "all-knowing" and "all-inclusive", an ambitious but unattainable goal, national libraries should work with other libraries with special areas of expertise and strength in a cooperative partnership and a division of labors. As we move toward "networked library" and "electronic library", the concept of "virtual library" should be the planning goal for every library.

D. Policy Maker

The development of national library and information systems and networks necessarily are guided by legislation and up-to-date national library and information policies. National libraries should advise the government on needed legislation and policies and help in drafting or revising these. There should be a close working relationship between the national library and the highest levels of national planning and policy-making bodies in the government to ensure that library development is given high priority and that libraries are empowered and adequately funded to carry out their functions.

E. Demonstrator and Trainer

To promote the adoption or adaptation of appropriate information technologies by libraries, national libraries should establish or support demonstration projects so that new technologies can be demonstrated and tested. The recently established National Demonstration Laboratory for Interactive Information Technology at the Library of Congress provides a model of such an undertaking. The Laboratory is equipped with some of the latest information technologies for exploration and testing. It helps both the public and librarians to "understand the technologies and their uses in library operations".①

In some instances, in the application of new technologies, national libraries should provide training to trainers from testing or participating libraries.

F. Promoter

Once a plan to use certain information technologies is made, active promotion is needed to induce libraries to follow. For example, the creation of an online national union catalog by means of cooperative cataloging will require the participation of all major libraries. This cooperative effort should be actively promoted within the library community to get maximum support and participation.

G. Coordinator

Because the programs of national libraries often have national implications affecting a wide spectrum of the country, extensive coordination with all concerned segments of the government, society, and library community is critical for success. Much of the coordination also involves the process of consultation to achieve a high degree of consensus and support.

H. Implementer

Nothing will happen until it is implemented. National libraries must work out most of the

---

① Kirti Withrow. "LC's Newest Addition to Its Vision for the Future. National Demonstration Laboratory to Open in March." *LC Information Bulletin.* Vol. 51, No. 4 (February 24, 1992): pp. 74–76.

operating details of an impending project with the participating libraries and then implement it.

I. Funding Source

At times, national libraries should act as a funding source for library projects as an incentive to induce library participation, to support innovative pilot projects which may have important national implications, or to encourage development in new directions. For example, for many years the Extramural Programs of the National Library of Medicine in the U. S. has provided financial support with good results through Medical Library Resource Grants, the Integrated Academic Information Management Systems program, and training grants in medical informatics and biotechnology. [①]

J. Research and Development Agent

To advance information technologies in a country, the research and development function of the national library must be emphasized. Through research and development, appropriate technologies and their applications can be identified, tested, and adapted to meet the needs of the country. Although not all the national libraries are well equipped to be totally responsible for the research and development tasks, they should work with other centers in and outside the country and should coordinate the resources and efforts within the country.

[①] Shirley Echelman, "Contributions to Networking at the National Libraries: The Last Three Years," In *The Role of the National Libraries in the Evolving National Networking* (Washington, D. C.: The Library of Congress, 1992. Network Planning Paper No. 22), p. 63.

网络化、电子化的虚拟图书馆
——20世纪90年代的图书馆①

Networked, Electronic and Virtual Library: Libraries of the 1990s

一、前言

目前，在全球范围内建立起来的互联网（Internet）以及为信息高速公路建设新做的一系列工作中一项最基础的工作便是积累大量的电子信息。图书馆和文献情报中心是采集、制作、存贮和提供电子信息资源的主要单位。我们可把图书馆的发展分为三个阶段。第一阶段是传统的以印刷信息为主的图书馆，在这类图书馆中，图书馆的藏书以印刷书刊资料为主，通过卡片目录和检索刊物来反映馆藏信息。第二阶段是自动化图书馆，在这种图书馆中，采用计算机与图书馆自动化管理系统辅助采购、编目、流通、检索、内部管理等，建立机读目录数据库和二次文献数据库，用户通过图书馆联机公共目录（OPAC）和联机情报检索系统查询书目与二次文献信息。第三阶段是电子图书馆，在电子图书馆中一切工作全部采用计算机，信息全部数字化，建立起采集、处理、存贮和提供电子信息的体系结构。电子图书馆形成后的服务方式、信息载体将发生重大变化，用户可以在图书馆、办公室、教室、实验室甚至家中利用联网查询一个或数个数据库，这些数据库中既有电子目录的信息，又有图像、声音、计算机文件、电子书刊等媒体。电子图书馆的实现将把我们带入"虚拟图书馆"的领地，因为在电子图书馆中，像文本、视频、声频等信息以数字化形式在网络上高速传递，使我们只要获取信息而不必关注信息存放在哪里。这一变化使物理存贮信息的图书馆这一概念向"虚拟"或没有围墙图书馆演变。电子图书馆是所有图书馆的发展方向，一些先进国家正在由自动化图书馆向电子图书馆转变。OCLC使许多图书馆进入自动化图书馆的行列，通过网络实现信息资源等的共享，OhioLINK则是向网络化电子化图书馆进军的一个尝试。网络化的图书馆与互联网的组合使我们看到了电子图书馆的未来。

二、OCLC的成功经验

当国会图书馆正编写机读目录格式MARCI时，俄亥俄州高校图书馆的经费却日益入不敷出。面对这种状况，1967年成立了俄亥俄州高校图书馆中心。1968年，国会图书馆改进机读目录标准，称之为MARC 1后，为OCLC的集中编目提供了依据，而且国会图书馆的书目数据磁带也为OCLC数据库提供了内容。1971年，OCLC装载了国会图书馆的数据磁带并实施它的重大改革——联机编目。1971年8月26日，俄亥俄大学图书馆成为世界上第一个进入OCLC数据库联机编目系统进行联合编目的图书馆。以后全美国及欧洲国家的图书馆纷纷加入这一联机编目组织。截止1995年4月，OCLC（现已改名为国际计算机图书馆中心）在世界范围内有2万个成员图书馆或加入联机编目、或参加检索、或加入馆际互借服务，已有三千二百余万条书目数据，馆际互借申请达五千八百万次，OCLC方法是成功的，其78%的记录是由成员馆贡献的，14%的记录由国会图书馆MARC磁带提供，还有的记录是由成员馆改编的国会图书馆记录（即所谓的准MARC资料）。

---

① 辛小萍、张海华编译自 Information Technologies and Information Services, Oct. 20 – 24, 1994, Collection B。

俄亥俄州高校图书馆一开始就以切实可行的实施过程向全美各图书馆表明，区域间共享信息是不可抗拒的。20世纪70年代中期，OCLC成为国家的一个非盈利性机构。虽然OCLC的成功运行使世界图书馆事业向前迈进了一步，但俄亥俄州高校图书馆的许多需求仍然尚未满足。馆际互借子系统的确是实现全美资源共享的革命，但OCLC不能满足成员图书馆各自的自动化管理集成系统的需要。所以OCLC最初的成员馆开始转向其他自动化系统，以满足其余的流通、采购等内部管理系统。实际上，80年代OCLC研制成功了LS2000自动化集成系统时，许多图书馆已从其他图书馆或公司那里购买并使用了自动化系统。LS2000提供了期刊验收和订购等多种功能，这一系统争取了一部分用户，但是大多数图书馆喜欢使用其他集成度高的自动化系统，到了九十年代，OCLC放弃了这一产品。

OCLC从联机共享编目网络向图书馆自动化的社会服务系统发展，并把这种发展从共享编目重点向参考服务重点转变。90年代，OCLC着重向两个方面发展，一是继续在联机编目（OUC）状态下共享编目，并且利用World Cat这个特殊资源推荐给用户可检的书目数据库。World Cat是FirstSearch的一部分，用主题词和关键词检索，这是OCLC从诞生起就开始追求的一个特点并把这一特点结合进联机共享书目库。OCLC向早期的回溯转换服务中加了编目合约，为那些仍以卡片目录为主而缺少技术和人力的图书馆提供回溯机读目录。另一方面，近年来，以自己联机联合目录数据库和巨大的远程联机通信网络为基础，加强参考服务功能，生产出多种二次文献信息产品，以适应用户对信息的需要。各种联机数据库与二三次文献传递服务系统相补充。除World Cat外，First Search提供大约8500多种期刊目次表内容、期刊原文和各种文献索引。为了更好地进行二三次文献服务，First Search已经开始出版电子期刊：The Online Journal of Current Clinic Trials。如对一些文献数据库检索，从1990年起检索Epic的次数已达84万余次，First Search自1991年10月起达到二千余万次。由此可以看出，OCLC已不仅仅是一个图书馆编目与联合目录系统，而且已成为交互式的情报检索系统，尤其是目前与互联网（Internet）相联，其信息资源更丰富。

当OCLC向既定方向逐渐过渡时，它的成员馆的需求常超出OCLC发展来满足图书馆的自动化需要。一份1988年关于俄亥俄州十三所州立大学和两个医科大学的调查报告可以说明这个情况。OCLC的这十五所成员馆中一个是自己研制出来的自动化系统，八个是从五个不同的自动化集成系统公司那里买下的系统，其余几所学院仍然处在选择或计划过程中。

三、OhioLINK图书馆系统

在这种背景下州立大学图书馆纷纷要求扩大图书馆馆舍。这就促使俄亥俄州议会在1986年设立了一个专家委员会负责审查图书馆的空间需要。委员会建议一方面集中建一场所，密集存贮大家不大用的出版物，另一方面，建议通过加强州内合作和通过全州高校图书馆系统网络实现高校图书馆的资源共享，称为OhioLINK网。专家委员会这一建议导致在1987年涌现出各种新委员会和项目组，全方位地开始定义该系统的未来，它不仅是面向俄亥俄州而且对世界信息环境建设具有参考意义。所有这些计划的制定人员包括来自大学的代表，其中有图书馆管理人员、计算机人员、教师、管理人员和大学领导。资料表明，现行的任何一个图书馆系统都不及现在的OhioLINK。

OhioLINK网的指导思想核心是：

（1）它应该是一个分布式系统，由各自图书馆自动化系统和一个中心系统分别承担一些功能。

（2）它提供各种资源，而不仅仅是 20 世纪 80 年代后期的联机公共目录查询系统（OPAC）。

（3）OhioLINK 成员机构要提供现存系统不能提供的不同范围的精细的功能。

（4）它的目的是尽可能地毫无遗漏地提供给用户多种多样的功能。

1990 年一份 200 多页的咨询建议说明书（OLIS，1989a）较为准确地评价了 OhioLINK 的能力。关于 OhioLINK 系统的一个重要协议是与加州的创新界面公司（Innovative Interface Inc.）签订的，由该公司负责系统软件部分。另一合约是与 DEC 公司签订的，由其负责系统的硬件部分。第一期工程于 1991 年开始，1992 年核心工程又增设了六个图书馆自动化系统作为中心系统，由于资金的延误，1993 年只安装到三个图书馆，1994 年末，OhioLINK 系统可以在十三个州立大学、二个私立大学、二个州立医科大学的图书馆和俄亥俄州图书馆内使用，预计到 1995 年完成 23 所社区和技术学院的系统安装。

四、OhioLINK 网的今天

1994 年 1 月，OhioLlNK 馆际互借功能正始开通，它创立了用户可使用的一种新的服务方式。它可以允许 OhioLINK 组织里的学生或者教师在他的区域寻找资料，找不到资料就转到中心系统的联合目录库中查询。如果发现所需要的书在州内的其他地方，这本书若是急需的，那么送书专车系统就把该书在两天之内送到借阅的那所图书馆。对论文的服务方式是直接用电子形式在网络传送而不是地面传送。OhioLINK 成员组织为了提供免费传真服务制定出合作协议，但尚未正式纳入系统。OhioLINK 打算用互联网络（Internet）作为传送信息的手段，但它还未决定使用图像系统（ARIEL）还是文本系统（CICnet），并将通过一个商业性公司传送文本和图像来完善这种服务方式进而将来取代这种方式。OhioLINK 所面临的不仅是采取各种手段提高效率而且还要考虑经济效益。

今天，学生和教师可以在终端和工作站前检索自己和其他成员馆里的许多文献数据库，例如报刊索引 和 ABI/lnform，现已装有国际最新刊登的学位论文文摘报道，这些文献数据库将会加上各个图书馆 和全州的馆藏信息，联机传送整篇文章的系统目前正在试验。到 1994 年下半年，一系列包括 Medline 在内的卫生与健康主题有关的数据库和心理学文摘库可在联网的光盘上供公共查询。一个图书目次数据库、一个新刊报导数据库和一系列多学科综合数据库计划在 1994 年 10 月投入使用。美国政府 出版物的详细记录和研究图书馆中心馆藏信息记录装载到某些图书馆自动化系统和中央图书馆数据库中会大大丰富原来传统的书目数据库。将来在同一个用户终端还可提供检索 Internet 资源的 功能，Gopher 服务器和客户器软件会加速检索 Internet 资源，一些图书馆正把 Gopher 服务器当成 各自图书馆自动化系统的组成部分。

OhioLINK 的公共特征是最重要的，它保证提供更多数量和各种类型信息以帮助成员图书馆去重新评价我们的贡献和服务，OhioLINK 发展有助于加速实现资源共享，已启用的馆际互借数据将提供良好的流量数据，使我们很快能了解到用户需要的资料是否马上就要，或者说用户使用资源只图方便或是研究所用。馆藏和馆际资源使用的数据将有利于合作馆藏发展和评价资源共享的实际可行性，在 1993 年 2 月对 10 所大学图书馆做的一次统计中显示，三百万种查询和借阅的出版物中只有 600 种由这 10 所大学图书馆收藏。

五、OhioLINK 的明天

作为联机馆际互借资源共享多种类型数据库和 Internet 互联网的分布式联合体，

OhioLINK 是现存图书馆系统和协作组织中重要革新组织。但它与之创立时的设想有一定的距离。OhioLINK 最有影响的两件事情是：

（1）在推动图书馆事业和信息服务中已取得了出色的进步。

（2）已得到认可，我们已踏上永无止境的旅程，等待最优成绩出现。

有关 OhioLINK 设想几乎与图书馆学一样悠久，用杜威的话来说就是在恰当的时间给需要的用户提供合适的图书。今天，这意味着全州大学图书馆藏书向所有学生和教职员工开放，一次检索就能确定该网络组织内的图书、论文、索引以及其他信息资源。

目前，OhioLlNK 继续增加一些数据库并尽量使查询界面一致。OhioLINK 将是一个直通式信息服务网络组织，将来在图书馆教师办公室、教师和学生的家里就可以开展信息查询并设法使信息检索更为简便、更为高效。

OhioLINK 积累了 OCLC 成员馆的 25 年的实践经验，它提供了具有自动化、网络化、电子化图书馆的特征，结合了 Internet 网资源和文献传递功能，充实了虚拟图书馆的定义。现在的这种图书馆对一位大学生来说是一种结构和物质资源，而虚拟图书馆总是以满足学生对信息需求这一目标而建设，因此现在的常规图书馆只是虚拟图书馆的一部分。学生不再需要关心他或她的图书馆是否拥有自己专业的信息。OhioLINK 虚拟图书馆中拥有权并不重要，因为学生能及时地在全州和全国获得信息，在校学生能够获取信息资源对拥有图书馆的大小无关要紧。

（原载《图书与情报》1995 年第 3 期，第 73－75 页。）

网络化、电子化的虚拟图书馆
——20世纪90年代的图书馆

Networked, Electronic and Virtual Library: Libraries of the 1990s[①]

Background

In the 1960s, publishers increasingly looked to computer-assisted composition in preparing indexes and bibliographies—a by-product of which was the availability of computer-readable data that could be distributed online. Simultaneously, libraries were turning to computers (usually mainframes) to deal with the increasing quantities of information and seemingly infinite cataloging backlogs that plagued most research libraries. Critical to this process was the adoption of the Machine Readable Catalog (MARC) standard by the Library of Congress (LC).

OCLC—Too Successful

While the Library of Congress was preparing its trial MARC format (known as MARC I), academic libraries in Ohio were confronting the perennial library problem of balancing rising costs with limited budgets. The result was the formation of the Ohio College Library Center (OCLC) in 1967. By 1968, the Library of Congress had refined the MARC standard (identified as MARC II) and this provided the basis of OCLC's early emphasis on shared cataloging and LC tapes provided the early content of the OCLC database. By 1971, OCLC was ready to move beyond loading LC tapes and undertake what was its great innovation—online shared cataloging. On August 26, 1971, Ohio University became the first library in the world to enter a cataloging record online—into the OCLC database (subsequently identified as the OCLC Online Union Catalog). That record, although it caused a hiccough in the OCLC system, was the snowflake that gave birth to an avalanche. In 1983, Ohio University was only one of nearly 10,000 members when it entered record 10,000,001. In October 1993, Ohio University entered record number 29,000,000, and the OCLC system (long since renamed the OCLC Online Computer Library Center) was serving more than 17,500 libraries around the world. Attesting to the success of OCLC's approach, based on data as of June 30, 1993, members had contributed 78% of the records, Library of Congress MARC tapes only 14%, and a further 8% were input by members adapted from LC copy (for pre-MARC materials).

What began as a vision and practical implementation by academic libraries in Ohio to respond to shared local problems proved irresistible to libraries across the United States. By the mid-1970s, OCLC became a national not-for-profit organization. While the world at large gained from OCLC's success, many needs of academic libraries in Ohio remained unmet. OCLC did introduce an equally successful Interlibrary loan subsystem that revolutionized resource sharing nationally, but it was much slower in addressing the needs of individual libraries for local library systems. Many founding members of OCLC began looking to other sources to supply local library systems. Indeed, by the time that OCLC entered the local system market in the 1980s, many of these institutions had already acquired systems from other vendors. (Described more fully in Lee, 1987)

Beyond marketing local systems, best known by the name LS 2000, OCLC also offered a variety of serials check-in and acquisitions functions. While each of these functions attracted a

---

[①] Presented at the International Seminar on Information Technologies and Information Services, October 20-24, 1994, Shanghai, China.

substantial number of users, many libraries—in the pursuit of integrated local systems—preferred to have such functions performed within a local system. By the 1990s, OCLC had relinquished the marketplace for these products (discontinuing its centralized acquisitions system and selling its local system operation to Ameritech) to other vendors.

In the 1990s, OCLC has emphasized two approaches. The first has been continuing its shared cataloging in the form of the Online Union Catalog (OUC) and capitalizing on this unique resource as WorldCat, offered as an end-user-searchable database. In WorldCat, which is offered as part of its FirstSearch ensemble, subject and keyword searching are available—a capability which libraries had sought from OCLC's inception. Also relying on its OUC, OCLC has added contract cataloging to its earlier retrospective conversion services to provide machine readable records for institutions lacking these for their collections. Where libraries have previously maintained a "copy cataloging" unit, which searched the OUC and added holdings information for often more than 80 percent of materials acquired, such acquisitions now can be reported to OCLC which will provide the searching and cataloging services.

Its other initiative is the offering of a variety of online databases—complemented by document delivery services. In addition to WorldCat, its FirstSearch offers Contents 1st (tables of contents of over 8,500 journals), Article 1st (articles from over 8,500 journals), and a large variety of other indexes. Related to document delivery services, it has begun an electronic journal publishing venture, featuring initially, *The Online Journal of Current Clinical Trials*.

While OCLC has moved in certain directions, its founding members frequently have looked beyond OCLC to meet core library automation needs. A 1988 survey of thirteen state-supported universities and two medical colleges in Ohio found that all were members of OCLC, one had a locally developed system, eight had acquired local systems from five different vendors, and those remaining were in the process of either selecting or planning local systems.

During the 1980s, local library systems available on the market made various claims of being integrated systems. Yet the available systems tended to be strong in some functional areas and weak in others. For example, some systems offered strong cataloging capabilities and interfaces with OCLC while others were much stronger in acquisitions or serials control. Of even greater importance for Ohio academic libraries, these local systems were developed to be largely or only local systems. As such, the systems were ill-designed to communicate with other systems and serve resource-sharing goals.

OhioLINK—Library Systems Redefined

Against this background, concern over many requests from state-supported university libraries in Ohio for new buildings to house ever-growing collections prompted the Ohio State Legislature to create a blue-ribbon panel in 1986 to examine academic library space needs. Beyond addressing the central theme in recommendations for shared high-density storage of little used materials, the committee recommended that the state increase cooperation and resource sharing among academic libraries through a statewide academic library system. (OBOR, 1987)

As often happens in academia, the blue-ribbon panel's recommendation gave birth in 1987 to a variety of new committees and task forces—all directed at defining a system for the future, not only of Ohio but of the world information community. (Lee, 1989) Importantly, all of these planning bodies included representation from across the academic spectrum—librarians, computer center staff, faculty, administrators, and university leaders. While several multi-institution systems were identified (e.g., in Illinois, Florida, and North Carolina) and offered desirable functionality, it became clear that no existing library system or approach was adequate to what came to be called the OhioLINK vision.①

Key concepts which guided OhioLINK planning were:

1. it should be a distributed system (with some functions performed by a local system and some by a central system);

2. it should provide a variety of resources rather than simply being an Online Public Access Catalog (OPAC) as was standard in the late 1980s;

3) no existing system could provide the diverse and sophisticated functionality demanded by OhioLINK member institutions; and

4) it should be aimed at providing this powerful functionality as seamlessly as possible to the user.

In 1990, after carefully evaluating responses to a Request for Proposal (OLIS, 1989a) of more than 200 pages of specifications, the prime contract for the OhioLINK system was awarded to Innovative Interfaces, Inc. (Ⅲ) of Berkeley for the software and a contract for hardware was awarded to the Digital Equipment Corporation of New Hampshire for hardware. The first installations began in 1991, and in 1992, the central site was added to six installed local sites. Due to delays in state funding (costs of initial installation are paid by the Ohio Board of Regents, with local institutions responsible for connectivity, maintenance, and local terminals), only three sites were installed in 1993; however, by the end of 1994, the OhioLINK system should be operational at thirteen state-supported universities, two private universities, and two state-supported medical colleges, and the State Library of Ohio. In 1994, installation will also begin at the first of 23 community and technical colleges to be completed by 1995.

OhioLINK Today

In January 1994, the most recent of OhioLINK's innovative services—user-initiated interlibrary borrowing—became operational. This allows a student or faculty member at an OhioLINK institution to search for materials at his/her local site, transfer the search to the union catalog at the central site, and—finding a desired book available elsewhere in the state—to immediately request it. Through a statewide courier service, the materials should be available at the requester's own library within two days. Similar service is planned for articles but using electronic rather than ground delivery. Cooperative agreements among OhioLINK participating institutions provide for free fax delivery but this has not yet been formally incorporated into the system. OhioLINK intends to use the Internet as the transmission medium but has yet to decide between an image system (represented by ARIEL) and a text system (represented by CICnet). Complementing this service (and possibly supplanting it in the future) will be the delivery of such text and images from a commercial provider. OhioLINK tests are expected to be revealing not only as to the effectiveness of the alternatives but also the economics.

In approaching a terminal or workstation today, students and faculty can search for materials in their own and all other participating libraries but also can choose from among many article databases (e.g., Periodicals Index, Newspapers Index, and ABI/Inform with the Dissertation Abstracts International currently loading). The article databases will be linked to local and statewide holdings, and a system for online delivery of the full-text of articles is currently being tested. Later in 1994, a variety of health databases (including *Medline*) and *Psych Abstracts* will be available at the same terminal but using a different search engine (developed by CD Plus). A book table-of-contents database, a journal current-awareness database, and a variety of multi-disciplinary databases are scheduled to be available by October 1994. Greatly enriching the traditional local online catalog will be full records for U. S. government documents and the holdings

---

① Initially formulated in: OLAS Steering Committee, 1988, but given more mature form in OLIS, 1989. OhioLINK originally was called the Ohio Library Access System (OLAS), then was changed—to avoid trademark infringements or challenges—to Ohio Library and Information System (OLIS) and, finally, to Ohio Library and Information Network, with the acronym OhioLINK.

of the consortia Center for Research Libraries will be loaded to local and central library databases. Still further, the same user terminal offers a connoisseur's selection of Internet resources. Gopher server and client software facilitate Internet navigation and some institutions are adding local Gopher servers as local options.

While the public features of OhioLINK are clearly most important, it also promises to provide increasing amounts and varieties of information that will help participating libraries (and, indeed, our profession) to reassess our contributions and services. OhioLINK is intended to facilitate resource sharing. Data on user-initiated borrowing will provide an excellent barometer as to whether users want materials immediately (i. e., available in their own library) or just expeditiously—in fact, the degree to which the use of resources is a convenience (such as needing any three articles on a particular subject—a familiar undergraduate request) or serious research (need for a specific book or article). Also, comparative data on collections and inter-institutional usage will be useful in pursuing collaborative collection development and in assessing the realities of resource sharing. One early statistic of interest is that, in February 1993, with 10 institutions loaded and a database of more than three million unique items, only 600 of the three million items were owned by all ten institutions.

OhioLINK Tomorrow

With the combination of distributed systems, online interlibrary resource sharing, multiple databases, and integral Internet access, OhioLINK is among the most innovative of existing library systems and cooperative efforts, but it is still a distance from the system envisioned at its creation. Two of the most encouraging things about OhioLINK are: 1) the exceptional progress that it has made in advancing librarianship and information service, and 2) the shared recognition that we have only embarked on an endless journey and the best is yet to come.

The OhioLINK vision is as old as librarianship—to paraphrase Melvil Dewey, getting the right information to the right person at the right time. Today that means opening the collections of the academic libraries in the state to all students and faculty (without library mediation), using a single search to identify books in participating collections, article and research indexes, and a variety of other resources. The delivery of full-text articles (as text or image) is being tested now. What more could be wished?

The answer, in part, lies in what is generically called a "scholar's workstation." This is presently being explored by a task force and solicitations are anticipated within the year—with the understanding that this will be a development project rather than an off-the-shelf product. Based on early discussions, it may well incorporate features of "the librarian" in Neal Stephenson's *Snow Crash* (Stephenson, 1993) a software capability to learn the type of information that the user usually seeks and to periodically check all available resources to advise the user if anything new is available in these subject areas. In essence, the user is freed from the tedium of periodically surveying the literature—the software does it without being asked. Typescript, announced by General Magic, Inc. in early 1994, would appear to offer this potential. (Ratcliffe, 1994, and Levy, 1994)

More immediately, OhioLINK continues to add databases and will continue to explore interfacing with different database search engines (exemplified by CD Plus) with the III system. OhioLINK will be a one-stop information service, available from the library, faculty offices, or the homes of faculty and students. It will continue to strive to make information-seeking as easy and as effective as possible.

OhioLINK has drawn on 25 years of experience among the members who participated in the founding of OCLC. It offers features of automated libraries, of networked and electronic libraries (both in incorporating Internet resources and document delivery), and is participating in the definition of the virtual library. The library apparent to a student at the University of Cincinnati, as a structure and material resources, represents only a fraction of the virtual library that has been crafted to serve that student's information needs and desires. The student no longer need be concerned with whether his or her library owns material on a particular subject. In the OhioLINK virtual library ownership is unimportant as that student will have timely access to resources from throughout the state and the nation. Students at campuses with the largest and the smallest libraries in the state will see little, if any, difference in their access to research resources.

The virtual library, like its predecessors, is a process rather than a fixed state of carefully defined characteristics. OhioLINK is part of the process and will continue to add to the definition to meet the information needs of students, faculty and the citizenry of Ohio.

References

1. Lee, Hwa-Wei. " Applications of Information Technology in an American Library— The Case of Ohio University Libraries. " *Proceedings of the First Pacific Conference on New Information Technology for Library and Information Professionals.* June 16 – 18, 1987, Bangkok, edited by Ching-Chih Chen and David I. Raitt. West Newton, MA: MicroUse Information, 1987: pp. 155 – 164.

2. Lee, Hwa-Wei. "Planning Process and Considerations for a State-Wide Academic Library Information System in Ohio. " Second Pacific Conference on New Information Technology for Library and Information Professionals and Educational Media Specialists and Technologists, Singapore, May 29 – 31, 1989. Published in Proceedings, edited by Ching-chih Chen and David I. Raitt. West Newton, MA: MicroUse Information, 1989: pp. 203 – 210, and in *The Journal of Educational Media and Library Sciences.* V. 27, No. 2 (Winter 1990): pp. 127 – 138

3. Levy, Steven. " Bill and Andy's Excellent Adventure II. " *Wired* No. 2. 04 (April 1994): pp. 102 – 107 and 131 – 133.

4. OBOR. Library Study Committee. *Academic Libraries in Ohio: Progress Through Collaboration, Storage, and Technology. Report of the Library Study Committee. Columbus, Ohio: Ohio Board of Regents*, 1987. OBOR (the Ohio Board of Regents) is the state agency charged with coordinating and overseeing the development of public higher education in Ohio.

5. OLAS Steering Committee. *Ohio Library Access System Planning Paper.* November 2, 1988. Columbus, Ohio: Ohio Board of Regents, 1988.

6. OLIS. *Connecting People, Libraries, & Information for Ohio's Future.* Columbus, Ohio: Ohio Board of Regents, 1989.

7. OLIS. "Request for Proposal for the Ohio Library & Information System (OLIS) on behalf of the Ohio Board of Regents and Ohio Library & Information System. " Columbus, Ohio: OLIS, August 4, 1989.

8. Ratcliffe, Mitch. "Let Your Agent Do the Walking. " *PC World.* V. 12, No. 2 (February 1994): pp. 56 – 58.

9. Stephenson, Neal. *Snow Crash.* NY: Bantam, 1993.

(Published in *Journal of Educational Media & Library Sciences.* V. 32, No. 2, Winter 1995: pp. 119 – 129.)

图书馆资源共享：OhioLINK 模式

Sharing of Library and Information Resources: The OhioLINK Model[①]

OhioLINK (the Ohio Library and Information Network) was established in 1990 in a statewide effort to more effectively share library and information resources among all major academic libraries and the State Library of Ohio. By using the same software system and hardware platform selected by the 18 initial participating libraries, OhioLINK is a distributed library network connecting some 45 individual library systems to a central system that consists of an online union catalog and numerous databases accessible to all authorized, library users through remote computers. Since its inception, many new services have been added and its usage and popularity have multiplied.

For resources sharing, an analysis of the duplication rate of titles held by member libraries in the central catalog reveals that 57.7% of all titles are held by only one library, 15.4% by 2 libraries, 7.8% by 3 libraries, and 19.1% by 4 or more libraries. Among the features of OhioLINK are: direct online interlibrary borrowing by library users during a search of the central catalog, up-to-the moment information on availability of any title in the network, rapid document delivery service, numerous bibliographic and full-text databases available through the central catalog, and electronic ordering and delivery of selected journal articles from full-text databases.

This paper introduces the history, network configuration, use information, resources descriptions, approaches to governance, and planned future development of OhioLINK as one successful models for library cooperation and resource sharing in the United States.

---

① This is an abstract of the paper presented at the Internatioal Conference on "1996 Information Resources and Society Development" (1996 信息资源与社会发展国际学术研讨会), Wuhan, September 3–6, 1996.

OhioLINK 网络化资讯获取和资源共享的成就[①]

The Success of OhioLINK for Information Access and Resources Sharing in a Networked Environment

介 绍

20 世纪 60 年代以来,全世界各种类型的图书馆已发生了许多变化。在美国,加快图书馆界变化步幅最显著的因素应属于在计算机、信息和电讯传播技术方面的革新。60 年代,图书馆在使用计算机技术方面有以下几项重要发展:

(1) 由国会图书馆开发的 MARC(机读目录)格式以促进计算机在合作编目方面的使用并确立机读目录的标准;

(2) 由国家医学图书馆创立的 (MEDLARS) 医学文献分析及检索系统用以便利医学文献的查询和获取;

(3) 为联机合作编目和资源共享所建立的俄亥俄州学院图书馆中心(OCLC,现已更名为计算机联机图书馆中心);

(4) 由一些主要索引和文摘出版机构利用计算机所建立的大型数据库(例如:化学文摘)。

此后,由于运算速度更快、效率更高的计算机不断涌现,专为图书馆应用所开发的计算机软件的不断改进,电讯传播和网络技术的提高,信息存储和检索技术的革新,互交媒体及多媒体技术应用的增加,电子出版的衍生,互联网络和全球网(www)的广泛使用等,使得图书馆界每五年至十年就要发生一次巨变。这些变化再加上"信息的爆炸",使图书馆从 60 年代以纸张和印刷品为主的机构转变为 70 年代以计算机为基础,八十年代以网络为基础,以至于 90 年代电子化、数字化和图书馆虚拟化。勿庸置疑,21 世纪的图书馆将在高科技,网络和数字化的环境中朝着综合发展的方向迈进。

图书馆面临的挑战

伴随着技术的演化,全球各地的图书馆同时也面临着以下的挑战:
(1) 人类知识以指数式的速度提高;
(2) 学术沟通与出版的迅速增长;
(3) 图书馆规模、职能、资源、服务和复杂性的扩大;
(4) 图书馆收藏品价格的飞涨;
(5) 信息载体的多样化;
(6) 图书馆经费的萎缩;
(7) 图书馆系统购置、维护、升级换代的高额价格;
(8) 对管理效率和责任的要求;
(9) 图书馆对于精通信息技术人员需求的增加;
(10) 图书馆藏书从"拥有"到"获取"这一本质性的变化;

[①] 本文为"1999 年现代图书馆的服务与管理讲习班"演讲稿,该讲习班由浙江大学图书馆承办,时间为 1999 年 9 月 13 – 15 日。

（11）读者的需求和指望也在增加；

（12）在扫除"信息盲"及终生教育所起的越来越重要的作用。

面对这多重挑战，美国图书馆把握机遇，在利用新兴技术、扩大资源以及通过合作和增加网络服务等诸多方面起到了带头作用。实际上，能够成功地对付这些挑战也对图书馆产生了激励的作用。

信息和知识超越地区和载体的获取已逐渐地取代了传统意义上的拥有。通过网络进行图书馆之间真正的资源共享已经成为共同的愿望和通用的手段。

OhioLINK 的探索

OhioLINK（俄亥俄州图书馆与信息网络）是于 1990 年开始在俄亥俄州学术图书馆之间形成。它已被证明是网络和资源共享方面具有成本效益的成功模式。本文将从以下各点对这一创举进行剖析：

（1）偶然的开端。

（2）OhioLINK 的构思。

（3）OhioLINK 的现状。

（4）OhioLINK 如何运作。

（5）OhioLINK 的未来走向。

（6）OhioLINK 的经验可否借鉴。

偶然的开端

OhioLINK 的形成，是由于俄亥俄州高校董事会在 1986 指定的一个特别小组，对俄亥俄州各州立大学图书馆的需求进行为期一年的研究的结果。在其《俄亥俄学术图书馆：通过协作、储藏与科技发展》的报告中，特别小组提出了若干的建议。其中最重要的一条是"从速建立起一个全州范围内的电子目录系统"。附带性建议还包括回溯性地将现存的卡片式目录记录转化为 MARC 格式；开发并实施在全州范围内的图书馆传递系统；以及一个合作性的图书维护及保存计划。

为了计划和实施这些建议，高校董事会设立了一个执行委员会，及一些由图书馆员、系统操作员、13 个州立大学教员代表、两间大的私立大学、两所单独的州立医学院以及俄亥俄州立图书馆代表所组成的工作小组和下属委员会。（见表一）

通过大量人力的投入及数百次的会议，一系列计划性的文件出台了。其中包括 1987 年 8 月颁布的《信息的征求》；1988 年 11 月颁布的《计划书》；1989 年 11 月《招标征求》；以及 1989 年颁布的一份概述：《为了俄亥俄州的未来，架起人、图书馆和信息之间的桥梁》；基于对《招标征求》所得到的回应，1990 年选用了 Innovative Interface 公司开发的图书馆系统，1991 年开始安装。

1992 至 1995 年该系统首先安装于 18 所最早参与的图书馆。之后，由州政府资助的两年制学院以及一些私立大专院校也陆续参加。在 1999 年 4 月，俄亥俄州内已有 74 家学术图书馆参加了 OhioLINK。有关会员馆资料，可查询 http://www.ohiolink.edu/members-info/。

OhioLINK 的构思

创建伊始，OhioLINK 的根本概念就是要利用已由 OARnet（俄亥俄州学术与研究网络）建立起来的全州范围内的电讯传播基础架构，用以连接参与的图书馆。每一个图书馆都拥有一个应用 Innovative Interface 图书馆系统的通用的计算机硬件和软件平台。

通过这个联接以及一个可供检索流通记录和图书馆藏书的中央联合目录，参与图书馆的使用者可以直接检索本馆及中央目录，并可以从其他图书馆借阅本图书馆无法提供的图书。由于有了 48 小时传递服务，在多数情况下，馆际图书借阅可以在两三天内完成。

一旦全州的网络建设完成，OhioLINK 就开始迅速地增加其他馆藏资源和服务用以便利其会员图书馆。这其中最重要的有：

（1）添置了许多高需求的电子数据库。
（2）扩大了全文数据库的数量。
（3）利用集体力量来争取到订购电子期刊的优惠折扣。
（4）发展新的查寻软件平台，以方便对多种数据库的同时查寻。
（5）采纳一个全州合作采购图书的方式来避免不必要的重复。
（6）扩大网上借阅范围——从图书拓展到其他种类的馆藏资料。
（7）建立一个电子期刊中心，并不断增加其刊物数量。
（8）利用俄亥俄州超级计算机中心几乎无限的存储空间来建立起一个数字化媒体中心，用来收藏会员图书馆或商业机构建立的数字化特藏。
（9）改善各个分校 OhioLINK 资源的使用。

OhioLINK 共有的构思可归纳为：

（1）将俄亥俄州内所有的学术图书馆在电子网络环境下联接起来。
（2）尽量利用现有的计算机和通讯基础结构。
（3）将所有图书馆的馆藏接合起来以便于利用和有效共享。
（4）通过多种途径来传送资料。
（5）以协作方式来发展馆藏。
（6）通过协作性的购买力对购买大型、昂贵的电子资源取得优惠价格。
（7）改变馆际合作和资源共享的形式。

图一显示出在 2000 万册集中的馆藏中（代表 710 万不同的书名），56% 的图书只有一所图书馆拥有，14% 由两所图书馆拥有，7% 由三所拥有，5% 由四所拥有，3% 由五所拥有，其余的 14% 由六所或更多的图书馆拥有。从大量的图书只有一所图书馆拥有这一事实说明了资源共享的益处和重要性，以及藏书总汇的巨大合力。

OhioLINK 的现状

虽然时至今日 OhioLINK 仍在不断发展，大力地扩大其馆藏资源和服务，但是它已经取得的具体成果很显著的。

（1）OhioLINK 以其业已被证明的集体功效和经济效益，得以获得更多的州政府经费补助以支援其网络中心的作业，传递服务，购买主要索引、参考和全文本数据库，以及其他新项目的开发。

（2）全州大约 46 万名大学生和 5 万名教职员工都可以共享由 74 所图书馆收藏、总数超过 2000 万册的图书。

（3）1993 年，对 OhioLINK 中央目录的查寻大约 45 万次，到 1998 年，这一数字增加到 275 万次。（见图二）

（4）1994 年，读者在网上直接借阅约为 7 万 5 千次，到了 1998 年，增加到 56 万次。从 1994 年元月至 1999 年 3 月，读者联机借阅积累次数已超过 200 万次。借阅成功率为 85%。（见图三）根据记录统计，由于读者直接借阅，馆际互借的成本已从运用传统方式每次 \$15 - \$30 锐减到如今的每次 \$8。

（5）在 1992 年 12 月，OhioLINK 只有两个可供检索的电子数据库，到了 1998 年 12 月已经增加到了 67 个。每年对 OhioLINK 参考数据库的查寻已由 1993 年的 50 万次增加到 1998 年的愈千万次。（见图四）每次查寻的成本由 1993 年的 \$3.90 减至 1999 年的 \$0.30。（见图五）

（6）在 1993 年读者还无法在网上获得期刊的全文，到了 1998 年，仅 11 月高峰期的一周之内，读者就可以从 UMI 公司的联机全文期刊数据库中打印出 3 万篇期刊文章的全文，总页数达 12 万 5 千页。每篇文章的平城费为 \$0.90。（见图六）

（7）经由联合订购，OhioLINK 参考数据库的订费比起单一图书馆的订费要便宜 30% 到 80%。

（8）OhioLINK 还从几家大的学术期刊出版商处，以现行支付纸张期刊的订费加上 5 - 10% 的费用以换取在网上无限制地使用这些出版商所出版的全部期刊的电子版（包括没有订阅的期刊在内）。这种优惠的协定使得每个图书馆的读者都可以免费使用近 2000 种学术性的电子期刊。

（9）自 1998 年 4 月建立伊始，OhioLINK 电子期刊中心就在不断扩大对电子刊物的收藏。至 1998 年 12 月止，在已订的 1325 种期刊中，读者从 1307 种中选用了 160713 篇文章。（见图七和八）

OhioLINK 如何运作

1. **系统架构**

OhioLINK 系统由 60 个区域性系统和一个中央系统构成。每个区域性系统均配备一台或多台 Digital 公司的计算机（服务器），以及数百个联网的工作站、打印机、扫描器等。图九显示了 OhioLINK 系统构成的最初设置，图十显示了目前 OhioLINK 中央系统的架构。

2. **管理**

OhioLINK 的董事会是由各参与机构的教务长、由图书馆馆长组成的图书馆顾问委员会的主席和副主席、俄亥俄州高校董事会的代表人员组成，直接属于州高校董事会。OhioLINK 董事会聘用一位执行长监督总部的财政及行政运行。

在制订政策及规划的层次上有一个图书馆顾问委员会（LAC），由 18 位创始图书馆的馆长，以及由两年制学院、私立大学和学院、法律、医学图书馆馆长所选出的代表组成。其主席、副主席及上届主席组成执行协作委员会（LACCC）。

在运作这一层上，有一个领导实施小组和四个常设工作小组。领导实施小组成员是由各参与图书馆的系统管理员或指定的专人构成。四个常设小组的成员由图书馆馆长提名，由执行长任命。这四个小组分别为：

（1）信息资源合作管理小组。

（2）读者服务小组。

（3）校际服务小组。
（4）数据库的管理与标准小组。
图十一列出了 OhioLINK 的大体组织结构。

3. 经费

OhioLINK 的主要经费来源于州政府的拨款。这需要俄亥俄高校董事会向州长办公室每两年一次提出预算申请，经俄亥俄州议会审核批准。这笔经费分为两种形式：运作经费和资本经费。运作经费用来支付经常性开销，例如：总部的职工薪水和福利，办公用品及设备，馆际图书传递费用，以及其他的运作支出。资本经费是用来支付总部计算机的软件和硬件及其升级换代，区域系统和数据库的启动经费，购置电子参考、全文本、期刊数据库（拥有而非租赁），俄亥俄学术与研究网络的特别设置费用，以及多媒体和全文本系统等费用。

在 1998—1999 财政年度里，运作经费预算为 515 万 7 千美元，资本经费预算为 250 万美元。图十二、十三、十四分别显示 OhioLINK 的实际拨款数，每两年按百分比的运作开销和 OhioLINK 资本经费的分配使用情况。

各高校系统的维护和升级，校园电讯及其他与 OhioLINK 相关的运作开销等，大部分都由各图书馆自行筹措。而下列开支则由中央资金支付：各校区最初系统的软件和硬件购买费，回溯性编目，名称和主题权威控制，电讯传播的主干线路，核心参考数据库，中央购置的电子图书，对于电子期刊集体购买的部分津贴，以及互借书刊资料的传递服务。从 1998 年开始，OhioLINK 会员馆已同意向各馆征收少量资金（占俄亥俄大学书刊购置费的 1%）来建立，为数 60 万美元的"专款"用来购买新的核心参考数据库。（以前购置的中心数据库乃将继续由 OhioLINK 的资本经费全额支付）

OhioLINK 的未来走向

随着 OhioLINK 的成功，许多人把 OhioLINK 当作在电子和网络环境中有效利用信息和资源共享的一个理想模式。然而以我们有利的地位，当我们在 21 世纪进入信息高速公路第一线时，我们有信心可以做得更多。我们已经认识到几个在不远的将来运作时要注意的战略重点：

（1）扩大现有的数据库——特别是像地图、数字数据、图表和各类的影像。
（2）开拓更加有效的合作收藏方式。
（3）增加新功能：例如通过一个整合的以全球网为基础的平台和文献的电子传播系统把所有的服务传递到个人计算机上。
（4）提供一个更加方便、好用的界面。
（5）把期刊和报纸数据库与实际的馆藏，流通记录和文献全文连接起来。
（6）鼓励、协调并开展更多的数字化项目。
（7）支持多种形式的电子出版，以控制价格，防止出版商侵占作者的知识产权。
（8）寻求与其他洲际、国内、国际的图书馆网络合作。例如"国际图书馆网络联盟"的组织。

综上所述，很明显 OhioLINK 的未来是丰富多彩、令人振奋的。

OhioLINK 的经验可否借鉴

OhioLINK 的成功大致可以归功于以下因素：

（1）人们已经认识到"任何图书馆都不能独自提供其读者所需的广泛的信息资源"。

（2）所有的图书馆，无论大小，都强烈要求合作，共享资源：这是俄亥俄州长久以来的传统，OCLC 即因此在 1967 年成立。

（3）有眼光的图书馆领导对馆际合作的决心和积极行动。

（4）政府部门（俄亥俄州高校董事会）的理解和支持，并愿意提供启动和运作经费。

（5）具备了图书馆自动化和网络化所需的更加成熟的图书馆和信息技术。

（6）越来越多的电子和数字出版物。

（7）所有图书馆都能全力参与 OhioLINK 这个组织健全的机构。能够达成共识，做出明智的及适时的决定。

如果具备上述条件的话，俄亥俄州能够做到的其他地方也能做到。实际上，如果必要的话有些因素是可以培养出来的。

此外，与 OhioLINK 这样的图书馆合作形式不一定要一模一样，发展中国家的图书馆有更急迫的需求来建立网络上的信息利用和资源共享，以便能充分利用极其有限的经费、物资、技术和人力资源。但是，由于各地的环境和条件不一，每一个图书馆合作都应该根据当地的需求来计划和发展，以建立具有其特点的合作方式。对于任何一组想要在网络环境中最大程度地利用信息和资源共享而合作的图书馆，OhioLINK 可以作为一个成功的实例。万事开头难，但是一旦开始，那显著的效益就会成为动力，促使其向前发展。

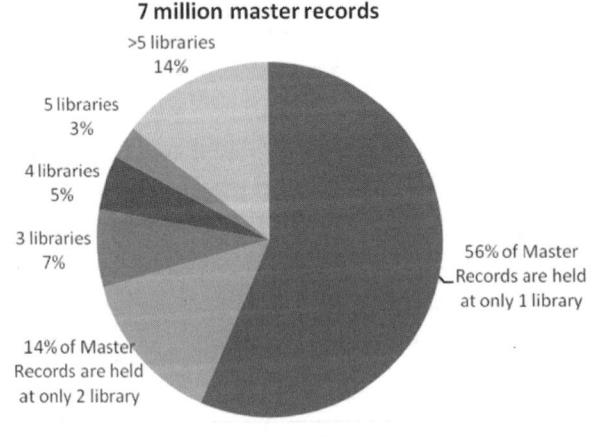

图 1　重复图书的百分比

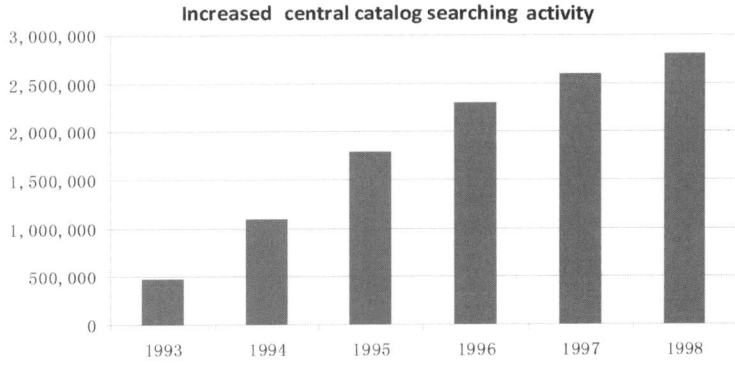

图 2　线上检索 OhioLINK 中央书目的年度统计

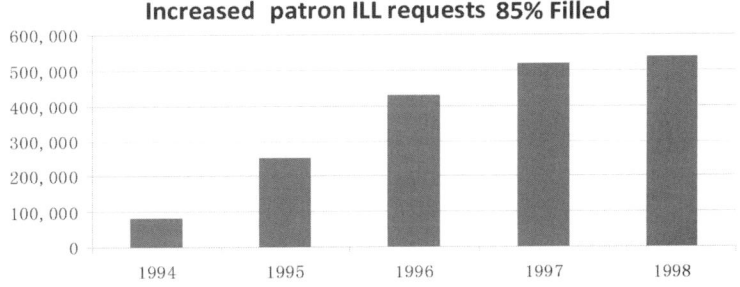

图 3　OhioLINK 由读者直接线上馆际借书的年度统计

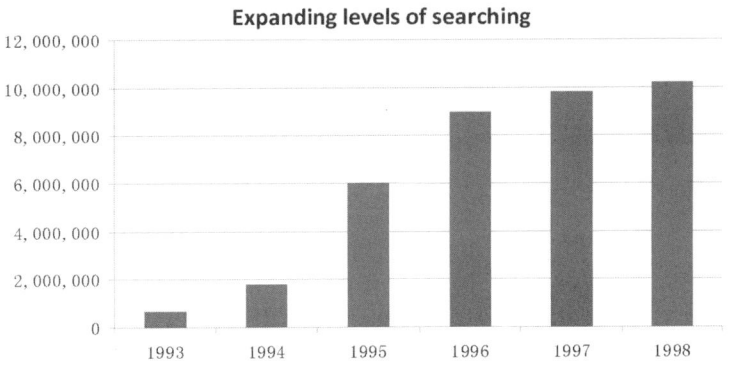

图 4　检索 OhioLINK 中央参考资料库的年度统计

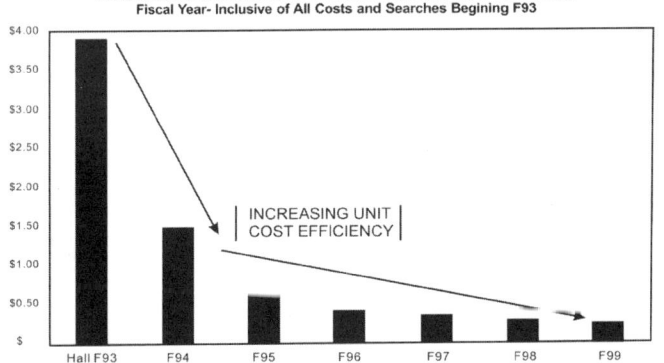

图 5　检索参考资料库的平均单元成本价格

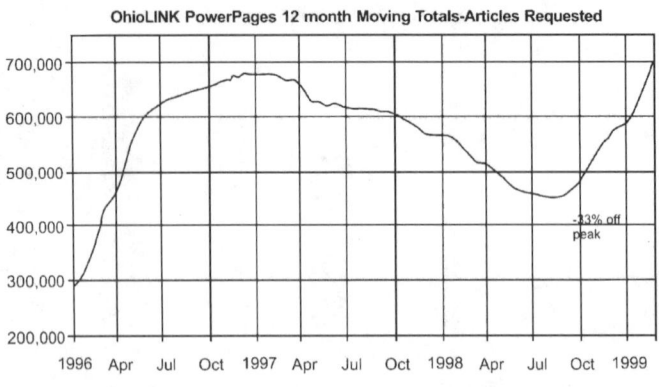

图 6　使用 UMI 期刊全文资料库打印文章的页数统计

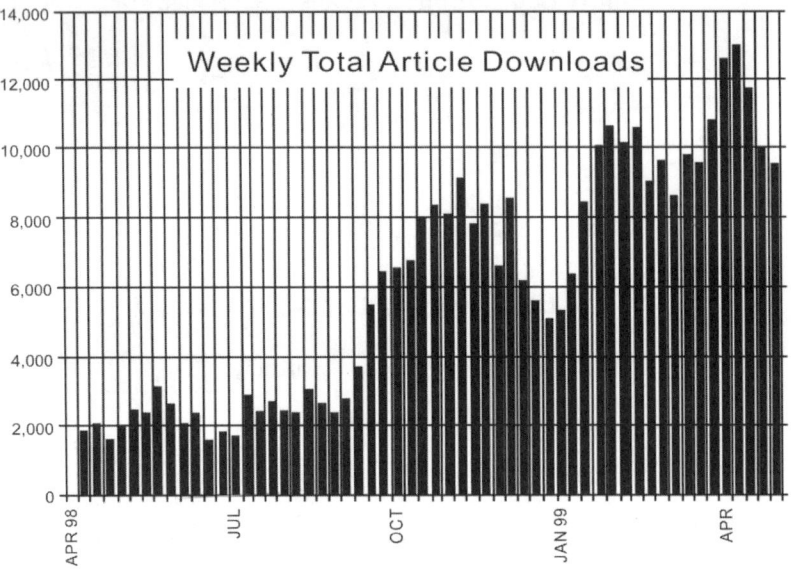

图 7　使用电子期刊中心文章的每周统计

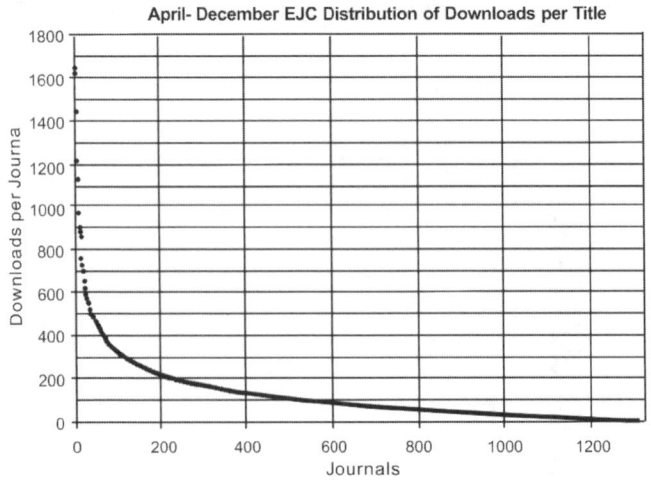

图 8　1998 年电子期刊中心期刊使用频率统计

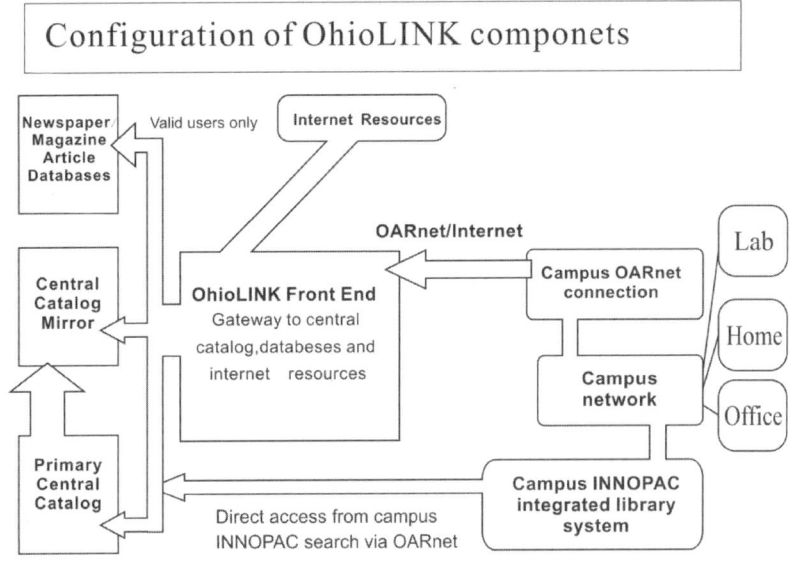

图 9　OhioLINK 主要部分的图示

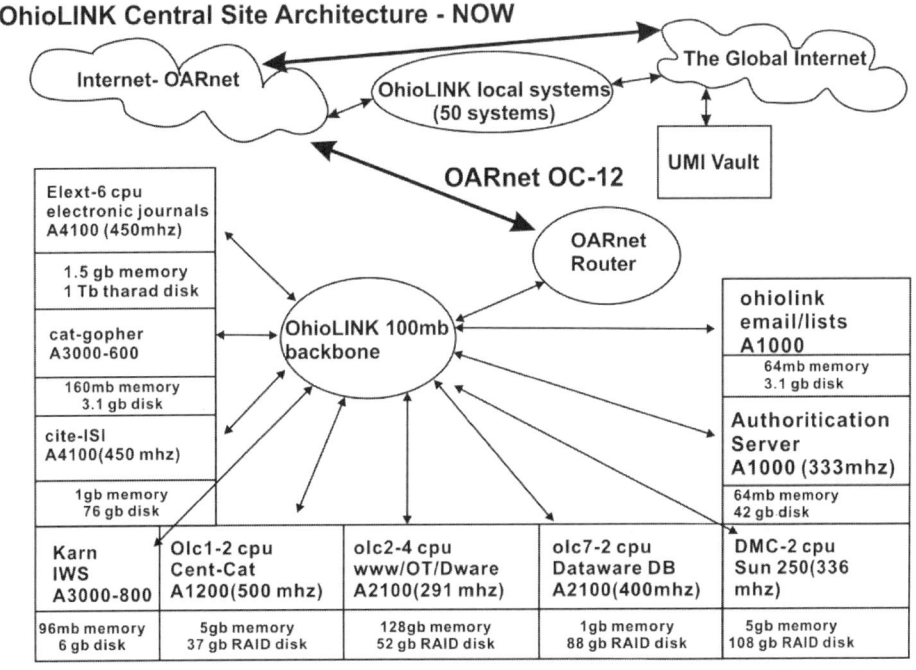

图 10　OhioLINK 中央系统结构图

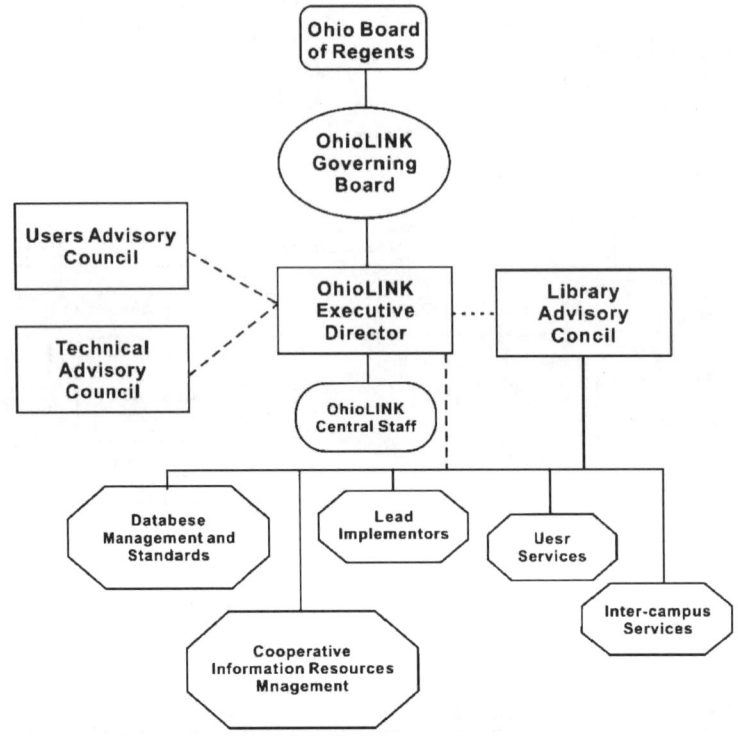

图 11　OhioLINK 组织图

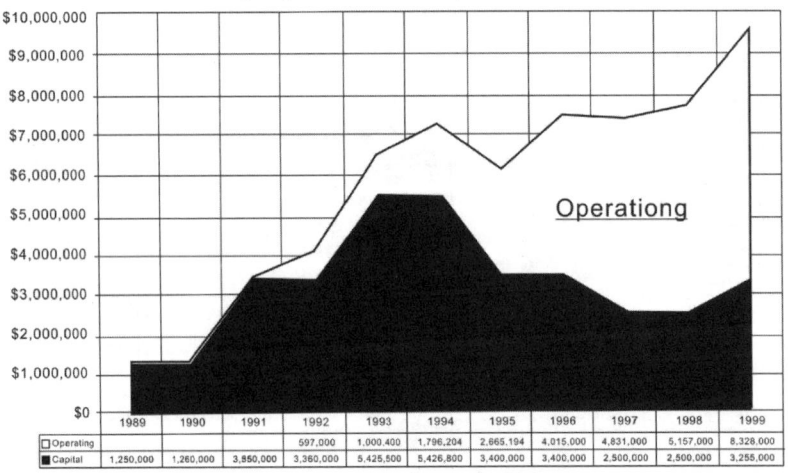

图 12　州政府对 OhioLINK 的年度拨款

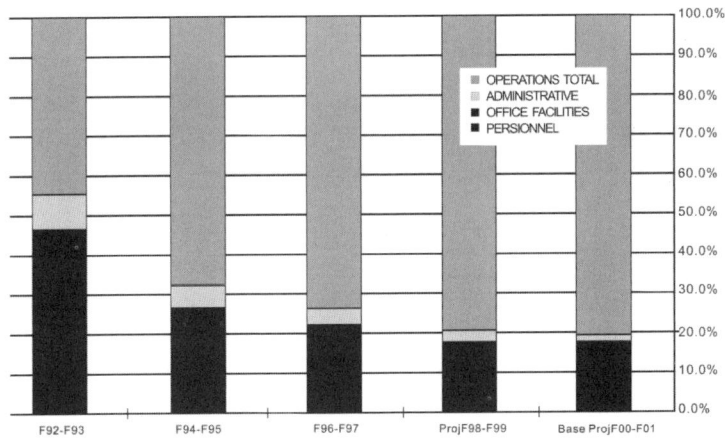

图 13 OhioLINK 双年度运作经费用途的百分比

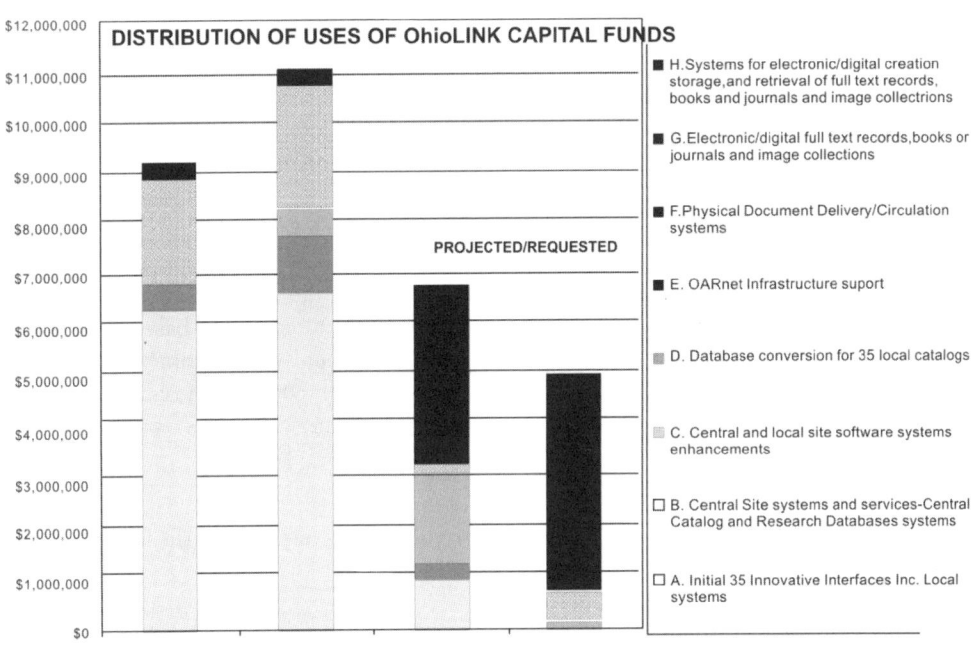

图 14 OhioLINK 双年度资本经费使用的分配

OhioLINK 网络化资讯获取和资源共享的成就

The Success of OhioLINK for Information Access and Resources Sharing in a Networked Environment

INTRODUCTION

Since the 1960s, many changes have taken place in libraries of all types throughout the world. In the U.S., the most significant force accelerating the pace of change in libraries has been the revolution in computer, information, and telecommunication technologies. In the 1960s several major applications of computer technology in libraries were introduced, including the development of the MARC (Machine-Readable Cataloging) Format by the Library of Congress to facilitate the use of computers in cataloging and to set record standards; the establishment of the Medical Literature Analysis and Retrieval System (MEDLARS) by the National Library of Medicine for easy search of and access to the large body of medical literature; the creation of the Ohio College Library Center (OCLC—now renamed as Online Computer Library Center) for online shared cataloging and resource sharing, and the compilation of large computer databases by major indexing and abstracting publishers (e.g., the Chemical Abstract Services).

Since, there have been dramatic changes every five to ten years brought about by a succession of much faster and more powerful computers, sophistication of software packages for library applications, improvements in telecommunications and networking technologies, innovations in information storage and retrieval techniques, growing uses of interactive hyper- and multi-media technologies, evolution of electronic publishing, widespread use of Internet and the World Wide Web (WWW), and others. These changes, coupled with the information explosion, have transformed libraries from paper-based institutions prior to 1960 to computer-based from the 1970s on, to networked since the 1980s, and on to electronic, digital and virtual library in the 1990s. It is clear that the direction of libraries in the 21st century will be a synthesis of these various developments in a high-tech, networked, and digital environment.

CHALLENGES TO LIBRARIES

In addition to the technological transformations, libraries everywhere also face the following challenges:
- Exponential growth of human knowledge;
- Rapid expansion in scholarly communication and publishing;
- Growth in libraries' sizes, functions, resources, services, and complexity;
- Skyrocketing costs of library materials;
- Growing diversity in information formats;
- Shrinking library funding;
- High costs of acquiring, maintaining, and upgrading library systems;
- Requirements for management accountability;
- Increasing demands for library staff skilled in information technologies;
- Changing nature of library collections from "ownership" to "access";
- Expanding user demands and expectations;
- Increasingly vital role in information literacy and lifelong learning.

Facing these multiple challenges, libraries in the U.S. have proactively responded to seize the opportunities available to them. They, in any ways, have played a leading role in the deployment of new and emerging technologies to broaden their resources and to expand their services through cooperation and networking. In fact, their successes have spurred the foregoing challenges.

The traditional concept of "ownership" in collection development is gradually being replaced by "access" to information and knowledge without regard to location and format. True resource sharing among libraries through networking has become the common desire and practice.

THE OhioLINK APPROACH

The formation of OhioLINK (Ohio Library and Information Network) among academic libraries in Ohio, beginning in 1990, for cost-effective networking and resource sharing has proven to be a successful approach. This paper will describe this initiative under the following themes:
- A Serendipitous beginning
- The OhioLINK vision
- Where does OhioLINK stand today?
- How does OhioLINK work?
- What's next for OhioLINK?
- Can the OhioLINK experience be replicated?

A SERENDIPITOUS BEGINNING

The formation of OhioLINK was a direct result of a year-long study by a blue-ribbon panel appointed in 1986 by the Ohio Board of Regents[①] to study library needs of state universities in Ohio. In its report *Academic Libraries in Ohio: Progress Through Collaboration, Storage, and Technology*[②], the panel made several recommendations. The most important of these was to implement "as expeditiously as possible a statewide electronic catalog system". Collateral recommendations included retrospective conversion of remaining paper cataloging records to the MARC format, development and implementation of a statewide delivery system for library materials, and a plan for a cooperative preservation program.

To plan and implement these recommendations, a Steering Committee was established by the Regents with a number of task forces and subcommittees composed of librarians, systems staff, and faculty members from the initial 13 state-supported universities, two large private universities, two independent state-supported medical universities, and the State Library of Ohio. (See Table 1)

Through the investment of thousands of person-hours in hundreds of meetings, several planning documents were completed, including a "Request for Information" issued in August 1988[③], a "*Planning Paper*" issued in November 1988[④], a "*Request for Propose*" issued in August 1989[⑤], and an overview, "*Connecting People, Libraries & Information for Ohio's Future*" issued in 1989.[⑥] Based on the responses to the "*Request for Proposal*", a commercially developed library system by Innovative Interfaces, Inc., was selected in 1990 and installations began in 1991.

After the system was installed in the 18 initial participating libraries between 1992 and 1995, OhioLINK was expanded to cover all state-supported two-year colleges and to an increasing number of private colleges and universities. As of this writing in April 1999, 74 academic libraries in Ohio have joined OhioLINK. Membership identification and information can be found at http://

---

① The Ohio Board of Regents is a state coordinating agency reporting to the Governor with the responsibility of planning and overseeing the general policies and funding of all state-supported institutions of higher learning.

② Ohio Board of Regents. Library Study Committee. "Academic Libraries in Ohio: Progress Through Collaboration, Storage, and Technology" in *Report of the Library Study Committee* (Columbus, Ohio: Ohio Board of Regents, 1987).

③ *Request for Information for the Ohio Library & Information System (fOLIS) on Behalf of the Ohio Board of Regents and Ohio Library & Information System* (Columbus, Ohio: OLIS, August, 1988).

④ OLAS Steering Committee. *Ohio Library Access System Planning Paper.* November 2, 1988 (Columbus, Ohio: Ohio Board of Regents, 1988).

⑤ *Request for Proposal for the Ohio Library & Information System (OLIS) on Behalf of the Ohio Board of Regents and Ohio Library & Information System* (Columbus. Ohio: OLIS, 1989).

⑥ Ohio Library & Information System, *Connecting People. Libraries. & Information for Ohio's Future* (Columbus, Ohio: Ohio Board of Regents, 1989).

www.Ohiolink.edu/members-info/.

Table 1　List of the Founding Libraries

Thirteen State-Supported Universities:
University of Akron
Bowling Green State University
Central State University
University of Cincinnati
Cleveland State University
Kent State University
Miami University
Ohio State University
Ohio University
University of Toledo
Shawnee State University
Wright State University
Youngstown State University
TWO Largest Private Universities:
Case Western Reserve University
University of Dayton
Two State-supported Medical Colleges:
Medical College of Ohio
Northeastern Ohio Universities College of Medicine
One State Library:
The State Library of Ohio

THE OhioLINK VISION

Since its inception, the basic concept of OhioLINK has been to exploit the existing statewide telecommunication infrastructure built by OARnet (Ohio Academic and Research Network) to link the library systems in all the participating libraries, each with a common computer hardware and a software platform—using the Innovative Interfaces Library System.

Through this linkage and a central union catalog capable of retrieving real-time circulation record and location information, users of all participating libraries can access both online local and central catalogs and can initiate borrowing requests for items not available locally from any of the other libraries which own the item. Through a 48-hour delivery service, interlibrary borrowing can be completed within two or three days in most cases.

Once the basic system-wide network was established, OhioLINK has been able to quickly add other resources and services to benefit its member libraries. Most important of these have been:
- the acquisition of many much-in-demand electronic databases,
- expanding the number of full-text databases,
- acquiring electronic journals through discounted pricing for a large consortium,
- developing a new search engine to ease the search of multiple databases,
- adopting a statewide approval plan to reduce unnecessary duplication,
- expanding online borrowing from books to other types of library materials,
- establishing an Electronic Journal Center with an increasing number of e-journals,
- establishing a Digital Media Center with virtually unlimited storage space available at Ohio Supercomputer Center for member created or commercially produced digital collections:
- improving off-campus access to OhioLINK resources.

The shared vision of OhioLINK can thus be summarized as:
- linking all major academic libraries in Ohio in an electronic network environment,

- tapping the existing computer and telecommunication infrastructure,
- pooling all library resources for easy access and effective sharing,
- delivering materials quickly by various means,
- cooperating for collection development,
- acquiring large and expensive electronic resources cost effectively through consortia purchasing power,
- transforming interlibrary cooperation and resource sharing.

Figure 1 shows that among the 20 million combined library holding of books (representing over 7.1 million individual titles) 56% were held by only one library, 14% by two libraries, 7% by three libraries, 5% by four libraries, 3% by five libraries, and the rest 14% by six or more libraries. The fact that a large percentage of books are held by only one library indicates the importance and benefit of resource sharing and the combined strength of a pooled collection.

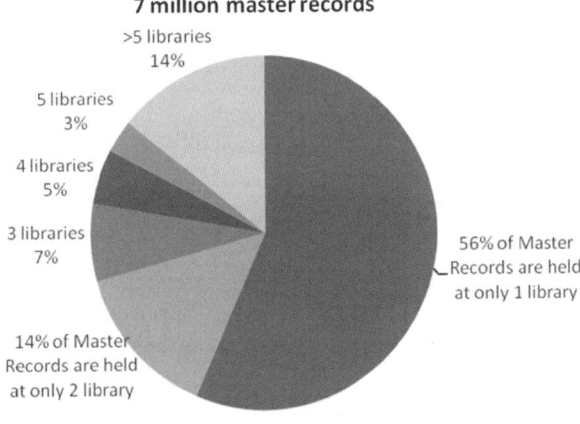

Figure 1　Percent of Items Held by Number of Libraries

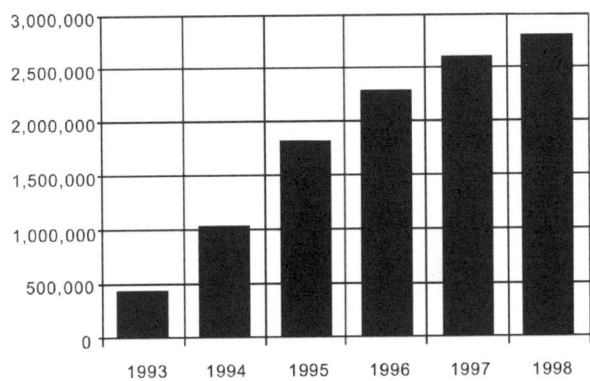

Figure 2　Annual Searches of the OhioLINK Central Online Catalog

WHERE DOES OhioLINK STAND TODAY?

Even though OhioLINK is still developing and expanding its resources and services, some concrete results have already been achieved.

- Demonstrated benefits and economies of scale have enabled OhioLINK to seek more State funding in support of its central operations, delivery services, acquisition of major bibliographic, reference, and full-text databases, and undertaking other new initiatives.

- More than 7.1 million individual titles representing 20 million volumes held by 74 libraries are now available to approximately 460,000 students and 50,000 faculty and staff.
- In 1993, there were nearly 450,000 annual searches of the OhioLINK central catalog. In 1998, this rose to more than 2.75 million searches. (See Figure 2).
- In 1994, about 75,000 requests for direct borrowing by patrons were initiated. By 1998, this jumped to 560,000 requests. Between January 1994 and March 1999, the cumulative patron online borrowing requests surpassed two million. The successfully filled rate was 85% of the requests. (See Figure 3) According to documented studies, patron-initiated borrowing has reduced the cost of an interlibrary loans from $15 - $30 per item by traditional methods to $8.00 per item.
- For statewide access to electronic information—in December of 1992, there were only two databases, but in December 1998, there were 67 databases. The annual searches of all OhioLINK reference databases have gone from 500,000 in 1993 to more than 10 million in 1998. (See Figure 4) The cost per search has been reduced from $3.90 per search in 1993 to less than $0.30 per search in 1999. (See Figure 5)
- For access to full-text —in 1993, nothing was available, but in a single week in the peak month of November 1998, 30,000 full-text journal articles of 125,000 pages were printed online by users from the UMI supplier. The average cost per article was $0.90. (See Figure 6)
- Using consortia purchasing power, OhioLINK's reference database licensing costs represent 30% to 80% discounts from individual library prices.
- OhioLINK has successfully negotiated license fees for electronic journals at +5% to +10% annual cost increases (compared to 10% to 15% increases historically) that deliver 5 to 10 times more titles than traditional print subscription levels.
- Since its inception in April 1998, OhioLINK's Electronic Journal Center has expended its collection of electronic journals. As of December 1998, 160,713 articles had been downloaded from 1,307 of the 1,325 available journal titles. (See Figures 7 & 8)

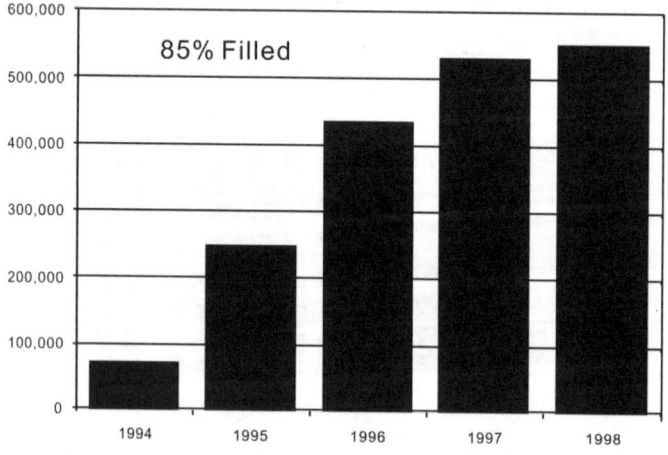

Figure 3 OhioLINK Patron Initiated Online Borrowing

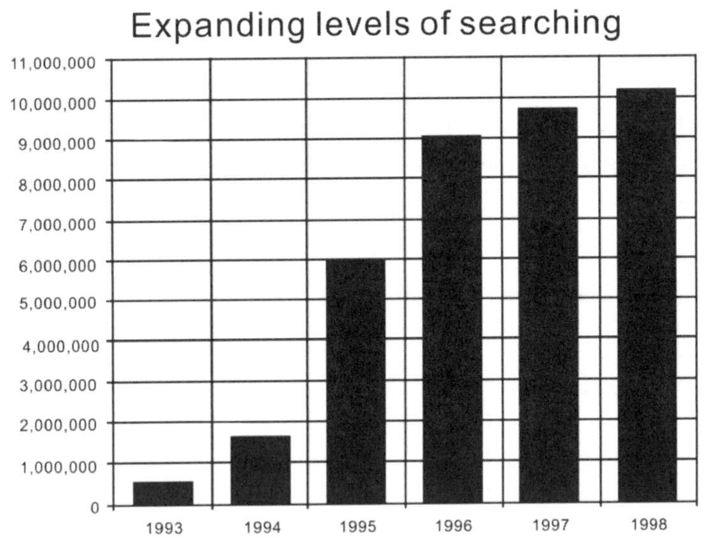

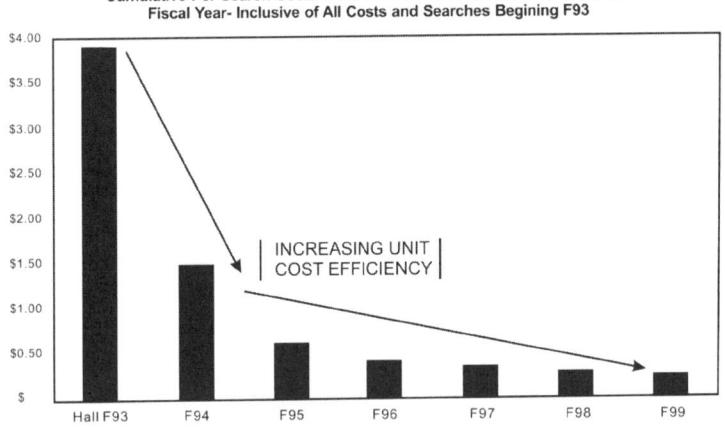

Figure 4 Searches of OhioLINK Central Reference Databases

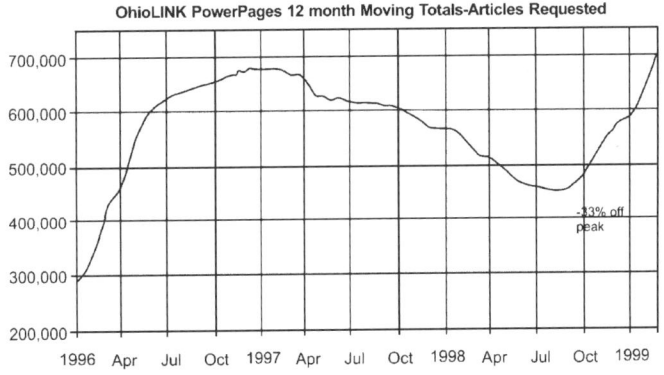

Figure 5 Cumulative Per Search Costs of Reference Databases

Figure 6 UMI Power Pages Article Downloads

HOW DOES OHIOLINK WORK?

1. Systems Architecture

The OhioLINK systems consist of 60 local systems and a central site system. Each local system has one or more Digital computers, servers, and up to several hundred networked workstations, printers, scanners, etc. Figure 9 below shows the initial configuration of OhioLINK system components. Figure 10 shows the current OhioLINK central site system architecture.

2. Governance

OhioLINK's Governing Board is made up of provosts or chief academic officers of participating institutions, the chair and vice chair of the Library Advisory Council, and the liaison staff from the Ohio Board of Regents. It reports directly to the Regents. The Governing Board hires the Executive Director and oversees the financial and administrative operations of the Headquarters.

At the policy-making and planning level, there is a Library Advisory Council (LAC) which consists of library deans/directors from the 18 initial libraries and representatives from the two-year colleges, private universities and colleges, law libraries, and medical libraries. The Chair, Vice Chair, and the immediate past chair constitute the executive Coordinating Committee (LACCC).

At the operational level, there are a Lead Implementers group and four standing committees. The Lead Implementers group is made up of systems librarians or designated staff of the participating libraries. The four standing committees, whose members are nominated by library directors and appointed by the Executive Director, are:

- Cooperative Information Resource Management
- User Services
- Inter-campus Services
- Database Management and Standards

Figure 11 illustrates the general organizational structure of OhioLINK.

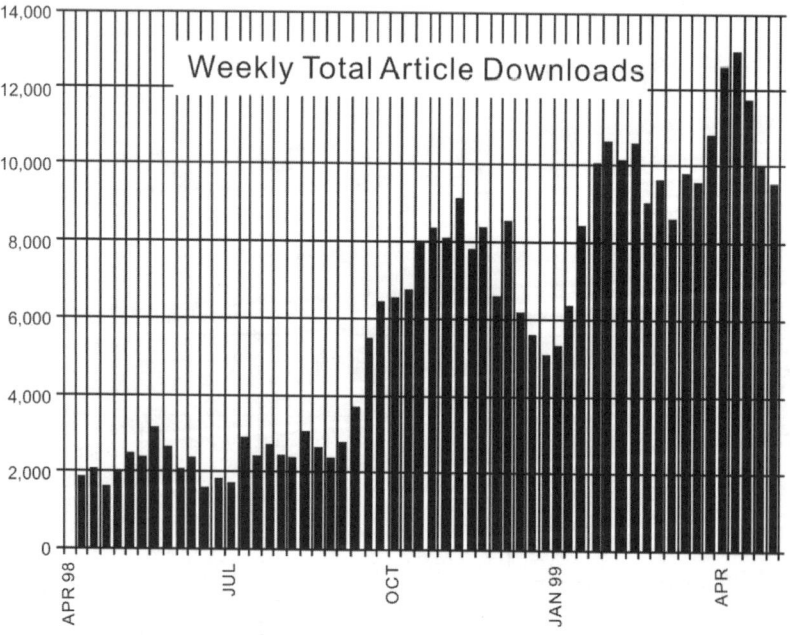

Figure 7   Electronic Journal Center (EKC) Downloads

3. Funding

OhioLINK's main funds have come from State appropriations based on requests submitted through the Ohio Board of Regents to the Governor's office and approved by the Ohio State Legislature. These are in two forms: Operating and Capital. Operating funds cover recurrent costs such as headquarters salaries, office facilities, and administrative and other operating costs of the central site. Capital funds cover such costs as the initial central-site computer hardware and software including upgrades and enhancements; initial costs of local systems and database preparation; purchase of electronic reference, full-text, and journal databases (that are owned rather than leased), infrastructure support of the Ohio Academic and Research Network, and multimedia and full-text systems.

In 1998/99 fiscal year, the Operating Budget is \$5.157 million and the Capital Budget is \$2.5 million. Figures 12, 13, and 14 below show the actual OhioLINK appropriations, biennium operating expenses by percentage, and the distribution of uses of OhioLINK capital funds.

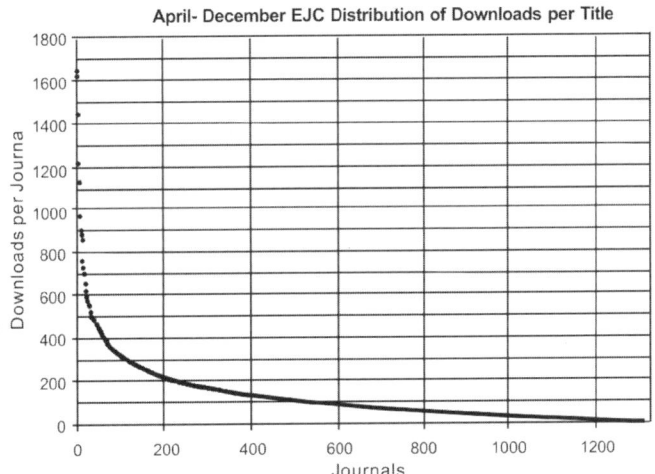

Figure 8 Electronic Journal Center Downloads Per Title

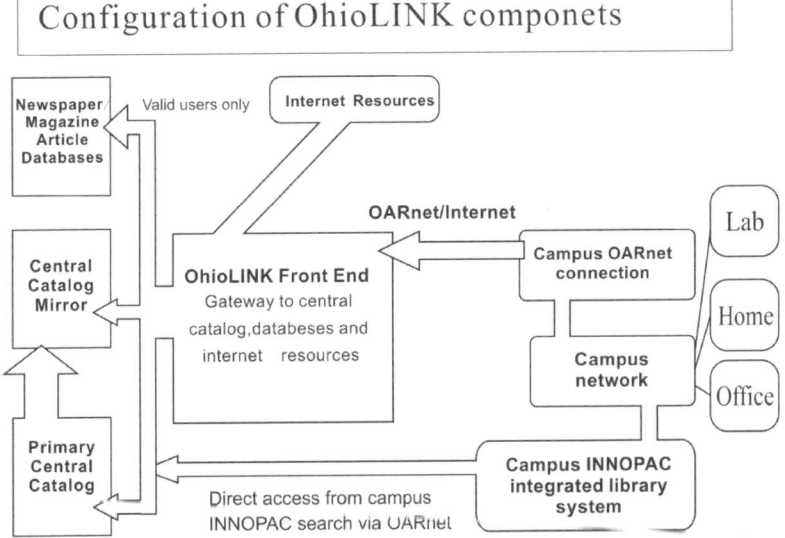

Figure 9 Configuration of OhioLINK Components

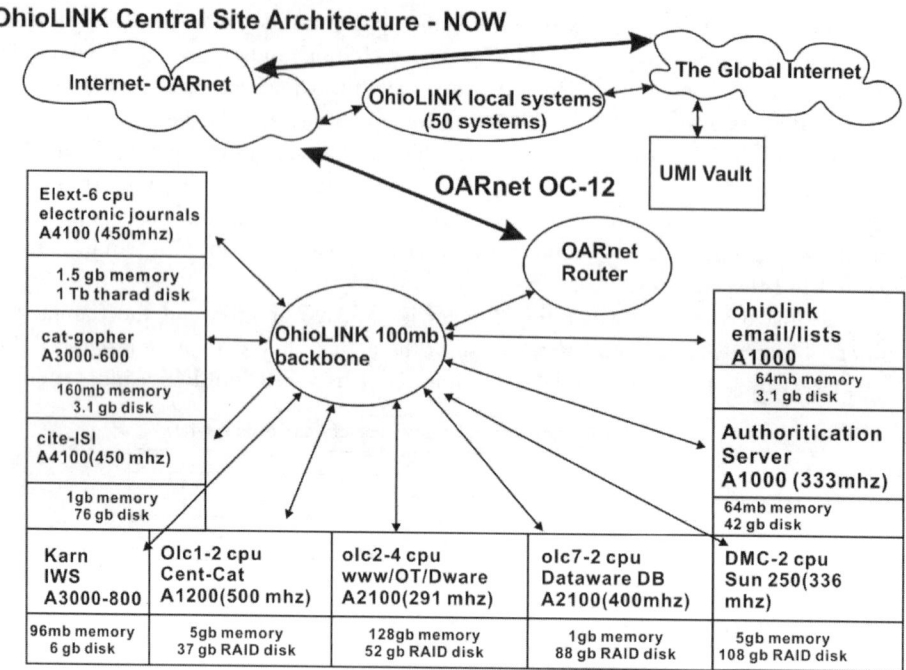

Figure 10   Ohio Central Site Architecture

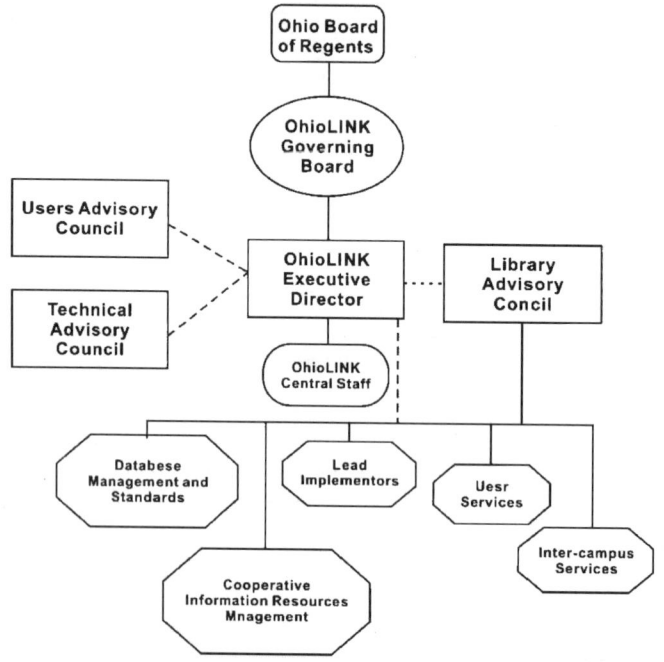

Figure 11   OhioLINK Organizational Structure

Most of the expenditures for maintaining and upgrading local systems, local campus telecommunications, and other local OhioLINK-related operating costs are the responsibility of each library with notable exceptions: the initial local system hardware and software, retrospective conversion, authority control, telecommunications backbone, core reference databases, centrally purchased electronic books, partial subsidies for a group licensed electronic journals, and contracted document delivery services—all of which have been paid by central funds. Beginning in 1998, OhioLINK libraries have agreed to be assessed a small amount (about 1% of acquisition funding for my university) to create an initial $600,000 "war chest" to expand the funding for the central acquisition of further core reference databases (previously purchased core databases have been and continue to be paid entirely by state funding to OhioLINK).

WHAT'S NEXT FOR OhioLINK?

With the demonstrated success of OhioLINK, many have viewed OhioLINK as an ideal model for effective information access and resource sharing in an electronic and networked environment. However, from our vantage point, we see opportunities to do even more as we enter the fast lane of the information superhighway in the 21st century. Several strategic priorities have been identified for actions in the immediate future. These are:

· Expanding current databases—especially full-text and non-text-based resources such as maps, numeric data, graphics, and images of all sorts.

· Promoting more effective means for cooperative collection development.

· Adding new capacities such as the delivery of all services to the desktop via an integrated WWW-based platform and electronic transmission of articles.

· Providing a more convenient and user-friendly interface.

· Linking journal and newspaper databases to actual holdings, circulation records, and full-text articles.

· Encouraging, coordinating, and hosting more digitization projects.

· Supporting alternative methods and strategies in electronic publishing to control costs and prevent publishers usurping control of the intellectual property rights of authors.

· Seeking alliances with other state, national and global networks, exemplified by the International Coalition of Library Consortia.

It is clear from viewing the list of strategic priorities, OhioLINK has a full and exciting agenda ahead.

CAN OhioLINK EXPERIENCE BE REPLICATED?

The successes of OhioLINK are due largely to the following elements:

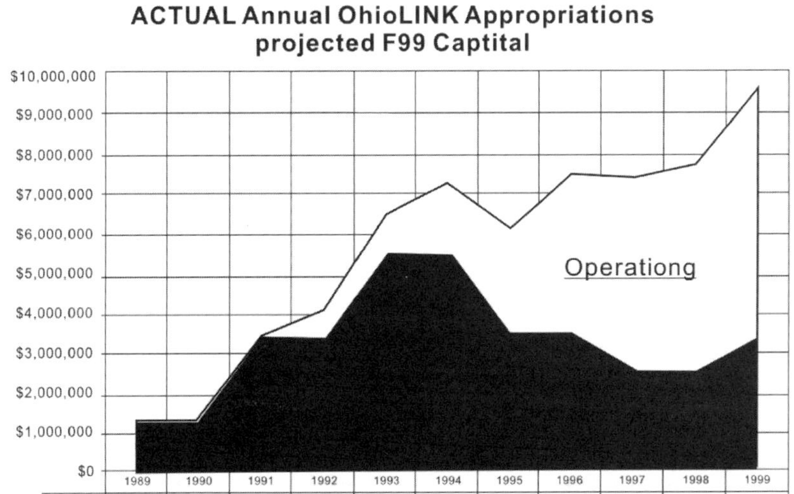

	1989	1990	1991	1992	1993	1994	1995	1996	1997	1998	1999
□ Operating				597,000	1,000,400	1,796,204	2,665,194	4,015,000	4,831,000	5,157,000	8,328,000
■ Capital	1,250,000	1,260,000	3.550,000	3,360,000	5,425,500	5,426,800	3,400,000	3,400,000	2,500,000	2,500,000	3,255,000

Figure 12 Actual Annual OhioLINK Appropriations

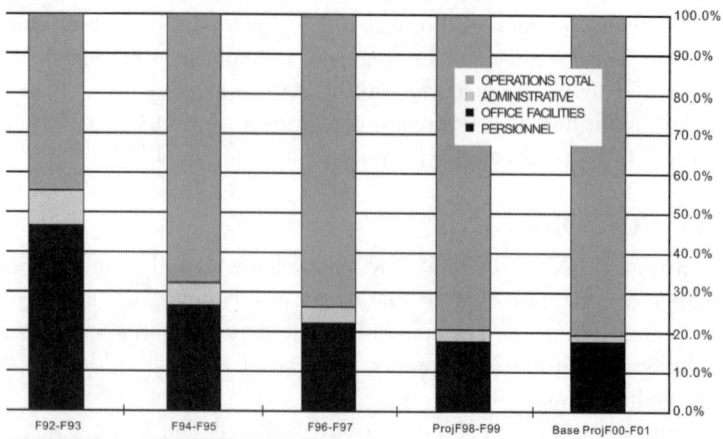

Figure 13　OhioLINK Biennium Operation Expenses by Percentage

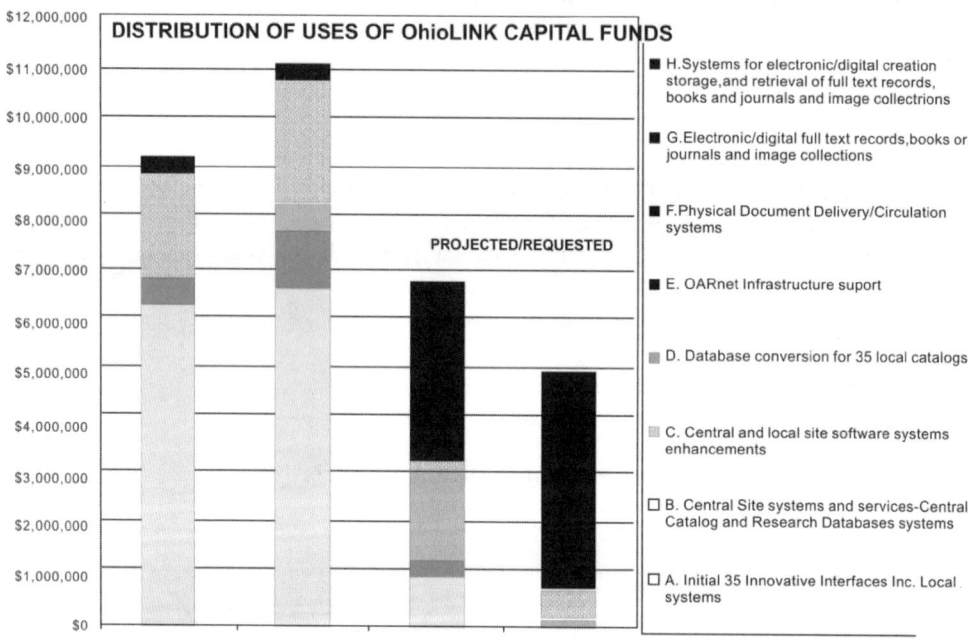

Figure 14　Distribution of Users of OhioLINK Capital Funds

· General recognition that no library can be self-sufficient in providing the wide-range of information sources needed to serve its users.

· Strong desire of all libraries, both large and small, to cooperate and share resources—a long-honored tradition among Ohio libraries which was a chief reason for founding OCLC back in 1967.

· Visionary library leadership committed to library cooperation.

· Understanding and support of a governing body (the Ohio Board of Regents) willing to provide initial and ongoing funding.

· Availability of more sophisticated library and information technologies for library automation and networking.

· Increasing availability of electronic and digital publications.

• Full participation of all libraries in a functional organizational structure which is able to build consensus and to make wise, judicious, and timely decisions.

What can be done in Ohio can also be done elsewhere if the abovementioned elements are present. In fact, some of these elements can be cultivated and nurtured if necessary.

Furthermore, an OhioLINK-like library consortium need not be identical. Libraries in developing countries have more impetus for networked information access and resource sharing to make the best use of rather limited financial, material, technical, and human resources. But because of the different local conditions, each library consortium should be planned and developed according to local and regional needs and should develop its own unique feature. The OhioLINK approach can serve as a successful working example in maximizing information access and resource sharing in a networked environment among any group of libraries with a desire to cooperate. Taking the first step may not be easy, but once begun, the obvious benefits will be a driving force to move forward.

(Published in *Bulletin of Library and Information Science*. V. 30, No. 8, 1999: pp. 1 – 17.)

网络时代的图书馆合作和资源共享[①]

Library Cooperation and Resource Sharing in a Networked Environment

介 绍
◇ 电脑、资讯和电讯传播技术的不断革新。
◇ 资讯爆炸、知识与创新、科教兴国。
◇ 图书馆受技术革新的冲击。
◇ 网际网络的发展。
◇ 高等教育的变化。
◇ 图书馆所面临的挑战。
◇ 从 OCLC 到 OhioLINK。

我们久所盼望的 21 世纪即将来临
◇ 除了大家所关心电脑 Y2K 是否可以过关的问题。
◇ 大家更关心的是随着 21 世纪所到来的新技术与新知识时代。

在这个新世纪里——
我们可以看到科学技术及人类知识会以更快的速度发展。
知识（Knowledge）是数位（Digit）、资料（Data）及资讯（Information）的合成（Synthesis）。
它必须渗入人类的智慧及创造力才会生机显现，造福社会。
所谓的"硅谷"精神就是包括了以科技及知识为基础的创造力、冒险犯险、竞争与创业奋斗。
21 世纪将会是一个知识不断更新的时代，而且这种更新的速度会越来越快。

20 世纪 60 年代图书馆在技术方面的主要应用
◇ 由国会图书馆开发的 MARC（机读目录）格式
◇ 由国家医学图书馆创立的（MEDLARS）医学文献分析及检索系统
◇ OCLC（俄亥俄州学院图书馆中心——现已更名为电脑联机图书馆中心）的建立
◇ 由一些主要索引和文摘出版机构利用电脑所建立的大型资料库（例如：化学文摘）

自从 20 世纪 60 年代以来技术的发展
◇ 运算速度更快、效率更强的电脑不断涌现。
◇ 专为图书馆应用所开发的电脑软件的不断改进。
◇ 电讯传播和网络技术的提高。

[①] 这是 1999 年在台湾图书馆学会"网际网络与图书馆发展研讨会"上的演讲文稿。

◇ 资讯储存和检索技术的革新。
◇ 互交媒体及多媒体技术应用的增加。
◇ 电子出版的衍生。
◇ 网际网络和全球网的广泛使用。

图书馆技术革新的演变

◇ 60 年代以前以纸张和印刷品为主的图书馆。
◇ 60 年代电脑化的图书馆。
◇ 70 年代网络化的图书馆。
◇ 80 年代电子化图书馆。
◇ 90 年代数位化和虚拟的图书馆。

高等教育的变化

◇ 经费来源的削减。
◇ 对于效率的责任和要求。
◇ 学生结构的改变。
◇ 多样化的校园。
◇ 新的课程。
◇ 新的学术沟通方式。
◇ 强调学习重于教学。
◇ 增加对技术的投入。
◇ 函授及终身的教育的发展。
◇ 对国际性的重视。

教学新模式

传统模式	新的模式
◇ 全时制	◇ 部分时间
◇ 校园内	◇ 校园外
◇ 连续的	◇ 不连续的
◇ 按顺序的	◇ 无顺序的
◇ 累积的	◇ 非累积的
◇ 全班的	◇ 单个的
◇ 单向的	◇ 互相的
◇ 同时进行的	◇ 非同时进行的

图书馆面临的挑战

◇ 人类知识以指数式的速度提高。
◇ 学术沟通与出版的迅速增长。
◇ 图书馆规模、职能、资源、服务和复杂性的扩大。
◇ 图书馆收藏品价格的飞涨。
◇ 资讯载体的多样化。

◇ 图书馆经费的萎缩。
◇ 图书馆系统购置、维护、升级换代的高额价格。
◇ 对管理效率和责任的要求。
◇ 图书馆对于精通资讯技术人员需求的增加。
◇ 图书馆藏书从"拥有"到"获取"这一本质性的变化。
◇ 读者的需求和期望也在增加。
◇ 在扫除"资讯盲"及终身教育上所起的越来越重要的作用。

对于挑战所做出的反应

◇ 为资源共享建立图书馆网络。
◇ 新技术的开发和使用。
◇ 强调图书馆员素质的提高。
◇ 招收具有资讯技术的馆员。
◇ 馆藏的多样化。
◇ 运用协作性购买力来取得优惠价格。
◇ 以协作方式来发展馆藏。
◇ 为远地的读者提供服务。

OhioLINK 的探索

◇ 偶然的开端。
◇ OhioLINK 的构思。
◇ OhioLINK 的形状。
◇ OhioLINK 如何运作。
◇ OhioLINK 的未来走向。
◇ OhioLINK 的经验可否借鉴。

偶然的开端

◇ 1986 年,成立了一个特别小组,对各州立大学图书馆的需求进行研究。
◇ 1987 年,提出通过一个全州范围的网络来增加合作和资源共享。
◇ 1989 年,颁布《招标征求》。
◇ 1990 年,挑选系统。
◇ 1991 年,首批安装。
◇ 1994 年,18 所最早参与的图书馆运营。
◇ 1994 年,OhioLINK 扩展到其他学术图书馆。

OhioLINK 的构思

◇ 连接俄亥俄州所有的学术图书馆。
◇ 集中所有的馆藏资料。
◇ 利用现有的网络通讯架构。
◇ 使读者很容易使用馆藏及资料。
◇ 快速传递。

◇ 最大限度地利用现有资源
　● 有效共享图书馆资源。
　● 以合作采购方式来发展馆藏。
　● 协作购买力。
◇ 成为馆际合作的楷模。

通过合作来扩大资源和服务范围

◇ 集中采购高需求的电子资料库。
◇ 扩大全文资料库的数量。
◇ 通过集体优惠价格购买电子刊物。
◇ 发展新的查寻软件平台，以方便对多种资料库的同时查寻。
◇ 采纳一个全州合作采购图书的方式来避免不必要的重复。
◇ 扩大网上借阅范围——从图书拓展到其他种类的馆藏资料。
◇ 建立一个电子期刊中心。
◇ 建立一个数位化媒体中心。

OhioLINK 的现状

◇ 为 74 所院校的 46 万学生提供服务。
◇ 图书收藏总数超过 2000 万册（700 万种）。
◇ 网上直接借阅。
◇ 电子参考资料。
◇ 全文本资料库。
◇ 电子期刊的联合订购契约。
◇ 电子期刊文章的传递。

OhioLINK 如何运作

◇ 系统架构。
◇ 组织与职员。
◇ 管理
　● 董事会
　● 图书馆顾问委员会
　　资料库的管理与标准小组
　　读者服务小组
　　资讯资源合作管理小组
　　校际服务小组
◇ 经费。

OhioLINK 的未来走向

◇ 扩大现有的资料库——特别是全文资料库。
◇ 增进更加有效的藏书发展合作。
◇ 增加新功能。

◇ 通过一个整合的以全球网为基础的平台，把所有的服务传递到个人电脑上。
◇ 文献的电子传播。
◇ 一个更加方便、好用的界面。
◇ 把期刊和报纸资料库实际的馆藏、流通记录和文献全文链接起来。
◇ 数位化项目的协调。
◇ 电子出版。
◇ 寻求与其他州际、国内、国际的图书馆网络合作。

OhioLINK 成功的因素

◇ 人们已经意识到"任何图书馆都不能独自提供所需资讯"。
◇ 所有的图书馆都强烈要求合作、共享资源。
◇ 有眼光的图书馆领导者对馆际合作决心和积极行动。
◇ 政府部门的理解和支持。
◇ 具备了图书馆网络化所需的资讯技术。
◇ 越来越多的电子和数位出版物。
◇ 能够达成共识，做出明智的及适时的决定。

OhioLINK 的经验可否借鉴

◇ 发展中国家的图书馆有更急迫的需求来建立网络上的资讯利用和资源共享。
◇ 这样的图书馆合作不一定要一模一样。
◇ 三个重要的成功因素。
- ● 共识
- ● 合作的愿望
- ● 政府的支持

（原载《网际网络与图书馆发展研讨会论文集》，台湾图书馆学会，1999 年，第 3－44 页）

21 世纪数位化及网络化知识时代中的图书馆[①]

Libraries in the Digital and Networked Knowledge Age of the Twenty-first Century

一、前言

从 20 世纪 50 年代起,科技更迭的速度大大地加速并带来人类知识以等级数速度成长,亦即资讯爆炸!保守预测,这种改变速度会持续到 21 世纪,我们的生活及社会将逐渐以知识为主导。虽然许多的改变是源自科技革命,尤其是在电脑、通讯及网络等方面,但是我们必须清楚了解所有这些科技的突破都是人类知识、才能、创造与智慧发展的结果。人类才是科技改变的驱动力。事实上,我们确认科技的进步将带给人类益处,并且迎接我们进入 21 世纪数位化及网络化的知识时代。

图书馆在这个知识昌明的时代所扮演的角色是本文重点,旨在探讨知识时代的特质、图书馆的角色及知识与创造间的关系。

美国国会图书馆馆长 James H. Billington 于 1989 年 1 月以国会图书馆发展新趋向为题对美国图书馆学会理事(the Council of the American Library Association)发表演说,在演说中他指出:"国会图书馆是一个主动、积极支持与鼓励获取及使用知识的地方;国会图书馆在资讯转换成知识、知识转换成智慧的过程中担任触媒者及参与者;国会图书馆支持、强化及提升美国人民生活智力与文化的基础。"[②] 虽然 Billington 的演说是针对国会图书馆的发展,但是对所有图书馆在知识昌明时代所扮演的角色无疑是强而有力的声明。

二、知识时代的特质

什么是知识时代?其一般的特质如何?这些问题需要提出并获得解答。

Daniel Bell 对知识的定义是:"知识是一组对事实或想法经过组织的陈述,呈现合理的评断或一项实验结果,这些评判或实验结果是以某种有系统的形式经由某种通讯媒体传布给其他人。"[③] 至于资讯(information)的定义,Marc Porat 认为"资讯就是经过组织与沟通的数据。"[④] 这两种定义似乎提示我们知识比资讯来得精炼。换言之,资讯只被视为数据与事实的报道,而知识则较复杂,它是数据、事实、想法、及经验的合成体。

在知识时代,我们看到人类的知识以史无前例的速度累增,这种速度影响我们的生活及社会的每一个层面。经由人类的智力、创造与智慧,我们的知识世界每一分秒都在增长。据估计,世界各地所出版的学术性出版品大约有 850,000 种,每年增长 2.5%。连续性出版品从 1972 年的 70,000 种增加到 1997 年的 118,500 种。全球每分钟就有一篇科技论文完成,这是知识时代的基本特质。知识时代这个词强调知识在新世纪所扮演的角色。

近年来电脑、通讯与网络等科技的进步是知识扩充一个重要的理由。我们越能快速传

[①] 本文由台中图书馆赖丽香翻译。
[②] From author's notes of the Council meeting.
[③] Bell, Daniel. *The Coming of Post-industrial Society: A Venture in Social Forecasting.* New York: Basic Books, 1973: p. 175.
[④] Porat, Marc. *The Information Economy: Definition and Measurement.* Washington, D. C.: U.S. Department of Commerce, Office of Telecommunications, 1977. (Publication 77-12).

递资讯与知识,知识就越发达。在7世纪末期发明印刷术的中国及15世纪的欧洲,都大大地促进人类知识的保存与传播。但是在1884年,只有Samuel Morse所发明的电传才能使资讯的传送速率比一匹马或一个人所能跑的速度还快。

现今,随着网际网络及全球资讯网的来临,我们真的处在一个世界地球村,在这里,资讯及知识能以光的速度传输,不受距离或社会、政治、经济、文化或种族等其他因素的限制。

三、机会与挑战

在21世纪的知识时代,我们有许多的机会,也面临许多的挑战。为了发展策略性的眼光及规划适当的行动方案以因应挑战,我们必须更严谨及更深入地检视这些机会与挑战。

(一)电脑及通讯科技的发展与整合

自从微电脑在80年代问世以来,每一代的电脑体积越来越小,价格也越来越便宜,但运算能力却大幅提升。按莫尔原理(Moore's Law)的推断,电脑的处理速度每十八个月增加一倍。由于方便、可携性及人们买得起,桌上型电脑、膝上型电脑、笔记型电脑、掌上型电脑及个人资料助理型电脑对越来越多的一般民众而言,已成为极为有用的必需品。不仅多数的办公室配有这些设备,越来越多的家庭及公共场所,例如图书馆、学校、大学、机场、会议中心及旅馆等,也都备有这些设备以供使用。每年有越来越多的人口具备电脑素养。这种情形在许多发展中国家也是如此。电脑与封包型电话的结合,使连结Internet更容易,因此更促进新知识与新发现的交流。

Evans电传公司的总裁及C-SPAN的联合创办人John D. Evans在一次演说中强调,"我们正处在一个史无前例的全球革命之中,我们正从长期以来的模拟化社会逐渐进入一个数位化的社会。这种革命的影响至少可以说是相当令人惊奇的。"①

根据Evans的说法,数位化时代的诞生是由于高速电脑、大量资料储存媒体、人造卫星、电缆、宽频传输、新的传播科技、及封包交换与路由发展等科技的会合。

Evans认为我们现在已经拥有:[Evens, *ibid.*]

➢ 区域及广域网络,
➢ 即时电子邮件,
➢ 每台低于美金800元的个人电脑,却具有70年代IBM360大型电脑的处理能力,
➢ 桌上型视讯会议,
➢ 语音辨识系统,能将笔记或报告转入电脑并自动校正文法及拼字,
➢ 提供检索数千个网站的资讯,
➢ 超过100,000个讨论园地供志同道合者互动与交流,
➢ 数千个新闻讨论群,提供新知及资讯,内容包括各种议题,从AIDS到最新的电影评论或Monica Lewinsky的录音带,
➢ 超过500个电视节目频道的电缆及人造卫星系统,
➢ 随选视讯,
➢ 人造卫星广播电视,
➢ 具文字与通信能力的无线数位电话。

---

① Evans, John D. "Worldwide Communications: Are You Ready?" ***Rocco C. Siciliano*** Forum: Second Annual Lecture, October 6, 1998. Salt Lake City, Utah: College of Social and Behavioral Science, University of Utah, 1999.

（二）网络化环境

三十年前，在 1969 年 10 月 29 日，有一群科学家聚集在加州大学洛杉矶分校，采用封包交换的技术传送一件电子讯息给史丹佛研究所（Stanford Research Institute）的一组研究人员。这种技术是由 UCLA 的工程教授 Leonard Kleinrock 所发展出来的，他就是广为流传的 Internet 之父。几年之内，Internet 传遍美国各州，也跨越到世界各地。

由于 Internet 的使用每个月以百分之十五的速率成长，因此已相当拥挤。在 2002 年以前，预估将有 328,000,000 人口连结 Internet，商业或其他用途将塞满原已非常拥挤的资讯公路。为克服这些瓶颈，一些研究型大学在 1996 年成立联盟以创造一个速度更快、专为学术和研究机构使用的 Internet。这个联盟的正式名称为 University Corporation for Advanced Internet Development（UCAID），超过 130 个研究型大学及单位加入这个联盟。这个扩展的 Internet 称为 Internet2，在 1999 年年底以前将其频宽扩充 100 倍。为了加大现有 Internet 的容量以供大众的使用，一个由民间团体参与和投入精力来创造的"下一代 Internet"也在积极发展中。

Internet 使用的成长确实是具有革命性的。各种线上资讯资源的快速扩充，从图书馆的线上公用目录、电子资料库、数位化资讯，以及来自世界各地的商情、政府、学术机构、其他组织、医药健康、运动、气象等各种资讯，在刺激 Internet 的使用。此外还有最新新闻、财经资讯以及通讯工具，例如 E-mail、BBS、电子会议等也都是促使 Internet 快速成长的因素。

虽然 Internet 有其重要的益处与贡献，但也有一些问题。Internet 不是我们所想象的万灵丹，大家对 Internet 有下列共同的抱怨：
➢ 资讯污染，
➢ 信息超载，
➢ 不适当的资讯及欺骗，
➢ 电脑病毒，
➢ 骇客入侵，
➢ 缺乏隐私，
➢ 缺乏安全，
➢ 缺乏归档，
➢ 滥用，
➢ Internet 犯罪。

对于 Internet 是否应设定使用规范有很多的争议。虽然 Internet 的先驱是美国国防部所设立的网络系统，目的在连结该部散置各地的电脑，但后来的发展，Internet 已不是官方正式的组织。至于现在，一般人仍认为这种自由放任形式的架构应该继续存在，因为它还是利多于弊。

从图书馆的观点来看，我们显然地倾向维持资讯自由流通，但关心资讯污染、不适当及有害资讯入侵的问题。我们并不希望设立检查制度，但是强调由具有能力与学科背景的馆员在 Internet 资讯环境中为图书馆使用者做一个领航员、筛选者、组织者及阅读指导者的重要性，就如他们在印刷资料与出版品环境中所做的一样。

（三）资讯与知识数位化

电脑与 Internet 的普及已刺激资讯与知识数位化的快速成长。化学摘要服务公司（Chemical Abstract Services）及工程索引公司（Engineering Index）在 60 年代首先使用电脑来加速大量书目资料的处理工作，以便出版纸本式索引及摘要。他们的努力所获得的副产品是70年代电脑可查询的资料库（computer searchable database）。当时的Dialog及BRS二个资讯检索服务公司首先提供线上资讯检索服务。

在80年代，许多出版商看到电子出版的利益，一些百科全书、期刊及图书开始以电子形式出现，包括CD-ROM。现在由于Internet的发展，数位化资讯及知识已充斥于网络中且毫无疑问地将大大地影响我们的日常生活，传统的学术交流模式将会快速地被取代了。

（四）版权与知识财权的保护

充分保护作品的版权所有及创作者的智能财产权是重要且必要的。世界智慧财产组织（WIPO）是联合国的一个机构，有167个代表国家，负责各种版权条款之发展与管理。

虽然图书馆是保护版权及智慧财产权的支持者，但促进资讯自由流通是图书馆主要的任务，在"合理使用"的原则下，允许图书馆提供资讯给读者，以非营利的态度在教育、学习及学术交流等方面做正当的使用，这是在美国宪法有关版权部分特别阐明的。为此，图书馆对印刷及数位化形式的出版品已付费。但是，许多学术出版商对图书馆索价比一般个人购买还高，这对期刊而言更是如此。事实上众所皆知图书馆是学术出版品出版商主要的财力来源。

许多研究者及学者也感觉到被一些出版商所剥削。他们必须交出作品的版权给这些出版商以换取自己的文章或论文出版的机会。这种情形，往往与研究者及学者的兴趣不兼容，这些研究者及学者很希望能及时且在较少限制的情况下与同道分享他们的新知识、创作或发现。

（五）出版界与学术交流

过去，研究者及学者经常透过在专业书刊中发表著作来分享他们的研究心得，也参与各种研讨会与同道面对面讨论及交换资讯。此外，学术研究者及学者为了升迁及获得终身聘任也需要出版他们的智慧结晶。30年代以前，多数的学术及专业期刊是由学术团体及专业组织来出版，提供他们的会员及图书馆较付得起的订购价格。自此之后，则有愈来愈多的期刊改由商业出版商出版，他们的订购价格根本无法控制。很讽刺的是，当出版商从中获利且图书馆必须支付超出预算的经费时，作者并未得到任何金钱的回报。

因学术期刊价格不断上涨、延误发行，及使用上种种的限制，使各学科领域的学者感到不满，因此在80年代开始试着在Internet上出版电子期刊。由研究图书馆学会（The Association of Research Libraries）在1997年出版的电子学术期刊，通讯及学术讨论组合指南（Directory of Electronic Scholarly Journals, Newsletters, and Academic Discussion List）上列有1,002种电子刊物。[①]

最近在研究图书馆学会的领导之下，一些主要的学术及研究图书馆采取另一个重要的措施，成立了一个学术出版及学术资源联盟（Scholarly Publishing and Academic Resources Coalition, SPARC），鼓励发展替代的出版方法，使能与商业出版者竞争，降低期刊价格，并减少出版商不合理的使用限制，将版权回归给原作者。有关SPARC将在下节中有更多的说明。

（六）教育与学习的改变

随着社会快速的变迁，教育的本质同样也已历经变革，这些改变有些是源自社会、经

---

① Mogge, Dru. "Forward." *Directory of Electronic Scholarly Journals, Newsletters, and Academic Discussion Lists.* (7th edition.) Washington, D. C.: Association of Research Libraries.

济及科技的转型，有些是因为教学法、全球化及国际竞争的改变。以美国高等教育为例，以下是一些明显的改变：
- 新课程及新主修。
- 强调学习重于讲授。
- 学生人口结构的改变。
- 校园多元化。
- 有限的经费资源。
- 对效率与负责任的要求。
- 网络化的校园。
- 增加科技投资。
- 电脑素养的需求。
- 新的学术交流模式。
- 扩展远距教学与终身学习。
- 重新重视全球意识及国际教育。

下表列举教学传递方法的改变

表 1 教学传递方法的改变

传统模式	新模式
*全时的	*部分时间的
*校园内	*校园外
*连续的	*不连续的
*顺序的	*非顺序的
*累增的	*非累增的
*教室的	*个别的
*单向的	*互动的
*同步的	*异步的

我们可以看到传统以教师为中心的模式已改变为以学生为中心及以能力为基础的学习经验模式。在以教师为中心的模式中，课堂学分数（或上课时间）成为教育成就的主要指标，而以学生为中心的模式则投注更多的心力在评量学习成果及学生的成就表现。在新的学习模式中，学生是资讯及知识的积极参与者而不是被动的接收者。

经由图书馆的努力，有些大学将资讯寻求的基础知识与技能列为大学部学生必备的能力，如此可以促进及扩展学生在学习和毕业后的教育经验。

除了多数的高等教育机构提供的传统继续教育与终身教育外，虚拟大学的概念也已浮现，将新科技带入远距教学的领域中。

四、图书馆的新角色

受社会及技术改变的影响，各类型图书馆也从 60 年代传统纸张或印刷式资料为主的图书馆快速转型为 70 年代的电脑化图书馆，以至 80 年代的网路化图书馆及 90 年代的电子或数位化图书馆。在迈入 21 世纪时，图书馆也面临挑战。图书馆在 21 世纪的第一季将结合传统以纸张为主的图书馆、电脑化图书馆、网络化图书馆、电子与数位化图书馆，及虚拟图书馆而成为一个超越围墙、馆藏、资讯媒体及时间等限制的综合型图书馆。

(一) 图书馆面临的特殊挑战

审视图书馆面临的特殊挑战，有很多是显而易见的，包括前面所提到的，这些挑战特别与学术及研究图书馆息息相关，但对世界各地其他类型图书馆也具同样的影响力。

➢ 因科学和技术发展及其交互影响的结果造成了人类知识快速的成长。
➢ 丰富的资讯资源，不论是好的或不好的在 Internet 上都可以取得。
➢ 各层次教育的发展、世界经济的成长、文化及生活水准的提升，及出版、通讯与大众媒体的蓬勃发展。
➢ 大学里新的课程、学科及研究领域在不断地增加。
➢ Internet 的快速成长、普遍化及全球化使学术交流及出版的形式有很大的改变。
➢ 图书馆规模、功能、资源、服务及复杂性的增长。
➢ 图书馆资料，特别是科学、科技及医学方面的期刊出版品费用暴增。这些出版品逐渐为少数具有权力及以高利润取向的国际商业出版商集团所垄断。
➢ 在保护版权及智能财产权中增加对"合理使用"原则的限制，带给图书馆负面的影响。
➢ 多元化资讯类型不断增长。
➢ 图书馆馆藏及服务国际化。
➢ 图书馆馆藏从"拥有"到"获取"的本质正在改变中。
➢ 图书馆的经费缩减。
➢ 图书馆系统的需求、维护及升级的费用很高。快速的科技发展似乎也使电脑及网络系统很快就过时，而经常性的更新费用尚未成为图书馆编列预算考虑的因素。
➢ 大众要求更有效率的管理。
➢ 对图书馆自动化、馆际合作、资源分享、员工发展、读者教育、现代化管理及服务品质等要求投入更多的心力。
➢ 对图书馆员的资讯技能的要求不断增加。
➢ 读者的需求及期望不断扩增，而图书馆满足这些需求的能力却在下降。
➢ 资讯素养及终身学习的重要性在不断提升。
➢ 快速改变所提升的压力。
➢ 政府及社会对图书馆的重要性还不够重视。
➢ 图书馆可能的崩解及不确定的未来所带来的威胁。

图书馆面临的挑战还有很多，不胜一一列举。

(二) 图书馆面对挑战的因应措施

图书馆面对这一大串的挑战，它的回应是什么？以下是图书馆主动采取的因应措施。

➢ 为了改进图书馆的合作、服务及资源分享等业务，图书馆应组织地方性、区域性、国家性、国际性及专门性的图书馆网，以满足读者的各种需求。OCLC 及 OhioLINK 是两个最成功的范例，下节将详细介绍。
➢ 每个图书馆在各自的特殊任务、目标及需求的基础上应该规划独特的资源发展计划，将各种可获得的资讯类型及其他合作图书馆现有馆藏资源的长处均列入考虑。
➢ 充分发挥电脑、资讯、通讯及网络等科技的潜能，经由电脑化及网络化作业来改善图书馆的服务、资源及管理。
➢ 强力支援 Intenet 2 及下一代 Internet 的发展，使资讯资源的发展、搜集、典藏、传布及学术交流更快速、更有效率。

➢ 图书馆人员应该经常并有系统地在 Internet 上探寻有用的资讯资源并让使用者易于获取这些资源。

➢ 图书馆应该使用联盟的力量，以获得购买图书及其他图书馆资料更好的价格，并与电子资料库、电子期刊及其他数位化资源出版商取得较有利的使用权协议。

➢ 图书馆应该汇聚力量发展或寻求学术交流新的替代方案，免受商业出版商不合理的抬价与使用限制。这是 SPARC 创立的一个很好的例子。SPARC 是由研究图书馆学会的会员所发起，这个学会的 122 个团体会员来自美加主要的研究图书馆及大学图书馆。

➢ 图书馆应合作或联合策划，对无版权限制或已取得版权所有者同意的馆藏选择性地进行数位化。这些数位化的馆藏将有助于实现 21 世纪数字图书馆的理想，并以过去无法达成的方式将图书馆带给远距离的读者。

➢ 为了提高馆员的技能与素质，图书馆应该对馆员继续教育与训练给予优先重视。

➢ 图书馆应该采取有效的措施来招聘具备资讯及应用技能的新馆员来为读者服务。

➢ 为使读者具备在知识时代生活所需之资讯获取技能，图书馆应该对读者教育投注更多的关注。

➢ 图书馆应该更进一步加强其终身学习场所的功能。公共图书馆更是适合扮演社区成人继续教育的中心的角色。

➢ 图书馆应该采用新的管理原则与实务做法，特别是那些适合于当地文化与环境的原则与做法。

➢ 图书馆应定期评估其任务、目标、策略方向并为组织更新与再生检视其组织架构。

➢ 图书馆必需通过不断改进资讯收集、组织及对读者服务的持续过程来发挥他们的价值与长处。唯有如此，才能获得读者的尊重及赢得政府与社会的支持。

➢ 图书馆应该为社区内较少获得服务的民众，包括贫民、未受教育者、少数族裔、新移民及残障者，规划适当的活动和服务。

➢ 生活在 21 世纪相互依赖的世界，图书馆必须将其馆藏、活动及服务国际化。

➢ 图书馆必须尽可能地进行研究与发展计划，来提升图书馆学与资讯科学的知识理论与实务作法。

以上这些回应在美国、欧洲、亚洲及世界各地的图书馆中被部分采用。下节将说明 OCLC、OhioLINK 及 SPARC 三个成功的回应例子。

（三）OCLC—线上电脑图书馆中心①

原 OCLC——俄亥俄学院图书馆中心（Ohio College Library Center），是由俄亥俄州学术图书馆在 1967 年成立。当时成立的主要目的是发展一套电脑系统，使参与的图书馆能做线上合作编目，并建立线上联合目录，透过馆际互借分享图书馆资源。在 OCLC 成立之前，大多数的图书馆必需对每一件图书馆所征得的资料进行原始编目，这是费时、费力且费钱的作业。图书馆参与线上合作编目，能减少重复的原始编目，同时能以最经济有效的方式编制线上馆藏联合目录。在 60 年代后期与 70 年代初期之间，很少有图书馆付得起大型电脑主机的费用，也很少有馆员能操作大型电脑主机。为图书馆作业所需的电脑软体也未存在，OCLC 的创立是俄亥俄州学术图书馆为迎接当时的挑战所迈进的革命性的一步。OCLC 在 1971 年成功地进行线上编目之后，吸引其他州的图书馆踊跃加入，在几年之内，

---

① *An Overview of OCLC Services: Look What You're Doing Now... With OCLC.* Dublin, Ohio: OCLC Online Computer Library Center, 1999.

OCLC 的参与图书馆已经遍及美国，也因此促使 OCLC 在 1977 年改变其管理架构及名称为 OCLC 公司（OCLC，Inc.），1981 年则更改其名称为 OCLC——线上电脑图书馆中心（Online Computer Library Center）。在管理架构改变后，使俄亥俄州以外的图书馆也成为 OCLC 的会员图书馆，具有使用者委员会代表的身份及参加董事会选举及被选的权利。

根据 OCLC 最近发布的消息，截至 1999 年 6 月 30 日，在 67 个国家及地区超过 34,700 个图书馆是 OCLC 各种服务的使用者。这些图书馆透过 OCLC 线上及批次载入的方式进行编目作业，他们使用 OCLC 的 WorldCat 系统内的书目记录进行资料编目，若在资料库内无相对应的书目记录，则输入原始书目记录。

OCLC 的线上目录称为 WorldCat 是，目前世界上最大的书目资料库。以下是截至 1999 年 6 月 30 日在 WorldCat 39,697,399 笔书目记录的分析表。OCLC 的会员图书馆以每 15 秒新增一笔记录的速度每年新增大约有两百万笔记录。这些记录包含超过 720,000,000 个馆藏信息，400 多种语言，跨越超过 4,000 年的知识记载。

表 2　OCLC 书目记录的来源

资料类型	国会图书馆的记录笔数	会员图书馆的记录笔数	国会图书馆的记录，经由会员图书馆修改的笔数	总笔数
图书	4,778,812	26,213,871	2,353,163	33,345,846
连续性出版品	205,682	1,767,981	53,171	2,026,834
视觉资料	102,006	1,016,215	27,009	1,145,230
地图	194,281	337,533	6,701	538,515
混合资料	240	286,846	422	287,546
录音资料	153,382	1,107,773	51,080	1,312,235
乐谱	55,328	814,958	53,009	923,295
电脑档	4,325	113,376	197	117,898
合计	5,494,056	31,658,571	2,544,772	39,697,399

OCLC 设立的目的是为了进一步检索世界知识及降低图书馆的费用。因为图书馆是非营利的机构[①]：
- ➢ OCLC 的经费是完全自筹，不依赖外来支持。
- ➢ 对图书馆的收费是依据各馆使用 OCLC 的服务及对 OCLC 的贡献而定。
- ➢ 通过使用者委员会及顾问委员会与 OCLC 会员图书馆一起检讨收费价格。
- ➢ 寻求降低图书馆每一单项运作成本成长的速率。
- ➢ 对于参与原始编目及资源分享的图书馆给予补偿。
- ➢ 资助研究、学术及教育。
- ➢ 寻求增加检索及使用世界各地的资讯。

除了提供各种编目服务外，OCLC 也提供一些非常有用的线上参考服务，其中最重要的是 OCLC FirstSearch 服务，这项服务提供超过 2,200 种电子期刊及 85 种资料库供检索，

---

① *Ibid.*, p. 3.

并且超过 5,500,000 篇的全文文献也可通过 FirstSearch 线上取得。使用者可在这个数量不断增加且含有馆藏讯息的资料库系统中提出馆际互借的需求。OCLC 自 1978 年开放馆际互借服务以来，已处理超过 94,000,000 件馆际互借服务。

OCLC 研究部（OCLC Office of Research）于 1978 年成立，是世界主要研究中心之一，致力于带领图书馆勇敢地面对知识时代所面临的问题与挑战，进而加以研究并寻求对策。过去 10 年间，OCLC 投资超过 1 亿美元来研究及发展新的服务。

自从 1997 年以来，OCLC 的一项新服务是建立 OCLC 学院（OCLC Institute），为图书馆在 21 世纪地球村及数位环境中提供高级教育与交换知识的机会。OCLC 学院所提供的课程，较受欢迎的是：

- 资源分享的持续与创新。
- 知识获取的管理。
- 知识管理：方法与系统。
- 快速改变时代的科技计划。
- 元数据 Metadata 在知识管理中的应用。

仅在 1999 年，就有 52 种高级研习会在 OCLC 俄亥俄州哥伦布市总部、美国其他地区及世界各国举行。

目前 OCLC 学院正在招募有意愿扩展新课程的兼任教师。2000 年的重点工作是将教育及训练的课程延伸到亚洲地区。

在迈入 21 世纪之际，OCLC 排订在 2000 年 7 月 1 日推出另一项新的服务，称为合作线上资源目录（Cooperative Online Resource Catalog，简称 CORC）。2000 年 1 月，超过 200 所各类型图书馆，包括 30 所非美国图书馆，已参与这项计划的发展与测试。这项计划将为合作图书馆建立下列工作的工具：

- 采用主要的国际标准建立电子资源的描述语，例如：
  ○ 元资料（Metadata）：都柏林核心集（Dublin Core）、英美编目规格则第二版及机读编目格式（AACR2/MAR）
  ○ 字集（Characters）：Unicode、美国图书馆学会字集（ALA Characters）
- 建立路径查询系统（网页书目，Webliographies）。
- URL 的维护（国际范围，全球使用）。
- 产生辅助分类表、标题及关键字（提供 Web 检索杜威分类号）。
- 联结式的权威档（建立权威名字的格式）。
- 指引式的查寻（只需 Web 浏览器供检索或使用）。
- CORC 两个主要的好处是结合地方资源及减少图书馆重复投入。

（四）OhioLINK（Ohio Library and Information Network）

在俄亥俄州，学术图书馆的创意与合作精神已远近驰名，而 OCLC 于 1967 年成立可谓迈开了一大步。尽管 OCLC 在改进世界书目记录的发展与检索方面有相当的成就，但在俄亥俄州的学术图书馆界仍觉得有必要成立一个全州性的学术图书馆联盟，以便全州图书馆与资讯服务的各个层面彼此有更密切的合作。俄亥俄州大专院校董事会（Ohio Board of Regents）于 1986 年指定一个特选的小组委员会，经过一年的研究后，发表一份报告——《俄亥俄州学术图书馆：经由合作、储存与科技的进展》（*Academic Libraries in Ohio*：

Progress Through Collaboration, Storage, and Technology)① 这份报告的建议是：
  ➢ 尽速建立全州电子目录系统，包括将仍存留之卡片式目录回溯转换成机读目录格式。
  ➢ 发展及建立一套全州各参与图书馆的资料传递系统。
  ➢ 规划合作保存计划。

从这份草创的报告及由俄亥俄州大专院校董事会所成立的推动委员会（Steering Committee）所采取的一连串行动下，OhioLINK 带着雄心壮志于 1989 年筹组成立。创始之初，有 18 个单位加入，其中 13 个是综合型的州立大学，2 个大型私立大学，2 个州立医学大学及俄亥俄州图书馆。截至 1999 年 11 月，参与的单位数已扩增到 79 个，包括全州所有两年制的州立社区学院、技术学院及大多数私立学院和大学。

OhioLINK 的网络是建立在俄亥俄州学术及研究网（Ohio Academic and Research Network，OAR net）上，是一个具集中式电脑系统的分布式图书馆网，它的中心电脑系统连接到各参与单位的电脑系统。通过规划，集中端（central site）及分散端（local site）都备有划一的电脑硬件及软件平台，使能达到最大极限之联结能力与兼容性。在集中端，有一个具有即时显示每一件图书馆资料馆藏现况的线上联合目录。OhioLINK 的特点之一是允许任何一馆的读者可在线上直接向其他所有的图书馆借书，包括所在图书馆未收藏、已借出或无法取得的图书资料。读者可以通过校园网络或 Internet，在办公室、实验室及家里提出借阅馆藏资料的需求，贷方图书馆将资料收集后经由特殊安排的传递服务送到读者所在图书馆，目标在 48 小时内完成传送，也就是多数的馆际互借可在二至三天内完成，这对读者而言是一大便利且无需花费金钱。目前 OhioLINK 的集中式线上联合目录包含超过七百万种的图书资料，约有两千万册/件，而百分之五十六的资料是不重复的。这个系统服务全州大约有 460,000 名学生及 50,000 名教职员。在 1998 年，查询联合目录的次数达到 2,800,000 次并且有 550,000 件的馆际借阅需求。

过去几年间，除了很受欢迎并且使用率高的馆际借阅服务外，OhioLINK 也推出其他的合作专案来扩展电子资源的分享，并且开创其他服务，兹举其荦荦者如下：
  ➢ 采购多种高度需求的电子书目资料库及全文资料库。
  ➢ 增加全文电子资料库的数量，特别是电子期刊。
  ➢ 以联盟采购的力量与出版商协商，取得较理想的折扣和达成有利的使用权协议。
  ➢ 采用一个全州选购图书的计划（a state wide approval plan），避免各馆采购不必要的复本。
  ➢ 扩大线上馆际借阅资料的范围，从图书到其他可外借的资料类型，例如微缩资料、录影带及 CD。
  ➢ 发展一套较完整的检索引擎，使易于同时检索多种资料库。
  ➢ 成立电子期刊中心（Electronic Journal Center），管理日益增加的电子期刊。
  ➢ 在俄亥俄州高速电脑中心（Ohio Supercomputer Center）成立一个可扩展储存空间的数位媒体中心（Digital Media Center），供各会员图书馆储存他们所开发的电子馆藏、其它非营利机构或商业公司开发的电子资源。
  ➢ 改善校外远距检索 OhioLINK 资源的品质。

到目前为止，OhioLINK 的会员图书馆已完成下列共同的目标：

---

① The Ohio Board of Regents is a state coordinating agency reporting to the Governor with the responsibility of planning and overseeing the general policies and funding of all state-supported institutions of higher education.

- 使用现有之电脑及通讯系统架构。
- 将俄亥俄州所有主要的学术图书馆连接在一个电子网络环境中。
- 集中所有图书馆资源使易于检索及有效分享资源。
- 以各种方式快速传递资料。
- 增购一般较常用且个别或小型图书馆负担不起的电子参考资料库。
- 合作及协调全州之馆藏发展以扩充馆藏并减少不必要的复本。
- 获得较佳之使用权协议。
- 降低资讯检索与传递的单价费用。

由于 OhioLINK 展示其利益及经济指标，在俄亥俄州政府及俄亥俄州大专院校董事会的支持下，每年可获得足够的经费。多数的经费用在支持集中作业、传递服务及主要书目、参考与全文资料库的采购、软体的持续发展、新开创事项及其他方面的支出。1999 年初，会员图书馆投票表决，决定每年从每个图书馆的采购经费中征集一部分基金供集中采购之用。

为了进行合作保存计划，建造了 5 座大型区域储存中心并且已在运作中。这些储存中心很有计划地分别设在俄亥俄州的中部、东北部、西北部、东南部及西南部，供全州州立大学及学院储存较少使用的馆藏资料。各中心高密度及低价格的储存设备舒缓了多数校园中总馆及分馆书库拥挤的情况，使这些图书馆能有宽畅的空间为他们的读者提供较好的服务。所有存放在储存中心的资料开放现场使用，也可以提借，在读者提出借阅需求当天或次日便将资料还回原图书馆或送到其他 OhioLINK 的会员图书馆供使用。

（五）学术出版及学术资源联盟（SPARC）

在面对，也许更正确的说是无法忍受科技与医学期刊费用的暴涨，以及少数控制学术期刊出版的出版商集团对期刊使用的诸多限制，使得图书馆界终于决定联合起来予以反击。

研究图书馆学会共有 122 个会员图书馆，包括美国及加拿大的国家图书馆、研究图书馆及大学图书馆，在该会的领导之下，一个新的联盟，称为学术出版及学术资源联盟（Scholarly Publishing and Academic Resources Coalition，SPARC）在 1998 年 6 月成立，其目的在开创与另外一些出版机构的"伙伴"关系，以发展高品质而低价格的出版物同高价的出版物竞争，它的目标如下:[1]

- 创造一个更具竞争力的市场，使期刊的采购与使用费用能降低，并奖励客户的需求予以合理回应的出版机构。
- 在加强保护财产权与作者权益时，仍能确保公平使用电子资源的原则。
- 应用科技，改善学术交流的过程，及降低制作与销售价格。

SPARC 提出合作伙伴的三种计划:[2]

- SPARC 替代计划：支持能直接与高价的科学、技术或医学期刊竞争的低价替代品。
- SPARC 前端计划：支持能使用新技术和有竞争力的商业模式来满足新兴或快速发展的新科学、技术和医学领域对资讯的需求。
- SPARC 科学社群计划：支持发展各学科非营利的专门出版品，以集合同侪评估过的研究结果及其他内容来满足个别学科社群的需要。

---

[1] Ohio Board of Regents. Library Study Committee. *Academic Libraries in Ohio: Progress Through Collaboration, Storage, and Technology. Report of the Library Study Committee.* Columbus, Ohio: Ohio Board of Regents, 1987.

[2] SPARC Fact Sheet, Washington, DC: SPARC, 1999.

以会员年费的收入，SPARC 已经设立基金提供开办各项计划所需费用，它的会员也同意订购 SPARC 所支持的期刊并且协助拓展期刊的销售市场。令人士气鼓舞的是在短短的时间内，前面所提到的三种合作伙伴计划都各有几个享有名望的伙伴团体加入。SPARC 的努力也得到美国、英国及澳大利亚等国主要学术机构的支持，它的成功不仅对图书馆有帮助，对研究者、作者、出版商伙伴及知识世界也都有益处。

SPARC 的壮举可以用 Richard K. Johnson 的话来总结，他说："只有创造有竞争力的市场才能改变现状，这就是 SPARC 的共同信念。这个简单但不单纯的想法说明了我们行动的范围，展示了我们已准备好采取一致的行动。"①

（六）图书馆角色的蜕变

虽然图书馆在过去三十多年已经历了相当大的改变，而且改变的速度仍持续加快，丝毫没有慢下来的征兆，但是图书馆的基本概念及目的大部分仍是一样的。正如图书馆与资讯资源委员会（The Council on Library and Information Resources）主席 Deanna B. Marcum 最近所断言的，"图书馆仍然是提供各种资源以满足教职员、学生的研究及查询的需求。同时，图书馆的实体空间仍是知识及其对社会重要性的社区象征。"② 目前，Marcum 所描述的传统图书馆的角色正与网络化、电子化及数位化环境的文化融合在一起。

在 1996 年，由纽约公共图书馆所策划之"21 世纪全球图书馆策略研讨会"③，是该馆一百周年馆庆一项重要的活动，约有来自 26 个国家 50 个领导者与会。诚如所报导的，虽然所有与会者都拒绝 Internet 将取代图书馆的想法，但他们都赞同 Internet 正深深地改变图书馆的角色。丹麦哥本哈根公共图书馆馆长 Borge Sorensen 说，"新图书馆的定义不是以她的馆藏来界定，而是以她能创造获取世界各地的资讯的潜力来界定。"图书馆将扮演知识的领航员，引领民众在资讯大海中前进。

在该次的研讨会中，其他的论点如下：

➢ 大家都赞同图书馆将继续存在，且成为文化与教育的中心。

➢ 根据 IBM 公司资深研究副总裁 Paul M. Horn 的观点，科技的确能帮助图书馆降低费用，因为过去十年中，资讯储存费用每一年降低了百分之四十。

➢ Horn 也指出，科技能使图书馆以指数方式增加他们的馆藏，但不需相对地扩充馆藏空间。

以上所有的论点足以提示我们，各类型图书馆都将继续存在并且繁荣发展。而能采用新的构想及运用科技的图书馆将会更好且更机敏。21 世纪图书馆的潜在能力是界限在图书馆员的想象力与巧智，以及社会的支持。

五、奠基石原则

由研究图书馆学会及 OCLC 联合召开的学术图书馆馆长策略问题讨论会于 1999 年 9 月 24－25 日在科罗拉多州的奠基石市（Keystone）举行，有 80 个学术图书馆的领导者参加。会中宣示三个基本原则作为 21 世纪数位知识时代图书馆的远景目标，称为奠基石原则。

原则一

学术及政府资讯是"公共财产"，个人使用者应能自由取得这些资讯，不受市场偏见、

---

① SPARC Fact Sheet, Washington, DC: SPARC, 1999. http://www.arl.org/sparc/factsheet.html
② Johnson, Richard K. **SPARC White Paper**. Washington, DC: SPARC, 1999. http://www.arl.org/sparc/whitepaper.html
③ Marcum, Deanna B. A Summary Comments, in **Technology and Scholarly Communication**, edited by Richard Ekman and Richard E. Quandt. Berkeley, CA: University of California Press, 1999: p.417.

商业动机及费用的限制。

原则二

图书馆负责开发、创新的资讯系统供传播及保存各种形式的资讯及新知识。

原则三

学术图书馆是社区的智慧公共食堂，在那里，现实与理想在真实环境与虚拟环境中交互相应，以扩展学习及创新知识。

奠基石原则的重要性是在于每一项原则的行动方案。其全文、理论基础及具体行动等详细资料可在网站中取得，网址为：http://www.oclc.org/institute/keystoneprinciples.htm.

六、知识与创意

本文讨论新知识时代的来临及其对我们的图书馆、社会及世界中所带来的影响。知识是事实、数据及资讯的合成体，知识与人类的创造力及智慧融合在一起时才能显现其重要性。20世纪的一个常被引用的成功例子是硅谷（Silicon Valley），这个词已超越地理名词，而成为新企业家、创造精神和以知识为主的冒险进取及竞争力的象征。1970年代半导体的发展，1980年代个人电脑的引进，1990年代网络科技的扩延等都跟硅谷有关，因此，硅谷这个词已成为创造的同义词。知识时代最重要的特质之一就是以不让知识停滞的方式使知识不断更新。如果我们要在21世纪知识时代的资讯高速公路上保持在第一车道的话，我们必须持续更新自己，并且站在创新的领先位置。

在知识更新的过程中，我们必须改变教育的系统，为有能力挑战旧时代并且能创造新时代的年轻人培养他们最佳的优点。我们必须创造正确的环境让年轻的心得以像花朵一样地盛开。图书馆应该携手合作创造这样一个良好的环境。

在知识时代，我们也必须极力改善"资讯拥有"（information haves）与"资讯缺乏"（information have nots）两者之间不平等的问题，以确保每一个人都有平等的机会获取所需的资讯与知识，这种概念也应延伸到第三世界的人民，如此才能达到人类和平、平等及繁荣的目的。因为知识是建立在知识的基础上，它的繁衍是没有界限的。图书馆应该同心协力，确保知识能自由流通以服务人群。

参考书目

1. Altschiller, Donald. (ed.) *The Information Revolution*. New York: H. W. Wilson, 1995 (*The Reference Shelf*, V.67, No.5).

2. Bell, Daniel. *The Coming of Post-industrial Society: A Venture in Social Forecasting*. New York: Basic Books, 1973: p.175.

3. Drucker, Peter Ferdinand. "The Rise of the Knowledge Society." *The Wilson Quarterly*. V.17 (Spring 1993): 52 – 65 + .

4. Dyson, Esther & others. "A Magna Carta for the Knowledge Age." *New Perspectives Quarterly*. V.11 (Fall 1994): 26 – 37.

5. Ekman, Richard & Quandt, Richard E. (eds.) *Technology and Scholarly Communication*. Berkeley, CA: University of California Press, 1999.

6. Evans, John D. "Worldwide Communications: Are You Ready?" Rocco C. Siciliano Forum: *Second Annual Lecture*, October 6, 1998. Salt Lake City, Utah: College of Social and Behavioral Science, University of Utah, 1999.

7. Koelsch, Frank. *The Information Revolution: How it is Changing Our World and Your Life.* New York: McGraw-Hill Ryerson, 1995.

8. Johnson, Richard K. *SPARC White paper.* Washington, DC: SPARC, 1999. http://www.arl.org/sparc/whitepaper.html

9. McClure, Charles R., Moen, William E. & Ryan, Joe. *Libraries and the Internet/NREN: Perspectives, Issues, and Challenges.* Westport, CT: Mecklermedia, 1994.

10. Negroponte, Nicholas. *Being Digital.* New York: Knopf, 1995.

11. Ohio Board of Regents. Library Study Committee. *Academic Libraries in Ohio: Progress Through Collaboration, Storage, and Technology. Report of the Library Study Committee.* Columbus, Ohio: Ohio Board of Regents, 1987.

12. Ohio University Libraries. *Shaping Our Future: A Strategic Plan. Ohio University Libraries 1998 - 2004.* Athens, Ohio: Ohio University Libraries, 1998.

13. *An Overview of OCLC Services: Look What You're Doing Now... With OCLC.* Dublin, Ohio: OCLC Online Computer Library Center, 1999.

14. Porat, Marc. *The Information Economy: Definition and Measurement.* Washington, D.C.: U.S.

15. Department of Commerce, Office of Telecommunications, 1977 (Publication 77 - 12): p.1.

16. Technology, Scholarship, and the Humanities: The Implications of Electronic Information. September 30 - October 2, 1992. *Summary of Proceedings.* Santa Monica, CA: The Getty Art History Information Program, 1993.

17. Weinberg, Nathan. *Computers in the Information Society.* Boulder, CO: Westview, 1990.

18. Wriston, Walter B. *The Twilight of Sovereignty: How the Mormation Revolution is Transforming Our World.* New York: Scribner, 1992.

(Published in *Proceedings of the Seminar on 21st Century Public Libraries: Vision and Reality.* Taichung, Taiwan: National Taichung Library, 2000: pp. 43 - 68.)

21 世纪数位化及网络化知识时代中的图书馆

Libraries in the Digital and Networked Knowledge Age of the Twenty-first Century[①]

Overview

   In the second half of the twentieth century, the rate of technological change has greatly accelerated, accompanied by exponential growth in human knowledge—the information explosion! It is safe to predict that the rapid rate of change will continue into the twenty-first century and our lives and societies will be increasingly knowledge-based. Although many of the changes have resulted from the technological revolution, especially in the area of computer, telecommunication, and network technologies—which are truly phenomenal to say the least, we must clearly understand that all of these technological breakthroughs have been the result of human knowledge, ingenuity, creativity, and wisdom. We are the driving forces of technological change. In fact, we can and will make certain that technological advances benefit mankind and usher us into the digital and networked **knowledge age** of the twenty-first century.

   The role of libraries in this enlightened knowledge age is the focus of this paper which discusses the characteristics of the knowledge age the many opportunities and challenges that come with it, the role of libraries, and the relationship between knowledge and creativity.

   In a speech to the Council of the American Library Association in January 1989 concerning new directions at the Library of Congress, James H. Billington, the Librarian of the Congress, said that it is a place that actively and aggressively supports and encourages access to and the creative use of recorded knowledge, that it serves as both catalyst and participant in the intellectual process that transforms information into knowledge and knowledge into wisdom, and that it supports, strengthens, and advances the intellectual and cultural foundation of American life.[②] Although Billington's remarks were directed at the Library of Congress, they are also a powerful statement of the role of libraries in general in the enlightened knowledge age.

The characteristics of the knowledge age

   What is the knowledge age and what are its common characteristics? These questions need to be defined and answered.

   Daniel Bell defines knowledge age a set of organized statements of facts or ideas. Presenting a reasoned judgment or an experimental result, which is transmitted to others through some communication medium in some systematic form...?[③] As for information, Marc Porat offers, Information is data that have been organized and communicated.[④] These two definitions seem to suggest that knowledge is more subtle, polished, and refined than information. In other words, information can be seen merely as the communication of organized data and facts. In comparison, knowledge is far more sophisticated in that it is the synthesis of data, facts, ideas, experience, and information.

   In a knowledge age, we see the accumulation of human knowledge at an unprecedented rate

---

   [①] Presented at the Seminar on 21st Century Public Libraries: Vision and Reality, May 1–3, 2000, Taipei, Taiwan, organized by the Central Taiwan Office of the Council for Cultural Development.
   [②] From author's notes of the Council meeting.
   [③]. Bell, Daniel. *The Coming of Post-industrial Society: A Venture in Social Forecasting.* New York: Basic Books, 1973: p. 175.
   [④] Porat, Marc. *The Information Economy: Definition and Measurement.* Washington, D.C.: U.S. Department of Commerce, Office of Telecommunications, 1977 (Publication 77-12): p. 1.

which affects every aspect of our life and society. It is through human ingenuity, creativity, and wisdom that our world of knowledge is compounded in the passing of every second, minute, and hour. It was estimated that about 850,000 publications of scholarly interest are published annually throughout the world, and this number is increasing by about 2.5 percent per year. Serials publications have grown from 70,000 titles in 1972 to 118,500 in 1997. Every two minutes, a scientific article is completed around the world. This is the basic characteristic of the knowledge age. The term of Knowledge age emphasizes the role that knowledge will play in the new millennium.

A major reason for the expansion of knowledge has been advances in computer, telecommunication, and network technologies in recent times. The faster we can communicate information and knowledge, the more knowledge will flourish. The invention of printing in China in the late seventh century and in Europe in the fifteenth century greatly facilitated the preservation and dissemination of human knowledge. But only with the invention of the telegraph by Samuel Morse in 1844, just 155 years ago, could information travel faster than a horse or a man could run.

Now, with the coming of the Internet and its World Wide Web, we are truly a global village where information and knowledge can be disseminated at the speed of light regardless of distance or other constraints—be they social, political, economic, cultural, or ethnic.

Opportunities and challenges

As we are about to enter into the enlightened knowledge age of the twenty-first century, there are many opportunities as well as challenges. In order to develop our strategic vision and to plan appropriate action, we need to examine these opportunities and challenges more critically and in depth.

Advances and convergence in computer and telecommunication technologies

Since the introduction of microcomputers in the 1980s, each computer generation computers have become smaller and cheaper while computing power has grown by leaps and bounds. It has been observed (Moore's Law) that processing speeds of computers double every 18 months. Because of convenience, portability, and affordability, tabletop computers, laptop computers, notebooks, palmtops, and personal data assistants (PDAs) have become valued possessions for more and more of the general public. Not only are they provided in most offices, but they are also available in more homes and public places, such as libraries, schools, universities, airports, convention centers, and hotels. Each year, a larger portion of the population becomes computer literate. This is also evident in many of the developing countries. The convergence of computers and cellular phones in some of the latest devices enables easy connection to the Internet, thereby further facilitating the communication of new knowledge and discoveries.

In a recent speech, the cofounder of C-SPAN and CEO of the Evans Telecommunications Company, John D. Evans observed that A We are in the midst of a global revolution unlike anyone has ever seen before. We are moving from being an analog society to becoming a digital society. The implications of this revolution are breathtaking, to say the least. ①

According to Evans, the digital age was spawned by the technological convergence of high speed computers; mass data storage; satellite, cable, fiber optic, and broadband transmissions; new broadcast technologies; and packet switching and routing developments.

Today we have, said Evans,
➢ local and wide area networks,
➢ instant e-mail,
➢ desktop PCs for less than $800 that have the power of the big IBM 360s of the 1970s,
➢ desktop video conferencing,

---

① Evans, John D. "A Worldwide Communications: Are You Ready" in *Rocco C. Siciliano Forum: Second Annual Lecture*. October 6, 1998. Salt Lake City, Utah: College of Social and Behavioral Science, University of Utah, 1999.

- speech recognition so you can dictate lab notes or term papers into a computer that corrects the grammar and spelling as you go along,
- access to thousands of Web sites,
- over 100,000 chat rooms where people with common interests interact,
- thousands of news groups that post news and information about every topic from AIDS issues to the latest movie reviews or the Monica Lewinsky tapes,
- cable and satellite systems with over 500 channels of video programming,
- near video on demand,
- satellite broadcast TV, and
- wireless digital phones with text and messaging. ①

The networked environment

The development of the networked environment is also highly significant. Thirty years ago, on October 29, 1969, a group of scientists gathered at the University of California in Los Angeles to send an electronic message to a group at the Stanford Research Institute using packet-switching developed by Professor Leonard Kleinrock, a UCLC engineering professor who is widely heralded as a father of the Internet. Within a few years, the Internet spanned the country and then extended to other parts of the world.

Because the use of Internet is growing at 15 percent per month, it is increasingly congested. By 2002, an estimated 328 million people will be connected to the Internet. Commercial and other uses will crowd the already congested information superhighway. To overcome this situation, a number of research universities got together in 1996 to form a consortium to create a much expanded Internet for exclusive use by the academic and research community. The official name of the consortium is the University Corporation for Advanced Internet Development (UCAID). The expanded Internet is named Internet 2. More than 130 research universities and institutions have joined the consortium with an aim to quickly expand the bandwidth of Internet 2 by 100 times by the end of 1999. Further expansion to 1,000 times is also anticipated. To expand the capacity of the current Internet for the use of a wider public, efforts have also been made to create the next generation of Internet with active participation of the private sector.

The growth of Internet use is truly revolutionary. This has been stimulated by the rapid expansion of a variety of information resources available online from libraries' online public access catalogs, electronic databases, digital information, etc. to information on business, companies, government offices, academic institutions, organizations, health, medicine, sports and weather, provided by a variety of sources worldwide. There are also up-to-date news, financial information, and a host of communication tools such as electronic mail, bulletin board systems, newsgroups, electronic conferences, and others.

Although the Internet has its obvious advantages and contributions, there are some problems as well. It is not a panacea as many would think. Some of the common complaints are:
- information pollution,
- information excess,
- undesirable information and deception,
- viruses,
- hacking,
- lack of privacy,
- lack of security,
- lack of archiving,
- misuse, and
- Internet crimes.

There have been arguments on whether or not the use of the Internet should be regulated. Although the forerunner of the Internet was set up by the U.S. Department of Defense in an effort

---

① Evens, ibid.

to network its widely dispersed computers, later development has been largely non-governmental with minimal formal organization. As of now, the general consensus is to let this laissez-faire type of structure continue because it yields more good than evil.

From the viewpoint of libraries, we obviously prefer the maintenance of the free flow of information but are concerned about information pollution and the intrusion of undesirable and harmful information. We are not in favor of censorship but see the importance of skilled and subject-competent librarians to act as navigators, selectors, organizers, and reader advisors of Internet information on behalf of library users just as they have been doing for printed materials and publications.

The digitization of information and knowledge

The popularization of computers and the Internet have stimulated rapid growth in the digitization of information and knowledge. The initial use of computers to speed up the work of compiling the very large bibliographic databases for publication of printed indexes and abstracts by the Chemical Abstract Services and the Engineering Index in the 1960s was the forerunners of digitalization. The byproducts of these efforts were computer-searchable databases in the 1970s when Dialog and BRS first offered the computerized information retrieval service. In the 1980s, many publishers saw the advantage of electronic publishing and a number of encyclopedia, journals, and books began to appear in electronic form, including CD-ROMs. Now, with the Internet, digitized information and knowledge have flooded cyberspace and will undoubtedly have far reaching impacts on our daily life. The traditional modes of scholarly communication have been drastically altered.

Issues on copyright and intellectual property protection

Adequate protection of copyrighted works and intellectual property rights of its creator(s) is both important and necessary. Representing 167 countries, the World Intellectual Property Organization (WIPO), an agency of the United Nations headquartered in Geneva, is responsible for developing and administering various copyright treaties.

Although libraries are supporters of copyright and the protection of intellectual properties, we feel that for the facilitation of free information flow which has been the chief mission of libraries and the reason for copyright articulated in the United States Constitution, there should be provision in any copyright law that, under the principle of fair use, libraries should be allowed to disseminate copyrighted information to their readers for legitimate use in education, learning, and scholarly communication in a not-for-profit manner. For this, libraries have paid the cost of publications in print and digital formats. Many academic publishers actually charge libraries a higher price to purchase, access, or subscribe to published information than are charged individual buyers. This is especially true for journals. In fact, it is well known that libraries provide the main financial support for publishers of scholarly publications.

Many researchers and scholars also feel that they have been exploited by some publishers by having to turn over the copyright of their works to these publishers in exchange for publication of their articles or papers. Such a practice is often contradictory to the interest of researchers and scholars who actually want to share their new knowledge, creative works, or discoveries with others in their respective fields in a timely and less restrictive way.

The publishing world and scholarly communication

In the past, researchers and scholars often shared their new discoveries through publishing their findings in professional journals and books. They also attended conferences to have face to face exchanges of information and discussions with others in the same field. For academic researchers and scholars, publishing of their intellectual works is necessary for promotion and tenure. Prior to the 1930s, most academic and professional journals were published by learned societies and professional associations at more affordable costs to their members and to libraries. Since then, more and more of these journals have been published by commercial publishers, and the costs of subscriptions are out of control. The irony is that, while publishers profited and libraries had to pay beyond their means, the authors received no monetary returns.

Unhappy both with the rising cost of journals and the delay and restrictions in distribution and access, scholars in many fields began to experiment with publishing of electronic journals over the Internet in the 1980s. The Association of Research Libraries' ***Directory of Electronic Scholarly Journals, Newsletters, and Academic Discussion Lists*** identified 1,002 refereed electronic journals in 1997. ①

Another major step undertaken recently by major academic and research libraries under the leadership of the Association of Research Libraries has been the establishment of an action group named **Scholarly Publishing and Academic Resources Coalition** (**SPARC**) to encourage the development of alternative methods of publishing that can compete with commercial publishers to bring the journal prices down, to reduce unhealthy use restrictions imposed by the publishers, and to return copyrights to the original authors. More will be said later in this paper about the SPARC initiative.

Changes in education and learning

Concurrent with the rapid changes in our societies, the basis of education has undergone major changes as well. Some of these changes are induced by social, economic, and technological transformations, others by changes in pedagogy, globalization, and international competition. Using American higher education as an example, the following are some readily identifiable major changes:

➢ New curricula and new majors.
➢ New emphasis on learning over teaching.
➢ Changing student demographics.
➢ Increased diversity on campus.
➢ Constrained funding sources.
➢ Demand for productivity and accountability.
➢ Wired campus.
➢ Growing investment in technology.
➢ Requirement of computer literacy.
➢ New patterns of scholarly communication.
➢ Expanding distance education and lifelong learning.
➢ Renewed emphasis on global awareness and international education.

The following table illustrates the change in methods of instructional delivery.

Table I Change in Methods of Instructional Delivery

Traditional Model	New Model
* Full-time	* Part-time
* On campus	* Off campus
* Continuous	* Discontinuous
* Sequential	* Non-sequential
* Incremental	* Non-cumulative
* Classroom	* Individual
* One-way	* Interactive
* Synchronous	* Asynchronous

We can see that the traditional teacher-centered paradigm in which classroom credit hours (or seat time) constitute the prime index of educational attainment has been altered towards a student-

---

① Mogge, Dru. Forward. ***Directory of Electronic Scholarly Journals, Newsletters' and Academic Discussion Lists.*** (7th edition). Washington, D. C. : Association of Research Libraries, 1997.

centered, competency-based learning experience in which more attention is paid to measurable outcomes and demonstrated achievement. In the new learning models, students are expected to be active participants rather than passive recipients of information and knowledge. ①

Through the efforts of their libraries, some universities have also made basic knowledge and skills in information seeking one of the necessary competencies required for all undergraduate students so that they can accelerate and broaden their education experience both in school and after graduation.

In addition to the traditional continuing education and lifelong learning offered by a majority of higher education institutions, the concept of virtual university has surfaced to bring new technology into the realm of distance education.

The new role of libraries

Affected by the social and technical changes, libraries of all types have also gone through rapid transformations from traditional paper-based or print libraries prior to the 1960s, to computerized libraries in the 1970s, to networked libraries of the 1980s, and to electronic or digital libraries of the 1990s. In entering the twenty-first century, libraries also encounter their own challenges. Most likely, libraries in the first quarter of the 21st century will be hybrids combining the virtues of the print-based library, the networked library, the electronic and digital library, and the virtual library—a library which is extending far beyond the confines of its walls, its collections, its information media, and its time span.

Library-specific challenges

In even a quick inventory of library-specific challenges, a dozen or more stand out, including some of those identified earlier. These challenges are especially relevant to academic and research libraries in the U. S. but have the same effects on libraries of other types and in other parts of the world.

➢ Exponential growth in human knowledge as a result of interaction with the advancement of science and technology.

➢ Abundant information resources, good or bad, available through the Internet.

➢ Development of education at all levels, growth of the world economy, rise in culture and standards of living, and booming publishing, telecommunications, and mass media.

➢ Addition of new curricula, fields of study, and research interests in universities.

➢ Changes in the pattern of scholarly communication and publishing caused by the rapid growth, popularity, and globalization of Internet.

➢ Growth in library size, functions, resources, services, and complexity.

➢ Skyrocketing costs of library materials, especially journal publications in the fields of science, technology, and medicine, which are increasingly concentrated among a few powerful, highly-profit-motivated international commercial publishing conglomerates.

➢ Negative impacts on libraries by increasing restrictions on fair use in copyright laws and intellectual property right protection.

➢ Growing diversity in information formats.

➢ Internationalization of library collections and services.

➢ Changing nature of library collections from ownership to access.

➢ Shrinking library funding.

➢ High costs of acquiring, maintaining, and upgrading library systems. Rapid technological advancement has also resulted in seemingly instant obsolescence of computer and network systems. Periodic replacement costs have not been factored into library budgets.

➢ Public demand for management accountability.

---

① *Shaping Our Future: A Strategic Plan Ohio University Libraries 1998 – 2004.* Athens, Ohio: Ohio University Libraries, 1998: p. 8.

- Need for libraries to further efforts in automation, interlibrary cooperation, resource sharing, staff development, reader education, modern management, and quality services.
- Increasing demands for library staff skilled in information technologies.
- Expanding user demands and expectations and decreasing ability for libraries to meet these demands.
- Increasingly vital role of information literacy and lifelong learning.
- Growing pressure from the accelerated rate of change.
- Inadequate recognition by governments and society at large of the importance of libraries.
- Threat of the demise of libraries and uncertainty of the future.

The listing of these challenges could continue still go on, seemingly without end.

Libraries responses

What then are the responses of libraries toward this long list of challenges? Below are some of pro-active responses that have been made by libraries:

- Libraries should form local, regional, national, international, and specialty library networks to improve library cooperation, services, and resource sharing.
- In order to meet a variety of needs of their users, two of the most successful models, OCLC and OhioLINK, will be described later.
- Based on its special missions, goals, and needs, each library should develop a unique plan for resources development, taking into consideration the wide array of information formats available and the existing strength of library resources in other cooperating libraries.
- Strive to fully realize the potentials of computer, information, telecommunication, and network technologies to improve library services, resources, and management through computerization and networking.
- Strongly support the development of **Internet 2** and the **Next-generation Internet** for faster and more effective information resource development, gathering, archiving, and dissemination, as well as for scholarly communication.
- Library staff should regularly and systematically surf for useful information resources on the Internet and make them available to users.
- Libraries should use consortia power to obtain better prices for the purchase of books and other library materials as well as to negotiate better licensing agreements for the access to electronic databases, journals, and other digital resources.
- Libraries should join forces to develop or seek new alternatives in scholarly communications and to free themselves from the unreasonable price dominance and use restriction imposed by some commercial publishers. One good example of this is the founding of the **SPARC** initiative (*Scholarly Publishing and Academic Resources Coalition*) by members of the Association of Research Libraries—a membership organization of 122 major research and university libraries in the U.S.A. and Canada.
- Libraries should participate in collaborative or coordinated projects to digitize selected collections which have no copyright restriction or have the permission of copyright holders. Such digitized collections will contribute to the realization of the digital library of the 21st century and bring the library to distant readers in a way not possible before.
- Libraries should give high priority to the continuing education and training of staff in order to raise competency and quality.
- Libraries should develop effective programs to recruit new staff skilled in information technology and its application in user services.
- Libraries should give further attention to user education in order to equip their users with the information-seeking skills necessary for living in the knowledge age.
- Libraries should further strengthen their function as the place for lifelong learning. Public libraries especially are situated to serve as community centers for continuing adult education.
- Libraries should adopt new management theories and practices, especially those that are suitable and sensitive to indigenous cultures and environment.

➤ Libraries should periodically reassess their mission, goals, and strategic directions and review their organizational structure for renewal and rejuvenation.

➤ Libraries must prove their value and usefulness by instituting a continuing process of improvement in information gathering, organization, and services to their users. Only in this way, can they gain the respect of their users and win the support of their government and society.

➤ Libraries should develop appropriate programs to serve the under-served population in their communities, including the poor, uneducated, ethnic minorities, new immigrants, physically disabled, etc.

➤ To live in an interdependent world of the 21st century, libraries must internationalize their collections, programs, and services.

➤ Whenever possible, libraries should conduct research and development projects to advance the knowledge and practice of library and information science.

It is true that many of these responses have already been implemented by libraries in America, Europe, Asia, and many other parts of the world. Three successful models of these responses, OCLC, OhioLINK, and SPARC will be featured below.

OCLC Online Computer Library Center

The original OCLC, the Ohio College Library Center, was established by a group of academic libraries in Ohio in 1967. The primary purpose at that time was to develop a computer system which would enable participating libraries to do online shared cataloging, to create an online union catalog, and to share library resources through online interlibrary loan. Prior to OCLC, most libraries had to perform original cataloging on every item of library materials acquired. It was a time-consuming, labor-intensive, and costly operation. By participating in online shared cataloging, libraries can reduce duplication in original cataloging and, at the same time, create an online union catalog of library holdings-all in a very efficient and cost-effective way. During the late 1960s and early 1970s, few libraries could not afford the cost of a mainframe computer, nor had they the staff to operate it. Computer software especially written for library operations was also non-existent. The creation of OCLC was a revolutionary step taken by Ohio academic libraries to meet the challenge of that time. The instant success of OCLC after its online cataloging went into operation in 1971 attracted libraries in other states to want to join. In a few years, OCLC's participating libraries had spread to the entire country, causing it to change its governance structure and its name to OCLC, Inc. in 1977, and to the OCLC Online Computer Library Center in 1981. The change in governance structure enabled libraries outside Ohio to become OCLC members, to have a representation in the Users Council, and to participate in the election of the Board of Trustees.

According to recent information released by OCLC, as of June 30, 1998, more than 34,000 libraries in 67 countries and territories were users of a variety of OCLC services. Among them 8,303 libraries were full OCLC members. These member libraries do all their cataloging with OCLC either online or via batchload. They use the records in OCLC's WorldCat to catalog materials and to input original cataloging records when there are no corresponding records in the database.

The online catalog of OCLC, which is called WorldCat, is by far the largest bibliographic database in the world. Below is a breakdown of the 37,504,394 bibliographic records in WorldCat as of June 30, 1998. About two million new records are added each year by OCLC member libraries at a rate of 15 seconds a record. These records contain over 700 million location listings, in 400 languages, and over a span of 4,000 years of recorded knowledge. ①

---

① *An Overview of OCLC Services*: **Look What You = re Doing Now... With OCLC.** Dublin, Ohio: OCLC Online Computer Library Center, 1999.

Table II The Sources of OCLC Bibliographic Records

Format	Records by the Library of Congress	Records by memberlibraries	Records by LC, edited by member libraries	Total records
Books	4,585,177	24,644,086	2,287,908	31,517,171
Serials	198,836	1,663,955	52,786	1,915,577
Visual Materials	101,577	938,115	23,515	1,063,207
Maps	188,594	310,414	6,510	505,518
Mixed Materials	240	278,896	442	279,578
Sound Recordings	147,860	1,038,774	49,929	1,236,563
Scores	52,274	775,468	52,185	879,927
Computer Files	3,881	102,814	158	106,853
Total	5,278,439	29,752,522	2,473,433	37,504,394

OCLC is organized for the public purpose of furthering access to the world's knowledge and reducing library costs. As a nonprofit corporation, OCLC:
➢ is entirely self-supporting and does not rely on outside funding agencies,
➢ charges libraries based on use of and contribution to OCLC services,
➢ reviews its pricing with the OCLC membership through the Users Council and advisory committees,
➢ seeks to reduce the rate of rise of per unit costs in libraries,
➢ provides libraries with credits for their original cataloging and resource sharing activities,
➢ supports research, scholarship and education, and
➢ seeks to increase access to and use of the ever expanding body of information worldwide. ①

In addition to the variety of cataloging services, OCLC also offers some very useful online reference services. The most important of these is the OCLC FirstSearch Service which provides easy access to more than 2,200 electronic journal titles and 85 databases. More than 5.5 million full-text articles are available online through FirstSearch. Users can also place interlibrary loan requests from this growing number of databases that include library holdings information. Since the inception of the OCLC Interlibrary Loan Service in 1979, it has processed over 94 million loans.

Established in 1978, the OCLC Office of Research is one of the world's leading centers devoted exclusively to confronting the problems and challenges of libraries in the knowledge age. During the past 10 years, OCLC has invested more than $100 million to research and develop new services.

The latest new service launched by OCLC since 1997 has been the establishment of the OCLC Institute to provide library professionals with opportunities for advanced education and knowledge exchange in the emerging global, digital environment of the 21st century. Some of the more popular courses offered by the Institute are:
➢ Continuity and Innovation in Resource Sharing
➢ Knowledge Access Management
➢ Knowledge Management: Methods and Systems

---
① *Ibid.*, p. 3.

➢ Technology Planning in a Time of Rapid Change
➢ Using Metadata for Knowledge Management

In 1999 alone, a total of 52 advanced seminars were conducted both at the OCLC Headquarters in Columbus, Ohio and in other parts of the USA and several regions of the world. Currently OCLC Institute is recruiting new adjunct faculty members with the intend to develop and expand new course offerings. A major focus for the year 2000 has been to extend the educational and training programs to Asia.

Entering the 21st Century, OCLC is scheduled to launch another new service on July 1, 2000, the "Cooperative Online Resource Catalog" (CORC). In January 2000, more than 200 libraries of all types, including about 30 non-U.S. libraries, have already participated in the development and testing of the project which will provide a tool to cooperative libraries for

➢ Creating descriptions of electronic resources using key international standards such as:
  Metadata: Dublin Core, AACR2/MARC
  Characters: Unicode, ALA Character Set
➢ Creating pathfinders (Webliographies)
➢ URL maintenance (international scope, global use)
➢ Assisted classification, subject heading and keyword generation (offers Web access to DDC)
➢ Linked authorities (established forms of names)
➢ Guided access (requires only Web-browser for access/use)

Two major advantages of CORC are the integration with local resources and the reduction of redundant effort by libraries.

OhioLINK (Ohio Library and Information Network)

Academic libraries in Ohio have been known for their innovative and cooperative spirit. The establishment of OCLC in 1967 was a giant step. Even with the tremendous success of OCLC to greatly improve the development of and access to the bibliographic records of the world's knowledge, academic libraries in Ohio still felt a need to form a statewide academic library consortium for a closer cooperation in many other areas of library and information services within the State. After a yearlong study by a blue-ribbon panel appointed in 1986 by the Ohio Board of Regents[1], a report entitled. ***Academic Libraries in Ohio: Progress Through Collaboration, Storage, and Technology*** was issued.[2] Among the recommendations of the report were:

➢ to implement as expeditiously as possible a statewide electronic catalog system which will include retrospective conversion of remaining paper cataloging records to the MARC (Machine-readable catalog) format,

➢ to develop and implement a statewide delivery system of library materials among participating libraries, and

➢ to plan for a cooperative preservation program.

From this initial report and a series of actions undertaken by a Steering Committee established by the Regents, OhioLINK—with ambitious plans and programs—was formed in 1989. The 18 participants in the initial group of libraries included the 13 comprehensive state universities, two large private universities, two state medical universities, and the State Library of Ohio. By November 1999, this number had expanded to 79, including all of the two-year state community and technical colleges and virtually all of the private colleges and universities.

Building on an existing statewide telecommunication infrastructure, OARnet (Ohio Academic and Research Network), OhioLINK is a distributed library network with a central computer system which is linked to the computer systems at each or combinations of participating campuses. By

---

[1] The Ohio Board of Regents is a state coordinating agency reporting to the Governor with the responsibility of planning and overseeing the general policies and funding of all state-supported institutions of higher education.

[2] Ohio Board of Regents. Library Study Committee. ***Academic Libraries in Ohio: Progress Through Collaboration, Storage, and Technology. Report of the Library Study Committee.*** Columbus, Ohio: Ohio Board of Regents, 1987.

design, both the central and local sites are equipped with a common computer hardware and a software platform to enable maximum connectivity and compatibility. At the central site, an online union catalog is constructed with real-time circulation and location status of each library item. One of the unique features of OhioLINK is allowing library users in any one of the libraries to check the library holdings of all other libraries and to initiate borrowing requests for items not owned or available in the borrower's library. This user-initiated borrowing can be done from offices, labs, and home via campus networks or the Internet. The requested materials are then collected and sent by the lending library to the requestor's library by the specially arranged delivery service which aims at a 48-hour delivery time. This means that most interlibrary borrowing can be completed within two to three days. It is a great convenience and at no cost to the users. Currently, OhioLINK's central online union catalog consists of more than seven million individual titles representing 20 million volumes. 56% of the seven million titles are held by one library only. It serves an estimated 460,000 students and about 50,000 faculty and staff statewide. In 1998, the number of searches made in the central catalog reached 2,800,000 times and there were 550,000 interlibrary borrowing requests.

Within the past few years, in addition to the very popular and heavily used interlibrary borrowing service, OhioLINK has also launched other cooperative activities to expand shared electronic resources and to initiate other services. Most important of these are:

➢ the acquisition of many much-in-demand electronic databases from bibliographic to full text;

➢ expanding the number of full-text databases, especially electronic journals;

➢ employing consortium-purchasing power to obtain large discounts and/or more favorable licensing agreements from publishers;

➢ adopting a statewide approval plan for library materials to avoid unnecessary duplication;

➢ expanding online interlibrary borrowing from books to other types of library materials which can be lent, such as microforms, videos, and CDs;

➢ developing a more sophisticated search engine to ease the search of multiple databases;

➢ establishing an Electronic Journal Center to manage the increasing number of electronic journals;

➢ establishing a Digital Media Center with a much expanded storage space available at the Ohio Supercomputer Center for digital collections created by members, other non-profit institutions, or commercial firms; and

➢ improving off-campus access to OhioLINK resources from a distance.

Thus far, OhioLINK member libraries have accomplished the following goals that were among their shared visions:

➢ Tapping the existing computer and telecommunication infrastructure.

➢ Linking all major academic libraries in Ohio in an electronic networked environment.

➢ Pooling all library resources for easy access and effective sharing.

➢ Delivering materials quickly by various means.

➢ Expanding commonly needed electronic reference databases some of which cannot be afforded by individual or small libraries.

➢ Cooperating and coordinating in a statewide collection development to broaden collections and reduce unnecessary duplication.

➢ Acquiring large and expensive electronic resources in a cost-effective way through consortia purchasing power.

➢ Getting much better deals in licensing agreements.

➢ Reducing the unit costs in information access and delivery.

Because of the demonstrated benefits and economies of scale, OhioLINK has been able to obtain adequate funding annually from the State with strong endorsement and support from the Ohio Board of Regents. Much of the state funding supports the central operation, delivery services, acquisition of major bibliographic, reference, and full-text databases, continuing software development, new initiatives, and others. Beginning in 1999, member libraries also voted to create a central fund for acquisitions through annual assessment from each library's acquisition budget.

For the implementation of a cooperative preservation program, five large regional storage centers have been built and are in operation. These centers are strategically located in the central, northeastern, northwestern, southeastern, and southwestern parts of Ohio for the purpose of storing lesser-used library collections of all the state universities and colleges. These high-density, low-cost storage facilities provide much needed relief for the congested shelving space in the main or branch library buildings on most of the campuses and allow these libraries to better serve their users. All stored library materials can be retrieved and returned to the library for use on the same day or the next day after a request or dispatched to other OhioLINK libraries. Stored materials also are available for use on site.

SPARC (Scholarly Publishing and Academic Resources Coalition)

Faced with and, perhaps more correctly, fed up with the sharp rise in the cost of scientific, technical, and medical journals (STM) and the increasing restrictions on use imposed by a small number of publishing conglomerates that dominate the publishing of these scholarly journals, library communities have finally decided to make a concerted effort to fight back.

Under the leadership of the Association of Research Libraries whose members consist of 122 major national, research, and university libraries in the U. S. and Canada, a new alliance, the **Scholarly Publishing and Academic Resources Coalition (SPARC)** was founded in June 1998. The expressed purpose of SPARC is to create partnerships with other publishers who are developing high-quality, economical alternative to existing high-price publications. The aims of this partnership are to:

➢ create a more competitive marketplace where the cost of journal acquisition and use is reduced, and publishers who are responsive to customer needs are rewarded,

➢ ensure fair use of electronic resources, while strengthening the proprietary rights and privileges of authorship, and

➢ apply technology to improve the process of scholarly communication and to reduce the costs of production and distribution. ①

Three categories of partnership collaboration are offered by SPARC:

➢ *SPARC Alternatives program*: Supports lower-cost, directly competitive alternatives to high-priced scientific, technical, or medical journals in important fields.

➢ *SPARC Leading Edge program*: Supports ventures that obtain competitive advantage through technology use or innovative business models, and/or address the information needs of an emerging or fast-growing STM field.

➢ *SPARC Scientific Communities program*: Supports development of nonprofit portals that serve the needs of a discrete scientific community by aggregating peer-reviewed research and other content. ②

Thus far, SPARC, through its annual membership fees, has created a capital fund to provide start-up money for SPARC projects. Its members will also subscribe and help to market SPARC supported journals. It is very encouraging to note that within its brief existence, several prestigious partners for each of the three abovementioned categories have been established. The efforts of SPARC have also received strong endorsement from leading academic organizations in the U. S., UK, and Australia. The success of SPARC will not only benefit libraries but also researchers, authors, publisher-partners, and the knowledge world.

The noble attempt of SPARC can best be summarized by the statement made by Richard K. Johnson: ASPARC's unifying ideology is that competitive market forces must be unleashed if the status quo is to be challenged. This simple, but not simplistic, idea is intended to give voice to a

---

① SPARC Fact Sheet, @ Washington, DC: SPARC, 1999.
② "SPARC Fact Sheet, @ Washington, DC: SPARC, 1999. < http://www.arl.org/sparc/factsheet.html >

range of actions, to demonstrate at last our readiness to act in concert.①

The new role of the libraries

Although libraries have gone through rather drastic changes in the last thirty or more years and the rate of change are still accelerating with no sign of slowing down, the basic concept and fundamental purpose of libraries have remained largely the same. The library still exists to provide whatever resources are necessary to meet the research and inquiry needs of students and faculty members. At the same time, the library as a physical place still serves as a community symbol of knowledge and its importance to society, as assured recently by Deanna B. Marcum, President of the Council on Library and Information Resources15. It is safe to predict, however, that this traditional role of libraries described by Marcum is being melded with the culture of networked, electronic, and digital environments.

At the 1996 conference on Global Library Strategies for the 21st Century organized by the New York Public Library as a key event in the Library's Centennial year, some 50 library leaders from 26 countries attended. As was reported, although all the conference participants rejected the idea that the Internet will replace libraries, they agreed that it is profoundly changing libraries' roles. The new library is defined not by its collections but by its possibilities—it's potential to create access to information from all over the world, said Borge Sorensen, Director of the Copenhagen (Denmark) Public Libraries. The library will act as a navigator, steering people through this mass of information.

Other points made at the conference are:
> All agreed that libraries would continue to exist as cultural and educational centers.
> Technology can actually help libraries reduce expenses for the reason that the cost of storing information (in bits and bytes) has been decreasing by 40 percent a year for the last ten years, according to Paul M. Horn, senior vice president for research at the IBM Corporation.
> "Technology can help libraries increase their collections exponentially without experiencing a corresponding expansion in square footage," Horn also pointed out.

It is sufficient to say that all of these comments suggest that libraries of all types will continue to exist and flourish. However, by adopting new ideas and technologies they will be better and smarter. Their possibilities in the 21st century can only be limited by the imagination and ingenuity of their librarians and by their societal supports.

The Keystone Principles

In a more recent gathering of eighty academic library leaders during a two-day Strategic Issues Forum of Academic Library Directors held in Keystone, Colorado, September 24 – 25, 1999, sponsored jointly by the Association of Research Libraries and OCLC, three basic principles were declared as the expanded vision for libraries in the digital knowledge age of the 21st century. These three principles are called the **Keystone Principles.**

Principle One

Scholarly and government information is a "public good" and must be available free of marketing bias, commercial motives, and cost to the individual user.

Principle Two

Libraries are responsible for creating innovative information systems for the dissemination and preservation of information and new knowledge regardless of format.

Principle There

The academic library is the intellectual commons for the community where people and ideas interact in both the real and virtual environments to expand learning and facilitate the creation of new knowledge.

The importance of the Keystone Principles is the listing of action items under each of these

---

① Marcum, Deanna B. "A Summary Comments" in **Technology and Scholarly Communication**, edited by Richard Ekman and Richard E. Quandt. Berkeley, CA: University of California Press, 1999: p. 417.

principles. The full text of the Keystone Principles, their rationales, and accompanying actions is available in the Website under: http://www.oclc.org/institute/keystoneprinciples.htm.

Knowledge and creativity

This paper thus far has discussed the coming of the new Knowledge age and its implications for our libraries, our society, and our world. Knowledge is the synthesis of facts, data, ideas, and information. Knowledge can only be useful if it is infused with human ingenuity, creativity, and wisdom. One of the often cited examples of the twentieth century success is the Silicon Valley, which has transcended from a geographical term to a symbol of new entrepreneurship, creative spirit, and knowledge-based risk-taking and competition. The development of semiconductors in the 1970s, the introduction of personal computers in the 1980s, and to the sprawl of network technologies in the 1990s are all related to Silicon Valley which has become the synonym for creativity. One of the most important characteristics of the knowledge age is the unceasing renewal of existing knowledge by not letting it stagnate! We must continue to regenerate ourselves and be at the leading edge of creativity if we want to stay in the fast lane of the information superhighway in the twenty-first-century Knowledge age.

In the process of knowledge renewal or rejuvenation, we need to reform our educational systems to bring out the best in our young people who are capable of challenging the old and creating the new. We need also to create the right environment for the young mind to blossom. Schools and libraries should join hand in hand to create such a favorable environment.

In the Knowledge age, we also need to address the issue of information haves and have nots to ensure that all people have equal access to needed information and knowledge. This concept should also be extended to people of the Third World so that the goal of peace, equality, and prosperity of all mankind can be achieved. Knowledge is built on knowledge. There is no boundary for knowledge to multiply. Libraries everywhere must work together to make sure that knowledge can flow freely to serve mankind.

References

1. Altschiller, Donald. (ed.) **The Information Revolution.** New York: H. W. Wilson, 1995 (**The Reference Shelf.** V.67, No.5).

2. Bell, Daniel. T**he Coming of Post-industrial Society: A Venture in Social Forecasting.** New York: Basic Books, 1973: p.175.

3. Drucker, Peter Ferdinand. "The Rise of the Knowledge Society." **The Wilson Quarterly.** V.17 (Spring 1993): 52 – 65 + .

4. Dyson, Esther & others. "A Magna Carta for the Knowledge Age." **New Perspectives Quarterly.** V.11 (Fall 1994): 26 – 37.

5. Ekman, Richard & Quandt, Richard E. (eds.) **Technology and Scholarly Communication.** Berkeley, CA: University of California Press, 1999.

6. Evans, John D. "A Worldwide Communications: Are You Ready?" Rocco C. Siciliano Forum: **Second Annual Lecture**, October 6, 1998. Salt Lake City, Utah: College of Social and Behavioral Science, University of Utah, 1999.

7. Koelsch, Frank. **The Information Revolution: How it is Changing Our World and Your Life.** New York: McGraw-Hill Ryerson, 1995.

8. Johnson, Richard K. **SPARC White paper.** Washington, DC: SPARC, 1999. < http://www.arl.org/sparc/whitepaper.html >

9. McClure, Charles R., Moen, William E. & Ryan, Joe. **Libraries and the Internet/ NREN: Perspectives, Issues, and Challenges.** Westport, CT: Mecklermedia, 1994.

10. Negroponte, Nicholas. **Being Digital.** New York: Knopf, 1995.

11. Ohio Board of Regents. "Library Study Committee." **Academic Libraries in Ohio: Progress Through Collaboration, Storage, and Technology. Report of the Library Study**

Committee. Columbus, Ohio: Ohio Board of Regents, 1987.

12. Ohio University Libraries. ***Shaping Our Future: A Strategic Plan, Ohio University Libraries 1998 – 2004***. Athens, Ohio: Ohio University Libraries, 1998.

13. ***An Overview of OCLC Services: Look What You're Doing Now ... With OCLC.*** Dublin, Ohio: OCLC Online Computer Library Center, 1999.

14. Porat, Marc. ***The Information Economy: Definition and Measurement.*** Washington, D. C.: U. S. Department of Commerce, Office of Telecommunications, 1977 (Publication 77 – 12): p. 1.

15. Technology, Scholarship, and the Humanities: The Implications of Electronic Information, September 30 – October 2, 1992. ***Summary of Proceedings.*** Santa Monica, CA: The Getty Art History Information Program, 1993.

16. Weinberg, Nathan. Computers in the Information Society. Boulder, CO: Westview, 1990.

17. Wriston, Walter B. ***The Twilight of Sovereignty: How the Information Revolution is Transforming Our World.*** New York: Scribner, 1992.

(Published in *Proceedings of the Seminar on 21st Century Public Libraries: Vision and Reality.* Taichung, Taiwan: National Taichung Library, 2000: pp. 43 – 68.)

亚洲图书馆：数位时代图书馆的新生

Libraries in Asia: New life for Libraries in the Digital Age

Culturally, Asia has played a key role in the development of civilization with its great diversity and variety of contributions. Techniques for papermaking and movable-type printing were invented in China long ago, and education and science also flourished in China, India and many Asian countries in their history. However, under various colonial rules and the conflict of the wars of the nineteenth and twentieth century, most Asian countries became underdeveloped countries despite their glorious past.

In the traditional cultural setting, education and learning were greatly revered in Asian societies and mindsets. This honorable tradition has not been deterred despite the wars, internal strife, racial conflicts, historical rivalries, population explosion, natural disasters, political instabilities, mismanagement, and the resulting poverty among a large segment of the population. After World War II, when colonial rulers were gone, most of the war-torn countries began to rebuild. This led to the economic boom in many of these countries in the 1970s, 1980s, and 1990s, until the recent worldwide economic crisis which has hit some countries harder than others, including the economic giant of Japan and the four "dragons" of Hong Kong, Korea, Singapore, and Taiwan. Since the early 1990s, however, China and India have become the new economic and industrial powers in Asia.

Historically, as a place where human knowledge was stored, have libraries existed as long as reading and writing. Just as the great Alexandria Library (the Bibliotheca Alexandrina) was built in the beginning of the century BC in Egypt, great libraries were known to exist in China and India about the same time. Most of them served the needs of rules, scholars, and those of the privileged classes.

The development of popular education which began in the later part of the nineteenth century brought about the development of modern libraries in most Asian countries. The process was often slow and uneven, but still it was real and visible. Libraries at all levels—from national libraries to local libraries—and of all types—from university libraries to public, school, and special libraries—have been established. The most important distinction between traditional libraries and modern libraries is the way that modern libraries make themselves freely accessible to the general public. Yearning for knowledge is everywhere in Asia—just see the growing numbers of very bright Asian students who flood the campuses of developed countries the world over. Many of them are well motivated and prepared for the highly competitive and demanding postgraduate education in the West. In fact, this phenomenon has contributed to the problem of a significant "brain drain" for most Asian countries which have invested heavily in the education of their most talented youngsters but have lost a sizable portion of them to the west.

The traditional reverence for education and learning prompted widespread educational reforms in most Asian countries, along with drastic changes in their libraries. In China, for example, among the first wave of students sent to the United States for studies in the beginning of the twentieth century, several returned with degrees in library science. They were pioneers in developing new types of libraries with the help of Mary Elizabeth Wood (1862 – 1931), a librarian of the Richmond Library in Batavia, New York and an English teacher, who arrived in China in 1899 and stayed until her death in 1931.

In India, the person who has done more than anyone else to modernize and professionalize library science in that country is Shiyali R. Ranganathan (1892 – 1972) who received his library science education in England. Ranganathan set up his famous Five Laws of Library Science:

1) Books are for use.

2) Every reader his book.
3) Every book its reader.
4) Save the time of the reader.
5) The library is a growing organism.

These five laws might seem self-evident today, but certainly were not to Asian librarians in the early part of the century. His five laws helped to put library work on a scientific basis and to ensure that libraries were service-oriented—unlike private collections for the glorification of a ruler or a state.

The most development of libraries in Asia came in the 1960s, however, when computers and information technology penetrated libraries, first in the US, Canada, and some of the European countries, and then into Asian countries. We have witnessed the accelerated changes from time-honored paper- and print-based libraries to computerized libraries in the 1970s, to networked libraries in the 1980s, to electronic and digital libraries in the 1990s, and now on to the globally linked virtual libraries supported by the World Wide Web backbones.

The greatest benefit of the Internet has been its power to transmit information and knowledge across the world—allowing information to flow freely at amazing speeds and low communication costs. In effect, the Internet has transcended geographical and political barriers and, in time, will narrow the gap between the "haves" and "have-nots" in terms of accessing information and knowledge. It is hopeful that such a gap can also be narrowed by the joint effect now undertaken by the scholarly community, learned societies, and libraries to move away from the dominance of a few commercial publishers who have monopolized the worldwide publication of scientific, technological, and medical journals, set high prices for their subscription, and placed unreasonable restriction on their use. Alternative approaches such as supporting the publishing of new scholarly journals at low-cost and with less restrictions for scholarly use, and establishing a system of open digital archives where researchers and scholars can deposit their preprints and other writings for easy online access either for free or for a nominal handling cost, are making progress.

To facilitate the sharing of library resources, libraries in many Asian countries have also established local, national, and regional consortia to create online union catalogs and to carry out cooperative projects such as collection development, interlibrary loans, staff exchange, networking, and so forth. OCLC, the On-line Computer Library Center headquartered in Dublin, Ohio, is a worldwide library cooperative which provides valuable services to many libraries in Asia.

There are more than two billion unique, publicly available web pages existing on the Internet and it is growing at a rate of seven million pages each day. Although the very size of this resource makes it difficult to handle, and its nature asks new questions, with advanced searching techniques, one can still discover a large amount of hidden treasures.

For many Asian libraries that cannot afford to purchase expensive books and subscribe to highly priced journals, the Internet has become an indispensable source of information. As more and more libraries in Asia have connected to the Internet, many libraries have become selectors, navigators, organizers, and providers of digital information on the web. An increasing number of teachers, students, researchers, and scholars of all fields have used the Internet as a new means for communication and knowledge exchange. Thus the "Digital Divide" between those who have access to the Internet and those who have not is also narrowing as more and more libraries in Asia are trying to provide Internet access to their users. In recent travel throughout Asia I also saw the fast spread of Internet "cafes" everywhere which are frequented by people of all ages, although students have made up the largest group of customers. The growing Internet literacy among an increasing number of people has in some ways reduced the severity of information illiteracy still existing in many of the less developed countries in Asia.

The advance of digital and networking technologies and the extremely fast expansion of digitized information—both "born digital" and created through the process of "digitization" — have led to the development of the "digital library" concept and brought new life to libraries across the globe. Libraries in Asia are especially happy to welcome the coming of the digital age in that it has in effect brought the world of information and knowledge close to home in real time and has emancipated both libraries and their users from the barrier of geographical isolation.

(Published by *Harvard Asia Pacific Review*. Fall 2002, V. 6, No. 2: p22 –24.)

陈钦智：华美图书馆与资讯学界的明星和典范

Ching-chih Chen: A Shining Star and Model of Chinese American Library and Information Science Professionals

INTRODUCTION

Dr. Ching-chih Chen (陈刘钦智) is a visionary leader and a shining star in the library and information science profession. We are especially proud of her pace-setting achievements as a Chinese American in the profession. I have known Ching-chih for nearly a quarter of a century and have never met anyone who possesses as many sparkling ideas and as much boundless energy as she. Our first meeting occurred in May 1979 when I enrolled in a Seminar on Management without Bias directed by Ching-chih with a grant from the U.S. Department of Education to Simmons College. Since then we have met at least once annually at ALA, CALA, and other conferences. When Ching-chih launched her first international conference on new information technology (NIT) in Bangkok in 1987, she invited me to assist her in making local arrangements because of my extensive contacts in Thailand. (I had worked there in connection with my appointment as Director of Library and Information Center at the Asian Institute of Technology under the sponsorship of the U.S. Agency for International Development.) Her contributions to the global community and to the profession are both extensive and impressive.

NIT Conferences

After years of consulting international organizations in bringing information technology to developing regions, in the mid-1980s Ching-chih felt she should develop a forum for international exchange. Since she believed the Asian Pacific Region was ready for this, in 1987 she organized the first NIT conference with the "the aim ... to give librarians and information specialists from the Asian and Pacific Region the opportunity to see for themselves some of the many information systems and products that are available in other parts of the world and to discuss their needs, interests, and requirements with other knowledgeable people". Ching-chih's trademark is a daring and aggressive way of facing challenges. The first NIT conference (called *First Pacific Conference on New Information Technology*) was a stunning success and gave Ching-chih motivation to organize eleven more such conferences around the world over a twelve-year span—Singapore in 1989, Guadalajara (Mexico) in 1990, Budapest (Hungary) in 1991, Hong Kong in 1992, Puerto Rico in 1993, Alexandria (Virginia) in 1994, Riga (Latvia) in 1995, Pretoria (South Africa) in 1996, Hanoi (Vietnam) in 1998, Taipei in 1999, and Beijing in 2001. Participants at these conferences came from some thirty countries. It was Ching-chih's goal that through these conferences library and information professionals from both developing and developed countries could be brought together to build a powerful, informal network for global cooperation and for sharing knowledge on new information technology. Also, NIT conferences were credited by several countries with being the first to bring a conference of this quality and scale to a country or region that was newly opened—for example, NIT '91 in Budapest after the fall of the former Soviet Union, NIT '95 in Latvia for the Baltic region, NIT '96 in South Africa after apartheid, and NIT '98 in Vietnam after the resumption of diplomatic ties with the U.S.

Whoever has organized international conferences knows well the great difficulties involved in planning and holding conferences in countries half way around the world. As the sole organizer, Ching-chih worked very hard on each of the twelve NIT conferences. She spent countless hours and days attending to details and reviewing and editing all the papers for publication as conference proceedings. It is fair to say that only Ching-chih's superior organizational skills, management talents, entrepreneur instinct, endless energy, and hard-rock work ethic could have achieved this! With all of these conferences, just as with other projects undertaken by Ching-chih, she insisted on nothing other than the best. This is one of the trademarks of Ching-chih's credibility and her recipe for success.

In her writing on "The History and Status of Chinese Americans in Librarianship", published in Library Trends (Summer 2000, Volume 49), Dr. Mengxiong Liu praised Ching-chih as one of the very few people in the library world who has done so much in advocating the application of new information technologies to libraries. "Standing at the forefront of cutting-edge library development, she is always one step ahead of everybody else," said Mengxiong Liu.

Education

Ching-chih was born in Fuzhou, Fujian Province, on the southeastern coast of China. She completed her elementary and secondary schooling in Taiwan and attended the Taiwan University as a Rotary Scholar, receiving a B. A. degree in foreign literature and language in 1959. According to Ching-chih, her original interest was not in English language and literature but rather in engineering or medicine. Circumstances, however, made her change her direction. Soon after graduation, Ching-chih came to the United States for graduate studies and was awarded a highly competitive and prestigious Barbour Scholar Fellowship by the University of Michigan where she completed an A. M. L. S. degree in 1961. While attending library school at Michigan, she also took courses in mathematics for "fun". This was an early indication, of her later concentrated interest in computer and technological areas and helps to explain her ease in working on R&D projects with high-level computer scientists. After ten years of library work experience and while starting her teaching career as a full-time faculty member at Simmons College, she enrolled in the doctoral program at Case Western Reserve University where in 1974 she was awarded a Ph. D. in Information Science. Even though Ching-chih's doctoral degree was earned from Case Western, her dissertation was under the supervision of Dr. Philip Morse at MIT, a distinguished physicist, operational researcher, and director of the first computer science center of MIT. Her thesis involved analyzing the circulation data of the Harvard Medical School Library by using the operational research method and then developing a model using new technology and probabilistic theory, referred to as the Morse-Chen Markovian Model. A modified version of her Ph. D. thesis, entitled *Applications of Operations Research Models to Libraries: A Case Study of the Use of Monographs in the Francis A. Countway Library of Medicine, Harvard University*, was published by the MIT Press as the first in her prolific publishing career of thirty-five books. This unusual combination was credited by Ching-chih as the beginning of her life-long interdisciplinary pursuit of R&D work.

Career

Ching-chih's illustrious career began in the 1960s with scientific, technical, and medical librarianship. After two years of professional experience with the University of Michigan and Windsor Public Library in Ontario, Canada, she became in 1963 the Head Science Librarian at McMaster University in Hamilton, Ontario, Canada. She was the Head of the Engineering, Mathematics, and Science Library at the University of Waterloo in Ontario, Canada, from 1965 to 1968. From 1968 to 1971, she served as the Associate Science Librarian at the Massachusetts Institute of Technology in Boston. She then joined the faculty of the Graduate School of Library and Information Science, Simmons College, where she was promoted in 1975 from an Assistant Professor to Associate Professor and to the rank of Professor and Associate Dean in Academic Affairs in 1979. She relinquished her administrative position in February 1997 when she accepted an appointment to the U. S. President's Information Technology Advisory Committee (PITAC) — a high-level committee composed of a very select group of world-class high-tech leaders in academics, computing, and industry. Created by a specific Presidential Executive Order, PITAC is charged with providing guidance and advice to the President on all areas of high performance computing, communications, and information technologies. When PITAC submitted its first-term report entitled *Information Technology Research*: *Investing in Our Future*, a new IT* 2 Initiative with $ 366 million was immediately introduced by the Clinton-Gore administration. In addition to serving on PITAC from 1997 to December 2001 when the Executive Order expired, she also served as a member of PITAC's PITAC /NGI (Next Generation Internet) and PITAC /IT* 2 Review Subcommittees and Panels on Digital Libraries, Digital Divide, Future of Learning, International Issues (co-Chair), and Individual Security. She also chaired the Subcommittee on Digital Divide for Smaller Institutions. Many recommendations resulting from these committees have prompted new or expanded federal programs.

Publications

Throughout her illustrious professional career, which is still flourishing, Ching-chih has authored and edited more than thirty-five books, published some 180 journal articles, written countless reports, and produced several award-winning multimedia works. By looking at the titles and dates of her books, we can easily perceive that Ching-chih is not only a productive and gifted writer but also a visionary thinker and pioneering researcher in the field of librarianship and information science. Representative scholarly works include *Application of Operations Research Models to Libraries* : *A Case Study of the Use of Monographs in the Francis A. Countway Library of Medicine* (MIT Press, 1976, based on her doctoral dissertation). *Scientific and Technical Information Sources* (MIT Press, 1977 and 1987, a 520-page reference tool for the 1977 edition and an 824-page monumental tool for the 1987 edition). *Quantitative Measurement and Dynamic Library Service* (Oryx Press, 1978), *Library Management without Bias* (JAI Press, 1980), *Zero-Base Budgeting in Library Management* : *A Manual for Library Administrators* (Oryx Press, 1981), *Health Sciences Information Sources* (MIT Press, 1981, a 770-page reference tool), *Information Seeking* : *Assessing and Anticipating User Needs* (co-author) (Neal-Schuman, 1982), *Microcomputers in Libraries* (co-author) (Neal-Schuman, 1982), *Numeric Databases* (co-author) (Ablex, 1984), *HyperSource on Multimedia / Hypermedia Technologies* (Library and Information Technology Association, 1989), *HyperSource on Optical Technologies* (Library and Information Technology Association, 1989), *Optical Discs in Libraries* : *Use and Trends* (Learned Information, 1991), *Planning Global Information Infrastructure* (Ablex Publishing Co., 1995), *Electronic Resources and Consortia* (STIC, Taiwan, 1999), *IT and Global Digital Library Development* (MicroUse Information, 1999), and *Global Digital Library Development in the New Millennium* : *Fertile Ground fori Distributed Cross-Disciplinary Collaboration* (Tsinghua University Press, Beijing, 2001). These monographic publications are indicative of her professional and R&D activities ranging from scientific, technical, and medical collections to management, from library evaluation to user information needs; from microcomputer applications to optical and multimedia technology applications; and, finally, in the last decade, from planning global information infrastructure to global digital libraries and international and cross-disciplinary collaboration.

In addition to her prolific publications, she has also been heavily involved in many journal publications. In order to promote the application of information technology in libraries, Ching-chih was the founding Editor-in-Chief of *Microcomputers for Information Management*: *Global Internetworking for Libraries*, a quarterly international journal published by the Ablex Publishing Company, from Volume 1 to 13 (1984—1996), and serves on the editorial board of several other key professional journals including Electronic Library.

Innovation and R&D

When the microcomputer was first introduced in the 1970s, Ching-chih began to concentrate her energy and professional activities on the application of new information technologies to libraries. During the years, she has worked on numerous high-tech projects, from interactive videodisc technology, to multimedia technology, to electronic publishing and CD-ROM desktop publishing, to digital imaging, to Internet-related applications, to the global information infrastructure, and to global digital libraries. The *First Emperor or of China*, her pioneering work with interactive videodiscs and multimedia CD-ROM, was a by-product of her PROJECT EMPEROR-I, the first large-scale technology project supported by the Humanities in Libraries Project of the National Endowment for the Humanities. The project was conducted at a time in the mid-1980s when few libraries except the Library of Congress were experimenting with such technology applications. As a result, her work was widely recognized with over sixty keynote and invited speeches in over twenty countries during the five-year period 1987 – 1991 alone. Not surprisingly, her initial invited speeches were mostly at such conferences as *leaser Active*, *Imagerie Electronique* in Paris, *Computer World*, etc. Recognition from library conferences took place in a big way several years later when she was invited to be the sole keynote speaker at the Library Information Technology Association's (LITA's) annual conference in Dallas, Texas, in 1989.

For her cutting-edge R&D activities, she received the LITA's prestigious LITA / Gaylord Award for Achievement in Library and Information Technology in 1990, and her multimedia product received a *Cindy Award* from the Association of Visual Communicators in 1991 and was chosen in 1994 by MacUser as one of the "Best 50 CD-ROMs". In the early 1990s, Ching-chih launched a Global Digital Library (GDL) Initiative that demonstrated how information repositories in various types of cultural and educational institutions, such as national libraries, national archives, major museums, networks, and research /academic libraries, could be linked together in one single global digital library system with a coherent and consistent interface. Although programs such as the National Science Foundation's (NSF) Digital Library Initiative Phase I (DLI – 1) started around 1994 and was followed by the DLI – 2, yet it was only after NSF introduced its International Digital Library Program (IDLP) in February 1999 that Ching-chih was able to seize the opportunity to apply for NSF support. Her proposal entitled *Chinese Memory Net* (*CMNet*): *US-Sino Collaborative Research Toward Global Digital Library in Chinese Studies* was one of the very first supported by the NSF /IDLP program. Since May 1999, she has worked tirelessly with both computer science and library researchers in the U. S. (Carnegie Mellon University and Penn State University), Mainland China (Peking University, Tsinghua University, and Shanghai Jiao-Tong University), and Taiwan (Taiwan Tsinghua University, Taiwan Taiwan University, and the Academia Sinica) to develop a collaborative model. Beginning in 2000, she has also been the co principal investigator with Dr. Raj Reddy of Carnegie Mellon University on the large-scale *China-U. S. Million Book Digital Library Project*. With the support of the Chinese Ministry of Education and the U. S. National Science Foundation, twelve of the largest and best universities in China will be involved in a massive scanning project to create terabytes of valuable digital information resources for universal access. Currently, she is active with several European digital library projects related to digital imagery and multimedia.

With Ching-chih's never-ending pursuit for better usage of current information technology, it is fair to speculate that her innovative ideas in digital library development are only beginning.

Speaking and Consulting

Because of her knowledge and expertise in the emerging field of information technology, Ching-chih has been a very popular and busily sought after keynote speaker for many national, regional, and international conferences in over forty countries. Over the last quarter century, she has been one of the most visible keynote speakers in various parts of the world extending over three dozens of countries. In the last five years alone, she has delivered about seventy speeches in over a dozen countries and regions besides the U. S., including Mainland China, Taiwan, Singapore, Korea, Vietnam, New Zealand, Austria, Germany, Italy, the United Kingdom, and Trinidad. Of these, twenty were keynote speeches and thirty-two invited speeches in numerous, diversified fields. Amazingly, as witnessed by her keynote speeches at the following, her expertise is recognized far beyond her main areas of library and information technology and digital libraries:

 I. *MERLOT*: *International Conference 2002—Academic Approaches to Technology*, Atlanta, GA
 II. *WebNet 2001*: *World Conference on the WWW and Internet*, Orlando, FL
 III. *I-Know'01*: *International Conference on Knowledge Management in Graz*, Austria,
 IV. International Conference on Computers in Education /International Conference on Computer Assisted Instruction 2000 (ICCE /ICCAI 2000), Taipei, Taiwan.

She is an energetic and dynamic speaker who has effectively used this forum to promulgate her ideas and concepts.

In spite of her many hundreds of speeches, she has often mentioned her very first speaking engagement in China in 1979 at the History Museum's auditorium to nearly a thousand librarians— an event organized by the National Library of China. Since then, she has established long-lasting relationships with countless library and information professionals in China. She must have been in China over twenty times since 1979; and in the year 2002 alone, she was there over six times and gave at least four keynote speeches at four international conferences.

Similarly, she has been an active and aggressive consultant to many international organizations such as the United Nations Educational, Scientific, and Cultural Organization (UNESCO), the World Health Organization (WHO), the United Nations Development Program (UNDP), the United States Information Agency (USIA), the World Bank, and the Soros Foundation. These consulting assignments took her to over three dozen countries. She is truly a world-class library and information science professional who has left her mark on every continent.

As a Chinese American, she has shared her knowledge and expertise generously in both Mainland China and Taiwan. In the 1980s, for both UNESCO and WHO, she offered many training courses on microcomputer applications in different parts of China. She also served as a consultant to the National Science Council (NSC) in the 80s and helped to establish the first Science and Technical Information Center of NSC. In the late 1990s, she served as consultant to the Vice Premier and the Chairman of NSC and helped to initiate Taiwan's "digital museum" program.

Awards and Recognition

Because of her extensive, innovative, and pace-setting contributions to librarianship and information science, Ching-chih has become one of the most decorated information professionals with numerous leading awards and recognitions. As early as 1980, her alma mater, the University of Michigan, honored her with the *Distinguished Alumni Award*. The citation appropriately stated, "As librarian, she worked with scientists; as scientist, she trained librarians... Space and time are scarcely dimensions to her... She is Newman's uncommon person, the discoverer and teacher caught in one."

In the last two decades, she has continued this legacy, collecting many more major awards. The Taiwan University, another alma mater, honored her with the *Distinguished Alumni Award* in 1983; and Case Western Reserve University, her other alma mater, recognized her with the *Grazella Sheperd Memorial Award for Excellence in Education* in 1999. She has received many major awards from professional associations, including the *Outstanding Information Science Teacher Award* in 1983 from the American Society for Information Science (ASIS then and ASIST now); the Library and Information Technology Association's (LITA) two highest awards—the *LITA / Gaylord Award for Achievement in Library and Information Technology* in 1990 and the *LITA / HiTech Award* in 1994; the American Library Association's *Humphry /OCLC /Forest Press Award on International Achievement* in 1996 and several ALA *Distinguished Service Awards*; the Association of Library and Information Science Educators' first *ALISE-Pratt / Severn National Faculty Innovation Award* in 1997; the *Emerson Greenauuay Award* from the New England Library

Association in 1994; the Cindy Award of the Association of Visual Communication in 1992; and the American Association of Higher Education's 2001 *Ernest A. Lynton Award for Faculty Professional Service and Academic Outreach*.

In recognizing her global and broad-based contributions to the library and information profession, CALA awarded its first *Distinguished Service Award* to her in 1982, and APALA honored her with its *Distinguished Service Award* in 1992. She also received the *Distinguished Service Award* from the Library Association of China in Taipei in 1986.

Ching-chih was one of the very few library professionals elected as a Fellow of the American Association for the Advancement of Science (AAAS) in May 1985. The world renowned AAAS defined its Fellow as "a Member whose efforts on behalf of the advancement of science or its applications are scientifically or socially distinguished". Specifically, she was cited "for contributions to information science, in particular for leadership in education". An interesting coincidence was that Ching-chih's husband, a professor in nuclear engineering and a solid-state physicist, was elected as an AAAS Fellow the same year.

Ching-chih's broad-based achievements are further indicated by these two major events:

1. In 1996, she became the first Asian American in the ALA's over 120-year history ever formally nominated by the ALA as a presidential candidate. Although she narrowly lost the election in a three-way run, history was made, and she has helped to open up more opportunities for Asian Americans in ALA.

2. As previously mentioned, in February 1997, she was appointed by President Clinton to serve as a member of the President's Information Technology Advisory Committee (PITAC). She was one of the very few whose interest was in broad-based societal needs, and she has played a significant role in this high-level federal committee.

For her leadership and accomplishments, *Avenue Asian* selected Ching-chih Chen as one of the 500 most influential Asian Americans in 1997 and 1998 consecutively.

Leadership

Leadership can be demonstrated in various ways in many different activities. Ching-chih has epitomized a well-rounded person who has consistently demonstrated her unusual and forceful leadership in all the areas previously described. Few librarians have been appointed to such U.S. Presidential Advisory Committees as PITAC in subject areas other than their own. With her participation on PITAC and on various PITAC panels and subcommittees, she has been able to make significant contributions to federal government information policies in information technology in areas of societal and international importance. In earlier days, her contributions to the *First White House Conference on Library and Information Services* on areas related to citizens' information needs had a significant impact on information, policies, and her publication on this topic is still a frequently-cited classic.

Ching-chih has been very active in many professional associations. These include the American Library Association (ALA), the American Society for Information Science and Technology (ASIST), the Association for Library and Information Science Education (ALISE), the American Association for the Advancement of Science (AAAS), and other regional, national, and international professional organizations.

In ALA, Ching-chih served three terms (nine years) as an elected Councilor-at-Large and was involved in a number of important committees, including chairing the Legislative Committee and the Subcommittee on Asia and the Pacific of the International Relations Committee, serving as a member of the Board of Directors of the Library Information and Technology Association (LITA), and serving as a member of the ALA Assembly of Planning and Budget. In 1996, because of her outstanding leadership and popularity, Ching-chih was the first Asian American to become a presidential candidate of ALA in its 120-year history.

For ASIST, Ching-chih has served in a variety of capacities, including Chair of the Special Interest Group / Education of Information Science (SIG / ED), one of the co-founders of the

Special Interest Group / International Information Issues (SIG / III), member of several committees including the Education Committee and the Standards Committee. She was elected to the Board of Directors in 1982-1984 and was the 1984 presidential candidate. For ALISE, Ching-chih chaired the Program Planning Committee in 1983 and was the 1985 presidential candidate. Other activities include her chairing of the Nominating Committee of Electorate T (Information, Computing, and Communication) of AAAS.

Her various formal nominations to run for President of ASIS, ALISE, and then ALA have signified her ability to be involved at the highest level of professional associations. Although she lost the elections, these processes have had much greater significance than the results. For example, in relation to ALA, some of her agenda for leading the association into the twenty-first century as well as her concepts for globalization can be traced in the association's activities following the election. To Asian Americans, and particularly Chinese Americans, she has truly been a role model.

In recent years, because of her shift in R&D interest to the area of digital libraries, she has asserted her leadership at an equally high level in various organizations and conferences related to digital libraries. For example, she has served on the Program Committee of the Association for Computing Machinery (ACM) and the Institute of Electrical and Electronic Engineers (IEEE) Joint Conferences on Digital Libraries in 2001, 2002, and 2003 and is the co-Conference Chair for the 2004 JCDL meeting. She is on the Advisory Committee of DELOS (European Union's Excellence in Digital Library Networks in Europe) and the co-Chair of the DELOS / NSF *Working Group in Digital Imagery for Significant Cultural, Heritage and Historical Materials* (see http: // dli2. nsf. gov / international projects / working _ group _ reports / digital _ imagery. html for the *Working Group Report*). She is currently the co-Program Chair for the DELOS / NSF Workshop in Multimedia in Digital Libraries in Crete, Greece, June 2 – 3, 2003. Clearly, the international digital library communities have benefited greatly from her leadership in these areas.

Family

It is difficult to sum up the incredibly impressive and successful career of Ching-chih. Perhaps some of the most important aspects may be her extraordinary intelligence and her unusual insightfulness, creativity, determination, perseverance, and ability to put ideas into action. But this article would not be complete without a few words regarding her family. Not only has Ching-chih been successful in her professional career both as a thinker and as a doer; she has also been very successful as a wife, a mother of three very gifted children—Anne, Cathy, and John—and a grandmother of three—Emily, Christopher, and Jason.

Ching-chih's husband, Dr. Sow-Hsin Chen, is a professor of nuclear engineering at MIT. Both Ching-chih and Sow-Hsin are global travelers, usually in connection with their professional activities. They manage to travel together whenever they can and be supportive of each other. Her three children, all graduates of MIT, have their own busy professional careers. Anne, who received her Ph. D. from UCLA, is a genetic scientist; Cathy, a graduate of Harvard Medical School, is a pediatric surgeon with Harvard Medical School and Children's Hospital in Boston; and John, who received his Ph. D. in material science from MIT, is with a biotech company. When the three children were young, they were often great helpers to their mother. I remember vividly that at both the NIT Conferences in Bangkok and Singapore, the children helped with registration and other conference activities. Sow-Hsin, too, was there to give his moral support. This is why she has thanked her family for their love and support in every book she has published. Until a few years ago, Ching-chih also managed to take care of her aging mother who lived to be 101 years old. According to Ching-chih, her mother, who was herself a teacher, was a great model and mentor for her. Truly, behind Ching-chih's success there is an incredible family.

Conclusion

In 1989, when Ching-chih was interviewed by Christina Allen for the publication of *Woman of Color in Librarianship* (ALA, 1989, pp. 135—148), Ching-chih stated that she has a tremendously high-level of concentration and can undertake many tasks at the same time ("multitasking," so to speak).

> Those are working habits. To be very productive in one's work, I think it's very important one understands conceptually what he or she is doing. I have a very full agenda in every single project I'm involved with. That agenda derives from a clear conceptual framework: Why on earth am I doing this project? What do I hope to get out of this thing? What do I hope to convey to people? There's a very strong sense of purpose, of wanting to do certain things; that's a driving force. When I speak, I speak very forcefully. When I talk about certain issues, I have very strong feelings. This is why oftentimes people have said I'm very enthusiastic about some things and that enthusiasm is contagious.

Ching-chih is also very good in time management and "knows how to block out the very limited amount of time in twenty-four hours a day". She admitted in the interview that she does not "sleep very much". According to Ching-chih,

> I like to sleep seven to eight hours, but the trouble is a lot of times I don't have the luxury. For instance, working on the *PROJECT EMPEROR-I* when we were doing postproduction at the studio in California, during that whole month I must have slept only two or three hours every single night for a solid month.

These statements from Ching-chih show that success does not come easily. It requires a great deal of hard work and personal sacrifice in addition to intelligence, ability, and other personal qualities. We all have much to learn from her, especially from those factors that have contributed to her amazing success. I am fortunate to have known her and to have her as a friend. She is a true, rare role model!

Many years after we first shared a podium in 1979, we were pleased to be together on another podium in 2002, when Ching-chih spoke at the *Knowledge Management: Opportunities and Challenges for the Library: International Conference*, Chinese Academy of Sciences in Beijing organized by me in celebration of the new building of the Chinese Academy of Sciences. I look forward to many more shared professional moments.

(原载《架起中美文化的桥梁——美国华人图书馆协会回眸三十年：1973 - 2003》. 沈志佳等编. 广西师范大学出版社 2004 年出版, 第 9 - 25 页。)

美国图书馆自动化五十年的主要里程碑[①]

Main Milestone in American Library Automation in Past 50 Years

美国图书馆自动化,尤其是在使用计算机(电脑)这一方面,早在20世纪的60年代即已开始,而且进展极快,对图书馆业务的发展、馆际合作、资源共享、信息数字化及个人化服务等起了极大的作用。最近两三年因为Web2.0及Lib2.0的快速发展,使图书馆开始使用社会化软件及社会化网络。由于第三代移动通讯技术的普遍化,图书馆也在积极发展"泛在图书馆"的概念,使图书馆服务无所不在,不受时空的限制。笔者在1957年进入美国匹兹堡大学教育研究所攻读,1959年开始在该大学图书馆工作,1999年从俄亥俄大学第一次退休,2009年从美国国会图书馆第二次退休,其间还在OCLC担任了3年的杰出访问学者和顾问,可以说亲身经历了近半个世纪图书馆自动化的整个过程。因此现身说法,把个人的经验与体会撰文向广大读者介绍及请教。

50来,美国图书馆自动化大概有以下10项主要的里程碑。其中有5项是在上一个世纪的60年代开始,可见当时图书馆界已经预见到图书馆自动化的可行性及在图书馆中所能发生的重要作用,进而促进了图书馆与时俱进、改革创新。

(1)第一个图书馆自动化的主要研究(1961年)。
(2)麻省理工学院信息传递试验计划(1965—1973年)。
(3)国会图书馆开发的机读目录格式(60年代)。
(4)大型数据库开始发展(60年代)。
(5)OCLC计算机联机图书馆中心成立(1967年)。
(6)各馆自行开发及厂商开发的自动化系统开始建立(70年代)。
(7)俄亥俄州大学及学院联网首先建立(1989年)。
(8)随着互联网及万维网的发展,数字资源大量出现(90年代)。
(9)国家数字信息基础设施及保护方案出炉(2000年)。
(10)机读目录MARC 21,统一编码,图书馆2.0及其他发展(2000年至今)。

本文将逐一介绍这10项主要的里程碑及其对图书馆界的影响。

1. 第一个图书馆自动化的主要研究

在1961年4月,美国的一个民间组织——图书馆资源委员会(Council on Library Resources)特别拨款资助美国的国会图书馆进行一项关于研究大型图书馆对信息组织、储存及检索使用自动化手段的可能性的调查。这种自动化的功能不仅要适用于单一的图书馆,而且要适用于与许多研究图书馆彼此之间有相互关联的活动上。

美国的国会图书馆为此特别邀请了一些专家,设立了一个研究小组进行研究,出版了一本"Automation and the Library of Congress"(自动化与国会图书馆)的报告,作出以下几点主要结论[②]:十年之内自动化可以加强及加快大型研究图书馆所提供的服务。对于书目处理、目录查寻及文献检索的自动化在技术上及经济效益上是可以做得到的。自动化可

[①] 本文根据作者在国内由毕通城资讯(北京)有限公司所主办的一系列有关"国际图书馆自动化历史回顾与未来展望研讨会"所作报告的讲稿改写而成。

[②] Automation and the Library of Gongress. Washington, DC: Library of Congress, 1963.

以加强图书馆在国家研究环境内的应变力及促成全国性图书馆系统的发展。这些结论后来都被印证是正确的。

2. 信息传递试验计划（Project INTREX-INformation TRansfer Experiment）

第二个主要的里程碑是美国著名的麻省理工学院从 1965 到 1973 进行的信息传递试验。这项试验是麻省理工学院对使用原始及二次信息所设计的早期图书馆自动化系统。它对用缩微印刷品（Microprint）及数字形式（Digital Farm-Binary Codes）的方法储存及传递图书馆信息进行试验[①]。

信息传递试验有三个基本目标：把自动化技术应用到图书馆作业上；促进图书馆及信息中心走向全国性网络化；向联机互动性图书馆自动化及信息检索的方向发展。

麻省理工学院的 INTREX 试验促成了往后各图书馆自动化系统的发展。

3. 机读目录格式（The MARC Format）的设计和推广

美国的国会图书馆曾经是图书馆编目的权威机构。在 20 世纪 60 年代以前它为众多其他的图书馆提供编目卡片以避免对书刊文献的重复编目，节省人工，并促成编目格式的标准化。在 60 年代初国会图书馆为了要把手工编目的卡片改为机器可以识别及操作的目录即开始发展适用于各种书目著录的格式（Machine-Readable Cataloging Format，简称为 MARC 格式）。这个格式在 1966 年开始被使用，由国会图书馆用磁带将机读目录分送给参加试验的图书馆试用。在 60 年代后期机读目录 MARC II 成为美国的书目格式及编目标准，而且为很多国家采用。

国会图书馆的机读目录格式被认为是图书馆自动化的先驱者和导因。在机读目录被普遍采用后，国会图书馆即开始回溯转换编目，将旧式的目录更新。为图书馆建立自动化系统及联合目录提供方便。

有关 MARC 的介绍、发展及标准可以访问以下两个网站：http：//en.wikipedia.oig/wiki/MARCstandards；http：//loc.gov/marc/development。

4. 信息储存及检索——早期的开拓者

就在国会图书馆开发机读目录格式的同时，美国的国家医学图书馆也开始设计该馆的医学文献分析及检索系统（Medical Literature Analysis and Retrieval System – 简称为 MEDLARS）。这个系统在 1964 年投入使用，成为美国图书馆界最早开发出来的大型图书馆自动化系统。在 1971 年它的联机系统：MEDLINE（MEDLARS Online）也正式启用[②]。

1966 年，美国政府的教育资源信息中心也推出了一个可供机器检索的教育资源信息数据库：The ERIC database of the Educational Resources Information Clearinghouse[③]。1967 年，美国的化学文摘社也把他们手工编排的大量化学文摘改用计算机编排并建立了可供机器检索的数据库[④]。

随后，在 1972 年，美国的罗克希火箭和太空公司（Lockheed Missiles & Space Company）推出了他们的 Dialog 检索服务，为图书馆提供了检索数据库最早的工具之一[⑤]。

---

① Carl F. Overhage &J. Francis Reintics. "Project Intrex：A general review." *Information Storage and Retrieval*. 10, 5/6 (May/June 1974)：pp. 157 – 188.

② http：//en.wikipedia.org/wiki/MECLARS 及 Frank B. Rogers. "The Development of MEDLARS." *Bulletin Medical Library Association*. 52（1）（January 1964）：pp. 150 – 151.

③ http：//www.eric.ed.gov/

④ http：//en.wikipedia.org/wiki/Chemical-Abstracts-Service 及 http：//www.cas.org/aboutcas/cas100/anniversary.html

⑤ Roger Smith. "Reflections on the beginnings of Dialog：The birth of online information access." http：//support.dialog.com/publications/chronolog/200206/1020628.shtml

5. OCLC 的开始及快速扩展

为了要试用国会图书馆提供的 MARC 编目数据以进行合作编目，建立联合目录，进而实行资源共享，俄亥俄州各大学图书馆在州政府的资助下于 1967 年建立了俄亥俄州学院图书馆中心（Ohio College Library Center OCLC）。这个中心最早设在俄州省会哥伦布市，1971 年开始运作，并由俄亥俄大学图书馆成功地输入第一条 MARC 编目数据。

自从 OCLC 联机系统在 1971 年成功地运作之后，很多不同形式的图书馆也从其他各州及一些国家纷纷加入。在 1977 年，OCLC 已成为全国及国际各型图书馆的联网组织[①]。为此，在 1981 年，OCLC 改名为计算机联机图书馆中心（OCLC Online Computer Library Center）并建立了美仑美奂的总部大楼。员工也由最初不到 10 人增加到上千人。根据 2008 年的年度报告，分布在全世界 112 个国家 69,840 个各种各样、大小不同的图书馆都在使用 OCLC。其中有 11,674 个是 OCLC 的会员图书馆。为了使全球各地的成员图书馆都能参与 OCLC 的管理和决策，OCLC 扩大了它的会员代表大会及董事会的组织。

OCLC 的愿景是要"经由创新及合作，OCLC 要作为全球图书馆领先的合作机构，帮助图书馆，以经济的方式，对读者提供知识信息"。（OCLC will be the leading global library cooperative, helping libraries serve people by providing economical access to knowledge through innovation and collaboration.）

目前，OCLC 的联机目录 WorldCat 是世界上最大的书目数据库。现有 108,200,000 条记录。从 2007 年 7 月 1 日到 2008 年 6 月 30 日，增加了 22,200,000 条新的书目记录。这些书目包括了 474 种语言及 6,808 年人类知识的记录。在同一年内，有 79,000,000 读者检索了 OCLC 的 FirstSearch 数据库及经由 OCLC 进行了一千万次的馆际互借[②]。

有关 OCLC 的十大主要文字及其书目记录的主要来源请看表 1 与表 2：

表 1　OCLC 的十大主要文字

英文 English	55,192,687
德文 German	12,311,742
法文 French	6,248,331
西班牙文 Spanish	3,602,529
荷兰文 Dutch	2,681,470
日文 Japanese	2,540,136
中文 Chinese	2,362,795
俄文 Russian	1,781,390
意大利文 Italian	1,693,616
瑞典文 Swedish	1,384,137

---

① OCLC 2007/2008 年度报告（OCLC Annual Report 2007/2008）. OCLC website：http://www.oclc.org/news/publications/annualreports/2008/2008.pdf

② OCLC2007/2008 年度报告（OCLC Annual Report 2007/2008）. OCLC website：http://www.oclc.org/news/publications/annualreports/2008/2008.pdf

表2　OCLC 书目记录的主要来源

格式	OCLC 提供的记录	参与图书馆提供的记录	OCLC 提供由参与图书馆修改过的记录	全部记录
书 Books	7,174,988	81,633,366	1,774,796	90,583,150
刊物 Serials	632,354	3,892,448	37,558	4,562,360
视觉资料 Visual Materials	180,293	3,369,556	18,239	3,568,088
地图 Maps	264,449	1,343,184	8,348	1,615,981
多媒体资料 Mixed Materials	49,403	807,437	4,255	861,095
音响录音 Sound Recordings	303,023	3,393,161	64,197	3,760,381
乐谱 Scows	88,063	1,788,448	55,715	2,401,070
电脑文档 Computer Files	10,383	828,018	424	838,825
全部记录	8,702,956	97,522,574	1,965,420	108,190,950

在20世纪70年代，除了OCLC之外，还有一些大型图书馆联网，例如：研究图书馆联网（RLIN-The Research Library Information Network）；华盛顿州图书馆联网（WLN-The Washington Library Network，name changed to Western Library Network）；多伦多大学图书馆自动化系统（UTLAS-The University of Toronto Library Automation System）。

RLIN 及 WLN 后来均与 OCLC 合并。UTLAS 也已不存在。

当 OCLC、RLIN、WLN 被称为书目服务机构（Bibliographic Utilities）时，很多州内或区域性图书馆联盟在70年代后期及80年代初开始发展。俄亥俄州学术图书馆联网（OhioLINK-Ohio Library and Information Network）就是州内图书馆联盟的一个好例子。它成立于1989年。是一个由俄亥俄州高等院校图书馆组成，用以加强图书馆合作及资源共享的图书馆联盟。现有89所学术图书馆及州图书馆参加。总藏书量超过47,900,000百万。其中11,400,000百万是单一本。它的服务也包括提供研究数据库、电子期刊、数字媒体、电子书及电子论文等集中订购的信息资源①。

OhioLINK 的合作项目可以用"多姿多彩"一词来形容。它包括以下各项：

* 各图书馆都采用同一的硬件及软件系统以发挥最大的连通性及互操作性。

* 建立一个包括实时的图书流通记录的联合目录，使得任何一个图书馆的读者可以向另外一个图书馆进行网上借书。

* 制定全州的书刊采购政策，以避免不必要的重复采购。

* 与州内公共图书馆系统和学校图书馆系统建立互借及资源共享的协定。

* 运用联盟的影响力，廉价购买高需求及高价格的电子数据库，并获得最有利的使用权。

* 提供给读者更多的全文数据库和电子期刊。

* 快速传递馆际互借的资料。

* 发展可同时检索多种数据库的检索引擎。

* 设立电子期刊中心，用以永久保存电子期刊的数据文档。

* 设立数字媒体中心，用以集中保存数字媒体资源。

* 使合格的读者能在校外或远处检索 OhioLINK 的各种信息资源。

---

① OhioLINK Snapshot 2008 Supporting Teaching, Learning & Research. http : //www.ohiolink.edu/about/snapshot2008.pdf

* 发展与 Google 检索引擎类似的 Quick Search@ OhioLINK 快速检索工具，具备图书馆所要求的可靠性及高质量结果。

OhioLINK 的另一项合作就是在州政府的资助下在，州内五个地区，即分别在东北、东南、西北、西南及中部地区，各建立一个图书文献资料书库，用以集中储存各馆少用的书刊资料，以疏解图书馆的空间，大量节省了各校每年增建新馆或扩建旧馆的费用。

6. 各馆自行开发及厂商开发的图书馆系统

在图书馆自动化发展的早期，一些大型研究图书馆和政府机构图书馆多自行开发馆内系统。像国家医学图书馆 National Library of Medicine、斯丹佛大学 Stanford University、加州伯克里大学 University of California at Berkeley、维吉利技术大学 Virginia Tech、西北大学 Northwestern University 等。有一些厂商开发的系统实际上是起源于大学图书馆已开发的系统，像 Inrovative Interfaces、VTLS 及 NOTTS 等[①]。

因为对图书馆自动化需求的不断增加，许多厂商涌入图书馆自动化的市场。这些厂商提供了流通、采购、书目检索、联机目录、计算机输出缩微胶卷目录等先进的图书馆自动化集成系统。为了便于图书馆使用，很多全套安装好的系统（Turnkey Systems）在 80 年代开始上市。客户机/服务器技术（Client/server technology）也在 90 年代为图书馆所采用[②]。

7. 机读目录的进展

随着计算机及网络技术的快速发展，国会图书馆推出了新一代的 MARC21，开始使用可扩展的标记语言的结构。其中也包括了以下一些新的措施[③]：

（1）使用新开发的协议及系统。

* 国际下一代 Z39.50—网络信息检索协议规范（SRW-Search/Retrieval Web service, such as Z39.50 International Next Generation）和查询/检索 web 的服务协议。

* 开放性文档先导计划的采集（OAI-Open Archives Initiative harvesting）。

* 元数据编码与传送标准（MET5-Meta Encoding & Transmission Standard）。

（2）寻求与其他新的 XML 模式之间的互操作性。

* 元数据事物描述模式 MODS（Metadata Object Description Schema）。

* 都柏林核心元数据集在 MARC 环境中的使用（DC-Use data from Dublin Core in MARC environment）。

* 联机信息交换格式在 MARC 环境中的使用（ONIX-Use data from ONIX-Online Information Exchange-in MARC environment）。

（3）实行统一编码（Unicode）。[④]

8. 数字文献内容的保存及 NDIIPP 的设立

当我们进入数字信息时代，大量的人类知识及创造活动是以数字的形式产生及储存的。但是大多数在几年以前或近期内设立的数字信息网站并没有被保存下来。因此有很多有价值的知识信息丢失了。

面对如何保存数字信息内容的挑战是要及早采取行动，建立合作机制，拟定可行的计划，设立标准，分头执行。目前开放式的 XML 和 PDF/A（可移植文档格式）已被认可为国际标准。

---

① James Rice. *Introduction to Library Automation*. Littleton, CO：Libraries Unlimited, 1984.
② Dennis Reynolds. *Library Automation：Issues and Applications*. New York：R. R. Bowker, 1985.
③ http://www.loc.gov/marc/development.html
④ http://en.wikipedia.org/wiki/Unicode 及 The Unicode Standard, Version 5.0, Fifth Edition, The Unicode Consortium. (Reading, MA：Addison-Wesley Professional, 27 October 2006. ISBN0-321-48091-0)

2000年12月美国国会 PL 106-554 法案授权国会图书馆设立国家数字信息基础设施及保护项目（National Digital Information Infrastructure and Preservation Program，简称 NDIIPP）。两年之后，国会图书馆颁布了"保存我们数字遗产：国家数字信息基础设施及保护项目计划"。这个计划召集全国的专家们针对数字保存及维护，提供全国性的政策、标准和技术的建议。

以下是 NDIIPP 的五个目标：
* 认定及收集面临危机的原始数字文献资料。
* 建立及支持一个全国性的由众多合作机构组成的数字文献资料储存网络。
* 开发及使用用以保存及维护的技术工具及服务。
* 鼓励有关公共政策以支持数字资源的保存及维护。
* 有关 NDIIPP 的发展及近况请访问该项目的网站：http://www.digitalpreservation.gov。

9. 国会图书馆网上资源的发展

为了加强网上信息资源的服务，跟很多其他图书馆一样，美国国会图书馆近年来也大力开发及提供网上信息资源服务。其中较为重要者有：

（1）建立大型的数字资源库。
* American Memory 美国的记忆，http://memory.loc.gov。
* Global Gateway：World Culture & Resources 全球的通路：世界文化与资源，http://international.loc.g3v/intldl/intldlhome.html。
* THOMAS Legislative Database 托马斯立法数据库，http://thomas.loc.gov。
* MINERVA（罗马神话里司智慧、工艺及战争的女神）根据事件与专题的收藏，http://www.loc.g3v/webcapture 及 http://loc.gov/minerva/。
* World Digital Library 世界数字图书馆：http://project.wdl.org/project/project/english/index.html。

（2）提供网上参考咨询服务。
* 国会图书馆网站上电子信件咨询。
* 询问图书馆员 Ask a Librarian http://www.loc.g3v/rr/askalib/及使用 OCLC 操作的全球图书馆馆际问答服务 QuestionPoint。
* 为个别读者提供实时发送信息服务（Introducing RSS-Really Simple Syndication-feeds）http://www.loc.gov/rss/。
* Webcasts http://www.loc.gov/today/cyberlc/，
* Podcasts http://www.loc.gov/podcasts/，
* Blog http://www.loc.gov/blog/，and
* YouTube http://www.youtube.com/user/LibraryOfCbngress。
* 与 Internet Archive，Alexa，WebArchivist.org 等机构的合作有选择地将网上面临危机的数字资源收藏存档。

10. 世界数字图书馆 The World Digital Library

这是国会图书馆一个新的项目，得到联合国教育、科学及文化组织（United Nation's Educational, Scientific, and Cultural Organization-UNESCO）的支持，要在互联网上提供一个免费及多种语言的，包含有关世界各种文化最重要原始资料的数据库。它的目的是要扩大互联网上非英语及非西方信息的内容，藉以推广国际及各文化间的相互了解（http://

pioject. wdl. oig/pioject/english/index. html）。

回顾半世纪来美国图书馆自动化的进展，路程虽然漫长，但大体上还是一帆风顺、成果丰硕。面对将来，难免有很多新的挑战。这些挑战，像以下开列的一些例子，很多是现有发展的延续，需要我们继续努力，百尺竿头，更进一步！

（1）处理及保存快速增加的电子文献内容（Electronic Contents）及数字媒体（Digital Objects）。

（2）改进与互联网的接口及其工具，如Web 2.0和图书馆2.0。

（3）适当地使用社会化软件及社会化网络。

（4）发展"泛在图书馆"概念，使用第三代移动通讯技术。

（5）加强全球图书馆的合作及交流。

（6）发展及采用新的国际标准。

（7）采用日新月异的新技术来改善图书馆服务。

（8）图书馆的发展要与时俱进，改革更新，以满足读者与社会持续发展的需要。

除了以上这些挑战之外，还希望图书馆的同仁能群策群力，集思广益，利用新的技术和理念，发挥图书馆在21世纪的新使命。

参考文献

1. Automation and the Library of Congress. Washington, DC：Library of Congress, 1963.

2. Carl F. Overhage &J. Francis Reintics. "Project Index：A general review." *Information Storage and Retrieval.* 10, 5/6（May/June 1974）：pp. 157 – 188.

3. http：//en. wikipedia. org/wiki/MECLARS 及 Frank B. Rogers. "The Development of MEDLARS." *Bulletin Medical Library Association.* 52（1）（January 1964）：pp. 150 – 1514. http：//www. eric. ed. gov/

5. http：//en. wikipedia. org/wiki/Chemical-Abstracts-Service 及 http：// www. cas. org/aboutcas/cas 100/anniversary. html

6. Roger Smith. "Reflections on the beginnings of Dialog：The birth of online information access." http：//support. dialog. com/publications/chro-nolog/200206/1020628. shtml

7. OCLC 2007/2008 年度报告（OCLC Annual Report 2007/2008）. OCLC website：http：//www. oclc. org/news/publications/annualreports/2008/ 2008. pdf

8. OCLC 2007/2008 年度报告（OCLC Annual Report 2007/2008）. OCLC website：http：//www. oclc. org/news/publications/annualreports/2008/ 2008. pdf

9. OhioLINK Snapshot 2008 Supporting Teaching, Learning & Research. http：//www. ohiolink. edu/about/snapshot2008. pdf

10. James Rice. *Introduction to Library Automation.* Littleton, CO：Libraries Unlimited, 1984.

11. Dennis Reynolds. *Library Automation：Issues and Applications.* New York：R. R. Bowker, 1985.

12. http：//www. loc. gov/marc/development. html

13. http：//en. wikipedia. org/wiki/Unicode 及 The Unicode Standard, Version 5.0, Fifth Edition, The Unicode Consortium.（Reading, MA：Addison-Wesley Professional, 27 October 2006. ISBN 0 – 321 – 48091 – 0）

（原载《高校图书馆工作》2010年第30卷第1期，第3-7页。）

4. 亚洲研究与区域研究资源
Resources for Asian Study and Area Study

杜肯大学图书馆的非洲收藏

Africana Collections at Duquesne University Library

Interest in African studies has long been an established tradition of Duquesne University and its founders, the Fathers of the Congregation of the Holy Ghost, who began missionary work in Africa in the year 1778. By this tradition, books on Africa have been treasured ever since the University Library came into existence.

In November 1956, with the inauguration of the new Institute of African Affairs at Duquesne, special efforts were made to develop the collection to include large quantities of government documents, serial publications and books, and to enlist the active interest and assistance of Holy Ghost Fathers in obtaining and preserving material on Africa. The initial steps taken were all well received. Invaluable source materials poured in from the continent of Africa and from all over the world. This greatly strengthened the original collection.

Beginning in 1960, an African Language and Area Center was launched as part of the Institute of African Affairs and was subsidized through a contract with the Department of Health, Education, and Welfare under the National Defense Act. The Federal Government thus provides part of the much needed funds for the collection.

When Duquesne University planned a new addition to the library building, a special room was provided for the African Collection, and a full time librarian was appointed to take charge of the planning, organization and further development of the collection and to extend its services to all interested persons.

The purpose of the African collection is twofold. First, it seeks to provide and to build up a collection of the source materials necessary for the program and research undertaken by the Institute of African Affairs and its African Language and Area Center. Second, it aims to become one of the major centers of African materials in this country, in order to give assistance to scholars and specialists in their research on cultural, social, economic and political conditions in the rapidly changing continent of Africa.

The collection now contains some 4,500 volumes of books and government publications, approximately 1,000 pamphlets, and some 217 periodicals and newspaper titles, more than two-thirds of which are acquired regularly.

Although major emphasis was previously given to materials on East Africa and to materials on linguistics, the expansion of the program of the Institute of African Affairs in recent years has made it necessary to broaden the collection's acquisitions to include important materials and standard works on other regions and subject areas. At present the collection possesses a good selection of materials on anthropology, ethnology, economics, history, politics, religions and sociology, with a wide coverage of all parts of the continent.

In addition to books, documents, periodicals, newspapers and pamphlets, there are also seventy-four reels of microfilm, many of which were made from the archives of the Missionaires de la Congregation du Saint-Esprit et du Saint-Coeur de Marie in Paris, eighteen records of both linguistics and music and nineteen reels of tapes recording the complete lessons of language instruction in Swahili and Gio. The former was made under the direction of Father A. Loogman assisted by Mr. Peter Kyara, the latter was made by Kenneth E. Griffes and William E. Welmers to accompany their language text. The collection also includes a small number of manuscripts including the English-Idoma Dictionary by Rev. John M. Schreier, Nomen und Verbum in afrikanischen Sprachen: Eine Strukturlehre by Robert Lessig, etc., and some two hundred photographs on North Africa, especially Algeria, collected by Mrs. L. E. Hubbell.

In order to keep pace with the expansion of the African Program in the Institute where classical Arabic and Hausa are now taught in addition to Swahili, materials on these two languages are being developed.

Special Features

For interested scholars and African specialists, the following specialties of the collection are worth noting:

There are some ninety-six African languages represented in the collection. About twenty of these are spoken by more than one million people Arabic, Swahili, Hausa, Amharic, Fula, Ibo, Malagasy, Yoruba, Luba, Somali, Sotho, Zulu, Kanuri, Mbundu, Shona, Xhosa, Fang-Bulu, Ganda, Kongo and Myamwezi-Sukuma. Most of the books in these languages are grammars, bilingual dictionaries, readers and books of religious teachings.

The collection possesses an almost complete set of the publications (nearly 400 titles) by the Academie Royale des Sciences d'Outre-mer in Brussels. It includes the Biographie Coloniale Beige, Bulletin des Seances, and the Memoires which are in three classes: sciences morales et politiques; sciences naturelles et medicales; and sciences techniques. Many of these Memoires begin with Tome I, fasc. 1 which were published as early as 1930 and present a most thorough study of the former Belgian Congo.

A great deal of attention is being devoted to the building, up of a good collection of bibliographies and catalogs. The notable ones include those on official publications of various countries or regions by the Library of Congress and the Catalog of African Government Documents and African Area Index Publications; Bibliographie du Congo Beige et du Ruanda-Urundi; and South African Bibliography; etc. The International African Institute's Africa Bibliography Series provides good bibliographic information on ethnography, sociology and linguistics. In the missionary field, there are two important bibliographies, the Bibliotheca Missionum by Robert Streit and the Bibliografia Missionaria. Perhaps the most up-to-date bibliography indexing books and periodical articles of social and economic interest is the Fiches Bibliographiques of the Centre de Documentation Economique et Sociale at Brussels. It is arranged on "3 × 5" cards. Some 1, 500 items are indexed each year with full bibliographic information.

The published catalogs of the African collections of both Northwestern University Library and Howard University Library are also sources of information to supplement the National Union Catalog for locating many rare items in Africana. Standard periodicals in the African field which regularly feature book reviews and abstracts are also received.

In addition to contributing regularly to the Joint Acquisitions List of Africana compiled by the African Department of Northwestern University Library, the collection also publishes a monthly acquisitions list of its own, which is distributed free upon request. Publication of a printed catalog of the collection is being considered. It is hoped that it will provide needed bibliographic assistance to scholars and specialists.

(Published in *African Studies Bulletin*. V. 6, No. 3, October 1963: pp. 25 – 27.)

中国近期的教育改革

The Recent Educational Reform in China

On Nov. 11, 1967, the *People's Daily*, an official newspaper of the Chinese Communist Party (CCP) published in Peking, carried the announcement that three institutions of higher learning in China—the Tungchi University in Shanghai, the Peking College for Forestry, and the Peking Normal University—had drafted simultaneously their initial plans for educational reform. ① In the following weeks, many other educational institutions, including both universities and high schools, had followed such examples and drafted their own programs of "educational revolution". An analysis of the various programs adopted reveals drastic changes in the educational system as compared with the one existing prior to the "Great Proletarian Cultural Revolution" and the "Red Guard Movement". It was because of the Red Guard Movement that all school classes in China were suspended in order that students might participate in the Proletarian Cultural Revolution. This suspension lasted from June, 1966, until the late summer of 1967, despite the repeated orders from the Central Committee of the Chinese Communist Party to reopen elementary schools by Feb. 20, 1967, to resume classes in secondary schools by Mar. 1, 1967, and for all college students and teachers to return to their own schools by Mar. 20, 1967. ②

Although, according to the source, the Great Cultural Revolution was aimed at "the maintenance of proletarian political power and the consolidation of dictatorship of the proletariat, and the prevention of a capitalist restoration"③, it was actually a bloody and cruel power struggle among communist political and military leaders, with the youth serving as the sacrifice in the midst of political turmoil. While the Red Guard Movement was in progress, one of the major targets was the turning of their schools into political battlegrounds for a struggle against "reactionary" classmates and teachers. ④ In the waged war against the "Four olds" —old ideas, old culture, old manners, and old customs—the "old" school system, which largely was unaltered from the pre-communist period up to the present, was attacked vigorously. The first of such major attacks was reported at Peking University, where Lu P'ing, the university president, was bitterly criticized as a promoter of bourgeois education discriminating against students of worker or peasant origin through the enforcement of false academic standards. ⑤

The bitterness of such criticism soon was spread to other universities and to secondary schools. To quote one crude expression in a pamphlet, July 20, 1966, by a Red Guard: "For 17 years our school has been ruled by the bourgeois class. We shall not tolerate this any longer! ... Old and young gentlemen, we tell you frankly, you all stink and you are nothing but rotten trash. ... Formerly you were in a privileged position, sat on our heads and let your excrement fall on us to show that you were superior. Today you are under dictatorship and you suffer. ... You thought you could make use of the temporary existing bourgeois education to climb higher up the ladder to become "white" experts, get into the university, join up with the "professors, experts". Your heart was set on a small car, a little modern house, a white coat, a laboratory... on enjoying comfort, affluence, a good reputation, a good salary. ... Really wicked eggs! We tell you: if you do not wish to change, if you remain reactionary, we will not spare you! ... Your class hatred

---

① *Jen-min Jih-pao* (*People's Daily*), Nov. 11, 1967.
② "The Anti-academic Year of 1966/67." *China News Analysis* (Hong Kong). 660: 4 – 5, May 19, 1967.
③ It was published as a joint New Year's editorial of the *Jen-min Jih-pao* (*People's Daily*) and *Hung Ch'i* (*Red Flag*), reprinted in *Peking Review*, Jan. 1, 1967. The editorial gave a brief review of the development of the Cultural Revolution.
④ John Israel. "The Red Guards in Historical Perspective: Continuity and Change in the Chinese Youth Movement." *China Quarterly*. 30: 12, April-June, 1967.
⑤ *Ibid.*, p. 7.

will stick to the points of our bayonets. Your guts will be dug out. . ."①

This furious condemnation of bourgeois education was only one of many examples. On June 13, 1966, a joint decision was made by the Central Committee of the CCP and the State Council to abrogate the old system of entrance examinations at institutions of higher learning. Enrollments for 1966 were postponed six months② to insure the "thorough and successful carrying out of the Cultural Revolution and to effect thorough reform of the educational system"③.

Besides the examination system, other phases of education also were criticized. On June 18, 1966, the *People's Daily* published an editorial entitled "Carry out the Cultural Revolution Thoroughly and Transform the Educational System Completely". In part it stated: "It is not only the system of enrollment that requires transforming, all the arrangements for schooling, for testing, for passing or not passing, and so on must be transformed, and so must the content of education. Further investigation must be made as to how to implement the policy of combining education with productive labor.

"We must relegate to the morgue all the old teaching materials that go against Mao Tse-tung's thought, that seriously depart from the three great revolutionary movements of class struggle, the struggle for production, and scientific experimentation, or that inculcate an exploiting class world outlook. New teaching materials must be compiled under the guidance of Mao Tse-tung's thought and the principle of placing proletarian politics in the forefront. ...

"The study of Chairman Mao's works should be listed as a required course in all schools, whether primary or intermediate or institutions of higher learning."④

In conjunction with this editorial, which reflected the Party's thinking and concern, point 10 of the 16-point pronunciamento on Proletarian Cultural Revolution, issued on Aug. 8, 1966, by the 11th Plenary Session of the Eighth Central Committee of the CCP, also dealt with educational reform. Point 10 reads: "The transformation of the old educational system and of the old teaching policy and method is a very important task of the current Proletarian Cultural Revolution. In the course of this cultural revolution, the phenomenon of domination of our schools by bourgeois intellectuals must be thoroughly transformed. Comrade Mao Tse-tung's policy of letting education serve proletarian politics and combining education with productive labor must be thoroughly implemented at the schools of various categories so that students can develop their moral, mental, and physical education simultaneously, and become workers with both socialist consciousness and cultural knowledge.

"The course of study should be shortened, and the courses should be simple and concise. Teaching materials should be thoroughly transformed, and part of them should be simplified first. Students should treat study as their main concern but learn other things at the same time. In other words, they should not only learn about literature but also about industry, agriculture, and military affairs. They should also participate in the cultural revolution struggle of criticizing the bourgeoisie."⑤

This party directive was published at the height of the Red Guard Movement, when most of the active Red Guards were roving across the map of China in "exchange of revolutionary experience", so no immediate action was taken on the reform. However, at the beginning of January, 1967, the Central Committee of the CCP issued, "for discussion", a draft plan for educational reform. It was not published in the official newspaper or announced over the radio, but only appeared on "big-character" posters (wall posters) and leaflets. This draft plan spelled out the basic principles of the educational reform that were approved by the party. "General standard education, from primary to senior middle school, should be a straightforward eight-year course, with the final curriculum reaching senior middle school level. After graduation, part of the

---

① *China News Analysis* (Hong Kong), 636: 2-4, Jan. 11, 1966.
② It was, in fact, a 16-month postponement for the majority of schools in Communist China.
③ *China Yearbook, 1966-67* (Taipei: China Publishing Co., 1967), p. 475.
④ *Jen-min Jih-pao* (*People's Daily*), June 18, 1966.
⑤ *China Yearbook, 1966-67*, op. cit., pp. 475-476.

students will go to universities, part of them to technical colleges and the rest to two-year professional institutions from which they will come out as workers and commune members. " Physical education classes should be converted into military training classes, and militia activities intensified. Destroy and abolish all old textbooks, compose and publish new ones. Foreign language textbooks should be reviewed and rewritten, and Chairman Mao's works, anti-revisionist articles or similar materials incorporated in them.

"All examinations, such as annual, terminal and primary school examinations, should be abolished. In short, there should be no examinations at all. School or academic results should be democratically discussed and decided by 'study sections', which is a 'living' way of doing things.

"The power of granting graduation should be handed over to the Party, to the workers, peasants and soldiers. Whether a student is allowed to graduate or not will depend on whether he has taken part in manual labor, the 'four-clean-ups movement'① and military service and has succeeded lastly in obtaining the 'ideology graduation certificate.' Only after having been granted graduation is a student then allowed to be promoted or assigned a job, which decision must be made by workers, peasants, and soldiers.

"Personal wishes should be disregarded because they are invariably and absolutely selfish. The needs of the Party should be taken as the personal wish. Both summer and winter vacations should be abolished, for they are specially introduced by the bourgeoisie and the revisionists for the enjoyment of the former 'lordly masters and their children'. Vacations should be changed into busy farming vacations. ...

"All university and middle school students should adopt the half-work and half-study system. Schools and academic institutions should be established within factory premises and moved to frontier provinces. ... Living conditions of university graduates and research students are extremely high. Food for all university students should be reduced to a lower level. "②

The half-work, half-study school system actually was introduced before the Cultural Revolution, and was endorsed by Mao as essential techniques for molding the "new man" in China. It was the belief that with students devoting half of their time to physical labor and half of their time to study, they would not become averse to manual labor and would not be prone to revisionism.

In his report to the First Session of the Third National People's Congress in December, 1964, Chou En-lai stated: "Part-work and part-study with part-farming and part-study schools are schools of a new type which integrate education with labor. These schools are capable of training people of a new type who are able to participate in physical labor and have culture and technique, creating conditions for the gradual elimination of the difference between mental and physical labor. These schools provide the direction for the long-range development of socialist and communist education. "③

In order to extend the half-work, half-study system to all schools, a definite timetable for implementation was established on Dec. 6, 1965. It was decided that, for the first five years, the system would be experimental in various technical middle schools and universities and then be implemented gradually throughout the entire educational system in the next 10 years. ④ But now, in light of the Cultural Revolution, the previous adopted timetable is considered not speedy enough; a faster pace for implementation is being sought.

Although the Red Guards, along with other students and teachers, were urged to return to

---

① The "four-clean-ups movement" includes "political clean-up", "ideological clean-up", "organizational clean-up", and "economical clean-up". It was launched 11th Plenary Session of the Eighth Central Committee of the CCP, held Aug. 1 – 12, 1966.

② "Quarterly Chronicle and Documentation". *China Quarterly*. 30: 200 – 201, April-June, 1967.

③ *Jen-min Jih-pao* (*People's Daily*), Dec. 31, 1964. See also, Donald J. Munro. "Maxims and Realities in China's Educational Policy: The Half-work, Half-study Model." *Asian Survey*. 7: 257, April, 1967.

④ *Ibid.*, Munro.

their schools in February and March of 1967, this "back-to-school campaign" did not have much success. Many rival groups of Red Guards still were engaging in bitter fighting among themselves. A lack of unity and anarchic conditions prevailed in most of the schools. Old school administrative organizations were dissolved and the friction and clashes among rival groups prevented the forming of new administrations. School buildings occupied by roving Red Guards, who lived in the schools wherever they went, were damaged badly and in need have repair. One newspaper in Shanghai described in its editorial the situation in schools: "Students are fighting teachers, students are fighting students. Many revolutionary teachers and students have been called counter-revolutionary. The Cultural Revolution has been suppressed."① It further stated: "In many schools the bourgeois influence has not been cleaned up yet. The Revolutionary Rebels (Red Guards) must get into action to extirpate all their poison, to distinguish true leftists and fake leftists, to pick out the 'ti-fu-fan-huai-yu' (landlords, kulaks, counter-revolutionaries, bad elements, and rightists) from among teachers and send them to corrective labor."②

The six-point urgent appeal, issued on Feb. 16, 1967, by three Shanghai Red Guard groups, suffices to illustrate the gravity of the situation. It said:

"1. The 'Revolutionary Rebel'③ parties of the city's secondary schools should stop roving and return to the schools to seize power, smash the devil king and become masters.

"2. Those branded counter-revolutionary by Party committees and Party branches in schools should be rehabilitated. Those who dare to oppose the instruction of the Party Central, oppose the rehabilitation, refuse to hand out black materials and plan revenge, are going the way of death! All doings under the title of 'blood doctrine'④ must come to an end; secret rivalries between groups must stop. All should unite against the 'small clique of capitalist-road men in power.'

"3. Teachers must return to the schools to make revolution, to study the instruction of the Party Central concerning the Cultural Revolution.

"4. Accusations against each other, 'you are a rightist', 'you joined the wicked spirits and evil devils', etc., must stop and all revolutionary teachers and students must unite.

"5. The writings of Chairman Mao, Correction of Error within the Party, and Against Liberalism, must be studied, and individualism, bragging, anarchism, personal ambitions, factionism, must stop.

"6. Teachers and students still in factories and in the villages must promptly return to the schools to take part in the seize-power, then go to work in a planned, organized way

"We swear that we stand on the side of the Shanghai People's Commune."⑤

In Peking, many serious clashes among different Red Guard groups persisted for much longer. A Japanese newspaper quoted from a big-character poster that on May 14, 1967, Hsieh Fu-chih, head of the Peking Revolutionary Committee, forbade fighting among Red Guards. The poster stated that, between Apr. 30 and May 10, 1967, 60,350 persons had taken part in fighting.⑥ Even in late September, according to a report by the People's Daily, in many instances, the People's Liberation Army had to be brought in to help establish unity among students in schools.⑦

The utilization of the People's Liberation Army to help maintain order in schools began on Jan. 27, 1967, when the army first was dispatched to Yenan Middle School in Tientsin. This was extended then to other schools by order of Mao Tse-tung on Mar. 7, 1967, to carry out military training and to help in the establishment of a provisional administration based on the principle of

---

① *Wen Hui Pao* (Shanghai), Feb. 17, 1967.
② *Ibid.*
③ Red Guard
④ A theory relating students with their family grounds. It was thought that students from bourgeois family background were reactionaries and could not be trusted.
⑤ *Wen Hui Pao* (Shanghai), Feb. 17, 1967. See also, *China News Analysis* (Hong Kong). 660: 5–6, May 19, 1967.
⑥ *Asahi* (Tokyo), May 20, 1967.
⑦ *Jen-min Jih-pao* (*People's Daily*), Sept. 22, 1967.

"three-way alliances", composed of representatives of Red Guards, revolutionary teachers and staff members, and party cadres. ① It was under this military supervision that the schools set out to draft programs for educational reform in line with the Party Central's directive- "back to schools to make revolution!"②

Three so-called "initial plans of educational revolution" made big headlines in the People's Daily on Nov. 2, 1967. These were the three experimental plans of the three institutions of higher learning in China-T'ungchi University in Shanghai, the Peking College of Forestry, and the Peking Normal University, respectively. ③

The draft drawn up by T'ungchi consisted of the following major changes: Following the organizational pattern of a people's commune, the entire university is to be transformed into a commune combining teaching and learning, designing, and labor and production into one "threeway alliance". The former division of departments is to be replaced by several vocational committees, each with a number of subordinate classes. Each class is to consist of teachers, students, workers, and technicians and is to be organized as a military unit. ④ Political instructions are to be given by political officers attached to each of the committees and classes. Teaching personnel will take turns in receiving corrective labor at regular intervals. The length of schooling is to be shortened from five or six years⑤ to three years without exception. Curriculum shall consist of the Thought of Mao Tse-tung, military training, and vocational courses of study. The vocational courses are of two types: theoretical and practical. The theoretical courses must be combined with practical courses. The proportion of theoretical courses over practical courses may increase gradually each year. But the emphasis always shall be with labor work and production.

The major changes contemplated in the Peking College of Forestry are similar to those proposed by T'ungchi. The former departmental organization of the college is replaced by vocational teams organized in military units. Each vocational team is controlled by a committee composed of revolutionary cadres, revolutionary teachers, and Red Guards.

The educational revolution of Peking Normal University is said to concentrate on reforms in the examination system, class promotion, and admission procedures. The entrance examination is to be replaced by a combination of recommendations and selections. Workers, peasants, and soldiers are to have high priority in being admitted to higher schools. There is to be no age limitation. Students with records of being both "red" and "expert" also are to be given special consideration. Open-book examinations and examination of practical experience in the form of discussion are to be permitted. There no longer will be any failures to pass to the next class because of academic failure.

Judging from the wide publicity they received, the aforementioned drafts, while not final, no doubt have official approval. It can be anticipated that more schools of various categories and levels soon will follow suit to adopt their own programs of educational reform. With the young Red Guards and their "alliances" having seized power in schools, the current educational revolution merely is beginning. How far will such fanatic changes be their effects? What be allowed to go? What will be the extent of the opposition and difficulties the new reforms will encounter? These are just a few of the many questions to which no immediate answers are available. The fate of present educational reform is tied closely to the fate of the Cultural Revolution and, moreover, to the result of the present power struggle. Available information shows that the power struggle is far from being settled, and Mao surely will step up the Cultural Revolution. One can be sure that there will continue to be more destructive changes in communist education before the Cultural Revolution is

---

① *Jen-min, Jih-pao* (*People's Daily*), Nov. 2, 1967. See also, *Central Daily News* (Taipei), Nov. 3, 1967.
② *Jen-min, Jih-pao* (*People's Daily*), Mar, 7, 1967.
③ *Jen-min, Jih-pao* (*People's Daily*), Nov. 2, 1967. See also, *Central Daily News* (Taipei), Nov. 3, 1967.
④ T'ungchi University was one of the well-known universities in pre-Communist China. It consisted of colleges of arts, science, law, engineering, and medicine. In 1952, it was changed to a single-purpose university offering program of study in civil engineering, architecture, and design. Only 10 departments remained prior to the present reform.
⑤ Prior to, the present reform, the length of schooling in T'ungchi was five years for all departments except for the department of architecture, where it was six years.

over.

Despite the several unpredictable variables in the current educational reform, there are some immediate and obvious problems that can be detected:

1. The lowering of educational standards. With the shortening of the length of schooling combined with proportional increase in political indoctrination, the study of Mao's thought, the military training, the productive labor, and the frequently required political activities, students are left very little time for genuine study. The attempts to simplify the contents of academic subjects, to abolish examinations, and to disregard academic failure are merely a few of the signs that the Chinese Communists do not want academic work to hamper political and ideological activities.

The admission of students on the basis of their political reliabilities and their family origins has excluded many intelligent students from entering the schools. There is a great diversity in the qualifications of students who do get in. Likewise, the teachers who advocated high academic standards, after being accused of taking the bourgeois road and condemned to make confession or sent to corrective labor, are replaced now by persons who are qualified politically, but not necessarily academically.

2. The lack of provision for advanced study and research. In addition to the lowering of educational standards, the absence of opportunities for advanced study and research is also obvious in the present system. At its best, the school system in China is capable only of turning out a large number of technicians. The shortage of highly trained specialists and researchers has not caused serious concern to the party. Since learned persons often are referred to as bourgeois "scholar-tyrants" in the present Cultural Revolution and are considered as class enemies not to be trusted, any concern shown about the deteriorating academic standards is regarded as an expression of bourgeois thinking. For the present generation of students, nothing is to be more important than inculcating in them a high degree of political consciousness and proficiency in productive labor.

3. The completely political and military controls. In order to affect complete control of all schools in the hands of revolutionary radicals, the old school administration has been replaced with a revolutionary committee founded mostly on the basis of "three-way alliances". The party control long has been present in the schools. But the addition of military control is new and is a direct result of the present power struggle in schools in which many of the turbulences were brought under control only by the presence of the People's Liberation Army. Now that the army is in, it is not likely to withdraw easily.

The new revisions of T'ungchi University to convert the entire school into a form of "people's commune", to experiment in collective living and to intensify military training indicate the wishes of the Communist Party to seek tighter political control of the individual student and teacher.

4. Resistance to the current educational reform. The present educational reform is not without opposition. As mentioned earlier, the entire Cultural Revolution is, in fact, a life and death power struggle between pro-Mao and anti-Mao elements. The struggle to "seize power" is far from settled. According to an editorial published in the *People's Daily*, it is recognized that the "overthrown class enemies still remain and they are not reconciled to their defeat"[①]. This situation is also valid on the educational front. When the three drafted plans for educational reform were announced in the *People's Daily*, it was acknowledged that the plans were drafted amidst severe opposition. Those against the educational reform included a handful of people within the party who are in authority and are taking the capitalist road, the reactionary teachers and students, and even some in the ranks of the revolutionary Red Guards, workers, and peasants. "These opponents to educational reform are trying at every opportunity to kill this infant while it is still in the cradle."[②]

(Published in *School & Society*. Nov. 9, 1968: pp. 395 – 400.)

---

① *Jen-min, Jih-pao* (*People's Daily*), Jan. 22, 1967. See also, "Quarterly Chronicle and Documentation." *China Quarterly*. 30: 212, April-June, 1967.
② *Central Daily News* (Taipei), Dec. 11, 1967.

第一百万册图书 (节选)

The Millionth Volume (extract)[1]

By happy coincidence, Ohio University Libraries has proudly acquired its millionth volume—a thirteenth century illuminated Bible manuscript—during the 175th Anniversary of the University. It took nearly 140 years for the Libraries to acquire the first 100,000 volumes, 165 years to assemble the first half million, and the last 10 years to double it! This is a true reflection of the rate of growth in knowledge and scholarship.

Although in recent years more and more academic libraries have reached the million-volume mark in their collections, it is still considered a major milestone for Ohio University Libraries to acquire the first one million volumes. It culminates a long-term commitment of the University to develop the strong library resources necessary for support of quality education. The addition of the Millionth Volume signifies not only the past accomplishments of the University and the Libraries but also the beginning of yet another phase of development toward greater maturity and excellence.

The purchase of the Millionth Volume, a work of devotion, faith, scholarship, beauty, and perfection, is the fruit of a very generous gift presented by the Carr Liggett Advertising, Incorporated in memory of its founder, the late M. Carr Liggett, a distinguished alumnus and a frequent donor to the Libraries. Owing to the initiative of many long-time supporters of the Libraries, the occasion is also marked by the formation of a Friend of the Ohio University Libraries for the first time in the 175 year history of the University. The attempt to broaden the base of library support beyond State funds is both necessary and a guarantee of maintaining a level of excellence in the years ahead.

(Published in *The Library Scene*. V. 8, No. 4, December 1979: p. 24.)

---

[1] This is a part of "The Millionth Volume" written by Dr. Lee, Ohio University Libraries, Alden Library, Athens, Ohio, 1979.

东南亚特藏在美国的成长：俄亥俄大学的经验

Southeast Asia Collection Growth in the United States: Ohio University's Experience[①]

Dedication

During my long years of association with Southeast Asia, I consider it as a great privilege to know and work with Dr. Donald Wijasuriya whose distinguished career in the library profession spans thirty years and whose outstanding contributions have affected every aspect of library development, within and outside the region. I pay tribute to Dr. Wijasuriya's on the occasion of his retirement as Director General of the National Library of Malaysia. Dr. Wirjasuriya's influence, on behalf of the Malaysian government, has extended to America's heartland, through the Malaysian depository in Ohio University Libraries.

A truly dedicated library leader, an able administrator, a teacher in word and deed, a highly respected scholar, and—above all—a gentleman and friend, Dr. Wijasuriya still has much to contribute after his retirement. His world vision of librarianship should continue to radiate far and wide. We are pleased to join others from the global community in acknowledging our debt and paying tribute with this paper.

National and Historical Background

Despite U.S. involvement in Southeast Asia dating back to the eighteenth century[②], academic study of Southeast Asia was an isolated undertaking until after the Second World War[③]. Only Yale University earlier had developed a substantial library collection[④]. In the post-war period, the

---

[①] Co-author: K. Mulliner.

[②] This has been best documented for the pepper trade between Sumatra and Salem, Massachusetts: for example, James Duncan Phillips, *Pepper and pirates: adventures in the Sumatra pepper trade of Salem* (Boston, Houghton Mifflin, 1949). James W. Gould's "American Interests in Sumatra, 1784 – 1873," Ph. D. diss., Fletcher School of Law and Diplomacy, 1955, and his *Americans in Sumatra* (The Hague, M. Nijhoff, 1961) a more complete, and bibliographically useful, picture. K. Mulliner and Lian The-Mulliner, "Americans in Early Singapore," (paper presented at Southeast Asian Studies Summer Institute, University of Michigan, August 3, 1985) reflects further resources. Raymond G. Nunn, ed. *Asia and Oceania: A Guide to archival and manuscript sources in the United States*, 5 vols. (London and New York, Mansell Publishing, 1985) has opened vast avenues for further exploration.

[③] Craig A. Lockard, *The Rise and changing status of the Southeast Asian history field in the United States: an analytical study* (Wisconsin papers on Southeast Asia; Madison: University of Wisconsin Center for Southeast Asian Studies, 1989), especially pp. 3 – 6, describes the neglect and slow development of even Southeast Asian history.

Doctoral research is one of the best evidences of this neglect. Prior to 1941, only 79 dissertations were written on Southeast Asia and nearly three-fourths of these were on the Philippines (three were on Malaya and one on Singapore). Lian The and Paul W. van der Veur, *Treasures and trivia: doctoral dissertations on Southeast Asia accepted by universities in the United States*, Ohio University papers in international studies, Southeast Asia series, No. 1 (Athens, Ohio University Center for International Studies, Southeast Asia Program, 1968), p. 126.

[④] Yale traces its Collection to the beginning of the Yale College Library, which included three books on Southeast Asia in its first published catalogue in 1742, but-except for nineteenth century journals and monographs of the leading colonial research societies, such as the Koninklijk Instituut voor Tall -, Land -, en volkenkunde and the Ecole Francaise d'Extreme Orient-real interest in the region probably dates from the hiring of Clive Day at the beginning of the 20th century. Information on Yale was graciously provided for this paper by Charles Bryant, Curator of the Southeast Asia Collection; however, this brief summary is solely the responsibility of the authors.

An exception to the generalization on the absence of specialized research resources can be found in the government document collections of research libraries at major state universities. With the U.S. occupation in the Philippines, substantial resources were produced by the U.S. Government and made available under its depository program. The nature and extent of these materials are evidenced in Daniel F. Doeppers, comp., *Union catalogue of selected bureau reports and other official serials of the Philippines, 1908 – 1941*. Wisconsin Papers on Southeast Asia, No. 4. (Madison: University of Wisconsin Center for Southeast Asian Studies, 1980)

formation of Cornell University's Southeast Asia Program and Modern Indonesia Project marked the beginning of wider but still scattered interest in teaching and research on Southeast Asia[①].

This small base produced the generation of scholars who launched Southeast Asia Studies programs (and justified Southeast Asia Collections) at other universities in the United States. Of the second-generation Southeast Asia centers, Ohio University was the youngest, dating from 1967. The 1980s have seen modest renewed academic interest with the creation of Southeast Asia programs at Arizona State University and in the Northwest (through a consortium consisting of the Universities of Oregon, Washington, and British Columbia). Today, besides the Library of Congress (LC), identifiable collections on Southeast Asia or with major focus on Southeast Asia include the name of the primary librarian:

Institution	Head/Curator
Arizona State University, Tempe	Dora Biblarz (Associate Dean for Collection Development)[②]
University of California, Berkeley	Peter Ananda
Cornell University, Ithaca	John Badgley
Northern Illinois University, DeKalb	Mai Kyi Win
Ohio University, Athens	Lian The-Mulliner
University of Hawaii at Manoa	Alan Kamida
University of Michigan, Ann Arbor	Fe Susan Go
University of Washington, Seattle[③]	Judith Henchy

The rarity of Southeast Asia collections encouraged increasing recognition of the importance of cooperation. Moreover, the few scholars and librarians with interests in the region prompted shared awareness of mutual advantage in improving research collections and access to resources. In contrast to collections for other areas[④], scholars and librarians in Southeast Asia studies combined to form the Committee on Research Materials on Southeast Asia (CORMOSEA). CORMOSEA subsequently, growing out of the Puntjak (Indonesia) Conference, began the Southeast Asia

---

① A brief history of Cornell's Southeast Asia Program can be found in Lauriston Sharp, "The Cornell Southeast Asia Program, 1950 – 1975," and of its Southeast Asia Collection in John Echols, "The Southeast Asia Collection," both in Cornell University Libraries, *Sotuheast Asia catalogue* (Boston: G. K. Hall, 1976), 1: xiii-xxi and xxiii-xxiv respectively. Sharp notes that the Southeast Asia Program may be traced to the 1919 gift of his library by Charles W. Wason. While the Collection focused on China and the Chinese, it did include those in the Nanyang (Southeast Asia; literally the South Seas). The Southeast Asia Collection was identified as part of the Wason Collection until 1977, when it was separately designated as the Echols Collection in honour of the distinguished scholar and Cornell faculty member. Additional information on the collection can be found in *The John M. Echols collection on Southeast Asia: Cornell assembles a national treasure* (Ithaca, n. p., 1982) and, most recently, Mohd. Razali Agus, "Koleksi Malaysia di John M. Echols Collection on Southeast Asia, Perpustakaan Universiti Cornell," *Kekalabadi*, Vol. 8, No. 2 (June 1989): 17 – 21.

The history of the Modern Indonesia Project (CMIP) is described in George McT. Kahin, "Cornell's Modern Indonesia Project," *Indonesia*, No. 48 (October 1989): 1 – 25. The CMIP made donations to the National Museum Library and the University of Indonesia as well as providing $4,000 to the Cornell Library for the purchase of Indonesian books and periodicals.

② ASU reported that its collection is still in the early stages. Hiring of a Southeast Asia specialist to oversee collection development is anticipated in the next couple of years.

③ As noted, Washington is part of a consortium which has complementary collections being developed at the Universities of Oregon and British Columbia. The library dimension of the consortium was highlighted in "Consortium Librarians Coordinate Their Backing of Academic Expansion," SEASPAN (Southeast Asia studies in the Pacific Northwest), V. III, No. 2 (Winter 1990): 1 – 2.

④ Librarians for East Asia and South Asia, for example, have formed separate library-focused organizations: CEAL (Committee on East Asian Libraries) and CONSALD (Committee on South Asian Libraries and Documentation).

Microforms Project (SEAM)①. With a wider membership than CORMOSEA (as SEAM has attracted additional libraries with Asian research interests and overseas associate members), SEAM is a separate dues-paying organization under the Center for Research Libraries in Chicago but continues to include a representative of CORMOSEA on its executive committee.

Formal Cooperation—NPAC

The most significant national activity, especially from a collection development perspective, was the establishment of a Library of Congress Field Office in Jakarta, Indonesia, in early 1963 and the implementation of a PL-480 program for acquisition of Indonesian materials②. In 1969, with PL-480 funding disappearing, participating libraries assumed the costs of materials, shipping, and some administrative overhead. This arrangement became the first participant-supporting National Program for Acquisitions and Cataloguing (NPAC)③. While NPAC initially continued to concentrate on Indonesia, in 1970 it extended coverage to Malaysia, Singapore, and Brunei through contracts with local dealers. Besides acquiring materials, the Jakarta Office produces preliminary records, which provide most of the descriptive information.

Among the problems encountered by NPAC were the difficulty in obtaining multiple copies of titles, the quality of copies of many documents (as they were printed on office duplicating machines), and the limited life-expectancy of the paper④. The remedy, microfiching materials from the Jakarta Office (initially at New Delhi), solved not only these problems but also afforded wider dissemination of materials (as individual fiche titles could be acquired by anyone), a means for dealing with quasi-fugitive materials such as pamphlets, and a dramatic decrease in the cataloguing arrearage at the Jakarta Office. Fiche titles were identifiable only through LC's *Accessions list, Southeast Asia*; however, with federal funding, Ohio University began the first of a series of major microforms projects⑤ to catalogue the fiche. Initially, the intent was to deal with the 1978–1981 titles and convert these to AACR2 as the Library of Congress intended to provide

---

① An article on the history, activities, and holdings of SEAM is presently being prepared by K. Mulliner (the current SEAM Chair) for the *Microforms Review*. The conception and gestation of SEAM were described in the proceedings of the "Puntjak" conference, see Fred W. Riggs, "Report on Chicago Meeting, January 2–4, 1969," *Conference on Southeast Asian research materials held at Puntjak, Indonesia, April 21–24, 1969* (Jakarta: Lembaga Ilmu Pengetahunan Indonesia, 1969). SEAM is one of a number of area microform collections at the Center for Research Libraries. The nature and operations of these programs were described in Ray Boylan and Cecelia L. Shores, "Collecting retrospective materials from developing countries: A cooperative approach through microforms," *Library acquisitions: practice and theory*. V. 6, No. 2 (1982): 211–219.

② Under Public Law 480 (Agricultural Trade Development and Assistance Act of 1954), the Library of Congress was authorized to acquire and catalogue materials from foreign countries for libraries and research centers in the United States. Funding for the program was provided by local currencies generated from U.S. food assistance, of which Indonesia was a major recipient (and, hence, currency generator), described in Alice L. Kniskern, "Library of Congress overseas offices: acquisition programs in the Third World," *Library acquisitions: practice and theory*. V. 6, No. 2 (1982): 87–101. A contemporary report on NPAC as it was expanding and moving into participant funding can be found in Frank M. McGowan, "The Library of Congress in Southeast Asia," in Cecil Hobbs, ed., *Conference on access to Southeast Asian Research Materials: proceedings* (Washington, D. C.: Library of Congress, 1971): 55–58.

③ Kniskern: 87–101. NPAC was a general program, derived from TitleII-C of the Higher Education Act in 1965, and the Jakarta-based program is now officially known as the Cooperative Acquisitions Program for Thailand. Participants, however, continue to refer to irt by its original, generic name, and that is the sense in which it is used here. See Edmond L. Applebaum, "Foreign Acquisitions Programs of the Library of Congress." In *Acquisition of foreign materials for U.S. libraries*, edited by Theodore Samore (Metuchen, N. J., Scarecrow Press, 1973): 23–25.

④ In 1970, the Library of Congress noted, "...microfilm which is authorized by PL-480 legislation, plays no part in the NPAC program and there is no particular reason why it should," McGowan, p. 58. Seven years later, these and other reasons were apparent. Microfiche programmes were introduced at other LC offices but the Jakarta Office was the first, Kniskern, p. 98.

⑤ The Major Microforms Projects (MMP) were developed by the Association of Research Libraries to provide machine-readable (MARC) cataloguing records for microformat collections. Under the projects, now handled by OCLC, records for a specific microform project are gathered together on a tape which can be loaded into local systems, at a fraction of the usual item cost (even without considering staff costs). For OCLC members, holdings symbols are added-thus facilitating interlibrary loan requests for individual titles by other libraries. In addition to the LC Jakarta Office fiche, Ohio University is preparing to catalogue most of the Indonesia microfiche produced by IDC as MMPs, and has a proposal pending for the fiche produced by the Dutch Royal Institute for Linguistics and Anthropology (KITLV) and the Indonesian Scientific Documentation Center (PDII).

cataloguing for fiche after the inception of AACR2—a plan later abandoned by LC. Subsequent projects added cataloguing for fiche produced between 1982 and late 1987 (when LC began making minimal level cataloguing records for the fiche available to the OCLC and RLIN bibliographic utilities). A separate microfiche program for mainland Southeast Asia (especially Burma and Thailand) has been ignored, for the most part, by Southeast Asia collections (in comparison to the number of standing orders for the Jakarta fiche).

In 1990 the NPAC program moved in exciting new directions. At the urging of Southeast Asia collections in the U. S. and financial support from the Henry Luce Foundation, a new NPAC program has opened for Thailand. It is hoped that this will provide a base for programs covering other mainland Southeast Asian countries. Also, the Library of Congress is exploring opening the NPAC programs to participants from other countries. In Indonesia, for example, the Dutch Koninklijk Institute (KITLV) operates acquisitions and fiche programs in cooperation with the Indonesian Scientific Documentation Center (PDII), and Australia also has had acquisitions programmes. While each of these efforts had developed unique capabilities, the need for (and value of) the substantial redundancy among them is questionable.

The support of the Henry Luce Foundation has not been limited to the NPAC program-that project developed out of a much larger commitment by the Foundation to revitalize Southeast Asia studies in the United States. The Foundation specifically identified library development as a priority and has awarded millions of dollars for preservation, collection development, staff, and other library needs. ①

Ohio University's Experiences

Against this broad background, it may be instructive to consider how one Southeast Asia Collection has defined its mission locally, nationally, and internationally②. When the Ohio University Southeast Asia Collection was conceived in 1967, the University wisely began by hiring the best librarian available, Ms Lian The (since The-Mulliner) then working in the Cornell Southeast Asia Collection. Beyond the unique contributions of Ms The, the decision to begin with a librarian assured a coherent approach to collection growth (rather than following the "Topsy" model ③ or reflecting the then few faculty members' interests). While Ms The found a number of volumes and a few journal titles on Southeast Asia④, in retrospect, she essentially began with a blank slate (except in comparison to Yale's beginnings). ⑤

In its early years, the Collection concentrated on simply acquiring current materials, standard reference works, and complete runs of major Western-language journals. As faculty interests and language instruction, from the beginning, concentrated on what was later defined as the Malay

---

① Commendably, after an initial cycle in which few library awards were made (because scholars were uncomfortable choosing among the myriad library proposals), the Henry Luce Foundation supported a working conference in May 1988 at which librarians were asked to identify significant national needs and priorities. Most library awards were made in a Fall1988 cycle, following those recommendations.

② A more complete history, focusing on economic issues, can be found in K. Mulliner and Hwa-Wei Lee, "Funding for the Southeast Asia Collection and Research Resources at Ohio University" [Paper presented at the 38th Annual Meeting of the Association for Asian Studies, Chicago, March 21, 1986-available from ERIC (Educational resources Information Center) in print or fiche, ED 285602].

③ "it just grew"

④ As a result of the tenure of Professor John Cady, who offered at Ohio University what was the first course on Southeast Asia history in the U. S. , Lockard *Rise and changing status*, p. 6. See also John F. Cady, Contacts with Burma: 1935–1949: a personal account (Athens, Ohio University Center for International Studies, Southeast Asia Series, No. 61, 1983): 106–107.

⑤ An unanticipated advantage, for the entire field of Southeast Asian Studies, of having a librarian from the beginning was the time that Ms The was able to give, while the Collection was still small, to significant bibliographic tools. In addition to her collaboration with Paul van der Veur on *Treasures and trivia*, they produced Verhandelingen vanhet Batagiaasch Genootschap : *an annotated content analysis* (Athens, Ohio University Center for International Studies, Southeast Asia Series No. 26, 1973) and she translated a report from the Hollandsch-Inlandsch Onderwijs-Commissie which appeared as "The Social and Geographic Origins of Dutch-Educated Indonesians." In Paul W. van der Veur, *Education and social change in colonial Indonesia* (Athens, Ohio University papers in international studies, Southeast Asia series, No. 12, 1969).

World (primarily Indonesia and Malaysia but also Brunei, the Philippines, Singapore, and Southern Thailand), this formed a natural early emphasis. It also provided the impetus for the Collection to become a participant in the NPAC program for Indonesia (and—coincidentally because of the timing—Brunei, Malaysia, and Singapore) in 1970①.

The Collection's growth was stimulated by federal support as a national center for Southeast Asia studies through most of the 1970s②. Throughout the first decade, collection development addressed retrospective gaps with concentration provided by the NPAC program.

Academic libraries confront a fundamental, three-horned dilemma: should library collections serve campus courses, faculty research, or national needs? The ideal answer, all three, is seldom budgetary realistic. Moreover, the dilemma is compounded by staff and curricular changes. It was within this context that the Southeast Asia Collection undertook the strategic planning represented by a collection development policy. Although the faculty with Southeast Asian interests continued, the Malay World focus emerging in the Collection, they and their courses were clearly slanted toward Indonesia.

Despite pressures to concentrate on Indonesia, it was clear that—even by concentrating expenditures—the Collection would never be more than a pale shadow of Cornell's John Echols Collection on Southeast Asia③. At the same time, while it had been widely believed that Cornell University was collecting comprehensively on all Southeast Asia, many recognized that Cornell had confronted the reality that all libraries have had to face: it is impossible for a single institution to collect everything on everything (even for a limited geographic area like Southeast Asia).

Faculty concerns were not ignored (and the Collection has maintained considerable strength on Indonesia). In dialectic between the faculty and the library, faculty members were reassured and educated about the importance of diverse and complementary collections nationally. Indeed, one virtue of a collection development policy is to chart a long-term plan which balances the needs of current faculty and students with those of future generations.

To address local demand while fulfilling a vital national function, the Southeast Asia Collection determined that no other collection was attempting to collect comprehensively on Brunei, Malaysia, and Singapore. As the collection was comparatively strong in resources from these countries, they represented a logical concentration. Not long after this decision, a national conference on the Malay World at Ohio University afforded an opportunity for an external assessment of the Southeast Asia Studies Program and the Collection. The late Professor John Echols was invited to provide such an assessment in conjunction with his contribution to the Conference. He reported:

This [a well-balanced library collection of monographs, serials and fugitive materials] the Southeast Asia collection has in Western languages and, thanks to a heavy emphasis on Malaysia and Indonesia, it also has strength in depth and breadth in the vernacular as well. ... The Southeast Asia librarian has pointed out, accurately, that no library in this country has placed its

---

① Fortunately, Indiana University was in the process of withdrawing from the program and offered to transfer the Indonesian serials which it had acquired and had yet to add to its collection. These were supplemented in the 1980s by the transfer from another major research library (anonymous by request) which had participated in the NPAC program from the beginning but had warehoused many of the serials and monographs received from Indonesia.

② Under Federal programs to encourage language and area studies, called NDEA (National Defense Education Act) Centers, grants were made to universities for a variety of functions including faculty, travel, library acquisitions, and others. An analysis of these grants for 1978 - 1979 revealed that Southeast Asian centers (then Cornell, Michigan, and Ohio) allocated a much larger portion of the grant budget to libraries than other areas. For example, 21.7 per cent of the average grant to Southeast Asia Centers were for library acquisitions, compared to 15 per cent for East Asia Centers 13 per cent or less for all other areas, documented in Ann Schneider, "NDEA Centers: How They Use Their Federal Money," in *President's commission on foreign language and international studies: background papers and studies* (Washington, D.C., Government Printing Office, 1979): 168 -174. At Ohio University, the Southeast Asia Center consciously recognized that federal support (or other "soft" money) can be fleeting but that library materials acquired would continue to be available to serve future generations of students and scholars.

③ The thinking behind the analysis has since been well articulated by Kenichi Ohmae: "Merely allocating resources in the same way as your competitors will yield no competitive advantage," in *The Mind of the strategist: business planning for competitive advantage* (New York, Penguin Books, 1983): 42.

primary attention upon Malaysian. The Ohio University plans to strive for primacy in Malaysian materials and should be given all possible support in this endeavour. It will be in the national interest to do so.

While Malaysia was the first focus, the Collection recognized that an attempt to collect Malaysian materials as opposed to Singapore materials or Brunei materials was historically blind. Professor Echol's remarks on Malaysia would have been equally applicable to Brunei and Singapore.

The concentration on Malaysia also was justified in terms of institutional history, if not primary faculty research interest. Virtually synchronous with the birth of the Southeast Asia Program and Collection, contacts with the Malaysian High Commissioner in Nigeria[1] resulted in a visit to Malaysia by the university president and provost. There, in March 1967, they met the Minister of Education and began a cooperative undertaking with the Mara Institute of Technology (ITM), which continues to the present, and has included the conferral of Ohio University degrees for work done at ITM with Ohio University faculty[2]. Manifest in a university president who regularly visits Malaysia, more than 100 faculty and staff who have visited or worked in Malaysia in official capacities, and hundreds of Malaysian alumni, the ties between the university and Malaysia are deep and enduring[3].

In 1985, during the First Tun Abdul Razak Chair Conference on Southeast Asian Studies[4], the Minister of Education (Datuk Abdullah bin Haji Ahmad Badawi) inaugurated the Malaysian Resource Center in Ohio University's Southeast Asia Collection. The goals of the Resource Center were manifold, including providing an information center on Malaysia of first resort for North America (serving scholars, corporations, government offices, and citizens) and serving thousands of Malaysians in universities in North America with the scholarly resources which would enable them to make their education and research relevant to Malaysia and its needs[5]. For the Resource Center, the Malaysian Government asked various government agencies to provide a copy of their publications. Not surprisingly, some departments were more responsive than others and even the most consistent did not really understand a research library's definition of comprehensive, or the need for, complete serial runs.

As the Center grew, the Malaysian Government came to appreciate that meeting scholarly needs and building a substantial collection required understanding and efforts which one could not expect from government officials who were not professional librarians. From this awareness, the

---

[1] The High Commissioner in the mid-1960s was elected the Yang DiPertuan Besar of Negeri Sembilan in 1967 and is the Timbalan Yang DiPertuan Agung (Deputy King) of Malaysia from June 1979, DYMM Tuanku Jaafar Ibni AlMarhum Tuanku Abdul Rahman from April 1989.

[2] A description of the first decade of cooperation was presented by Felix Galiano (currently Associate Provost for International Programs), "The Malaysia connection: Ohio University's link to the world's other side is a decade old," *The Ohio University alumnus magazine*, No. 10 (March 1977): 8 – 13.

[3] On the occasion of the conferral by Ohio University of a Doctorate of Laws and Public Service in 1981 on Malaysia's third Prime Minister, Tun Hussein Onn, he noted that "this relationship is securely anchored upon the principles of mutual understanding and mutual respect". In 1979 the University and Malaysia embarked on a unique joint venture, the Tun Abdul Razak Chair in Southeast Asia Studies. With initial funding from the government and U. S. corporations doing business in Malaysia, this permanently endowed Chair brings prominent Malaysian scholars to the United States to teach at the University, consult with professional American colleagues, attend and sponsor conferences, and to better inform the American citizens about Malaysia. The Chair was also exemplary in designating a part of the earnings to support the acquisition of Malaysian library resources. Regarding the Tun Razak Chatir, with words that would equally apply to the later development of the Malaysian Resource Center and depository, Tun Hussein Onn stressed:

Acknowledging that education is always a two-way street, Ohio University has acted upon its conviction that the United States has much to learn about and from Malaysia as well as the other way round.

[4] Since that time, two additional Tun Razak Conferences have been held, focusing on the special concerns of the Chair holder. Copies of the papers from these conferences have been provided to the National Library of Malaysia and academic libraries in Malaysia—as a courtesy and service to scholars.

[5] The role of the Malaysian Resource Center and related activities of the University's Southeast Asia Collection were described in K. Mulliner and Hwa-Wei Lee, "Educating for international interdependence: the role of the academic library—Ohio and Malaysia" (Paper presented at the first Tun Abdul Razak Conference on Southeast Asia Studies, Athens, Ohio, May 10, 1985—available through ERIC in print or fiche, ED 285602).

Government wisely designated the National Library (under the table leadership of Dr. Donald Wijasuriya) as the focal point when, in a 1987 cabinet decision, it designated Ohio University as the North American Depository for Malaysian materials. From that action, the nature and consistent flow of materials were transformed.

Beyond looking to identify a unique niche on which to focus the Collection, complementary activities were underway. The most significant have been emphases on accessibility and service[①]. As a founding member of OCLC[②] and the first OCLC member institution to input a record online, the Ohio University Library has emphasized access to its resources as the basis for cooperation and resource sharing[③]. The Southeast Asia Collection has amplified these commitments in striving to enter its entire collection into the OCLC system and regularly publishing a bibliography of new materials[④]. For resource sharing, the Southeast Asia Collection now lends hundreds of items each year[⑤], demonstrating the strength of its resources and its commitment to the free exchange of information (by not charging for interlibrary loans, except in reciprocity).

Just as access rather than ownership is a solution to the information explosion, libraries today must emphasize service rather than warehousing. Reflecting a library-wide commitment to service[⑥], the Southeast Asia Collection has recognized that merely "owning" nationally important resources is insufficient. With the addition of a Research Bibliographer position (with seed money from the Henry Luce Foundation), the Collection is providing reference service and assistance in using resources for researchers nationally. This has been especially important in assisting graduate students from Malaysia engaged in doctoral research throughout North America.

Just as the evaluation by Professor John Echols was a major impetus to the decision to develop the Malaysian concentration, a 1987 evaluation by Professors R. S. Milne and Diane K. Mauzy attested to the success of the selective excellence strategy:

> The Southeast Asia Collection has an international reputation among scholars and it is rightfully regarded as one of the best libraries for Southeast Asian research in North America. Its Malaysia collection, and its designation by the Malaysian government as the official repository of Malaysian materials, makes it the best library facility in North America for research on Malaysia.

Cooperating to Serve a World of Learning

As the 1970s progressed, most Southeast Asia collections in the United States conceded that comprehensive coverage of all subjects for all countries in the region was impossible for a single institution because of the cost, staffing, and expertise required. Whether stimulated by example or necessity, collections increasingly looked to "distributed collection development" to address the

---

① The Southeast Asia Collection has also been a focal point in the international internship for professional librarians, inaugurated by Ohio University Libraries in 1979. This has been described in Hwa-Wei Lee, "Library internships: a new approach to cooperation," in *Areas of cooperation in library development in Asian and Pacific regions*, edited by Sally Tseng, el al. (Athens, Ohio University Libraries for Asian/-Pacific American Librarians Association and Chinese-American Librarians Association, 1985): 21 – 27.

② Today identified as OCLC Online Computer Library Center but originally the Ohio College Library Center—from its conception by academic libraries in Ohio.

③ Background on Ohio University's commitment to automation and technology to improving access to its resources is provided in Hwa-Wei Lee, "Trends in automation in American libraries: Ohio University's experiences," *Journal of educational media and library sciences*, V. 27, No. 1 (Autumn 1989): 1 – 23.

④ Since 1983, the Southeast Asia Collection has produced a regular 20 – 25 page "Malaysia-Singapore-Brunei-ASEAN bibliography" in *Berita: newsletter of the Malaysia/Singapore/Brunei Studies Group*. ASEAN has been added to the title for the past year.

⑤ In contrast to a decade ago, when fewer than 100 interlibrary loan requests were filled. For only the first six months of the 1989 – 1990 year, more than 300 requests were handled. Such requests include a good number of technical and scientific publications, from individuals with little knowledge of the area-evidencing the sophistication of education and research among the ASEAN nations.

⑥ Providing "effective, efficient Library service" is the primary goal in "Ohio University Libraries: mission, goals and objectives for 1990 and beyond" (Athens, Ohio University Libraries, 1990): 1.

national need for access to resources for Southeast Asia Studies. Under this concept, collections undertake to coordinate and develop complementary strengths. A study in the late 1970s which attempted to identify collection strengths[1] provoked strong reactions which led most collections to conclude that closer cooperation was needed on collection assessment and development issues: resulting in the creation of a collection development subcommittee of CORMOSEA[2].

The major accomplishment of the new Subcommittee has been the division of collecting responsibility for Indonesia. Where it was possible for Ohio University to identify, and pursue comprehensive collecting for Malaysia, Singapore, and Brunei (with a combined population of about 20 million), Indonesia's size and ethnic, geographic, and linguistic diversity demanded the resources and attention of several collections[3]. The division of responsibilities is:

Cornell	Jakarta, Kalimantan, Sulawesi, and West Java[4]
Hawaii	East Indonesia, including Irian Jaya
Michigan	Yogyakarta and Central Java
Northern Illinois	Bali
Ohio	East Java, Jambi, Riau, and South Sumatra
Yale	North Sumatra

Like its more universal predecessor, the Farmington Plan, distributed collection development depends on candour and commitment. Whether it will prove more successful than the Farmington plan has yet to be proven, but clearly such an approach is needed in the absence of bottomless pockets at a single institution. Consideration is underway for extending the distributed approach to other countries of Southeast Asia (especially Thailand and the Philippines).

(Published in *the Information Challenge: A Festschrift in Honor of Dr. Donald Wijasuriya*. Edited by Ch'ng Kim See. Kuala Lumpur: Knowledge Publishers, 1995: pp. 87 – 103.)

---

[1] Giok Po Oey, *Survey of Southeast Asia collections: November 1977-January 1978* (Ithaca, Cornell University Libraries, 1982). The study looked only at the collections of Cornell, Yale, the Library of Congress, Michigan, California, and Hawaii.

[2] With a formal membership of the heads/curators of collections, this subcommittee followed the Technical Processing Subcommittee which, under the able leadership of Ms Lian Tie Kho, has promoted standardized cataloguing of Southeast Asian materials nationally. Despite the progress described for collection development, collection assessment remains largely unaddressed. A draft model by Peter Ananda and LeRoy D. Ortopan, "Analysis of Southeast Asian Materials at the University of California, Berkeley, 1985" (Berkeley, General Library, University of California, 1985) indicated how the LC classification schedule could be used in an assessment of collection strengths but has yet to be implemented. The Ananda and Ortopan analysis could provide the basis for a Southeast Asia Conspectus. The use of a conspectus to guide South Asian acquisitions was described in Pauline Tina Lesnik, "The Research Libraries Group's Cooperative Acquisitions Program for South Asia," *Library acquisitions: practice and theory*. V. 6, No. 2 (1982): 233 – 238.

[3] From the Subcommittee report in *CORMOSEA Bulletin*, V. 16, No. 1 (June 1987): 3.

[4] Cornell has indicated that it would prefer to have Kalimantan and Sulawesi transferred to another institution(s), and this was discussed at the Subcommittee meeting in April 1990.

俄亥俄大学邵友保博士
海外华人文献和研究中心十周年 (1993—2003)

First Decade of the Dr. Shao You Bao Overseas Chinese Documentation and Research Center at Ohio University (1993 – 2003)[①]

The Dr. Shao You Bao Overseas Chinese Documentation and Research Center (邵友保博士海外华人文献研究中心, the Shao Center) at Ohio University Libraries was established in 1993 with a generous endowment from Dr. Shao You Bao (邵友保博士), a well-known Hong Kong banker, business and civic leader, former member of the Preparatory Committee of the Hong Kong Special Administrative Region, current member of the Chinese People's Political Consultative Conference, and Advisory Professor of Peking University and Tsinghua University. In 1999, Dr. Daniel Kung-Chuen Shao (邵公全博士), son of Dr. Shao You Bao and an alumnus of Ohio University, donated an additional gift to endow the Shao Center Curatorship.

The establishment of the Shao Center at Ohio University was in recognition of both the strategic location in North America for the research on Overseas Chinese around the world and the favorable conditions for such research existing at Ohio University. During the first ten years of its existence, the Shao Center has made great strides in the promotion of document collection and research on Overseas Chinese.

The Strategic Location in North America for the Research of Overseas Chinese around the World

The development of Overseas Chinese studies in various parts of the world is not balanced at the present. In terms of government support, China appears to have the most. With the government's encouragement, China has more institutes and scholars engaging in Overseas Chinese studies than any other countries in the world. It enjoys the advantage of possessing a large quantity of official archives and other public information sources on Overseas Chinese at both the national and the local levels. It also holds a wealth of genealogical materials related to Overseas Chinese in private collections. In addition, it is very convenient for scholars who are interested in ancestral villages of Overseas Chinese (侨乡, qiao xiang) or Overseas Chinese investments in China to conduct their field work locally. Because of these advantages, Chinese scholars are in the leading positions in the studies of Overseas Chinese migration history (华侨出国史), of Overseas Chinese investments in China (海外华人投资), and of qiao xiang (侨乡研究). Nevertheless, Chinese scholars have so far not been able to broaden the geographic scope of their research. As a result of difficulties in language barriers, research funding, and visa approval for the study of Chinese residing outside China, more often than not Chinese scholars have not been able to travel overseas to gather first-hand information themselves. Their research thus has had to rely on second-hand sources from foreign scholars and accordingly has only scratched the surfaces of issues.

Southeast Asia is the place most Overseas Chinese reside. Therefore, studies of Overseas Chinese in Southeast Asia also had an early start. Initially, European, American, and Japanese scholars were the main forces in the study of Overseas Chinese in Southeast Asia. But in recent decades, many local Chinese scholars in Southeast Asia have begun to play a key role and their contributions have been quite unique. However, owing to the narrow nationalism practiced by the governments of many newly independent Southeast Asian countries since the end of the Second

---

[①] Co-author: Liren Zheng.

World War, which either restricted or totally prohibited Overseas Chinese studies, many important and rare historical materials on Overseas Chinese were destroyed or forced to be evacuated to countries outside of Southeast Asia. One example of this is the archives of the Chinese Council (中华公馆) in Batavia / Jakarta, Indonesia. The Chinese Council, Tiong Hwa Kong Koan in Fukien pronunciation, was founded in 1775 and continued to keep its official records right up to 1950. In the earlier days, the Tiong Hwa Kong Koan in Batavia / Jakarta served as a quasi-government of the Chinese community to administer Chinese community affairs such as birth, death, and marriage registrations, mediation and arbitration of legal disputes, management of the finance and charitable activities of Chinese temples, maintenance of public cemeteries, etc... Its archives therefore contained a rich source of demographical, economic, legal and other original information relating to the Chinese in the Dutch East Indies, which are undoubtedly invaluable for the study of the history of Overseas Chinese in Jakarta[①]. But out of consideration for their safety, some one hundred boxes of these documents were moved to the University of Leiden in the Netherlands for safe keeping and became the special collection of that university. Under these circumstances, studies on Overseas Chinese have become a sensitive issue or even worse a political taboo, in many Southeast Asian countries. Local scholars of Overseas Chinese studies have to be very cautious in order not to "step on a land mine".

Researchers of Overseas Chinese studies in Japan have largely concentrated their attention on the economic aspects of Overseas Chinese in Southeast Asia, Japan, and their ancestral villages in China. Their strengths are in the breadth of their material collections and the details of their analyses. The key weakness of their research has been the lack of outreach since more than 95 percent of their publications are in Japanese. For researchers who do not read Japanese, there is no way for them to learn the fine points of their studies.

Many European countries such as Britain, France, and Netherlands, being the former colonial rulers of Southeast Asian countries, possess a large amount of historical archives of the previous colonial governments. Researchers in these countries have therefore been tending towards the studies of the history of Overseas Chinese in Southeast Asia prior to the Second World War. They have done relatively little in the study of Overseas Chinese outside Europe and Southeast Asia.

In Comparison, North America Has a Greater Advantage in the Study of Overseas Chinese

First of all, North America is the region that has had the fastest growth in the Chinese population. In recent decades, due to the continuing revisions of the immigration laws by the United States and Canada, North America has become the main destination for new migrants from mainland China, Taiwan, and Hong Kong, and for re-migrants of Chinese origins from Southeast Asia. Take the United States as an example. In 1930 there were only 102,000 Chinese in the United States. In 1943, the Chinese Exclusion Act, in effect since 1882, was repealed by the U. S. Congress. According to the new regulation, each year a total number of 105 Chinese was permitted to immigrate into the United States with the exception of students, professors, and missionary workers who were not subject to this quota limitation. In 1960, the Chinese population in the U. S. increased to 237, 000. In 1965, a new immigration law (the Immigration Act of 1965) was passed by the Congress that increased the annual quota for Chinese immigrants to 20, 000. In 1970, the Chinese population expanded to 435, 000. In 1979, as a result of the diplomatic rapprochement between the U. S. and China, the immigration quota of 20,000 for the Chinese that had been given to Taiwan since 1965 was transferred to mainland China. In 1980, the Chinese population grew to 806, 000. In 1981, the Congress passed legislation assigning a separate 20,000 immigration quota to Taiwan. In 1987, the Congress increased the annual quota

---

① Leonard Blusse, Cheng Shao gang, Wu Fengbin: Kong Koan Betawi——*Inventaris van het archief van de Chinese Raad of Kongkoan te Batavia (1775 – 1950)* (Institute for the History of European Expansion, Leiden, 1996).

for immigrants from Hong Kong from the original 600 to 5,000. In 1990, the total Chinese population in the U.S. reached ail all time high of 1,645,000, which accounted for 23.8% of the entire Asian American population and exceeded the populations of Filipinos (20.4%), Japanese (12.3%), Indians (11.8%), Koreans (11.6), and Vietnamese (8.9%), making the Chinese the largest ethnic group among all Asians.① During this period of thirty years between 1960 and 1990, the Chinese population in the U.S. nearly doubled every ten years. The 2000 Census has revealed that a total of 2,432,585 Americans identified themselves as ethnic Chinese. If those who indicated that they were partially ethnic Chinese had been included, the Chinese population in the United States in 2000 was 2,879,636.②

In Canada, the Chinese Immigration Act of 1923, which was very similar to the Chinese Exclusion Act in the U.S., was also repealed in 1943. Beginning in the 1960s, the Chinese population in Canada also doubled every ten years from 58,000 in 1961, to 118,000 in 1971, to 289,000 in 1981, and to 586,000 in 1991.③ Due to the drastic increase in the Chinese population, the Chinese language has become the third most commonly used language in Canada after English and French.④

In terms of numbers, North America, second only to Southeast Asia, has become the region where Overseas Chinese are most concentrated. If the current trend continues, in the foreseeable future, the United States will surpass Indonesia to be the country that has the largest population of ethnic Chinese.

Secondly, North America has advantages in the study of Overseas Chinese not just because it has had the fastest growth in the Chinese population but also because its Chinese population represents the new direction of Overseas Chinese development in terms of the population quality.

Again, let's use the U.S. as an example. In 1940 about 71% of the Chinese population in the U.S. engaged in such industries as mining, laundry business, restaurant business, garment manufacturing, and grocery; only 29% were considered professionals.⑤ The professional structure of the Chinese population in the U.S. has since changed dramatically. The 1990 Census indicates that 46.7% of Chinese American males and 35% of Chinese American females aged 25 years and over held at least a bachelor's degree or higher.⑥ It is obvious that the rise in the educational level of community members has had a profound effect on the professional composition of the Overseas Chinese society in the United States. This has been confirmed by the statistics furnished by the 1990 Census. The 1990 Census indicates that, among the Chinese American working population, 67.1% are professionals engaging in engineering and technology, business management, government services, marketing and sales, health and dental care, academia and education, etc.⑦

---

① U.S. Bureau of the Census: *Historical Statistics of the United States*: *Colonial Times to 1970* (Washington, D.C.: U.S Government Printing Office, 1975);
U.S. Bureau of the Census: *1990 Census of Population*: *Asians and Pacific Islanders in the United States* (Washington, D.C.: U.S. Government Printing Office, 1993); U.S. Department of Commerce, Economics and Statistics Administration, Bureau of the Census: *We the Americans*: *Asians* (Washington, D.C.: U.S. Government Printing Office, 1993);
杨国标等:《美国华侨史》(广东高等教育出版社, 1989), pp. 538 – 541;
刘汉标等:《世界华侨华人概况(欧洲、美洲卷)》(暨南大学出版社, 1994), pp. 169 – 174.
② U.S. Census Bureau: American FactFinder, http://factfmder.census.gov/
③ 刘汉标等:《世界华侨华人概况(欧洲、美洲卷)》(暨南大学出版社, 1994), pp. 140 – 141; David Chuen-Yan Lai: *Chinatowns*: *Towns within Cities in Canada* (Vancouver: University of Columbia Press, 1988); Canada Bureau of Statistics: Census of Canada, 1991: Population (Ottawa: 1992).
④ Lynn Pan: *The Encyclopedia of the Chinese Overseas* (Singapore: Archipelago Press, 1998), p. 234.
⑤ 张希哲:《美国华侨史略与美国华侨社会之发展》(华侨协会总会, 1997), pp. 191.
⑥ U.S. Bureau of the Census: *1990 Census of Population*: *General Population Characteristics* (U.S. Government Printing Office, 1992); U.S. Bureau of the Census: *1990 Census of Population*: *Asians and Pacific Islanders in the United States* (U.S. Government Printing Office, 1993); U.S. Department of Commerce, Economics and Statistics Administration, Bureau of the Census: *We the Americans*: *Asians* (Washington, D.C.: U.S. Government Printing Office, 1993).
⑦ U.S. Bureau of the Census: *1990 Census of Population*: *General Population Characteristics* (U.S. Government Printing Office, 1992); U.S. Bureau of the Census: *1990 Census of Population*: *Asians and Pacific Islanders in the United States* (U.S. Government Printing Office, 1993).

The quality of the Chinese population in the United States has been further uplifted by the influx of new immigrants from China as a significant percentage of them are equipped with higher academic degrees. With the entry of large numbers of Chinese college graduates from China into American science and technology professions, the influence of Chinese Americans in the scientific and technological world can now be well felt.

The influx of new Chinese immigrants with higher academic degrees started during the 1950s and has continued to the present. According to a report by the Ministry of Education of the, from 1950 to 1980, the Ministry approved 63,061 college graduates from Taiwan in China to pursue their graduate study abroad; most of them went to the United States. Only 7,240 of these students eventually returned to Taiwan. In 1980 a total of 5,572 students from Taiwan went to study in the U.S. while in the same year only 331 students returned to Taiwan after the completion of their study in the U.S. [1] According to another statistic, from 1967 to 1974, a total of 54,382 Chinese were granted permanent U.S. residence status, of whom over 22,000 were students from Taiwan. [2] As early as 1962, based on the statistics provided by the then "Cultural Counselor's Office of the Embassy" (Taiwan) in the U.S., there were a total of 1,571 Chinese who held either a teaching position or a research position at American universities or research institutes. [3]

The students from mainland China soon joined this trend. According to the statistics published by the State Education Commission of the People's Republic of China (now renamed the Ministry of Education) in October 1996, a total of 250,000 students from mainland China had gone to study abroad since 1979. [4] Like their forerunners from Taiwan, most of these students from mainland Chinese chose to study in the United States. From 1979 to 1998, based on the incomplete statistics provide by the Chinese Embassy in the U.S., approximately 160,000 students from mainland China came to study in the U.S. [5] Statistics provided by the National Science Foundation, a U.S. organization based in Arlington, Virginia, indicates that, during the academic year of 1995 – 1996, 82% of all the students from mainland China were graduate students. [6] In 1993, over 50,000 students from mainland China obtained permanent U.S. residence status. [7]

Beginning in the late 1980s, a large number of graduate students from mainland China started to enter science and technology professions in the United States. This new development can be well illustrated by two set of statistics. The first set is comprised of the significant percentage of all the doctorates in science and engineering granted by American universities that were occupied by students from mainland China. According to National Science Foundation statistics, from 1988 to 1996, a total of 219,643 doctorates in science and engineering were awarded by American universities, of which 16,550, or roughly 7.5%, were awarded to students from mainland China. [8] The breakdown of the science and engineering doctoral degrees awarded to mainland

---

[1] Yuigui Guo: "The Eventual Tendency: To Integrate Chinese Scientists and Engineers into International Community of Science" in *International Conference of Institutes and Libraries for Overseas Chinese Studies—Papers and Abstracts* (Athens, Ohio, USA, March 24 – 25, 2000), p. 173. Sources: Ministry of Education, *Educational Statistics of the ROC*, 1997, pp. 54, 56 – 57, 60; Li Chen-ching: "Returning Home after Studying in the USA: Reverse Brain Drain in Taiwan" in *Cultural & Educational Digest*, 1995a, pp. 20 – 24.

[2] 张希哲:《美国华侨史略与美国华侨社会之发展》(华侨协会总会, 1997), p. 190.

[3] 张希哲:《美国华侨史略与美国华侨社会之发展》(华侨协会总会, 1997), p. 191.

[4] "跨世纪中国的人才资源" 载《华声月刊》(No. 6, 1996).

[5] Yuigui Guo: "The Eventual Tendency: To Integrate Chinese Scientists and Engineers into International Community of Science" in *International Conference of Institutes and Libraries for Overseas Chinese Studies—Papers and Abstracts* (Athens, Ohio, USA, March 24 – 25, 2000), p. 171.

[6] United States National Science Board: *Science and Engineering Indicators 1998* (Washington, D. C.: National Science Foundation, 1998).

[7] Lynn Pan: *The Encyclopedia of the Chinese Overseas* (Singapore: Archipelago Press, 1998), p. 267.

[8] Another statistic by the National Science Foundation indicates that, from 1986 to 1998, over 21,600 Chinese students from mainland China earned their doctoral degrees in Science and engineering in the U.S. Source: National Science Foundation, Division of Science Resources Studies, *Science and Engineering Doctorate Awards: 1998* (Arlington, VA., 1999).

Chinese recipients by selected fields is as follows:①

Field	Total	Mainland Chinese	Percentage (mainland Chinese)
Mathematics	9,173	1,354	14.8
Physics	32,897	4,278	13.0
Engineering	48,109	4,377	9.1
Earth/ATM/ Oceanographic Sciences	6,934	622	9.0
Biology & Agriculture	52,928	4,442	8.4
Computer Science	7,202	421	5.8

The second set of statistics is comprised of the numbers of students from mainland China who, after completing their doctorates in science and engineering, joined the science and technology professions in the United States. As mentioned above, from 1988 to 1996, a total of 16,550 Chinese students completed their doctorates in science and engineering in the U.S. In the peak year of 1996 alone, about 3,000 such degrees were awarded to mainland Chinese students. Of these mainland Chinese science and engineering doctorate holders, 31% received a firm offer of a postdoctoral appointment in science and engineering following their graduation and thus constituted a crucial force in the research enterprise of American universities and national laboratories.② In addition to postdoctoral appointments, about 17% of the new mainland Chinese science and engineering doctorate holders received offers from industry (11%), institutions of higher education (5%), and government agencies or non-profit institutions (1%). The statistics also reveal that, during this period of 8 years, American corporations totally recruited 1,138 mainland Chinese who received their doctorates in engineering, 491 mainland Chinese who received their doctorates in physics, and 400 mainland Chinese who received their doctorates in mathematics.③ In his retrospective study of the employment situation of mainland Chinese doctorate recipients in engineering, American scholar Michael Finn found that, among 4,010 mainland Chinese doctorate recipients in engineering who earned their degrees between 1992 and 1993, 92% had been hired in the U.S. by 1997.④

Because of the influx of a large number of students from China into science and technology professions in the U.S., China has become one of the top six countries of origin of scientists and engineers making exceptional contributions to U.S. science. The other five countries are: Austria, Canada, Germany, Britain, and India.⑤ In American institutions of higher education, for example, there were a total of 224,707 science and engineering faculty members in 1997, and 20% of them were foreign-born. Within foreign-born science and engineering faculty members, the number of Chinese-born faculty members (6,650) ranks second, making up 2.9 percent of

---

① Jean M. Johnson: "Collaboration in Information Exchange between the United States and China" presented to CIES 2000 Conference (San Antonio, Texas, March 7 – 11, 2000). Sources: National Science Foundation, Division of Science Resources Studies: *Statistics Profiles of Foreign Doctoral Recipients in Science and Engineering: Plans to Stay in the United States* (Arlington, VA., 1998) and Susan T Hill: *Science and Engineering Doctorate Awards: 1996* (Arlington: National Science Foundation, 1997).
② The statistics provided by the National Science Foundation also indicate that, from 1986 to 1998, over 6,000 mainland Chinese scientists and engineers accepted firm offers of postdoctoral appointments in the United States. Jean M. Johnson, *ibid*.
③ Jean M. Johnson, *ibid*.
④ Michael Finn: *Stay Rates of Foreign Doctorate Recipients from U.S. Universities, 1997* (Oak Ridge, TN: Oak Ridge Institute for Science and Education, 2000).
⑤ Paula E. Stephan and Sharon G. Levin: *Exceptional Contributions to U.S. Science by the Foreign-Born and Foreign-Educated*—a research paper supported by the Alfred P. Sloan Foundation.

the science and engineering faculty in U. S. higher education (mainland China 2.1% and Taiwan 0.8%), next only to that of India-born faculty members (3.1%).① In that same year, based on statistics by the National Science Foundation, a total of 78,963 Chinese-born persons with science and engineering degrees were employed in the U. S.; among them, 32,660 held bachelor's degrees, 28,970 held master's degrees, and 17,333 held doctoral degrees.② By far, Chinese Americans, who only comprise roughly 1% of the total American population (275,562,673 in July 2000), have had six Nobel Prize laureates (Chen Ning Yang 杨振宁, Tsung-Dao Lee 李政道, Samuel Chao-Chung Ting 丁肇中, Yuan-Tseh Lee 李远哲, Steven Chu 朱棣文, and Daniel C. Tsui 崔琦), 27 American Academy of Sciences members (Ching-Wu Chu 朱经武, Chia Chiao Lin 林家翘 etc.), and 35 American Academy of Engineering members (Chang-Lin Tien 田长霖, Tung Yen Lin 林同炎 etc.).③ As each year thousands of Chinese college graduates from China are continuing to come to the U. S. for graduate study in the fields of science and engineering, and thousands of current Chinese graduate students complete their graduate degrees and enter science and technology professions, the influence of Chinese Americans in science and technology will certainly continue to grow.

Thus far, the strength of Overseas Chinese has been demonstrated mainly in the worlds of business and science/technology. Its economic muscles are represented by the business giants of ethnic Chinese in Southeast Asia, while its muscles in science and technology are represented by Chinese American scientists and engineers. As the make-up of the Overseas Chinese population in North America symbolizes the new quality of the Overseas Chinese population in general, the academic interest shown in Overseas Chinese in North America should soon catch up with that previously shed lavishly on their counterparts in Southeast Asia, thus making North America, abreast of Southeast Asia, the major geographic focus in Overseas Chinese studies.

Finally, the advantage of North America in Overseas Chinese studies is closely associated with, its strong academic ability and unlimited potential in pursuing such studies. Unlike Southeast Asia, the United States and Canada are very keen about multicultural studies 多元文化研究. Therefore the research on ethnic Chinese, a minority of increasing importance, has the prospect to receive broad support from a wide range of academic institutes in North America. In the United States, 55 universities have programs in teaching or research on the Asian American population. Of these universities, 25 have research centers for Asian American studies; 18 have departments of Asian American studies; and 12 offer courses on Asian Americans.④ The study of Chinese Americans is an intrinsic component of these programs. The study of ethnic Chinese in Southeast Asia is largely undertaken by centers for Southeast Asian studies in many universities. A total of 15 universities in the United States possess centers for Southeast Asia studies.⑤ Interest in East Asia has long been a tradition among American academia. Currently 47 American universities have programs related to East Asian studies.⑥ These East Asian programs are also interested in Overseas Chinese studies, especially on the topics concerning Overseas Chinese business networks 海外华人经济圈 and China's policies towards Overseas Chinese. Furthermore, centers for Latin American studies, centers for African studies, and centers for European studies, etc. in American universities all have the abilities to study Overseas Chinese in the regions under their care. As the Chinese Diaspora is now the most widespread ethnic group around the world, the topics related to ethnic Chinese in their respective regions could naturally become the objects of their concerns. It is evident that, in comparison with mainland China, Southeast Asia, Japan, or Europe, the

---

① Jean M. Johnson, op. cit.
② *Ibid*.
③ See A Global Network for Chinese Professionals 全球华人专业人士网络 website: http://www.networkchinese.com/.
④ Asian American Studies Program, Cornell University: *Directory of Asian American Studies Program* (Ithaca, New York: 1999).
⑤ Virginia Jing-yi Shih: International Directory of Southeast Asia Librarians & Catcilogers (University of California, Berkeley, 2001).
⑥ See CEAL website: http://staff.washington.edu/rrbritt/ceal/.

U. S. possesses the unexcelled ability and potential for extensive research on Overseas Chinese wherever they reside.

North America is also a major center in the world for international scholarly exchange. Owing to its solid academic strength, highly developed information resources and communication services, and convenient transportation, many international conferences of scholarly importance have selected the U. S. as their venues. Since 1990, several large scale international conferences on Overseas Chinese studies have been held in the U. S., including the Symposium on the Roles of the Indonesian Chinese in Shaping Modern Indonesian Life organized by Cornell University in 1990, the Loudi-Shenggen (落地生根) International Conference on Legal, Political and Economic Status of Chinese in Diaspora organized by the University of California at Berkeley in 1992, the International Conference on Chinese Population in Contemporary Southeast Asian Societies organized by the University of Illinois at Urbana-Champaign in 1997,[①] and the International Conference of Institutes and Libraries for Overseas Chinese Studies organized by Ohio University in 2000. In addition, the well-attended annual conferences of the U. S. Association for Asian Studies often have had sessions on Overseas Chinese.

In terms of research organizations and academic societies for Overseas Chinese studies, North America can boast of owning the second largest number next only to mainland China. The research organizations and academic societies for Overseas Chinese studies in North America are geographically widespread. They include the Chinese Historical Society of New England (新英格兰华人历史学会)[②] and the Greater Boston Chinese Cultural Association (GBCCA) (大波士顿华人文化协会)[③] in Boston, the Museum of Chinese in the Americas (纽约华人博物馆)[④] and the Society for the Study of the History of Chinese with an American Education (华族留美史学会) in New York City, the Organization of Chinese Americans (华美协会)[⑤] in Washington, D. C., the Dr. You Bao Shao Overseas Chinese Documentation and Research Center at Ohio University Libraries[⑥] in Athens, Ohio, the Mai Wah Society 美华学会[⑦] in Butte, Montana, the Chinese Historical Society of Pacific North-West (美国西北华人历史学会) in Seattle, the Chinese Historical Society of America (美国华人历史学会)[⑧] and the Chinese Cultural Center of San Francisco (旧金山中华文化中心)[⑨] in San Francisco, the Chinese American Museum (Los Angeles) (罗省华美历史博物馆)[⑩] and the Chinese Historical Society of Southern California (南加州华人历史学会)[⑪] in Los Angeles, the Chinese Historical Society of Greater San Diego and Baja California (大圣地亚哥华人历史学会)[⑫] and the San Diego Chinese Historical Museum (圣地亚哥中华历史博物馆)[⑬] in San Diego, the Dr. Sun Yat-Sen Foundation of Hawaii (夏威夷孙中山基金会)[⑭] in Honolulu, the Chinese Cultural Centre of Greater Vancouver and its Museum and Archives (大温哥华中华文化中心博物档案馆)[⑮] in

---

① Hwa-wei Lee (李华伟): "Dr. You-Bao Shao Overseas Chinese Documentation and Research Center" presented at Special Conference of the Evolving Research Library and East Asian Studies (Beijing, 1996).
② See the Chinese Historical Society of New England website: http://yerkes.mit.edu/mbta/Chinatown/chsne.html.
③ See The Greater Boston Chinese Cultural Association (GBCCA), 大波士顿华人文化协会 website: www.anewnet.com/gbcca.htm.
④ See 纽约华人博物馆 website: http://www.ny.com/niuseums/chinatown.history.museum.html.
⑤ See Organization of Chinese Americans website: www.ocanatl.org.
⑥ See the Shao Center website: www.library.ohiou.edu/subjects/shao/main.htm.
⑦ See 美华学会 website: www.maiwah.org.
⑧ See the Chinese Historical Society of America website: www.chsa.org.
⑨ See the Chinese Cultural Center of San Francisco website: www.c-c-c.org/.
⑩ See the Chinese American Museum in Los Angeles website: www.camla.org/.
⑪ See the Chinese Historical Society of Southern California website: www.chssc.org.
⑫ See the Chinese Historical Society of Greater San Diego and Baja California, Inc. website: www.sandiego-online.com/forums/chinese/htmls/museum.htm.
⑬ See San Diego Chinese Historical Museum website: www.sandiego-online.com/forums/chinese/htmls/museum.htm.
⑭ See Dr. Sun Yet-Sen Foundation of Hawaii website: http://sunyatsen.hawaii.org/.
⑮ See the Chinese Cultural Centre of Greater Vancouver and its Museum and Archives website: www.cccvan.com/musarc.htm.

Vancouver, and the Chinese Cultural Centre of Greater Toronto (大多伦多中华文化中心)① in Toronto. With the exception of the Shao Center at Ohio University Libraries, which is devoted to the studies of Overseas Chinese worldwide, all the others focus their attention on the ethnic Chinese in North Americans, especially on the history of their local Chinese communities.

The Favorable Conditions for the Research on Overseas Chinese at Ohio University

In addition to the overall favorable conditions for research on Overseas Chinese in North America, Ohio University has its own particular advantages conducive to the pursuit of Overseas Chinese studies.

Founded in 1804, Ohio University is one of the oldest and finest universities in the United States.② Ohio University's connection with Chinese can be traced back to 1909 when the first Chinese student from Guangdong, China was admitted. Since then thousands of Chinese students from mainland China, Taiwan, Hong Kong, Southeast Asia, and the U.S as well have come to study at Ohio University. Dr. Daniel K. C. Shao, a major supporter of the Shao Center, graduated from Ohio University in the early 1970s. Currently, over 400 Chinese students are enrolled at Ohio University, and around 50 faculty and staff members are ethnic Chinese. These Chinese students, faculty, and staff members, along with their families, constitute the largest ethnic minority on the Ohio University campus.

Interest in Overseas Chinese at Ohio University is innately affiliated with its focus on Southeast Asian studies. Ohio University initiated its Southeast Asian studies in 1967 when it established the Center for Southeast Asian Studies in conjunction with the inauguration of the Southeast Asia Collection at Ohio University Libraries.③ The Center for Southeast Asian Studies at Ohio University was soon designated by the U. S. Government as one of the National Resource Centers for Southeast Asian Studies. With the firm commitment of the University and the strong support from the U. S. Government and private gifts, the Center for Southeast Asian Studies at Ohio University and the Southeast Asia Collection at Ohio University Libraries have quickly developed into a world-class research institute and library collection on Southeast Asia.

At present, the Center has 15 faculty members and scholars involved in studying a wide range of issues related to Southeast Asia. Through academic cooperation and exchange programs, the Center maintains close working relationships with educational and research institutions and scholars throughout Southeast Asia. The Southeast Asia Collection at Ohio University Libraries currently occupies the first floor of the Vernon R. Alden Library building with a size of more than 20,000 square feet. The Collection contains 218,000 bound volumes, 45,000 microfilms, and 90,000 active serials, and adds more than 11,000 additional pieces each year. The strengths and services of the Collection have attracted scholars and other patrons from across North America, Southeast Asia, and the world to the Athens campus. The total number of the services requested, including loans of books and reference assistance, is in the neighborhood of 10,000 per year.

In recognition of the strength and reputation of the Southeast Asia Collection at Ohio University Libraries, the Malaysian Government selected it to be the Malaysian Resource Center in North America in 1985. Two years later, the Malaysian Government further named it as its sole United States Depository for materials published in Malaysia. As far as we know, this was the first such designation of its kind ever done by a foreign country to any American university. The Malaysian Government and several U. S. corporations in Malaysia also jointly set up and find a unique Tun Abdul Razak Chair in Southeast Asian Studies at Ohio University in honor of the second Prime Minister of Malaysia. The endowed professorship, with a two-year residency at Ohio University, has been filled by Malaysian scholars selected by the Malaysian Ministry of Education

---

① See the Chinese Cultural Centre of Greater Toronto website: www.cccgt.org/.
② See the website of Ohio University: www.ohiou.edu.
③ See the website of the Southeast Asia Studies of Ohio University: http://www.ohiou.edu/seas/index.html.

in consultation with the Razak Council and Ohio University. Over the past 20 years, 10 well-known Malaysian scholars have come to Athens, teaching at the Center for Southeast Asian Studies and using resources of the Southeast Asia Collection for their research. The current Tun Abdul Razak Professor is Dr. Zakaria Bin Ahmad, Dean of Social Sciences and Humanities at the National University of Malaysia. Both the Center for Southeast Asia Studies and the Southeast Asia Collection maintain close contacts with Ohio University alumni and alumni associations throughout Southeast Asia, which number over 1,000, and receive their substantial support.

Concurrent to promoting Southeast Asian studies, Ohio University has paid exceptional attention to the study of Overseas Chinese in the region. The Southeast Asian Collection has made particular efforts to extensively collect materials on Overseas Chinese in Southeast Asia published in mainland China, Taiwan, and Western countries. It has also worked with the Field Office of the Library of Congress in Jakarta to secure books, periodicals, and other materials on Overseas Chinese published in Southeast Asian countries. All of these extraordinary endeavors laid a sound foundation for the establishment of the Shao Center at Ohio University in 1993. From this launch point, the Shao Center has greatly expanded its coverage to include Overseas Chinese in North America and elsewhere as the objects of its concern.

Shao Center's Efforts in the Promotion of Overseas Chinese Studies

Since its inception in 1993, the Shao Center has made consistent efforts to promote Overseas Chinese studies and has achieved considerable accomplishments.

1. Document Collection

One of the Shao Center's missions is to collect, organize, and preserve relevant documents and other information resources related to Overseas Chinese, such as monographs, periodical articles, official archives, private manuscripts, genealogies, epigraphic materials, and oral records. The Shao Center has exploited a variety of channels to effectively secure publications on Overseas Chinese. It orders Western-language publications mainly through regular book dealers that have signed agreements with Ohio University Libraries. It enlists the assistance of the Field Office of the Library of Congress in Jakarta to extensively amass materials on Overseas Chinese published in Southeast Asian countries. To purchase Chinese-language materials on Overseas Chinese published in mainland China, the Shao Center has established a partnership with the Center for Overseas Chinese Documents and Information Data at Jinan University Library, Guangzhou, PRC. Meanwhile, through an international exchange program with the National Central Library in Taipei, the Shao Center is able to collect materials published in Taiwan. Finally, the Shao Center also can rely on the Chubu University Library, which has a long-standing relationship with Ohio University Libraries, to acquire Japanese-language materials on Overseas Chinese.

Despite the invaluable contributions of the Overseas Chinese to economic and cultural developments in Southeast Asia and elsewhere, their historical roles and evidence of that have often been neglected, ignored, or actively suppressed. Many valuable historical documents scattered in various parts of the world have not been properly cared for and are now in grave danger of deteriorating or vanishing entirely. This situation has resulted from narrow nationalism, ethnic jealousies, or ignorance combined with inadequate resources to effectively preserve such documents. In the light of this situation, securing and preserving historical documents on Overseas Chinese has become an urgent task that calls for immediate action.

Realizing the long-term neglect of historical documents on Overseas Chinese in Indonesia, the Shao Center is paying special attention to the salvage of materials on Indonesian Chinese. In 2001, the Center acquired 1,415 microfiche copies of Dr. Myra Sidharta's personal collection on Indonesian Peranakan literature, which cover Peranakan literature works published between 1884 and 1976, thus making Ohio University Libraries one of only two libraries in the United States that possess this valuable resource. The Shao Center also gives a special emphasis to preserving materials on Overseas Chinese in North America. In 2002, the Shao Center paid over 10,000 dollars to secure the complete microfilm set of The Young China Daily (少年中国晨报) (1910 – 1991). The Young China Daily is a Chinese-language newspaper, which was founded by Dr. Sun Yat-Sen in San Francisco in 1910 as the official newspaper of his revolutionary organization, the Tung Meng Hui. With over 82 years of publication, The Young China Daily has the longest history among all of the Chinese newspapers ever published in North America, which enables it to provide researchers with rich information in regard to the Chinese communities in the United States and Canada. The Shao Center holds the distinction of being the only library collection in North America that holds the complete set of this important newspaper.

2. Databases

In order to provide scholars around the world with easy access to bibliographical and digital resources on Overseas Chinese through modern library networks and information systems, the Shao Center has been actively working on building databases. A major project, which is now under construction and will soon be available on the Internet, is the Database on Overseas Chinese Publications (海外华人文献数据库). This database will be the first comprehensive database on Overseas Chinese publications for the global academic society. It will include publications on Overseas Chinese in Western languages, Chinese, Japanese, Indonesian/Malay, and other Southeast Asian languages. It will include thousands of items published since the early 20th century. Data can be searched by authors, titles, subjects, and keywords via the Internet.

In the process of constructing this database, the Shao Center has received active assistance from Jinan University Library and Shenzhen Library in China. By means of an on-going cooperative program, The Center for Overseas Chinese Documents and Information Data at Jinan University Library has sent two experienced library staff members to Ohio University to assist in the project. Meanwhile, the Shenzhen Library has generously donated a software system to the Shao Center for the project. The Shenzhen Library has developed the Integrated Library and Information System (ILAS), which has now been widely adopted by libraries in mainland China. The Shenzhen Library specifically modified the system to meet the requirements of the Shao Center's project.

3. Teaching

The Shao Center has offered regular courses on Overseas Chinese for the graduate students from the Center for International Studies at Ohio University. Graduate seminar Studies of Overseas Chinese in Southeast Asia (东南亚海外华人研究) surveys major themes of Overseas Chinese studies in Southeast Asia: the history of Overseas Chinese migration to Southeast Asia, the changing relationship between China and Overseas Chinese, social structures and business networks of Overseas Chinese communities, identity issues, and the problems Overseas Chinese are facing in various countries in Southeast Asia. It is a 5-credit course that meets for 4 hours a week. The Shao Center has also provided independent study courses for graduate students who conducted their interdisciplinary study on Overseas Chinese. These courses were well received by international students, especially those from Asian countries. After graduating and returning to his country, Ehsanul Haque, a Fulbright scholarship student from Bangladesh, wrote to the Shao Center Curator:

"I have resumed my teaching duties at the University of Dhaka, Bangladesh. I am teaching two classes: one on Southeast Asian Affairs and the other one on International Relations of South Asia. I strongly feel (that) my participation in your class on Overseas Chinese has broadened my knowledge and I am using the reading materials you gave in the class. I really appreciate your approach to teaching."

Thus far, students from the U.S., China, Japan, Korea, Vietnam, Indonesia, Singapore, Malaysia, Bangladesh, and Mexico have taken these courses on Overseas Chinese. A number of undergraduate students have also audited the graduate seminar. The Center for International Studies requires that all students should have one major and two minor fields for their comprehensive examination in order to receive their Master's degrees. Many students, who had taken courses on Overseas Chinese, selected Overseas Chinese studies as one of their minor fields. In addition to regular teaching, the Shao Center also provided academic advice and bibliographic support to graduate students who presented their research papers at international conferences on Overseas Chinese.

In view of the fact that only very few universities in North America are now offering courses on Overseas Chinese studies, the Shao Center has played a pioneering role in accumulating teaching experience on Overseas Chinese studies and developing Overseas Chinese curriculum.

4. International Conferences

Since its inception, the Shao Center has actively promoted scholarly exchange in the field of Overseas Chinese studies through international conferences. It has sponsored, hosted, or participated in many important international conferences on Overseas Chinese.

In 1996, the Shao Center sponsored the International Conference on Hakkaology (客家学国际学术会议) held in Singapore. In 1997, the Shao Center again sponsored the International Conference on Chinese Population in Contemporary Southeast Asian Societies held at the University of Illinois at Urbana-Champaign. The proceedings of the Urbana-Champaign conference have recently been published by prestigious Curzon Press in London.①

In 2000, the beginning of a new century, the Shao Center initiated, organized, and hosted The First International Conference of Institutes and Libraries for Overseas Chinese Studies (海外华人研究与收藏机构国际合作会议) at Ohio University in Athens, Ohio. A total of 53 institutes and libraries from mainland China, Taiwan, Hong Kong, Japan, Southeast Asia, Australia, Europe, and North America sent representatives or papers to participate in this conference. A cooperation organization The World Confederation of Institutes and Libraries for Overseas Chinese Studies was also launched during the conference. This ground-breaking conference was financially sponsored by Ohio University, Dr. Shao You-Bao, the Chiang Ching-Kuo Foundation (蒋经国基金会), the Cultural and Charity Foundation of the United World Chinese Commercial Bank (世界华人联合商业银行文化慈善基金会), the Fong Shu Fook Tong Foundation (方树福堂基金会), and the Fong's Family Foundation (方润华基金会). This inaugural conference received worldwide attention and was subsequently reported in detail by the People's Daily (Overseas Edition) (人民日报) (海外版) in mainland China, the Chiaohsieh Tsachih (侨协杂志) in Taiwan, the Kangao Chihyou Tunghsun (港澳之友通讯) in Hong Kong, the Rippon Kyopo (日本侨报) in Tokyo, the Diaspora in Russia, and the Collection Building in the U.S.

As a sequel to the successful *First International Conference of Institutes and Libraries for Overseas Chinese Studies*, Ohio University and the Chinese University of Hong Kong (CUHK) will jointly host The Second International Conference of Institutes and Libraries for Overseas Chinese Studies on March 13 – 15, 2003 in Hong Kong. The Shao Center will continue to make efforts to develop *The International Conference of Institutes and Libraries for Overseas Chinese Studies* into a regular and important international forum for the global academic society to share their scholarly accomplishments.

In addition to sponsoring and hosting the above international conferences, the Shao Center has presented papers at and participated in the following important international events: The Roundtable on *Collecting Overseas Chinese Sources* at the International Convention of *Asian Scholars* (Noordwijkerhout, The Netherlands, 1998), the *International Conference for Qiaoxiang Studies* (Quanzhou, PRC., 1998), the Joint Working Meeting of Research Institutes for Overseas Chinese Studies (Guangzhou, PRC. 1998), the *International Conference on the Ethnic Chinese-Inter-cultural Relations and Cultural Transformation of Ethnic Chinese Communities* (Manila, The

---

① M. Jocelyn Armstrong, R. Warwick Armstrong, Kent Mulliner, ed.: *Chinese Population in Contemporary Southeast Asian Societies—Identities, Interdependence and International Influence* (London: Curzon Press, 2001).

Philippines, 1998), the *International Conference on Chinese in Japan* (Nagasaki, Japan, 1999), the *Roundtable on Primary Overseas Chinese Sources at the Annual Meeting of The Association for Asian Studies* (San Diego, U. S. A., 2000), the *Overseas Chinese Studies Session* at the 2000 Symposium of the Ohio Chinese Academic and Professional Association (Athens, Ohio, U. S. A., 2000), and the *17th World Hakka Conference* (Jakarta, Indonesia, 2002).

5. Information and Reference Services

The most important services provided by the Shao Center to the public since its establishment have been its information and reference services, which have been and continue to be widely used.

To provide information services, the Shao Center has set up two websites:

www. overseaschineseconfederation. org

www. library. ohiou. edu/subjects/shao/main. htm

With these two websites, the Shao Center is able to provide the public with an abundance of digital information on Overseas Chinese studies through the Internet. The information furnished by these two websites includes databases, directories of institutes and scholars in the field of Overseas Chinese studies, resource guidance (libraries, archives, museums, public and individual collections, etc.), curriculum syllabuses and references, selected research papers, links to relevant websites, and announcements of conferences, new publications, new videos, and exhibitions, etc.

The publicity created by the Shao Center's websites and other external activities has resulted in a greater demand of reference services from the Shao Center. The Shao Center provides its reference services mainly though electronic mail, facsimiles, telephone, and regular mail services as most of the requests for assistance has come from outside the campus. The number and scope of inquiries has considerably increased in recent years. Geographically the patrons are widely distributed, including individuals from the United States, Canada, Britain, Italy, France, Sweden, Australia, New Zealand, Russia, Japan, Korea, Malaysia, Singapore, The Philippines, Thailand, Indonesia, Hong Kong, Taiwan, and mainland China. The requests have varied from bibliographic guidance, reference assistance, statistics and historical information, academic consultation to thesis advice. There were also requests for help to contact overseas Chinese organizations, research institutes, or individual scholars in order to conduct surveys or other research projects. The Shao Center has done its best to respond to inquiries, and its services were well appreciated by its patrons. After receiving assistance in securing information on Overseas Chinese benevolent associations in Mexico, Vietnam, Madagascar, and New Zealand, Ms. Julie Hand, a senior East Asian Studies major at Middlebury College, Vermont, who was applying for a Watson Fellowship to spend one year in the above countries studying local Overseas Chinese cultures, wrote to the Shao Center:

"*Thank you so much for the plethora of information you have provided for me. I feel as if I have struck a goldmine. It is wonderful to know that there are such valuable resources in this field.*"

Ms. Julia Hand has successfully received a Watson Fellowship; she is now doing her field work abroad. Ms. Alessia Borin, a student at Ca'Foscari University in Venice, Italy, wrote to the Dean of Ohio University Libraries, expressing her gratitude for the assistance she received while she was writing her graduate thesis on Chinese Vietnamese refugees:

"*I made contact with Doctor Liren Zheng. His collaboration and his invaluable piece of advice have been a very very very precious gift for me. So, I feel flattered by the honor of writing you, to appreciate this Library's devotion to Overseas Chinese Studies.*"

The study of Overseas Chinese is a new and rapidly developing academic discipline. As a Chinese maxim stating "The burden is heavy and the way ahead is long (任重而道远)", it will be a great challenge for the Shao Center to become a key mover in Overseas Chinese studies in North America. In the next ten years, the Shao Center will stay the course set by its missions. It will continue to collect documents and archives, expand research and teaching, and promote international cooperation in order to push Overseas Chinese studies forward for the purpose of exalting the history of struggles and contributions of Overseas Chinese. This history is not only an important element in the history of those countries where Overseas Chinese resided, but is also the extension and glorification of the long lasting Chinese civilization.

(Published in *the Proceeding of the Second International Conference of Institutes & Libraries for Chinese Overseas Studies*. "*Transnational Networks: Challenges in Research and Documentation of the Chinese Overseas.*" March 13 – 15, Hong Kong, 2003: p. 17. Also published in *Chinese Overseas: Migration, Research and Documentation*. Edited by Tan Chee-Beng, Colin Storey, and Julia Zimmerman. Hong Kong: The Chinese University Press, 2007: pp. 275 – 295.)

美国国会图书馆为区域研究、文化保存、全球共识和知识创新建立世界级的亚洲馆藏

Building a World-Class Asian Collection in the Library of Congress for Area Studies, Culture Preservation, Global Understanding, and Knowledge Creation

The Beginning

The first acquisition of an Asian collection in the Library of Congress can be traced back to 1865 when the Smithsonian Institution transferred a collection of books on Southeast Asia and Pacific islands that had been gathered in Singapore by the Wilkes Exploring Expedition from 1838 to 1842. Four years later, in 1869, the Emperor of China (Tung-Chih 同治皇帝) presented to the Library of Congress 10 major Chinese works in 933 volumes. This was soon followed by the exchange of government publications with the Japanese government initiated in 1875. [1] From these early beginnings, the collection of Asian publications from all parts of Asia and in all major and some minor Asian languages have grown to more than 2.5 million items in a variety of formats. In addition to the holdings in the Asian Division, important Asian collections of legal materials, maps, music, motion pictures, prints, and photographs are housed and cared for by other divisions in the Library of Congress in collaboration with the Asian Division. These other units include the Law Library, the Geography and Map Division, the Prints and Photographs Division, the Motion Picture, Broadcasting and Recorded Sound Division, the Performing Arts Division, the Manuscript Division, etc. Other Asia-related publications not in Asian languages are also housed in the Main Reading Room, Microform Reading Room, Newspaper and Current Periodical Reading Room, Performing Arts Reading Room, Science Reading Room, and in some of the other area studies and special collections.

The name of Asian Division has gone through several changes since 1928 when the Division of Chinese Literature was established for the first time through the effort of Herbert Putnam, Librarian of Congress (1899–1939). Three years later, in 1931, the name was changed to the Division of Chinese and Japanese Literature. In 1932, it was renamed the Division of Orientalia. This was changed again to the Asiatic Division in 1942 and changed back to Orientalia Division in 1944. Finally, the name of Asian Division was formally adopted in 1978. [2]

The Vision and Mission

Guided by the mission statement of the Library of Congress—The Library's mission is to make its resources available and useful to the Congress and the American people and to sustain and preserve a universal collection of knowledge and creativity for future generations[3] 3—the vision and mission of the Asian Division are:

Vision of the Asian Division:

To establish the collections of the Asian Division as the premier research and scholarly resource of all formats and times on Asia and in Asian languages that is compatible with the

---

[1] *The Asian Division*. Washington, DC: The Library of Congress, 2002: pp. 1, 2, 4, 8.
[2] Chi Wang. *The Chinese Collection in the Library of Congress: A Brief Introduction*. Washington, DC: Chinese Section, Asian Division, Library of Congress, 2001: pp. 5–6.
[3] *The Mission and Strategic Priorities of the Library of Congress: FY 1997–2004*. Washington, DC: Library of Congress, 1997.

dynamics of knowledge and creativity of the 21st Century-frequently referred to as the "Asian Century".

Mission of the Asian Division:

The mission of the Asian Division is to make comprehensive collection resources and information services related to Asia available and useful to the Congress, American people, and the scholarly research community nationally and internationally. [①]

The Organization

Although the Library of Congress is the library of the American Congress, it has also served as the national library of the United States of America. For the discharge of its mission as the library of the Congress, there is a unit called Congressional Research Service. The chief responsibility of this unit is to provide the Congress with research and analysis on the full range of legislative policy issues. For carrying out the functions of the national library, there is another unit called Library Services, headed by an Associate Librarian. The position is now held by Dr. Deanna Marcum. There is another unit named Law Library, which holds the world's largest law collections covering U. S., foreign, and international law.

The Asian Division is one of the four area studies divisions (African and Middle Eastern Division, Asian Division, European Division, and Hispanic Division) reporting to the Assistant Librarian for Library Services and Director for Area Studies Collections. Dr. Carolyn Brown is in charge of this part of Library Services. She is also in charge of the Federal Research Division and the Office of Scholarly Programs.

Within the Asian Division, under the general leadership and management of the Chief, there is a plan for a Head of Collection Services and a Head of Scholarly Services. The professional staff members of the division, who are either area specialists or reference librarians, are divided into five area teams: China and Mongolia, Japan, Korea, Southeast Asia, and South Asia. A coordinator of each team is appointed from the team members by the Chief. The Chief is also assisted by an Administrative Officer, an Information Technology Specialist, and a Secretary. Hopefully, another position with the responsibility for outreach and special events can be added soon.

Division of Labor

When it was first founded, the Asian Division was largely responsible for the selection, acquisition, and maintenance of its rapidly growing Asian collections. In the subsequent years, the work of acquisitions has been undertaken by the African/Asian Acquisitions and Overseas Operations Division and the Serial Record Division of the Directorate for Acquisitions. The entire work of cataloging is done by the Regional and Cooperative Cataloging Division of the Directorate for Cataloging, while the work of binding, conservation, and microfilming is the responsibility of the Directorate for Preservation. The Automation Planning and Liaison Office take care of the needs of computer applications and system operations. The Asian Division works very closely with all these and other units in the Library of Congress to carry out its responsibilities and daily operations.

Building Comprehensive Asian Collections

Recognizing the importance of Asia in the 21st century the Library of Congress has devoted great effort to building a comprehensive collection of Asia. Today, after 138 years of painstaking work by generations of Asian area specialists, librarians, and scholars, a vast storehouse of

---

① ***The Strategic Plan of the Asian Division, 2003 to 2008.*** Washington, DC: Asian Division, the Library of Congress, 2003.

knowledge and culture about the diverse nations, languages, and peoples has been assembled. It is perhaps the best of such collections outside Asia. With the foresight of Dr. James Billington, the current Librarian of the Congress, an exquisite Asian Reading Room has been provided as a gateway to this world-class collection. Below are brief descriptions of the key collections by countries or geographic regions:

The Chinese and Mongolian Collection

The Chinese and Mongolian Collection consists of 900,000 volumes and physical pieces. Besides works in the Chinese language, it also includes several thousand volumes in Manchu, Mongol, Naxi (Moso), Tibetan, and other minority languages. The collection covers all subjects and is especially strong in the humanities and social sciences, among them, classical Chinese literature, archival materials of the Qing (清) dynasty (1644 – 1911) and Republican (民国) period (1911 – 1949), traditional Chinese medicine, local and regional histories (gazetteers), and contemporary publications of Mainland China, Hong Kong, and Taiwan.

The collection also contains some of the most valuable rare books from China, and Mongolia. The rare books from China cover Song (宋) dynasty (960 – 1279), Jin (金) dynasty (1115 – 1234), Yuan (元) dynasty (1271 – 1368), Ming (明) dynasty (1368 – 1644), and Qing (清) dynasty (1644 – 1911). It includes a Buddhist invocation sutra (一切如来, (Yi qie ru lai) printed in 975 A. D. that was recovered from the hollow bricks of the foundation of the Thunder Peak Pagoda (雷峰塔, Lei feng ta) when it collapsed in 1924, 41 surviving volumes of the Great Encyclopedia of the Ming Emperor Yongle (《永乐大典》, Yongle da dian), and the 1895 – 1898 printing of the Imperial Encyclopedia of China (《古今图书集成》, Gu jin tu shu ji cheng) in 5,044 volumes.

Examples of other unique collections are the 3,337 pictographic manuscripts from the Naxi 纳西 minority group in Yunnan province, the Gamble collection of a 19th-century American missionary printer that includes Christian publications in Chinese and translations of Western works, and the Arthur W. Hummel collection of rare Chinese maps.①

The Library of Congress is one of the world's leading centers for Tibetan publications with holdings that are representative of the entire body of Tibetan literature from the 8th century to the modern day. These include religious texts, history, biography, traditional medicine, astrology, iconography, musical notations, grammars, social sciences, and secular literature.

Since religion plays a major role in Tibetan society, the holdings of Tibetan Buddhist scriptures in the Asian Division are especially strong. The Tibetan Buddhist canon is contained in the Kanjur, in over a hundred volumes of sutras, and the Tanjur, most editions totaling some 225 volumes of commentaries. The Tibetan canonical texts are accurate translations of the original Buddhist texts, written in Sanskrit between 500 BC. and 900 AD. Among the individuals who were responsible for the early periods of development of the Tibetan collection are William Woodville Rockhill, the American diplomat and Tibetologist who travels in Mongolia and Tibet between 1888 and 1892 and again in the 1900s; Berthold Laufer, another leading Tibetologist in the late 1800s; and Joseph Rock, the colorful explorer, adventurer, and scientist who lived and traveled in China's rugged west for 27 years in the early 1900s.②

The Japanese Collection

After the initial arrangement for the exchange of government publications established in 1875 between the two governments, the Japanese collection began to grow in 1905 when a significant gift was received from Crosby Stuart Noyes, journalist and editor of the **Washington Evening Star.** The Noyes collection included 658 illustrated books produced from the mid-18-century to the late-

---

① **The Chinese Collection.** Washington, DC: Asian Division, the Library of Congress, n. d.
② **The Tibetan Collection.** Washington, DC: Asian Division, Library of Congress, April 2002.

19th century. In 1907, a systematic effort was undertaken by Kan'ichi Asakawa of Yale University to purchase Japanese books for the Library of Congress. Because of his effort, some 9,072 volumes on the subjects of Japanese history, literature, Buddhism, Shinto, geography, music, and the arts were added. In 1930, the Library appointed Dr. Shiho Sakanishi as the Chief Assistant of the Japanese Section to further develop the collection. During her tenure from 1930 to 1941, the collection tripled in size. Today, the Japanese collection has grown to 1.1 million volumes of monographs and serials as well as extensive microfilm and microfiche holdings-the largest collection in the Asian Division-through purchase, gift, exchange, and other avenues of acquisition.

Among the wealth of rare items are approximately 5,000 titles of publications and manuscript copies of works produced before the end of the Tokugawa Shogunate in 1868 and the beginning of the Meiji period (1868 – 1912). Included are the **dharani** (百万搭陀罗尼) prayer charms, which date to 770 A. D. and are among the world's earliest surviving printed material. Also noteworthy are a complete edition of the Japanese literary masterpiece Genji monogatari (《源氏物语》, The Tale of Genji) published in Kyoto in 1654 and the **Yoshitsune azuma kudari monogatari** printed on movable type between 1624 and 1643. A complete catalogue of the rare books in the Library of Congress was published in 2003 by Yagi Shoten in Tokyo.① At the end of World War II, a large number of historical documents such as the former Japanese Imperial Army and Navy, the South Manchuria Railway Company, and the East Asian Research Institute were given to the Library by the Washington Document Center. Much of the materials from the latter two are pre-World War II studies on such areas as Korea, Taiwan, Mainland China, Mongolia, and the Pacific Islands. The Library also has a microfilm copy of the archives of the Japanese Foreign Ministry from 1868 to 1945 and pre-1945 records of the Police Bureau of the Ministry of Home Affairs-some of these are censored wartime publications. ②

Another important collection is the "Inoh Maps" —the first modern maps of Japan created originally by Tadataka Inoh between 1800 and 1821. Copies of 207 of the Inoh's original 214 sheets large-scale set (1∶36,000) that cover the Japanese archipelago from Hokkaido to Kyushu were discovered in the map collection of the Library of Congress in the spring of 2001 and have caused great excitement in Japan. In order to make these maps available for exhibition and for online access, all of them have been digitized and sent to the Japan Map Center. A selection of the actual-size reproductions of these maps is now on exhibition at the Tokyo National Museum from October 31 to December 14, 2003. Some of the original maps will also be loaned and exhibited in Kobe, Sendai, Atami, and Nagoya in 2004.

The Korean Collection

The Korean collection began in the 1920s with the generous gift of Korean books from Dr. James S. Gale, a Canadian missionary who spent 40 years in Korea from 1888 to 1928. Dr. Gale also helped the Library to acquire a number of Korean classics, including rare books from the estate of the Korean scholar Kim To-hui. Systematic development of the Korean collection was started in the early 1950s during the period of the Korean War. Today, the Korean collection in the Library totals 210,000 volumes in the Korean language, as well as 20,000 Japanese language books and 8,000 English language books on Korea. Coverage of North Korea is also strong, with some 10,000 items.

There are 480 titles of Korean rare books, in 3,000 volumes. They were all written in Chinese characters and printed on mulberry paper. Although China was the first county to use movable type made of clay, Korea was the first one to use movable metal type for printing. Several good examples of this type of printing are in the collection. These are the collected writings of the

---

① *Beikoku Gikai Toshokan zo Nihon Kotenseki Mokuroku* (Catalog of Japanese Rare Books in the Library of Congress). Tokyo: Yagi Shoten, 2003.
② *The Japanese Collection*. Washington, DC: Asian Division, the Library of Congress, n. d.

renowned 16th-century Confucian scholar and statesman Yi I printed in 1744 and the 1834 reprint of the works of the "father of Korean literature", Ch'oe Ch'i-won (857 – 915). Other rare books printed by woodblock include the **History of the Koryo Dynasty** (高丽史), printed in 1590, and the **Law Code of the Yi Dynasty** (《经国大典》), printed in 1630. ①

The Southeast Asian Collection

As was mentioned in the beginning of this paper, the earliest acquisition of the Southeast Asian collection in the Library of Congress began in 1865, which predates the beginning of all other Asian collections. The collection was acquired in Singapore in 1842 by the U. S. Naval Exploring Expedition led by Lt. Charles Wilkes. Wilkes and the Expedition s philologist, Horatio Hale, collected Malay manuscripts and early printed books with the assistance of Alfred North, an American missionary in Singapore. The collection went first to the Smithsonian Institutions which later transferred the collection to the Library of Congress in 1865. Included in this earliest acquisition are a unique collection of manuscripts written in the Buginese script of South Sulawesi; an account of the 19th-century Malay world written in Jawi, the **Hikayat Abdullah** (The Story of Abdullah); and an 1840 Mission Press edition of the **Sejarah Melayu** (Malay Annals), an important Malay history written in 1612, also in Jawi, the Malay language in Arabic script.

The Southeast Asian collection contains many palm leaf manuscript copies of the **Tipitaka**, the basic text of Theravada Buddhism which is the majority religion of Cambodia, Laos, Myanmar (Burma), and Thailand. In 1905, a special Thai **Tipitaka** was presented to the Library of Congress by King Chulalongkorn (Rama V) of Thailand. In 1949, an especially fine collection of Burmese manuscripts in the Pali language as well as a **Tipitaka** in Pali using Burmese script was presented to the Library of Congress as a part of a large Burmese donation. The donation also included an important Burmese history, **The Glass Palace Chronicle**, written by a group of scholars in 1829.

The Asian Division also holds rare materials from the Philippines and Vietnam. Of special note is a set of inscribed bamboo tubes, with lettering in the old Indic script similar to the ancient scripts used in neighboring Indonesia. The collection of 55 bamboos in prose and 22 in verse provides a fascinating glimpse into Mangyan (Hampangan) and Tagbanua society. Several examples of Vietnamese dynastic histories are also represented, including texts printed from early woodblocks at the former imperial palace at Hue.

In 1938, the Library of Congress launched the Indic Project in order to improve its collections from Southeast and South Asia, particularly publications in local languages. Following World War II, as U. S. interest in the region increased, the collection grew dramatically and today consists of holdings from Brunei, Cambodia, Indonesia, Laos, Malaysia, Myanmar, the Philippines, Singapore, Thailand, Vietnam, and many of the South Pacific island nations such as Papua New Guinea, etc. The establishment of the Library's overseas offices in New Delhi, India, in 1962, in Jakarta, Indonesia, in 1963, and in Islamabad, Pakistan, in 1965 has provided a continuous flow of books, newspapers, and periodicals from the region in a variety of formats. ②

The South Asian Collection

The foundation for the South Asian collection was laid in 1904 when a collection of over 4,000 books and pamphlets from the German Indologist, Dr. Albrecht Weber, was purchased. Included were texts in Sanskrit of India's sacred Hindu works—the **Vedas**, **Brahmanas**, and **Upanisads**—as well as the stories of the Puranas and the great epics in the **Mahabharata** and the Ramayana. In addition, there are a number of Weber's notebooks with his handwritten transcriptions of rare Indian texts for his pioneering critical editions.

---

① ***The Korean Collection***. Washington, DC: Asian Division, the Library of Congress, n. d.
② ***The Southeast Asian Collection***. Washington, DC: Asian Division, Library of Congress, April 2002.

In 1938, the Library received a grant from the Carnegie Corporation to develop the South Asian collection systematically, and it initiated the Indic Project— "Project F-Development of Indic Studies". During the 1950s the collection continued to expand and growth accelerated even further with the opening of the Library's New Delhi Overseas Office in 1962. Under the Public Law (PL) 480 program, the New Delhi office used rupees from Indian purchases of U. S. agricultural products to buy books and other materials from India and other countries of South Asia. An overseas office in Karachi, Pakistan, was opened in 1965 to oversee the acquisition of publications from Pakistan and neighboring areas. Later, the office was moved to the capital city, Islamabad.

Today, the South Asian collection holds materials in over 100 modern languages used in India, Pakistan, Bangladesh, Sri Lanka, and Nepal. The majority of the publications are in Hindi (20 percent), Bengali (15 percent), Urdu (13 percent), and Tamil (11 percent). Other languages represented in large numbers include Marathi, Telugu, Malayalam, Gujarati, and Kannada.

An example among the many rare books and manuscripts in the South Asian collection is a 1452 manuscript of the Jaina **Kalpasutra** from Gujarat in western India. This illustrated text tells the story of Mahavira, the founder of the Jaina religion. The "Crosby Khotan fragments" are also among the more unusual rare items. During a 1903 journey to Central Asia, Oscar Terry Crosby, an American who later became Assistant Secretary of the Treasury, purchased these manuscripts in Sanskrit at the Taklamakan oasis town of Khotan. [1]

Between 1990 and 2000, a very important project undertaken by the New Delhi Overseas Office was the Microfilming of Indian Publications Project (MIPP). This project was a joint collaboration between the Government of India and the Library Congress, aimed at preserving and making accessible out-of-print works listed in the **National Bibliography of Indian Literature: 1901 – 1953.** Some 22,686 titles in 15 languages were microfilmed from 67 repository libraries in India and 3 libraries outside India (the Library of Congress, University of Chicago, and British Library). These titles were selected by Indian scholars as being central to the understanding of India. [2]

Overseas Offices

The accelerated growth of the library collections from South and Southeast Asia since the 1960s should be credited to the efforts of the overseas offices in New Delhi, Jakarta, and Islamabad. In addition to these three, the African/Asian Acquisitions and Overseas Operations Division of the Library of Congress also operate overseas offices in Cairo, Nairobi, and Rio de Janeiro.

One of the unique features of the three Asian overseas offices is the offering of their service to other libraries who want to acquire publications from countries and regions covered by these offices. For example, the 44 academic and research libraries, mostly from North America, that participated in the South Asia Cooperative Acquisitions Program (SACAP) receive publications of their choice from the New Delhi office and its many sub-offices. Being the largest and the oldest of the six overseas offices, the New Delhi office covers India, Bangladesh, Bhutan, the Maldives, Nepal, and Sri Lanka—as well as Burma, Mongolia, and the Mongolian and Tibetan Autonomous Regions of China. The New Delhi office performs a wide range of services to SACAP libraries, including acquisitions, cataloging, bibliographic control, and preservation of publications acquired in some 65 languages and 25 different scripts. Another service of the New Delhi office is the maintenance of an extensive program for official and informal exchanges of publications with key institutions and libraries in South Asia. [3]

---

[1] *The South Asian Collection.* Washington, DC: Asian Division, Library of Congress, April 2002.
[2] *The Library of Congress in South Asia, 1960 –2002. Celebrating 40 Years of Bibliographic and Cultural Exchanges.* New Delhi: Library of Congress Office, n. d. p. 16.
[3] *The Library of Congress in South Asia, 1960 –2002. Celebrating 40 Years of Bibliographic and Cultural Exchanges.* New Delhi: Library of Congress Office, n. d.

Scholarly services

The Asian Division and its Asian Reading Room, located in the Thomas Jefferson Building, across the street from the U. S. Capitol, is the primary public access point for researchers seeking to use the most comprehensive Asian Collection. In order to provide special guidance and service to researchers and scholars from near and far, a team of well trained and highly qualified reference librarians and area studies specialists who have extensive knowledge of the various collections are ready to be of assistance.

Besides on-site visits by scholars, which are essential to fully explore the wealth of the treasured Asian collection, readers are encouraged to search the Library of Congress online public access catalog for library holdings (http://catalog.loc.gov). In order to save their valuable time, researchers may telephone or email ahead of their visits so that needed materials may be available for use upon arrival. Researchers in remote locations may also request items through interlibrary loan from their nearby libraries. Some rare materials may only be available for on-site use.

There is another advantage for on-site visits and that is the accessibility to a variety of online electronic databases. Because of the licensing agreement and other restrictions imposed by publishers these databases can only be searched and used onsite. In the digital age, the Asian Division is moving ahead in supplementing its printed collections by a growing body of electronic resources from e-books, e-journals, e-newspapers, to a wide range of e-materials, both digitized from printed version or born digital.

As a part of the Library's effort to provide more and more specialized digital resources online, such as the **American Memory** (http://memory.loc.gov/), the Global Gateway (http://international.loc.gov/intldl/intldlhome.html), etc., the Library's portals now serve as a gateway to selected web resources on a variety of subjects and world areas (http://www.loc.gov/rr/international/portals.html). The portals of the Asian Division (http://www.loc.gov/rr/asian/area_AD.html) are increasingly a useful source on all the Asian countries and regions. We invite you to visit our website and use the portals. You will do us a great favor by recommending more high quality and relevant websites so that we can continue to add and update our Asian portals.

Being a leader in the development of **QuestionPoint**—a worldwide online reference service operating on a 24-hours-a-day and 7-days-a-week schedule—now operated by the OCLC Online Computer Library Center, library users anywhere can now send their reference questions through OCLC online global network to the Library of Congress for reply by our reference librarians and area studies specialists (http://www.oclc.org/questionpoint). Library users may also use the service of Asking a Librarians (http://www.loc.gov/rr/askalib-asian.html) to get reference assistance from librarians in the Asian Division.

Kluge fellowships and other funding opportunities

Through the generous gift of $60 million from Mr. John W. Kluge, the John W. Kluge Center was established in 2000 in the Jefferson Building with funding from the Kluge endowment. The endowment also funds a number of Kluge Chair holders, distinguished visiting scholars, and Kluge post-doctoral fellows each year. A number of other fellowship opportunities funded by other private foundation gifts is also administered by the Kluge Center and the Office of Scholarly Programs. Recipients of Kluge fellowships may spend from six to twelve months at the Center with a monthly stipend which is sufficient to cover transportation and living expenses in the Washington, D C., area. Selected researchers and scholars are expected to use the extensive collections and resources of the Library of Congress for their research.

The Kluge Center especially encourages humanistic and social science research that makes use of the Library's large and varied collections. Interdisciplinary, cross-cultural, or multi-lingual research is particularly welcome. For information about the Kluge Center and its fellowships, please visit the website: http://www.loc.gov/Kluge or send email to: scholarly@loc.gov.

International cooperation

In order to further develop the Asian collections two important international roles of the Asian Division have been identified. They are:

1. Expand international relations for Asian librarianship, scholarship, and network.
2. Develop collaborative projects with organizations and institutions at the national and international levels.

For the first international role, the Asian Division endeavors to develop regular contacts with libraries and librarians in Asian countries in a joint effort to advance librarianship and scholarship. Being the world's largest library, the Library of Congress has been a frequent place of visit by many Asian librarians and information professionals. We want to extend our warmest welcome to all our visitors and hope that through such visits a mutually beneficial relationship can be established. Furthermore, it is our sincere hope that external funding may be found to support an internship program for Asian librarians who wish to pursue training and internship at the Asian Division.

For the second international role, we would like to develop collaborative projects with national libraries and international organizations for the purpose of sharing our resources to facilitate mutual understanding, international education, and scholarly research. One such project is the **Global Gateway Project** undertaken by the Library of Congress in collaboration with other national libraries in a joint effort to convert unique items from the collections of each into digital form and to share these at no cost over the Internet with the people of both countries and the world. Each of the projects is built around a broad theme that focuses on the culture and history of the respective partner country and in particular its interactions with the United States. The URL for **Global Gateway** is http://international.loc.gov. Currently, the Asian Division and the International Research Center for Japanese Studies (Nichibunken) are engaged in discussion for a joint digitization project for collections relating to Japan on the eve of its opening to the Western world and the subsequent development of U.S.-Japan relations. The project will include digitizing some of the rare Japanese collections in the Library of Congress.

Building a World-Class Asian Collection in the Library of Congress

Hwa-Wei Lee
Chief, Asian Division, Library of Congress, USA
hlee@loc.gov

November 2003 — Hwa-Wei Lee — 1

The Beginning

- The first acquisition of an Asian collection in the Library of Congress can be traced back to **1865** when the Smithsonian Institution transferred a collection of books on Southeast Asia and Pacific islands that had been gathered in Singapore by the Wilkes Exploring Expedition from 1838 to 1842.

November 2003 — Hwa-Wei Lee — 2

The Beginning

- Four years later, in **1869**, the Emperor of China (Tung-Chih 同治皇帝) presented to the Library of Congress 10 major Chinese works in 933 volumes.
- This was soon followed by the exchange of government publications with the Japanese government initiated in **1875**

November 2003 — Hwa-Wei Lee — 3

The Size of Asian Collection

- Collections in Asian languages – 2.5 million volumes.
  - Japanese: 1,100,000
  - Chinese: 900,000
  - Korean: 210,000
  - Southern Asian: 350,000
- Covering all Asian countries and major languages.
- All subjects from ancient to modern.

November 2003 — Hwa-Wei Lee — 4

Asian Collections in Other Formats

- Legal materials, maps, music, motion pictures, prints, and photographs are housed and cared for by other divisions in the Library of Congress in collaboration with the Asian Division:
  - the Law Library,
  - the Geography and Map Division,
  - the Prints and Photographs Division,
  - the Motion Picture, Broadcasting and Recorded Sound Division,
  - the Performing Arts Division,
  - the Manuscript Division, etc.

Collections not in Asian Languages

- Other Asia-related publications not in Asian languages are also housed in:
  - the Main Reading Room,
  - the Microform Reading Room,
  - The Newspaper and Current Periodical Reading Room,
  - The Performing Arts Reading Room,
  - the Science Reading Room, and
  - in some of the other area studies and special collections.

The Asian Reading Room

- The Asian Reading Room, located in the historical Thomas Jefferson Building, is the focal point where services for materials of and about Asia will be provided.
- Readers and researchers can also go to any other reading rooms for service of non-Asian language materials or materials in non-book formats.

Photo of the Jefferson Building

Photo of the Main Reading Room

Photo of the Asian Reading Room

Name Changes of the Asian Division

- 1928 - the Division of Chinese Literature was established for the first time.
- 1931 - the name was changed to the Division of Chinese and Japanese Literature.
- 1932 - it was renamed the Orientalia Division.
- 1942 - this was changed to the Asiatic Division.
- 1944 – it was changed back to Orientalia Division.
- 1978 - the name of Asian Division was formally adopted.

Mission of the Library of Congress

- *The Library's mission is to make its resources available and useful to the Congress and the American people and to sustain and preserve a universal collection of knowledge and creativity for future generations.*

Vision of the Asian Division

- *To establish the collections of the Asian Division as the premier research and scholarly resource of all formats and times on Asia and in Asian languages that is compatible with the dynamics of knowledge and creativity of the 21st Century – frequently referred to as the "Asian Century."*

Mission of the Asian Division

- *The mission of the Asian Division is to make comprehensive collection resources and information services related to Asia available and useful to the Congress, American people, and the scholarly research community nationally and internationally.*

The Organization

- Although the Library of Congress is the library of the American Congress, it has also served as the national library of the United States of America.
  - Congressional Research Service - to provide the Congress with research and analysis on the full range of legislative policy issues.
  - Library Services - to carry out the functions of the national library. (Headed by Dr. Deanna Marcum, Associate Librarian.)
  - Law Library - the world's largest law collections covering U.S., foreign, and international law.

Area Studies Collections

- Asian Division is one of four area studies divisions:
  - African and Middle Eastern Division
  - Asian Division
  - European Division
  - Hispanic Division
- Dr. Carolyn Brown is the Director for Area Studies Collections.
- She is also in charge of
  - Federal Research Division
  - Office of Scholarly Programs.

The Asian Division

- The planned reorganization is underway.
- It is a combination of functional and matrix models.

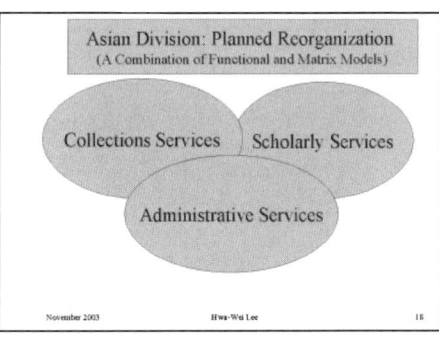

Area Teams

- China (and Mongolia)
- Japan
- Korea (North and South)
- Southeast Asia
- South Asia

Notes:
1. Each staff is encouraged to join more than one team.
2. A coordinator for each team may be elected, appointed, or rotated.
3. Team coordinator's term is normally for one year and is renewable.

Overall Goals for the Restructure

- A flattened structure.
- A team-based and task-oriented organization.
- Highly efficient, flexible, and responsive.
- Maximum interaction and communication across areas and tasks.

Division of Labor

- The Asian Division works closely with all other units in the Library to carry out its responsibilities and daily operations.
    - The African/Asian Acquisitions and Overseas Operations Division and the Serial Record Division of the Directorate for Acquisitions.
    - The Regional and Cooperative Cataloging Division of the Directorate for Cataloging.
    - The Directorate for Preservation.
    - The Automation Planning and Liaison Office.

Building Comprehensive Asian Collections

- Recognizing the importance of Asia in the 21st century, the Library of Congress has devoted great effort to building a comprehensive collection of Asia.
    - The Chinese and Mongolian Collection.
    - The Japanese Collection.
    - The Korean Collection.
    - The Southeast Asian Collection.
    - The South Asian Collection.

The Chinese & Mongolian Collection

- Major languages covered:
    - Chinese
    - Manchu
    - Mongol
    - Naxi
    - Tibetan
    - Others
- Periods:
    - Song Dynasty (960-1279)
    - Jin Dynasty (1115-1234)
    - Yuan Dynasty (1271-1368)
    - Ming Dynasty (1368-1644)
    - Qing Dynasty (1644-1911)
    - Republican Period (1911-1949) & Taiwan (1949-)
    - PRC Period (1949-)

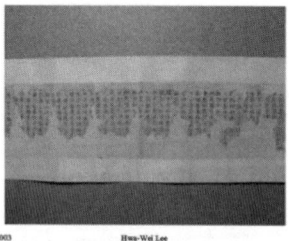

Selected Samples of the Treasured Chinese Collection
A Buddhist Sutra from the Thunder Peak Pagoda
975 AD

Selected Samples of the Treasured Chinese Collection
Discovered from the Thunder Peak Pagoda in 1924

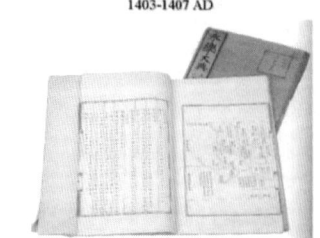

Selected Samples of the Treasured Chinese Collection
The Great Encyclopedia of the Emperor Yongle
1403-1407 AD

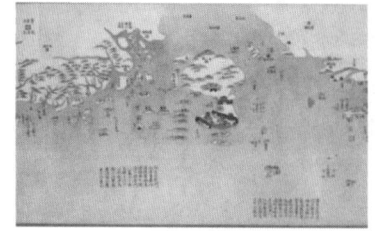

Selected Samples of the Treasured Chinese Collection
An 18th century Chinese Scroll Map

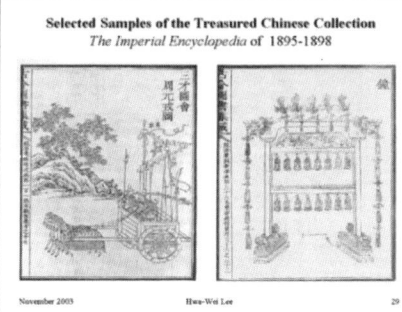
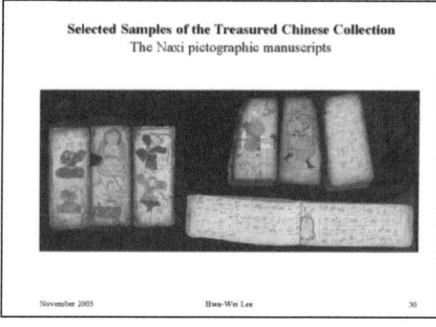
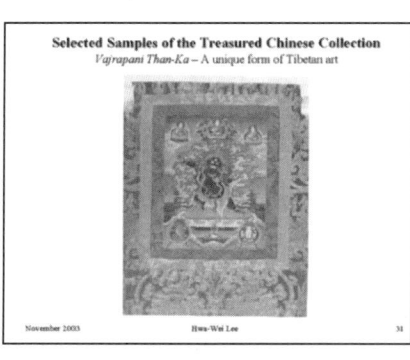

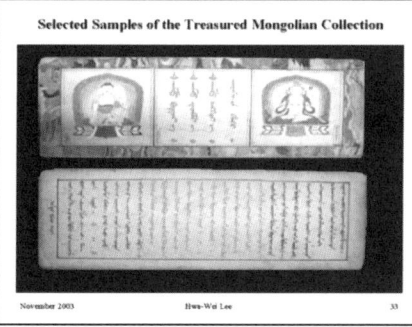

The Japanese Collection

- Begun in 1875 with the exchange of government publications between the two countries.
- In 1905, a significant gift of 658 illustrated books, mostly produced from the mid-18th century to the late-19th century, was received from Crosby Stuart Noyes.
- Since 1907, a systematic effort has been made to expand the Japanese collection.
- Some 5000 titles are considered rare materials.

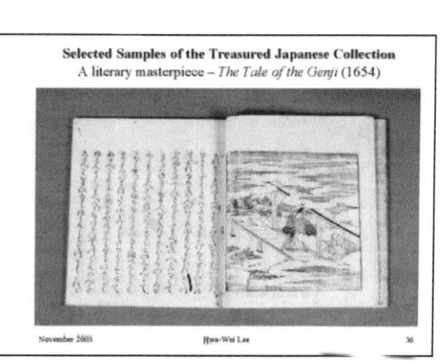

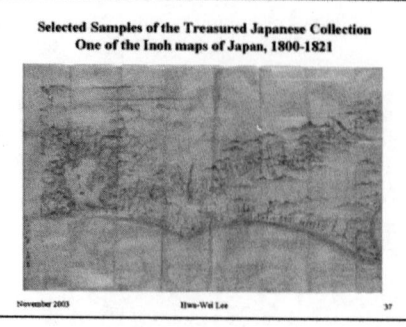
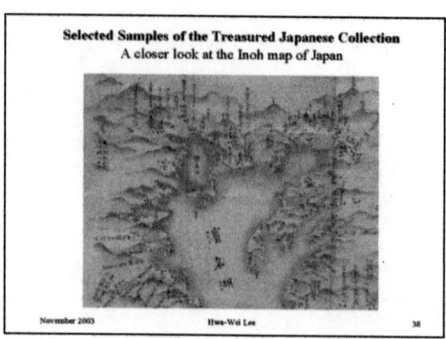

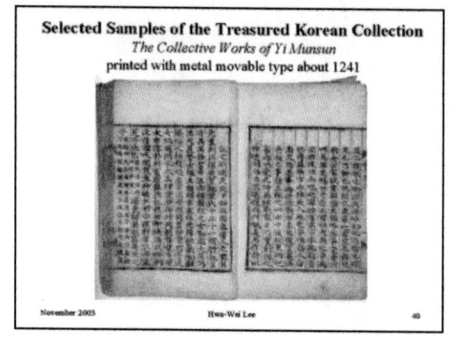
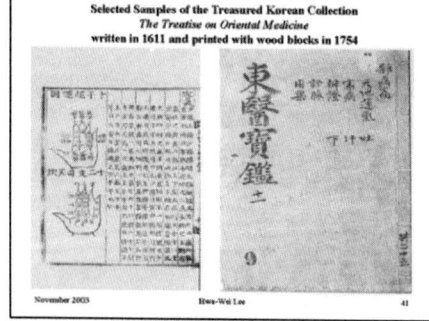
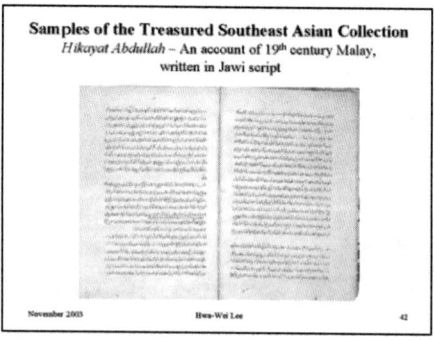

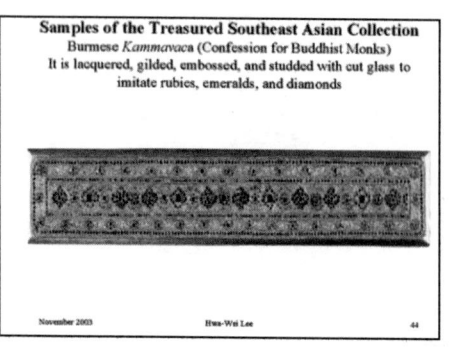

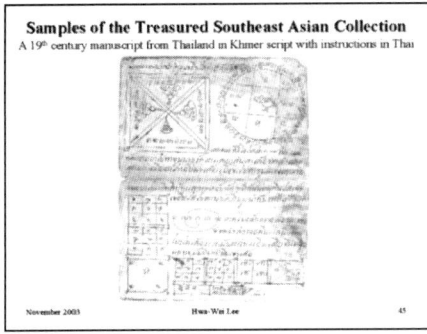
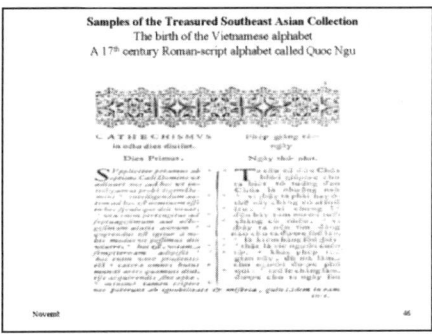
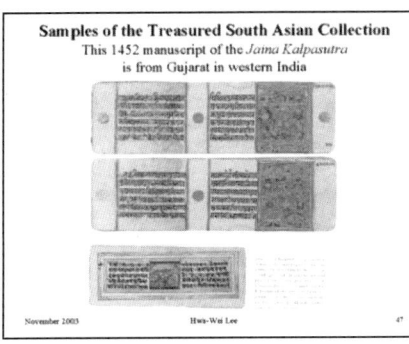
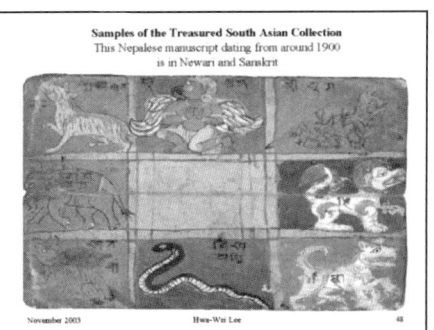

Overseas Offices

- The accelerated growth of the library collections from South and Southeast Asia since the 1960s should be credited to the efforts of the overseas offices in New Delhi, Jakarta, and Islamabad.
- In addition to these three, the LC's African/Asian Acquisitions and Overseas Operations Division also operates overseas offices in Cairo, Nairobi, and Rio de Janeiro.

Cooperative Acquisitions Programs

- One of the unique features of these overseas offices is the offering of their service to other libraries who want to acquire publications from countries and regions covered by these offices.
- For example, the 44 academic and research libraries, mostly from North America, that participated in the South Asia Cooperative Acquisitions Program (SACAP) receive publications of their choice from the New Delhi office and its many sub-offices.

The New Delhi Office

- Being the largest and the oldest of the six overseas offices, the New Delhi office covers India, Bangladesh, Bhutan, the Maldives, Nepal, and Sri Lanka – as well as Burma, Mongolia, and the Mongolian and Tibetan Autonomous Regions of China.
- The New Delhi office performs a wide range of services to SACAP libraries, including acquisitions, cataloging, bibliographic control, and preservation of publications acquired in some 65 languages and 25 different scripts.

Scholarly Services

- Asian Reading Room, located in the Thomas Jefferson Building, is the primary public access point for researchers seeking to use the most comprehensive Asian Collection.
- In the digital age, the Asian Division is moving ahead in supplementing its printed collections by a growing body of electronic resources from e-books, e-journals, e-newspapers, to a wide range of e-materials, both digitized from printed version or born digital.

Online Services Available

- The Library's online public access catalog. http://catalog.loc.gov
- Interlibrary loan through local libraries.
- *American Memory*. http://memory.loc.gov/
- *Global Gateway*. http://international.loc.gov/intldl/intldlhome.html
- The portals of the Asian Division http://www.loc.gov/rr/asian/area_AD.html
- *Asking a Librarian*. http://www.loc.gov/rr/askalib/ask-asian.html

The Portals of the Asian Division

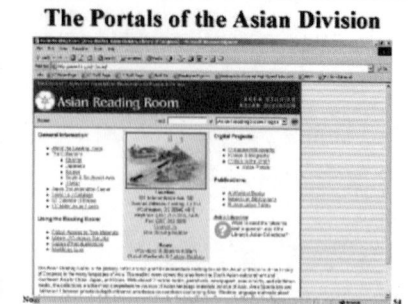

Asking a Librarian

Research Fellowships

- The Library encourages humanistic and social science research that makes use of the Library's large and varied collections.
- A variety of fellowship opportunities are available each year to qualified researchers, including Kluge Chair holders, distinguished visiting scholars, and Kluge post-doctoral fellows.
- For information about the Kluge Center and its fellowships, please visit the website: http://www.loc.gov/Kluge

International Cooperation

- Two important international roles of the Asian Division:
  - Expand international relations for Asian librarianship, scholarship, and network.
  - Develop collaborative projects with organizations and institutions at the national and international levels.

Expand International Relations

- Develop regular contacts with libraries and librarians in Asian countries in a joint effort to advance librarianship and scholarship.
- Find external funding to support an internship program for Asian librarians who wish to pursue training and internship at the Asian Division.

Develop Collaborative Projects

- Develop collaborative projects with national libraries and international organizations for the purpose of sharing our resources to facilitate mutual understanding, international education, and scholarly research.
- One such project is the *Global Gateway Project* undertaken by the Library of Congress in collaboration with other national libraries.

Questions and Discussion

Thank You

(Published in the *Proceedings of the Symposium*: "The New Horizon of Library Services Toward the Better Understanding of Asia," November 19, 2003. Kyoto, Japan: National Diet Library, Kansai-kan, 2004: p. 179.)

共享美国国会图书馆的亚洲文献宝库

Sharing the Treasures of the Asian Collection in the Library of Congress

The Beginning

The first acquisition of an Asian collection in the Library of Congress can be traced back to 1865 when the Smithsonian Institution transferred a collection of books on Southeast Asia and Pacific islands that had been gathered in Singapore by the Wilkes Exploring Expedition from 1838 to 1842. Four years later, in 1869, the Emperor of China (Tung-Chih 同治皇帝) presented to the Library of Congress 10 major Chinese works in 933 volumes. This was soon followed by the exchange of government publications with the Japanese government initiated in 1875. From these early beginnings, the collection of Asian publications from all parts of Asia and in all major and some minor Asian languages has grown to more than 2.5 millions items in a variety of formats. In addition to the holdings in the Asian Division, important Asian collections of legal materials, maps, music, motion pictures, prints, and photographs are housed and cared for by other divisions in the Library of Congress in collaboration with the Asian Division. These other units include the Law Library, the Geography and Map Division, the Prints and Photographs Division, the Motion Picture, Broadcasting and Recorded Sound Division, the Performing Arts Division, the Manuscript Division, etc. Other Asia-related publications not in Asian languages are also housed in the Main Reading Room, Microform Reading Room, Newspaper and Current Periodical Reading Room, Performing Arts Reading Room, Science Reading Room, and in some of the other area studies and special collections.

The name of Asian Division has gone through several changes since 1928 when the Division of Chinese Literature was established for the first time through the effort of Herbert Putnam, Librarian of Congress (1899—1939). Three years later, in 1931, the name was changed to the Division of Chinese and Japanese Literature. In 1932, it was renamed the Division of Orientalia. This was changed again to the Asiatic Division in 1942 and changed back to Orientalia Division in 1944. Finally, the name of Asian Division was formally adopted in 1978.

1. The Vision and Mission

Guided by the mission statement of the Library of Congress —*The Library's mission is to make its resources available and useful to the Congress and the American people and to sustain and preserve a universal collection of knowledge and creativity for future generations*—the vision and mission of the Asian Division are:

Vision of the Asian Division:
To establish the collections of the Asian Division as the premier research and scholarly resource of all formats and times on Asia and in Asian languages that is compatible with the dynamics of knowledge and creativity of the 21st Century—frequently referred to as the "Asian Century".

Mission of the Asian Division:
The mission of the Asian Division is to make comprehensive collection resources and information services related to Asia available and useful to the Congress, American people, and the scholarly research community nationally and internationally.

2. The Organization

Although the Library of Congress is the library of the American Congress, it has also served as the national library of the United States of America. For the discharge of its mission as the library of the Congress, there is a unit called Congressional Research Service. The chief responsibility of this unit is to provide the Congress with research and analysis on the full range of legislative policy issues. For carrying out the functions of the national library, there is another unit called Library Services, headed by an Associate Librarian. The position is now held by Dr. Deanna Marcum. There is another unit named Law Library, which holds the world's largest law collections covering U. S. , foreign, and international law.

The Asian Division is one of the four area studies divisions (African and Middle Eastern Division, Asian Division, European Division, and Hispanic Division) reporting to the Director for Collections and Services. Dr. Carolyn Brown is in charge of this part of Library Services.

Within the Asian Division, under the general leadership and management of the Chief, there are two section heads: the Head of Collection Services and the Head of Scholarly Services. The professional staff members of the division, who are either area specialists or reference librarians, are divided into five area teams: China and Mongolia, Japan, Korea, Southeast Asia, and South Asia. A coordinator of each area team is appointed from the team members by the Chief. The Chief is also assisted by an Administrative Officer, an Information Technology Specialist, a special assistant, and a Secretary.

3. Division of Labor

When it was first founded, the Asian Division was largely responsible for the selection, acquisition, and maintenance of its rapidly growing Asian collections. In the subsequent years, the work of acquisitions has been undertaken by the African/Asian Acquisitions and Overseas Operations Division, the Serial Record Division, and the Regional and Cooperative Cataloging Division of the Directorate for Acquisitions and Bibliographic Control. The work of binding, conservation, and microfilming is the responsibility of the Directorate for Preservation. The Automation Planning and Liaison Office take care of the needs of computer applications and system operations. The Asian Division works very closely with all these and other units in the Library of Congress to carry out its responsibilities and daily operations.

4. Building Comprehensive Asian Collections

Recognizing the importance of Asia in the 21st century the Library of Congress has devoted great effort to building a comprehensive collection of Asia. Today, after 138 years of painstaking work by generations of Asian area specialists, librarians, and scholars, a vast storehouse of knowledge and culture about the diverse nations, languages, and peoples has been assembled. It is perhaps the best of such collections outside Asia. With the foresight of Dr. James Billington, the current Librarian of the Congress, an exquisite Asian Reading Room has been provided as a gateway to this world-class collection. Below are brief descriptions of the key collections by countries or geographic regions :

4.1 The Chinese and Mongolian Collection

The Chinese and Mongolian Collection consists of 900, 000 volumes and physical pieces. Besides works in the Chinese language, it also includes several thousand volumes in Manchu, Mongol, Naxi (Moso), Tibetan, Uyghur, and other minority languages. The collection covers all subjects and is especially strong in the humanities and social sciences, among them, classical Chinese literature, archival materials of the Qing (清) dynasty (1644 – 1911) and Republican (民国) period (1911 – 1949), traditional Chinese medicine, local and regional histories (gazetteers), and contemporary publications of Mainland China and Taiwan.

The collection also contains some of the most valuable rare books from China, Mongolia, and Tibet. The rare books from China cover Song (宋) dynasty (960 – 1279), Jin (金) dynasty (1115 – 1234), Yuan (元) dynasty (1271 – 1368), Ming (明) dynasty (1368 – 1644), and Qing (清) dynasty (1644 – 1911). It includes a Buddhist invocation sutra (一切如来, Yi qie ru lai) printed in 975 A. D. that was recovered from the hollow bricks of the foundation of the

Thunder Peak Pagoda (雷峰塔, Lei feng ta) when it collapsed in 1924, 41 of the 400 surviving volumes of the 1560 copy of **the Great Encyclopedia of the Ming Emperor Yongle** (《永乐大典》, Yongle da dian), and the 1895 - 1898 printing of **the Imperial Encyclopedia of China** (《古今图书集成》, Gu jin tu shu ji cheng) in 5044 volumes.

Examples of other unique collections are the 3344 pictographic manuscripts from the Naxi (纳西) minority group in Yunnan province, the Gamble collection of a 19th-century American missionary printer that includes Christian publications in Chinese and translations of Western works, and the Arthur W. Hummel collection of rare Chinese maps.

The Library of Congress is one of the world's leading centers for Tibetan publications with holdings that are representative of the entire body of Tibetan literature from the 8th century to the modern day. These include religious texts, history, biography, traditional medicine, astrology, iconography, musical notations grammars, social sciences, and secular literature.

Since religion plays a major role in Tibetan society, the holdings of Tibetan Buddhist scriptures in Asian Division are especially strong. The Tibetan Buddhist canon is contained in the Kanjur, in over a hundred volumes of sutras, and the Tanjur, most editions totaling some 225 volumes of commentaries. The Tibetan canonical texts are accurate translations of the original Buddhist texts, written in Sanskrit between 500 BC. and 900 AD. Among the individuals who were responsible for the early periods of development of the Tibetan collection are William Woodville Rockhill, the American diplomat and Tibetologist who travels Mongolia and Tibet between 1888 and 1892 and again in the 1990s; Berthold Laufer, another leading Tibetologist in the late 1800s; and Joseph Rock, the colorful explorer, adventurer, and scientist who lived and traveled in China's rugged west for 27 years in the early 1900s.

4.2 The Japanese Collection

After the initial arrangement for the exchange of government publications established in 1875 between the two governments, the Japanese collection began to grow in 1905 when a significant gift was received from Crosby Stuart Noyes, journalist and editor of the Washington Evening Star. The Noyes collection included 658 illustrated books produced from the mid-18th century to the late-19th century. In 1907, a systematic effort was undertaken by Kan'ichi Asakawa of Yale University to purchase Japanese books for the Library of Congress. Because of his effort, some 9072 volumes on the subjects of Japanese history, literature, Buddhism, Shinto geography, music, and the arts were added. In 1930, the Library appointed Dr. Shiho Sakanishi as the Chief Assistant of the Japanese Section to further develop the collection. During her tenure from 1930 to1941, the collection tripled in size. Today, the Japanese collection has grown to 1.1 million volumes of monographs and serials as well as extensive microfilm and microfiche holdings—the largest collection in the Asian Division through purchase, gift, exchange, and other avenues of acquisition.

Among the wealth of rare items are approximately 5000 titles of publications and manuscript copies of works produced before the end of the Tokugawa Shogunate in 1868 and the beginning of the Meiji period (1868 ~ 1912). Included are the **dharani** 百万搭陀罗尼 prayer charms, which date to 770 A. D. and are among the world's earliest surviving printed material. Also noteworthy are a complete edition of the Japanese literary masterpiece **Genji monogatari** 源氏物语 (The Tale of Genji) published in Kyoto in 1654 and the **Yoshitsune azwna kudari monogatari** printed on movable type between 1624 and 1643. A complete catalogue of the rare books in the Library of Congress was published in 2003 by Yagi Shoten in Tokyo. At the end World War II, a large number of historical documents such as the ones from former Japanese Imperial Army and Navy, the South Manchuria Railway Company, and the East Asian Research Institute were given to the Library by the Washington Document Center. Much of the materials from the latter two are pre-World War II studies on such areas as Korea, Taiwan, Mainland China, Mongolia, and the Pacific Islands. The Library also has a microfilm copy of the archives of the Japanese Foreign Ministry from 1868 to 1945 and pre-1945 records of the Police Bureau of the Ministry of Home Affairs—some of these are censored wartime publications.

Another important collection is the "Inoh Maps" —the first modern maps of Japan created originally by Tadataka Inoh between 1800 and 1821. Copies of 207 of Inoh's original 214 sheets large-scale set (1∶36 000) that cover the Japanese archipelago from Hokkaido to Kyushu were discovered in the map collection of the Library of Congress in the spring of 2001 and have caused great excitement in Japan. In order to make these maps available for exhibition and for online access, all of them have been digitized and sent to the Japan Map Center. A selection of the actual-size reproductions of these maps was on exhibition at the Tokyo Nation Museum from October 31 to December 14, 2003. Some of the original maps will also be loaned and exhibited in Kobe, Sendai, Atami, and Nagoya in 2004.

4.3 The Korean Collection

The Korean collection began in the 1920s with the generous gift of Korean books from Dr. James S. Gale, a Canadian missionary who spent 40 years in Korea from 1888 to 1928. Dr. Gale also helped the Library to acquire a number of Korean classics, including rare books from the estate of the Korean scholar Kim To-hui. Systematic development of the Korean collection was started in the early 1950s during the period of the Korean War. Today, the Korean collection in the Library totals 210,000 volumes in the Korean language, as well as 20,000 Japanese language books and 8000 English language books on Korea. Coverage of North Korea is also strong, with some 10,000 items.

There are 480 titles of Korean rare books, in 3,000 volumes. They were all written in Chinese characters in printed on mulberry paper. Although China was the first country to use movable type made of clay, Korea was the first one to use movable metal type for printing. Several good examples of this type of printing are in the collection. These are the collected writings of the renowned 16th-century Confucian scholar and statesman Yi I printed in 1744 and the 1834 reprint of the works of the "father of Korean literature", Ch'oe Ch'i-won (857 – 915). Other rare books printed by woodblock include **the History of the Koryo Dynasty** (高丽史), printed in 1590, and the **Law Code of the Yi Dynasty** (《经国大典》), printed in 1630.

4.4 The Southeast Asian Collection

As was mentioned in the beginning of this paper, the earliest acquisition of the Southeast Asian collection in the Library of Congress began in 1865, which predates the beginning of all other Asian collections. The collection was acquired in Singapore in 1842 by the U.S. Naval Exploring Expedition led by Lt. Charles Wilkes. Wilkes and the Expedition's philologist, Horatio Hale, collected Malay manuscripts and early printed books with the assistance of Alfred North, an American missionary in Singapore. The collection went first to the Smithsonian Institutions which later transferred the collection to the Library of Congress in 1865. Included in this earliest acquisition are a unique collection of manuscripts written in the Buginese script of South Sulawesi; an account of the 19th-century Malay world written in Jawi, the **Hikayat Abdullah** (The Story of Abdullah); and an 1840 Mission Press edition of the **Sejarah Melayu** (Malay Annals), an important Malay history written in 1612, also in Jawi, the Malay language in Arabic script.

The Southeast Asian collection contains many palm leaf manuscript copies of the **Tlpitaka**, the basic text of Theravada Buddhism which is the majority religion of Cambodia, Laos, Myanmar (Burma), and Thailand. In 1905, a special Thai **Tipitaka** was presented to the Library of Congress by King Chulalongkorn (Rama V) of Thailand. In 1949, an especially fine collection of Burmese manuscripts in the Pali language as well as a **Tipitaka** in Pali using Burmese script was presented to the Library of Congress as a part of a large Burmese donation. The donation also included an important Burmese history, **The Glass Palace Chronicle**, written by a group of scholars in 1829.

The Asian Division also holds rare materials from the Philippines and Vietnam. Of special note is a set of inscribed bamboo tubes, with lettering in the old Indie script similar to the ancient scripts used in neighboring Indonesia, The collection of 55 bamboos in prose and 22 in verse provides a fascinating glimpse into Mangyan (Hampangan) and Tagbanua society. Several examples of Vietnamese dynastic histories are also represented, including texts printed from early woodblocks at the former imperial palace at Hue.

In 1938, the Library of Congress launched the Indic Project in order to improve its collections from Southeast and South Asia, particularly publications in local languages. Following World War II, as U.S. interest in the region increased, the collection grew dramatically and today consists of holdings from Brunei, Cambodia, Indonesia, Laos, Malaysia, Myanmar, the Philippines, Singapore, Thailand, Vietnam, and many of the South Pacific island nations such as Papua New Guinea, etc. The establishment of the Library's overseas offices in New Delhi, India, in 1962, in Jakarta Indoneda, in 1963, and in Islamabad, Pakistan, in 1965 has provided a continuous flow of books, newspapers, and periodicals from the region in a variety of formats.

4.5 The South Asian Collection

The foundation for the South Asian collection was laid in 1904 when a collection of over 4000 books and pamphlets from the German Indologist, Dr. Albrecht Weber, was purchased. Included were texts in Sanskrit of India's sacred Hindu works—the **Vedas**, **Brahmanas**, and **Upanisads**—as well as the stories of the Puranas and the great epics in the **Mahabharata** and **the Ramayana**. In addition, there are a number of Weber's notebooks with his handwritten transcriptions of rare Indian texts for his pioneering critical editions.

In 1938, the Library received a grant from the Carnegie Corporation to develop the South Asian collection systematically, and it initiated the Indie Project— "Project F-Development of Indie Studies". During the 1950s the collection continued to expand and growth accelerated even further with the opening of the Library's New Delhi Overseas Office in 1962, Under the Public Law (PL) 480 program, the New Delhi office used rupees from Indian purchases of U.S. agricultural products to buy books and other materials from India and other countries of South Asia. An overseas office in Karachi, Pakistan, was opened in 1965 to oversee the acquisition of publications from Pakistan and neighboring areas. Later, the office was moved to the capital city, Islamabad.

Today, the South Asian collection holds materials in over 100 modern languages used in India, Pakistan, Bangladesh, Sri Lanka, and Nepal. The majority of the publications are in Hindi (20 percent), Bengali (15 percent), Urdu (13 percent), and Tamil (11 percent). Other languages represented in large numbers include Marathi, Telugu, Malayalam, Gujarati, and Kannada.

An example among the many rare books and manuscripts in the South Asian collection is a 1452 manuscript of the Jaina **Kalpasutra** from Gujarat in western India. This illustrated text tells the story of Mahavira, the founder of the Jaina religion. The "Crosby Khotan fragments" are also among the more unusual rare items. During a 1903 journey to Central Asia, Oscar Terry Crosby, an American who later became Assistant Secretary of the Treasury, purchased these manuscripts in Sanskrit at the Taklamakan oasis town of Khotan.

Between 1990 and 2000, a very important project undertaken by the New Delhi Overseas Office was the Micro filming of Indian Publications Project (MIPP). This project was a joint collaboration between the Government of India and the Library Congress, aimed at preserving and making accessible out-of-print works listed in the **National Bibliography of Indian Literature: 1901—1953**. Some 22,686 titles in 15 languages were microfilmed from 67 repository libraries in India and 3 libraries outside India (the Library of Congress, University of Chicago, and British Library). These titles were selected by Indian scholars as being central to the understanding of India.

5. Overseas Offices

The accelerated growth of the library collections from South and Southeast Asia since the 1960s should be credited to the efforts of the overseas offices in New Delhi, Jakarta, and Islamabad. In addition to these three, the African/Asian Acquisitions and Overseas Operations Division of the Library of Congress also operate overseas offices in Cairo, Nairobi, and Rio de Janeiro.

One of the unique features of the three Asian overseas offices is the offering of their service to other libraries who want to acquire publications from countries and regions covered by these offices. For example, the 44 academic and research libraries, mostly from North America, that participated in the South Asia Cooperative Acquisitions Program (SACAP) receive publications of their choice from the New Delhi office and its many sub-offices. Being the largest and the oldest of the six overseas offices, the New Delhi office covers India, Bangladesh, Bhutan, the Maldives, Nepal, and Sri Lanka—as well as Burma, Mongolia, and the Mongolian and Tibetan Autonomous Regions of China. The New Delhi office performs a wide range of services to SACAP libraries, including acquisitions, cataloging, bibliographic control, and preservation of publications acquired in some 65 languages and 25 different scripts. Another service of the New Delhi office is the maintenance of an extensive program for official and informal exchanges of publications with key institutions and libraries in South Asia.

6. Scholarly Services

The Asian Division and its Asian Reading Room, located in the Thomas Jefferson Building, across the street from the U.S. Capitol, is the primary public access point for researchers seeking to use this most comprehensive Asian Collection. In order to provide special guidance and service to researchers and scholars from near and far, a team of well trained and highly qualified reference librarians and area studies specialists who have extensive knowledge of the various collections are ready to be of assistance.

Besides on-site visits by scholars, which are essential to full explore the wealth of the treasured Asian collection, readers are encouraged to search the Library of Congress online public access catalog for library holdings (http://catalog.loc.gov). In order to save their valuable time, researchers may telephone or email ahead of their visits so that needed materials may be available for use upon arrival. Researchers in remote locations may also request items through interlibrary loan from their nearby libraries. Most rare materials may only be available for on-site use.

There is another advantage for on-site visits and that is the accessibility to a variety of online electronic databases. Because of the licensing agreement and other restrictions imposed by publishers these databases can only be searched and used onsite. In the digital age, the Asian Division is moving ahead in supplementing its printed collections by a growing body of electronic resources from e-books, e-journals, e-newspapers, to a wide range of e-materials, both digitized from printed version or born digital.

As a part of the Library's effort to provide more and more specialized digital resources online, such as the ***American Memory*** (http://memory.loc.gov/), the ***Global Gateway*** (http://international.loc.gov/intldl/intldlhome.html), etc., the Library's portals now serve as a gateway to selected web resources on a variety of subjects and world areas (http//www.loc.gov/rr/international/portals.html). The portals of the Asian Division (http//www.loc.gov/rr/asian/area_AD.html) are increasingly a useful source on all the Asian countries and regions. We invite you to visit our website and use the portals. You will do us a great favor by recommending more high quality and relevant websites so that we can continue to add and update our Asian portals.

Being a leader in the development of ***QuestionPoint***—a worldwide online reference service operating on a 24-hours-a-day and 7-days-a-week schedule—now operated by the OCLC Online Computer Library Center, library users anywhere can now send their reference questions through OCLC online global network to the Library of Congress for reply by our reference librarians and area studies specialists (http://www.oclc.org/questionpoint). Library users may also use the service of ***Asking a Librarians*** (http://www.loc.gov/rr/askalib-asian.html) to get reference assistance from librarians in the Asian Division.

7. Kluge Fellowships and other Funding Opportunities

Through the generous gift of $60 million from Mr. John W. Kluge, the John Kluge Center was established in 2000 in the Jefferson Building with funding from the Kluge endowment. The endowment also funds a number of Kluge Chair holders, distinguished visiting scholars, and Kluge post-doctoral fellows each year. A number of other fellowship opportunities funded by other private foundation gifts is also administered by the Kluge Center and the Office of Scholarly Programs. Recipients of Kluge fellowships may spend from six to twelve months at the Center with a monthly stipend which is sufficient to cover transportation and living expenses in the Washington, D. C, area. Selected researchers and scholars are expected to use the extensive collections and resources of the Library of Congress for their research.

The Kluge Center especially encourages humanistic and social science research that makes use of the Library's large and varied collections. Interdisciplinary, cross-cultural, or multi-lingual research is particularly welcome. For information about the Kluge Center and its fellowships, please visit the website: http://www.loc.gov/Kluge or send email to: scholarly@loc.gov.

8. International Cooperation

In order to further develop the Asian collections two important international roles of the Asian Division have been identified. They are:

(1) Expand international relations for Asian librarianship, scholarship, and network.

(2) Develop collaborative projects with organizations and institutions at the national and international levels.

For the first international role, the Asian Division endeavors to develop regular contacts with libraries and librarians in Asian countries in a joint effort to advance librarianship and scholarship. Being the world's largest library, the Library of Congress has been a frequent place of visit by many Asian librarians and information professionals. We want to extend our warmest welcome to all our visitors and hope that through such visits a mutually beneficial relationship can be established. Furthermore, it is our sincere hope that external funding may be found to support an internship program for Asian librarians who wish to pursue training and internship at the Asian Division.

For the second international role, we would like to develop collaborative projects with national libraries and international organizations for the purpose of sharing our resources to facilitate mutual understanding, international education, and scholarly research. One such project is the Global Gateway Project undertaken by the Library of Congress in collaboration with other national libraries in a joint effort to convert unique items from the collections of each into digital form and to share these at no cost over the Internet with the people of both countries and the world. Each of the projects is built around a broad theme that focuses on the culture and history of the respective partner country and in particular its interactions with the United States. The URL for Global Gateway is http://international.loc.gov. Currently, the Asian Division and the International Research Center for Japanese Studies (Nichibunken) are engaged in discussion for a joint digitization project for collections relating to Japan on the eve of its opening to the Western world and the subsequent development of U. S. -Japan relations. The project will include digitizing some of the rare Japanese collections in the Library of Congress. Discussions are also underway with the National Central Library in Taiwan and the Academia Sinica in Taiwan to digitize selected Chinese rare books and pre-1900 Chinese maps held by the Library of Congress for worldwide access by scholars and researchers.

References

1. ***The Asian Division.*** Washington, DC: The Library of Congress, 2002: pp. 1, 2, 4, 8.

2. Chi Wang. ***The Chinese Collection in the Library of Congress: A Brief Introduction.*** Washington, DC: Chinese Section, Asian Division, Library of Congress, 2001, pp. 5 – 6.

3. ***The Mission and Strategic Priorities of the Library of Congress : FY 1997—2004.*** Washington, DC: Library of Congress, 1997.

4. ***The Strategic Plan of the Asian Division, 2003 to 2008.*** Washington, DC: Asian Division, the Library of Congress, 2003.

5. ***The Chinese Collection.*** Washington, DC: Asian Division, the Library of Congress, n. d.

6. ***The Tibetan Collection.*** Washington, DC: Asian Division, Library of Congress, April 2002.

7. ***Beikoku Gikai Toshokan zo Nihon Kotenscki Mokuroku*** (Catalog of Japanese Rare Books in the Library of Congress). Tokyo: Yagi Shoten, 2003.

8. ***The Japanese Collection.*** Washington, DC: Asian Division, the Library of Congress, n. d.

9. ***The Korean Collection.*** Washington, DC: Asian Division, the Library of Congress, n. d.

10. ***The Southeast Asian Collection.*** Washington, DC: Asian Division, Library of Congress, April 2002.

11. ***The South Asian Collection.*** Washington, DC: Asian Division, Library of Congress, April 2002.

12. ***The Library of Congress in South Asia, 1960—2002.*** *Celebrating 40 Years of Bibliographic and Cultural Exchanges.* New Delhi: Library of Congress Office, n. d. p. 16.

13. ***The Library of Congress in South Asia, 1960—2002.*** *Celebrating 40 Years of Bibliographic and Cultural Exchanges.* New Delhi: Library of Congress Office, n. d.

（原载《第二届国际图书馆论坛——城市发展与图书馆服务论文集》，上海科学技术文献出版社2004年版，第157-165页。）

海外华人与海外华人研究
——兼介绍美国俄亥俄大学邵友保博士海外华人文献研究中心

Overseas Chinese and Overseas Chinese Studies
—Dr. Shao You Bao Overseas Chinese Documentation and Research Center at Ohio University, U. S. A.

一、海外华人

（一）海外华人的概念和总数

研究海外华人，首先必须廓清有关海外华人两个不准确的概念，从而确定海外华人的总数。

在英文中，海外华人和华侨均译为"overseas Chinese"，不少人也因之将海外华人等同于华侨。其实不然，海外华人应包括华侨（overseas Chinese with Chinese Citizenship）和外籍华人（overseas Chinese with Foreign Citizenship）两部分。

"华侨"一词始于清末。此前，海外定居的华人自称"唐人"，因盛唐时，华人开始往海外经商定居，遂得此称。1883年，郑观应在给李鸿章呈文中首用"南洋各埠华侨"一词，[1] 时值清政府力图开拓海外财源以支持洋务运动，因而一改排斥政策，认同定居海外的华人为侨民，"华侨"一词便成为定居海外华人之通称。1909年清政府颁布《国籍法》，采血统主义原则，界定凡有华人血统，不论居住海内外，均为中国国民。1929年南京国民政府另颁《国籍法》，仍沿续前清之国籍原则[2]。

"二战"之后，东南亚诸国纷纷独立，定居这些国家的华人便面临是否与其所居国认同而加入其国籍的抉择。新成立的中华人民共和国政府为发展与东南亚国家的友好关系，乃决定放弃血统主义国籍原则。1952年，中华人民共和国华侨事务委员会在《关于海外侨民工作的指示》中明示：华侨是保留中国国籍的侨民，入当地国籍者不能算华侨[3]。此后，中国政府便与印尼政府等签约放弃双重国籍。1984年，中国国务院侨办在《关于华侨、归侨、华侨学生、归侨学生、侨眷、外籍华人身份的解释》文件中更进一步明确区分：华侨必须是合法定居海外的中国公民，入外籍者则为外籍华人[4]。

故海外华人不等于华侨，而应包括外籍华人。目前，在海外华人中，约百分之十为华侨、百分之九十为外籍华人。海外华人研究之范畴除华侨、外籍华人外，也涵盖侨眷，其定义按国务院侨办《关于华侨、归侨、华侨学生、归侨学生、侨眷、外籍华人身份的解释》为：华侨和外籍华人（包括回国定居者）在中国国内的眷属[5]。

关于海外华人的另一不准确概念是将海外华人之范畴扩及港、澳、台的居民，由此产生了关于海外华人人口总数的两个不同数字。其一是西方学者常采用的，以1992年7月份伦敦《经济学人》的一篇评论海外华人经济实力的著名文章为代表。该文章将两千一百万台湾居民和六百万香港居民纳入海外华人，由此得出五千五百万海外华人拥有一点五至

---

[1] 郑观应："禀北洋通商大臣李傅相为招商局与怡和、大古定合同"（1883），后辑入郑观应著《盛世危言后编》。相关考证文章见庄国土：《中国封建政治的华侨政策》（厦门大学出版社，1989年版）。
[2] 毛起雄，林晓东：《中国侨务政策概述》中国华侨出版社1993年版，第3-4页。
[3] 同上，第4-5页。
[4] 同上，第5-6页。
[5] 同上，第13页。

两兆美元流动资产的结论①,此数字以后便被广泛引用②。其二是中国内地和台湾地区的统计数字。一九九七年,内地暨南大学图书馆华侨华人文献信息中心、汇总《华人经济年鉴》,各地海外华人报纸报道及外交部和侨务部门报告等不同资料来源,得出海外华人总数为三千四百余万③。一九九九年,台湾侨务委员会发布的各方统计数字则是三千三百万④。这两个数字相近且都不包括港、澳、台的居民。西方学者采用两分法,以海外华人(overseas Chinese)相对于祖国大陆华人(Mainland Chinese),因而将港、澳、台居民列入海外华人。祖国大陆和台湾则明确海外华人系居于中国领土之外的华人(Chinese Abroad)。港、澳、台为中国领土,其居民当然不属海外华人,因此海外华人总数应当为三千三百万至三千四百万人之间。

(二)海外华人分布的特点

海外华人的分布有以下几个特点:

其一,海外华人是目前世界上地理分布最广的一个族裔。

据统计,海外华人现已散布全球一百四十个国家和地区,按数量多少排列为:

亚洲三十四个国家,两千八百一十七万人,占海外华人总数的百分之八十二点六;

美洲三十三个国家,三百五十七万人,占海外华人总数的百分之十点五;

欧洲二十六个国家,一百六十一万人,占海外华人总数的百分之四点八;

大洋洲十四个国家,五十七万人,占海外华人总数的百分之一点七;

非洲三十三个国家,十三万人,占海外华人总数的百分之零点四⑤。

其二,海外华人主要集中于东南亚地区。

由于历史和地理的原因,东南亚地区成为海外华人最主要的居住地。

目前,东南亚共有华人一千一百五十九万,占全球海外华人总数的百分之六十三,其中印尼又以其六百万华人而居全球之首。但近年来,在这一地区的一些国家,华人数目剧减。以越南为例,1975 年,据估计越南有一百八十万华人。此后,由于越南政府的排华政策,二十八万越南华人被遣返中国大陆、五十七万逃离越南,以难民身份定居于美国、法国和澳大利亚。至 1989 年 4 月 1 日人口普查时,越南华人仅剩九十万零二百人,锐减约百分之五十⑥。在另一些国家,虽然华人人口绝对总数增加了,但在总人口中所占的比例却不断下降。比如在马来西亚,1980 年普查数字显示,华人仍占全部人口的百分之三十四点七⑦,至 1999 年,在马来西亚人口和家庭发展局的最新人口统计中,华人比例已降至百分之二十六⑧。

其三,在美国、加拿大、澳大利亚等发达国家,华人人数迅速增长。

近数十年来,由于美国、加拿大、澳大利亚等西方发达国家陆续修改了移民法案,这

---

① "The Overseas Chinese—A Driving Force" in The Economist (July 18 - 24, 1992), p. 21。

② 见 Louis Kraar:"Importance of Chinese in Asian Business" in Journal of Asian Business, Vol. 9, No. 1 (Winter 1993), p. 87。

③ 暨南大学图书馆华侨华人文献信息中心:《1946—1997 中国华侨侨务信息资源库》,电子工业出版社,CD 光盘。

④ 张希哲:"国际合作研究'海外华人'的新境界——参加俄亥俄大学'海外华人研究机构国际合作会议'记略",载于《侨协杂志》第六十九期(2000 年夏季刊),第 2 页。

⑤ 以上数据引自暨南大学图书馆华侨华人文献信息中心:《1946—1997 中国华侨侨务信息资源库》,电子工业出版社,CD 光盘。

⑥ 王士录:《当代越南》,四川人民出版社,1992 年版,第 264 页。方雄普,谢成佳:《华侨华人概况》,中国华侨出版社,1993 年版,第 18 - 19 页。

⑦ 黄露夏:《马来西亚的华人》,福建人民出版社,1999 版,第 27 页,数据引自香港《华人》月刊,1984 年第 9 期,第 15 页。

⑧ 《联合早报(电子版)》,2000 年 7 月 11 日:"从 1991 年至 1999 年马国华人人口比例减少 1.4 个百分点"。

些国家便成为中国大陆、台湾、香港新移民和东南亚地区华人再移民的主要目的地。以美国为例，1930年，全美华人仅十万两千人。1943年，美国国会废除排华法案，每年准许全球华人移民美国一百零五名，留学生、教授、传教士不受此限。至1960年，华人人口增至二十三万七千人。1965年美国国会通过新移民法案，华人移民配额增加到两万，1970年，华人人口增至四十三万五千。1979年，中美建交，原属台湾的两万名移民名额转给大陆，1980年华人人口增至八十万六千。1981年，美国总统签署国会法案，每年另拨两万移民配额给台湾，1987年，美国国会将香港移民配额由原来的六百名增至五千名，1990年，全美华人人口已达到一百六十四万五千名①。从1960年至1990年的三十年间，全美华人人口几乎每隔十年就增长一倍。加拿大也在1943年废除排华法案。从60年代开始，加拿大华人人口也每十年翻一番，从1961年之五万八千，增至1971年之十一万八千，再增至1981年二十八万九千，直至1991年的五十八万六千②。1966年，澳大利亚放弃白澳政策时，该国华人人口仅二万六千。1986年，华人人口增至十九万六千，二十年间增长七点五倍③。

（三）海外华人构成的变化

早期海外华人社会的构成有以下几个特点：一是早期移民海外的华人主要来源于广东、广西，和福建的贫困农民，他们以契约劳工身份出国，出卖血汗，在东南亚开垦锡矿和橡胶园，在美国修铁路，在加勒比海种植甘蔗。略有积蓄，转而从事商贩，劳工和商人遂成为海外华人社会的主体。二是在华人社会中，男女比例严重失调。三是在一个特定的国家，海外华人的祖籍大多源于同一省，同一地区，甚至同一县。以美国为例。1940年，百分之七十一的华人从事采矿业、洗衣业、车衣业、餐馆业和杂货业，仅有百分之二十九属专业人士④。同年，美国华人中男性为四万八千六百三十三人，而女性仅为一万两千四百六十三人⑤。美国早期华人百分九十五以上原籍广东，其中又以台山、开平、新会、恩平四邑为最⑥。

这些早期海外华人社会的构成特点已发生了重大的变化。仍以美国华人为例。早期华人移民的第二代或第三代在美普遍受到较好的教育。1990年的人口统计显示，在二十五岁以上的美国华人中，百分之四十点七以上拥有学士或更高的学位，美国总人口中仅百分之二十点三拥有学士以上学位⑦。另一方面，由中国来美的新移民中，受良好教育者也占很大比例。据统计，从1967年至1974年，全美共有五万四千三百八十二名华人调整身份取

---

① 以上资料数据来源：
U. S. Bureau of the Census：*Historical Statistics of the United States：Colonial Times to 1970*（Washington, D. C.：U. S Government Printing office, 1975）.
U. S. Bureau of the Census：*1990 Census of Population：Asians and Pacific Islanders in the United States*（Washington, D. C.：U. S. Government Printing office, 1993）.
杨国标等：《美国华侨史》（广东高等教育出版社，1989年版），第538—541页。
刘汉标等：《世界华侨华人概况（欧洲，美洲卷）》（暨南大学出版社，1994版），第169—174页。

② 资料数据来源：
刘汉标等：《世界华侨华人概况（欧洲，美洲卷）》（暨南大学出版社，1994版），第140—141页。
David Chuen-Yan Lai：*Chinatowns：Towns within Cities in Canada*（Vancouver：University of Columbia Press, 1988）, Canada Bureau of Statistics：Census of Canada, 1991：Population（ottawa：1992）.

③ Lynn Pan：*The Encyclopedia of the Chinese overseas*（Singapore：Archipelago Press, 1998）, p. 276.

④ 张希哲：《美国华侨史略与美国华侨社会之发展》（华侨协会总会，1997年版），第191页。

⑤ 同上，第188页。资料来源：Stanford M. Lyman：*Chinese Americans*（New York，Random House, 1974）.

⑥ 刘汉标等：《世界华侨华人概况》（欧洲，美洲卷），（暨南大学出版社，1994年版）第168页。

⑦ U. S. Bureau of the Census：*1990 Census of Population：General Population Characteristics*（U. S. Government Printing office, 1992）.
U. S. Bureau of the Census：1990 Census of Population：Asians and Pacific Islanders in the United States（U. S. Government Printing office, 1993）.

得绿卡，其中二万一千多人是来自台湾的留学生①。大陆方面，按中国国家教委 1996 年 10 月公布的数字，自 1979 年以来，共有一十五万人自大陆出国留学②，其中按中国驻美大使馆的不完全统计，约十六万留学美国③。在 1998 年至 1999 学年度，按美国教育部统计，在美国各大学就读的大陆学生达五万一千零一人，占外国留美学生总数的百分之十，居第一位④。在大陆留美学生中，按美国国家科学理事会 1995 至 1996 学年度统计，百分之八十一为研究生⑤。1993 年有五万名以上中国大陆学生在美调整身份取得绿卡⑥。

教育程度的提高对海外华人社会的影响是很明显的。1990 年美国人口统计显示，在美国华人中，专业人士（包括科技人员、管理人员、行政人员、经销人员、医生、教师等）已占华人从业人员的百分之六十七点一。男女比例也发生了逆转，美国华人女性总人口现已超过美国华人男性总人口零点七个百分点⑦。同时美国华人社会再也不是以广东人为主的社会了，国语或普通话已取代了四邑话成为美国华人社会的通用语言⑧。

（四）海外华人的经济和科技人才实力

海外华人的实力主要体现在经济方面和科技人才方面。其经济实力以东南亚海外华人财团为代表；其科技人才实力则以美籍华人科技力量为代表。

二次世界大战后，特别 20 世纪 60 年代后，海外华人经济实力大幅增长的主要标志是出现了众多的华人财团，而海外华人财团主要集中在东南亚。根据《FORBES 资本家》1995 年 6 月报道，东南亚地区总资产在一亿美元以上的华人财团计有一百五十三个，总资产二千零十七亿美元，分别为泰国七百二十三点五亿美元，印度尼西亚四百七十一亿美元，马来西亚三百三十七点五亿美元，新加坡二百三十七点五亿美元，菲律宾二百四十八亿美元⑨。这些华人财团均成为当地国民经济的骨干。比如泰国的五大财团，除王室财团外，其余四大财团，即梭逢帕尼财团（盘谷银行）、兰三财团（泰华农民银行）、叻达那勒财团（大城银行）和德差派汶财团（京华银行），均为华人财团。新加坡三大财团也皆为华人财团，此即大华、华侨、华联银行集团。印度尼西亚最大的四十个企业集团中，三十家为华人财团，也包括实力强大的沙林集团、阿斯特拉集团、金光集团和力宝集团。马来西亚有华人财团四十个，包括财力雄厚的郭氏兄弟集团、云顶集团和丰隆集团。菲律宾华人财团二十四个，包括总资产五十亿美元以上的郑周敏财团、四十亿美元以上的陈永栽财团、三十亿美元以上的许寰哥财团，以及二十亿美元以上吴亦辉财团、施至成财团、郑少坚财团⑩。

海外华人财团的一个重要特点是实现了投资的国际化和经营的多元化。以马来西亚的

---

① 张希哲：《美国华侨史略与美国华人社会之发展》，华侨协会总会 1997 年版，第 190 页。
② "跨世纪中国的人才资源"，载《华声月刊》（1996 年第 6 期）。
③ Yuigui Guo: "The Eventual Tendency: To Integrate Chinese Scientists and Engineers into International Community of Science" in *International Conference of Institutes and Libraries for overseas Chinese Studies—Papers and Abstracts* (Athens, ohio, USA, March 24 – 25, 2000), p. 171.
④ Institute of International Education: *Open Doors 1998/1999: Report on International Educational Exchange* (New York: 1999).
⑤ United States National Science Board: *Science and Engineering Indicators 1998* (Washington, D. C.: National Science Foundation, 1998.
⑥ Lynn Pan: *The Encyclopedia of the Chinese overseas* (Singapore: Archipelago Press, 1998), p. 267.
⑦ U. S. Bureau of the Census: *1990 Census of Population: General Population Characteristics* (U. S. Government Printing office, 1992).
U. S. Bureau of the Census: *1990 Census of Population: Asians and Pacific Islanders in the United States* (U. S. Government Printing office, 1993).
⑧ 张希哲：《美国华侨史略与美国华人社会之发展》（华侨协会总会，1997 年版），第 189 页。
⑨ 世界华商经济年鉴编辑委员会：《世界华商经济年鉴 1996/1997》，企业管理出版社 1996 年版，第 356 页。资料出处：《FORBES 资本家》（1995 年 6 月刊）。
⑩ 方雄普，谢成佳：《华侨华人概况》，中国华侨出版社 1993 年版，第 38 – 39 页。

郭氏兄弟集团为例。郭民兄弟集团从70年代开始朝投资国际化和经营多元化的方向发展。为此，1976年集团总部由马来西亚的吉隆坡迁往香港。至1995年，郭氏兄弟集团总财富达六十亿美元，旗下二百余家公司和企业，分布于十八个国家和地区，涉足进出口、蔗糖、食品、油脂、化工、矿产、酒店、航运、房地产、新闻出版、影视、金融保险诸行业。郭氏兄弟集团同时与印度尼西亚的沙林财团、泰国的梭逢帕尼财团、香港的李嘉诚、邵逸夫财团等，形成了合伙、融资或合作参股关系①。海外华人财团的投资国际化和经营多元化使之成为推动亚太经济乃至世界经济发展的一股重要力量。

美籍华人科技力量是随着大陆和台湾的留学生大量进入美国科技界而崛起的。据台湾"教育部"报告，从1950年至1980年，台湾"教育部"共核准六万三千零六十一名大学毕业生到国外攻读研究生课程，其中大部分赴美，然只有七千二百四十人返台。以1980年为例，当年赴美就读的各类台湾学生共计五千五百七十二人，然而当年学成回台的仅三百三十一人②。因而早在1962年，据当时台湾驻美使馆文化参赞处的统计，即有一千五百七十一名华人在美国大学任教或研究机构任职③。

从80年代起，祖国大陆来的研究生也开始成批进入美国的科技界，这可由两个统计资料来说明：一是大陆留学生取得美国理工科博士学位的人数占美国各大学颁发理工科博士学位总数的比例。美国国家科学基金会的统计资料表明，从1988年至1996年，美国各大学共授出二十一万九千六百四十三个理工科博士学位，其中一万六千五百五十个学位系授予大陆留学生，占授出理工科博士学位总数的百分之七点五。以具体学科分计，大陆留学生在这期间所获得的博士学位，占美国各大学同期授出数学博士学位总数的百分之十四点八，物理学的百分之十三，工程学的百分之九点一，地球海洋科学的百分之九，农业生物科学的百分之八点四，计算机科学的百分之五点八④。二是大陆留学生取得理工科博士学位后随即加入美国科技界的人数。美国国家科学基金会的另一个统计资料显示，从1986年至1998年，在美国获得理工科博士的大陆留学生共计两万一千六百名，其中最高峰的是1996年，当年计有三千名左右的大陆学生在美获得理工科博士学位。这些大陆留美理工科博士中，有百分之三十，亦即六千余人随即进入博士后，成为美国高等院校和国家实验室的一支重要力量。另百分之十七随即受雇于美国工业界，高等院校，政治或私人机构。其中，高等院校聘用了百分之二，政府或私人机构聘用了百分之一，余下多为美国公司的研究和发展部门所雇佣。据统计，在这十二年间，美国公司从大陆留学生中共雇佣了一千一百三十八名工科博士，四百九十一名物理博士，和四百名数学博士⑤。就工科博士单项而言，美国学者麦克·芬在去年发表的追踪调查报告表明，在1992年和1993年取得

---

① 世界华商经济年鉴编辑委员会：《世界华商经济年鉴1996/1997》，企业管理出版社1996年版，第438－439页。

② Yuigui Guo："The Eventual Tendency: To Integrate Chinese Scientists and Engineers into International Community of Science" in *International Conference of Institutes and Libraries for overseas Chinese Studies—Papers and Abstracts* (Athens, ohio, USA, March 24－25, 2000), p. 173. 资料来源：Li Chen-ching: "Returning Home after Studying in the USA: Reverse Brain Drain in Taiwan" in *Cultural & Educational Digest*, 1995a, pp. 20－24.

③ 张希哲：《美国华侨史略与美国华侨社会之发展》，华侨协会总会1997年版，第191页。

④ Jean M. Johnson: "Collaboration in Information Exchange between the United States and China" presented to CIES 2000 Conference (San Antonio, Texas, March 7－11, 2000). 资料来源：National Science Foundation, Division of Science resources Studies: *Statistics Profiles of Foreign Doctoral Recipients in Science and Engineering: Plans to Stay in the United States* (Arlington, VA, 1998) and Susan T Hill: *Science and Engineering Doctorate Awards: 1996* (Arlington: National Science Foundation, 1997).

⑤ Jean M. Johnson，同上。

美国工科博士学位的四千零一十名大陆留学生中,到 1997 年百分之九十二已在美国就职①。

大量的大陆和台湾留学生加入美国科技界,使中国与奥地利、加拿大、德国、英国和印度并列,成为美国六个最主要的外部科技人才来源②。以高等院校为例。1997 年,美国共有理工科教授二十二万四千七百零七名,其中百分之二十非原籍美国。在这百分之二十非原籍美国的理工科教授中,原籍印度的居第一位,占百分之三点一,大陆和台湾居第二位,占百分之二点九(大陆百分之二点一,台湾百分之零点八),共六千六百五十人③。同年,据美国国家科学基金会统计,原籍中国,在美取得理工科学士、硕士、博士学位后就职于美国的科技人员总数是七万八千九百六十三人,其中学士三万二千六百六十人,硕士二万八千九百七十人,博士一万七千三百三十三人④。由于每年继续有数万名来自大陆和台湾的留学生赴美攻读研究生,美籍华人科技力量还将不断地壮大。目前,从这些美籍华人科技精英中已涌现出六名诺贝尔奖获得者(杨振宁,李政道,丁肇中,李远哲,朱棣文,崔琦)、二十七名美国国家科学院院士(朱经武,林家翘等)和三十五名美国国家工程院院士(田长霖,林同炎等)⑤。

二、海外华人研究

(一) 海外华人研究的重要性

海外华人研究的重要性可以从全球经济文化的发展、具体国家多元化社会的形成和促进中华民族现代化三个角度来分析。

从全球的角度来讲,海外华人是目前世界上人数最多、分布最广的一个族裔,其在世界各地传播并发展的中华文明极大地丰富了所居住国家的历史文化,其所积累的数千亿美元流动资产对亚太地区,乃至整个世界经济有着举足轻重的影响,因而海外华人对今日世界文明的繁荣和人类社会的进步是有巨大贡献的。

从具体国家的角度来说,华人是其所居住国家多元化社会的一个重要组成部分。由于悠久的中华民族文化传统,海外华人在不同的国家和文化背景下,并没有简单地被同化,而是形成了当地多元化社会中的一个族裔,如华裔美国人、华裔加拿大人、华裔澳大利亚人、华裔泰国人、华裔菲律宾人、华裔印度尼西亚人等。在美国,加拿大,澳大利亚等这些西方多种族的国家里,保护少数族裔的权益和文化已成了民间和政府的共识。他们认识到多元文化是一个客观存在的事实,正确引导多元文化的发展不但有利于各族裔间的团结,而且还有利于整个社会经济文化的繁荣。因此在美、加和澳洲的主要大学里设置了亚裔研究中心。在东南亚国家里,华人在当地的人口结构中占相当大的比例,形成了主要的少数民族,甚至多数民族。许多东南亚国家政府也逐渐认识到狭隘的种族排他主义政策并不利于社会稳定、种族团结和经济文化的繁荣进步,转而开始承认华族的权利并尊重其文化传统。泰国、菲律宾、马来西亚、越南都朝着这个方向发展,而印度尼西亚的排华骚动则受到世界舆论的普遍谴责,连其政府也不得不承认是个国家耻辱。

从中华民族这个角度来分析,海外华人是中国现代化进程中的一个重要推动力。自 19

---

① Michael Finn: *Stay Rates of Foreign Doctorate Recipients from U. S. Universities*, 1997 (Oak Ridge, TN: Oak Ridge Institute for Science and Education, 2000).
② Paula E. Stephan and Sharon G. Levin: *Exceptional Contributions to U. S. Science by the Foreign-Born and Foreign-Educated*—A research paper supported by the Alfred P. Sloan Foundation.
③ Jean M. Johnson, 同上。
④ 同上。
⑤ 见全球华人专业人士网络http://www.networkchinese.com/.

世纪中叶以来，海外华人即积极投资国内，从 1862 年至 1949 年的八十余年间，海外华人在国内一共创设了两万五千余家企业①。从 1949 年至 1966 年，海外华人又投资一亿美元于大陆，支持新中国的建设②。"文革"后中国大陆实行对外开放，海外华人投资便成了大陆引进外资中的主体部分。据统计从 1979 年至 1994 年，大陆共引进外资九百五十五亿美元，其中六百六十五亿美元，亦即约百分之七十来自境外华人③。许多海外华人财团是经由香港投资大陆的，如从 1985 年至 1993 年，马来西亚的郭氏兄弟财团即经由香港嘉里集团在大陆投资逾十亿美元，其投资的三十五个项目遍布中国十四个省和直辖市④。海外华人在促进中国与先进国家的科技交流中也发挥了不可取代的重要作用。中国对外开放以来，大量的海外华人学者即络绎不绝地往大陆进行学术交流和讲学，至 1993 年，据不完全统计，已有近八百名外籍华人学者往大陆进行学术活动。此外，包括诺贝尔奖金获得者杨振宁、李政道、丁肇中等一百余名杰出的外籍华人学者应邀担任了国内高等院校的讲座教授或顾问⑤。

（二）海外华人研究的课题

海外华人研究的课题也可由三个层面来分类。

在全球的层面上，海外华人研究包括三大课题：一是研究其历史文化，亦即研究海外华人如何向全球移民，如何将华夏文化传播到全球的每一个角落，又如何在不同的背景下发展起各地独特的海外华人文化圈；二是研究其经济现状，亦即研究当前海外华人的全球经济网络及其对整个世界经济和各地区经济圈的影响；三是研究其发展趋势，亦即通过对海外华人新移民群体，包括留学生移民群体、技术移民群体、投资移民群体、贸易移民群体、东南亚华人再移民群体、乃至非法移民群体等的研究，探讨海外华人在人口总数、区域分布、职业构成、总体实力等质和量上的变化。

在各具体国家的层面上，海外华人研究也包括三大课题：一是研究各具体国家华人的经济、文化、历史、社区结构、社团组织；二是研究在各具体国家多元化社会中，华人作为一个少数族裔（新加坡例外）的地位，其中包括该国对华人的政策、族裔关系、华人融入主流社会的程度和政治参与的深度等；三是对不同地区和国家的华人社会作横向的比较研究，如比较泰国华人与印尼华人对当地文化认同上的差异等。

最后在与中国的关系上，海外华人研究的三大课题包括：一是中国政治的华侨华人政策，其中包括中国外交政策中对华人问题的考量等；二是海外华人在中国历史进程中特别是中国现代化进程中所扮演的角色；三是侨乡研究。

（三）海外华人研究机构

海外华人研究是非常有意义而且有极大发展前景的一项事业，其研究成果不但具有重要的学术价值而且具有现实意义，因而海外华人研究目前已成为国际学术界的一项热门课题，研究海外华人的机构在世界各地陆续成立。

中国研究海外华人始于 1903 年梁启超著《记华工禁约》，记述美国华侨历史。1928 年，上海暨南大学成立"南洋文化事业部"，是中国第一家研究东南亚和海外华人的机构。1956 年，"厦门大学南洋研究所"成立，是中国第一所由国家支持的研究东南亚和海外华人的机构。1959 年，"华侨博物院"在厦门落成，成为大陆首家系统展示海外华人历史的

---

① 方雄普，谢成佳：《华侨华人概况》（中国华侨出版社，1993 年版），第 65 页。
② 同上，第 66 页。
③ 世界经济年鉴编辑委员会：《世界华商经济年鉴 1996/1997》（企业管理出版社，1996 年版），第 205 页。
④ 同上，第 439 页
⑤ 方雄普，谢成佳：《华侨华人概况》（中国华侨出版社，1993 年版），第 160 页。

专业博物馆。"文革"后,中国第一个全国性的海外华人研究学术团体"中国华侨华人历史学会"于1981年成立。此后,各地陆续成立了地方性的海外华人研究学术团体,至1991年,全国共有二十七个县级以上华侨华人研究学会①。"文革"后建立的专业海外华人研究机构则有:全国侨联的"中国华侨华人历史研究所"、中国社会科学院民族研究所的"海外华人研究中心"、福建社会科学院的"华侨华人研究所"、北京大学的"海外华人经济研究中心"、暨南大学的"华侨华人研究所"②、暨南大学图书馆的"华侨华人文献信息中心"③、华侨大学的"华侨华人研究所"、浙江师范大学的"华侨华人研究所"、山东大学历史文化学院的"华侨华人研究所"④、厦门大学的"陈嘉庚研究室"、厦门大学人文学院的"东南亚华文文学研究中心"和汕头大学的"港台及海外华文文学研究中心"。此外,广西社科院的"东南亚研究所"、云南社科院的"东南亚研究所"、中山大学的"东南亚研究所"⑤、暨南大学的"东南亚研究所"⑥、汕头大学的"东南亚研究中心"以及"中国海外交流协会"⑦ 等也都涉猎海外华人研究。

台湾的海外华人机构主要有成立于1942年的"华侨协会总会"、成立于1981年的"海外华人研究学会"⑧ 和成立于1992年的"'中央'研究院近代史研究所海外华人研究群"⑨。此外,"中央研究院"中山人文社会科学研究所的"历史与思想组"⑩、"中央研究院"的"东南亚区域研究计划"⑪、淡江大学国际研究学院的"东南亚研究所"⑫、暨南国际大学的"东南亚研究中心"⑬、中山大学的"东南亚研究中心"⑭ 也都有海外华人研究的项目。

香港的海外华人研究机构计有:香港中文大学的"海外华人研究中心"⑮、香港大学图书馆的"华侨华人文献研究中心"⑯、香港浸会大学图书馆的"当代中国研究资料部"⑰和岭南大学的"族群与海外华人经济研究部"⑱。以香港为基地的"陈嘉庚国际学会"和"国际客家学会"也以赞助海外华人学术研究活动为主要宗旨。

东南亚地区历史最悠久的海外华人研究机构是1940年成至于新加坡的"南洋学会"⑲,此后,新加坡便成为研究东南亚华人的最主要基地。目前新加坡的海外华人研究机构有:"华裔馆"⑳、新加坡国立大学中文图书馆的"海外华人特藏库"㉑ 和南洋理工大

---

① 巫乐华:《华侨史概要》,中国华侨出版社1994年版,第1-3页;
丁炯淳、谢美华:"华侨博物院介绍" in Papers and Abstracts—*International Conference of Institutes and Libraries for overseas Chinese Studies* (Athens, ohio, USA, March 24-25, 2000), p. 24。
② 暨南大学华侨华人研究所网页:www.inu.edu.cn"华侨华人"。
③ 暨南大学图书馆华侨华人文献信息中心网页:www.inu.edu.cn"图书馆"。
④ 山东大学历史文化学院华侨华人研究所网页:www.sdu.edu.cn/csdu/yx/history.html。
⑤ 中山大学东南亚研究所网页:www.zsu.edu.cn/english/southasian.htm。
⑥ 暨南大学东南亚研究所网页:www.inu.edu.cn/yxis.center/cdnv.html。
⑦ 中国海外交流协会网页www.coea.org。
⑧ 海外华人研究学会网页:www.cca.gov.tw/Culture/resources/cartgroup/misc/index113.htm。
⑨ "'中央研究院'近代史研究海外华人研究群"网页:http://w2.world.net.tw/~overseas/。
⑩ "中央研究院"中山人文社会科学研究所历史与思想组网页:www.issp.sinica.edu.tw/。
⑪ "中央研究院"东南亚区域研究网页:www.sinica.edu.tw/%Eproseaw3/
⑫ 淡江大学国际研究学院东南亚研究所网页:www2.tku.edu.tw/~tibx/homepage.htm。
⑬ 暨南国际大学东南亚研究中心网页:www.dseas.ncnu.edu.tw/。
⑭ 中山大学东南亚研究中心网页:www2.nsvsu.edu.tw/cseas/。
⑮ 香港中文大学海外华人研究中心网页:www.cuhk.edu.hk/proj/oca/oca.htm。
⑯ 香港大学图书馆华侨华人文献研究中心网页:www.hku.hk/lib/FpsLib/。
⑰ 香港浸会大学图书馆当代中国研究资料部网页:www.hkbu.edu.hk/lib。
⑱ 岭南大学族群与海外华人经济研究部网页:www.ln.edu.hk/eocb/intro.htm。
⑲ 许苏吾:《南洋学会与南洋研究》(Singapore: South Seas Publishers, 1977),第2页。
⑳ 华裔馆网页:www.huavihome.org。
㉑ 新加坡国立大学中文图书馆海外华人特藏库网页:www.lib.nus.edu.sg/chz/chineseoverseas。

学图书馆的"海外华人文库"①。此外，新加坡国立大学的"东亚研究所"、"新加坡亚洲研究学会"和"新社"也进行海外华人研究。"新加坡国家档案馆"、"新加坡国家档案馆口述历史中心"、"新加坡东南亚研究所图书馆"和"新加坡宗乡会馆联合总会"②则保存有丰富的海外华人研究资料。

东南亚地区其余国家的海外华人研究机构有马来西亚的"华社研究中心"③、"南方学院马华文学馆"④和"砂拉越华族文化协会"⑤。菲律宾的"华裔青年中心"⑥和"菲中发展资源中心"。此外，印尼的"中国研究中心"，泰国朱拉隆功大学亚洲研究院的"亚洲移民研究中心"⑦和越南的"东南亚研究所"也进行海外华人研究。

日本是华人圈之外最积极进行海外华人研究的国家。早在1915年，日本即成立了"南洋协会"，研究东南亚和居住在该地区的华人。此后，为配合其侵略东南亚的南进政策，台湾总督府外事部、台湾银行总务部调查课、满铁东亚经济调查局、拓殖学会、南方协会、太平洋协会都将南洋华侨研究列为主要课题之一，发表了大量的调查报告和研究著作。战后，从60年代开始，随着日本经济向东南亚扩张，日本再次重视对东南亚华人研究，其中尤为重点的是对东南亚华人经济的研究。日本研究东南亚华人的学术机构有："亚洲经济研究所"、"亚非语言文化研究所"、"京都大学东南亚研究所"、"东京大学东洋文化研究所"、"东南亚学会"和"华侨经济研究会"⑧。从80年代开始，在日本华人的推动下，一些以研究日本华人为主的学术团体产生了，其中包括"长崎华侨华人研究会"、"神户华侨华人研究会"、"九州华侨华人研究会"和"神户孙中山纪念馆"。九十年代，随着留日中国学生群体的壮大，便产生了以研究和收集华人新移民群体资料为主的"在日中国人文献资料中心"⑨和"创意综合研究所"⑩。

韩国对华人进行研究的有汉城延世大学的"国际研究中心"。

澳大利亚最主要的海外华人研究机构是设在澳大利亚国立大学亚太学院的"南方华裔研究中心"⑪。澳大利亚华人设立的研究机构则有墨尔本的"澳华博物馆"⑫。

在美国，除设在俄亥俄大学的"邵友保博士海外华人文献研究中心"⑬和设在旧金山的"世界华人联盟"⑭以研究全球海外华人为目标外，其余的均以研究美国的华人为目标。此类的机构包括："华族留美史学会"、"美华学会"⑮、"华美协会"⑯，"美国华人历史学会"⑰、"美国西北华人历史学会"、"新英格兰华人历史学会"⑱、"南加州华人历史学

---

① 南洋理工大学图书馆海外华人文库网页：www.ntu.edu.sg/library/overseass/chinese.htm。
② 新加坡国立大学新加坡宗乡会馆联合总会网页：www.sfcca.org.sg/。
③ 马来西亚华社研究中心网页：http://huayan.net.my。
④ 南方学院马华文学馆网页：www.southern.edu.my/mahua/index.html。
⑤ 砂拉越华族文化协会网页：www.inet.com.mv/scca/。
⑥ 菲律宾华裔青年中心网页：www.kaisa.org.ph。
⑦ 泰国朱拉隆功大学亚洲研究院亚洲移民研究中心网页：www.chula.ac.th/institute/arcm/。
⑧ 郭梁："近代以来日本的华侨华人研究（1914—1996）"，载于庄国土等主编：《世纪之交的海外华人》，福建人民出版社1998年版，第109—125页。
⑨ 在日中国人文献资料中心网页：www.cf.net/cpj/ch/index.html。
⑩ 创意综合研究所网页：www.sovi.co.jp/。
⑪ 南方华裔研究中心网页：http://rspas.anu.edu.au/cscad/。
⑫ 澳华博物馆网页：http://home.vicnet.net.au/%7Emcah/welcome.htm。
⑬ 美国俄亥俄大学邵友保博士海外华人文献研究中心网页：www.ibrary.ohiou.edu/subjects/shao/main.htm。
⑭ 世界华人联盟网页：www.huren.org/。
⑮ 美华学会网页：www.montana.com.maiwah/。
⑯ 华美协会网页：www.ocanatl.org。
⑰ 美国华人历史学会网页：www.chsa.org。
⑱ 新英格兰华人历史学会网页：http://yerkes.mit.edu/Chinatown/morechsne.html。

会"①、"大圣地亚哥华人历史学会"②、"圣地亚哥中华历史博物馆"③、"罗省华美历史博物馆"④、"纽约华人博物馆"⑤、"旧金山中华文化中心"⑥，和"大波士顿华人文化协会"⑦。

保存有较多海外华人资料的美国大学图书馆有：哈佛大学"燕京图书馆"、康奈尔大学"华氏文库"、华盛顿大学"东亚图书馆"、密执安大学"东南亚图书馆"、耶鲁大学"东南亚图书馆"和俄亥俄大学图书馆的"李华伟博士国际特藏部"。设在盐湖城的"尤他州族谱学会"⑧在收集全世界族谱的同时也重视收集海外华人的族谱。此外，以大陆留美学者为主的"中国旅美社会科学教授协会"、"美国中国历史学家学会"、"美国中国经济学会中国资料中心"，以及"全美中文学校协会"也鼓励其成员进行海外华人研究。美国大陆之外的夏威夷有研究孙中山先生海外活动的"夏威夷孙中山基金会"⑨。

加拿大华人建立的海外华人研究组织有："大温哥华中华文化中心博物档案馆"⑩、"大多伦多中华文化中心"⑪和"温城中华文化中心"⑫。加拿大"人类文明博物馆"的亚洲部则有关于加拿大华裔的丰富展品。⑬

拉丁美洲和加勒比海对华人进行研究的有古巴哈瓦那大学的"费南多·奥地兹高级研究中心"、特立尼达与多巴哥的"西印度群岛大学"历史系，以及设在加拿大温哥华专事研究圭亚那华人的"圭亚那华人之根"⑭。

欧洲有如下对海外华人进行研究的机构：俄国国家科学院的"东方研究所"主要兴趣在于对俄国华人新移民的研究，荷兰的"莱登大学汉学院"主要兴趣对印尼华人的研究，荷兰"中华公馆档案之友协会"主要整理雅加达中华公馆档案资料，荷兰"国际亚洲学会"的主要海外华人项目是研究侨乡⑮，英国牛津大学"中国研究所"目前的项目是研究在欧洲的福州新移民⑯，英国国家档案馆的"公共档案部"和大英图书馆的"远东和印度收藏部"拥有大量新马华人资料，伦敦大学的"东方和非洲学院"亦对海外华人的历史和现状进行研究，法国的"当代中国研究中心"则设办公室于香港，研究华南和东南亚海外华人⑰。

南非对华人进行研究的有比勒陀利亚大学的历史文化系。

世界性的海外华人研究组织有两个。一是成立于1992年，总部设于美国加州大学伯克利分校族裔研究系的"世界海外华人研究学会"⑱。二是成立于2000年，总部设于美国俄亥俄大学邵友保博士海外华人文献研究中心的"世界海外华人研究与文献收藏机构联合

---

① 南加州华人历史学会网页：www.chssc.org。
② 大圣地亚哥华人历史学会网页：www.Sandiego-online.com/forums/chinese/htmls/museum.htm。
③ 圣地亚哥中华历史博物馆网页：www.sandiego-online.com/forums/chinese/htmls/museum.htm。
④ 罗省华美历史博物馆网页：www.camla.org/。
⑤ 纽约华人博物馆网页：http://fargo.itp.tsoa.nvu.edu/~chin/mca.info.htm。
⑥ 旧金山中华文化中心网页：www.c-c-c.org/。
⑦ 大波士顿华人文化协会网页：www.anewnet.com.gbcca.htm。
⑧ 尤他州族谱学会网页：www.familysearch.org。
⑨ 夏威夷孙中山基金会网页：http://sunvatsen.hawaii.org/。
⑩ 大温哥华中华文化中心博物馆档案馆网页：www.cccvan.com/musarc.htm
⑪ 大多伦多中华文化中心网页：www.cccgt.org/。
⑫ 温城中华文化中心网页：www.pangea.ca/~wccc/index2.html。
⑬ 加拿大人类文明博物馆亚洲部网页：www.civilization.ca/cmc/cmceng/welcmeng.html。
⑭ 圭亚那华人之根网页：http://CGRoots.tripod.com。
⑮ 国际亚洲学会侨乡研究网页：http://iias.leidenuniv.nl/iias/research/qiaoxiang/index.htm
⑯ 英国牛津大学中国研究所欧洲福州新移民研究项目网页：www.transcomm.ox.ac.uk/wwwroot/pieke.htm。
⑰ 法国当代中国研究中心网页：www.cefc.com.hk。
⑱ 世界海外华人研究学会网页：http://socrates.berkeley.edu/~ethnicst/issco。

会"①。前者主要是研究海外华人学者的联合组织,约每两年举行一次学术会议,探讨海外华人学者共同感兴趣的学术问题。后者为研究海外华人的学术研究机构与文献收藏机构的联合组织,也每两年举行一次会议,讨论国际上有关海外华人研究与文献收藏的合作问题。

综上所述,目前在全世界范围,研究海外华人或涉及海外华人研究的机构共约有一百四十六个。其中以中国大陆为最多,计四十八个。美国次之,二十六个。以下按数量排列为:东南亚地区十九个,日本十二个,欧洲九个,台湾八个,香港六个,加拿大四个,拉丁美洲和加勒比海地区三个,澳大利亚两个,韩国和南非各一个。另外,世界性的组织两个。

三、邵友保博士海外华人文献研究中心

(一)邵友保博士海外华人文献研究中心的缘起

美国俄亥俄大学邵友保博士海外华人文献研究中心是在1993年由香港著名银行家、全国政协委员、香港特别行政区筹委会委员邵友保博士赞助下于美国俄亥俄大学成立的。之所以在北美大陆的俄亥俄大学建立一个海外华人文献研究中心是基于以下两点考虑的。

其一,北美大陆有研究海外华人的巨大优势

目前世界各地区海外华人研究力量的发展状况并不平衡。以政府投入的力量论,当首推中国大陆。中国大陆所设立的海外华人研究的机构最多,从事海外华人研究的专业人员的数量也最大。中国大陆的优势是拥有大量中央和地方有关海外华人的官方档案资料,民间亦存有丰富的海外华人的族谱,同时对侨乡和海外华人对大陆投资的调查又有地利之便,因此中国大陆学者在华侨出国史、海外华人投资、侨乡研究等方面都居领先地位。但对于居位在中国境外的华人,由于语言、经费以及获得签证方面等存在的困难,大陆学者往往不能作实地考察和资料收集,其研究便多依赖于国外学者之二手资料,有"隔靴搔痒"之弊。

东南亚是海外华人的集中居住地,对当地华人的研究也起步最早。原来研究东南亚海外华人的主力是欧美和日本的学者,近数十年来,当地的海外华人学者开始崛起,对东南亚华人的研究做出许多独特的贡献。然而,自"二战"结束以来,当地新独立国家以主体民族为主的政府往往推行狭隘的种族排他主义,限制甚至全盘禁止对海外华人的研究,许多珍贵的海外华人史料被毁,或被迫转移到其他国家。比如印尼雅加达的"中华公馆"成立于1775年,时至1950年该组织均保有完整的会议记录、审案通告、公共簿记、公墓和寺院清册,以及户籍、婚姻和死亡登记等,是研究雅加达华人历史极其宝贵的原始资料②。但基于安全的考虑,成百箱的公馆档案已于数年前运往荷兰的莱登大学,成为该校的特藏。在这一气氛下,海外华人研究便成了学术敏感课题或政治禁忌,令当地华人学者小心翼翼,害怕误触雷区。

日本海外华人研究学者的注意力多集中于东南亚华人圈、日本华社和中国大陆侨乡,尤其是对经济方面的调查感兴趣。日本学者以对材料收集的广泛和对分析的细腻见长。缺点是日本学者喜欢自成体系,百分之九十五以上的论著以日文发表,不谙日文的外国学者

---

① 世界海外华人研究与文献收藏机构联合会网页:www.overseaschineseconfederation.org。
② Leonard Blusse, Cheng Shaogang, Wu Fengbin: Kong Koan Betawi—Inventaris van het ar chief van de Chinese raad of Kongkoan te Batavia (1775 – 1950) (Institute for the History of European Expansion, Leiden, 1996)。

无从得其精髓①。欧洲的英国、法国、荷兰原为东南亚国家的宗主国，保有大量当时殖民地政府的档案资料，因而这些国家的学者也往往偏重对战前东南亚华人历史的研究，对欧洲和东南亚之外的海外华人则较少关注。

同以上地区比较，北美拥有研究海外华人的诸多优势。

首先，北美是海外华人数量增长最快的地区。据估计，至90年代中期，美国华人总数已达二百万人，超过日裔、韩裔、菲裔，成为美国亚裔人口中数量最大的族裔②。在加拿大，由于华人数量的剧增，华语已成为仅次于英语和法语的第三大通用语言③。目前，北美已仅次于东南亚，成为海外华人最集中的居住地；而且，如按目前的增长速度，在可预见的未来，美国将超过印尼成为海外华人数量最多的国家。同时，北美华人不仅在量上，而且在质的构成上也代表着海外华人发展的新趋向。因此，对北美华人的研究很快将与对东南亚华人的研究齐驱，成为海外华人研究的两大重点课题。

其次，同东南亚地区不同，美国和加拿大重视对多元文化的研究。北美华人作为一个日显重要的少数民族族裔也因之日益受到学术界的广泛重视。美国拥有数量仅次于中国大陆的海外华人研究机构与团体便是一个很好的证明。

第三，北美具有研究海外华人的雄厚学术力量。在美国，总共有五十五所大学进行有关亚裔的研究和教学，其中二十五所大学设有亚裔研究中心，十八所大学设有亚裔研究系，此外还有十二所大学开设亚裔课程④。这些亚裔中心和亚裔系大多也包括对北美华人的研究。对东南亚的华人研究，则由高校中的东南亚研究中心进行。在美国，共有十五所大学设有东南亚研究中心⑤。美国大学的东亚研究中心也致力于海外华人研究，特别是对海外华人经济圈以及中国大陆海外华人政策的研究。美国共有四十七所大学设有亚洲或东亚研究中心或系⑥。此外，美国大学的拉美研究中心、非洲研究中心、欧洲研究中心等也都有能力对这些地区的华人进行研究。因此，与中国大陆、日本、欧洲等相比较，美国具有全方位研究海外华人的巨大潜力。

第四，北美是国际学术交流的主要中心。由于1990美国学术力量雄厚、资讯发达、交通便捷，因而国际学术会议多选在美国举办。从1990年以来，已有多次有关海外华人的大型国际学术会议在美国举行，其中包括1990年在康奈尔大学召开的有关印尼华人现状的国际学术会议，1992年在加州大学伯克利分校召开的有关海外华人"落地生根"的国际学术会议，1997年在伊州大学香槟—乌布拉分校召开的有关东南亚华人人口的国际学术会议⑦，和2000年在俄亥俄大学召开的有关海外华人研究机构国际合作的会议。此外，每年一度极其盛大的美国亚洲学会年会也多有关于海外华人的专题讨论。

其二，俄亥俄大学有研究海外华人的优越条件

俄亥俄大学立校于1804年，是美国历史最悠久的大学之一⑧。俄亥俄大学与华人的联系可溯源至1909年，是年俄大招收了第一名来自中国广东的学生。此后，有数以千计来

---

① 福崎久一：《华人、华侨关系文献目录》，アジア经济研究所，1996年版日文部分。
② Lynn Pan: The Encyclopedia of the Chinese overseas (Singapore: Archipelago Press, 1998), p. 269.
③ 同上，第234页。
④ Asian American Studies Program, Cornell University: Directory of Asian American Studies Program (Ithaca, New York: 1999).
⑤ Virginia Jing-yi Shih: International Directory of Southeast Asia Librarians & Catalogers (Uuniversity of California, Berkeley, 2001).
⑥ CEAL 网页：http://staff.washington.edu/rrbritt/ceal/。
⑦ Hwa-wei Lee（李华伟）: "Dr. You-Bao Shao overseas Chinese Documentation and research Center" presented at Special Conference of the Evolving research Library and East Asian Studies (Beijing, 1996).
⑧ 俄亥俄大学网页：www.ohiou.edu。

自中国大陆、台湾、香港，以及东南亚和美国本地的华人学生就读于俄大，"邵友保博士海外华人文献研究中心"的主要赞助人邵公全博士便是俄大70年代的毕业生。目前，俄大有五百余名华人学生，华人教职员工亦有数十名，二者连同家属构成俄大校园最大的少数族裔。

俄亥俄大学的海外华人研究与该校的东南亚研究联系密切。俄大的东南亚研究始于1967年，当年该校建立了跨学科的东南亚研究中心和图书馆东南亚收藏部[①]。俄大的东南亚研究不久就被美国政府指定为美国国家的东南亚研究基地（National resource Center for Southeast Asian Studies）。在联邦政府数百万美元支持下，俄大的东南亚研究中心和图书馆东南亚收藏部迅速发展，成为世界闻名的东南亚研究重镇之一。目前，俄大校内有十数名教授和学者致力于东南亚问题的研究，学校与东南亚的教育研究机构和学者之间保持着紧密的交流合作关系。同时，俄大图书馆东南亚收藏部成为世界上最重要的东南亚资料收藏库之一。该部目前占地两万平方英尺，计有藏书和装订期刊二十一万八千册，微缩胶片四万五千卷，常年期刊、报纸和研究报告系列九千余种。每年新增藏书一万一千余册。有鉴于俄大图书馆东南亚收藏部的实力和名誉，1985年马来西亚联邦政府特别指定其为马来西亚在北美的资讯中心。两年之后，马来西亚联邦政府又进一步指定该部为马来西亚出版物北美收藏点，由马来西亚国家图书馆负责提供各种出版物。

俄大在发展其东南亚研究项目的同时，十分重视对该地区海外华人的研究。俄大图书馆东南亚收藏部除广泛收集中国大陆、台湾和欧美国家关于东南亚华人的出版物外，亦委托美国国会图书馆设在东南亚的采购中心大量收集当地华人的出版物。俄大东南亚研究中心和图书馆东南亚收藏部在研究和收集东南亚华人资料方面所付出的努力为"邵友保博士海外华人文献研究中心"的建立奠定了坚实的基础。"邵友保博士海外华人文献研究中心"遂以东南亚为起点，进而扩大收藏并研究北美乃至全球的海外华人文献资料。

（二）邵友保博士海外华人文献研究中心的宗旨与目标

邵友保博士海外华人文献研究中心的宗旨是充分利用北美大陆和俄亥俄大学优越的学术条件，通过收集全球海外华人文献资料，开展有关海外华人的研究和教学，以及推动国际的学术合作等来再现海外华人奋斗与贡献的历史。此历史不仅是海外华人所居国家历史发展的重要组成部分，亦是悠久中华文明在海外的延伸与光大。

邵友保博士海外华人文献研究中心的工作目标具体分述如下：

1. 文献资料的收集

海外华人对东南亚以及世界各地的经济文化发展贡献巨大，然而由于一些国家狭隘的种族排他主义对海外华人研究所设的种种限制，海外华人的历史文献资料未得到应有的重视，零散于世界各地的许多珍贵文献日益流失，老一辈华人领袖及重要历史事件见证人亦逐渐辞世，征集文字手稿和口述历史资料之工作备显急迫。

邵友保博士海外华人文献研究中心的工作目标之一便是广泛地收集、整理和保存有关海外华人的文献资料，其中包括政府档案、私人手稿、家谱、碑铭、口述记录，以及重要报刊文章等。同时为使世界各地的学者能方便而有效地通过现代化图书馆网络与资讯系统使用文献资料，邵友保博士海外华人文献研究中心亦积极地开展建立数据库的工作。目前正在建立的有《海外华人文献数据库》。该数据库将输入百余年来以中、日、英、法、西班牙、印尼、马来等语种出版或发表的有关海外华人的书籍，报刊文章和论文。数据库将

[①] 俄亥俄大学东南亚研究中心网页http://www.ohiou.edu/seas/index.html。
俄亥俄大学图书馆东南亚收藏部网页：www.library.ohiou.edu/libinfo/depts/sea/sea.htm。

通过国际互联网提供给世界各地研究海外华人的学者使用。邵友保博士海外华人文献研究中心还准备与其他的海外华人研究机构和团体合作,共同建立"世界各地海外华人研究机构与学者资源库"、"美国知名华人数据库"、"世界知名华人数据库"、"世界各地华人社团数据库"和"世界各地华人工商企业数据库"等。

2. 研究与教学

邵友保博士海外华人文献研究中心努力推动国际上对海外华人的研究。自成立以来,邵友保博士海外华人文献研究中心赞助了1996年在新加坡召开的"客家学国际学术会议",1997年在伊州大学香槟—乌布拉分校召开的"东南亚华人人口国际学术会议"和1998年在广州暨南大学召开的"中国各海外华人研究所所长联合工作会议";独立主办了2000年在俄亥俄大学举行的首届"海外华人研究机构国际合作会议"。

与此同时,邵友保博士海外华人文献研究中心出席了1998年6月在荷兰莱登召开的"国际亚洲学会"年会中关于海外华人原始资料的研讨会,1998年10月在福建晋江由厦门大学南洋研究院主持召开的关于侨乡研究的国际学术会议,1998年12月在马尼拉由"世界海外华人研究学会"召开的"华人国际研讨会"和2000年3月在加州召开的"美国亚洲学会"年会中的关于海外华人原始资料的研讨会。邵友保博士海外华人文献研究中心向以上各国际学术会议均提交了论文。

邵友保博士海外华人文献研究中心还负责主持了1999年10月由日本九州华侨华人研究会主办的"长崎唐人街立埠三百周年国际学术会议"中关于日本与福建海上贸易的研讨会和2000年五月在俄大召开的"俄亥俄州华人学者和专业人士学术年会"中的海外华人探讨会。

在研究方面,邵友保博士海外华人文献研究中心还准备以电子刊物的形式发表海内外学者有关海外华人的学术文章,此后,经过充分的准备,再创办一份国际性的海外华人学术研究刊物(暂定名《海外华人研究学刊》)以发表世界各地学者在海外华人研究方面有分量的文章。

在教学方面,邵友保博士海外华人文献研究中心已为俄大国际研究中心开设了"东南亚海外华人研究"的研究生课程,讲述中国海外华人政策之沿革、东南亚华人之历史、经济、社会结构、与主体民族的关系及东南亚各国华社之现状和面临的问题等。此课程很受研究生好评,已列为俄大国际研究中心东南亚专业研究生班的常设课程。除研究生课程外,中心亦指导研究生和本科生关于海外华人的论文。

3. 推动国际合作

海外华人研究的发展势必要求全球各海外华人研究机构共同加强合作。为推动海外华人研究机构之间的国际合作,邵友保博士海外华人文献研究中心在2000年三月发起并主办了首届"海外华人研究机构国际合作会议"。来自中国大陆、台湾、香港、日本、东南亚、澳洲、欧洲和北美的五十多个研究所、图书馆、学会、高校教学单位、博物馆和民间后援会派负责人或代表参加了这次会议。此次开创性的会议在海外华人学术界中影响弥远,大陆的《人民日报(海外版)》(2000年4月12日)[①]、台北华侨总会的《侨协杂志》(总第六十九期)、香港的《港澳之友通讯》(总第三十一期)、东京的《日本侨报》(2000年夏季刊)和俄国国家科学院的《族裔研究(Diaspora)》2000年夏季刊)均对会议作了详尽报道。目前,邵友保博士海外华人文献研究中心正与香港中文大学图书馆、香港大学

---

① 《人民日报(海外版)》(2000年4月12日)。

图书馆、香港浸会大学图书馆、香港岭南大学图书馆共同积极筹备2002年在香港举行的更大规模的第二届"海外华人研究机构国际合作会议"。

在首届"海外华人研究机构国际合作会议"期间，与会的代表发起并成立以俄亥俄大学邵友保博士海外华人文献研究中心为基地的"世界海外华人研究与文献收藏机构联合会"。联合会由从事海外华人研究与文献收藏的研究中心、图书馆、学会、高校教学单位、博物馆、档案馆和学者个人组成。其宗旨是综合机构与学者的集体力量来推动海外华人研究。联合会通过探讨、规划和实施在研究与文献收集方面的联合项目来促进成员间的国际合作[1]。联合会将在第二届"海外华人研究机构国际合作会议"召开的同时举行成员大会。

俄亥俄大学邵友保博士海外华人文献研究中心是邵友保博士慷慨捐赠五十万美元得以建立，又承知名实业家邵公全博士慷慨赞助二十八万美元设立了中心主任职。该中心甫成立，任重而道远。我们正努力从支持海外华人研究事业的热心人士中募集两百万美元作为永久基金，以使中心发展为世界第一流的海外华人收藏与研究机构。

资料来源
中文部分
1. 丁炯淳，谢美华："华侨博物院介绍"in International Conference of Institutes and Libraries for overseas Chinese Studies—Papers and Abstracts（Athens，Ohio，USA，March 24 – 25，2000）
2. 郭梁："近代以来日本的华侨、华人研究（1914—1996）"载于庄国土等主编：《世纪之交的海外华人》，（福建人民出版社，1998年版）。
3. 方雄普，谢成佳：《华侨华人概况》，中国华侨出版社1993年版。
4. "跨世纪中国的人才资源"载《华声月刊》（1996年第6期）
5. 黄露夏：《马来西亚的华人》，福建人民出版社1999版。
6. 暨南大学图书馆华侨华人文献信息中心：《1946—1997中国华侨侨务信息资源库》（电子工业出版社，CD光盘）
7. 联合早报（电子版）》（7/11/2000）："从1991年至1999年马国华人人口比例减少1.4个百分点"
8. 刘汉标等：《世界华侨华人概况》（欧洲，美洲卷），暨南大学出版社1994年版。
9. 毛起雄，林晓东：《中国侨务政策概述》（中国华侨出版社，1993年版）
10. 世界华商经济年鉴编辑委员会：《世界华商经济年鉴1996/1997》，企业管理出版社1996年版。
11. 许苏吾：《南洋学会与南洋研究》（Singapore：South Seas Publishers，1977）
12. 王士录：《当代越南》，四川人民出版社1992年版。
13. 巫乐华：《华侨史概要》，中国华侨出版社1994年版。
14. 杨国标等：《美国华侨史》，广东高等教育出版社1989年版。
15. 张希哲："国际合作研究'海外华人'的新境界——参加俄亥俄大学'海外华人研究机构国际合作会议'记略"，载于《侨协杂志》第六十九期（2000年夏季刊）
16. 张希哲：《美国华侨史略与美国华侨社会之发展》，华侨协会总会1997年版。
17. 郑观应：《盛世危言后编》。

---

[1] 见世界海外华人研究与文献收藏机构联合会网页www.overseaschineseconfederation.org。

18. 庄国土：《中国封建政府的华侨政策》，厦门大学出版社 1989 年版。

日文部分

1. 福崎久一：《华人·华俸关系文献目录》，アジア经济研究所 1996 年版。

英文部分

1. Asian American Studies Program, Cornell University: *Directory of Asian American Studies Program* (Ithaca, New York: 1999).

2. Canada Bureau of Statistics: *Census of Canada, 1991: Population* (Ottawa: 1992).

3. Finn, Michael: *Stay rates of Foreign Doctorate recipients from U. S. Universities, 1997* (Oak ridge, TN: Oak ridge Institute for Science and Education, 2000).

4. Guo, Yuigui Guo: "The Eventual Tendency: To Integrate Chinese Scientists and Engineers into International Community of Science" in *International Conference of Institutes and Libraries for overseas Chinese Studies*—Papers and Abstracts (Athens, Ohio, USA, March 24 – 25, 2000).

5. Hill, Susan T.: *Science and Engineering Doctorate Awards: 1996* (Arlington: National Science Foundation, 1997).

6. Institute of International Education: *Open Doors 1998/1999: report on International Educational Exchange* (New York: 1999).

7. Johnson, Jean M.: "Collaboration in Information Exchange between the United States and China" presented to CIES 2000 Conference (San Antonio, Texas, March 7 – 11, 2000).

8. Kraar, Louis: "Importance of Chinese in Asian Business" in *Journal of Asian Business*, V. 9, No. 1 (Winter 1993).

9. Lai, David Chuen-Yan: Chinatowns: *Towns within Cities in Canada* (Vancouver: University of Columbia Press, 1988).

10. Lee, Hwa-Wei (李华伟): "Dr. You-Bao Shao overseas Chinese Documentation and research Center" presented at Special Conference of the Evolving research Library and East Asian Studies (Beijing, 1996).

11. Li, Chen-ching: "returning Home after Studying in the USA: reverse Brain Drain in Taiwan" in *Cultural & Educational Digest*, 1995a.

12. Lyman, Stanford M.: *Chinese Americans* (New York, random House, 1974).

13. National Science Foundation, Division of Science resources Studies: *Statistics Profiles of Foreign Doctoral recipients in Science and Engineering*: Plans to Stay in the United States (Arlington, VA, 1998).

14. Pan, Lynn: *The Encyclopedia of the Chinese overseas* (Singapore: Archipelago Press, 1998).

15. Shih, Virginia Jing-yi: *International Directory of Southeast Asia Librarians & Catalogers* (University of California, Berkeley, 2001).

16. Stephan, Paula E. and Sharon G. Levin: *Exceptional Contributions to U. S. Science by the Foreign-Born and Foreign-Educated*-a research paper supported by the Alfred P. Sloan Foundation.

17. "The overseas Chinese—A Driving Force" in T*he Economist* (July 18 – 24, 1992).

18. United States *National Science Board*: *Science and Engineering Indicators 1998* (Washington, D. C.: National Science Foundation, 1998.

19. U. S. Bureau of the Census: *Historical Statistics of the United States*: *Colonial Times to 1970* (U. S. Government Printing office, 1975).

20. U. S. Bureau of the Census: *1990 Census of Population*: *Asians and Pacific Islanders in the United States* (U. S. Government Printing office, 1993).

21. U. S. Bureau of the Census: *1990 Census of Population*: *General Population Characteristics* (U. S. Government Printing office, 1992).

荷文部分

1. Leonard Blusse, Cheng Shaogang, Wu Fengbin: Kong Koan Betawi—*Inventaris van het archief van de Chinese raad of Kongkoan te Batavia* (*1775 – 1950*) (Institute for the History of European Expansion, Leiden, 1996).

网络资源

1. 澳华博物馆网页: http: //home. vicnet. net. au/%7Emcah/welcome. htm
2. CEAL 网页: http: //staff. washington. edu/rrbritt/ceal/
3. 创意综合研究所网页: www. sovi. co. ip/
4. 大波士顿华人文化协会网页: www. anewnet. com. gbcca. htm
5. 大多伦多中华文化中心网页: www. cccgt. org/
6. 大圣地亚哥华人历史学会网页: www. sandiego-online. com/forums/chinese/htmls/museum. htm
7. 大温哥华中华文化中心博物档案馆网页: www. cccvan. com/musarc. htm
8. 淡江大学国际研究学院东南亚研究所网页: www2. tku. edu. tw/~ibx/homepage. htm
9. 俄亥俄大学网页: www. ohiou. edu
10. 俄亥俄大学东南亚研究中心网页: http: //www. ohiou. edu/seas/index. html
11. 俄亥俄大学图书馆东南亚特藏部网页: www. library. ohiou. edu/libinfo/depts/sea/sea. htm
12. 法国当代中国研究中心网页: www. cefc. com. hk
13. 菲律宾华裔青年中心网页: www. kaisa. org. ph
14. 圭亚那华人之根网页: http: //CGroots. tripod. com
15. 国际亚洲学会侨乡研究网页: http: //iias. leidenuniv. nl/iias/research/qiaoxiang/index. htm。
16. "国立"暨南国际大学东亚研究中心网页: www. dseas. ncnu. edu. tw/
17. "国立"中山大学东南亚研究中心网页: www2. nsysu. edu. tw/cseas/
18. 海外华人研究学会网页: www. cca. gov. tw/Culture/resources/cartgroup/misc/index113. htm
19. 旧金山中华文化中心网页: www. c-c-c. org/
20. 华美协会网页: www. ocanatl. org

21. 华裔馆网页：www.huayihome.org/
22. 暨南大学东南亚研究所网页：www.jnu.edu.cn/yxjs.center/cdny.html
23. 暨南大学华侨华人研究所网页：www.jnu.edu.cn"华侨华人"部分
24. 暨南大学图书馆华侨华人文献信息中心网页：www.jnu.edu.cn"图书馆"部分
25. 加拿大人类文明博物馆亚洲部网页：www.civilization.ca/cmc/cmceng/welcmeng.html
26. 岭南大学族群与海外华人经济研究部网页：www.ln.edu.hk/eocb/intro.htm
27. 马来西亚华社研究中心网页：http://huayan.net.my
28. 南方学院马华文学馆网页：www.southern.edu.my/mahua/index.html
29. 罗省华美历史博物馆网页：www.camla.org/
30. 美国俄亥俄大学邵友保博士海外华人文献研究中心网页：www.library.ohiou.edu/sub亚cts/shao/main.htm
31. 美国华人历史学会网页：www.chsa.org
32. 美华学会网页：www.montana.com.maiwah/
33. 南方华裔研究中心网页：http://rspas.anu.edu.au/cscad/
34. 南加州华人历史学会网页：www.chssc.org
35. 南洋理工大学图书馆海外华人文库网页：www.ntu.edu.sg/library/overseass/chinese.htm
36. 纽约华人博物馆网页：http://fargo.itp.tsoa.nyu.edu/~chin/mca.info.htm
37. 全球华人专业人士网络：http://www.networkchinese.com/
38. 砂拉越华族文化协会网页：www.inet.com.my/scca
39. 山东大学历史文化学院华侨华人研究所网页：www.sdu.edu.cn/csdu/yx/history.html
40. 圣地亚哥中华历史博物馆网页：www.sandiego-online.com/forums/chinese/htmls/museum.htm
41. 海外华人研究学会网页：http://socrates.berkeley.edu/~ethnicst/issco
42. 世界海外华人研究与文献收藏机构联合会网页：www.overseaschineseconfederation.org
43. 世界华人联盟网页：www.huren.org/
44. 泰国朱拉隆功大学亚洲研究院亚洲移民研究中心网页：www.chula.ac.th/institute/arcm/
45. 温城中华文化中心网页：www.pangea.ca/~wccc/index2.html
46. 夏威夷孙中山基金会网页：http://sunyatsen.hawaii.org/
47. 香港大学华侨华人文献研究中心网页：www.hku.hk/lib/FpsLib/
48. 香港浸会大学图书馆当代中国研究资料部网页：www.hkbu.edu.hk/lib
49. 香港中文大学海外华人研究中心网页：www.cuhk.edu.hk/proi/oca/oca.htm
50. 新加坡国立大学中文图书馆海外华人特藏库网页：www.lib.nus.edu.sg/chz/chineseoverseas/
51. 新加坡宗乡会馆联合总会网页：www.sfcca.org.sg/
52. 新英格兰华人历史学会网页：http://yerkes.mit.edu/Chinatown/morechsne.html
53. 英国牛津大学中国研究所欧洲福州新移民研究项目网页：www.transcomm.ox.ac.uk/wwwroot/pieke.htm
54. 尤他州族谱学会网页：www.familysearch.org
55. 在日中国人文献资料中心网页：www.cf.net/cpi/ch/index.html

56. 中国海外交流协会网页：www. coea. org
57. 中山大学东南亚研究所网页：www. zsu. edu. cn/english/southasian. htm
58. "中央研究院"东南亚区域研究网页：www. sinica. edu. tw/％Eproseaw3/
59. "中央研究院"近代史研究所海外华人研究群"网页：http：//w2. world. net. tw/？overseas/
60. "中央研究院"中山人文社会科学研究所历史与思想组网页：www. issp. sinica. edu. tw/

美国国会图书馆建立世界级亚洲馆藏

Building a World-Class Asian Collection in the Library of Congress

The Beginning

The first acquisition of an Asian collection in the Library of Congress can be traced back to 1865 when the Smithsonian Institution transferred a collection of books on Southeast Asia and Pacific islands that had been gathered in Singapore by the Wilkes Exploring Expedition from 1838 to 1842. Four years later, in 1869, the Emperor of China (Tung-Chih 同治皇帝) presented to the Library of Congress 10 major Chinese works in 933 volumes. This was soon followed by the exchange of government publications with the Japanese government initiated in 1875. [1] From these early beginnings, the collection of Asian publications from all parts of Asia and in all major and some minor Asian languages have grown to more than 2.5 million items in a variety of formats. In addition to the holdings in the Asian Division, important Asian collections of legal materials, maps, music, motion pictures, prints, and photographs are housed and cared for by other divisions in the Library of Congress in collaboration with the Asian Division. These other units include the Law Library, the Geography and Map Division, the Prints and Photographs Division, the Motion Picture, Broadcasting and Recorded Sound Division, the Performing Arts Division, the Manuscript Division, etc. Other Asia-related publications not in Asian languages are also housed in the Main Reading Room, Microform Reading Room, Newspaper and Current Periodical Reading Room, Performing Arts Reading Room, Science Reading Room, and in some of the other area studies and special collections.

The name of Asian Division has gone through several changes since 1928 when the Division of Chinese Literature was established for the first time through the effort of Herbert Putnam, Librarian of Congress (1899–1939). Three years later, in 1931, the name was changed to the Division of Chinese and Japanese Literature. In 1932, it was renamed the Division of Orientalia. This was changed again to the Asiatic Division in 1942 and changed back to Orientalia Division in 1944. Finally, the name of Asian Division was formally adopted in 1978. [2]

The Vision and Mission

Guided by the mission statement of the Library of Congress—*The Library's mission is to make its resources available and useful to the Congress and the American people and to sustain and preserve a universal collection of knowledge and creativity for future generations*[3]—the vision and mission of the Asian Division are:

Vision of the Asian Division:

To establish the collections of the Asian Division as the premier research and scholarly resource of all formats and times on Asia and in Asian languages that is compatible with the dynamics of knowledge and creativity of the 21st Century-frequently referred to as the "Asian Century".

Mission of the Asian Division:

The mission of the Asian Division is to make comprehensive collection resources and information services related to Asia available and useful to the Congress, American people, and the scholarly

---

[1] *The Asian Division*. Washington, DC: The Library of Congress, 2002: pp. 1, 2, 4, 8.

[2] Chi Wang. *The Chinese Collection in the Library of Congress: A Brief Introduction*. Washington, DC: Chinese Section, Asian Division, Library of Congress, 2001: pp. 5–6.

[3] *The Mission and Strategic Priorities of the Library of Congress: FY 1997–2004*. Washington, DC: Library of Congress, 1997.

research community nationally and internationally. ①

The Organization

Although the Library of Congress is the library of the American Congress, it has also served as the national library of the United States of America. For the discharge of its mission as the library of the Congress, there is a unit called Congressional Research Service. The chief responsibility of this unit is to provide the Congress with research and analysis on the full range of legislative policy issues. For carrying out the functions of the national library, there is another unit called Library Services, headed by an Associate Librarian. The position is now held by Dr. Deanna Marcum. There is another unit named Law Library, which holds the world's largest law collections covering U. S., foreign, and international law.

The Asian Division is one of the four area studies divisions (African and Middle Eastern Division, Asian Division, European Division, and Hispanic Division) reporting to the Assistant Librarian for Library Services and Director for Area Studies Collections. Dr. Carolyn Brown is in charge of this part of Library Services. She is also in charge of the Federal Research Division and the Office of Scholarly Programs.

Within the Asian Division, under the general leadership and management of the Chief, there is a plan for a Head of Collection Services and a Head of Scholarly Services. The professional staff members of the division, who are either area specialists or reference librarians, are divided into five area teams: China and Mongolia, Japan, Korea, Southeast Asia, and South Asia. A coordinator of each team is appointed from the team members by the Chief. The Chief is also assisted by an Administrative Officer, an Information Technology Specialist, and a Secretary. Hopefully, another position with the responsibility for outreach and special events can be added soon.

Division of Labor

When it was first founded, the Asian Division was largely responsible for the selection, acquisition, and maintenance of its rapidly growing Asian collections. In the subsequent years, the work of acquisitions has been undertaken by the African/Asian Acquisitions and Overseas Operations Division and the Serial Record Division of the Directorate for Acquisitions. The entire work of cataloging is done by the Regional and Cooperative Cataloging Division of the Directorate for Cataloging, while the work of binding, conservation, and microfilming is the responsibility of the Directorate for Preservation. The Automation Planning and Liaison Office take care of the needs of computer applications and system operations. The Asian Division works very closely with all these and other units in the Library of Congress to carry out its responsibilities and daily operations.

Building Comprehensive Asian Collections

Recognizing the importance of Asia in the 21st century the Library of Congress has devoted great effort to building a comprehensive collection of Asia. Today, after 138 years of painstaking work by generations of Asian area specialists, librarians, and scholars, a vast storehouse of knowledge and culture about the diverse nations, languages, and peoples has been assembled. It is perhaps the best of such collections outside Asia. With the foresight of Dr. James Billington, the current Librarian of the Congress, an exquisite Asian Reading Room has been provided as a gateway to this world-class collection. Below are brief descriptions of the key collections by countries or geographic regions:

---

① *The Strategic Plan of the Asian Division, 2003 to 2008*. Washington, DC: Asian Division, the Library of Congress, 2003.

The Chinese and Mongolian Collection

The Chinese and Mongolian Collection consists of 900,000 volumes and physical pieces. Besides works in the Chinese language, it also includes several thousand volumes in Manchu, Mongol, Naxi (Moso), Tibetan, and other minority languages. The collection covers all subjects and is especially strong in the humanities and social sciences, among them, classical Chinese literature, archival materials of the Qing (清) dynasty (1644 – 1911) and Republican (民国) period (1911 – 1949), traditional Chinese medicine, local and regional histories (gazetteers), and contemporary publications of Mainland China, Hong Kong, and Taiwan.

The collection also contains some of the most valuable rare books from China and Mongolia. The rare books from China cover Song (宋) dynasty (960 – 1279), Jin (金) dynasty (1115 – 1234), Yuan (元) dynasty (1271 – 1368), Ming (明) dynasty (1368 – 1644), and Qing (清) dynasty (1644 – 1911). It includes a Buddhist invocation sutra (一切如来, Yi qie ru lai) printed in 975 A.D. that was recovered from the hollow bricks of the foundation of the Thunder Peak Pagoda (雷峰塔, Lei feng ta) when it collapsed in 1924, 41 of the 400 surviving volumes of 1560 copy of the *Great Encyclopedia of the Ming Emperor Yongle* (永乐大典, Yongle da dian), and the 1895 – 1998 printing of the **Imperial Encyclopedia of China** (古今图书集成, Gu jin tu shu ji cheng) in 5,044 volumes.

Examples of other unique collections are the 3,334 pictographic manuscripts from the Naxi 纳西 minority group in Yunnan province, the Gamble collection of a 19th-century American missionary printer that includes Christian publications in Chinese and translations of Western works, and the Arthur W. Hummel collection of rare Chinese maps. ①

The Library of Congress is one of the world's leading centers for Tibetan publications with holdings that are representative of the entire body of Tibetan literature from the 8th century to the modern day. These include religious texts, history, biography, traditional medicine, astrology, iconography, musical notations, grammars, social sciences, and secular literature.

Since religion plays a major role in Tibetan society, the holdings of Tibetan Buddhist scriptures in the Asian Division are especially strong. The Tibetan Buddhist canon is contained in the **Kanjur**, in over a hundred volumes of sutras, and the **Tanjur**, most editions totaling some 225 volumes of commentaries. The Tibetan canonical texts are accurate translations of the original Buddhist texts, written in Sanskrit between 500 BC. and 900 AD. Among the individuals who were responsible for the early periods of development of the Tibetan collection are William Woodville Rockhill, the American diplomat and Tibetologist who travels in Mongolia and Tibet between 1888 and 1892 and again in the 1900s; Berthold Laufer, another leading Tibetologist in the late 1800s; and Joseph Rock, the colorful explorer, adventurer, and scientist who lived and traveled in China's rugged west for 27 years in the early 1900s. ②

The Japanese Collection

After the initial arrangement for the exchange of government publications established in 1875 between the two governments, the Japanese collection began to grow in 1905 when a significant gift was received from Crosby Stuart Noyes, journalist and editor of the **Washington Evening Star**. The Noyes collection included 658 illustrated books produced from the mid-18th-century to the late-19th century. In 1907, a systematic effort was undertaken by Kan'ichi Asakawa of Yale University to purchase Japanese books for the Library of Congress. Because of his effort, some 9,072 volumes on the subjects of Japanese history, literature, Buddhism, Shinto, geography, music, and the arts were added. In 1930, the Library appointed Dr. Shiho Sakanishi as the Chief Assistant of the Japanese Section to further develop the collection. During her tenure from 1930 to 1941, the collection tripled in size. Today, the Japanese collection has grown to 1.1 million volumes of monographs and serials as well as extensive microfilm and microfiche holdings-the largest collection in the Asian Division-through purchase, gift, exchange, and other avenues of

---

① *The Chinese Collection*. Washington, DC: Asian Division, the Library of Congress, n. d.
② *The Tibetan Collection*. Washington, DC: Asian Division, Library of Congress, April 2002.

acquisition.

Among the wealth of rare items are approximately 5,000 titles of publications and manuscript copies of works produced before the end of the Tokugawa Shogunate in 1868 and the beginning of the Meiji period (1868 – 1912). Included are the **dharani**(百万搭陀罗尼) prayer charms, which date to 770 A. D. and are among the world's earliest surviving printed material. Also noteworthy are a complete edition of the Japanese literary masterpiece **Genji monogatari**(《源氏物语》, The Tale of Genji) published in Kyoto in 1654 and the **Yoshitsune azuma kudari monogatari** printed on movable type between 1624 and 1643. A complete catalogue of the rare books in the Library of Congress was published in 2003 by Yagi Shoten in Tokyo.① At the end of World War II, a large number of historical documents such as the former Japanese Imperial Army and Navy, the South Manchuria Railway Company, and the East Asian Research Institute were given to the Library by the Washington Document Center. Much of the materials from the latter two are pre-World War II studies on such areas as Korea, Taiwan, Mainland China, Mongolia, and the Pacific Islands. The Library also has a microfilm copy of the archives of the Japanese Foreign Ministry from 1868 to 1945 and pre-1945 records of the Police Bureau of the Ministry of Home Affairs—some of these are censored wartime publications.②

Another important collection is the "Inoh Maps"—the first modern maps of Japan created originally by Tadataka Inoh between 1800 and 1821. Copies of 207 of the Inoh's original 214 sheets large-scale set (1∶36,000) that cover the Japanese archipelago from Hokkaido to Kyushu were discovered in the map collection of the Library of Congress in the spring of 2001 and have caused great excitement in Japan. In order to make these maps available for exhibition and for online access, all of them have been digitized and sent to the Japan Map Center. A selection of the actual-size reproductions of these maps is now on exhibition at the Tokyo National Museum from October 31 to December 14, 2003. Some of the original maps will also be loaned and exhibited in Kobe, Sendai, Atami, and Nagoya in 2004.

The Korean Collection

The Korean collection began in the 1920s with the generous gift of Korean books from Dr. James S. Gale, a Canadian missionary who spent 40 years in Korea from 1888 to 1928. Dr. Gale also helped the Library to acquire a number of Korean classics, including rare books from the estate of the Korean scholar Kim To-hui. Systematic development of the Korean collection was started in the early 1950s during the period of the Korean War. Today, the Korean collection in the Library totals 210,000 volumes in the Korean language, as well as 20,000 Japanese language books and 8,000 English language books on Korea. Coverage of North Korea is also strong, with some 10,000 items.

There are 480 titles of Korean rare books, in 3,000 volumes. They were all written in Chinese characters and printed on mulberry paper. Although China was the first county to use movable type made of clay, Korea was the first one to use movable metal type for printing. Several good examples of this type of printing are in the collection. These are the collected writings of the renowned 16th-century Confucian scholar and statesman Yi I printed in 1744 and the 1834 reprint of the works of the "father of Korean literature", Ch'oe Ch'i-won (857 – 915). Other rare books printed by woodblock include the **History of the Koryo Dynasty**(高丽史), printed in 1590, and the **Law Code of the Yi Dynasty**(经国大典), printed in 1630.③

The Southeast Asian Collection

As was mentioned in the beginning of this paper, the earliest acquisition of the Southeast Asian collection in the Library of Congress began in 1865, which predates the beginning of all other Asian collections. The collection was acquired in Singapore in 1842 by the U. S. Naval

---

① *Beikoku Gikai Toshokan zo Nihon Kotenseki Mokuroku* (Catalog of Japanese Rare Books in the Library of Congress). Tokyo: Yagi Shoten, 2003.
② *The Japanese Collection*. Washington, DC: Asian Division, the Library of Congress, n. d.
③ *The Korean Collection*. Washington, DC: Asian Division, the Library of Congress, n. d.

Exploring Expedition led by Lt. Charles Wilkes. Wilkes and the Expedition's philologist, Horatio Hale, collected Malay manuscripts and early printed books with the assistance of Alfred North, an American missionary in Singapore. The collection went first to the Smithsonian Institution which later transferred the collection to the Library of Congress in 1865. Included in this earliest acquisition are a unique collection of manuscripts written in the Buginese script of South Sulawesi; an account of the 19th-century Malay world written in Jawi, the **Hikayat Abdullah** (The Story of Abdullah); and an 1840 Mission Press edition of the **Sejarah Melayu** (Malay Annals), an important Malay history written in 1612, also in Jawi, the Malay language in Arabic script.

The Southeast Asian collection contains many palm leaf manuscript copies of the **Tipitaka**, the basic text of Theravada Buddhism which is the majority religion of Cambodia, Laos, Myanmar (Burma), and Thailand. In 1905, a special Thai **Tipitaka** was presented to the Library of Congress by King Chulalongkorn (Rama V) of Thailand. In 1949, an especially fine collection of Burmese manuscripts in the Pali language as well as a **Tipitaka** in Pali using Burmese script was presented to the Library of Congress as a part of a large Burmese donation. The donation also included an important Burmese history, **The Glass Palace Chronicle**, written by a group of scholars in 1829.

The Asian Division also holds rare materials from the Philippines and Vietnam. Of special note is a set of inscribed bamboo tubes, with lettering in the old Indic script similar to the ancient scripts used in neighboring Indonesia. The collection of 55 bamboos in prose and 22 in verse provides a fascinating glimpse into Mangyan (Hampangan) and Tagbanua society. Several examples of Vietnamese dynastic histories are also represented, including texts printed from early woodblocks at the former imperial palace at Hue.

In 1938, the Library of Congress launched the Indic Project in order to improve its collections from Southeast and South Asia, particularly publications in local languages. Following World War II, as U. S. interest in the region increased, the collection grew dramatically and today consists of holdings from Brunei, Cambodia, Indonesia, Laos, Malaysia, Myanmar, the Philippines, Singapore, Thailand, Vietnam, and many of the South Pacific island nations such as Papua New Guinea, etc. The establishment of the Library's overseas offices in New Delhi, India, in 1962, in Jakarta, Indonesia, in 1963, and in Islamabad, Pakistan, in 1965 has provided a continuous flow of books, newspapers, and periodicals from the region in a variety of formats. ①

The South Asian Collection

The foundation for the South Asian collection was laid in 1904 when a collection of over 4,000 books and pamphlets from the German Indologist, Dr. Albrecht Weber, was purchased. Included were texts in Sanskrit of India's sacred Hindu works—the **Vedas**, **Brahmanas**, and **Upanisads**—as well as the stories of the Puranas and the great epics in the **Mahabharata and the Ramayana**. In addition, there are a number of Weber's notebooks with his handwritten transcriptions of rare Indian texts for his pioneering critical editions.

In 1938, the Library received a grant from the Carnegie Corporation to develop the South Asian collection systematically, and it initiated the Indic Project— "Project F-Development of Indic Studies". During the 1950s the collection continued to expand and growth accelerated even further with the opening of the Library's New Delhi Overseas Office in 1962. Under the Public Law (PL) 480 program, the New Delhi office used rupees from Indian purchases of U. S. agricultural products to buy books and other materials from India and other countries of South Asia. An overseas office in Karachi, Pakistan, was opened in 1965 to oversee the acquisition of publications from Pakistan and neighboring areas. Later, the office was moved to the capital city, Islamabad.

Today, the South Asian collection holds materials in over 100 modern languages used in India, Pakistan, Bangladesh, Sri Lanka, and Nepal. The majority of the publications are in Hindi (20 percent), Bengali (15 percent), Urdu (13 percent), and Tamil (11 percent). Other languages represented in large numbers include Marathi, Telugu, Malayalam, Gujarati, and

---

① *The Southeast Asian Collection*. Washington, DC: Asian Division, Library of Congress, April 2002.

Kannada.

An example among the many rare books and manuscripts in the South Asian collection is a 1452 manuscript of the Jaina ***Kalpasutra*** from Gujarat in western India. This illustrated text tells the story of Mahavira, the founder of the Jaina religion. The "Crosby Khotan fragments" are also among the more unusual rare items. During a 1903 journey to Central Asia, Oscar Terry Crosby, an American who later became Assistant Secretary of the Treasury, purchased these manuscripts in Sanskrit at the Taklamakan oasis town of Khotan. ①

Between 1990 and 2000, a very important project undertaken by the New Delhi Overseas Office was the *Microfilming of Indian Publications Project* (MIPP). This project was a joint collaboration between the Government of India and the Library Congress, aimed at preserving and making accessible out-of-print works listed in the ***National Bibliography of Indian Literature: 1901-1953***. Some 22,686 titles in 15 languages were microfilmed from 67 repository libraries in India and 3 libraries outside India (the Library of Congress, University of Chicago, and British Library). These titles were selected by Indian scholars as being central to the understanding of India. ②

Overseas Offices

The accelerated growth of the library collections from South and Southeast Asia since the 1960s should be credited to the efforts of the overseas offices in New Delhi, Jakarta, and Islamabad. In addition to these three, the African/Asian Acquisitions and Overseas Operations Division of the Library of Congress also operate overseas offices in Cairo, Nairobi, and Rio de Janeiro.

One of the unique features of the three Asian overseas offices is the offering of their service to other libraries who want to acquire publications from countries and regions covered by these offices. For example, the 44 academic and research libraries, mostly from North America, that participated in the South Asia Cooperative Acquisitions Program (SACAP) receive publications of their choice from the New Delhi office and its many sub-offices. Being the largest and the oldest of the six overseas offices, the New Delhi office covers India, Bangladesh, Bhutan, the Maldives, Nepal, and Sri Lanka—as well as Burma, Mongolia, and the Mongolian and Tibetan Autonomous Regions of China. The New Delhi office performs a wide range of services to SACAP libraries, including acquisitions, cataloging, bibliographic control, and preservation of publications acquired in some 65 languages and 25 different scripts. Another service of the New Delhi office is the maintenance of an extensive program for official and informal exchanges of publications with key institutions and libraries in South Asia. ③

Scholarly services

The Asian Division and its Asian Reading Room, located in the Thomas Jefferson Building, across the street from the U.S. Capitol, is the primary public access point for researchers seeking to use the most comprehensive Asian Collection. In order to provide special guidance and service to researchers and scholars from near and far, a team of well trained and highly qualified reference librarians and area studies specialists who have extensive knowledge of the various collections are ready to be of assistance.

Besides on-site visits by scholars, which are essential to fully explore the wealth of the treasured Asian collection, readers are encouraged to search the Library of Congress online public access catalog for library holdings (http://catalog.loc.gov). In order to save their valuable

---

① *The South Asian Collection*. Washington, DC: Asian Division, Library of Congress, April 2002.
② *The Library of Congress in South Asia, 1960-2002. Celebrating 40 Years of Bibliographic and Cultural Exchanges*. New Delhi: Library of Congress Office, n. d. p. 16.
③ *The Library of Congress in South Asia, 1960-2002. Celebrating 40 Years of Bibliographic and Cultural Exchanges*. New Delhi: Library of Congress Office, n. d.

time, researchers may telephone or email ahead of their visits so that needed materials may be available for use upon arrival. Researchers in remote locations may also request items through interlibrary loan from their nearby libraries. Most rare materials may only be available for on-site use.

There is another advantage for on-site visits and that is the accessibility to a variety of online electronic databases. Because of the licensing agreement and other restrictions imposed by publishers these databases can only be searched and used onsite. In the digital age, the Asian Division is moving ahead in supplementing its printed collections by a growing body of electronic resources from e-books, e-journals, e-newspapers, to a wide range of e-materials, both digitized from printed version or born digital.

As a part of the Library's effort to provide more and more specialized digital resources online, such as the **American Memory** (http://memory.loc.gov/), the **Global Gateway** (http://international.loc.gov/intldl/intldlhome.html), etc., the Library's portals now serve as a gateway to selected web resources on a variety of subjects and world areas (http://www.loc.gov/rr/international/portals.html). The portals of the Asian Division (http://www.loc.gov/rr/asian/area_AD.html) are increasingly a useful source on all the Asian countries and regions. We invite you to visit our website and use the portals. You will do us a great favor by recommending more high quality and relevant websites so that we can continue to add and update our Asian portals.

Being a leader in the development of **QuestionPoint**—a worldwide online reference service operating on a 24-hours-a-day and 7-days-a-week schedule—now operated by the OCLC Online Computer Library Center, library users anywhere can now send their reference questions through OCLC online global network to the Library of Congress for reply by our reference librarians and area studies specialists (http://www.oclc.org/questionpoint). Library users may also use the service of **Asking a Librarians** (http://www.loc.gov/rr/askalib-asian.html) to get reference assistance from librarians in the Asian Division.

Kluge fellowships and other funding opportunities

Through the generous gift of $60 million from Mr. John W. Kluge, the John W. Kluge Center was established in 2000 in the Jefferson Building with funding from the Kluge endowment. The endowment also funds a number of Kluge Chair holders, distinguished visiting scholars, and Kluge post-doctoral fellows each year. A number of other fellowship opportunities funded by other private foundation gifts is also administered by the Kluge Center and the Office of Scholarly Programs. Recipients of Kluge fellowships may spend from six to twelve months at the Center with a monthly stipend which is sufficient to cover transportation and living expenses in the Washington, D C., area. Selected researchers and scholars are expected to use the extensive collections and resources of the Library of Congress for their research.

The Kluge Center especially encourages humanistic and social science research that makes use of the Library's large and varied collections. Interdisciplinary, cross-cultural, or multi-lingual research is particularly welcome. For information about the Kluge Center and its fellowships, please visit the website: http://www.loc.gov/Kluge or send email to: scholarly@loc.gov.

International cooperation

In order to further develop the Asian collections two important international roles of the Asian Division have been identified. They are:

1. Expand international relations for Asian librarianship, scholarship, and network.
2. Develop collaborative projects with organizations and institutions at the national and international levels.

For the first international role, the Asian Division endeavors to develop regular contacts with libraries and librarians in Asian countries in a joint effort to advance librarianship and scholarship. Being the world's largest library, the Library of Congress has been a frequent place of visit by many Asian librarians and information professionals. We want to extend our warmest welcome to all our visitors and hope that through such visits a mutually beneficial relationship can be established. Furthermore, it is our sincere hope that external funding may be found to support an internship program for Asian librarians who wish to pursue training and internship at the Asian Division.

For the second international role, we would like to develop collaborative projects with national libraries and international organizations for the purpose of sharing our resources to facilitate mutual understanding, international education, and scholarly research. One such project is the **Global Gateway Project** undertaken by the Library of Congress in collaboration with other national libraries in a joint effort to convert unique items from the collections of each into digital form and to share these at no cost over the Internet with the people of both countries and the world. Each of the projects is built around a broad theme that focuses on the culture and history of the respective partner country and in particular its interactions with the United States. The URL for **Global Gateway** is http://international.loc.gov. Currently, the Asian Division and the International Research Center for Japanese Studies (Nichibunken) are engaged in discussion for a joint digitization project for collections relating to Japan on the eve of its opening to the Western world and the subsequent development of U.S.-Japan relations. The project will include digitizing some of the rare Japanese collections in the Library of Congress.

（原载《跨越数字时代的信息服务：张鼎钟教授七秩荣庆论文集》，张鼎钟教授七秩荣庆筹备小组编，台北市：文华图书馆管理资讯股份有限公司2004版，第17－30页。）

美国国会图书馆的汉学资源 ①

Sinological Resources in the Library of Congress

美国国会图书馆的现况

美国国会图书馆创办于公元 1800 年。今天它不仅是美国国会的图书馆,同时也是服务美国人民的国家图书馆。它的馆藏总数是 1.28 亿册②,每天新增加 7,000 册③。是世界上最大、馆藏增加量最高的图书馆。其中包括不同类型的文献资料和 470 种不同的语言,大概有 3 千余万种书刊文献的书目资料可以在图书馆的网上目录中 (http://catalog.loc.gov/) 查到。除此之外,不同的部门也编印了一些特别的馆藏目录供读者使用。从创馆之初,国会图书馆就以保存全人类的知识为目标,致力于建立一个包罗世界各国、各地的文明和知识精华的馆藏。

美国国会图书馆总的使命

"本图书馆的使命是要向美国国会及美国人民提供它的馆藏资源,以供所用,同时也要为后代子孙维持及保存全人类知识和创新的纪录。"

(The Library's mission is to make its resources available and useful to the Congress and the American people and to sustain and preserve a universal collection of knowledge and creativity for future generations.) ④

在这个总的使命指引之下,美国国会图书馆亚洲部拟定自己的使命如下:

"亚洲部的使命是要使亚洲部的馆藏资源成为有关亚洲地区及亚洲语言各种类型和时代的首要研究和学术资源,使之能配合 21 世纪知识和创新的驱动力;同时也要向美国国会、美国人民,以及全国甚至于全世界的学术界提供它的馆藏资源及资讯服务,以供所用。"

(The mission of the Asian Division is to establish the collections of the Asian Division as the premier research and scholarly resource of all formats and times on Asia and in Asian Languages that is compatible with the dynamics of knowledge and creativity of the 21st Century; and to make these resources and information services available and useful to the Congress, American people, and the scholarly research community nationally and internationally.) ⑤

请注意最后一个词语"全世界的"(Internationally)。这表明了国际上的学术研究者虽然并非美国国会图书馆的首要服务对象,但国会图书馆人员也乐意为他们提供馆藏资料及服务。美国国会图书馆是美国纳税人供养的国家图书馆,然而有足够的胸襟,大公无私地服务全世界的学者。这符合中国的古老说法"学术为天下之公器"。

美国国会图书馆的馆藏当中,三分之一是英文资料,三分之二是英文以外其他语言的

---

① 本论文宣读于数字时代汉学研究资源国际研讨会,2004 年 12 月 7-9 日,台北:汉学研究中心。
② 这是取其约数。根据最近的馆藏年报,2003 年的藏品数字是 127,720.880。见 Annual Report of the Librarian of Congress for the fiscal year ending September 30, 2003. (Washington, DC: Library of Congress, 2004), p. 242。
③ 这是把 2003 年新增加的 1,802,914 项藏品的数字除以 2003 年的日数得出的。出处同上。
④ The Mission and Strategic Priorities of the Library of Congress: FY 1997 – 2004. Washington, DC: Library of Congress, 1997.
⑤ The Strategic Plan of the Asian Division, 2003 to 2008. Washington, DC: Asian Division, Library of Congress, 2003.

资料。它可以说保存着全世界每一个国家、地区、种族、语种的文献。它收藏的各国的书刊资料,其数量常常可以和资料来源的该国所藏的相匹敌,有时甚至比他们本国的还要多。

举例说,中文、俄文、日文、韩文、波兰文的文献,是中国、俄罗斯、日本、韩国、波兰以外最多的;亚拉伯文文献是埃及以外最多的;世界上最丰富的犹太文献也被收藏在美国国会图书馆;[1] 这里也有世界上最多的纳西文献。

能够履行"保存全人类知识"这个重大使命,当然首先是因为美国国力雄厚。但文献的积累,除了财政因素之外,还有历史因素。美国国会图书馆的先驱者高瞻远瞩,很早便定下了搜罗国外书刊文献的远大目标,经过长时间辛勤的收集,才有今天的成绩。

亚洲部中文藏书的开始

美国国会图书馆中文藏书的开始可以追溯到1869年。在1867年国会通过了国际书籍交换法案之后,中国清朝的同治皇帝在1869年就首先赠送了933册中文线装书。六年之后,1875年,日本政府也正式与美国国会图书馆建立了政府出版书籍的交换。

目前主管亚洲书刊文献及服务的部门是亚洲部,它是在1928年成立的。最早称为中文部,1931年改称为中日文部,1932年扩大为东方部,1942年改名为泛亚部,到1978年才正式定名为亚洲部。亚洲部现在有中国及蒙古、日本、韩国(南北韩)、东南亚和南亚五个组,总藏书量(已编目的)有260万册。

除了亚洲部的收藏外,法律图书馆,地理及地图部,图片及照片部,电影及录音部,音乐部,手稿部,西文馆藏部及特类书籍部也收藏了很多关于亚洲的文献资料。其中包括不同类型的文献资料和大约160种不同的亚洲语言。

美国国会图书馆收藏中文资料的过程,本身便是一部中美文化交流史。70年代初,余秉权教授将1898至1971年美国国会图书馆馆长年报中关于中文书的部分搜辑出来,编成洋洋三巨册的一套大书[2]。此外,胡述兆教授的博士论文亦以美国国会图书馆中文藏书历史为课题[3]。

投入巨大的人力、物力,经过长时间的搜罗,国会图书馆的中文收藏现况是:950,258册[4],包罗广泛的学科领域,以人文科学及社会科学为主,而文集、清朝文献、民国书刊、医书最为丰富[5]。在2003年中文馆藏了17,600种。中文期刊总数量是14,657种(其中持续订购的期刊有5,500种)。此外,中文微缩胶卷大约有15,500卷。

国会图书馆的中文善本珍藏

中国近年经济兴旺、发展蓬勃,文化需求甚殷,使中国成为出版大国。尽管新书层出不穷,种数繁多,到底是能够购藏得到的。比较之下,那些木版印刷的线装古籍,才是"千金难买"的。这令我们联想到,汉学图书馆中,最有价值的收藏部分应该是古籍,尤

---

[1] 见国会图书馆网页 About the International Collections 主页:http://www.loc.gov//rr/international/int-about.html.
[2] *Chinese Collection in the Library of Congress: Excerpts from the Annual Report (s) of the Librarian of Congress, 1898 – 1971.* Complied by Ping-kuen Yu. Washington, D. C.: Center for Chinese Research Materials, Association of Research Libraries, 197.
[3] *The Development of the Chinese Collection in the Library of Congress.* By Hu Shu Chao. Boulder, Colorado: Westview, 1979.
[4] 2003年6月30日公布的数字,见 Council on East Asian Libraries 的调查 Holdings of North American Institutions as of June 30, 2003: http://www2.lib.ku.edu/ceal/stat/。
[5] 见国会图书馆网页的中文藏书介绍:http://www.loc.gov/rr/asian/collections.html。

其是善本古籍了。

国会图书馆有幸是中国善本古籍的渊薮。到底有多少古籍，谁也说不清楚，因为美国国会图书馆从来没有投放大量资源在中国文献的整理上，而且在美国能够整理古籍的人才也很难找。早年曾经从中国请来专家帮忙，譬如朱士嘉教授协助整理方志，王重民教授协助整理善本；以至近年得到李孝聪教授协助整理古地图，朱宝田教授整理纳西文献等。他们都在个别专题上考订鉴别、出版专著，做得很出色。但是，要深入而且全面地整理目录和撰写提要，必须有具备这方面学识特长的专家长期服务才行。因为美国国会图书馆的中国古籍实在非常多，可以说比一家普通汉学图书馆的非古籍还要多，而且珍品无数，许多罕有文献甚至不为人所知，更不必说能够充分利用了。下面摘要介绍一些特藏。

善本书

20世纪40年代初期，国会图书馆邀请到王重民教授负责考订善本，并且编有目录。这个目录的稿本在战后的1945年由王教授带回中国，准备由北京大学排印出版。后来由于中国内战，美国国会图书馆跟王教授和北京大学再也联络不到，出版计划无法实现。王教授的目录稿本当时留有缩微胶片，便由袁同礼博士校订后，在华盛顿用手抄本影印的形式出版了。这便是我们现在看到的《国会图书馆藏中国善本书录》①。里面包括宋版11种、金版1种、元版14种、明版1,518种、清初版70种、抄本140种、高丽版汉籍11种、日本刻汉籍11种、拓本1种，共1777种。

但王教授其实并未全部完成善本书的整理工作。况且，40年代以来，善本书的定义也有所放宽②。所以，王教授的目录未能全面反映美国国会图书馆的善本收藏情况。该目录未收已经编目的善本起码有近千种。此外，还有一大批数目不详、从来没有编过目的古籍深藏在国会图书馆的书库，其中也有许多善本。粗略估计，王氏编目的书，加上不在其中的已编、未编的书，国会图书馆的善本书应该接近五千种，这比起一般汉学图书馆的普通本线装书还要多。

方志（约4,000种，60,000册）

国会图书馆很早即着力搜集中国方志，甚至曾经托人在中国刊登广告，公开征集。大规模的入藏则要归功于施永高博士（Dr. Walter T. Swingle）。他是农林学专家，有志于把中国的优良蔬果种子移植到美国，他发现中国地方志有关于土壤和植物的记载，于是向美国政府建议扩大对中国方志的收集。他在1918年代表美国国会图书馆到中国各省去采访地方志，成绩良好。回国以后他仍继续为美国国会图书馆间接地采购，直到1928年为止。美国国会图书馆现藏的中国古方志，有一半以上是1928年以前入藏的。

1928年美国国会图书馆正式成立中文部，由恒慕义博士（Dr. Arthur W. Hummel）担任该部的主任。恒慕义曾经委托 Dr. Joseph F. Rock 为美国国会图书馆访购方志。因为 Dr. Rock 研究云南地区，长期待在中国西南一带，所以他所访购的以西南各省的方志为多，尤其是四川的方志。到1934年，恒慕义也亲自到中国采购了三百来种。随后又设法在日本访求中国方志，也得到好几种珍本。

---

① 王重民：《国会图书馆中文善本书录》，华盛顿：美国国会图书馆1957年版。部分提要也收进他后来出版的《中国善本书目提要》中。王重民：《中国善本书目提要》，台北明文书局1984年版。

② 王教授考订国会图书馆善本书时，一般以明代以及以前版本为善本，清代善本只收70种。现在善本书的定义，单以年代计，包括清乾隆及以前的版本。

美国国会图书馆收集中国方志，最值得大书特书的是1933年一次入藏几乎全部的山东方志。这批方志原本的主人是山东一位县长高鸿裁（1851—1918）。高鸿裁字翰生，山东潍县人，是一位研究金石学的学者。当时知名之士如缪荃孙、孙薛田和他都有往来。他用了二十多年的精神财力收集该省的志书，所以内中有许多极不易见的版本。他的藏品有"潍高翰生收辑山东全省府州县志印记"的印章，可见他的立志所在。根据我们所藏的旧档案，知道当时德国驻青岛领事馆曾经派员接洽，要购买这批方志。美国国会图书馆通过当时清华大学图书馆王文山馆长的介绍，这次搜购行动比当时掌管山东的德国人领先了一步，得到了这批极具价值的山东方志。

后来其他著名的藏书家如抱经楼卢址、稽瑞楼陈扑、铁琴铜剑楼瞿镛，他们收藏的方志也曾一鳞半爪地流传到美国国会图书馆来。根据恒慕义博士在1954年所做的报告，方志收藏数目已经达到3,600种。这一年以后，还陆续有所增添，不过以后再没有专门就方志做统计了。

根据朱士嘉教授考订本馆方志时（见下文）的统计，修于宋代的有23种，修于元代的有9种，修于明代的有68种，修于清代的有2,376种，修于民国的有463种，总计2,939种。（朱教授之后，我们再没有做这种方志地域统计了。）出版年代不是评定一部方志价值的关键标准。同样要列入考虑的，是各方志所涉及的地区在中国文化上的地位，和该方志的罕见程度。

从前收集方志，比较侧重省志。比较小的行政区域，他们的方志便流传不广。美国国会图书馆所藏方志，遍及各省、府、州、县、乡镇，而且十分齐备，有不少是他馆难得一见的。

如果按地区分，美国国会图书馆所藏方志最多的是河北282种，其次是山东279种，然后是江苏和四川各有252种，山西234种，此外，浙江、陕西、江西、广东、湖北、安徽各省的方志为数也很可观。

版本种类方面，也很多样化，有永乐大典本、刻本、稿本、精钞本。此外，我们还注意到有许多出于清代学者编修的方志。它们体例谨严、取材宏富，具有学术著作的规格，是编纂方志的范本。

总而言之，在中国以外的汉学图书馆中，方志收藏能够和美国国会图书馆比肩的，实在不多。在王重民教授考订善本的同时，美国国会图书馆得到朱士嘉教授所考订方志，编有《国会图书馆藏中国地方志目录》，1942年用手稿影印的形式在华盛顿出版。

《永乐大典》（41册）

1923年在美国国会图书馆中文藏书历史上是重要的一年，因为在这一年的春天购藏29册《永乐大典》。连同先前已经拥有的4册，一共是33册。后来又再陆续得到8册，所以美国国会图书馆总共藏有41册《永乐大典》，公认是中国以外收藏最多的了。

《永乐大典》一般误会是1900年6月八国联军攻陷北京时连同翰林院一起烧掉的，但据近人考证，当时翰林院内只有数百册《永乐大典》。这部22,877卷、11,095册的大书，早已经因为典藏不善，散失殆尽了。翰林院内数百册《永乐大典》，有很少数是当时居住在附近的外国人抢救出来的，但是美国国会图书馆收藏的《永乐大典》，都没有烟熏火燎的痕迹，所以推论不属于这批抢救出来的劫余。

2002年4月，在北京召开"《永乐大典》编纂600周年国际研讨会"时，统计现在散藏在8个国家和地区的《永乐大典》零本一共有400余册。美国国会图书馆大概藏有全世界现存《永乐大典》的十分之一。

美国国会图书馆所藏《永乐大典》，其中有 3 册（卷 11956—11960）详细描述了商周"鼎"的形制，有插图 78 幅，是考古学的珍贵资料。此外，有 12 册（29 卷）是关于宋宁宗（1195—1225 年在位）的史料，这无疑是研究宋史的一手材料。

《古今图书集成》（2 套 6,672 册）

《古今图书集成》是 10000 卷 5044 册的大书，编成之后，于康熙 6 年（1728 年）用铜活字印制。但是美国国会图书馆所藏的《古今图书集成》2 套，都不是铜活字原版。

1908 年，清朝政府为了答谢美国政府退还庚子赔款，赠送一套《古今图书集成》给美国国会图书馆，并且派遣特使唐绍仪（1874 年清廷选派赴美留学幼童之一）带来华盛顿。这套《古今图书集成》5044 册，是 1895—1898 年影印本。

十多年后，美国国会图书馆派遣施永高博士（Dr. Walter T. Swingle）到中国访求古书，前后几年，买了大批古籍。其中最大部头的书，便是现藏的第二套《古今图书集成》。这部和前一部的版本不一样，是上海 Major Brothers 于 1884 年铅活字排印本，分订 1628 册。

虽然这两部《古今图书集成》都不是铜活字原版，但其价值不可低估。第一套因为是清朝政府赠书，而具备特别意义。

古地图

美国国会图书馆的中文地图收藏，从古地图、近现代实测地图，到近年的航空、航天照片，多达几万幅。

这里单说古地图，美国国会图书馆地图部藏有大约 300 幅中国古地图，这些地图或是绘画的，或是木刻印刷的，包括长卷地图、扇子地图和石刻地图的拓本等。纯以数量来说，是西半球最丰富的收藏。几乎每个省的地图都有，以河南省、山东省、湖北省数量最多。其中年代最早的是 1136 年石刻《禹迹图》的拓本（拓本是 19 世纪做的）。还有几幅明代舆图和清朝康熙、乾隆年间的彩色绘本图。

有一幅清朝康熙年间绢本彩绘的《台湾舆图》，用鸟瞰实景画的形式描给台湾岛和澎湖列岛的山川地理景致、城镇、村社以及生活场景，形象生动。在中国大陆也未有比之更早的台湾地图。

还有一幅清朝乾隆年间彩色绘画的《热河行宫全图》，也是用鸟瞰式全景画的形式描绘热河行宫（即避暑山庄）和周围的山水、庙宇，绘画非常精细。据考订为 1775 年以前的地图，比中国大陆所藏的任何热河行宫地图都要早。

此外，还有一些很有研究价值的海防图、驻防图、运河图、运河工程图、黄河工程图等。其中运河和黄河的工程图刚好是同一系列中，是中国图书馆所缺失的部分。2002 年，由居蜜博士和地图部主任共同主持一项中国古地图整理计划，邀请到北京大学的李孝聪教授到来做过考订、解题。今年十一月，印刷精美的《美国国会图书馆藏中文古地图叙录》由中国北京的文物出版社出版。

在古地图的资源共享方面，我们的地图部将迈出阔步。已经和台北的"中央研究院"签约，由他们组织人力、物力，来国会图书馆扫描馆藏的古地图，以便公之于世。还有一点要特别指出，地图资源不但限于地图部收藏的、单张或成册的地图。更丰富的还有和亚洲部的中文藏书并行，或加插在书中的地图。书中加插地图，以方志为最多，但绝对不限于方志。譬如有一部明版《武备志》，书中附有长达 24 叶的郑和航海地图，标示了郑和船队到过的地方。美国国会图书馆地图部已经扫描了这些地图，正准备上网。

清季试卷

美国国会图书馆藏有一批清末科举考卷，是江亢虎博士于 1920 年捐赠给美国国会图书馆的。江亢虎在民国初年的政坛非常活跃，是中国无政府主义的创始者，曾经组织政党，是一位很有才华的人。有一段时期他在伯克莱加州大学教中国语言文学，每年夏天到美国国会图书馆协助编书。现在美国国会图书馆的藏书和卡片上，还有他的手迹。

江氏是考试世家，一连几代中科名者不绝，尤其中进士、举人的非常多。这批清季试卷原是江氏家族所收藏，共分两类。首先是分册刊印的个别考生的试卷（含小量题名录等材料）、零散的个别试卷（含课艺、习作及小量诗文零篇）。

刊印的试卷列举考生的履历、家世、师辈、益友、名次（间有任官资料）、考官、考试篇题及答卷、评语。不但在科举史上是重要的一手材料，也因为其中的家世资料有时比族谱还要详尽，所以也是家族史的重要文献。

这批试卷中，有些光绪后期以至宣统年间的考卷，已经引入一些西学的试题，答卷中也不乏在当时相当前进的思想表现，在中国近代思想史上很有研究价值。

北美洲汉学图书馆中，藏有科举试卷的不多，据我们所知只有洛杉矶加州大学有一个特藏。美国国会图书馆的这个试卷特藏，一直无人整理，到今年初才由居蜜博士和潘铭燊博士合作编出一个目录。

太平天国印书

太平天国立国之初，就开始编写、刻印书籍，用来宣示立国制度、宣传思想、记录事件等。当时太平天国自己称之为"诏书"，编有一部"旨准颁行诏书总目"。太平天国失败后，这些书籍被清朝政府尽数销毁。但当年和太平天国有过接触的西方传教士、外交官等，往往得到赠书，带回本国，使这些书得以保存下来。

美国国会图书馆藏有太平天国印书 10 种 10 册，都是上述"总目"之内的书。它们原是顾盛藏书的一部分。顾盛（Caleb Cushing）是 19 世纪 40 年代在澳门望厦村和清朝政府订立第一个中美条约"望厦条约"的美国外交官，他和太平天国好像没有联系，这些书是签订"望厦条约"时的翻译、传教士裨治文（Elijah Coleman Bridgman）赠送给他的。

美国国会图书馆藏太平天国印书有历法、诏书、礼制、启蒙读本等，对于研究太平天国有一定的参考价值。北美洲的汉学图书馆除了耶鲁大学有一个简又文太平天国特藏以外，似乎也没有很多这方面的史料。

1999 年前后，应居蜜博士邀请，中国社会科学院近代史研究所的王庆成教授来到美国国会图书馆考订太平天国印书，已经编成目录，准备在适当时机发表。

少数民族古籍

研究中国少数民族，尤其是少数民族古籍，应该可以算做汉学研究的一部分。在这方面，美国国会图书馆无疑是一个重镇。

我们收藏的少数民族古籍，以藏文为最丰富，已经编目的有 4,000 种，未编目的尚未知有多少。亚洲部常有喇嘛高僧到访，借阅藏文经典。藏文以外，还有很多满文和蒙文的古籍。

不过，我们收藏的少数民族语文文献当中，最为人所津津乐道的，应该是纳西文献了。纳西文字是世界上仅有的、仍然有生命力的象形文字，在云南丽江地区仍然有少数人在使用着。

1999年前后，我们邀请到云南省博物馆的朱宝田教授来美国国会图书馆考订纳西文献。他认为美国国会图书馆所藏的3038件纳西写本虽然并非全世界最多（最多是在中国），但却是全世界最好的纳西文献。

朱教授和本馆居蜜博士共同研究纳西文献的成果，最近放上国会图书馆的网页，请大家参看。①

中国东北与日本之历史文献

当第二次世界大战在1945年结束时，大量的日本战时文献，其中包括政府公文、书刊、电影及其他文件等，被联军统帅部在1945—1952年间没收。这些书刊资料及文献大部分是从日本外务省、陆军省、海军省、内务省的思想控制警察局、东京警视厅、南满洲铁道株式会社东京分社、东亚经济调查局及东亚研究所等机构收集来的。那些从南满洲铁道株式会社东京分社、东亚经济调查局及东亚研究所的大部分书刊资料都是研究关于中国东北（满洲）、中国大陆别的地区，（包括台湾地区）、韩国、蒙古及太平洋地区的。大部分日本政府的公文档案后来多归还日本政府。

然而，在归还前一年，一个特别的微缩胶卷制作小组仓促成立，由哥伦比亚大学的教授 C. Martin Wilbur 担任组长。这个小组的目的是将一小部分经过挑选的档案做成163卷胶卷（约四十余万页）②。文件被制成胶卷的有日本对中国义和团运动以及1911—1912年革命的情报报告、日本陆海军在不同冲突和战役中的活动及日本政府在发动太平洋战争时的行动。其他有价值的历史文献如明治天皇（1868—1912年在位）时期的军事记录、1919年韩人暴动事件、1931年的沈阳事件及后来在东北延续发生的事件和1939年洛门汉事件（Nomonhan Incident）。这些文献当时多半被日本政府视为秘密文件。在1960年代和1970年代，美国国会图书馆继续将大量的文献做成微缩胶卷。在1974年11月20日，日本议会图书馆和美国国会图书馆签订了合约，订定互相交换这些文献资料的微缩胶卷。

南满洲铁道株式会社

南满洲铁道株式会社（满铁）是在1906年成立的。成立的原因是根据日俄战争（1904—1905）的停战协定将由俄国占有的中国东部铁路权转交给日本。这铁路原有1,128公里的轨道，因迅速的扩张，满铁变成在中国东北规模最大的经济企业，也是日本深入中国的大本营。从一开始，日本政府就紧紧掌握满铁。同时日本的关东军有权控制满铁的警察及铁路监管。在整个满铁的存在期间，它实际上控制了东北的经济命脉，如铁路、煤矿、工业等。在战争期间满铁更发展到东北以外的地方。③

---

① 居蜜博士主持国会图书馆纳西文献研究历经数年，最近将研究成果浓缩在纳西网页中。该网页可以通过国会图书馆亚洲部的网页链接（http://www.loc.gov/rr/asian > Naxi Manuscript Collection），或直接登录以下的网址亦可：http://international.loc.gov/inteldl/naxihtml/naxihome.html。

② 吉村敬子（Yoshiko Yoshimura）编《1956年前被查禁的日文期刊：微缩胶卷馆藏目录清单（Censored Japanese Serials of the Pre – 1946 Perios: A Checklist of the Microfilm Collection）》华盛顿：国会图书馆亚洲部日文组，1994，第225页。该委员会的委员有：哥伦比亚大学的Martin Wilbur和James Morley，耶鲁大学的Chitoshi Yanaga，哈佛大学的Edwin O. Reischauer，乔治城大学的杨觉勇及国会图书馆的艾允表（Edwin G. Beal）

③ Young, John（杨觉勇）. *The Research Activities of the South Manchruian Railway Company, 1907 – 1945: A History and Bibliography*. New York: East Asian Institute, Columbia Universtiy, 1966. p. 1。

对这些满铁文献作过极为详细调查的学者杨觉勇（John Young）用英文写了一本《南满铁道株式会社研究项目，1907—1945：历史与书目》(*The Research Activities of the South Manchurian Railway Company, 1907–1945: A History and Bibliography*)，由哥伦比亚大学东亚研究所在1966年出版。

据估计在1945年日本投降时，满铁在东京的分社共藏有十万册的书刊资料，其中有三万册是西文书刊，来到国会图书馆的大约有六万册，其中25,000册已归纳入日本藏书，其他35,000册多半是中文、韩文及西文书刊，送去了中文、韩文及西文组收藏。有些还分配给法律图书馆、地理及地图部、图片及照片部、电影及录音部等。其他多余的版本则送到美国及琉球的东亚图书馆去收藏。

根据杨觉勇（John Young）书中的报道，对满铁当时有三种研究。第一种是研究日本很感兴趣的地方的经济、社会及文化，这些地方包括中国、西伯利亚及其他亚洲地区。第二种包括自然科学及应用科学如物理学、化学、地质学、农业、植物学、卫生学、气象学及细菌学。第三种是与满铁业务有关的商业及统计题材。满铁的研究中心最盛时期有300多位研究人员，完成了6,200多项研究报告及内部文件，代表了20世纪顶尖的知识库之一。在1945年"二次大战"末期，满铁经过一个短暂的俄军占领时期，满铁在中国东北的书刊资料及其他资产几乎被掠夺一空。满铁主权最后由中国收回。依照当年亚洲部日文组组长黑田（Andrew Y. Kuroda）在1967年7月6日的报告说："在1942年3月大连图书馆及三个满铁分社的馆藏共有524,396册。这些馆藏在东北被俄军于1945年8月控制期间，都被运去了俄国。这些书刊资料的质与量都远比东京分社的书刊资料好得多。尽管如此，在中国东北很多图书馆中仍然保留了相当数量的满铁书刊资料。"

善本数位化计划

国会图书馆不愿这些善本、古籍秘而不宣，而希望本着学术为天下之公器的原则，将资料公开。以此之故，将和国家图书馆达成协议，短期内进行"国会图书馆善本扫描计划"，由国家图书馆筹措经费、组织人力，派员到国会图书馆进行扫描，然后送到国家图书馆加工。但为数五千种（册数十万至二十万）的善本，不可能全部扫描。现正由居密博士、潘铭燊博士协力甄选，未编目的补作编目，无提要的补撰提要。这样规模庞大的汉学资源数位化计划，在北美洲的汉学界无疑是一项空前创举。期望计划完成之后，能够为汉学研究开辟一些新的路向，也为未来的数位化工程起到一定的借鉴作用。

（原载台湾《师大校友》2005年2月第325期，第4–12页。）

美国国会图书馆有关郑和研究的中文收藏

Chinese Resources for Zheng He Studies in the Library of Congress[1]

Opening remarks

From a recent book on Zheng He studies written by Louise Levathes entitled *When China Ruled the Seas: The Treasure Fleet of the Dragon Throne, 1405 – 1433*, published in 1994, the author praised the Library of Congress in her acknowledgements:

"Most of the research and writing of the book was done in Washington D. C. where I had a study facility at the Library of Congress and was able to obtain most of the Ming manuscripts and other research materials I needed. I was continually amazed at the breadth and depth of the library resources in every department and feel privileged to have been able to work there."[2]

Inspired by Dr. Joseph Needham, the great scholar in the study of the history of Chinese science and technology, Louise Levathes dedicated herself to writing a book on Zheng He. She began by collecting historical documents in the Library of Congress. Then she visited Cambridge, Singapore, Malaysia, East Africa, Nanjing, Beijing, Fujian and Taipei to supplement what she found. Finally, she came back to the Library of Congress to do the actual writing. We, At the Library of Congress, take it as an honor for being able to serve researchers who come to use the wealth of its resources.

As the National Library of the United States and the depository of knowledge for the whole of humanity, the Library of Congress devotes itself to collecting all materials of research value in any language. This effort results in the ability of the Library of Congress to provide researchers in almost all topics in the humanities and social sciences with relevant resources. Such is the case in the study of Zheng He. The following paper will report briefly on what research materials we have on the great admiral of the Ming Dynasty.

Ming Dynasty records

Zheng He was undoubtedly a great admiral. He was also a navigator and a diplomat. Much to our regret, he was not a writer. If he were, he would have left to us voluminous records of his epochmaking voyages. These records would have changed the world outlook of the Chinese people after him, and researchers on his achievements would not be limited by the scarcity of information. According to the practice of navigators, Zheng He should have maintained logbooks. Unfortunately, his navigational records were all destroyed. Not only was this a calamity for the study of Ming history, but also an irretrievable loss in the records of the civilization of humankind.

Needless to say, the most important type of resources consists of documents contemporary with Zheng He. The only such documents still extant include the three travel records by Zheng He's entourages and a navigational map. The three entourages were Ma Huan (马欢), Fei Xin (费信) and Gong Zhen (巩珍). They participated in one to four voyages. Ma Huan, who wrote *Yingya Shenglan* (《瀛涯胜览》) (Panoramic View of the Landscapes of the Remotest Places on Earth), was selected because he was a Muslim who could interpret the Arabic languages. Fei Xin, who wrote *Xingcha Shenglan* (《星槎胜览》, Panoramic View of the Landscapes as seen from the Fleet of Envoy), was selected because: the political essay he wrote on the significance of the

---

[1] Paper presented at the Third International Conference of Institutes and Libraries for Chinese Overseas Studies held in Singapore on August 18 – 21, 2005 under the theme "Maritime Asia and the Chinese Overseas, 1405 – 2005."

[2] Levathes, Louise (1994). *When China Ruled the Seas: The Treasure Fleet of the Dragon Throne, 1405 – 1433*. New York and Oxford: Oxford University Press. See page 234.

voyages. Gong Zhen, who wrote *Xiyang Fanguozhi* (《西洋番国志》, Records of Alien Nations of the Western Seas) started out as a soldier but was promoted to an aide because of his literary talent. These three were small books, hardly publishable as independent works. Rather, they were preserved because of their inclusion in *congshu* (丛书, collectanea). The Library of Congress has early congshu editions of *Yingya Shenglan* (《瀛涯胜览》) and *Xingcha Shenglan* (《星槎胜览》), but only a modern version of X*iyang Fanguozhi* (《西洋番国志》).

The navigational map of Zheng He (《郑和航海图》) was preserved as the last *juan* (卷) (chapter) of *Wubeizhi* (《武备志》, Encyclopedia of Military Science) compiled by Mao Yuanyi (茅元仪). The Library of Congress has 4 sets (3 editions) of *Wubeizhi* (《武备志》), with the navigational map intact in all 4 sets. The navigational map was the topic of discussion in the papers presented by Asian Division colleagues Dr. Mi Chu Wiens (居蜜)[①] and Dr. Ming Sun Poon (潘铭燊)[②] in the one-day conference *An International Symposium on the Significance of Admiral Zheng He's Voyages (1405 – 1433)* held at the Library of Congress on May 16 this year. The symposium was organized by the Asian Division of the Library of Congress in collaboration with a number of local organizations in the Greater Washington DC region.

It is to be noted that in Zheng He's navigational map, many details were given, quite accurately, for the regions around present-day Malaysia and Sumatra because this region was among those in which Zheng He's fleets were most active. Place-names were different 600 years ago, but they are mostly identified with their modem equivalents by studying phonetic similarities and descriptions in the travel records. We know, for example, *Danmaxi* "淡马锡" is present-day Singapore, *Longyamen* "龙牙门" is present-day Singapore Strait, *Manlajia* "满剌加" is present-day Malacca, and *Sumendala* "苏门荅剌" is present-day Samalanga (please note that the name Sumendala didn't refer to the entire island of Sumatra during the Ming Dynasty). Also, we can see from the map that two enormous *guanchang* "官厂" (official warehouses) were built in *Manlajia* and *Sumendala* respectively, evidence of the fact that diplomacy wasn't the only mission of Zheng He's voyages but commerce might have been an even greater driving force.

Among the official historical records of the Ming Dynasty, researchers on Zheng He should first of all consult *Ming Shilu* (《明实录》, True Records of the Ming Dynasty) which was archived by court historians on a daily basis and has been known for its comprehensiveness and reliability. This voluminous compilation has never been printed, but was preserved in the palace in the form of manuscripts. In the 1960's the Institute of History and Philology, Academia Sinica in Taiwan, published a facsimile edition from microfilm printouts. The Library of Congress has one set of this facsimile edition. Zheng He scholars have long recognized the research value of *MingShilu* (《明实录》) and efforts were made to collect every piecemeal of information directly related to Zheng He. However, there is still indirect information useful for the study of Zheng He waiting to be explored. For example, the emperors (most notably Emperor Yongle 永乐) in the early Ming period dispatched incessant diplomatic delegations to foreign countries (Zheng He was only the most famous leader of these missions) while kings and envoys paying tributes to the Ming court came in continuous streams. It is interesting to find out the underlying reasons for this upsurge in diplomatic activities and the essential substance of the exchanges. Such findings will help us to understand better the historical background of Zheng He's voyages. It is very likely that there are still unexplored materials buried in *Ming Shilu* (《明实录》) waiting to be unearthed.

Activities of such magnitude as these epoch-making voyages were too important to ignore. Although official records were destroyed, there must be mentions of these voyages here and there in collected works, literary sketches and works of creation. Over a dozen Ming Dynasty works had been identified to contain information relating to Zheng He directly or indirectly. For example, *Qianwen Ji* (《前闻记》) (A Book of Old Records) by Zhu Yunming (祝允明) contains a

---

[①] Wiens, Mi Chu. (2005) *Map section (Juan 240) of* (武备志, *Wubeizhi*): *Zheng He's Voyages*.

[②] Poon, Ming Sun. (2005) *Comparative study of Zheng He's navigational map and three 15th century travel records of Zheng He's voyages*.

paragraph depicting Zheng He's last voyage in great detail. The Library of Congress has good editions of *Qianwen Ji* (《前闻记》) and many, many other works by Ming Dynasty authors. ①

In the area of literary creation, *Sanbao Taijian Xia Xiyang Ji* (《三宝太监下西洋记》, The West Seas Voyages of Eunuch Sanbao) by Luo Maodeng (罗懋登) is the most important. It is unmistakably a novel, with imaginative and supernatural components. But it is also known to contain fragments that can supplement, even rectify, historical records. The author should have seen some of the materials that are no longer extant. This novel, therefore, should be of value to historians who exercise discrimination on the information contained in it. The Library of Congress has the next best edition of the novel (《新刻全像三宝太监西洋记通俗演义》)②.

Compared to the novel, a Ming Dynasty play on Zheng He's voyages is much more obscure. Few people know about the play *Feng Tian Ming Sanbao Xia Xiyang* (《奉天命三保下西洋》, Sanbao's Voyages to the West Seas under Imperial Orders). It was preserved in a collection of plays that appeared in 1615. The Library of Congress does not have this collection. But we do have the modern version *Xia Xiyang Zaju* (《下西洋杂剧》, Poetic Drama on the Voyages to the West Seas) collated by Xu Yunqiao (许云樵)③, This play offers very scanty information to historians, but it reflects the mentality the Ming people had on Zheng He's voyages

Awaiting our exploration are also local gazetteers (方志), Local gazetteers contain a wealth of information not found in dynastic histories or historical works on a national scale. *Longjiang Chuanchang Zhi* (《龙江船厂志》, Gazetteer of the Longjiang Shipyard) was a Ming Dynasty record of the shipyard where Zheng He's ocean-going vessels were built. This important work is preserved only in *Xuanlan Tang Congshu Xuji* (《玄览堂丛书续集》, Collectanea of the Hall of Subtle Reading: Supplement) and the Library of Congress is among the few libraries that have this collectanea. Furthermore, have we scanned through the leaves of local gazetteers of Yunnan (云南) (where Zheng He was born), Nanjing (南京), (where Zheng He spent most of his time when he was not sailing), and Fujian (福建) (where Zheng He's fleet anchored and were supplied)? The Library of Congress prides itself for unparalleled holdings of Chinese local gazetteers in the West. *A Catalog of Chinese Local Histories in the Library of Congress* (《国会图书馆藏中国方志目录》, Washington DC: U. S. Government Printing Office, 1942) compiled by Zhu Shijia (朱士嘉) in the 1930's, listed 2939 titles of local gazetteers. It is still a useful bibliographic tool for the collection because the majority of early local gazetteers were added to the Library of Congress before the 1930's.

What this paper has mentioned so far are materials that are already known. How about information that has never been discovered by scholars? Do we have a chance of unveiling resources never before mentioned? Yes, in the Library of Congress the voluminous collection renders these chances into likelihoods. A few months ago, my colleague Dr Ming Sun Poon (潘铭燊) came across in the Library of Congress a unique copy of *Taiyang Xiaohou Miao Zhi* (《太洋萧侯庙志》, Gazetteer of the Temple of Xiaohou in Taiyang) in which he found records of Zheng He's fleet having been saved from drowning by a sea-god Xiaohou (萧侯) in one of the return voyages. With this information Dr. Poon wrote an interesting and original article *Zheng He De Baohushen* (《郑和的保护神》, The god who safeguarded Zheng He in his voyages). This example leads us to believe that there still are many topics unexplored, many articles unwritten by researchers. The information is there, buried in the tens of thousands of obscure, sometimes unique, books never before read, let alone used, by researchers. The Library of Congress has a multitude of these unread books and we welcome scholars from around the world to come and use them. In the 1930's and 1940's, when Professor Wang Zhongmin (王重民) worked as cataloger in the Library of Congress, he selected 1777 titles of rare books and wrote annotations on them

---

① These other works include 陆容《菽园杂记》、黄省曾《西洋朝贡典录》、罗懋登《三宝太监下西洋记》、茅元仪《武备志》、何乔远《名山藏》、《国榷》、《皇明四夷考》、《殊域周咨录》、《东洋考》和《皇明象胥录》, and others.

② The Library's edition is 步月楼翻刻明万历本.

③ Xu, Yunqiao (许云樵). (1962) *Xiao Xiyang zaju* (《下西洋杂剧》). Singapore: 星洲世界书局.

(including 1518 titles of Ming editions). These annotations were published as *A Descriptive Catalog of Rare Chinese Books in the Library of Congress* (《国会图书馆藏中国善本书录》, Washington DC, 1957). After Professor Wang died in Beijing in 1975 his colleagues and students put together his annotations on 4200 titles of Chinese rare books and published it as the posthumous *Zhongguo Shanbenshu Tiyao* (《中国善本提要》, Annotated Catalog of Chinese Rare Books). The 1777 annotations he wrote in the Library of Congress were also included. For researchers in Zheng He studies or other disciplines who intend to use the Chinese rare books held by the Library of Congress, please consult either of these two catalogs first. But please be aware that the number of Chinese rare books in the Library of Congress far exceeds 1777 titles by two-fold, even three-fold. Many of them have not even been cataloged.

Dispersed in libraries around the globe, there may be numerous imprints of the Ming Dynasty that have not been seen by researchers in Zheng He studies. Much information on Zheng He's voyages may still be left unnoticed. In the Western world, Princeton University is famous for its rich holdings in Ming literature and records. But according to the assessment by professors and library experts of Princeton University, the Library of Congress surpasses them in holdings in the same area. From my viewpoint as a librarian, no library can be totally self-sufficient in any specific branch of studies. Librarians now believe that we should be interdependent and achieve relative completeness through resource sharing.

Qing Dynasty records

You might have already questioned why I didn't mention *MingShi* (《明史》, Ming Dynastic History) up to this point. Ming Shi of course is an absolute necessity for any topics relating to the Ming Dynasty. But I would like to point out that there is not much information on Zheng He in *Ming Shi* other than those sections on *Chengzu Benji* (《成祖本》, Records of Emperor Chengzu), *Huanguan Zhuan* (《宦官传》, Biographies of Eunuchs), and *Waiguo Zhuan* (《外国传》, History of Foreign Countries), etc. And we should bear in mind that all dynastic histories were written by historians of the next dynasty, hence tainted with the prejudice of the new sovereigns towards the defeated regime. Take for instance, the official *Ming Shi* which was written by historians of the Qing Dynasty (清朝) that explained Emperor Yongle's motive for supporting Zheng He's voyages as a hidden plan to trace the whereabouts of the thrown-out Emperor Huidi. This explanation obviously grew out from prejudice.

Talking about *Ming Shi* (《明史》) I wish to introduce to you a particular copy of *Ming Shi* which is the draft prepared by Wan Sitong (万斯同). Wan Sitong devoted the latter half of his lifetime to the compilation of *Ming Shi* in the Qing Imperial Academy of History. As a draft, Wan Sitong's *Ming Shi* of course differs from the final, official version, and contains greater details in some areas. It should be interesting to do a comparative study of Wan's version and the official version, and records on Zheng He in Wan's version might have some extra information. So far we haven't seen any report on this comparative study, presumably because Wan's *Ming Shi* isn't easily accessible. I am glad to say that the Library of Congress has a set of Ming Shi by Wan Sitong, hand-copied from the original manuscript in Beijing in the early Republican period. This handwritten book on fine paper, though more than 70 years old, is still in excellent condition. As far as I know, Princeton University through special arrangement acquired the microfilms of this set. The reason for compiling *Gujin Tushu Jicheng* (《古今图书集成》, Collection of Ancient and Modern Books) in the early Qing period was no different than other similar efforts in the beginning of a new regime. In order to pride themselves of cultural achievement after military success the early emperors of dynasties often sponsored the compilation of large encyclopedias and anthologies. Despite their ulterior motives, the end products were usually beneficial to the preservation of Chinese culture. Furthermore, there was an inevitable trend of book loss in any of dynasty so that only about one-tenth the books relating to the previous dynasty were extant at the end of that dynasty compared to the conditions when the dynasty began. The inevitable trend brought out the chief value of *Gujin Tushu Jicheng*, so although it was a book produced by transcribing and rearranging information only it now contains a lot of fragments of lost works. We have every reason to believe that information on shipbuilding and on foreign countries, for example, preserved by *Gujin Tushu Jicheng* cannot be found anywhere else now. The Library of Congress is blessed with 3 sets of old editions of *Gujin Tushu Jicheng* and wishes to extend an invitation to researchers to use them.

Two or three centuries after Zheng the influences of his expeditions were still felt in the early Qing period. The world outlook of the people in early Qing and their knowledge about foreign countries still carried the reflections of Zheng He's voyages. For this reason alone, it may be helpful to further our understanding of Zheng He by reading books produced in the early Qing Dynasty. Take for example, some passages in *Bahong Yishi* (《八纮译史》, Interpreted History of the Eight Directions), authored by Lu Shiyun (陆士云) who was intensely interested in foreign countries although he didn't travel outside of China himself, contain information which can verify and supplement that in the three travel records mentioned earlier in this paper. I believe many similar works are waiting to be explored.

Qing Dynasty works are present in abundance in the collections of the Library of Congress. Bibliographic control of these works, however, still has room for improvement. The collections are of course accessible, but some patience is needed on the part of the users.

Works by modern and contemporary scholars

Discussions on Zheng He's historical significance began to surge in the late Qing Dynasty, apparently because of the bitter feelings of the weak government. The eminent opinion-leader Liang Qichao (梁启超) (1873 – 1929) wrote a biography of Zheng He, *Zuguo Tahanghaijia Zheng He Zhuan* (《祖国大航海家郑和传》) in 1901 which he concluded with the following statement: "There were innumerable Columbuses after Columbus and innumerable Da Gamas after Da Gama. But in China, there was only one Zheng He. Alas, it is certainly not Zheng He who is to blame."[①] This outstanding remark had been quoted over and over again. The Library of Congress, of course, has the works of Liang Qichao (梁启超) in its holdings-just as any other library.

The study of China-foreign relations in history became a scholarly trend in the 1920's and 1930's. Such study inevitably included Zheng He in the agenda. A pioneering attempt was *Zhongxi Jiaotongshi* (《中西交通史》, History of Foreign Relations between China and the West) by Xiang Da (向达) published in Shanghai in 1934. Chapter 6 of this founding work dealt with Zheng He.

The first lengthy study devoted entirely to Zheng He was in French. The 216-page article *Les grands voyages maritimes chinois au debut du Xve siecle* (1933) by Paul Pelliot (1878 – 1945) was a book by itself. It was translated into the first Chinese book on Zheng He, *Zheng He Xia Xiyang Kao* (《郑和下西洋考》, A Critical Study of Zheng He's Voyages to the West Seas) by Feng Chengjun (冯承钧) and was published in Shanghai in 1935.[②] Pelliot made a thorough and meticulous comparative study on the three travel records mentioned earlier together with *Xiyang Chaogong Dianlu* (《西洋朝贡典录》, Records of Tributes Presented by Nations of the West Seas). He was undoubtedly the first non-Chinese Zheng He scholar. Towards the end of China's Anti-Japanese War, there appeared two books on Zheng He written by Chinese scholars and published in 1943. Both *Zheng He Hanghai Tukao* (《郑和航海图考》, A Critical Study of the Navigational Map of Zheng He) by Fan Wentao (范文涛) and *Zheng He Jiapu Kaoshi* (《郑和家谱考译释》, Zheng He's Family Record: a Textual Study and Explanation) by Li Shihou (李士

[①] Liang, Qichao (梁启超). (1998) *Zuguo Tahanghaijia Zheng He Zhuan* (《祖国大航海家郑和传》). In his *Liang Qichao Xue Shu Lunzhu Ji: Zhuan Ji Juan* (《梁启超学术论著集：传记集》). Shanghai: 华东师范大学出版社 (pp. 499 – 510).

[②] Feng, Cheng jun (冯承钧). (1935) *Zheng He Xia Xiyang Kao* (《郑和下西洋考》, A Critical Study of Zheng He's Voyages to the West Seas). Shanghai: 商务印书馆.

厚) initiated an interest in Zheng He studies among Chinese scholars.

Another Zheng He scholar, Zheng Hesheng (郑鹤声) (1902 - ?) lived in Nanjing (南京) before the Anti-Japanese War in 1934 - 1935. He made many investigations to sites relating to Zheng He in the vicinity and took pictures of them. Unfortunately, he left Nanjing in haste without bringing with him the pictures together with his manuscripts on Zheng He studies when the war broke out. He wasn't able to reconstruct the old manuscripts in totality while living as a refugee in Sichuan (四川) Province. But he managed to finish the first Chinese book embodying systematic research. This book, entitled *Zheng He* (《郑和》), was published in Chongqing (重庆) in 1945① and proved to be very influential. Many scholars were inspired by this book and produced many books and articles on the same topic.

A companion book to this one, by the same author, was a monumental collection of primary sources relating to Zheng He. Published in Shanghai in 1947, *Zheng He Yishi Huibian* (《郑和遗事汇编》, Source Book on Zheng He)② arranged the primary sources that he painstakingly collected in a thorough classification scheme. Incidentally, the historical background in which Zheng Hesheng (郑鹤声) carried out his Zheng He studies was similar to what surrounded Mao Yuanyi (茅元仪) when he included the Zheng He navigational map in his military encyclopedia *Wubeizhi* (《武备志》) —both were periods when the Chinese people were being invaded. The study of Zheng He therefore, has something more than pure scholarship—it can arouse patriotism and exhilarate the people.

The decade following the publication of these two books had seen a relative dormancy in the study of Zheng He. Not until 1955 do we see another book. *Hanghaishi Shang Diyiren* (《航海史上第一人》, The First Man in the History of Navigation), written by Xie Juntao (谢君韬). and published in Taipei in 1955③ to celebrate the 550th anniversary of Zheng He's voyages and the official designation of July 11 each year as the "Ocean-going Festival" (航海节). In chapter 4 of this book, the author pointed out that "the traditional mainland mentality is the archenemy of navigational achievements." The statement was indeed concise and penetrating.

In mainland China, a monograph devoted to Zheng He appeared the next year. Entitled *Zheng He* (《郑和》, published in Beijing in 1956)④, this book by Zhu Xie (朱偰) presented a comprehensive treatment of Zheng He as a historical figure together with an evaluation of his contributions. The book contained special features, like representing Zheng He's routes of navigation by modem cartography and comparing old place-names with new ones, which influenced future writings.

In 1958 Xiang Da (向达), a professor in China's history of foreign relations at Peking University (北京大学), planned the publication in Beijing of *Zhongwai Jiaotong Shiji Congkan* (《中外交通史籍丛刊》, Collectanea of Historical Works on China's Foreign Relations) and prepared the initial three books for the series. Two of these three books, published in 1960, related directly to Zheng He and the other was indirectly relevant. Unfortunately, the closed-door policy of China during the Cultural Revolution preempted the continuation of the series. Xiang Da himself died in 1966. It was not until the end of the 1970's that Beijing resumed the publication of this important series.⑤

During this period, in Taiwan, the most important scholars in China's history of foreign

---

① Zheng, Hesheng (郑鹤声). (1945) *Zheng He* (《郑和》). Chongqing (重庆): 胜利出版社. The main theme of this book is on Zheng He's "出使". There are four appendixes ("本传"、"碑记"、"诗赋"、"海外诸国释地"). It contains many original sources.
② Zheng, Hesheng (郑鹤声). (1947) *Zheng He Yishi Huibian* (《郑和遗事汇编》, Source Book on Zheng He). Shanghai (上海): 中华书局.
③ Xie, Juntao (谢君韬) (1955) *Hanghaishi Shang Diyiren* (《航海史上第一人》, The First Man in the History of Navigation), Taipei (台北): 航海出版社.
④ Zhu, Xie (朱偰). (1956) *Zheng He* (《郑和》). Beijing (北京): 三联书店.
⑤ Xiang, Da (向达). (1960) *Zhongwai Jiaotong Shiji Congkan* (《中外交通史籍丛刊》, Collectanea of Historical Works on China's Foreign Relations). Beijing (北京): 中华书局, 1960. (Xiang Da's book was reprinted in 2000 by 中华书局)

relations and in Zheng He studies were Fang Hao (方豪) and his student Xu Yuhu (徐玉虎). *Zhongxi Jiaotongshi* (《中西交通史》, History of China's Foreign Relations) by Fang Hao (方豪)① surpassed his predecessors, and its chapter 13 was devoted to Zheng He. Xu Yuhu (徐玉虎) wrote *Zheng He Pingzhuan* (《郑和评传》, Critical Biography of Zheng He)② was another systematic treatment of Zheng He as a man and as a navigator. The three appendices at its end were useful too.

A very important work on Zheng He appeared in 1980. It is *Zheng He Xia Xiyang Ziliao Huibian* (《郑和下西洋资料汇编》, Cyclopedia of Source Materials on Zheng He's Voyages to the West Seas) published in Jinan in 4 volumes.③ This voluminous work was more than a compilation. A whole structure of "Zheng Xue" (郑学, the science of Zheng He studies) was presented in an elaborate classification scheme. The authors, Zheng Hesheng (郑鹤声) and his son Zheng Yijun (郑一钧) spent great efforts to put together numerous primary source information for use by researchers.

The year 1985 saw the 580th anniversary of Zheng He's voyages. A couple of years before that a "Preparatory Committee to Celebrate the 580th Anniversary of the Voyages to the West Seas Led by the Great Navigator Zheng He" (纪念伟大航海家郑和下西洋580周年筹备委员会) was formed with the Society for the Study of the Chinese History of Navigation (中国航海史研究会) as one of the key organizers. The convocation of conferences and publication of anthologies were among the achievements.

The 29 papers presented in the Jiujiang (九江) Conference was later collected into volume 1 of *Zheng He Xia Xiyang Lun Wenji* (《郑和下西洋论文集》, Papers on Zheng He's Voyages to the West Seas) (第一集); those in the Nanjing (南京) Conference, volume 2 (《郑和下西洋论文集》) (第二集). The former has a focus on the technological aspects.

There were at least 3 books on Zheng He published in 1985 by Renmin Jiaotong Chubanshe (北京人民交通出版社, People's Transportation Press). *Zheng He Xia Xiyang* (《郑和下西洋》, Zheng He's Voyages to the West Seas) was a systematic treatise. Topics discussed included historical background, organization of the fleet, ocean-faring technology, details of the 7 voyages, achievements attained, archaeological sites, and the reasons for stopping the expeditions after Zheng He. The text came with a handful of useful illustrations, maps and charts. The portrait of Zheng He specially designed for this book became the widely accepted, standard portrait of Zheng He.

Zheng He Jiashi Ziliao (《郑和家世资料》, Sourcebook on the Family of Zheng He) put together the documents relating to Zheng He's family.④ Knowledge of Zheng He's family history will shed light on our understanding of Zheng He's character, psychological orientation, and religious belief.

Zheng He Shiji Wenwu Xuan (《郑和史迹文物选》, Selections of Remains and Relics Relating to Zheng He)⑤ contains 32 reports with relevant photographs. It is a graphic representation of what we can trace based on which the life and contributions of Zheng He can be reconstructed. It is unfortunate that the printing of this book is in inferior quality and should be reprinted if feasible.

For people who prefer to read works of creativity, the novel *Zheng He* (《郑和》) by Tian Mu

---

① Fang, Hao (方豪). (1959) *Zhongxi Jiaotongshi* (《中西交通史》, History of China's Foreign Relations). Taipei: 中华书局.

② Xu, Yuhu (徐玉虎). (1958) *Zheng He Pingzhuan* (《郑和评传》, Critical Biography of Zheng He). Taipei: 中华文化出版事业委员会.

③ Zheng, Hesheng (郑鹤声) and Zheng, Yijun (郑一钧). (1980) *Zheng He Xia Xiyang Ziliao Huibian* (《郑和下西洋资料汇编》, Cyclopedia of Source Materials on Zheng He's Voyages to the West Seas). Jinan (济南): 齐鲁书社, 4 vols.

④ These documents includes several of Zheng He's family histories such as: 《郑和家谱》,《南京郑和家谱首序》,《宝典赤家谱》, and 《马氏家乘》.

⑤ *Zheng He Shiji Wenwu Xuan* (《郑和史迹文物选》, 1985, Selections of Remains and Relics Relating to Zheng He). Beijing (北京): 人民交通出版社.

(田木) and (Jin Ke) 靳柯 (published in Kunming (昆明) in 1987)① is recommended. Using the voyages as the main theme, the novel weaves together activities in the imperial court, among the local people, on the land, on the seas, and in and outside of China. The novel excels in characterization, psychoanalysis, and descriptions of foreign lands and navigational knowledge.

Although Xinbian *Zheng He Hanghai Tuji* (《新编郑和航海图集》, A New Atlas of the Voyages of Zheng He)② was published a bit later, it is unmistakably a product of the 580-year-anniversary celebration. This atlas reproduced with modem cartography the navigational routes of Zheng He, comparing the new maps with the old ones. Careful study of the old place-names was made and their modem equivalents explained in a gazetteer of place-names. It is certainly a work of scholarship.

In Taiwan, the 580-year-anniversary celebration was not openly advocated, but a few books on Zheng He were published in the late 1980's. Notably among them was *Zui Zao De Zhongguo Dahanghaijia Zheng He* (《最早的中国大航海家——郑和》, Zheng He, the Earliest Great Navigator of China) published in 1986.③ It is the only book written in both Chinese and German by the author Jiang Hong (江鸿). It investigates historical and geographical questions using engineering charts. One important point raised by the author was that Zheng He made eight expeditions instead of seven, which was the common belief. He also proposed the collection and preservation of cultural relics relating to Zheng He outside of China. He was truly one of the first advocates of the globalization of Zheng He studies.

Another novel on Zheng He that warrants our attention is Su Shangyao's (苏尚耀), *Zheng He Xia Xiyang* (《郑和下西洋》, Zheng He's Voyages to the West Seas) published in 1987.④ It reduced the Ming Dynasty novel *Sanbao Taijian Xia Xiyang Ji* (《三宝太监下西洋记》) to one-quarter its length, removed the weird and uncanny contents, and gave prominence to the customs and produce of the alien countries visited by Zheng He's fleets.

A new direction of research was launched in the late 1980's. In 1987, Ma Wenkuan (马文宽) and Meng Fanren (孟凡人) wrote *Zhongguo Ciqi Zai Feizhou De Faxian* (《中国古瓷在非洲的发现》, The Discovery of Chinese Porcelains in Africa).⑤ This imparted the thought of introducing archaeological findings to Zheng He studies. Given that documentary evidences are insufficient, could archaeological excavations join in?

In her popular book *When China Ruled the Seas*, Louise Levathes, after on-site investigations along the East African coast, declared that the Famao tribe (法茂族) in the island of Pate, off the coast of Kenya (东非肯亚帕帖), consists of descendants of Chinese sailors. Following her footsteps, Nicholas D. Kristof, a reporter of the *New York Times*, did interviews and researches on the island. He confirmed that the Famao tribe has features and complexion reflecting a Chinese ancestry. From the porcelains that the tribesmen use and the form of their graves he noted further some hints of Chinese civilization. There was also an oral tradition among the tribesmen, he held, that their ancestors were sailors of Zheng He's fleet who swam on-shore after their ships were wrecked. Their stories include the tribute of giraffes by the African chiefs to the Ming emperor.

We know very well that in Malaysia there are descendants of interracial marriages between Chinese and Malays. These descendants are called *niangre* (娘惹), and *baba* (峇峇) in the Chinese language. It is very likely that the Pate tribesmen are the East African version of niangre and *baba*.

---

① Tian, Mu (田木) and Jin, Ke (靳柯). (1987) *Zheng He* (《郑和》). Kunming (昆明): 云南出版社.
② *Xinbian Zheng He Hanghai Tuji* (《新编郑和航海图集》, A New Atlas of the Voyages of Zheng He) (1988). Beijing (北京): 人民交通出版社.
③ Jiang, Hong (江鸿). (1986) *Zui Zao De Zhongguo Dahanghaijia Zheng He* (《最早的中国大航海家——郑和》, Zheng He, the Earliest Great Navigator of China). Taipei (台北): 台湾中华书局.
④ Su, Shangyao (苏尚耀). (1987) *Zheng He Xia Xiyang* (《郑和下西洋》, Zheng He's Voyages to the West Seas). Taipei (台北): 东方出版社..
⑤ Ma, Wenkuan (马文宽) and Meng, Fanren (孟凡人). (1987) *Zhongguo Ciqi Zai Feizhou De Faxian* (《中国古瓷在非洲的发现》, The Discovery of Chinese Porcelains in Africa). 北京: 紫禁城出版.

From the navigational map of Zheng He, we know for certain that his fleets visited East Africa. But had they gone beyond East Africa? The retired British submarine commander Gavin Menzies believes that Zheng He's fleet went round the Cape of Good Hope and reached America, and even circumscribed the globe. His monumental work *1421: The Year China Discovered the World*[①] ignited global interest in Zheng He. Since he is so well-known, I think I need not go into details here.

The Library of Congress has all of the modern and contemporary writings on Zheng He mentioned in this paper. Because of their multitude, I cannot possibly discuss them one by one. I wish to conclude this paper with reference a few Chinese journals.

The earliest Chinese journal containing articles on Zheng He was *Hai Jiao Shi Yanjiu* (《海交史研究》, Studies on China-foreign Relations). A brief statistics study I made reveals that in the first 40 issues (1978–2001) of *Hai Jiao Shi Yanjiu* there were 27 articles directly relating to Zheng He. The most prolific year of production was 1985 when 9 articles were published in one year. This of course was the result of the 580-year-anniversity celebration. Then the role of *Hai Jiao Shi Yanjiu* in this respect was taken over by the journal I am going to mention below.

One of the fruits of the 580-year-anniversary celebration was the launching of a journal specifically on Zheng He. *Zheng He Yanjiu* (《郑和研究》, Studies of Zheng He) edited by Nanjing Zhenghe Study Association (南京郑和研究会) which started out to be a semi-annual publication. It was changed to a quarterly in 1994, and changed back to semi-annual in 2000. For reasons unknown to me, it became a nei bu ziliao (内部数据 "internal circulation only" publication) since the latter half of 2003. Appearing in this journal are some very interesting articles, like comparing *Zheng He with Columbus* (《郑和与哥伦布航海之比较》) and discussing the heritage of *Zheng He's and its implication for logistics of a modern navy* 《略论郑和船队后勤保障对海军后勤建设的启示》, and so on. I wish also to raise a point here about an obscure but interesting book reviewed in the 1995 issue of *Zheng He Yanjiu*. The topic of this book, entitled *Zheng He Yu Yindunixiya* (《郑和与印度尼西亚》, Zheng He and Indonesia), intrigued me but I could not find it from any of the electronic library databases I consulted. In my opinion, this kind of topic is among the most desirable in future research and writing on Zheng He. I look forward eagerly to reading more publications on the "footprint" of Zheng He's fleets and their influences in countries along the "West Seas" (西洋) because Zheng He's heritage is more than a Chinese heritage, certainly a heritage of global scale.

In 2001, we saw the publication of *Zheng He Yanjiu Yu Huodong Jianxun* (《郑和研究与活动简讯》, Newsletter on Researches and Activities on Zheng He) in Taiwan. This newsletter contains reports of the most recent publications, conferences, etc.

The Asian Division of the Library of Congress has in its holdings the three journals mentioned above. Besides Chinese books and journals, the Division also has publications relating to Zheng He in Japanese, Korean, Malay, Indonesian, Hindu and other Asian languages. The Library of Congress is, of course, very rich in Western language collections. However, discussion on publications in languages other than Chinese is beyond the scope of this paper and may be the topic of another paper in the future.

Acknowledgement

This paper couldn't have been written without the expert advice and assistance of Dr. Ming Sun Poon. His contributions to writing of this paper are gratefully acknowledged.

---

① Menzies, Gavin. (2002) *1421: The Year China Discovered the World.* London: Bantam Press. Another title: *1421: The Year China Discovered America.* New York: HarperCollins Publishers, 2004.

美国国会图书馆建立世界级的数位时代亚洲馆藏

Building a World-class Asian Collection in the Digital Age at the Library of Congress[①]

The Universality of the Collection

The Library of Congress was established by an act of American Congress in 1800. After the initial collection was destroyed by the invading British troops in 1814, the Congress acquired the personal collection of 6,487 books from the retired President Thomas Jefferson a year later. In offering his collection to Congress, Jefferson provided justifications about the scope of his collection, which included books in foreign languages and volumes of philosophy, science, literature and other topics not normally viewed as part of a legislative library, "I do not know that it contains any branch of science which Congress would wish to exclude from their collection; there is, in fact, no subject to which a member of Congress may not have occasion to refer."[②] It was this concept of universality and belief that all subjects are important to the library of the American legislature that led the Library of Congress to develop its comprehensive collecting policies and adhere to this basic guiding principle.

From the core of Jefferson's library in 1815, the size of today's collection has grown to 130 million items of which 29 million are printed collections. Others are in a variety of formats including manuscripts, maps, motion pictures, photographs, prints, sheet music, sound recordings, videos, etc. About 34 million of all these are included in the Library's online catalog. In the year of 2004 alone, a total of 2.5 million new items were added, making it the largest and fastest growing library collection in the world.[③] It is important to note that more than one half of the entire collection is in languages other than English.

Below is the mission statement of the Library:

The Library's mission is to make its resources available and useful to the Congress and the American people and to sustain and preserve a universal collection of knowledge and creativity for future generations[④]

Serving as the National Library

Although the Library of Congress is the library of the American Congress, it has also been serving as the national library of the United States of America. For the discharge of its mission as the library of the Congress, there is a unit called Congressional Research Service. The chief responsibility of this unit is to provide the Congress with research and analysis on the full range of legislative policy issues. For carrying out the functions of the national library, there is a major unit called Library Services, headed by an Associate Librarian. The position is now held by Dr. Deanna Marcum. There is another unit named Law Library, which holds the world's largest legal publications covering U.S., foreign, and international law. In addition, the Library of Congress is also in charge of copyright registration and protection. The unit that is responsible for this is the U.S. Copyright Office. By law, two copies of all publications published in the U.S. must be deposited at the Copyright Office. In 2004, over 600,000 items were deposited and about half of

---

[①] Presented at the Symposium on Library Collection in the Digital Age, January 16 – 17, 2006, Taichung, Taiwan: Graduate Institute of Library and Information Science, Chung Hsing University & Chung Hsing UniversityLibrary.

[②] The Thomas Jefferson Building of the Library of Congress Washington, DC: Library of Congress, 2003: pp. 1 – 2.

[③] The Annual Report of the Librarian of Congress for the Fiscal Year Ending September 30, 2004. Washington, DC: Library of Congress, 2005: pp. 211 – 215.

[④] The Library of Congress Strategic Plan: Fiscal Years 2004 – 2008. Washington, DC: Library of Congress, 2003: p. 13.

them were selected and added to the Library's collection.

Collection Development in the Digital Age

Because of the rapid change in information creation, storage, and dissemination brought about by the revolutionary change in information technology, electronic publishing, the creation of the Internet, proliferation of web-based resources, and powerful search engines, etc. more and more human knowledge and creativity are now accessible in digital form. Increasingly, a larger portion of funding for library acquisitions has shifted to the acquisition of digital resources. The most recent statistics compiled by the Association of Research Libraries shows that in 2003 – 2004 expenditures for all types of electronic resources (computer files, electronic serials, bibliographic utilities and networks, and computer hardware and software) were increased substantially. For example, the expenditures for electronic serials alone as reported in 1994 – 1995 by 63 ARL libraries was $11,847,577, but it went up to $270 million in 2003 – 2004 as reported by 100 ARL libraries. ①

Below is the table adapted from the Kyrillidou and Young report:

Expenditures for Electronic Materials in ARL University Libraries, 2003 – 2004②

Expenditures	Sum	Number Reporting
Computer Files (one time/monographic)	$32,098,404	102
Electronic Serials	$269,601,241	110
Bibliographic Utilities, Networks, etc. (Library)	$25,985,819	105
Bibliographic Utilities, Networks, etc. (External)	$17,420,498	52
Hardware and Software	$65,802,192	110

These amounts may not include expenditures for in-house digitization or digital conversation.

The expansion of the Web has also revolutionized the way libraries are providing and delivering their services. Remote access to online catalogs, electronic bibliographic tools, and full-text digital resources-either born digital or digitized-are just a few of the value-added services that can be offered by libraries through the Internet. Increasingly libraries are moving toward a virtual library model no longer confined by their physical space and walls. These profound changes have prompted many libraries to reconsider their collection policies and refine their roles.

In the Library of Congress, a digital strategic plan was issued in March 2003. ③ The plan is an evolution of the digital future's strategy and was developed in the context of the Library's core missions and vision and provides a consistent, institution-wide approach to ensuring the continued collection, protection, organization, preservation of, and access to, historically significant materials in their evolving digital formats.

In addition to the internal LC initiatives, the Library's digital strategy also provides for leadership of the National Digital Information Infrastructure and Preservation Program (NDIIPP). The mission of NDIIPP is to develop a national strategy to collect, archive, and preserve the burgeoning amounts of digital contents, especially materials that are created only in digital

---

① Martha Kyrillidou and Mark Young. "ARL Library Trends" in ***ARL Statistics 2003 – 2004***. See http://www.arl.org/stats/arlstat/04pub/04intro.html

"*ARL Statistics 2003 – 2004* is the latest in a series of annual publications that describe collections, staffing, expenditures, and service activities for the 123 members of the Association of Research Libraries (ARL). Of these, 113 are university libraries and 10 are public, governmental, and nonprofit research libraries. ARL member libraries are the largest research libraries in North America, representing 16 Canadian and 107 U. S. research institutions. The academic libraries, which comprise about 92% of the membership, include 14 Canadian and 99 U. S. libraries"

② Kyrillidou and Young. *Ibid*.

③ *Library of Congress Digital Strategic Plan*, March 2003. (PDF) http://www.loc.gov/staff/deog/deog-home.shtml

formats, for current and future generations.

The Beginning of the Asian Collection

The first acquisition of an Asian collection from Asia by the Library of Congress can be traced back to 1865 when the Smithsonian Institution transferred a collection of books on Southeast Asia and the Pacific islands that had been gathered in Singapore by the Wilkes Exploring Expedition from 1838 to 1842. Four years later, in 1869, the Emperor of China (Tongzhi 同治皇帝) presented to the Library of Congress 10 major Chinese works in 933 volumes. This was soon followed by the exchange of government publications with the Japanese government initiated in 1875.[①] From these early beginnings, the collection of Asian publications from all parts of Asia and in all major and some minor Asian languages has grown to nearly 2.8 million monographic volumes and 15,000 active serial titles. In addition to the holdings in the Asian Division, important Asian collections of legal materials, maps, music, motion pictures, prints, and photographs are housed and cared for by other divisions in the Library of Congress in collaboration with the Asian Division. These other units include the Law Library, the Geography and Map Division, the Prints and Photographs Division, the Motion Picture, Broadcasting and Recorded Sound Division, the Performing Arts Division, the Manuscript Division, etc. Other Asia-related publications not in Asian languages are also housed in the Main Reading Room, Microform Reading Room, Newspaper and Current Periodical Reading Room, Performing Arts Reading Room, Science Reading Room, and in some of the other area studies and special collections.

The name of Asian Division has gone through several changes since 1928 when the Division of Chinese Literature was established for the first time through the effort of Herbert Putnam, Librarian of Congress (1899 – 1939). Three years later, in 1931, the name was changed to the Division of Chinese and Japanese Literature. In 1932, it was renamed the Division of Orientalia. This was changed again to the Asiatic Division in 1942 and changed back to Orientalia Division in 1944. Finally, the name of Asian Division was formally adopted in 1978.[②]

The Organization of the Asian Division

The Asian Division is one of the four area studies divisions (African and Middle Eastern Division, Asian Division, European Division, and Hispanic Division) reporting to the Director for Collections and Services. Dr. Carolyn Brown is in charge of this part of Library Services.

Within the Asian Division, under the general leadership and management of the Chief, there are two section heads: the Head of Collection Services and the Head of Scholarly Services. The professional staff members of the division, who are either area specialists or reference librarians, are divided into five area teams: China and Mongolia, Japan, Korea, Southeast Asia, and South Asia. A coordinator of each area team is appointed from the team members by the Chief. The Chief is also assisted by an Administrative Officer, an Information Technology Specialist, a special assistant, and a Secretary.

Vision of the Asian Division

To establish the collections of the Asian Division as the premier research and scholarly resource of all formats and times on Asia and in Asian languages that is compatible with the dynamics of knowledge and creativity of the 21st Century-frequently referred to as the "Asian Century".

Mission of the Asian Division

The mission of the Asian Division is to make comprehensive collection resources and information services related to Asia available and useful to the Congress, American people, and the scholarly

---

① *The Asian Division*. Washington, DC: The Library of Congress, 2002: pp. 1, 2, 4, 8.
② Chi Wang. *The Chinese Collection in the Library of Congress: A Brief Introduction*. Washington, DC: Chinese Section, Asian Division, Library of Congress, 2001: pp. 5 – 6.

research community nationally and internationally. ①

Building a Comprehensive Asian Collection

Recognizing the importance of Asia in the 21st century the Library of Congress has devoted great effort to building a comprehensive collection of Asia. Today, after 140 years of painstaking work by generations of Asian area specialists, librarians, and scholars, a vast storehouse of knowledge and culture about the diverse nations, languages, and peoples has been assembled. It is perhaps the best of such collections outside Asia. With the foresight of Dr. James Billington, the current Librarian of the Congress, an exquisite Asian Reading Room has been provided as a gateway to this world-class collection. Below are brief descriptions of the five key collections:

The Chinese and Mongolian Collection

The Chinese and Mongolian Collection, as of November 18, 2005, consists of 981,931 monographic volumes, 4,149 active serial titles, and 10,953 inactive serial titles. Besides works in the Chinese language, it also includes several thousand volumes in Manchu, Mongol, Naxi (Moso), Tibetan, Uyghur, and other minority languages. The collection covers all subjects and is especially strong in the humanities and social sciences, among them, classical Chinese literature, archival materials of the Qing (清) dynasty (1644 – 1911) and Republican (民国) period (1911 – 1949), traditional Chinese medicine, local and regional histories (gazetteers), and contemporary publications of Mainland China and Taiwan.

The collection also contains some of the most valuable rare books from China, and Mongolia. The rare books from China cover Song (宋) dynasty (960 – 1279), Jin (金) dynasty (1115 – 1234), Yuan (元) dynasty (1271 – 1368), Ming (明) dynasty (1368 – 1644), and Qing (清) dynasty (1644 – 1911). It includes a Buddhist invocation sutra (《一切如来》, (Yi qie ru lai) printed in 975 A. D. that was recovered from the hollow bricks of the foundation of the Thunder Peak Pagoda (雷峰塔, Lei feng ta) when it collapsed in 1924, 41 of the 400 surviving volumes of the 1560 copy of the *Great Encyclopedia of the Ming Emperor Yongle* (《永乐大典》, Yongle da dian), and the 1895 – 98 printing of the *Imperial Encyclopedia of China* (《古今图书集成》, Gu jin tu shu ji cheng) in 5,044 volumes.

Examples of other unique collections are the 3,344 pictographic manuscripts from the Naxi 纳西 minority group in Yunnan province, the Gamble collection of a 19th-century American missionary printer that includes Christian publications in Chinese and translations of Western works, and the Arthur W. Hummel collection of rare Chinese maps. ②

The Library of Congress is one of the world's leading centers for Tibetan publications with holdings that are representative of the entire body of Tibetan literature from the 8th century to the modern day. These include religious texts, history, biography, traditional medicine, astrology, iconography, musical notations, grammars, social sciences, and secular literature.

Since religion plays a major role in Tibetan society, the holdings of Tibetan Buddhist scriptures in the Asian Division are especially strong. The Tibetan Buddhist canon is contained in the *Kanjur*, in over a hundred volumes of sutras, and the *Tanjur*, most editions totaling some 225 volumes of commentaries. The Tibetan canonical texts are accurate translations of the original Buddhist texts, written in Sanskrit between 500 BC. and 900 AD. Among the individuals who were responsible for the early periods of development of the Tibetan collection are William Woodville Rockhill, the American diplomat and Tibetologist who travels in Mongolia and Tibet between 1888 and 1892 and again in the 1900s; Berthold Laufer, another leading Tibetologist in the late 1800s; and Joseph Rock, the colorful explorer, adventurer, and scientist who lived and traveled in China's rugged west for 27 years in the early 1900s. ③

---

① *The Strategic Plan of the Asian Division, 2003 to 2008*. Washington, DC: Asian Division, the Library of Congress, 2003.
② *The Chinese Collection*. Washington, DC: Asian Division, the Library of Congress, n. d.
③ *The Tibetan Collection*. Washington, DC: Asian Division, Library of Congress, April 2002.

The Mongolian collection also includes 80 books in traditional script and format acquired in the early 20th century and complete reprint editions of the Mongolian Kanjur and Tanjur, the Buddhist canonical texts and their commentaries. In recent years, the Library's New Delhi Field Office has been actively acquiring current publications from Mongolia.

The Japanese Collection

After the initial arrangement for the exchange of government publications established in 1875 between the two governments, the Japanese collection began to grow in 1905 when a significant gift was received from Crosby Stuart Noyes, journalist and editor of the *Washington Evening Star*. The Noyes collection included 658 illustrated books produced from the mid-18th century to the late-19th century. In 1907, a systematic effort was undertaken by Kan'ichi Asakawa of Yale University to purchase Japanese books for the Library of Congress. Because of his effort, some 9,072 volumes on the subjects of Japanese history, literature, Buddhism, Shinto, geography, music, and the arts were added. In 1930, the Library appointed Dr. Shiho Sakanishi as the Chief Assistant of the Japanese Section to further develop the collection. During her tenure from 1930 to 1941, the collection tripled in size. Today, the Japanese collection has grown to 1,149,833 volumes of monographs, 6,334 active serial titles, and 9,451 inactive serial titles-the largest collection in the Asian Division-through purchase, gift, exchange, and other avenues of acquisition.

Among the wealth of rare items are approximately 5,000 titles of publications and manuscript copies of works produced before the end of the Tokugawa Shogunate in 1868 and the beginning of the Meiji period (1868 – 1912). Included are the *dharani* (百万搭陀罗尼) prayer charms, which date to 770 A. D. and are among the world's earliest surviving printed material. Also noteworthy are a complete edition of the Japanese literary masterpiece Genji monogatari (《源氏物语》, The Tale of Genji) published in Kyoto in 1654 and the **Yoshitsune azuma kudari monogatari** printed on movable type between 1624 and 1643. A complete catalogue of the rare books in the Library of Congress was published in 2003 by Yagi Shoten in Tokyo.①

At the end of World War II, a large number of historical documents such as the ones from the former Japanese Imperial Army and Navy, the South Manchuria Railway Company, and the East Asian Research Institute were given to the Library by the Washington Document Center. Much of the materials from the latter two are pre-World War II studies on such areas as Korea, Taiwan, Mainland China, Mongolia, and the Pacific Islands. The Library also has a microfilm copy of the archives of the Japanese Foreign Ministry from 1868 to 1945 and pre-1945 records of the Police Bureau of the Ministry of Home Affairs-some of these are censored wartime publications.②

Another important collection is the "Inoh Maps" —the first modern maps of Japan created originally by Tadataka Inoh between 1800 and 1821. Copies of 207 of Inoh's original 214 sheets large-scale set (1:36,000) that cover the Japanese archipelago from Hokkaido to Kyushu were discovered in the map collection of the Library of Congress in the spring of 2001 and have caused great excitement in Japan. In order to make these maps available for exhibition and for online access, all of them have been digitized and sent to the Japan Map Center. A selection of the actual-size reproductions of these maps was on exhibition at the Tokyo National Museum from October 31 to December 14, 2003. Some of the original maps were also loaned and exhibited in Kobe, Sendai, Atami, and Nagoya in 2004.

The Korean Collection

The Korean collection began in the 1920s with the generous gift of Korean books from Dr. James S. Gale, a Canadian missionary who spent 40 years in Korea from 1888 to 1928. Dr. Gale also helped the Library to acquire a number of Korean classics, including rare books from the estate of the Korean scholar Kim To-hui. Systematic development of the Korean collection was

---

① *Beikoku Gikai Toshokan zo Nihon Kotenseki Mokuroku* (Catalog of Japanese Rare Books In the Library of Congress). Tokyo: Yagi Shoten, 2003.
② *The Japanese Collection*. Washington, DC: Asian Division, the Library of Congress, n. d.

started in the early 1950s during the period of the Korean War. Today, the Korean collection in the Library totals 220,000 volumes in the Korean language, as well as 20,000 Japanese language books and 8,000 English language books on Korea. Coverage of North Korea is also strong, with some 10,000 items.

There are 480 titles of Korean rare books, in 3,000 volumes. They were all written in Chinese characters and printed on mulberry paper. Although China was the first country to use movable type made of clay, Korea was the first one to use movable metal type for printing. Several good examples of this type of printing are in the collection. These are the collected writings of the renowned 16th-century Confucian scholar and statesman Yi I printed in 1744 and the 1834 reprint of the works of the "father of Korean literature", Ch'oe Ch'i-won (857 – 915). Other rare books printed by woodblock include the *History of the Koryo Dynasty* (《高丽史》), printed in 1590, and the *Law Code of the Yi Dynasty* (《经国大典》) printed in 1630. ①

The Southeast Asian Collection

As was mentioned earlier, the earliest acquisition of the Southeast Asian collection in the Library of Congress began in 1865, which predates the beginning of all other Asian collections. The collection was acquired in Singapore in 1842 by the U.S. Naval Exploring Expedition led by Lt. Charles Wilkes. Wilkes and the Expedition's philologist, Horatio Hale, collected Malay manuscripts and early printed books with the assistance of Alfred North, an American missionary in Singapore. The collection went first to the Smithsonian Institution which later transferred the collection to the Library of Congress in 1865. Included in this earliest acquisition are a unique collection of manuscripts written in the Buginese script of South Sulawesi; an account of the 19th-century Malay world written in Jawi, the *Hikayat Abdullah* (The Story of Abdullah); and an 1840 Mission Press edition of the *Sejarah Melayu* (Malay Annals), an important Malay history written in 1612, also in Jawi, the Malay language in Arabic script.

The Southeast Asian collection contains many palm leaf manuscript copies of the *Tipitaka*, the basic text of Theravada Buddhism which is the majority religion of Cambodia, Laos, Myanmar (Burma), and Thailand. In 1905, a special Thai *Tipitaka* was presented to the Library of Congress by King Chulalongkorn (Rama V) of Thailand. In 1949, an especially fine collection of Burmese manuscripts in the Pali language as well as a *Tipitaka* in Pali using Burmese script was presented to the Library of Congress as a part of a large Burmese donation. The donation also included an important Burmese history, *The Glass Palace Chronicle*, written by a group of scholars in 1829.

The Asian Division also holds rare materials from the Philippines and Vietnam. Of special note is a set of inscribed bamboo tubes, with lettering in the old Indic script similar to the ancient scripts used in neighboring Indonesia. The collection of 55 bamboos in prose and 22 in verse provides a fascinating glimpse into Mangyan (Hampangan) and Tagbanua society. Several examples of Vietnamese dynastic histories are also represented, including texts printed from early woodblocks at the former imperial palace at Hue.

In 1938, the Library of Congress launched the Indic Project in order to improve its collections from Southeast and South Asia, particularly publications in local languages. Following World War II, as U.S. interest in the region increased, the collection grew dramatically and today consists of holdings from Brunei, Cambodia, Indonesia, Laos, Malaysia, Myanmar, the Philippines, Singapore, Thailand, Vietnam, and many of the South Pacific island nations such as Papua New Guinea, etc. The establishment of the Library's overseas offices in New Delhi, India, in 1962, in Jakarta, Indonesia, in 1963, and in Islamabad, Pakistan, in 1965 has provided a continuous flow of books, newspapers, and periodicals from the region in a variety of formats. ②

The South Asian Collection

The foundation for the South Asian collection was laid in 1904 when a collection of over

---

① *The Korean Collection*. Washington, DC: Asian Division, the Library of Congress, n. d.
② *The Southeast Asian Collection*. Washington, DC: Asian Division, Library of Congress, April 2002.

4,000 books and pamphlets from the German Indologist, Dr. Albrecht Weber, was purchased. Included were texts in Sanskrit of India's sacred Hindu works-the *Vedas*, *Brahmanas*, and *Upanisads*-as well as the stories of the Puranas and the great epics in the *Mahabharata and the Ramayana*. In addition, there are a number of Weber's notebooks with his handwritten transcriptions of rare Indian texts for his pioneering critical editions.

In 1938, the Library received a grant from the Carnegie Corporation to develop the South Asian collection systematically, and it initiated the Indic Project— "Project F-Development of Indic Studies". During the 1950s the collection continued to expand and growth accelerated even further with the opening of the Library's New Delhi Overseas Office in 1962. Under the Public Law (PL) 480 program, the New Delhi office used rupees from Indian purchases of U. S. agricultural products to buy books and other materials from India and other countries of South Asia. An overseas office in Karachi, Pakistan, was opened in 1965 to oversee the acquisition of publications from Pakistan and neighboring areas. Later, the office was moved to the capital city, Islamabad.

Today, the South Asian collection holds materials in over 100 modern languages used in India, Pakistan, Bangladesh, Sri Lanka, and Nepal. The majority of the publications are in Hindi (20 percent), Bengali (15 percent), Urdu (13 percent), and Tamil (11 percent). Other languages represented in large numbers include Marathi, Telugu, Malayalam, Gujarati, and Kannada.

An example among the many rare books and manuscripts in the South Asian collection is a 1452 manuscript of the Jaina **Kalpasutra** from Gujarat in western India. This illustrated text tells the story of Mahavira, the founder of the Jaina religion. The "Crosby Khotan fragmants" are also among the more unusual rare items. During a 1903 journey to Central Asia, Oscar Terry Crosby, an American who later became Assistant Secretary of the Treasury, purchased these manuscripts in Sanskrit at the Taklamakan oasis town of Khotan. ①

Between 1990 and 2000, a very important project undertaken by the New Delhi Overseas Office was the *Microfilming of Indian Publications Project (MIPP)*. This project was a joint collaboration between the Government of India and the Library of Congress, aimed at preserving and making accessible out-of-print works listed in the **National Bibliography of Indian Literature: 1901 – 1953**. Some 22,686 titles in 15 languages were microfilmed from 67 repository libraries in India and 3 libraries outside India (the Library of Congress, University of Chicago, and British Library). These titles were selected by Indian scholars as being central to the understanding of India. ②

Overseas Acquisition Offices

The accelerated growth of the library collections from South and Southeast Asia since the 1960s should be credited to the efforts of the overseas acquisition offices in New Delhi, Jakarta, and Islamabad. In addition to these three, the African/Asian Acquisitions and Overseas Operations Division of the Library of Congress also operate overseas offices in Cairo, Nairobi, and Rio de Janeiro.

One of the unique features of the three Asian overseas offices is the offering of their service to other libraries which want to acquire publications from countries and regions covered by these offices. For example, the 44 academic and research libraries, mostly from North America, that participated in the South Asia Cooperative Acquisitions Program (SACAP) receive publications of their choice from the New Delhi office and its many sub-offices. Being the largest and the oldest of the six overseas offices, the New Delhi office covers India, Bangladesh, Bhutan, the Maldives, Nepal, and Sri Lanka—as well as Burma and Mongolia. The New Delhi office performs a wide range of services to SACAP libraries, including acquisitions, cataloging, bibliographic control,

---

① *The South Asian Collection.* Washington, DC: Asian Division, Library of Congress, April 2002.
② *The Library of Congress in South Asia, 1960 – 2002. Celebrating 40 Years of Bibliographic and Cultural Exchanges.* New Delhi: Library of Congress Office, n. d. p. 16.

and preservation of publications acquired in some 65 languages and 25 different scripts. Another service of the New Delhi office is the maintenance of an extensive program for official and informal exchanges of publications with key institutions and libraries in South Asia. ①

Building the Asian collection in the digital age

Throughout the 20th century the building of Asian collections were focused mainly on printed materials. However, the trend has begun to change in the past five years with attention gradually shifting to electronic and web resources. Large-scale digitization of rare materials has also being launched to make some of the treasured collections, which have no copyright restriction, freely accessible to researchers via the Internet. The approaches taken thus far include the subscription to selected electronic bibliographic databases; the acquisition of digitized full-text databases of e-books, e-journals, e-newspapers, and others; the digitization of selected rare books and other collections, and the capture of relevant web sites for the Library's Asian portals which are constructed and maintained by the Asian Division.

Subscription to selected electronic bibliographic databases

At present forty-five of the Library's 219 subscription databases deal with Asia or Asian studies. These databases, such as Aardvark (Asian resources for librarians), *Asian Development Bank Economics & Statistics* (of Economics and Research Department of Asian Development Bank), *Asian Law Bibliographic Database* (from the University of Melbourne), *Bibliography of Asian Studies* (from Association for Asian Studies), *Country Studies* (produced by Federal Research Division, the Library of Congress), and *Treaties and International Agreements* (by Oceana Publications), are all accessible in the Library's reading rooms.

Acquisition of digitized full-text databases

Since 2003, special efforts have also been made to acquire a number of most important digitized full-text databases from Mainland China, Japan, Korea, and Taiwan.

In the Mainland China and Taiwan areas we have acquired *Ren min ri bao dian zi ban* (人民日报电子版 *The People's Daily Electronic Version*), 1946 – 2004; China Data Online; *China Journals Full-text Database* (中国期刊全文数据库 – 7240 *titles*) and *Chinese Core Newspapers Databases* (中国重要报纸数据库 – 1,000 *titles*) of the *China National Knowledge Infrastructure* (CNKI 中国国家知识基础架构); and most recently we gained access to a 100,000-title monograph database from *Superstar Digital Library* (超星电子图书馆). We have also acquired *Si ku quan shu* (*Wen yuan ge Edition* 四库全书文渊阁版) – a professional standalone version, the Academia Sinica's Geographic Information Systems (GIS) of *Chinese Civilization in Time and Space* (CCTS 中国文明之时空基础架构) and *Taiwan History and Culture in Time and Space* (THCTS 台湾历史文化地图系统) and the *Encyclopedia of Taiwan* (台湾百科全书).

For the Japanese collection the Library has acquired two important subscription databases: *Directory of Japanese Scientific Periodicals* (from National Diet Library, covering 13,875 serial titles on science and technology published in Japan) and *Kodansha Encyclopedia of Japan* (based on the 1993 publication entitled *Japan: an Illustrated Encyclopedia*, with 11,000 entries). Several Japanese rare books have also been digitized and are available from the Library's OPAC. In addition, the Library currently subscribes full-text databases of five major Japanese newspapers including Mainichi, Sankei, Chunichi, Tokyo and Yomiuri Newspapers through a U.S. based commercial aggregator/vendor, www.factive.com.

In the Korea area the recent acquisitions were *Chosun Daily Newspaper Archive* (covering articles from the Chosun Ilbo, the most widely read newspaper in South Korea), *Korean Studies Database* (by KRPIA, covering history, literature, and traditional medicines), *Korean Studies Information Service System* (KISS, a database of full-text articles from 6,000 journals published by 1,200 Korean academic institutions), and *Law n B-Korean Law Database* (Law and business,

---

① *The Library of Congress in South Asia, 1960 – 2002. Celebrating 40 Years of Bibliographic and Cultural Exchanges.* New Delhi: Library of Congress Office, n. d.

available for access in the Law Library reading room only).

Digitization of selected rare books and other collections

In recent years, Asian Division has undertaken several major collaborative projects to digitize its unparalleled Asian collections. With a three-year grant from the Chiang Ching-kuo Foundation (1998 – 2001) the Chinese and Mongolian Section was able to hire an expert to review and prepare a detailed description for the 3,344 Naxi manuscripts in the collection and subsequently digitized a portion of this unique collection. This digitized collection is now accessible from LC's website: http://international.loc.gov/intldl/naxihtml/naxihome.html

On October 1, 2004, the Library and the Academia Sinica (Taipei) signed an agreement for the digitization of China-related maps. Through two working visits of the subject and digital experts from the Academia Sinica in 2004 and 2005, digital images of 21,000 maps and 840 aerial photos were made and transported to Taiwan for post-digitization processing. This digital file will be incorporated into the *Chinese Civilizations in Time and Space* (CCTS) database and supported by a historical geographic information system with spatial-temporal applications.

In May 2005, the Library and the National Central Library (Taipei) signed an agreement for the digitization of Chinese rare books. A team of technical specialists from Taiwan is now working onsite at the Library of Congress for two years to digitize selected titles in the Chinese rare book collection, which have been reviewed by Chinese rare book experts for the authentication and annotation of the Chinese rare books, and by the Library's Conservation Division. The two experts are funded by Chiang Ching-kuo Foundation for 2005 and 2006. The goal of this collaborative project is for the two libraries to share each other's digitized databases of Chinese rare books and make them easily and freely accessible to researchers worldwide.

In close collaboration with the International Research Center of Japanese Studies (Nichubunken), the Asian Division digitized the Nara Ehon collection, four titles of *Shizuka, Homyo Doji, Shigure, and Soga Monogatari* and made over 2,000 digital images including 173 color illustrations available online through the Library's OPAC. Nara Ehon is a type of colorfully illustrated manuscript books or hand-printed books of stories and tales produced in the Muromachi period (1333 – 1573) through the mid-Edo period (1615 – 1868). It is considered to be the earliest popular picture books in Japan. Another Japanese rare book, *The Tale of Genji*, a sixty-volume set is in the process of being digitized. This set is a rare and complete set of the 1654 edition.

Japanese Ukiyo-e collection in the Prints and Photographs Division also benefited from collaboration with Nichubunken. Under the agreement signed by the Library and Nichubunken in February 2005, a team of Japanese Art historians visited the Library for three weeks and completed their work in identifying and describing some 3,000 prints. The Library has finished the scanning of the Ukiyo-e prints collection with financial support from Nichibunken and will make the collection available through the Library of Congress and Nichubunken websites in 2006.

In cooperation with the Japan Map Center of the Geographical Survey Institute in Japan, the Geography and Map Division digitized the only surviving set of 207 large-scale Japanese maps (made in 1816 – 1819) by the famous map maker, Inoh Tadataka, and made it available in June 2005 through the Library's webpage: http://www.loc.gov/rr/geogmap/.

Capture of relevant web sites

As a part of the Library's effort to provide more and more specialized digital resources online, such as the *American Memory* (http://memory.loc.gov/), the Global Gateway (http://internationaLloc.gov/intldl/intldlhome.html), etc., the Library's portals now serve as a gateway to selected web resources on a variety of subjects and world areas (http://www.loc.gov/rr/international/portals.html). The portals of the Asian Division (http://www.loc.gov/rr/asian/area_AD.html) are increasingly a useful source on all the Asian countries and regions.

Online reference services

Being a leader in the development of QuestionPoint-a worldwide online reference service operating on a 24-hours-a-day and 7-days-a-week schedule-operated by the OCLC Online Computer Library Center, library' users anywhere can now send their reference questions through OCLC online global network to the Library of Congress for reply by our reference librarians and area studies specialists (http://www.oclc.org/questionpoint). Library users may also use the service of Asking a Librarians (http://www.loc.gov/rr/askalib-asian.html) to get reference assistance from librarians in the Asian Division.

The World Digital Library-the latest digital initiative of the Library

In November 2005, the Librarian of Congress, Dr. James H. Billington, launched a new project to create a World Digital Library (WDL) for the purpose of bringing people all over the world closer together "by celebrating the depth and uniqueness of different cultures in a single global understanding". The concept for the WDL came from a speech that Billington delivered to the newly established U.S. National Commission for UNESCO on June 6, 2005, at Georgetown University in Washington, DC.[①] In his speech, Billington proposed the public research institutions and libraries work with private funders to begin digitizing significant primary materials of different cultures from institutions across the globe. Billington said that the World Digital Library would bring together online "rare and unique cultural materials held in U.S. and Western repositories with those of other great cultures such as those that lie beyond Europe and involve more than 1 billion people: Chinese East Asia, Indian South Asia and the worlds of Islam stretching from Indonesia through Central and West Asia to Africa."

On November 22, 2005, Google Inc. was the first private-sector company that responded with an initial funding of $3 million. Google Co-Founder and President of Technology said, "Google supports the World Digital Library because we share a common mission of making the world's information universally accessible and useful."

To lay the groundwork for the WDL, the Library will develop a plan for identifying technology issues related to digitization and organization of WDL collections, including presentation, maintenance, standards and metadata, and the selection of primary materials representing all of the world's cultures.

The Library of Congress has extensive pioneering experience building digital libraries. Two of the most important examples are:

American Memory

In 1994 the National Digital Library Program was instituted at the Library to offer American historical treasures online; today more than 10 million rare and unique materials from the Library and those of its partners are available free of charge in the American Memory Web site (http://www.loc.gov/memory). The content of WDL, like that of American Memory, will be primarily one-of-a-kind materials, including manuscript and multimedia materials of the particular culture.

Global Gateway

In 2000, the Library launched its Global Gateway Web site (http://international.loc.gov/intldl/find/digital collaborations.html) to present international collections of the Library and materials from major libraries of the world. Current contributors to the site are repositories from Russia, Spain, Brazil, the Netherlands, and France. The bilingual, multimedia presentations in Global Gateway concentrate on the historical intersections and parallels between the United States and the site are contributing nations. The new WDL will focus the other nations' own culture and history and will broaden the geographic scope by including non-Western nations and cultures. To further clarify this point, Dr. Deanna Marcum, Associate Librarian of Congress for Library Services, stated in her internal communication "It is important that WDL be viewed as a world-wide effort, not a project of the Library of Congress, so we have asked IFLA to support and participate in the effort."

---

① The full text of the speech is available at http://www.loc.gov/about/welcome/speeches.

The current large-scale digitization project undertaken by the Asian Division in collaboration with the National Central Library in Taiwan to digitize the Chinese rare book collection will be among the first group of projects which will make up the World Digital Library.

(Published in the Proceedings on *the Symposium on Building Collection in the Digital Age*. Taichung, Taiwan: Chung Hsing University, January 2006: pp. 11-29.)

美国国会图书馆数字时代的亚洲馆藏

Asian Collections in the Digital Age at the Library of Congress[①]

1. The Universality of the Collection

The Library of Congress was established by an act of American Congress in 1800. After the initial collection was destroyed by the invading British troops in 1814, the Congress acquired the personal collection of 6,487 books from the retired President Thomas Jefferson a year later. In offering his collection to Congress, Jefferson provided justifications about the scope of his collection, which included books in foreign languages and volumes of philosophy, science, literature and other topics not normally viewed as part of a legislative library, "I do not know that it contains any branch of science which Congress would wish to exclude from their collection; there is, in fact, no subject to which a member of Congress may not have occasion to refer."[②] It was this concept of universality and belief that all subjects are important to the library of the American legislature that led the Library of Congress to develop its comprehensive collecting policies and adhere to this basic guiding principle.

From the core of Jefferson's library in 1815, the size of today's collection has grown to 132 million items of which 30 million are printed collections. Others are in a variety of formats including manuscripts, maps, motion pictures, photographs, prints, sheet music, sound recordings, videos, etc. About 35 million of all these are included in the Library's online catalog. In the year of 2005 alone, a total of 2,088,905 new items were added, making it the largest and fastest growing library collection in the world.[③] It is important to note that more than one half of the entire collection is in languages other than English.

Below is the mission statement of the Library:

The Library's mission is to make its resources available and useful to the Congress and the American people and to sustain and preserve a universal collection of knowledge and creativity for future generations[④]

2. Serving as the National Library

Although the Library of Congress is the library of the American Congress, it has also been serving as the national library of the United States of America. For the discharge of its mission as the library of the Congress, there is a unit called Congressional Research Service. The chief responsibility of this unit is to provide the Congress with research and analysis on the full range of legislative policy issues. For carrying out the functions of the national library, there is a major unit called Library Services, headed by an Associate Librarian. The position is now held by Dr. Deanna Marcum. Other major units of the Library of Congress are the Law Library, which holds the world's largest legal publications covering U. S., foreign, and international law, and the U. S. Copyright Office, which annually transfers to the Library about 1 million copies in various formats, including 562,588 items that were received from publishers in 2005 under the mandatory deposit provisions

---

① Keynote speech for 20th anniversary of Shenzhen Library, December 15, 2006, Shenzhen, Guangdong, China.
② The Thomas Jefferson Building of the Library of Congress. Washington, DC: Library of Congress, 2003: pp. 1 – 2.
③ The Annual Report of the Librarian of Congress for the Fiscal Year Ending September 30, 2005. Washington, DC: Library of Congress, 2006: pp. 222 – 227.
④ The Library of Congress Strategic Plan: Fiscal Years 2004 – 2008. Washington, DC: Library of Congress, 2003: p. 13.

of the copyright law.① About half of them were selected and added to the Library's collection.

3. The Beginning of the Asian Collection

The first acquisition of an Asian collection from Asia by the Library of Congress can be traced back to 1865 when the Smithsonian Institution transferred a collection of books on Southeast Asia and the Pacific islands that had been gathered in Singapore by the Wilkes Exploring Expedition from 1838 to 1842. Four years later, in 1869, the Emperor of China (Tongzhi 同治皇帝) presented to the Library of Congress 10 major Chinese works in 933 volumes. This was soon followed by the exchange of government publications with the Japanese government initiated in 1875.② From these early beginnings, the collection of Asian publications from all parts of Asia and in all major and some minor Asian languages has grown to nearly 2.8 million monographic volumes and 15,000 active serial titles. In addition to the holdings in the Asian Division, important Asian collections of legal materials, maps, music, motion pictures, prints, and photographs are housed and cared for by other divisions in the Library of Congress in collaboration with the Asian Division. These other units include the Law Library, the Geography and Map Division, the Prints and Photographs Division, the Motion Picture, Broadcasting and Recorded Sound Division, the Performing Arts Division, the Manuscript Division, etc. Other Asia-related publications not in Asian languages are also housed in the Main Reading Room, Microform Reading Room, Newspaper and Current Periodical Reading Room, Performing Arts Reading Room, Science Reading Room, and in some of the other area studies and special collections.

The name of Asian Division has gone through several changes since 1928 when the Division of Chinese Literature was established for the first time through the effort of Herbert Putnam, Librarian of Congress (1899 – 1939). Three years later, in 1931, the name was changed to the Division of Chinese and Japanese Literature. In 1932, it was renamed the Division of Orientalia with a much expanded geographic and language coverage. This was changed again to the Asiatic Division in 1942 and changed back to Orientalia Division in 1944. Finally, the name of Asian Division was formally adopted in 1978.③

4. The Organization of the Asian Division

The Asian Division is one of the four area studies divisions (African and Middle Eastern Division, Asian Division, European Division, and Hispanic Division) reporting to the Director for Collections and Services.

Within the Asian Division, under the general leadership and management of the Chief, there are two section heads: the Head of Collection Services and the Head of Scholarly Services. The professional staff members of the division, who are either area specialists or reference librarians, are divided into five area teams: China and Mongolia, Japan, Korea, Southeast Asia, and South Asia. A coordinator of each area team is appointed from the team members by the Chief. The Chief is also assisted by an Administrative Officer, an Information Technology Specialist, and a special assistant.

In the 2003 – 2008 Strategic Plan of the Division the following vision and mission statements were adopted:

Vision of the Asian Division

To establish the collections of the Asian Division as the premier research and scholarly resource of all formats and times on Asia and in Asian languages that is compatible with the dynamics of knowledge and creativity of the 21st Century-frequently referred to as the "Asian

---

① The Annual Report of the Librarian of Congress for the Fiscal Year Ending September 30, 2005. Washington, DC: Library of Congress, 2006: p. 18 – 19.
② The Asian Division. Washington. DC: The Library of Congress, 2002: pp. 1, 2, 4, 8.
③ Chi Wang. The Chinese Collection in the Library of Congress: A Brief Introduction. Washington, DC: Chinese Section, Asian Division, Library of Congress, 2001: pp. 5 – 6.

Century."

Mission of the Asian Division

The mission of the Asian Division is to make comprehensive collection resources and information services related to Asia available and useful to the Congress, American people, and the scholarly research community nationally and internationally. ①

5. Building a Comprehensive Asian Collection

Recognizing the importance of Asia in the 21st century the Library of Congress has devoted great efforts to building a comprehensive collection on Asia. Today, after 140 years of painstaking work by generations of Asian area specialists, librarians, and scholars, a vast storehouse of knowledge and culture about the diverse nations, histories, languages, and peoples has been assembled. It is perhaps the best of such collections outside Asia. With the foresight of Dr. James Billington, the current Librarian of the Congress, an exquisite Asian Reading Room has been provided as a gateway to this world-class collection. Below are brief descriptions of the five key collections:

The Chinese and Mongolian Collection

The Chinese and Mongolian Collection, as of September 30, 2006, consists of 1,000,289 monographic volumes, 4,789 active serial titles, and 10,961 inactive serial titles. Besides works in the Chinese language, it also includes several thousand volumes in Manchu, Mongol, Naxi (Moso), Tibetan, Uyghur, and other minority languages. The collection covers all subjects and is especially strong in the humanities and social sciences, among them, classical Chinese literature, archival materials of the Qing dynasty (1644 – 1911) and Republican period (1911 – 1949), traditional Chinese medicine, local and regional histories (gazetteers), and contemporary publications of Mainland China and Taiwan.

The collection also contains some of the most valuable rare books from China, Mongolia, and Tibet. The rare books from China cover Song dynasty (960 – 1279), Jin dynasty (1115 – 1234), Yuan dynasty (1271 – 1368), Ming dynasty (1368 – 1644), and Qing dynasty (1644 – 1911). It includes a Buddhist invocation sutra (《一切如来》, Yi qie ru lai) printed in 975 A.D. that was recovered from the hollow bricks of the foundation of the Thunder Peak Pagoda (雷峰塔, Lei feng ta) when it collapsed in 1924, 41 of the 400 surviving volumes of the 1560 copy of the Great Encyclopedia of the Ming Emperor Yongle (《永乐大典》, Yongle da dian), and the 1895 – 1998 printing of the Imperial Encyclopedia of China (《古今图书集成》, Gu jin tu shu ji cheng) in 5,044 volumes.

Examples of other unique collections are the 3,344 pictographic manuscripts from the Naxi (纳西) minority group in Yunnan province, the Gamble collection of a 19th century American missionary printer that includes Christian publications in Chinese and translations of Western works, and the Arthur W. Hummel collection of rare Chinese maps. ②

The Library of Congress is one of the world's leading centers for Tibetan publications with holdings that are representative of the entire body of Tibetan literature from the 8th century to the modern day. These include religious texts, history, biography, traditional medicine, astrology, iconography, musical notations, grammars, social sciences, and secular literature.

Since religion plays a major role in Tibetan society, the holdings of Tibetan Buddhist scriptures in the Asian Division are especially strong. The Tibetan Buddhist canon is contained in the Kanjur, in over a hundred volumes of sutras, and the Tanjur, most editions totaling some 225 volumes of commentaries. The Tibetan canonical texts are accurate translations of the original Buddhist texts, written in Sanskrit between 500 BC and 900 AD. Among the individuals who were responsible for the early periods of development of the Tibetan collection are William Woodville

---

① The Strategic Plan of the Asian Division, 2003 to 2008. Washington, DC: Asian Division, the Library of Congress, 2003.

② The Chinese Collection. Washington, DC: Asian Division, the Library of Congress, n. d.

Rockhill, the American diplomat and Tibetologist who traveled in Mongolia and Tibet between 1888 and 1892 and again in the 1900s; Berthold Laufer, another leading Tibetologist in the late 1800s; and Joseph Rock, the colorful explorer, adventurer, and scientist who lived and traveled in China's rugged west for 27 years in the early 1900s.①

The Mongolian collection also includes 80 books in traditional script and format acquired in the early 20th century and complete reprint editions of the Mongolian Kanjur and Tanjur, the Buddhist canonical texts and their commentaries. In recent years, the Library's New Delhi Field Office has been actively acquiring current publications from Mongolia.

The Japanese Collection

After the initial arrangement for the exchange of government publications established in 1875 between the two governments, the Japanese collection began to grow in 1905 when a significant gift was received from Crosby Stuart Noyes, journalist and editor of the Washington Evening Star. The Noyes collection included 658 illustrated books produced from the mid-18th century to the late-19th century. In 1907, a systematic effort was undertaken by Kan'ichi Asakawa of Yale University to purchase Japanese books for the Library of Congress. Because of his effort, some 9,072 volumes on the subjects of Japanese history, literature, Buddhism, Shinto, geography, music, and the arts were added. In 1930, the Library appointed Dr. Shiho Sakanishi as the Chief Assistant of the Japanese Section to further develop the collection. During her tenure from 1930 to 1941, the collection tripled in size. Today, the Japanese collection has grown to 1,155,668 volumes of monographs, 5,614 active serial titles, and 9,451 inactive serial titles—the largest collection in the Asian Division—through purchase, gift, exchange, and other avenues of acquisition.

Among the wealth of rare items are approximately 5,000 titles of publications and manuscript copies of works produced before the end of the Tokugawa Shogunate in 1868 and the beginning of the Meiji period (1868 – 1912). Included are the dharani (百万搭陀罗尼) prayer charms, which date to 770 A.D. and are among the world's earliest surviving printed material. Also noteworthy are a complete edition of the Japanese literary masterpiece Genji monogatari (《源氏物语》, The Tale of Genji) published in Kyoto in 1654 and the Yoshitsune azuma kudari monogatari printed on movable type between 1624 and 1643. A complete catalogue of the rare books in the Library of Congress was published in 2003 by Yagi Shoten in Tokyo.②

At the end of World War II, a large number of historical documents such as the ones from the former Japanese Imperial Army and Navy, the South Manchuria Railway Company, and the East Asian Research Institute were given to the Library by the Washington Document Center. Much of the materials from the latter two are pre-World War II studies on such areas as Korea, Taiwan, Mainland China, Mongolia, and the Pacific Islands. The Library also has a microfilm copy of the archives of the Japanese Foreign Ministry from 1868 to 1945 and pre-1945 records of the Police Bureau of the Ministry of Home Affairs-some of these are censored wartime publications.③

Another important collection is the "Inoh Maps" — the first modern maps of Japan created originally by Tadataka Inoh between 1800 and 1821. Copies of 207 of Inoh's original 214 sheets large-scale set (1:36,000) that cover the Japanese archipelago from Hokkaido to Kyushu were discovered in the map collection of the Library of Congress in the spring of 2001 and have caused great excitement in Japan. In order to make these maps available for exhibition and for online access, all of them have been digitized and sent to the Japan Map Center. A selection of the actual-size reproductions of these maps was on exhibition at the Tokyo National Museum from October 31 to December 14, 2003. Some of the original maps were also loaned and exhibited in

---

① The Tibetan Collection. Washington, DC: Asian Division, Library of Congress, April 2002.
② Beikoku Gikai Toshokan zo Nihon Kotenseki Mokuroku (Catalog of Japanese Rare Books in the Library of Congress). Tokyo: Yagi Shoten, 2003.
③ The Japanese Collection. Washington, DC: Asian Division, the Library of Congress, n. d.

Kobe, Sendai, Atami, and Nagoya in 2004.

The Korean Collection

The Korean collection began in the 1920s with the generous gift of Korean books from Dr. James S. Gale, a Canadian missionary who spent 40 years in Korea from 1888 to 1928. Dr. Gale also helped the Library to acquire a number of Korean classics, including rare books from the estate of the Korean scholar Kim To-hui. Systematic development of the Korean collection was started in the early 1950s during the period of the Korean War. Today, the Korean collection in the Library totals 253,829 volumes in the Korean language, as well as 20,000 Japanese language books and 8,000 English language books on Korea. Coverage of North Korea is also strong, with some 10,000 items. There are also 1,389 active serial titles and 5,598 inactive serial titles.

Included in the Korean collection are 480 titles of Korean rare books, in 3,000 volumes. They were all written in Chinese characters and printed on mulberry paper. Although China was the first country to use movable type made of clay, Korea was the first one to use movable metal type for printing. Several good examples of this type of printing are in the collection. The most important one is the Collective Works of Yi Munsun (in 8 volumes) printed with metal movable type about 1241. Others include the collected writings of the renowned 16th-century Confucian scholar and statesman Yi I printed in 1744 and the 1834 reprint of the works of the "father of Korean literature", Ch'oe Ch'i-won (857 – 915). Other rare books printed by woodblock include the History of the Koryo Dynasty (《高丽史》), printed in 1590, and the Law Code of the Yi Dynasty (《经国大典》), printed in 1630. ①

The Southeast Asian Collection

As was mentioned earlier, the earliest acquisition of the Southeast Asian collection in the Library of Congress began in 1865, which predates the beginning of all other Asian collections. The collection was acquired in Singapore in 1842 by the U. S. Naval Exploring Expedition led by Lt. Charles Wilkes. Wilkes and the Expedition's philologist, Horatio Hale, collected Malay manuscripts and early printed books with the assistance of Alfred North, an American missionary in Singapore. The collection went first to the Smithsonian Institution which later transferred the collection to the Library of Congress in 1865. Included in this earliest acquisition are a unique collection of manuscripts written in the Buginese script of South Sulawesi; an account of the 19th-century Malay world written in Jawi, the Hikayat Abdullah (The Story of Abdullah); and an 1840 Mission Press edition of the Sejarah Melayu (Malay Annals), an important Malay history written in 1612, also in Jawi, the Malay language in Arabic script.

The Southeast Asian collection contains many palm leaf manuscript copies of the Tipitaka, the basic text of Theravada Buddhism which is the majority religion of Cambodia, Laos, Myanmar (Burma), and Thailand. In 1905, a special Thai Tipitaka was presented to the Library of Congress by King Chulalongkorn (Rama V) of Thailand. In 1949, an especially fine collection of Burmese manuscripts in the Pali language as well as a Tipitaka in Pali using Burmese script was presented to the Library of Congress as a part of a large Burmese donation. The donation also included an important Burmese history, The Glass palace Chronicle, written by a group of scholars in 1829.

The Asian Division also holds rare materials from the Philippines and Vietnam. Of special note is a set of inscribed bamboo tubes, with lettering in the old Indic script similar to the ancient scripts used in neighboring Indonesia. The collection of 55 bamboos in prose and 22 in verse provides a fascinating glimpse into Mangyan (Hampangan) and Tagbanua society. Several examples of Vietnamese dynastic histories are also represented, including texts printed from early woodblocks at the former imperial palace at Hue.

In 1938, the Library of Congress launched the Indic Project in order to improve its collections from Southeast and South Asia, particularly publications in local languages. Following World War II, as U. S. interest in the region increased, the collection grew dramatically and today consists of

---

① The Korean Collection. Washington, DC: Asian Division, the Library of Congress, n. d.

holdings from Brunei, Cambodia, Indonesia, Laos, Malaysia, Myanmar, the Philippines, Singapore, Thailand, Vietnam, and many of the South Pacific island nations such as Papua New Guinea, etc. The establishment of the Library's overseas offices in New Delhi, India, in 1962, in Jakarta, Indonesia, in 1963, and in Islamabad, Pakistan, in 1965 has provided a continuous flow of books, newspapers, and periodicals from the region in a variety of formats. ①Today, the total collection for Southeast Asia in major Southeast Asian languages includes 179,357 monographic volumes 2,736 active serial titles, and 8,462 inactive serial titles.

The South Asian Collection

The foundation for the South Asian collection was laid in 1904 when a collection of over 4,000 books and pamphlets from the German Indologist, Dr. Albrecht Weber, was purchased. Included were texts in Sanskrit of India's sacred Hindu works-the Vedas, Brahmanas, and Upanisads-as well as the stories of the Puranas and the great epics in the Mahabharata and the Ramayana. In addition, there are a number of Weber's notebooks with his handwritten transcriptions of rare Indian texts for his pioneering critical editions.

In 1938, the Library received a grant from the Carnegie Corporation to develop the South Asian collection systematically, and it initiated the Indic Project— "Project F-Development of Indic Studies". During the 1950s the collection continued to expand and growth accelerated even further with the opening of the Library's New Delhi Overseas Office in 1962. Under the Public Law (PL) 480 program, the New Delhi office used rupees from Indian purchases of U. S. agricultural products to buy books and other materials from India and other countries of South Asia. An overseas office in Karachi, Pakistan, was opened in 1965 to oversee the acquisition of publications from Pakistan and neighboring areas. Later, the office was moved to the capital city, Islamabad.

Today, the South Asian collection holds materials in over 100 modern languages used in India, Pakistan, Bangladesh, Sri Lanka, and Nepal. The majority of the publications are in Hindi (20 percent), Bengali (15 percent), Urdu (13 percent), and Tamil (11 percent). Other languages represented in large numbers include Marathi, Telugu, Malayalam, Gujarati, and Kannada. As of September 30, 2006, the collection consists of 233,829 monographic volumes 1,616 active serial titles, and 2,120 inactive serial titles.

An example among the many rare books and manuscripts in the South Asian collection is a 1452 manuscript of the Jaina Kalpasutra from Gujarat in western India. This illustrated text tells the story of Mahavira, the founder of the Jaina religion. The "Crosby Khotan fragments" are also among the more unusual rare items. During a 1903 journey to Central Asia, Oscar Terry Crosby, an American who later became Assistant Secretary of the Treasury, purchased these manuscripts in Sanskrit at the Taklamakan oasis town of Khotan. ②

Between 1990 and 2000, a very important project undertaken by the New Delhi Overseas Office was the Microfilming of Indian Publications Project (MIPP). This project was a joint collaboration between the Government of India and the Library of Congress, aimed at preserving and making accessible out-of-print works listed in the National Bibliography of Indian Literature: 1901 – 1953. Some 22,686 titles in 15 languages were microfilmed from 67 repository libraries in India and 3 libraries outside India (the Library of Congress, University of Chicago, and British Library). These titles were selected by Indian scholars as being central to the understanding of India. ③

6. Overseas Acquisition Offices

The accelerated growth of the library collections from South and Southeast Asia since the 1960s should be credited to the efforts of the overseas acquisition offices in New Delhi, Jakarta,

---

① The Southeast Asian Collection. Washington, DC: Asian Division, Library of Congress, April 2002.
② The South Asian Collection. Washington, DC: Asian Division, Library of Congress, April 2002.
③ The Library of Congress in South Asia, 1960 – 2002. Celebrating 40 Years of Bibliographic and Cultural Exchanges. New Delhi: Library of Congress Of ce, n. d. p. 16.

and Islamabad. In addition to these three, the African/Asian Acquisitions and Overseas Operations Division of the Library of Congress also operate overseas offices in Cairo, Nairobi, and Rio de Janeiro.

One of the unique features of the three Asian overseas offices is the offering of their service to other libraries which want to acquire publications from countries and regions covered by these offices. For example, the 44 academic and research libraries, mostly from North America, that participated in the South Asia Cooperative Acquisitions Program (SACAP) receive publications of their choice from the New Delhi office and its many sub-offices. Being the largest and the oldest of the six overseas offices, the New Delhi office covers India, Bangladesh, Bhutan, the Maldives, Nepal, and Sri Lanka—as well as Burma and Mongolia. The New Delhi office performs a wide range of services to SACAP libraries, including acquisitions, cataloging, bibliographic control, and preservation of publications acquired in some 65 languages and 25 different scripts. Another service of the New Delhi office is the maintenance of an extensive program for official and informal exchanges of publications with key institutions and libraries in South Asia. ①

7. Building the Asian Collection in the Digital Age

Throughout the 20th century the building of Asian collections was focused mainly on printed materials. However, the trend has begun to change in the past five years with attention gradually shifting to electronic and web resources. Large-scale digitization of rare materials is also being launched to make some of the treasured collections, which have no copyright restriction, freely accessible to researchers via the Internet. The approaches taken thus far also include the subscription to select electronic bibliographic databases; the acquisition of digitized full-text databases of e-books, e-journals, e-newspapers, and others; the digitization of selected rare books and other collections; and the capture of relevant web sites for the Library's Asian portals which are constructed and maintained by the Asian Division.

Subscription to selected electronic bibliographic databases

At present forty-five of the Library's 219 subscription databases deal with Asia or Asian studies. These databases, such as Aardvark (Asian resources for librarians), Asian Development Bank Economics & Statistics (of Economics and Research Department of Asian Development Bank), Asian Law Bibliographic Database (from the University of Melbourne), Bibliography of Asian Studies (from Association for Asian Studies), Country Studies (produced by Federal Research Division, the Library of Congress), and Treaties and International Agreements (by Oceana Publications), are all accessible in the Library's reading rooms.

Acquisition of digitized full-text databases

Since 2003, special efforts have also been made to acquire a number of most important digitized full-text databases from Mainland China, Japan, Korea, and Taiwan.

In the Mainland China and Taiwan areas we have acquired Ren min ri bao dian zi ban (人民日报电子版 The People's Daily Electronic Version), 1946 – 2004; China Data Online; China Journals Full-text Database (中国期刊全文数据库 – 7240 titles) and Chinese Core Newspapers Databases (中国重要报纸数据库 – 1,000 titles) of the China National Knowledge Infrastructure (CNKI 中国国家知识基础架构); the Wanfang Chinese Conference Proceedings Database (万方中国学术会议全文数据库 400,000 papers); the Wanfang Chinese Theses and Dissertations Databases (万方中国学位论文数据库 450,000 titles); and the 100,000-title monograph database from Superstar Digital Library (超星电子图书馆). We have also acquired Si ku quan shu (Wen yuan ge Edition 四库全书文渊阁版)—a professional standalone version, the Academia Sinica's Geographic Information Systems (GIS) of Chinese Civilization in Time and Space (CCTS 中国文明之时空基础架构) and Taiwan History and Culture in Time and Space (THCTS 台湾历史文化地图系统), and the Encyclopedia of Taiwan (台湾百科全书).

---

① The Library of Congress in South Asia, 1960 – 2002. Celebrating 40 Years of Bibliographic and Cultural Exchanges. New Delhi: Library of Congress Of ce, n. d.

For the Japanese collection the Library has acquired two important subscription databases: Directory of Japanese Scientific Periodicals (from National Diet Library, covering 13,875 serial titles on science and technology published in Japan) and Kodansha Encyclopedia of Japan (based on the 1993 publication entitled Japan: an Illustrated Encyclopedia, with 11,000 entries). Several Japanese rare books have also been digitized and are available from the Library's OPAC. In addition, the Library currently subscribes full-text databases of five major Japanese newspapers including Mainichi, Sankei, Chunichi, Tokyo and Yomiuri Newspapers through a U.S. based commercial aggregator/vendor, www.factive.com.

In the Korea area the recent acquisitions were Chosun Daily Newspaper Archive (covering articles from the Chosun llbo, the most widely read newspaper in South Korea), Korean Studies Database (by KRPIA, covering history, literature, and traditional medicines), Korean Studies Information Service System (KISS, a database of full-text articles from 6,000 journals published by 1,200 Korean academic institutions), and Law n B-Korean Law Database (Law and business, available for access in the Law Library reading room).

Digitization of selected rare books and other collections

In recent years, Asian Division has undertaken several major collaborative projects to digitize its unparalleled Asian collections. With a three-year grant from the Chiang Ching-kuo Foundation (1998 – 2001) the Chinese and Mongolian Section was able to hire an expert to review and prepare a detailed description for the 3,344 Naxi manuscripts in the collection and subsequently digitized a portion of this unique collection. This digitized collection is now accessible from LC's website:
http://international.loc.gov/intldl/naxihtml/naxihome.html

On October 1, 2004, the Library and the Academia Sinica (Taipei) signed an agreement for the digitization of China-related maps. Through three working visits of the subject and digital experts from the Academia Sinica between 2004 and 2006, digital images of 21,000 maps and 840 aerial photos were made and transported to Taiwan for post-digitization processing. This digital file will be available online from the website of the Geography and Map Division of the Library of Congress as well as incorporated into the Chinese Civilizations in Time and Space (CCTS) database and supported by a historical geographic information system with spatial-temporal applications.

In May 2005, the Library and the National Central Library (Taipei) signed an agreement for the digitization of Chinese rare books. A team of technical specialists from Taiwan is now working onsite at the Library of Congress for three years to digitize selected titles in the Chinese rare book collection, which have been reviewed by Chinese rare book experts for the authentication and annotation of the Chinese rare books, and by the Library's Conservation Division. The two experts are funded by Chiang Ching-kuo Foundation for 2005 and 2006. The goal of this collaborative project is for the two libraries to share each other's digitized databases of Chinese rare books and make them easily and freely accessible to researchers worldwide.

In close collaboration with the International Research Center of Japanese Studies (Nichubunken), the Asian Division digitized the Nara Ehon collection, four titles of Shizuka, Homyo Doji, Shigure, and Soga Monogatari and made over 2,000 digital images including 173 color illustrations available online through the Library's OPAC. Nara Ehon is a type of colorfully illustrated manuscript book or hand-printed book of stories and tales produced in the Muromachi period (1333 – 1573) through the mid-Edo period (1615 – 1868). It is considered to be the earliest popular picture book in Japan. Another Japanese rare book, The Tale of Genji, a sixty-volume set is in the process of being digitized. This set is a rare and complete set of the 1654 edition.

Japanese Ukiyo-e collection in the Prints and Photographs Division also benefited from collaboration with Nichubunken. Under the agreement signed by the Library and Nichubunken in February 2005, a team of Japanese Art historians visited the Library for three weeks and completed their work in identifying and describing some 3,000 prints. The Library has finished the scanning of the Ukiyo-e prints collection with financial support from Nichibunken and will make the collection available through the Library of Congress and Nichibunken websites in 2006.

In cooperation with the Japan Map Center of the Geographical Survey Institute in Japan, the Geography and Map Division digitized the only surviving set of 207 large-scale Japanese maps (made in 1816 – 1819) by the famous map maker, Inoh Tadataka, and made it available in June 2005 through the Library's webpage: http://www.loc.gov/rr/geogmap/.

Capture of relevant web sites

As a part of the Library's effort to provide more and more specialized digital resources online, such as the American Memory (http://memory.loc.gov/), the Global Gateway (http://international.loc.gov/intldl/intldlhome.html), etc., the Library's portals now serve as a gateway to selected web resources on a variety of subjects and world areas (http://www.loc.gov/rr/international/portals.html). The portals of the Asian Division (http://www.loc.gov/rr/asian/area AD.html) are increasingly a useful source on all the Asian countries and regions.

Planning is also underway to begin web harvesting and archiving on special topics or events of importance such as the tsunami disaster, etc.

Online reference services

Being a leader in the development of QuestionPoint—a worldwide online reference service operating on a 24-hours-a-day and 7-days-a-week schedule—operated by the OCLC Online Computer Library Center, library users anywhere can now send their reference questions through OCLC online global network to the Library of Congress for reply by our reference librarians and area studies specialists (http://www.oclc.org/questionpoint). Library users may also use the service of Ask a Librarian (http://www.loc.gov/rr/askalib-asian.html) to get reference assistance from librarians in the Asian Division.

8. Research Fellowships Established

In order to encourage the use of the Library's collections for serious research, the Library has established a number of research fellowships. Many of these research fellowships are administered by the John W. Kluge Center of the Library. Detailed information about the various Kluge Center fellowships, such as the applicant eligibility, tenure and stipend, and applications, can be found from the website: http://www.loc.gov/loc/kluge/kluge-fenowships.html

Beginning in 2006, through the generosity of Ms. Florence Tan Moesen, the Asian Division has begun offering up to 10 Florence Tan Moesen Fellowships each year to researchers who will use the Asian collections for her/his research. Detailed information about the Florence Tan Moeson fellowship are provided on the website: http://www.loc.gov/rr/asian/2007FYM.html

(Published in *Shenzhen Library Newsletter* (《深图通讯》). No. 14, January 2007: pp. 3 – 11.)

美国国会图书馆的亚洲馆藏：历史概览

Asian Collections in the Library of Congress: A Historical Overview[①]

The Universality of the Collection

The Library of Congress was established by an act of the American Congress in 1800. After the initial collection was destroyed by invading British troops in 1814, the Congress acquired the personal collection of 6,487 books from the retired President Thomas Jefferson a year later. In offering his collection to Congress, Jefferson provided justifications about the scope of his collection, which included books in foreign languages and volumes of philosophy science, literature and other topics not normally viewed as part of a legislative library, "I do not know that it contains any branch of science which Congress would wish to exclude from their collection; there is, in fact, no subject to which a member of Congress may not have occasion to refer."[②] It was this concept of universality and belief that all subjects are important to the library of the American legislature that led the Library of Congress to develop its comprehensive collecting policies and adhere to this basic guiding principle over its entire history.

From the core of Jefferson's library in 1815, the size of today's collection has grown to 132 million items of which 30 million are printed collections. Other items are in a variety of formats including manuscripts, maps, motion pictures, photographs, prints, sheet music, sound recordings, videos, etc. About 35 million of these are included in the Library's online catalog. In the year of 2005 alone, a total of 2,088,905 new items were added, making it the largest and fastest growing library collection in the world.[③] It is important to note that more than one half of the entire collection is in languages other than English.

Below is the mission statement of the Library:

The Library's mission is to make its resources available and useful to the Congress and the American people and to sustain and preserve a universal collection of knowledge and creativity for future generations[④]

Serving as the National Library

Although the Library of Congress is the library of the American Congress, it has also been serving as the national library of the United States of America. For the discharge of its mission as the library of the Congress, there is a unit called Congressional Research Service. The chief responsibility of this unit is to provide the Congress with research and analysis on the full range of legislative policy issues. For carrying out the functions of the national library, there is a major unit called Library Services, headed by an Associate Librarian. The position is now held by Dr. Deanna Marcum. Other major units of the Library of Congress are the Law Library which holds the world's largest legal publications covering U. S., foreign, and international laws, and the U. S. Copyright Office which annually transfers to the Library about 1 million copies of publications in various formats, including more than 500,000 items that are received annually from publishers under the

---

[①] Presented at the Conference on *Over a Hundred Years of Collecting: The History of East Asian Collections in North America*, held at the University of California, Berkeley, October 18 – 19, 2007.

[②] *The Thomas Jefferson Building of the Library of Congress*. Washington, DC: Library of Congress, 2003: pp. 1 – 2.

[③] *The Annual Report of the Librarian of Congress for the Fiscal Year Ending September 30, 2005*. Washington, DC: Library of Congress, 2006: pp. 222 – 227.

[④] *The Library of Congress Strategic Plan: Fiscal Years 2004 – 2008*. Washington, DC: Library of Congress, 2003: p. 13

mandatory deposit provisions of the copyright law. ① About half of them were selected and added to the Library's collection.

The Beginning of the Asian Collection

The first major acquisition of an Asian collection from Asia by the Library of Congress can be traced back to 1865 when the Smithsonian Institution transferred a collection of books on Southeast Asia and the Pacific islands that had been gathered in Singapore by the Wilkes Exploring Expedition from 1838 to 1842. Four years later, in 1869, the Emperor of China (Tongzhi 同治皇帝) presented to the Library of Congress 10 major Chinese works in 933 volumes. This was soon followed by the exchange of government publications with the Japanese government initiated in 1875. ② From these early beginnings, the collection of Asian publications from all parts of Asia and in all major and some minor Asian languages has grown to nearly 2.8 million monographic volumes and 15,000 active serial titles. In addition to the holdings in the Asian Division, important Asian collections of legal materials, maps, music, motion pictures, prints, and photographs are housed and cared for by other divisions in the Library of Congress in collaboration with the Asian Division. These other units include the Law Library, the Geography and Map Division, the Prints and Photographs Division, the Motion Picture, Broadcasting and Recorded Sound Division, the Performing Arts Division, the Manuscript Division, American Folk life Center, etc. Other Asia-related publications not in Asian languages are housed in the Main Reading Room, Microform Reading Room, Newspaper and Current Periodical Reading Room, Performing Arts Reading Room, Science Reading Room, and in some of the other area studies and special collections.

The name of Asian Division has gone through several changes since 1928 when the Division of Chinese Literature was established for the first time through the efforts of Herbert Putnam, Librarian of Congress (1899 – 1939). Three years later, in 1931, the name was changed to the Division of Chinese and Japanese Literature. In 1932 it was renamed the Division of Orientalia with a much expanded geographic and language coverage. This was changed again to the Asiatic Division in 1942 and changed back to Orientalia Division in 1944. Finally, the name of Asian Division was formally adopted in 1978. ③

The Organization of the Asian Division

The Asian Division is one of the four area studies divisions (African and Middle Eastern Division, Asian Division, European Division, and Hispanic Division) reporting to the Director for Collections and Services.

Within the Asian Division, under the general leadership and management of the Chief, there are two section heads: the Head of Collection Services and the Head of Scholarly Services. The professional staff members of the division, who are either area specialists or reference librarians, are grouped into five area teams: China and Mongolia, Japan, Korea, Southeast Asia, and South Asia. A coordinator of each area team is appointed from the team members by the Chief. The Chief is assisted by an Administrative Officer, an Information Technology Specialist, and a Special Assistant.

In the 2003 – 2008 Strategic Plan of the Division the following vision and mission statements were adopted:

Vision of the Asian Division

To establish the collections of the Asian Division as the premier research and scholarly resource of all formats and times on Asia and in Asian languages that is compatible with the dynamics of

---

① *The Annual Report of the Librarian of Congress for the Fiscal Year Ending September 30, 2005.* Washington, DC: Library of Congress, 2006: pp. 18 – 19.

② *The Asian Division.* Washington, DC: The Library of Congress, 2002: pp. 1, 2, 4, 8.

③ Chi Wang. *The Chinese Collection in the Library of Congress: A Brief Introduction.* Washington, DC: Chinese Section, Asian Division, Library of Congress, 2011: pp. 5 – 6.

knowledge and creativity of the 21st Century-frequently referred to as the "Asian Century".

Mission of the Asian Division
The mission of the Asian Division is to make comprehensive collection resources and information services related to Asia available and useful to the Congress, American people, and the scholarly research community nationally and internationally. ①

Building a Comprehensive Asian Collection

Recognizing the importance of Asia in the 21st century the Library of Congress has devoted great efforts to building a comprehensive collection on Asia. Today, after 142 years of painstaking work by generations of Asian area specialists, librarians, and scholars, a vast storehouse of knowledge about the diverse nations, histories, cultures, languages, and peoples has been assembled. It is perhaps the best of such collections outside Asia. With the foresight of Dr. James Billington, the current Librarian of the Congress, an exquisite Asian Reading Room has been provided as a gateway to this world-class collection. Below are brief descriptions of the five key collections:

The Chinese and Mongolian Collections
The Chinese and Mongolian Collection, as of September 30, 2006, consists of 1,000,289 monographic volumes, 4,789 active serial titles, and 10,961 inactive serial titles. Besides works in the Chinese language, it also includes several thousand volumes in Manchu, Mongol, Naxi (Moso), Tibetan, Uyghur,② and other minority languages. The collection covers all subjects and is especially strong in the humanities and social sciences, among them, classical Chinese literature, archival materials of the Qing dynasty (1644 – 1911) and Republican period (1911 – 1949), traditional Chinese medicine, local and regional histories (gazetteers), and contemporary publications of Mainland China and Taiwan.

The collection also contains some of the most valuable rare books from China, Mongolia, and Tibet. The rare books from China cover Song dynasty (960 – 1279), Jin dynasty (1115 – 1234), Yuan dynasty (1271 – 1368), Ming dynasty (1368 – 1644), and Qing dynasty (1644 – 1911). It includes a Buddhist invocation sutra (《一切如来》, *Yi qie ru lai*) printed in 975 A. D. that was recovered from the hollow bricks of the foundation of the Thunder Peak Pagoda (雷峰塔 Lei feng ta) when it collapsed in 1924, 41 of the 400 surviving volumes of the 1560 copy of the Great Encyclopedia of the *Ming Emperor Yongle* (《永乐大典》, *Yongle da dian*), and the 1895 – 1898 printing of the *Imperial Encyclopedia of China* (《古今图书集成》, *Gu jin tu shu ji cheng*) in 5,044 volumes.

Examples of other unique collections are many. These include the 3,344 pictographic manuscripts from the Naxi (纳西) minority group in Yunnan province that were acquired by Joseph Rock and Quentin Roosevelt, the William Gamble collection of the 19th century American Presbyterian Missionary Press established by Gamble in Ningbo and Shanghai in 1858 – 1860 that produced Christian publications in Chinese and translations of Western works, and the Arthur W. Hummel collection of rare Chinese maps. ③

The Library of Congress is one of the world's leading centers for Tibetan publications with holdings that are representative of the entire body of Tibetan literature from the 8th century to the modern day. These include religious texts, history, biography, traditional medicine, astrology, iconography, musical notations, grammars, social sciences, and secular literature.

Since religion plays a major role in Tibetan society, the holdings of Tibetan Buddhist scriptures in the Asian Division are especially strong. The Tibetan Buddhist canon is contained in

---

① *The Strategic Plan of the Asian Division, 2003 to 2008*. Washington, DC: Asian Division, the Library of Congress, 2003.
② Collection of Uyghur materials is kept in the Near East Section of the African and Middle Eastern Division.
③ *The Chinese Collection*. Washington, DC: Asian Division, the Library of Congress, n. d. Most of the rere Chinese maps are kept in the Geography and Map Division of the Library.

the *Kanjur*, in over a hundred volumes of sutras, and the *Tanjur*, most editions totaling some 225 volumes of commentaries. The Tibetan canonical texts are accurate translations of the original Buddhist texts, written in Sanskrit between 500 BC and 900 AD. Among the individuals who were responsible for the early periods of development of the Tibetan collection are William Woodville Rockhill, the American diplomat and Tibetologist who traveled in Mongolia and Tibet between 1888 and 1892 and again in the 1900s; Berthold Laufer, another leading Tibetologist in the late 1800s; and Joseph Rock, the colorful explorer, adventurer, and scientist who lived and traveled in China's rugged west for 27 years in the early 1900s. ①

The Mongolian collection also includes 80 books in traditional script and format acquired in the early 20th century and complete reprint editions of the Mongolian Kanjur and Tanjur, the Buddhist canonical texts and their commentaries. In recent years, the Library's New Delhi Field Office has been actively microfilming Mongolian newspapers and serials. New publications are currently being acquired by the Library's bibliographic representative in Ulaanbaatar.

The Japanese Collection

After the initial arrangement for the exchange of government publications established in 1875 between the two governments, the Japanese collection began to grow in 1905 when a significant gift was received from Crosby Stuart Noyes, journalist and editor of the *Washington Evening Star*. The Noyes collection included 658 illustrated books produced from the mid-18th century to the late-19th century. In 1907, a systematic effort was undertaken by Kan'ichi Asakawa of Yale University to purchase Japanese books for the Library of Congress. Because of his effort, some 9,072 volumes on the subjects of Japanese history, literature, Buddhism, Shinto, geography, music, and the arts were added. In 1930, the Library appointed Dr. Shiho Sakanishi as the Chief Assistant of the Japanese Section to further develop the collection. During her tenure from 1930 to 1941, the collection tripled in size. Today, the Japanese collection has grown to 1,155,668 volumes of monographs, 5,614 active serial titles, and 9,451 inactive serial titles-the largest collection in the Asian Division—through purchase, gift, exchange, and other avenues of acquisition.

Among the wealth of rare items are approximately 5,000 titles of publications and manuscript copies of works produced before the end of the Tokugawa Shogunate in 1868 and the beginning of the Meiji period (1868 – 1912). Included are the *dharani* (百万搭陀罗尼) prayer charms, which date from 770 A. D.

10 The Tibetan Collection. Washington, DC: Asian Division, Library of Congress, April 2002.

and are among the world's earliest surviving printed material. Also noteworthy is a complete edition of the Japanese literary masterpiece *Genji monogatari* (《源氏物語》, The Tale of Genji) published in Kyoto in 1654 and the *Yoshitsune azuma kudari monogatari* printed on movable type between 1624 and 1643. A complete catalogue of the rare books in the Library of Congress was published in 2003 by Yagi Shoten in Tokyo. ②

At the end of World War II, a large number of historical documents such as the ones from the former Japanese Imperial Army and Navy, the South Manchuria Railway Company, and the East Asian Research Institute were given to the Library by the Washington Document Center. Much of the materials from the latter two are pre-World War II studies on such areas as Korea, Taiwan, Mainland China, Mongolia, and the Pacific Islands. The Library also has a microfilm copy of the archives of the Japanese Foreign Ministry from 1868 to 1945 and pre-1945 records of the Police Bureau of the Ministry of Home Affairs-some of these are censored wartime publications. ③

Another important collection is the "Inoh Maps" —the first modern maps of Japan created

---

① *The Tibetan Collection.* Washington, DC: Asian Division, Library of Congress, April 2002
② **Beikoku Gikai Toshokan zo Nihon Kotenseki Mokuroku** (Catalog of Japanese Rare Books in the Library of Congress). Tokyo: Yagi Shoten, 2003
③ **The Japanese Collection.** Washington, DC: Asian Division, the Library of Congress, n. d.

originally by Tadataka Inoh between 1800 and 1821. Copies of 207 of Inoh's original 214 sheets large-scale set (1∶36,000) that cover the Japanese archipelago from Hokkaido to Kyushu were discovered in the map collection of the Library of Congress in the spring of 2001 and have caused great excitement in Japan. In order to make these maps available for exhibition and for online access, all of them have been digitized and sent to the Japan Map Center. A selection of the actual-size reproductions of these maps was on exhibition at the Tokyo National Museum from October 31 to December 14, 2003. Some of the original maps were also loaned and exhibited in Kobe, Sendai, Atami, and Nagoya in 2004.

The Korean Collection

The Korean collection began in the 1920s with the generous gift of Korean books from Dr. James S. Gale, a Canadian missionary who spent 40 years in Korea from 1888 to 1928. Dr. Gale also helped the Library to acquire a number of Korean classics, including rare books from the estate of the Korean scholar Kim To-hui. Systematic development of the Korean collection was started in the early 1950s during the period of the Korean War. Today, the Korean collection in the Library totals 264,400 volumes in the Korean language, as well as 20,000 Japanese language books and 9,000 English language books on Korea. Coverage of North Korea is also strong, with some 10,000 items. There are also 1,389 active serial titles and 5,598 inactive serial titles.

Included in the Korean collection are 480 titles of Korean rare books in 3,000 volumes. They were all written in Chinese characters and printed on mulberry paper. Although China was the first country to use movable type made of clay, Korea was the first one to use movable metal type for printing. Several good examples of this type of printing are in the collection. The most important one is the Collective Works of Yi Munsun (in 8 volumes) printed with metal movable type about 1241. Others include the collected writings of the renowned 16th-century Confucian scholar and statesman Yi I printed in 1744 and the 1834 reprint of the works of the "father of Korean literature," Ch'oe Ch'i-won (857–915). Other rare books printed by woodblock include the *History of the Koryo Dynasty* (《高丽史》), printed in 1590, and the *Law Code of the Yi Dynasty* (《经国大典》), printed in 1630.①

The Southeast Asian Collection

As was mentioned earlier, the earliest acquisition of the Southeast Asian collection in the Library of Congress began in 1865, which predates the beginning of all other Asian collections. The collection was acquired in Singapore in 1842 by the U.S. Naval Exploring Expedition led by Lt. Charles Wilkes. Wilkes and the Expedition's philologist, Horatio Hale, collected Malay manuscripts and early printed books with the assistance of Alfred North, an American missionary in Singapore. The collection went first to the Smithsonian Institution which later transferred the collection to the Library of Congress in 1865. Included in this earliest acquisition are a unique collection of manuscripts written in the Bugis script of South Sulawesi; an account of the 19th-century Malay world written in Jawi, the *Hikayat Abdullah* (The Story of Abdullah); and an 1840 Mission Press edition of the *Sejarah Melayu* (Malay Annals), an important Malay history written in 1612, also in Jawi, the Malay language in Arabic script.

The Southeast Asian collection contains many palm leaf manuscript copies of the Tipitaka, the basic text of Theravada Buddhism which is the majority religion of Cambodia, Laos, Myanmar (Burma), and Thailand. In 1905, a special Thai Tipitaka was presented to the Library of Congress by King Chulalongkorn (Rama V) of Thailand. In 1949, an especially fine collection of Burmese manuscripts in the Pali language as well as a Tipitaka in Pali using Burmese script was presented to the Library of Congress as a part of a large Burmese donation. The donation also included an important Burmese history, The Glass Palace Chronicle, written by a group of scholars in 1829.

The Asian Division also holds rare materials from the Philippines and Vietnam. Of special note is a set of inscribed bamboo tubes, with lettering in the old Indic script similar to the ancient

---

① *The Korean Collection*. Washington, DC: Asian Division, the Library of Congress, n. d.

scripts used in neighboring Indonesia. The collection of 55 bamboos in prose and 22 in verse provides a fascinating glimpse into Mangyan (Hampangan) and Tagbanua society. Several examples of Vietnamese dynastic histories are also represented, including texts printed from early woodblocks at the former imperial palace at Hue.

In 1938, the Library of Congress launched the Indie Project in order to improve its collections from Southeast and South Asia, particularly publications in local languages. Following World War II, as U. S. interest in the region increased, the collection grew dramatically and today consists of holdings from Brunei, Cambodia, East Timor, Indonesia, Laos, Malaysia, Myanmar, the Philippines, Singapore, Thailand, Vietnam, and many of the South Pacific island nations such as Papua New Guinea, etc. The establishment of the Library's overseas offices in Jakarta, Indonesia in 1963 has provided a continuous flow of books, newspapers, and periodicals from the region in a variety of formats. The office has recently started collecting grey literature documenting the growth of civil societies, local music in minority languages in Laos and Indonesia, early histories of the Islamic kingdoms of Pattani, environmental works, and literature by and about Chinese in Southeast Asia. Today the total collection for Southeast Asia in major Southeast Asian languages includes 179,357 monographs, 2,736 active serials, and 8,462 inactive serials.

While the Southeast Asia team did not exist as such prior to 2003, this does not mean that Southeast Asia was completely ignored within the Asian Division between 1865 and 2003. On the contrary, there were numerous important developments during the twentieth century such as the organization of the Southeast Asia collection, the development of important research tools and the discovery of lost treasures. For example Cecil Hobbs, a former missionary in Burma and head of the Southern Asia section from 1958 to 1972, and Kohar Rony, Indonesian area specialist from 1962 until 2000, used their complimentary expertise to organize the Southeast Asian collections and bring them under better bibliographic control. They both published numerous finding aids and promoted the collections by participating in national and international professional organizations. The twentieth century also witnessed the "discovery" of lost treasures. One example of these is the Farquhar correspondence. In 1990 reference librarian Dr. Allen Thrasher found the Farquhar correspondence in a bound volume in the mixed arrearages then kept on the 4th Floor of the Adams Building. Examples of these original letters from the rulers of various states in and around the Malay penninsula to the British Resident in Singapore Farquhar, were recently put on display in Singapore. The Southeast Asian team is very active in promoting its collections and works closely with the Vietnamese-, Lao-and Philippine-American communities in particular.

The South Asian Collection

The foundation for the South Asian collection was laid in 1904 when a collection of over 4,000 books and pamphlets from the German Indologist, Dr. Albrecht Weber, was purchased. Included were texts in Sanskrit of India's sacred Hindu works-the *Vedas*, *Brahmaas*, and *Upanisads*-as well as the stories of the Puranas and the great epics of the *Mahabharata* and the *Ramayana*. In addition, there are a number of Weber's notebooks with his handwritten transcriptions of rare Indian texts for his pioneering critical editions.

In 1938, the Library received a grant from the Carnegie Corporation to develop the South Asian collection systematically, and that initiated the Indie Project- "Project F-Development of Indie Studies." During the 1950s the collection continued to expand and growth accelerated even further with the opening of the Library's New Delhi Overseas Office in 1962. Under the Public Law (PL) 480 program, the New Delhi office used rupees from Indian purchases of U. S. agricultural products to buy books and other materials from India and other countries of South Asia. An overseas office in Karachi, Pakistan, was opened in 1965 to oversee the acquisition of publications from Pakistan and neighboring areas. Later, the office was moved to the capital city, Islamabad.

Today, the South Asian collection holds materials in over 100 modern languages used in India, Pakistan, Bangladesh, Sri Lanka, and Nepal. The majority of the publications are in Hindi (20 percent), Bengali (15 percent), Urdu (13 percent), and Tamil (11 percent). Other languages represented in large numbers include Marathi, Telugu, Malayalam, Gujarati, and

Kannada. As of September 30, 2006, the collection consists of 233,829 monographic volumes, 1,616 active serial titles, and 2,120 inactive serial titles.

An example among the approximately 1000 rare books and manuscripts in the South Asian collection is a 1452 manuscript of the Jaina Kalpasutra from Gujarat in western India. This illustrated text tells the story of Mahavira, the founder of the Jaina religion. The "Crosby Khotan fragments" are also among the more unusual rare items. During a 1903 journey to Central Asia, Oscar Terry Crosby, an American who later became Assistant Secretary of the Treasury, purchased these manuscripts in Sanskrit at the Taklamakan oasis town of Khotan. ①

Between 1990 and 2000, a very important project undertaken by the New Delhi Overseas Office was the Microfilming of Indian Publications Project (MIPP). This project was a joint collaboration between the Government of India and the Library of Congress, aimed at preserving and making accessible out-of-print works listed in the National Bibliography of Indian Literature: 1901–1953. Some 22,686 titles in 15 languages were microfilmed from 67 repository libraries in India and 3 libraries outside India (the Library of Congress, University of Chicago, and British Library). These titles were selected by Indian scholars as being central to the understanding of India. ②

Overseas Acquisition Offices

The accelerated growth of the library collections from South and Southeast Asia since the 1960s should be credited to the efforts of the overseas acquisition offices in New Delhi, Jakarta, and Islamabad. In addition to these three, the African/Asian Acquisitions and Overseas Operations Division of the Library of Congress also operate overseas offices in Cairo, Nairobi, and Rio de Janeiro.

One of the unique features of the three Asian overseas offices is the offering of their services to other libraries which want to acquire publications from countries and regions covered by these offices. For example, the 44 academic and research libraries, mostly from North America, that participate in the South Asia Cooperative Acquisitions Program (SACAP) receive publications of their choice from the New Delhi office (with its many sub-offices) and from the Islamabad office. The Jakarta office administers the Cooperative Acquisitions Program for Southeast Asia (CAP-SEA). The largest and the oldest of the six overseas offices, the New Delhi office covers India, Bangladesh, Bhutan, Burma, the Maldives, Nepal, and Sri Lanka. The Jakarta office covers all the countries of Southeast Asia with the exception of Burma. The Islamabad office covers Pakistan, and in addition, several other countries in Central Asia and the Near East. All three offices perform a wide range of services to CAP libraries, including acquisitions, cataloging, bibliographic control, and binding materials in many languages and scripts. The New Delhi and Jakarta offices also have microfilm and microfiche units for preservation of newspapers and fragile publications. In addition all the offices maintain extensive programs of exchanges of publications with key institutions and libraries in South and Southeast Asia. ③

Building the Asian Collection in the Digital Age

Throughout the 20th century the building of Asian collections focused mainly on printed materials. However, the trend has begun to change in the past five years with attention gradually shifting to electronic and web resources. Large-scale digitization of rare materials is also being launched to make some of the treasured collections, which have no copyright restriction, freely accessible to researchers via the Internet. The approaches taken thus far also include the subscription to select electronic bibliographic databases; the acquisition of digitized full-text

---

① *The South Asian Collection*. Washington, DC: Asian Division, Library of Congress, April 2002.

② *The Library of Congress in South Asia, 1960–2002. Celebrating 40 Years of Bibliographic and Cultural Exchanges*. New Delhi: Library of Congress Office, n. d. p. 16.

③ *The Library of Congress in South Asia, 1960–2002. Celebrating 40 Years of Bibliographic and Cultural Exchanges*. New Delhi: Library of Congress Office, n. d.

databases of e-books, e-journals, e-newspapers, and others; the digitization of selected rare books and other collections; and the capture of relevant web sites for the Library's Asian portals which are constructed and maintained by the Asian Division.

Subscription to selected electronic bibliographic databases

At present forty-five of the Library's 219 subscription databases deal with Asia or Asian studies. These databases, such as Aardvark (Asian resources for librarians), Asian Development Bank Economics & Statistics (of Economics and Research Department of Asian Development Bank), Asian Law Bibliographic Database (from the University of Melbourne), Bibliography of Asian Studies (from Association for Asian Studies), Country Studies (produced by Federal Research Division, the Library of Congress), and Treaties and International Agreements (by Oceana Publications), are all accessible in the Library's reading rooms.

Acquisition of digitized full-text databases

Since 2003, special efforts have also been made to acquire a number of most important digitized full-text databases from Mainland China, Japan, Korea, and Taiwan.

In the Mainland China and Taiwan areas we have acquired *Ren min ri bao dian zi ban* (人民日报电子版 *The People's Daily Electronic Version*), 1946-to date; *China Data Online*; *China Journals Full-text Database* (中国期刊全文数据库 – 7240 *titles*) and *Chinese Core Newspapers Databases* (中国重要报纸数据库 – 1,000 *titles*) of the *China National Knowledge Infrastructure* (CNKI 中国国家知识基础架构); the *Wanfang Chinese Conference Proceedings Database* (万方中国学术会议全文数据库 400,000 *papers*); the *Wanfang Chinese Theses and Dissertations Databases* (万方中国学位论文数据库 450,000 *titles*); and the 100,000-title monograph database from *Superstar Digital Library* (超星电子图书馆) We have also acquired *Si ku quan shu* (*Wen yuan ge Edition* 四库全书文渊阁) a professional standalone version, the Academia Sinica's Geographic Information Systems (GIS) of Chinese Civilization in Time and Space (CCTS 中国文明之时空基础架构) and *Taiwan History and Culture in Time and Space* (THCTS 台湾历史史文化地图系统 *Taiwan Electronic Periodicals* (台湾电子期刊 – 500 *titles*), and the *Encyclopedia of Taiwan* (台湾百科全书).

For the Japanese collection the Library has acquired two important subscription databases: Directory of Japanese Scientific Periodicals (from National Diet Library, covering 13,875 serial titles on science and technology published in Japan) and Kodansha Encyclopedia of Japan (based on the 1993 publication entitled Japan: an Illustrated Encyclopedia, with 11,000 entries). Several Japanese rare books have also been digitized and are available from the Library's OPAC. In addition, the Library currently subscribes full-text databases of five major Japanese newspapers including Mainichi, Sankei, Chunichi, Tokyo and Yomiuri Newspapers through a U.S. based commercial aggregator/vendor, www.factive.com.

On May 21 2007, The Korean Team signed the exchange agreement with the Korean National Assembly Library (KNAL) to acquire access to KNAL full text Database free of charge. The KNAL databases contain over 8 million items. The full-text databases include monographs, government publications, dissertations in all fields, social science journals, historical newspapers, White papers, Periodicals Index (1910 –), and others.

In addition to the latest acquisition, the Korean Team also acquired the Chosun Daily Newspaper Archive (covering articles from the Chosun llbo, the most widely read newspaper in South Korea), Korean Studies Database (by KRPIA, covering history, literature, and traditional medicines), Korean Studies Information Service System (KISS, a database of full-text articles from 6,000 journals published by 1,200 Korean academic institutions), DBPia (Searchable database of full-text articles in about 700 scholarly journals published in Korea), and Law n B-Korean Law Database (Law and business, available for access in the Law Library reading room).

The acquisition of nine subscription databases pertaining to South and Southeast Asia is pending.

Digitization of selected rare books and other collections

In recent years, Asian Division has undertaken several major collaborative projects to digitize its unparalleled Asian collections. With a three-year grant from the Chiang Ching-kuo Foundation (1998 – 2001) the Chinese and Mongolian Team was able to hire Prof. Zhu Baotian of the Yunnan Museum to review, categorize, and prepare a detailed description for the 3,344 Naxi manuscripts in the collection and subsequently digitized a portion of this unique collection. This digitized collection is now accessible from LC's website: http://international.loc.gov/intldl/naxihtml/naxihome.html

On October 1, 2004, the Library and the Academia Sinica (Taipei) signed an agreement for the digitization of China-related maps. Through three working visits of the subject and digital experts from the Academia Sinica between 2004 and 2006, digital images of 21,000 maps and 840 aerial photos were made and transported to Taiwan for post-digitization processing. This digital file will be available online from the website of the Geography and Map Division of the Library of Congress as well as incorporated into the *Chinese Civilizations in Time and Space* (CCTS) database and supported by a historical geographic information system with spatial-temporal applications.

In May 2005, the Library and the National Central Library (Taipei) signed an agreement for the digitization of Chinese rare books. A team of technical specialists from Taiwan is now working onsite at the Library of Congress for three years to digitize selected titles in the Chinese rare book collection, which have been reviewed by Chinese rare book experts for the authentication and annotation of the Chinese rare books, and by the Library's Conservation Division. The two experts are funded by Chiang Ching-kuo Foundation for 2005 and 2006. The goal of this collaborative project is for the two libraries to share each other's digitized databases of Chinese rare books and make them easily and freely accessible to researchers worldwide.

In close collaboration with the International Research Center of Japanese Studies (Nichubunken), the Asian Division digitized the Nara Ehon collection (four titles: *Shizuka*, *Homyo Doji*, *Shigure*, *and Soga Monogatari*) and made over 2,000 digital images, including 173 color illustrations, available online through the Library of Congress Online Catalog at http://catalog.loc.gov/. Nara Ehon is a type of colorfully illustrated manuscript book or hand-printed book of stories and tales produced in the Muromachi period (1333 – 1573) through the mid-Edo period (1615 – 1868). It is considered to be the earliest popular picture book in Japan. Another Japanese rare book, *The Tale of Genji*, a rare and complete sixty-volume set of the 1654 edition was also digitized in 2007. The digital files are currently available via the Library of Congress Online Catalog or at http://lcweb4.loc.gov/seivice/asian/asian0001/2005/2005html/20050415toc.html.

Japanese Ukiyo-e collection in the Prints and Photographs Division also benefited from collaboration with Nichibunken. Under the agreement signed by the Library and Nichibunken in February 2005, a team of Japanese Art historians visited the Library for three weeks and completed their work in identifying and describing some 3,000 prints. The Library completed the scanning of the Ukiyo-e prints collection in 2006 with financial support from Nichibunken and made the collection available through the Library's Prints & Photographs Online Catalog (http://lcweb2.loc.gov/pp/pphome.html) and Nichibunken websites.

In cooperation with the Japan Map Center of the Geographical Survey Institute in Japan, the Geography and Map Division digitized the only surviving set of 207 large-scale Japanese maps (made in 1816 – 1819) by the famous map maker, Inoh Tadataka, and made it available in June 2005 through the Library's webpage: http://www.loc.gov/rr/qeoqmap/.

As recently as May 2007, the Library of Congress also signed an agreement with the National Library of Korea (NLK) on a collaborative project which involves the preservation of the Library's rich and rare Korea-related maps and atlas holdings in its Geography and Map Division. The Library's Korean maps and atlas collections include both manuscript copies and woodblock impressions; interestingly, woodblock impressions are generally more uncommon and valuable than manuscript copies. The collections range in date from circa 1760 to 1896, with many becoming brittle due to age. The National Library of Korea has agreed to support the conservation of the maps and atlases. After treatment, the Library will digitally scan the selected maps and atlas and provide free Internet access to these electronic versions via the Library's website.

Also, the Library is in the final review of the agreement with the NLK to digitize selected rare Korean books in the Asian Division.

Capture of relevant web sites

As a part of the Library's effort to provide more and more specialized digital resources online, such as the American Memory (http://memorv.loc.gov/), the Global Gateway (http://internationalJoc.gov/intldl/intldlhome.html), etc., the Library's portals now serve as a gateway to selected web resources on a variety of subjects and world areas (http://www.loc.gov/rr/international/portals.html). The portals of the Asian Division (http://www.loc.gov/rr/asian/area AD.html) are increasingly a useful source on all the Asian countries and regions.

Planning is also underway to begin a cooperative web capture project for at-risk content. This project addresses the problems that web content that will be important for future research is disappearing before it can be collected and that many smaller institutions may not have resources and/or budgets for collecting web sites. The Library of Congress will be working with select partner institutions to identify web sites for content preservation. The Asian Division is currently focusing on two specific topics: North Korea and Islam in Asia. The collaborative effort will ensure that on-line information needed by researchers is preserved for posterity.

Online reference services

Being a leader in the development of Question Point—a worldwide online reference service operating on a 24-hours-a-day and 7-days-a-week schedule—operated by the OCLC Online Computer Library Center, library users anywhere can now send their reference questions from their local libraries through the OCLC online global network to the Library of Congress for reply by our reference librarians and area studies specialists (http://www.oclc.org/questionpoirit). Library users may also use the service of Ask a Librarian (http://www.loc.gov/rr/askaHb-asian.html) to get reference assistance from librarians in the Asian Division.

Research Fellowships Established

In order to encourage the use of the Library's collections for serious research, the Library has established a number of research fellowships. Many of these research fellowships are administered by the John W. Kluge Center of the Library. Detailed information about the various Kluge Center fellowships, such as the applicant eligibility, tenure and stipend, and applications, can be found from the website: http://www.loc.gov/loc/kluqe/kluqe-fellowships.html

Beginning in 2006, through the generosity of Ms. Florence Tan Moesen, the Asian Division has begun offering up to 10 Florence Tan Moesen Fellowships each year to researchers who will use the Asian collections for her/his research. Detailed information about the Florence Tan Moeson fellowship is provided on the website: http://www.loc.gov/rr/asian/FTM.html.

Friends Society and Outreach Programs

Established in January 2004, the Asian Division Friends Society has a very significant mission that is to facilitate a joint effort with all individual and organization members to build a world-class Asian collection as the premier research and scholarly resource on Asia and in Asian languages.

From April 2005 to present, ADFS has organized and/or co-hosted 52 outreach programs, including 7 major symposia, 34 lectures/presentations/film screening/cultural performances, 3 Asian literature club meetings, 4 highlight collection tours, and 4 annual membership meetings and open houses. Most of these programs were free and open to the public. They covered the subject fields of East, South, and Southeast Asian studies and have successfully reached out to the diverse community that the Asian Division serves. Through these scholarly and cultural programs, ADFS also formed closer partnership and friendship with academic institutions, embassies, and Asian Pacific American organizations.

Currently, ADFS has over 280 individual and 20 corporate members. All donations are tax-deductible and are being used for the Asian Division's outreach purposes. Information about ADFS, its upcoming programs, and membership benefits is available on www. lcasianfriends. org

Bibliography of Relevant Publications

The great breadth and depth of the Asian collections cannot be adequately described in this brief paper. Researchers who are interested in knowing more about these treasured and unparalleled collections are advised to consult some of the published bibliographies, finding tools, and papers listed below.

ASIAN

1. Hummel, Arthur W. "The Growth of the Orientalia Collections." *Library of Congress Quarterly Journal of Current Acquisitions.* V. 11, No. 2 (February 1954): pp. 69 – 87.

2. Lee, Hwa-Wei. "Building a World-class Asian Collection in the Library of Congress for Area Studies, Culture Preservation, Global Understanding, and Knowledge Creation." *Proceedings of the Symposium on "The New Horizon of Library Services Toward the Better Understanding of Asia."* November 19, 2003. Kyoto, Japan: National Diet Library, Kansai-kan, 2004. Japanese translation, pp. 57 – 67. English paper and slides, pp. 150 – 169.

3. *Library of Congress Asian Collections: An Illustrated Guide.* Written by Harold E. Meinheit. Washington, D. C.: Library of Congress, 2000: p. 80. (An updated 2007 electronic edition will be accessible from the Division's website: http://www. loc. gov/rr/asian/quide/)

CHINESE

1. Chu, Mi. "LC's Chinese Collection is Largest in Western World: Growth Tied to Political Changes." *Library of Congress Information Bulletin.* V. 53 (September 5, 1994): p. 16.

2. Chu, Mi. "World Digital Library and E-Resources in the Asian Division, Library of Congress." *Journal of East Asian Libraries.* No. 138 (February 2006): pp. 1 – 4.

3. Hu, Shuzhao. *The Development of the Chinese Collection in the Library of Congress.* Boulder, Colo.: Westview Press, 1979.

4. Huang, Hanzhu and David Hsü. *Chinese Periodicals in the Library of Congress.* Washington, D. C.: Library of Congress, 1988.

5. Huang, Hanzhu, and Hseo-chirn Jen. *Chinese Newspapers in the Library of Congress.* Washington, D. C.: Library of Congress, 1985.

6. Lee, Hwa-Wei. "Chinese Resources for Zheng He Studies in the Library of Congress" presented at the Third International Conference of Institutes and Libraries for Chinese Overseas Studies held in Singapore on August 18 – 21, 2005. In Proceedings on *"Maritime Asia and the Chinese Overseas, 1405 – 2005."* To be published in Singapore by the National Library of Singapore in 2007.

7. Lee, Hwa-Wei. "Historical Resources on Northeast China and Japan in the Library of Congress," unpublished paper presented at the International Conference of the Historical Resources for the Studies of Northeast China and Japan, held at Niigata University in Japan, October 27 – 30, 2004. (In Chinese and Japanese)

8. Lee, Hwa-Wei. "Sinological Resources in the Library of Congress," unpublished paper presented at the International Conference on Sinological Resources in the Digital Era, December 7 – 9, 2004. Taipei: National Central Library, 2004.

9. Li, Xiaocong. *Descriptive Catalogue of the Traditional Chinese Maps in the Library of Congress (Meiguo guo hui tu shu quan cang zhong wen gu di tu xu lu).* Beijing: Wen Wu Publishing Co., 2004.

10. Library of Congress, Asian Division. *Commemorating the Two-Hundredth Anniversary of Robert Morrison's Arrival in China* (compiled by Mi Chu and Man Shun Yeung, assisted by Ariele

Bernard). Taipei: eHanism Global, 2007.

11. Lu, Judy S. "The Contemporary China Collection in the Asian Division, The Library of Congress." *Journal of East Asian Libraries*. No. 141 (Feb. 2007): pp. 19 – 28.

12. Lu, Judy S. and Meinheit, Harold. "Hong Kong: From Fishing Village to Financial Center." *Library of Congress Information Bulletin*. V. 56 (1977): pp. 272 – 275.

13. Matsumura, Jun. *A Catalogue of the Manchu Materials in the Library of Congress: Xylographs, Manuscripts, Archives*. Tokyo: Toyo Bunko, produced by the University of Tokyo Press Production Center, 1999.

14. Matsumura, Jun. "A Catalogue of the Manchu Books in the Library of Congress, Washington, D. C.." *The Tokyo Gukuho*. V. 57, Nos. 1 – 2 (January 1976): pp. 36 – 60.

15. Soong, James Chu-yul. Chinese Materials on Microfilm Available from the Library of Congress. Washington, D. C.: Center for Chinese Research Materials, Association of Research Libraries, 1971.

16. Sumiyoshi, Tomohiko. "Beikoku Gikai Toshokanzo Nihon Denrai Kanseki Mokuroku Kaidai Choheri." *Shido Bunko Ronshu*. V. 41 (2007): pp. 201 – 270.

17. Wang, Chi. "Development of the Chinese Collection in the Library of Congress and Its Utilization by Researchers." *Proceedings of the International Conference on National Libraries-Towards the 21st Century*. Taipei: National Central Library, 1993: pp. 645 – 653.

18. Wang, Zhongmin. *A Descriptive Catalog of Rare Chinese Books in the Library of Congress*. 2 vols. Washington, D. C.: Library of Congress, 1957.

19. Young, John. *The Research Activities of the South Manchurian Railway Company, 1907 – 1945: A History and Bibliography*. New York: Columbia University Press, 1966.

20. Zhu, Shijia. *A Catalog of Chinese Local Histories in the Library of Congress*. Washington, D. C.: Library of Congress, 1942.

MONGOLIAN

1. Farguhar, David M. "A Description of the Mongolian Manuscripts arid Xylographs in Washington, D. C." *Central Asiatic Journal*. V. 1, No. 3 (1955): pp. 161 – 218.

2. Meinheit, Susan. "The Tibetan and Mongolian Collections in the Asian Division, Library of Congress." *Journal of East Asian Libraries*. No. 139 (June 2006): pp. 27 – 35.

TIBETAN

1. Buescher, John B. "Tibetan Materials in the Asia Rare Book Collection of the Library of Congress." *Journal of the International Association of Buddhist Studies*. V. 13, No. 1 (1990). (Lists xylographs and manuscripts acquired between 1900 and 1928 by William Rockhill, Berthold Laufer, and Joseph Rock.)

2. Kapstein, Matthew. "Inventory of Tibetan Works Acquired Under 0199431: The Acquisition of Tibetan Books Published in the People's Republic of China, June 14-August 11, 1990; Report Submitted to the Library of Congress. August 28, 1990." (Titles and sometimes detailed contents of 340 volumes of current xylographs acquired from Tibetan printers in the People's Republic of China.)

3. Maurer, Walter. "List of Tibetan Materials with Identification Numbers, 1962 (?)." (Lists works in Laufer collection and other miscellaneous works, with occasional notes on the subject matter of the text.)

4. Meinheit, Susan. "The Tibetan and Mongolian Collections in the Asian Division, Library of Congress." *Journal of East Asian Libraries*. No. 139 (June 2006): pp. 27 – 35.

5. Meinheit, Susan. "Tibetan Classical Literature and the U. S. Library of Congress: Preservation of Knowledge." Paper presented at the First Beijing Tibetology Conference, Beijing, September 13 – 16, 1991. *China Tibetology* (Special Issue, 1992): pp. 361 – 372.

6. Robinson, Hanna. *First Cumulative Dictionary Catalog of Tibetan Works in the Library of*

the Institute of Advanced Study of World Religions. Stony Brook, N. Y.: IASWR, 1985. (Catalog of PL 480 Tibetan collections.)

7. Rockhill, William Woodville. "Catalogue of Tibetan Books in the Library of Congress, 1902." (A handwritten list of sixty-two titles in Tibetan script followed by transliteration, with brief descriptive annotations as to subject matter and physical features.)

8. Tachikawa, Murashi, Tshulkrim Kelsang, and Shunzo Onoda. *A Catalogue of the United States Library of Congress Collection of Tibetan Literature* In Microfiche. 2 vols. Tokyo: International Institute for Buddhist Studies, 1983 – 1988 (Bibliographica Philologica Buddhica. Series maior, III).

9. *Woodblock to Laser. Library of Congress Tibetan Listings.* Asian Classics Input Project. Washington, D. C.: Library of Congress, 1993. cd-rom. (Available in Microform Reading Room.)

JAPANESE

1. *Catalog of Japanese Rare Books in the Library of Congress (Beikoku Gikai Toshokan zo Nihon Kotenseki Mokuroku).* Tokyo: Yagi Shoten, 2003.

2. Honda, Shojo. *Pre-Meiji Works in the Library of Congress: Japanese Literature, Performing Arts, and Reference Books.* Washington, D. C.: Library of Congress, 1997.

3. Honda, Shojo. *Pre-Meiji Works in the Library of Congress: Japanese Mathematics.* Washington, D. C.: Library of Congress, 1982.

4. Kuroda, Andrew. "A History of the Japanese Collection in the Library of Congress, 1874 – 1941." *Senda Masao Kyoju Koki Kinen Toshokan Shiryo Ronshu.* Tenri, Senda Masao Kyoju Koki Kinenkai, 1970: pp, 281 – 327.

5. Nagao, Philip. *Japanese Local Histories in the Library of Congress.* Washington, D. C.: Library of Congress, 1988.

6. *The Floating World of Ukiyo-e: Shadows, Dreams, and Substance.* Essays by Sandy Kita... [et. al]. New York: Abrams in association with the Library of Congress, 2001.

7. *The Noyes Collection of Japanese Prints, Drawings, Etc., Presented by Crosby Stuart Noyes.* Washington, D. C.: Library of Congress, 1906.

8. Ohta, Thaddeus. *Japanese National Government Publications in the Library of Congress.* Washington, D. C.: Library of Congress, 1980.

9. Tanaka, Hiromi. *A Comprehensive Catalogue of Publications of the Former Imperial Army and Navy.* Tokyo: Toyo Shorin, 1995.

10. Tanpo, Keisuke and Yasuhiro Honda. *Kyu Taiwan Sotokufu Kankei Shiryo Mokuroku: Beikoku Gikai Toshokan Shozo = Bibliography of Materials Related to the Taiwan Government General: Collection at the Library of Congress in the United States.* Naruto, Japan: Yagi Insatsujo, 1996.

11. Uyehara, Cecil. *Checklist of Archives in the Japanese Ministry of Foreign Affairs Tokyo, Japan, 1868 – 1945: Microfilmed for the Library of Congress, 1949 – 1951.* Washington, D. C.: Photoduplication Service, Library of Congress, 1954.

12. Yoshimura, Yoshiko. *Censored Japanese Serials of the Pre-1946 Period: A Checklist of the Microfilm Collection.* Washington, D. C.: Library of Congress, 1994.

13. Yoshimura, Yoshiko. *Japanese Government Documents and Censored Publications: A Checklist of the Microfilm Collection.* Washington, D. C.: Library of Congress, 1992.

14. Yoshimura, Yoshiko. *Pre-1956 Japanese Documents and Censored Materials: / Checklist of the Microfilm Collection of the Library of Congress.* Washington, D. C., 2002, 2006.

15. Young, John. *Checklist of Microfilm Reproductions of Selected Archives of the Japanese Army, Navy, and Other Government Agencies.* Washington, D. C.: Georgetown University Press, 1959.

16. Young, John. *The Research Activities of the South Manchurian Railway Company, 1907 – 1945: A History and Bibliography.* New York: Columbia University Press, 1966.

KOREAN

1. Cho, Sung Yoon. *Law and Legal Literature of North Korea*: *A Guide*. Washington, D. C.: Library of Congress, 1988.

2. Ch'on Hye-bong et al. *Mi Uihoe Tosogwan sojang Han'gukpon Mongnok* (List of Korean Rare Books in the Library of Congress). Seoul: Han'guk Soji Hakhoe, 1994.

3. "An Inventory of English-language Publications on Korea in the Library of Congress as of 1994." *Asian Division*, *Library of Congress*. Washington, D. C., 1997. Photocopy.

4. *Korea*: *An Annotated Bibliography of Publications in Far Eastern Languages*, comp. by Edwin G. Beal, Jr., and Robin L. Winkler. Washington, D. C.: Library of Congress, 1950.

5. *Korea*: *An Annotated Bibliography of Publications in the Russian Language*, comp. by Albert Parry et al. Washington, D. C.: Library of Congress, 1950.

6. *Korea*: *An Annotated Bibliography of Publications in Western Languages*, comp. by Helen D. Jones and Robin L. Winkler. Washington, D. C.: Library of Congress, 1950.

7. Yang, Key P. *Ch'uryoso yokkun Miguk Kukhoe Tosogwan sojang Pukkoe Charyo Mongriokchip* (Selected North Korean Source Materials Held in the Library of Congress). Seoul: Kukt'o T'ongirwon, 1970.

8. Yang, Key P. *Korean War Bibliography*. Washington, D. C.: Library of Congress, 1990.

9. Yang, Key P. "Reference Guide to Korean Materials, 1945 – 1959." Master's thesis, Catholic University of America, Washington, D. C., 1960.

SOUTH ASIAN

1. "Archive of World Literature on Tape." Recorded Sound Section, Motion Picture, Broadcasting, and Recorded Sound Division, Library of Congress. Audio recording. (Chiefly poets reading selections from their own work. Especially strong for Indian and Pakistani poets.)

2. "Card Catalog of 466 South Asian Manuscripts in the Southern Asia Section." Library of Congress. Handwritten. (Most of the manuscripts are in Sanskrit. This catalog does not cover approximately fifty other uncataloged South Asia manuscripts in Sanskrit, Sinhalese, Tamil, Oriya, Gujarati, and Urdu.)

3. "Card Catalog of the Holdings of the South Asia Microform Project." Southern Asian Section, Library of Congress. (A dictionary card catalog of the film and microfiche acquired by the South Asia Microform Project, 1970 – , and housed at the Center for Research Libraries, Chicago. Issued in book format as *SAMP Catalog*.)

4. "Card Catalog of the South Asia Microfiche Collection." Southern Asian Section, Library of Congress. (A card catalog of titles acquired on microfiche in the New Delhi South Asia Fiche Program since its inception in 1981. Closed in 1994 when newly cataloged microfiched serials began to be put on line on LOCIS. Microfiched monographs already on line for several years.)

5. "Discovery and Exploration Footage in the Library of Congress." Motion Picture, Broadcasting, and Recorded Sound Division, Library of Congress, 1991 (?). Printout. [Lists video collections, films, newsreels, short subjects, and television programs in the custody of the Motion Picture, Broadcasting, and Recorded Sound Division. Includes films of Tibet (1930, 1938 – 1939) and expeditions to Himalayan sites, including Ladakh (1923), Hunza (n. d.), Kanchenjuriga (1930), Nanga Parbat (1934), Dhaulatagiri (1960), and the Everest region (1953, 1955). Margaret Mead's films of Bali and New Guinea and footage of Burma and the Indian Ocean are listed. Also includes other films of New Guinea and several South Pacific islands.]

6. Korom, Frank J. "South Asian Recordings in the Archive of Folk Culture." Library of Congress Folk Archive Finding Aid: LCFAFA No. 5, August 1987. Typescript.

7. New Delhi Field Office, Library of Congress. *Accessions List*, *South Asia*. 16 Vols. New

Delhi: E. G. Smith, 1981 – 1996. (Combines earlier, separate Accessions Lists for India, Pakistan, Sri Lanka, Nepal, Bangladesh, and Afghanistan.)

    8. Poleman, Horace I. *A Census of Indic Manuscripts in the United States and Canada.* New Haven, Conn.: American Oriental Society, 1938. (Includes South and Southeast Asian manuscripts in the LC collection acquired up to 1938.)

    9. "*Southern Asia Accessions List.*" 9 Vols. Southern Asian Section, Library of Congress, 1952 – 1960. Photocopy. Reprint, New York: Arno Press, 1971.

    10. Weber, Albrecht. *Katalog der Bibliothek des verstorbenen Professors des Sanskrit an der Uriiversitat zu Berlin.* Gutersloh: Gedruckt bei C. Bertelsmann, 1902. (Lists the titles in the Weber Indological Library, now in LC. Includes sixty volumes of manuscripts, many of which contain transcriptions of several texts, sometimes in transliterated form. The originals of some no longer exist. Texts are presented which are not identified in other sources.)

SOUTHEAST ASIAN

    1. "*Accessions List, Southeast Asia.*" 19 Vols. Jakarta Field Office, Library of Congress, January/March 1975-November-December 1993 (monthly). Photocopy. [Continues "Accessions List, Indonesia" (1964 – 1970) and "*Accessions List, Indonesia, Malaysia, Singapore, and Bruner* (1971 – 1974).]

    2. Asma Ahmat. "*Malay Manuscripts and Malay Nineteenth-century Printed Books in the Library of Congress.*" Asian Division, Library of Congress, 1990. Photocopy. (Describes fifteen Jawi manuscripts, twenty-nine early printed books in Jawi, and a collection of forty-six handwritten letters from local principates to the British Resident of Singapore, 1819 – 1823, William Farquhar.)

    3. Fiedler, Lien Huong. "Adapting the Chinese model: Han Nom script and the development of Vietnamese literature =汉模越用：汉喃文字和越南文学." Unpublished paper presented at "The International Conference of Han Literature and Popular Cultures of the Southeast Asian Countries = Hội Thảo Khoa Học Quốc Tế vềVăn Học Chữ' Hán và Văn Hóa Dân Gian Khu Vữ'c Đong Nam Á" at Chengkung University, Tainan, Taiwan, March 22 – 24, 2007. 20 pages.

    4. Frederick, William H., and A. Kohar Rony. *Indonesia: A Select Reading Guide in English.* New York: Festival of Indonesia Foundation, 1991. (A subject guide for the nonspecialist reader. Includes books in English focused exclusively on Indonesia published within the last thirty years.)

    5. Gardner, Fletcher, and lldefonso Maliwanag. *Writings of the Mindoro-Palawan Axis.* 3 Vols. San Antonio: Witte Memorial Museum, 1939 – 1940. (Transliterates and translates texts on bamboo strips.)

    6. Harun Mat Piah. "Manuskrip-manuskrip Melayu dalam Koleksi Library of Congress Amerika." *Sari* (1987). pp. 3 – 15.

    7. Hibler, Anita, and William P. Tuchrello. *Burma: A Selective Guide to Scholarly Resources.* Washington, D. C.: Woodrow Wilson International Center for Scholars, 1986.

    8. Hibler, Anita, and William P. Tuchrello. *Burma: A Study Guide.* Washington, D. C.: Woodrow Wilson International Center for Scholars, 1987.

    9. Hobbs, Cecil C. *Southeast Asia Subject Catalog, Library of Congress.* 6 Vols. Boston: G. K. Hall, 1972. (A record of twenty-five years of LC acquisitions of Southeast Asian materials in the form of photocopied catalog cards containing descriptions of books, periodical titles, pamphlets, and other printed material.)

    10. Hobbs, Cecil C. *Indochina: A Bibliography of the Land and People.* Washington, D. C.: Library of Congress, 1950, index, pp. 367.

    11. "Indochina Studies Program Grants Collection: A Finding Aid." Processing Section, Motion Picture, Broadcasting, and Recorded Sound Division, Library of Congress, 1989 – .

Loose-leaf binder. (Indexes contents of audio and video records of interviews with recent immigrants from Indochina drawing upon their experiences in their homelands and their cultural heritage. Studies were sponsored by the Social Sciences Research Council beginning in 1983. Audio and video records are archived in the Library's Motion Picture, Broadcasting, and Recorded Sound Division.)

12. Johnson, Victoria E. "Vietnam on Film and Television: Documentaries in the Library of Congress." Motion Picture, Broadcasting, and Recorded Sound Division, Library of Congress, July 1989. Printout. (About four hundred items, chiefly American television programs and features. A few 1940 Nippon News programs from the Japanese collection. Some material dates from as early as 1901.)

13. Meinheit, Harold E. "Unveiling Vietnam: The Maps of Alexandre de Rhodes." *The Portolan*, 65 (Spring 2006), pp. 28 – 41.

14. Library of Congress Netherlands Studies Unit, *Netherlands East Indies: A Bibliography of Books Published After 1930 and Periodical Articles After 1932*. Washington, D. C.: Library of Congress, 1945, index, pp. 208.

15. Poe, Mya Thanda. "The Library of Congress Experience in Coordinating the Development of Collections in the United States." *JIAS Newsletter*. V. 15 (1998): pp 70 – 71.

16. Pruitt, William. "Addition to the Burmese Manuscripts in the Library of Congress, Washington, D. C." *Journal of the Pali Text Society*. V. 24 (1998): pp. 171 – 183. (Lists and describes an additional thirty-six manuscripts.)

17. Pruitt, William. "Burmese Manuscripts in the Library of Congress, Washington, D. C." *Journal of the Pali Text Society 1989*. pp. 1 – 31. (Lists and describes 124 Burmese Pali manuscripts.)

18. Rony, A. Kohar. "Malay Manuscripts and Early Printed Books at the Library of Congress," *Indonesia*. (1991) pp. 123 – 134.

19. Rony, A. Kohar. *Philippine Holdings in the Library of Congress, 1960 – 1987: A Bibliography*. Washington, D. C.: Library of Congress, 1992.

20. Rony, A Kohar. *Southeast Asia: Western-language Periodicals in the Library of Congress*. Washington, D. C.: Library of Congress, 1979.

21. Rony, A. Kohar. *Unveiling Indonesia, Indonesian Holdings in the Library of Congress: A Bibliography*. Washington, D. C.: Library of Congress, 1996.

22. Rony, A. Kohar. *Vietnamese Holdings in the Library of Congress: A Bibliography*. Washington, D. C.: Library of Congress, 1982.

23. Rony, A. Kohar. *Vietnamese Holdings in the Library of Congress, Supplement 1979 – 1985: A Bibliography*. Washington, D. C.: Library of Congress, 1987.

24. Rony, A. Kohar, and leda Siqueira Wiarda. *The Portuguese in Asia: Malacca, Moluccas, East Timor*. Hamburg: Abera Publishing House, 1997.

25. Teeuw, A. "Korte Mededelingen: Malay Manuscripts in the Library of Congress." *Bijdragen tot de taal-, land-, en volkenkunde* (1967). pp. 517 – 520.

26. Wellen, Kathryn Anderson. "Searching for the Malay World at the Library of Congress." Unpublished paper presented at an international colloquium ("Libraries and the Construction of Knowledge about the Malay World"), National University of Malaysia, August 2 – 3, 2004.

27. Wellen, Kathryn Anderson. "On Distant Shores: Library of Congress Collections Pertaining to the Pacific Islands." Unpublished paper presented at an international conference ("Hidden Treasures: Assessing Riches in Pacific Islands Collections") Center for Pacific Islands Studies, University of Hawaii at Manoa, Honolulu, March 15 – 16, 2007.

他山之石——向海外推广中文书的秘籍

Promotion of Chinese Books Outside China: Important Lessons

我演讲的内容是华文出版物在北美洲的市场预计，北美洲的市场包括美国和加拿大两个比较大的市场。在北美一般需要华文出版物的都是一些图书馆、学者、专家等等。现在在美国的东亚图书馆一共有78家，基本上都是大学的图书馆，在加拿大有8家。在这些图书馆里，北美洲最大的中文藏书，一个是美国国会图书馆有70多万册，哈佛有65万册左右，耶鲁大学有40多万册，哥伦比亚大学有30多万册，加州、洛杉矶大学有20多万册，这些数字可以大概地表明中文藏书的数量。在美国有一个机构叫图书馆人文机构，是属于美国的亚洲研究学会的一个附属机构。

除了刚才讲的大学图书馆之外，这几年因为在北美州的华文图书比例大量增加，美国的宪法修改以后，每年运到美国去的一些畅销的华文图书，都在一些大型的公共图书馆出现，比如波士顿的公共图书馆，还有洛杉矶、纽约等，都开始收集更多中文资料。政府机构的图书馆包括美国国会图书馆，还有一些国家农业图书馆、国家医学图书馆等。

现在很多留学生的父母担心自己孩子会忘记母语，他们很希望在外国能有更多的中文书籍出现，还有一些在外国工作的华人或者是懂中文的外国人、在外国出生的儿童。据统计，现在在美国的华人三四百万，在美国学中文的人超过了十万，并且这个数字还在不断地增加。还有中文的教学在美国越来越受欢迎，需要大量的教授中文的学者和机构。现在推广华文的教育已经越来越全面，很多美国的学校愿意接受中国政府提供给他们的基金，来提高从事中文教学的老师的中文水平。据我的了解，在国内也有很多关于中文教学的出版商，包括北京大学出版社、外语教学与研究出版社等。中国的外研社在2005年，推出了一个非常大的计划，这使对外汉语教育有了很大的提高。它计划在美国投入大约一千万人民币用于汉语的国际推广，使中国文化走出国门。

对国外选择华文图书来讲，是以图书馆来作为选择的标准，专门选择一些大家有兴趣的书籍。这是根据不同的图书馆自己对应的不同的读者来选择书籍的。第一选择社会科学、人文、历史等方面的资料；第二看作者的名字；第三看出版商、出版社的声誉。另外一个选书的依据是根据可靠的书评，有很多新书的书评都会在学术刊物上刊登。我知道还有两个可供选择的标准，就是在中国出版物推广到世界上去时，最好加上英文书名的解释和拼音，这样对选书的人来说如果不懂中文的话也可以凭着英文解释或者拼音来选择书籍；还有就是在书中最好用英文配上内容简介或者作者介绍，这样选书的人在选择书籍的时候能够更加了解这本书的内容。图书馆基本上是通过出版社或者书商来选择书籍的，图书馆会事先通知购书机构，说明所需要的书名或者书籍的类型，然后由书商帮忙购买并送到图书馆，图书馆也通过网上的一些资料来选择书籍。另外，图书馆也会通过派遣一些专家到国内来参加书展，挑选适合自己图书馆的书籍，所以我们也很希望国内举办大型书展的时候能够尽早通知我们，免得我们错过了机会。因为国外的图书馆在购买书籍之前都会做一个预算，所以我们如果能早点得知书展的时间，就能够早点做好预算。一般来讲美国的图书馆对书籍都会有这样几点要求：一是需要书中都有英文翻译或者注以拼音，二是图书馆希望中国的出版商在出版的时候，对书籍的纸张和简介都能够做得再精致一些；还有就是在这本书的扉页上最好能够提供这本书的相关的信息,那就可以为图书馆节省很多编务的工作。现在也有很多著名的期刊为了打进北美市场,不仅在期刊名字上打上拉丁文的名字,也打进了英文的名字。

下面我要讲一讲合作和沟通的重要性。中国出版商、出版社如果想走进北美,就要多多参加国际书展,对于美国来说对中文书比较感兴趣的,一个是美国图书馆年会的一个书展,一般在每年的六月份的第三个星期。我们中国来参加这个年会的很少,一般都只有两到三家,如果中国出版商想把华文出版物推进北美市场的话,那么希望多来参加这类书展。还有一个就是亚洲研究学会的年会,一般在每年的三月底四月初,出席这个年会的人员一般都是研究亚洲书籍的学者专家,所以多参加这类书展也可以对亚洲的华文出版有一个更好的了解。现在我发现国内已经有很多很大型的网上购书商店,一般人买书要是在书店买不到自己想要的书,他们就会上网寻找,而且价格更便宜,还能送货到家,现在比较有名的是"当当网上书店"、"卓越网上书店"。但是我认为中国的几个网上书店的取名和宣传不够,所以导致很多人都不是很明白有这样一个大型的购书网。

大家知道,在美国现在有三四百万华人,并且每年在增加,所以对外推广华文图书也是迫在眉睫。现在中国也在推广中国的文化,不仅在国内,最重要的是要面向世界。对这方面的推广我有个建议,希望在向国外推广的时候不仅有中文的文字推广,还应该加上英文的文字推广,因为在国外懂中文的人毕竟不多,所以如果只有中文推广的话,那么效果肯定不好。在美国出版的《出版商》,最近刊出世界排名前四十五位的出版商名单,中国只有一家出版社排在第 44 位。但我发现在这 45 家中有五家是日本的,希望下次我们中国的出版商能够排到世界的前列。但是也有另外的原因导致排名落后:第一是因为我们中国出版物的价格相对比较便宜;第二是我们的出版商基本规模都很小,竞争力不够,所以我希望我们的出版商能够团结起来,到国外去开拓市场。

我们中国的文化能够推广到国外去,这是一件很有意义的事情。我们要在不知不觉中把中国文化推广出去。我们中国的出版商要联合起来,一起来为中国文化的推广打造一个很好的团队,把握时机、开拓创新。同时也要让国外知道我们国内有很好的网上书店,让国外的人士能很方便的购买中文书籍。同时,政府的支持也是非常重要的。最后希望华文出版物能够走出国门,走向世界!

(原载《编辑学刊》2007 年第 6 期,第 6 - 8 页。)

美国国会图书馆建立全美的亚太美裔特藏

Building a National Asian Pacific American Collection in the Library of Congress, USA[①]

A New Initiative by the Library of Congress

In October 2007, a distinguished group of scholars in the field of Asian Pacific American Studies gathered in Washington D. C. to discuss and implement the establishment of a National Asian Pacific American Collection in the capitol of the United States. The historic deliberation was both a powerful statement and a determined rectification of what can be deemed as the country's profound neglect in gathering for historical posterity the scattered documentation of its Asian and Pacific Islander peoples, many of whom are in their 4th or 5th generation of residing in the United States of America.[②]

Ever since the late 18th century, there have been many waves of immigration of Asian Pacific people to Hawaii and the West Coast of the United States. In 1763, Filipinos established the small settlement of Saint Malo in present-day Louisiana. In 1778, many Chinese sailors came to Hawaii, the same year that Captain James Cook stumbled upon the island. During the 19th century, a number of Chinese, Korean, Japanese, and Filipino laborers were brought in to work on sugar plantations in Hawaii. In the mid-19th century, a larger number of Chinese and Japanese began immigrating to the U. S. to work in the gold mines and as laborers on the transcontinental railroad.

Ironically, a number of laws to curtail the influx of Asian immigrants were adopted by the government during those years, including, particularly, the Chinese Exclusion Act of 1882. There were also frequent anti-Chinese and anti-Asian violence as well as discriminatory taxation and treatment during that period. Despite the many negative factors, these early immigrants had not only endured the hardships, but also had made great contributions to the development of the American West.

The first Chinese Exclusion Act enacted by the U. S. Congress was in 1882. It was renewed for another 10 years in 1892 and when revisited in 1902, the Act was to remain law for an indefinite period. The Act was finally repealed in 1943 allowing a restricted number of 105 Chinese annually to enter the U. S. The long and bitter effects of this "yellow peril" attitude, the only one of its kind enacted towards a single immigrant group, ended in 1965. The year became the watershed year for Asians when the Immigration and Nationality Act Amendments of 1965 were enacted. The Amendments eliminated the highly restrictive "national origins" quotas and replaced all previous exclusionary immigration rules, thus allowing Asians to immigrate to the U. S. without prejudice.

A New Chapter in APA History

In a mere span of four and a half decades since 1965, the country is experiencing unprecedented growth in its Asian Pacific American population. Issues concerning Asian Pacific Americans have gained prominence within the U. S. Congress and the general public.

The 1990 Census was the first to have a separate "Asian or Pacific Islander" category. In the 1993 census report—***We the Americans: Asians***—the number of Asian and Pacific Islander

---

[①] 论文发表于《第四届海外华人研究与文献收藏机构国际合作会议——互动与创新：多维视野下的华侨华人研究》，由中国暨南大学与美国俄亥俄大学合办，2009年5月9-11日在广州暨南大学举行。

[②] Asian Pacific Americans (APA) is defined as the population living in the U. S. who self identify as having Asian or Pacific Islander ancestry, in whole or in part, regardless of whether they are U. S.- or foreign-born, a U. S. citizen or not, or length of residence.

population in the United States doubled from 1.5 million in 1970 to 3.7 million in 1980 to 7.3 million in 1990. The percentage of Asians and Pacific Islanders in the total population also nearly doubled during the 1980s, from 1.5 percent to 2.9 percent. ① According to the 2000 Census, 11.9 million people reported themselves as having either full or partial Asian heritage. This ethnic group comprised 4.2% of the U.S. population. 3 The latest figures released by the U.S. Census Bureau showed that in July 2007 there were 15.2 million Asians (about 5% of the total population② and 1 million Native Hawaiians and other Pacific Islanders (about 0.3% of the total population). Among the 15.2 million Asians, 3.54 million were Chinese, 3.05 million were Filipinos, 2.77 million were Asian Indians, 1.64 million were Vietnamese, 1.56 million were Koreans, and 1.22 million were Japanese. ③

Even though the Asian Pacific American population is the smallest of the four major ethnic groups in the country, their contributions to the country is far reaching and fast growing as the population expands. Asian Pacific Americans as a whole have the highest educational attainment and median household and median personal income of any racial demographic in the United States. Many of them have excelled in government, education, medicine, science/technology, business, military, arts, architecture, and sports. It is unprecedented that in the present administration, President Barack Obama appointed two prominent Chinese Americans to his cabinet.

As conditions improved, scholarly and archival interest in gathering and preserving historical records of Asian Americans and writings by and about them increased. A number of these early records and publications, be it comparatively small in number, began to be collected by the Library of Congress and by local historical societies, museums, ethnic associations, and centers for Asian American studies. In fact, since the establishment of the first Asian American Study program in San Francisco State University in 1969, many more followed. Currently there are 53 such programs in American colleges and universities. Most of them have made serious attempts to collect historical materials on Asian Pacific Americans.

In the 209 years' history of the Library of Congress, the number of publications relating to Americans of Asian ancestry and of Pacific Islander heritage has begun to grow after the 1960s. However, there has not been an organized effort nor a systematic approach to ensure that the Library has in its holdings historical records and primary materials of what is now collectively called "Asian Pacific Americans". In fact, some of the scattered archival documentations in private hands are at risk of being lost if they are not promptly identified, acquired, organized, and preserved.

Today, at the Library of Congress the Asian American Pacific Islander Collection is finally among the permanent designated collections housed in both the Library's Asian Division and in other areas of the Library according to their languages and formats. The entire collection is now under the overall coordination of the curator of the Asian Pacific American Collection who reports directly to the Chief of the Asian Division.

The Library's initiative on a nationwide level is to rectify the historical invisibility of a major segment of the U.S. population that has been growing rapidly in recent decades. The creation of an Asian Pacific American Collection will address the vacuum in American history and recognize the importance of Asian Pacific American contributions not merely at the state level or even at a regional level, East Coast or West Coast, but at the national level.

The Library of Congress: A Treasure House

The Library of Congress occupies a very special place in the nation's history. It is the nation's oldest federal cultural institution and functions both as the primary research arm of the United States Congress as well as the national library. The Library also operates the Copyright Office and

---

① Source: 1993 We the Americans: Asians. http://www.census.gov/apsd/wepeople/we-3.pdf
② Source: The Asian Population 2000. http://www.census.gov/prod/2002pubs/c2kbr01-16.pdf
③ Source: 2007 American Community Survey. http://factfinder.census.gov

the Nation's Law Library.

Its universal collections consist of 135 million items that include more than 34 million books and other printed materials, 6.2 million moving images, sound recordings and related documents, 13 million photographs, 5 million maps, and 59 million manuscripts. Through its Copyright Office and extensive overseas acquisitions, the Library adds more than two million items to its collection each year. More than 2.8 million of the 34 million books and other printed materials are in some 100 or more major Asian languages. The Asian Division of the Library of Congress, established in 1928, is the custodial and service division for this comprehensive research collection, which is the largest Asian collection in Asian languages outside of Asia.

The Library's mission is "to make its resources available and useful to the Congress and the American people and to sustain and preserve a universal collection of knowledge and creativity for future generations"①. Researchers and scholars from any part of the world are welcome to use the Library collections and its wide-range services, both onsite and online.

The Current Scope of the APA Collection

Most of the items in the Library's collections by and about Asian and Pacific Islander Americans are cataloged and classified with the Library of Congress classification numbers and subject headings, same as for other publications. Some of them may have different location designations in accordance with their languages and specific formats. Because the APA collection is scattered throughout the entire Library, it is difficult to have a precise count.

Furthermore, there are extensive non-classified APA holdings that can be located in some 26 areas, centers, divisions, or reading rooms of the Library. Some of these areas, including the Asian Division Reading Room and the Main Reading Room, are:

1. African & Middle Eastern Division Reading Room http://www.loc.gov/rr/amed/
2. American Folk Life Center http://www.loc.gov/rr/folklife/
3. American Memory http://memory.loc.gov/
4. Asian Division Reading Room http://www.loc.gov/rr/asian/
5. Business Reading Room http://www.loc.gov/rr/business/
6. Children's Literature Center http://www.loc.gov/rr/child/
7. Copyright Records Room http://www.copyright.gov/circs/circ23/
8. European Division Reading Room http://www.loc.gov/rr/european/
9. Federal Research Division http://www.loc.gov/rr/frd/
10. Geography & Map Division Reading Room http://www.loc.gov/rr/geogmap/
11. Hispanic Division Reading Room http://www.loc.gov/rr/hispanic/
12. Law Library http://www.loc.gov/rr/law/
13. Local History & Genealogy Reading Room http://www.loc.gov/rr/genealogy/
14. Main Reading Room http://www.loc.gov/rr/main/
15. Manuscript Division Reading Room http://www.loc.gov/rr/mss/
16. Microform Reading Room http://www.loc.gov/rr/microform/
17. Motion Picture & Television Reading Room http://www.loc.gov/rr/mopic/
18. National Audio-Visual Conservation Center http://www.loc.gov/avconservation/collections/
19. Performing Arts Reading Room http://www.loc.gov/rr/perform/
20. Prints & Photographs Division Reading Room http://www.loc.gov/rr/print/
21. Rare Book & Special Collections Reading Room http://www.loc.gov/rr/rarebook/
22. Recorded Sound Reference Center http://www.loc.gov/rr/record/
23. Science & Technology Reading Roo http://www.loc.gov/rr/scitech/
24. Serial & Government Publications Reading Room http://www.loc.gov/rr/news/

---

① Source: http://www.loc.gov/about/

25. Veterans' History Project http://www.loc.gov/vets
26. Virtual Programs & Services http://www.loc.gov/rr/program/

As a general rule, those cataloged and classified collections can be located by a search of the Online Catalog of the Library (http://catalog.loc.gov) by means of a variety of access points such as authors/creators, titles, subject headings, keywords, series/uniform titles, call numbers, ISSN, and ISBN, etc. The Library's Asian Division holds numerous publications in Asian languages specifically concerned with Asian migrations to the United States. In the general microform collections, there are a large number of monographs and serials, and hundreds of doctoral dissertations, in the microformat by and about Asian Pacific Americans.

For the many uncataloged items in many of the reading rooms, there exist finding tools, some of which are online bibliographies or lists. Interested readers are advised to visit the websites of these reading rooms as provided above and to examine the extent of the relevant collections; especially those related to Asian Pacific American subjects.

For digital collections and services, by searching the Library's website: http://www.lQc.gov/libary/libarch-digital.html, one can find a list of "Featured Digital Collections & Services", included among them is the historical documentation of the "Chinese in California-Multiformat – 1850 – 1945", As the description says:

The Chinese in California, 1850 – 1925 illustrates nineteenth and early twentieth century Chinese immigration to California through about 8,000 images and pages of primary source materials. Included are photographs, original art, cartoons and other illustrations; letters, excerpts from diaries, business records, and legal documents; as well as pamphlets, broadsides, speeches, sheet music, and other printed matter. These documents describe the experiences of Chinese immigrants in California, including the nature of inter-ethnic tensions. They also document the specific contributions of Chinese immigrants to commerce and business, architecture and art, agriculture and other industries, and cultural and social life in California. Chinatown in San Francisco receives special treatment as the oldest and largest community of Chinese in the United States. Also included is documentation of smaller Chinese communities throughout California, as well as material reflecting on the experiences of individuals. Although necessarily selective, such a large body of materials presents a foil spectrum of representation and opinion. The materials in this online compilation are drawn from collections at The Bancroft Library, University of California Berkeley; The Ethnic Studies Library, University of California Berkeley; and The California Historical Society, San Francisco.

Some Finding Tools for Chinese American Sources

If one were to begin from the beginning, so to speak, the Library of Congress provides some genealogical tools for Chinese Americans, but one needs to enter the right surname to find them. The tool for finding common Chinese surnames and their transliterations is:

http://www.loc.gov/rr/genealogy/bib_guid/sumames-country.htm

A bibliography prepared by the Library staff to help readers who seek guidance on how to approach genealogical research in one of the Asian countries is

http://www.loc.gov/rr/genealogy/bib_guid/foreignasia.htm

The following are two important works on Chinese American genealogy with their corresponding Library of Congress call numbers:

(i) ***China Connection: Finding Ancestral Roots for Chinese in America*** by Jeanie W. C. Low. 2nd ed. San Francisco: published by J. W. C. Low, c1993. E184. C5 L69 1993b. Call numbers for other editions are: E184. C5 L69 1993, E184. C5 L69 1994.

(ii) ***A Student's Guide to Chinese American Genealogy*** by Colleen She. Phoenix, Ariz.: published by Oryx Press, 1996. E184. C5 S47 1996.

Also available are some Chinese American genealogical works with local interest such as:

(i) ***From Kwang Tung to Kohala: Lineage of the Luke Family of Kohala, Hawaii*** by

Lillian Awai Lum, Warren K. K. Luke. [Hawaii]: published by LUKEs of Kohala, 1989. CS71. L953 1989.

(ii) ***Ewry and Cook Account Books, 1870 to 1876: a Portland, Oregon Undertaking Firm*** by Connie Lenzen. Portland, OR: published by C. Lenzen, [1989] F884. P853 A28 1989.

(iii) ***The Chinese in Astoria, Oregon, 1870 – 1880: a Look at Local Newspaper Articles, the Census, and Other Related Materials*** by Lisa Penner. Astoria, Oregon: published by L. Penner, 1990. F884. A8 P46 1990

Genealogical works for Chinese in other parts of the world and local histories as well, may provide useful information on Chinese Americans, too, as the latter may have ancestral links in these places.

(i) ***Major Genealogical Records Sources in Taiwan***, the Genealogical Department of the Church of Jesus Christ of Latter-Day Saints. Salt Lake City, Utah: The Department, 1976. CS1169. 5. M35 1976.

(ii) 台山县侨乡志, 原台山县志编写组编 陈田军, 黄仁夫, 黄仲楫执笔 [台山县]: 中共台山县委宣传部, 中共台山县委党史研究办公室, 台山县档案馆, published in 1985. DS793. T33C47 1985

Personal reminiscences about Chinese emigrants can be found in wenshi ziliao (文史资料) published in the districts mentioned above. There are index tools available for this group of limited-circulation (sometimes internal) publications.

In recent years, a number of Chinese genealogical works, ancestral hall records, and family documents were published in districts from where overseas Chinese originated (mainly in Guangdong and Fujian provinces). These publications were usually in small print-runs for limited circulation. They hardly find their way to libraries in the West.

Also in the Library of Congress are Chinese American family histories. "***Immigrant Arrivals: a Guide to Published Sources***" is an important guide prepared by the staff of the Library's Local History & Genealogy Reading Room. There is a publication listed in this guide that is relevant to Chinese American genealogy, entitled ***Chinese American Portraits. Personal Histories, 1828 – 1988***, authored by Ruthanne Lum McCunn and published in 1996 by the University of Washington Press. E184. C5 Ml 95 1996.

Another publication of interest is 从华侨到华人·二十世纪美国华人社会发展史 written by 麦礼谦 (H. Mark Lai) and published in Hong Kong by 三联书店 1992. E184. C5L35 1992.

Electronic Resources for Chinese Americans

A partial listing of electronic resources on genealogy and immigrants in the Library of Congress that may include Chinese entries are:

(i) Roger Daniels' ***Coming to America: a History of Immigration and Ethnicity in American Life*** contains a lengthy Selected Bibliography, http://www.loc.gov/catdir/toc/becities/genealogy/immigrant/89046524.refs.html Thirteen entries are directly related to Chinese Americans.

(ii) The table of contents of Lingchei Letty Chen's ***Writing Chinese: reshaping Chinese cultural identity*** can be accessed in http://www.loc.gov/catdir/enhancements/fy0625/2005053900-t.html

(iii) There is also an electronic version of ***Four Hundred Years of American Life and Culture: a List of Titles at the Library of Congress*** with a section on Asian immigrants at pages 90 – 94. http://www.loc.gov/rr/genealogy/bib_guid/400years.pdf

(iv) The table of contents of Mary Ellen Snodgrass' ***Amy Tan: a literary companion*** can be accessed at http://www.loc.gov/catdir/toc/ecip0419/2004014713.html

(v) The table of contents of Chieh Chieng's ***A long stay in a distant land: a novel*** is accessible at http://www.loc.gov/catdir/toc/ecip0419/2004015078.html

Americana Focus

Absent in other research centers in the U. S. and unique to the Library of Congress is its Asian American and Pacific Islander holdings found in the American Folk Life Center and in the Recorded Sound Division. Finding aids are in (SONIC), the Sound Online Inventory and Catalog. http://www.loc.gov/rr/record//Sonicmtro.html

In these two divisions, the growing cultural contributions and oral experiences expressed by Asian American and Pacific Islanders are retained by way of presentations, such as ethnic dance, music, performance, oral history, and poetry readings in conjunction with the Smithsonian Institute's annual Folk Life Festival.

The Topical Overview in American Memory covers the Chinese during the Westward Expansion; San Francisco's Chinatown: Architectural Space; San Francisco's Chinatown: Business & Politics; and San Francisco's Chinatown: Community Outsiders Looking In on Chinese Communities.

The Library's Asian Pacific American collection is also especially strong in the areas of history, ethnicity, and immigration studies, particularly for the larger Asian American groups: Chinese Americans, Filipino Americans, Japanese Americans and Korean Americans. Extensive collections of government documents-historical, legal and contemporary-provide useful primary data.

Accessible in the Library of Congress at http://www.loc.gov/rr/law/ are legal resources on Chinese immigration, immigration administration, Chinese exclusion, racial anxiety in the United States during 1848 – 1882, Chinese legal status, laws, cultural assimilation, emigration and immigration in California, race relations, San Francisco's anti-Chinese ordinances, 1850 – 1900.

The APA Primary Holdings Initiative

There is now a concerted effort to increase the Library's Asian Pacific American primary data holdings through an extensive outreach to individuals, families, communities and cultural organizations nationwide. Significant acquisitions of private collections have increased since the National Conference to Establish the Asian Pacific American Center at the Library of Congress, Oct. 4 – 5, 2007.

Little is known of the personal lives in the early Chinese communities in the U. S. Pacific Northwest or in the West Coast. Most of the data available are from government documents and Census reports that relate to agricultural migrant labor statistics of who worked the sugarcane harvest in Hawaii, and temporary recruits who manned the canneries in Alaska.

In fiction writing and in the familiar language of the memoir, the ordinary lives of Asians are underscored by the early knowledge that they were different; that their existence was separated from those of their Caucasian counterparts; and that Asian families prized the value of educational achievement to its highest levels. The outbreak of the Second World War became the great leveler: It broke down racial barriers due to the Army's need for new recruits and the marginalized groups' need to prove their patriotism towards their new homeland.

Since 2007, the Library has been very pleased to receive several major donations of great importance to the APA collection. The most notable one is **the Betty Lee Sung Collection.**

Betty Lee Sung, Professor Emerita and former Chair of the Department of Asian Studies at City College of New York, is the chair of the Asian American/Asian Research Institute and a recognized pioneer and leading authority on Chinese Americans studies. Throughout her distinguished career in teaching and research, Prof. Sung has written many books on Chinese Americans. Her first book, **Mountain of Gold**, published by Macmillan in 1967, pioneered the study of the history of the Chinese in America and is regarded as a classic in Asian American studies.

Prof. Sung followed with seven other books on Chinese Americans, among them: ***The Story of the Chinese in America* (1971) *The Chinese in America* (1973), *Survey of Chinese American Manpower and Employment* (1976), *Album of Chinese Americans* (1977),**

Statistical Profiles of the Chinese in the United States (*1979*), *Adjustment Experience of Chinese Immigrant Children in New York City* (*1987*), *and Chinese American Intermarriage* (*1990*). In 1994, two years after her retirement from City College, she completed a database of the Chinese immigrant records in the New York Region National Archives. The database enables scholars to recreate the early history of the Chinese in this country and has become a fertile source for genealogical research.

In support of the idea of establishing an Asian Pacific American Collection at the Library of Congress, Prof. Sung decided to donate to the Library her Asian American collection which she accumulated during the last 50 or so years. The collection consists of approximately 600 monographs, including her own publications, 100 or so conference proceedings, and yearbooks, directories, historical photographs, newspapers and newspaper clippings (before the onset of the Internet) and articles, dated as early as the beginning of the 20th century up to 2005. Also included in the collection are the early newsletters of Asian American organizations. The scarcity of some of the early newspapers from various cities, which had only very short runs, or had only the first issues, may represent the only records from the early periods and the only clues to scholars providing a glimpse of Asian American, especially Chinese American, activities of the times.

Prof. Sung's collection as a microcosm of the Chinese American experience is evident. It focuses on the sociological impact of Chinese assimilation into America's mainstream by inclusion of discussions and reports tangential to the intermarriage issue, generational conflicts, the proliferation of Chinatowns as either conclaves, communities or ghettos, the fight to include Asian American studies into the university curricula, empowerment through social and fraternal organizations and the Chinese American contributions to the U. S. economy.

Other notable collections are: The Jade Snow Wong Collection, The Carlos Bulosan Archives, The James Miho Conceptual Diaries, The Royal Morales Collection, and the records of U. S. -bound refugees contained in VOICE (Vietnamese Overseas Initiative for Conscience Empowerment).

Plan of Actions

In order for the Library of Congress to serve as the national APA collection, planning is underway to launch a series of coordinated actions:

· Consult with all interested parties to develop national and regional strategies for the creation of a distributed and networked national APA collection.

· Build partnership with APA studies programs, library collections, archives, museums, organizations, communities, and individuals.

· Develop effective communication and outreach programs.

· Conduct a nationwide survey of all APA collections and create an online directory.

· Work with OCLC (Online Computer Library Center) to create an online union catalog of all APA collections held by OCLC member libraries worldwide. It will be a subset of OCLC's WorldCat.

· Develop a comprehensive collection development policy and procedure.

· Plan to acquire all available and relevant APA resources including ephemera, personal papers, community records, organization archives, and oral histories in various formats.

· Establish a workable plan for cooperative acquisitions, preservation, digitization, and resource sharing among all APA collections.

· Participate in the Library's "American Memory", "American Chronicle: Historical American Newspapers", "American Veterans", and "American Folklife" projects to ensure more APA materials are included.

· Investigate the possibility of launching an APA oral history project across the country.

· Increase the on-line presence to include texts, videos, audio clips, photographs and research aids as well as state-of-the-art media that facilitate the use and interpretation of APA historical documents.

· Launch a concerted fund-raising effort to raise major endowment funds in support of APA projects and collection.

Above is a current "to-do" list envisioned by the APA Collection of the Library of Congress. Additional action items will be added as dictated by new opportunities and needs.

The building of the nation's Asian Pacific American Collection cannot be delayed nor procrastinated over for a more propitious time. It is imperative that Asians and Pacific Islanders as communities are made aware of the importance of legacy-building for the generations who will be eager to unearth the hidden history of their forefathers who arrived as immigrants and struggled to make permanent their rights as citizens of the United States of America.

(原载《第四届海外华人研究与文献收藏机构国际合作会议——互动与创新：多维视野下的华侨华人研究文集》，由中国暨南大学与美国俄亥俄大学合办，2009年5月9－11日.)

美国国会图书馆藏有关中国东北与日本的历史文献①

Historical Resources on Northeast China and Japan in the Library of Congress

美国国会图书馆创办于1800年。今天它不仅是美国国会的图书馆，同时也是服务美国人民的国家图书馆。它的馆藏总数是1.38亿册，是世界上最大、馆藏增加量最高的图书馆。从创馆之初，国会图书馆就致力于建立一个包罗世界各国、各地文明和知识精华的馆藏。

国会图书馆中文和日文藏书的开始可以追溯到1869年及1875年。在1867年国会通过了国际书籍交换法案之后，中国清朝的同治皇帝在1869年就首先赠送了933册中文线装书。六年之后，1875年，日本政府也正式与国会图书馆建立了政府出版书籍的交换。

从1869年到现在，经过了140年的努力，国会图书馆亚洲部目前拥有在中国大陆、台湾及日本之外最好的中文及日文藏书。这两个藏书的总数是221多万。根据2009年6月最新的统计，馆藏中文书有1,035,164册，馆藏日文书有1,175,498册。中文期刊总数量是16,170种（持续订购的期刊有5,208种），日文期刊总数量是15,794种（持续订购的期刊有6,343种）。中文缩微胶卷17,739卷，日文11,901卷，中文缩微平片23,199片，日文缩微平片21,345片。除此以外，中日文组还订购了很多主要的全文数据库。

亚洲部及书目提要

国会图书馆的亚洲部成立于1928年，早期名为中文部，三年以后改为中日文部。1932年再改为东方部并作地域上的扩充。最后于1978年定名为现在的亚洲部。亚洲部的藏书目前分为五个地区：中国及蒙古、日本、韩国（韩国与朝鲜）、东南亚及南亚。除了亚洲部的收藏外，法律图书馆、地理及地图部、图片及照片部、电影及录音部、音乐部、手稿部、西文馆藏部及特类书籍部也收藏了很多关于亚洲的文献资料。总馆藏1.38亿册/件中包括了不同类型和470种不同的语言的文献资料。大概有3,700万种书目可以在图书馆的网上目录中（http://catalog.loc.gov/）查到。除此之外，不同的部门也编印了一些特别的馆藏书目供读者使用。下面是几个关于中国东北和日本在20世纪上半期文献资料的目录：

《旧满洲国关系资料》（Kyu Manshukoku Kankei Shiryo）②

《韩国：远东文字资料解题书目》（Korea：An Annotated Bibliography of Publications in Far Eastern Languages）③

《满洲：解题书目》（Manchuria：An Annotated Bibliography）④

---

① 此文曾于2004年10月27-30日在日本新潟大学举办的中国东北与日本研究的历史文献国际研讨会上宣读，正式发表时有部分更改。

② Imura, Tetsuo. Ky Manshkoku kankei shiryo [Shinky, etc.：Manshkoku, etc. 1932-1944].

③ Beal Edwin George. Korea：an annotated bibliography of publications in Far Eastern languages（Washington：Library of Congress. Reference Dept, 1950）

④ Berton, Peter. Manchuria：an annotated bibliography（Washington：Library of Congress. Reference Dept., 1951）.

《日本外务省档案目录清单，1868—1945. 国会图书馆制作的缩微胶卷，1949—1951》（Checklist of Archives in the Japanese Ministry of Foreign Affairs, Tokyo, Japan, 1868—1945. Microfilmed for the Library of Congress 1949—1951）①

《日本政府文件及被查禁的出版物：缩微胶卷馆藏目录清单》（Japanese Government Documents and Censored Publications：A Checklist of the Microfilm Collection）②

《1946年前被查禁的日文期刊：缩微胶卷馆藏目录清单》（Censored Japanese Serials of the Pre-1946 Period：A Checklist of the Microfilm Collection）③

除了以上由国会图书馆出版的关于中国东北与日本的文献资料目录之外，以下是一些由其他机构出版的目录：

《日本共产党：日文解题书目》（Japanese Communism：An Annotated Bibliography of Japanese Publications）④

《东南亚：日文书籍解题选目》（Southeast Asia：Selected Annotated Bibliography of Japanese Publications）⑤

《日本左倾社会运动：解题书目》（Leftwing Social Movements in Japan：An Annotated Bibliography）⑥

《日本陆、海军及其他政府机构档案选目，1868—1945：缩微胶卷目录清单》（Check List of Microfilm Reproductions of Selected Archives of the Japanese Army, Navy and other Government Agencies 1868—1945）⑦

《南满铁道株式会社研究项目，1907—1945：历史与书目》（The Research Activities of the South Manchurian Railway Company, 1907—1945：History and Bibliography）⑧

《旧殖民地关系机关刊行物总合目录》（Union Catalogue of Publications by the Former Colonial Institutions）⑨

《米国议会图书馆所藏战前亚洲关系日本语逐次刊行物目录》（An Annotated List of Japanese Periodicals on Pre-War Asia：The Holdings of the Library of Congress）⑩

《满洲关系和汉书件名目录》（A Catalogue of Manchu Relations and Chinese Books）⑪

《米国议会图书馆所藏满洲语文献目录》（A Catalogue of Manchu Materials in the Library

---

① Uyehara, Cecil H. Checklist of archives in the Japanese Ministry of Foreign Affairs, Tokyo, Japan, 1868—1945. Microfilmed for the Library of Congress 1949 – 1951（Washington：Library of Congress, Photoduplication Service, 1954）.

② Yoshimura, Yoshiko. Japanese government documents and censored publications：a checklist of the microfilm collection（Washington：Library of Congress, 1992）.

③ Yoshimura, Yoshiko. Censored Japanese serials of the pre-1946 period：a checklist of the microfilm collection（Washington：Library of Congress, 1994）.

④ Langer, Paul F. Japanese communism：an annotated bibliography of works in the Japanese language, with a chronology, 1921 – 52（New York, International Secretariat, Institute of Pacific Relations, 1953）.

⑤ Irikura, James K. Southeast Asia：selected annotated bibliography of Japanese publication（New Haven：Southeast Asia Studies, Yale University, in association with Human Relations Area Files, 1956）.

⑥ Uyehara, Cecil H. Leftwing social movements in Japan：an annotated bibliography（Tokyo, Rutland, Vt., C. E. Tuttle Co., 1959）.

⑦ Young, John. Checklist of microfilm reproductions of selected archives of the Japanese Army, Navy and other government agencies, 1868—1945（Washington, Georgetown University Press, 1959）.

⑧ Young, John. The research activities of the South Manchurian Railway Company, 1907— 1945：a history and bibliography（New York, ：East Asian Institute, Columbia University, 1966）.

⑨ 《旧殖民地関係機関刊行物総合目録》（Union Catalogue of Publications by the Former Colonial Institutions）アジア経濟研究所図書資料部編纂.（東京：アジア経濟研究所 Institute of Developing Economies, 1973—1979）5卷.（卷1：台湾編；卷2：朝鮮編；卷3：満洲国—关东州編；卷4：満鉄編；卷5：索引編）.

⑩ Imura, Tetsuo. 米国議会図書館所藏戰前期アジア関係日本語逐次刊行物目録（東京：アジア経済研究所, 1995）.

⑪ 満鉄図书馆業務研究会, 満洲関係和漢書件名目録（大連：満鉄図书馆業務研究会, 1935）.

of Congress：Xylographs-Manuscripts-Archive5）①

中国东北与日本之历史文献

当第二次世界大战在 1945 年结束时，大量的日文战时文献，其中包括政府公文、书刊、电影及其他文件等，被联军统帅部在 1945—1952 年间没收。这些书刊资料及文献大部分是从日本陆军省、海军省、内务省的思想控制警察局、东京警视厅、南满州铁道株式会社东京分社、东亚经济调查局及东亚研究所等机构收集来的。

另外，在占据期间，近 7,000 多种日本出版品被认为是宣传军国主义、扩张主义的都从出版商、书商、发行商、批发商及其他商业性机构全部没收。可是没有从任何大学、学校、公家或私人图书馆、私人住宅没收书刊②。

那些从南满洲铁道株式会社、东亚经济调查局及东亚研究所拿到的大部分书刊资料都是研究关于中国东北（满洲）、中国别的地区、（包括台湾地区），及韩国、蒙古和太平洋地区的。

在 1945 年，这一批数量颇大的书刊资料最初是由美国陆海军的华盛顿文献中心（Washington Document Center-WDC）在东京的先头部队收纳整理。这个项目是在当时美国作战部的军事情报单位及美国海军部海军情报室作为情报分析和收集有关战犯的资料以作为审判战犯的根据。在 1946 年，华盛顿文献中心开始将这些书刊资料运回华府并将其中一部分送交国会图书馆，同时也将档案文献送去国家档案馆。据记录，从 1946 到 1950 年，国会图书馆收到 40 万本书刊资料，其中一些重复书刊则转赠给耶鲁大学、哥伦比亚大学、密歇根大学、西北大学、加州大学伯克利校区、斯坦福大学、克拉蒙学院及琉球大学等。另外一些是过时无甚研究价值的自然科学和技术书刊，只能作为历史参考。最后剩下的 16.5 万册是这批书刊资料中最好的一部分③，这些书刊资料的大部分都已经整理编目，由日文组收藏。在整理过程中发现有几百袋档案文件，亦移交至国家档案馆。

在 1958 年美国国家档案馆把部分档案资料归还日本政府。在没有归还前一年，一个特别的缩微胶卷制作小组仓促成立，由哥伦比亚大学的教授韦慕庭（Clarence M. Wilbur）担任组长。这个小组的目的是将一小部分经过挑选的档案做成 163 卷胶卷（约四十余万页）④。文件被制成胶卷的有日本对中国义和团之乱和 1911 至 1912 年革命的情报报告、日本陆海军在不同冲突和战役中的活动及日本政府在发动太平洋战争时的行动，其他有价值的历史文献如明治天皇（1868—1912 年在位）时期的军事记录、1919 年韩人暴动事件、1931 年的沈阳事件及在东北延续发生的事件和 1939 年洛门汉事件（Nomonhan Incident）。这些文献当时多半被日本政府视为秘密文件⑤。在 20 世纪 60、70 年代国会图书馆继续将大量的文献做成缩微胶卷。在 1974 年 11 月 20 日，日本议会图书馆和国会图书馆还签了合约，订定互相交换馆藏华盛顿文献中心的文献资料的缩微胶卷。

关于国会图书馆馆藏华盛顿文献中心的胶卷可参考吉村敬子的《日本政府文件及被查禁的出版物：缩微胶卷馆藏目录清单》及《1946 年前被查禁的日文期刊：缩微胶卷馆藏

---

① 松村潤，米國議會圖書館所藏滿洲語文獻目錄（東京：東北アジア文獻研究會，1999）
② 吉村敬子（Yoshiko Yoshimura）编．1956 年前被查禁的日文期刊：微缩胶卷馆藏目录清单（Censored Japanese Serials of the Pre-1946 Period：A Checklist of the Microfilm Collec-tion）华盛顿：国会图书馆亚洲部日文组．1994，第 219 页。
③ 日文组组长清水修（Osamu. Shimizu）1958 年 6 月 9 日的公文。
④ 吉村敬子（1994）．第 220 页。该委员会会员有：哥伦比亚大学的 Martin Wilbur 和 James Morley，耶鲁大学的 Chitoshi Yanaga、哈佛大学的 Edwin O. Reischauer、乔治城大学的杨觉勇及 LC 的艾允表（Edwin G. Beal）。
⑤ 吉村敬子（1994）．第 225 页。

目录清单》。这两本目录前面已经提过，以下是扼要大纲：

第一个目录是国会图书馆馆藏1954年之前日本政府文件及被政府查禁出版物的缩微胶卷，这部分馆藏主要包括日本内务省思想控制警察局的档案和查禁的书刊，同时也包括几千册南满铁路的资料①。

第二个目录是1946年之前被查禁的日文期刊缩微胶卷。这部目录分成两部分，并有两个附录及四个索引。

第一部分包括华盛顿文献中心期刊目录及个别期刊介绍。这些期刊已于1990年分类编目并做成缩微胶卷。这些期刊原来是在内务省的馆藏里并在1946年以前经过政府审查。这些期刊缩微胶卷的编号是"MOJ76"（44卷胶卷，包括1924到1944年出版的976期、742种期刊）。这些期刊都是在日本出版的，其中两个期刊是中文，一个期刊是韩文，其他都是日文。这些期刊多半有政府检查印章，可分成四类："审查通过或没有疑问"、"警告"、"除去用词或段句"和"禁止流通"。虽然这些期刊的内容非常广泛，但经常讨论的是政治、行政、日本与其他国家之间的外交和军事关系及现代日本的经济、贸易等议题②。

第二部分包括其他1946年前被政府查禁的期刊。这些期刊是曾经被国会图书馆在不同时间根据不同需要做成缩微胶卷的华盛顿文献中心资料。胶卷号码MOJ16及MOJ75则列于1992年的《日本政府文件及被查禁的出版物：缩微胶卷馆藏目录清单》，胶卷号码MOJ73，共八卷，内含76种期刊，记载了右倾人士的思想与活动。而胶卷号码MOJ74共八卷，内含90种期刊，大部分则记载了左倾人士的政治思想与活动③。

附录I是一份修改过的华盛顿文献中心的描述以及在日文组收藏的该中心的文献资料。附录II分为两部分，第一部分包括从弗吉尼亚州诺福克市（Norfolk）的麦克阿瑟将军纪念馆挑选出联军统帅部部分文献档案所制作的缩微胶卷。第二部分包括从东京日本议会图书馆缩微胶片馆藏中挑选出来再复制的缩微胶卷。这些复印版的原件则藏于美国国家档案馆马里兰州瑞兰市（Suitland）的咨询部④。

至于这个目录的四个索引则是：人名索引、出版单位索引、主题索引及刊名索引。

值得注意的是，这两个目录中所记载的书刊文献都备有35毫米的缩微胶卷。胶卷可外借也可以在国会图书馆的复印部购买。

南满洲铁道株式会社（或满铁会社）

另外一个华盛顿文献中心重要的收藏就是当年半官方机构南满洲铁道株式会社东京分社的书刊文献，对这些文献作过极为详细调查的学者杨觉勇（John Young）用英文写了一本《南满铁道株式会社研究项目，1907—1945：历史与书目》（The Research Activities of the South Manchurian Railway Company, 1907—1945: A History and Bibliography），由哥伦比亚大学东亚研究所在1966年出版。

据估计，在1945年日本投降的时期，满铁在东京的分社共藏有10万册的书刊资料，其中有3万册是西文书刊。来到国会图书馆的大约有6万册，其中2.5万册已归纳入日文组藏书，其他3.5万册多半是中文、韩文及西文书刊，已送去了中文、韩文、及西文组收藏。有些还分配给法律图书馆、地理及地图部、图片及照片部、电影及录音部等。其他多

---

① 吉村敬子（1994）。第vii页。
② 吉村敬子（1994）。第vii—viii页。
③ 吉村敬子（1994）。第viii—ix页。
④ 吉村敬子（1994）。第ix页。

余的版本则送到美国及琉球大学的东亚图书馆。

在这些满铁资料中，凡有中、韩文字的文件夹在日文中的，都已分别送到中、韩组。根据1959及1960的两个馆内文件，共有1,141册中文及89册韩文资料分别送到中、韩文组收藏，其中有两个中文文件是很有历史价值的：

《中国共产党扩大执行委员会决议案，中国现时的政局与共产党的职任议决案（1925年10月）》（Resolution of the Expanded Executive Committee of the Chinese Communist Party. Resolution on the Current Chinese Political Situation and the Responsibilities of the Communist Party. October 1925）油印件。

《中国共产青年团中央局扩大会议的经过与意义（1928年1月13日）》，弼时记录。(The Process and Meaning of the Expanded Meeting of the Central Bureau of the Chinese Communist Youth Corp, January 13, 1928)。油印件。

满铁是在1906年成立的。成立的原因是根据日俄战争（1904—1905）的停战协定将由俄国占有的中国东部铁路权转交给日本。这段铁路原有1,128公里的轨道，因迅速的扩张，满铁变成在中国东北规模最大的经济企业，也是日本深入中国的大本营。从一开始，日本政府就紧紧掌握满铁，供给满铁一半的基金，同时又有权力制定规则控制其财政。日本政府又有权任命总裁及副总裁。如必要又可发令决定满铁的商务，考察其行政人员的行动。同时日本的关东军有权控制满铁的警察及铁路监管。在整个满铁的存在期间，它实际上控制了东北的经济命脉，如铁路、煤矿、工业等。在战争期间满铁更发展到东北以外的地方[①]。

根据杨觉勇书中的报道，对满铁当时有三种研究。第一种是研究日本感兴趣的地方的经济、社会及文化。这些地方包括中国、西伯利亚及其他亚洲地区。第二种包括自然科学及应用科学，如物理学、化学、地质学、农业、植物学、卫生学、气象学及细菌学。第三种是与满铁业务有关的商业及统计题材。满铁的研究中心最盛时期有三百多位研究人员，完成了6,200项研究报告及内部文件，代表了20世纪顶尖的知识库之一[②]。在1945年二次大战末期满铁经过一个短暂的俄军占领时期，书刊资料及其他资产被掠夺一空，满铁主权最后终由中国收回。

依照当年日文组组长黑田（Andrew Y. Kuroda）在1967年7月6日的报告说："在1942年3月大连图书馆及三个满铁分社的馆藏共有524,396册。这些馆藏在东北被俄军于1945年8月控制期间，都被运去了俄国。这些书刊资料的质与量都远比东京分社的书刊资料好得多"[③]。

国会图书馆所收藏的满铁书刊资料是从东京分社转来的。日本国家议会图书馆在1984年已将在日本找不到的3,270种文献做成缩微胶卷，让两馆读者使用。

其他关于中国东北与日本的馆藏

国会图书馆的日文组除了收藏由华盛顿文献中心转来大量有关中国东北与日本及南满铁道的书刊文献之外，本身也收藏了很多这方面的日文书刊资料。其他的部门像中文组、韩文组及西文部等也收藏了很多中、韩、西文关于20世纪上半叶中国东北与日本及南满铁道的书刊资料。大部分这类的书刊资料可以在国会图书馆的联网目录上查到（网址：

---

① 杨觉勇（John Young）南满铁道株式会社之研究，1907—1945：历史及书目，(1966)。第1页。
② 杨觉勇（1966）。第1页。
③ 吉村敬子（1994）。第222页。

http://catalog.loc.gov)。另外,读者也可以在 OCLC(Online Computer Library Center)的联合目录上(http://www.worldcat.org)查寻国会图书馆及其他图书馆所收藏的有关资料。

(原载《北美中国学:研究概述与文献资源》(*Chinese Studies in North American-Research & Resources*),张海惠主编,中华书局 2010 年出版,第 787-794 页。)

美国国会图书馆东亚收藏的历史：书目指南

A History of the East Asian Collections in the Library of Congress: A Bibliographic Guide

The Library of Congress was established by an act of the United States Congress in 1800. One year after invading British troops destroyed the initial collection in 1814, the Congress acquired the personal collection of retired president Thomas Jefferson, totaling 6,487 books. In offering his collection to the Congress, Jefferson addressed the great scope of his collection, which included English and foreign language editions of books on a number of topics in the humanities, social sciences, and physical sciences, when he wrote, "I do not know that it contains any branch of science which Congress would wish to exclude from their collection; there is, in fact, no subject to which a member of Congress may not have occasion to refer."[1] It was with this spirit of inclusiveness that the Library of Congress later began to develop its comprehensive East Asian collections.

In 1869, the Tongzhi emperor of China presented the Library of Congress with 10 major Chinese works in 933 volumes. This was soon followed by an exchange of government publications with the Japanese government in 1875.[2] From these early beginnings, the East Asian holdings have expanded to include East Asian monographs and periodicals, important collections of legal materials, maps, music, motion pictures, prints, and photographs of East Asia. Many of these materials are collected and cared for by the Asian Division in collaboration with other divisions within the Library of Congress, including the Law Library, the Geography and Map Division, the Prints and Photographs Division, the Motion Picture, Broadcasting, and Recorded Sound Division, the Performing Arts Division, the Manuscript Division, and the American Folklife Center.

In 1928, Herbert Putnam, then librarian of Congress (1899 – 1939), helped establish the Division of Chinese Literature. Three years later, in 1931, the name was changed to the Division of Chinese and Japanese Literature, and in 1932, it was renamed the Division of Orientalia, and the geographic and linguistic scope of its holdings was expanded. The division was renamed the Asiatic Division in 1942, and again changed, to the Orientalia Division, in 1944. Finally, its current name, Asian Division, was adopted in 1978.[3] Arthur W. Hummel Sr. (1884 – 1975) served as the division chief from 1928 to 1954.

The Chinese and Mongolian Collection consists, as of September 30, 2008, of 1,011,816 monographic volumes and 5,090 current serial titles. In addition to Chinese language works, it includes several thousand volumes in Manchu, Mongol, Naxi (Moso), Tibetan, and other minority languages in China[4]. The collection covers a comprehensive range of subjects and is especially strong in the humanities and social sciences, including classical Chinese literature, archival materials of the Qing dynasty and Republican period, traditional Chinese medicine, local and regional histories (gazetteers), and contemporary publications of Mainland China and Taiwan.

The collection also contains some of the most valuable rare books from China and Mongolia. Chinese rare holdings date back to the Song, Jin, Yuan, Ming, and Qing dynasties, and include such items as the Buddhist invocation sutra *Yi qie ru lai* (《一切如来》), a 975 C. E.

---

[1] *The Thomas Jefferson Building of the Library of Congress* (Washington, D. C.: Library of Congress, 2003), 1 – 2.
[2] *The Asian Division* (Washington, D. C.: Library of Congress, 2002), 1, 2, 4, 8.
[3] Chi Wang, *The Chinese Collection in the Library of Congress: A Brief Introduction* (Washington, D. C.: Chinese Section, Asian Division, Library of Congress, 2001), 5 – 6.
[4] The collection of Uyghur materials is kept in the Near East Section of the African and Middle Eastern Division.

manuscript discovered in 1924 in the foundation of the Thunder Peak Pagoda (雷峰塔); 41 of the 400 extant volumes of the 1560 edition of *Yongle dadian* (《永乐大典》, Great Encyclopedia of the Ming Emperor Yongle era); and the 1895 – 98 *Gu jin tu shu ji cheng* (《古今图书集成》, Complete collection of illustrations and writings past and present). Other unique holdings include 3,344 pictographic manuscripts from the Naxi minority group of Yunnan Province, acquired by Joseph Rock and Quentin Roosevelt; the Arthur W Hummel collection of rare Chinese maps; and the Willam Gamble collection of the nineteenth-century American Presbyterian Missionary Press, which was established by Gamble in Ningbo and Shanghai in 1858 – 1860 and which produced Christian publications in Chinese as well as translations of Western works. [1]

The Library of Congress is one of the world's leading centers for Tibetan publications, with holdings covering Tibetan literature from the eighth century to the present day, including religious texts, biographies, musical notations, grammars, secular literature, and works on history, traditional medicine, astrology, iconography, and social sciences. Holdings of Tibetan Buddhist scriptures are especially strong, with over 10 volumes of Kanjur texts and approximately 225 volumes of Tanjur commentaries. The individuals who developed the earliest Tibetan collection include William Woodville Rockhill, the American diplomat and Tibetologist who travels in Mongolia and Tibet in the late nineteenth and early twentieth century, Berthold Laufer, another leading Tibetologist in the late 1800s, and Joseph Rock, the colorful explorer, adventurer, and scientist who lived and traveled in China's rugged west for twenty-seven years in the early 1900s. [2]

The library's Mongolian collection includes complete reprint editions of the Mongolian Kanjur canonicl texts and Tanjur commentaries. Maintenance of the Mongolian collection is a multinational effort, with new acquisitions managed by Ulaanbaatar bibliographic representatives, and microfilming of periodicals handled by the library's New Delhi field office.

The Japanese collection began to expand offer the Library of Congress arranged an exchange of government publications with the Japanese government in 1875. In 1905, a significant gift from Crosby Stuart Noyes, a journalist and editor of the *Washington Evening Star*, established the Noeys collection, which includes 658 illustrated books produced from the mid-eighteenth century to the late nineteenth. In 1907, Kan'ichi Asakawa (朝河贯一) (1873 – 1948) of Yale University launched a systematic effort to purchase Japanese books for the Library of Congress. Thanks to his work, the library acquired approximately 9,072 titles on Japanese history, literature, Buddhism, Shinto, geography, music, and the arts. Under the stewardship of Shiho Sakanishi, appointed in 1930 as chief assistant in the Japanese Section, the collection tripled in size from 1930 to 1941. As of 2008, the Japanese collection contained 1,172,234 volumes of monographs and 6,102 current serial titles, making it the largest collection in the Asian Division.

Among Japanese rare holdings are approximately 5,000 titles of publications and manuscripts produced before 1868 Meiji Restoration, including *Hyakumantō darani* (百万搭陀罗尼) prayer charms, printed in 770 CE, making them among the world's earliest surviving printed materials. Also noteworthy is a complete edition of *Genii monogatari* (《源氏物语》, Tale of Genji) published in Kyoto in 1654, and the *Yoshitsune azuma kudari monogatari* (义经东下り物语) printed with movable type between 1624 and 1643. A complete catalog of the Japanese rare books in the Library of Congress was published in 2003 by Yagi Shoten (八木书店) in Tokyo. [3]

At the end of World War II, the Washington Document Center donated a large number of historical documents confiscated from the former Japanese Imperial Army and Navy and the South Manchurian Railway Company, many of them pre-World War II Japanese studies of Korea, Taiwan, Mainland China, Mongolia, and the Pacific islands. The library also acquired a microfilm

---

[1] *The Chinese Collection* (Washington, D. C.: Asian Division, Library of Congress, n. d.). Most of the rare Chinese maps are kept in the Geography and Map Division of the library.

[2] *The Tibetan Collection* (Washington, D. C.: Asian Division, Library of Congress, 2002).

[3] *Beikoku gikai toshokan zō Nihon kotenseki mokuroku* (Catalog of Japanese Rare Books in the Library of Congress) (Tokyo: Yagi shoten, 2003).

collection of Japanese Foreign Ministry archives from 1868 to 1945, as well as the pre-1945 records of the Police Bureau of the Ministry of Home Affairs of Japan. Some of these documents were censored wartime publications.①

The Inoh Maps Collection contains early modern maps of Japan created by *Tadataka Inoh* (伊能忠敬) between 1800 and 1821, with 207 of the original 214 sheets of Inoh's large-scale set (1∶36,000), which covers the Japanese archipelago from Hokkaido to Kyushu. The discovery of these maps in the spring of 2001 caused great excitement in Japan. In order to make them available for exhibition and online access, all of them have been digitized and are now under the care of the Japan Map Center.

The Korean collection began in the 1920s with a gift from James S. Gale, a Canadian missionary who spent forty years in Korea, from 1888 to 1928. Gale helped the Library acquire rare books from the estate of the Korean scholar Kim To-hui. A more systematic development of the Korean collection began in the early 1950s, during the Korean War. As of 2008, the Korean collection had 263,732 monographic volumes, 1,689 current serial titles, as well as 20,000 Japanese-language and 9,000 English-language books on Korea. A separate North Korea collection includes about 10,000 items, with 1,389 current and 5,598 noncurrent periodicals.

The Korean collection contains 480 Korean rare books in 3,000 volumes printed on mulberry paper. Examples of Korean movable type printing are found in the eight-volume *Collected Works of Yi Munsun*, printed circa 1241. Other rare holdings include the 1744 printed edition of the collected writings of the renowned sixteenth-century Confucian scholar and statesman Yi I (李珥) (1536–1584), the 1834 reprint of the works of Ch'oe Ch'i-wǒn (崔致远) (857–915), the 1590 print edition of *Koryǒ sa* (《高丽史》, History of the Koryǒ dynasty), and a 1630 print edition of Koryǒngguk taejǒn (《经国大典》, Law code of the Yi dynasty).②

The development of the various collections in the Library of Congress's Asian Division has been a cooperative effort spanning more than a century. This process has involved many librarian, scholars, and donors. Much has been written about this long and complicated development. Those who are interested in knowing more about the history of East Asian collections in the Library of Congress are advised to consult the bibliography below.

(A) Publications that provide an overview of the history of East Asian collections of the Library of Congress

Hummel, Arthur W. "The Growth of the Orientalia Collections." *Library of Congress Quarterly Journal of Current Acquisitions* 11. No. 2 (February 1954): 69–87.

Lee, Hwa-Wei. "Building a World-Class Asian Collection in the Library of Congress for Area Studies, Culture Preservation, Global Understanding, and Knowledge Creation." In *Proceedings of the Symposium on "The New Horizon of Library Services toward the Better Understanding of Asia,"* November 19, 2003. Kyoto: National Diet Library, Kansai-kan, 2004. (There is a Japanese translation on pages 57–67. The English paper and illustrations appear on pages 150–69.)

Meinheit, Harold E. *Library of Congress Asian Collections: An Illustrated Guide*. Washington, D.C.: Library of Congress, 2000. (An updated electronic edition is available on the Asian Division's Web site, http://www.loc.gov/rr/asian/guide2007/.)

(B) Publications that discuss the Chinese collections of the Library of Congress

Hu, Shuzhao. *The Development: of the Chinese Collection in the Library of Congress*. Boulder: Westview, 1979.

Huang, Hanzhu, and David Hsü. *Chinese Periodicals in the Library of Congress*. Washington, D.C.: Library of Congress, 1988.

---

① *The Japanese Collection* (Washington, D.C.: Asian Division, Library of Congress, n.d.).
② *The Korean Collection* (Washington, D.C.: Asian Division, Library of Congress, n.d.).

Huang, Hanzhu, and Hseo-chin Jen. *Chinese Newspapers in the Library of Congress.* Washington, D. C.: Library of Congress, 1985.

Lee, Hwa-Wei. "Chinese Resources for Zheng He Studies inthe Library of Congress." In *Maritime Asia and the Chinese Overseas*, 1405 – 2005. Singapore: National Library of Singapore, 2005.

————. "Historical Resources on Northeast China and Japan in the Library of Congress." Paper presented at the international conference Historical Resources for the Studies of Northeast China and Japan, Niigata University, October 27 – 30, 2004. In Chinese and Japanese.

————. "Sinological Resources in the Library of Congress." Paper presented at the international conference Sinological Resources in the Digital Era, National Central Library, Taipei, December 7 – 9, 2004.

Li, Xiaocong (李孝聪). *Meiguo guohui tushuguan cang Zhongwen gu ditu xulu* (《美国国会图书馆藏中文古地图叙录》, *Descriptive Catalogue of the Traditional Chinese Mapsin the Library of Congress*). Beijing: Wenwu chubanshe, 2004.

Library of Congress, Asian Division. *Commemorating the Two-Hundredth Anniversary of Robert Morrison's Arrival in China.* Compiled by Mi Chu and Man Shun Yeung, assisted by Ariele Bernard. Taibei: eHanism Global, 2007.

Lu, Judy S. "The Contemporary China Collection in the Asian Division, the Library of Congress." *Journal of East Asian Libraries* 141 (February 2007): 19 – 28.

Lu, Judy S., and Harold Meinheit. "Hong Kong: From Fishing Village to Financial Center." *Library of Congress Information Bulletin* 56 (1977): 272 – 75.

Matsumura, Jun. *A Catalogue of the Manchu Materials in the Library of Congress: Xylographs, Manuscripts, Archives.* Tokyo: Tōyō Bunko, 1999.

————. "A Catalogue of the Manchu Books in the Library of Congress, Washington, D. C." *Tōyō gakuhō* (东洋学报) 57, Nos. 1 – 2 (January 1976): 230 – 53.

Soong, James Chu-yul. *Chinese Materials on Microfilm Available from the Library of Congress.* Washington, D. C.: Center for Chinese Research Materials, Association of Research Libraries, 1971.

Sumiyoshi Tomohiko (住吉朋彦). "Beikoku gikai toshokan zō Nihon denrai Kanseki mokuroku kaidai chōhen" (米国议会图书馆藏日本伝来汉籍目录解题长编). *Shidō bunko ronshū* (《斯道文库论集》) 41 (2007): 201 – 70.

Wang, Chi. "Development of the Chinese Collection in the Library of Congress and Its Utilization by Researchers." In *Proceedings of the International Conference on National Libraries: Towards the Twenty-first Century*, 645 – . 53. Taipei: National Central Library, 1993.

Wang, Zhongmin. *A Descriptive Catalog of Rare Chinese Books in the Library of Congress.* Washington, D. C.: Library of Congress, 1957.

Wiens, Mi Chu. "LC's Chinese Collection Is Largest in Western World: Growth Tied to Political Changes." *Library of Congress Information Bulletin* 53 (September 5, 1994): 16.

————. "World Digital Library and E-Resources in the Asian Division, Library of Congress." *Journal of East Asian Libraries* 138 (February 2006): 1 – 4.

Young, John. *The Research Activities of the South Manchurian Railway Company, 1907 – 1945: A History and Bibliography.* New York: Columbia University Press, 1966.

Zhu, Shijia. *A Catalog of Chinese Local Histories in the Library of Congress.* Washington, D. C.: Library of Congress, 1942.

(C) Publications that discuss the Tibetan and Mongolian collections of the Library of Congress

Buescher, John B. "Tibetan Materials in the Asia Rare Book Collection of the Library of Congress." *Journal of the International Association of Buddhist Studies* 13, No. 1 (1990): 1 – 15. Lists xylographs and manuscripts acquired between 1900 and 1928 by William Rockhill, Berthold Laufer, and Joseph Rock.

Farquhar, David M. "A Description of the Mongolian Manuscripts and Xylographs in Washington, D. C." *Central Asiatic Journal* 1, No. 3 (195S): 161-218.

Kapstein, Matthew. "Inventory of Tibetan Works Acquired under 0199431: The Acquisition of Tibetan Books Published in the People's Republic of China, June 14-August 11, 1990: Report Submitted to the Library of Congress, August 28, 1990." Available in the Asian Division Reading Room, Library of Congress. Titles and sometimes detailed contents of 340 volumes of current xylographs acquired from Tibetan printers in the People's Republic of China.

Maurer, Walter. "List of Tibetan Materials with Identification Numbers, 1962 [?]." Lists works in the Laufer collection and other miscellaneous works with occasional notes on the subject matter of the text. Available in the Asian Division Reading Room, Library of Congress.

Meinheit, Susan. "The Tibetan and Mongolian Collections in the Asian Division, Library of Congress." *Journal of East Asian Libraries* 139 (June 2006): 27-35.

————. "Tibetan Classical Literature and the U. S. Library of Congress: Preservation of Knowledge." *China Tibetology*. special issue (1992): 361-72.

Robinson, Hanna. *First Cumulative Dictionary Catalog at Tibetan Works in the Library of the Institute of Advanced Study of World Religions*. Stony Brook, N. Y.: Institute of Advanced Study of World Religions, 1985. Catalog of PL 480 Tibetan collections.

Rockhill, William Woodville. "Catalogue of Tibetan Books in the Library of Congress, 1902." A handwritten list of 62 titles in Tibetan script followed by transliteration with brief descriptive annotations as to subject matter and physical features. Available in the Asian Division Reading Room, Library of Congress.

Tachikawa, Murashi, Tshulkrim Kelsang, and Shunzo Onoda. *A Catalogue of the United States Library of Congress Collection of Tibetan Literature*. Bibliographic Philological Buddhica, series major, No. 3. Tokyo: International Institute for Buddhist Studies, 1983-1988. Microfiche.

Woodblock to Laser: Library of Congress Tibetan Listings. Washington, D. C.: Library of Congress, 1993. Asian Classics Input Project, CD-ROM. Available in Microform Reading Room, Library of Congress.

(D) Publications that discuss the Japanese collections of the Library of Congress

Beikoku gikai toshokan zō Nihon kotenseki mokuroku (《米國議會図書館藏日本古典籍目錄》) (*Catalog of Japanese Rare Books in the Library of Congress*). Tokyo: Yagi shoten, 2003.

Honda, Shojo. *Pre-Meiji Works in the Library of Congress: Japanese Literature, Performing Arts, and Reference Books*. Washington, D. C.: Library of Congress, 1997.

————. *Pre-Meiji Works in the Library of Congress: Japanese Mathematics*. Washington, D. C.: Library of Congress, 1982.

Kita, Sandy, et al. *The Floating World of Ukiyo-e: Shadows, Dreams, and Substance*. New York: Abrams in association with the Library of Congress, 2001.

Kuroda, Andrew Y. *A History of the Japanese Collection in the Library of Congress, 1874-1941*. Washington, D. C.: Library of Congress, 1970.

Nagao, Philip. *Japanese Local Histories in the Library of Congress*. Washington, D. C.: Library of Congress, 1988.

The Noyes Collection of Japanese Prints, Drawings, Etc., Presented by Crosby Stuart Noyes. Washington, D. C.: Library of Congress, 1906.

Ohta, Thaddeus. *Japanese National Government Publications in the Library of Congress*. Washington, D. C Library of Congress, 1980.

Tanaka, *Hiromi. A Comprehensive Catalogue of Publications of the Former Imperial Army and Navy*. Tokyo: Toyo Shorin, 1995.

Tanpo Keizō (田甫桂三) and Honda Yasuhiro (本多泰洋) Taiwan Sōtokufu kankei shiryō mokuroku: Beikoku gikai toshokan shozō (《旧台湾総督府关系数据目录: 米国议会图书馆所藏》) (*Bibliography of Materials Related to the Taiwan Government General: Collection at the*

Library of Congress in the United States). Naruto: Yagi insatsujo, 1996.

Uyehara, Cecil. *Checklist of Archives in the Japanese Ministry of Foreign Affairs, Tokyo, Japan, 1868 – 1945: Microfilmea for the Library of Congress, 1949 – 1951.* Washington, D. C.: Photoduplication Service, Library of Congress, 1954.

Yoshimura, Yoshiko. *Censored Japanese Serials of the Pre-1946 Period: A Checklist of the Microfilm Collection.* Washington, D. C.: Library of Congress, 1994.

————. *Japanese Government Documents and Censored Publications: A Checklist of the Microfilm Collection.* Washington, D. C.: Library of Congress, 1992.

————. *Pre-1956 Japanese Documents and Censored Materials: A Checklist of the Microfilm Collection of the Library of Congress.* Washington, D. C., (2002) 2006.

Young, John. *Checklist of Microfilm Reproductions of Selected Archives of the Japanese Army, Navy, and Other Government Agencies.* Washington, D. C.: Georgetown University Press, 1959.

————. *The Research Activities of the South Manchurian Railway Company, 1907 – 1945: A History and Bibliography.* New York: Columbia University Press, 1966.

(E) Publications that discuss the Korean collections of the Library of Congress

Cho, Sung Yoon. *Law and Legal Literature of North Korea.* A Guide. Washington, D. C.: Library of Congress, 1988.

Haeoe chŏnjŏk munhwajae chosa mongnok: Mi ŭihoe tosŏgwan sojang Han'gukpon mongnok (《海外典籍文化财调查目: 美议会图书馆所藏韩国本目录》) (*List of Korean Publications in Foreign Countries: List of Korean Rare Books in the Library of Congress*). Seoul: Han'guk sŏji hakhoe, 1994.

"An Inventory of English-Language Publications on Korea in the Library of Congress as of 1994." Washington, D. C.: Asian Division, Library of Congress, 1997. Photocopy.

Korea: An Annotated Bibliography of Publications in Far Eastern Languages. Compiled by Edwin G. Beal Jr. and Robin L. Winkler. Washington, D. C.: Library of Congress, 1950.

Korea: An Annotated Bibliography of Publications in the Russian Language. Compiled by Albert Parry. Washington, D. C.: Library of Congress, 1950.

Korea: An Annotated Bibliography of Publications in Western Languages. Compiled by Helen D. Jones and Robin L. Winkler. Washington, D. C.: Library of Congress, 1950.

Lee, Sonya. "The Korean Collection in the Library of Congress." *Journal of East Asian Libraries* 142 (June 2007): 37 – 43.

Yang, Key P. 량기백 Ch'uryŏsŏ yŏkkŭn Miguk kukhoe tosogwan sojang pukkoe charyo mongnokchip 추려서 역은 미국 국회도서관 소장 북괴자료 목록집 (*Selected North Korean Source Materials Held in the Library of Congress*). Seoul: Kukt'o T'ongirwon, 1970

————. Korean War Bibliography. Washington, D. C.: Library of Congress, 1990.

————. "Reference Guide to Korean Materials, 1945 – 1959." Master's thesis, Catholic University of America, Washington, D. C., 1960.

(Published in *Collecting Asia: East Asian Libraries in North America, 1868 – 2008.* Edited by Peter X. Zhou, published by Association for Asian Studies, 2010. Also published in *Asian Past & Present: New Research from AAS.* No. 4: pp. 22 – 31.)

美国国会图书馆亚洲部进展报告

Progress Report of the Asian Division, Library of Congress[①]

Asian Division

The Asian Division, founded in 1928, is one of four area studies divisions under the Directorate of Collections and Services in the Library Services:
- African and Middle Eastern Division
- Asian Division
- European Division
- Hispanic Division

Reorganization Completed

Two sections:
- Collection Services
- Scholarly services

Five Area Collections:
- China and Mongolia
- Japan
- Korea (South and North)
- South Asia
- Southeast Asia

Vision of the Asian Division

To establish the collection of the Asian Division as the premier research and scholarly resource on Asia, in most Asian languages, that is compatible with the dynamics of knowledge and creativity of the Asian people.

Mission of the Asian Division

The mission of the Asian Division is to make comprehensive collection resources and information services related to Asia available and useful to the Congress, the American people, and the scholarly community nationally and internationally.

The Size of Asian Collections (03/31/2006)

Area	Monographs (volumes)	Serials (Active titles)	Serials (Inactive titles)
China/Mongolia	985,701	4,235	10,953
Japan	1,151,267	5,421	9,451
Korea	249,102	1,193	5,598
South Asia	227,866	1,616	2,120
Southeast Asia	174,969	2,736	8,462
Total	2,788,905	15,201	36,584

---

① This is a PPT version

Asian Collections in Other Formats

Legal materials, maps, music, motion pictures, prints, and photographs are housed and cared for by other divisions in the Library in collaboration with the Asian Division:
- the Law Library
- the Geography and Map Division
- the Prints and Photographs Division
- the Motion Picture, Broadcasting and Recorded Sound Division
- the Performing Arts Division
- the Manuscript Division, etc.

Collections not in Asian Languages

Other Asia-related publications not in Asian languages are also housed in:
- the Main Reading Room
- the Microform Reading Room
- The Newspaper and Current Periodical Reading Room
- The Performing Arts Reading Room
- the Science Reading Room
- some of the other area studies and special collections

Building Asian Digital Resources

In the digital age, the Asian Division is moving ahead in supplementing its printed collections by a growing body of electronic resources from e-books, e-journals, e-newspapers, to a wide range of e-materials, both digitized from printed version or born digital.

Types of Digital Resources

Subscription of e-bibliographic databases.
Acquisition of digitized full-text databases.
Digitization of rare books and other collections.
Capture of relevant web sites.
Online access and reference services.

Subscribed to E-Bibliographic Databases

At present forty-five of the Library's 219 subscription databases deal with Asia or Asian studies. Some of these are:
- Aardvark (Asian resources for librarians)
- Asian Development Bank Economics & Statistics (Economics and Research Department of Asian Development Bank)
- Asian Law Bibliographic Database (University of Melbourne)
- Bibliography of Asian Studies (Association for Asian Studies)
- Country Studies (Federal Research Division, the Library of Congress)
- Treaties and International Agreements (Oceana Publications)

Acquired Digitized Full-text Databases (From Mainland China and Taiwan):
- People's Daily 人民日报电子版 – 1946–2004.
- China Data Online.
- Chinese Journals 中国期刊全文数据库 – 7,240 titles.
- Chinese Core Newspapers 中国重要报纸数据库 – 1,000 titles.

– SuperStar Digital Library 超星电子图书馆 – 100,000 titles.
– Si Ku Quan Shu 四库全书文渊阁版.
– the Academia Sinica's Chinese Civilization in Time & Space 中国文明之时空基础架构 and Taiwan History & Culture in Time & Space 台湾历史文化地图系统.
– The Encyclopedia of Taiwan 台湾百科全书.

Acquired Digitized Full-text Databases (From Japan):

– Directory of Japanese Scientific Periodicals (from National Diet Library, covering 13,875 S/T serial titles).
– Kodansha Encyclopedia of Japan (11,000 entries, based on the 1993 publication: Japan: an Illustrated Encyclopedia).
– Several Japanese rare books have been digitized and are available in full text from the Library's OPAC.
– Full-text databases of five major Japanese newspapers including Mainichi, Sankei, Chunichi, Tokyo and Yomiuri Newspapers.

Acquired Digitized Full-text Databases (From Korea):

– Chosun Daily Newspaper Archive (covering articles from the Chosun Ilbo, the most widely read newspaper in South Korea)
– Korean Studies Database (by KRPIA, covering history, literature, and traditional medicines)
– Korean Studies Information Service System (KISS, a database of full-text articles from 6,000 journals published by 1,200 Korean academic institutions)
– Lawn B-Korean Law Database (Law and business, available for access in the Law Library reading room)

Digitized Rare Books & Other Collections

The digitized Naxi (纳西) collection is now accessible online: http://international.loc.gov/intldl/naxihtml/naxihome.html

In collaboration with the Academia Sinica, some 21,000 maps and 840 aerial photos have been digitized and will be incorporated into the historical geographic information system: Chinese Civilizations in Time and Space (中国文明之时空基础架构).

In collaboration with the National Central Library in Taiwan a three-year project to digitize the Chinese rare books in the Library of Congress has been launched since May 2005.

Digitized Rare Books & Other Collections

In collaboration with the International Research Center of Japanese Studies (Nichibunken) in Japan four rare books in the Nara Ehon collection were digitized and are accessible online through LC's OPAC.

Also in collaboration with Nichibunken some 3,000 prints from the Japanese Ukiyo-e collection were digitized and will be available online in 2006.

The complete set of 207 large-scale maps of Japan made by Inoh Tadataka (伊能忠敬) (1816 – 1819) were digitized and is now accessible from the Library's webpage: http://www.loc.gov/rr/geogmap/

Capturing Relevant Web Sites

The portals of the Asian Division are increasingly a useful web resource on all the Asian countries and regions. http://www.loc.gov/rr/asian/area_AD.html

Planning is being made to begin web harvesting and archiving on special topics or events of importance. Example: the tsunami disaster.

Providing Online Access and Services

The Library's online public access catalog. http://catalog.loc.gov
American Memory. http://memory.loc.gov/
Global Gateway. http://international.loc.gov/intldl/intldlhome.html
The portals of the Asian Division http://www.loc.gov/rr/asian/area_AD.html
QuestionPoint. http://www.oclc.org/questionpoint
Asking a Librarian. http://www.loc.gov/rr/askalib/ask-asian.html

The World Digital Library

Proposed by Dr. James Billington in June 2005.

To bring together online rare and unique cultural materials held by libraries and repositories in all parts of the world.

Digitization will be done through public and private collaboration.

On November 22, 2005, Google Inc. responded with an initial funding of $3 million.

The World Digital Library

The current large-scale digitization projects undertaken by the Asian Division in collaboration with major libraries in Asia will be the first group of projects which will make up the World Digital Library.

Published Report on E-Resources

Dr. Mi Chu Wiens' article, "World Digital Library and E-Resources in the Asian Division, Library of Congress," published in the February 2006 issue of the Journal of East Asian Libraries, No. 138: pp. 1-4.

The Friends Society of Asian Division

It was established on January 20, 2004 as a mean of outreach to a broader user community.

We now have more than 200 individual and corporate members.

Through the generosity of Florence Tan Moeson, up to 15 research fellowships will be awarded each year.

For information about the Friends Society, please visit the website: http://www.lcasianfriends.org.

The Florence Tan Moeson Research Fellowship

Established through the generosity of Florence Tan Moeson, the Moeson Fellowship provides individuals with the opportunity to pursue research on East, Southeast, or South Asia (including the overseas Asian communities), using the unparalleled Asian collections of the Library of Congress in Washington, DC.

Scholarly Programs Launched

An International Symposium on the Significance of Admiral Zheng He's Voyages (1405-1433).

In the Footsteps of Marco Polo: An International Symposium on Italy-China Cultural Exchangein the 13th—17th Centuries.

America Is in the Heart for the 21st Century: The Carlos

Bulosan Symposium—In Commemorating the Centennial of the First Wave Migration to Hawaii by Filipino Nationals.

An International Symposium On the Significance of Admiral Zheng He's Voyages (1405 – 1433) In Commemoration of the 600th Anniversary of Zheng He's First Voyage
Monday, May 16, 2005, 8:30 a.m. ~4:30 p.m.
Mumford Room (6th floor)
Madison Building
The Library of Congress

Asian Division, The Library of Congress
Embassy of Italy/Italian Cultural Institute, Washington D. C. & The Honorable Henry E. Brown, Jr. Present In the Footsteps of Marco Polo: An International Symposium on Italy-China Cultural Exchange in the 13th—17th CenturiesThursday, March 23, 2006
8:30am ~12:00pm
Members Room
LJ-162, Jefferson Building
Sponsored by: The National Italian American Foundation—Frank J. Guarini Public Policy Forum
Alitalia

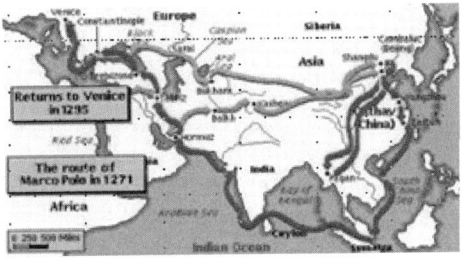

The Asian Division Friends Society
The Embassy of The Republic of The Philippines
Our Own Voice
Invite You to Attend
America Is in the HeartFor the 21st CenturyThe Carlos Bulosan Symposium—In Commemorating the Centennial of the First Wave Migration to Hawaii by Filipino Nationals
Friday

April 28, 2006
9:15am~5:00pm
Room LJ-119
Jefferson Building

Carlos Bulosan is the literary icon of early Filipino migrant experience in the United States.
SPONSORS: Philippine American Writers and Artists, Inc. (PAWA, Inc.) / The Asian Pacific American Labor Alliance (APALA AFL-CIO) / Carayan Press, San Francisco / Remedios G. Cabacungan

5. 序言与书评
Preface and Review

《图书馆新技术应用国际学术讨论会论文集》序

Preface of *the Proceedings of the International Symposium on New Techniques and Applications in Libraries*[①]

Seeing the International Symposium on New Techniques and Application in Libraries under the joint sponsorship of Xi'an Jiaotong University and Ohio University become a reality has given us profound pleasure and satisfaction. The spirit of cooperation and hard work among the organizing staffs of both institutions paved the way for a successful symposium which has attracted leading experts and library professionals from many countries.

Although the purpose of this Symposium is to provide a forum for participants from China and abroad to meet and share information on recent development in library and information technologies, the high quality of participants and the wide-range of expertise may spawn new ventures and directions in innovative information services. This is especially important as the pace of technological change has accelerated in recent years and shows no sign of abating. Many of the new technologies suitable for library applications such as microcomputers, compact discs, video discs, artificial intelligence, etc. have world-wide implications and applicability.

The Symposium was organized in part to coincide with the dedication of the new library building at Xi'an Jiaotong University. It is, therefore, our wish to dedicate this Symposium to this important occasion. The new library serves not only as a symbol of learning and scholarship for a most distinguished university but, hopefully, will lead in library automation and innovation in the years to come.

The success of this Symposium is the result of contributions by many individuals and organizations. The cooperation of Kanazawa Institute of Technology in Japan from the inception has been tremendously valuable. The participation of featured speakers who willingly accepted the invitation is especially appreciated. All of the paper contributors who share their knowledge and experience are equally appreciated. To other participants, from near and far, including exhibitors; we want to extend to them our heartfelt thanks. The generous financial support of many sponsors and vendors has helped to cover part of the expenses. Special acknowledgement is also due to the President and officials of both Xi'an Jiaotong University and Ohio University for their encouragement and support. All of these contributions were necessary ingredients for a fruitful Symposium providing a unique opportunity for information sharing which transcends geographical and national barriers.

Founded in 1804, Ohio University was the first public university west of the Ohio River. At its main campus in Athens, Ohio, the University enrolls 15500 students in its colleges (Arts and Sciences, Business Administration, Communication, Education, Engineering and Technology, Fine Arts, Health and Human Services, Honors Tutorial, Osteopathic Medicine, and University College). Through its five regional campuses in Southeastern Ohio, it serves an additional 6300

---

① Co-author: James Bryant.

students. The University has a strong tradition in international education and cooperation. Currently, about 1400 foreign students representing 90 countries are enrolled in the Athens campus. Furthermore, the University has actively participated in cooperative programs in Africa, Asia, and Latin America.

As the center for learning and research activities, the libraries of Ohio University play a key role in academic excellence. As one of the founding institutions of OCLC (Online Computer Library Center), and the member library to catalog online into the OCLC shared cataloging system, Ohio University Libraries have been active in library automation and networking. Using the VTLS software, its local ALICE system has become an online, fully integrated library system, interlibrary loan. The Libraries' Southeast Asia Collection and International Librarian Internship Program are well known throughout the world. The support of Ohio University for this Symposium is a part of our continued commitment to international program and cooperation.

(Published in *The Proceedings of the International Symposium on New Techniques and Applications in Libraries*, edited by Zhang Zhiyou and Hwa-Wei Lee. Xi'an: Xi'an Jiaotong University Press, 1988: p. 576.)

《海外华人研究机构国际合作会议论文与摘要集》序

Preface of *International Conference of Institutes and Libraries for Overseas Chinese Studies Papers and Abstracts*

A New Milestone Reached and a New Chapter Opened

The establishment of the Dr. You Bao Shao Overseas Chinese Documentation and Research Center at Ohio University Libraries in 1993 was a major milestone in an attempt to systematically collect, organize, and preserve the valuable historical documents to facilitate research on the origin, reasons, patterns, struggle, ingenuity, culture, society, economic impacts, politics, and contributions of Overseas Chinese in Southeast Asia. This attempt is the result of the foresight of Dr. You Bao Shao who saw the importance and growing interest in the study of Overseas Chinese as a new academic and multi-discipline field. At the Ohio University Libraries, we saw that such an undertaking complements our effort to further expand our world-renown Southeast Asia Collection. Over the years, even under financial and staffing constraints, we have devoted major efforts to strengthen the research resources and have made significant progress in this far-reaching, monumental work.

Now, the convening of the International Conference of Institutes and Libraries for Overseas Chinese Studies held for the first time on the Ohio University campus is another giant step toward furthering our aim to promote international cooperation among all institutes and libraries for Overseas Chinese studies in the world with an emphasis on identifying and implementing cooperative endeavors.

We are most grateful for the overwhelming response and support received. This conference proceeding represent the papers and reports from scholars and practitioners in the field from institutes and libraries around the world. It is a truly international gathering for scholarly exchange of information on works in progress.

It is our sincere hope that this Conference will not only be a beginning of our joint efforts on a worldwide scale but also be an important step to set a strategic agenda for close cooperation and coordination in the 21st century. The Conference is seen as the opening of a new chapter in the cooperative and coordinated development of worldwide resources for Overseas Chinese studies.

I am honored to be asked to write this preface for the proceedings. It is only appropriate that I also acknowledge the contributions of many individuals at Ohio University who have strongly supported the Center over the years. President Robert Glidden is to be thanked especially for his unyielding support throughout the years. Ms. Julia Zimmerman, Dean of the University Libraries, has seen the importance of the Center and has been very supportive ever since assuming the Deanship last August. Ms. Lian The-Mulliner, Curator of the Center for International Collections and founding Head of the Southeast Asia Collection, has done much to build the Overseas Chinese collection long before the Shao Center was established. Dr. Liren Zheng, the Daniel Shao Endowed Curator of the You Bao Shao Center for Overseas Chinese Documentation and Research Center, is responsible for the planning, development, and operations of the Center and is instrumental in organizing this Conference.

To Dr. You Bao Shao, our founder, and his son, Dr. Daniel Shao, both of Hong Kong, we are most grateful for their most generous gifts to endow the Center as well as the Curatorship.

Also, our gratitude should be extended to many of the other unsung heroes who have worked hard behind the scenes to make this Conference successful. To all the invited speakers and participants, we want to express a heartfelt welcome and our appreciation.

(Published in *International Conference of Institutes and Libraries for Overseas Chinese Studies Papers and Abstracts*. (《海外华人研究机构国际合作会议论文与摘要集》) By the Dr. You Bao Shao Overseas Chinese Document and Research Center, Athens, Ohio: Ohio University Libraries, 2000: pp. 1 – 2.)

《持守中正：易经的介绍》序

Foreword of *The Centered Life*: An Introduction to I Ching—Book of Changes the Universal Principles of Living and Its Amazing Oracle

About two years ago, I had the pleasure of reading the first draft of Mr. Franklin Hum Yun's writing on *I Ching* (*The Book of Changes*). It is widely known that *I Ching* is perhaps the oldest of the ancient Chinese classics written by a number of sages over a period of three thousand years. The ancestor-king *Fu Hsi* (c. 3000 B. C.), who invented the trigrams (the *pa kua*), began it and then it went through numerous editions and interpretations by Chinese scholars in the ensuing two thousand years. However, few of us, even among contemporary learned Chinese, have read it in its entirety or understand the essence of it. I was one of them until I had the opportunity of reading Mr. Yun's writing.

Throughout Mr. Yun's teaching and other professional careers in Korea and California, he has been very attracted to the *I Ching*, which is also highly regarded and respected in Korea, and he has devoted a great deal of time to studying it. This longtime devotion and love have enabled Mr. Yun to write this profound and scholarly book of *I Ching* in English, which is very easy to read and understand for those readers who may not be able to read the texts in Chinese or Korean.

I Ching is generally known as a book on the ancient Chinese method of divination that uses the symbols for the two opposing forces in the universe, *yin* and *yang*. Today, it remains a popular medium of divination for predicting the future and for obtaining direction for a future course of action. Some scholars also study it for clues to the development of the Chinese language. Dr. Everett Kleinjans, a contemporary scholar of East Asian philosophies, regards *I Ching* as a basis for reflective wisdom, theoretical understanding, and pragmatic application. He sees that *I Ching* can be used (1) for one's own spiritual growth regardless of the religion one adheres to; (2) for an understanding of medicine, management, communication, conflict, and other human thoughts and activities; and (3) for providing insight into everyday decisions. [1]

According to Mr. Yun, what makes *I Ching* a respected and enduring classic is its scope and depth beyond the realm of divination. It presents a philosophy of life based on *Tao* (nature's way), and it provides universal principles of human conduct to follow. These principles have greatly influenced Asian philosophies and religions (Taoism, Confucianism, Buddhism, etc.) as well as other aspects of Asian cultures.

The sages who developed *I Ching* present the conceptualization of the universe, from how the universe was created to how the universe operates through continual interaction of all its forces and elements. These interactions result in constant changes in recurring cycles.

In the midst of constant changes, it is essential to strive for the center to maintain equilibrium or balance. *I Ching* affirms maintaining the center as the integral force in the universe, and it emphasizes the importance of having human conduct follow that mode. The *I Ching* divination is based on the fundamental truths of the universe; thus, its predictions will be reliable, and one's conduct will be proper and propitious if the principle of being in the center is applied to everyday living.

Mr. Yun's book on *Centered Life* is an introductory book of *I Ching*. It presents the key aspects *of I Ching* within the context of their original meanings, including historical and cultural perspectives. These aspects are covered in sufficient depth so that the reader can gain basic but

---

[1] Everett Kleinjans. *Living in Harmony with the I China*. (Singapore: The Institute of East Asian Philosophies, National University of Singapore, 1989) p. 12.

comprehensive understanding of this classic.

I Ching consists of sixty-four hexagrams representing the whole universe. Through the analysis of the individual lines and sets of lines and the interpretation of its symbols, images, and movements, one can obtain predictions of good or bad fortune and guidance in living a virtuous life. The teachings and divination of *I Ching* have relevance in today's world for those who seek wisdom and a virtuous life.

Mr. Yun's book is a significant contribution to the understanding of *I Ching*. It is also an important guide to our way of life and thinking in the rapidly changing world of the new millennium. I hope all readers of this great Chinese classic will find it to be intellectually and spiritually stimulating.

(Published in ***The Centered Life: An Introduction to I Chine-Book of Changes The Universal Principles of Living and Its Amazing Oracle.*** Yun, Franklin Hum. Raleigh, North Carolina: Pentland Press, 2001: p. 367.)

《英汉图书馆情报学词汇》序

Preface for *An English – Chinese Dictionary of Library and Information Science*

世界正在经历着一场巨变，由工业时代迈向信息时代、知识经济时代，人类面对的是一个由信息支持的社会，一个由知识推动的世界。通信网络的延伸，信息资源的激增，技术平台的开发，信息的交流和知识的传播促进了人们对信息和知识的渴求，增强了人们对服务于存取和管理文献信息的图书馆的关注和需要。网络文化的传播，数字图书馆的出现，虚拟资源中心的发展使得图书馆学、信息学和文献学及其相关学科从传统走向未来。

《英汉图书馆情报学词汇》具有时代气息。它的编撰和出版顺应了全球信息化发展的潮流，满足广大读者学习图书信息相关知识的要求，帮助读者了解有关文献信息和知识的生产、搜集、组织、检索、传播及评价的各种理论和方法，从而应对信息超载的局面。

《英汉图书馆情报学词汇》具有实用性。它广泛地收录图书馆学、信息学和文献学学科的大量术语，涵盖了与其相关的编辑、出版印刷、文化、教育、语言等领域的词汇，同时加入了与所涉学科相关的重要院校、主要研究项目和一些系统、软件的名称。借助本词汇，读者不仅可以方便地阅读所涉学科的英文专著、教材，而且可以顺利地浏览网上的英文信息资源，进而可以准确地理解原文并翻译相关领域的文献资料。

《英汉图书馆情报学词汇》具有可靠的编撰质量。其编者有着长期从事大学图书馆工作和教育工作的实践经历，有着广博的人文和科技知识，熟悉专业并跟踪学科的发展，同时具备文献信息教学和专业英语教学的丰厚经验和底蕴，对学科的英文术语有较深的理解和研究。本书编者曾编撰过多本教材和词典，为本书的撰写打下了扎实的基础。编者本着严谨、细致的态度，从各种不同的渠道搜集所涉学科领域的术语，在注意引入最新词汇的同时，也将国际标准（ISO 5127：2001（E））和中国国家标准（GB 4894—85）中的内容收入其中。

《英汉图书馆情报学词汇》的编撰是件很有意义的工作，它的出版一定会给广大读者带来学习和工作上的便利。衷心希望本书在使用和评价中不断总结提高，更新版本，成为一本较完善和成熟的并与时俱进的词汇工具书。

李华伟

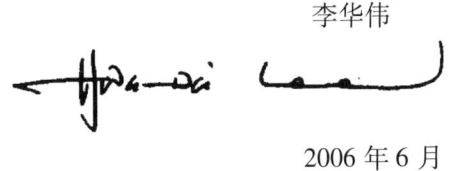

2006 年 6 月

（原载《英汉图书馆情报学词汇》 (*An English-Chinese Dictionary of Library and Information Science*)，孙平著，清华大学出版社 2006 出版）

《养生之道》序

Preface for *The Guide to a Healthy Life*

我和史勇伟先生是多年的老朋友了，与他相识是看了他所拍摄并印制的中国56个民族的画册开始的。这是一位才华横溢、有所作为、不断奋进的青年。25年前，他居然独自一人走遍中华大地，拍摄了大量珍贵的56个民族的照片，包括台湾的高山族所属9个支系的照片。至今看来，这些照片依然亲切、生动感人，散发着强烈的民俗风情风味。

他是中国第一个用照相机拍摄全56个民族的人！由此可见，史先生毅力超强，意志非凡。

史先生在华盛顿经营着一家最大最气派的中国餐馆——Hunan Dynasty，席座200人，酒会可容纳300人。因工作关系，我也是这家餐馆的常客，每次去餐馆用餐，史先生总是亲自掌勺、照顾有加，难能可贵的是，史先生同时也是这家餐馆的大厨师。这家餐馆的大部分客人是美国国会参、众两院的议员，他们对史先生所烹制的美式中国菜赞不绝口。

在美国，最高法院终身大法官地位崇高，当国家、总统遇到难以解决的麻烦事，都由大法官们来拍板定案。而9名大法官中，资深大法官肯尼迪先生非常欣赏史先生所烹制的美式中国菜。当他品尝了史先生亲手所做的菜后，相当满意。为此，大法官还寄了一封精致的热情洋溢的感谢信给史先生。可见史先生烹调美式中国菜已达炉火纯青的境界。这家餐馆的所有用料和菜都是由史先生从营养学的角度加以科学配制，深受客人喜欢。纽约州参议员希拉里（前总统克林顿的夫人）和舒默是这家餐馆的常客。今年2月，希拉里和舒默还在这家餐馆举行了新闻发布会，宾客云集，达300多人。美国杂志《纽约客》做了专题报道，CNN电视台做了转播介绍。美国《华盛顿邮报》也曾介绍过这家餐馆。前美国众议院议长海斯特是这家餐馆的常客。而众议院议长是美国的第三号人物，当总统和副总统遇有不测，议长将直接行使代总统的权力。现任众议院议长南茜·佩洛西也经常光顾这家餐馆。今年3月26日，史先生亲自为众议院议长南茜·佩洛西举行迷你生日晚会，并与议长合影留念。

史先生经常亲自为我烹制的一道菜是"西洋参枸杞炖甲鱼"，这道菜的色、香、味、形俱全，可贵的是，他对火候掌握精准，所炖甲鱼酥而不烂，入口即化，味道鲜美。最令我感动的是，上个月我刚做完胆囊切除手术，出院后，史先生即给我列一张手术后的饮食宜忌及注意事项，看后我终于领略到史先生在养生方面的深厚功力。没想到，时过几月，史先生要出版《养生之道》一书，读过手稿，感慨万千。史先生在养生方面的独到见解、与众不同的养生理念，值得推广介绍。这是一本对大众有益的书，对整个社会有益的书，值得一读。

美国国会图书馆亚洲部主任
李华伟博士

2007年夏于华盛顿

（原载《养生之道》，史勇伟著，文化艺术出版社2007年出版，第134页）

《图书馆与信息科学年鉴》书评

Book Reviews in *Library and Information Science Annual*

1999

188. Wei, Wu Guang; and Lili Zheng with Liu Suya and Shao Youliang. **Education for Librarianship in China.** Herndon, Va., Mansell/Cassell, 1997. 250p. index. (Education of Library and Information Professionals: An International Series) $99.50. ISBN 0-7201-2193-0.

 This book, with chapters by several authors, provides a general introduction to education for librarianship in China yet suffers in both conception and execution. Divided into 2 parts and 10 chapters, the 1st part covers the history of library science education, programs offered by institutions of higher education, employment conditions of library school faculty members, other forms of training, current development, and achievements and problems. Many of the chapters lack depth, ignore scholarly standards, and are little more than lists. Citations do not indicate whether sources were published in Chinese journals or in the Chinese language (citations are in English) and omit page numbers. Although an editor is credited, there is little evidence of her work. For example, some of the personal names are not in their correct pinyin romanization; for example, professor Nian Yiming should have been Yan Yiming (p. 111) and Mrs. Tong Shiaoying should have been Dong Xiaoying (p. 121).

 The 2nd part, chapters 7 to 10, covers Hong Kong, Taiwan, and Macau. Even though library science education in Taiwan is more developed than in Hong Kong and Macau, it receives scant treatment, offering a single chapter on only the National Taiwan University. Three appendixes, a note on contributors, and an index conclude the book. Appendix 1 is a directory of library and information programs but also includes a list of faculty members of the Department of Library and Information Science at Peking University, with the specialization and publications of each. No reason is given why faculty members of other universities are not similarly listed. Appendix 2 is a list of professional conferences held in China between 1990 and 1994. Appendix 3 is identified as a "comprehensive bibliography of Chinese literature on library science"; however, the citations are given in English. Such a list serves neither Chinese readers, who will have difficulty identifying the actual titles, nor those who do not read Chinese, as the bibliography omits numerous works in English and other languages that have been published outside of China.

222. Corson-Finnerty, Adam, and Laura Blanchard. **Fundraising and Friend-Raising on the Web.** Chicago, American Library Association, 1998. 122p. illus. index. $50.00pa. ISBN 0-8389-0727-X.

 The rapid development and widespread use of the Internet and the World Wide Web in recent years offers new tools for fundraising. Since 1995 the University of Pennsylvania Library has been using the Web for public relations, constituency building, and solicitation of gifts. This book and CD-ROM describe the experiences of the University of Pennsylvania Library with a strong conviction that the Internet and its friendly face (the Web) possess great potential for enhancing fundraising initiatives and improving results.

 The book includes 3 parts—an epilogue, two appendixes, and an index. Part 1 discusses, among other things, traditional fundraising, Web-enhanced fundraising, making a difference, creative use of the Internet to solicit and acknowledge major gifts, electronic plaguing, and online pledges. Part 2 introduces several successful Websites. Part 3 shows how to get started with simple design tips for building a Website and the benefits and techniques of publishing online pages on a CD-ROM disc for wider distribution. The 2 appendixes, "Fundraiser's Choice: Cool Sites" and "The Web Developer's Bootstrapping Toolkit" are full of useful suggestions. The accompanying Web enabled CD-ROM provides tips, tools, ideas, and signposts for setting started.

The coauthors emphasize that: "A wired development office is not an office that uses the Web exclusively to communicate with its constituency. Rather, it is an office that uses the Web to plan, organize, design, and advance an entire communications strategy." This resource set (book and CD-ROM) is an excellent beginning for such a strategy. It is highly recommended for library administrators, fundraisers, and public relations officers. [1]

(Published in *Library and Information Science Annual*, 1999.)

---

[1] R: BL, 15 Oct 98: p. 398

《美国参考书年鉴》书评

Book Reviews in *American Reference Books Annual*

1981

297. Dewe, A., and J. Deunette. (eds.) **EURIM 3: A European Conference on the Contribution of Users to Planning and Policy Making for Information Systems and Networks.** Presented by Aslib in association with Association Nationale de la Recherche Technique, Bibliothèque Royale de Belgique, Consiglio Nazionale delle Ricerche, Deutsche Gesellschaft für Dokumentation, NOBIN, NORDFORSK, 25 – 27 April 1978, Künstlerhaus, Munich, Germany. London, Aslib, 1980. 100p. illus. price not reported. pa. ISBN 0 – 85142 – 133 – 4.

　　There have been three conferences in the EURIM series: The first EURIM on research into the management of information services and libraries was held in Paris in 1973; EURIM 2 on the application of research in information services and libraries was held in Amsterdam in 1976 (see ARBA 78, entry 267); and EURIM 3, the latest one, with an emphasis on the users and their effects on information systems and networks, was held in Munich in 1978.

　　Unlike its predecessors, EURIM 3 had fewer papers but devoted more time to discussions. Of the 12 paper presented there were 2 each on networks and users; operations; compatibility and standards; finance, pricing and cost effectiveness; education and training; and international cooperation. Except for one in German and one in French, a majority of the papers are in English. The only non-European speaker was Martha E. Williams of the United States. The papers as a whole, together with the transcription of the discussions, provide an overview of the latest developments in information systems and networks in Europe. These 100 pages contain much useful information..

1982

270. Baker, Leigh R. **Development of University Libraries in Papua New Guinea.** Metuchen, NJ, Scarecrow, 1981. 399p. illus. maps. Bibliog. index. $20.00. LC 80 – 26936. ISBN 0 – 8108 – 1393 – 9.

　　University libraries in developing countries faced mangy problems in the building up of their collections and services. Those in Papua New Guinea were no exception. This book is a detailed survey of the two Papua New Guinea university libraries, as well as a comprehensive survey of university libraries in English-speaking, former British colonial counties. Problems in the areas of resources, staffing, organization, funding, services, and buildings are highlighted. The work concludes with a list of 107 recommendations for the improvement of the university libraries, some of which are solutions used in libraries in other developing countries.

　　The survey of university libraries in several developing countries is of international interest, and the many intriguing little facts that emerge from the comparison whet the reader's appetite for more details. Fortunately, the author has provided bibliographical notes at the end of each chapter to lead to further reading.

　　The survey covers the period between 1955 and 1975, that period being considered the time when much progress was seen in the university libraries in developing countries. However, significant and rapid developments have occurred since then, especially in the field of library automation. One project that springs to mind is the Malaysian MARC Project (Malmarc), a cooperative computerized cataloging project among the university libraries and the National Library of Malaysia. What is needed now is another work to bring this one up to date.

This book should be a useful source for students of comparative librarianship and those interested in libraries and librarianship in developing countries.

1983

206. **Directory of Chinese Libraries**. Wang Enguang, Wu Renyong, and Xie Wanruo. (eds.) Beijing, China, China Academic Publishers; distr., Detroit, Gale, 1982. 428p. illus. (part col.). index. (Word Books Reference Guide, No. 3) $45.00.

Claimed by the distributor, Gale Research, to be the first such compilation ever published in China, this bilingual directory covers nearly 3,000 libraries in the People's Republic of China. After a brief (one and one-half pages) description of library services in China and 24 pages of photographs (8 in colors) of selected libraries, the first 162 pages offer brief descriptions of 658 selected libraries with foreign holdings. This is followed by 182 pages listing Chinese libraries with addresses. As addenda, descriptions of an additional 73 libraries received too late for inclusion among the libraries with foreign holdings complete the volume.

Both the select descriptive section and the lengthier (2,887 entries) list of libraries with addresses are organized as to whether public libraries, academic and special libraries, or college and university libraries, with group designator and an institutional number assigned each. Locating a specific library is possible through an index. Each of the entries in the address list and most of the descriptions of the libraries with foreign holdings are in both Chinese characters and English. The index, however, is only in English with Chinese names in pinyin in the roman alphabet. Rounding out the volume is an appendix listing 126 libraries with holdings greater than 500.000 volumes, arranged in order of size.

While the remainder of the volume may be of some limited use, the most useful section is the descriptions of libraries with foreign holdings, supplemented by the 73 additional institutions in the addenda. The descriptions provide detailed if succinct information on each library, including the year of its founding, overall holdings and special foci of collections, user services, publications, staffing, and address and telephone number. The directory should be of interest and value to anyone wishing to do research in China as well as to publishers, libraries, suppliers, and others seeking to contact Chinese libraries.

1986

564. Li Heng. **Dictionary of Library and Information Sciences: English-Chinese/ Chinese-English**. Munich, New York, K. G. Saur, 1984. 327p. $41.00. ISBN 3-598-10532-0.

Claimed to be the first bilingual dictionary for library and information sciences in English-Chinese, Chinese-English, this dictionary is a useful tool for translating selected library and information science terms to Chinese. The English and Chinese definitions of terms are very helpful. The main body of the dictionary is the English-Chinese section which provides, in alphabetical order, English terms with corresponding Chinese characters. The second section is Chinese-English index using the Pinyin system for the Chinese language. Added at the end of the book are a list of acronyms and abbreviations, three appendices explaining the Chinese phonetic alphabet and a bibliography.

Although the dictionary claims to contain more than 1.800 entries, it includes fewer terms than the pocket-sized English-Chinese dictionary *English-Chinese Dictionary of Library Science* (Beijing: Commercial Press, 1982). A random comparison of the two finds that the Li dictionary lacks many important terms such as *CODEN*, *PRECIS*, *precision ratio*, *recall ratio*, *Project INTREX*, *UNISIST*, and others which are in the pocket-sized dictionary. Another similar dictionary. *English-Chinese Library and Information Sciences Terminology* by Lucy Te-Chu lee, published in Taipei in 1981 contains 5,480 entries, about three times as many as the title reviewed. For comprehensive coverage, all three dictionaries are needed. The pocket-sized dictionary, however, is probable the best of the three.

1991

603. **Information Science Abstracts. Volume 25, NO. 2: February 1990.** Harry Alcock, ed. New York, Plenum, 1990. 1v. (various paging). Index. $425.00pa. (12 issues) ISSN 0020-0239.

Formerly *Documentation Abstracts*, this publication contains bibliographic citations and abstracts of selected books, journals, conference proceedings, reports, and patents relevant to the broad field of information science. It is a joint project of the American Society for Information Science, the Division of Chemical Information of the American Chemical Society, and the Special Library Association. The current editorial board also includes representatives from the American Library Association, the American Society of Indexers, the Association of Information and Dissemination Centers, the Association of Library and Information Science Education, and the Medical Library Association. The ISA database is available for online searching through DIALOG.

Each issue includes some 800 citations with abstracts divided among 8 broad subjects and over 70 subsections. All issues have author and subject indexes, with the final issue of a volume cumulating each of the indexes. Extensive cross-references direct attention to related items included in the same or previous issues. Although rather expensive for many libraries, this publication is recommended for large library and information science collections as well as for reference collections in very large libraries.

2001

651. **Knowledge Management for the Information Professional.** T. Kanti Srikantaiah and Michael E. D. Koenig. (eds.) Medford, NJ., Information Today, 2000. 598p. illus. index. $35.60 (ASIS members); $44.50 (nonmembers). ISBN: 1-57387-079-X.

The term knowledge management, which has emerged in the business community only recently, has now been acknowledged by the library and information science profession. This book is the result of a graduate course developed by a library school for students who want to be information professionals and managers. This book is divided into 5 major areas: an overview of knowledge management.

This book is divided into 5 major areas: an overview of knowledge management, background and issues in knowledge management, creating the culture of learning and knowledge sharing in the organization, the tools of knowledge management, and the applications of knowledge management. In each of these major areas a number of chapters are written by different authors. Altogether there are 28 chapters with well-selected topics. In addition to the 5 major areas, a 6th area contains 4 appendixes. Appendix A is a course syllabus for knowledge management. Appendix B is a comprehensive bibliography on knowledge management. Appendix C is a thematic model in information-driven management. The last appendix is about the contributors. Both editors are also contributors and are authors of several key chapters and the appendixes.

Unlike most of the other books on knowledge management that address the subject almost exclusively in the context of a firm or an organization, this book looks at knowledge management in a broader transorganizational context. The comprehensiveness of this book and its rich context will be useful for all library and information professionals, not merely for graduate students. If one wonders just what is knowledge management, this is the book to read. [R: JAL, Sept 2000: pp. 368 – 369]

2002

592. Ravid, Ruth, and Marianne G. Handler. **The Many Faces of School-University Collaboration: Characteristics of Successful Partnerships.** Englewood, Colo., Libraries Unlimited, 2001. 2001. 263p. index. $ 36.0pa. ISBN 1 – 56308 – 792 – 8.

This book on collaboration between schools and universities in a variety of models offers useful information and suggestions for establishing good working partnerships and avoiding common mistakes. Each of the four major models described in this book are illustrated through real-life projects and perspectives of educators from participating schools and universities. Also included are the advantages and disadvantages of each model.

Divided into 2 sections and 17 chapters, the first 3 chapters in section 1 provide an introduction. Chapter 1 describes the 4 major models: the university and professional development school (PDS) model, the consultation model, the one-to-one collaborations model, and the umbrella model. Chapter 2 discusses the process of change in school-university collaboration. Chapter 3 discusses what makes partnerships work. Chapters 4 to 17 in section 2, "Collaboration Through the Eyes of the Partners" were put together under the specific collaboration model that the partners embraced and used. This book will be very useful for educators wanting to develop meaningful and successful collaborative relationships between schools and universities as well as for those who want to better understand of further improve existing partnerships.

621. Gong, Yitai, and G. E. Gorman. **Libraries and Information Services in China.** Lanham, Md., Scarecrow, 2000. 317p. index. $ 65.00. ISBN 0 – 8108 – 3782 – X.

This latest book on libraries and information services in China is a welcome addition to available publications concerning the rapid development of library and information services in China in recent decades. It complements well the two other publications on, or related to, the subject: Sharon Chien Lin's *Libraries and Librarianship in China* (Greenwood Press, 1988) and Guangwei Wu & Lili Zheng's *Education for Librarianship in China* (Mansell, 1977). Both authors of the latest book are well qualified and knowledgeable and have done an admirable job in a balanced review and insight on the subject.

The book consists of eight chapters and six appendixes. Chapter 1 provides historical perspectives. Chapter 2 describes the present scenario. Chapters 3 to 6 deal with the key functions of library and information services, such as collection development and resource sharing; cataloging, classification, and universal bibliographic control; reader and information services; and automation and information technology. Chapter 7 expresses the authors' reflections on the future of libraries and information services in China. Chapter 8 is an introduction to selected libraries in China. The six appendixes provide additional information on the chronology of Chinese library materials, fields in a full CN MARC record, schedule for the creation of the bibliographic database during the Eighth Five Year Plan, and schedule for the creation of factual databases and union catalogs during the Eighth Five Year Plan.

A number of omissions were found, but they do not diminish the total value of the book. The first is that there is no mention on modern library development between 1930 and 1949, which is the period under the Republic of China, in chapter1. The second is that in chapter 3 to 5 no mention was made on CALIS (China Academic Library and Information System), the most important development among academic libraries in recent years. The third is the omission in chapter 6 of the ILAS (Integrated Library Automation System) developed by Shenzhen Library that is now used by more than 1,700 libraries of all types and sizes in China.

650. Cravey, Pamela J. **Protecting Library Staff, Users, Collections, and Facilities: A How-To-Do-It Manual.** New York, Neal-Schuman, 2001. 175p. index. (How-To-Do-It Manuals for Librarians, no. 103) $55.00pa. ISBN 1-55570-392-5.

　　Library security is a complicated and important issue faced by libraries of all sizes, types, and ages. It requires a comprehensive and library-wide program and process to effectively deal with this multifarious issue. This How-To-Do-It manual provides a step-by-step guide to libraries on measures that should be taken to ensure staff and patron safety; to secure general and special collections, electronic files, and systems; and to cope with the legal issues. The book consists of seven chapters and a conclusion. Chapter 1 provides an overview of today's library security. Chapters 2 to 7 discuss the various security measures, such as general collections, users and employee, electronic files and systems, special collections, special events, and legal and personnel considerations. In the conclusion, the author suggests a series of actions to develop an overall security plan for each individual library that includes a disaster preparedness and implementation program. Written from the perspective of an experienced library administrator and front-line library security officer, this easy-to-read and practical guide is a valuable addition to the How-To-Do-It Manuals for Librarians series. ①

654. Reed, Sally Gardner. **Making the Case for Your Library: A How-To-Do-It Manual.** New York, Neal-Schuman, 2001. 143p. index. (How-To-Do-It Manual for Librarians, no. 104) $45.00pa. ISBN: 1-55570-399-2.

　　This very easy-to-read manual is intended to help library leaders, staff, and supporters assertively advocate, promote, defend, and ensure funding for their libraries at a time when libraries of all types and sizes are facing critical challenges, from misconceptions about the relevance of libraries in the new digital age to decreasing funding and public support. *Making the Case for Your Library* is divided into three parts. Part 1 discusses ways to develop and share a politically powerful message. Part 2 focuses on the ongoing campaign for support, such as how to keep the profile of a library high and viewed as important by the decision makers in its community or on its campus. Part 3 discusses how to develop an effective campaign for a specific purpose, such as passing a bond referendum or getting a significant increase in the operating budget. A wealth of selected library promotional materials that send a powerful message for support are included as samples in both parts 2 and 3. This 143-page manual covers all the basics for planning, targeting, and implementing advocacy campaigns and fulfills a very important need in professional library literature. It is highly recommended for all libraries. ②

657. Turner, Anne M. **Vote Yes for Libraries: A Guide to Winning Ballot Measure Campaigns for Library Funding.** Jefferson, N.C., McFarlan, 2000. 142p. index. $35.00pa. ISBN 0-7864-0855-3.

　　Winning ballot campaigns for library funding has been an important concern for public libraries throughout the country as most of them are facing increased demands for services that are more expensive to provide. More frequently than not, many of these libraries must go to their voters for operating levy approvals or for building funds. Even in the best financial times, persuading voters to support new taxes for libraries is not all easy.
　　Written by an experienced library director who has gone through both losing and winning

---

① R: RUSQ, Fall 01, p. 89.
② R: RUSQ. Fall01, pp. 88-89.

campaigns, this book is a very useful guide to any public library that is contemplating such a move and wants to win. Through the 14 chapters, the author provides easy-to-follow advice and examples from actual experiences. Among the titles of these chapters are: "In the Begging"; "Getting Organized and Making It Official"; "Will They Support It?"; "Campaign Consultants"; "Strategy: Part One of the Campaign Plan"; "Adding Up and Counting Backward"; "The Fundraising Plan"; "Ask, Ask, and Ask Again"; "Campaign Tactics: One-on-One Voter Contact"; "More Campaign Tactics"; "The Campaign and the Media"; "The Opposition"; and "And If You Lose". Although written as a practical guide for library campaigns, this book is also useful for library public relations, marketing, and politics. It is highly recommended for all public libraries. ①

2003

636. Hayes, Robert M. **Models for Library Management, Decision-Making, and Planning.** San Diego, Calif., Academic Press, 2001. 278p. index. (Library and Information Science) $99.95 (w/CD-ROM). ISBN 0-12-334151-5.

Models for Library Management, Decision-Making, and Planning, written by a distinguished information science professor, is a much-welcomed addition to the list of professional publications on library management. By scanning through the detailed table of contents, readers cannot help being impressed with the wide scope of coverage on all topics of modern library management. The purpose of this book, as stated by the author, is to provide an overview of models, mostly quantitative but with some qualitative and descriptive ones when applicable, that are of utility for library management.

There are nine chapters divided under three parts. Part 1, "Scientific Management and the Library Planning Model" consists of chapters 1 through 3. It provides a general introduction to the concepts and methods of modeling and an overview of the Library Planning Model (LPM) —a theoretical and practical model for library management. Part 2, "Library Operational and Tactical Management Contexts" consists of chapters 4 through 6. It deals with all major operational and tactical issues in library internal management. Part 3, "Library Strategic Management Contexts" consists of chapters 7 through 9. It discusses those strategic issues that are essentially external to the library, but that must be considered in library management.

Another important feature of this book is the enclosed CD-ROM on the LPM that includes most of the quantitative, qualitative, and descriptive models presented in the text in the form of a computer spreadsheet that enables readers to interrelate and bring together several models for application to specific libraries and policy contexts. At a time of rapid and profound changes taking place in the library and information profession in the digital, network, and knowledge age of the twenty first century, this book should be of special interest to all of those who are in library management positions as well as to those who aspire to it.

640. Reed, Sally Gardner. **Small Libraries: A Handbook for Successful Management.** 2d. ed. Jefferson, N. C., McFarland, 2002. 170p. index. $35.00pa. ISBN 0-784-1238-0.

This 2d edition of a very successful handbook on managing small public libraries should be of interest to anyone who is working or wishes to work in a small library. As was suggested by the author, managing a small library can be both a very challenging and rewarding experience in that one has to know the operations and services of the entire library, not just a part of it. Small libraries in small towns and communities are also the center of the neighborhoods they serve. They are an integral part of their respective communities.

---

① R: RUSQ. Spring01, pp. 300-301.

This concise handbook, written by an experienced librarian and a writer of several books on library management during the past decade, covers the whole range of library management in five chapters—from creating a political base, to personnel matters, collection development, library building, and service. Since the publication of the 1st edition 10 years ago must has changed on the library scene. This fully revised and updated edition provides current information on library automation and information technology and on advocacy to help small public libraries. The *Handbook* also includes many useful appendixes, such as sample documents for library friends groups, worksheets for job descriptions and personnel policies, a volunteer application form, the American Library Association's Library Bill of Rights and Code of Ethics, Internet use policy, a building program, and more. Following these appendixes are an annotated bibliography of other related books and an index.

2004

668. **Cooperative Efforts of Libraries.** William Miller and Rita M. Pellen, eds. Binghamton, N. Y, Haworth Press. 2002. 273p. index. $59.95; $34.95pa. ISBN 0-7890-2187-0; 0-7890-2188-9pa.

This book on library cooperation, co-published simultaneously as *Resource Sharing and Information Networks* (V. 16, Nos. 1 and 2, 2002) by Haworth Information Press, is a collection of 17 original articles on a variety of cooperative efforts undertaken by libraries in various states and regions of the United States. Three of these articles deal with some aspects of international cooperation.

The coverage of this collective work on selected cooperative initiatives are quite comprehensive, including virtual reference work in a multitype consortium, a consortia approach to cooperative cataloging and authority control, a joint information competence initiative, a state-wide cooperative collection development, resource sharing, cooperative preservation, shared storage facilities, and cross-border interlibrary loan and document deliver. Just as in most collective works, these are obvious omissions of other successful cooperative models. One such example is OhioLINK, the forerunner of many other state-wide library cooperatives. Although OCLC Online Computer Library Center was cited by several articles, it is definitely a serious omission to not have a separate article on OCLC, a pioneering effort in library cooperation and networking started in the late 1960s.

The two short introductions, one for each of the two parts of the book, are almost identical, differing only in the description of its articles. It would have been more useful with just one introduction that could have included an in-depth overview of the recent development in library cooperation in order to provide a historical background and perspective. Despite the shortcomings, this collective work does contribute to the library literature on the very important topic of library cooperation and networking.

2005

639. Christopher, Connie. **Empowering Your Library: A Guide to Improving Service, Productivity, & Participation.** Chicago, American Library Association, 2003. 75p. index. $30.00pa.; $27.00pa. (ALA members) ISBN: 0-8389-0858-6.

This how-to manual is a convenient and easy-to-read motivational book for beginners or junior managers who seek ideas or reinforcement for improving library service, productivity, and participation. The book covers topics on empowerment rationale, learning organization, motivation, communication, shared vision, trust, interpersonal and team skills, emotional intelligence, and library leadership. It is divided into three parts and nine chapters. Part 1 is on empowerment rationale. Part 2 is on making it happen. Part 3 is on building for the future. At the end of each chapter a number of notes are given. The book also includes a bibliography and an index.

The goal of this book, according to the author, is for readers to "learn how and why to empower the library, its teams, and individual employees; overcome resistance to change and other obstacles; encourage risk-taking, creativity, and innovation; access proven tools to motivate, communicate, and envision a new future; and build library leaders throughout the organization." Being one of the many management books published in recent years, this one may be considered a beginner's book. ①

2006

638. Gordon, Rachel Singer. **The Accidental Library Manager.** Medford, NJ. Information Today, 2005. 362p. index. $29.50pa. ISBN: 1-57387-210-5.

There have been a number of good books on library management. It is a pleasure to review another such book with a comprehensive coverage of general practice and theoretical background in library management. Even though many library managers may find themselves in the managerial position accidentally, to become a good library manager is by no means accidental! This is the reason that this book can be very useful.

The book is divided into 13 chapters. Chapter 1 discusses making the transition into library management. Chapter 2 addresses different levels of management and their usual responsibilities. Chapters 3–5 talk about managing people, communication, and leadership. Chapter 6 discusses some of the potential managerial pitfalls and desired behaviors from the perspective of library staff. Chapter 7 deals with such issues as library facilities and technology. Chapter 8 discusses managing change in today's library environment. Chapter 9 covers issues from budgeting to fundraising. Chapter 10 talks about building relationships. Chapter 11 provides a brief overview of management theories and principles. Chapter 12 discusses philosophical, legal, and ethical issues. Finally, chapter13 addresses the question of where to go from here in one's management career. The footnotes and recommended readings at the end of each chapter are also helpful features for readers. This work is recommended reading for all practicing librarians, whether managers or not. [R: LJ, 15 May 05, p. 152.]

2007

103. Gunawardcna. C. A. **Encyclopedia of Sri Lanka.** 2d rev. cd. Elgin. Ill., New Dawn Press Group: distr., Chicago. Independent Publishers Group. 2005. 399p. illus. $49.95. ISBN 1-932705-48-1.

This 2d edition of a one-volume encyclopedia of Sri Lanka has included a few revised, expanded, and new entries to reflect the changes that have taken place since its 2003 edition. It has also corrected the many omissions of the 1st edition. For a country that is less known to the outside world other than the famous "Ceylon tea", which was the country's chief agricultural export, this encyclopedia is a very important reference tool for readers who want to learn more about Sri Lanka. It would have been more useful if this encyclopedia also included an introductory chapter with a general history of the country instead of the very brief one-page "key facts" as well as the entry under the heading "History" listing only the "Important Events and Dates". It is also unfortunate that this encyclopedia does not include many important entries such as "Culture", "Government", and "People", to name just a few. However, one important feature of this

---

① R: LJ, 15 Nov 03, p. 104.

encyclopedia is its extensive coverage of biographical information, which takes up almost one-third of the total 1,200 entries and can serve as a Sri Lankan who's who.

"The merit of this book", as one reviewer put it "is its comprehensive range of subjects and the style in which it is communicated". Having a background as a journalist, the author of this encyclopedia has applied his skill in reporting to make this reference book very readable to the general readers who seek information on Sri Lanka. The short bibliography at the end of this book helps to provide leads to additional in-depth scholarly sources on Sri Lanka for serious readers who wish to learn more about the country. The book also contains over 100 photographs, including 20 in color, and a number of tables for easy reference.

2008

549. **The Impact of Technology on Asian, African, and Middle Eastern Library Collections.** R. N. Sharma, ed. Lanham, MD., Scarecrow, 2006. 278p. index. (Libraries and Librarianship: An International Perspective) $50.00pa. ISBN: 0-8108-5448-1.

Library development in Asia, Africa, and the Middle East, especially in the area of technology applications, varies by countries and regions. This book about the impact of technology on Asian, African, and Middle Eastern library collections consists of an introduction and 15 papers written by some of the most knowledgeable library professionals who are very familiar with the topic or geographical area about which each was invited to write. Under the editorship of R. N. Sharma, the 15 papers are grouped in five parts: "Worldwide", "Asia", "Africa", "Middle East", and "Barriers".

The leading paper in part 1 on the Global Memory Net, written by Ching-chih Chen, describes the application of cutting-edge technologies to link global cultural, historical, and heritage multimedia contents over a distributed network. There are five papers in part 2 led by Andrew Wang's article on "OCLC Library Information Services and Libraries in Asia and the Pacific Region". The other four papers describe the situations in India, Vietnam, China, as well as South Asian collections and services in U.S. libraries. There are also five papers in part 3 covering information poverty in Africa, academic libraries in Botswana and Francophone Africa, collections and services in Nigeria, and African collections in the United States. The lead paper in part 4 is on the Arab countries of the Middle East and North Africa written by Mohammed M. Aman. There are two other papers, one on Egypt and another on Middle Eastern collections and services in the United States. The last part, written by R. N. Sharma, lists a number of barriers in the application of technology in less developed or developing countries in Asia, Africa, and the Middle East. As a way of conclusion, Sharma also offer his suggestions for improvement.

As the first publication in the new series, Libraries and Librarianship: An International Perspective, this book is a useful addition to the literature on comparative librarianship with special focus on the application of information technology by countries in Asia, Africa, and the Middle East. It is also a very important information source for learning about some of the area study collections in the United States.[①]

(Published in *American Reference Books Annual*, 1978-2008.)

---

① R: LJ. 15 Oct 06, p. 90.

附录1：李华伟著述系年①

Appendix I: A Chronicle of Hwa-Wei Lee's Writing

1963 年

1. Hwa-Wei Lee. Africana at Duquesne University Library. *African Studies Bulletin*. V. 6, No. 3 (October 1963): pp. 25 – 27.

2. Hwa-Wei Lee. Africana—A Special Collection at Duquesne University. The Catholic Library World. V. 35, No. 4 (December 1963): pp. 209 – 211. Also in *Librarianship in World Perspective: Selected Writings, 1963 – 1989*. Taipei: Student Book Company, 1991.

1964 年

3. Hwa-Wei Lee. Educational Development in Taiwan under "Nationalist Government", 1945 – 1962. Ph. D. dissertation, University of Pittsburgh, 1964.

1966 年

4. 李华伟. 留美学生所面对的实际问题及其认识——出席美国中西部各大学中国留学生申请入学审查研讨会记要. 中国一周, 第834期, 1966年4月18日, 第12 – 15页.

1968 年

5. Hwa-Wei Lee. The Recent Educational Reform in "Communist China". *School and Society*. V. 46, No. 2311 (November 9), 1968: pp. 395 – 400.

1969 年

6. Hwa-Wei Lee. Computer Application in Library and Information Services: The Current AIT Experiments and Future Plans. Paper presented at the First Computer Applications Symposium jointly sponsored by the Computer Science Laboratory, Chulalongkorn University and U. S. Educational Foundation in Thailand, Bangkok, June 23 – 25, 1969. （因未找到原文，本文集暂未收录）

7. Hwa-Wei Lee. Planning for Computer Applications in the AIT Library. Paper presented at the 1969 annual conference of the Thai Library Association, Bangkok, December 15 – 19, 1969. （因未找到原文，本文集暂未收录）

1971 年

8. Hwa-Wei Lee. Proposal for a Regional Information Center for Science and Technology at the Asian Institute of Technology. Bangkok, Thailand: Asian Institute of Technology, January 1971.

---

① 共164条，含20条书评，40条会议论文；本文集未获取原文10篇。

9. Hwa-Wei Lee. Fragmentation of Academic Library Resources in Thai University Libraries. *International Library Review*. V. 3, No. 2 (April 1971): pp. 155 – 167. Also in *Librarianship in World Perspective: Selected Writings, 1963 – 1989*. Taipei: Student Book Company, 1991.

10. Hwa-Wei Lee. Library Mechanization at the Asian Institute of Technology. *International Library Review*. V. 3, No. 3 (July 1971): pp. 257 – 270.

11. Hwa-Wei Lee. A New Engineering Library Emerging in Asia. *Libraries in International Development*. No. 41 (December 1971): p. 103. Also in *Librarianship in World Perspective: Selected Writings, 1963 – 1989*. Taipei: Student Book Company, 1991.

1972 年

12. Hwa-Wei Lee. An Approach to Regional Cooperation In Scientific and Technical Information Services For Southeast Asia. *Proceedings of the Conference on Scientific and Technical Information Needs for Malaysia and Singapore*. Kuala Lumpur: Persatuan Perpustakaan Malaysia and Library Association of Singapore, 1972: pp. 97 – 105. In a revised form, also in *A Survey of Automated Activities in the Libraries of Asia and the Far East*. (World Survey Series, V. 5). Peoria, Illinois: The Larc Press, 1974: pp. 11 – 17. Also in *Librarianship in World Perspective: Selected Writings, 1963 – 1989*. Taipei: Student Book Company, 1991.

1973 年

13. Hwa-Wei Lee. The Information Technology—New Tools and New Possibilities for Information Storage, Retrieval and Dissemination. Paper presented at the Regional Seminar on Information Storage, Retrieval and Dissemination, organized by Asian Mass Communication Research and Information Centre in cooperation with the National Research Council of Thailand, Bangkok, March 26 – 30, 1973. Also in *Librarianship in World Perspective: Selected Writings, 1963 – 1989*. Taipei: Student Book Company, 1991.

14. Hwa-Wei Lee. Asian Information Center for Geotechnical Engineering. Progress Report, January to June 1973. Bangkok, Thailand: Asian Institute of Technology, July 1973. （因未找到原文，本文集暂未收录）

15. Hwa-Wei Lee. Partner for School Library Development in Thailand. *T. L. A. Bulletin*. V. 17, No. 5 (September/October 1973): pp. 443 – 448.

1974 年

16. 李华伟. 建立全国图书资料网刍议. "中央日报"（台北）. 1974 年 2 月 26 ~ 27 日. 又见: 李华伟著. 图书馆学的世界观. 台北: 学生书局. 1991.

17. Hwa-Wei Lee. Possibilities in Employing Computer and Other Information Technologies to Further Library and Information Services in Southeast Asia. *Network*. V. 1, No. 3 (March 1974): pp. 10 – 12, 24 – 28.

18. Hwa-Wei Lee & S. W. Massil. Library Automation at the Asian Institute of Technology—Bangkok. *The Larc Reports*. V. 7, No. 3, 1974.

19. Hwa-Wei Lee. The Application of Information Technology to Close the Information Gap. Paper presented at the First Conference on Asian Library cooperation. Tamsui, Taipei, August

19-22, 1974. Also in *Librarianship in World Perspective*: *Selected Writings*, *1963-1989*. Taipei: Student Book Company, 1991.

20. Hwa-Wei Lee. User and Use Analysis: A Case Study of the Information Utility by Geotechnical Engineers in Asian Countries. *Information Utilities*: *Proceedings of the 37th Annual Conference of the American Society for Information Science*. Edited by Pranas Zunde. Washington, D. C.: 1974, V. II: pp. 133-136. Also in *Librarianship in World Perspective*: *Selected Writings*, *1963-1989*. Taipei: Student Book Company, 1991.

21. Hwa-Wei Lee & S. W. Massil. Proposal for Library Development at Prince of Songkla University in Southern Thailand. Prepared at the request of the University Development Project Office, Prince of Songkla University. Bangkok: Asian Institute of Technology, 1974.（因未找到原文，本文集暂未收录）

1975 年

22. S. W. Massil & Hwa-Wei Lee. Scholarly Publications: Considerations on Bibliographic Control and Dissemination. *Scholarly Publishing in Southeast Asia*. Edited by Beda Lim. Kuala Lumpur: 1975: pp. 212-218. Also in *Librarianship in World Perspective*: *Selected Writings*, *1963-1989*. Taipei: Student Book Company, 1991.

23. 李华伟, 杨黄晴. 国际图书刊物统一编号及著录的标准. 图书馆学与资讯科学, 1975年第1卷第1期, 第60-66页. 又见: 李华伟著. 图书馆学的世界观. 台北: 学生书局. 1991.

24. Hwa-Wei Lee. The Experience of a Specialized Information Service in Asia—AGE. Paper presented at the Round Table Conference on Documentation Problems in Developing Countries, Khartoum, Sudan, April 10-11, 1975 sponsored by FID/DC and FID National Member in Sudan. Also in *Journal of Library and Information Science*. V. 1, No. 2 (Oct. 1975), pp. 82-93. Also in *Librarianship in World Perspective*: *Selected Writings*, *1963-1989*. Taipei: Student Book Company, 1991.

25. 李华伟. 国际图书馆界最近的重要发展. 中华图书馆协会会报. 1975年第27期, 第34-36页.

1976 年

26. Hwa-Wei Lee. *The Possibility of Establishing a Regional Centre for the International Serials Data System in Thailand*. (SC-76/WS/7). Paris: UNESCO, 1976.

27. Hwa-Wei Lee. The Third Conference of Southeast Asian Librarians. *Leads*. V. 18, No. 1 (March 1976): pp. 3-4.

28. Hwa-Wei Lee. Proposal for the Establishment of an ISDS Regional Center for Southeast Asia in Thailand. *Leads*. V. 18, No. 2 (July 1976): pp. 4-5.

1977 年

29. Hwa-Wei Lee. Regional Cooperation for ISDS. *Proceedings of the Third Conference of Southeast Asian Librarians*. Edited by Luwarsih Pringgoadisurjo and Kardiati Sjahrial. Jakarta: PDIN-LIPI for Ikatan Pustakawan Indonesia (Indonesian Librarians Association), 1977: pp. 159

–166. Also in *Librarianship in World Perspective*: *Selected Writings*, *1963 – 1989*. Taipei: Student Book Company, 1991.

30. Hwa-Wei Lee. Cooperative Regional Bibliographic Projects in Southeast Asia. Paper presented at the Library Seminars of the International Association of Oriental Librarians held in conjunction with the 30th International Congress of Human Sciences in Asia and North Africa, Mexico City, August 3 – 8, 1976. Also in *UNESCO Bulletin for Libraries*. V. 31, No. 6 (Nov. – Dec. 1977): pp. 344 – 351, 370. Also in *Librarianship in World Perspective*: *Selected Writings*, *1963 – 1989*. Taipei: Student Book Company, 1991.

1978 年

31. Hwa-Wei Lee & Marjorie Rhoades. Approaches to Development of Water Resources Scientific Information Systems. *Water Knowledge Transfer*: *Proceedings of the Second International Conference on Transfer of Water Resources Knowledge*. Fort Collins, Colorado: Water Resource Publications, 1978, V. 2: pp. 625 – 644. Also in *Librarianship in World Perspective*: *Selected Writings*, *1963 – 1989*. Taipei: Student Book Company, 1991.

32. Hwa-Wei Lee. Sharing Information Resources Through Computer-assisted Systems and Networking. *Journal of Library and Information Science*. V. 4, No. 1 (April 1978): pp. 14 – 24. Also in *Resource Sharing of Libraries in Developing Countries*: *Proceedings of the 1977 IFLA/ UNESCO Pre-Session Seminar for Librarians from Developing Countries*. Munchen: K. G. Saur, 1979: pp. 208 – 216. Also in *Librarianship in World Perspective*: *Selected Writings*, *1963 – 1989*. Taipei: Student Book Company, 1991.

33. Hwa-Wei Lee. Impact of International Information System and Programs on NATIS. Paper presented at the 4th Congress of Southeast Asian Librarians on Regional Co-operation for the Development of National Information Services, June 5 – 9, 1978, Bangkok, Thailand. In a revised form, also in *Proceedings of Regional Cooperation for the Development of National Information Services*. Bangkok: Thai Library Association, 1981: pp. 133 – 146.

1979 年

34. Hwa-Wei Lee. The Millionth Volume. *The Library Scene*. V. 8, No. 4 (December 1979): p. 24.

35. Hwa-Wei Lee. The Current Status of Academic Library Administration in the U. S. Paper presented at the Annual Meeting of Directors of Academic and Research Libraries, Taipei, December 1, 1979. （因未找到原文，本文集暂未收录）

1980 年

36. 李华伟. 线上作业与图书馆. 见：台湾师范大学图书馆编. 图书馆规划与媒体技术：图书馆实务研讨会会议记录. 1980 年，第 14 – 17 页.

37. K. Mulliner, Lian The-Mulliner and Hwa-wei Lee. International Information Exchange and Southeast Asia Collections—A View from the U. S. Paper presented at the 1980 Meeting of the International Association of Orientalist Librarians, Manila, August 17 – 23, 1980. Also in *Journal of Educational Media Science*. V. 18, No. 2 (Winter 1980): pp. 3 – 18. Also in *Librarianship in*

World Perspective: *Selected Writings*, *1963 – 1989*. Taipei: Student Book Company, 1991.

1981 年

38. Hwa-Wei Lee. A Sketch for a Computerized National Library and Information Network. Paper presented at the International Workshop on Chinese Library Automation, Taipei, February 14 – 19, 1981. Also in *Librarianship in World Perspective: Selected Writings*, *1963 – 1989*. Taipei: Student Book Company, 1991.

39. Hwa-Wei Lee. Book Review. *American Reference Books Annual*. V. 12. 1981: p. 140.

1982 年

40. K. Mulliner & Hwa-Wei Lee (Editor and Compiler). *Acquisitions from the Third World*, special thematic issue of *Library Acquisitions: Practice and Theory*. V. 6, No. 2 (1982): pp. 79 – 238.

41. K. Mulliner & Hwa-Wei Lee. Library Acquisitions from the Third World: An Introduction. *Library Acquisitions: Practice and Theory*. V. 6, No. 2 (1982): pp. 79 – 85. Also in *Librarianship in World Perspective: Selected Writings*, *1963-1989*. Taipei: Student Book Company, 1991.

42. Hwa-Wei Lee. Recent Breakthroughs in Library Automation in Taiwan. *Journal of Educational Media Science*. V. 19, No. 2 (Winter 1982): pp. 119 – 136. Also in *Librarianship in World Perspective: Selected Writings*, *1963 – 1989*. Taipei: Student Book Company, 1991.

43. Hwa-Wei Lee & K. Mulliner. International Exchanges of Librarians and the Ohio University Internship Program. Paper presented to the International Relations Round Table of the American Library Association at the ALA Conference in Philadelphia, July 1982. Also in *College & Research Libraries News*. V. 43, No. 10 (November 1982): pp. 345 – 348. Also in *Librarianship in World Perspective: Selected Writings*, *1963 – 1989*. Taipei: Student Book Company, 1991.

44. Hwa-Wei Lee. Book Review. *American Reference Books Annual*. V. 13. 1982: p. 153.

1983 年

45. Hwa-Wei Lee. Challenges for the Library and Information Profession. *Bulletin of the Library Association of China*. No. 35 (1983): pp. 235 – 246. Also in *Librarianship in World Perspective: Selected Writings*, *1963 – 1989*. Taipei: Student Book Company, 1991.

46. Hwa-Wei Lee. Book Review. *American Reference Books Annual*. V. 14. 1983: pp. 97 – 98.

1984 年

47. Hwa-Wei Lee, K. Mulliner, E. Hoffmann-Pinther, and Hannah McCauley. ALICE at One: Candid Reflections on the Adoption, Installation, and Use of the Virginia Tech Library System (VTLS) at Ohio University. Paper presented at the Integrated Online Library Systems Second National Conference, September 13 – 14, 1984, in Atlanta, Georgia. Also in the Proceedings. Canfield, Ohio: Genaway & Associates, 1984: pp. 228 – 242. Also in

Librarianship in World Perspective: Selected Writings, 1963 – 1989. Taipei: Student Book Company, 1991.

48. M. Beckman, Hwa-Wei Lee and Jianyan Huang. Management of Scientific and Technical Information Centres: Aspects of Planning a Course Sponsored by IDRC (Canada) and ISTIC (China). Paper presented at the International Federation for Documentation (FID) Pre-Congress Workshop on Curriculum Development in a Changing World, The Hague, September 3 – 4, 1984.

1985 年

49. Sally C. Tseng, Hwa-Wei Lee and K. Mulliner (Editor). *Areas of Cooperation in Library Development in Asia and Pacific Regions.* Papers presented at the 1983 Joint Annual Program of the Asian/Pacific American Librarians Association and Chinese American Librarians Association, June 28 – 29, 1983, Los Angeles, California. Athens, Ohio: Chinese American Librarians Association, 1985.

50. Hwa-Wei Lee. International Library Internships: An Effective Approach to Cooperation. Paper presented to the annual program of the Asian/Pacific American Librarians Association and the Chinese American Librarians Association, in conjunction with the annual American Library Association conference, Los Angeles, June 28 – 29, 1983. Also in *Areas of Cooperation in Library Development in Asian and Pacific Regions.* Athens, Ohio: Chinese-American Librarians Association, 1985: pp. 21 – 27. In a revised form, in the *International Library Review.* V. 17, No. 1 (1985), pp. 17 – 25. Also in *Librarianship in World Perspective: Selected Writings, 1963 – 1989.* Taipei: Student Book Company, 1991.

51. Hwa-Wei Lee. *Lecture Notes and Suggested Readings on Modern Library Management and Automation.* Athens, Ohio, 1985.（因未找到原文，本文集暂未收录）

52. K. Mulliner & Hwa-Wei Lee. Educating for International Interdependence: The Role of the Academic Library—Ohio University and Malaysia. Paper presented at the First Annual Tun Abdul Razak Conference in Malaysia, Athens, Ohio, May 10, 1985. Also see *Librarianship in World Perspective: Selected Writings, 1963 – 1989.*

1986 年

53. K. Mulliner & Hwa-Wei Lee. Funding for the Southeast Asia Collection and Research Resources at Ohio University. Paper presented at the Annual Meeting of the Association for Asian Studies in Chicago, Illinois, March 21, 1986. Also see *Librarianship in World Perspective: Selected Writings, 1963 – 1989.*

54. Hwa-Wei Lee. International Exchanges and Internships for Librarians. Paper presented at the LACUNY (Library Association of the City University of New York) Institute '86, New York City, April 4, 1986.（因未找到原文，本文集暂未收录）

55. 李华伟. 美国图书馆现状及其发展动向. 福建省图书馆学会通讯. 1986 年第 1 期, 第 34 – 38 页.

56. Hwa-Wei Lee. Book Review. *American Reference Books Annual.* V. 17. 1986. pp. 216 – 217.

1987 年

57. Hwa-Wei Lee. Principles and Issues on National Library and Information Policy. *Papers of the Library Cooperation and Development Seminar*. Taipei: National Central Library, 1987: pp. 5.1 – 5.22. Also in *Journal of Library and Information Science*. V. 13, No. 1 (April 1987): pp. 1 – 16. Also in *Librarianship in World Perspective: Selected Writings, 1963 – 1989*. Taipei: Student Book Company, 1991.

58. Hwa-Wei Lee. Applications of Information Technology in an American Library—The Case of Ohio University Libraries. *Proceedings of the First Pacific Conference on New Information Technology for Library and Information Professionals*. Edited by Ching-Chih Chen and David I. Raitt. West Newton, MA: MicroUse Information, 1987: pp. 155 – 164.

59. Hwa-Wei Lee. Library Automation at Ohio University Library: Past, Present and Future. Published in *Collection of Essays Honoring Chiang Wei-Tang on His Ninetieth Birthday*. Taipei, Taiwan, Library Association of China, 1987: 47 – 72.

1988 年

60. Zhang Zhiyou & Hwa-Wei Lee (Editor). *Proceedings of the International Symposium on New Techniques and Applications in Libraries*. Xi'an: Xi'an Jiaotong University Press, 1988.

61. James Bryant & Hwa-Wei Lee. Preface by Ohio University. *Proceedings of the International Symposium on New Techniques and Applications in Libraries*. Edited by Xi'an: Xi'an Jiaotong University Press, 1988: pp. 3 – 4.

1989 年

62. Hwa-Wei Lee. Trends in Automation in American Academic Libraries: Ohio University's Experience. By Educational Resources Information Center, ED 315 081, ERIC Clearinghouse, May 1989. Also in Journal of *Educational Media & Library Sciences*. V. 27, No. 1 (Autumn 1989): pp. 1 – 23. Also in *Librarianship in World Perspective: Selected Writings, 1963 – 1989*. Taipei: Student Book Company, 1991.

63. 李华伟. 美国图书馆自动化六十年代以来的重要里程碑. 台湾"中央图书馆"馆讯, 1989 年 11 月第 11 卷第 4 期第 4 – 7 页.

64. Hwa-Wei Lee. Planning Process and Considerations for a State-Wide Academic Libraries Information System in Ohio. *Proceedings of the Second Pacific Conference on New Information Technology for Library and Information Professionals and Educational Media Specialists and Technologists*. Edited by Ching-chih Chen and David I Raitt. West Newton, MA: MicroUse Information, 1989: 203 – 210. Also in *Journal of Educational Media & Library Sciences*. V. 27, No. 2 (Winter 1990): pp. 127 – 138. Also in *Librarianship in World Perspective: Selected Writings, 1963 – 1989*. Taipei: Student Book Company, 1991.

65. 李华伟. 图书馆服务的新观念与新技术. 见: 图书馆学讲座专辑之十. 高雄, 台湾: 中山大学图书馆, 1989.

1990 年

66. Hwa-Wei Lee. *Final Report of the INNERTAP Project Review*. Consultant Report on the Information Network on New and Renewable Energy Resources and Technologies for Asia and the Pacific, commissioned by the International Development Research Centre. Ottawa, Canada: IDRC, 1990.（因未找到原文，本文集暂未收录）

1991 年

67. Hwa-Wei Lee. *Librarianship in World Perspective: Selected Writings, 1963 – 1989*. Taipei: Student Book Company, 1991.

68. Hwa-Wei Lee. *Library Development, Resource Sharing, and Networking among Higher Education Institutions in Papua New Guinea. Final Report and Recommendations*. Port Moresby, Papua New Guinea: Commission for Higher Education, 1991.

69. Hwa-Wei Lee & Anne S. Goss. Medical Librarianship in China: Recent Developments. *Asian Libraries*. V. 1, No. 1 (March 1991): pp. 80 – 84.

70. Hwa-Wei Lee. The 1991 White House Conference Participant Observations. *ALAO Newsletter*. V. 10, No. 1 (September 1991): pp. 6 – 7.（因未找到原文，本文集暂未收录）

71. Hwa-Wei Lee. Book Review. *American Reference Books Annual*. V. 22. 1991: pp. 240.

1992 年

72. Hwa-Wei Lee & Gary Hunt. *Fundraising for the 1990s: The Challenge Ahead—A Practical Guide for Library Fundraising: From Novice to Expert*. Canfield, Ohio: Genaway and Associates, 1992.

73. Hwa-Wei Lee. New Visions in Library Automation and Networking—Ohio's Approach to the 1990s. Paper presented at the International Conference on New Frontiers in Library Information Services, May 8 – 12, 1991 *Proceedings*. 2 vols. Taipei, Taiwan: National Central Library, 1992: pp. 361 – 382.

74. 李华伟. 图书馆自动化和网络化的新境界——俄亥俄走向九十年代. 鲍平，张晓艳译. 大学图书馆学报，1992 年第 1 期第 38 – 45 页.

75. Hwa-Wei Lee. The Future Begins Now: Ohio's Library Automation, Information Services and Networking. Presented at "the International Seminar on Collection Development and Resource Sharing in Modern Library"（现代图书馆藏书建设与资源共享国际研讨会），May 17 – 20, 1992, Xi'an, China. Published in *The Proceedings of the International Seminar on Collection Development and Resource Sharing in Modern Library*, edited by Chen Yu, published by Shanghai Scientific & Technical Publishers, 1992: pp. 59 – 60.

76. Judith Sessions, Hwa-Wei Lee and Stacey Kimmel. OhioLINK: Technology and Teamwork Transforming Ohio Libraries. *Wilson Library Bulletin*. V. 66, No. 10 (June 1992): pp. 43 – 45.

77. Hwa-Wei Lee & John Evans. Developing Higher Education Libraries in Papua New Guinea. *Information Development: The International Journal for Librarians, Archivists and Information Specialists*. Vol. 8, No. 2 (November 1992): pp. 221 – 227.

78. Hwa-Wei Lee & Gary Hunt. The Ten Principles for Successful Fundraising. *The Bottom Line*. V. 6, No. 3/4 (Winter 1992/Spring 1993): pp. 27 – 33.

79. Hwa-Wei Lee & Gary Hunt. Contributions of International Faculty to International Education on Campuses. Paper presented at the 1992 Ohio Chinese Academic and Professional Association, Columbus, Ohio, April 1992.

1993 年

80. Hwa-Wei Lee. Advancing Information Technologies: The Role of National Libraries. Paper presented to the International Conference on National Libraries: Toward the 21st Century, sponsored by the National Central Library, Taiwan, April 20 – 24, 1993.

81. Hwa-Wei Lee. Ohio Academic Libraries Prepare for the 21st Century. *Library in the 90's, Selected Papers of the International Symposium on the Latest Development in Technologies of Library Service*. Beijing: International Academic Publishers, 1993: pp. 292 – 308.

82. Hwa-Wei Lee. Managing Information Technology—The Experience of Ohio Academic Libraries. Paper presented to the IX Congress of Southeast Asian Librarians (CONSAL) in Bangkok, May 2 – 7, 1993, and the Seminar on National Academic Library Networking, May 12, – 14, 1993, Chiang Mai, Thailand. *CONSAL IX Papers: Future Dimensions and Library Development*. Bangkok: CONSAL IX Secretariat, 1993: pp. B45 – B62.

83. Angela Lew & Hwa-Wei Lee. *Workshops and Consultation on the Management of Libraries and Information for the Institutes of Education in China*. (A World Bank Funded Teacher Training Project, held in Tianjin, Beijing, and Shanghai, July 11 to August 8, 1993). August 15, 1993.

84. Hwa-Wei Lee. Expanding Ties between Ohio and Chinese Libraries. *Ohio Libraries*. V. 6, No. 4 (Fall 1993): pp. 22 – 23.

85. 李华伟. 管理资讯技术——俄亥俄州大学图书馆之经验. 政大图资通讯, 1993 年 11 月第 7 期第 1 – 11 页.

1994 年

86. Hwa-Wei Lee. Managing Information Technology—the Experience of Ohio Academic Libraries. *Chiang Mai University Library Journal*. V. 4. 1994: pp. 20 – 43.

87. Hwa-Wei Lee. Networked, Electronic and Virtual Library—Libraries of the 1990s. *Proceedings of the International Seminar on Information Technologies and Information Services*. Beijing: China Social Sciences Publishing House, 1994. V. 2, pp. 167 – 172. Also in *Journal of Educational Media & Library Sciences*. V. 32, No. 2 (Winter 1995): pp. 119 – 129.

88. Hwa-Wei Lee. Book Review. *American Reference Books Annual*. V. 25. 1994: pp. 272.

1995 年

89. 李华伟. 网络化、电子化的虚拟图书馆——20 世纪 90 年代的图书馆. 图书与情报. 辛小萍, 张海华编译. 1995 年第 3 期第 73 – 75 页.

90. Kent Mulliner & Hwa-Wei Lee. Southeast Asia Collection Growth in the United States: Ohio University's Experience. *In the Information Challenge. A Festschrift in Honor of Dr. Donald Wijasuriya*. Edited by Ch'ng Kim See. Kuala Lumpur: Knowledge Publishers, 1995: pp. 87 – 103.

91. Hwa-Wei Lee. Global Information Access: Libraries as Citizens' Gateway to the World. Paper presented at the Chubu University-Ohio University Conference on Lifelong Learning for the 21st Century: Local and Global Dimensions, October 4 – 6, 1994. Kasugai, Japan. Also in *The Proceedings of Chubu University-Ohio University Conference on Lifelong Learning for the 21st Century: Local and Global Dimensions*. Kasugai: Chubu University, 1995: pp. 75 – 82.

92. Hwa-Wei Lee. Program *CPR/91/420 Basic Education: Administration and Teachers Training. Consultant Report*, submitted to United Nations Educational, Scientific and Cultural Organization, June 30, 1995.

1996 年

93. 李华伟. 现代化图书馆管理. 台北: 三民书局, 1996.

94. Hwa-Wei Lee. American Contributions to Modern Library Development in China: A Historic Review. Paper presented at the China—US Conference on Global Information Access: Challenges and Opportunities, held in Beijing, China, August 21 – 23, 1996. Also in *Journal of Information, Communication, and Library Science*. V. 4, No. 4 (Summer 1998): pp. 10 – 20.

95. Hwa-Wei Lee. Sharing of Library and Information Resources: the OhioLink Model. Presented at the International Conference on "1996 Information Resources and Society Development" (1996 信息资源与社会发展国际学术研讨会), Wuhan, September 3 – 6, 1996.

1997 年

96. Hwa-Wei Lee & Gary Hunt. The Ten Principles for Successful Fundraising. *Sponsoring fur Bibliotheken*. Edited by Rolf Busch. Berlin: Deutsches Bibliotheksinstiut, 1997: pp. 130 – 141.

1998 年

97. Hwa-Wei Lee. Maximizing Information Access and Resource Sharing: The OhioLINK Experience. Paper presented at the 10th International Conference on New Information Technology, March 24 – 26, 1998, Hanoi, Vietnam. Also in the *Proceedings*. Edited by Ching-Chih Chen. West Newton, MA: MicroUse Information, 1998: pp. 149 – 156.

98. Hwa-Wei Lee. Maximizing Information Access and Resources Sharing: The OhioLINK Approach. Paper presented at the International Conference on New Missions of Academic Libraries in the 21st Century, October 25 – 28, 1998, Beijing, China. Also in the *Proceedings*. Beijing: Peking University Press, 1998: pp. 283 – 287.

1999 年

99. 刁维汉, 王行仁, 李华伟. OCLC 联机与光盘编目概论. 上海: 华东师范大学出版社, 1999.

100. 李华伟. 图书馆编目的自动化（Automated Cataloging in Libraries）. 见: 刁维汉、王行仁、李华伟编著. OCLC 联机与光盘编目概论（第二章）. 上海: 华东师范大学出版社, 1999: 47 – 64.

101. Hwa-Wei Lee. Library Cooperation and the Development of a Library Network—The

OhioLINK. Paper presented at the Seminar on Library Cooperation, Resource Sharing and the Development of Networks, August 19 – 20, 1999, Bangkok, Thailand, organized by the Rajabhat Institute Bansomdejchaopraya. Also in the *Proceedings*. Bangkok: Rajabhat Institute Bansomdejchaopraya, 1999: pp. 1 – 27. （因未找到原文，本文集暂未收录）

102. Hwa-Wei Lee. The Success of OhioLINK for Information Access and Resources Sharing in a Networked Environment. Published in *Bulletin of Library and Information Science*. V. 30, No. 8, 1999: p. 1 – 17.

103. 李华伟. 网络环境中 OhioLink 在信息获取和资源共享方面所取得的成就. 在 "1999 现代图书馆的服务与管理讲习班" 上发表, 1999 年 9 月 13 – 15 日, 浙江大学图书馆.

104. 李华伟. 网络环境中的图书馆合作和资源共享. 见：网际网路与图书馆发展研讨会论文集, 台北, 台湾图书馆学会, 1999 年, 第 3 – 44 页.

105. Hwa-Wei Lee. *Ohio University Libraries 1998 – 99 Annual Report*. Athens, Ohio: Ohio University Libraries, 1999.

106. Hwa-Wei Lee. Book Review. *Library and Information Science Annual*. V. 7. 1999: pp. 113 – 114.

2000 年

107. Hwa-Wei Lee. A New Milestone Reached and a New Chapter Opened. *International Conference of Institutes and Libraries for Overseas Chinese Studies Papers and Abstracts*. Published by Dr. You-Bao Shao Overseas Chinese Document and Research Center. Athens, Ohio: Ohio University Libraries, 2000: pp. 1 – 2.

108. Hwa-Wei Lee. Libraries in the Digital and Networked Knowledge Age of the Twenty-First Century. Paper presented at the Seminar on 21st Century Public Libraries: Vision and Reality, May 1 – 3, 2000, Taipei, Taiwan, organized by the Central Taiwan Office of the Council for Cultural Development of ROC. Also in the *Proceedings*. Taichung, Taiwan: National Taichung Library, 2000: pp. 43 – 68.

109. 李华伟. 21 世纪数位化及网路化知识时代中的图书馆. 见：台中图书馆编印. 新世纪・新理念——公共图书馆发展事务研讨会论文集. 赖丽香译, 2000 年, 第 69 – 88 页.

110. Hwa-Wei Lee. Knowledge Management and the Role of Libraries in the New Century. Published in *Prospects of the 21st Century*, Taichung, Taiwan: Feng Chia University and Liao Ying-Ming Cultural and Educational Foundation, 2000: pp. 397 – 436.

2001 年

111. Hwa-Wei Lee. Does Library have a Role in Knowledge Management. Paper presented at the 12th International Conference on New Information Technology, May 29 – 31, 2001, Beijing, China. Also in *Global Digital Library Development in the New Millennium*. Edited by Ching-Chih Chen. Beijing: Tsinghua University Press, 2001: pp. 145 – 152.

112. Hwa-Wei Lee. Foreword. *The Centered Life: An Introduction to I Chine-Book of Changes. The Universal Principles of Living and Its Amazing Oracle*. Raleigh, North Carolina: Pentland Press, 2001: pp. XV-XVI.

113. Hwa-Wei Lee. Book Review. *American Reference Books Annual*. V. 32. 2001：p. 294.

2002 年

114. 李华伟. 知识管理与图书馆在 21 世纪所扮演的角色. 见：李华伟，董小英，左美云著. 知识管理的理论与实践（第十四章）. 北京：华艺出版社，2002.

115. Hwa-Wei Lee. Strategic Direction of Libraries in Knowledge Management. Published in *New Technology of Library and Information Service*（《现代图书情报技术》，S1，2002：13-17.

116. Ratana Na-Lamphun & Hwa-Wei Lee. Focusing on Information and Knowledge Management：Redesigning the Graduate Program of Library and Information Science at Chiang Mai University. *Information Development*. V. 18，No. 1（March 2002）：pp. 47-58.

117. 李华伟. 实施知识管理，提供优质服务，促进知识创新. 见：知识管理：图书馆的机遇与挑战学术研讨会录，北京：中国科学院出版，2002，第 90-94 页. 又见：图书情报工作动态，2002 年第 4 期第 2-6 页.

118. 刘淑德，李华伟. 非营利组织在电子期刊出版营销的合作模式：以 SPARC 与 OCLC 合作 BIO-ONE 为例. 中国图书馆学会会报，2002 年 6 月第 68 期第 14-25 页.

119. Hwa-Wei Lee. Who should be in Charge of Knowledge Management，Librarians/Libraries or Someone else Presented in the International Seminar on Digital Library Age：Current Situation and Development Trend（"数字图书馆时代：现状与发展趋势"国际学术研讨会），Beijing，China，October 23-25，2002. Published in *Journal of Academic Libraries*，supplement issue（增刊），2002：pp. 79-84.

120. Hwa-Wei Lee. Libraries in Asia：New Life for Libraries in the Digital Age. *Harvard Asia Pacific Review*（Fall 2002）：pp. 22-24.

121. Hwa-Wei Lee. Book Review. *American Reference Books Annual*. V. 33. 2002：p. 266.

122. Hwa-Wei Lee. Book Review. *American Reference Books Annual*. V. 33. 2002：p. 279.

123. Hwa-Wei Lee. Book Review. *American Reference Books Annual*. V. 33. 2002：p. 292.

124. Hwa-Wei Lee. Book Review. *American Reference Books Annual*. V. 33. 2002：p. 293-294.

125. Hwa-Wei Lee. Book Review. *American Reference Books Annual*. V. 33. 2002：p. 295.

2003 年

126. 李华伟. 知识管理：图书馆的作用. 津图学刊. No. 78. 2003（1）：1-5.

127. Hwa-Wei Lee & Liren Zheng. First Decade of the Dr. Shao You Bao Overseas Chinese Documentation and Research Center at Ohio University（1993-2003）. *Proceeding of the Second International Conference of Institutes & Libraries for Chinese Overseas Studies*. "*Transnational Networks：Challenges in Research and Documentation of the Chinese Overseas.*" March 13-15，2003，Hong Kong，organized jointly by the Chinese University of Hong Kong Libraries and Ohio University Libraries. Hong Kong：2003. Also in *Chinese Overseas：Migration，Research and Documentation*. Edited by Tan Chee-Beng，Colin Storey，and Julia Zimmerman. Hong Kong：The Chinese University Press，2007：pp. 275-295.

128. 楼宏青，李华伟. 关于图书馆服务效益评估的若干问题 大学图书馆学报，2003 年第 21 卷第 5 期第 18-22 页.

129. Hwa-Wei Lee. Libraries in Rapid Transition: Information Management vs Knowledge Management. Paper presented at the International Conference on Challenges and Opportunities for Libraries and Information Professionals in Knowledge Management and the Digital Age. 20 – 22 March 2003, Chiang Mai, Thailand. Organized by Department of Library Science, Faculty of Humanities, Chiang Mai University, Chiang Mai, Thailand, 2003: pp. 1 – 9.

130. Hwa-Wei Lee. Library Cooperation and Resources Sharing. Paper presented at the International Conference on Challenges and Opportunities for Libraries and Information Professionals in Knowledge Management and the Digital Age. 20 – 22 March 2003, Chiang Mai, Thailand. Organized by Department of Library Science, Faculty of Humanities, Chiang Mai University, Chiang Mai, Thailand, 2003: pp. 29 – 32.

131. Hwa-Wei Lee. Steps in Implementing Knowledge Management. Paper presented at the International Conference on Challenges and Opportunities for Libraries and Information Professionals in Knowledge Management and the Digital Age. 20 – 22 March 2003, Chiang Mai, Thailand. Organized by Department of Library Science, Faculty of Humanities, Chiang Mai University, Chiang Mai, Thailand, 2003: pp. 84 – 93

132. Hwa-Wei Lee. Promoting Positive Changes in Scholarly Communication: The SPARC Initiative. Paper presented at the International Conference on Challenges and Opportunities for Libraries and Information Professionals in Knowledge Management and the Digital Age. 20 – 22 March 2003, Chiang Mai, Thailand. Organized by Department of Library Science, Faculty of Humanities, Chiang Mai University, Chiang Mai, Thailand, 2003: pp. 118 – 121.

133. Hwa-Wei Lee. Measuring Library Service Quality: The LibQUAL + Tool. Paper presented at the International Conference on Challenges and Opportunities for Libraries and Information Professionals in Knowledge Management and the Digital Age. 20 – 22 March 2003, Chiang Mai, Thailand. Organized by Department of Library Science, Faculty of Humanities, Chiang Mai University, Chiang Mai, Thailand, 2003: pp. 122 – 128.

134. Hwa-Wei Lee. Book Review. *American Reference Books Annual*. V. 34. 2003: p. 289.

135. Hwa-Wei Lee. Book Review. *American Reference Books Annual*. V. 34. 2003: p. 291.

2004 年

136. Hwa-Wei Lee. Building a World-class Asian Collection in the Library of Congress for Area Studies, Culture Preservation, Global Understanding, and Knowledge Creation. *Proceedings of the Symposium "The New Horizon of Library Services Toward the Better Understanding of Asia"*. Kyoto, Japan: National Diet Library. 2004: pp. 57 – 67; 150 – 169.

137. 李华伟. 美国国会图书馆建立世界级的亚洲馆藏（Building a World-class Asian Collection in the Library of Congress）（英文论文）. 见：张鼎钟教授七秩荣庆筹备小组编. 跨越数位时代的资讯服务：张鼎钟教授七秩荣庆论文集. 台北：文华图书馆管理资讯股份有限公司, 2004: 17 – 30.

138. Hwa-Wei Lee. Ching-chih Chen: A Shining Star and Model of Chinese American Library and Information Science Professionals. 见：沈志佳等编. 架起中美文化的桥梁 美国华人图书馆协会回眸三十年：1973 – 2003. 桂林：广西师范大学出版社, 2004. 6: 9 – 25.

139. Hwa-Wei Lee. *Sharing the Treasures of the Asian Collection in the Library of Congress.*

在"第二届国际图书馆论坛——城市发展与图书馆服务"上发表. 2004 年 10 月 12 – 15 日, 上海图书馆. 又见: 第二届国际图书馆论坛——城市发展与图书馆服务论文集. 上海: 上海科学技术文献出版社, 2004: 157 – 165.

140. 李华伟. 美国国会图书馆有关中国东北与日本的历史文献. 中国东北与日本研究的历史文献国际研讨会演讲论文, 日本新潟大学, 2004 年 10 月 27 – 30 日 (参见 162).

141. Hwa-Wei Lee. Book Review. *American Reference Books Annual*. V. 35. 2004: p312.

142. 李华伟. 海外华人与海外华人研究——兼介绍美国俄亥俄大学邵友保博士海外华人文献研究中心. 2004 年.

2005 年

143. 李华伟. 美国国会图书馆的汉学资源. 论文宣读于数字时代汉学研究资源国际研讨会, 2004 年 12 月 7 – 9 日, 台北: 汉学研究中心. 又见: 师大校友, 2005 年 2 月第 325 期第 4 – 12 页.

144. Hwa-Wei Lee. Sinological Resources in the Library of Congress. *Culture Communication*. No. 17 (July/August 2005, p. 2) and No. 18 (September/October 2005, p. 3)

145. Hwa-Wei Lee. Chinese Resources for Zheng He Studies in the Library of Congress. Paper presented at the Third International Conference of Institutes and Libraries for Chinese Overseas Studies, held in Singapore on August 18 – 21, 2005.

146. Hwa-Wei Lee. Book Review. *American Reference Books Annual*. V. 36. 2005: p311.

2006 年

147. Hwa-Wei Lee. Building a World-class Asian Collection in the Digital Age at the Library of Congress. Presented at the Symposium on Building Collection in the Digital Age, January 16 – 17, 2006, Taichung, Taiwan: Graduate Institute of Library and Information Science, Chung Hsing University & Chung Hsing University Library. Published in *the Proceedings on the Symposium on Building Collection in the Digital Age*, Taichung, Taiwan: Chung Hsing University, January 2006: pp. 11 – 29.

148. 李华伟. 序. 见: 孙平编. 英汉图书馆情报学词汇. 北京: 清华大学出版社, 2006 年.

149. Hwa-Wei Lee. Book Review. *American Reference Books Annual*. V. 37. 2006: pp295 – 296.

2007 年

150. Hwa-Wei Lee. Asian Collections in the Digital Age at the Library of Congress. Published in *Shenzhen Library Newsletter* (《深图通讯》). No. 14, January 2007: pp. 3 – 11.

151. 李华伟. 序. 见: 史勇伟著. 养生之道. 北京: 文化艺术出版社. 2007 年.

152. 李华伟. 他山之石——向海外推广中文书的秘籍. 编辑学刊. 2007 年第 6 期第 6 – 8 页.

153. Hwa-Wei Lee. Asian Collections in the Library of Congress: A Historical Overview. Paper presented at the Conference on Over a Hundred Years of Collecting: The History of East Asian Collections in North America, held at the University of California, Berkeley, October 18 – 19, 2007.

154. Hwa-Wei Lee. Book Review. *American Reference Books Annual*. V. 38. 2007：p. 52.

2008 年

155. 李华伟. 美国国会图书馆中文馆藏与汉学研究资源. 新世纪图书馆. 2008 年第 1 期第 86 – 30 页.

156. Hwa-Wei Lee. Book Review. *American Reference Books Annual*. V. 39. 2008：pp. 255 – 256.

2009 年

157. Hwa-Wei Lee. Building a National Asian Pacific American Collection in the Library of Congress，USA. 见：第四届海外华人研究与文献收藏机构国际合作会议——互动与创新：多维视野下的华侨华人研究. 中国暨南大学与美国俄亥俄大学合办，2009 年 5 月 9 – 11 日，广州暨南大学.

158. 李华伟. 促进中美文化交流的中美图书馆员专业交流合作项目. 公共图书馆，2009 年第 4 期第 57 – 58 页.

2010 年

159. Hwa-Wei Lee. A History of the East Asian Collections in the Library of Congress：A Bibliographic Guide. *Collecting Asia：East Asian Libraries in North America，1868 – 2008*. (Asian Past & Present：New Research from AAS, No. 4). Edited by Peter X. Zhou. Ann Arbor，Michigan：Association for Asian Studies, 2010：pp. 22 – 31.

160. 李华伟. 美国图书馆自动化五十年主要里程碑. 高校图书馆工作，2010 年第 30 卷第 1 期第 3 – 7 页.

161. 李华伟. 美国国会图书馆中文馆藏的发展与影响. 见：张志强，周原主编. 图书为媒 沟通中西：中美文化交流与图书馆发展国际学术研讨会暨钱存训图书馆开馆典礼会议论文集. 南京：南京大学出版社 2010 年版，第 189 – 201 页.

162. 李华伟. 美国国会图书馆收藏有关中国东北与日本的历史文献. 见：张海惠主编. 北美中国学：研究概述与文献资源. 北京：中华书局 2010 年版.

163. 李华伟. 大学图书馆实行知识管理的新理念. 见：全球化视野——大学图书馆馆长论坛会务手册. 上海：上海财经大学图书馆, 2010.

164. 李华伟. 分享中文数位资源的契机与探讨. 见：第八次中文文献资源共建共享合作会议暨图书馆中文资源与数位典藏学术研讨会会议手册. 台北，汉学研究中心, 2010 年.

附录2：李华伟研究资料

Appendix II：Research Materials about Hwa-Wei Lee

（1）书　评 ·· （1354）
Book Reviews

　　一位美籍华人的精心之作——《现代化图书馆管理》读后 ············ 钟守真（1354）
　　图书馆管理空间的新拓展——评《现代化图书馆管理》 ······ 付立宏　邱均平（1357）
　　一部融汇现代管理思想的杰作——评《现代化图书馆管理》 ······ 吕红　李悦（1360）
　　Fundraising for the 1990s：The Challenge Ahead ················ Joan M. Hood（1363）

（2）记　述 ·· （1364）
Articles

　　亚洲理工学院 ·· 聂　玲（1364）
　　Alden Director：Lee Brings Varied Career to New Job，Sees Opportunity for
　　　　Changes ··· Teri Krimm（1367）
　　教育系四三级李华伟校友盛赞母校图书馆资料新颖 ··························· （1369）
　　美国俄亥俄大学图书馆馆长李华伟先生在京作学术报告 ············ 李晓明（1370）
　　Alden Library Grows in Size and Stature ················ Dwight Woodward（1372）
　　Ohio's Top Librarian：Lee Is Surprised by OLA Award ········· Nancy Roe（1374）
　　OU's Dr. Lee Named Ohio's Librarian of the Year ····························· （1375）
　　Alden Director Named Librarian of the Year ·················· Anne Hiller（1376）
　　John Ames Humphry/Forest Press Award Recipient Announced ········· （1377）
　　李华伟博士及其领导下的美国俄亥俄大学图书馆 ····················· 卢素心（1378）
　　美国第一个华人图书馆馆长——访李华伟博士 ························ 李晓晶（1380）
　　享有盛誉的海外华人学者——李华伟博士简介 ································ （1381）
　　经纬枢纽　美华桥梁——李华伟博士印象 ···························· 徐国定（1383）
　　不变的中国心——记美国俄亥俄大学图书馆馆长李华伟博士 ········ 吕　红（1386）
　　甘作美中文化交流的桥梁——记美籍华人李华伟博士 ················ 吕　红（1388）
　　一位海外华人的特殊贡献——记美国俄亥俄大学图书馆馆长李华伟博士
　　　　··· 吕　红（1390）
　　现代化图书馆管理的新探索——李华伟博士学术报告总结 ········ 苏颖怡（1397）
　　美国图书馆界的头号华人 ··· 景　星（1405）
　　美国俄亥俄大学图书馆馆长李华伟博士剪影 ·························· 徐国定（1416）
　　我们的良师益友李华伟先生 ·· 闵凡林（1418）
　　跨越时空的追寻与奉献——记俄亥俄大学图书馆馆长李华伟博士 ······ 吕　红（1420）
　　Modern Library Development in China：An Interview with Dean Hwa-Wei Lee
　　　　··· Ron Chepesiuk（1443）

For 21 Years, Lee Has Charted Libraries' Stellar Course ………… Richard Heck (1447)
End of Era for University Libraries: Dean Lee Retires After 21 Years
　……………………………………………………………… Alice Sachs (1449)
Alden Returns for Library Celebration—Weekend's Events Honor Others at Library
　……………………………………………………………… Monica Neeporte (1451)
Ohio University Honoring Dr. Hwa-Wei Lee …………………… Marian Chou (1452)
李华伟博士访谈录 ………………………………… 封学绛　程小澜　贾晓东 (1453)
Tributes to Dr. Hwa-Wei Lee's Retirement ……………………………………… (1458)
给著名图书馆学家李华伟博士的信 …………………………………… 张白影 (1460)
李华伟博士简介 ……………………………………………………… 汪雁秋 (1462)
OLC Honors Its Own ………………………………………………………… (1465)
Hwa-Wei Lee Named OCLC Visiting Distinguished Scholar ………………… (1466)
图书馆界之巨擘　海外华人之骄傲——美国最著名的华人图书馆馆长
　李华伟博士 ………………………………………………………… 潘燕桃 (1467)
国际图书馆界的亲善大使——李华伟博士专访 ………… 林呈潢　黄倩如 (1470)
李华伟（1933－）……………………………………………………… 汪雁秋 (1474)
天下谁人不识君——记美国 OHIO 大学图书馆长李华伟博士 ……… 张白影 (1477)
Hwa-Wei Lee Named Chief of Asian Division ………………………………… (1479)
国会图馆亚洲部　首见华裔当主任 …………………………………… 谭焕瑛 (1480)
二十一世纪知识管理者所扮演的角色
　　——专访美国国会图书馆亚洲部主任李华伟博士 ……………… 吕　红 (1481)
国会图书馆亚洲部开放日涌人潮 ……………………………………… 谭焕瑛 (1485)
Dr. Hwa-Wei Lee's Success Story at Library of Congress ………… Jennie L. Ilustre (1486)
Hwa-Wei Lee: Pride and Role Model of Librarians ⋯ Rush Miller & Zhijia Shen (1489)
国会图书馆中文部将开放电子书库 …………………………………… 于茂芬 (1495)
《亚裔年鉴》第二辑在国会图书馆举行发表会 ………………………………… (1496)
美国国会图书馆亚洲部中文组的改弦更张
　　………………………… 居蜜（Dr. Mi Chu Wiens）& 陈家仁（Lily Kecskes）(1497)
国会图书馆亚洲部之友会积极活跃：李华伟冀华人社区踊跃参与 ………… (1500)
李华伟任满三年建树多
　　——国会图书馆亚洲部主任推动公图合作　创设亚洲部之友会 ⋯ 谭焕瑛 (1501)
让书籍"活"起来——专访美国国会图书馆亚洲部主任李华伟 …… 李　焰 (1502)
华人的骄傲——访美国国会图书馆亚洲部主任李华伟 ……………… 罗露西 (1505)
华盛顿美国国会图书馆纪行 …………………………………… 王　威　郭怡红 (1507)
Interview: Dr. Hwa-Wei Lee, Ph. D. ………………………………………… (1512)
国会图书馆扩大收藏亚美作品 ………………………………………… 黄美惠 (1515)
Asian Pacific American Collection Added to Library of Congress Data
　……………………………………………………………… Reme Grefalda (1516)
The Hwa-Wei Lee Annex: A Model of Efficiency ………… Julia Zimmerman (1518)
国图馆欢送李华伟　离情依依 ………………………………………… 于茂芬 (1519)
The Quiet Life ………………………………………………… Mike Magner (1520)

李华伟：图书馆把知识变成智慧 …………………………………… 李怀宇（1521）
以智慧和毅力构架希望之桥 ——访本刊顾问李华伟博士 ……… 弘　晓（1525）
"图书馆，丰富人们的生活"——李华伟博士在合肥接受记者专访……
　　………………………………………………………………… 孔　华（1529）
让图书馆的服务无所不在 ………………………………………… 刘思敏（1531）
原美国国会图书馆亚洲部主任李华伟：资源共享是图书馆发展趋势
　　………………………………………………………………… 刘　琼（1532）
李华伟：经纬枢纽，美华桥梁 …………………………………… 赵　晶（1534）
访前美国国会图书馆亚洲部主任前俄亥俄大学图书馆馆长李华伟博士
　　………………………………………………………………… 韩淑举（1539）
图书、图书馆和图书馆长——感怀三篇，赠李华伟博士 ……… 王汉川（1551）
Hwa-Wei Lee ………………………………………………… Mengxiong Liu（1552）

（3）信　函 …………………………………………………………………（1553）
Letters

Letter from James H. Billington ……………………………………………（1553）
Letter from Carolyn T. Brown ………………………………………………（1555）
Letter from Elaine Chao（赵小兰）…………………………………………（1557）
Letter from Michael M. Honda ………………………………………………（1558）
Speech of Hon. Michael M. Honda of California in the House of Representatives
　　………………………………………………………………………（1559）
Letter from Deanna Marcum ………………………………………………（1560）

(1) 书 评
Book Review

一位美籍华人的精心之作
——《现代化图书馆管理》读后

钟守真[①]

美籍华人李华伟博士在中外图书馆界享有盛誉,是我国图书馆界众所熟知的学者。1991年李博士受聘为南开大学信息资源管理系客座教授,使我有机会与他相识,此后,我们一直保持联系。在与李博士的接触中,他对图书馆经营、管理的执着思考,他的种种颇为新鲜的见解,以及他对中华民族图书馆事业的真挚热爱,深深地感染了我。特别在1996年62届IFLA会后,李博士再次应邀到南开大学讲学,笔者有幸得其惠赠《现代化图书馆管理》新作,读后备感亲切,深受启发,由此撰写此文,以期传播李博士的图书馆管理与经营的新观念。

李华伟博士早年就读于台湾师范大学教育系,毕业后赴美深造,先后取得美国匹兹堡大学教育学硕士、图书馆学硕士学位。1964年获匹兹堡大学哲学博士学位。1966—1968年在美国宾州爱丁堡大学图书馆任馆长和该校图书馆学系助理教授。1968—1975年赴泰国任亚洲理工学院图书馆及信息中心主任。1975—1978年任美国科罗拉多州大学教授及图书馆副馆长。1978年至今任美国俄亥俄大学教授及图书馆馆长。李博士还是一位国际图书馆事业活动家,曾当选为国际图联(IFLA)的大学及研究图书馆委员会委员、美国图书馆学会及俄亥俄图书馆学会理事等。在联合国教科文组织的倡议下,李博士多次担任该组织在中国、印尼、泰国等国家和地区的图书馆顾问及基金会顾问。由于李博士的突出贡献,曾获俄亥俄州1987年最杰出图书馆员奖,以及1991年美国图书馆学会国际关系卓越贡献奖等项荣誉。大家知道,李博士极为关心中国的教育与图书馆事业,为中外图书馆事业的沟通与发展作出了突出的贡献。他受聘担任了中国科学院、南开大学、西安交大、武汉大学、兰州大学等单位的客座教授及学术顾问。

李博士长期居住在美国,近30多年来一直从事图书馆工作并担任行政职务。他对西方图书馆有种种切近的观察与直接的体验,所形成的图书馆管理与经营思想,凝聚于《现代化图书馆管理》一书。该书系李华伟博士近著,1996年4月由台北三民书局出版发行。全书资料新颖、体例独特、内容丰富、论证透彻、融理论与实务为一体,堪称是现代图书馆管理领域上乘之作。《现代化图书馆管理》一书作为图书馆管理专著,表现出以下几个鲜明的特点:

第一,主线清晰。全书以现代化图书馆管理与经营为主线,划分成八章,进而再分节,书后附有索引。该书第一章绪论;第二章20世纪西方管理学的发展;第三章图书馆

[①] 任职于南开大学信息资源管理系。

的规划;第四章图书馆的组织;第五章图书馆人力资源管理;第六章图书馆的领导和作业;第七章图书馆的控制与评估;第八章跨世纪的图书馆发展。在绪论里,作者阐述了现代化图书馆的任务与使命,勾画了现代图书馆的发展轨迹,剖析了管理科学与图书馆学的交叉、渗透、移植的关系,逻辑地导出了以下各章的结构顺序。该书以 20 余万字的篇幅论述现代化图书馆管理这样复杂的内容,附表 17 个,图 23 张,参考文献 111 篇,始终条理清晰而不冗长,给人以耳目一新之感。该书内容涵盖面相当广泛,涉及图书馆的规划、组织、人力资源管理、领导和作业、控制和评估五大管理功能,读后能使我们了解现代化图书馆管理与经营的基本知识,掌握其方法。

第二,探索性。图书馆管理是一门致用性很强的学科,但也是一门具有创新性的学科。我们知道,当前图书馆事业正处于重大突破的阶段,由于人类知识及信息业的发展,计算机技术、通讯技术、多媒体技术及电子出版物的不断涌现,再加上国际信息网络的畅通,图书馆正处于"急剧锐变"和"重新定位"的"紧要关头"。在现代图书馆管理中已出现许多难点和热点问题,这就要求我们吸取现代管理科学的理论与方法,结合图书馆实务,对这些问题作出回答。作者正是在这一方面作了有益的探索。正如作者在自序中所言:"图书馆和资讯中心已从传统式以纸张印刷品为主的"纸张图书馆"(Paper-based Library)进展到 70 年代的"自动化图书馆"(Automated Library),80 年代的"网络化图书馆"(Networked Library)及 90 年代的"电子化图书馆"(Electronic Library)。21 世纪的图书馆和资讯中心将无疑的朝向"虚拟图书馆"(Virtual Library)这个方向发展。虚拟图书馆是融合了各期图书馆的特色和优点,破除了图书馆人为的栅篱,使得图书资讯的服务能无远弗届,不受空间和距离的限制。这本探讨现代化图书馆管理的书是尽可能地配合这个发展的趋势。"这一段话,表明了作者正是针对世纪之交,现代化图书馆管理中的问题进行探讨。从内容上看,该书既有现代化图书馆管理理论与实务的阐述,又有对未来图书馆管理与经营的探索,在现代化图书馆的研究方面具有开创意义。

第三,兼容性,融理论与实务于一体。《现代化图书馆管理》虽是一本理论专著,但它并不是从理论到理论,而是力求理论联系实际。如在第二章论述 20 世纪西方管理学的发展时,不仅介绍了西方现代管理科学的新理论、新观点,而且紧密地结合图书馆管理的实际情况,集中论述了在现代化图书馆管理中,已见实效的三种理论,即图书馆结构的观点、图书馆人际关系的观点、图书馆政治运用的观点,使读者深切地感受和认识现代管理科学对图书馆管理的影响。难能可贵的是,该书还紧密结合大量的现代化图书馆管理实例,进行了透彻确凿的分析。例如,在第七章第二节财务的控制中,作者在介绍成本效益的分析时,指出"像图书馆的馆际互借,假设每一次的实际平均费用是十五美元,假如有一本常用的书,在一年之内要向别馆去借三次,倒不如去买一本来得便宜及方便。"接着又指出:"亦有些图书馆为了向读者催付在美金三元以下逾期还书的罚款,其所花的人工及手续费远超过三块钱,是否值得?若是从成本效益的观点来看,凡是罚款在三元以下者,不必立刻催付。使用自动化的图书流通系统,读者在下次借书时,电脑系统会显示读者还有未清的罚款,那时候再催还欠款。另外,图书馆也可以等到读者欠款超过十美元时再采取行动。"显然,这些见解很能引起读者的共鸣,在我们的图书馆管理中,不计成本消耗的"管理行为"随处可见,如果我们图书馆各级管理者增强成本效益分析意识,掌握、应用成本效益分析方法,那么,图书馆的效益将会不断提高。此外,该书还提出一些观点,如全品质管理、图书馆员工的考绩方法,以及建立、加强图书馆管理信息系统等,都直接涉及现代化图书馆经营之道,均结合实例作了分析和介绍。在图书馆现代化不断发展的情况下，作者适时地推出这样一本著作，无疑将对现代化图书馆的管理与经营有很大的现实指导作用。

第四，启迪性。一部著作问世，不必期望它能教会读者多少不知道的东西，重要的是看它能否启迪读者思考得更深更远些，是否能够拓展读者的思考空间。从这一角度看，《现代化图书馆管理》一书，达到了这一水平。在论著中，作者对现代化图书馆管理的一系列问题不仅进行了阐述，而且注意到给肯于思考的读者提供一个进一步思考的空间。例如，在作为结论的第八章第五节，题为"跨世纪的挑战"里，作者认为："在20世纪即将结束，而21世纪即将来临的今天，因为受了知识爆炸、资讯技术发展和资讯社会的需求种种影响，图书馆遭遇了空前未有的激荡和挑战。"作者列举了图书馆面临的各种挑战，描绘了跨世纪的图书馆，指出："……虚拟图书馆将是21世纪图书馆的特色，它综合了纸张图书馆、自动化图书馆、网络化图书馆及电子化图书馆的优点，扩大了图书馆的资源，使得图书馆的服务能无远不及，超越了时空的限制，真正做到了馆际的资源共享，撤除了图书馆间人为的栅篱和障碍。"在这里，作者提醒人们，书刊资料转成数位化（Digitized）供读者使用时，将出现知识产权的保护问题。接着作者提出一连串值得人们思考的问题："除了智慧产权之外，使用这些资料的费用如何决定？对于图书馆会发生何种影响等？是否会造成资讯使用者之间贫富差异的不公平现象？（Disparity Between the Information Rich and Information Poor）诸如此类的很多问题……"明确表示："有待对于今后发展的观察和大家的探讨。"

显然，《现代化图书馆管理》一书具有鲜明的时代感，特性非常明显，既注重理论性、学术性，又突出实践性、可操作性；既吸取现代管理科学的理论与方法，又实现与图书馆管理的结合；既有西方的图书馆理论与实务，又融合了中国式管理的精华，要达到这一步是相当不容易的，可以看出作者"精心"的程度，正因如此，这本书才显得十分珍贵，值得我们认真研究。

（原载《津图学刊》1977年第1期，第34－38页。）

图书馆管理空间的新拓展
——评《现代化图书馆管理》

付立宏　邱均平[①]

　　1996年4月，台湾三民书局股份有限公司出版了李华伟博士的力作《现代化图书馆管理》。现任美国俄亥俄大学图书馆馆长（院长级）兼教育学院教授的李华伟博士，是一位学识渊博、经验丰富的图书馆学者和管理专家。他早年毕业于台湾师范大学教育系，1957年赴美深造，曾先后获得匹兹堡大学教育学硕士、图书馆学硕士及哲学博士学位，历任匹兹堡大学、都肯大学、宾州爱丁堡大学、科罗拉多州大学等多所大学图书馆的行政职务，为华裔中担任美国大学图书馆馆长最早的一人。1968年，他由美国政府国际发展总署派往泰国担任亚洲理工学院图书馆及信息中心主任，达七年之久。这本关于现代化图书馆管理的专著，是李博士融汇了三十多年的图书馆管理经验，历时五载才完成的一部理论与实践相结合的典范之作。笔者有幸拜读了这部大作，细细品味，获益匪浅。与同类著作相比，它确有许多独出机杼之处，不愧为世界图书馆管理领域的经典著作。

1. 博采众长，理论精深

　　李博士的这部著作，广泛涉猎了行为科学、社会学、心理学、人类学、经济学、技术科学、工程学、应用数学、系统论、信息论和控制论等学科的理论与方法，但又有所扬弃、有所消化。李博士密切联系图书馆管理活动的实际，把所吸取的科学养分化成了自己理论体系的有机组成部分。例如，作者在简要介绍了科学管理学派、一般管理学派、行为学派、数量学派、程序学派、系统学派和情境学派等学派的主要代表人物及其观点后，并不急于将其理论和方法直接植入图书馆管理活动中，而是先分析各学派管理思想的长处和短处，再明确指出对图书馆管理实践较有参考价值的主要是三种理论，即结构的观点、人际关系的观点和政治运用的观点。对于这三种理论，作者也不赞成全盘接受，而是坚持作价值评判。作者认为，结构理论有助于了解组织的目的、技术与结构间的关系，但忽视机构中人的地位及权力和冲突因素；人际关系理论虽然强调人在组织中的重要性，但忽视结构的约束和权威等作用；政治运用的观点强调组织内外各种政治因素的作用，但也有管中窥豹之弊。通过价值评判后，作者在书中对上述理论综合采用或择优选用。又如，作者简析了当前管理学中关于激励作用的八种理论（即需求层次理论、X和Y理论、双因素理论、三需求理论、目标设定理论、强化理论、公平理论及期望理论）之后，又从注意事项、"高品质工作生活"的界定、目标管理、高品质工作生活计划、"品质圈"、"全品质管理"等方面，详细讨论了这些理论在图书馆管理活动中的实际应用价值。再如，作者在第一章第四节中指出，管理学家一般把规划、组织、用人、领导与控制看做是管理的五大功能，现代管理学即是研究这些现象与规律的科学。接着，作者用大量篇幅（三、四、五、六、七，共五章），分别讨论了图书馆的规划、图书馆的组织、图书馆人力资源管理、图书馆的领导和作业、图书馆的控制与评估等管理功能，因地制宜地将管理的五项一般功能移植到图书馆活动之中，毫无雕琢之嫌。由上述可见，作者真正是"拿来"了，并消化、吸收了。对于一位图书馆学者和管理专家而言，这无疑是一种走向学术成熟的境界。

[①] 任职于武汉大学信息管理学院。

2. 内容新颖、详细，实用性强

李华伟博士在此书中着墨最多的，就是通过对图书馆管理具体功能的阐述，通过对当代世界图书馆变革大趋势的揭示，重新界定图书馆管理，从而给人们一个关于图书馆管理的崭新而科学的概念——"有效的图书馆管理"。在作者看来，现代图书馆管理活动，只要选择合理的体制模式、组织形式、经营方式、激励手段以及制定正确的战略、规划和策略等，就能把一切潜在的能量释放出来，并将其转变为现实的财富和效益，由此展现图书馆的活力，促进图书馆事业的发展和社会的进步。在作者的这一思维过程中，自始至终都贯穿着一根主线，即知识的实用性和可操作性，力戒夸夸其谈和泛泛而论。具体来说，作者主要是通过以下两种手法来把握这一要旨的。

第一，论证严谨而细密。例如，作者在论述策略性的规划时，首先界定了策略性规划的涵义，并将其与传统性规划进行了比较；接着探讨了策略性规划的门径；最后从使命说明、策略分析、目的及目标、作业计划、执行、评估等方面，顺次说明了策略性规划的流程。又如，围绕组织的设计和结构问题，作者从组织的部门化和层级化、集中或分散、矩阵式的组织、对角线的考虑、权威与授权、非正式的组织、参与式的管理等视角切入，进行了深入而细致的探讨，给读者一个清晰而完整的印象。再如，作者在该书第五章第一节中，详细地叙述了人员的甄选和任用程序，即人力资源规划、工作分析、甄选、考试、背景调查、面谈等。其中，对某些环节作了更细密的分解，如从工作分析的四种方法、工作说明书的格式、工作说明书和职务问卷的主要用途、职位评审和分类的三个标准等层面，将"工作分析"展示得淋漓尽致，从而增强了该书的实用性和可操作性。

第二，材料翔实而新颖。这一特色主要体现在书中添附了大量的图表资料。全书共附插图 23 幅，表 12 个。其中，俄亥俄大学图书馆组织图、俄亥俄大学图书馆编目及图书馆系统部矩阵式组织图、OCLC 在 1993—1994 会计年度服务统计表、OCLC 目录资料库按媒体分类表、OCLC 目录资料库按出版年代分类表、OCLC 目录资料库按语言分类表、俄亥俄大学图书馆 1994—1995 会计年度业务预算分类表等图表，均为一般著作中所罕见。这些图表资料对图书馆管理人员具有重要的实际参考价值，对广大用户利用图书馆的文献信息资源也具有导引功能。

3. 大力倡导图书馆精神

图书馆精神是图书馆管理活动中的一种无形的、重要的激励因素。它能激发图书馆员的进取心、责任感、事业心、求知欲和献身精神，而且有持久效应；它能引导人们目光远大、心胸开阔、志趣高尚，把长远利益和眼前利益、国家利益与集体利益、个人利益有机结合起来。正因为如此，作者在书中大力倡导图书馆精神，指出图书馆在其组织、收藏、管理、流通、服务各方面，应具备发展民智、服务社会的精神。由于各国的国情不同，加上各类图书馆及信息中心内外环境有别，其组织与管理体制是有明显差异的。作者认为，不论体制如何，图书馆和信息中心内部的组织管理层均须具备现代化的精神，力求创新，以适应时代发展的需要；同时，在管理上必须采用新的观念，强调图书馆服务于社会的宗旨，重视情境因素的互动关系，尊重个体差异和需求，运用科学和民主的方法，发扬协调合作的精神，完成图书馆的历史使命。书中表述的这些思想，充分体现了一位管理专家勇于探索的创新精神。

4. 中国式管理思想的深刻阐发

图书馆管理要在正确管理理论的指引下，充分考虑到社会环境和人文因素，创造性地运用计划、组织、人事、领导及控制等职能，对人力、物力资源进行最佳配置，从而实现最大效益。在该书中，李华伟博士将图书馆管理视为一种创新活动，并紧密结合文化传统、社会环境与人文因素，对富有中国特色的图书馆管理模式和思想进行了深刻的发掘、梳理、阐释和描述。作者认为，有效的图书馆管理应掺入中国式管理的特质，并符合中国的文化背景和国情，维护中国传统，吸收西洋精华，力求自我创造。在书中，作者对富有中国特色的图书馆管理思想极为赞赏，如"管理的意义是修己安人"，"管理的有效力量是感应"，"管理的最佳原则是'情、理、法'"，等等。

5. 紧紧扣住了时代的脉搏

当今时代，由于电脑、电讯、多媒体、电子出版、密集存贮、国际互联网等新兴信息技术飞速发展，加快了高新技术对人类生活刚性介入的速度，人类生存方式已进入了高度技术化的阶段。与此同时，图书馆也面临着严峻的挑战，正处于一个急剧变化和重新定位的非常时期。面对这种形势，图书馆界的众多有识之士正在认真思考。李华伟博士以超人的学术勇气，站在当代科技发展的前沿，深入思考和探索最新科学技术给图书馆事业带来的新挑战和新机遇，试图设定 21 世纪的图书馆的位置，为传统图书馆管理向现代化图书馆管理的过渡寻找良策。在书中，作者大胆地提出了一系列精辟的见解，如"图书馆的组织必须打破传统的金字塔式架构而趋向扁平化"，"图书馆的人力、财力和物力也应该按照策略性的规划予以重新分配和组合"，"注重员工的素质"，"发挥团队精神"，"加强馆际合作"等等，从而为 21 世纪图书馆管理蓝图的设计指明了方向，同时也提供了一个具有重要参考价值和启发意义的思维框架。

毋庸讳言，《现代化图书馆管理》一书也并非完美无瑕，它在某些方面还存在不足。例如，该书对图书馆管理学的个别基本问题的探讨还重视不够，对如何处理电子出版物及多媒体的专利权和复制权，以及信息使用者之间贫富差异的不公平现象等问题的探讨也还不够深入，似有浅尝辄止之嫌。然而，瑕不掩瑜。从总体上看，李华伟博士的这部新作不愧为现代图书馆管理领域的"精心制作"（王振鹄先生语）和"经典之作"（周宁森先生语）。它对图书馆管理空间的积极拓展和对图书馆事业的重大贡献，将永载光辉的史册！

（原载《图书情报知识》1998 年 12 月第 4 期，第 74－76 页。）

一部融汇现代管理思想的杰作
——评《现代化图书馆管理》

吕红 李悦

现代管理科学发展迅猛、交互渗透，业已影响到各个行业，以人类知识信息保存和传播为己任的图书馆也不例外。

地处"信息之州"，有着近 200 年历史的美国俄亥俄大学图书馆素以管理卓越著称。现任馆长李华伟先生，已在此位 20 年。此前他曾先后任美国宾州匹兹堡大学、都肯大学、爱丁堡大学、科罗拉多大学等数所美国高校图书馆的行政要职。他深谙美国高校图书馆的管理工作，加之李华伟先生是一位善于思考、治学严谨的学者型管理专家，所以他对现代化图书馆的管理理论有着独到的见解。他的新作《现代化图书馆管理》，系多年来在中国各地多所大学讲学的结晶，以现代化图书馆管理与经营为主线，内容涉及规划、组织、人力资源管理、领导和作业、控制和评估等五大功能，吸纳了东西方管理科学的最新成果，加以比较和评述，并附有统计数据及其他各类图表资料，大多采用俄亥俄大学图书馆近年正式公布的文件，故本书也是理论和实践的结合，是一个全面了解美国大学图书馆实际运作过程及效果的窗口。

1. 管理的最终目的在"安人"

人皆有不安与躁动的一面，尤其是在我国对社会主义商品经济理论有了新认识之后，人们的不安与躁动更是日趋表面化，反映在教科文系统及图书馆尤为明显。从目前来看，我国高校图书馆的地位尚未得到明显提高，人员的不稳定、不安心是一个客观事实。然而就局部而言，在管理者中也确有一些对管理的目的不甚明了。笔者以为《现代化图书馆管理》一书可以在这方面给我们一些启示。

李华伟先生在该书第一章绪言中写道："21 世纪的图书馆不管是以何种形式出现，在促进知识发展、资讯传递、生活素质和文化水平上会承担更重要的任务与使命。"

图书馆管理者首先要使员工对图书馆的社会使命产生深切的认同。在员工认识了共同的使命之后，还必须让他们直接参与使命与目标的达成，通过直接参与获得成就感。员工有了成就感，就会认识到个人对集体的存在价值，这对员工的安心是至关重要的。"从图书馆的观点来看，它与一般企业机构有不同之点，因为它是服务性及非营利性的，虽然在经营上图书馆也要讲求现代化的管理及效率，但在与企业机制比较起来应该是非常民主及透明的。因此在制定目标时，图书馆的主管不仅要允许员工参与，而且应该创造机会，鼓励员工积极地参加。"作为一种组织，"它是一个有机体的系统，重视分工合作及经由有协调的交互影响，以满足员工的需要和希望。"只有兼顾了员工的这两方面的心理要求，才可能真正让他们安心安定地做好自己的工作。

李华伟先生在《现代化图书馆管理》一书中对"安人"的论述，可以说是贯穿始终的，他认为管理的本质是"有效地透过一个组织中的成员去完成一些工作的过程。"而人是完成任何组织之使命的决定性因素。所以，有关"安人"的思想精髓无疑渗透到他认为应该渗透的几乎所有各个环节中。

以上论述对我们颇有启示：当前我国的图书情报观念及技术手段正处于新旧交替、变革分化、逐步向现代信息社会演进阶段，任何手段的更新离不开人的能动因素。"安人"

是现代化管理很重要的一环，明确目的和使命，尊重个别的差异和需要，就能够达到"安人"的效果，从而推动图书馆工作现代化的发展。

2. 管理的最佳原则是"情、理、法"

作者认为"情、理、法"也就是管理的人性化和制度化。

一个现代化图书馆管理者在他整个管理程序中必须透过员工，对信息进行各种有效的操作。管理者一般是将操作规程制度化，任何一个图书馆都有工作条例，或许区别仅仅在于繁简详略不同而已。然而，是不是光凭条例或规程就能够把工作做好呢？答案显然是否定的。尤其是现代图书馆作为信息时代信息业的重要一支，面对繁多杂乱无章的信息，图书馆员工必须要有责任感和对信息工作特有的热情，才可能胜任其职责。因此，对员工的管理应主要是合理使用人才，充分调动员工的积极性和创造性，对他们的管理要情、理、法三者适时、适当、适度地运用。

作者认为，情、理、法在中国的管理思想中有其先后次序。"理"居于中，有驾驭"情"与"法"的作用，使管理合理化。"法"是人定的，但它是依理而定，也可依"理"来修改。另外，"理"与"法"都要有人性，也就是说管理要"人性化"，否则，"安人"之道将无从谈起。人之不安，则说明"理"与"法"都难以实行。

我们对作者"情理"重于"法"的管理原则，可以从书中得到更好的理解。"政策、规则、标准和程序是将规划付诸实施的重要规范，它的目的不在于约束，而是对各个层次的员工在自己的职权范围内经常出现的情况所能自行作主的授权，它亦能协助各层次的管理人员在遭遇困难时，知道应该采取任何措施，或选择解决问题的途径，好的政策及规则要有员工参与，共同制定，它可以引发员工的积极性及促成各单位间工作的和谐一致性，以求有效地达成机构的目的和目标。"从上面这段话中，我们可以看到作者对员工的管理原则因势利导。同时在他的具体而有效的运作上，我们可以看到作为一个卓越的管理者的思维方式，即："在奖与罚中，我们要多选择奖励；在鼓励与责备之间，我们要多选择鼓励；在松绑与约束中，我们要多选择松绑，不让员工把规章制度作为束缚，而是作为一种情理交融，能够最大限度调动员工积极性的最佳管理原则。"

充分而适当地授权下属，鼓励员工参与管理，是作者在重视员工"情理"交融式的管理思想的发挥，他在该书中阐述道："有些主管喜欢自己总揽全权，紧握不放；或者是对部属不够信任，怕授权太多会失去对部属的控制。有些部属因为怕失败而受责不敢承担较大的职责。以上这些情况会造成授权的障碍，为了要破除这些障碍，上级主管应该设法创造一种互相信赖，上下和谐，不怕冒险犯错的组织文化。另外，对于工作努力、绩效优越的部属，也应该给予适当的奖励。这种奖励不一定必须是金钱的，举凡褒奖、晋升、更好的工作条件、更有挑战性的职责或同事的认可都能发生鼓励作用。"

由此想到，现在国内有些单位的员工积极性没有充分被调动起来，与长期的大锅饭体制上的弊病形成的工作惰性、思想观念的封闭性、人才缺乏流动、竞争机制不够健全有很大关系。实际上，一个催人奋发向上的环境的造就，比多发一点奖金更为重要。一个单位搞得好不好，与其是否"人尽其才、才尽其用"有很大关系。当然，有关部门已经开始注意这个问题，目前各地都纷纷进行人才招聘考试等等，说明各个行业在管理体制上正在进行一场深刻的变革。尽管图书馆一般属于相对稳定保守的部门，但也不可能不受到影响和冲击。

3. 管理的最高境界是"无为而治"

该书在比较早期西方科学管理及一般管理学派的特点时指出，结构观点的理论有助于我们了解组织的目的、技术和结构间的关系，其缺点在于忽视人在机构中的地位及权力和冲突在组织中的因素。人际关系的理论虽然强调人在组织中的重要性，但却忽视结构的约束和权威等作用。政治运用的观点强调内外各种政治因素的作用，利用协调的方式以化解矛盾冲突，达成明智的决策，使有限资源得到合理的分配。作者认为上述观点应该综合采用，并因情况不同而作出适当的选择。

从广义上讲，管理也是一门艺术，特别是要把人员管理好，没有高超的管理艺术和深厚的知识修养，很难达到成功的境界。书中比较了中、日、美三国不同的管理特点后，提出管理的最高境界在于"无为而治"。

所谓"无为而治"系指选择性的"有为"，有所为，有所不为，"有所不为才能有所为"，"无为故能使众为"。作者在实际工作中，正是通过授权、目标管理、控制与评估等等有选择、有重点的工作来"有为"，以实现"无为"。

"无为而治"的管理思想融合了东西方管理思想的精髓，是对管理思想的一个创造。要想达到"无为而治"的境界，必须处理好"有为"与"无为"的辨证关系。"无为"是以"有为"为前提的，管理者必须具备组织才能、决策才能、与员工进行沟通和化解冲突的能力，否则"无为"就成了无所作为。管理者除了吸收西方管理科学的精华，还要有深厚的中国文化修养，并将外来的管理思想与中国国情相结合，创造性地运用现代化的管理方法，这是一种复杂而有意义的探索，也是《现代化管理思想》一书带给我们的深刻启示。

（原载《大学图书馆学报》1998年第1期，第74－75页。）

Fundraising for the 1990s: The Challenge Ahead

Joan M. Hood[①]

The subtitle for this book is *A Practical Guide for Library Fundraising: From Novice to Expert*. The authors explain that the book is a practical guide written for novices who need a "how-to" or "do-it-yourself" type of approach. They also state that "unlike most published guides on fundraising, which were written by development professionals, this is written by librarians and intended for librarians, library trustees, and volunteers". Although this is true, the book draws heavily on previously published material written by development professionals and librarians. While the book does not add much new information or research to the fundraising body of literature, it does draw together, in a very readable and clear style, the fundamentals of fundraising and sources of support. The authors present straight-forward information concerning the planning for fundraising, the sources of funds from the public and private sectors, and the organization of one's library for success in fundraising.

Chapter 4, "Sources of Funds, the Private Sector" will be beneficial to librarians and newcomers in the library development field. It outlines the differences between corporations and foundations, addresses the importance of research, and concludes with a well-structured section on individuals and the types of giving one encounters in fundraising.

Chapter 6 recounts two successful fundraising programs. The first case study describes the Brandeis University National Women's Committee, a highly successful fundraising organization working on behalf of the Brandeis Library. Although the program is eminently successful and the study makes interesting reading, it is a program that would be impossible for most libraries to emulate.

The second case study, from the University of Kentucky Library, is also interesting reading and underscores the importance of high-level administrators' involvement. The author, Paul A. Willis, Director of Libraries at the University of Kentucky, states: "During the entire campaign it was the President who was the key... he made it clear that the new library building and endowment were his first priorities. This obviously was important to potential major donors."

In Chapter 8, "The Conclusion," the authors list 12 principles for successful fundraising. Although these principles have been pointed out in the past by numerous writers, it is a good list for people to remember.

The appendices list professional fundraising organizations, sources of information on government grants and foundations, as well as information on corporate and individual prospects. I recommend reading many of the original source references cited on the suggested reading list. They will be helpful to people new to library development and to library professionals. The major strength of this volume is its compilation and clear organization of basic development information.

(Published in *The Journal of Academic Librarianship*. No. 1, V. 21, 9940: p. 34.)

[①] Director of Development and Public Affairs, The Library System, University of Illinois, 227 Main Library, 1408 W. Gregory, Urbana, IL61801.

（2）记　述
Articles

亚洲理工学院

聂　玲

念理工科的人要出国留学，总是到美国、加拿大或欧洲去，很少人想到泰国去深造的。事实上，也很少人知道泰国有一所杰出的、被誉为"亚洲麻省理工学院"的高等学府。

这所学校就是亚洲理工学院（Asian Institute of Technology）简称 AIT，它是世界上唯一的一所地域性国际学府。它设在泰国的首都曼谷，却不属于泰国所有，它是独立的。许多人不知道它，可能是因为它的历史太短。它是 1967 年 11 月 24 日成立的，到现在还不足两年。

训练亚洲工程人才

真正说来，要讲它的历史短，是不正确的。早在 1959 年 6 月 30 日它已经存在了，不过那时候的名称不是亚洲理工学院，只是隶属于东南亚公约组织的一个研究所。设立这个研究所的目的，在培养公约国家的工程建设人才，所以那时候只有水利工程一系，第一班的研究生只有十九个人。

亚洲国家最头痛的事，是人才外流；亚洲地区的留学生最伤脑筋的事，是学成归国后，发现自己在国外所学的，和国内所需要的不相吻合。亚洲理工学院就是要解决这些问题。

亚洲理工学院的校长弥尔顿·班德曾经说过，他们创校的目的，"是为亚洲地区开发中的国家提供工程技术发展所急需的专门人才，它也是针对着亚洲国家人才外流的缺点设立的。"该校的课程是实际重于理论，几乎所有的课程全在配合亚洲国家的实际需要。

目前只有硕士班

现在，该校有六个研究所：水利工程、土壤工程、结构工程、运输工程、环境工程和海岸工程。目前，他们只开硕士班，没有大学部，也不设博士学位。将来，他们计划增开博士班。

该校的最高决策机构，是一个由二十五人组成的董事会，现任董事长是泰国银行总裁——华裔黄培谦博士。董事会其他的成员多半是东南亚公约组织国选派的代表。现在，这个限制已经取消，新的董事也可以是非会员国的代表。经费的来源，是由美、英、加、澳、纽、泰、菲和其他亚洲国家的政府和私人基金会捐助的。目前，大部分的经费是靠美国国际开发总署用美援方式透过美国科罗拉多州立大学补助的。现在该校改制后，许多非会员国家都有意给予经济支持。新加坡李氏基金会已捐了一笔奖学金，供十位星马地区的学生在该校求学的两年全部费用。

来自十四个国家地区

十年来，从这个学校毕业的学生有二百二十七人。其中百分之八十七都回到他们的本国服务去了。现在，在学校的学生有一百六十四人，他们是来自十个国家：巴基斯坦、阿富汗、印度、韩国、马来西亚、土耳其、菲律宾、泰国、英国和越南，以及中国的台湾和香港地区。从今年八月开始，还增加了新加坡和印尼的学生。

这些学生里，有半数是泰国的学生，其次是来自菲律宾和巴基斯坦的。从台湾去的学生相当多，目前在校的中国学生有二十九位，占五分之一。中国学生大半是来自台湾大学、成功大学和中原理工学院的毕业生。

中国教授和学生

该校初成立的时候，几乎没有中国学生，因为中国不是公约会员国。1962年起，才允收中国学生。该校独立以后，从中国去的学生每年都在增加。

中国学生在亚洲理工学院都表现得很杰出。教授们说，中国学生都能勤学竞业，学业成绩非常好。他们还组织了一个中国同学会，经常聚餐、郊游、开庆生会和比赛球类。

该校共有三十四位教授和研究助理。学生和教授的比例是五比一。这些教授是从不同的国家聘来的。其中一部分是亚洲地区的学者专家，一部分是从赞助国延聘的。特别的是，教授们的薪俸并不统一，都是比照他们本国的薪俸折算的。

目前，在校任教的教授们，从美国聘请的最多，共有十二人，校长班德就是其中之一。泰国和英国教授各有四人，现任教务长约翰·罗拔便是英国人。

中国籍教授，都是从美国聘去的。前任教务长张翘林博士，曾任美国匹兹堡大学土木工程教授。土壤工程研究所主任莫若楫博士，出身于美国麻省理工学院，曾任耶鲁大学教授。在结构工程系任教的李成立博士，原来在美国西北大学任教。他的一位学生，现在已经得到博士学位，也在亚洲理工学院执教。

学费相当贵

该校的费用并不比欧美国家低，每学期的学费是美金一千二百元，寒暑假期间的学费是美金八百元。还要加研究费和医药费，两年算下来，美金六千五百元。

成绩好的学生可以申请到奖学金。泰国以外地区的学生，如果申请到了全部的奖学金，可以得到：来回飞机票（一般为美金二百元），学费和生活费美金一千五百七十五元，书籍费美金二百二十五元。全部的奖学金额是美金八千五百元。得到了奖学金的人，如果成绩下滑，就会停发奖学金。

还有一部分学生可以申请到助教奖学金，在学校里工作，每小时可以得到泰币二十元的报酬。每个月的工作时间，不能超过二十小时。

英文程度必须好

在亚洲理工学院读书，很容易遭到淘汰。每门功课都以六十分算及格，第一学期的平均成绩不能低于六十五分，以后每学期的平均成绩都不得低过七十分。

英文程度不好的学生，最好不要进这个学校。该校重视英文的程度，比美国的许多学校有过之而无不及。不论是授课、讨论、研究、写作都用英文。英文程度差的学生，根本就跟不上。

该校常派教授到亚洲各地，直接和申请入校的学生面谈，就是为了要测验他们的英文程度。去年，班德校长和张翘林到台湾来，曾有许多学生直接向他们申请入学，张翘林都先测验他们的英文程度，英文不佳的学生，根本不作进一步的考虑。

该校的课程是偏重在实用方面。学生每上一小时课，要在研究室做三小时的实验。对学生来说，寒暑假几乎是不存在的，他们只有几天的假期，然后，就要接着上课。

每一个学生，平均一星期要上十小时课。其余的时间，总可以在实验室或图书馆找到他们。挑灯夜读，对他们而言，是家常便饭。

女生只有几个人

每年，学生最盼望的，是圣诞节。这时候，学生代联会就举办一年一次的嘉华年会。这是学生们最轻松的时刻，他们可以参加各种社团活动，艺术表演，聚餐和舞会。各国的同学会都趁这个机会，互相别苗头。

有趣的是，这个学校的男女生比例相差悬殊，五十五个男生中，才有一个女生。每到开舞会的时候，一个女生很可能有五十五次被邀请的机会。据说，中国男生在这方面最有办法，他们不知用什么方法，把仅有的一些女生都变成了他们的舞伴。

曼谷的生活水准，要比台湾高两倍。住宿费一个月泰币四百元，合新台币八百元。住学校宿舍就便宜得多，一个月泰币一百五十元，也就是新台币三百元就够了。如果把伙食费也一起算入，平均每个月的生活费是泰币一千五百元（合新台币三千元）。

图书馆，设备一流

亚洲理工学院的学生，大部分都寄宿在学校里。男女生的宿舍距离不远，离学校大约都是十分钟的路程。每间宿舍只住两个人。

最令学生满意的是学校的伙食。如果学生不喜欢泰国的食物，可以在委托餐厅包饭。委托餐厅可以做各国的食物。中国的米饭，印度、巴基斯坦的锅饼，泰国的龙煎，都有。

该校最骄傲的是他们的图书馆和一般设备，这些在亚洲都是首屈一指的。图书馆馆长是华籍的李华伟博士，他原任美国宾州爱丁堡学院图书馆馆长兼图书馆学系教授。

图书馆有工程学藏书两万多册，专门期刊六百多种。各种出版物都以英文为主，其他各种文字的书刊也相当多。最近，他们计划在短期内设立一个东南亚地域工程资料中心，促进本地区资料的流通和交换。他们并计划用电子计算机来处理图书馆的资料，这个计划如能实现，将成为亚洲地区的创举。

将建新的校本部

该校的每一系科，都有供教学研究的实验器材和其他设备。大的如河道水流的实验模型，小的如土壤检定和分类仪器。工程和电子仪器部门常常自制实验器材，测量实验结果。他们并有一套自备的电子计算机，可供工程研究。

去年，该校董事会通过了美金一千八百多万元的建校计划，这个计划，要十年完成。泰国政府指拨了一块土地做校址，占地四百英亩。新厦完成后，学生人数将可扩充到六百八十四人，教授也将增加到九十六人，并将增设机械和电机工程两系。

（原载《综合月刊》，1969 年 10 月，第 76－81 页。）

Alden Director: Lee Brings Varied Career to New Job, Sees Opportunity for Changes

Teri Krimm

When Hwa-Wei Lee was shelving books and working behind the circulation desk during evenings and weekends at the University of Pittsburgh's library, he had no aspirations to set up a graduate study library in Bangkok, Thailand, or to work for a cooperative program between university libraries.

All Lee wanted to do was earn enough money to pay his living expenses while he completed his master's degree in education. Then it would be back to Taiwan and to a teaching job.

Instead Lee moved on to Carnegie Mellon University on a special library science scholarship. It was a giant step to a rich and varied career in the library field, both in the United States and abroad.

His change-of-career plans in midstream have left the new Alden Library director with no regrets. Besides seeing a great deal of transformation within the library system, Lee has initiated changes of his own.

He seems particularly proud of his work in Southeast Asia as the director of the library and information center at the Asian Institute of Technology in Bangkok, Thailand. Initially a one-year project supported by the U. S. government, the challenge of the job, Lee said, inspired him to work in Asia for seven years.

As a faculty member in the department of library science at Chulaiongkorn University and the director of the Asian information center for geotechnical engineering at the Asian Institute of Technology, Lee says he saw "brain waste" among the country's U. S. educated graduate students.

"Their training in the United States was not directly related to the situation in their own country," he explained. The courses at the Asian Institute of Technology, however, became tailored to the needs of the country. "The school itself," he said, "was a very new concept."

And Lee thrives on new concepts—he said he hopes to initiate positive changes in Alden Library, which has suffered a cutback in funds because of declining enrollment in the early '70s. While other college libraries were experimenting with computerization and information technology, "we were standing still," Lee said.

"I see the opportunity for improvement," he said. "I think this is the most exciting aspect (of my job)." A computer research service is part of the opportunity possibilities Lee speaks so highly of. The research tool will be available to students and faculty by November 1, he said.

Lee said he wants to change the image of the word library.

"I don't see our job here as (just) keeper of the collections," he said. It is necessary, he explained, to make the library "more attractive" to students and faculty by extending its hours during examination weeks and setting up a coffee and snack area for late-night studiers.

"I think we have to market ourselves in order to stay in business," he said. As part of this marketing plan, he hopes to make students more aware of the library's special collections and to offer the assistance of his staff as subject bibliographers.

Some members of the library staff, he explained, are specialists in certain fields since they have master's degrees in dual areas.

But his prime emphasis as director will be to expand the library's Collection.

"I put a lot of importance on collection development," he said, "I think we have to have a quality collection."

The university can have a quality collection, however, without going to a drastic expense. "We just have to be more cooperative," Lee explained.

A proponent of resource sharing, Lee says participating in state and nation-wide library sharing networks is essential.

"Sharing resources is no longer something you just talk about," he said. "It's reality."

(Published in *The Post* (Ohio University). October 4, 1978: p. 5.)

教育系四三级李华伟校友盛赞母校图书馆资料新颖

母校四三级教育系系友李华伟,日前返台参加第二次建设研讨会,并赞扬母校图书馆的设备和管理方法都很新颖。

李华伟目前是美国爱丁堡州立大学视听教育教授兼图书馆馆长,曾于去年十一月间回台湾参加第二次建设研讨会,同时担任文教小组的召集人,也顺便参加图书馆事务研讨会。

由于本身学图书馆,所以李校友特别关心岛内的图书馆教育。他认为,目前台湾的图书馆专门的书籍还嫌不够,即使有,也多半是外文的,即使有部分已翻译为中文,但自己著述的专门书籍仍然不多。

社会一般民众可能对图书馆的重要性了解不深,所以使用的并不普遍。但是大学生利用图书馆资料的习惯未养成,则是遗憾。

在美国,教授制定作业,而由学生自己收集资料,在课堂上详讲,使得学生比较主动。

以他自己担任馆长的爱丁堡州立大学而言,这个学校已有一百七十五年的历史,目前有十个学院一万三千多学生,图书资料已高达一百万册,并拍摄有缩微片五十万个。图书资料可说相当的丰富。

在参观母校图书馆的设备之后,又听说母校图书馆已使用电脑作业,方法非常新颖时,他特别赞扬馆长张鼎钟是个人才!但也同时寄望母校师生更支持图书馆的活动。

李华伟,四十三年自母校毕业后,曾在台北师专附属小学担任训导处之训导员,不久即赴美匹兹堡大学攻读教育硕士,在研修教育博士的同时因在该校东方图书馆担任采购编目而兼修图书馆学。

1968 年到 1975 年,李博士曾为美国国务院援外总署礼聘到泰国。在泰国设立亚洲理工学院,帮助泰国推展图书馆教育扩充当地图书馆,直至计划完成后才又回到美国。

目前他在美国爱丁堡大学任课视听教育,兼图书馆馆长,指挥部分学生撰写论文。他的著作有图书馆自动化、东南亚地区期刊资料中心的计划等六、七十篇,多半是以英文写成的。同时,他也拥有一个"大"家庭。李夫人是美国人,同为图书馆学专家,是他在匹兹堡大学的研究所的同学,目前则在家里相夫教子。六个小孩的脸上都有外国血统,李博士后来也没有忘记教他们说中文,告诉他们是中国人,最大的儿子今年读大三……李博士滔滔地谈着家庭和事业的时候,在旁四三级教育系的老系友们则提醒他别忘了一点钟的飞机起飞时间,并嘱咐记者如还有问题,问他们好了,因为他们还等着他聚餐呢!

(原载《师大校友月刊》1980 年第 189 期,第 6 页。)

美国俄亥俄大学图书馆馆长李华伟先生在京作学术报告

李晓明

1982年12月28日上午，由北京大学图书馆学系、北京大学图书馆和北京地区高校图书馆学会联合举行学术报告会，邀请回国讲学路过北京的美国俄亥俄大学图书馆馆长李华伟先生介绍美国大学图书馆的现状和发展趋势。

关于美国大学图书馆的现状，李华伟先生谈到了六个方面。

一、藏书

过去美国大学图书馆的藏书每年增加5%–7%，约十六年增加一倍。二十世纪六十年代由于经费足，各馆买书很多，尽可能做到自足，把馆际互借的观念放在了一边。到了七十年代由于书价上涨，图书馆藏书由量的增加转向质的提高；重质不重量的另一个原因是馆容饱和，新盖的大楼越来越少。自动化的两个结果也影响图书馆藏书：1. 网络化使馆际互借发展起来；2. 资料库的发展使得读者从终端查到的资料线索超出了图书馆所能提供的资料，增加了图书馆的负担，没有一个图书馆能独立满足读者的全部要求。因此，在70年代至80年代，馆际互借与图书流通重新受到重视。

美国大学图书馆的采购经费一般占全馆经费的25%–30%，占全校经费的1%–2%。

二、图书资料分类编目的标准化

由于IFLA和UNESCO等国际组织的努力和大力推动，一些国际标准已经得到了广泛的应用。由于采用统一的格式，建成资料库以后，磁带的交换与使用就非常方便。过去一些大的图书馆由于藏书多、标准化的起步较晚，现在也不得不做相应的改变。这对中国来说有值得借鉴的地方，即标准化可能会带来某些不方便，它需要有些学校改变原有的工作程序，可是从长远来看是值得的。

三、自动化与网络化

由于计算机与通讯技术的发展，近十几年来，图书馆自动化和网络化的发展速度越来越快，效果也越来越好。自动化包括索引与文摘的自动化，以及图书馆管理的自动化。自动化在图书馆的发展可以俄亥俄大学图书馆中心（OCLC）为例。OCLC买来国会图书馆的机读目录磁带，存入计算机，供各国图书馆共同使用。开始时，买回的新书在资料库中可以查到编目数据的仅占30%–40%，现在已经上升到94%。OCLC的另一个有效服务项目是馆际互借，成功率超过90%。OCLC还有采购、外借、期刊控制等系统，但效果不是顶好，所以有的图书馆不用这些系统。但OCLC也有一些缺点：由于网络是星状的，所有的作业都要经过中心，这对于地方性的作业不很经济有效，有的图书馆另外配置小型计算机来弥补星状系统的这一缺陷；不能用主题的途径来检索。

四、图书馆员的培训与专业范围的扩大

70年代以来由于经费的增加率赶不上工资的增加率，有的图书馆雇用的工作人员数实际上在减少，很多图书馆系的毕业生找不到工作。对于图书馆来说，结果是提高了馆员

素质，现在只有一个图书馆专业的硕士学位就不够了。另外一个趋势是图书馆的工作越来越复杂，科学管理的要求越来越迫切，"专业人员"的概念扩大了。现在美国大学图书馆员的培训有在职培训与技术教育两种形式，在职培训指提高馆员的工作能力，是图书馆的责任；而技术教育不一定与图书馆工作有关，是图书馆员自己的事。

五、图书馆行政与管理的民主化、公开化与科学化

大学图书馆做到人事公开、财物公开，例如人员补缺需要组织征选委员会，对应征人员进行考核，决定初步的人选，再由馆长最后确定聘用。

六、服务观念的加强

大学图书馆与社会的关系越来越密切，大学图书馆成为当地图书馆资源的中心。大学图书馆对社会服务，可以从州政府得到补助，这是一种很好的服务方式，使得大学图书馆的资源得到充分的利用。美国的大学图书馆每周开放106小时，星期一至星期五从8：00开到24：00，服务项目应有尽有，包括对残疾人服务。

关于今后的发展趋势，李华伟先生概括为五个方面：
（1）网络之间、系统之间加强联系。
（2）中小型计算机大量应用。
（3）馆际合作的加强，系统、网络使馆际合作变得迅速有效。
（4）图书馆进一步重视情报工作。
（5）成本效益的观念受到重视。

（原载《大学图书馆通讯》1983年第1期，第93－94页。）

Alden Library Grows in Size and Stature

Dwight Woodward

Classes, professors, sports, Greek life, taverns, and various other facets of the university are images that come to mind when thoughts turn to undergraduate life on a college campus. But the backbone of the institution—the library—is often overlooked.

Alden Library, built in 1968—two wings were added in 1972 completing the building—replaced Chubb Hall as Ohio University's book depository.

Alden is the fourth largest library in the state behind Ohio State, Cincinnati and Kent, not including public libraries which stock numerous copies of the same book at branch libraries.

The seven-story structure, designed to hold 1.4 million volumes, now houses 1.3 million volumes, including books, bound periodicals and government documents. That doesn't include an equal number of items available on microfiche and microforms, according to Director Hwa-Wei Lee.

A native of Guang Zhou, China, Lee fled to Taiwan during the Communist revolution in China. He completed his undergraduate degree at Taiwan Normal University and went on to a doctorate in education at the University of Pittsburgh. With stints at libraries in Pennsylvania, Bangkok, Thailand and Colorado State University, Lee said he was attracted to OU by President Charles Ping's strong stance on international education and Alden's impressive Southeast Asian Collection.

Lee came to Alden in 1978. He said his main accomplishment has been informing university faculty of what the library offers and the importance of maintaining a strong acquisitions budget. The result has been stronger support of the university's base acquisitions budget which topped $1 million in academic 1985–1986 for the first time. All told, with grants and gifts, the acquisition budget was $1.5 million, more than double the $660,000 of 1978–1979.

Lee points to the On-line Computer Library Center as an asset the university can be particularly proud of. The center began in 1971 when OU put the first entry into the computerized system—never mind that the system immediately crashed. The on-line computer system allows users to review the catalogues of more than 7,000 other participating libraries in the United States and overseas.

More than 15 years since it began, the system has more than 15 million entries and is adding another million every seven to eight months. That is nearly four times the number of accessible volumes at the Library of Congress, making the system by far the largest in the world, Lee said.

Increased use of the center has increased the use of the interlibrary loans. OU loaned 23,844 of its volumes in 1985–1986, compared to only 3,283 a decade before.

ALICE—not an acronym, just a nice name—allows students to access the library's holdings by subject, author or title. Based on the Virginia Tech Library System, ALICE now has 80 percent of Alden's holdings in memory.

With Alden reaching its capacity, Lee is making plans for a "long-term, low-cost storage facility on campus." In fact, the Innovation Center now houses about 10,000 volumes; other state universities which built libraries about the same time are facing similar space problems.

President Ping is serving on a committee, appointed by the Board of Regents, to research and establish a centralized storage facility for state universities, Lee said.

The total value of the holdings of Alden, including books, microforms, posters, cassettes, slides, manuscripts, equipment and other items was estimated at $115 million in 1986 by Lee.

But Lee said the library staff is now planning a "Third Century" fund drive in an effort to raise a $10 million library endowment.

"It will put us in a better position for future potential growth," Lee said.

As for the one complaint often heard about the library —its heating system always leaves it too hot or too cold —Lee says $500,000 in improvements, including a backup air conditioner, will keep temperatures more comfortable and even.

Alden Library served 1.32 million people in 1985 – 1986 while circulating 285,244 volumes, with the library staff fielding 193,425 questions, according to library statistics.

(Published in *The Athens Messenger.* March 15, 1987: p. D – 1.)

Ohio's Top Librarian: Lee Is Surprised by OLA Award

Nancy Roe

Director of University Libraries Hwa-Wei Lee is no stranger to awards and honors, but his recent selection as Ohio Librarian of the Year nevertheless came as a surprise.

Lee, who received the Ohio Library Association (OLA) award Nov. 6, was particularly pleased that the ceremony marked the second time a University librarian had been singled out for recognition by the profession.

"It's quite an honor For Ohio University to have two librarians of the Year," he says, noting that Hannah McCauley, head of the Ohio University-Lancaster Library, received the award in 1980.

Lee came to campus in 1978 and believes he was fortunate "to come at the right time".

"By then, library funds had been cut to the bone and the staff was demoralized," he recalls.

"We sought—and got—strong support and leadership from President Ping and first Provost Neil Bucklew and then Provost James Bruning. The result is that we've made a comeback. We've seen enormous change here in-the last 10 years."

Lee looks on the OLA award as "an honor for the entire Library staff", saying, "They go out of their way to make the best use and do the most with our available resources."

The Lee era of intense change in the Library has seen:

· Automation of Alden Library and extension of an integrated system to the regional campuses.

· Steady growth in development of library collections, improvement of services and library beautification.

· Emergence of the Ohio University Libraries as a major resource for 11 public libraries throughout Southeast Ohio.

· Creation of innovative internship programs that have brought professionals from Asia and Europe to campus for training in computer technology and modern management practices.

· Success in gaining outside funding for library programs, acquisitions and special collections from the National Endowment for the Humanities and other federal, state and private sources.

· Extensive staff development programs and exchange programs with international libraries.

· Long-range planning to meet future library space and funding needs.

Lee, the driving force behind the library success story, has also brought international recognition to Ohio University and its libraries through his work with library and professional associations around the globe.

(Published in *Ohio University Outlook '87*, November 1987.)

OU's Dr. Lee Named Ohio's Librarian of the Year

Ohio University's library director, Dr. Hwa-Wei Lee, has been selected as Ohio Librarian of the Year by the Ohio Library Association.

"I feel great," Lee said after learning of the award. The award recognizes distinguished service to the profession and innovative leadership in the development of libraries and improvement of library services.

Lee said winning the award means he's going to have to work harder. "There's a greater expectation of me now that I've won the award."

Lee came to OU in 1978 and has overseen the automation of Alden Library, development of the library's collections and improvement of library services. He also created internship programs that bring librarians from Europe and Asia to campus to train in computer technology and management practices.

He said the award is more than recognition of his personal achievements, but rather reflects on the university as a whole.

"It's definitely going to help Ohio University," Lee said, adding the school could get some national publicity from the award.

Lee said the library still has a lot of things to accomplish, and fund-raising is going to play a key role.

"State income can only keep us at a level we consider adequate," he explained. "To be excellent, we have to find more private endowments."

The citation specifically commended Lee on his fund-raising efforts.

(Published in *The Athens Messenger*, November 12, 1987.)

Alden Director Named Librarian of the Year

Anne Hiller[①]

The man who implemented a variety of improvements in the past 10 years at Alden Library doesn't claim all the credit to himself.

But these improvements resulted in Dr. Hwa-Wei Lee, director of libraries, being named the best librarian in the state.

Lee was selected as Ohio Librarian of the Year last week at the Midwest Federation of Library Association's Conference in Indianapolis.

Lee said the library's computer automation and improvements in book collections help to make Alden "one of the better (libraries) throughout the state".

"I think the library has a very strong collection and a strong staff," Lee said. "The faculty and students also help to make the library a better place."

Lee came to OU in 1978 and he has made considerable improvements since then.

"**WE ARE** very fortunate to have library beauty," he said. "A lot of improvements have been made to the building."

Those improvements are the work of the Library Beautification Project which Lee helped create.

"It has helped to make the library an environment more conducive to studying," he said.

He said when he first came to OU, cutbacks in funding had taken their toll on the library.

"We really needed to raise the staff morale and establish credibility," Lee said.

"We also needed to be more responsive to needs like being open for more hours," he added.

Lee was nominated for the Ohio Librarian award after the Ohio Library Association's Board of Directors nominated him for a nationwide award.

WHILE HE didn't win the national award, Lee said it was "quite an honor".

"I was surprised, but I'm also pleased," he said. "We have a very good university and very sound leadership so I am pleased with it."

Lee said OU's library is just now being established among the library community, but it is "one of the better throughout the state".

Lee was awarded the Outstanding Administrator Award by Administrative Senate in 1982 and has lectured throughout the world, according to OU News Services.

He has also created an international exchange program between Alden and other libraries.

OU's international program is one of the reasons Lee first came to Alden.

Lee is very modest about his success, though.

"I don't take the credit all to myself," he said. "In order to do a good job, it takes a lot of effort from everyone."

(Published in *The Post* (Ohio University), November 12, 1987.)

---

① Staff writer

John Ames Humphry/Forest Press Award Recipient Announced[1]

Hwa-Wei Lee, director of libraries at Ohio University in Athens, is the recipient of the American Library Association (ALA) International Relations Committee John Ames Humphry/Forest Press Award.

The award, $1,000 donated by Forest Press, is given to an individual for significant contribution to international librarianship.

"Dr. Lee has contributed to international librarianship as an educator, consultant, and innovator," said Helen Maul, chair of the Humphry/Forest Press Award for International Librarianship Jury. "His work with UNESCO, USAID, FAO, and IFLA, has resulted in improved access to information and library resources in Southeast Asia. As director of libraries at Ohio University, he has set up an internship program for foreign librarians at the University Library and has been an active supporter of international networking as a member of the OCLC Users Council. His dedication to the development of international librarianship represents the very best in our profession."

Lee is an honorary professor at the National Taiwan College of Education and previously served as a consulting professor at Xi'an Jiaotong University in China. He is also a consultant for the Food and Agriculture Organization (FAO), UNESCO and USAID in Mainland China, Hong Kong, Indonesia, Taiwan and Thailand.

He has a bachelor's degree from the Taiwan Normal University in Taipei, two master's degrees from the University of Pittsburgh and Carnegie Mellon University and a doctoral degree from the University of Pittsburgh.

A member of the ALA Council, Lee is also the ALA representative on the Section of University Libraries and Other General Research Libraries of the International Federation of Library Associations and Institutions (IFLA). Lee is a member of both the Advisory Council on Federal Library Programs for the State Library of Ohio, and Advisory Council of the School of Library Science at Kent State University. He is past president of the Chinese Academic and Professional Association in Ohio and received the Distinguished Service Award in 1983 from the Chinese-American Librarians Association.

Lee will receive his award on Tuesday, July 2, 1991, during the International Assembly from 2 p.m to 4 p.m., during the ALA Annual Conference in Atlanta.

(Published in *American Library Association News*, May 1991.)

---

[1] From: Pamela Goodes Linda Wallace 312-280-5043. 5042.

李华伟博士及其领导下的美国俄亥俄大学图书馆

卢素心[①]

我作为一名中国图书馆工作者，在参加由美国图书馆学会（American Library Association）和美国新闻总署（United State Information Agency）联合举办的"交换图书馆员计划"项目中，被安排在李华伟博士领导下的俄亥俄大学图书馆工作。在近两个月的学习、工作和考察中，我见到了该馆所达到的自动化技术程度、对读者提供的高水准的服务以及具有特色的藏书体系，领略了李博士的渊博学识、丰富阅历和开拓精神。现谨以此拙文，将我所了解的李华伟博士以及他领导下的美国俄亥俄大学图书馆（下称俄大图书馆）介绍给我国图书馆同仁。

1. 全美高等院校图书馆中职位最高的华人

李华伟博士是美国华裔中最早担任美国大学图书馆馆长的人，也是当前全美高等院校图书馆中职位最高的华人。从1978年至今，任俄大图书馆院长级馆长兼教育学院教授的李华伟博士，曾先后获得匹兹堡大学教育硕士、图书馆学硕士及高等教育的哲学博士学位。在他风华正茂、面临多种前途的时候，他选择了图书馆这一平凡而又高尚的事业，并在这一事业中坚持不懈地奋斗了30多年，历任匹兹堡大学、都肯大学、宾州爱丁堡大学、科罗拉多州立大学等图书馆行政职务。由于李博士在图书馆领导工作中表现出了卓越才能，1968年美国政府国际发展总署选派他前往泰国担任亚洲理工学院图书馆及资料中心主任，长达7年之久。李博士在美国图书馆界极为活跃，曾当选为美国图书馆学会及俄亥俄州图书馆学会理事、国际图书馆联盟的大学及研究图书馆委员会委员。在学术上，他具有专深的造诣，曾著有《图书馆学的世界观》和《90年代图书馆募款指引》，发表学术论文60余篇，并多次担任联合国教科文组织及其他国际机构与基金会的顾问。

李博士不仅对美国图书馆事业敬业勤勉，而且积极为发展和推动世界各国的图书馆事业做出努力。他曾多次参与组织图书、信息、新技术国际学术会议，经常应邀为世界各国图书馆界作学术报告，其中包括为我国武汉、福州、兰州、北京、长沙等地的图书馆同仁作学术报告。他具有代表性的学术报告有《现代图书馆管理和图书馆行政管理自动化》、《科技信息中心管理》等。需要特别提出的是，李博士设立了"国际图书馆实习项目"，该项目的宗旨是提供俄大图书馆作为世界各国图书馆员实习的学习、工作与研究的基地；自1979年至今，该馆先后共接收来自中国图书馆的馆员70多名。

由于李博士对图书馆事业作出了卓越贡献，他曾获得俄亥俄州1987年"最杰出图书馆员奖"及1991年美国图书馆学会"国际关系卓越贡献奖"等多种荣誉。

2. 俄亥俄大学图书馆的概况

俄大图书馆的历史，可追溯到1804年。现有一个总馆和五个分馆，总馆和分馆形成了既有分工又有合作、在藏书建设上既各有侧重又资源共享的统一体系。总馆——阿尔顿图书馆（Vernon R. Alden Library）坐落在总校园中心，环境幽静，花木茂盛，洁白色的七层楼的现代化建筑使人们直接感受到知识殿堂的气氛，分馆分别设在五所分校的校园

[①] 任职于深圳图书馆。

之中。

在藏书建设上，俄大图书馆坚持把满足和适应院校领导、专家、教授和师生员工的需要作为其工作原则。因此，它既要照顾到普通藏书的合理性，又要突出形成自己特色的藏书体系。至1993年，该馆共有藏书165万册，期刊1.1万多种，缩微胶片200多万件，声像、光盘等非书刊资料30多万件。其中，丰富的东南亚文献资料是该馆藏书的主要特色之一，现有12万多册藏书并以每年递增1.1万多册藏书的东南亚文献收藏部，已成为全世界著名的东南亚文献资料收藏中心之一。有鉴于该部实力雄厚及其服务声望，马来西亚政府于1988年将其作为北美地区马来西亚信息中心，并指定该部为北美地区负责入藏马来西亚出版物的收藏点，由马来西亚国家图书馆免费提供书刊资料。此外，体现藏书特色的文献还有政府出版物、特藏和档案资料、地图和缩微资料、绘画美术资料、音乐舞蹈资料及医学文献资料等。

采用新技术是俄大图书馆的突出特点。该馆不仅是美国高等院校图书馆中采用电脑技术最早的图书馆之一，而且是1971年建立的国际性的图书馆电脑系统网络（OCLC）的创建者之一。如今该馆已拥有一整套高水准的图书馆自动化系统网络，其中包括一个CD-ROM光盘数据库系统网络；一个联合编目及馆际互借系统网络，可经由OCLC的国际网络与北美及世界各地的1.4万多家图书馆建立合作编目及馆际互借关系。此外，该馆的采购、流通、办公系统都全面实现了电脑化管理，缩微技术、视听技术、复印技术、电讯技术也到达相当高的水准。

为读者提供高质量的服务，是该馆奉行的宗旨。可共享的丰富的文献资源、大量的CD-ROM光盘数据库、完善的新技术设施、高素质的参考咨询人员，是他们提供高质量服务的保证。该馆除了提供传统的阅览、外借服务外，还提供参考咨询服务、检索服务，并有专门的专业人员辅导读者使用CD-ROM系统网络、Internet系统、缩微阅读机、教学媒体技术，并每年为新读者开设有关图书馆知识方面的课程。此外，由于俄大馆所处地区的公共图书馆系统规模较小，该馆还担负着为本地区公众服务的任务，并从学术上辅助和指导地方公共图书馆系统的工作，成为该地区传播信息、知识和资源共享的中心。就该馆的功能而言，可归结为：（1）院校领导、专家、教授、教师、博士生、研究生的参考咨询和研究中心；（2）院校教育的辅助中心；（3）学生的第二课堂；（4）地方图书馆行业的学术研究中心；（5）地方公众索取资料、获取信息和阅读的中心。

3. 结语

一所图书馆要健康发展，既取决于图书馆所制定的方针、政策，又取决于领导者的魄力和领导才能。俄大图书馆能够取得今天的成就，跻身于世界图书馆的前列，正是李博士将他的毕生精力和卓越才干奉献给图书馆事业的写照。作为图书馆界的元老，李博士为同仁树立了敬业的典范，他的学术成就是全世界图书馆事业发展的宝贵财富。

（原载《图书情报知识》1995年第4期，第46-47页。）

美国第一个华人图书馆馆长
——访李华伟博士

李晓晶

我在武汉大学参加"信息资源与社会发展国际学术研究研讨会"时,曾与美国俄亥俄大学图书馆馆长李华伟博士不期而遇,他的一席之谈,至今仍给我留下深刻印象。

65岁的李华伟先生平易近人,待人彬彬有礼,谈吐儒雅,颇有学者风度。李先生祖籍福州,2岁时随家人离开老家,高中毕业前一年去台湾,在台湾读完高中,考入台湾师大学习教育行政专业,毕业后在台湾工作了两年。1957年赴美国深造,在匹兹堡大学读书7年,获得教育硕士、图书馆学硕士、教育哲学博士三个学位。1966年,李先生毕业时,刚好赶上美国高等教育在扩充,就被州立学院聘为图书馆馆长,在那之前还没有过华人成为美国大学图书馆馆长。1978年他开始担任俄亥俄大学图书馆馆长兼教育院教授。

从此,李先生几乎每年都有机会回到祖国讲学,与国内一些大学和中国社会科学院图书馆建立了合作关系,前后为中国图书馆界培训了很多图书馆员,在李先生帮助下,国内有近70位图书馆员曾到俄亥俄大学图书馆接受了短期训练。李先生还曾与中国的国家图书馆及中国图书馆学会合办了第一届中美图书馆合作会议,得到了圆满的结果。美国方面的参加单位有美国图书馆学会、国会图书馆、美国国家图书馆、信息科学委员会、华美图书馆学会。这的确是李先生在中美图书馆合作的历史上做了一件很有意义的事。

据李先生介绍,美国的联机图书馆自动化中心已正式宣布与清华大学合作设立在中国的服务中心。这所目前世界上最大的信息服务公司,简称OCLC,如今在世界上有64个国家23000多个图书馆参加,说到这里,李先生又进一步介绍:"1994年开始,国家教委决定由清华大学牵头建立中国的教育科研网络,以便与世界的网际联网。虽然有了这个中国的信息高速公路,但必需要引进一些有价值的国际信息资源,原因在于OCLC已有60几种数据库,首先考虑把OCLC的数据库引进到中国来,经过我在中间穿针引线,这件事情发展顺利,OCLC除了为中国提供它现有的信息资源外,还要在技术上帮助中国,建立中国的数据库及全国性的合作编目,以及管机附件系统,使中国的图书信息能够为中国的读者所使用,并且与国际接轨进而推广。这件事我已做了三年,这对宣扬中国文化及学术上的成就会发生很大的作用,同时,国外进来的信息资源对中国来讲是非常及时的。"

说起俄亥俄大学"海外华人文献研究中心"的创立、规划、目标等,李先生侃侃而谈。海外华人不仅对所居住的地区国家的经济文化发展作出了巨大贡献,还对中国的经济发展与教育建设提供了强大有力的帮助,但是他们的历史作用并未得到应有的重视。应保存海外华人的文献与遗产,系统地、原始地记载分散于世界各地有成就的海外华人的事迹资料,使学者们有效而充分地利用这些资料来评价海外华人的历史贡献。俄亥俄大学的"海外华人文献研究中心"作为世界上第一所类似的机构,其目标是通过收集、整理、保存、介绍及研究有关海外华人的文献史料,再现他们奋斗与贡献的历史。这不仅是海外华人居住国发展的一个重要组成部分,也是悠久的中华文明在海外的延伸与发扬光大。

"我是炎黄子孙,虽然身居海外,但我还是希望能为祖国文化和学术的发展贡献一份力量。"李先生这样说,也是这样做的。那次会议刚结束,第二天一早就马不停蹄地赶往成都去讲学了。为了中国图书馆事业的发展,李华伟博士确是尽了自己的力。

(原载《读书周报》第631号,1997年3月29日。)

享有盛誉的海外华人学者
——李华伟博士简介

自 1978 年以来担任美国俄亥俄大学图书馆馆长的李华伟博士原籍是福建省福州市。1933 年 1 月 25 日生于广东四会，抗日战争时期以前在南京度过幼年的岁月。1937 年日军入侵，随父母迁往广西桂林及四川重庆，念毕小学及初中二年级，1945 年胜利后，回到南京进入南京一中，完成了初中的学业。1947 年又迁回桂林，进入国立汉民中学高中部。1949 年随家迁往台湾，在台中市立第一中学毕业，1950 年考入当时的台湾省立师范学院攻修教育学。1954 年毕业后，前后在"陆军军官及政工干部学校"接受了一年的预备军官训练。1955 年分配到台北省立师范专科学校的附属小学担任训导主任一年，次年被已升格为台湾师范大学的母校聘为助教，派往训导处担任主管学生社团活动的训导员。

1957 年，因获得美国匹兹堡大学的入学许可及奖学金，在 9 月 1 日动身赴美进修，以七年的时间，念毕教育硕士，图书馆学硕士及哲学博士的学位。在此期间，除一面攻读及研究外，还在匹兹堡大学图书馆勤工俭读，在 1959 年由该馆正式聘用，首先担任培训馆员。两年后升为采访部第一助理，1962 年，由在匹兹堡城的都肯大学图书馆聘为采访部主任兼该馆极为著名的非洲特藏部主任。

1965 年在匹兹堡大学完成主修教育及副修图书馆学的哲学博士学位以后，即由当时宾州的爱丁堡州立学院聘为图书馆副馆长兼图书馆系助理教授，次年升为馆长。为中国人在美国高等院校担任图书馆馆长最早的一人，在此期间还一度兼任图书馆学系系主任职。

1968 年，在一个偶然的机遇下，由美国国际发展总署向宾州爱丁堡州立学院借调派往泰国的亚洲理工学院担任该院首任的图书馆及信息中心的主任。

一年后，因为工作的需要辞掉爱丁堡的工作，在泰国停留了七年，直到 1975 年美国支援亚洲理工学院的项目圆满结束，当在亚洲理工学院服务时，还应泰国朱拉隆功大学图书馆学系之邀，自 1970 年至 1975 年在该系讲授"图书馆自动化"的课程，这在亚洲还是最早开设的图书馆课程。除此之外，还多次担任联合国教科文组织，联合国发展计划，世界粮农组织，加拿大国际发展及研究中心等机构有关图书馆发展项目的顾问。

1975 年返回美国后即应聘担任美国科罗拉多州大学图书馆教授级副馆长，三年以后转任俄亥俄大学图书馆馆长一职至今。

李博士在美国图书馆界极为活跃，曾经担任过美国图书馆学会理事、国际关系委员会亚洲太平洋地区小组主席、俄亥俄图书馆学会理事、美国华美图书馆员学会会长及理事、OCLC 会员代表大会俄州代表、国际图联大学及研究图书馆委员会委员等职务。因为他的卓越成就，李博士曾得到很多奖励，其中主要的有：俄亥俄大学最杰出行政人员奖（1982年）、华美图书馆员学会杰出服务奖（1983 年）、俄亥俄州最杰出图书馆员奖（1987 年）、台湾图书馆学会杰出贡献奖（1989 年）、美中华人学术及专业学会杰出服务奖（1991年）、美国图书馆学会国际关系卓越贡献奖（1991 年）、亚美及太平洋地区图书馆员学会杰出服务奖（1991 年）、美国新闻署杰出服务奖状（1992 年）、美国图书馆学会杰出理事奖状（1992 年）、俄亥俄图书及信息网感谢奖状（1993 年）等。

另外，李博士还陆续地被选载在《世界名人传》、《美国名人传》、《美国教育界名人传》等年鉴上。

即使在极为忙碌的工作中，李博士仍然不忘教学、研究与写作，在他近四十年的图书馆生涯中，曾经发表过六十多篇文章，出版了三本专著，编过两本会议录及先后担任了六种学术期刊的编辑委员，他的著作是《图书馆学的世界观》（1991年台湾学生书局出版）、《九十年代图书馆的筹款指引》（与盖里·汉博士合著，1992年由美国坚那位公司出版）、《现代化的图书馆管理》（1996年由台湾三民书局出版）。

李博士曾经主持或协办过多次国际会议，其中包括，1983年6月28日在洛杉矶由亚美及太平洋图书馆员学会与华美图书馆员学会合办"亚太地区图书馆的发展及合作的途径"的年会、1988年9月8日至11日在西安由俄大图书馆与西安交大图书馆合办的"图书馆新技术应用国际学术讨论会"、1994年10月20日至24日在上海由中国科学院上海图书馆主办的"信息技术与信息服务国际研讨会议"、1996年8月21日至23日在北京举行的"第一届中美图书馆合作会议"、1996年9月3日至6日由武汉大学及上海师范大学等合办的"信息资源与社会发展国际学术研讨会"。

在俄亥俄大学，李博士除了担任图书馆馆长之外，还兼任了该大学教育学院的教授，先后担任了十余位博士的学位论文指导老师。

除此之外，自1982年以后，李博士还每年应邀前往中国各地讲学，近年来还应中国国家教委之邀多次在世界银行贷款项目及联合国发展基金项目下，对国内师范院校的图书馆长开办图书馆管理的培训班，由于他孜孜不倦的教学活动，国内很多大学都邀请他担任访问教授或客座教授，包括西安交通大学、南开大学、湖南医大、武汉大学、四川联合大学、东北师范大学、天津理工学院。中国科学院武汉文献信息中心及兰州文献信息中心也聘请李博士担任学术顾问。

作为一个美籍华裔的图书馆从业人员，李博士极为关心中国图书馆的发展，除了经常回国讲学外，从1980年起，还在俄亥俄大学图书馆设立了一个国际图书馆员培训计划，曾先后为中国培训了近百名的图书馆员，包括北大、清华、北师大、南开、邮电大、三〇一医院图书馆、重大、浙江医科大学、中国科学院文献情报中心、中国科技信息研究所等，其中很多位是馆长、副馆长及部门主任。

面对21世纪的信息时代，发展现代化的图书馆信息事业是每一个发展中国家当务之急，李博士认为："中国要加速科技、经济、政治、教育、文化及社会的发展，必须加速现代化图书馆及信息工作的发展"。目前正在兴建的中国教育科研网是国家信息基础建设的一个主要部分。有了这个教研网，中国的高等学府才能与国际上的国际联网衔接交流，吸取世界上最先进的知识。要为中国学术界的信息高速公路引进世界上一些最重要的信息源，经过李博士的穿针引线，居中协调，美国最大的信息机构（OCLC——联网计算机图书馆中心）在1996年正式与清华大学签订了长期互惠合作的协定，这个协定将会加速中国图书馆界现代化的发展。

（原载《世界科技研究与发展》1997年第19卷第4期，第46—47页。）

经纬枢纽　美华桥梁
——李华伟博士印象

徐国定[1]

美国俄亥俄大学图书馆馆长李华伟先生，在他近40年的图书馆生涯中，曾经发表过60多篇论文，出版了3本书，先后担任6种学术期刊的编辑委员。他的《图书馆的世界观》（1991年台湾学生书局出版）、《90年代图书馆的筹款指引》（与蓝里博士合著，1992年由美国坚那位公司出版）和《现代化的图书馆管理》（1996年台湾三民书局出版），在国际图书馆界影响很大。特别是《现代化的图书馆管理》一书，对当今图书馆进行现代化管理有指导意义。这本书荟集了他几十年来在国内外尤其是在中国大陆讲学的精髓，花了近五年时间才完成的。这部书是在当今图书馆大变革时期，人类信息大爆炸，计算机技术、通讯技术、密集储蓄技术、多媒体技术、电子出版技术等快速发展和国际信息网络日渐畅通、现代化管理思想逐日深化的情况下定稿的。它吸取了传统式的"纸张图书馆"、70年代"自动化图书馆"、80年代"网络化图书馆"、90年代"电子化图书馆"的各个历史时期管理思想的理论，是一部适应21世纪图书馆和信息中心朝向"虚拟图书馆"方向发展需要的佳作。书中不仅就现代化的任务与使命加以阐释，就20世纪西方管理的发展、图书馆的规划、组织、人力资源、领导与作业、控制与评估等作了剖析，并附有大量管理操作的实例、统计及罕见的资料，最后，以跨世纪的图书馆的发展需要作为结论，系统完整地总结了图书馆发展的理论和实践经验。绪论中还提到"图书馆在组织、收藏、管理、流通、服务等各方面应具备的崇尚民主、发展民智、服务社会并具有公正不偏的精神"。这实际是当代图书馆在管理观念上所遵循的原则。他认为管理的意义在"修己安人"，管理的基本精神在"中道"。因此，说明他提倡图书馆实行科学化、制度化与人性化的综合管理的方式，使图书馆成为开放的、自由的、为社会大众提供公正服务的信息和教育中心。《图书信息学丛书》主编周宁森博士称赞说："华伟兄的这部大作不但深入浅出、思维细密、巨细不遗，可作为图书馆管理学的课本；更是图书馆从业人员应参考的经典之作。这部书足以传世。"

李华伟先生之所以这样成功，是与他丰富的阅历，曲折的道路和坚实的社会实践分不开的。他读过小学、中学、师范，当过兵受过训，做过小学的训导主任，当过师范大学的社团活动训导员；取得了教育硕士、图书馆硕士及教育哲学博士学位，还曾获得美国匹兹堡大学的入学许可证及奖学金。从事图书馆工作后，他先后勤工俭学，担任过培训馆员、采访部助理、采访部主任、非洲特藏部主任、图书馆系助理教授、系主任、教授级副馆长，直至馆长。他是美国高校图书馆最早担任馆长的华人。还担任过泰国亚洲理工学院图书馆和信息中心主任，并在泰国国立米拉隆功大学图书馆开讲"图书馆自动化"课程，这是当时亚洲开设最早的图书馆课程。

这些经历说明了他的理论知识的丰厚，这些职务说明他实践知识的广博，对他著书立说无疑奠定了坚实的基础。再加上他对事业的全心奉献、孜孜不倦的精神，自然成果累累，业绩斐然。有一次我问其夫人："李博士很忙很累，按美国人习惯，你应该陪伴他照顾他，陪他出访旅游，为什么不……"话还没说完，夫人便风趣地说："他爱图书馆胜过

---

[1] 任职于海南大学图书馆。

爱我，走到哪儿就到哪儿看图书馆，把我甩在一边，显然我没有他那个图书馆重要。"她的玩笑话，证明了华伟馆长的敬业精神。正是这种精神，他先后得到的奖状奖励和荣誉称号甚多，仅在1982年—1993年间就夺得9项大奖：俄亥俄大学最杰出行政人员奖（1982年）、华美图书馆员学会杰出服务奖（1983年）、俄亥俄最杰出图书馆员奖（1987年）、美中华人学术及专业学会杰出服务奖（1991年）、美国图书馆学会国际关系卓越贡献奖（1991年）、亚美及太平洋地区图书馆员学会杰出服务奖状（1991年）、美国新闻署杰出服务奖状（1992年）、俄亥俄图书及信息网感谢奖（1993年）等。他的名字被载入《世界名人传》、《美国名人传》、《美国教育界名人传》等。

李华伟博士还积极参与国际图书馆界的活动，并十分关注国内图书馆事业的发展。多年来，他奔走于海峡两岸，教学、讲演及参加各有关会议，宣扬图书馆经营的新理念。

可以说，他是当今外籍华人中在这方面所作的贡献最大的一个。这可从他所担任的下列职务得到证实：1978年以来，他担任美国图书馆学会理事的同时，还担任了国际关系委员会亚洲太平洋地区小组主席；在做着俄亥俄图书馆学会理事的时候，又做着华美图书馆员学会会长及理事；他是OCLC会员代表大会俄州代表，又多次担任联合国教科文组织、联合国发展计划、世界粮农组织、加拿大国际发展及研究中心等机构有关图书馆发展项目的顾问；等等。他主持和协办过的国际会议就有：1983年6月28日在洛杉矶由亚美太平洋图书馆学会与华美图书馆员学会合办的"亚太地区图书馆的发展及合作的途径"年会、1988年9月8日在西安由俄大图书馆与西安交大图书馆合办的"图书馆新技术应用国际学术讨论会"、1994年10月20日至24日在上海由中国科学院上海图书文献情报中心主办的"信息技术与信息服务国际研讨会议"、1996年8月21日至23日在北京举行的"第一届中美图书馆合作会议"、1996年9月3日至6日由武汉大学与上海师范大学等合办的"信息资源与社会发展国际学术研讨会"。

自1982年后，李华伟馆长还每年应邀前来中国各地讲学。国内很多大学都邀请他担任访问教授或客座教授，如西安交通大学、南开大学、湖南医大、武汉大学、四川联合大学、北京师范大学、东北师范大学、天津理工学院等。中国科学院武汉文献信息中心及兰州文献信息中心也聘请李博士担任学术顾问。清华大学图书馆及中国新技术开发公司也分别邀请李博士担任顾问。近年来，他还应中国国家教委之邀，多次在世界银行贷款项目及联合国发展基金项目下，对国内师范院校的图书馆长开办图书馆管理的培训班。

从1980年起，他还在俄亥俄大学图书馆实施一项国际图书馆员培训计划，先后为北大、清华、北师大、南开、中国科技情报所等单位培训了近百名图书馆员，其中很多是馆长、副馆长及部门主任。他为中国图书馆事业的发展呕心沥血，千方百计，飞越大洋不知多少次，日程总是满满的：1996年7月他在美国忙于筹备ALA大会，接待我们这些人；8月在北京忙于筹备中美图书馆合作会议大会，9月在武汉主持召开"信息资源与社会发展国际学术研讨会"……李华伟馆长认为：面对21世纪的信息时代，发展现代化的图书信息事业是每一个发展中国家当务之急，"中国要加速科技、经济、政治、教育、文化及社会的发展，必须加速现代化图书馆及信息工作的发展"。因此他十分重视中国教育科研网建设，认为这是中国信息基础建设的一个主要部分。有了这个教育科研网，中国的高等学府才能与国际上的国际联网衔接交流，吸取世界上最先进的知识。因而他积极地穿针引线，居中协调，为中国学术界的信息高速公路引进世界上一些最重要的信息源。如1996年8月美国最大的信息机构——OCLC（联网计算机图书馆中心）正式与清华大学签订了长期互惠合作的协定。在这个隆重的协定签字仪式上，他被称为OCLC与清华大学联姻的

"红娘",引起了当时在北京召开的 IFLA 大会代表们的关注,更引起国内图书馆界人士的关注。因为他是为中国图书界和信息界全面走向网络化的牵线人之一,是中美乃至全世界信息相通、心心相连的桥梁。

1996 年 8 月 27 日下午,在清华大学图书馆的大厅里,他胸前佩戴着悦目的"贵宾"花带,接受着参与大会的所有代表及清华大学师生们的谢礼。在北京五洲大酒店的宴会厅里,在《友谊地久天长》的音乐声中,大家频频向他敬酒,他举杯一一回敬了大家。当他走到我跟前的时候,我觉得"红娘"这个词还不够味儿,于是悄悄地在他耳边朗读着我送给他的那幅题词:"经纬枢纽,美华桥梁。"他高兴地碰了我的杯,激动地说:"谢谢!不敢当,我还要继续努力!"

(原载《书与人》(Books and People) 1997 年第 5 期,第 152 - 155 页。)

不变的中国心
——记美国俄亥俄大学图书馆馆长李华伟博士

吕 红[①]

还没到美国,我已经听过许许多多关于他的故事。有称他为信息产业联姻"红娘"的;有赞他是中美文化交流桥梁的;有提他为人处事"比雷锋还雷锋的";还有夸他"不是亲人胜似亲人的好馆长"的……几乎有口皆碑。——他,就是在中美图书馆界享有盛誉的美籍华人李华伟博士。

"浮云游子意,落日故人情"这是一副悬挂在李华伟先生客厅中的墨迹,也是李先生身居海外的一生写照。

现任俄亥俄大学图书馆馆长兼教育学院教授的李华伟博士,祖籍福州,早年毕业于台湾师范大学教育系,1957年来美深造,先后获得匹兹堡大学教育硕士、图书馆学硕士及高等教育的博士学位。为华裔中担任美国大学图书馆馆长最早的人。

在美国四十年的奋斗生涯中,李馆长曾荣获十多种奖励和称号,如俄州1987年杰出图书馆员奖;1991年美国图书馆学会国际关系卓越贡献奖等多种殊荣;并被连续载入《世界名人传》、《美国名人传》、《美国教育界名人传》等历史年鉴上。

自80年代以来,李馆长几乎每年都要到中国各地的大学、图书馆讲学,并应国家教委之邀,多次利用世界银行贷款项目和联合国发展基金项目,为国内的图书馆开办图书馆管理培训班,先后有近百人在这里接受过系统培训。大家说:"如果要写改革开放以来的中国图书馆事业史,特别是中美图书馆交流合作史,李华伟馆长定是不可缺少的重要人物。"

孜孜不倦致力于中美之间图书情报牵线搭桥,热衷于东西方文化交流与合作的李华伟先生,在1996年全力促成了一件值得一提的大事,在他事业的里程碑上刻下深深的一笔:首届中美图书馆合作会议在北京隆重召开。两国近百位图书馆馆长和专家学者聚集一堂,就会议主题展开热烈的讨论:"全球的信息存取——挑战与机遇"。会议取得了圆满的成功,其意义不同凡响。用北京图书馆馆长任继愈教授的话说,"在迈向信息社会的今天,各国图书馆之间加强了解与合作,互相学习新技术、新方法,实现资源共享的愿望越来越强烈"。李华伟博士在会上作了重要报告,总结了中美图书馆合作的历史经验,以及在今后的发展重点。有意借国际图联大会的契机,积极促成中美图书馆界的密切合作。在中美图书馆发展史上写下新的篇章!

这次会议对中美及世界图书馆的合作与发展产生积极而深远的影响。会议之后又有多个图书馆相继结为姊妹馆。

在俄亥俄大学里,师生们都知道图书馆有个六十多岁、豁达热情的馆长。特别是中国留学生感触极深——每当他们生活上有了困难,学习上遇到了问题,首先第一个就找李馆长。有的同学刚下了飞机找不到车接,或者尚未联系好住处的,哪怕半夜三更到了,也是第一个拨他家的电话;还有的同学刚到异国他乡,面临着学习上、经济上的压力很大,心里一时受不了,向他诉苦。他以一个长者、过来人的身份对他们说:"有很多人以为到了美国就什么问题都解决了,其实,这只是奋斗的开始。"有同学表示畏难情绪,说在国内

[①] 任职于中国武汉广播电视报社。

是铁饭碗，什么都不用愁，而到了这里，感觉精神上的负担很重，经济的压力，学业的压力，文化背景不同的压力，实在受不了，可是又没面子回去，不知怎么办才好。李华伟博士说："大家都想到美国来，来了，就要有思想准备，咬咬牙拼一下。你现在还没有拼就想打退堂鼓，这可不行。"然后他把自己的学习方法或过去读书的有关技巧等一一告诉大家，那些同学听了很受鼓舞，三个月学期考试后，大家都是笑嘻嘻地来看望他，向他报喜。

作为教育学院兼职教授、华裔馆长，除了在学业上给予留学生指导帮助外，还尽可能提供经济方面的支持。他说，我过去从台湾出来赴美求学时吃过苦，尝过经济拮据的滋味。对有生活困难的人，他总是帮忙想办法安排在图书馆工作，对中国大陆来的尤其关照。最令人感动的，是他把这些都看作是份内的事，有求必应，事必躬亲，没有一丝名人的架子。有时他半开玩笑说：同样是中国人，可是台湾来的我要收他们的培训费；你们来，我不仅不收，还在各方面给予照顾，恐怕人家要说我偏心了。

1989年，一个来美国学习的中国女生刚下飞机，突然晕倒在机场，初来乍到人生地不熟，又身患急性肝炎，当时可以说是陷入了困境……李馆长知道这件事后，忙为她询医找药，联系住处，花费了他不少时间精力，直到那个女生完全康复并且顺利完成了学业。

还有一次，李华伟馆长刚刚从机场上接人回来，中途在一家中国餐馆就餐，忽然遇上了在餐馆打工的女生向他求助。原来，她是我国一位著名演员的女儿，在美国进修时与人结婚并生下了孩子，谁料感情变化，那个美国人竟要抛弃她，还要驱她出境，情形很可怜。李馆长闻知此事，马上找到在该城颇具声望的俄亥俄大学副校长白礼恩博士夫妇，请他们陪同出庭，出面力争，几经周折，通过法律程序，终于维护了那女子的合法权益。事后有人问道：李馆长，你怎么想着要帮助一个非亲非故的人？他说：一个弱女子在异国他乡受了欺负，正好又求到了我，我怎么能不尽力去帮助她呢？

曾经有人问：李华伟先生，很多人到国外后都会取一个英文名字，您怎么没有取一个？他笑吟吟地说："华伟这名字能让我时时想到祖国，想到我身上流着的华族的血，更有特殊意义。"言语之间流露出他热爱故乡，一生不变的中国心！

（原载《长江日报》1997年9月1日第6版。）

甘作美中文化交流的桥梁
——记美籍华人李华伟博士

吕 红

在美国俄亥俄大学里，师生们都知道图书馆有个豁达热情的馆长。每当留学生生活上有了困难，学习上遇到问题，首先就找他。还有的同学刚到异国他乡，面临压力，向他诉苦，他以一个长者身份说："有很多人以为到了美国就什么问题都解决了，其实，这只是奋斗的开始。"他，就是在中外图书馆界享有盛誉的美籍华人李华伟博士。李博士说："大家都想到美国来，既然来了，就要有思想准备，咬咬牙拼一下。你现在还没有拼就想打退堂鼓，这可不行。"作为教育学院兼职教授、华裔馆长，除了在学业上给予留学生指导帮助外，还尽可能提供经济方面的支持，对中国来的学生尤其关照。

李华伟博士早年毕业于台湾师范大学教育系，1957年来美深造，曾先后获得匹兹堡大学教育硕士、图书馆学硕士及高等教育的哲学博士学位；历任匹兹堡大学、都肯大学、宾州爱丁堡大学、科罗拉多州立大学等图书馆行政职务，为华裔中担任美国大学图书馆馆长最早的人。在美国40年的奋斗生涯中，他曾荣获十多种奖励和称号，如1991年美国图书馆学会国际关系卓越贡献奖等多种荣誉。

自80年代以来，李馆长每年都要来中国各地多所大学讲学，还应国家教委之邀多次在世界银行贷款项目及联合国发展基金项目下，对国内师范院校的图书馆员开办图书馆管理的培训班。由于他孜孜不倦的教学活动，国内很多大学都邀请他担任访问教授或顾问教授，包括西安交通大学、南开大学、湖南医大、武汉大学、四川联合大学、东北师范大学、天津理工学院、中国科学院武汉文献信息中心及兰州文献信息中心都聘请李博士担任顾问。其讲学精髓汇聚成书——《现代化的图书馆管理》，作为图书馆管理专著，内容涉及图书馆的规划、组织、人力资源管理、领导和作业、控制和评估五大功能，融会了他在美国几十年的管理思想体系……去年在成都讲学时，他就是用这本散发着油墨香的新书作教材的。

如果说过去他工作的着眼点在现代信息管理、自动化技术观念的传播与推广等方面的话，那么现在他的发展计划又有了更高意义的拓展。1993年，在香港银行家邵友保博士的赞助下，"海外华人文献研究中心"正式创立，作为全世界第一所类似的机构，通过收集、整理、保存、介绍及研究有关海外华人的文献资料，再现他们奋斗与贡献的历史。这一历史不仅是居住国发展的一个重要组成部分，而且也是悠久的中华文明在海外的延伸与发扬光大。

提起俄亥俄大学"海外华人文献研究中心"，它不仅凝聚了诸多海外赤子的心血与智慧，而且也体现了一个华裔专家的拳拳回报故国之心。

李华伟先生具有凡事不落人后、力争第一的天性，又是他第一个设立国际图书馆员培训计划，在联合国教科文组织等赞助下，先后有来自亚洲及世界各地的160多为馆员来此完成了培训工作，光中国就有近百人，包括北大、清华、北师大、南开、邮电大、三〇一医院图书馆、重庆大学、浙江医科大学、科学院图书馆、中国科技情报所等，其中很多位是图书馆馆长、科学院副院长及部门主任。这一计划以及该馆与亚洲图书馆的多种合作项目，皆已成为全美图书馆的典范。

要知道，那些资助培训费用是他多方奔走、四处筹集而来的呀！难怪有人送他"经纬枢纽，美华桥梁"的题字呢！

(寄自美国)

(原载《人民日报》海外版第3983号，1997年10月10日第1版。)

一位海外华人的特殊贡献
——记美国俄亥俄大学图书馆馆长李华伟博士

吕 红

一、前言

还没到美国,我就已经听过许许多多关于他的故事。有称他为信息产业联姻"红娘"的;有赞他是中美文化交流桥梁的;有提他为人处事"比雷锋还雷锋的";还有夸他"不是亲人胜似亲人的好馆长"的……几乎有口皆碑。而说得最多的,还是他对推进中国图书馆现代化的贡献。

他,就是在中外图书馆界享有盛誉的美籍华人李华伟博士。

最近,作为访问学者我有机会来到美国,在短短几周内接触了方方面面的人物,收集到大量第一手材料。从一些直接或间接的采访中对他了解更多、更深。碰巧,我在俄亥俄大学遇见的第一人,是正在探亲的、原北京大学图书馆的庄守经馆长,他与李华伟博士交往已久,提到高校系统图书馆发展的历史时,他侃侃而谈:

"概括地说,从80年代到现在的十多年是国内图书馆发展最重要的时期,是从传统的向现代的图书馆迈进的一个关键的十年。在这些年的变革过程中,李华伟先生起了相当大的作用。开始,我们对什么是图书馆的现代化,如何实现现代化,既无经验,也缺乏有关的知识。这就必须学习,必须走出国门,必须借鉴外国的特别是美国的经验。学习美国经验,对我们十分有利的条件就是有大批的华人在美国图书馆界工作,他们十分关心祖国图书馆事业的发展,从多方面给予了热情的帮助,李华伟先生就是他们中最突出的代表。"

"就我个人和北京大学图书馆来说,李馆长的帮助有十分重要的意义。这种帮助首先是在观念方面、知识更新方面。通过讲学、研讨以及个别交谈,他系统地向我们介绍了美国近几十年图书馆发展过程与发展趋势,这就是:60年代以前是传统纸张型的,60年代至70年代是计算机自动化,70年代至80年代是网络化、资源共用,80年代至90年代是电子化、资讯化、无围墙的虚拟图书馆。国情虽然不同,但图书馆现代化的过程与趋势是大体一致的,最后会形成资讯业的全球一体化。这些对我们启发很大,使我们当前办馆思想更加明确、坚定。其次在人才培养方面,在李馆长的直接帮助关怀下,从80年代中到90年代中,北大图书馆先后到俄大图书馆培训的有近20人次,包括图书馆自动化、西文编目、情报服务、采访工作和期刊管理等各业务领域,他们学习回国后都在各自业务岗位以及国际交往中发挥了骨干作用。"

"李馆长对海峡两岸图书馆界的交流合作也十分关注;1988年、1989年间,他曾多次与我商议,拟筹备在美国或香港的双方都能参加的图书馆学术研讨会,以打破两岸图书馆界长期的封闭隔膜状态,连具体人员、地点、经费等都作了考虑,后因两岸解冻,可以直接交往了。这会议便没再举行。由于李馆长的介绍,使我对台湾图书馆的情况、包括一些专家教授都有印象,如原台湾'中央图书馆'馆长王振鹄教授,我们有一见如故之感,有很多共同的话题。"

"就我所知,李华伟馆长与国内许多大学图书馆、图书馆学系,如清华、北师大、南开、西安交大以及中国科技情报所系统、中科院图书情报系统、公共图书馆系统等都有密切关系,都给予了许多帮助,他参与组织了多次在国内举办的大型图书馆学术研讨会,多次应邀在培训班系统讲学。十多年来，李馆长对国内图书馆方面的贡献，以及他的热情诚挚的态度、严谨的工作作风，得到了国内图书馆界一致的敬仰钦佩。大家说：'如果要写改革开放以来的中国图书馆事业史，特别是中美图书馆交流合作史，李华伟馆长是不可缺少的重要人物。'"

"我感到近十多年来国内图书馆事业的发展确实得到海外华人十分有效的帮助，如果说香港的包玉刚、李嘉诚、邵逸夫是在硬件方面在建设新图书馆方面给予了有力的支持，那么李华伟馆长以及在美的许多华裔图书馆员则是在软件方面、在思想观念以及人才培养方面，给予了有效的帮助。这方面的意义日渐重要和深远了。"

"我觉得我们要佩服他，同时要学习他，要学习他凝结在大大小小事情中的那种优秀的品德和可贵的精神。"庄馆长如是说。

二、一位美籍华人的情怀

李华伟先生平易近人、风度儒雅，举止谈吐间融学者的见识和管理者的才智于一体。在他家啊，墙壁上悬挂着中国书法，窗台上、案头上及书架上摆放着朴拙或精美的工艺品，那些让人赏心悦目的工艺品，不仅是他足迹的记录，更是他交游甚广、朋友遍天下的证明。

"浮云游子意，落日故人情"几笔饱满酣畅的大字，是否是他一生的真实写照呢？我长久地品味壁上的书法寻思着……

现任俄亥俄大学图书馆院长级馆长兼教育学院教授的李华伟博士早年毕业于台湾师范大学教育系。1957年来美深造，曾先后获得匹兹堡大学教育硕士、图书馆学硕士及高等教育的哲学博士学位。历任匹兹堡大学、都肯大学、宾州爱丁堡大学、科罗拉多州立大学等图书馆行政职务，为华裔中担任美国大学图书馆馆长的最早一人。1968年由美国政府国际发展总署派往泰国担任亚洲理工学院图书馆资讯中心主任七年。李博士曾当选美国图书馆学会及俄亥俄图书馆学会理事，国际图书馆学会联盟的大学及研究图书馆委员会委员等职务，曾出版《图书馆学的世界观》、《90年代图书馆募捐指引》及《现代化的图书馆管理》等书，发表学术论文六十余篇，曾多次担任联合国教科文组织，其他国际机构及基金会顾问。由于他的人品及出色的工作，在美国及亚洲乃至中国图书馆界都很有名望。在美国四十年的奋斗生涯中，他曾荣获十多种奖励和称号，如俄州1987年最杰出图书馆员奖及1991年美国图书馆学会国际关系卓越贡献奖等多种荣誉。并被连续载入《世界名人传》、《美国名人传》、《美国教育界名人传》等历史年鉴上。

曾经有人问他：李华伟先生，很多人到国外都会取一个英文名字，你怎么没有取一个？为什么？他笑吟吟回答说："华伟这名字能让我时时想到祖国，想到我身上流着华族的血，更有特殊意义。"言语之间流露出他一生不变的中国心。

自从80年代以来，李博士每年都要到中国各地多所大学去讲学。还应国家教委之邀多次在世界银行贷款项目及联合国发展基金项目下，对国内师范院校的图书馆员开办图书馆管理的培训班，由于他孜孜不倦的教学活动，国内很多大学都聘请他担任访问教授或顾问教授，包括北京大学、西安交通大学、南开大学、湖南医大、武汉大学、四川联合大学、北京师范大学、东北师范大学、天津理工学院。清华大学图书馆，北图新技术开发公司，中国科学院武汉文献资讯中心及兰州文献资讯中心也聘请李博士担任顾问。

博士每次讲学前都要认真准备，百忙中仍抽出时间来浏览吸收世界管理科学最新成果。其讲学精髓汇聚成书——《现代化的图书馆管理》，作为图书馆管理专著，内容涉及图书馆的规划、组织、人力资源管理、领导和作业、控制和评估五大功能,该书高屋建瓴,学贯中西,既得益于他多年从事馆长工作的经验,又融汇了他在美国几十年的管理思想体系,对当今图书馆进行现代化管理颇有指导意义。深刻表明在当今大变革时期人类资讯大爆炸、计算机技术、通讯技术、密集储蓄技术多媒体技术、电子出版技术等迅猛发展和国际资讯网络日渐畅通的状况下,图书馆的现代化管理愈显重要。他总结了各个历史时期的管理思想,以适应21世纪"虚拟图书馆"的发展方向。剖析与阐释,系统而完整地总结发展进程的理论和实践经验,表明当代图书馆在管理观念所应遵循的原则,即:"在民主、自由、开放及重视基本人权的社会中,图书馆在组织、收藏、管理、流通服务等各方面应具备的崇尚民主、发展民智、服务社会,并保持公正不偏的精神。"他认为管理的意义在于"修己安人",管理的基本精神在"中道",由此说明他所提倡的图书馆管理应该是科学化、制度化与人性化的综合管理方式。因而他所期望的图书馆,实际上是一所开放的、自由的、为社会大众提供公正服务的资讯和教育中心。该书问世后,引起学术界的重视。……去年在成都讲学时,他就是用这本散发着墨香的新书作教材的。据反映,效果相当不错。所以专家评价说,"李华伟先生对国内的贡献不是物质上的,更主要是精神层面的。"体现在更新观念上、在人才培养上及教育软件方面,这位美籍华人的贡献尤其显得突出。在现代社会中,所谓竞争说到底也就是人才的竞争。教育的根本就是培养人才,人才在现代化事业中就是一批活生生的力量。而现代化图书馆应该相当于人才培养基地。无论是送出国去培训也好,还是他到国内来讲学也罢,这对于图书馆管理人才、专业技术人才的成长,对于图书馆软硬环境的改善是大有好处的。

如果说过去他工作的着眼点在现代资讯管理、自动化技术观念的传播与推广等方面的话,那么现在他的发展计划又有了更新意义的拓展。1993年,在香港银行家邵友保博士的赞助下,"海外华人文献研究中心"正式创立,作为全世界第一所类似的机构,通过收集、整理、保存、介绍及研究有关海外华人的文献资料,再现他们奋斗与贡献的历史。这一历史不仅是居住国发展的一个重要组成部分,而且也是悠久的中华文明在海外的延伸与发扬光大。

提起俄亥俄大学"海外华人文献研究中心",它不仅凝聚了诸多海外赤子的心血与智慧,而且也体现了一个华裔专家的拳拳报国之心。

李华伟馆长说:"放眼世界,中国人祖先的事迹到处都可以探寻到。华人移民海外已有一千多年的历史。尤其是自从19世纪中期以来,华人侨居他国的现象更为显著。他们对居住国社会经济的发展有着不可磨灭的贡献,与此同时,他们关注中国的进步与繁荣,早在辛亥革命以及抗战时期,海外华侨都给予了积极的支持和帮助,因此,被孙中山先生誉为'革命之母'。优良传统延续至今,海外华人对中国的经济发展与教育建设也提供了强有力的帮助。"

据统计,总数为五千五百万的海外华侨,拥有价值两千亿美元的流动资产。一权威学者评述道,如果这些华人居住在一个国家的话,其国民生产总值将超过五百亿美元。可以预见,海外华人对中国、亚洲以及世界的未来都将产生积极而重大的影响。然而,长期以来他们的历史作用未得到应有的重视,学术界对此问题的研究也不够深入普及。这不仅归咎于一些国家目光短浅的民族排外主义,也因为许多专门性的图书馆缺乏充分的财力和物力去收集保存海外华人的文献与遗产。大量的原始记载分散于世界各地,学者们无法有效而系统地利用这些资料来评价海外华人的历史贡献。另一方面,目前个人、家庭及社会对海外华人的历史记录的保存每况愈下,许多宝贵的文献逐渐散失。随着老一辈华人领袖以及其他重要人物逐渐离开历史舞台,向他们征集个人传记、手稿、口述历史资料的迫切性也更为突出。俄亥俄大学的"海外华人文献研究中心"正是在这一背景下创立的。

作为全世界第一所海外华人的研究中心,它的创立已经引起了世人的关注。

三、甘作中美文化交流的桥梁

李华伟先生从来就具有凡事不落人后,偏要争第一的天性,这从他发奋求学的青少年时期就已经显露出来……作为美国第一个华人图书馆馆长,被国际发展总署派出赴东南亚的亚洲理工学院担任第一任馆长,第一个开始在亚洲讲授资讯自动化的课,第一个把大学图书馆变成一些外国政府指定为该国出版物的收藏中心。还有,第一个设立国际图书馆员培训计划,在联合国教科文组织等赞助下,先后有来自亚洲及世界各地160多位馆员在此完成了培训工作,光中国大陆的就有近百人,包括北大、清华、北师大、南开、邮电大、三〇一医院图书馆、重庆大学、湖南医科大学、科学院图书馆、中国科技情报所等,其中很多位是图书馆馆长、副馆长及部门主任。这一计划以及该馆与亚洲图书馆的多种合作项目皆已成为全美图书馆的典范。虽然,这种国际文化教育交流工作在美国做的华裔不止他一人,但是像他这样有目标有计划的、大规模的、长时间持续不断的、不受外界干扰影响的为中美文化发展牵线搭桥,呕心沥血倾尽全力的,的的确确少有!

要知道,不仅那些资助培训费用是他多方奔走、四处筹集而来,而且他还根据不同的人安排不同的培训计划,甚至包括培训人员的生活起居他都关心到了。

中国驻纽约总领事馆徐敦潢参赞、高超领事说:"有的人有他这份心,没有他的身份和地位做不成这些事;也有人有了地位身份,却不见得愿意做这些事。唯他两者兼有,所以他做得有声有色,颇受好评。"

难怪有人送他"经纬枢纽,美华桥梁"的题字呢!

孜孜不倦致力于中美之间牵线搭桥,热衷于东西方文化交流与合作的李华伟先生,在1996年全力促成了一件值得一提的大事,在他事业的里程碑上刻下深深的一笔:首届中美图书馆合作会议在北京隆重召开。两国近百位图书馆馆长和专家学者聚集一堂,就会议主题展开热烈的讨论:"全球的资讯存取——挑战与机遇"。会议取得了圆满的成功,其意义不同凡响。用北京图书馆馆长任继愈教授的话说,"在迈向资讯社会的今天,各国图书馆之间加强了解与合作,互相学习新技术、新方法,实现资源共用的愿望越来越强烈"。美国图书馆学会主席图罗克女士认为,"最重要的是电子资讯的流通和交换,发挥图书馆最大作用"。李华伟博士在会上作了重要报告,总结了中美图书馆合作的历史经验以及在今后的发展重点。有意借国际图联大会的契机,积极促成中美图书馆界的密切合作,在中美图书馆发展史上写下新的篇章!

这次会议对中美两国及世界图书馆界的合作与发展产生积极而深远的影响,会议之后又有多个图书馆相继结为姊妹馆。从观念改变到具体措施;从人员培训到文化交流;从技术引进到信息传播;等等。

海外传媒报道:"自从中国1869年向美国国会图书馆捐赠1000册图书后,相隔一百多年,中美两国近百位馆长和专家学者站在中国国家图书馆的台阶上。"这一幕载入了历史。美国国会图书馆副馆长泰伯评价道:"这不仅是行业合作,也加强了两国人民彼此的了解"。

事后了解,当初为筹备这个会议,李华伟馆长在一年前就积极倡议,并频频与北京电信往来,从经费的筹集到会议资料的印刷,还有大会期间的组织及翻译工作、包括一些词汇提法的相互切磋，大到两国学术界高层的接触交流，小到代表餐宿人员安排，他都一一落实。说实在的，尽管李博士曾经主持或协办过多次国际会议，其中包括1983年在美国举办的"亚太地区图书馆发展及合作途径"年会、1988年由俄大图书馆与西安交大图书馆合办的"图书馆新技术应用"国际学术讨论会、1994年在上海举办的"资讯技术与资讯服务"国际会议、1996年武大的"信息资源与社会发展"国际学术研讨会。但从第一次在中国举办这种大型的两国间高层图书馆合作会议的方面看，中美双方从语言交流、文化背景、工作方式都有诸多的不适，如果没有一个热衷于这项事业的、同时又具有地位和能力的人来操办，很难想象，会取得如此的成功。大家感动地说："从早到晚，忙个不停，李馆长真是太累了！"尤其对一个已是60多岁的并患有腰疾人来说，更为不易。可他笑呵呵地说："身为华人，我乐于作个桥梁。"

中国图书馆的孙蓓欣副馆长称颂道："李华伟先生为图书馆事业所作的努力是令人感佩的！"

1996年8月北京清华大学与美国OCLC联机计算机图书馆中心合作成立服务中心，意味着中国教育科研网有了丰富的资讯源，OCLC是目前世界上最大的资讯服务公司，有64个国家23000多个图书馆参加。已进入这一网络的中国百余所高等学府从此便可以迅速查阅世界的文献资料。在揭幕典礼上，清华大学校长王大中对一位"红娘"的独特贡献表示衷心的感谢，他，就是李华伟馆长。

原来，两年前清华大学图书馆馆长与李馆长谈起"资讯公路尚缺高校所需的一些文化教育科技等资讯"的情况，李馆长闻知立即着手联系，穿针引线，积极地促成双方的合作，他的基本观点是："面对21世纪，发展现代化的图书信息事业是每个发展中国家的当务之急。与世界的网络接轨将有助于宣扬中国文化及成就，同时也将及时引进国外最新的资讯资源。"与国际资讯网络接轨，不仅丰富了资讯资源，而且完善了技术手段，使中国迅速建立数据库及联合编目系统。

李华伟博士认为，"中国要加速科技、经济、政治、教育、文化及社会的发展，必须加速现代化图书馆及资讯工作的发展。"科技网是国家资讯基础建设的一个主要部分，有了这个教研网，中国的高等学府能与国际上的国际联网衔接交流，吸取世界上最先进的知识，从而加速高级人才的培养。

1997年的李博士更加忙碌，除了为筹集"海外华人文献研究中心"200万美元经费而奔波外，还要与中国国家图书馆联手合作，为促进全国公共图书馆资讯网络系统的建立，继续牵线搭桥。

不久前，国家教委"211工程"高等教育文献保障体系项目考察团来美国访问，李博士对他们全面介绍了OhioLink的成功经验，教委条件装备司的李英惠司长以及有关专家非常感兴趣，准备回国进一步完善方案，并正式聘请李华伟博士为CALIS项目的高级顾问。李博士欣然应允，他说，一步步地引进世界最先进的网络系统，吸取成功的合作与管理经验，必将全面推动资讯现代化建设，加速中国文化教育现代化的发展。

与此同时，有关国际学术会议的新主题也在与同仁酝酿商议中。

最近，他在中科院成都文献中心《世界科技》期刊上开辟"海外华人专栏"，准备系统地介绍卓有成就的海外华裔，这将是国际文化交流的又一个视窗。

在耳闻目睹了李华伟先生大量的事迹后，有不少人提出想给他作传记，他都婉言谢绝了，他很谦逊地说："我是个平凡的人，还不够立传的资格。"

这句话使中国科学院武汉文献情报中心的张万萍馆长大为感动，她说，她常常在李华伟馆长身上看到一种闪光的精神，如果不把他写出来教育青年一代，将是莫大的遗憾！他们与李华伟先生所领导的俄亥俄大学图书馆合作十多年，学习、交流、培训，可以说获益匪浅。

中国国家图书馆周和平副馆长感慨道："李先生长年累月忙于联系、接待、推动、奔波……他图的是什么？图名吗？在美国多年，他早已功成名就、誉满华美学术界；图利吗？可他干这些事，不仅没有分文回报，相反还要赔进大量的时间精力和金钱；那么，他到底为了什么？值得人去好好挖掘。"

我就此采访李馆长，他说："一是出于对图书馆事业的热爱，因为图书馆本身是没有国界的；再一个自己作为炎黄子孙，多年身居海外，也总是想着为中华民族做点实实在在的事情。"

多么朴素的语言，多么真挚的情感！还有什么东西比这更无价、更可贵的呢？在世界政治经济急速发展变化、东西方文明交互渗透的今天，这种良好的精神品格不正是我们民族强大所需要保存和延续的吗？

四、在美国，有这样一位留学生的指导教授

凡是从美国访问回来的，与他有过交往的人，没有一个不称他是个好人的，可想而知，在这褒誉评价后面无穷无尽的付出，既不是一时一事的表现，更不是三言两语能说得清的简单事例。他体现的是一种精神内涵和人格魅力，并在人与人之间的交往中，他塑造了自己诚信、助人、宽容、理解、谦虚、务实等优秀品质。

在俄亥俄大学里，师生们都知道图书馆有个豁达热情的馆长。特别是中国留学生感触极深——每当他们生活上有了困难，学习上遇到问题，首先第一个就找李馆长，有的同学刚下飞机找不到车接，或者尚未联系好住处的，哪怕半夜三更到了，也是第一个拨他家的电话；还有的同学刚到异国他乡，面临着学习上、经济上的压力很大，心里一时受不了，向他诉苦，哭哭兮兮的，他以一个长者、过来人的身份对他们说："有很多人以为到了美国就什么问题都解决了，其实，这只是奋斗的开始。"有同学表示畏难情绪，说在国内是铁饭碗，什么都不用发愁，而到了这里，感觉精神上的负担很重，经济的压力、学业的压力、文化背景不同的压力，实在受不了。可是又没面子回去，不知怎么办才好。李华伟博士说："大家都想到美国来，既然来了，就要有思想准备，咬咬牙拼一下。你现在还没有拼就想打退堂鼓，这可不行。"然后他就把自己的学习方法或过去读书的有关技巧等一一告诉大家，那些同学听了很受鼓舞。三个月学期考试后，个个都是笑嘻嘻的来看望他，向他报喜。

作为教育学院兼职教授、华裔馆长，除了在学业上给予留学生指导外，还尽可能提供经济方面的支援，他说，我过去从台湾出来赴美求学时吃过苦，尝过经济拮据的滋味，所以和学生们还能谈到一起，有共同语言。对生活有困难的人，他总是帮忙想办法安排在图书馆工作，包括许多来培训的人，时时处处能感受到他的帮助。大家自觉不自觉地就会把他当作精神支柱。最令人感动的，是他把这些都看作是份内的事。有求必应、事必躬亲。没有一丝名人的架子。他常常说："中国人应该帮助中国人。"

他给别人带来方便，却给自己找了太多的麻烦。在他家住过的访问学者也是一批接一批，从衣食起居到学术活动安排，亲身感受到他无微不至的关照。有一年来美参加国际学术会议的中国代表一下子到了好几个，统统住在他家，好像他家成了招待所似的，把他的夫人也忙坏了。代表们很过意不去，向他致谢，他却笑道："没关系，反正我的6个孩子都大了走了，正好也有空房。"谁都知道，家中来客是最麻烦的事，尤其在喜欢清静的美国，一般人是从不把外人往家里带的，况且还有许多素不相识、仅是熟人朋友介绍的客人，他都以诚相待。所以他的家经常高朋满座，汇聚了方方面面的人物，基本上相当于一个中美文化交流中心。

据几位在他家住过的馆长说："他下班在家也没好好休息，有时给各地的人回电子邮件；有时筹划交流合作事项；还有时，他忽然想起一些中国留学生缺少生活用具，比如张三刚来还没有褥子，李四还缺锅碗瓢勺什么的，就赶忙把自己家里的东西拿上一些，开着车送上门去。像这样助人为乐的事对他来说已属家常便饭，他把别人的事样样放在心上，可是夫人或医生叮嘱他按时吃药的事早忘到九霄云外。叫他的夫人啼笑皆非。"

1989年，一个来美国学习的中国女生刚下飞机，突然晕倒在机场，初来乍到，人生地不熟，又身患急性肝炎，当时可以说是陷入了绝境……李馆长知道这件事后，忙为她询医找药、联系住处，花费了他不少时间精力，直到那个女生完全康复并且顺利完成了学业。

还有一次，李华伟馆长刚刚从机场接人回来，中途在一家中国餐馆就餐，忽然遇上了在餐馆打工的女生向他求助。原来，她是我国一位著名演员的女儿，在美国进修时与人结婚并生了孩子，谁料感情变化，那个美国人竟要抛弃她，还要驱她出境。情形很可怜。李馆长闻知此事，马上找到在该城颇具声望的俄亥俄大学的副校长白礼恩博士夫妇，请他们陪同出庭，出面力争，几经周折通过法律程序，终于维护了那女子的合法权益。事后有人问道："李馆长，你怎么想着要帮助一个非亲非故的人？"他说："一个弱女子在异国他乡受了欺负，正好又求到了我，我怎么能不尽力去帮助她呢？"

像这样的事大大小小还有很多，从中可以看出，在李华伟先生的身上还保留着相当多的中华民族传统的美德。

这，也许就是他一贯所倡导的精神体现吧。

我深信：他的学术成就及他科学化、制度化与人性化综合管理方式的精髓，应该而且正在成为人类文明世界的宝贵财富。

（原载《资讯传播与图书馆学》1997年第4卷第2期，第67—73页。）

现代化图书馆管理的新探索
——李华伟博士学术报告总结

苏颖怡①

随着我国图书馆网络化和自动化进程的深入推进，必然对图书馆管理提出更高的要求。这种要求不是简单地在原基础上的改进和提高，而是一种对全新的、现代化的管理理念的呼唤。这是由网络化和自动化所赋于的时代特性所决定，不由人为的意志所阻挠。我国当前图书馆资源共享及网络化工作的步履维艰，正是一个生动的注脚。他山之石，可以攻玉，美国俄亥俄大学图书馆馆长李华伟博士带来了他的成功经验。

李华伟博士于1997年11月23日至12月6日在中山大学进行了为期两周的访问讲学。在李博士所作的题为"现代化图书馆的管理"、"迈向21世纪之图书馆——俄亥俄网络模式"、"美国最常用的三种图书馆管理工具"等多场学术报告中，其重心都是围绕图书馆管理现代化这一主题。李博士的报告浓缩了他在美国图书馆界服务三十多年之经验、一位有着卓越贡献的成功馆长之体会，赋有魅力和说服力；它们渗透着李博士对图书馆管理的执着思考和精辟见解，不仅于我们有可借鉴学习的东西，而且颇多值得回味、启人深思之处。为此，笔者试将李博士讲学内容之大体加以反映，公诸同好；又因篇幅所限，不能尽录，故选择其有特色、具探索性的，归纳整理辑录如下。

1. 现代化图书馆管理的滥觞与契机

现代化图书馆管理观念的提出，不是赶时髦之作，是基于对图书馆发展历史，尤其是20世纪60年代以来种种社会冲击给图书馆所带来影响的考察，并结合管理学的研究成果而作出的必然选择。

1.1 20世纪以来图书馆发展的重要转折点

1900年——由为少数人服务的藏书楼变为大众化的图书馆。国家图书馆、公共图书馆、大专院校图书馆等都开始快速地发展。

1940年——特殊图书馆和科技资讯中心开始发展茁壮，成为各类图书馆中重要的一支。

1960年——由以印刷品及人工为主的"纸张图书馆"开始向"自动化图书馆"发展。

1970年——开始向"网络化的图书馆"发展。

1980年——开始向"电子化的图书馆"发展。

1990年——因为国际电脑资讯联网的普遍化，使得图书馆开始向 ''虚拟的图书馆"发展。

2000年——结合了纸张图书馆、自动化图书馆、网络化图书馆、电子化图书馆及虚拟图书馆特色的综合图书馆。

1.2 20世纪60年代以后的重要发展

（1）60年代的几个重要的发展——多以大型计算机为主

美国国会图书馆开始设计及推广机读目录标准格式（Machine—Readable—Catalog—MARC Format）。

---

① 任职于中山大学信息管理系。

俄亥俄州一些大学及学院图书馆联合设立俄亥俄学院图书馆中心（Ohio College Library Center-OCLC）。

美国国家医学图书馆建立医学文献分析及检索系统（Medical Literature Analysis and Retrieval System-MEDLARS）。

美国的化学文摘社及一些大规模的文摘索引机构开始用计算机作业并建立大型数据库

（2）70年代的重要发展——配合迷你型计算机（Mini Computer）及电讯技术（Telecommunication Technology）的发展

以迷你型计算机为主的，个别图书馆自动化系统开始出现。

Dialog等数据库检索服务中心提供联机检索。

（3）80年代的重要发展——配合个人计算机（Personal Computer或Desk-top Computer），专为图书馆设计的软件系统、密集储存技术、光盘技术等的发展

以个人计算机为主的图书馆自动化系统，促进了小型图书馆的自动化。

在迷你型或大型计算机上作业的一些单一功能图书馆开始朝集成化系统的方向发展。

光盘数据库的出现逐渐取代了印刷的数据库，缩微媒体的数据库及Dialog等数据检索中心的功能以个人计算机组成的馆内光盘数据库网开始建立，图书馆自动化系统和光盘检索系统开始与校园网联网。

电讯传真（Telefacsimile）与光学辨认字（Optical Character Recognition）等技术被图书馆所普遍采用。

以个人计算机为主的图书馆自动化系统促进了小型图书馆自动化。

（4）90年代的重要发展——结合各型计算机的优势，多媒体技术的发展及国际计算机联网（Internet）的信息高速公路（Information Superhighway）建设

电子出版物及大型全文数据库的发展——书刊资料的数位化（Digitized）。

国家信息基础架构（National Information Infrastructure）的建立。

大型图书馆合作网的建立——像OhioLINK国际计算机联网的普遍使用电子信息及数据库的大量出现。

1.3 图书馆的共同任务

图书资料的搜集、整理、存储。

图书信息的流通和使用。

读者服务、指导和教育（包括对文盲及老弱残疾民众）。

馆际合作和资源共享。

配合社会发展所需，包括促进教育、文化、经济及工商业发展等所提供的特殊服务。

图书馆员素质的提升，包括在职训练和继续教育的加强。

有关图书馆和资讯服务技术、方法等的研究、发展、引进及使用。

1.4 图书馆的共同使命

人类知识和文化的收集、保存、传递和发扬光大。

人类精神和文化生活的充实。

配合国家与地方的建设与发展。

满足社会大众对资讯、职业、教育、休闲和文化生活的需要。

配合时代改变、科技进步、知识发展所因应的各种新服务及措施。

1.5 图书馆相应的改变

藏书的数量急剧增加，收藏知识的媒体也日新月异，图书馆服务的项目变得多样化及

大众化。

图书馆员的素质和专业教育不断地提高。

图书馆的组织结构、人员编制及经费随着扩大。

引进各种新技术以增加对读者服务的效能。

进行现代化管理。

1.6　20世纪西方管理学的发展

管理学理论在图书馆中的应用主要有以下几种观点：

图书馆结构的观点。

图书馆人际关系的观点。

图书馆政治运用的观点。

2. 图书馆的规划

目前，图书馆所面临的困难是如何将有限的资源做最合理及有效的分配于应用，规划可以在众多要做的工作中，分别轻重前后，帮助图书馆在这一方面做理性的选择及决定。为全体员工指导行动方向，使大家能为共同的目标而努力。规划是管理的基础，而在现代化图书馆的管理中，应采取策略性规划，它有别于传统式的管理。

2.1　策略性规划（Strategic Planning）

（1）定义

策略性规划是要使一个机构了解它现在所处的地位及情况，确认它将来希望达到的境界以及设计如何达到此境界的最佳途径。

（2）策略性规划的流程（见下图）

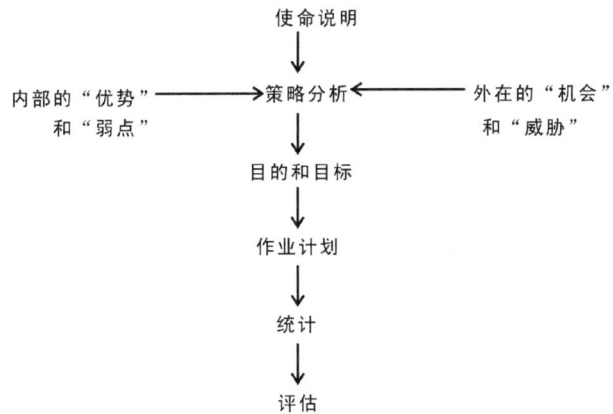

（3）策略性规划的特征

面对将来的（Futuristic）。

以服务对象为导向的（Clientdriven）。

重视行动的（Action-oriented）。

有弹性的（Flexible）。

对文化敏感的（Cultural Sensitive）。

（4）"策略性规划"与"传统性规划"不同点

传统性规划是由近而远。先有一个长远目标，再规划达成的策略和步骤；以推演方式从近程目标伸延到远程目标，容易犯故步自封的毛病，不易突破现状。

策略性规划是由远而近。先有一个长程的目标，再规划达到的策略和步骤：能突破现状，开创新的境界。其特点是具有前瞻性（Forward Looking）及冒险性（Risk-taking）。但它的冒险是经过慎重考虑以下各种情况及应变措施后，才大胆作出决定：

了解本身的优势和弱点。

调查外在的威胁和机会。

认知可能的限制和参数。

为此，主持策性规划的人必须具备以下素质：

策略性的眼光（Strategic Vision）：大胆假设，而且眼光远大。

策略性的思想（Strategic Thinking）。

策略性规划不仅可以"应变"，而且可以"防患于未然"，发挥"洞悉先机"的效果。

3. 图书馆的组织

3.1 为达到共同的使命，完成共同的任务而存在的图书馆组织，是随着环境及需要的变动而进行调整有机系统，它跟环境有着交互作用。

（1）图书馆组织的外在环境

一般环境（一般情况下不能改变的）：包括当前的政治、经济、社会、教育、科技发展等。

特定环境（可以主动加以改变的）：每一个图书馆个别的上级机构，服务的社区和对象，地方上的压力团体。

有关的法令规章等。

要了解图书馆外在环境的四个步骤：

要了解环境的特质及本身的任务。

要了解图书馆与其特定环境中其他机构的关系。

要了解图书馆与其他图书馆间的交流合作关系。

要了解环境对图书馆内外结构和操作的影响。

3.2 组织的设计和结构

"组织设计"是指如何经由设计以建立最合适当前情况及需要的结构。它将组织内的员工及其他资源做最合理的分配和利用。其中矩阵式的组织是一种新的尝试。（见图1、图2）：

图1　矩阵式的组织图

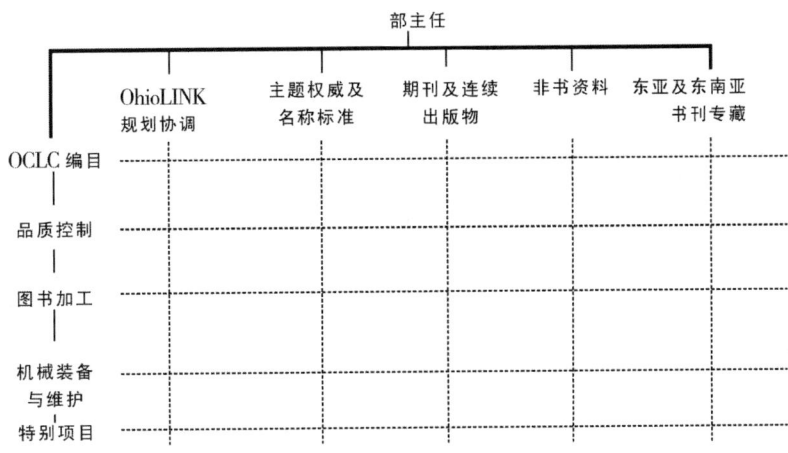

图 2 俄亥俄大学图书馆编目部及图书馆系统矩阵式组织图

这种方法最早在工厂出现,近几年开始应用于图书馆管理,它的最大特点是灵活性强。能把部门人员根据实际情况随时调配,组织任务的完成,又可适时解散,改变以前一些工作有许多人做,一些工作却没有人做的状况,充分利用了资源,提高了工作效率。

4. 图书馆人力资源管理

科学的人力资源管理,包括人员的甄选和任用、薪酬、福利和安全、员工的训练和发展、考绩及激发动机。

4.1 工作分析

为了明确工作人员的职责,避免工作上的互相推诿,每一职位都应有"工作说明书"（Job Description）,其内容包括:

工作职称	部属	功能	专长
工作单位	职位编号及分类	职责	其他
直属主管	等级薪酬	最低学经历要求

4.2 考绩

客观公平的考绩,能增进一个机构的效率以达到机构的目标;协助员工的自我发展及成长,使能更胜任所担任的工作;为员工提供有关各人在工作上的表现和成就的评估和及时的回馈;辅导员工改正工作上的缺点;作为决定薪酬及升迁的依据;加强员工与上司之间的沟通与了解。这种评估应该是双向的,即既有由上而下,亦有由下而上的。

考绩评分表的样式

比重分（1-5 分）　特征　　　　　　　　　　评分　　总分

工作的质与量

专业的知识与技能

适应能力

可靠性

主动性和理解力

合作和人品

行政和管理能力

　　　　　　　　　图书馆专业和大学内的服务
　　　　　　　　　专业的发展

总比重分　　　　　　　　　　　　　　　　　　总评分　　　总积分
总积分
―――――― = 平均分数（或绩效分数）
总比重分

5. 图书馆的领导和作业

每一个有效能的机构都必需有它的领导者，否则这个机构将会变得"群龙无首"、"不知所从"。当此人类知识和信息技术急速发展的时代，我们所面临的环境可以说是"变幻莫测"和"瞬息万变"，包括图书馆在内的很多机构都遭遇到严重的考验。这些机构必需有卓越的领导者。他们具有丰富的专业知识、崇高的人品、过人的精力，能够团结员工，把握机会，发挥潜能，塑造一种适合环境的组织文化，以完成机构的使命与目的

5.1 管理者与领导者的区别

领导者的着眼是长程的，管理者所关心的是现状的；领导者的立场是战略性的，管理者的立场多半是战术性的。

领导者的考虑是全盘的。管理者的眼光多半是局部的；管理者以一己的利害做决策。领导者则应该是大公无私的。

5.2 领导模式

体制型领导模式是设立一个以任务为中心的工作机制，以分工合作和分层负责的方式，按工作的要求和特征来达成目标。其内容可归纳为：分配工作，制定目标，按期完成。

体谅型领导模式是建立一个以员工为主导的社会气氛，鼓励员工能自发自动地尽其所能。领导者重视人际关系，关心部属的需求。

图书馆应该采用那种模式，可参考豪斯所提出的四点假设：

对于那些能自发自动的部属，领导者应该采用"体谅型"；

对于那些缺乏自发自动的部属，领导者应该采用"体制型"；

当任务的例行性、群体规范性以及控制活动已经使得目标和达成目标和路径明朗化时，"体制型"的程度要降低；

当部属对工作感到不满、疲乏、挫折或者逼迫感的时候。领导者应给予"体谅"。

6. 图书馆的全品质管理

全品质管理是为了达到顾客的最高满意程度所进行的长期的、全面的和彻底的内部改进，使整个机构各个功能和过程，从服务到考核能够推到整体一贯的配合、规划、组织、执行，以形成追求最高品质的组织文化。

由目标管理（Management By Objective）、参与式管理（Participative Management）发展到全品质管理（Total Quality Management），这是一个管理不断走向现代化的过程，它不是一个时髦的口号。它的目的是在满足服务对象的需求，它的方法是动员全体员工从改良工作的过程着手，在整个制度、观念和作法上进行改革，以提供最令人满意的服务。图书馆和信息中心是一个服务的专业，追求和提供全品质的服务也是"当仁不让"的努力目标。

6.1 全品质管理的特征

基于一种新的管理观念所导致的组织文化的改变（Cultural Change），这种观念是采用持续的改进来满足顾客的要求。

这种管理概念所形成的管理行为（Management Behavior）包括了以身作则，设计高品质的生产或服务过程，使用优良的工具，鼓励沟通，提供回馈，及建立相互依赖支持的工作环境。

改变的方式（Mechanisms Of Change）包括有训练、沟通、认可（Recognition），协调合作和使顾客满意的计划。

在执行（Implementing）时要确定机构的使命，预期的成果，顾客和服务的对象，了解顾客的要求，设计产品和服务的标准和品质以及采取必需的行动。

测量达成高品质的标准与不达成高品质的差价和后果。

6.2 实行全品质管理的十四个要点

要与机构的目标一致：使员工充分了解机构的使命与目的。

采用新的观念来改善品质：培养认真负责的精神，尽量做到零错误。

停用依靠对产品的查验做为提高品质的方法：着重对整体作业的改进。

在选购材料时不要以价格为标准：以高品质为标准。

对于作业过程的改进应该持续不断：要不满足现状，具有"日日新"和"更上一层楼"的精神。

加强对员工的训练。

培养领导的才能；鼓励员工自动自发，发挥各人的才干。

驱除恐惧感：增加员工的信心，敢于面对困难。

撤除各部门的阻碍，互相合作，团结无间。

少用口号、劝诫等指标：这些方法的效果不佳造成员工的被动性。

取消数量定额制度：重质不重量。

使员工对自己的知识技能感到自豪：提供优良的工作环境、设备，材料等，以发挥所长。

创造自我改进的机会：协助员工在工作中成长，吸取新知识和学习新的方法。

建立全品质管理制度并全力推行：有计划地实行，让全体员工都能参与。

7. 总结

现代化的中国式的管理应该是"修己安人"。其最终目的在于让员工安分乐业、无忧无惧。其管理的最佳原则是"情、理、法"：即管理的人性化、合理化，制度化。而管理的基本方法则是"经权法"："经"指的是"万变不离其宗"的法则；"权"时"通权达变，或"一本万殊"的法则，一个机构要能"守经达变"才能历久而长新，配合时代的改变。此外，管理的最高境界在"无为而治"：放手支持部属去做，部属的"有为"。正是主管的"无为"。无为而治的现代化功能是要使机构内的员工都能自发自动地发挥潜能，以达成工作的目标。

正如文章开头所言，我国图书馆的现代化必然包括图书馆管理的现代化。与此同时，在当前我国不断开放的社会中，图书馆的管理模式及整个行政架构无疑也正在走向开放，当人们不断抱怨自动化、网络化流于形式而无实际成果时，我们首先该做的是从内部着手，改革现有的图书馆管理，时代呼唤这样一种开放式的现代化管理模式：一个灵活、富于冒险精神、强有力的馆长,他既是图书馆学家,又是外交家,担负着整个图书馆发展规划、资金来源等重责;懂多种业务、富有奉献精神、有魄力的馆长,他既是图书馆学家,又是实干家,全身投入图书馆各项具体工作的开展;一支精干的、富有专业素养、有创造力的馆员队伍,能在各个岗位发挥其潜能,他们各司其责,各尽其职,是所谓的"智者尽其谋,勇者竭其力,仁者播其惠,信者效其忠"。国内一些图书馆的成功经验表明了这种管理模式在我国的有益尝试,是一种新的探索。诚如李博士所期望的:虽然美国的经验不一定完全适合中国的国情,但有益的借鉴学习是必不可少的,希望中国图书馆管理在改革过程中逐步迈向科学化和现代化。

(原载《高校文献信息学刊》1998年第5卷第1期,第19-24页。)

美国图书馆界的头号华人

景 星

他图的是什么？图名吗？在美国多年他早已功成名就，誉满华美学术界；图利吗？他干这些事情，不仅没有分文回报，相反还要搭进大量的时间，精力和金钱。那么，他到底为了什么呢？

大洋彼岸。午夜，万籁俱寂。一位年逾花甲的教授，支撑着有伤病的腰端坐在电脑前，开始认真地回复每一件来自故乡的电子信函。

夜以继日，教授不知疲倦地忙碌着。此情此景，多年来已经成为他生活中不可缺少的一部分。

为了加快中国图书馆事业现代化进程。为了中国知识分子和年轻一代的学业进步，自1982年相隔33年首次返回祖国大陆之后，他每年至少归来一次（最多时达到3次）——教授以自己的赤诚之心和顽强毅力，亲手架起了连接过去与未来的桥梁。这座科学与文明之桥跨越重洋，把中美两国图书馆学界紧密联系在一起了。

在海外，他是华人担任美国著名大学图书馆长的第一人，自1978年至今已有20载。

在祖国，作为外籍学者，他是北大、清华等著名学府和中国国家图书馆——北京图书馆同时聘为客座教授和荣誉顾问的第一人。

这位诚信热情、和蔼可亲的老人名叫李华伟，博士、教授，美籍华人，美国俄亥俄大学图书馆院长级馆长，今年65岁。

自1869年中国皇帝向美国国会图书馆捐赠1000册图书馆之后，相隔127年，中美两国近百位图书馆馆长和专家学者首次坐到了一起，李华伟博士是这一载入史册事件的积极促成者。

1998年5月4日，中国著名高等学府北京大学迎来百年校庆。百年庆典活动将延续一年，其间举办一系列庆祝活动和穿插几十个国际会议。

作为海外的外籍学者和北大客座教授，李华伟博士荣幸地应邀参加百年庆典，前来出席将于今年10月举行的百年校庆活动之一——北大图书馆新馆开幕典礼。届时，北大图书馆还将召开国际会议，主题是"21世纪大学图书馆新使命"。七八十位世界著名大学图书馆馆长都将与会，李华伟博士也是该国际会议的组织者之一。

李博士于1997年10月20日被北大聘为客座教授。当时，北京大学将此称为一件"大喜事"并专门举行聘任仪式。仪式上，北大信息管理系表示："衷心期望李教授今后能在我系与美国图书馆学、情报学、教育界之间架起密切合作的桥梁，在扩大我系和国际图书馆情报学的学术交流与合作等方面作出贡献。"

1997年10月，北京，金秋送爽。10月15日，中国国家总书库和国家图书馆——北京图书馆举行新馆开馆10周年暨建馆85周年馆庆。党和国家领导人江泽民、李鹏等纷纷为北图明日的腾飞，题写了满怀期待之情的题词。江总书记的题词是："保护文明遗产，开发信息资源，服务改革开放，发挥北京图书馆在两个文明建设中的作用。"

北图披上了节日的盛装。新馆嘉言堂内，鲜花在主席台、会议桌和来宾胸前交相辉映，李华伟博士作为北图的荣誉顾问，专程前来参加庆典。来宾席上李博士胸佩鲜花，笑容满面。他目光深邃地对笔者表示："迎接21世纪，北图应努力开拓新业务，满足各类读者的新需求。"他认为，北图还应同时拉动全国图书馆信息化建设，比如建立全国图书目录系统，提供图书馆编目，做到资源共享——他乐于为此效力。

此前一天，李博士接受了北图颁发的正式聘书："鉴于您30年来在图书馆界所取得的卓越成就和为中美两国图书馆交流与合作作出突出贡献，中国国家图书馆为了更方便移樽就教及恭请指导，特荣幸地聘请您为本馆顾问。"

1996年8月27日下午，清华大学图书馆大厅，此时正值'96国际图联大会（IFLA）在京开会期间，IFLA委员之一的李华伟博士精神焕发，参加了清华大学OCLC服务中心开通仪式。这一天，是美国最大的文献信息服务机构之一的OCLC（联机计算机图书馆中心）和清华大学长期合作的开端。隆重的仪式上，已被聘为清华大学顾问的李华伟博士，被称为双方联姻的"红娘"。开通典礼上，清华大学校长王大中对"红娘"的贡献表示衷心感谢。

"红娘"的功绩在于：通过OCLC，清华大学图书馆的读者甚至包括100多所国内高校，从此以后可以通过OCLC，迅速进入全球的2.2万个图书馆和科研机构查阅文献，检索信息。"红娘"的功绩还在于：清华大学的OCLC是开放式的，在当月即已有国内315个单位通过清华的OCLC中心在总部注册，并可免费使用美国OCLC的信息资源3个月。

笔者是采访IFLA大会期间结识李华伟博士的。IFLA大会前夕，8月21日，首届中美图书馆合作会议在北京图书馆召开。当时，我在美国《侨报》撰写的文章写道："自从中国皇帝1869年向美国国会图书馆捐赠1000册图书之后，相隔127年，中美两国近百位图书馆馆长和专家学者，站到了中国国家图书馆——北京图书馆的台阶上。"这次会议，"将意味着两国图书馆界的合作迈入了以光电为文字载体的新时代。"

当时，笔者注意到：开幕式主席台上有两位美籍华人引人注目。其一即是李华伟博士。会议期间，李博士非常活跃，甚至当我请他为我作翻译，采访美国图书馆学会主席图罗克女士时，他也是一口应承。事后了解到，热情助人是他一贯的行事准则。

首届中美图书馆会议得以在京成功召开，李博士是积极的促成者。从美国筹集会议经费到审阅会议论文，他都以责无旁贷的态度参与。当时他对笔者表示："中美图书馆界的合作，虽然开始得很早，但中间有过挫折。随着中美关系的改善，目前国际图联大会又提供了一个新的机会。这次美国图书馆界高层领导都来到北京，我们华人乐于当桥梁。"

李华伟博士还在会上作报告指出了中美图书馆开展合作在今后的发展重点。事实证明，李博士借IFLA大会契机促成中美图书馆界密切合作的意图得到具体的成功体现。业内专家认为：这次会议对中美两国及世界图书馆界的合作与发展，将产生积极而深远的影响。会议期间，全美最大图书馆——美国国会图书馆副馆长威斯顿·泰伯强调："这不仅是行业合作，也加强了两国人民彼此的了解。"此后，中美两国又有多个图书馆陆续结为姐妹馆。双方从人员培训到文化交流、从引进技术到信息传播等多方面开始了密切合作。

李华伟博士在首届中美图书馆合作会议召开的一年前，就积极倡议着手进行此会议的筹备。他与北图电信往来频频，包括两国学术界高层次交流内容以及具体到会议的组织、翻译、文件印刷，甚至一些细节如某些词汇提法的表达切磋，与会代表的餐宿安排，李博士都关心到并一一落实，还亲自为会议筹款数万美元。他深知：第一次在中国举办中美两国高层次大型的图书馆合作会议，双方从语言交流、文化背景到工作方式等都需要适应和磨合，如不投入相当精力则很难保证会议达到预期效果。

那期间，李博士周围的工作人员感叹：从早到晚不停地忙，李馆长真是太累了！北京图书馆副馆长孙蓓欣则由衷赞颂："李博士为中国、为中国图书馆做事尽心尽力，他的精神和努力令人感佩！"

至于李华伟博士本人，他却认为这是应当做的："一是出于对图书馆事业的热爱，因为图书馆是没有国界的。而是作为炎黄子孙，多年身居海外，总想着为中华民族做点实实在在的事情。"

1982年，面对改革开放之初的祖国，李华伟博士发现：中国图书馆界对外界信息闭塞，迫切希望获取外部世界的新信息。他强烈地意识到："中国要加速科技、经济、政治、教育、文化及社会的发展，必须加速现代图书馆及信息工作的发展。"此后，李华伟把它当作了自己义不容辞的义务和为故土做实事的唯一的目标。

李华伟生于1933年，父亲李圣述，参见国民革命后改名李干军，跟随李宗仁先生从军从政，曾任省训练团教育长和北京行辅参议，到台湾后在中兴大学教书。

1949年，中国大陆解放前夕，李华伟的兄长驾着轰炸机把李华伟他们一家载到台湾。李华伟祖籍福建，他两岁起，跟随父母先后辗转南京、桂林、重庆等地。16岁去台湾后完成高中毕业。1954年毕业于台湾师范大学教育学系。

大学毕业之后，李华伟接受了一年军训，教过两年书。1957年，他申请到奖学金赴美国宾夕法尼亚州匹兹堡大学攻读教育学和图书馆学硕士学位。

留美深造，改变了李华伟的人生轨迹。1959年李华伟硕士毕业，与玛丽小姐结婚。他在匹兹堡大学图书馆工作3年，1962年转往在匹兹堡市都肯大学的图书馆担任非洲特藏部主任，并在匹兹堡大学继续进修高等教育行政，副修图书馆学的博士学位。

1965年，李华伟拿到博士学位，受聘于宾州爱丁堡州立学院任图书馆副馆长，翌年任馆长。33岁的李博士，当时是美籍华人做馆长的第一人。

1968年，由美国、英国出资在泰国曼谷建起的亚洲理工学院需要一专家任图书馆信息中心主任。美政府国际发展总署派李华伟博士远渡重洋担任此职。学院后来为亚洲包括中国在内培养了很多工程技术人员。

在泰国工作期间，李华伟博士与联合国、世行、亚行、世界粮农组织等建立起密切联系，担任了一些国际组织的顾问，经常为亚洲地区的图书馆建设出谋划策，参与项目合作。

在泰国工作7年之后，李华伟博士1975年回美国，先在科罗拉多州立大学图书馆当副馆长，1978年任俄亥俄大学图书馆院长级馆长至今。

80年代初期的中国，刚刚结束了"文革"的噩梦，确立了一切以经济建设为中心的工作重心，建设社会主义现代化强国的宏图初展。当时，国门初开，人们睁大眼睛望着异彩纷呈的外部世界；同时，与祖国隔绝多年的海外炎黄子孙，也以极大的热忱关注着故土的改革开放和社会进步。

"少小离家老大回，乡音无改鬓毛衰"，这恰似李华伟博士的真实写照。1982年，年近知天命的李华伟博士返回到了阔别33年的祖国。这一年，他还回到自两岁起离开就没再回去过的福建祖籍寻根。

"浮云游子意，落日故人情"。在深切感受浓郁乡情的同时，李华伟博士也感受到了故乡的巨变以及和他第二祖国——美国在多方面的巨大差距。

第一次故乡行，李华伟博士是应聘为昆明一个情报中心管理培训班做讲师授课。培训班由中国科技情报所和加拿大国际发展研究中心合办。

李华伟博士由此开始，参观了解了故乡众多各类型的图书馆，包括科研院所、大学和公共图书馆。他从经验丰富、业绩显著的学者视角，审视当时中国的图书馆现状。他看到：无论是"硬件"或"软件"，国内图书馆与美国相比都落伍很多，差距达到二三十年。他感到：中国的图书馆最需要的，是引进现代化图书馆的管理方式方法，引进技术并推广使用。与此同时，李华伟博士也被中国图书馆工作人员的敬业精神所感动：图书馆经费紧缺，专业人员地位低，收入少，但大家不抱怨，工作勤奋努力。从他们身上，李博士看到了振兴中国图书馆事业的希望，他决心"尽力牵线搭桥"，把建设好故土的"人才培养基地"——现代化的图书馆，作为他回报故土，鼎力相助的奋斗目标。

从那时起，李华伟博士身体力行，在日常繁忙的管理、教学工作之余，每年都要抽暇到祖国大陆各地图书馆讲学。他孜孜不倦，乐此不疲，目的就是推动和促进国内图书馆跟上世界潮流。应国家教委之邀，他利用世行贷款项目和联合国发展基金项目，多次开办国内师范院校图书馆培训班。他的足迹遍至北京大学、清华大学、武汉大学、四川联大、北京师大、东北师大等，这些高等学府纷纷聘请他担任访问教授或顾问教授。中国科学院武汉和兰州的文献信息中心也聘请他担任顾问。

十几年来，李华伟博士的不倦身影和慈祥面容，频频出现在国内众多大学、科研院所和公共图书馆的讲坛上。他参与组织了多次大型学术研讨会，多次应邀在培训班系统讲学。他以5年的讲课内容汇集成一本专著——《现代化的图书馆管理》，内容覆盖图书馆的规划、组织、人力资源管理，领导和作业，控制和评估5个方面，书中汇集了他当馆长多年的宝贵经验和管理思想，重点在现代信息管理和自动化技术的应用。他在总结各个历史时期图书馆的管理思想的基础上，提出今后的图书馆应适应社会发展变化，发展为社会大学，成为大教室，应发展为开放的、自由的、为社会大众提供公正服务的信息和教育中心等一系列先进思想，对当今国内图书馆进行现代化建设和管理颇有指导意义。行家评论是："这部大作深入浅出，思维缜密，钜细不遗，可作为图书馆管理学的课本，更是图书馆从业人员应参考的经典之作。这部书足以传世。"

进行了数年穿梭巡回讲学之后，李华伟博士意识到：还应更进一步，应当创造机会与条件，把中国的图书馆员们"请出去"。百闻不如一见：他们亲眼看一看世界先进图书馆的运行模式，并亲身实践一番，收获一定更大，对推动国内图书馆事业的进步将更加有益。

一个宏伟的中国图书馆馆员培训计划，开始萦绕在李华伟博士心间。此时约在80年代末，他开始为计划的实现多方奔走。

十多年来，李华伟馆长对国内图书馆方面的贡献，以及他的热情诚挚的态度，严谨的工作作风，得到了国内图书馆界一致的敬仰钦佩。大家说：如果要写改革开放以来中国图书馆事业史，特别是中美图书馆交流合作史，李华伟馆长是不可缺少的重要人物。

俄亥俄大学坐落在美国俄亥俄州雅典城郊。从因特网上，国内人们可以查阅到该大学和图书馆的多种信息。

李华伟博士供职的俄亥俄大学，是美国最古老的公立大学之一，建于1804年，也是现代美国重要的大学之一，有在校生2.7万名。大学关注亚洲的社会发展，半数外国留学生来自东亚和东南亚。

　　俄亥俄大学具有优良的学术传统和声誉。这与该校国际一流水准的图书馆系统密不可分。7层楼高的阿尔顿图书馆拥有200多万册藏书及期刊，以及200多万缩微卷片、30多万种非书刊资料。图书馆有120名工作人员，是全美图书馆电脑化的先驱、也是创建于1971年的国际性OCLC图书馆电脑网络的创建单位之一。在李华伟馆长极具远见的领导下，如今，该馆拥有一个联网的光盘资料库系统，一套整体的图书馆系统网络，一个全州图书馆资源共享网络，还可以经由OCLC与北美及世界各地的2万多家图书馆实现馆际互借、建立合作编目。

　　"李博士在图书馆界是一位学养深厚，经验丰富的图书馆学者管理专才。"李馆长先后担任了美国图书馆学会理事、美国华美图书馆学会会长、国际图联大会及研究图书馆委员会委员，同时身兼联合国教科文组织、联合国发展计划，世界粮农组织等机构有关图书馆发展项目顾问。

　　毫无疑问，李华伟博士在所从事的专业领域，已经达到了炉火纯青的境界。他曾发表过60多篇学术论文、著有《图书馆学的世界观》、《90年代图书馆筹款指引》、《现代化的图书馆管理》等多部学术著作。因其贡献突出、成绩卓著，他曾荣获美国华美图书馆员学会杰出服务奖、美国图书馆学会国际关系卓越贡献奖、亚太地区图书馆学会杰出服务奖、美国图书馆学会杰出理事奖、美国新闻署杰出服务奖、台湾中国图书馆学会杰出贡献奖等众多褒奖。他的名字被列入《世界名人传》、《美国名人传》、《美国教育界名人传》。

　　同时，李华伟博士还兼任俄亥俄大学教育学院教授、博士生导师。现在还在带7个博士生，其中有几个中国人。行政事务、教学科研、社会工作头绪繁杂，任务繁重、紧张繁忙可以想见。就是在如此高负荷的工作状态下，李华伟博士16年来又以满腔热忱和执着的精神，日夜为祖国图书馆事业的发展运筹谋划，呕心沥血。

　　北京大学教授庄守经，1983年至1993年任北大图书馆馆长。他80年代初结识了李华伟，从此两人友谊日深，谈起李华伟博士，他感触颇深，滔滔不绝："在我当馆长的期间，是国内图书馆发展最重要的时期，是从传统图书馆向现代图书馆过渡与迈进的一个关键10年。在这10年的变革过程中，李华伟博士起了相当大的作用。"

　　"开始，我们对什么是图书馆的现代化，如何实现现代化，既无经验，也缺乏有关的知识。这就必须学习，必须走出国门借鉴外国特别是美国的先进经验。学习美国经验，对我们十分有利的条件就是有大批华人在美国图书馆界工作。他们十分关心祖国图书馆事业的发展，从多方面给予了热情的帮助。李华伟先生就是他们中最突出的代表。"

　　庄守经以自己亲身体会，讲述李馆长对他和北大图书馆的热情帮助具有十分重要的意义："这种帮助首先体现在观念方面、知识更新方面。通过讲学、研讨以及个别交谈，他系统地向我们介绍了美国近几十年图书馆发展过程和发展趋势：60年代以前是传统纸张型的，六七十年代是计算机自动化，七八十年代是网络化、资源共享，八九十年代是电子化、信息化，今后是无围墙的'虚拟图书馆'。各国国情虽然不同，但图书馆现代化的过程，趋势大体会一致的，最后将形成信息业的全球一体化。"

　　庄馆长谈到：李华伟博士给他们讲述的这些情况，对他们启发很大，使他们办馆思路更加明确，决心也更坚定。他还指出，李博士的热情帮助还体现在，经李华伟直接相助，从80年代中到90年代中，北大图书馆先后有近20人次到俄亥俄大学图书馆接受业务培训，培训涉及图书馆自动化、西文编目、情报服务、采访工作和期刊管理等领域。这些专业人员回国后都在各自的业务岗位和国际交往中发挥了骨干作用。

庄守经强调："如果说香港的包玉刚、李嘉诚、邵逸夫是在硬件方面、在建设国内新图书馆馆舍方面给予了有力的支持，那么李华伟馆长以及在美的许多华裔图书馆员则在软件方面，在思想观念以及人才培养方面，给予了有效的帮助——这方面的意义日渐重要和深远了。"

1993 年，萦绕李华伟博士心头多年的夙愿得以实现：在他校友邵公全的资助下，俄大成立了专门用于培训亚洲地区图书馆馆员的基金。这意味着每年可以有 4 名来自中国大陆的图书馆馆员，免费赴美接受为期 3 个月的业务培训。该基金使得建于 1980 年，由联合国教科文组织和美国国际发展总署及一些基金会赞助下设立的俄亥俄大学图书馆"国际图书馆馆员短期培训计划"项目，更加充实和更加具针对性。

李华伟博士谈到此事，欣慰之情溢于言表："包括其他方式，过去 15 年，俄大图书馆为祖国大陆培训了 10 多位中国馆员。其中多是馆长、副馆长和部门主任。"笔者了解到：俄大图书馆的该培训计划以及与亚洲图书馆的多种合作项目，如今已成为全美图书馆的典范。

为了接待好祖国大陆来的同胞——赴美培训和访问交流的中国图书馆界专家学者，李华伟博士卖掉了自己的福特牌小轿车，专门购置了一辆 8 座雪佛兰面包车。他汲取华夏民族传统文化和现代美国开放社会道德标准的精髓，形成了自己独特的人格魅力。人们称赞他："真心待人，不图回报；有求必应，事必躬亲"，"是世界上最好的馆长"。

"比雷锋还雷锋"，"不是亲人胜似亲人的好馆长"，在美国与李华伟博士交往回国归来的人，总是用各种誉美之词赞颂李华伟博士。

在李华伟博士任教的俄亥俄大学，很多师生都知道图书馆有个诚信豁达、热情助人的好馆长，尤其是中国留学生感触较深。常常是，当他们在学习，生活中遇到了难题，首先想到就是——去找李馆长。初到美国，当有的同学向李馆长哭泣，诉说面临的学习、经济上的压力时，他会一个长者和过来人的经历耐心劝慰："这只是奋斗的开始，既然来了，就要咬咬牙拼一下，还没有拼就想打退堂鼓可不行。"

除了在学业上帮助指导，李华伟博士还对这些青年人尽可能提供经济支持。他常说："我早年赴美求学时吃过苦，尝过经济拮据的滋味。"他想方设法安排生活困难的学生在图书馆工作，对中国大陆来的格外关照。许多从国内来此接受培训的馆员、学者，也经常能感受到他的热情帮助。更为难得的是，对这些琐事或付出，李博士视为自己的分内事，有求必应。还开玩笑地解嘲："同样是中国人，台湾来的我要收培训费。你们来，我不仅不收、还在各方面给予照顾，恐怕人家要说我偏心了。"实际上，李博士对台湾图书馆事业的发展同样关注和支持。为此，他于 1989 年获得了台湾"图书馆事业特殊贡献奖"，以表扬"他所展现的全心奉献和全力投入的专业精神"。

中国海南大学图书馆馆长徐国定，便亲自体会到了李馆长关照的无微不至："在我决定赴俄亥俄大学学习的半年准备时间里，我和他的电话、传真、通信就有 20 次之多。他传达的信息细致、准确、细腻到让我乘什么飞机，走哪条线路停何站，带什么行李、办什么手续，怎么接我……我到纽约，他还忙于一个会议，仍不忘派认识我的人到机场举着牌子迎候。为了节约我们的开支，他安排我们住在他家中。"

初到纽约，徐国定不慎遗失了联系人电话及一些物品。李博士甚至比徐本人还着急，不顾腰有病东跑西问，终于帮徐找到了徐的朋友家电话，并从自己的电话联系本中，为徐一路行程物色好了联系人、电话，让徐以他的名义去寻求帮助。还说："你是我请来的朋友，初来美国，又在很乱的纽约丢了东西，我这心里也不好受！"当徐国定找到了护照和身份证时，李博士高兴得如同找到了自己遗失的东西一样，连说三声："这太好了！"

回国以后，有人问徐国定：你到美国最大的收获是什么？徐当即毫不犹豫地说："我认识了一位世界上最好的馆长！"

徐国定强调，这不仅是他个人的结论：他从俄亥俄大学图书馆工作人员包括秘书、馆长助理及办公室职员的言行中，也看到了大家对李馆长的尊敬、敬佩和爱戴。甚至俄亥俄大学校长也这样评价李华伟馆长。校长有时不在学校，便授权李华伟博士代表他或者副校长出席一些重要会议并讲话。徐的感触是：一个华人被美国人上级如此确认并多年不变、诚属不易。

1989年，一个来美国学习的中国学生刚下飞机就晕倒在机场，经诊断患有急性肝炎。初来乍到，人地生疏又疾病缠身，女学生几近绝望。李华伟博士闻知此事，赶忙为她联系住所，寻医问药，热情帮助，直到女学生康复并顺利完成学业。

李华伟博士对图书馆界同仁和学生热情关照是有口皆碑的。同时，他对素不相识的人也是尽力相帮。有一次他在途中的一家中国餐馆吃饭，在餐馆打工的一个中国年轻妇女向他求救："您是中国人吧。我希望得到您的帮助。"她是我国一位著名演员的女儿，在美进修时与美国人结婚并生了孩子。这时那美国丈夫要遗弃她，还威胁要驱逐她出境。这位女子面对婚变无法可想，精神快要崩溃了。富于同情心的李华伟博士答应帮助她，他出面请学法律出身的俄亥俄大学副校长白礼恩博士帮忙。经过白博士法庭上的据理力争，打赢了官司，维护了弱女子的权益。有人问他为何这样做，他的回答是："第一她是中国人，第二是弱女子，能帮尽量帮。"

李华伟博士有一个幸福美满的家庭。夫人玛丽是他大学同学，文学硕士，比他小6岁，夫妇育有4男2女，都已长大，事业有成。李博士已有5个孙子辈的子女。说到他的家庭，他脸上笑意盈盈，夸他的美国夫人是个"贤内助"，在事业上对他帮助非常大。而她的夫人玛丽女士则很风趣："他爱图书馆胜过我，走到哪里都看图书馆，把我甩在一边。显然我没有他那个图书馆重要。"

自1990年开始，因为经常去机场接从祖国大陆来的中国同胞，他新买了一辆8座面包车，连人带行李，一个车全装了。他还经常自己开着车，假期拉着中国同行们到处参观游览，去华盛顿、纽约、大瀑布，单程一去就是6到8小时，甚至12小时。这两年由于年纪大了，腰又不好，才改为由他的学生开车代陪。

去过他家的大陆同胞都知道，他的家简直就是一个中美文化交流中心。李博士的家中经常住着一批又一批的访问学者，大家的衣食住行、学术交流，事无巨细，他都细致入微地予以关照。

有一年，几位赴美参加国际学术会议的中国代表都被李博士接到家中，他家成了一个"接待站"，夫人玛丽也跟着忙前忙后。代表们多次向他致谢，对搅乱他的家庭生活表示歉意。李华伟听了总是连连摆手："没关系。我的6个孩子都大了走了，正好也有空房。"实际上，来他家的"房客"，不少人与他并不相识，只是熟人朋友介绍来找他而已。他总是来者不拒，以诚相待。

几位在他家住过的馆长们回忆，李华伟博士的业余时间，也常常被这类事情占据，很少能闲着。他或是给国内各地有求于他的人回电子邮件，或筹划交流、谋划合作，或联系捐助。有时，他会突然想起一些刚来的中国留学生缺少生活用具如卧具等，就匆匆从家中带上一些，亲自开车送过去。

乐于助人，能做就做，不图回报。就像一只辛勤吐丝的春蚕，李博士从小事入手，精心编织着连接中美图书馆界的牢固纽带。面对各方面各种各样美誉之词，李华伟博士的反应很坦然，他谦虚地对笔者表示："平易近人，有求必应，也许是我的一个长处。尽管费时费力，我还会做下去。现在太忙，有心无力，我做得还很不够。"

李华伟博士以一片赤子之心为故土做事，也博得了我国驻美使领馆官员的高度评价和赞扬。中国驻纽约总领馆徐敦璜参赞、高超领事的话一语中的："有的人有他这份心，没有他的身份和地位，做不成这些事；也有人有了地位身份，却不见得愿意做这种事。唯他两者兼有，所以做得有声有色。"

在李华伟博士崇高的精神境界中，他所做的一切都是为了"大家"——整个中华民族的兴旺和强盛。他以自己的行动，把"小我""小家"融入他乡之献身的事业中去。他向笔者讲述了他家中一段鲜为人知的不幸往事——那也是我们中华民族的悲哀。而他晚年致力创立的世界上第一家"海外华人文献研究中心"，更是他崇高理想和高风亮节的切实展现。

李华伟共有兄妹7人，他排行老三。当年，李的大哥为了抗日，参加了国民革命军空军，曾远赴印度、美国受训。但回国后却派驻东北，参加了国共两党的内战。

电闪雷鸣，乌云翻滚。一架漆有国民党军徽的美制轰炸机在海面低空飞行。那是李华伟长兄驾驶飞机，把他们全家接出大陆。1949年，在解放战争的隆隆炮声中，李华伟全家——父母和兄妹7人同机飞抵台湾。

从大陆到台湾到美国。1949年至1959年，李华伟一直在上学读书。而李的大哥则一直在台湾服役。朝鲜战争结束后，美国希望仍能获取远东尤其是中国大陆的军事情报。台湾军方迎合需求，与美方合作，将李华伟长兄所在的轰炸机大队改派执行空中摄影和收集电子信息任务。这在当时台湾军队内部也是一项保密度很高的"军事机密"。李华伟一家当然毫不知情。

李华伟当时根本想象不到，就在他远赴重洋上学深造以不负家人期望的年月，他的长兄却从事着家人所不知情的特殊任务。

1959年，李华伟拿到硕士学位的前两天，李华伟长兄驾驶的飞机在大陆被击落。飞机撞上了广东恩平的金鸡山，机上14人全部殉命。多年以后，李华伟回大陆后得知，在美台此项军事合作项目中，李长兄驾驶的飞机是被击落的第一架。此后，又有14架飞机照样被一一击落在大陆。

李华伟1982年首次归国时，李年迈的父母还在世，当年他们只被告知大儿子驾机在大陆失事，一直还心存侥幸，让李华伟打听是否被俘在押。"这么多年了，如果人死了，也找找是否有个坟墓。"

对双亲的嘱托，李华伟一直铭记在心。直到1993年12月，在广东恩平当地政府的帮助下，李华伟博士才找到了他大哥的遇难地点。

当地人告诉李华伟，当时14人的尸体全被埋到一个大坑里。事隔34年，他们居然还找到了埋尸的地点。李华伟经过多方打听，获悉该机另一飞行员的女儿是台湾《联合报》的副主编，便告诉其父的长眠之地。于是，她便在《联合报》上刊出消息，讲述该事情的结局。消息见报后，14名当事人的亲属都先后取得了联系。他们相约从美国、台湾组团到香港，然后一起进入广东，找到亲人埋葬之处，祭奠完后将遗体火化了。

"这是一个悲剧。但结果还算完满。"李华伟博士以此作为故事的结尾。然而，令他非常遗憾的是，李华伟的父母生前一直没能得悉他们长子的明确下落。1993年李华伟找到其长兄飞机的坠落地点时，二老已仙逝多年。这留给李华伟的岂止是惆怅？

一方面惦念家事的了结；另一面，李华伟博士还惦记着海峡两岸同胞间的和解、交流与沟通。家事、国事，李华伟博士的思想境界和宽阔胸怀，绝不是能用"以德报怨"的层次所能概括和包容的。

1988年到1989年间，李华伟博士对打破海峡两岸图书馆界长期隔绝的状态非常关注。通过交流，李华伟博士得知，北大图书馆馆长庄守经教授与他颇有同感，海峡两岸的图书馆界同行专家学者应聚在一起，就编目、主题、汉字处理标准化等问题共同研讨。同时，通过探询，李华伟博士还获悉，台湾"中央图书馆"馆长王振鹄教授也有此心。

于是，当时双方决定将重任托付李华伟博士：由他选定在香港或美国召开海峡两岸的学术研讨会，从此推开封闭的大门，促成两岸图书馆界的联系，增进两岸专业人员的了解合作。李华伟博士积极负责地对参加研讨会的具体人员、经费、地点等进行了考虑和安排。

恰恰在此之后不久，两岸关系缓和，民间可以直接交往了，筹划中的会议就没付诸实现，留下了佳话一段。由于有此作为基础，不久以后，王振鹄馆长率团来大陆直接与同行们见面，成员包括了台湾图书馆界的高层人士。从那以后，两岸同行间来往密切，1997年大陆这边有30多人赴台湾访问。

庄守经馆长回忆：由于李华伟馆长那次牵线，"使我对台湾图书馆界的情况，包括一些专家教授都有印象。例如对王振鹄教授，我们有一见如故之感，有很多共同的话题。"

作为一个心系中华民族的海外游子，李华伟博士的爱国不仅体现在为祖国图书馆事业的明天尽心尽力，还体现在率先为海外华人昨天奋斗与贡献的历史，进行系统的收集整理和保存。

1993年，李华伟博士通过他的校友邵公全，联系到邵父邵友保博士捐资50万美元，创立了世界上第一家"海外华人文献研究中心"。邵友保博士是位香港银行家，港事顾问，《香港基本法》起草人之一。

海外华人文献研究中心设在俄亥俄州大学图书馆内，研究的区域重点是东南亚。因为半数以上的海外华人集中于此，也由于俄亥俄大学图书馆拥有世界一流的东南亚资料收藏部。中心的目标是"通过收集、整理、保存、介绍及研究有关海外华人的文献资料，再现他们奋斗与贡献的历史——这一历史不仅是海外华人居住国发展的一个重要组成部分，而且也是悠久的中华文明在海外的延伸与发扬光大"。

李华伟博士深知中国人移民海外的个中滋味。为了生计和发展，炎黄子孙揖别故土移民海外，已有逾千年的历史。海外华人对居住国特别是东南亚国家的社会经济发展做出了不可磨灭的贡献。20世纪初，英国驻马来西亚联邦总署弗兰克·瑞天威指出："马来西亚各个州所以会有今天，全靠中国人的精神和事业。"

海外华人心系故土，他们虽生活在异国土地上，生计艰辛，仍然关注祖国的进步与发展繁荣。他们曾对辛亥革命和抗日战争做出巨大贡献和牺牲。"革命之母"是孙中山先生对华侨的由衷赞誉。华侨们更对新中国投入了空前的热忱。

进入当代，海外华人在各居住国已成为一支经济实力雄厚的少数族裔。据统计，现今总人数约为5500万的海外华人，拥有价值总额为2000亿美元的流动资产，相当于日本人的三分之二。海外华人对中国、亚洲及世界的未来都将产生积极而重大的影响。

作为业内杰出的专家学者，李华伟博士看到了收藏与研究海外华人文献的迫切性：多少年来，海外华人的历史作用并未得到应有的重视，学术界对海外华人问题的研究也欠深入普遍。李华伟博士强调的是："这不仅归咎于一些国家目光短浅的民族排外主义，也因为许多专门性的图书馆缺乏充分的财力和物力保存海外华人的文献和文化遗产。"

"这就造成了当前亟待解决的问题：学者们无法有效、系统地利用分散在世界各地的海外华人的原始记载分析、评价海外华人的历史贡献；另一方面，目前个人、家庭及社会对海外华人的历史记录的保存每况愈下，许多宝贵的文献正逐渐散失。"

"尤其是，随着老一辈华人领袖等各类重要人物逐渐离开历史舞台，向他们征集个人传记、手稿以及口述历史资料的迫切性显得更为突出。"

仿佛听到了历史的召唤，李华伟博士出于"能做就做，不图回报"的崇高思想境界，责无旁贷地承担起了筹建海外华人文献研究中心的重任。他打算在1999年退休离任后，把晚年全部精力都用在中心的建设发展和研究上。按照他的构想，中心今后还将扩大收藏与分析北美华人的文献资料。因为近年来，北美地区已逐渐成为海外华人定居的主要目的地。他预计，"这一趋势将海外华人社会的未来发展产生不可低估的影响"。李博士期望：中心今后将发展成为北美地区研究海外华人问题的一所重镇。

在国外，许多华人大都会取一个当地"洋"名字。李华伟博士则一直坚持他的这个称谓。他说：华伟这名字能让我时时想到祖国，想到我身上流着的是中华民族的血液，更有特殊意义。

李华伟博士最感欣慰的，是自他1982年回祖国大陆后，到1998年十几年间，祖国大陆图书馆事业的"进展非常大"。他认为标志主要有二：一是馆员素质提高了。当初只有少数几个高校如北大、武大等设有图书馆学系，现在已有59所大学开设了图书馆与信息学系，专门培养图书馆员，队伍好多了。二是图书馆开始了自动化信息化集成。这方面尽管财力有限，但正在一步步与国际先进水平接近和接轨。虽然与最先进水平相差10年，但过去则是差20年、30年。

"我做的是很有意义的工作，心甘情愿、义不容辞。"说起来，也真有点"舍我其谁"的意味——在全美约有4000多华裔图书馆员，当大学图书馆馆长的却只有3人。李在美图书馆界有相当的影响力。

李华伟博士还谦虚地表示："过去做了一些工作，但做得不够。退下来后，有很多事情是可以做的，还应会有所作为，如北大、北图的事情。"

谈到图书馆界近年来的发展变化，李华伟博士高屋建瓴，富于远见："过去的40年，是图书馆界空前的变革时期，每5年即有小变化，10年有大变化，而以往的几百年一直很少变化。40年内发生如此巨变，我们赶上了，应感到幸运。随着最新技术的迅速应用，电子通信、电子出版、多媒体、密集储存技术等，对图书馆冲击非常大。现在的图书馆借助电脑和网络，已向虚拟图书馆发展，堪称'无远不及，无所不在'。这已经远非以往意义的图书馆，至少已经改头换面了。图书馆前景光明，还会有很多机会和机遇，我们现在还不能看得很清楚。但无疑,整个变化将给图书馆业带来从未有过的勃勃生机。"

在谈到现代化的图书馆如何与发展着的社会相适应时,李华伟博士认为:"今日美国社会,图书馆开始发挥社会大学和大教室的作用。美国现在的教育正从正规教育趋向非正规教育。过去上大学年龄是18到22岁,现在平均是23岁。不少青年人先就业、生育子女,然后再回校读书。这样更成熟,求知欲也高。另外社会发展变化快,人们需要终身教育,因此图书馆自然变成了'社会大学'。美国大学图书馆对社会是开放的。"

"同时,美国的大学现在还展现一种趋向:教师的传授不再为主,成为辅助的。学生自己学习,在教室外学习比在教室内学更为重要。图书馆也自然而变成'大教室'。"

"在这种背景下,图书馆作用更显重要了。国内图书馆怎样更加充分发挥功能,也应当未雨绸缪,早做规划和准备。"

作为该领域的权威,李博士的提示显然非常重要和富于针对性。

改革开放以后,中国走出封闭,百业待兴。李华伟博士对中国图书馆事业走向现代化,所起到的推动和促进作用,毫无疑问是外籍华人中贡献最为卓著的一个。

北京图书馆副馆长周和平感概:李华伟博士长年累月奔波,忙于联系、接待、推动……他图的是什么?图名吗?在美国多年他早已功成名就,誉满华美学术界;图利吗?他干这些事情,不仅没有分文回报,相反还要搭进大量的时间,精力和金钱。那么,他到底为了什么呢?

谁言寸草心,报得三春晖。他以自己的言行向故乡的父老乡亲展示着:李华伟博士,有一颗宽宏务实、追求卓越、报效故土、真诚可贵的闪闪发亮的中国心!

(原载《中华儿女》1998年第7期,第60-67页。)

美国俄亥俄大学图书馆馆长李华伟博士剪影

徐国定

1996年7月,我赴美参加ALA(美国图书馆学会)年会回来,总有一种冲动,想写一写李华伟。

李华伟博士1978年任美国俄亥俄大学图书馆馆长兼教育学院教授。

在他近40年的图书馆生涯中,曾经发表过60多篇论文、出版了3本书,写过2本会议录,先后担任6种学术期刊的编辑委员。他的《图书馆学的世界观》(1991年台湾学生书局出版)、《90年代图书馆的筹款指引》(与蓝里博士合著,1992年由美国坚那位公司出版)和《现代化的图书馆管理》(1996年台湾三民书局出版),在图书馆界影响很大。特别是《现代化的图书馆管理》一书,荟集了他几十年来在国内外尤其是在中国大陆讲学的精髓,花了近5年时间才完成。它吸取了传统式的"纸张图书馆"、70年代"自动化图书馆"、80年代"网络化图书馆"、90年代"电子化图书馆"的各个历史时期管理思想的理论,是一部适应21世纪图书馆和信息中心向"虚拟图书馆"方向发展需要的佳作。书中不仅就现代化的任务与使命加以阐释,就20世纪西方管理的发展、图书馆的规划、组织、人力资源、领导与作业、控制与评估等作了剖析,且在最后,还以跨世纪的图书馆发展的需要作为结论,十分系统而完整地总结了图书馆的历史发展进程中的理论和实践经验,书中还附有大量的管理操作的实例、统计以及罕见的资料。

李华伟馆长先后得到的奖状奖励和荣誉称号甚多,仅在1982—1993年间就夺得9个主要巨奖:俄亥俄大学最杰出行政人员奖(1982年)、华美图书馆学会杰出服务奖(1983年)、俄亥俄最杰出图书馆员奖(1987年)、台湾中国图书馆学会杰出贡献奖(1989年)、美中华人学术及专业学会杰出服务奖(1991年)、美国图书馆学会国际关系卓越贡献奖(1991年)、亚美及太平洋地区图书馆员学会杰出服务奖状(1991年)、美国新闻署杰出服务奖状(1992年)、俄亥俄图书及信息网感谢状(1993年)等。他的名字被载入《世界名人传》、《美国名人传》、《美国教育界名人传》。

他是美国图书馆学会理事、华美图书馆员学会会长及理事;担任了国际关系委员会亚洲太平洋地区小组主席;他同时并多次担任联合国教科文组织、联合国发展计划、世界粮农组织、加拿大国际发展及研究中心等机构有关图书馆发展项目的顾问。

作为一个美籍华裔的图书馆从业人员,李华伟博士极为关心中国图书馆的发展,从1980年起,他在俄亥俄大学图书馆设立了一个国际图书馆员培训计划,曾先后为中国培训了近百名图书馆员,包括北大、清华、北师大、南开、邮电大、三〇一医院图书馆、重庆大学、浙江医科大学、科学院图书馆、中国科技情报所等,其中很多是馆长、副馆长,及部门主任。

自1982年以后,李华伟馆长还每年应邀前往中国各地讲学。国内很多大学都邀请他担任访问教授或客座教授,包括西安交通大学、南开大学、湖南医大、武汉大学、四川联合大学、北京师范大学、东北师范大学、天津理工学院等。中国科学院武汉文献信息中心及兰州文献信息中心也聘请李博士担任学术顾问。清华大学图书馆及中国新技术开发公司也分别邀请李博士担任顾问。近年来他还应中国国家教委之邀多次在世界银行贷款项目及联合国发展基金项目下,对国内师范院校的图书馆馆长开办图书馆管理培训班。

李华伟馆长为中国图书馆事业的发展呕心沥血，千方百计，飞越大洋不知多少次，日程总是满满的：1996年7月在美国他忙于筹开ALA大会，接待我们这些人；8月在北京忙于筹开中美图书馆合作会议大会，为清华与OCLC合作牵线；9月在武汉，主持召开"信息资源与社会发展国际学术研讨会"。李华伟馆长认为：面对21世纪的信息时代，发展现代化的图书信息事业是每一个发展中国家当务之急，"中国要加速科技、经济、政治、教育、文化及社会的发展，必须加速现代化图书馆及信息工作的发展"。因此，他十分重视中国教育科研网建设，认为这是中国信息基础建设的一个主要部分。有了这个教育科研网，中国的高等学府才能与国际上的国际联网衔接交流，吸取世界上最先进的知识。因而他积极地穿针引线，居中协调，为中国学术界的信息高速公路引进世界上一些最重要的信息源。如1996年8月美国最大的信息机构OCLC（联网计算机图书馆中心）正式与清华大学签订了长期互惠合作的协定。在这个隆重的协定签字仪式上，他被称作为OCLC与清华大学联姻的"红娘"，引起了当时在北京召开的IFLA大会代表们的关注，更引起国内图书馆界人士的关注。因为他是为中国图书界和信息界全面走向网络化的牵线人之一，是沟通中美乃至全世界信息相通、心心相连的桥梁。

（原载《图书馆杂志》1998年第4期，第63-64页。）

我们的良师益友李华伟先生

闵凡林

今年3月18日收到大洋彼岸李华伟先生于3月10日写给我的来信。他说："今年十月下旬我将到北京，参加为庆祝北大100周年校庆及新图书馆落成所举办的一个国际会议。我已应北图之邀，在会后开一个为期一周的图书馆馆长培训班，希望到时候我们能够在北京见面。"这封大洋彼岸的来信，令我十分激动。几年来我与李先生结识的那种令人愉悦、令人感动的美好情景又一一浮现在我的眼前。

李华伟教授现任美国俄亥俄大学图书馆馆长，俄亥俄大学领导成员之一，院长级馆长。他祖籍福建，在台湾读完大学，在美国获博士学位，是第一位任美国大学图书馆馆长的美籍华人，是政治上有影响，学术上有造诣，国际图书馆界有声望的知名人士。

我结识李先生是在1993年暑期，国家教委决定在天津举办全国教育学院图书馆馆长培训班。李华伟先生作为主讲人，我作为主要组织者之一，与李先生共同度过了两周的时光。在朝夕相处的日子里，我和同志们感到了他品格的高尚；在聆听了李先生的生动讲演之后，我和同志们认知了他学识的渊博。有的同志既风趣又认真地说："我们都是馆长，却不是等量级的，李先生一人可抵得上我们几十位馆长"。"李先生的学问够我们学一辈子的"。这绝非自谦者对李先生的溢美之词，而确属真切的感受。

培训班上，李先生介绍了世界各国图书馆发展建设的历史，讲述了美国大学图书馆自动化的现状和未来发展远景，以及馆长如何对图书馆进行科学、规范的管理。特别讲到在美国，大学图书馆的重要地位、作用以及人们对这一崇高事业的敬仰。李先生渊博的学识，精湛的讲演，拓宽了我们的眼界，增强了大家做好图书馆工作的信心，使我们进一步认识到图书馆作为高等院校三大支柱之一的不可替代性，自慰事业的神圣。

李先生的人品更强烈地感染着我们。记得在培训班集体参观南开大学新图书馆时，要乘电梯上楼，由于人多，组织者号召年轻的同志最好爬楼梯走上去，否则会耽误时间。李华伟先生当时已年过半百，又是请来的美国专家，理应是第一个坐电梯，可他却喊着"我还年轻"就随同年轻人跑着爬上了楼梯。这意外的举动，使许多同志放弃了电梯，纷纷跟着李先生奔向了现代化的演播厅。

在培训班期间，我们组织大家到海河船上俱乐部联欢。开始，大家由于陌生，而显得拘谨，面对舞池，彼此相望，就是不敢投足。李先生也本不善舞，为了鼓动大家，率先进入舞池，顿时将沉寂的场面变得热烈，继而推向了高潮。风度儒雅的李先生以其人格的魅力和巨大的感召力，征服了我们这些天南地北聚集而来的馆长们。他当之无愧是我们的良师益友。

两周的学习时光就要结束了，此时对于我们，显得格外的短暂。对李先生的依依不舍之情笼罩着整个培训班。大家在商量，用什么形式来表达我们对李先生的拥戴和惜别之情？商量再三，最后决定送李先生一张条幅，条幅上每个学员写上一句最能表达自己真情的话，之后再签上自己的名字，以此作为最好的纪念。有一位女学员，因为对李先生的"领舞"印象太深，于是她在两米多长的条幅上，选择了一个显要的位置，写下了"何日再起舞"五个大字。好一个"何日再起舞"！多数不会跳舞的我们，真想尽早地再一次地与李先生起舞，为我们的人生起舞；为我们的事业起舞！为我们的友情起舞！我馆的孙新同志在条幅上纪录下了李先生的那句话："我还年轻"。好一个"我还年轻"！我们的岁月年轻，我们的事业年轻，我们愿跟随着李华伟先生永远以年轻的心境奔向新的世纪，攀登科学的高峰。我写的是："中美文化交流的伟大使者"！愿这位中美友好使者永远年轻，永远活跃在中美文化交流的舞台上。

在告别仪式上，李先生接过这蕴含着深情的条幅，激动地对大家说："我回到美国，将它挂在我的办公室里，看到它，就会想起你们，想起在天津的这些美好日子"。

李先生回国后不久，就给我们来了信，并寄来了为我们所拍的照片。我们在给他的回信中说："看看您和我们在一起的照片，就觉得您仍在中国，仍在我们中间，大洋隔开了我们，鸿雁又连结了我们，我们从事的事业是一个整体，我们的心是永远贴在一起的"。后来，李先生又两次给我们寄来了外文原版图书百余册。对此赠书义举，我们在回信中写道："李先生赠书给我们，小而言之，是为我们天津教育学院图书馆的发展建设；大而言之，则是一位美籍华人为中华民族的振兴发达竭尽自己的所能。"

1995年5月，国家教委在武汉再次举办培训班，培训全国教育学院图书馆自动化方面的人才，李先生是主讲人之一，我们得到通知后，除派我馆技术部主任李凤来同志参加外，院长又派我代表学院，专程去武汉看望李先生，以表达我们对李先生的谢意。到了湖北教育学院，我和凤来就去拜见李先生，不巧，他被武汉大学请走了。当他回来听说我们来了，就在我们住宿的走廊里大声呼唤我们，我和凤来赶紧出来应道："我们住在这里，在这里！"两年后的相见，真是：执手相看泪眼，竟无语凝噎！

我在武汉的两天，没有上街，没有访友，白天认真听李先生讲课，晚上与李先生交谈，以求更多收获。李先生热心灼人，这期间经他介绍，我又结识了北京师范大学图书情报系教授王酉梅先生。李先生在武汉讲完课又到郑州、长春考察，最后回到北京，为清华大学的国际联网，进入信息高速公路牵线搭桥。在李先生离开北京之前，在清华大学外宾招待所，他又与我畅谈了许久……

1996年9月2日华北地区高校图协第十届年会在天津召开。李华伟先生在参加第62届国际图联大会之后，被邀请到会作了《美国大学图书馆的现代化管理》的报告，受到与会代表们的欢迎，反响热烈。休息时，我走到讲坛前与李先生见面，并邀请李先生，结果被大会一位工作人员挡驾，他说："李教授来天津时间很紧，不能再做安排。"我恳望利用晚上时间，这位同志一边打手势让我离开，一边毫不客气地对我说："晚上也安排满了，另外李教授还要休息，不要见了。"这时李先生说："他是我的朋友，我来天津很想见见他。"然后对我说："你晚上10点到纺织工学院外宾楼找我。我10点前一定赶回来。"

晚上10点我们相见时，李先生告诉我，他9点半就不顾南开大学的挽留而提前回来了。李先生对我的这份非同寻常的感情，使我深为感动。他对我，从大处说，是看到天津教育学院图书馆步履维艰，要无私的帮助我们；从小处说，他把我当成兄弟，都是炎黄子孙，都是黄皮肤，血管里流淌的都是一样的血。

今天，当我接到李先生的来信，约我在今年十月与他在北京相见时，我的心情是难以平静的，这位良师益友带给我的深情厚谊是很难用语言表达出来的，我耐心地等待着这个金秋十月里的吉日良辰，在首都北京与李先生会晤的激动时刻。

（原载《天津师范学院通讯》1999年第2页。）

跨越时空的追寻与奉献
——记俄亥俄大学图书馆馆长李华伟博士①

吕　红

开篇：凡是有太阳的地方就有华人。

远离故乡亲人在异国他乡定居，他不仅成为所在国的新公民，而且通过自身努力成为学界宗师，中西文化交流的桥梁，一个备受不同肤色不同血统不同政见的各方人士爱戴的学者。在美国图书馆学会颁奖大会上；在IFLA国际图书馆联合会上；在华美图书馆员协会上……他以灵活有度的管理方式、业精于深的学术成就为华人争得了荣誉。他的举手投足、侃侃言谈均洋溢着民族的自豪感。

他，心理素质极好。不亢不卑，堂堂正正。真诚坦荡地带着他黄皮肤的小弟兄们进入以白人占优势的主流社会。凭自己的本领和智慧做出斐然成绩，直至终于赢得大家的尊敬，赢得优秀馆长称号，赢得会场上的掌声雷动，哗——如暴风雨，长时间回响激荡在每个人的胸膛……

在这气氛隆重热烈的会议上，他结交了许多新朋友，同时他也为更多的人所认识，人们记住了他的名字：李华伟。

人们记住他，是因为他战胜了傲慢与偏见，赢得了承认与尊重。

他为人家付出了很多，而他自己不求任何回报。他不是伟人和奇人，他却有坚如磐石的信念，博大仁爱的胸怀和不拘地域的气度。

他爱才惜才重才，用不同的方式、通过不同的管道，力所能及地帮助了许多人，让别人的创造力得以更好的施展，并充分给予他人建功立业的机会。他的家，无形中已成了一个温暖温馨的沙龙，一个让所有到过那儿的人久久怀念的地方。

他的话语很浅显易懂，内涵却令人品味再三。他说："我希望每个接触过我们的人都能由衷地道一句，中国人很好！"

对人对事他始终保持良好的感受力和反应力，对新的知识新的观念始终学而不倦，竞争意识磨练了思维和行动。

总之，他的追求就是，集刚强柔韧于一身，化不利为有利，变困境为顺境，帮助自己和他人立身于广大的世界。行游寰宇，广闻博识，方能高瞻远瞩，纵横比较，这样，对于人世间的许多问题，往往能看得更远、想得更深。与此相关的，是他孜孜不倦在东西方国家牵线搭桥，推动事物向好的方向转化，推动一个又一个合作专案的完成，且总是精神饱满、充满干劲，他的敏捷矫健让人羡慕。他虽已不年轻，但他的心永远年轻！

我们的生活的空间远不是完美无缺，但多一个好人存在就多一分光明。至少可以避免陷阱和弯路。而且，只要有这样的好人在坚持乐观地前行，在我们的身边循循引路，想必许多困窘也一定能够迎刃而解吧！

柳绿枫红　春华秋实

我认识李华伟先生的年头应该说是不短了。屈指一算竟已十来个春秋。有时想想，人和人之间的相互联系，远近疏密，似乎就起始于那一面之缘的偶然。

---

① 此为长篇传记文学部分篇章节选。

1982年，他穿过33年的风雨路，从大洋彼岸回到故土，以外籍专家之誉在春城昆明为中国科技情报所的管理者们授课，之后，便不断收到来自学术界的邀请。

1985年秋，他前来中国科学院武汉分院讲学并代表美国俄亥俄大学与文献资讯中心签署合作协定。签署仪式完毕便与全体工作人员合影留念（那会儿，我是一个阅历尚浅、不大起眼的中文期刊管理员。）。是日当晚，领导召集大家和李博士座谈，开个Party营造欢乐气氛，正巧我和他是邻座，李博士拿出全家合影让大家看，我第一次看到他的妻子——一个金发碧眼的贤妻良母，还有6个中西合璧、健康可爱的孩子。我忍不住称赞了一声："您夫人真漂亮！""哦，谢谢。"他笑容满面地回答。初次的对话给我留下一个旅美多年、礼貌习俗亦西化的学者印象。

次年6月，他携夫人回国讲学，同时以特约嘉宾身份参加馆庆30周年活动。那一段前后，我作为初露头角的撰稿人和武汉电视台首次合作了专题片《在过去和未来之间》以及一些新闻片。在展览室我们偶然相遇，一位同行拍下照片，他说，"你们总是为别人留下纪念，而忽略了自己。"此轻轻一言，尤其令人感动。

再见他已是数年之后。我在报刊上出现频率渐多并出了点集子，且在新闻圈里混饭吃。那日，趁李华伟博士在湖北教育学院讲学的间隙，赶去面谈组团文化交流事宜，临走时顺便送了他两本小书。没想到，时隔不久他特地从美国发来传真，称"在武汉承您赠送大作《红颜沧桑》，我已拜读。对您的文学才华极为钦佩。我馆将会把您的大作编目收藏，以供更多的读者阅读。"——再没有比这更高的奖励了！对一个喜欢和笔墨打交道的人来说，还有什么能比千山万水之外传来的资讯更有价值、更鼓舞人心的呢？

组团访美之事因故搁浅，然而两年后，作为访问学者的我，飞到美利坚合众国。

在山清水秀、景致迷人的俄亥俄大学拜访这位赫赫有名的美籍华人、资深的国际图书馆学家，许多有关他的身世和他的家庭、他的事业、他在中美之间的桥梁作用、他和祖国血脉相连的故事，渐渐被发掘出来……

经纬枢纽　华美桥梁
一位美籍华人的情怀

李华伟先生平易近人、风度儒雅，举止谈吐间融学者的见识和管理者的才智于一体。在他家和办公室里，墙壁上悬挂着中国书法，窗台上、案头上及书架上摆放着朴拙或精美的工艺品，那些让人赏心悦目的工艺品，不仅是他足迹的记录，更是他交游甚广、朋友遍天下的证明。

有趣的是，我无意中在他几十本相册里找到了十多年前他为我和同行拍下的照片：当时的我，笑得多么开心！而他与我们全体工作人员的大幅合影，赫然醒目地挂在他的书房里。

"浮云游子意，落日故人情"几笔饱满酣畅的大字，是否是他一生的真实写照呢？我长久地品味壁上的书法寻思着……

现任俄亥俄大学图书馆院长级馆长兼教育学院教授的李华伟博士，早年毕业于台湾师范大学教育系。1957年来美深造，曾先后获得匹兹堡大学教育硕士、图书馆学硕士及高等教育的哲学博士学位。历任匹兹堡大学、都肯大学、宾州爱丁堡大学、科罗拉多州立大学等图书馆行政职务，为华裔担任美国大学图书馆的首位馆长。并由美国政府国际发展总署派往泰国担任亚洲理工学院图书馆资讯中心主任七年。在那一期间，他与联合国、世行、亚行、世界粮农组织等建立起密切的联系，为他日后成为信息领域及国际舞台上活跃的领导角色奠定了良好的发展基础，为有关亚洲地区图书馆建设出谋划策、参与专案提供了理论与实践的依据。90年代，李华伟博士曾经作为专家被邀请到白宫参与讨论有关资讯管理发展方面的问题。

由于李华伟博士在国际图书情报界享用很高的声誉，被选举连任两届（4年一任）美国图书馆学会理事，该学会是全世界最大的学会，有会员5.7万名。同时他还担任国际图书馆学会联盟的大学及研究图书馆委员会委员等职务。出版了《图书馆学的世界观》、《九十年代图书馆募捐指引》及《现代化的图书馆管理》等书，发表学术论文六十余篇。多次担任联合国教科文组织及其他国际机构及基金会顾问。因其贡献突出，成绩卓著，他曾荣获十多种奖励和称号，如美国华美图书馆员学会杰出服务奖，美国图书馆学会国际关系卓越贡献奖，亚太地区图书馆员学会杰出服务奖，美国图书馆学会杰出理事奖，美国新闻总署杰出服务奖，台湾图书馆学会杰出贡献奖等多种荣誉，并被连续载入《世界名人传》、《美国名人传》、《美国教育名人传》等历史年鉴上。

在中国改革开放的强劲之风吹动下，诸多海外赤子怀着满腔热情或以资财或以才学报效祖国。李华伟博士便是其中最突出的代表。

身为大学教育学院兼任教授、博士生导师，他带了7个博士生，其中有几个是中国人。行政事务、科研教学、社会工作头绪繁杂，其紧张状态可想而知。用一句中国教育领事的话来说，"李馆长的时间安排是以分钟计算的。"即使在如此高负荷的工作状态下，仍把祖国的事放在心头。他多次应中国国家教委之邀，以世界银行贷款专案及联合国发展基金项目，对国内图书馆管理者开办培训班。孜孜不倦、广结善缘，名气越来越大，越来越多的大学聘请他担任访问教授或顾问教授，包括北京大学、清华大学、北京师范大学、北京邮电大学、西安交通大学、南开大学、武汉大学、四川联合大学、东北师范大学、天津理工学院等。中国科学院武汉文献资讯中心及兰州文献资讯中心、中国国家图书馆以及台湾"中央图书馆"也聘请李博士担任顾问。

所以专家评价说，"李华伟先生对国内的贡献不是物质上的，更主要是精神层面的。"体现在更新观念上，在人才培养上，即教育软件方面，这位美籍华人的贡献尤其显得突出。

在现代社会中，所谓竞争说到底也就是人才的竞争。教育的根本就是培养人才。人才在现代化事业中就是一批活生生的力量。而现代化图书馆应该相当于人才培养基。无论是送出国去培训也好，是他到国内来讲学也罢，这对于图书馆管理人才、专业技术人才的成长，对于图书馆软硬环境的改善是大有好处的。

为了加速中国图书馆事业现代化进程，为了年轻一代中国知识分子的成长，自1982年开始，李华伟博士每年都要往返奔波于中美之间——以赤诚之心和顽强毅力，亲手架起一座连接东方西方、过去与未来的桥梁！

在美国，他是华人担任高等院校图书馆长的第一人。在这个科学与文明交互渗透的领域，他呕心沥血勤勉奋斗至今已40载。

在祖国，他的德才人品及学术成果享誉大学、科学院、情报所、公共图书馆等几大系统，并竞相被所有著名的大学所聘请，堪称绝无仅有的第一人。

李华伟先生从来就具有凡是不落人后，偏要争第一的天性，又是他第一个设立国际图书馆员培训计划，在联合国教科文组织等赞助下，先后有来自亚洲及世界各地160多位馆员在此完成了培训工作，光祖国大陆的就有近百人，包括北大、清华、北师大、南开、邮电大、三〇一医院图书馆、重庆大学、湖南医科大学、科学院图书馆、中国科技情报所等，其中很多位是图书馆馆长、副馆长及部门主任。这一计划以及该馆与亚洲图书馆的多种合作方式皆已成为全美图书馆的典范。虽然搞国际文化交流的人，在美国远不止他一个，但像他这样有目标有计划的、大规模的、长时间持续不断的、且不受外界干扰影响的，忙前跑后竭尽全力去牵线搭桥的人，的的确确难得，少有！

要知道，不仅那些资助培训费用是他多方奔走、四处筹集而来，并且他还根据各人不同情况安排培训计划，甚至包括其生活起居都关心到了。

中国驻纽约总领事馆徐敦潢参赞和领事说："有的人有他这份心，没有他的身份和地位做不成这些事；也有人有了地位身份，却不见得愿意做这些事。惟他两者兼有，所以他做得有声有色，颇受好评。"

难怪有人送他"经纬枢纽，美华桥梁"的题字呢！

看着眼前那一幅幅奖状、一份份聘书，我思绪浮动，感慨万千。忽然问了一个似乎不搭界的问题："李华伟先生，很多人到国外都会取一个英文名字，你怎么没有取一个？为什么？"

他笑吟吟回答说："华伟这名字能让我时时想到祖国，想到我身上流着是中华民族的血，更有特殊意义。"言语之间流露出他一生不变的中国心。

长年累月致力于中美之间牵线搭桥，热衷于东西方文化交流与合作的李华伟先生，在1996年全力促成了一件值得一提的大事，在他事业的里程碑上刻下深深的一笔：首届中美图书馆合作会议在北京隆重召开。两国近百位图书馆馆长和专家学者聚集一堂，就会议主题展开热烈的讨论："全球的资讯存取——挑战与机遇"。会议取得了圆满的成功，其意义不同凡响。用北京图书馆馆长任继愈教授的话说，"在迈向资讯社会的今天，各国图书馆之间加强了解与合作，互相学习新技术、新方法，实现资源分享的愿望越来越强烈"。美国图书馆学会主席图罗克女士认为，"最重要的是电子资讯的流通和交换，发挥图书馆最大作用"。李华伟博士在会上作了重要报告，总结了中美图书馆合作的历史经验，以及在今后的发展重点。有意借国际图联大会的契机，积极促成中美图书馆界的密切合作，在中美图书馆发展史上写下新的篇章！

这次会议对中美两国及世界图书馆的合作与发展产生积极而深远的影响。会议之后又有多个图书馆相继结为姐妹馆。从观念改变到具体措施；从人员培训到文化交流；从技术引进到资讯传播；

海外传媒报导："自从中国1869年向美国国会图书馆捐赠1000册图书后，相隔一百多年，中美两国近百位馆长和专家学者站在中国国家图书馆的台阶上。"这一幕载入了历史。美国国会图书馆副馆长泰伯评论道："这不仅是行业合作，也加强了两国人民彼此的了解"。

事后了解，当初为筹备这个会议，李华伟馆长在一年前就积极倡议，并频频与北京电信往来，从经费的筹集，到会议资料的印刷，还有大会期间的组织及翻译工作、包括一些词汇提法的相互切磋，大到两国学术界高层的接触交流，小到代表餐宿人员安排，他都一一落实。说实话的，尽管李博士曾经主持或协办过多次国际会议，其中包括1983年在美国举办的亚太地区图书馆与西安交大图书馆合办的"图书馆新技术应用"国际学术讨论会、1994年在上海举办的"资讯技术与资讯服务"国际会议、1996年武大的"资讯资源与社会发展"国际学术研讨会。但在中国举办这种大型的两国间高层图书馆合作会议确属

"大姑娘上轿——头一遭"，中美双方从语言交流、文化背景、工作方式都有诸多的不适，如果没有一个热衷于这项事业的、同时又具有地位和能力的人操办，很难想象，会取得如此的成功。大家感动地说："从早到晚，忙个不停，李馆长真是太累了！尤其对一个已是60多岁的并患有腰疾人来说，更为不易。可他笑呵呵地说："身为华人，我乐于作个桥梁。"

中国图书馆的孙蓓欣副馆长称颂道：李华伟先生为图书馆事业所作的努力是令人感佩的！

还有一个细节值得一提：据当时担任翻译的张沙丽女士说，会议之后有人纷纷写报告争功论赏不亦乐乎，可是李华伟先生却退居幕后，以极为淡然的态度看待功名荣誉。知情者挺为他抱不平，李先生一笑，"只要事情能办成功，谁获得什么这并不重要。"

可谓"正其义，不谋其利；明其道，不计其功"。当人家忙于争成果时，他却在为一笔专为会议筹集的数万美金经费的其中一部分账目不清、花得不明不白而追查。当他搞清是美国学会里一位掌权者所为，没有就此甘休。我劝他说，凡事别太认真了。我说这话是因为我知道：哪儿都有贪官污吏，无论东方还是西方，都不例外。我的见怪不怪的神情与他气忿忿、涨红了脸的神情形成对比，既显出他的正直也显出了他坦荡天真的一面。其实，凡和他交往的人都领略过他热情好客、慷慨大方的秉性，对国内来访者他总是尽量安排在自己家，请客吃饭全掏自家腰包，从未吝啬过。然而对公家的事，他如此的认真，这也是我从不曾想到的。我总开玩笑说我老公太廉洁，造成我的家像"清水衙门"。他再三表示他欣赏这样的人，如果国家多一点这样廉洁无私的官，那么社会也能进步得更快。

1997年6月一个傍晚，我和中国图书馆副馆长周和平在俄亥俄大学美丽的校园漫步，周先生刚刚与李华伟博士就今后双方合作达成共识。此刻他对我感慨道："李先生长年累月忙于联系、接待、推动、奔波……他图的是什么？图名吗？在美国多年他早已功成名就、誉满华美学术界；图利吗？可他干这些事，不仅没有分文回报，相反还要搭进大量的时间精力和金钱；那么，他到底为了什么？值得人去好好挖掘。"

我就此采访李馆长，他说："一是出于对图书馆事业的热爱，因为图书馆本身是没有国界的；再一个自己作为炎黄子孙，多年身居海外，也总是想着为中华民族做点实实在在的事情。"

多么朴素的语言，多么真挚的情感！还有什么东西比这更无价，更可贵的呢？在世界政治经济急速发展变化、东西方文明交互渗透的今天，这种良好的精神品格不正是我们民族强大所需要保存和延续的吗？

激励鼓舞　永恒祝愿

1997年10月31日，对李华伟博士来说，应该是一个不同寻常的日子。

马不停蹄风尘仆仆地刚从北京讲学返回美国的他，甚至来不及休整一下长途奔波的劳累，一回俄亥俄大学即赶到办公室处理各种函件。他首先看到的，是中国驻纽约领事馆发来的通知，邀请他作为俄亥俄州的华人代表，去纽约参加一个大型会见：即正在美国进行国事访问的中国国家主席江泽民，接见他们这些有名望有成就的美籍华人。

消息不胫而走，迅速传开，在当地引起了轰动，尤其是引起了校园华裔师生的羡慕和不少美国人士的关注。俄亥俄大学电视台、爱森市电台和报社，州府所在地《哥伦布信使报》的记者等纷纷采访了李华伟博士，请他谈谈观感。而他的情绪似乎还沉浸在两周前……

在金风送爽的紫禁城，国家总书库北京图书馆新馆10周年暨建馆85周年馆庆。国家最高领导人纷纷题词致贺寄予了新的期望。盛装彩披，交相辉映。北图给这位睿智和蔼的教授的最高荣誉——"鉴于您30年来在图书馆界所取得的卓越成就和为中美两国图书馆交流与合作作出的突出贡献，中国国家图书馆为了更方便移樽就教及恭请指导，特荣幸地聘请您为本馆顾问。"差不多与此同时，著名的高等学府北京大学也为他专门举行聘任仪式，北大学生为他戴上校徽并献上鲜花，感谢、景仰、还有期待，尽在其中！

于是他对记者感慨道："我刚刚结束了一个对中国为时两周的访问，在周日晚才到家，所以对马上又不得不再次旅行没有思想准备，但当我意识到自己是一小部分经过挑选的人去参加这个会面时，我又欣然接受了邀请。"

在那段时间"中国"成为各传媒使用频率最高的词汇，连普通的美国人似乎对中国也开始感兴趣了。报纸的标题是——"俄亥俄大学图书馆的馆长和江泽民会面"，除了李华伟博士的个人小照外，另还在标题上方配以美联社记者拍摄的大幅图片：江泽民主席与克林顿总统微笑着向大家招手致意，非常醒目。

报道中说：俄亥俄大学的图书馆馆长李华伟在这个星期的早些时候接到一份邀请，请他赴纽约与中国国家主席江泽民见面。接到这份邀请之后他考虑再三，他的担心并不是由于具有争议的人权或是政治问题，相反是考虑旅程问题。

李先生从1978年以来就担任俄亥俄大学的图书馆馆长，他是一位国际公认的图书馆专家，是这次全美范围内受邀请与江泽民会面的优秀华人学者之一。他说，作为大约30名华裔美国学者和领导人之一，能够被邀请，我甚感荣幸。因为我非常希望中国和美国之间关系有更好更大的发展，而这种建立在两个伟大国家的领导人之间互相理解和信任的关系，对世界和平的意义非同寻常。李先生说，他想他之所以被邀请参加会面，是因为自己在中国的图书馆现代化事业上起到了他本人所应起的作用。李先生说，中国在图书馆的技术方面比美国要落后10—15年，他们正在迅速地赶上来。传媒称在为中国图书馆所做的事情当中，有关李先生做的是，使中国图书馆能够通过国际互联网与国外相联系。

从李先生周一收到的这份传真来看，这个3小时的会面将包括：江泽民的一次演讲，一个提问和回答的时间段落和一个非正式的招待会。江泽民在纽约时，还预期将访问证券交易所。李先生说："我昨天试图和中国大使馆领事馆的官员联系，了解一下有关周末会面等情况，但是并不成功。"李先生出生在中国，1949年前夕，他还是一个少年，和家人一起离开了祖国大陆，在此后的几十年内未能回去，一直到1982年他被邀请赴中国大陆讲学，内容是"图书馆的管理"。自从那个时候，就有不断的邀请。他几乎每年都要回去（有时甚至一年去三次），到世界上人口最多的大学图书馆讲学和提供咨询。他这个月的访问当中，应邀参加了中国国家图书馆85周年的庆典，并受邀担任顾问，中国国家图书馆在亚洲地区是最大的图书馆，在世界范围内排名第五。据李先生近次从中国主要的大学获得的荣誉称号包括：北京大学客座教授资格，北京邮电通讯咨询教授资格。在过去的30年当中，李先生是一个世界范围的图书馆的咨询专家和演讲教授；联系最紧密的是那些东南亚国家。正由于他和中国强有力的联系，才导致他建立了邵友保博士海外华文文献研究中心。这个中心位于图书馆的东南亚收藏室内，保存和记录了华侨的一些书面资料。他力求使之变为最大的海外华人资料库，以便让这些资讯能够对学者们开放使用。

但这个期间美国的各种媒体反映不一，显得十分复杂。除了正面的报导，亦有不少杂音。因为从10月10日开始，美国各地电影院都在放映一部好莱坞的影片《西藏七年》。从技术上来说，影片的导演和演员都是相当棒的。该片加深了一些不了解实际情况的美国公众对于中国的想象,让人误解西藏是被中国强行兼并的。在江泽民访美之前大放特放这么一部片子,似乎显得别有用心。

一时间,沸沸扬扬,对中国西藏敏感问题成为公众舆论的焦点。几乎所有看过该片的美国人都在谈论,连李夫人玛丽都对此表示特别关注,和丈夫进行了一番讨论。李华伟跟她解释了半天西藏的历史背景及有关情况。尽管中国的问题比较复杂,不是三言两语能讲清楚并让西方人明白的。他还是尽力而为之。

因为美国传媒一向关心中国的人权问题、台湾问题和西藏问题,有的记者就希望他对此发表看法,他说最好不要谈论政治(新华社记者也曾经就几个敏感话题采访他,他虽然没有回避,但亦谈的不多)。他从来都是以一个教育界的资深学者身份来参与各种活动的;他始终把民族的利益看得高于党派或者国家。这大概是他40年来在异邦立足的处世之道吧。

一位学新闻专业的留学生在和他谈及舆论现象时,李华伟博士说,美国新闻界在对中国的报道上确实有失偏颇,尤其表现在江泽民访美之事上。他说,中美两国首脑能坐在一起交换各自的看法本身就是一件好事,是两国关系的一大进步。美国新闻界应该多报道这方面,但是没有,在江主席来以前就造成一种围攻的声势。……大家都说21世纪是亚洲的世纪,亚洲的世纪又不能不提到中国,美国传媒在中美关系中应起到什么作用呢?答案应该是不言而喻的。

也正由于他出色的才学和人品,以及为推动中美文化交流、海峡两岸关系改善所作出的不懈努力,所以才得到许多嘉奖和高层政要的注意。

在纽约参加会见前,李华伟博士和另一位州立大学的华裔教授相遇,闲聊时,那位教授说起担任行政工作的压力和劳累,想以后放弃主任职位,埋头搞搞专业算了。

李馆长说:"华人在美国奋斗不容易,特别像你这样取得这样的成就和地位更是难得,所以我觉得你还是不要轻易放弃系主任的位置。不是为你自己,而是为更多的中国人。让人家看看,华人在美国大学里同样做得很好!"

他们一行集合从纽约领事馆乘车出来,到江泽民主席下榻的达华尔道夫旅馆,在三楼宴会大厅等候。大约上午11时,江泽民主席开始与华人、华侨及留学生代表会面。随即,江主席发表了热情洋溢的讲话。他说:"我首先代表中国政府与人民向你们并通过你们向旅居美国的所有侨胞、留学生人员和华人朋友,以及来自香港特别行政区和澳门、台湾的同胞,致以亲切的问候和良好的祝愿。"

他说,"这次我与美国总统克林顿达成了一项很好的共识,就是中美两国不应因各自历史文化、社会制度和发展水准的不同而影响双方友好的合作关系的发展……"

他说,"我刚刚参观了IBM公司,感受到科技发展的突飞猛进。在这样的资讯时代,要想国家的发展,必须把重视科技、尊重人才放在第一位。江主席祝愿各界华人、华侨在各自的工作岗位上继续作出突出的贡献。他讲话轻松,常常夹着一些英语,充满了幽默和风趣,讲话经常被掌声和欢笑声打断。他的访美之行,所到之处遇到无数欢迎面孔,同时也像他所讲的"有些噪音进入耳朵"。但他泰然自若,表现出了一个大国首脑的风范,亦算实地亲身感受了什么是西方式的"民主和自由"吧。"

开始合影了,李华伟馆长就站在江主席身后,心想,真看不出来已是71岁的人,头上连一根白发都没有,显得比自己还要年轻呢。

李馆长向记者表示,在苦难深重的20世纪,中国人民经历了各种磨砺和考验,才终于在世界上挺起了胸膛昂起了头，尽管迈向未来的路仍很漫长，但随着经济的进一步发展和文化水准的进一步提高，我们华人无论在哪里、做何种工作，都有充分的信心与祖国一道完成21世纪的跨越！

第一篇　峥嵘岁月

1. 历史动荡　波云奇诡

箴言："上帝给你的仁爱很少，但上帝给你的希望却很多。"

在碧波万顷的台湾海峡西岸，有一座美丽的城市——福建省的省会、中国历史文化名城福州。

福州是一座拥有2200年历史的古城，"因州北有福山而得名"，唐开元十三年设福州都督始称福州。五代梁开平二年闽王审知扩建城池，就将风景秀丽的乌山、于山、屏山圈入城内，使福州成为"山在城中，城在山中"的独特城市，所以"三山"成了福州的别名；又因古时全城遍植榕树，福州又称"榕城"。福州四面环山，水流量超过黄河的闽江穿城而过，构成了"三山两塔一江流"的空间格局。

一方水土养育一方人。

提到李华伟的今天，不能不提到父亲对他的许多影响。李华伟祖籍福建福州，曾祖父李顺卿经商，祖父李祖和是前清秀才，一直从事师教。也许，这即成为李家后来三代人命运都与教育有关的开始。

父亲李圣述身处那个动荡的年代，一生可以说是大波大澜跌宕起伏。少年受到福州英华书院的正科教育，在北京燕京大学获得文学学士学位后，又在燕京大学研究院读教育学硕士，毕业后又赴美国阿利根大学攻读心理学硕士，起初他的志向就是毕生从事教育。回国受聘于福建协和大学，任副教授、教授，调入福州师范学校任校长。

青年时代的李圣述颇有一股冲劲。受当时进步思潮的影响，他改变了教育救国的初衷。1928年8月，他毅然辞去福州协和大学和师范学校校长的职位，弃文从戎，跑到国民革命军第十一军政治部宣传科担任了中校科长，第二年就调任陆军第六十师政治训练处主任，并且升为上校军衔，不过仍然属于文官性质。他甚至把自己的名字都改了——"李干军"，表明他立志从军、革命到底的决心。

……

他们一家搬到南京仅一年多，局势就紧张起来了，国民政府开始撤退。他们又回到广西。蒋介石和李宗仁闹翻了，蒋介石下台后实际上并没有放权，李宗仁代总统，却没有实权。同时，整个国府"兵败如山倒"，全面崩溃了。

大陆解放前夕，李干军原是不打算去台湾的，就留在广西，但他的长子这时已经是国民党空军军官，蒋介石的计划是把军人精英带到台湾去，因为台湾作为一个岛便于防守。上面说军官可以携家眷。于是在乌云密布的一天，他的长子亲驾飞机接一家老小飞往台湾，飞机沿海面低空飞行，操作难度相当大，但人心惶惶，也顾不上许多了。就这样，全家到了台湾。

李干军深知官场凶险，再加上自己与桂系的关系，所以他到台湾后决心不问政治。好在他是搞教育出身，过去间断地教过书，于是乎重操旧业教书去了。他是教会学校培养出来的，加上还留过学，英文功底很好，便在大学里教英文。从此一教20年，直到退休。

他常常对二儿子李华伟说,这是他人生中最轻松愉快的一段时光。晚年时候的父亲不仅喜欢给人谈经论道,而且在信仰上也有了大的转变。他完全脱离政界,皈依宗教,最后成了一个很虔诚的基督教徒。

李华伟一生都记得父亲对他说过的话,政治太黑暗,你将来无论如何都不要去干这个,最好是从事教育工作,作点学问或选择其他比较超脱的职业。许多年后,父亲的教诲仍然深深地影响着他。凡是与政治沾边的事他是能躲就躲,尽量少打交道。这也使他避免了许多麻烦,当然,或许也失掉了一些出人头地、升官发财的机会。

这里还有一个小插曲:前几年,美国国务院有人打电话给他说,"联合国图书馆馆长出缺,我们希望能推荐你出来担任馆长。"

李华伟大吃一惊,问:"你是谁?"对方告诉了自己名字。李华伟觉得似曾相识,但不记得哪里见过。

那人说:"你不记得——你的儿子是我的棒球队队员,我是教练,义务的。想起来了吗?"

李华伟仔细想了想,恍然大悟说,"噢,你是上校!"他说:"是,我就是。"李华伟问:"你到国务院来工作了?"

"上校"说,"我现在负责向美国国际机构推荐合适的人到联合国机构去工作,因为各国都有固定人选,他希望美国人多一点,能有影响力。过去联合国图书馆总部都是苏联人,现最后一个人任期已满,所以美国希望找一个自己人,但要有第三国家支持的。譬如像你,既是华裔又是美国人,同时还在亚洲做了那么久,我想是比较合适的。"

李华伟说:"你怎么知道我这么清楚?"

他说:"我清楚的不得了,我现在也不瞒你,我是中央情报局驻泰国负责人。"

原来儿子"棒球教练"竟是……李华伟大吃一惊。他万万没想到的是,1966年到1975年,正好是越战升级阶段,美国国内闹得凶,而他在泰国理工学院埋头教学,与越南挨得很近反倒没感觉。实际上美国的军事后援在泰国,军方空运基地也在那里。尽管李华伟工作在教育系统,跟他们几乎没打什么交道,却也难免被"盯"住。

"上校"说:"你在泰国工作,美国政府都有记录,我们每年都要做安全调查,你不知道,可是你的记录我这里全有,你回到美国我还有你的记录。要不我怎么会觉得你非常合适呢?"

李华伟一听出了点冷汗。他心想:"我幸亏没做什么坏事。"以后对人谈到此事还大笑道:"有一天我要用"资讯自由"的法案,去把我的资料调出来,去看看究竟有些什么东西。"不过经"上校"这么一提醒,倒把前前后后的事联系起来了:

在泰国,教授们都住在一个公寓里,那个公寓有联合国机构派出人员,有日本做生意的,也有美国人,意大利人,还有印度人。看门的门房就是个印度人。一天,李华伟正要出门——那个门房和他们一家处的很好——他悄悄告诉李华伟说:"刚才,有人向我来调查你的情况。他问你的生活情况,问了很多事情,问得很仔细,好像是美国政府什么单位的。"

李华伟觉得很奇怪。他想:"我是美国援外总署派来的,并没有什么政府色彩,没有什么机密工作。只是在图书馆做自己份内的事而已。"他把疑问向门房表露,门房却只能摇摇头,耸耸肩作了个莫名其妙的手势。于是这件事便成了他心中的一个解不开的迷,渐渐地,随着岁月流逝他差不多已经淡忘。谁知道冒出个"上校"来把"谜底"揭穿。他说:"每年我们要做一个安全调查,有的安全调查要求高一点,有的比较低。不过你的记录好极了。所以这次又选上你。"

李华伟说:"给我时间让我考虑一下吧。"他再三权衡,自己在俄亥俄大学已经做了很久,工作环境很好,各方面关系相处得不错。干事业的条件也不错,他不想轻易放弃。另外,他对联合国图书馆也很熟悉,知道里面很复杂,政治的因素非常强。他有熟人在联合国里面工作。李华伟博士就通过熟人打听了一下内情,知道他们待遇非常好,可是有些福利上并没有俄大好,算一下划不来,这是其一;第二个原因就是,自己本质还是个学者型的管理人,搅到派别斗争的漩涡里去,或是从父辈身上吸取的经验教训所致,不愿意从政。况且搞教育的人本质都比较清高。如果进了联合国机构,就代表了政府,难免给牵涉到这种情报机构去。

这么一想,他就说要跟夫人商量商量。玛丽也说不要去,认为"如果到了那样机构,你就变成了政治的一种工具,美国政府希望你去,他们认为你可靠,能为其做事,很有可能情报局第一个就把你吸收去了。那么你整个人生观及准则都要改变。"

另外从现实利益来讲,如很多国际机构一样,联合国的工作也是有任期的,隔几年就要轮换,大概4年一任,可以续任。

似乎为了打消李华伟的种种顾虑,"上校"一再保证说:"你没有问题,这个机构相当大,只要上任后,应该是长久的。当然他也不否认每次都要经过严格的审察。"

考虑再三,李华伟还是决定推辞这个跳槽机会。过了几天,他给"上校"打电话,表明了选择。

2. 历经磨砺　冶炼成才

1933年1月25日,在广东新会——李家二儿子呱呱落地,这孩子一出世显得特别气足。李干军望着妻子怀里的新生婴儿,欣喜而感慨,期望儿子将来有出息,像自己一样不作庸庸碌碌之辈,他沉吟片刻,提笔写下"华伟"二字。

在李华伟孩提时代,父亲给他最大的影响就是为人正派、秉公认真。他严宽并济,在家庭中的威信亦很高,孩子们多少都有一点怕他。只要有他在,小哥俩地喧哗都要轻一些。李华伟小时候挺调皮,不免要挨父亲的骂,有时还被打手心,但他从没有感觉过分。他从那双期待的目光中逐渐体会到了一个父亲对子女的关爱。

自然地,因为母亲和他们在一起时间比较多的缘故,孩子们要和她更接近一些。母亲王晓辉出生于书香门第,她还有一个哥哥、一个妹妹也都受到很好的教育。(姨妈在美国伊利利诺大学拿到图书馆学位。从来没有回去,就在匹兹堡大学图书馆做部门主任。李华伟后来进入图书馆界,她非常高兴,认为是受了她的影响。)王晓晖早年则毕业于华南女子文理学院。为人秀外慧中,温柔淡雅。母亲给予他们的最好的影响是——待人真诚,和邻居们关系相处融洽。正因为母亲慈祥、富有牺牲精神、全心爱着孩子们、李华伟感觉与母亲更贴近些。而父亲则很少与外人交谈。他做新会县县长时,李华伟尚小。抗战前还有一段好日子,但之后就东奔西走逃难、调工作,日子很艰难,很清苦。

李华伟开始独立生活得很早,从少年到青年时代都在战乱和动荡中,独自求学亦很少和家人在一起,许多事还是留美回台探亲才知道的。母亲见他回家常常高兴地忙前忙后,真是不知怎样才好。有时母亲在厨房为他烧几个好菜,他就帮着打下手,陪母亲说说话,回忆回忆往事。他说他不记得自己去过福州老家,他那时太小了,什么印象也没有。然而老家的人却记得他……说他两岁曾经来过这里,他的叔叔还带他到处游玩。

半个多世纪以后,已双鬓染霜的李华伟仍深深怀念自己童年时代度过的一段快乐的时光。那时,父亲在忙于公务还能偕眷携子去公园拍两张照片,有小哥俩捉迷藏的,有母亲搂着小儿女微笑的，尤见其乐融融。

小华伟还与比他大几岁的哥哥一起跟着父亲的卫兵，悄悄跑到广西的山野里去打老虎。那会儿，他们头上戴着灯，一发现老虎后就突然打开，让强光把老虎照傻，等老虎的眼睛也发出光亮，再开枪击中老虎，这时还不能马上跑过去看，怕受伤的老虎更凶猛；要等到第二天再顺着老虎流血的痕迹去找，然后几个人把这个垂死的，或者已死的庞然大物拖回家，剥皮、剔肉、烧烤，饱餐一顿。小华伟一开始真是怕得不得了，因为他们夜间常常在那片鬼火荧荧的坟地或密林里穿行和躲藏，小华伟心里直打颤，不知道会发生什么事。但随着打猎次数增多，他的胆子也慢慢变得大起来。他记得他还吃了不少老虎肉呢！

也许是父辈们的影响，也许是少年生活的磨难，或者还有其他因素铸成，李华伟能够日后在旅美华人中崛起而成为佼佼者，的确经历了一个痛苦漫长的过程。

3. 战乱往事　不堪回首

抗日战争以前他在南京度过幼年的岁月。1937年日军入侵，国土不断地沦丧，人民不断地沦亡，神州变成人间地狱，惨绝人寰。凡是在那个年代出生的人，都无可避免地与无数中国人一道经历了那段悲壮惨痛的历史。中国军民以血肉之躯奋起抗战，艰苦绝伦。日寇铁蹄踏至腹地，南京等地相继沦陷……

李华伟一家也开始逃难，从南京辗转到桂林，一路上颠沛流离，经历艰难困苦。好容易到了广西，刚刚稍微安定一点，日本鬼子又打过来，飞机天天轰炸，搞得人心惶惶。空袭警报一响，老百姓便携儿带女四下逃生。

广西有很多山洞可以藏身，只要空袭警报一响，人们就纷纷躲到山洞里。等轰炸过后出来，才发现洞口有不少人被炸死了，血肉模糊，尸体遍地，实在惨不忍睹。小华伟被大人牵着往洞口走，一不留神就踩着软软的尸体，情景极为恐怖。

老百姓经常是早上起来带干粮到郊外躲难，夜晚回去，一看房子都烧光了，已成断垣残壁的一片废墟。路边常常有衣衫褴褛的人在为亲人的惨遭不幸和家园的丧失而哀号。

战争的残酷在李华伟幼小的心灵刻下了深深的烙印。

李华伟说，当时父亲并不是什么大官，只是一个中级的公务人员，非常辛苦。他担任广西省训练团的教务长，这是专门为培训地方县级干部的机构。由于情势紧张，父亲没有办法照顾家人，只能由随从人员带家人过境。他们从广西桂林到南宁、柳州，然后又到龙州，后又过境到镇南关——一根扁担两个筐，挑着小华伟和弟弟，而母亲怀着身孕，拖着几个幼小的儿女风餐露宿、一路颠簸逃到了越南，在苦难中挣扎，数月后生下华伟最小的妹妹华宙，暂居在越南河内附近的地方——海防，在那儿住了一年多。就这样，一个母亲带着五男二女，尽管日子过得紧紧巴巴，但华伟的兄弟姐妹七个总算是活下来了。

那年对日抗战方酣，许多有血性的中华男儿，选择了他们认为消除"国仇家恨"最有效最直接的路——从军，李华伟的哥哥也不例外，书未读完就考取了空军军官学校。从"李华星"改名为"李瞖"。"瞖"取义字经书，即不怕死的意思。表明时刻准备用自己的年轻生命与日本鬼子血战到底的决心（见其在印度受训的照片，年轻的李瞖，是那么的意气风发，身后的大门题着谁的墨宝——"贪生怕死莫入此门，升官发财请走别道"）。学员们先在昆明后到印度再到美国受训。等到受训完成回国，抗战已经胜利了。当时他被调到东北驻防，接着内战开始了。他亦卷入其中，留下一段悲剧性的结局……

1945年抗战胜利后，李华伟回到南京进入南京一中，完成了初中的学业。他依稀还记得抗战胜利时，国民党政府从重庆回到南京的一些情景。

当时还有日本军人没有撤退完。那些兵在码头上走来走去，等待遣返。那天下着大雨，那些兵排着队，小孩子们看见就朝他们扔石头。他们低着头不理，使劲踢他们也不动。过往的百姓有高声怒骂的、有冲过去打的……可想而知人人那个恨哪！败兵们垂头丧气站在江边雨中，仿佛成了一具具僵尸，早已麻木。

饱经战乱之苦的少年华伟，似乎显得比同龄人成熟。他忽然沉思般地对同学说：这帮家伙不过是日本天皇的战争工具，是军国主义的牺牲品，而真正犯下滔天大罪的，是那些制定战争计划的杀人恶魔。

李华伟是一个个性相当强的人。他的强不在表面，而是在骨子里。在师大念书时他就喜欢抱打不平，曾经与一位同学干了一架。当时班上有个男生非常霸道，一贯欺负弱小。同学们恨他，但总是敢怒不敢言。李华伟那天实在忍耐不住，忽地站出来，慷慨激昂指责他不应该欺负别人。

谁料那人根本没有把身板儿瘦瘦的李华伟放在眼里。一家伙操起墨水瓶向他砸过来，墨水洒了一身。李华伟愤怒地一拳出去，揍得那人呲牙咧嘴，顿时门牙缺了。李华伟的手也划破一个口子，鲜血直流。

有生以来这是他唯一的一次打架事件。他理直气壮，兴奋而紧张。

然而校方才不管他们是为什么打架，君子动口不动手，动手就是错。不管原由、不分青红皂白地责罚他，还要他赔偿医药费，并给予处分。

要赔钱，他上哪去找这笔钱呢？要知道当时台湾很穷，许多人就是为缓解家庭经济拮据才报考师范学院。他当然不愿意告诉家人，让辛苦一生的父母背包袱。可是违反校规就得受罚，否则会面临更严重的后果——这真叫他为难了。

可是班上大多数同学们却欣赏、钦佩他，为他的勇气叫好。这个给五块那个凑十块的，鼎力相助。他自己也利用家教所得，凑齐了医药费。

刚刚从内战中过来的台湾岛仍然处在高度紧张状态。一直搞备战，无论是谁，每个大学生都要参加军训，毕业后还要接受预备军官训练。几乎等于"全民皆兵"。

1954年，李华伟大学本科毕业，前后在"陆军军官"及"政工部学校"接受了一年的预备军官训练。他在一年军训时，头半年是入伍训练，很难，一点时间都没有。后半年是专长训练，根据每个人不同的情况分到不同的兵种。因为他是学教育的，又善于搞学生活动，就把他派到"政工干部学校"去。他整天就是上课，接受思想教育，譬如三民主义呀、五权宪法呀等等。上课时他就把复习要看的书摆在下面，老师台上讲政治，他在下面拼命看自己的专业书。他只能充分抓紧每一分钟时间，去全力拼搏、去抓住命运的手——

他将面临着四个考试：留学考试、就业考试、教育行政公务员资格高等考试和研究所考试。院长录取了李华伟，给了他读研究生的机会。但没过多久美国匹兹堡大学也给他发来录取通知书。他当然毫不犹豫作了去国外读书的选择。而对院长的器重也心怀感激，多少年不忘。每次回国还专程去拜访看望老院长。

院长望着已经功成名就的李华伟博士点点头，乐呵呵地说："啊哈，知道你去国外喝洋墨水了，也好，听说更严？"

李华伟很谦虚地说："也不一定，只因为我语言不好，在别人轻而易举的事，我就费了不少力、吃了不少苦。"

李华伟记得中学高三的英文老师学问还可以，但发音不行，以致后来他到美国很久还改不过来，老是错误发音，要纠正还很困难。而且感到以往教学法陈旧，中翻英，英翻中；背单词，记文法；然而听和讲都不行，一到美国就成了聋子哑巴的"半残疾人"。哎，那时真苦！

所以军训的唯一的好处是，给了他半年温习功课的时间，使他抓住了机会奋力一搏。1957 年，李华伟获得美国匹兹堡大学的入学许可及奖学金，在九月一日动身赴美进修。

第二篇　求学之路

路漫漫其修远兮　吾将上下而求索

1. 体验打工　甜酸苦辣

母体文化与客体文化差异所带来的，是情趣盎然、啼笑皆非的插曲；是兼收并蓄、适者生存的经典著作。痛苦与欢乐从来就是孪生姐妹。人生在世入乡随俗，矛盾的产生和解决都是自身力量潜能的最好的证明。

在匹兹堡大学研究所的第一课，李华伟心里没底，不敢坐在前面，就在最后一排悄悄找了个位子坐下来。就在教授将要进教室时，一位披着金黄色长头发的女生匆匆进门，也坐在后排，正好就坐在李华伟旁边，这个时候大概谁都没想到是命运的安排吧。

许多留学生都有这个体会，头几回听课，只听老师在上面叽里呱啦，犹如听天书，那滋味够呛。对于听力基础稍差的学生就更不知所云。虽然李华伟是个性子比较急、内心也比较好强的人，到这时，也真正感到精神上的压力了。

下了课，教授有意走到李华伟身边，和颜悦色地问道：“我讲的课你听得懂吗？”李华伟老老实实地回答：“你讲的内容我大致知道，但确实听不懂。”教授看了看他的课堂笔记，居然都是用中文写的，便摇摇头说这样不行。又向坐在李华伟旁边的金发女生说道：“密斯玛丽，这位密斯特李大概需要你帮忙，你可不可以帮他？”玛丽很美丽的一笑，说："当然可以。"

"当然可以，"李华伟听到旁边女生答应的如此爽快，心里一喜，不禁大着胆多看了她两眼。这是一个生得十分秀美的西方女子，她不仅有着飘然如瀑布般的金发，而且，皮肤非常嫩白透明，几乎都能看得见纤细的蓝色血管的纹路。高高的鼻梁、深深的眼窝，虽然戴着眼镜，但神采仍时时从一双绿色的大眼睛里映出来。玛丽被这位中国小伙子看得有点不好意思了，又是嫣然一笑。然后她就主动把自己上课记得很详细的笔记借给了他。

那时，李华伟的生活非常紧张，每天只能睡三四个小时，需要看的专业书和其他参考书堆积如山，加上英语程度的限制，要大量地查字典，根本看不完。只有少睡觉——有时真恨不得效法古人"头悬梁、锥刺股"的精神来对付没完没了的作业和应接不暇的考试。

李华伟因自小生活在战乱中，再加上长年累月孤身在外，特别能吃苦的性格业已磨炼出来。他总是在最艰难的时候想想抗战时期，就能咬牙挺住。最要命的是吃饭。一开始李华伟的生活费是由教会资助的，但并不固定，时有时无，再加上他自尊心又强，不愿意多向人开口。有相当一段时间，经济上、学业上的压力把这个初到异国他乡的年轻人压得够呛，最倒霉的是，他出国前，住处被小偷光顾，箱子被人提走，眨眼之间，除了身上穿的，几乎一无所有。那小偷不仅偷光了他的衣物，甚至连他父亲赠给他的大衣都毫不留情地顺手牵了羊，他当时浑身冷汗，简直快气晕了。

进入秋季，位于美国中东部的匹兹堡，比台湾气温显然要低得多，尤其是早晚，风吹得人身上一阵阵发寒，他本来人就瘦，没有大衣，更加弱不禁风。下课了，他饥肠辘辘又心情沮丧地走在回去的路上，已经有一个多月没见到牧师，听说是生病了。自己好几天没吃饱肚子，仅仅靠一点洋面包胡乱对付。身上连一分钱都没有，怎么办呢？他觉得应该去打工，最起码要解决温饱问题。当然，那也不是容易的事……

突然，他发现眼前有什么东西一闪：美元，而且还是一张 10 美元的绿色钞票。他以为是自己看花了眼，莫非是饥饿导致的？忙揉揉眼睛再看，的确没错，就是 10 美元！哇——对他来说真是"久旱恰遇及时雨"，他高兴极了，自语道："这就叫做天无绝人之路啊！"当时的 10 美元简直是一笔大款，相当于现在的 100 美元，他立马用这"上天"给他的美元去买了一些吃的，煮了一大锅面，美美地饱餐一顿，总算继续维持了一段日子。

在他匹兹堡的住处，小窗上经常咕咕叫着停着许多野鸽子，大概它们从未遇到过危险，所以神态安详，旁若无人地嬉戏。听它们咕咕咕叫，看着它们悠然的样子，他不由得想起抗战时期，也是因为饥饿难忍，几个小伙伴约着去打麻雀，一打就是一大串，然后架起篝火烧烤，那味儿真香啊！在美国想起这些往事真是别有一番滋味在心头。好几次他肚子咕咕咕叫，下课回去路上都在想："真想把它们打下来，做一餐美味呀！"但他咽了咽口水，终于还是克制了自己，没有这么做。

在匹兹堡大学第一年，他和另一男生共住一间房。楼里其他人都是美国匹兹堡大学足球队队员，他们吃香喝辣，出尽风头，女孩子都追得挺欢。尤其是他们的生活方式颠三倒四，与台湾来的穷学生大不一样。李华伟歇息了他们还在外面胡闹，而等到他们睡觉时李早已起来。特别是周末晚上，有女孩打电话来找足球健将，那些男生早就跑光了，只有李华伟在用功，电话一响都是他接。

女孩子问："你是足球队员吗？"

李说："不是，我是学生。"

"噢，那你是真不错！"女孩子说，"我请你约会行吗？"

李华伟哭笑不得。不过，这样也促使他第一年就把美国足球搞清楚了，因为那些队员也送票给他，请他去观看比赛。但宿舍总感觉很杂乱，生活极不规律的球队队员们闹哄哄的。以后，李华伟还是想办法搬到另一个地方去了。

为解决生活费的问题，他在美国的第一个暑假是在教会的一个夏令营度过。在那里他除了在餐厅工作之外，还参加唱诗班等活动，体会了打工的滋味。

第二年开始，他又在图书馆打工，从最基础做起：在书库上架书籍。他慢慢走上了经济上的自立，也逐步开始了与女同学玛丽的浪漫交往。

2. **异国之恋　振翅双飞**

爱情的浪漫给他带来羽翼，带着年轻的心翱翔在自由自在的世界。

世界上的大学里最高建筑是 43 层莫斯科大学，匹兹堡大学 42 层。图书馆就在 4、5、6 层，教育学院位于 26、27、28 层。李华伟每上完课或是打工间隙就到一层休息餐厅去喝点咖啡吃点东西，歇一歇，喘口气。李华伟去了好几次，都看见玛丽在那儿独自看书（这个形象已深深刻进他脑海。直到今天，玛丽仍喜欢捧一本书，躺在沙发上静静地阅读半天，她的精神世界丰富而深邃，而李华伟是扎扎实实踏在现实中的。但这并不妨碍他们相濡以沫走过人生）。

李华伟就走过去和她聊聊天。他心里有几分惊讶：怎么别的女孩都去交朋友去散心，她没有，还这么用功——这是怎样的一个美国女孩呢？李华伟走近她，问道："可以吗？"玛丽抬起脸，那覆盖长睫毛的绿色大眼睛在笑，轻轻颔首："请"。他一坐下来就聊开了，且越聊越有劲。

玛丽很坦率，告诉李自己是有男朋友的，不过他似乎很忙，也不常见（反倒是李华伟和玛丽见面更多一些）。看得出男朋友对她不大好，她少不了会抱怨几句，李华伟还帮助她分析,去怎么对付。

交流当然是用英语,李华伟的英语生硬一点,有时感到词不达意他也不怕。他说:"美国这个社会就是这样,比英国好。在英国规范用语,稍不好便可能被取笑。可是在美国只要你能表达,不要怕就行。我这人就是不怕,慢慢地讲,人家给你纠正纠正,慢慢就讲好了。"起初,李华伟由于口语不行,人家跟他讲一大串,他只会说"Yes""No",以至于后来玛丽一开玩笑就称他为"Yes,No"先生。其实,自从与玛丽交往后,他的口语提高得很快,常常令玛丽刮目相看。

他知道既然都要经过这个过程,就得多念书,因为有很多生词在书里。头一年里,他翻破了两三本字典,每一个字都要弄清楚。要看的书太多,时间太紧,所以觉睡得很少。后来他学到了诀窍,知道教授指定的书是看不完的,只看主要的书而且专挑重点章节看。很多书是大同小异,把要领掌握住就能够考出好成绩。况且他又遇到玛丽这么好的同学加英语老师。玛丽的笔记做得整洁,李华伟就借来抄下;有时他做作业,玛丽还帮他作语法修改。可特别让她吃惊的是,李华伟反而每次考试成绩居然还考得比她好。她开始怎么也不能明白是怎么一回事,生气地说:"这怎么可能呢?老师是不是搞错了?"李华伟笑嘻嘻说:"没错,教育学本来就是我的老本行嘛!"

事实上也是这样,在台湾,李华伟本身就是学教育的(包括教育哲学、教育心理学、教育历史、教育法和教育统计学等课程),基础打得不错。唯一的区别是:在台湾学的是中国教育历史,也学西方教育史,不过没有那么深。到美国后,他加大西方哲学的阅读量;教育心理学自然也比台湾学得深多了;还有的观点和研究比较新,对他更新知识结构颇有作用。虽然一开始他英文不够熟练,但专业内容还可以掌握,知道哪本书是重点,抓重点挑着看,效率很高。中国人一向以聪明勤奋著称于世,能够考出国的更是"人尖子"。再加上李华伟从小养成的好习惯:作业认真,字迹整整齐齐的,每篇作业都肯下功夫,尽力做到自己最满意的程度。教授们都喜欢这样的学生,觉得比美国人要强。以至今天去大陆演讲仍是那么一丝不苟,每次都要提早把重点概念、主要章节、段落都做成投影片,让听者一目了然,方便笔记,便于理解消化。所以李华伟的成绩能够遥遥领先,也就毫不奇怪了。

玛丽忍不住被这个聪明的中国男同学逗得哑然失笑了。他以其素有的禀赋才干赢得了玛丽的芳心。

3. 家园何处　处处家园

第一次,李华伟要想吻她,她说"No"。并举起纤细的手轻轻做了一个拒绝的手势。

你猜他说什么?他本来想说"我不喜欢这个字",却说成了"我不喜欢这个世界"。因为英文这个"word"(字)跟"world"(世界)发音很相似。事后玛丽大笑道:"当时想,噢,他真是怪可怜的,多么悲观!居然不喜欢这个世界了。"玛丽现在一想起这些因为语言不通所产生的误会,就忍不住发笑。她觉得他们虽然不像电影小说里的爱情那么罗曼蒂克,但也充满了温馨,充满了各种甜酸苦辣的小插曲。

他们天天在一起,习惯成自然。哪天不看见,都会觉得缺了什么。玛丽在感恩节时带李华伟到家里,发现他对很多东西过敏,不能吃,于是只好另外给他做。早上吃米饭,中午吃米饭,晚上还是吃米饭。她第一次带华伟是到乡下哥哥家里,她主人一样殷勤地招待他。尽量让他感觉自然放松和舒适。那里是一片田园风光,屋前屋后有幽静的树林和清凉的河水,有连绵起伏的山坡和肥沃平整的草场,风景美极了,像是有谁在渲染一幅色彩斑斓、深浅浓淡不一的水彩画。在这片风光中,她感觉到对方的心跳和激荡的热血,感到一阵阵涌动的激情，感到自己是真正地爱上了他。

即便在教会的夏令营，他俩的热线电话联系亦很频繁。男同学们纷纷对他打趣说："密斯特李有很多的电话，哇——都是一个美国女孩子打来的。"

教会的夏令营是在威斯康辛州，那地方风景非常好，牧师们在那里进行传教活动。他们请了四五十个学生帮忙。作为研究生，李华伟年龄显得比其他人大一点。他什么活都干，包括在餐厅洗碗、参加合唱团、做礼拜，还有话剧表演，等等，各种各样的工作，使他从早到晚忙个不停。

玛丽几乎每天要给她的华伟打长途电话，十分温馨体贴。惹得大家都开李华伟的玩笑，毕业做纪念册时，给他的临别语是——"电话最多的一个"。李华伟后来挺得意："是玛丽追求我。"有人调侃道："恐怕是你先把人家追到手，然后又让人家追你吧？"他只好笑道："对，对。"

"看来这位东方小伙子还是挺有心计的嘛！"玛丽事后也悟出来了。等悟出来，她和他已无法分离。

草长莺飞，万木吐蕊。时间过得真快，在美国，一转眼就过了快两年。李华伟和玛丽的婚期定在1959年3月14日，当时他俩还在读书，时间较紧，匆匆忙忙就利用春假举办了婚礼。三个月后双双取得了硕士学位。

第三篇　初出茅庐

1. 命运转折　全力冲刺

如果说他们俩相遇是一次命运的相互改变的话，那么，与图书馆女馆长打交道，对李华伟来说，则意味着一次人生的转折——

在匹兹堡一共七年，读了三个学位。除一面攻读及研究外，还在匹兹堡大学图书馆勤工俭学。李华伟在图书馆打工一开始是在书库里上架，那几个月他干得不错，部门头儿就把他调出来，在一楼专门开辟一个本科生专用图书馆，精选近10万册书刊，就让他管理。他那时没有图书馆学位，只是个研究生，除了上课之余，他就到那个阅览室打工，按小时计。

那时候馆长权力相当大，说要雇佣谁就是谁，说炒谁没人敢说个"不"字。况且这个馆长又是个独生老太太，在图书馆干了很多年头，对人很严格，甚至都有点儿严厉，几乎人人都怕她。一天，他正在书库上架，突然听到扩音器里传来通知："李华伟，请马上到馆长办公室来一下。"听到这个通知他也吓一跳，"馆长为什么要找自己？我干错了什么事吗？"他心里直打鼓，七上八下，不知道要发生什么事，但他还是不得不硬着头皮进了馆长办公室。女馆长正在等他。看见李华伟进门，竟露出平时难得一见的笑容，还扶着他的肩膀说："请坐，请坐。"立马解除了李华伟的紧张情绪。馆长说："我听不少人反映你很不错，聪明能干，工作非常认真，现在我馆有一个正式职位你愿意申请吗？"

李华伟喜出望外，忙说："愿意，我当然愿意。"馆长说他们馆准备设立一个亚洲研究中心，需要一个能够懂得中文的馆员来进行选购、编目工作，他们觉得李华伟不错，打算培养他做训练馆员，接着又对他提了一个要求，希望他半工半读再拿一个图书馆硕士的学位，学费由馆里支付。他也一口应允下来。因为他的教育硕士学位已经拿到，刚读博士，同时也可以读图书馆硕士学位，况且他已经与玛丽结婚，正需要经济支援和稳定的工作，女馆长的赏识给了他升迁的机会，他怎么能不高兴呢？那一段生活真是忙碌而充实。当时李华伟不仅读书辛苦，而且还是全职工作。人家不愿意晚上工作、周末工作——他全都包下来。他所有闲置时间几乎全泡在图书馆，他觉得自己运气挺不错，特别是一年后他就转为正式馆员并去读图书馆学位了。再以后他的命运就是"三年跳一个台阶"步步高升，从副主任升主任，从副馆长升馆长，而且是第一个华人馆长！别说很多中国人没有他这样的机会，就连一些美国人也没遇到他这样好的机会，而他，凭的是什么呢？后来有不少华人都希望从他的成功中吸取一些经验，找到一些诀窍。成功的经验是多方面的。说的简明一点，就是他的执着，他的韧性，他那相容了东方式的柔中有刚、外圆内方的性情。人际关系是一个重要因素，虽然那时他觉得自己还没有磨练到炉火纯青的地步。但作为一个中国人，基本是做人态度是比较好的，待人诚恳。除此之外，还有一个更重要的原因，就是他做事认真，富于主动精神，非常有责任感。这是所有行政主管都很看重的良好品格。

另一个原因是他的专业准备非常好。拥有教育硕士、图书馆学硕士及哲学博士的学位，再加上当时机会很多，正赶上美国教育大发展，扩建学校、扩建图书馆，各个学校都急需高层次的专业人才。爱丁堡州立学院，要改成州立大学，规定一定要有多少教工是博士学位，可是那时州立学院有博士学位的不到20%。于是他的指导教授就作了推荐。推荐信写明了他刚刚拿到学位又有实际工作的经验。既有博士学位，又有两个硕士学位，同时图书馆的经验又很丰富，校长一看正中下怀，马上就聘了李华伟博士，并给他的薪水又加了一倍。在匹兹堡大学时候，他月薪不到3千元，到都肯大学是6千元，到爱丁堡学院9千元，还是几十年以前的薪水，相当可观。在那个期间李华伟还兼图书馆学系主任，他那时才33岁左右！

"我觉得美国人有种族歧视，是无形中的，在北方较好一点。美国人都会对来做他们领导的外国人表示怀疑，毕竟你母语不是英语，说起来也不怎么流畅，所以总抱观望态度，你要使他们对你有信心，第一步就是要做出成就来。他们要求很高，你做的跟美国人一样还不够，一定要做得比他们好得多，人家才能接受，他们一旦接受了你那就没有问题，那就没有种族歧视，一视同仁了。所以每到一个新地方，要把这个突破，让人家很快对你有信心。"

他那时真觉得很困难，英文表达不够好，沟通能力差，跟美国人没有办法接近。所以总是要想用别的方式来弥补缺陷。他说，"我们华人做馆长，怎么样发挥你的优点，怎么样想办法用长处来弥补缺点，使得你的优点让大家看见并慢慢把缺点压住，隐瞒住。我当初作馆长时，也是经过了这样一个很痛苦的过程，并不是说得到这个职位就什么都来了。最初两三年，美国人还是有这个观念，外国人来领导我们，你究竟有多大的本领？看看你的本领怎么样？你要是做得没有他们好的话，他早就把你轰下去了，所以要能够压住他们，真要做得使他们服贴。经过三年后，情况大不一样。美国人这点很好，一旦服气了，他就完全支持你。"李华伟对此深有体会。

2. 朋友绝命　诗才陨落

初到异邦，谁都免不了要全力以赴，在各种角色的矛盾中力求平衡。感受中西文化的碰撞、相容与互补，体会在新的土地上落脚之不易，开始阶段的跌跌撞撞、漂泊不定，磨炼过五关斩六将、百折不挠的恒心及毅力。考试人生，磨炼人生，对正在美国奋斗的年轻人来说，毕竟生活在浓厚的西方文化氛围之中，唯有容纳其思想价值观念和知识体系，方能立于不败之地。

1967年的秋天，在李华伟的生活圈子中发生一桩令人震惊的事：他的最要好的朋友陈慧自杀了（二十多年后，他周围也有个熟人因为精神压力而自杀）。这个事件对李华伟的震动是很大的,要知道,他们是从最青春年少、最真挚的年华开始的友谊,说来,李华伟在学校一直喜欢组织参与社会活动,在同学们中颇得人缘。从他大量的青少年时期的照片中可以看到他性情合群,并且也相当活跃。唯一一张与男同学单独合影的就是陈慧。照片上,他和陈慧并头仰卧在青青的草地上,面向蓝天舒展纯净的笑容,踌躇满志的样子。虽然他们所学的专业不同,但彼此欣赏,相互信赖,情同手足。后来李华伟赴美求学,天各一方,仍保持着频繁的书信往来。

1963年,李华伟已经拿到学位、找到工作并结婚生子,生活趋于安定,老朋友陈慧才从台湾动身赴美,开始了坎坷的奋斗里程。陈慧原本是学中文的,才华横溢。可惜英语不怎么好,在美国求学感到十分困难,再加上经济压力,非常苦恼,经常与李华伟通信倾谈。一次,他忽然来信说有人偷他的笔记本,有人要陷害他,疑神疑鬼。李华伟觉察到他有类似精神分裂的前兆,就劝告他说,如果学习压力实在太重受不了,就该考虑先回台湾休养休养身体,以他的条件,找个中学教教书是不成问题的;再不然,亦可以考虑先打工一段时间,既可以练习一下英语,又可以有点钱应付生活。

然而,像大多数出国的年轻人一样,他没有急流勇退回台湾,却跑到纽约打工去了。在餐馆洗盘子,受尽老板的呵斥;到外面送匹萨饼,一路跌跌撞撞;尽管赚得几个钱,日子却过得并不舒心。然而最让他痛苦的,是在台湾的女朋友琵琶别抱,又跟别人结了婚。陈慧素来心高气傲,睥睨一切,结果却在现实中接连碰壁,对其自尊心、自信心是个极大的挫伤。于是,他情绪倏然起伏,极不稳定。苦闷中他拼命写诗,宣泄情怀,咏叹一番。然后就寄给自己要好的朋友。李华伟收到诗信后,常常很为其担忧,不断的写信给他以安慰、打气、加油,希望他振作起来,开拓自己的新领域。可是,没想到他的心境最后突然急转直下,终于走上了自杀一途。

自杀前一年,即1966年的秋天,他又寄来两首诗,他的诗是这样写的——

(一) 无题

大好阳光滚滚尘沙,
人生能有几回任性的豪赌,
输定年华,挫钝多少棱骨?!

偶捡得,几粒参悟,一叶悲壮,
敏感如含羞草,亦恒介乎,
坚忍与麻木。

匆匆,为赶路,也为和
时间赛跑,
尘沙滚滚中,路路都如旋螺。

正午已过,阳光大好。

一年后的秋天,11月6日上午10时左右,在纽约洛克菲勒中心的RAC大厦第四十五层楼上,他从容地把鞋子脱下,抬手最后一次梳理了一下纷乱的头发,吟哦着自己用血写的诗,然后,从一间办公室敞开的窗户纵身一跃,像一片树叶,轻轻飞了出去……

（二）写在时间如漩之夜

过去未来，如风吹落叶，
在这没有秋季的秋夜，
飘荡的如雪，翻卷的飞沙走石。

台北，新加坡，愈来愈远了，
时间真像流水；
故乡，童年，更是渺貌不可见，
极目望去，几如神话。

从广播电视上闻知、从亲友的电话中证实老朋友自杀的消息后，好多天来李华伟心情沉痛，昼夜难眠，他想起陈慧那天来电话语无伦次，情绪波动很大，曾经希望他去纽约一叙，当时他有实在脱不开身的难处，且想就是临时订票飞去救人也来不及，于是赶紧打电话请妹妹、妹夫去开导。他们火速赶到陈慧住处，敲门不开、喊又无人答应，一下子急了，报警找警员把门踹开——里面却空无一人。正狐疑间，陈慧从外面回来。原来他出去散心了，把妹妹、妹夫吓出一身冷汗。后来他们打电话告诉李华伟，说："没事了，我们把他接到家，包饺子给他吃，劝说了半天，看他情绪平稳了才送走。"李华伟说还是要多注意他，关心他的心理动向。妹妹妹夫答应说隔天再接他到家来，谁知他第二天竟走了绝路……

（三）

现在低陷，而复浮凸起来，在汪洋的时空大海，
我，赤足的鲁宾逊，奔逐于这汪洋的孤岛。
浩浩乎时空无涯，纵横聚散，
此古战场也，自有人类以来，
孤独如生，寂寞如死，
风从古老处吹来，往渺茫处吹去。

今夜，
记忆不寐，感情哭泣，意志愤怒，
我但仰卧风潮，不数萧瑟！

李华伟翻阅过去的书信和照片，脑子里像放电影，一点点地重播他们多年相处的日子……睹物思人，内心极不平静。于是奋笔疾书，写下悼文一篇投寄《联合》杂志（留美中国同学会联合会主办的季刊），并附上陈慧的遗作。既为老朋友的去世感到悲哀，又对杜绝此类现象提出建设性的意见，他写道："与陈慧曾在台湾师大同学四年，虽非同系，但彼此过往甚密，对其卓越才华与诗人禀赋，素表钦佩。在同学中，他以思想敏锐与情感丰富见称，是一位易受感情支配的人。……"从诗里我们可以看出他年来的处境与心情是相当苦涩的。但这并不仅是他一人的不幸遭遇；在留学生中，除了少数幸运儿之外，都多多少少受过若干折磨的滋味，能够艰苦奋斗有所成就者，究竟不多。"

他从自己和他人的经历中体会到，目前国内一般青年仍然抱有一种错误观念——以为只要能够来到美国，一切就有办法。因此，对自己的英文程度如何？经济状况怎样？以及应选择何种学科？生活能否适应等基本问题，事前毫不加以慎重考虑，结果，到了美国之后，处处碰壁，进退失据，痛苦难堪。而英文基础太差者，吃亏最大。事实上，很多美国

大学对外国学生的英文能力，不但不予从宽优待，反而格外苛求，对学文法学科者尤为严格。在此种情景之下，如果经济上再有问题，其惨况可以想见。接着，李华伟概括道："课业加打工，精疲力竭；卒子过河，有进无退；政府机构，请多照顾。"这些认识是他留美多年的真切感受，不知道究竟是否有警世作用。

3. 胸怀大家　情系中华

20世纪是一个充满了苦难、纷扰、动荡和急剧变化的世纪，国家和民族在这样的历史阶段中，无不饱经磨难与沧桑。生活在这个时期的人或多或少都会领略各种思潮的冲击、各个派别的较量，经受各种考验和洗礼。所幸的是，坚冰已经打破，道路正在开通。

对于李华伟来说，在横跨亚洲和北美，穿梭于东方与西方的半个多世纪中，亦在这大转折大变动中受到深刻影响。但是无论环境怎样变化，他的中国心始终不变，为整个中华民族的强盛贡献力量又是他孜孜不倦、无怨无悔的主旋律。

李华伟兄弟姐妹七人，除了哥哥英年早逝，其他都在各自的领域学有所成。李华伟压根儿就没想到，就在他远渡重洋奋力拼搏以不负家人期望之时，他的兄长却在从事一个危险的、家人所无法知情的特殊任务。

1959年5月29日午夜11时，天空乌云密布，细雨蒙蒙。广东恩平县的乡民多半已安寝，进入梦乡。突然，上空传来隆隆飞机声，由远而近，扰乱了夜的宁静。紧接着，一道火光，夹杂着嘭嘭的炮声，飞机抖动一下，顿时火光熊熊，一扇机门先掉下来，紧接着机身向西南县境俯冲，轰隆一声巨响，坠落在金鸡村旁边的大旺山上。

事后查明：这架被击落的飞机是隶属台湾空军34中队、编号为"815"的B—17侦察机，机队由飞行官李暋等14人组成，任务是深入到大陆西南一带进行侦察活动。34中队也称"蝙蝠"中队，队徽的上方是一只蝙蝠图，下方是七颗星星，意思是它像蝙蝠一样专门在夜间出动，主要是从事电子侦察。午夜11时10分，飞机行踪被广州的雷达站所发现。中国空军18师值班指挥员李宪一声令下，中尉蒋哲伦驾驶米格—17战斗机从佛山沙堤机场腾空而起，追踪到恩平上空迅速接近目标，他果断地按下炮钮，B—17机立刻中弹着火，这时，着火飞机冲入厚云层，蒋哲伦很担心它逃脱，就赶紧和地面联系，请求引导，终于见到一团火光在云层闪现，于是继续发射一阵机关炮，震天动地，"815"号机全身着火，映红了夜空，火球般地拖着浓烟坠落山谷……

80年代初期的中国，结束了"文革"噩梦，并确立了一切以经济建设为中心的工作重心。国门初开，人们睁大眼睛观望着异彩纷呈的外部世界，与此同时，远隔重洋的海外侨胞也以极大的热忱关注着故土的开放和发展。别离故乡数十载的海外游子，不能不为这沧桑巨变而百感交集。1982年，李华伟应聘为昆明一个情报中心管理培训班授课，这是中国科技情报所和加拿大国际发展研究中心合办的。当他把消息提前告诉了父亲，80多岁的老父激动地写信给儿子说："现今我们从台湾是无法去大陆的，你以美国公民的身份去反而比较方便。你到大陆一定想法子打听打听你哥哥的下落。如果他真的已不在人世，也要找到葬身之地，做个墓也是好的。"

"少小离家老大回，乡音未改鬓毛衰"。年近知天命的李华伟带着父亲的嘱托，回到阔别33年的祖国。第一次故乡行，他就有心托福建省社会科学院副院长、林则徐的后裔林子东打听情况（她的丈夫是福州市长）但没有成功。

自从李华伟博士第一次回国之后，结识了不少图书馆系统或学术界的人物。而他在国际图书馆界所享有的名望及成就也逐渐引起了高等学府的关注和兴趣，几乎每年都有不少院校邀请他回国讲学。每次踏上故国的热土，他都感到十分激动。

随着时间的推移，长期封冻的海峡两岸关系逐渐被民族统一的热潮所融化，人们通过探亲访问或经贸往来，过去多少年的积怨在化解，"相逢一笑泯恩仇"成为海峡两岸同胞的共同心声与真实写照。1987年两岸关系在急剧升温，台湾解除戒严后两个月，台湾《自立晚报》两位记者违反台湾有关禁令到大陆采访两周，成为两岸关系史上的大事。再后，台湾当局放宽来大陆政策，始有大批台胞有回大陆探亲的机会。接待台胞省亲一时成为祖国大陆有关部门新的任务。通过关系，李华伟家人终于和北京市政协全国统一工作组的张纯一副主任取得联系。张纯一是原国民党高级将领张治中的二公子，也是广东人。当他南下广东出差时，便向省政协转达了李华伟博士的愿望。

几经周折，终于在1992年12月11日，他们分别从台湾及美国两地结集起"815"号飞行员家属一行14人，从广州向恩平进发，到荆棘丛生、山势陡峭的金鸡山寻找亲人遗骨。一路上大家心情沉重，未知结果如何。好在抵达恩平后，受到有关官员的热情接待，问寒问暖，同胞备受感动。次晨即驱车行路前往坠机地点。那里是一座荒山，根本无路可走，只好请人开路而进。因为灌木杂草缠绕，很不好走，真是费了九牛二虎之力，才算寻到埋尸地点。当接近炭窑时，个个百感交集，几至不能自持。

然而，相距三十多个春秋，霜侵水蚀，是否还有完整的骨头呢？谁也不敢保证……终于，在亲属们的虔诚感召和农民的努力下，总算圆满达成海峡同胞"千里寻亲骨"的心愿。家属们把遗骨遗物捧在胸前，热泪盈眶，感慨万千。过去，李华伟每次回到祖国大陆，他父亲都要问问情况怎么样了，并非常关心大陆的一切。没想到时隔多年，待找到长兄飞机坠落地点时，二老早已仙逝作古。无怪有人感叹：留给后人的岂止是惆怅？

从这件事也反映了两岸之间关系在改善。几经周折、多方努力，终于促成了此事的圆满解决。了却了一桩心愿，也算告慰了在天之灵。家属事后纷纷撰文书写各自的心情和感受。傅依萍女士在《联合报》发表文章说："爸爸回来了，离他出门三十三年，是化成灰给捧回来的。我没有哭，只是感到欣慰。"

人们在思索：在中国这块丰饶而又灾难重重的土地上，有多少白骨是历史误会的牺牲品呢？我们活着的人，是否应该警惕，保证悲剧不再发生。李暋的侄儿李书超写道："身为一个中国人，今天在国际上仍要面对两岸的敏感局面。虽情势和多年前已有了大幅度的改善，两岸的百姓在私下也建立了良好的关系，但无人能够出面保证中国人自斗的悲剧从此结束。我诚心祈望诸位在天之灵，能够带引中国走向和平富强之道，还有他们的无谓牺牲，也能成为中国人从此后必须团结之警戒。"后代们都不希望再有同胞自相残杀的悲剧出现。李华伟博士感叹道："这是一个悲剧，但结果还算完满。"他以一个过来人的眼界和胸怀看待人生，看待历史的一切。在他的学术活动中，凡是有助于增进两岸同胞的情谊、有助于消除历史造成的隔阂、有利于祖国统一大业的事，他都不遗余力，尽心去做。作为一个身在异国他乡的炎黄子孙，他更牵挂着的是中华民族的崛起、是千千万万个同胞的苦乐，是有着悠久文化的东方古国的富强！

唯此，"穷则独善其身，达则兼济天下"，古代先哲的遗训始终未敢忘怀。这里，我很想补充一点，李先生在台湾大学时代曾经受到蒋氏父子的接见，留美后又曾经三次受到台湾"国建会"的邀请，商讨教育改革的大计。他用自己的专长、学术地位和影响力，在海外和海峡两岸穿梭奔波。原北京大学图书馆馆长庄守经先生说，"李馆长对海峡两岸图书馆界的交流合作十分关注；1988年和1989年间，他曾多次与我商议，拟筹备在美国或香港等地举办双方都能参加的学术研讨会，以打破两岸图书馆界长期封闭隔膜状态，连具体人员、地点、经费等都作了考虑。后因两岸解冻，可以直接交往了，这会议便没再举行。

但由于李馆长的介绍，使我对台湾学界的情况、包括一些专家教授都有印象，如原台湾"中央图书馆"馆长王振鹄教授，我们有一见如故之感，有很多共同的话题。"

4. 珠联璧合　水乳交融

鸟需要有窝，人岂能无家。家和万事兴。夫唱妇随和谐稳定的家庭是他事业有成的基本保证。在亚洲一住7年，5个孩子变成了6个，小姑娘变成了亭亭玉立的少女。在泰国，那些日本太太都羡慕玛丽找了个好丈夫。

李华伟第一次回台湾探望双亲，是来美留学七八年之后。他已拿到博士学位并有了固定的职务，可以说是衣锦还乡，并且已是儿女成群的人了。他到美国后与父亲通信比较多。父亲嘴里不说什么，心里还是很为这个儿子自豪的。因为他是李家第一个拿到博士学位的，不仅如此，他还尽力帮助兄弟姐妹都到了美国。

李华伟与玛丽的婚姻确实得到了老人坚定而有力的支持。当时，整个台湾的经济状况不怎么好，政治上也相当保守，父亲认为还是在国外更有发展前途。当儿子在美国结婚的时候，父母他们也在台湾请了亲朋好友，摆了两桌酒，热闹地庆贺一番。

李华伟升为爱丁堡大学副馆长后，曾经把父母接到美国探亲，同住了一年。玛丽非常孝顺，公婆喜欢这个洋媳妇，像待自己女儿一样，逢人便夸这个儿媳不错，虽然是金发碧眼的洋人，但她最招人疼也最疼人。玛丽与李华伟结婚时没有条件去台湾。不像现在台湾出来留学的学生，几个月就回去，经济条件好，不在乎几个路费钱。那时旅费很贵，李华伟的手头也不宽裕，想吃甜食没钱，现在有钱了又不能吃了。

三年之后他们到了泰国，途经台湾——玛丽才第一次带着5个孩子来到这个东方的宝岛！玛丽有一双绿色的眼睛，故喜欢选择绿色服饰来搭配。那时她很年轻，不喜欢老呆在某一个小地方，她要去大世界看看、走走。她说不一定非选择宗教，她也许想做教会的看护，后来又觉得这不是她所要的，自己并不真正适于作看护，所以她又到了教育系。当她第一次走出省界和国界来到外国，颇感紧张、兴奋和新鲜。不过，并非像她年轻时幻想的那样是以传教士身份，而是一个贤妻良母的身份！

初到台湾，她抱着孩子从飞机上下来，第一个感受就是：这地方什么东西都长锈了。台湾的潮湿使她大为吃惊，什么自行车啦、生活用具啦，都生锈了，连房顶也是锈迹斑斑。据说有的地方一年有200多天是雨季。他们去看了华伟年老的双亲。李华伟的父亲英文好，他们常常通信。玛丽还给他寄了日本式的尖尖的筷子。

在台北机场，他们一家相当引人注目。据说当时美国男人娶中国太太的多，但中国男人娶美国太太的还不多见。尤其是玛丽又长得很漂亮，金黄色的头发，长长的飘在身后，身材苗条，一双会说话的眼睛，笑起来很纯。孩子活泼可爱，个个都聪明漂亮，只要走在大街上，人们都会驻足观望，啧舌羡慕：好幸福的一家！李华伟觉得挺不好意思，生怕别人评头论足，他走得快快的，心里希望别人不要看他。

玛丽还记得一件趣事：他们全家几口回台湾时，小孩全都穿一样的衣服，因为担心机场人太多，容易走散，同样的衣服便于辨认。每当去海滩、车站、公园等人多的公共场合，她就给孩子们穿一样花色的衣服，免得她找不到他们。有一次在买东西时，东转西转，杰克忽然不见了，她心急得要命。那卖东西的人看见她身边的孩子都穿一样的衣服，就问她，"那边有一个也穿一样衣服的男孩，是不是你的孩子？"她赶紧说，"正是正是。"终于找到了杰克。

作为两个不同文化背景的一对男女结合，一个要多了解东方文化，一个要多了解西方文化，同时彼此也要接受对方，尽管观点不同，但仍然要调解。说起来很容易，做起来就难了。如果说，建立生活的家园已属不易，那么建立精神的家园则更为艰难复杂。作为海外的学子、游子及侨居在美的华人，即使是英文相当好，已入乡随俗，但东西方文化的差异，无论怎样也难以使他们离开祖国五千年的优秀传统和光辉灿烂的文化，更不待说那些语言不通的新移民和寂寞在家的老人。

在海外生活几十年，超过了在本土生活的时间，然而永难忘怀的是母语。他教妻儿学汉语，亦是一种文化认同，寻求心灵的归属感。比如当初家里特别请了泰国华人教中文，让玛丽和孩子一起学习。也许孩子太多、太小，她无法集中精力，再加上中文比较难学，后来就放弃了。那个老师也感到比较吃力，不过与玛丽和孩子相处得很好。李华伟只是觉得有些可惜。在泰国7年，老师至少教了4年，大一点的孩子都会一些基本会话。因为玛丽不说，孩子们也都没坚持下去。玛丽认为既然生活在西方，还是应该以西方文化为主。李华伟不同意这个观点。孩子在美国，在西方文化氛围下长大，自然应该多了解学习东方文化，对他们的成长发展有好处。但李华伟还是将就了妻子，因为自己工作忙，顾不上教孩子，孩子跟谁多自然就受谁的影响多了。

他的家毕竟与一般的美国家庭不同，他和玛丽毕竟给予了子女不同血缘的一半——这比什么都重要！孩子们成人之后，对此极为铭感。在一次父亲节和母亲节时，大女儿谢莉和女婿分别给父母一份珍贵的礼物：一本精心制作的相册，还有一封情真意切的信……

大儿子与小儿子也分别寄来贺卡……

二女儿帕姆长得最像东方人，她身上流淌着父亲的血液，继承了父辈倔强好胜、活跃乐观的秉赋与天性；喜欢旅行、擅长摄影艺术，尤其是她体育极佳，一直担任学校的棒球教练；并得到了印第安那大学的奖学金，在学业上继续深造……

1997年的耶诞节我和他们伉俪、6个儿女、几个孙子女，热热闹闹一大家子欢聚一堂，在品尝圣诞大餐时，我笑着给他们出了个题目：谈谈你们心目中的父亲，并举一两件印象最深刻的事情。二儿子说，他记得小时候父母带他们回台湾探亲，有一次在公园观猴子，正看得起劲，没提防那猴子忽然调皮，竟伸出毛爪，一把揪住他的头发不放，顿时把他吓坏了，而他爹地急得——他模仿他爹地当时的举动，手掌朝那猴子的头啪啪猛拍……一番维妙维肖的讲述，让大家听得前仰后合哈哈大笑。他们知道我是记者和作家，都不想"露怯"，说，待我们回去好好回忆一下，然后再写给你好吗？这，再好不过。我当然是没有什么意见喽！

（原载《美华文学》(*The Literati*)，1999年1-2月，第25期第24-43页。）

Modern Library Development in China:
An Interview with Dean Hwa-Wei Lee

Ron Chepesiuk

Dr. Hwa-Wei Lee, Dean of University Libraries and Professor of Education at Ohio University, has had a distinguished relationship with libraries in the People's Republic of China since 1982, 6the year the International Development Research Centre (IDRC) of Canada invited him to the country to lecture at a two-week seminar on "Management of Information Centers in China". Since then, Dr. Lee has been invited to China every year to teach and consult by various universities as well as the Chinese Academy of Sciences, the Ministry of Education, the National Library, and the Shenzhen Library. Sponsors have included the Chinese government, OCLC, Ohio University, UNDP, UNESCO, the United Board of Christian Higher Education in Asia, and the World Bank.

Besides giving lectures, organizing conferences, and advising on library management, Dr. Lee has brought some 150 Chinese librarians to Ohio University as part of an International Librarians Internship Program he established in 1979. His 1996 book, *Modern Library Management*, was written in Chinese and published in Taiwan, and it is currently being used by several library schools in China as a textbook.

Dr. Lee's long relationship with China has given him a unique perspective on that country's library development as it struggles to become what many experts believe will be the superpower of the twenty-first century.

What kind of role do libraries play in the country's development?

Historically, China always has had a very high regard for libraries, even though their missions and functions have gone through many changes over the times.

Throughout the twentieth century, even with the negative effects of successions of wars and periods of political instability, libraries in China have managed to grow, modernize, and play a key role in national development.

Despite inadequate funding, libraries of all levels and types have expanded rapidly since 1978 when China began major economic, educational, social, and political reforms.

The 1996 IFLA General Conference in Beijing demonstrated the Government's support of libraries. Mr. Li Peng, Premier of China at that time, spoke at the opening ceremony on the importance of libraries in national development in China. He also urged more cooperation and exchange of information among libraries of the world.

During my last trip to China in October 1998, I was received by two deputy ministers of the Ministry of Culture, who consulted with me in lengthy discussions as to the proper course of action in China's plan to launch a national digital library project.

Does the current Chinese leadership view libraries as important in its efforts to modernize the country?

The opening speech given by Premier Li Peng at the 1996 I FLA General Conference clearly pointed out the important role played by libraries in national development. He pledged the government's strong support to further library development as China strives to build a modern socialist country with an open-market economic system based on education, science, and technology.

Even though funding and human resources for libraries are still very limited, a great deal of development has taken place in China in recent years due to a greater recognition and support given by various levels of the Chinese government to libraries.

What has been the biggest change in Chinese library development since your association with China began?

Many significant changes have taken place in Chinese library development since the early 1980s. Most important of these was the rebuilding of libraries ruined by the Cultural Revolution. Because of a serious shortage of trained librarians, the number of library schools has grown from four before the Cultural Revolution to over fifty in 1998.

A large number of continuing education programs have also been developed during this period. Over the past twenty years, not only has the number of libraries of all kinds increased, but so has the size of library collections and the variety of services offered.

Many new library buildings have been built to replace small and out-moded facilities. Modern library concepts and practices have also been adopted, including the conversion by an increasing number of libraries from a close-stack system to an open-stack system. Noticeable progress also has been made in other areas.

Could you give some more examples?

These include the development of library standards in cataloging, subject headings, and classification; the compilation of a National Bibliography; the implementation of the cataloging in publication (CIP); the establishment of a national microfilming center; wide dispersion of library automation applications and networking; increasing numbers of professional publications; substantial efforts in library research; the rapid growth in Internet connectivity and use; and international cooperation.

What are some important issues facing the library profession in China?

Even though libraries are recognized as very important in national development, funding for libraries has been inadequate to meet the needs. Salaries for librarians and support staff are not attractive, and this has caused a serious brain-drain problem.

The high costs of publications, especially those from the West, increasingly place them beyond the reach of most Chinese libraries, and this contributes to a paucity of foreign information resources in Chinese libraries. The use of more sophisticated information technologies by libraries has also drained the limited library funding.

The concepts of library cooperation and resource sharing have been much discussed among Chinese librarians, but little has been done. Government intervention through funding and other incentives may be necessary to jump-start such efforts.

Disparities in economic development among different regions of China also have caused imbalances in library development. In Beijing, Shanghai, and Guangdong Province, for example, modern library facilities and services are readily available but not in poorer regions, especially those in the inland western provinces.

How important is the copyright issue to our colleagues in China?

Chinese libraries are very much aware of the copyright issue. Since 1990, the Chinese government has also promulgated a series of laws and regulations including the 1991 Copyright Law and the 1994 Regulations for the Punishment of Copyright Violators.

After China joined the Paris Universal Copyright Convention and the Berne Convention for the Protection of Literary and Artistic Works, a Regulation on the Implementation of International Copyright Agreement was issued in September 1992.

In July 1994, the State Council promulgated additional measures to protect the intellectual property rights. On September 29, 1994, the Supreme Court of China also issued a set of directives to lower courts to enforce the protection of intellectual property rights.

In my recent visits to China, I have been pleased to find that the previous practice of reproducing foreign journals and reference publications for redistribution in China without authorization has ceased. Because most libraries in china cannot afford to acquire highly priced foreign publications, either in print or electronic format, they are starving for the latest foreign information sources. To alleviate this grave situation, more publications in Chinese, which have been written by Chinese authors and published in China, are quickly filling the void.

How is the position of librarian viewed in China?

The positions of librarians and information workers are viewed as equal with professional people in other fields. This is especially true in universities and research organizations. It is quite common to find competent librarians with subject specialization in science, engineering, or medicine, who are willing to work in libraries or documentation and information centers.

In recent years, professionally trained librarians have filled increasingly more library positions. Library directors are required to be scholars or senior professionals before being appointed.

Is the pay commensurate with the librarian's new-found status?

With the progress toward an open-market economy, the salary gap between employees in the public and private sectors is widening every day. The situation has made the positions of librarians and information specialists, who are mostly in the public sector, less attractive due to low pay.

For the first time in the last twenty years, library schools now find it difficult to attract the best students to apply for admission. Libraries, too, are having a hard time retaining their best staff members.

What kind of relationship have Chinese librarians developed with their foreign colleagues?

In my frequent contacts with Chinese librarians, I have found a strong desire among Chinese libraries and librarians to establish cooperative relationships with foreign libraries and librarians to exchange professional knowledge, publications, and staff visits. Chinese librarians also are interested in learning the latest changes and development in librarianship in other countries from foreign colleagues.

In response to this need, the Ohio University Libraries and many other American libraries have set up exchange programs and internships for Chinese librarians. Many more such opportunities are needed.

How far along is China in connecting to the Internet?

China started to connect with the Internet in the beginning of 1994. Since then, the rate of growth, both in terms of the number of computers and the number of users connected to the Internet, have been dramatic. According to a news report on October 20, 1998, by the official China Xinhua News Agency, the number of people who plug in to the Internet in China doubled in the first half of 1998, reaching 1.17 million by the end of June.

There were 542,000 computers connected to the Internet and 3,700 websites. It was estimated by the China Internet Information Center that the number would reach 2.5 million by the end of 1998 and 5 million by the year 2000.

How does this state of affairs compare to other Third World countries?

As a newcomer to using the Internet, China was ranked low in terms of its long-term potential of information technology in Asia and the Pacific region, according to a 1996 Gartner Group report. It ranked Mainland China behind Japan, Hong Kong, Singapore, South Korea, Taiwan, Malaysia, Thailand, Indonesia, and the Philippines. But recent developments in China, coupled with strong economic performance (and the economic decline in other parts of Asia), may change this ranking in the near future.

To increase the usefulness of the Internet as an important resource for Chinese information, a Web-based Chinese information service, ChinaInfo, has been established by the Institute of Scientific and Technical Information of China (ISTIC) and operated by Wangfang Data Corporation. Regarded as a comprehensive Chinese "Yahoo" service, ChinaInfo intends to build a comprehensive and dynamic information service, combining both public and commercial information into one unified information source.

How important is it that China hook up to the Internet?

The decision by the Chinese government in late 1993 to connect China to the Internet was a major recognition of the importance for China to be a part of the worldwide information flow and exchange. Internet users, both in China and abroad, have greatly benefited from the availability of

Internet connectivity.

What are some of the problems that the Chinese face in connecting to the Internet?

Taking full advantage of the Internet for the growing number of Internet users in China requires that China quickly expand its national information infrastructure and lower user fees. A concerted effort will also be needed to coordinate the creation and maintenance of all important and relevant Chinese information databases on line.

Is there any concern on the part of the Chinese leadership about the freedom the individual enjoys on the Internet?

Initially, there were concerns by the Chinese Government that the Internet might subject China to much undesirable information, some of which could have negative political, social, cultural, or moral effects. But, the decision-makers felt that the advantages far out-weighted the disadvantages in connecting to the Internet.

Has the Chinese government tried to censor the Internet?

In February 1996, the State Council did issue a policy statement: "The Contemporary Rules of Computer Networks Connected with the Internet," which stated that only state-owned telecommunication companies could provide Internet international connections. It also required that any other ISP or ICP be registered with government agencies before their operation.

There was fear then that the Chinese Government would introduce some measures to ban pornography and politically sensitive content. The new rules threaten potential offenders with jail terms. So far, other than this policy, the Chinese Government has not taken any obvious action to censor the use of the Internet.

What can librarians in other countries do to further the Internet connection and a more open China?

Libraries in China have been in the forefront of the country's move to connect to the Internet. We need to give our Chinese colleagues more encouragement and recognition for their achievements and offer our technical help if needed, although China's level of technical expertise is high.

What are some of the things you plan to do in the future vis a vis China?

The greatest need in China, as I see it, is to establish more library linkages with other countries for information and staff exchange. I will continue to be a facilitator for these types of linkages. In addition, I will continue to conduct workshops on modern library management in China as long as there is such a need.

Reprinted with permission of the editor, from *International Leads*, Volume 13, Number 1, March 1999.

(Published in *Library Times International*. V. 15, No. 4, April 1999: pp. 37, 40 – 41.)

For 21 Years, Lee Has Charted Libraries' Stellar Course

Richard Heck[①]

After 40 years of working in the library profession, including 21 years at Ohio University, Dean of Libraries Hwa-Wei Lee plans to retire in August.

But despite his retirement, one of the university's most internationally recognized administrator's plans to remain an ambassador for OU.

"It's time to retire and pass on to someone younger who can bring the Libraries to its next level of excellence," Lee said of his decision to step down after a distinguished career that included steering OU's library system into becoming a world-class institution.

"I've done the best I can, and 40 years in the library profession seem like a good number to leave on," Lee said.

Under Lee's tenure, OU's collections have grown to 2.1 million bound volumes, more than 15,032 periodical subscriptions, 3.2 million other materials and more than 1.3 million users annually.

Even more impressive and important in today's global economy, Alden Library on OU's main campus is ranked in the top tier of university research libraries in the world, home to the national depositories of four countries: Malaysia, Botswana, Swaziland and Guatemala.

Although Lee will officially retire this August, he is not severing his ties with OU. In fact, just days after his official retirement, Lee plans an extended trip to Asia to lecture and serve as an ambassador for the university.

"I have a good number of lectures scheduled in Mainland China, Taiwan and Thailand," Lee said. "People must like my lectures because I've received a number of invitations. I've already lined up six of them."

Lee plans to use his lecture trips, and other such ventures, to promote OU and help with university fundraising efforts overseas.

"This university has been so good to me, I would like to continue to help," Lee said.

With his extensive network of contacts across Asia, Lee plans to meet with alumni, potential students and library donors and sponsors abroad to promote OU, making him an obvious candidate for a role as a university recruiter. Lee helped formed the university's Thailand Alumni Association.

"The university doesn't have a full-time recruiter for international students, but I can do that easily," Lee said. "We've seen a decline in international students the last two or three years, and since I'll be traveling, I can also recruit students. I'll be in a perfect setting to talk about OU."

Lee's international reputation and contacts have played an important role in the rising stature of the OU libraries.

Serving as the national depositories for the four countries in three continents benefits those countries as well as OU, Lee noted.

"They benefit because we catalogue all of their documents, and we benefit because we become a window on their countries," Lee said.

Researchers no longer have to travel to Asia, Africa or Central America to find information about the four countries, but come to OU instead, Lee explained. The depository designation has made Alden Library an important aspect of the university's international reputation, he added.

Alden Library also has become a training site for librarians from other countries, while Alden employees are able to visit and train at libraries in other countries.

Asked about his most satisfying accomplishments at OU, Lee cited the library's international

---

[①] Messenger staff writer

reputation and ties, and the fact that the library has kept pace with the growing role of new technology in providing library services to the campus community.

OU has played a central role in the continuing development of the Online Computer Library Center, a joint venture of Ohio libraries that catalogues collections and provides a central system for library users across the state to locate materials.

Since coming to OU, Lee has seen the extensive card catalogues where library users searched for books evolve into computerized data banks.

"Library science has changed so much over the past 40 years," Lee said.

"Computer technology, network technology, all of these things have been very challenging, but have enabled us to do our job better," Lee said. "But it has not come cheaply, and you have to know how to use them effectively. That has been a major challenge, making good use of the technology."

Lee also has overseen the development of a permanent endowment for the library, now at more than $10 million, which has enabled the library to keep up with changing technology and staff development.

"I've been really fortunate. This is a great university, and I feel fortunate that I have had the support of my staff who is wonderful people, the faculty and administration," Lee said.

Lee will be honored by the university with a community reception May 21 as part of the library's 30th anniversary celebration, followed by a dinner the next day.

(Published in *Athens Messenger*, May 9, 1999.)

End of Era for University Libraries: Dean Lee Retires After 21 Years

Alice Sachs

For Dean of Libraries Hwa-Wei Lee, retirement means the opportunity to travel more frequently to Southeast Asia to lecture on modern library management and time to revise his book on the same topic.

While Lee is not officially leaving his position until the end of August, the campus community is hosting a series of events this month to honor his 21 years of service to the university. Among the celebrations is the naming of the Hwa-Wei Lee Library Annex on Columbus Road on May 21.

Since Lee took over in 1978, the university library has gained national and international recognition. In the 1998 national ranking compiled by the Association of Research Libraries, Ohio University was ranked 68th among the top 111 academic research libraries in the United States and Canada.

Under Lee's leadership, Alden Library's book collection has increased from about 1 million to nearly 2.1 million volumes, and the microfilm collection has grown from less than 650,000 units to more than 2.8 million. Today, the library is home to several well-regarded international collections, including the Southeast Asian Collection, ranked as one of the best of its kind in the world.

"Dean Hwa-Wei Lee has a remarkable record of achievement in his leadership of the Ohio University libraries," said President Robert Glidden. "He has brought us to membership in the prestigious Association of Research Libraries and his vision and diligence have helped us to establish some very impressive and important special collections."

Lee also has been a strong advocate of new technology. When he arrived on campus, he launched a concerted effort to automate the library's circulation system and to create an online public access catalog, a feat accomplished in 1980.

Under his leadership, Ohio University became a founding member in 1990 of OhioLINK, a consortium of 74 college and university libraries that share a pooled library collection of 21 million volumes and growing electronic reference databases and journals.

Another achievement has been the growth of the library's endowment fund from less than $10,000 to more than $8 million.

"Dean Lee is the founder of the library as we know it today," said Provost Sharon Brehm.

A native of China, Lee's family fled to Taiwan in 1949. He arrived in the United States in 1957 to pursue graduate study at the University of Pittsburgh, and his first library job was working as a student in the stacks. He later was hired full time by the library and went on to complete a master's degree in library science and a doctorate in education.

"In those days the library was primarily paper-based," Lee said. "The stacks were closed and library employees had to run around getting the books people had requested. There was no automation and everything had to be done manually. I always thought that there had to be an easier way to do things."

In his search for less time-intensive procedures, Lee became interested in emerging technologies and experimented with basic computer programming as a way to streamline book acquisitions, cataloging and circulation records.

When he arrived in Athens, Lee remembers finding the Alden Library building half empty. Two decades later, the library's collection has more than doubled and the facility continues to add an average of 60,000 volumes a year. To alleviate congestion, a new library annex, to be named in Lee's honor this May, opened in 1997 to house lesser-used items.

During Lee's tenure, the library has become an official U.S. depository for the publications of

Malaysia, Botswana, Swaziland and Guatemala. Lee also has traveled to Asia to lecture on modern library management and overseen the International Librarian Internship Program, which has brought more than 150 information professionals to campus.

"Hwa-Wei has been a most effective ambassador for Ohio University throughout Asia," Glidden said. "We will miss Hwa-Wei as our library dean, but we also will miss his cordial and effective representation of us in other parts of the world."

While he is stepping down as dean, Lee will continue to call Athens home and help with the library's fundraising efforts. He also plans to continue lecturing.

"In my 40 years as a librarian, I have never had a dull moment. The library has become a dynamic place with an accelerated rate of change," Lee said. "I have been fortunate to have dedicated colleagues who have worked hard together with a common goal to better serve the information needs of the university community. None of the accomplishments of the last decades can be attributed to one person; they are the result of teamwork."

(Published in *Ohio University Outlook*, May 1999, p. 4.)

Alden Returns for Library Celebration
Weekend's Events Honor Others at Library

Monica Neeporte[①]

In August 1961, it was just a vision for soon-to-be Ohio University President Vernon Alden. He looked at the inadequate Chubb Hall library and realized that if the university was going to aspire to distinction, it would need a library to support its undergraduate and graduate programs.

It was the one building that Alden spoke of in his 1962 inaugural address, and it took seven years for his dream to become a reality. But in February 1969, the yet unnamed library opened its doors.

Today, Ohio University's Vernon R. Alden Library contains more than two million volumes, two million units of microfilm and is the official repository for four foreign countries. It is ranked 68th by the Association of Research Libraries.

On Saturday, Alden returned to the library to mark its 30th anniversary.

He said his goal is to see the library ranked among the top 30 research libraries within his lifetime. He credits much of the library's success to its dean, Dr. Hwa-Wei Lee, who is retiring this August after 21 years at OU and 40 years in the library profession.

The growth of the library's collections can largely be attributed to Lee's tenure, Alden said, noting that the library's endowment has dramatically increased from $10,000 to $9 million.

Because of Lee's connections, Alden said, he has brought the Pacific Rim to Ohio University and expanded the library's outreach internationally.

But Lee and Alden are not alone in their longtime dedication to the institution. Five employees of Alden Library were honored Saturday in recognition of 30 years or more of service. Lee presented certificates to Theodore Foster, Elizabeth Hoffman-Pinther, David Miller, Lian The-Mulliner and Nancy Rue.

A ribbon-cutting ceremony followed at the Hwa-Wei Lee Library Annex on Columbus Road. Former OU President Dr. Charles Ping and current President Robert Glidden both gave remarks prior to the event.

A dinner honoring Dr. Lee was held Saturday night at Ohio University's Baker Center.

(Published in *Athens Messenger*, May 24, 1999.)

---

① Messenger staff writer

Ohio University Honoring Dr. Hwa-Wei Lee

Marian Chou

Dr. Hwa-Wei Lee retires on August 31, 1999, after twenty one years as Dean of Libraries at Ohio University. In recognition of his outstanding accomplishments, Ohio University has named a new library Annex as the Hwa-Wei Lee Library Annex on May 22, 1999. (Picture 1)

Lee's retirement marked the culmination of a distinguished 40-year career in academic libraries, beginning at the University of Pittsburgh, then Duquene University, Edinborg University of Pennsylvania, Asian Institute of Technology at Bangkok, Thailand, Colorado State University and Ohio University.

He has served the American Library Association (ALA) in a variety of capacities, including as a Councilor at Large 1988 – 1991 and 1992 – 1997, the Chair of the Subcommittee on East Asia and the Pacific International Relations Committee. For his significant contributions to international librarianship, he was the recipient of the John Ames Humphry Award in 1991 presented by ALA International Relations Committee and the Forest Press OCLC.

Lee also served actively at the Ohio Library Association, being recognized as Ohio Librarian of the Year in 1987, elected as a board director 1990 – 1993, and was appointed as a delegate to the White House Conference on Library and Information Services, July 9 – 13, 1991.

Dr. Lee was a past president of the Chinese American Librarians Association (CALA), 1978 – 1979, and was the recipient of the CALA Distinguished Services Award in 1984. For his contribution to the Asian pacific Librarian Association (APALA), he was presented the APALA Distinguished Services Award in 1983.

Lee was also very active in IFLA, and has been a much sought after lecturer and consultant in many Asian countries. He has published three books and more than sixty papers, and was the organizer of five international library conferences.

CALA Midwest Chapter sends its warmest congratulations to Dr. Lee on this occasion for his remarkable accomplishments. We sincerely wish Dr. Hwa-Wei Lee for a very enjoyable and active retirement.

(Published at the Website of Ohio University: http://www.uic.edu/depts/lib/projects/resources/calamw/lee)

李华伟博士访谈录

封学绛　程小澜　贾晓东[②]

程：李博士，上午您参观了我们图书馆，您能给我们谈谈看法吗？

李：可以。整个馆舍建筑的设计、布局，尤其是按大学科分类符合下个世纪的发展潮流。在中国还很少看到这样的馆。可以说，你们的馆舍、布局和你们的服务观念与国外同类型、同规模图书馆相比已毫不逊色。新馆建成以后整个布局规划，尤其是藏书建设要多加考虑。我希望你们把眼光瞄向21世纪，在建馆百年之际对社会发展作出更大贡献。

程：这几年您多次回国作学术报告，您认为国内外图书馆的主要差距是什么？

李：过去我觉得差距比较大，主要有两方面。一是经费上，国内图书馆的经费与国外同类型图书馆在经费上相比，确实少得多。可是这几年差距在逐渐地缩小。二是对读者服务的观念上差距比较大。过去吃大锅饭，多做少做对一般工作人员来说没什么两样。可是这两年，在服务观念方面已经有很大的改变。我觉得要归功于国内图书馆的领导，能够有更开放的思想，能够接收国外图书馆的经验。当然还有一个问题就是馆员素质的问题。因为在国外公共图书馆进去的馆员都受过相当的图书馆学方面的训练，而国内受过专业图书馆学训练的馆员人数还是偏少了一点。这几年有了很大的进步。我们要朝着这个方向努力下去，我想我们图书馆，尤其是公共图书馆还是非常有希望的。

程：您在上午的报告中谈到，浙江省的公共图书馆、大学图书馆和科技情报文献馆可以互相联系，实现资源共享。您觉得我们目前的情况实现资源共享可借鉴哪些经验？

李：第一，我觉得OCLC是个成功的模式，还有OhioLINK这二个都是从俄亥俄州高等院校图书馆发展而来的。现在已成为国际性合作较好的成功范例。我想在浙江省来说，有浙江图书馆、浙江大学图书馆、浙江省科技情报所，这些馆尽管隶属的系统不一样，可是每一个馆都有它特别的功能、长处和特点。如果把它们结合起来，这个服务就能做得很全面，很好。你们可以合作编目、建立联合目录。有了目录以后，才知道每个馆的收藏特点。读者要找某种资料时通过联合目录来进行查找，实现馆际互借。第二，我想国内图书馆包括情报所，其经费都是比较有限的。而国外的许多科技、医学期刊的订费非常昂贵。我们可以根据各个馆的需要和特长进行分工，合作采购，这样可以尽量避免不必要的重复。使我们的资料起到更好的作用。我们应当认识到图书馆藏书从以往强调"拥有"到目前强调"获取"这一本质性变化。第三，在人员上可以互相支援。比如某个馆的馆员在某个方面有特长，有的馆在其他方面有特长，馆员之间可以彼此合作与交换，对馆员进行合作培训，甚至开展一些合作研究项目，这些对馆员素质的提高都会有所帮助。

程：李博士，您谈到文献要强调"用"的观点，请问国外相当于我们国内的省级图书馆是如何处理文献藏与用的关系？

李：在这方面大学图书馆与公共图书馆有比较显著的差别。大学图书馆的功能要求收藏有价值的、有代表性的学术性书刊。而公共图书馆除了本地文献和特藏之外，一般收藏比较通俗性的、满足一般读者需要的文献。公共图书馆藏书的主要作用就是怎样让读者充

---

① 本文为封学绛、程小澜、贾晓东根据李华伟于1999年9月在浙江省图书馆所作《展望21世纪图书馆》演讲录音编辑整理而成。

② 任职于浙江省图书馆。

分使用。公共图书馆的藏与用关系是以用作为导向的，它收集的资料要是不用的话就失掉了藏的意义，这一点对公共图书馆来讲是非常重要的。可是对大学馆、科技馆来讲有时候用不是收藏的第一导向，而是要看有没有长期保存的价值。所以不同图书馆就有不同的侧重点。就公共馆来讲，尤其省馆跟一般的公共馆又有不同，因为省馆还有一个兼具研究和提高读者阅读兴趣的功能。对省馆来讲根据自己的需要，拟定一个馆藏发展的计划或规则，根据这个计划来进行藏书的发展。对绝大部分书的采购与收藏的指导性原则就是用。用得越多，图书馆藏书的效果就越好。

程：李博士，您在报告中谈到，美国的公共图书馆开展许多特色服务，开展这些活动经费有没有困难？

李：在美国每个州都不一样，我们这个州是比较幸运的。大概在十五年前我们州议会特别通过一个法案，规定本州所得税的6.5%作为公共图书馆的经费。根据这个法案，现在公共馆的经费可以说是非常的充裕。因为所得税在不断增加，每年政府所得税收入都保持很大幅度的增加。这个6.5%的所得税对公共图书馆的发展起了非常大的作用。所以目前我们州图书馆的经费一般来讲是非常充足的。另外，地方上图书馆如果有需要的话，还可以动用地方上的税收。美国有联邦政府税、州政府税，还有地方税。地方税是由老百姓投票决定的。很多地区觉得这6.5%还不够，还希望增加一些税收来支持公共图书馆，所以有些地方还有额外的税收支持。所以美国公共图书馆的发展一般都非常好。因为有钱，他们服务的面就非常广，几乎能想到的事情他们都做到了。国内图书馆在这方面还受到经费的限制，没有完全发挥公共图书馆的功能。不过今天我看了你们馆以后，我觉得在很多方面已经具备了开展各种主要服务项目的条件。而且一般公共图书馆该做的主要项目你们也都具备了。假设你们经费更充裕的话，还有很多项目可以推行。比如，把图书馆的服务项目从馆内推广到馆外去。在美国一些城市，公共图书馆有流动书车，大型公共客车里面经过特别装饰，有书库、有电脑，每天定时地将车子开到边远地区去，为边远地区的读者服务。那儿的读者就不需要到图书馆来，他们可以在流动书车所到之处去挑选他们想要借的书。还有可以做的就是用邮寄的方式、专门送书上门的方式，满足各种各样读者的要求。这些服务在美国图书馆都做到了。我想你们馆可以根据经费情况做一些符合国情，适合本地居民需要的服务。

程：李博士，现在国际上数字化图书馆的研究进展很快，我们也正在拟定这方面的计划。您认为像我们这样的图书馆在数字化图书馆建设方面首先应该做哪些工作？

李：数字化图书馆的主要根据就是数字化信息资源的收集和开发。有些馆有自己比较特殊的收藏，也有技术力量和资金，他们自己可以把一些收藏做成数字化，使之成为数字化资源的一部分。另外，有很多图书馆购买由商业机构或其他图书馆完成的电子数据库或数字化数据库。只要是配合我们的馆藏范围的都可以购买。这样有个好处，因为一个图书馆开发资源丰富的电子数据库，这种费用是很高的。所以能够买一些比较现成的，就像买书刊一样。要是我们自己去写一本书，自己把它印刷出版、发行，那么一本书的成本就会很高。要是由书商出版，印刷很多本，图书馆去买一本，这个费用就容易承担。第三就是进行馆际合作。利用互联网的优势，大家在网上分工地去查询、检索已经在网上现有的电子或数字化图书信息资源，把它下载到图书馆主页上，让读者使用。有很多电子信息数据是免费的。同时更新速度很快，可以说是取之不尽。但这需要受过专业训练的、有学科背景的图书馆馆员在网上经常查寻。查寻到合适的，把它引用下载。也可以借用别的馆已经查寻过的电子数据，比如说，你可以查寻俄亥俄州立大学图书馆的网页，其中有一个电子图书馆数字资源的项目，进入到这里，您可以找到一些有用的信息资源，可以把它引用下来，不需要另外再花时间去查寻。这些都是在数字图书馆建设方面可以做的一些很有意义的工作。

程：李博士，现在电子出版物越来越多，互联网也在迅速扩展，但是传统的印刷型出版物由于它一些不可替代的优点，仍然是读者获取信息的重要载体。您认为图书馆如何兼顾这两方面收藏和服务才是比较合适的？

李：我想，图书馆收藏多样化是现在我们发展的一个必然趋向。过去传统印刷型书刊，还是有它存在的价值，还是有它受读者欢迎的因素。它的费用比较便宜。所以我们图书馆在这方面的收藏和服务还是不能够忽视的。同时也要兼顾其他的信息资源的载体。现在电子化、数字化的资源越来越多了，不能忽视。两方面都要有所考虑。可是图书馆的资金有限，有时候也不能面面俱到。这方面要拟定一个周详的馆藏发展规划，根据这个规划来进行馆藏的发展。但这个规划每一二年要修订一下，才能适合当时、当地的特点和情况。

贾：您认为图书馆未来印刷型出版物会不会消失？

李：五十年之内不会消失，同时还会继续增长。除此之外，其他的出版物也会越来越多。这对我们图书馆是一个很大的问题，经费有限，可是要买的东西却越来越多，这就需要我们去考虑规划，考虑资源共享。

程：李博士，请问一下美国图书馆在开展一些深层次信息服务时，是否要向读者收取费用？

李：在美国，不管大学图书馆也好、公共图书馆也好，都尽量不收取读者的费用。因为我们认为，尤其是公共图书馆，它的经费来源已经很充裕了，没有必要再另外向读者收费。它的主要目的是鼓励读者到图书馆来使用图书馆的收藏。要是收费的话，会造成贫富机会不均的问题。就是说，有钱的人可以使用钱来利用图书馆的信息资源，没有钱的人就不敢来。所以公共图书馆满足为大众服务的要求最好不收费。大学图书馆基本上也是不收费的，可是因为美国大学图书馆是对校外、对社会开放的，校外有些企业的图书馆希望大学图书馆能够为他们提供一些专门的信息查询服务。在这种情况下，图书馆就要专门为他们做这项工作，这是信息加值的工作，就要收一些适当的费用。主要目的是大学图书馆并没有对读者做这种加值服务的功能，而这种服务需要图书馆员特别利用时间去做。我们的馆员在做此工作时无形中把对读者服务时间减少了，那么，我们专门要收费，但费用并不贵，是社会可以承担的。这是在美国的基本情况，其他一般不收费，因为要是收费的话，究竟要收多少才是比较合适的？根据我们的经验，图书馆依靠收费来支付部分开销是以小失大。因为所收的钱实在很有限，但对图书馆来讲，作为社会教育文化公益性机构会造成一个不好的形象。但在美国的私立大学，如哈佛大学、耶鲁大学图书馆接待学校以外的读者都是要收费的，有的要收300美元一年的服务费。

程：李博士，您谈到专业馆员的招聘很重要，你认为图书馆员应该具备怎样的知识结构？

李：在美国，图书馆员必须受过图书馆信息方面的专业教育。图书馆专业人员的教育程度至少具备图书馆学或者信息科学的硕士学位。在大学图书馆，甚至规定了要两个硕士学位，一个是图书馆学的，一个是学科方面的。这样，一方面具备图书馆的专业知识，另一方面也具备一门学科的专业知识，这样可以为读者做更好的服务。

程：李博士，您谈到你们的馆员都很勤奋敬业，那么管理者是否也采取一些激励的措施？

李：在美国，就我所在的图书馆来说，因为经常有许多国内的图书馆馆员来参观或者短期培训，他们一致的结论就是对我们馆工作人员勤奋敬业的精神、高度负责任的精神印象很深，这是一个事实。因为，我自己也觉得，在美国，一般工作人员工作的时候很认真；工作之后，下班的时间，这是他自己的时间，可以充分使用，做好自己的事。公私分得很清楚，工作时候他一定是很卖力地把自己的工作做好。当然在美国，有时候每个馆也并不都一样。有些馆也有内部的纠纷，馆员之间的摩擦，馆员士气不高的情况。但是一般来讲美国人做事是比较负责的。工作时间他会尽量地把工作做好，工作之外的时间我们很少去干涉他。比如说，我们让一个员工加班要付给他150%的加班费，相当可观，所以我们也尽可能地不要求加班。

贾：有没有我们国内的措施，比方说奖勤罚懒措施？

李：也有，也有。在美国，一般馆员包括专业馆员和非专业馆员每一年都要有年终考核。有的图书馆实行目标管理，在年度开始之前，制定全馆的工作目标，也就是说一个总的工作目标。这是经过馆员大家的参与，由各阶层的馆员代表用各种不同的形式来拟定全馆的远期目标、近期目标。然后根据这个目标，每个部门建立自己部门的目标，那就要求比较具体，有些指标规定一年要完成多少工作项目。根据这个部门的工作目标，每个工作人员也要有自己个人的工作目标。每个年度结束时，我们要对他们进行考核。这个考核，每个部门都不一样，基本上是看你个人的目标究竟达到多少。要是超过了你个人的目标，在评价上就给予特别高的分数；要是没有达到目标，又没有很能说服人的理由，他的评价结果就比较差。这个评价结果对他的加薪有直接关系。在美国根据生活指数的调整，经费好的时候在指数之外还有一些加薪。每一个人的加薪都不一样，是根据你的考绩结果来决定加薪的多少。工作做得好、考绩好，每年加薪的幅度就比较大；工作不好、考绩差，加薪幅度就比较小。这就是一种激励员工的方式。钱的奖励并不是激发员工工作的唯一因素，很多人很自觉地把工作做好。根据心理学家马斯洛五个需求的层次来讲，第一个层次、第二个层次要想调动员工的积极性一定要把员工的基本生活需求给予满足。要是他饭吃不饱，没有住的地方，也没有好的交通工具，用别的方式激励他工作的积极性也激励不出来，只有条件达到了基本要求，他自己就会主动地向上一层的目标去追求。比如说，他要追求在社会的成就感，认为我要得到我的同事的认可比其他因素更重要，同事说我好，我自己就会感觉很愉快。这就是调动人的积极性，要满足他基本生活的要求，然后要用群体的、员工彼此之间的监督和督促力，这种力量是很大的。大家都在这个地方，这个环境，大家都会互相比较，因此压力很大，他自己会调动自己的积极性。要是连续几年不加薪或少加薪，他自己就会觉得不好意思，提出辞职去另外地方。自己把事情做好了，就能满足工作的荣誉感，自己觉得对社会有所贡献。这些因素对于一个员工积极性的发挥是重要的因素。因此一般来讲，我们是用各种各样的方式，而不是用单一的方式来鼓励大家的积极性。

程：李博士，刚才看了您的生平介绍，知道您是美国3000多名华裔图书馆工作人员中的出类拔萃者，您认为您事业的成功主要是依靠什么？

李：我想，我的成功与我们中国的很多文化传统有着密切关系。中国人是很厚道的，对人很诚恳。我觉得要能够跟人相处得到大家的支持和爱戴，一定要对人以诚相待，这是中国人待人接物的道理和传统。美国人有时不大讲人情味，公事公办，上班来了，下班走了，大家没有什么来往。中国人就很注重人与人之间的关系和感情的培养。同事生病了，去医院看看他，出于真心的而不只是表面上的。平时，能够跟周围的同事多接触，了解一些他们的实际情况，他家庭有些什么事情呀，这些我们都很关怀。虽然都是小事情，但做起来不容易，您能够做得到，多半都有影响。另外，就是用人，一定要用能干的人，这是做好工作的根本。在美国有一个好的规则，就是如果我们有职位空缺，可以在全州、甚至在全国公开性地招聘，从中挑选最好的、最合适的工作人员。这样一来，新进的人员都是非常优秀的，再在工作上加强训练、培养。这样有了好的工作人员，有了好的干部，事情就可以做得很好。所以应该说有很多因素在这里面。当然我们自己也要不断充实自己，提高自己。做馆长的，像我有很好的机会做了馆长，我觉得我好像是一个掌舵的人。在海上行舟的时候，自己一定要把握住方向，否则就误导了。所以我们要不断充实自己，掌握好方向。有时候不一定一个人就是绝对都是对的，所以我很主张参与式的管理，让同事都有机会参与决策的过程。馆长要作最后的决定，但在过程里面，我们要尽量让同事发表和参与意见，这样作出的决定，一方面大家都了解，因为他们都参与了，让大家有机会发言，而我们馆长要对决定的结果负最后的责任。我认为同事参与管理是很重要的。另一个就是目标管理，在做目标管理的时候，大家讨论策略性的规划，战略性的规划，怎么样看远一点，有所突破，就要用策略性的规划作长期的目标，然后再规划怎么样能达到这个目标。传统的规划是逐渐从现在走向将来，所以要渐进，一步一步来，一步一步向前走。现在是快速发展的信息时代，要求我们要突破现状，迎合新技术快速发展的需要，所以要作战略性规划。做好规划之后呢，采用目标管理的方式来执行。而这是一个参与式的管理，让大家都参与。第三个我认为是全品质管理。下午，杨教授也讲了要从用户，从服务对象的观点来看，怎么样能最大限度满足他们的需求，而不是我们自己设想到的，而是要从他们的立场来看，满足他们的要求。从这个角度来规划我们图书馆，做到能有最好的服务。这三点都是很重要的，以我个人过去的经验都得益于以上三个方法。另外，再配以我们中国人这种厚道的管理思想。中国还有一个就是不知是好还是坏的"中庸之道"，因为有很多事情还是非常复杂的，怎么样能够听从大家的意见，这里要找一个大家都能接受的折衷方法，有时候折衷的方法不一定是最好的方法，因为我们要突破，不要折衷。可是，折衷的方法，在一些比较有矛盾性的问题方面还是比较好的。没有矛盾以后，你再跳跃、再突破。中国人的这种技术还是有它的用处的。待人以诚，我觉得这个诚很重要。你如果不相信人家或人家不相信你，就比较麻烦。我觉得我已经尽了我的力量了，看人家怎样反馈，我问心无愧了。如果你待人以诚的话，人家就多半会有相对好的对应和交流。

程：李博士，您原来是学教育学的，一个偶然的机会开始走上从事图书馆事业的道路，而且做得非常出色。您认为这项工作很有意义吗？

李：是的。我从事图书馆工作已四十年，在今年8月底我退休之前，我们学校为我举行盛大的退休欢送大会，他们问我有什么感想，我觉得我精神上一直是非常愉快的。我从来没有感觉到我走错了路。当初我并不是学图书馆学的，我是学教育学的，很偶然的机会进入图书馆这一行，可进入以后我觉得非常适合我的个性，适合我的需求。我个人有一个很重要的观点，就是人生以服务为目的，记得孙中山先生讲过这话。而真正要做到这一点，我觉得图书馆是个最好的地方。真正为社会服务，是很有价值的。虽然我们的回报不多，可是你自己觉得你做的事情对别人有用、有价值。我对我毕生从事这项事业没有任何后悔，觉得很光荣、很愉快。国内也好，国外也好，这项工作都是十分有意义的，十分有价值的。

（原载《图书馆研究与工作》1999年第4期，第11-15页。）

Tributes to Dr. Hwa-Wei Lee's Retirement

(**Editor's notes**: Dr. Hwa-Wei Lee was one of founders of CALA. During his long time commitments to CALA, he served as a CALA President and was a recipient of the CALA Distinguished Award. Dr. Lee's significant contributions were recognized at his retirement ceremony at Ohio University, ALA, and other places. The Editor for this issue is pleased to present the following news to our readers. —Sha Li Zhang)

From Friends of Hwa-Wei Lee Committee

This year Dean Lee will retire after 21 years of exemplary service to Ohio University and Ohio University Libraries. Under his careful guidance and skillful leadership, the libraries have experienced unprecedented growth and progress in every facet of its operations and programs.

Dean Lee's tenure at Ohio University is credited with library reorganization that has resulted in more efficient service, founding membership in Ohio Link—a statewide system pooling materials of all major academic libraries into one unified entity; library endowments grew to over $8 millions, major renovations were accomplished, and a regional annex was constructed, the first digitization project was secured, library acquisitions exceeded two million volumes, and membership was achieved in the elite Association of Research Libraries—recognizing Ohio University Libraries as one of the top 121 research libraries in the United States and Canada.

We also acknowledge Dr. Lee's model for international service. He is and has been a remarkable friend and adviser to international students. Under his tenure, a program for international librarian exchange was established, the library received the unique designation as an official depository for four countries, the Southeast Asia Collection grew to national and international prominence, and the Chubu University Commemorative Japanese and You-Bao Shao Overseas Chinese Documentation and Research Center were established.

Dr. Lee has worked in academic libraries for over 35 years and has left his footprints in five continents as a library consultant and lecturer, has chaired or organized seven international conferences, and is a member, councilor, delegate, director, consultant, and president of 13 national and international councils and committees. He is a world citizen and a remarkable role model to students and colleagues alike. His career has advanced scholarship and human understanding while setting unparalleled standards of service, loyalty, honor, honesty, and integrity. (**Contributed by Attorney Charlotte Coleman-Eufinger**, *Chair of Friends of Hwa-Wei Lee Committee at Ohio University.*)

From Ohio University News Release

In recognition of his outstanding achievements Ohio University's Board of Trustees adopted a resolution naming a new library building the "*Hwa-Wei Lee Annex*" By a separate action, the Board also conferred on Dr. Lee the title of *Dean of Libraries Emeritus*. A permanent office in the Library Annex has been provided to Dr. Lee for his use after retirement.

The Resolution reads:

Whereas, Dr. Hwa-Wei Lee will retire as Dean of Ohio University Libraries on August 31, 1999, having served 21 years as the head of university libraries,

Whereas, under Dean Lee's skillful leadership, the Ohio University Libraries have grown from edifice to interface, experiencing unprecedented growth and progress in every facet of its operations, programs, and endowments, and has become one of the top 121 research libraries in the United States and Canada, achieving membership in the highly competitive and prestigious Association of Research Libraries,

Whereas, Dean Lee has worked in academic libraries for over 35 years, leaving footprints in five continents as a library consultant and lecturer, and

Whereas, under Dean Lee's administration, an international librarian exchange program was created and developed, and the unique status of depository for four countries was achieved,

Now, therefore be it resolved that staff of the Ohio University Libraries and Friends of Hwa-Wei Lee Committee formally request the Ohio University Board of Trustees to name the library annex on Columbus Road in honor of retiring Dean of Ohio university Libraries, Dr. Hwa-Wei Lee.

Be it further resolved that the official name shall be **Hwa-Wei Lee Library Annex.**

At the retirement party held on May 22, 1999 hosted by the university President and Mrs. Robert Glidden, it was announced that through a generous gift by Dr. and Mrs. Vernon R. Alden, President Emeritus and for whom the main library building is named, the first floor of the Vernon Alden Library will be completely renovated this summer and be named as **Hwa-Wei Lee Center for International Collections.**

In an interview to a local newspaper reporter, Dr. Lee was quoted as saying that after his retirement he will spend his time in international traveling, lecturing in Mainland China, Taiwan, and Thailand, and with his extended families of six children who reside in many parts of the U. S. He will also serve as unofficial ambassador for Ohio University in some of its international programs. (*Ohio University News Release, June 22, 1999.*)

From an ALA Committee

Whereas, Hwa-Wei Lee retires on August 31, 1999, after twenty one years as Dean of Libraries at Ohio University; and

Whereas, in recognition of his outstanding accomplishment, Ohio University has named a new library annex as the Hwa-Wei Lee Library Annex on May 22, 1999; and

Whereas, his retirement marked the culmination of a distinguished 35-year career in academic libraries, beginning at the University of Pittsburgh then on to Duquesne University, Edinboro University of Pennsylvania, the Asian Institute of Technology (Bangkok, Thailand), Colorado State University, and Ohio University; and

Whereas, he has served the American Library Association in a variety of capacities, including as a Councilor at Large (1988 – 1991, 1992 – 1997), the chair of the Subcommittee on East Asia and the Pacific, International Relations Committee, etc. ; and

Whereas, for his significant contributions to international librarianship, he was the recipient of the John Ames Humphry Award in 1991 presented by ALA International Relations Committee and the Forest Press OCLC; and

Whereas, he also served actively at the Ohio Library Association as a board director (1990 – 1993), was recognized as the Ohio Librarian of the Year in 1987, and was appointed as a delegate to the White House Conference on Library and Information Services, July 9 – 13, 1991; and

Whereas, he was a past president of the Chinese American Librarians Association (1982) and was the recipient of the CALA Distinguished Services Award in 1984; and

Whereas, for his valuable contributions to the Asian/Pacific American Librarians Association he was the recipient of the APALA Distinguished Services Award in 1983; and

Whereas, he has been a much sought after lecturer and consultant in many Asian countries, has published three books and more than sixty papers; and was the organizer of five international library conferences;

Now, therefore, be it Resolved, that the American Library Association send its warmest congratulations to Dr. Hwa-Wei Lee on this occasion for his remarkable accomplishments and to wish him an enjoyable and active retirement. (*Contributed by Yu-Lan Chou, Chair, ALA / IRC East Asia and the Pacific Subcommittee, June 1999.*)

(Published in *Chinese American Librarians Association Newsletter.* September 1999: pp. 7 – 8.)

给著名图书馆学家李华伟博士的信

张白影

尊敬的李华伟馆长：

您好！

去年11月9日，尽管您在广州暨南大学曾告诉我将于明年离开图书馆馆长岗位，但今天接到贵校惠函，称"在模范地服务于美国俄亥俄大学及其图书馆21年之后，李华伟馆长将于年内退休"时，我的心中仍顷刻之间涌动一股惆怅与失落，慨叹不已。每当看到你奔走于美国、中国及五大洲各图书馆之间的匆匆步履和不无倦容的身影时，我们多么希望您能享有应得的休闲、安适和清静，但许许多多图书馆界同仁后学，又几乎是永无满足地渴望得到您对事业发展的热情促进和谆谆指教。您作为学者、长者、人友、人师，其敬业、勤业、精业的品格和风范，"为同行和学生树立了一个世界公民的模范榜样。"

山包海汇、博大精深的图书馆内，古今学者共聚，千代贤哲同堂，门庭挨着门庭，智慧之光绵绵。留连于此，天人合一，身心飘腾，时空永恒，那份人类精神与知识的厚重，是不可以言"休"也不能语"退"的，您为图书馆这方沃土，在春天精心撒下的种子，在夏天辛勤留下的汗珠，在秋季无私奉献的果实，在冬日真诚传播的祝愿，将给世界范围内的朋友和学生们注入永恒的激励和温情。

我初识阁下于80年代末之仲春，那天，您与高斯馆长来到长沙岳麓山下湖南大学图书馆。这座源于公元976年中国宋代岳麓书院御书楼的书城，依山伴岭，檐角飞天，湘江如带，一水拖兰，十纪连绵，弦歌不绝，我们共同于此品味华夏文明源远流长的淳香，又展望图书馆未来的灿烂。之后，您不时赠我大著，我也偶奉习作；我的心中从此多了一位良师益友，大洋彼岸，牵系着万里关山隔不断的真诚云树之思。

1992年7月，受阁下盛邀，我与湖南财经学院图书馆左大铖馆长趋贵校访问。您和您的同事让我们在俄亥俄渡过了充实而愉快的一周时光。在您主持的图书馆里，在您服务的大学校园中，在您热情邀集华人学者聚会的餐桌上，在您周到安排的清澈雅洁的湖水旁，友谊，像一束温暖的阳光，像一股和煦的春风，像一只快乐的小鸟，像俄亥俄随处可见的艳丽鲜花和沁人心脾的青青草坪，始终环绕在我们的身旁。随后，我们到了华盛顿，到了纽约，到了洛杉矶，不论走到哪里，我们的眼前都会不时浮现您儒雅温文亲切的言谈笑貌音容。1996年在北京IFLA大会上，我见过您忙碌的身影；1998年在暨南大学讲坛上，我见过您演讲的神情。朋友们的来信经常通报您在中国大陆西北、西南、华北、华东的匆匆之旅，为祖国图书情报事业的发展，您无私地奉献着满腔赤诚。

如果说您离开图书馆长的岗位后，时间将会更自由和从容，那么，我们——您在中国所有的朋友和学生，都热忱地欢迎您随时来讲学，来团聚，来旅游，来品茗饮酒，来看神州大地看不够的黄河、长江、华山、泰山和万里长城，来侃故乡亲朋侃不尽的松、竹、梅、兰、风花雪月和海阔天空。北京的庄守经先生等您来，甘肃的潘寅生先生等您来，武汉的彭斐章先生等您来，广东的谭祥金先生等您来……有一位从湖南西部山区走出来名叫宋祖英的青年歌唱家，唱过一首脍炙人口的歌《等你来》，她那像山涧溪流一样甜润清纯的嗓音，人听人醉。我暂时抽去歌词中年轻人爱情的汁液，加进浓浓的友谊和乡情，我们也在唱《等您来》，等您来，您听到了吗？

祝您永远年轻、健康!
祝您全家快乐、幸福!

您真挚的朋友　白影
1999年3月8日于广州

(原载《图书馆论坛》1999年第3期第86页,又载于《书城人事两依依》,长沙:湖南大学出版社2003版,第54-57页。)

李华伟博士简介

汪雁秋

李华伟博士今年8月退休，俄亥俄大学对他在促进国际文化交流与合作，尤其中美（包括台湾与大陆）给予极高的评价及肯定。为表彰他的贡献，该校董事会特将新建的图书馆分馆命名为"李华伟图书馆分馆"，另在总馆第一层楼重新装修命名为"李华伟国际藏书中心"还特为他设置一间永久性的办公室。华人在国外得到如此殊荣，李华伟博士还是第一人，深感到美国比我们更富人情味，也重视退休人员的贡献及其专长，充分利用人力的资源。

今年6月美国图书馆学会年会在美国纽奥良市举行，我代表团一行十三人，由本会张理事长鼎钟领队，前往参加，会中遇到李华伟博士，谈到他将退休，及退休后的生涯规划。俄亥俄大学仍请他继续为该校服务，拓展国际合作。我们同时参加美国华人图书馆员协会晚宴，在晚宴中华人图书馆员协会由前任会长于钱莉娜女士代表表扬李华伟杰出贡献。张理事长代表本会赠送银盘一座，感谢他过去对台湾图书馆界的协助及交换人员的支援，并当面邀请他今年12月参加本会年会。本来计划为他作一专访，因时间匆忙，只有请他提供他的资料，藉会讯的园地，以供同道分享他的荣誉。

自1978年到现在一直担任美国俄亥俄大学图书馆院长级馆长的李华伟博士将在今年8月底退休。李华伟博士是极少数华人在美国大学图书馆担任图书馆馆长者之一。因为他的卓越成绩，俄亥俄大学董事会亦破例把一座新建的图书馆分馆命名为"李华伟图书馆分馆"。在该馆中还特别为他设置了一间永久性的办公室。除此以外，为了表彰他在发展国际合作，促进图书馆藏书全球化方面所做出的贡献，还特别将总馆的第一层楼重新装修，命名为"李华伟国际藏书中心"。

李华伟博士原籍是福建省福州市。1933年1月25日生于广州，抗日战争以前在南京渡过幼年的岁月。1937年日军入侵，随父母迁往广西桂林及四川重庆，念毕小学及初中二年级，1945年胜利后，回到南京进入南京一中，完成了初中学业。1947年又迁回桂林，进入国立汉民中学高中部。1949年随家迁往台湾，在省立台中第一中学毕业，1950年考入当时的台湾省立师范学院攻修教育系。1954年毕业后，前后在陆军军官及政工干部学校接受了一年的预备军官训练。1955年分配到台北省立师范专科学校的附属小学担任训导主任一年，次年被已升格为台湾师范大学的母校聘为助教，派往训导处担任主管学生社团活动的训导员。

1957年，因获得美国匹兹堡大学的入学许可及奖学金，在9月1日动身赴美进修，以七年的时间，念毕教育硕士、图书馆学硕士及哲学博士的学位。在此期间，除一面攻读及研究外，还在匹兹堡大学图书馆勤工俭读，1959年由该馆正式聘用，首先担任培训馆员，两年后升为采访部第一助理，1962年，由在匹兹堡城的都肯大学图书馆聘为采访部主任兼该馆极为著名的非洲特藏部主任。

1965年在匹兹堡大学完成主修教育及副修图书馆学的哲学博士学位以后，由当时宾州的爱丁堡州立学院聘为图书馆副馆长兼图书馆系助理教授，次年升为馆长，为中国人在美国高等院校担任图书馆馆长最早的一人，在此期间还一度兼任图书馆学系系主任一职。

1968年，在一个偶然的机遇下，由美国国际发展总署向宾州爱丁堡州立学院借调，派往泰国的亚洲理工学院担任该院首任的图书馆及资讯中心主任。一年后，因为工作的需要辞掉爱丁堡的工作，在泰国停留了七年，直到1975年美国支援亚洲理工学院的项目圆满结束。在亚洲理工学院服务时，还应泰国朱拉隆功大学图书馆学系之邀，自 1970 年至 1975 年在该系讲授"图书馆自动化"的课程，这在亚洲还是最早开设的课程。除此之外，还多次担任联合国教科文组织、联合国发展计划、世界粮农组织、加拿大国际发展及研究中心等机构有关图书馆发展项目的顾问。

1975 年返回美国后即应聘担任美国科罗拉多州立大学图书馆教授级副馆长，三年以后转任俄亥俄大学图书馆馆长一职至今。

李博士在美国图书馆界极为活跃，曾经担任过美国图书馆学会理事、国际关系委员会亚洲太平洋地区小组主席、俄亥俄州图书馆学会理事、美国华人图书馆员协会会长及理事、OCLC 会员代表大会俄州代表、国际图联大学及研究图书馆委员会委员等职务，因为他的卓越成就，李博士曾得到很多奖励，其中主要的有：俄亥俄大学最杰出行政人员奖（1982 年）、华人图书馆员协会杰出服务奖（1983 年）、俄亥俄州最杰出图书馆员奖（1987 年）、台湾中国图书馆学会杰出贡献奖（1989 年）、美中华人学术及专业学会杰出服务奖（1991 年）、美国图书馆学会国际关系卓越贡献奖（1991 年）、亚美及太平洋地区图书馆学会杰出服务奖（1991 年）、美国新闻署杰出服务奖状（1992 年）、美国图书馆学会杰出理事奖（1992 年）、俄亥俄图书及信息网感谢状（1993 年）等。

另外，李博士还陆续的被选载在《世界名人传》、《美国名人传》、《美国教育界名人传》等年鉴上。

即使在极为忙碌的工作中，李博士仍然不忘教学、研究与写作，在他近四十年的图书馆生涯中，曾经发表过六十多篇文章，出版了三本书，编过两本会议录及先后担任了六种学术期刊的编辑委员。他的著作是《图书馆学的世界观》（1991 年台湾学生书局出版）、《90 年代图书馆的筹款指引》（与盖里·汉博士合著，1992 年由美国坚那位公司出版）、《现代化图书馆管理》（1996 年由台湾三民书局出版）。

李博士曾经主持或协办过多次国际会议，其中包括，1983 年 6 月 28 日在洛杉矶由亚美及太平洋图书馆员学会与华人图书馆员协会合办"亚太地区图书馆的发展及合作的途径"会议、1988 年 9 月 8 日至 11 日在西安由俄大图书馆与西安交大图书馆合办的"图书馆新技术应用国际学术讨论会"、1994 年 10 月 20 日至 24 日在上海由中国科学院与上海图书馆主办的"资讯技术与资讯服务国际研讨会"、1996 年 8 月 21 日至 23 日在北京举行的"第一届中美图书合作会议"、1996 年 9 月 3 日至 6 日由武汉大学及上海师范大学等合办的"资讯资源与社会发展国际学术研讨会"及 1998 年 10 月 25 日至 28 日在北京大学为了庆祝北大建校一百周年及新图书馆大楼落成所举办的"21 世纪大学图书馆的新使命"国际学术研讨会。

在俄亥俄大学，李博士除了担任图书馆馆长之外，还兼任了该大学教育学院的教授，先后担任了十余位博士学生的论文指导老师。

李博士除了专长大学图书馆行政外，还积极参与俄亥俄大学的策略规划、课程设计及更新、新讲学技术的采用、校园计算机及电讯网路的建立、远距离教育的发展、教育的国际化、人力资源管理的革新、建教合作，以及对外募捐等。在李博士任内，通过他优越的人际关系，他曾为俄亥俄大学筹募了上千万美元，其中八百多万是图书馆的专用基金，在美国的公立大学中名列前茅。

除此之外，自 1982 年以后，李博士还每年应邀前往中国大陆和台湾各地讲学，近年来还应中国国家教委之邀多次在世界银行贷款项目及联合国发展基金项目下，对大陆师范院校的图书馆长开办图书管理的培训班。由于他孜孜不倦的教学活动，大陆很多大学都邀请他担任访问教授或客座教授，包括北京大学、北京师范大学、北京邮电大学、西安交通大学、南开大学、湖南医大、武汉大学、四川联合大学、东北师范大学、天津理工学院。中国科学院武汉文献资讯中心及兰州文献资讯中心也聘请李博士担任学术顾问。中国的北京图书馆、清华大学图书馆及台湾"中央图书馆"也礼聘李博士担任顾问。

作为一个美籍华裔的图书馆从业人员，李博士极为关心中国图书馆的发展，除了经常回国讲学外，从1980起，还在俄亥俄大学图书馆设立了一个国际图书馆员培训计划，曾先后为中国大陆及台湾培训了百余名的图书馆员，大陆方面包括中国国家图书馆、北京大学、清华大学、北京师范大学、南开大学、北京邮电大学、三〇一医院图书馆、重庆大学、浙江医科大学、中山大学、中山医科大学、科学院图书馆、中国科技文献中心、东北师范大学、华中师范大学、深圳图书馆，台湾方面有"中央图书馆"、中山大学、淡江大学、逢甲大学和一些省市图书馆等，其中很多位是馆长、副馆长，及部门主任。

在李馆长退休的前夕，美国图书馆学会特别由理事会决议表扬。美国的华人图书馆员协会、亚太美裔图书馆员学会、俄亥俄州的 OHIOLINK 及 OHIONET、还有台湾图书馆学会及"中央图书馆"等都分别颁赠奖状，祝贺李馆长的荣退。

（原载《"中国图书馆学会"会讯》1999年9月30日出版的第7卷第3期，第1-3页。）

OLC Honors Its Own

At OLC's Annual Conference in Dayton the following members were honored for their achievements and dedication to library service in Ohio.

Dr. Hwa-Wei Lee completed twenty-one years as Dean of Libraries at Ohio University in August of 1999. During his tenure, the holdings of the Vernon R. Alden Library doubled from 1 million to 2 million print volumes, and library endowments rose to more than $7 million. The library's southeast Asia collection is ranked as one of the best of its kind in the world. Under his guidance, Alden Library has been instrumental in providing library service to the general public through direct contact and through their local public and school libraries. He has been an active supporter of the Ohio Library Association serving as an OLC Board member and encouraging his staff to participate in library affairs statewide.

...

Hall of Fame Librarian

Dr. Hwa-Wei Lee completed twenty-one years as Dean of Libraries at Ohio University in August of 1999. In this position. Dr. Lee provided exceptional service to all types of libraries in southeastern Ohio and throughout the state.

Dr. Lee's accomplishments at Ohio University are noteworthy. During his tenure the holdings of the Vernon R. Alden Library doubled from 1 million to 2 million print volumes, and library endowments rose to more than $7 million. The library's Southeast Asia collection is ranked as one of the best such in the world.

While these achievements are remarkable. Dr. Lee deserves recognition also for his commitment to sharing this tremendous resource with all the people of southeast Ohio. Under his guidance Alden Library has been instrumental in providing library service to the general public through direct contact and through their local public and school libraries.

Alden Library was an active participant from the beginning in the Ohio Valley Area Libraries regional system, and was the only academic library in the state to function as a reference and interlibrary loan resource library for public libraries. Dr. Lee has always welcomed field trips by area school children, welcoming them as eagerly as he hosted visits by professional librarians from around the world.

He has been an active supporter of Ohio Library Association, serving as an OLA Board member and encouraging his staff to participate in library affairs statewide.

For his outstanding leadership and superior achievement in library service throughout his career, both locally and at the state, national, and international levels, we name Dr. Hwa-Wei Lee to the Ohio Librarian Hall of Fame.

(Published in Access: *A Monthly Newsletter for Members of Ohio Library Council*. November 1999: p. 1.)

Hwa-Wei Lee Named OCLC Visiting Distinguished Scholar

Hwa-Wei Lee, dean emeritus, Ohio University Libraries, has been named OCLC Visiting Distinguished Scholar for a one-year term beginning Jan. 1.

The Visiting Distinguished Scholar program is sponsored by the OCLC Office of Research to bring experienced educators and administrators to OCLC.

Dr. Lee will be working with the OCLC Institute to help extend its program internationally, with a focus on the Asia Pacific region. The institute promotes the evolution of libraries through advanced education and knowledge exchange.

"I consider it a great privilege to continue my association with OCLC in a much closer relationship this coming year," said Dr. Lee. "I am especially pleased that I will be working in my new role to strengthen OCLC's professional education and training programs in Asia through the OCLC Institute and OCLC Asia Pacific. The new initiative of the OCLC Institute in Asia is well timed and will expand the tie between OCLC and the fast-developing Asian library community."

"Dr. Lee brings a deep personal and professional commitment to the role of libraries in the countries and in the lives of the people of the Asia Pacific region," said Martin Dillon, executive director, OCLC Institute. "We expect his knowledge and insight to be instrumental as the OCLC Institute expands globally."

Since 1970, Dr. Lee has served as a library consultant and lecturer under the sponsorship of various organizations and agencies, including the Asia Foundation, the Food and Agricultural Organization of the United Nations, the Japan Foundation Center for Global Partnership, the International Development Research Centre of Canada, and the U. S. Agency for International Development.

Dr. Lee was dean of University Libraries, Ohio University, from 1978 to 1999. He served as the OHIONET delegate on the OCLC Users Council from 1985 – 1991, and as delegate-at-large to the Second White House Conference on Library and Information Services in July 1991.

Dr. Lee has received distinguished service awards from the American Library Association as Councilor for 1988 – 1992 and 1993 – 1997, the Ohio Library and Information Network, the Chinese Academic and Professional Association in Mid-America, and the Library Association of China (Taiwan). He was recognized in 1991 with the John Ames Humphry Award for International Librarianship.

During the past decade, Dr. Lee has been appointed advisor to the National Library of China and consultant to the Central Library in Taiwan and to the Peking University Library Foundation. He has served as visiting professor to nine Chinese universities. He is 1999 Ohio Hall of Fame Librarian.

Author of three books and some 60 articles, conference papers and consultant reports, Dr. Lee has organized eight international conferences. Currently, he is a member of the Advisory Board of the American Association of Universities/Association of Research Libraries Global Resources Program. More information is available on Dr. Lee's personal home page < http: // www. library. ohiou. edu/libinfo/staff/personal/leeh/leeh. htm > .

Dr. Lee earned a bachelor's degree in education from National Taiwan Normal University; a master's degree in education as well as a master's in library science, both from the University of Pittsburgh; and a doctoral degree in foundations of education and library science, also from the University of Pittsburgh.

(Published in *OCLC Newsletter*. No. 243, January/February 2000: p. 19.)

图书馆界之巨擘　海外华人之骄傲
——美国最著名的华人图书馆馆长李华伟博士

潘燕桃[①]

李华伟博士,第一位美国著名大学图书馆的华人馆长,第一位受到中国最高领导人亲自接见的海外图书馆杰出人士[②],第一位同时应聘为北京大学、清华大学等著名学府客座教授和中国国家图书馆荣誉顾问的美国图书馆学家。他是一位才华横溢、成就卓著的图书馆管理专家,一位学贯中西、著作等身的学者,一位诚信热情、和蔼可亲的老人;一座华人在美国图书馆历史上矗立的丰碑,一座飞架中美图书馆之间交流与合作的桥梁……是他令美国人折服敬佩,是他令举世华人骄傲自豪。

1999年8月,李华伟博士在服务图书馆事业40年之后光荣退休。为了表彰李华伟博士的杰出贡献、弘扬李华伟博士的卓越成就,美国图书馆界以命名图书馆的独特方式在美国图书馆史上刻上了"李华伟"这个光辉的名字,而中国图书馆界则以鸿雁和专文的传统方式遥寄对李华伟博士无限的美好祝福。

李华伟博士生于1933年,祖籍福建,自两岁起随父母先后辗转南京、桂林、重庆等地。1949年随父母迁往台湾后完成高中学业。1954年毕业于台湾师范大学教育学系。1957年赴美国宾夕法尼亚州匹兹堡大学攻读教育学和图书馆学硕士学位。1959年硕士毕业,与玛丽小姐结婚之后,在匹兹堡大学图书馆工作。1962年转至匹兹堡市都肯大学图书馆,担任采访部主任兼非洲特藏部主任,并在匹兹堡大学攻读主修高等教育行政、副修图书馆学的博士学位。1965年博士毕业后受聘于宾夕法尼亚州爱丁堡大学,任图书馆副馆长兼图书馆学系助理教授,次年晋升为馆长,当时年仅33岁的李博士是美籍华人担任美国大学图书馆馆长的第一人。1968年美国国际发展总署派遣李博士到泰国曼谷担任亚洲理工学院图书馆及信息中心主任,期间李博士还担任一些国际组织与机构的顾问,经常为亚洲地区的图书馆建设出谋划策,参与有关项目合作。1975年李博士回到美国,在科罗拉多州立大学图书馆任副馆长。自1978年起担任俄亥俄大学图书馆馆长,兼任俄亥俄大学教育学院教授、博士导师。

李博士在担任俄亥俄大学图书馆馆长期间,领导该馆建立一整套高水平的图书馆自动化系统网络,其中包括联网书目数据库系统网络(Alice Online Catalog)、电子文体系统网络(Electronic Texts)、联合编目及馆际互借系统网络(OhioLINK,此网络可经由OCLC的国际网络与世界各地的1.4万多家图书馆建立合作编目及馆际互借关系),从而使俄亥俄大学图书馆跻身于美国大学图书馆的前列。此外,李博士还积极参与俄亥俄大学的发展规划、课程设计及更新、采用新教学技术、建立校园网络、发展远距离教育、教育国际化、改革人力资源管理以及对外募捐等多项工作,成就卓著。

李博士在美国乃至世界图书馆界都非常活跃,历任美国图书馆学会理事及国际关系委员会亚洲太平洋地区小组主席、华美图书馆员学会会长及理事、国际图联大学及研究图书馆委员会委员、俄亥俄州图书馆学会理事、OCLC会员代表大会俄州代表;同时还多次兼任联合国教科文组织、联合国发展计划、世界粮农组织、加拿大国际发展及研究中心等机

[①] 任职于中山大学资讯管理学院。
[②] 江泽民主席在1998年访美时曾亲切接见数位华人诺贝尔奖金获得者与李华伟博士等十余位杰出美籍华人。

构有关图书馆发展项目的顾问。

　　李博士在为美国图书馆事业、世界图书馆事业奉献其卓越才干的同时，为中美图书馆架起了合作交流的桥梁，为祖国图书馆事业的发展运筹谋划，日夜奔忙，尽心尽力。1982年李博士应中国科技情报所和加拿大国际发展研究中心的邀请，首次回国到昆明一个情报中心管理培训班讲学。自此之后，李博士在日常繁忙的图书馆管理、教学工作之余，每年都要抽空应邀到中国大陆各地讲学，足迹遍及大江南北，中国国家图书馆、深圳图书馆等一批著名图书馆纷纷聘请李博士担任荣誉顾问和顾问，北京大学、清华大学、中山大学、西安交大、南开大学、湖南医大、武汉大学、四川联大、北京师大、东北师大等高等学府纷纷聘请他担任访问教授或顾问教授。李博士还利用世界银行贷款项目和联合国发展基金项目，多次开办国内师范院校图书馆管理培训班，多次参与组织了中国多所大学、科研院所和公共图书馆的大型图书馆学术研讨会。由于李华伟博士的不懈努力，从1980年起，联合国教科文组织和美国国际发展总署及一些基金会赞助俄亥俄大学图书馆设立了一个"国际图书馆员培训计划"，曾先后为中国培训了100多位图书馆员，其中多数是馆长、副馆长和部门主任。1993年，李博士又说服他的校友邵公全先生出资赞助俄亥俄大学图书馆成立了专门用于培训亚洲地区图书馆员的基金。该基金每年资助4名来自中国大陆的图书馆员赴美进修培训3个月。

　　李华伟博士不但是一位经验丰富的图书馆管理专家、热情诚挚的图书馆活动家，更是一位学养深厚的图书馆学家。他曾发表过60多篇学术论文，著有《图书馆学的世界观》、《90年代图书馆筹款指引》、《现代化图书馆管理》等学术著作。

　　李华伟博士贡献突出、成绩卓著，曾荣获俄亥俄大学"最杰出行政人员奖"、美国新闻署"杰出服务奖"、美国图书馆学会"国际关系卓越贡献奖"和"杰出理事奖"、美国华美图书馆员学会"杰出服务奖"、亚太地区美国图书馆员学会"杰出服务奖"、美中华人学术及专业学会"杰出服务奖"、俄亥俄州"最杰出图书馆员奖"、台湾"中国图书馆学会""杰出贡献奖"，以及俄亥俄图书及信息网络感谢状等众多褒奖。他的名字被列入《世界名人传》、《美国名人传》和《美国教育界名人传》。

　　1999年8月退休之后，李博士又获得了一系列的殊荣，俄亥俄大学为了表彰李博士的突出贡献，将新建的俄亥俄大学贮存图书馆命名为"李华伟图书馆"（Hwa-Wei Lee Library Annex），把重新装修一新的俄亥俄大学图书馆总馆阿尔登图书馆（Alden Library）首层命名为"李华伟国际藏书中心"（Hwa-Wei Lee Center for International Collections）。俄亥俄图书馆委员会授予李博士"荣誉图书馆员"的称号。此外，美国图书馆学会、美国华美图书馆员学会、亚太地区美国图书馆员学会、中国国家图书馆、台湾"中国图书馆学会"、俄亥俄图书馆网络（OhioNET）、俄亥俄图书馆在线（OhioLINK）、俄亥俄峡谷地区图书馆等机构纷纷以不同方式表彰李博士为图书馆事业所作出的杰出贡献。OCLC（Online Computer Library Center）聘请李博士为2000年杰出访问学者。

　　在致力图书馆事业40年、服务俄亥俄大学图书馆21年之后的今天，李华伟博士在享受丰富多彩的退休生活的同时，仍然奔走于中国大陆、台湾和泰国等地进行著述、讲学和顾问活动。

参考文献

1. 封学绛等. 李华伟博士访谈录. ［J］. 图书馆研究与工作［J］, 1999（4）: 11-15
2. 卢素心. 李华伟博士及其领导下的美国俄亥俄大学图书馆［J］. 图书情报知识,

1995（4）：46-47.

3. 景星. 美国图书馆界的头号华人［J］. 中华儿女，1998（7）：60-67.

4. http://www.library.ohiou.edu/libinfo/staff/personal/leeh/leeh.html

（原载《图书馆论坛》2000年第20卷第5期，第95-96页。）

国际图书馆界的亲善大使——李华伟博士专访[①]

林呈潢　黄倩如

赤子般的温暖笑颜是我们初见到李华伟馆长的第一印象。深冬的清晨，李馆长特别从紧凑的行程中拨冗接受本刊的专访，与我们分享他四十年来在美国图书馆界服务的经验与心得。

水道渠成、学业与事业兼顾

"其实我本来想当个"国中"校长的…"，1950 年进入台湾省立师范学院（台湾师范大学之前身）就读的李馆长认为当一名校长是最自然的安排，然而一九五七年获得美国匹兹堡大学（University of Pittsburgh）的入学许可及奖学金出国就学却使得他转换跑道，进入图书馆界服务。李馆长虽然主修教育，但为了减轻父母的经济负担，主动争取到该校图书馆"工读"的机会，一面工作，一面攻读学位，1959 年毕业后，因该校图书馆计划发展东亚藏书部门，以优越的条件聘请勤勉有加的李馆长留下来工作，并让他进入卡内基米伦大学的图书馆学院攻读图书馆学的硕士学位，两年内便升任采访部第一助理，为该校图书馆东亚部门奠定良好的基础。

"我的指导老师 Dr. Sarah Vann 曾半开玩笑对我说：换工作有两个要件，其一是薪水比原有的高，其二是职位比现有的高，把握机会才能获得较快的升迁。"1962 年，匹兹堡城内另一所学院杜肯大学图书馆馆长欲借重李馆长的专才，说服他前往该校担任采访部主任兼该馆著名之非洲特藏部主任，在公余继续在匹兹堡大学进修博士学位，主修教育，副修图书馆学。博士班的学习让李馆长扩大了图书馆学专业视野，并培养敏锐之分析、推理及研究的能力，配合大学图书馆的实务经验，奠定日后 40 年大学图书馆行政管理及教学研究工作深远的根基。

1965 年，李馆长取得博士学位后，即由当时宾州的爱丁堡州立学院聘为图书馆副馆长兼图书馆学系助理教授，次年升任馆长，是中国人在美国高等院校担任图书馆馆长最早的一人。

图书馆界国际亲善大使

李馆长丰富的专业生涯中，1968 年起前往泰国亚洲理工学院（Asian Institute of Technology AIT Thailand）服务的偶然机缘，造就他成为一位图书馆界的国际亲善大使："1968 年，由美国国际发展总署向宾州爱丁堡州立学院借调，我被派往泰国的亚洲理工学院担任该院首任图书馆及资讯中心主任，尔后七年一直参与亚洲理工学院建校与扩展，直到 1975 年美国支援该学院任务圆满结束为止。"

建立四个专业资讯中心及开设自动化课程是其泰国七年任内最重要的贡献，当时为了教学及研究上的需要，李馆长筹设了包括环境系统资讯中心（Environmental Systems Information Center, ENSIC）、国际地质工程资源中心（Geotechnical Engineering International Resources Center, GEIRC）、国际机构资讯中心（International Ferrocement Information Center, IFIC）、区域能源资讯中心（Regional Energy Resources Information Center, RERIC）

[①] 林呈潢、黄倩如采访，黄倩如整理撰稿。

等四个重要的资讯中心，该校以此四个中心，为整个亚洲地区培育相当多杰出的学者及研究人员。

1970年，李馆长更应泰国朱拉隆功大学图书馆学系之邀请，在该系讲授图书馆自动化课程，首创亚洲风气之先，直到1975年李馆长回国担任美国科罗拉多州立大学图书馆教授级副馆长，该课程才停止开设。回美国之后，李馆长并未停止教书及国际亲善交流的工作。1978年转任俄亥俄大学图书馆长后，他同时兼任教育学院教授，先后指导了十余位学生完成博士论文，三十余年来应亚洲地区中国大陆、台湾、香港和印度尼西亚、巴布亚新几内亚、菲律宾、南韩、泰国等国家和地区的机构团体之邀请，担任图书馆发展之顾问，更多次担任联合国教科组织、联合国发展计划、世界粮农组织、加拿大国际发展及研究中心等机构有关图书馆发展项目之顾问。

似乎就在不知不觉当中，亲切的李馆长成了国际图书馆界亲善大使，不但在美国图书馆界极为活跃，曾担任美国图书馆学会理事、国际关系委员会亚洲太平洋地区小组主席、俄亥俄州图书馆学会理事、美国华美图书馆员学会会长及理事、OCLC会员代表大会俄州代表、国际图联大学及研究图书馆委员会委员等职务。更因卓越的成就，得到许多学会团体颁赠之奖项，其中主要的有：俄亥俄州大学最杰出行政人员奖（1982年）、华人图书馆员协会杰出服务奖（1983年）、俄亥俄州最杰出图书馆员奖（1987年）、台湾"中国图书馆学会"杰出贡献奖（1989年）、美国图书馆学会国际关系卓越贡献奖（1991年）、亚美及太平洋地区图书馆员学会杰出服务奖（1991年）、美国新闻署杰出服务奖状（1992年）、美国图书馆学会杰出理事奖（1987—1992及1993—1997年）、俄亥俄州图书及资讯网感谢状（1993年）等。俄亥俄大学更为了表彰李馆长21年来对该校图书馆的贡献，特将新建的图书馆分馆命名为"李华伟图书分馆"，也另将总馆一楼重新装修命名为"李华伟国际藏书中心"。俄亥俄州图书馆学会也特别授予"终生荣誉图书馆员"（Ohio Hall of Fame Librarian）的称号。

开花结果　不解之缘

1978年李馆长至俄亥俄大学担任图书馆长，至1999年间荣退，这一段长达二十一年的岁月，是其事业的黄金期，"经过了图书馆学方面的学术研究以及多年图书馆专业工作的历练，在俄亥俄大学，我得以组织一个竞争力强的工作团队，引进图书馆界的各种新资讯技术，加强图书馆的资源及服务。"具体而言，这些贡献可以分为以下六点：

（1）应用资讯科技使图书馆持续创新与进步。

（2）持续建立丰富之馆藏，尤其是拓展国际出版品方面，俄亥俄大学拥有之东南亚区域书刊文献是世界上首屈一指；1993年亦成立海外华人文献及研究中心，同时也是全世界所有大学图书馆中，唯一被波札那（Botswana），危地马拉（Guatemala），马来西亚（Malaysia）及史瓦济兰（Swaziland）等四个国家政府指定为该国出版品之寄存图书馆。

（3）由于国际出版品丰富之馆藏量，俄亥俄大学于1996年成为美国研究图书馆学会之会员，该协会目前拥有美加地区122个大型学术图书馆；且自1996年来加入以后，排名由82名上升至68名，这些成果都是自李馆长任职以来全力推动的。

（4）李馆长在善募款项方面最为成功。当1978年李馆长刚至俄亥俄大学就职时，外界对图书馆之捐款不到2万美元，到了1999年6月，透过他优越的人际关系，已经募集了超过1千万美元之经费，其中8百多万是图书馆的专用基金。

（5）积极参与OCLC及建立俄亥俄州图书及资讯网（OhioLink），使俄亥俄大学以成功的馆际合作模式、合作网路的规划与建置扬名国内外。

（6）推动俄亥俄大学设立一个国际图书馆员培训计划，此计划赞助了来自各国超过175名馆员在俄亥俄大学接受专业继续教育，成为高级图书馆管理人才。

幸福大家庭

谈起位于俄亥俄州的美丽家园，李馆长的笑容更灿烂，从随身的公事包中拿出全家福照片，与我们分享家居生活美好的片段。1957年李馆长初抵美国后，在学校中认识了当时是同班同学的夫人，两年硕士班同窗生涯，培养了相知相惜的默契，1959年组成美满家庭，成为李馆长成功事业生涯中最大的助力。看着照片中健康而活泼的6名子女及5名孙子女，个个有着不同外貌，但其神采奕奕的眼神和亲切和蔼的笑容，正是这个大家庭最明显的徽记，也是李馆长自信的泉源。

专业自信　坚定不移

对于在图书馆界工作，李馆长四十年来没有丝毫的动摇，"我个人很荣幸能够在图书馆界服务，身为大学图书馆经营管理者，有机会参与1959至1999年间四十年图书馆事业快速转变的阶段，实在非常幸运。1960年代初任图书馆员时，图书馆仍是纸本馆藏为主，图书馆作业开始自动化的阶段，1970年代网路化图书馆开始成形，1980年代迈向电子图书馆，1990年，朝向数位及虚拟图书馆发展，这些转变都是图书馆成为21世纪网际网路世纪主流的前奏。面对接踵而至的机会和挑战，图书馆专业显得生趣处处，趣味盎然"。

多年来，李馆长对于教学及研究之热情不曾稍减，除了发表三本专著，六十多篇文章，又先后担任了六种学术期刊的编辑，更奔走各地主持重要的国际会议，为两岸图书馆事业投注相当多的心血。近几年来，李馆长更抽空回国讲学，将所擅长的图书馆观念及做法，如目标管理、参与式管理、全品质管理介绍给国内图书馆界，期盼图书馆事业更加革新与进步。

图书馆从业人员应有的价值观及服务观

当我们提到了国内近年来成立多所图书资讯学系所，图书馆专业人员应建立何种专业价值观及服务观之问题，李馆长表示特别的重视，"我以数天前美国图书馆学会（The American Library Association）所草拟的专业宣言与大家互勉，图书馆员应自许：①成为人类观念交换的桥梁；②使人们不受限制地接受新知；③从各项知识中学习与淬炼；④确保所有人类自由地构筑、拥有、表达自己之信念；⑤尊重每一个人；⑥保存人类之纪录；⑦维持资讯专业及机构之独立自主；⑧能达成以上所有目标之专业内涵。其中最后一项更贯穿了图书馆与资讯专业的核心，愿此成为带领大家之信念"。

提携后进　作育英才

关于国内图书馆界人才培养的问题，李馆长乐观的表示其实台湾图书馆界的人才素质高，是大陆图书馆界所没有的优势，高素质的图书资讯人员可使图书馆发展更进步，所提供的服务更能配合时代的需要。不过此次回国访问期间，仍观察到某些图书馆仍有馆员培养不易、无法留住优秀馆员的问题。

从个人的经验出发，李馆长倡导生涯规划的观念，他认为每位图书馆从业人员，都应该好好地计划自己的事业生涯，了解自己应该学习的方向。身为图书馆的领导者，必须奖励所属同仁进修、参与图书馆界的各项活动。当优秀的馆员另有高就时，虽有不舍仍然应该大力促成，因为大多数图书馆的组织还是金字塔型，若有机会向上发展，将可造就更多的图书馆管理人才。

乐在工作　乐在生活

惊见时光的流逝，访问尾声李馆长应我们的要求谈谈个人的特质，他谦虚地表示其实自己也是普罗大众之一员，或许在他人眼中，李馆长是一名工作狂，"人们常视我为一位工作狂，其实是其来有自，我常以我的专业为荣，总是为自己设定更高的标准，或许可以说是倾向当一名改革者及创新者。乐观的个性使我对于各种事物抱持着肯定积极的态度，有志者事竟成，乐与人们以互信为基础，组成团队完成工作，就是我多年来秉持的信念"。

结　语

步出了饭店大厅，忙碌的台北街头又充斥着热闹的人声与车行，返校的车程中，我们抛开了访谈内容，开心的闲话家常。这就是李馆长，虚怀乐取，推群独步，带领大家一起乐在工作、乐在生活，共同为喜爱的图书馆事业展望一个美好的未来。

（原载《图书与资讯学刊》2000年第5期，第96–100页。）

李华伟（1933 - ）

汪雁秋

现任美国国会图书馆亚洲部主任的李华伟博士原先是美国俄亥俄大学图书馆院长级馆长。他是极少数华人在美国大学图书馆担任图书馆总馆馆长者之一。因为他的卓越成绩，俄亥俄大学董事会破例地把一座新建的图书馆分馆命名为"李华伟图书馆分馆"。除此以外，为了表彰他在发展国际合作，促进图书馆藏书全球化方面所做出的贡献，还特别将总馆的第一层楼重新装修，命名为"李华伟国际藏书中心"。

李华伟博士原籍是福建省福州市。1949年随家迁往台湾，在省立台中第一中学毕业，1950年考入当时的台湾省立师范学院攻修教育系。1955年毕业后分配到台北省立师范专科学校的附属小学担任训导主任一年，次年被已升格为台湾师范大学的母校聘为助教。

1957年，因获得美国匹兹堡大学的入学许可及奖学金，在九月一日动身赴美进修，以七年的时间，念毕教育硕士，图书馆学硕士及哲学博士的学位。在此期间，除一面攻读及研究外，还在匹兹堡大学图书馆勤工俭读，1959年由该馆正式聘用，首先担任培训馆员，两年后升为采访部第一助理，1962年，由匹兹堡城的都肯大学图书馆聘为采访部主任兼该馆极为著名的非洲特藏部主任。

1965年在匹兹堡大学完成主修教育及副修图书馆学的哲学博士学位以后，由当时宾州的爱丁堡州立学院聘为图书馆副馆长兼图书馆系助理教授，次年升为馆长，为中国人在美国高等院校担任图书馆馆长最早的一人，在此期间还一度兼任图书馆学系主任一职。

1968年，在一个偶然的机遇下，由美国国际发展总署向宾州爱丁堡州立学院借调，派往泰国的亚洲理工学院担任该院首任的图书馆及资讯中心主任。一年后，因为工作的需要辞掉爱丁堡的工作，在泰国停留了七年，直到1975年美国支援亚洲理工学院的项目圆满结束。在亚洲理工学院服务时，还应泰国朱拉隆功大学图书馆学系之邀，自1970年至1975年在该系讲授"图书馆自动化"的课程，这在亚洲还是最早开设的课程。除此之外，还多次担任联合国教科文组织，联合国发展计划，世界粮农组织，加拿大国际发展及研究中心等机构有关图书馆发展专案的顾问。

一九七五年返回美国后即应聘担任美国科罗拉多州立大学图书馆教授级副馆长，三年以后转任俄亥俄大学图书馆馆长。

李博士在美国图书馆界极为活跃，曾经担任过美国图书馆学会理事、国际关系委员会亚洲太平洋地区小组主席、俄亥俄州图书馆学会理事、美国华美图书馆员学会会长及理事、OCLC会员代表大会俄州代表、国际图联大学及研究图书馆委员会委员等职务；因为他的卓越成就，李博士曾得到很多奖励，其中主要的有：俄亥俄大学最杰出行政人员奖（1982年）、华美图书馆员学会杰出服务奖（1983年）、俄亥俄州最杰出图书馆员奖（1987年）、台湾"中国图书馆学会"杰出贡献奖（1989年）、美中华人学术及专业学会杰出服务奖（1991年）、美国图书馆学会国际关系卓越贡献奖（1991年）、亚美及太平洋地区图书馆员学会杰出服务奖（1991年）、美国新闻署杰出服务奖（1992年）、美国图书馆学会杰出理事奖（1992年）、俄亥俄图书及资讯网感谢状（1993年）等。

另外，李博士还陆续的被选载在《世界名人传》，《美国名人传》，《美国教育界名人传》等年鉴上。

即使在极为忙碌的工作中，李博士仍然不忘教学、研究与写作，在他近四十年的图书馆生涯中，曾经发表过七十多篇文章，出版了五本书，编过三本会议录及先后担任了七种学术期刊的编辑委员。他的著作是《图书馆学的世界观》（1991年台湾学生书局出版）、《90年代图书馆的筹款指引》（与盖里·汉博士合著，1992年由美国坚那位公司出版）、《现代化图书馆管理》（1996年由台湾三民书局出版）、《OCLC联机与光碟编目概论》（与刁维汉、王行仁合著，1999年由上海华东师范大学出版社出版）、《知识管理：理论与实践》（与董小英、左美云合著，2002年在北京由华芝出版社出版）。

李博士曾经主持或协办过多次国际会议，其中包括，1983年6月28日在洛杉矶由亚美及太平洋图书馆员学会与华美图书馆员学会合办"亚太地区图书馆的发展及合作途径会议"、1988年9月8日至11日在西安由俄大图书馆与西安交大图书馆合办的"图书馆新技术应用国际学术讨论会"、1994年10月20日至24日在上海由中国科学院上海图书馆主办的"资讯技术与资讯服务国际研讨会"、1996年8月21日至23日在北京举行的"第一届中美图书馆合作会议"、1996年9月3日至6日由武汉大学及上海师范大学等合办的"资讯资源与社会发展国际学术研讨会"、1998年10月25日至28日在北京大学为了庆祝北大建校一百周年及新图书馆大楼落成所举办的"21世纪大学图书馆的新使命国际学术研讨会"、2001年8月11日至16日在New York和Washington, D.C.举行的"第二届中美图书馆合作会议"、及2002年5月19日至22日在北京由中国科学院图书馆为了庆祝新图馆大楼落成所主办的"知识管理：图书馆的机遇与挑战学术研讨会"。

在俄亥俄大学，李博士除了担任图书馆馆长之外，还兼任了该大学教育学院的教授，先后担任了十余位博士学生的论文指导老师。在李博士任内，通过他优越的人际关系，他曾为俄亥俄大学筹募了上千万美元，其中八百多万是图书馆的专用基金，在美国的公立大学中名列前茅。

除此之外，自1982年以来，李博士还每年应邀前往中国大陆和台湾各地讲学。由于他孜孜不倦的教学活动，大陆上很多大学都邀请他担任访问教授或客座教授，包括北京大学、北京师范大学、北京邮电大学、西安交通大学、南开大学、湖南医大、武汉大学、四川大学、东北师范大学、天津理工学院、深圳职业技术学院。中国科学院武汉文献资讯中心及兰州文献资讯中心也聘请李博士担任学术顾问。中国的国家图书馆、中国科学院图书馆、清华大学图书馆、深圳图书馆、浙江图书馆、及台湾的"中央图书馆"也礼聘李博士担任顾问。

作为一个美籍华裔的图书馆从业人员，李博士极为关心中国大陆及台湾图书馆的发展，除了经常回国讲学外，从1980年起，还在俄亥俄大学图书馆设立了一个国际图书馆员培训计划，曾先后为中国大陆及台湾培训了近两百名的图书馆员，包括中国国家图书馆、台湾"中央图书馆"、北京大学、清华大学、北京师范大学、南开大学、北京邮电大学、三〇一医院图书馆、重庆大学、浙江医科大学、中山大学、中山医科大学、湖南医科大学、科学院图书馆、中国科技资讯中心、东北师范大学、华中师范大学、华南理工大学、暨南大学、深圳图书馆、及台湾中山大学、淡江大学、逢甲大学和一些省市图书馆等，其中很多位是馆长、副馆长、及部门主任。

在1999年底李馆长从俄亥俄大学退休的前夕，美国图书馆学会特别由理事会决议表扬。美国的华美图书馆员学会、亚太美裔图书馆员学会、俄亥俄州的Ohio LINK及Ohio

NET、还有台湾图书馆学会及"中央图书馆"等都分别颁赠奖状,祝贺李馆长的荣退。俄亥俄州图书馆学会还特别授予他终身荣誉馆员的称号(Ohio Hall of Fame Librarian)。闻名全球的 OCLC 图书馆电脑中心也特别聘请李博士为杰出的访问学者。

(原载"中国图书馆学会"出版委员会主编《图书馆人物志(一)》,2003年,第213–216页。)

天下谁人不识君
——记美国 OHIO 大学图书馆长李华伟博士

张白影

  1999年3月8日，星期一，广州。阳光融融的早晨。上班伊始，我拆阅收发员递过来的一封寄自大洋彼岸的信，一行文字跃入眼帘："在模范地服务于美国俄亥俄大学及其图书馆二十一年之后，李华伟博士将于年内退休"。尽管去年11月9日，李博士在暨南大学时曾告诉过我，他明年将离开图书馆馆长的岗位，但看到这种事实真的出现时，我的心中仍顷刻之间涌起一股惆怅与失落，慨叹不已。我想起暨南大学那次见面：他仍是那么热情，那么慈蔼，仍然慷慨地给予别人帮助，仍在谋求跨越国界的互助合作。但时隔几年再度握手，毕竟人生易老天难老。每当看到李博士奔走于美国、中国及五大洲各图书馆之间的匆匆步履和不无倦容的身影时，我多么希望这位仁厚的老人能享有应得的休闲、安适和清静，而许许多多图书馆界同仁后学，又几乎是永无满足地渴望得到他对事业发展的热情促进，谆谆教导和知识滋润。他作为学者、长者、人友、人师，其敬业、勤业、精业的品格和风范，堪称一代楷模。

  在美国，李华伟博士是华人图书馆员的骄傲。在其担任俄亥俄大学图书馆馆长期间，他重组图书馆系统，使图书馆的捐赠基金达到800万美元，使藏书规模增至200万册，他成功地领导俄大图书馆参与创建OhioLINK工程，从而俄州各大学的图书馆联网；俄亥俄图书馆因其卓越的专业建设和服务成绩，被吸收为"研究图书馆协会"成员，并跻身北美第一流的121家研究图书馆行列。李博士为促进国际文化、学术和图书馆界交流作出了突出的贡献，他是俄大国际学生、特别是中国学生的知心朋友和导师。

  李博士在他服务于不同大学图书馆的35年间，把他的知识、智慧、精力和爱心撒播到全世界。他曾为五大洲的图书馆提供咨询和讲学，曾主持了7次国际学术会议，是13个全美或全球性组织的成员、评议员、代表、理事、顾问，乃至主席，他以他的热情、忠诚、信用、正直，为同行和学生树立了一个世界公民的模范榜样。

  山包海汇、博大精深的图书馆内，古今学者共聚，千代贤哲同堂，门庭挨着门庭，智慧之光绵绵。留连于此，天人合一，身心飘腾，时空永恒，那份人类精神与知识的厚重，是永远也不言"休"也不会语"退"的。李博士为图书馆这方沃土在春天精心撒下的种子，在夏天辛勤流下的汗珠，在秋季无私奉献的果实，在冬日真诚传播的祝愿，将给世界范围内的朋友和学生们注入永恒的激励和温情。

  我初识李博士是80年代末的仲春，他与他同事高斯女士来湖南大学图书馆参观指导。这座源于公元976年中国宋代岳麓书院御书楼的书城，依山伴岭，檐角飞天，湘江如带，一水拖兰，十纪连绵，弦歌不绝，我们在此一起品味华夏文明源远流长的醇香，又展望图书馆未来的灿烂。之后，他不时赠我华章大著，我也偶奉习作小品；聚时欢，别时难，天地悠悠人久长。我的心中从此多了一位良师益友，大洋彼岸，牵系着万里关山隔不断的真诚的云树之思。

  1992年7月，受李博士盛邀，我与湖南省教委主任季益贵先生赴美访问，他和他的同事让我们在OHIO渡过了充实而愉快的一周时光。在他主持的图书馆里，在他服务的大学校园中，在他热情邀集华人学者聚会的餐桌上，在他周到安排的CAS清澈洁净的湖水旁，友谊，像一束温暖的阳光，像一股和煦的春风，像一只快乐的小鸟，像俄亥俄随处可见的艳丽鲜花和沁人心脾的青青草坪，始终环绕在我们的身旁。漫步在俄亥俄大学，优雅静谧，空气清新，绿荫如盖，一幢幢教学楼红砖墙面上藤蔓舒展，表现出年岁的沧桑，校门上那两盏仿如中国宫灯似的照明，闪现着上个世纪的慈祥柔润的光亮。随之，我们惊讶而叹服地发现，俄亥俄州的历史，俄亥俄大学的历史，都被浓缩并生动地表现在他主持的图书馆里，他为这片土地和土地上的先民，树立了一尊永远的里程碑，我由此感叹图书馆工作乃是一种艺术。也许我来自被称为"千年学府"的湖南大学，特别容易陶醉在这种历史与现代的巧妙结合之中。

我们十分幸运，离开 OHIO 的前一天，恰恰赶上俄州一年一度的音乐艺术节，一片开阔的草地上，来自全州和其他州的几万人喜气洋洋地聚集于此，临时搭建的舞台像一张巨鲸的嘴巴，两旁是同样巨型的电子显示屏，演员表演清晰在目。人们和着熟悉的歌声与台上一同吟唱，老人孩子姑娘们踏着拍节，摆动身体，原地舞蹈；台上和台下交融一片，草地上回荡着演员和几万观众的声情。我们深受感染，不会唱，用手轻击拍节，也情不自禁地舞蹈起来。每个人都是演员，每个人都是观众，每个人都全情投入，每个人都尽情地享受着节日的欢欣，李博士独具匠心地让我们感受了一种西方大众祥和温馨的节日文化气氛。音乐节散去已很晚了，他仍坚持自己开车把我们送到机场旅店，依依话别。我们接着到了华盛顿，到了纽约，到了洛杉矶，不论走到哪里，我们的眼前都会不时浮现他儒雅温文亲切的言谈笑貌音容，念叨着刚刚和他在一起的渡过的日子。后来，1996 年在北京 IFLA 大会上，我见过他忙碌的身影；1998 年暨南大学讲坛上，我见过他演讲的神情。朋友们的来信，经常通报他在中国大陆西北、西南、华北、华东的匆匆之旅，为促进祖国图书情报事业的发展，他无私地奉献着满腔赤诚。

如果离开图书馆长的岗位后，时间将会变得自由和从容，那么，我们——他在中国所有的朋友和学生，都会热忱地欢迎他随时来讲学，来团聚，来旅游，来品茶饮酒，来看神州大地那看不够的黄河、长江、华山、泰山和万里长城，来侃故乡亲人侃不尽的松、竹、梅、兰、风花雪月和海阔天空。北京的庄守经先生，甘肃的潘寅生先生，武汉的彭斐章先生，东北的金恩晖先生，南京的卢子博先生，广东的谭祥金先生……我知道他朋友遍天下，遍天下的朋友都欢迎他。在即将结束这篇短文时，我想向李华伟博士的夫人表达敬意，这是一位慈祥的美国老太太，她以与李博士相濡以沫几十年的深厚爱情和宽阔胸怀，成就了丈夫遍及全球的足迹，共同编织了她丈夫与图书馆界广泛的友谊。像人们通常讲的，她操持的家是李博士生命之旅的港湾，回这里休养生息，从这里出发远航。

（原载《书城人事两依依》，湖南大学出版社 2003 年出版，第 54-57 页。）

Hwa-Wei Lee Named Chief of Asian Division

Hwa-Wei Lee has been appointed chief of the Asian Division of the Library.

"We are privileged to have Dr. Lee join us as chief of the Asian Division, " said Carolyn Brown, director for Area Studies Collections. " He is well-known in the field of international librarianship, having served as a library consultant and lecturer in countries throughout Asia under the sponsorship of organizations such as the Asia Foundation, the Food and Agricultural Organization of the United Nations, the Japan Foundation for Global Partnership, UNESCO and others. "

Lee graduated from National Taiwan Normal University and earned master's degrees in education and library science and a doctorate in education and library science from the University of Pittsburgh. He has had more than 40 years of experience in academic libraries including the University of Pittsburgh, Duquesne University, Edinboro University of Pennsylvania, Colorado State University, and Ohio University, where he held the position of dean of libraries for more than 21 years until his retirement in 1999.

During his tenure at Ohio University, he transformed a modest library system into one that achieved membership in the Association of Research Libraries. He developed international collections for Southeast Asian Studies as well as for other parts of the world. Lee was also a founding member and advisor to OhioLINK, a statewide system pooling materials of all major academic libraries into one unified entity.

In 1979, Lee initiated a highly successful internship program that brought librarians from Africa, Asia, the Middle East, and Central America to the university. To date, more than 175 librarians have participated in the program. Under his leadership, the endowments of the Ohio University libraries grew to more than $8 million and other grants reached an excess of $2.5 million.

Upon his retirement, Lee received awards for distinguished service from the American Library Association, Asian/Pacific American Librarians Association, Chinese American Librarians Association, Library Association of China (Taiwan), OhioLINK, Ohionet and others. In 1999, Ohio University named the first floor of the Vernon R. Alden Library (the main library) the Hwa-Wei Lee Center for International Collections, and by resolution of the Board of Trustees of the university, a new library building was named the Hwa-Wei Lee Library Annex. He served as dean emeritus at Ohio University until his recent appointment to the Library of Congress.

The Library of Congress is a central repository for all types of Asian publications that are not broadly available at other locations in the United States. Initiated in 1869 with a gift of 10 works in 934 volumes offered to the United States by the Emperor of China, the Library's Asian collection of more than 2 million items is the largest and most comprehensive outside of Asia.

(Published in *Library of Congress*: *The Gazette.* June 20, 2003: p. 3. Also published in *The Library of Congress Information Bulletin.* V. 62, No. 6, June 2003: p. 137.)

国会图馆亚洲部　首见华裔当主任

谭焕瑛

美国国会图书馆宣布，在空悬一年多之后，聘任华裔图书馆管理专家李华伟博士（Hwa-Wei Lee）出任亚洲部主任。他是该部门首位华裔主任。

已于日前正式上任的李华伟毕业自台湾师范大学，1957年来美，先后获得匹兹堡大学教育硕士、图书馆管理硕士、高等教育及图书馆管理博士学位，他曾在多所大学负责图书馆行政工作，也曾任俄亥俄大学（Ohio University）图书馆馆长，是美国大学图书馆的第一位华人馆长。

在担任俄亥俄大学图书馆馆长时，李华伟创办了第一个国际图书馆员培训计划，并率先设立海外华人研究，搜集海外华人文献。1971年与其他单位联合创建了国际性的OCLC（Online Computer Library Center）图书馆电脑网路。

尽管有扎实的专业基础与丰富的工作经验，李华伟说，新职对他仍是项挑战。

他指出，国会图书馆与大学图书馆和地方公共图书馆不同之处在于国会图书馆注重宝藏，服务对象以高层专业研究为主，加以书籍不外借，给人"藏而不用"的感觉。

李华伟计划加强与地方公共图书馆合作。让诸君可透过地方公共图书馆，向国会图书馆借书，图书目录可上网 www.loc.gov 查阅。

李华伟也计划增加亚洲部工作人员，整理书库，加强与其他部门合作，为亚洲部争取更多资源。

此外，他计划举办专题展览，介绍国会图书馆的珍藏；举办专题演讲，推动族裔间的文化交流。

李华伟表示也将尽力加强中文藏书。目前亚洲部藏书以日文最丰富，达110万册，其次是中文，有90万册。

（原载《世界日报》2003年6月3日）

21世纪知识管理者所扮演的角色
——专访美国国会图书馆亚洲部主任李华伟博士

吕 红

近年来,知识管理逐渐变成企业界一个通用的"口头禅",这个转变与新世纪的社会发展瞬息万变、信息技术突飞猛进、以及人们对知识的创造及使用有关。虽然知识管理在学术界已行之有年,但凭心而论还没有达到企业界所倡导的程度。美国国会图书馆亚洲部主任李华伟博士表示,在21世纪的知识时代里,信息专业人员必须要面对的诸多挑战及正视其扮演的角色。同时要在新知识的获取、处理、传播、创造性的使用及创新方面,能用他们的专长来促进知识管理,造福人类。

知识的创造及使用是一个从数据转变为信息,信息转变为知识,及由知识驱动所支持的人类行为和决策的一个连续的流程。

李华伟博士认为,之所以知识管理成为企业界一个时髦的术语,是因为企业界首先意识到知识在知识时代"全球经济"中的重要性。在新知识经济中,特别是当人们能共享及创造性地使用知识时,知识就是力量。拥有并不断地更新相关及策略性的知识会使企业在竞争上获得优势。

李华伟博士强调,信息专业人员长久以来被训练成为信息和知识查询、选择、获取、组织、储存、再包装、传播和服务的专家。而知识管理不仅仅是信息和数据的管理,也不仅仅是指信息技术。知识管理的一个目标是识别有用的、相关的知识,去组织,吸收及综合知识,及促进创造性地使用知识。信息技术为实现这一目标提供了技术工具。因为知识是通过人们的大脑来加工、使用、更新、扩展的,是人类智慧的产物,所以人是知识管理的最重要部分。

李华伟博士不仅现任美国国会图书馆亚洲部主任,同时也是俄亥俄大学图书馆荣誉馆长、OCLC图书馆计算机联网中心资深顾问和杰出访问学者。

李华伟博士以一系列翔实的数据和论证表示,从20世纪的后半叶到21世纪,科技更迭的速度大大地加快并带来人类知识以指数速度的增长,亦即信息爆炸!虽然许多几乎是史无前例的变化来源于技术革命,特别是计算机领域,通讯领域和网络技术领域的变化,但我们必须清楚地了解所有这些技术的突破都是人类知识、才能、创造与智慧发展的结果。人们才是技术变化的驱动力。正因为如此,我们必须保证技术的发展会造福于人类,并引导我们进入21世纪数字化和网络化的"知识时代"。

什么是知识时代?其一般的特质为何?李华伟博士表示,在知识时代,我们看到人类的知识以史无前例的速度累增,它影响到我们的生活及社会的每一个方面。近年来计算机、通讯与网络等科技的进步是知识扩充的一个重要理由。我们越能快速传递信息与知识,知识就越发达。在七世纪的中国和15世纪的欧洲所发明的印刷术大大地促进了人类知识的保存与传播。但是,只有在1884年,当山谬·摩尔斯(Samuel Morse)发明了电传,才使信息的传播速度比一匹马或一个人所能跑的速度快。

现今,随着因特网(Internet)及万维网(World Wide Web)的全球化,我们处在一个真正意义的地球村里,在这里,信息及知识能以光速的速度传播,不受距离或其他因素的限制。

由于人类的智力、创造力和智慧，我们的知识界每一小时、每一分、甚至每一秒都在增长。据估计，世界各地每年出版学术刊物大约有 850,000 种，年增长率为 2.5%。连续性出版品从 1972 年的 70,000 种增加到 1997 年的 118,500 种。全球每两分钟就有一篇科技论文完成。这种人类"显性"知识快速积累，只是能够看得到的一个更大的、存在人的大脑及经验里的"隐性"知识冰山所露出水面的一部分。这是知识时代的基本特性，知识时代这个词强调知识（显性知识和隐性知识）在新世纪所扮演的角色。

李华伟博士归纳总结说，21 世纪是以知识为基础，高度竞争的时代。美国的经济大师彼德·杜鲁克（Peter F. Drucker）曾经说过，知识的创造将会变成一个国家、企业、或公司竞争力的决定因素。早在 1965 年，杜鲁克就指出知识将要代替土地、劳力、资金、机械；等等，而成为主要的生产力。他的远见当时并没有得到适当的重视。直到 1991 年，当 Ikujiro Nonaka 提出了"隐性"知识和"显性"知识的概念，以及在《哈佛商业评论》上发表的"螺旋式知识"理论时，知识为主导的竞争时代才真正到来。1993 年，杜鲁克在他的《后资本主义社会》一书中阐述了知识工作者的支配地位，使得知识的重要性成为全球讨论的话题。从此知识管理变得越来越受重视，越来越多的关于如何提高知识管理的书和文章出现了。

微软的老板比尔·盖茨（Bill Gates）在他 1999 年出版的《数字化神经系统》一书中进一步指出知识和网络将会成为所有未来企业的基础。另一位专家利博维茨则指出："在走向现代知识管理的行动中，很多机构正设法平衡其组织内部的知识和其顾客及股东之间外部知识的关系。他们设法扩大其自身的组织智能来保证其竞争能力。知识管理的结果是为更好地平衡内部知识和外部知识而创造一个重视机构无形知识财产的程序。因此，知识管理指的是知识的创造、保护、获取、协调、统合、查寻以及传播。其目的是在建立一个知识共享环境，在这个环境中知识共享是力量，而不像老格言说的那样知识是力量。"

由于知识管理仍然是一个比较新的概念，不同的作者从不同的角度给予不同的定义，对于什么是知识管理？简妮佛·罗利（Jennifer Rowley）所给的定义为："知识管理是对一个有志于扩展其目标的组织在知识财产方面的开发和发展。需要管理的知识包括显性的、记录的知识，和隐性的、主观知识。管理是一个要经过所有与知识的识别、共享和创造的有关过程。这需要知识库的创立和维护系统，及知识共享和组织学习的培养和促进。那些知识管理很成功的组织通常把知识当作一种资产来发展该组织的模式和价值，这些模式和价值又反过来帮助知识的创造和享受。"然而，其他人却寻求用发展过程的观点来定义知识管理。例如：简·达菲（Jan Duffy）把知识管理定义为"通过重用组织的智慧和经验来推动革新的过程"。甘勒集团（Gartner Group）把知识管理定义为"一个以整合及协作方式来促进信息资产的创造、捕获、组织、获取和使用过程的一种学科"。

李华伟博士表示，当企业界在新知识经济和数字化时代中进行变化的时候，各种类型的图书馆也在经历着猛烈的改变。从 20 世纪 60 年代起，每五年到十年，图书馆和信息专业就会发生一次显著的变化，60 年代以前，大多数图书馆以纸张或者印刷式资料为主，发展的步伐缓慢，而且平静。然而，到了 60 年代，我们就看到了图书馆自动化的开始、机读目录格式的标准化，以及图书馆合作机构（OCLC—俄亥俄州学院图书馆中心）的建立。在 70 年代，开始出现联机信息查寻和检索，CD-ROM 也开始使用。80 年代，图书馆网络开始普遍化，图书馆的集成自动化系统也趋于成熟。90 年代，电子出版，多媒体，因特网，数字化得到重视。当我们进入 21 世纪时，图书馆向着综合的、虚拟的、及数字化方向迈进，数字化的世界深深地受着因特网（Internet）、万维网（World Wide Web）和知识时代的影响。诠释资料（Meatdata）、都柏林核心集（Dublin Core）、网上资源合作编目（Cooperative Online Resources Catalog），以及知识管理都受到图书馆和信息专业内外的广泛关注。

由于信息爆炸，因特网和万维网的扩展，我们的社会面临着更多的问题。问题之一是当我们淹溺在信息的汪洋大海里，我们仍然缺乏所需求的知识。另一个问题是"信息拥有"和"信息缺乏"之间距离的加大，这也是区分"信息富有"和"信息贫乏"的个人和国家的标志。这些问题对那些注重信息品质和平等使用知识的图书馆来讲是非常严重的。

面对挑战，管理者必须采取恰当的因应措施，甚至需要图书馆联合起来，同心协力去迎接这些挑战。例如：为了改进图书馆的合作、图书馆应组织地方性、区域性、国家性、国际性及专门性的图书馆网，以满足读者的各种需求。图书馆计算机联网中心 OCLC（Online Computer Library Center）及俄亥俄州高校图书馆联网（Ohio LINK）是两个最成功的范例。

充分发挥电脑、信息、通讯及网路等科技的潜能，经由电脑化及网络化作业改善图书馆的服务、资源及管理。强力支持 Internet 及下一代 Internet 的发展，使信息资源的发展、搜集、典藏、传播及学术交流更快速、更有效率。

由于各种类的知识按指数速度增长，这就需要图书馆的资源获取策略从纸张印刷型发展到电子和数字型，能够与它们的使命和职能保持一致。因为受到有限的资金、人员和空间的限制，图书馆必须要仔细地分析其使用者的需求，寻找发展一个合作选购的计划来满足这些要求。从"拥有"（Ownership）到"获取"（Access），从"万一"（Just in Case）到"及时"（Just in Time）这种概念的变化应该是一个健全的资源发展目标。

同时，互联网络的功能也应该用来为用户、知识者（教授、研究员和课题专家等）、出版商、政府机构、商业和工业以及其他组织之间作为知识交流之用。

李华伟博士表示，在企业组织所新创立的职位之中，如：主要知识官员（Chief Knowledge Officer）、知识管理专家、知识经理等，主要知识官员常常是一个公司的高级主管，一个比主要信息官员（Chief Information Officer）高的职位。在过去的二十年中，许多主要信息官员的职位是由受过信息技术训练的人来做，而不是由受过图书馆和信息专业训练的人来做，因为主要信息官员更具有技术性。现在，除非我们想要躲避 21 世纪图书馆在知识管理方面所担当的新角色，否则，随着知识管理的到来和主要知识官员职位的设立，具备远大目光、领导才能及专业知识的图书馆员及信息专家应该是最适合主要知识官员职位的。

李华伟博士强调，尽管知识管理已经成为管理上新近的"口头禅"，它是否会像以前的许多"口头禅"一样逐渐消失，将取决于我们怎样让它起作用。

李华伟博士（Hwa-Wei Lee，Ph. D）简介

美国国会图书馆亚洲部主任李华伟博士，俄亥俄大学图书馆荣誉馆员，OCLC 图书馆计算机联网中心杰出访问学者。

李华伟，祖籍福建，出生于广州。1949 年随家人到台湾。早年毕业于台湾师范大学教育系。1957 年来美深造，曾先后获得匹兹堡大学教育硕士、图书馆学硕士及高等教育的哲学博士学位。历任匹兹堡大学、都肯大学、宾州爱丁堡大学、科罗拉多州立大学等图书馆行政职务。俄亥俄大学图书馆任馆长 20 年，为华裔担任美国大学图书馆的首位馆长。

李博士曾经由美国政府国际发展总署派往泰国担任亚洲理工学院图书馆信息中心主任七年。在那一期间，他与联合国、世行、亚行、世界粮农组织等建立起密切的联系，为他日后成为信息管理领域及国际学术界活跃的领导角色奠定了良好的发展基础。为有关亚洲地区图书馆建设出谋划策、参与项目提供了理论与实践的依据。

由于李华伟博士在国际图书信息界享有很高的声誉，被选举连任两届（4 年一任）美国图书馆学会理事。该学会是全世界最大的学会，有会员 5.7 万名。同时他还担任国际图书馆学会联盟的大学及研究图书馆委员会委员等职务。出版了《图书馆学的世界观》、《90 年代图书馆募捐指引》，《现代化的图书馆管理》及《知识管理的理论与实践》等书，发表学术论文七十余篇。多次担任联合国教科文组织及其他国际机构及基金会顾问。因其贡献突出、成绩卓著，他曾荣获十多种奖励和称号。如美国华美图书馆员学会杰出服务奖；美国图书馆学会杰出国际服务奖；亚太地区图书馆员学会杰出服务奖；美国图书馆学会杰出理事奖；美国新闻总署杰出服务奖、台湾"中国图书馆学会"杰出贡献奖等多项荣誉。并被连续载入《世界名人传》、《美国名人传》、《美国教育界名人传》等年鉴上。

李华伟博士多次应中国国家教委之邀，以世界银行贷款项目及联合国发展基金项目开办信息专家及管理者培训班。多所大学聘请他担任访问教授或顾问教授，包括北京大学、清华大学、北京师范大学、北京邮电大学、西安交通大学、南开大学、武汉大学、四川联合大学、东北师范大学、天津理工学院等。中国科学院、中国国家图书馆，以及台湾"中央图书馆"也聘请李博士担任顾问。

所以专家评价，李华伟先生对国内的贡献不是物质上的，更主要是精神层面的。体现在更新观念上，在人才培养上即教育软体方面，这位美籍华人的贡献尤其显得突出。

为了加速图书馆事业现代化进程，为了年轻一代知识分子的成长，李华伟博士每年都要往返奔波于亚洲美洲之间——以赤诚之心和顽强毅力，亲手架起了一座连接东方与西方、过去与未来的桥梁。

在美国，他是华人担任国会图书馆亚洲部的首位主任，高等院校图书馆馆长的第一人。在这个科学与文明交互渗透的领域，他呕心沥血勤勉奋斗已逾 40 载。在祖国，他的德才人品及学术成果享誉大学、科学院、中信所、公共图书馆等各大系统，并被著名的大学聘请。

长年累月致力于东西方文化交流与合作的李华伟先生，在 1996 年全力促成了一件值得一提的大事，在事业的里程碑上刻下深深的一笔——首届中美图书馆合作会议在北京隆重召开。近百位图书馆馆长和专家学者聚集一堂，就会议主题"全球的信息存取——挑战与机遇"展开热烈的讨论。会议取得了圆满的成功，其意义不同凡响。李华伟博士在会上作了重要报告，总结了中美图书馆合作的历史经验，以及在今后的发展重点。这次会议对世界图书馆界的合作与发展产生积极而深远的影响。会议之后又有多个图书馆相继结为姊妹馆。从观念改变到具体措施，从人员培训到文化交流，从技术引进到信息传播，从……海外传媒报导："自从中国 1869 年向美国国会图书馆捐赠 1000 册图书后，相隔一百多年，中美两国近百位馆长和专家学者站在中国国家图书馆的台阶上。"

"这一幕载入了历史。"当时担任美国国会图书馆副馆长泰伯评价道，"这不仅是行业合作，也加强了两国人民彼此的了解。"中国图书馆的孙蓓欣前副馆长称颂道，"李华伟先生为图书馆事业所作的努力是令人感佩的，足可谓之'正其义，不谋其利。明其道，不计其功。'"

（原载《硅谷时报》（*The Sillicon Valley Times*) 2003 年 7 月 20 日，第 6 – 10 页。）

国会图书馆亚洲部开放日涌人潮
陈香梅、李祥甫谈阅读重要性　叶娜介绍中国传统音乐

谭焕瑛

美国国会图书馆亚洲部日前举行阅览室开放招待会，吸引大批读者，将阅览室挤得水泄不通。

招待会由亚洲部主任李华伟博士主持，中国近代研究专家卢雪乡筹划图书馆多位同仁负责接待，为来宾介绍重要收藏品、指导示范上网查阅亚洲部藏书目录。

除了开放参观，当天并邀请华府资深作家陈香梅、退休教授李祥甫谈阅读与图书馆的重要，民俗音乐研究专家叶娜则介绍中国传统音乐与乐器。

曾出版中、英文著作 40 余种的陈香梅表示，阅读不仅能增加知识、丰富心灵，也能保持健康与年轻，相当重要。她鼓励大家多读书，多利用图书馆。同时，她并将多部近作赠送给国会图书馆。

李祥甫自教职退休后专心译著，利用计算机出版著作，并在网络上发行，成绩不错。他出版的译著计有《论语》及《孙子兵法》英译本，讨论中国象棋与麻将的英文著作等。他说，他能够顺利完成这些译著，全赖国会图书馆帮忙。

叶娜拥有音乐博士学位，对中国音乐与乐器有深入研究。她指出中国音乐有八音，是根据乐器材料来分。如石钟、石铃；铜制的铜钟、铜铃、锣、铙、钹等；陶土制的蛋型乐器与球型笛；竹制的箫和笛；葫芦制的口琴；木制的击板、木鱼与木笛；丝制的筝、笙、琵琶、胡琴；皮革制的鼓等。叶娜一面以图片解说，一面播放不同的乐音，让听众辨别八音的不同。她说，音乐能美化心灵，是生活中不能缺少的。

李华伟除了鼓励读者多利用国会图书馆的收藏资料，并宣布组织国会图书馆亚洲之友协会，集思广益，共同为加强亚洲部的收藏与服务努力。他欢迎有意加入协会者与他联络，电话（202）707-5917；或电子信箱 hlee@ loc. gov。他同时提醒民众，如欲借阅国会图书馆馆藏，可接洽地区公共图书馆，图书目录可上网 www. loc. gov 查阅。

（原载《世界日报》2003 年 7 月 22 日）

Dr. Hwa-Wei Lee's Success Story at Library of Congress

Jennie L. Ilustre

After working for 40 years among books, one would think that Dr. Hwa-Wei Lee has had his fill. But then the Library of Congress came knocking.

"My children were all shaking their heads," recalled Dr. Lee, laughing. "They wanted me to enjoy my retirement instead." At 69, this author of three books is the new chief of the Asian Division of the Library of Congress.

How could he refuse such a dream job? The Library of Congress is a national institution with a prestigious history, not to mention a crucial role in the nation's present and future. It was established by an act of Congress in 1800 as a reference library for lawmakers.

In 1814, invading British troops set fire to the Capitol Building, burning the library's contents. Former President Thomas Jefferson offered his 50-year collection of books. His concept of universality is behind the institution's comprehensive collecting policies today.

Dr. Carolyn T. Brown, Assistant Librarian for Library Services and Acting Director of Area Studies Collections, is Dr. Lee's boss. It's obvious that in Dr. Brown's book, he's tops.

"Dr. Lee brings great experience and enormous stature in the American library and international library communities," she told *Asian Fortune*.

The Library of Congress conducted a nationwide search. Dr. Brown said a panel pruned down the list of 69 applicants to 19. The panel was composed of the chief of the European division, the chief of the federal research division, who is also a China scholar, and Dr. Brown.

"Dr. Lee was clearly the most outstanding candidate," said Dr. Brown. "He has had a forty-year career in professional library positions at several universities, including Pittsburgh, Duquesne, Edinboro in Pennsylvania, Colorado State, and for 21 years at Ohio University, where he was the Dean of University Libraries."

"He is well-known in international librarianship, having served as a library consultant and lecturer in 'countries' throughout Asia," she added. She cited Mainland China, Hong Kong, Indonesia, Japan, Papua New Guinea, the Philippines, South Korea, Taiwan, and Thailand.

Shelving books

Dr. Lee chuckled as he recalled he started his career shelving books. He graduated from the National Taiwan Normal University, and came to the United States in the late 50s, egged on by his civil servant father. By his second week at the University of Pittsburgh, his pocket money was down to $200.

He said: "I sought any job for graduate students. I was conscious of my accent, so when the librarian asked me what I could do, I told them I could shelf books. But even if that was all I did, I did my best."

The head librarian was impressed. Lee was given a full-time job, from a 20 hour-a-week part time. Added responsibilities came swiftly: selecting and ordering books. "You might as well get a library degree," he was told. Lee earned master's degrees, and a doctorate, in education and library science from the University of Pittsburgh, and never looked back.

"I believe I succeeded because in this field, we care about people," he said. "We don't just collect books, but we also enrich lives."

At Ohio University, Dr. Lee transformed a modest library into a library that gained membership in the Association of Research Libraries. He developed international collections for Southeast Asian Studies and for other parts of the world. Under his leadership, the endowments of the Ohio University libraries grew to over $8 million, with some grants exceeding $2.5 million.

He was a founding member and advisor to OhioLINK. The statewide system pooled materials of all major academic libraries into one unified entity. In 1979 he initiated a highly successful internship program, bringing to the university librarians from Africa, Asia, the Middle East, and Central America.

When he retired in 1999, Ohio University named the first floor of the Vernon R. Alden Library (the main library) the Hwa-Wei Lee Center for International Collections. A new library building was named the Hwa-Wei Lee Library Annex.

His vision

The Asian Division serves the Library of Congress and the public nation-wide. Dr. Lee wants to expand services electronically, making them available 24 – 7 (24 hours, seven days a week). "We also constantly look for websites and then we link, we have to keep on updating our data," he said. He's also for microfilming and digitizing database.

"All these would result in expanded, up-to-date information and easy access for many people, because we're closed on Saturdays," he said. "Also, longer life span for books because they wouldn't be subject to too much handling."

He wants to add five more reference libraries (current total is 27) and digitize them: Chinese, Japanese, Korean, Indonesian and Indian. Digitizing Chinese books in the vernacular from 1994 to the present would cost $250,000. Afterward, "maybe $35,000 for 10,000 new titles every year".

He said the Asian publications and resources of the Asian Division are among the best in the world. In announcing Dr. Lee's July 12 "Open House" of the Asian Reading Room, Area Specialist for China Judy Lu noted that "the collection of every Asian country in their vernacular languages, and numbering over 2.5 million volumes, represents the best knowledge and creativity of these nations, each with a rich and unique cultural heritage".

Acquisition of rare books, preferably through donations by individuals or children of scholars, is also in Dr. Lee's agenda. He also envisions productive community relationships, starting with the Open House.

Leadership

Those who know him don't doubt he will succeed. Remarked Dr. Robert Glidden, President of Ohio University, "I miss him at the university, but I know he's doing a wonderful job at the Library of Congress."

He added: "Dr. Lee gives entirely of himself to his institution, his colleagues and his profession. I'm very proud of him, of course. I can't imagine anyone in the U.S. more qualified or capable for the job. He's a consummate professional and a wonderful person. I have never heard him say anything negative about anyone or any situation. He gave outstanding leadership to the university libraries for two decades. I'm pleased with his appointment, but I'm also proud for Ohio University that he has been asked to accept this appointment."

Said Dr. Jeremy Wu, Communications Chair of the Asian American Government Executives Network (AAGEN): "AAG EN warmly welcomes Dr. Lee's appointment at the Library of Congress. He's another example of the excellent qualifications and valuable experience Asian Pacific Americans consistently bring to the executive ranks of the federal government."

Lien Huong Fiedler, president of the Library of Congress Asian American Association, stressed: "Dr. Lee is a true model for all Asian Pacific Americans and other federal employees at the Library of Congress. I knew I was meeting a great leader in Dr. Lee when I first met him in the Summer Conference of the American Library Association in 1998. For a person who has earned many honors and become one of the most esteemed international librarians, he has always been personable and caring, treating everyone equally with dignity and respect."

Family

As touched as he is by his achievements in his career, he positively glows at speaking about his family.

"My wife Mary, after receiving her Master's degree in education from the University of Pittsburgh, gave up her teaching career in order to raise our six children," he said. "She is truly a wonderful wife and most caring mother to our wonderful children."

Eldest daughter Shirley Kennedy was, until July 3, an administrative assistant in the President's Office at Ohio University. Her husband, Jay Kennedy, recently landed a new job in Jacksonville, Florida and the whole family moved there recently. Shirley and Jay have two children: Kristen, 14 and Kyle, 9.

Jim is the president and CEO of Eagle Registrations Inc. in Dayton, Ohio. He and his wife, Lisa, have three boys: Christopher, 13; Tyler, 10 and Austin, 8. Pam Lee is a Physical Therapist at the orthopedic surgery department of the University of Iowa Hospitals and Clinics.

Edward is a Facilities Planning Specialist at the Kimberiy-Clark Company in Neenah, Wisconsin with wife Amy, they have a daughter, Hannah, 2. Charles is a senior consultant at Blackboard Inc. in this capital. His wife, Erika, is a lawyer working at the Federal Trade Commission. Bob worked in the National Football League for five years in media relations and video production. He's currently the publications and web coordinator for the Ohio University athletics.

Remarked son Jim, "We're all very proud of Dad. He has worked extremely hard his entire life and has given so much. Dad could never retire and just relax, he's always got to be going and doing something."

He added: "Dad's traits, hard work and integrity, have been instilled in all his kids. What amazing is, even working long hours and traveling frequently, he managed to spend quality time with us. He took the time to make frequent family trips to cultural events or to visit different places.

"Dad is a very giving person. Always willing to help, sometimes too much. He never asks for anything in return."

Bob agreed: "Dad cares genuinely about others. Besides us six kids, he almost always had an international student staying with us. Even those students who didn't stay with us always came to my father for guidance with their problems."

Indeed, at the end of Dr. Lee's email messages are the words of Winston Churchill: "We make a living by what we get, but we make a life by what we give."

(Published in *Asian Fortune*. V. 11, No. 11, August 2003.)

Hwa-Wei Lee: Pride and Role Model of Librarians

Rush Miller[1] & Zhijia Shen[2]

Dr. Hwa-Wei Lee, Chief of the Asian Division at Library of Congress and Dean of Libraries Emeritus of Ohio University, is a name familiar to many librarians across cultural and national boundaries. He is known widely in the library world as a visionary leader, cultural communicator, mentor and role model for younger generations of librarians. Many also know him dearly as a caring teacher and good friend.

In his over 40 year career as a librarian, Dr. Lee has held many positions, working through the ranks from an acquisitions librarian at the University of Pittsburgh to become the first among very few Chinese American librarians to serve as the dean of a major academic library. After his retirement from Ohio University, Dr. Lee assumed the position of chief of the Asian Division of Library of Congress, bringing a life-long commitment to bring cross-cultural issues to libraries around the world.

His library career

In the late 1950s when the cold war was just starting and with the end of the Korean War, the field of Chinese studies was growing rapidly thanks to the influx of federal funding. The University of Pittsburgh, like many other universities, was designated a resource center for Asian studies. Soon Hwa-Wei's library job evolved from shelving books to include more professional responsibilities, such as selecting and acquiring Chinese language books to build a Chinese collection from scratch. Hwa-Wei became the first librarian specializing in East Asian materials at the University of Pittsburgh and the collection he developed and so meticulously cataloged has now become one of the top East Asian libraries in North America.

As Hwa-Wei's job responsibilities increased, his library colleagues suggested that he should pursue a "library degree". Hwa-Wei took this advice and enrolled in the library science mater's program at Pitt, receiving his degree in 1959. Upon graduation, Hwa-Wei married Miss Mary Frances Kratochvil, his American sweetheart with whom he has built a wonderful family. For the next three years, Hwa-Wei worked hard to build the Chinese collection at the University of Pittsburgh Library.

In 1962, Hwa-Wei assumed the position as head of the Special Collections for African materials at Duquesne University. While working at Duquesne, Hwa-Wei enrolled in the doctoral program in education and library management at University of Pittsburgh. Upon completing his Ph. D. degree, Hwa-Wei took the position as the associate director of the library at Edinboro University of Pennsylvania in 1965, and was then promoted to the position of director of that library a year later.

In 1968, a great opportunity came to Dr. Lee. Under a contract with the U. S. Agency for International Development, Colorado State University established the Library and Information Center for the newly founded Asian Institute of Technology (AIT). They were looking for an able and dynamic director to lead this operation and Dr. Lee was chosen for it. Dr. Lee took his family with him to Bangkok and spent the next seven years (1968 – 1975) in Thailand.

While in Thailand, Dr. Lee secured funding from the International Development Research Center of Canada to establish the Asian Information Center for Geotechnical Engineering and the

---

[1] Works for University of Pittsburgh Library
[2] Head, East Asian Library, University of Colorado

International Information Center for Ferro-Cement as a part of the outreach program of the AIT Library and Information Center. This institute later trained many technical people for Asia including China. During his tenure in Thailand, Dr. Lee also developed good relationship with many international organizations such as the United Nations, World Bank, the Asia Foundation, and the Food and Agriculture Organization of the United Nations and became actively involved in many of their consulting work.

Dr. Lee returned to the United States from Thailand in 1975 and assumed the position of Associate Library Director and Professor of Library Administration at Colorado State University. Then in 1978, Dr. Lee was appointed Dean of the Libraries at Ohio University, a position he held for the next twenty-one years.

Building a world class university library At Ohio University

The Ohio University Library in 1978 was a mediocre, little known, unranked, and geographically isolated university library. However by 1999, when Dr. Lee retired as the dean of the library, he left behind a major research library that had gained its place among the members of the prestigious Association of Research Libraries, ranking among the top 70 academic research libraries in North America. During twenty-one year tenure as its dean, the library of Ohio University more than doubled its collections from less than one million volumes in 1978 to over two millions in 1999, with unique and internationally-known research resources. The number of serial publications and microform titles had a four-fold increase over the same period.

It is no easy task to double the collection of a university library and quadruple its serials collection, especially during a period when book and subscription price increases were in double digits.

The first project Dr. Lee undertook on at Ohio University was to increase the funding resources of the library. He worked tirelessly to expand the library' endowment, increasing it from less than $20,000 in 1978 to over $8 million in 1999. He also initiated major projects through grants and was highly successful with consecutive awards from very competitive sources such as the Title II-C of the Higher Education Act and the Challenge Grants of the National Endowment of Humanities, with the total grants amount exceeding $2.5 million. Supported by grants and other funding he raised, Dr. Lee initiated many significant projects and brought national and international visibility to Ohio University and its library.

One of such initiatives was to build on his international experience both with East and Southeast Asia by developing collections for Southeast Asian Studies and other countries. As a result of Dr. Lee's outreach efforts, Ohio University Library became the officially designated depository of publications of Botswana, Guatemala, Malaysia, and Swaziland. In conjunction with the Malaysian depository, the Library's world renowned Southeast Asia Collection became the only Malaysia Resources Center outside Malaysia. Such designations are unique in American universities and have greatly strengthened the international research resources in support of international studies.

In 1993, Dr. Lee was the architect of the Dr. Shao You Bao Overseas Chinese Documentation and Research Center with special focus on historical and research resources in Southeast Asia. This is the first-of-its-kind resources centers and the result of Dr. Lee's longtime work in cultivating donor relationship with the Shao family, a family of a distinguished Ohio University alumnus in Hong Kong. Dr. Shao and his son, Dr. Daniel Shao, established a generous endowment designated for the center at Ohio University.

Another major outreach program Dr. Lee initiated at Ohio University was the establishment in 1979 of a well-recognized International Librarians Internship Program, bringing to Ohio University librarians from Africa, Asia, the Middle East, and Central America. Through this program, over 175 middle and upper level managers of libraries and information services from various developing countries were trained at Ohio University Library. This training program provided learning opportunities for international librarians to learn about America, as well as for Ohio university librarians and students to learn about these countries, opening a door between America and the third world and promoting communication among different cultures.

Dr. Lee made a special effort to bridge understanding between American libraries and libraries of foreign countries, especially Asian countries. He organized or played a key role in organizing numerous major international conferences, among which are the two China-US library conferences held in 1996 in Beijing and in New York and Washington, D. C. in 2001, the Open Session of "the Impact of Computerized Systems and Networks in Resources Sharing of Libraries" at the International Federation of Library Associations (IFLA) / United Nations Educational, Scientific and Cultural Organization (UNESCO) Pre-Session Seminar on Resources Sharing of Libraries in Developing Countries, held at Antwerp University, Belgium in 1977; the First Pacific Conference on New Information Technology for Library and Information Professionals in Bangkok, Thailand in 1987; the first Korea-US library conference held in San Francisco in 1998 and the first Thai-US library conference held in Bangkok in 1999, organized by the ALA/IRC Subcommittee on East and Southeast Asia that Dr. Lee chaired.

Dr. Lee also has been a sought-after library consultant and has lectured widely in Mainland China, Hong Kong, Indonesia, Japan, Papua New Guinea, the Philippines, Singapore, South Korea, Taiwan, and Thailand, sponsored by various foundations such as the Asia Foundation, the Council for International Exchange of Scholars, the Food and Agricultural Organization (FAO) of the U. N. , Freidrich Ebert-Stiftung, the International Development Research Center (IDRC) of Canada, OCLC Online Computer Library Center, the Library Bureau of the Ministry of Education of the People's Republic of China, the United Board for Christian Higher Education in Asia, United Nations Development Program, UNESCO, U. S. Agency for International Development (AID), U. S. Information Agency, World Bank, and others. His consultant mission for UNESCO in 1976 resulted in the establishment of a Regional International Serials Data System (ISDS) Center for Southeast Asia in Bangkok, Thailand.

As the Dean of the Library of Ohio University, Dr. Lee made a special effort to play an active role in the local library community in the state of Ohio. Under his leadership, Ohio University Libraries became one of the original founding members of Ohio Academic Library and Information Network (Ohio Link), a model statewide resource sharing system pooling materials of all major academic libraries in Ohio. Dr. Lee was involved in the design and implementation of OhioLINK beginning in 1988.

Dr. Lee also made special efforts to assist the public libraries in the Southeastern part of Ohio, a part of the Appalachian Region, where library services were not well developed because of inadequate funding and poor economic conditions. Dr. Lee worked closely with the Ohio Valley Area Libraries (OVAL), a regional library cooperative. As a result, the Ohio University Libraries became the resource library for poorly funded local libraries in the eleven counties in Southeastern Ohio for over twenty years during his tenure as Dean and until the changed state funding formula enabled more state funds to go to this region.

Dr. Lee was an active member of the Ohio Library Association, the state library association in Ohio. He joined the effort of other Ohio librarians in seeking to change the sources of library funding from being based on an intangible tax to being a fixed six-and one-half-percent of income tax. This change has placed the public libraries in Ohio among the best funded in the country. He was also a strong campaigner for library collaboration in his role as a member of the OLA Board of Directors. For his active participation and other outstanding professional contributions, Dr. Lee was elected the Ohio Librarian of the Year in 1981, the 1983 Outstanding Administrator of Ohio University, the 1991 ALA John Ames Humphrey Award winner for contributions to International Librarianship, selected Honorary Alumni of the Year of Ohio University, and was inducted into the Ohio Hall of Fame of Librarians in 1999.

An ardent advocate for Sino-American library exchange

The 1980s witnessed major and historic changes in China. After the end of the Cultural

Revolution, China embarked on economic reform and was re-opened to the rest of the world. Recognizing the huge gap between China and the developed world in the library field, Chinese librarians looked to the United States for models of advanced management for modern libraries.

Invited as a lecturer for a training program at an information center in Kunming sponsored by the Chinese Institute of Scientific Information and Canadian International Development Center in 1982, Dr. Lee returned to China for the first time in thirty-three years, during the time when China was still closed to the rest of the world. On this trip, he visited many different types of libraries in China to examine their status. It was shocking to him to see the serious gap created by the thirty years of isolation between the Chinese and American libraries both in the "hardware and software", i. e. library facilities and skills of librarians. He saw clearly that the most urgent needs for Chinese libraries at that time were modern library management and new technologies. Meanwhile, Dr. Lee was also touched by the dedication of Chinese librarians, who worked hard under poor working conditions and low pay with very limited resources. It was on this trip, Dr. Lee made up his mind to serve as a bridge between Chinese and American libraries.

Since this trip in 1982, Dr. Lee has visited China every year and initiated numerous major programs to train Chinese librarians and to implement collaborative projects between American and Chinese libraries. With funding from World Bank and UNESCO, Dr. Lee ran several training workshops for librarians from the normal universities in China. His collaborative projects took place between American academic libraries and numerous Chinese university libraries and he served as advisor and honorary professor for many Chinese universities. Based on his teaching and conference presentations, Dr. Lee published a book on library management, *Management for Modern Libraries*. This book was published in Chinese and highly received by librarians in China, who believe Dr. Lee's book provides them with guidance in the directions for Chinese libraries. This significant book in simple terms explains profound issues and can be used as textbook for library management and as a basic reference book for library professionals.

Dr. Lee also introduced China to many of his library colleagues in the United States, who have hence become bridges between Chinese and American cultures. In 1991, for example, Hwa-Wei organized an exchange between six library directors in the People's Republic of China under the auspices of the Tianjin Bureau of Higher Education and the library directors/deans from selected Ohio institutions. This program introduced the Ohio librarians to Chinese libraries in Tianjin, Beijing, Chongqing and Wuhan. One of these Ohio deans was Dr. Rush Miller, who later became Director of the University Library System at the University of Pittsburgh. Hwa-Wei's influence led Dr. Miller to seek out ways to enhance the East Asian Library's involvement in China and to develop programs to enhance library services for China scholars in the United States. As a result, the University Library System of the University of Pittsburgh established the Gateway Service Center for Chinese Journal Articles, a major training program for Chinese librarians, and other collaborations with Chinese university libraries that continue to have a significant impact on the field today. Dr. Miller has visited China eight times since 1991 and credits his good friend Hwa-Wei with his interest in China.

He gives his best to the library profession

Throughout his professional career, Dr. Lee has been an enthusiastic contributor to professional organizations. He has served as presidents and board member, chaired committees and task forces, and provided consultation to numerous professional organizations, such as International Federation of Library Associations, American Library Association, OCLC Users Council, the Second White House Conference on Library and Information Services, Chinese Academic and Professional Association of Ohio, State Library of Ohio; Advisory Council on Federal Library Programs of State Library of Ohio, Ohio Library Association Board director, just to name a few.

He has been a loyal and active member of ALA with a continuing membership since 1966 and served in various ALA divisions, committees, task forces, and sub-committees, including two terms as a Councilor-at-Large (1988 – 1992 and 1993 – 1997). In 1991 he received the ALA John Ames Humphrey/Forest Press Award for Significant Contributions to International Librarianship. Also in 1991, he was chosen as a Delegate-At-Large to attend the second White House Conference on Library and Information Services held in Washington, D. C. on July 9 – 13, 1991.

Dr. Lee is an active participant, supporter, and advocate of Asian American librarians. An active member of the Asian/Pacific American Librarians Association since its inception, he was the recipient of the APALA Distinguished Services Award in 1991. A founder of the Chinese American Librarians Association, Dr. Lee served numerous offices of CALA as its president, board member, and committee chair for many terms over the past thirty years. Through his long-term dedication and hard work, Dr. Lee has helped create and shape the organization to what it is today. In 1983, he was awarded the CALA Distinguished Service Award.

Dr. Lee is recognized internationally for his contributions to bridging cultures between the United States and many other countries. He has been appointed to honorary and consulting professorship at many prestigious universities in China and other areas in Asia, such as the National Taiwan College of Education, Peking University, Beijing Normal University, Nankeen University, and Wuhan University of China, just to name a few. He also have been invited to serve as an advisor to the Central Library in Taiwan, the National Library of China, China Academic Library and Information System, Peking University Library, Tsinghai University Library, and City University of Hong Kong, among many.

While working in the field as a library practitioner and educator, Dr. Lee is also a diligent library researcher and has published four monographs in the English and Chinese languages, and over eighty articles and conference papers. He also edited conference proceedings, served on editorial board of library journals, and reviewed more than one hundred books.

He can never retire (Retirement and beginning a new journey)

After serving the library profession for forty years, Dr. Lee retired as dean of the library in 1999. To recognize his great contributions to the university, Ohio University named the first floor of the Vernon R. Alden Library the Hwa-Wei Lee Center for International Collections, and the new library building the Hwa-Wei Lee Library Annex. This honor speaks for the contributions that Dr. Lee has made for Ohio University in the two decades of his tenure as Dean. He richly deserves these honors. As Dr. Robert Glidden, president of Ohio University, pointed out in honoring him, "Dr. Lee gives entirely of himself to his institution, his colleagues and his profession. I'm very proud of him... He's a consummate professional and a wonderful person. I have never heard him say anything negative about anyone or any situation. He gave outstanding leadership to the university libraries for two decades."

Dr. Lee did not rest on the laurels of his honors. After his retirement from Ohio University, he became even more active serving as a library consultant and visiting lecturer. Invited by OCLC, he served as a distinguished visiting scholar to advise the OCLC Institute in extending its highly acclaimed educational seminars to Mainland China, Hong Kong, Korea, the Philippines, Taiwan, and Thailand, and to the OCLC Asia Pacific Section in expanding its library services and programs to the Asia and Pacific Region. He also was selected to be a Fulbright Senior Specialist to Chiang Mai University, Chiang Mai, Thailand. At Chiang Mai, Dr. Lee advised the Department of Library Science in reviewing and redesigning its graduate program in library and information science.

Dr. Lee retired life was as busy as before retirement, and finally in 2002 when the Library of Congress was searching for a new chief of its Asian Division, Dr. Lee was persuaded to apply and take on the assignment.

The Asian Division serves the Library of Congress and the public nation-wide. After taking office as its chief, Dr. Lee makes it a priority to expand services electronically and to improve the use of its world-class Asian collections. Dr. Lee understands that the Asian publications and resources of the Asian Division are among the best in the world, and the collections of every Asian country in their vernacular languages numbering over 2.7 million volumes represent the best knowledge and creativity of these nations, each with a rich and unique cultural heritage. Expanded library services will allow these rich information resources to benefit more users.

Family

As proud as he is of his achievements in his career, Dr. Lee always glows when speaking about his family. "My wife Mary, after receiving her Master's degree in education from the University of Pittsburgh, gave up her teaching career in order to raise our six children," he said. "She is truly a wonderful wife and most caring mother to our wonderful children." Mary and Hwa-Wei are the proud parents of six successful children and grandparents of eight lovely grandchildren. Remarked son Jim, "We're all very proud of Dad. He has worked extremely hard his entire life and has given so much. Dad could never retire and just relax, he's always got to be going somewhere and doing something." He added: "Dad's traits, hard work and integrity, have been instilled in all his kids. What's amazing is, even working long hours and traveling frequently, he managed to spend quality time with us. He took the time to make frequent family trips to cultural events or to visit different places." "Dad is a very giving person. Always willing to help, sometimes too much. He never asks for anything in return... Dad cares genuinely about others. Besides us six kids, he almost always had an international student staying with us. Even those students who didn't stay with us always came to my father for guidance with their problems."

When interviewed by *Asian Fortune*, Dr. Lee remarked, "I believe I succeeded because in this field, we care about people.... We don't just collect books, but we also enrich lives." Dr. Lee's long-time endeavor, contributions to the library profession, and his high qualities as wonderful human being is a testimony of this statement. And truly Hwa-Wei Lee has enriched the lives of all of us who have come to know him as mentor and friend, and to love him for the wonderful man he is.

(Published by Chinese American Librarians Association, *Bridging Cultures: Chinese American Librarians and Their Organization: A Glance at the Thirty Years of CALA, 1973 – 2003*. Edited by Zhijia Shen, Liana Hong Zhou, and Karen T. Wei. Guilin: Guangxi Normal University Press, 2004: pp. 51 – 63.)

国会图书馆中文部将开放电子书库

于茂芬

国会图书馆亚洲部首位华裔主任李华伟表示，国会图书馆除与中国大陆清华大学合作，引进丰富的电子版期刊外，目前正全力试办电子书数据库，可望数月后即可开放供民众使用，是该馆中文部在电脑数据服务上的一大里程碑。

李华伟日前应"陶陶时事座谈"之邀，向听众介绍国会图书馆的服务和藏书，这也是他首度走入华府华人社区，直接与使用者面对面，畅谈他计划将该馆建成世界顶级亚洲藏书处的期望。

他将国会图书馆的历史细说从头，包括该馆最初在1865年获史密松宁学会转赠有关亚洲的收藏，后来1869年中国同治皇帝大量赠书，不过早年该馆搜集重点放在中国的草药和农政方面的书籍。今日的收藏除图书外，尚包括手稿、地图、音乐、影片、录音、照片及各种印刷品等，已是中国以外中文收藏最丰的图书馆。

去年上任后，李华伟积极充实中文藏书，尤其最近与中国大陆清华大学合作，将引进共有五千余种期刊的电子期刊系统；另外目前正在试办阶段的电子书数据库，读者可以到馆内将所要阅读的书籍全文下载到光盘里，有如将书本携回家，皆是李华伟到任后的新突破，预计两个月后陆续启用，对读者是一大利好消息。

查阅资料除可利用网站 www.loc.gov 外，还可事先打电话到阅览室查询，电话是（202）707-5426。

李华伟指出，国会图书馆的功能除服务国会，同时扮演"国家图书馆"的角色，然而馆方朝九晚五的开放时间，使同时间上班的大众根本无法利用。另外，国会图书馆书籍不外借，但透过馆方最新实施的馆际互借新措施，可以让民众先上网查阅所需书籍，再到地方图书馆申请馆际互相借书，可以稍稍弥补其中之不足。

李华伟表示，国会图书馆不断丰富其收藏，亚洲部最古老的收藏是在雷峰塔地下发现的佛教经典，最近该馆以10万多美元购入公元前二世纪的印度手抄本佛书，将是最古老的收藏。

李华伟表示，来华府任职后，便想从"公共图书馆"的角度经营，为民众服务，不仅举办开放日，还不时举办各种座谈会服务读者。最近计划成立国会图书馆中文部董事会，已经内部审查通过，目前正招募有兴趣的侨胞加入成为创会会员。

有意参加或欲知详情，可电询中文部专员卢雪乡（202）707-2385。

（原载《世界日报》2004年1月17日）

《亚裔年鉴》第二辑在国会图书馆举行发表会

3月1日（星期二）晚上六时，由 TIYM 出版公司编辑发行的《亚裔年鉴》（ASIAN AMERICAN YEARBOOK 2005/2006）在美国国会图书馆同读者见面。当晚，TIMY 公司在美国国会图书馆亚洲部举行新书发表会，宣布该年鉴正式发行。美国联邦众议员 Michael Honda 到会祝贺。他还用中文祝大家"鸡年快乐"。美国劳工部财务长莫天成等一百余人出席了酒会。TIYM 公司向每一位来宾赠送了这本《亚裔年鉴》。人们在书中看到，华人关颖山、李昌玉、赵小兰的条目列在其中。

晚间，国会图书馆 Thomas Jefferson Building，从大门到亚洲部的通道上站立着多位酒会的服务人员，她们为来宾们引路，欢迎大家的到来。每一位酒会的受邀者能准时地到达现场。国会图书馆亚洲部主任李华伟及卢雪乡、中国科主任居蜜等，身着盛装，热情款待来到亚洲部的客人。看到李华伟的着装，众议员 Michael Honda 开玩笑说"有人会把你当成印度尼西亚人"。酒会的客人中间有近十位身穿军服的美国海岸警卫队成员，他们的公关形象照片登载于《亚裔年鉴》的封底，他们对《亚裔年鉴》的出版给予了帮助。国际中国文化出版社社长赵小明、亚奇人文艺术中心的李峰夫妇出现在酒会上。

李华伟说，美国的亚裔人口与日俱增，他十分高兴地看到《亚裔年鉴》的再度出版，展现美国多元文化的一面。

《亚裔年鉴》西班牙裔的编辑 Angela E. Zavala 在酒会的致词中说，"去年首度发行《亚裔年鉴》，今年又再度发行。这本年鉴是具有名人鉴和工具书功能的读物，也是全美国最完整的亚裔年鉴"。

这是《亚裔年鉴》在华府第二辑发行，内容收集了许多的实用资料。包括八十多个国家涉及亚洲地区的基本资料，全美亚裔社团组织，名人鉴，亚太裔活动，媒体机构，学生申请奖学金与财务支持资料，等等。

晚间的酒会，华裔、韩国裔、印度裔社区的人士来了不少。大家一起在国会图书馆亚洲部的办公区享用了水果、饮料、烤牛肉、小卷饼等食品，聆听贵宾及专家们发表高见，大家在愉快中渡过美好的黄昏。

（原载《华盛顿新闻》2005年3月5日）

美国国会图书馆亚洲部中文组的改弦更张

居蜜（Dr. Mi Chu Wiens）& 陈家仁（Lily Kecskes）[①]

1. 昔日的辉煌

国会图书馆收藏中文书刊起源于清同治年间。1869 年 6 月，同治皇帝以明、清刻书十种赠予美国政府。"同治赠书"主题包括经学、性理、医书、农书、算数、类书等方面，合共 905 册。1904 年清廷参与"圣路易斯万国博览会"，参展图书及地图展会后全部赠给国会图书馆。

早期收藏过程中值得一提的有下列二项。1909 年清廷特使唐绍仪（为 1874 年来美留学幼童，届时 14 岁）赠送 1728 年铜版活字印刷《古今图书集成》一套五千零四十册。这是为感谢美国退还一千两百七十八万五千银两的庚子赔款。另一项是美同政府各部会委员会（U. S. Government Interdepartmental Committee）收购的 1938 年至 1945 年在重庆、成都、云南等地大后方生活纪录，包括文学、艺术、戏剧、歌谣、政治、经济等五千种。这批图书是研究中国抗战时期的珍贵资料。

美国国会图书馆通过传教士，外交官等各种途径，收到善本珍藏、地方志、少数民族文献及古地图等。有系统的大量收集得力于施永格和恒慕义。施永格主修植物学，1891 年入美国农业部工作，定居华盛顿。由于他酷爱研究中国植物，利用福建、广东一带地方志记载，研究柑桔的生长规律。为此施永格为国会图书馆收集了大量中国方志。1910 年至 1941 年，施永格通过商务印书馆张元济在华购书，为中国本土外奠立最辉煌的中文书库。

恒慕义 1915 年以公理会教士身份到中国传教。在山西汾州（今汾阳）明义中学教英文，长达十年之久。1928 年国会图书馆成立中国文献部（后易名为中、日文献部，东方部的中文组，最后改名为亚洲部的中文组），恒慕义任职 27 年，中文藏书由 100,000 册增至 291,000 册。各地学者每年络绎不绝地来到中文组查考资料，撰写博士、硕士论文。当时东方部的中文组也成为中国研究文化沙龙，凡知名的中国研究学者，均来中文组查书，引用馆藏文献资料在他们专著中发表。

恒慕义卸任后，Edwin Beal、吴光清、王冀继任中文组组长，而亚洲部主任则由日裔美籍 Warren Tsuneishi、缅甸裔美籍 Helen Poe 担任。

2. 衰败时期

1928 年中国文献部成立时，中文典藏何等风光。随后，日文，韩文，继而东南亚、南亚各国典藏相继成立，中文组在整个亚洲部中仍然保持领先地位。

到了 20 世纪 80 年代，中文组内部走向专制的体制，组长自视甚高，以管、控的方式来稳定自己的地位。组内上下层沟通不良，缺乏合作。与他组之间，亦不相往来。到了 90 年代，整个亚洲部在馆内地位日渐衰退。

1992 年南亚组组长提出把西藏藏书归入该组，而该组组员对藏文有兴趣。藏文精品均为 19 世纪时与中文藏书同时购入国会图书馆，而西藏专题研究，必须用中文史料和著作。在中文组日益老化、僵化和衰败的情况下，只得任其宰割。

[①] 任职于美国国会图书馆亚洲部。

在过去十年，因中国在亚洲崛起，中文藏书受到各方重视。中文组的收藏虽然在数量上有所增多，但是在品质上显然落后，受到国会关注及学者专家的批评。像 University of Miami 的 June Teufel Dreyer 教授，George Washington University 的 David L. Shambaugh 教授，Brookings Institution 的经济学专家学者 Nicholas R. Lardy 等都分别著文批评。June Teufel Dreyer 教授也是国会美中经济和安全审查委员会的委员。

3. 中文组改弦更张

中文组一蹶不振也和亚洲部缺乏有力领导有关。国会图书馆副馆长 Winston Tabb 和主管藏书和服务的 Carolyn Brown 求才若渴，认定要有真正的领袖人才，方能拯救危亡。2003 年国会图书馆延聘李华伟博士为亚洲部主任，为自 1928 年亚洲部成立以来第一位华裔主任。李博士为难得一见的行政长才，人称他是图书馆界最具声望的酋长（Guru）。在短短的两年半内，把濒亡的中文组带到生气蓬勃、举世瞩目的地位。

李主任首先透视到，在这极有限的人力资源下，一定要做到"人尽其才，物尽其用，货畅其流"，把丰富珍贵的中国藏书全力整理和开放，供世人使用。在这前提下，必需做内部组织调整，他把以往的中文组改成中文与蒙文组，西藏资料归回中国，蒙古文献（包括现在蒙古共和国出版品）扩张纳入此组，亚洲部各组组长是由主任从各组中挑选合适人材担任。经过此番调整，传统纵的服从，变成横的联盟，各组之间齐心共事，为亚洲部的使命和项目，全力投入。

在李主任组织结构的分配、人力资源的运用、分工授权的执行、团队精神的发挥和国际合作的调配下，中文组各方面的业务都一一展开。为了方便读者，亚洲部阅览室的开放也从每周五天延伸到六天。

横的合作推广到馆内其他部门。2003 年与地图部合作，邀请北京大学李孝聪教授鉴定馆藏中国古地图。2004 年出版《美国国会图书馆中文古地图叙录》（北京文物出版社）。同年与台湾"中央研究院"合作，扫描西人所制有关中国地图八百余幅。2005 年"中央研究院"工作团队再度来华盛顿，第二次携手合作。国会图书馆收藏将纳入"中央研究院"最大网站"中国文明之时空基础架构"。

2004 年亚洲部与馆内自动化小组合作，将珍藏的纳西文献依"美国记忆（American Memory）"的模式扫描后在国会图书馆网上推出，三千多件纳西经书，经云南博物馆朱宝田教授整理三年，通过网站，公诸世界。

2005 年亚洲部与台湾"中央图书馆"合作，开始中文善本书数位化项目。通过"蒋经国基金会"资助，善本书藏先由潘先生、范邦瑾两位专家进行版本鉴定，撰写解题及查考他馆收藏情况，开列扫描清单，再由台湾汉世纪公司承担数位化工作。预定今年进度可达乾隆以前刊刻本三百种。

购书方面，在配合国会对中国问题的重视下，中文组加强了有关现代中国书籍的收集。自 2000 年以来，中文组在鲁斯基金会的资助下把收集范围扩大到商业、财政、法律、科学技术以及环保等方面，并特别专注有关中国共产党党史、中国的美国研究、国际关系、经济改革、军事国防等出版物，增强了中文藏书的实力。

同时，中文组也继续加强对电子数据库的重视。随着中国出版事业的发展及中国期刊种类的大量增加，为了尽力满足读者对中文期刊和报纸所需，中文组在这方面作了不少努力，并获得一定的成绩，得到很多读者的欢迎。

从 2004 年起到目前为止，中文组已订购了五种数据库，例如《人民日报电子版》，提供从1946年到2004年在此报刊中登载的全文文章;"China Data Online"专门以中英文提供有关中国全国、省市等各类统计材料;"CNKI"包括《中国期刊全文数据库》及《中国报刊全文数据库》,提供六千多种学术性杂志及五百种左右报刊的全文文章;以及SuperStar《超星数字图书》,提供十万种以上的全文图书。

中文组目前正在继续努力增加电子版出版物的收集。最近又购买了《四库全书电子版》,不久即可使用。其他数据库的购买也正在进行中。

亚洲部与国际中国文化出版社、美国亚洲文化学院等众多机构、组织合作,不断推出与中国文化、历史现况有关的活动。5月16日,举办了庆祝郑和下西洋六百周年的国际学术讨论会;7月19日,由陈钦智教授讲述她所发展的Global Memory Net;9月21日,由亚洲学会举办有关国会图书馆亚洲部馆藏的介绍;11月14日,新任东方法律部主任白瑞教授讲述他在中国及香港工作经验;11月17日,"中央研究院"两位专家作专题演讲;12月1日,中国音乐家傅华根国乐演奏。

鉴于亚洲部中文组的业务蒸蒸日上,曾在国会图书馆工作过的谭翠荣女士捐赠亚洲部三十万美元,成立各种奖助、补助基金,让各地学者研究员能来到亚洲部,分享宫殿之美,所藏之富。

新成立两年的亚洲部之友会加强了亚洲部对外的发展和联系。

中国文化,自唐宋以来已超越所谓"中原"的政治和地缘定义,成为东亚和东南亚许多地区共同参与的一个文化体系。展望中文组的未来,不囿于中国大陆、香港和台湾,而是对整个亚洲,甚至于推广在全世界的华裔文献收藏和文化研究,前景是不可限量的。

(原载《新世界时报》2005年12月9日)

国会图书馆亚洲部之友会积极活跃：
李华伟冀华人社区踊跃参与

国会图书馆亚洲部之友会（ADFS）自 2004 年成立以来，在亚洲部李华伟主任的带领之下，积极地与亚裔社区加强互动关系。从推动周六开放亚洲部阅览室到募款成立谭翠荣亚洲研究奖学金，成绩相当可观；亚裔社区也更意识到亚洲部馆藏的珍贵和可利用的价值。

谭翠荣亚洲研究奖学金（Florence Tan Moeson Fellowship for Asian Studies）是由谭翠荣女士慷慨捐款所设立。谭女士在国会图书馆从事编目工作达四十五年，退休之后一心希望能回馈社会，尽其能力培养更多人才来报答社会对她的造就之恩。她捐款给国会图书馆亚洲部的三十万美金，分为十年赠与。

亚洲部利用该笔捐款成立亚洲研究奖学金、购买特别藏书基金，和作为国际图书馆员交流之用。2006 年度共有六十余人申请；预估 2007 年人数将会倍增。

2007 年度的奖学金申请将于九月公布，欢迎上国会图书馆网站：www.loc.gov 查询。

前不久日本日立公司（Hitachi）也加入支持亚洲部的阵容，成为亚洲部之友会第一个企业会员。日立向来对文化保存与建设工作不遗余力，其驻美事务总代表大出隆先生在参加李主任主讲的一场介绍国会图书馆的演讲上，对亚洲部有了更进一步的认识后，积极地向主管争取加入亚洲部之友会，成为永久会员。去年捐款五千美元；今年度将提升为一万美元，并计划继续和亚洲部进行其他多项大型文化和学术合作项目，捐赠款项也将用来举办更多的学术演讲和文化活动。

值得一提的是，为纪念今年菲律宾移民美国一百周年，亚洲部与美菲裔团体也将合作举办相关学术研讨会，为协助亚洲部筹经费办数项意义重大的活动，菲裔社区名人、高龄 98 岁的 Remy Cabacungan 女士在生日庆祝会上，宣布将所收到的礼金 1,700 美元全数捐给亚洲部，慷慨的情操令人感动。

对 ADFS 的成长，李主任表示高兴。他说亚洲部将会越来越活跃。本年度接下来，已订有多项与其他机构合办的国际性学术研讨会。他解释，一般观念认为国会图书馆已有国会拨款补助，何需向民间募款，但国会款项只负责购买一般藏书和人事费用，对于推广使用藏书办活动所需费用无法支持。

不举办活动提高大众对国会图书馆的认识，如何能与社区拉近距离？因此，李主任表示民间募款和支持是极重要的工作，具有文化上重大的意义。他希望华人社区能不落在其他亚裔之后，增加与亚洲部互动。欢迎公司和个人加入 ADFS 的行列，会费可抵税。

会员可直接收到活动和奖学金申请通知，享有图书馆礼品部 10% 的折扣，和同图书馆推荐购书的权利。详情请参阅：www.lcasianfriends.org.

（原载《星岛日报》2006 年 2 月 28 日 B1 版"大华府"）

李华伟任满三年建树多
——国会图书馆亚洲部主任推动公图合作 创设亚洲部之友会

谭焕瑛

美国国会图书馆亚洲部首位华裔主任李华伟，就任届满三年，日前受访畅谈他的工作、计划，以及对支持者的感激。他说，审视过去三年的工作成绩，虽非完美，但在经费渐减的情况下，仍存堪称满意的成果，确是不易，但也令人鼓舞。他将成果归功于亚洲部全体工作人员通力合作的团队精神，和社会人士的大力支持。

拥有图书馆管理博士学位的李华伟，除拥有多年的图书馆行政经验，在学术、行政上建树颇多，是国际知名的图书馆专家。尽管他有丰富经验和专业背景，李华伟表示，亚洲部主任一职对他仍深具挑战性，因为国图地位高，又属政府机构，制度、人事、性质自与其他图书馆相异，加上他是亚洲部第一个华裔主任，工作既不轻松，更不容许失败。他就任后对外做的第一件事，是与地方公共图书馆合作，让一般读者能通过公共图书馆借阅国会图书馆的书，图书馆目录可上网 www.loc.gov 查阅，改变了国图只服务高层、图书藏而不用的形象；对内则加强与其他部门合作，为亚洲部争取更多资源。

李华伟说，工作推动有赖相关人员合作，合作又需团队精神支持。为此，他以企业管理方式将亚洲部组织稍作更改，增设馆藏科和学术服务科，与各语文组直接互动，经公开甄选，由卢雪乡和居蜜分别担任科长，负专业职责。

他又将原有中、日、韩、越、南亚五组的亚洲部扩充为六组，将东南亚自南亚分出，并将中文组增列蒙文。李华伟说，10多年前南亚组组长曾以西藏流亡政府在印度为由，将原属中文组的藏文文献全部纳入南亚组内，中文组扩大后，他终将藏文文献重新纳回中文组怀抱。

李华伟另一创举为成立了亚洲部之友会。李华伟指出，该会团结了亚洲部与亚裔社区的力量。他说，三年前他就任不久，即发生了伊拉克战争，国会经费大受影响，使他的文化交流、研究培训等计划受阻，幸得亚洲部之友会及时支援，会员谭翠荣慨捐30万美元，将分10年，用于设立亚洲研究奖学金、购买特别藏书和国际图书馆员交流活动。

另外，企业会员日本日立公司（Hitachi）连续两年共捐款1万5000美元作学术演讲与文化活动之用。98岁菲裔人士为纪念菲裔移民美国一百周年，捐出生日礼金1700美元给亚洲部，这些都令李华伟深为感动。

对华人关注的中文组，李华伟表示，该组馆藏日益扩大充实，并与国外多个图书馆及研究机构合作，又获中国国家图书馆选为五年赠书计划对象之一。去年9月，中文组更为中美经济国家安全委员会听证会公开肯定与赞许。对亚洲部各方面的进步，李华伟强调是大家共同努力的结果，阅览室扩充服务周六全日开放，更是同仁不辞辛劳的表现，对此，李华伟深表欣慰。他希望更多人利用阅览室，利用亚洲部的资源，也欢迎更多社区人士加入亚洲部之友会，一起为推动文化活动努力。详情可浏览网页 www.lcasianfriends.org。

（原载《世界日报》2006年4月4日）

让书籍"活"起来
——专访美国国会图书馆亚洲部主任李华伟

李 焰

第一个华裔图书馆馆长

祖籍福建的李华伟1949年随家人移居台湾。在台湾师范大学获得教育学士两年后拿到了美国匹兹堡大学的奖学金,赴美攻读教育行政学硕士。说到与图书馆业结缘,恰恰是因为当时拿到的奖学金并不包含生活费,于是他跑去学校图书馆打工,专门负责为书库"归架"——重新整理归还的图书。连他自己也没想到,这份看似枯燥的工作却开启了他在美国图书馆界40多年的历程。

硕士毕业的时候,李华伟面前摆着两条前景看好的道路,要么回台湾当中学校长;要么留在匹兹堡大学继续攻读教育学博士。就在此时,图书馆馆长找到了他,希望李华伟能为即将组建的图书馆"亚洲研究所"进行中文书目的采购和编目工作。同时,馆长愿意推荐他就读匹兹堡大学的图书馆系硕士。

"采购、编目图书对很多人而言是繁琐而枯燥的工作。"李华伟回忆说,"你要阅读大量的新书介绍,学术书评,还要经常和各专业的教授交流,让他们推荐本学科的好书、新书;编目就更费功夫了,中文馆藏从无到有,所有书籍的描述、分类、作者姓名规范,都要你亲力亲为……但是,我却干得津津有味,乐在其中。"

李华伟自认坚持下来的动力是"年轻"和"愿意投入"。他说:"我从学生时代就有这样的想法:要做好一件事虽然很花时间,但却能培养一个人的才干和吃苦精神。"

这份兴趣和执着让李华伟留在了匹兹堡大学,他一边工作,一边攻读学位,每天只能睡四五个小时,但仍然无怨无悔。

1962年李华伟被聘为美国杜肯大学(Duquesne Unniversity)图书馆的技术部兼非洲部主任,主管书籍的采购和编目。两年后,拿到教育学博士学位的他又被导师推荐到宾州爱丁堡大学(Edinboro University of Pennsylvania)担任图书馆馆长。于是,他成为该校第一位拥有博士学位的图书馆馆长。

"如果说我在图书馆界的东亚经验是在匹兹堡大学积累的,那么东南亚方面的经验就要归功于东南亚七年的亲身实践了。后来我能入选会图书馆亚洲部主任就是依靠这两大优势。"李华伟说。

1968年,李华伟赴泰国主管美国国务院援外总署的东南亚图书馆专案。"越战"结束后才回到美国,并在克罗拉多州立大学(Colorado State University)当了三年副馆长。

"我1978年来到俄亥俄大学(Ohio University)图书馆是看中了它在东南亚馆藏方面的雄厚实力,这恰恰是我的特长所在。俄亥俄州共有13所州立大学。最大的俄亥俄州立大学(Ohio State University)图书馆以东亚馆藏见长。"李华伟说。结果他在俄亥俄大学做图书馆馆长一做就是21年,继续着重于发展东南亚方面的资料和研究。

21年间,俄亥俄大学图书馆的藏书总量从60万册发展到200多万册。当初李华伟刚到俄亥俄大学图书馆的时候,只容纳110名会员的美国图书馆界权威机构"研究图书馆协会"(Association of Research Libraries)根本不把俄亥俄大学图书馆放入考虑之列。1996年,他们却正式邀请俄亥俄大学图书馆加入。到1999年,俄亥俄大学图书馆在这个协会的排名也从三年前的第82名跃居为第70名。

活用书籍的管理之道

"要想管好图书馆,首先收藏要好,有特色;其次是服务要做好。有好书却不能物尽其用,那就会留下遗憾。"专业经验十分丰富的李华伟如数家珍地说。为了发挥俄亥俄大学图书馆的东南亚典藏特长,他建立了全世界第一所海外华人文献研究中心,收集东南亚华人的历史、资料,并与中国暨南大学、新加坡华裔馆合作,将资讯通过资料和网路方式,供全世界所有有兴趣的读者查阅。

"移居到东南亚的海外华人最初是依靠会社、同乡会等组织发展壮大起来的。这些团体积累了很多华侨们早年的奋斗史和生活记录。但是他们的下一代并没有祖辈那样珍惜这些历史资料,很多东西都由于年代久远而消失了。"他说,"当时,我有种将之收集起来的紧迫感。印度尼西亚的华侨组织名叫'公馆',连曾殖民那里的荷兰人都很重视,希望能获取其资料以飨本国学者。于是,我想,我们也应该收藏这笔历史财富。"

然而,无论要将收藏做好,还是要活用资源,都离不开一个字——钱。李华伟为图书馆募到900万美元的基金,放入俄亥俄大学基金会,每年从中抽取6%的利息,即54万多美元用于图书馆的建设。显然这笔经费是不够的。虽然州政府也有拨款,但是公家的钱要专款专用,限制很多,如"海外华人文献研究中心"这样的专案根本不要想沾上边了。

"其实,现在很多图书馆招聘馆长时,募款能力也是很重要的一条。"他说,"我们对外接触的管道很广,企业家、私人收藏家,乃至书商、善心人士,都是主要的资金捐款人。华人研究中心的建立就多亏了香港的银行家邵友保100万美元的支票。"

"然而,人脉并不是充分条件,最后决定你是否能募到款的要素是你要把图书馆管好。"他说,"有了'家底'之后,还要对外宣传,物尽其用。如今在国会图书馆,我们也经常和外界的组织一起搞活动,最近日本驻美国大使就主动找到我们,要来国会图书馆做演讲。"

李华伟的"活用"思路帮助俄亥俄大学图书馆提高了知名度,1999年他宣布退休时,校方送给他一份惊喜:用他的名字为图书馆命名,可谓开了美国图书馆界的先河。

华人:与图书馆业一起成长

李华伟近半个世纪的旅美过程让图书馆界的华裔后辈们都很憧憬,常常问其心得体会。

"肯干、认真是我的经验之谈。"他说,"白人总觉得行政工作是他们垄断的行业,华人由于语言和表达能力的劣势,没有竞争力。但我以为:我们首先不能小看自己。我们的天然不足是可以克服的。比如英语发音不好,可以用坚实的写作功底来弥补。当美国人从你的文字中看到你言之有物时,他们是会认可你的。相反,我们对于亚洲、中国的了解比美国人要多,发挥这些长处就能让你在同行间立足。但有时,中国人的缺点就是太谦虚了,不肯力争。"

寄语后辈之余,李华伟也不忘幽默地说:"我进入图书馆界也是拜天时所赐。人们说,1960年代的华人在美国就从事三大行业:餐饮业、洗衣业和图书馆。朝鲜战争结束后,美国感到自己不了解亚洲,因此在很多大专院校中设立了亚洲研究中心。于是,众多赴美学习语言、历史和教育的中国人看到了就业机会,转入图书馆业。"

李华伟说华人几十年来在美国图书馆界的地位已经有不小的提高。他说:"我1990年代任图书馆馆长时,和我同样在美国大学当馆长的可能只有一两人,现在应该增加到三四人了。另外,我们业界的华人组织'华美图书馆协会'的注册会员如今是1000多人,但是估计实际的数字可能超过5000人。"

经常回国参加学术活动的李华伟认为中国的图书馆业发展很迅速。

"我1982年第一次到祖国大陆时,那里的图书馆还非常落后,但是90年代的中国则出现了迅速的发展。一座座图书馆大楼都建得很漂亮,从业人员也有专业背景,50多所大学开设了图书馆专业。现在,国内的中文图书数位化比我们做得好,也比日本等很多亚洲国家要强。"李华伟对《华盛顿观察》周刊说。

国会图书馆亚洲部改革

"民主化、透明化和人性化是(在美国)管好图书馆的三大要素。如果说我在这个行当几十年来最大的成就,或许就是一直在尝试这三者有机地融合于管理工作当中。"李华伟对《华盛顿观察》周刊说,"与前两个要素不同,人性化带有我们中国人的理念。美国的规章制度非常严,往往缺少点人性的东西。但是'人性'太多了,就会变成'人情'。因此还要辅之以'理',才是管理的最高境界。"

美国没有国家图书馆,国会图书馆就担当了这种职能。从200多年前,杰弗逊总统将它的私人图书收藏卖给国会图书馆时,就树立起这样一种理念:国会图书馆是面向世界的。美国人的知识有限,图书馆应该尽量收集世界各国的图书资源。

"美国国务院、教育部、劳工部下只设有小型图书馆,馆藏极不全面。需要查阅中文典籍时,他们都会采用我们的资源。政府部门之外,美国还有70多所大学有东亚馆藏,但即使是哈佛大学燕京学院,中文书籍也不如我们。"李华伟说,"世界范围内,著名的大英图书馆在中文收藏,甚至亚洲收藏上,数量也在我们之下。"

"美国国会图书馆是政府部门,官僚气很重。因此,我来之后就做了一些改组。目前的亚洲部下直接设以图书收藏科和学术服务科两大纵向分支再辅以横向的五大语言组,包括中文、蒙文、日文、韩文、东南亚组和南亚组。虽然语言组别比以前模糊了,但在购书决定和服务上更有弹性,更有效率。"李华伟说。

在国会图书馆亚洲部工作了27年的居蜜(Mi Chu Wiens)拥有哈佛大学历史系的博士学位,如今是亚洲部学术服务科科长。她对《华盛顿观察》周刊说:"李博士是难得一见的行政人才。在短短两年半内,把一蹶不振的中文组带到了生气蓬勃的境地。"

原载《华盛顿观察》(*Washington Observer*)周刊,又载于《美国通》(*How2USA*). V. 7, No. 5, May 2006, pp. 8 – 10.

华人的骄傲
——访美国国会图书馆亚洲部主任李华伟

罗露西

4月的华盛顿碧空万里，鲜花盛开。从纽约罗切斯特到华盛顿旅游，我特地到美国国会图书馆拜访了久仰大名的亚洲部主任——李华伟博士。

美国国会图书馆，是美国国家图书馆，世界最大的图书馆，藏书近一亿。图书馆位于华盛顿东南一街，由三座分别以三位美国总统命名的宏伟建筑组成。亚洲部设在最早建于1800年欧洲古典风格的杰斐逊大楼二层。

走进亚洲部阅览大厅，一股东方文化的风迎面吹来，慢慢地浏览一排排图书索引架，体会到一种穿越历史、穿越不同文化的厚重感。不同年代，不同版本，不同主题的中文、日文、韩文、蒙文，以及东南亚各语种的图书分类保存。中国古籍出版社的赠书仪式，不久前在这里举行，中间的台子上还摆着出版社赠给图书馆的样书，那些印刷精致的图书，代表了中国图书的最高水平。

经过阅览大厅向右拐，就看到主任办公室。敲门进入，只见李华伟博士正在打电话，他示意我在他办公桌对面的沙发上坐下。等待的时刻，我注意到他办公桌上的台灯古色古香，底座是白色的中国古瓷，上面布满了殷红的梅花，中间加着几朵淡黄色的菊花，静静地表述着东方艺术的精髓，韵味十足，意境深远。侧面的墙上，有一幅巨大的中国书——"书"字，笔触苍劲有力，且融合了秀雅之气，"书"挂在这里真是再贴切不过了。李华伟博士放下电话，向我走来，坐在旁边的椅子上，我们像老朋友一样地聊起来……

博学长才智

被誉为"经纬枢纽华美桥梁"的李华伟博士风度儒雅，平易近人，融学者的才智和管理者的气度于一体。

他1933年生于广东新会，父亲是公务员，母亲生于书香门第。他有一个哥哥，一个妹妹，也都受到很好的教育。李华伟1945年在南京完成初中学业，1949年随父母到台湾，1954年在台湾师范大学毕业，1957年被美国匹兹堡大学录取，赴美留学。在匹兹堡大学一共七年，读了三个学位。当时，他像所有留学生一样，靠打工维持学业。他在匹兹堡大学图书馆打工时，负责书库上架。由于学习刻苦，工作勤奋，深得馆长的赏识，在他毕业时，为他提供了在图书馆正式工作的机会。从此，他就"三年跳一个台阶"步步高升，从副主任升主任，再从副馆长升馆长。曾历任匹兹堡大学、都肯大学、宾州爱丁堡大学、科罗拉多州立大学、美国国会图书馆的行政职务，并成为全美第一位华人馆长。

作为一个中国人，在西方的土地上获得成功，他靠的是执着和韧性，是他柔中有刚、外圆内方的东方性格。他待人诚恳热情，做事一丝不苟，有强烈的责任感，这些品质造就他成为强者。同时，他广博的学识储备，拥有的教育硕士、图书馆硕士及哲学博士学位，为他成为世界一流人才奠定了基础。

由于他在国际图书情报界享有很高的声誉，曾连续两届担任美国图书馆学会理事，并担任国际图书馆学会联盟大学及研究图书馆委员会委员职务，还多次担任联合国教科文组织顾问。他的专著有：《图书馆学的世界观》、《现代化图书馆管理》等，发表了大量学术论文。

激情报祖国

中国改革开放吸引了无数海外赤子回到故土，他们以不同的方式报效祖国。1982年，李华伟博士以外国专家身份第一次回到久别的祖国，他结识了许多图书馆界的同行，这激发了他要用自己在海外多年的经验，为中国的图书馆发展尽力的激情。他在国际图书馆界的名望和成就很快引起许多高校的关注和兴趣，几乎每年都有不少院校邀请他回国讲学。他先后受聘为北京大学、清华大学、北京师范大学、北京邮电大学、西安交通大学、南开大学、武汉大学、四川联合大学、东北师范大学、天津理工学院等院校的客座教授，同时，担任中国科学院武汉文献信息中心、兰州文献信息中心以及中国国家图书馆顾问。

他利用自己的影响力，在联合国教科文组织的赞助下，设立了国际图书馆员培训计划，先后有来自世界各地160多位学员完成培训，其中近百人来自中国大陆。他们都是图书馆长、副馆长及部门主任。这一培训计划成为国会图书馆国际合作的典范。

在李华伟博士的倡导下，首届中美图书馆合作会议于1996年在北京举行，两国近百位图书馆长和专家学者就"全球的信息存取——挑战与机遇"，展开热烈讨论。会议取得圆满成功，中美图书馆界的合作从此开始。李华伟博士做了大量牵线搭桥的事，很多时候是成就他人，他并没有得到什么。我问他："你为什么这样做？"他说："身为华人，我乐于作个桥梁。"他所做的一切的确是令人敬佩的。

（原载《人民日报》海外版2006年5月18日）

华盛顿美国国会图书馆纪行

王　威　郭怡红[①]

美国国会图书馆，是我们向往已久的地方。

2008年中国新年前夕，我们从纽约驱车五个小时，抵达首都华盛顿。

《世界日报》华盛顿的女记者谭焕英叮嘱我们，不要像以前那样驾车到市区。当我们进入市中心后才感觉到她的告诫多么英明。同过去来这里相比，华盛顿多了几分"战时"的紧张气氛，很多道路禁止通行。白宫一带行政区的周边街道和政府建筑旁，布满了各式现代化路障，随处可见荷枪实弹的军警在巡逻和检查过往车辆。显然这都是911之后反恐的举措，深感美国面临着世界上最严峻的恐怖袭击的威胁。华盛顿的人对此习以为常，可从纽约来的我们仍感到些许不习惯。

这天一早，在谭焕英的陪同下，我们来到大名鼎鼎的美国国会图书馆。图书馆亚洲部的负责人热情地接待了我们，他们是亚洲部主任李华伟先生，馆藏主任、中国近代研究专家卢雪乡女士，学术研究主任、哈佛大学历史学博士居蜜女士，以及主任助理郝安琦博士等。这些学识渊博、谦逊友善又风度翩翩的华裔学者，向我们详细介绍了国会图书馆和亚洲部，讲述了很多有趣的故事。

享誉世界的知识宝库

宏伟的美国国会图书馆位于国会大厦对面，由三座各以一位美国总统名字命名的精美建筑组成。它们是1897年落成的汤玛斯·杰弗逊大厦，1939年落成的约翰·亚当斯大厦，和1983年落成的詹姆斯·麦迪森大厦。藏书量高达一亿三千四百万册，每年为200万读者和大批的参观者提供服务。

国会图书馆规模宏大、历史悠久，是全世界最大的图书馆。它是国会的直属机构之一，拥有三重身份：美国的国会图书馆、国家图书馆、国家版权局。

国会图书馆成立于1800年。

1800年4月24日，亚当斯总统签署法案，拨款5000美元购置国会所需的图书及设备，虽然当时只有740册图书和三张地图，但国会图书馆由此诞生了。

一般认为杰弗逊总统是国会图书馆的创始人。1802年1月，这位有远见的政治家签署了界定国会图书馆任务与职能的法案，并由总统任命馆长。1814年，国会大厦连同图书馆被英军焚毁。后来，杰弗逊总统建议重建国会图书馆，并将自己的6487册私人藏书，以23950美元的价格"出售"给图书馆，于是国会图书馆重新有了图书收藏。讲到这里，李华伟先生笑道，那个时候当总统也是很穷的，但今天这批书籍已经成了"镇馆之宝"。

杰弗逊的这批书籍五花八门各类都有，有人提出国会图书馆主要供政府官员使用，收藏的都是政治方面的书籍，不该收藏像百科全书那样的书籍。而杰弗逊认为，民主来源于知识，作为立法者，需要任何一门学科的广泛知识。一个政治家必须了解所有的领域，而不仅是政治方面，他建议以后的收藏要包括各个领域的图书。此后，国会图书馆就遵照这样的宗旨，大量收藏世界各国各门类的图书资料了。

[①] 任职于《彼岸》杂志社。

1914年起,图书馆还成立了法律、教育、公共福利、环境与自然科学、外交和贸易与国防等五个研究室。

卢雪乡女士告诉我们,国会图书馆现有17个部门,包括按媒体特点划分的电影多媒体部、地图部、图片部、音乐部等,按地区和语言划分的亚洲部、非洲和中东部、拉丁美洲部、东欧部等;有28个宽阔华丽的阅览室,包括国会议员的专用阅览室。全馆有4000多位工作人员,仅在麦迪森大厦为国会服务的就有700人。值得一提的是,还有100多位华裔专家分布在各个部门,过去他们多来自台湾香港,今天已有半数来自中国大陆。所有员工和专家都属于联邦政府的雇员。

李华伟先生说:国会议员要讨论事情,我们就要为他们整理材料,做背景报告,议员们根据这些在国会里提出议案。有些议案甚至是我们替他们起稿。

国会图书馆的经费来自联邦政府的拨款,也接受社会各界的捐赠。2000年建馆200周年时,它收到了有史以来最大的一笔捐款:来自麦迪森委员会主席约翰·克鲁斯的6000万美元。

国会图书馆的收藏非常丰富,像收藏有最古老印刷的古登堡圣经等世界级珍品。仅地图部的收藏就达2000万件,是世界上最多的。全馆每年还要增加200万件新收藏。作为版权局,美国每件出版物都要向这里赠送两本,仅此项每年就增加60万种图书。它还大量购进各国的电子版图书和资料库等,收藏日臻全面。

国会图书馆既向国会议员和政府官员提供服务,也免费开放给全世界所有普通读者。美国公民用驾驶执照,外国公民用护照,做个简单登记,就可获得两年有效的会员证,凭此证就能自由出入国会图书馆各阅览室,使用这里的图书资料。

国会图书馆建立起资料库,图书资料经电子扫描等技术手段,放在它的网站上,供读者无偿使用。

引人入胜的亚洲部和中文收藏

国会图书馆有一个著名的亚洲部,尤其是它的中文组,在美国乃至世界都颇有地位。它的中文收藏除中国以外,在世界排名第一。著名的哈佛燕京图书馆的中文收藏,也仅为它的三分之二。

亚洲部在杰弗逊大厦内,创立于1928年,被誉为"国会图书馆的宝藏",设有中文、日文、韩文和东南亚四个部门。李华伟先生则是亚洲部成立以来的第一位华裔主任。

亚洲部收藏了300万册图书,涵括亚洲160种语言文字。

亚洲部的中文收藏始于清朝同治年间,1850年根据中美图书交换协定,同治皇帝赠送给国会图书馆10套书,933种。今天它的中文收藏超过100万件,古代善本达5万多册。还有4000多种6万余册的中国地方志,其中100多本为海内外孤本。还收藏了大量藏文、满文甚至东巴文的中国少数民族文献。

美国著名汉学家费正清教授抗战期间在中国收集的5000余种当时的各种资料,也保存在这里。

如今,国会图书馆每年都从中国大陆和台港澳地区采购15000册图书、2400种期刊、50种报纸,不断充实中文资料。

亚洲部的读者,2006年比2005年增加10%,2007年比2006年增加17%。他们做过一个调查,75%的在美国研究中国问题拿到博士学位的人,都使用过这里的中文资料。

李华伟告诉我们,你轻易不能小觑来这里的金发碧眼的美国人,他们很多人中文好得不得了，可以毫无障碍地阅读大公报文汇报，甚至可以流利地阅读古书的文言文。他笑道，此时华人讲话一定要注意，他们可都是中国通。

李华伟说：亚洲部有个多方位的发展规划。比如现在同台湾"中央图书馆"合作，把我们的古籍全部扫描，他们已在这里工作了三年，扫描了700多部，先做的都是大陆台湾都没有的世界性孤本。

亚洲部收藏了很多珍贵中文古籍。像《永乐大典》，已知全世界仅存400本，这里就有43本。

亚洲部曾请中国北京大学古地图专家李孝聪教授帮助整理收藏的中国古地图。他们看后说这里有太多宝贝，非常激动，回去后出了一本书《美国国会图书馆收藏中文古地图叙录》。这些古地图很清晰很形象，都经过地图部的技术人员处理，保存得相当好。

卢雪乡女士介绍：我们还有一部《妙法莲华经》，出自杭州雷峰塔，是公元975年用中国的古法印出来的。1924年雷峰塔倒塌后，发现了这部在塔里压了千年的佛经，这是我们收藏的最早的中文古籍。当时的馆长买回来后，进行了很好的修补，放在一个盒子里。此外还收藏了多部珍贵的敦煌写经。

但亚洲部收藏最多的不是中文书籍，而是日文的。这是因为二战后美国占领了日本，为了审判日本战犯，需要收集资料，美军在日本收集和没收了很多书籍资料，后来大多运到美国国会图书馆保存，仅这一项就高达60多万册。

书海中的故事

卢雪乡女士和居蜜女士专门调出珍藏的敦煌写经等古籍，请我们过来阅览大厅观看并拍照。

亚洲部宽敞的阅览大厅一尘不染，高大的书架上摆满了中文书籍。卢雪乡女士小心翼翼地展开泛黄的古经卷，自言自语念道：这个是残卷，唐末写本，敦煌出，经字第十号，大般若波罗蜜多经……

那手写经卷上的小楷，字迹清晰，娟秀工整，让人爱不释手赞叹不已。见到故国的瑰宝在这里珍藏得如此完好，心里有种说不出的欣慰和酸楚。

居蜜女士说，我们有敦煌写经11种，数量不多，却非常精彩。她举例告诉我们，图书馆当年曾用一万美元，从一位著名的中国收藏家手中一次性买来他的全部收藏1000件，其中就包括一些珍贵的古籍。

展开第237卷敦煌古卷。卢雪乡说，近代的书籍纸比较脆，含酸，不好保存，而中国古籍的宣纸材料非常好，保存很久也不会变质。

居蜜女士如数家珍地告诉我们：这里还有一个1931年王姓收藏家的敦煌高昌写经，过去人们得到高昌写经就会把它切成一段段地卖出去，你可以看到这部写经是一个很长的长卷，非常珍贵。

在国会图书馆不计其数的中文收藏中，交织着不少鲜为人知的故事。李华伟先生向我们讲述了若干。

当年，美国有个传教士在中国教书传教20多年。他有个收集中国古地图和地方志的嗜好，退休后回到美国，找到国会图书馆馆长，说我有很多中国的古地图和地方志，想送给国会图书馆，你们有没有兴趣？馆长马上回答，我们不仅愿意接受，还要成立一个中文组，请你来做第一任中文组组长。这个人一下就做了20多年的中文组组长，他的中文名字叫韩慕玉。后来，他的儿子当上了美国驻中国的大使。

上世纪20年代，美国农业部有个专家斯明戈，他认为中国同美国的环境气候很相似，中国有很多好的植物美国却没有。他就跑到中国去，发现在地方志里，记载了很多中国的植物和农作物，他就把一些物种介绍到美国。今天佛罗里达州和加州盛产的柑橘，就是当年他从中国引进的。有一年美国发生了很大的病虫害，大批果树都死了。斯明戈想起在中国看到果农把蚂蚁放在果树下消灭害虫，他又把中国的蚂蚁带来繁殖，结果把美国果树的病虫害消灭了，很多果树至今还长得好好的。斯明戈同国会图书馆馆长的关系很好，他把收集的中国地方志送给图书馆，后来图书馆就专门委托他帮助在中国买地方志。

有一次，台湾的教育官员来到国会图书馆，指名要看中国古地图。他有备而来，带了很多记者。图书馆把明代的地图拿出来，他立刻大做文章对记者说：你们看，这上面的中国版图里根本就没有标明包括台湾。图书馆马上又给他另一幅地图说：这张清代的地图里，就清楚地标明有台湾在中国版图里。讲到这里，李华伟和卢雪乡都面带不悦地说：后来这位"部长"回到台湾搞了个中学校长讨论会，他不提这张清代的地图，只拿那张明代地图说，"你看连美国国会图书馆的中国古地图上都没有台湾"。他们太政治了，我们都觉得被利用了。

亚洲部还存档有两类非常珍贵的资料：日本731部队二战期间在中国东北做人体实验的原始资料和照片，和日本研制原子弹的资料。

李华伟先生说：这些资料本该是可以提供给所有学者的，日本人曾来找过，我们担心会毁坏这些珍贵资料，所以非常谨慎。下礼拜沈阳要来几位专家，他们要盖一个"二战"期间日本侵略中国的博物馆，需要很多资料。我们愿意把这批尚未公开的照片和资料提供给他们，很好地保留起来，就毁不掉了。而另一个日本研究原子弹的资料，也是珍贵的原始文献，我们有当年日本研究人员的手稿和图。所以他们如果今天说没有这些事情，就可以拿出真正的证据来。

有一位上海的退休教授，他父亲是当年国民政府派遣参加审判日本战犯的中国代表团团长。岁月流逝，今天没有多少人还知道这段历史了。他专程来国会图书馆寻找父亲的痕迹，通过对这里资料的查询，了解了很多情况。当时由于国民政府比较穷，送不起很多人去东京参加审判日本战犯。结果他们到了东京一看，日本光为战犯们辩护的律师就有成百人，而中国只有两个。在这种情况下，他们必须整理出强有力的资料，只能拼命工作，最终完成了这个艰巨的历史使命。这位教授在此找到他父亲参与东京审判的大量资料，非常兴奋，决心要用这些资料写出书来，让更多的人了解这段历史。

与中国的书缘

看到亚洲部阅览大厅的台子上摆放着很多展览的中文书籍，原来当天下午中国的前文化部长孙家正要来访问，亚洲部专门摆上各种相关图书。

如今，国会图书馆与中国图书界有着广泛的联系与合作。他们在北京大学、武汉大学、广州中山大学等地建立代理，推荐和采购中国的书籍。我们多次看到媒体报导李华伟先生和卢雪乡女士等，亲自前往中国选购图书，参加学术活动。

李华伟说，国会图书馆不是情报机构，有一个只采购公开发行的书籍和论文，不买任何内部档的原则。现在每年用30万美元在中国采购书籍。还买了许多大学和研究机构的资料库，像清华大学7000种中国期刊杂志的资料库，中国科技情报所80万学术论文的资料库。

国会图书馆每年还为中国国家图书馆培训十名专业人员。中国国家图书馆每年向世界百家大图书馆赠送百套大陆精品图书，而国会图书馆得到的赠送则是上千种大陆的精选书籍。

亚洲部还协助中国艺术研究院与美国民俗中心建立合作，参与中国非物质文化遗产的发掘保护。

国会图书馆大量参与社会活动。亚洲部每月都要举办两次以上的文化活动。最近一次是邀请大陆和台湾的专家研讨孔子学说在当代的意义。

李华伟任职亚洲部后，发现176箱被封存半个世纪的中文书籍。这是日本占领中国东北时收集的情报，内容包括城乡、道路、产业等非常全面，很多都用到日后对中国的侵略战争中。战后，美国从南满铁路株式会社东京图书馆没收，送到这里。李华伟派专人已整理出10000多种，包括明清的古籍。

李华伟感叹地说，至今我们还有25万册图书没来得及整理和扫描，这项工作至少还需要五六年的时间。而李华伟这位学贯中西的长者，四个礼拜后就要退休了……

让李华伟先生感到遗憾的是，至今还有很多人以为国会图书馆是只为国会议员服务的机构。专访结束前，我们遵照李华伟先生的建议，去麦迪森大厦的读者登记处各自办理了一份国会图书馆会员证。真的那么简单，仅仅十分钟，不花一分钱，就得到了自由进入这个文化圣殿的权利。

国会图书馆渐行渐远了，华盛顿渐行渐远了。我们同李华伟先生一样，同卢雪乡女士一样，同居蜜女士一样，同国会图书馆所有勤奋的华裔专家一样，渴望更多的华人朋友来使用这个世界上最大的图书馆，让更多的人了解它、爱护它。

（原载《彼岸》（*Coastide Magazine*）2006年6月，第48-54页。）

Interview: Dr. Hwa-Wei Lee, Ph. D.
(Chief of the Asian Division Library of Congress)

Hwa-Wei Lee. Chief of the Asian Division, Library of Congress, and Dean Emeritus of Ohio University Libraries, was born in China, did his undergraduate studies in Taiwan, and completed his M. Ed. , and Ph. D. degrees at the University of Pittsburgh. During his library career, he worked in various library administrative positions in American universities, including a seven-year assignment in Thailand. Among the many honors he received were the 1987 Ohio Librarian of the Year, the 1991 American Library Association Award for Contributions to International Librarianship, and the 1999 Ohio Half of Fame Librarian. Upon his retirement in 1999, Ohio University named a new library building the Hwa-Wei Lee Library Annex and the first floor of the main library as Hwa-Wei Lee Center for International Collections.

AsAY: How is the Asian Division ensuring the preservation of Asian heritage and literary works?

Lee: The Library of Congress was established by an act of the American Congress in 1800. After the initial collection was destroyed by the invading British troops in 1814, the Congress acquired the personal library of 6.487 books from the retired President Thomas Jefferson. In offering his collection to Congress. Jefferson provided justifications about the scope of his collection, which included books in foreign languages and volumes of philosophy, science, literature and other topics not normally viewed as part of a legislative library. He wrote, "I do not know that it contains any branch of science which Congress would wish to exclude from their collection; there is in fact, no subject to which a member of Congress may not have occasion to refer." It was this concept of universality and belief that all subjects are important to the library of the American legislature that led the Library of Congress to develop its comprehensive collecting policies and adhere to this basic guiding principle. This basic principle is also reinforced by the Library's mission statement:

"The Library's mission is to make its resources available and useful to the Congress and the American people and to sustain and preserve a universal collection of knowledge and creativity for future generations."

The first acquisition of a major Asian collection from Asia can be traced back to 1865 when the Smithsonian Institution transferred a collection of books on Southeast Asia and the Pacific Islands that had been gathered in Singapore by the Wilkes Exploring Expedition from I83S to 1842. Four year later, in 1869. the Emperor of China (Tongzhi) presented to the Library 10 major Chinese works in 933 volumes. This was soon followed by the exchange of government publications with the Japanese government initiated in 1875. Since then, through intensive efforts of acquisition, more than 2.8 million volumes and 15,000 serials titles, in 160 Asian languages, have been acquired and preserved from all sources. Currently, the Asian Collection of the Library is among the best of such collections outside Asia.

In the 1960s, the Library established three field offices, one each in Jakarta, Indonesia; New Delhi. India; and Islamabad. Pakistan, to acquire publications in local languages from South and Southeast Asia.

AsAY: As the "research arm" of Congress, in what ways does the Library of Congress support our nation's policy makers?

Lee: Being the Library of Congress, the Library has a special unit named "Congressional Research Service" which is charged with the special responsibility of providing the Congress with research and analysis on the full range of legislative policy issues.

Throughout the year, staff lumbers of the Asian Division have also been contacted directly by

Congressional member and their staff to provide reference, consultation, and translation services by using Asian language materials and expert knowledge on Asia.

AsAY: What do you value most about your experience at the Library of Congress?

Lee: It has been a great privilege for me to work at the Library of Congress, which is not only the world's largest library, but as also known for its rich and unparalleled collections. I came to the Library four years ago after retiring from my previous position as the Dean of Ohio University Libraries. My strong credentials as an university library administrator, where I helped to build one of the best Southeast Asian Collections and started the first Chinese Overseas Documentation and Research Center, my seven years experience in Thailand as the Director of library and Information Center of the Asian Institute of Technology under the sponsorship of the U.S. Agency for International Development, and my earlier life in Mainland China and Taiwan have all prepared me well for my position as the Chief of Asian Division.

In the past four years, I reorganized the Asian Division by establishing five area teams—China and Mongolia, Japan, Korea (both South and North), South Asia, and Southeast Asia; expanding the acquisition program for more contemporary Asian materials (both printed and digital); developing collaborative programs with Asian countries to digitize some of our rare books so that they can be accessible to researchers online; continually finding ways to improve reader service; expanding library hours for the Asian Reading Room from regular weekdays to Saturdays; establishing the Asian Division Friends Society to expand outreach programs in order to publicize our treasured collections, and by establishing the Florence Tan Moeson Research Fellowship for researchers in the use of our Asian collections.

AsAY: In your opinion, what is the greatest challenge facing the Asian Pacific American community in the United States?

Lee: The significant contributions made by the Asian Pacific American community will continue to grow in all sectors of American society and in every branch and at every level of The government. However, until the enactment of the U.S. Immigration Act of 1965, Asian and Pacific Americans were discriminated against and stripped of their civil rights in the U.S. Because of this Act. Asian Pacific Americans are now able to enjoy their civil rights in the "Land of Opportunities" where they have excelled as citizens of this country.

In recent years, in a new era of historical and political consciousness of ethnic groups in the U.S. Asian American studies and ethnic studies have been recognized as legitimate fields of academic study by major American universities. There are now some 150 such programs engaged in teaching and research of the history of Asian Pacific immigrants and their subsequent acceptance as equal in the U.S. To collect the recorded historical documents of the waves of immigration of Asian Pacific Americans and their contributions is, in my view, a very important challenge. It is my hope that the library of Congress would take lead in developing such a collection and in working with the Asian Pacific American community and Asian Pacific American studies programs to plan for a coordinated approach in building such a national collection for historians and researchers and for future generations of Asian Pacific Americans.

AsAY: What aspect(s) of your own heritage are you most proud of?

Lee: Being an Asian Pacific American I am very proud of my Chinese heritage, As a young child. I endured hardship during the Sino-Japanese War and the Chinese civil war in China. Even during the most difficult time, my parents never gave up hope and wanted to make certain that I got a good education. During my graduate studies at the University of Pittsburgh I had to work full time in order to support my full-time study in Education and Library Science I have learned from my heritage drat hard work, endurance, lifelong learning, commitment to public services. care and respect for others, and leadership are all essential ingredients for success. I can find all these deeply rooted in Chinese culture and tradition.

AsAY: What rote will the Asian Pacific American community play in shaping the general direction of the country?

Lee: Asian Pacific Americans have much to contribute to our new homeland. First and foremost in importance is to be a good citizen by doing our best in our chosen vocation/ profession. Second in importance is to share the best of our cultural heritage to enrich the American way of life. America should be both a "melting pot" and a "salad bowl" so that the best of all cultures can be merged and integrated into a higher level of national culture.

In order to shape the general direction of this country. all Asian Pacific Americans should be actively taking part in the political process by running for offices at the local, state, and national levels, both in government services and the legislature.

A recent study by Lorraine H. Tone of the Congressional Research Service shows that from 1903 to 2005, only 20 Asian Pacific Americans were elected to Congress (excluding 13 Resident Commissioners from the Philippine Islands front 1907 to 1946).

Their ancestry has included Chinese, Chamorro. Filipino. Asian Indian. Japanese. Korean. Native Hawaiian, and Samoan. During the 108th Session, there were only five House Representatives and two Senators who were Asian Pacific Americans. This number must be expanded in the years to come as the Asian Pacific American community has become one of the fastest growing ethnic groups in this country.

AsAY: What has been the Asian Pacific American community's greatest achievement in recent years?

Lee: In terms of individual achievements, Asian Pacific Americans are doing very well Secretary of Tabor Elaine L Cbao. former Secretary of Transportation Norman Yoshio Mineta, Senators Daniel Kahikiua Akaka and Daniel Ken Inouye, Congressmen Eni F. H. Faleomavaega, Michael M. Honda. Robert Takeo Matsui, Robert C. Scott, and David Wu all have served our Cotentin well. Their achievements are inspirational for Asian Pacific Americans.

It is to be recognized also Thai in almost all fields of specialization from the arts, architecture. athletics, business, commerce, education, engineering. films, government, law, literature, medicine, military, music, sciences, to technology, there are numerous top achieves who are Asian Pacific Americans.

In order to celebrate the history, contributions and achievements of Asian Pacific Americans, President George H. W. Bush, on October 23, 1992, signed into law H. R 5572 (P. L. 102 – 450) —an act designating May of each year as Asian Pacific American Heritage Month. This important milestone was accomplished after the nearly 15 years of effort led by Representative Frank Hoiton and Senator Daniel Inouye, joined later by many others. Through this annual national event, Asian Pacific Americans can reflect on the past, revisit the rich and diverse culture and heritage, and work together to create a better future for the. . . .

(Published in *Asian American Yearbook*, *2007/2008*. McLean, VA: TIYM Publishing Co., 2007: pp. 27 –29.)

国会图书馆扩大收藏亚美作品

黄美惠

美国国会图书馆亚洲部主任（Chief, Asian Division, Library of Congress）李华伟（Dr. Hwa-Wei Lee）因柏克莱加大史达东亚图书馆开幕来到湾区，趁此行和湾区人士分享国会图书馆典藏亚太裔美国人出版品大计。

难得的是，在国会最支持国会图书馆增强亚洲及亚美资料扩充的联邦众议员麦克·本田也与会，在自己选区迎接来自华府的稀客。当天负责介绍李华伟的则是美国国会图书馆亚洲部之友会的理事成员安黄傅宁（Linda HuangAn）。

不论是李华伟、本田或者当天其他与会者，一个共同的强烈感受就是："针对美国国内亚裔出版品的典藏工作，老早该做了！"

李华伟刚刚才于4日和5日在国会图书馆召开过两天的研讨会，主题就是国会图书馆如何成立亚太裔数据收藏，包括柏克莱加大王灵智在内的学者专家多人与会，成果丰硕。

"19世纪是欧洲的世纪，20世纪是美国的世纪，21世纪应是亚洲的世纪了，"李华伟说，亚美裔的研究在美国渐形重要是必然趋势。他说，国会图书馆亚洲部共分五大部门：中国及蒙古、日本、南北韩、南亚、东南亚。每年预算采购约两百万美元、人事费约三百万美元。

现有的亚洲图书及各种媒材资料约280万件，分属160种语言。这些图书采自海外，方向是亚洲。如今谈的新增方向是在美国的亚裔。

当焦点转到"亚裔"这方向，才知国会图书馆里就连现有收编的总数都不清楚。下工夫后初步得知，书约五千种；非书刊的各种媒体如电影、录像带、音乐、档案、文献条目一一列出约50页，均可上网 www.loc.gov/rr/Asian 查到。

既然今后较用心搜罗，李华伟说，国会图书馆仍有其便利性。每年，国会图书馆收到新出版品60多万笔，通常出版者送来都是一式双份，其中一份正可供亚洲部拣选，从中找出和亚美相关者。其实，每年60万种出版品当中，国会图书馆留下约仅30万，饶是如此，也是相当大的搜罗基础了。

本田说，海峡两岸的关系是最近相当敏感的话题，国会要深层了解两岸的议题，依赖国会图书馆之处多矣，国会图书馆亚洲部任重而道远。

（原载《世界日报》2007年10月23日）

Asian Pacific American Collection Added to Library of Congress Data

Reme Grefalda

The Library of Congress has established an Asian Pacific American Collection, a move heralded by Asian American officials and leaders as both his and timely. Currently, the Library of Congress houses reference material from various Asian countries, referred to at the conference as "home-land", in contrast with the Asian Pacific American "home grown" literature.

At the opening of the conference on October 4 and 5, U. S. Secretary of Labor Elaine Chao praised the historic undertaking. She added: "It is time for a conference like this one. Asians and Pacific Islanders have been coming to America for hundreds of years and are a proud part of the American experience.... One critical link is between the Library's collections and the rapidly growing number of Asian American studies programs at American universities." She also underscored that America's "diversity is core strength".

Secretary Chao was joined by members of the Congressional Asian Pacific American Caucus. As chair of the APIA Caucus, U. S. Rep. Michael Honda (D-CA) commended the attendees for "recognizing the need to develop and coordinate such a national collection". He added to such a collection "is a necessary and appropriate progression for the Library, one that will centralize the APIA experience".

In his remarks at the opening of the afternoon session, Rep. David Wu (Oregon) likened the conference by quoting Thomas Jefferson in describing the attendees as "a small band of people who made a bold move", adding the conference "is worthy of inspiration for subsequent generations". Rep. Mazie K. Hirano (D-HI) said, "Our stories must be collected to make others aware of our presence in this country."

Both Wu and Hirano, members of the Congressional Asian Caucus, praised the coming together of Asian Studies scholars, researchers and noted members from academe to explore what Dr. Hwa-Wei Lee, Chief of the Asian Division described in his action plan as a "national distributed and networked APA collection".

Dr. Lee also announced the active partnership between the Library's Asian Division with the University of Maryland, College Park, Asian American Studies Program in the future development and direction of the national APA collection.

Dr. Frank Wu, Dean of Wayne State University Law School and formerly of Howard University, reminded the audience of the racial violence that resulted in the death of Vincent Chin. He spoke of changing the racial paradigm from just black and white issues to include a "panoramic racial world". He also urged Asian Americans to reject the conventional response to racial issues and instead encouraged the "diversity among us". Asian Americans have a unique "bridging role" between blacks and whites and should be wary of cultivating an "Anglo-Asian over-class".

Present at the two-day conference were: Dr. Betty Lee Sung of the Asian American/ Asian Research Institute; Dr. Franklin Odo, Director, Asian Pacific American Program, Smithsonian Institution; Prof. L. Ling-chi Wang of University of California, Berkeley; Prof. Don Nakanishi and Librarian Majorie Lee of UCLA; Dr. Kent Ono, University of Illinois, Urbana Champaign; Dr. Larry Shinagawa, Director, Asian American Studies, University of Maryland; Prof. Evelyn Hu-deHart of Boston University; Dr. Prema Kurien, Syracuse University; Dr. Krystyn R. Moon, University of Mary Washington; Gen, John Fugh (Ret.) of the Committee of 100; Ms. Ginny Gong and Dr. Michael Lin of the Organization of Chinese Americans; Ms. Katy Goring of the U. S. Indonesian Society; Dr. Juanita Tamayo-Lott and Dr. Jeremy Wu of the U. S. Census Bureau; Dr. Frank Joseph Schulman, President of the Library of Congress Asian Division Friends Society;

Ms. Rama Deva of the Indian American community, former publisher of Indic Magazine; and this writer, cultural activist from the Filipino American community.

(Published in *Asian Fortune*. November 2007, p. 18.)

The Hwa-Wei Lee Annex: A Model of Efficiency

Julia Zimmerman

These words are not often used to describe state government or, for that matter, higher education. But in Ohio these two entities have created a system of state-wide library depositories that has saved millions of dollars, while serving the scholarly needs of students and faculty all over the state.

The depository system includes five facilities: one centrally located near the Ohio State University campus in Columbus and one in each quadrant of the state. In southeastern Ohio, Ohio University hosts the Southeastern Ohio Library Depository facility, which is located at the Hwa-Wei Lee Annex on Columbus Road.

What is a depository? It's a place to store lesser-used library books and journals in higher densities, freeing up space in central library facilities—like Alden Library—for study space, library services, and high-use materials. Although the depositories resemble warehouses, they are designed expressly for their unique purpose.

At Ohio University's depository, some 736,000 books and journals are stored in boxes on 20-foot-high shelves in high-bay, climate-controlled storage areas. A "cherry picker" is required to retrieve books from the highest shelves. The materials are sorted by size, not subject matter, in order to squeeze the maximum number of books into the available space. Each book has a unique identifying number that is stored in the book's bibliographic record. This number tells staff members in which shelving range and box a book is located.

When students and faculty need a book from the Annex, they locate it in Alice, the library's online catalog, and with a few additional keystrokes, request it. Within a few hours the Annex staff will have retrieved the book and sent it to campus—Alden Library or the Music-Dance Library—where it waits for the requestor to pick it up.

Ohio's five depositories are connected through OhioLINK. The books are listed in OhioLINK's Central Catalog, making it easy for students and faculty around the state to find what they need and request delivery of materials to the user's home library, wherever it may be. As with other OhioLINK books, it usually takes three or four days for the book to be delivered.

Library users may also use the Annex reading room to do their research. This option is popular among researchers who want to peruse a large number of volumes and request additional materials on the spot. Because of the way the books are arranged for storage, and, of course, the giant-scale shelving, browsing is not possible, but with the help of the Annex staff, researchers can work effectively.

The Depository building contains more than just books. Official Ohio University records are housed there, as well as manuscript collections such as the papers of former Ohio Governor George Voinovich. The second floor of the Annex is the home of the Libraries' Preservation Department, where fragile or damaged library materials are treated.

So what about efficiency? Counting both initial construction and annual operating costs, storing one volume in a standard library configuration such as Alden Library costs $6.64 per year. In the Annex, storage costs only 49 cents per volume each year. The Annex cost only $2.3 million to build and equip. If Alden Library were expanded to accommodate 736,000 books, it would have cost $12.5 million. Multiply these savings by five depositories and thirteen cooperating universities, and it's easy to see that Ohio's libraries have hit upon a marvelously designed system that gets maximum bang for taxpayer's bucks.

Ohio University plans to build an addition to the Annex to accommodate ongoing growth in library collections. The new module will have 30-foot-high shelves, using space even more efficiently.

(Published in *Gatherings*, *Ohio University Libraries*, Winter 2007: pp. 12 – 13.)

国图馆欢送李华伟　离情依依

于茂芬

"五年前，中文部像是只睡着的狮子，直到被李华伟博士的魔杖一点，这只熟睡的狮子豁然惊醒……"，国会图书馆馆藏主任卢雪乡在该馆亚洲部主任李华伟的欢送宴上，道出大家对李华伟的感谢与惜别之情；而馆长毕灵顿（James H. Billington）则表示，这场欢送宴弥漫着哀伤气氛，诉说着大家对李华伟即将退休的不舍，他并盛赞李华伟任内以其高超的领导力，将国图馆的触角扩及全世界。

李华伟的欢送宴 15 日中午在国会图书馆举行，该馆高阶主管如毕灵顿及众多图书馆界人士均参加。

在朗读国会众议员本田及劳工部长赵小兰的信函后，毕灵顿致词表示，李华伟的个性使他任内完成多重任务。他倾听任何人的声音，不论对方的位阶大小；与台湾"中央图书馆"合作善本古籍数位化，使台湾成为首个与国会图书馆合作的亚洲国家和地区，其后陆续与中国、韩国和日本合作，将各种文化以不同形态展现给读者和观众。

主管图书馆服务的副馆长迪艾娜·麦肯（Deanna Marcum）则说，她与李华伟是旧识，当初李华伟接下该职，就言明只做五年，如何在五年内完成他要做的事，是重大考验。

李华伟任内进行部门重组，展现他魔术般的特质，他让所有下属有归属感，使大家团结为共同目标奋斗，同时创办亚洲部之友会协会，会务蓬勃发展，并为国会图书馆搭建舞台，建盖桥梁与世界接轨，均相当不易。

卢雪乡表示，李华伟是救援者，把没人理会的中文部点醒，带着大家学习走路、跑步，到真正地呈现在全世界的面前。李华伟以其管理长才，驯服难以驯服者，克服挫折，并为推行图书馆服务民众的理念，实施周六开放制度，使读者倍增。此外，争取到 25 万元推行图书馆的杂志学报资料上线，也于两个月内完成。在李华伟带领大家的五年里，让下属学到许多。

该馆亚洲部学术研究主任居蜜说，30 年馆龄的她目睹众多变迁，但李华伟任内带来的变化最大。他以有限的经费进行诸多工作，为此与"六楼"主管周旋谈判，百忙中仍四处演讲、宣扬亚裔文化及作专业著述。新创的亚裔馆藏部，更是深具使命的任务。她表示能为李华伟做事，是她的荣幸。

李华伟致词简短，不忘提及当初鼓励他应征这份工作的学术计划及库鲁奇中心主任凯洛琳·布朗（Carolyn Brown），并强调从学术机构转任联邦政府机关是很大的转折，对布朗一步步引领表示感谢。

此外，他表示自己一人无力完成这许多事，感谢五年来同仁的帮忙和协助。他有六个孩子及成群孙辈，退休后将把时间还给家庭，不过仍将留在顾问委员会上与大家共同推动计划。

李华伟将于 3 月底离任。李华伟对新创的亚裔馆藏部推动甚力，目前展开积极募款，全球华人图书馆协会特为他捐赠一千元给该基金会，而当天餐会收益及募款上万元，亦将并入该基金会。

（原载《世界日报》（北美版）2008 年 2 月 19 日"大华府新闻"）

The Quiet Life

Mike Magner

They named a library annex for **Hwa-Wei Lee** when he retired as Ohio University's dean of libraries in 1999. No such honor is likely to come with Lee's most recent retirement, after five years at the library of Congress, but you never know.

Since taking charge of the LOC's Asian Division in February 2003, Lee has revamped and reorganized its staff and its vast resources to ensure it had one of the finest Asian collections in the United States.

"He introduced innovative programs designed to improve and expand the division's resources, collections, services and outreach," said Rep. Mike Honda, D-Calif., chairman of the Congressional Asian Pacific American Caucus.

When Lee was named its chief, the Asian Division director's job had been vacant for three years; staff morale was low, funding was tight and the collection was disorganized.

Lee started an overhaul, securing funds for seven new positions, improving the process for selecting materials and reorganizing the collection's 2.8 million volumes and 16,000 periodicals into five areas: China-Mongolia, Japan, Korea, Southeast Asia and South Asia.

The China collection was made "more contemporary". Lee said. And, at Honda's urging, an Asian Pacific American Collection was started last year and is headed by Reme Grefalda, a cultural activist from the Filipino American community.

After a library career that started in 1959 at the University of Pittsburgh, Lee feels he has capped off his life's work nicely on Capitol Hill and at age 75, retired last month with his life, Mary, in Jacksonville, Fla.

"As anyone who has met Dr. Lee can attest, his boundless, enthusiastic spirit will not allow him to stay idle," Honda said.

(Published in *Congress Daily AM*, April 28, 2008.)

李华伟：图书馆把知识变成智慧

李怀宇

1932年生于广州，1957年赴美留学，在匹兹堡大学一共七年，读了三个学位。曾历任匹兹堡大学、都肯大学、宾州爱丁堡大学、科罗拉多州立大学、美国国会图书馆的行政职务，为全美第一位华人馆长。著有《图书馆学的世界观》、《现代化图书馆管理》等。

● 他在匹兹堡大学留学七年，共读了三个学位。
● 他任职多家图书馆，是全美第一位华人馆长。
● 他是美国国会图书馆亚洲部第一位华人主任。

华盛顿下过大雪之后，的士司机竟找不到国会图书馆杰斐逊大楼，在雪中等了几分钟，李华伟先生便到了我的面前，热情地带我穿过漫长的地下通道。来到他的办公室，首先入眼的是一个中国书法的"书"字。李先生主动谈起他跟广州的渊源："我父亲曾在四会县做县长，我后来找到四会县志，上面有他的介绍。我在广州出生一年多后才到南京。我的阿姨做过岭南大学图书馆馆长，她的广东话讲得很好，常跟我说：你是广东仔，一定要学广东话。"

李先生的太太是美国人，他们是匹兹堡大学的同学。"我们1959年结婚，当时白人男子跟亚洲人结婚倒是有，可是亚洲人娶白人女子几乎没有。所以我是很幸运的，我太太很好，我们结婚已经快50年了。"李先生回忆，"她的名字叫Mary，她父亲是捷克人，母亲是爱尔兰人，其实那时候美国多半都是从欧洲移民来的，还是比较保守。当初她父母反对，觉得这个婚姻不好，认为他们的女儿都没有出过宾州，如果跑到台湾去，这对他们来讲是不可思议的，就对我太太说：为什么要嫁给一个从亚洲来的穷小子？我们本来是要在学校的教堂结婚，可是她的父母认为在学校结婚不行，还是回到他们家乡的教堂。他们住在匹兹堡附近30里的乡下，改变主意，让我们到他们家乡的教堂结婚，我太太说：我父母开明。后来他们一直对我非常好，我很感谢。"

谈起生活习惯，李先生说："刚来美国时我最喜欢吃意大利面，因为跟中国的炸酱面很像。我太太也喜欢吃中国菜，但是有些东西是有选择性的，一些奇怪的东西不吃。"而对于中美文化的碰撞，他说："中国文化对我来讲并没有减色。中国文化博大精深，到美国以后改不过来，当然也吸收外国的文化。中国人讲情，美国人讲法，可是儒家的思想是把情与法协调成理。我们在美国久了，比较能协调这两个。我有时候也要学得折中一点。"

李先生告诉我，在华盛顿有几百个中国的社团，经常有活动。他还经常回台湾，"不过台湾现在的政治情况很复杂，'台独'很厉害，去中国化。"他也经常回祖国大陆，"大陆改革的速度非常快，中产阶级的数量在增加。问题是有，但是发展很快。"

今年已经七十多岁了，李先生并没有退休的念头。他自嘲地说："如果要找一个典型的工作狂的话，我就是。我没有爱好，爱好就是我的工作。"他现在几乎跑遍了全世界，可是太太说他："人家去看风景，你去看图书馆。"

李华伟1932年在广州出生，1937年一家搬到广西桂林，1949年从广西到台湾。1954年，李华伟在台湾师范大学毕业。

南方都市报：小时候受的教育是怎么样的？

李华伟：那时候生活很艰苦，吃的不多。我们兄弟姐妹七个人，家中没有办法养活我们七个人，我是老三，在重庆的时候，我和大哥就分配到国立第二华侨中学。那时候政府成立很多中学来收留流亡学生，我们在那里全部公费，可是一天只能吃两顿，早餐一顿，晚餐一顿，我们正在成长的时候，根本不够，整天都在饿肚子。可是那时候熬过来以后，什么苦都不觉得是苦了。

南方都市报：抗战胜利到南京，对国内的形势了解吗？

李华伟：那时候有一点了解，可是一知半解。因为我父亲原来在燕京大学跟司徒雷登学哲学和神学。可是他毕业以后认为宗教是西方侵略中国的一种手段，后来完全跟宗教脱离，参加政府工作。他是跟李宗仁先生，李宗仁后来竞选总统，然后做了副总统，我父亲在国内政界还算比较活跃，做过李宗仁的参军，我家里人曾经住在中南海，我一个人留在南京念书。那时候我们孩子对政治的了解都是从父亲的活动中获得的。我们本来没有想去台湾，准备留在广西。可是，我的大哥在抗战时恨日本人恨得不得了，就虚报岁数投报空军，在印度、美国受训后回到中国，他就在东北，后来调到台湾。当时台湾的政策就是，所有的军人家属必须弄到台湾去，我哥哥开了一架轰炸机到桂林，给我们24小时的时间，叫我们赶快整理一下东西上他的轰炸机，从桂林飞到台湾。当时台湾的天气很坏，山雾很大，我哥哥叫我们从窗子往外看，看到海的时候赶快告诉他，他才慢慢从海上降低，最后飞到台湾的空军基地。飞机上什么都装不了，我们全家空手的，就这样到了台湾。

南方都市报：到了台湾后你报考了师范大学，那个学校怎么样？

李华伟：我在台湾读了师范大学，那时候进师范大学也是因为经济的问题，公费，我从初一开始就是公费的。那时候兄弟姐妹很多，我父亲到台湾改行教书了，我考师范大学是因为可以拿到政府的公费。那时候师范大学的老教授都是北京师范大学过去的。我是教育系，中文系和哲学系的老师都是非常有名，我选过几个老师的课。我的恩师是孙邦政，他是系主任，是一个老教育家。我们的校长是刘真，胡适也在这里开过课。

南方都市报：在教育系主要读什么？

李华伟：我们那时候主要是学教育行政，为了培养中小学的校长。我觉得我的兴趣在行政这方面，就进了教育系。我父亲因为跟李宗仁的关系，去到台湾完全改行了。他在燕京大学跟司徒雷登学神学，英文非常好，就到台中农学院教英语课，一直教了二三十年到退休。他后来跟我讲：我这辈子前半辈子走错了路，后半辈子很高兴，培养了很多学生，你们以后千万不要搞政治。我也是受他的启发，后来进了师范学院。

1957年，李华伟赴美留学，在匹兹堡大学一共七年，读了三个学位。毕业时在图书馆正式工作。此后，他"三年跳一个台阶"，成为全美第一位华人图书馆馆长。

南方都市报：1957年怎么到美国留学？

李华伟：我的阿姨王肖珠一直鼓励我去留学，我当初的目的是读了硕士学位以后，到台湾去做中学校长。我连飞机票都买不起，当时从台湾飞到旧金山，单程需要400块美金，在台湾来讲是天文数字。那时候台湾的薪水大概是一个月700块台币，维持吃饭大概可以，剩下的钱就买套西装。所以我父亲到处去向朋友借钱，借了600块美金，400块美金买了机票，200块美金是零用钱，其他自己奋斗去吧。学校是给我学费，其他要自己去找。

我到了学校一个星期，我阿姨在医学院图书馆工作，她让我到总馆找某某人。那个人认识我阿姨，问我给书上架会不会，我想应该没有问题。那时候图书馆是封闭式的，不是开放的，学生要借书，拿一个条子，我赶快拿这个条子把书取下来，大概是因为我跑得快的关系，做了一年。那个馆长对我很欣赏，第二年我就到图书馆工作，至少比在饭馆里工作好一点。1959 年，我拿到硕士学位，馆长来找我。那时候美国政府对亚洲事务不懂，所以花钱在每个大学设立亚洲研究课程，可是图书馆要买书，没有一个人懂得中文的，就找我去："听说你跑得很快，我对你的工作非常满意，我现在给你换一个工作，让你去选书，买书，编目录，这个工作需要有一个图书馆学的硕士，你有没有兴趣去念？我们现在就可以雇用你，可是你要利用自己的时间，在两年内念一个硕士学位，你如果念不到这个学位，我们就要解雇你了。"我当时已经报了教育学的博士学位，每个学期都选课，也报了图书馆学硕士，就这样一直在图书馆做下来了。

南方都市报：那时候为什么对图书馆感兴趣？

李华伟：其实开头并不是兴趣，主要是为了谋生，可是后来就觉得图书馆本身有很大的意义。把书跟知识合起来，这是很有意义的工作。我做了一些工作，觉得这个工作比我想象的更好，后来就全力在做。那时候我运气很好，不仅亚洲学很热，整个大学教育在 60 年代都在扩展，有很多机会。

后来为什么很多中国人都到图书馆去呢？就是因为那时候机会很好。我在匹兹堡大学是做采购，后来另外一个教会大学请我去，不仅仅是做采购，还是做采购和编务的头，薪水加一倍，3000 块加到 6000 块。做了三年，我拿到了博士学位，宾州一个师范学院请我去做副馆长，从 6000 块加到 9000 块。这些是跳跃式的。那时候我其实刚刚出道，英文还是很差劲，可是我做得还不错，1967 年就升为馆长，那时候亚洲人在美国做馆长的，我是第一个。做了三年，泰国有一个亚洲理工学院，是美国国务院办的，就请我去把亚洲理工学院的图书馆办起来。1968 年，我到泰国去了，结果一去 7 年。1975 年才回到美国，先到科罗拉多州立大学做了三年副馆长，然后就到俄亥俄大学做馆长，做了 21 年，1999 年从那边退休。退休以后，本来以为可以轻松地做顾问的工作，2003 年国会图书馆就找我了，所以就到亚洲部来。

南方都市报：公共图书馆的制度是如何建立起来的？

李华伟：整个世界公共图书馆系统的发展，真正做得最好的还是美国。欧洲的历史很悠久，可是欧洲的许多图书馆还是比较封闭式的，并不完全开放。美国在开放方面做得比较好，因为美国在 19 世纪末就一直宣传一些私人图书馆让大家来使用，参加一个读者会，花一点钱，就可以使用这些图书。可是很快这些图书馆就被公共图书馆所取代了。美国最早很重视图书馆教育，图书馆教育在欧洲是学徒制，没有受到多少专业的训练。所以中国图书馆界很多先辈都是到美国来学习。

南方都市报：美国图书馆在亚洲部对中国的研究是如何发展的？

李华伟：国会图书馆最早在 1868 年跟清朝的同治皇帝设立一个交换协定。这是 1867 年美国国会图书馆设立的向全世界图书馆交换的关系，第一个就是跟同治皇帝，牵线的是美国早期的一些外交官、传教士，很多外交官找传教士做他们的智囊团。通过这种渠道，最早收藏的中国图书是 933 本，这是大批收藏中国图书的开始，从那以后，每一个时期，中国就赠送一些书，当然美国也回赠给中国一些书。当时外交官到中国的一个任务是收集中国的图书资料，因为战乱的关系，中国很多书流失在民间，很多国家就借这个机会很便宜地买了一大批中国书。这些中国的宝贝就流失到国外去了，很可惜。

1982 年，李华伟以外国专家身份第一次回到中国，此后几乎每年都有高校邀请他回国讲学。2003 年，美国国会图书馆聘请李华伟任亚洲部主任。

南方都市报：1982年回国，当时的图书馆给你什么样的印象？

李华伟：1982年回去的，看到图书馆实在是非常落后的，像员工中午吃饭的时候，图书馆就关门了，到下午5点钟又下班。开放的时间很短，图书馆的资料很少，收藏也很有限。我们现在再回去看，简直不可想象。现在国内图书馆越改越漂亮，比美国大学图书馆还盖得好。从软件来讲，中国现在也是出版大国，国内图书馆的购买力相当高。还有一点，中国图书馆不管在美国还是亚洲都是非常先进，就是数字化图书馆的工作。因为早期中国政府的干预，凡是新书期刊都要上交到国家图书馆去，国家图书馆就把它数字化，最早做得非常大，可是不好。做得好的是清华大学，清华早期做了两个数据库，一个是全国学术期刊的数据库，全中国大概7000种最重要的期刊，全文扫描进入数据库，所以图书馆不需要订全部的期刊，只要订数据库，就可以全文找到；第二个是报纸的数据库，从中央到地方的1000种报纸都有了。

南方都市报：你们馆的中文藏书在美国是最多的？

李华伟：我们最多。可是中文图书在我们部门来讲是第二位的，第一位是日文图书，现在有120多万册，中文图书刚刚超过100万册。其次是韩文、东南亚。中文为什么比日文少呢？有两个原因：一个是中国在"文革"时断层，没有什么出版；第二个是日本在战后被美军没收的60万件东西有10多万还是由政府收藏。可是，现在每年购进的东西，中文远远超过日文，再过两三年总量会赶上。

南方都市报：在你心目中，图书馆对社会发展的意义何在？

李华伟：图书馆的地位非常重要，美国早期的图书馆观念是从欧洲过来的，欧洲是以藏为主。最早从欧洲移民过来的人比较有自由思想，求知的欲望非常高，比欧洲的开放。美国有一个好处就是没有一个政府管制的机构，美国图书馆是下面管上。老百姓有很大的发言权，大学图书馆的主人是教授和学生。图书馆是要把知识变成智慧。

（原载《南方都市报》2008年9月3日 GB07版）

以智慧和毅力构架希望之桥
——访本刊顾问李华伟博士

弘 晓

2009年应该说是一个重要的年份，全球面临经济困境，东西方国家首脑纷纷出马出招、为加强合作、共创双赢而寻求最佳途径。而中美之间如何更进一步凝聚信心、扭转危机、加强经济文化等多方面合作，当是主旋律。因而，这年亦将成为转折与跨越之年。

在纪念中美两国建交30周年之际，5月18日上午9时，"2009—2010中美图书馆员专业交流项目"中国启动仪式暨图书馆专业研讨会在中国国家图书馆隆重举行。启动仪式上，文化部社会文化司副司长刘小琴、中国国家图书馆副馆长张雅芳和美方项目代表莫藤森国际交流中心副主任苏珊·希努尔女士先后致辞。张雅芳副馆长代表承办单位向美方项目代表赠送了纪念品。启动仪式由中国图书馆学会秘书长汤更生主持。

在项目合作签字仪式过程中，一位风度儒雅、笑容和蔼、鹤发童颜的长者格外令人瞩目，他就是美国国会图书馆前亚洲部主任、在图书馆界奋斗多年、声名卓著的李华伟博士，作为"中美图书馆员专业交流项目"美方审核与评估专家，他欣然而来。

很少有人在退休之年被一而再、再而三的聘请，并且继续运用自己的专长来服务社会、为国际文化交流而孜孜不倦亲力亲为。退而不休的李华伟博士曾是美国俄亥俄大学图书馆院长级馆长。是极少数华人在美国大学图书馆担任图书馆总馆馆长者之一。更是华人担任美国国会图书馆亚洲部主任的第一人。在知识与资讯管理领域，他呕心沥血勤勉奋斗已逾50载。而在祖国，他的德才及学术成果享誉大学、科学院、中信所、公共图书馆等各大系统，并竞相被著名的大学所聘请。

在社会上，也许有的人理想宏大，但却缺乏做人做事的实在和踏实，只能是好高骛远的幻想家；有的人大事做不来，小事又不愿做，终成为碌碌无为一辈；也有的人既聪明又有才智，但终因未能持之以恒，而成为三天打鱼两天晒网之人。唯有像李华伟博士那样，实实在在做人，踏踏实实做事，才能攀登事业的顶点、实现了宏伟愿望。

启动仪式结束后，"2009—2010中美图书馆员专业交流项目"举办了在中国的首场交流活动"图书馆专业研讨会"。美方专家张沙丽和苏珊·希努尔就"美国公共图书馆的管理体制与运营机制"发表了专题演讲，她们从美国公共图书馆的行政管理、经费管理、资金筹措途径及策略和公共图书馆的标准及统计等四个方面进行了详细阐述。美方专家罗伯特·威廉·佛勒克斯以"图书馆评估"为主题演讲。随后，中美图书馆同行们进行了热烈的现场互动。中国图书馆学会和中国国家图书馆向6位美国专家颁发了荣誉证书。

中美图书馆员专业交流项目（2009—2010）是中美两国政府文化交流活动的重要组成部分，是中美两国图书馆界的首个政府级合作项目。项目的主办单位是中华人民共和国文化部和美国总统人文艺术委员会与美国图书馆及博物馆服务机构（IMLS），由中国文化部专项资金和IMLS"放眼全球行诸全球"项目的劳拉·布希"21世纪图书馆员"专款联合资助。项目的承办单位是中国图书馆学会和美国伊力诺依大学厄本那香槟校区图书馆及其合作者美国华人图书馆员协会。该项目由图书馆馆长专题交流、图书馆职业教育专题交流、图书馆技术专题交流、图书馆专业普及交流和中文资讯共用平台试点等5个子项目组成。在未来的两年中，将有3批30位中国图书馆员赴美与美国图书馆同行进行专业交流，

9批约40位美国图书馆专家来华交流。预计国内受众省份20余个,图书馆员近千名。

该项目自筹备始,得到了文化部外联局和社会文化司的直接指导,2008年5月,中国图书馆学会接受文化部的委托,与美方承办机构密切合作,共同完成了项目的策划和可行性论证。2008年11月16日,中国图书馆学会理事长、中国国家图书馆馆长詹福瑞与美国伊力诺依大学图书馆馆长波拉·考夫曼在美国国会图书馆共同签署了《中美图书馆员专业交流项目协议书》。文化部部长蔡武和美国总统人文艺术委员会主席阿黛尔·玛戈女士出席了签字仪式。2009年5月至10月间,中美图书馆专业研讨会在南京、西安、兰州和南宁等地陆续举办。中美图书馆员专业交流项目的实施,对于提高图书馆从业人员的业务素质和管理水准,增强中美图书馆之间的相互了解,增进中美图书馆人之间的交流和友谊,推动图书馆事业发展具有重要意义。

"经纬枢纽,美华桥梁"

说来话长,在美国最早与中国图书馆界开展合作与培训计划的,正是李华伟博士。自80年代以来,李馆长到中国各地多所大学去讲学,还应国家教委之邀多次在世界银行贷款项目及联合国发展基金项目下,对国内师范院校的图书馆员开办图书馆管理的培训班。国内很多大学都邀请他担任访问教授或顾问教授,包括西安交通大学、南开大学、湖南医大、武汉大学、四川联合大学、东北师范大学、天津理工学院等,中国国家图书馆、中国科学院、中国科学院武汉文献资讯中心兰州文献资讯中心、清华大学图书馆、深圳图书馆、浙江图书馆,以及台湾的"中央图书馆"均聘请李博士担任顾问。其讲学精髓汇聚成书——《现代化的图书馆管理》,作为图书馆管理专著,内容涉及图书馆的规划、组织、人力资源管理、领导和作业、控制和评估五大功能,融会了他在美国几十年的管理思想体系……李华伟博士强调,因为知识是通过人们的大脑来加工、使用、更新、扩展的,是人类智慧的产物,所以人是知识管理的最重要部分。具备远大目光、领导才能,及专业知识的图书馆员及资讯专家应该是最适合担任主要知识主管(Chief Knowledge Officer)职位的。

所以专家评价说:李华伟先生的贡献不是物质上的,更主要是精神层面的。体现在更新观念上,在人才培养上即教育软件方面,这位美籍华人的贡献尤其显得突出。

长年累月致力于中美之间牵线搭桥,热衷于东西方文化交流与合作的李华伟先生,在1996年全力促成了一件值得一提的大事,在事业的里程碑上刻下深深的一笔——首届中美图书馆合作会议在北京隆重召开。两国近百位图书馆馆长和专家学者聚集一堂,就会议主题"全球的资讯存取——挑战与机遇"展开热烈的讨论,会议取得了圆满的成功,其意义不同凡响。李华伟博士在会上作了重要报告,总结了中美图书馆合作的历史经验,以及在今后的发展重点。有意借国际图联大会的契机,积极促成中美图书馆界的密切合作。这次会议对中美两国及世界图书馆界的合作与发展产生积极而深远的影响。会议之后又有多个图书馆相继结为姊妹馆。在中美图书馆发展史上写下新的篇章。

海外传媒报道:自从中国1869年向美国国会图书馆捐赠1000册图书后,相隔一百多年,中美两国近百位馆长和专家学者站在中国国家图书馆的台阶上。这一幕载入了历史。中美图书馆高层评价道,这不仅是行业合作,也加强了两国人民彼此的了解。而李华伟先生为图书馆事业所作的贡献更令人感佩。足可谓之:正其义,不谋其利。明其道,不计其功。

在1999年底李馆长从俄亥俄大学退休的前夕,美国图书馆学会特别由理事会决议表扬。美国的华美图书馆员学会、亚太美裔图书馆员学会、俄亥俄州的 Ohio LINK 及 OhioNET、还有台湾的"中国图书馆学会"及"中央图书馆"等都分别颁赠奖状，祝贺李馆长的荣退。俄亥俄州图书馆学会还特别授予他终身荣誉馆员的称号（Ohio Hall of Fame Librarian）。闻名全球的 OCLC 图书馆计算机中心也特别聘请李校友为杰出的访问学者。当他从俄亥俄大学退休时，该校董事会破例将一座新建的图书馆分馆命名为"李华伟图书馆分馆"。除此以外，还特别将总馆的第一层楼重新装修，命名为"李华伟国际藏书中心"。

2001 年 9 月，他应美国福尔伯来计划（Fulbright Program）的邀请，以资深专家的身份派去泰国的清迈大学协助该校的图书馆系设计及制定研究所的课程。

2003 年 2 月，美国国会图书馆特别聘请李馆长出任该馆亚洲部主任，赋予重任，进行多项重大改革：包括机构及人事重整，馆藏发展现代化，引进大量数位化资源，加强读者服务，延长开放时间，组织亚洲部之友会，举办学术活动，设立谭翠荣研究补助金，建立全国性的亚太裔文献资料特藏，加强与亚洲各国图书馆间的交流，并与亚洲一些国家图书馆及研究机构合作共建及共用彼此的古籍和特藏的数据库。在任务完成后，李馆长在 2008 年 4 月第二次荣退，得到美国国会及美国国会图书馆的表扬，中国图书馆学会也颁给名誉会员称号。

就在他第二次退休后不久，美国联邦政府的博物馆及图书馆服务局与中国政府的文化部，为了要推动两国之间的文化交流，特别设立了一个为期两年的中美图书馆合作项目，聘请李博士为该项目美方的评审员。因此李博士又三次复出，退而不休，继续为图书馆事业的发展而努力。

李博士原籍福建省福州市。抗日战争期间从南京随家迁往广西桂林及四川重庆等地。1949 年迁往台湾，先进入台中一中高三攻读，次年考进当时的台湾省立师范学院，后更名为台湾师范大学，攻修教育系。回顾个人的事业生涯，李华伟博士觉得在师大四年的学生生活，对他后来出国深造、就业、及做人有深远的影响。因为抗日战争的灾害，他童年及青少年的岁月几乎都是在战火和逃难的日子中度过。生活艰苦，学业经常中断，没能安心学习，但也培养了他能吃苦耐劳的性格。一直到了台湾，进入师大，才能有比较安定的求学环境。当时师大的师资都是一时之选。有了良师的教诲，学业才有较大的进展。当时的师大还鼓励学生参与课外活动，以培养学生的领导能力。李博士正是这样，担任了很多学生社团的骨干分子，学到了很多在书本知识以外做人处世的宝贵经验。这对他后来在事业上的发展，颇有助益。2004 年，李博士得到美国华府区师大校友会推荐，被选为第四届师大杰出校友。李华伟先生从事图书馆及教育工作五十年如一日，秉承师大"诚正勤朴"的校训，作为他日常为人处世的座右铭，兢兢业业，身体力行。

有人说，每个人所能达到的高度，始于一种内心的状态。当自己渴望有所作为的时候才能冲破种种束缚。一个人有进取心，才可以充分发掘自己的潜能；才能在生命中时刻充满激情和朝气；才能实现人生的价值，享受人生的甘美。在近半个世纪的图书馆生涯中，李华伟博士发表过八十多篇文章，出版了五本书，编过三本会议录及先后担任了七种学术期刊的编辑委员。由于李华伟博士在国际图书信息界享有很高的声誉，被选举连任两届（4 年一任）美国图书馆学会理事。该学会是全世界最大的学会，有会员 5.7 万名。同时他还担任国际图书馆学会联盟的大学及研究图书馆委员会委员等职务。多次担任联合国教科文组织及其他国际机构及基金会顾问。因其贡献突出、成绩卓著，他曾荣获十多种奖励和称号。并被连续载入《世界名人传》、《美国名人传》、《美国教育界名人传》等年鉴上。

为了加速中国图书馆事业现代化进程，为了年轻一代中国知识分子的成长，自 1982

年开始,李华伟博士每年都要往返奔波于中美之间——以赤诚之心和顽强毅力,亲手架起了一座连接东方与西方、过去与未来的桥梁。如果说过去数十年李华伟博士是中美文化交流尤其是信息管理合作的开创者,那么在当今全球化、东西方合作逐渐加强的趋势下,他退而不休进行合作交流项目,正以其智慧和毅力,将跨越时空的文化和希望之桥建构得更加坚固完美!

(原载《红杉林:美洲华人文艺》2009年第4卷第2-3期,第6-9页。)

"图书馆，丰富人们的生活"
——李华伟博士在合肥接受记者专访

孔 华

24日下午，受合肥市图书馆邀请，最具影响的华人图书馆馆长、前任美国国会图书馆亚洲部主任、现任美国总统文化基金项目——中美图书馆馆员交流的美国评审、从事了50年图书馆工作的李华伟博士来合肥讲学。讲座间隙，本报记者独家专访了李华伟博士，他向记者介绍了"图书馆，丰富人们的生活"的理念及未来图书馆将"走出馆舍限制，无所不在"的发展远景。

两次退休，现任中美文化交流"使者"

75岁的李华伟博士出生于广东新会，1949年随父母到台湾，1957年被美国匹兹堡大学录取攻读教育学硕士学位。次年，由于勤奋好学，常年泡在图书馆，他请求在图书馆打工获得批准。"那个时候，想借书，就写一张小纸条，图书馆馆员拿着这张纸条按图索骥到书库里找，经常需要两三个小时，有时找到的书还不是读者需要的，又要花时间重找。我呢，熟悉图书馆，经常把读者想借的书的同类图书多拿几本出来（相当于现代计算机书目查询），向读者推荐，得到学生及教授的好评。传到了校图书馆馆长那里，他告诉我，图书馆正好有个空缺，问我愿不愿意干，我答应了，从此就开始步入图书馆界。"

从小小的校图书馆馆员一直做到俄亥俄大学图书馆馆长，2003年李华伟博士退休后，又被美国国会图书馆聘为亚洲部主任，到2008年第二次退休，李华伟博士从事了50年的图书馆工作。他是美国第一位华人图书馆馆长，俄亥俄州东南边的一个书库以他的名字命名；他也是最具影响的华人图书馆馆长，在促进中美图书馆界交流甚至文化交流方面做出了卓越的贡献，他培训的中国图书馆馆长、主任超过了100位。如今，虽然退休，他仍然担任美国总统文化基金项目——中美图书馆馆员交流的美国评审，继续为中美文化交流贡献自己的力量。

"图书馆，丰富人们的生活"

"跟二三十年前相比，中国的图书馆发展真是巨大。"李华伟博士举例说，比如，在美国还不多见的24小时无人服务自动借书、还书图书馆站，在深圳已经有很多，而且陕西省图书馆也正在推广。相信未来这种不需要走进图书馆、不受时间限制就可以在家门口借还书的图书站会越来越多。"图书馆一方面要通过各种活动和宣传让人们走进来；另一方面也要大胆走出去，成为市民的书房，成为无所不在，无刻不在提供服务的公益场所。"李华伟博士介绍说"在美国，有医疗结构证明行动不便的老人，可以享受图书馆提供的专门个性化服务，比如送书上门，上门收书，老人只要一个电话即可将享受借书还书；家长可以把孩子放在图书馆写作业。"

资源共享：不同图书馆图书可以通借通还

50年图书馆工作经历李华伟博士充分感受到了科技带来的便利，他同时提出应该保护数字遗产。"我们有的图书馆搞专家、名人讲座，来听的人很少，效果也不大，为什么不把这些讲座录下来，整理好放在网站让更多的人享用呢！"李华伟博士告诉记者："图书馆除了提供传统的图书报刊服务，还应该提供个性化的、专题化的服务，而且图书馆管理也应该更人性化。以前图书馆不允许人们交谈、喝水、吃东西，后来美国的一些图书馆就专门提供区域供人们交谈，甚至提供咖啡等便利服务。"

资源共享是目前中国图书馆难以企及的一个话题。李华伟博士告诉记者：美国俄亥俄州的86个图书馆集体采购图书，这样可以避免重复采购、浪费金钱，而且在任何一个图书馆都可以借、还该馆没有其他馆有的图书，大学图书馆也向附近居民开放，资源开放形成了极大的便利。

"没有一家图书馆能满足所有读者的需要，资源共享则是最大程度满足人们需要的捷径。资源共享是图书馆发展的趋势。"李华伟博士告诉记者。

（原载合肥市图书馆网站 http：//www.hflib.gov.cn/News/News_show.php? ID=428，2009年9月26日。）

让图书馆的服务无所不在

刘思敏

今年76岁的美籍华人李华伟博士是本次公共图书馆国际高峰论坛的嘉宾,然而在昨天的会场上,这位慈眉善目的老人俨然成了半个主人:为嘉宾们互相介绍甚至在接受采访时充当临时翻译。李博士笑着告诉记者:"我和深圳有很深的渊源,我对深圳特别有感情。"

六年前,当李华伟成为美国国会图书馆亚洲部主任时,他成为这个世界上最大的图书馆自1928成立以来担任这个职位的第一位美籍华人。除此之外,他还是第一位华人高校图书馆馆长,第一位有幸被美国图书馆命名的馆长,俄亥俄大学将新建图书馆分馆命名为"李华伟图书馆分馆"……多年来,在推动中国图书馆与国际的合作与交流方面,李博士做出了卓越的贡献。

"我很骄傲为深圳图书馆自动化系统尽了绵薄之力"

和深圳的交情是从上个世纪80年代中期就开始了。李博士说,当时中国国内的图书馆发展还相对比较落后,然而深圳已经在自主研发图书馆自动化系统,这给他留下了特别深刻的印象。早在那个时候,深圳图书馆就派人到俄亥俄大学图书馆学习先进经验,从那以后直到1999年李博士退休,每年双方都会互派馆员进行交流学习。上个世纪90年代初,深圳图书馆在全国率先成功研发出了图书馆自动化系统ILAS,目前为止,这个系统已在全国几万家图书馆使用。讲到这里,李博士非常自豪,"我很高兴,也很骄傲为深圳图书馆自动化系统的研发尽了一点点力。"

"公共图书馆研究院的成立是个创新"

对于刚刚成立的公共图书馆研究院,李博士给予了高度的评价。他说,世界上还没有哪个国家成立过这样的专门研究公共图书馆事业发展的机构,这是一个创举。"对于这个研究院,我有着很大的期望。"李博士说,"我的愿望是让图书馆的服务无所不在。"

讲到中国公共图书馆相比发达国家的差距,李博士很客观地说,有一点是中国可以借鉴的:这就是建立图书馆联盟,将各种类型的图书馆的信息共享。李博士很早之前讲过这样一句话:没有一家图书馆能满足所有读者的需要。而如果建立这样的联盟问题就迎刃而解了,当然,要达到这一目标,还需要培训专业人员,加强信息管理。

李博士说,公共图书馆的具体动作情况其实是跟国情和每个社区的具体情况紧密相关的。他很欣喜的是,深圳政府对图书馆事业高度重视,公共图书馆配合深圳社区的具体需要发挥了相当重要的作用。李博士说,深圳提出的许多理念和构想都很新颖、细致,比如"自助图书馆",即使在美国也运用得相当少。不过,李博士也指出,中国的公共图书馆事业也存在着地区发展不平衡的问题。在很多发达城市越来越完善,而在偏远的地方才刚刚起步。

(原载《深圳特区报》2009年11月17日第B09版)

原美国国会图书馆亚洲部主任李华伟：
资源共享是图书馆发展趋势

刘 琼

77岁高龄的李华伟身上有很多"光环"：美国国会图书馆亚洲部自1928年成立以来第一位华裔主任，美国第一位华人高校图书馆馆长，同时他还是世界上最大的联机图书馆中心和俄亥俄州图书馆联盟的发起者和创办人。

自1982年首次回国后，李华伟曾多次来到深圳，对深圳建设"图书馆之城"提出了很多宝贵意见。昨日，李华伟来深参加公共图书馆国际高峰论坛，接受记者采访时说："深圳虽然是座成立仅30年的城市，但对文化建设却不遗余力，尤其在建设公共图书馆方面，取得了很大的成绩。但没有一家图书馆能满足所有读者的需要，资源共享将是图书馆的发展趋势，深圳应加强与国内国际的合作，在数字图书馆的建设和跨国合作方面积累资源。"

自助图书馆系统是一大创举

回忆起20多年前首次回国的情景，李华伟颇为感慨。他说，那时候，国内图书馆现代化的事业刚刚起步，与国外相比还有很大的差距。但经过20多年的发展，国内图书馆事业发展很快，像北京、上海、深圳等地的公共图书馆并不比美国差。如深圳的自助图书馆系统就是中国图书馆建设的一大创举。该系统配合中国文化背景、由深圳自主开发，能提供24小时的无人服务。这种在美国也不多见的自助借书、还书图书站，在深圳已有很多，并还在不断扩建中。

"但是，我们也要看到，中国图书馆事业的发展极不平衡。好的地方非常好，有些地方则非常落后。"李华伟说，近年来，他到各地调查研究，发现图书馆事业发展的地域性局限很大，尤其是一些偏远的农村地区，图书馆建设还处于空白状态。他希望政府和相关专业学者能重视这种差距，积极推动落后地区图书馆建设。

李华伟说，昨日在深成立的公共图书馆研究院就是一个很好的机构。"这样的机构在国外还没有，中国率先成立，集合国内外专家资源，在一个公共的平台上对话，并提供专业的调查研究，为图书馆事业的发展提供理论支持"。

资源共享，打造开放式图书馆

"资源共享是图书馆的发展趋势"，李华伟曾在多个场合反复强调他的这一观点。此次接受记者采访时，他依然不厌其烦地强调"资源共享"的重要性。

"任何一家图书馆的馆藏都是有限的，只有促进馆与馆之间的合作，共享彼此的资源才能节省成本，让馆藏运用最大化。"李华伟说，在美国，图书馆间会集体采购图书，这样可以避免重复购买。同时，各个城市间的任何图书馆都可以互借，极大地方便了各地读者。在中国，国内城市间的合作还应该进一步加强，通过建立数字图书馆、打造数字化网络等措施加强城市图书馆间的联系，打造"开放式"的图书馆。

李华伟认为，要打造数字化图书馆，图书馆员的专业素质非常重要。为了进一步提升图书馆员的素养，李华伟利用自己在图书馆界多年的影响力，在联合国教科文组织的赞助下，设立了国际图书馆员培训计划，培养了数百位图书馆馆长、副馆长和部门主任。目前，他正忙着"中美两国图书馆员专业交流项目"。他告诉记者，这是中国文化部和中国图书馆学会极为重视的专业交流项目，对公共图书馆今后的发展有深远的影响。作为该项目的评审员，他希望能培养出更多优秀的图书馆员。

（原载《深圳商报》2009年11月17日第C02版）

李华伟：经纬枢纽，美华桥梁

赵 晶

李华伟其人

李华伟博士早年毕业于台湾师范大学教育系，1957年来美深造，曾先后获得匹兹堡大学教育硕士、图书馆学硕士及高等教育的哲学博士学位。早在1962年就被聘为美国杜肯大学（Duquesne University）图书馆的技术部兼非洲部主任。两年后，他拿到博士学位，成为宾州爱丁堡大学（Edinboro University）第一位拥有博士学位的图书馆馆长。1968年，李华伟赴泰国主管美国国务院援外总署的东南亚图书馆项目，直至"越战"结束后才回到美国，并在科罗拉多州立大学（Colorado State University）当了三年副馆长。1978年到俄亥俄大学（Ohio University）图书馆，做了21年的图书馆馆长，为华裔中担任美国大学图书馆馆长最早的人。因为他的卓越成绩，俄亥俄大学董事会破例把一座新建的图书馆分馆命名为"李华伟图书馆分馆"。除此以外，为了表彰他在发展国际合作、促进图书馆藏书全球化方面所做出的贡献，还特别将总馆的第一层楼重新装修，命名为"李华伟国际藏书中心"。

在极为忙碌的工作中，李博士仍然不忘教学、研究与写作。在俄亥俄大学，李博士除了担任图书馆馆长之外，还兼任了该大学教育学院的教授，先后担任了10多位博士生的论文指导老师。在他40多年的图书馆生涯中，曾经发表过80多篇文章，出版了《图书馆学的世界观》、《现代化图书馆管理》等5本书，编过3本会议录及先后担任了7种学术期刊的编辑委员。他的《图书馆学的世界观》（1991年台湾学生书局出版）、《90年代图书馆的筹款指引》（与盖里·汉博士合著，1992年美国出版）和《现代化的图书馆管理》（1996年台湾三民书局出版），在图书馆界影响很大。特别是《现代化的图书馆管理》一书，花了近5年时间才完成，作为图书馆管理专著，内容涉及图书馆的规划、组织、人力资源管理、领导和作业、控制和评估5大功能，融会了他在美国几十年的管理思想。

目前，李华伟博士是美国国会图书馆亚洲部自1928年成立以来的第一位华人主任。他还曾连续两届担任美国图书馆学会理事，在国际图书情报界享有很高的声誉；并且多次担任联合国教科文组织、联合国发展计划署、世界粮农组织、加拿大国际发展及研究中心等机构有关图书馆发展项目的顾问。在美国40年的奋斗生涯中，李博士曾得到很多奖励，其中主要有：俄亥俄大学最杰出行政人员奖（1982年）、华美图书馆员学会杰出服务奖（1983年）、俄亥俄州最杰出图书馆员奖（1987年）、台湾图书馆学会杰出贡献奖（1989年）、美中华人学术及专业学会杰出服务奖（1991年）、美国图书馆学会国际关系卓越贡献奖（1991年）、亚美及太平洋地区图书馆员学会杰出服务奖（1991年）、美国新闻署杰出服务奖（1992年）、美国图书馆学会杰出理事奖（1992年）、俄亥俄图书及信息网感谢状（1993年）、中国图书馆学会荣誉会员（2005年）等。另外，李博士还被选载在《世界名人传》、《美国名人传》、《美国教育界名人传》等年鉴上。

自20世纪80年代以来，李馆长每年都要到中国各地多所大学去讲学，还应国家教委之邀多次在世界银行贷款项目及联合国发展基金项目下，对国内师范院校的图书馆员开办图书馆管理的培训班。由于他孜孜不倦的教学活动，国内很多大学都邀请他担任访问教授或顾问教授，包括西安交通大学、南开大学、湖南医大、武汉大学、四川联合大学、东北师范大学、天津理工学院；中国科学院武汉文献信息中心及兰州文献信息中心都聘请李博士担任顾问。

图书馆生涯

李华伟博士在图书馆界的东亚经验是在匹兹堡大学积累的，东南亚方面的经验就要归功于他在东南亚7年的亲身实践了。后来他能入选国会图书馆亚洲部主任就是依靠这两大优势。1968年，由美国国际发展总署向宾州爱丁堡州立学院借调，李博士被派往泰国的亚洲理工学院担任该院首任的图书馆及信息中心主任，在泰国停留了7年，直到1975年美国支援亚洲理工学院的项目圆满结束。在亚洲理工学院服务时，还应泰国朱拉隆功大学图书馆学系之邀，自1970年至1975年在该系讲授"图书馆自动化"的课程，这在亚洲还是最早开设的课程。

李华伟说："我1978年来到俄亥俄大学图书馆是看中了它在东南亚馆藏方面的雄厚实力，这恰恰是我的特长所在。俄亥俄州共有13所州立大学，最大的俄亥俄州立大学图书馆以东亚馆藏见长，而俄亥俄大学图书馆则以东南亚馆藏见长。"结果他在俄亥俄大学做图书馆馆长一做就做了21年。21年间，俄亥俄大学图书馆的藏书总量从60万册发展到200多万册。当初李华伟刚到俄亥俄大学图书馆的时候，只容纳110名会员的美加两国图书馆界权威机构"研究图书馆协会"根本不把俄亥俄大学图书馆放入考虑之列。1996年，他们才正式邀请俄亥俄大学图书馆加入。到1999年，俄亥俄大学图书馆在这个协会的排名也从三年前的82名跃居第70名。

李华伟博士不单单研究在现代信息管理、自动化技术观念的传播与推广等方面，现在他的发展计划又有了更高意义的拓展。1993年，在香港银行家邵友保博士的赞助下，正式创立的"海外华人文献研究中心"，成为全世界第一所这样的机构，通过收集、整理、保存、介绍及研究有关海外华人的文献资料，再现他们奋斗与贡献的历史。这一历史不仅是居住国发展的一个重要组成部分，而且也是悠久的中华文明在海外的延伸与发扬光大。俄亥俄大学"海外华人文献研究中心"，它不仅凝聚了诸多海外赤子的心血与智慧，而且也体现了一个华裔专家的拳拳回报故国之心。

李华伟先生凡事不落人后、力争第一的天性，促使他第一个建立国际图书馆员培训基地，在联合国教科文组织等赞助下，先后有来自亚洲及世界各地的160多位馆员来此完成了培训工作，光中国就有近百人，包括北大、清华、北师大、南开、邮电大学、三〇一医院图书馆、重庆大学、浙江医科大学、科学院图书馆、中国科技情报所等，其中很多位是图书馆馆长、科学院副院长及部门主任。这一计划的实施以及该馆与亚洲图书馆的多种合作项目，皆已成为全美图书馆的典范。而那些资助培训费用是他多方奔走、四处筹集而来的。当年他在俄亥俄大学当馆长时，国内图书馆来过很多访问图书馆员，平均每月6个，他为了方便大家专门买了一个面包车，利用自己的时间开车几小时到Columbus接送，还想办法让她（他）们到各处参观访问，并赠送准备好的礼物。不仅仅是国内的业内同仁，亚洲国家许多图书馆员也都受到过他的接待和帮助。到泰国去时连皇室都要接见他，但他低调、谦逊、对别人十分尊敬，十分超脱。他对每一个人都是那么亲切，不论对方的职位大小。东南亚的华人视他为亚洲文化的传播人，捐助巨款创建亚洲文化馆藏，他离开俄亥俄大学时已经为俄亥俄大学图书馆筹集了几百万美元的赞助，俄亥俄大学有一个新建的分馆和一条路以他的名字命名。

作为一名华人，李博上对于留学生的照顾也是无微不至的。每当留学生生活上有了困难,学习上遇到问题,首先就找他。还有的同学刚到异国他乡,面临压力,向他诉苦,他会以一个长者身份说"有很多人以为到了美国就什么问题都解决了,其实,这只是奋斗的开始。"李博士说:"大家都想到美国来,既然来了,就要有思想准备,咬咬牙拼一下。你现在还没有拼就想打退堂鼓,这可不行。"作为教育学院兼职教授、华裔馆长,除了在学业上给予留学生指导帮助外,还尽可能提供经济方面的支持,对中国来的学生尤其关照,难怪有人送他"经纬枢纽,美华桥梁"的题字。

与国会图书馆亚洲部

成立于1800年4月24日的美国国会图书馆是世界上最大的图书馆,其藏书近1.28亿册,每天新增加10,000种。国会图书馆从1865年起,开始收集亚洲图书资料,1869年首次获得中国清朝政府同治皇帝赠送的933册书籍。1928年,国会图书馆设立"中国图书部"。这个部门1931年改称"中国及日本图书部",1932年改称"东方部",1978年改称"亚洲部"。

特别是经历了长达135年的艰辛与努力,美国国会图书馆亚洲部目前已拥有中国大陆和台湾、日本之外最好的中文、日文藏书。这两种文字的藏书总数达200多万册。2003年,馆藏统计中文图书是17,600种,日文7,000种。中文期刊总数量14,657种(持续订购的期刊有5,000种)。日本期刊总数量19,474种(持续订购的期刊有5,800种)。此外,中文微缩胶卷大约有15,500卷。

李华伟主任在很多场合都详细介绍过国会图书馆亚洲部。亚洲部的中文馆有包罗广泛的学科领域,以人文及社会科学为主,其中以历代文集、清朝文集、民国书籍、医书最为丰富。此外,它收藏的中国方志,内容包括各省、府、州、县和乡镇,十分齐备。

美国国会图书馆收集的中国方志,最值得大书特书的是1933年一次入藏几乎全部山东方志。这批方志原本的主人是山东一位县长高鸿裁(1851—1918),他用将近20年的心血收集本省的志书,所以内中有许多极不易见的版本。在亚洲部的档案中,得知当时德国驻青岛领事曾派人要购买这批方志。而最终这批极具收藏价值的中国山东地方志现藏于美国国会图书馆亚洲部。1954年,据恒慕义博士所作的报告,方志的收藏数已达到3,600种。过去,一般的收集方志,侧重于省志。比较小的行政区域,方志流传不广。美国国会图书馆所藏方志,遍及各省、府、州、县和乡镇,而且十分齐备,有不少的中国方志是其它馆难得一见的。

同时,亚洲部收藏的古今图书集成、中国古地图、清末科举考卷、太平天国印书、少数民族古籍、中国东北与日本之历史文献、南满洲铁道株式会社文献等都是极具价值的古籍甚至是善本图书。除了中国以外,美国国会图书馆收藏的41册《永乐大典》是世界上收藏最齐全的。另外,亚洲部收藏的少数民族文献中,还藏有极具历史艺术价值的纳西文献。纳西文字是世界上仅有的、仍然有生命力的象形文字,在云南丽江地区仍然有少数人在使用着。1999年前后,中国云南省博物馆的朱宝田教授来美国国会图书馆考订纳西文献。朱教授认为美国国会图书馆收藏的3,038件纳西写本不是全世界最多(最多在中国),但是全世界最好的纳西文献。亚洲部中文资料的收藏过程,本身就是一部中美文化交流史。李华伟博士强调,国会图书馆并不希望这些善本、古籍文献束之高阁,秘而不宣。而是本着"学术为天下之公器"的原则将这些资料公开。因此,借助于信息科技的高度发达和数字化手段的广泛应用,国会图书馆应时提出了"善本数字化计划",希望早日实现图书资源共享。

中国近年来经济发展非常迅猛，文化的需求也与日俱增，各种形式的文化书籍大量出现使中国成为出版大国。虽然新书层出不穷，种数繁多，但这些书籍的购买并非很困难。相比较之下，那些木版印刷的线装古籍，才是"千金难买"。特别是在汉学图书馆中，最有价值的收藏部分应该是古籍，尤其是善本古籍。美国国会图书馆的中文古籍非常多，而且确有许多珍品，不少罕见的文献甚至不为人知。到底有多少古籍，到目前为止谁也无法说清楚，因为美国国会图书馆从来没有将大量的人力、物力和资源投放在中国文献的整理上，而且在美国能够整理古籍的人才也非常难找。早年，国会图书馆曾从中国请来专家帮忙，比如朱士嘉教授协助整理方志，王承民教授协助整理善本，近年李孝聪教授协助整理古地图，朱宝田教授整理纳西文献等。他们都在个别专题上考订鉴别，出版专著。

1999年在俄亥俄大学担任了21年的图书馆总馆长的李华伟博士退休之后，被聘任为美国国会图书馆亚洲部主任。目前，他负责国会图书馆亚洲部的所有日常事务。亚洲部是原来的中文组发展起来的，早在1928年中文组就已经成立。李华伟到亚洲部之前，该部有5个部门，分组混乱，相互之间并无什么总的协调，只有中文组有组长，其他各部门只是各自做自己的工作。所以，李主任到任的第一件事就是负责组织和协调各个部门。当时的分组中，西藏脱离中国被划在了南亚一组，蒙古与中国划分为一组，李华伟主任到任后，觉得这样的划分不行，在他的努力协调之下，把西藏划归为中国组。当时的蒙古要划分出去，他说，"亚洲大大小小那么多的国家，如果每一个国家都分为一组，那这样要分多少个组？"于是蒙古保持原样，被改名为中国及蒙古组。亚洲部学术服务科科长、哈佛大学历史系博士密洙雯（Mi Chu Wiens）曾对《华盛顿观察》说："李博士是难得一见的行政人才，在短短的两年半时间之内，把一蹶不振的中文组带到了生机勃勃的境地。"业内人士对李博士5年的亚洲部主任工作给予了充分肯定："5年前，亚洲部像是只睡着的狮子，直到被李华伟博士的魔杖一点，这只熟睡的狮子豁然惊醒……"，"李华伟任内以其高超的领导力，将国会图书馆的触角扩及全世界"。

在整个亚洲部的280万册藏书中，日文的藏书目前有115万册，而中国和蒙古文藏书只有大约100万册。李博士说，这大概有两个方面的历史原因：其一是中国的"文革"10年，图书发行数量极少；另外一个方面，第二次世界大战结束以后，美军占领日本的6年时间，没收过大量的日本文献、情报以及其他外务部门的资料，这大大丰富了日本的藏书。但是现在，中国的出版量很大，大约再过几年中文的馆藏就能超过日本。

李博士在谈到网络媒体发展对于图书馆的影响时说"其实图书馆本身就在改变，只是以前都是印刷品，现在很多材料都在网上，网上的东西有时候查找起来更快、更方便。以前要查资料，通常要翻整本的书，而电子版的材料，只要输入几个关键字就可以找到你想要的东西。之前什么都没有，我来了（亚洲部）之后，这方面的工作做得比较多。现在通过与国内合作，我们慢慢地填充了这方面的空白。中国的超星公司现在大约有218万册电子书，全部是电子全文扫描。他们的'读秀'系统，不仅有书、唱片，还有CD等都是一个非常有用的数据库。日本在这方面起步较早，但是它的商业化程度也很高。不仅价格昂贵、而且使用上也有太多的限制，所以我们买的很少。现在韩国看到中国做的这样好，在近4年间，也把书刊、会议录等进行扫描，但是数量上还是很少。从一个国家来讲，中国的学术传播是做得最好的。当然，这也是一个长远费力的工程。"

李华伟博士对于自己多年的图书馆工作有着自己的见解："图书馆工作是默默无闻的，不是一下子可以出名的，但是这是一项很重要的工作。如果没有人来做这项工作，那么人类的历史文化将会很可惜地流失。所以，从长远意义上来讲，这是非常重要的一项工作。

我自己愿意献身这一工作中，愿意将人类的历史文化保存下来并且希望它能够不断的发展，人类的知识才能不断的创新，人类才会不断进步。所以，我一直鼓励大家使用图书馆资源，并一直坚守这个信念。现在美国国会图书馆给了我这个机会，能够在全世界最大的图书馆工作，我自己是能多做一点就多做一点，也算是自己给自己一点安慰。并且不断培养年轻人才，那些有乐业、敬业精神的，我希望把他们培养成专业人才，建立新的团队，用中国的话来说叫'老中青结合'，发挥团队精神。这是一件值得做的事情。19世纪是欧洲的世纪，20世纪是美国的世纪，21世纪是亚洲的世纪，现在21世纪才刚刚开始，已经可以看出亚洲在全世界举足轻重的地位。中国、印度在将来的十几、二十年间会变得越来越重要。这是一个很好的机会，我们应该多做些事情。"李华伟博上回顾了自己50年的图书馆馆员生涯，提出了"为保存和传播人类知识的美好事业作贡献"的人生理想，并将自己定位为"一个非常敬业的馆员"，其儒雅睿智的学者风范和奉献专注的职业素养，令人感佩。

以一份默默无闻的工作，完成一个传承历史的接力，成就一项平凡而伟大的工程。这就是李华伟贡献其40多年的青春的伟大事业。他以自己的勤奋努力和对图书馆事业的深深热爱，成为第一位入主美国高校图书馆的华人，成为第一位被美国图书馆命名的馆长，成为全世界华人的骄傲。

（原载《图苑名家访谈录》，赖雪梅、姜火明主编，海洋出版社2010年4月出版，第83－91页。）

访前美国国会图书馆亚洲部主任
前俄亥俄大学图书馆馆长李华伟博士[①]

韩淑举[②]

韩淑举（以下简称韩）：李老师，您好！十分感谢您能接受我们的采访。在中国大陆图书馆界尽管近几年来介绍美国图书馆价值观、图书馆学术研究和工作实践的论文不断见诸图书馆学专业刊物，但是对美国图书馆学家的介绍文章却很少，以至大陆同行对美国专家的读书、治学、研究著述情况了解不多。借这次您到山东来的机会，我们想就您个人的学习、研究著述和促进国际图书馆界交流等方面的成就采访几个问题。从资料得知，您原籍福建福州，1957年获得美国匹兹堡大学的奖学金赴美进修。您的中小学在哪里完成的？匹兹堡大学的奖学金好申请吗？

李华伟博士（以下简称李）：在我读中小学的时候正好是中日战争时期，因此经常搬迁及换学校。我的小学基本上是在广西桂林断断续续读完的。初一初二是在四川江津的国立第二华侨中学攻读的。抗日战争结束后，复员到南京，在南京一中读完初三。以后又到桂林进入国立汉民中学读完高一及高二。1949年去了台湾，在台中一中读完高三，然后考进了台湾师范大学教育系，在那里毕业。当时申请美国大学研究所的奖学金并不容易。我是比较幸运的，获得匹兹堡大学的奖学金，并通过留学考试，得以顺利出国。

韩：在匹兹堡大学您先后修毕教育硕士、图书馆学硕士及哲学博士学位。当时为什么会选择修图书馆学位？匹兹堡大学图书馆学硕士需要学习些什么课程？这对您以后从事图书馆工作与研究有什么样的影响？

李：当我在匹兹堡大学攻修教育硕士时，为了挣生活费，还一边在大学图书馆打工，当学生助理。正好当时匹兹堡大学图书馆要建立东亚图书馆，觉得我是个可造之才，希望培养我为图书馆员，要我去读一个图书馆学的学位，并为我付学费。因此我又去读了一个图书馆学的硕士学位，并在图书馆中担任实习馆员。因为是全工半读，花了两年的时间，但也学得很全面。课程包括了图书馆学的方方面面，从理论到实际业务，非常充实。这对我以后从事图书馆工作与研究打下了极好的基础。后来，因为得到我在教育学院恩师的鼓励，我又全工半读，继续完成了主修教育副修图书馆学的哲学博士。

韩：李老师曾担任宾州的爱丁堡州立学院图书馆馆长、泰国亚洲理工学院图书馆及信息中心主任、科罗拉多州立大学图书馆副馆长、俄亥俄大学图书馆馆长，那么，您在美国的图书馆馆长任上需要做些什么工作？这一点与中国有何不同？您有什么管理经验？

李：作为一个图书馆馆长实在是很有挑战性的。只要是跟图书馆有关的业务都需要处理。在60年代，我还是一个新移民，英语也很差，因此做馆长更为困难。当我在1966年第一次做学院图书馆馆长时，当时在美国华人中可能是第一人。对我来说，压力很大。因为我要为所有的华人及少数族裔争口气，证明白人可以胜任的工作我们也可以做。幸好我在台湾念大学时喜欢课外活动，学到了很多做人处世的经验。在匹兹堡大学图书馆工作时又学到了图书馆的专业知识和经验。这些经历都被派上了用场。回想起来，在美国图书馆界我总算为美国华人争了一口气。尽管中美两国图书馆的体制不一样，图书馆馆长的工作

[①] 这是在山东省烟台市举办的"中美图书馆员交流项目——山东省图书馆馆长研修班"上的采访。
[②] 仼职于山东省图书馆。

性质却大同小异，有很多可以彼此借鉴的地方。

韩：李老师在近五十年的图书馆生涯里，出版了5本书，发表过八十余篇论文。可以说成果丰硕。请您简单介绍一下您的主要著述的内容。您是如何做到在繁忙的工作之余，研究著述不辍的？在图书馆学研究方面有什么心得和经验？

李：作为美国大学图书馆的馆长，不仅要掌握图书馆新的动向，而且要不断更新自己的知识，与时俱进。因此我的主要研究课题和著述内容也是根据工作的需要而改变。在我1991年出版的《图书馆学的世界观》一书中即收集了我的一些早期的中英文作品，包括了以下七大类：地区研究藏书，书目控制，国际交换及合作，图书馆与信息服务，图书馆自动化，图书馆发展，图书馆网络化等。1992年，我因对图书馆募款颇有心得，应美国一位出版商的邀请，与我的同事 Gary Hunt 用英文合写了一本《90年代图书馆如何募款》的书，当时很受图书馆的欢迎。1995年，我应台湾图书馆界的邀请，用中文写了一本《现代化图书馆管理》的书。这本书总结了我多年来担任图书馆行政的经验。到了21世纪，我开始思考图书馆重新定位的问题，因此与北大光华管理学院的董小英教授和左美云教授合写了一本《知识管理的理论与实践》的书，2002年在北京出版。除此以外我还发表了近一百篇有关图书馆的文章。这些作品都是在百忙之中，利用休闲时间完成的。

韩：我注意到李老师在美国图书馆界极为活跃，担任的社会职务很多，比如曾任美国图书馆学会理事、俄亥俄州图书馆学会理事、美国华美图书馆员学会会长及理事、国际图联大学及研究图书馆委员会委员等，并因此得到很多奖励，可以说是图书馆活动家。我想知道，博士为什么会热心于这些工作？做这些工作您最大的收获是什么？

李：我是一个比较内向的人，但为了工作的关系，必须加入各种校内外的活动。职位越高，活动的层面越广。我一向比较认真，既然参加了就全力以赴，希望以一己之力，为图书馆事业的发展有所贡献。参加这些活动也让我认识了不少图书馆界的朋友，并学到了很多为人处世的经验。

韩：2003年您在担任美国国会图书馆亚洲部主任后，进行了哪些改革性工作？

李：美国国会图书馆亚洲部的亚洲馆藏非常丰富，包括了亚洲各国近60种亚洲语言及从古代到现代的书刊资料。中日文的出版物超过200万件，其中颇多珍品。在上世纪末，该部因人事及管理方面的一些问题，受到馆内外的批评，馆长决定进行改革。我很幸运被选上该部的新主任，授予改革的重任。在重组的过程中，我首先将西藏从南亚划归中国；新聘12位亚洲各国学科馆员，建立新的服务架构（包括学术服务及馆藏服务两个组，及中国和蒙古，日本，南北韩，东南亚，南亚五个地区团队）；与编目部门合作使用亚洲文字编目；大量采购当代书刊文献及数字化中日韩文数据库，有系统的将中日韩文古籍善本进行数字化；与东南亚和南亚地区采购中心合作加强采购东南亚和南亚的文献资料，成立亚洲部之友会；延长阅览室开放时间，增加学术及交流活动；与国会亚太裔委员会合作建立新的亚太裔收藏，募到私人捐款30万美元以建立每年十个名额的研究补助金等。在短短五年内有此成绩，总算不负馆长的期望。

韩：自1982年以后，您每年应邀到中国大陆讲学，北京大学等名校邀您担任客座教授，国家图书馆、中国科学院图书馆、清华大学图书馆、深圳图书馆、浙江图书馆聘请您为顾问。并且不顾年事已高，亲自到中国各地参加"中美图书馆员专业交流项目"的授课。为促进中美图书馆界交流和中国图书馆事业的发展做出了很大贡献，请问李老师为什么如此关注中国的图书馆事业发展？您对大陆的图书馆同行有什么建议和希望？

李：在过去28年的岁月里，我能亲眼看到中国图书馆界突飞猛进的发展，并且直接和间接的参与了这一个发展的过程,感到十分高兴。当时我不仅经常回国讲学,还先后安排了近 150 位中国图书馆员前往俄亥俄大学图书馆接受短期培训。为了促进中美图书馆的合作,我还在 1996 年召开了第一届中美图书馆合作会议。当时是在北京举行的。以后每三、四年举办一次,今年是第五届,9 月间又要在北京举行。我一直认为中美图书馆合作能促进中美两国之间的文化交流和相互间的了解。目前我所参加的"中美图书馆员专业交流项目"是由中美两国政府正式建立的,其意义极为重大。我万分希望中国图书馆的同行能珍惜这个难得的机会,继续为发展中国图书馆事业而努力。

李华伟主要著述书目

一、书（Books）

1. Educational Development in Taiwan under Nationalist Government, 1945 – 1962 (Ph. D. dissertation, University of Pittsburgh. 1964). 333 p.

1 图书馆学的世界观. 台北：学生书局, 1991, 332 p.

2. Library Development, Resource Sharing and Networking among Higher Education Institutions in Papua New Guinea. Final Report and Recommendations. Port Moresby, Papua New Guinea; Commission for Higher Education, 1991. 48 p.

4. With Gary Hunt, Fundraising for the 1990s：The Challenge Ahead—A Practical Guide for Library Fundraising：From Novice to Expert Canfield, Ohio; Getaway and Associates, 1992. 183 p.

5. 现代化图书馆管理. 台北：三民书局, 1996. 257 p.

6. OCLC 联机与光盘编目概论. 上海：华东师范大学出版社, 1999. 222 p. （与刁维汉、王行仁合著）

7. 知识管理的理论与实践. 北京：华艺出版社, 2002. 471 p. （与董小英、左美云合著）

二、文章，报告和演讲（Papers, reports, and presentations：）

1. "Africana at Duquesne University Library." *African Studies Bulletin*. V. 6, No. 3 (October 1963)：pp. 25 – 27.

2. "Africana-A Special Collection at Duquesne University." *The Catholic Library World*. V. 35, No. 4 (December 1963)：pp. 209 – 211.

3. "Report of the Workshop on Admission of Students from Taiwan and Hong Kong." 中国一周. No. 834 (April 18, 1966)：pp. 12 – 15.

4. "The Recent Educational Reform in Communist China." 学校与社会. V. 46, No. 2311 (November 9, 1968)：pp. 395 – 400.

5. "Computer Application in Library and Information Services：The Current AIT Experiments and Future Plans." Paper presented at the First Computer Applications Symposium jointly sponsored by the Computer Science Laboratory, Chulalongkorn University and U. S. Educational Foundation in Thailand, Bangkok, June 23 – 25, 1969.

6. "亚洲理工学院 Asian Institute of Technology." *The Scooper Monthly*. October 1969：pp. 76 – 81. (In Chinese)

7. "Planning for Computer Applications in the AIT Library." Paper presented at the 1969

annual conference of the Thai Library Association, Bangkok, December 15 – 19, 1969.

8. "Fragmentation of Academic Library Resources in Thai University Libraries." *International Library Review.* V. 3, No. 2 (April 1971): pp. 155 – 167.

9. "Library Mechanization at the Asian Institute of Technology." *International Library Review.* V. 3, No. 3 (July 1971): pp. 257 – 270.

10. "Regional Cooperation in Scientific and Technical Information Service." *Proceedings of the Conference on Scientific and Technical Information Needs for Malaysia and Singapore.* Institute Teknoloji Mara, Kuala Lumpur, September 24 – 26, 1971. Kuala Lumpur; Persatuan Perpustakaan Malaysia and Library Association of Singapore, 1972: pp. 97 – 105.

11. "A New Engineering Library Emerging in Asia." *Libraries in International Development.* No. 41 (December 1971): pp. 103.

12. "The Information Technology—New Tools and New Possibilities for Information Storage, Retrieval and Dissemination." Paper presented at the Regional Seminar on Information Storage, Retrieval and Dissemination, organized by Asian Mass Communication Research and Information Centre in cooperation with the National Research Council of Thailand, Bangkok, March 26 – 30, 1973: p. 10.

13. "Partner for School Library Development in Thailand." *T. L. A. Bulletin.* V. 17, No. 5 (September/October 1973): pp. 443 – 448.

14. "Proposal for the Establishment of a National Library and Information Network." *Central Daily News* (Taipei). February 26 – 27, 1974. (In Chinese)

15. "Possibilities in Employing Computer and Other Information Technologies to Further Library and Information Services in Southeast Asia." *Network.* V. 1, No. 3 (March 1974): pp. 10 – 12, and 24 – 28.

16. With S. W. Massil, Library Automation at the Asian Institute of Technology—Bangkok. *The Larc Reports.* V. 7, No. 3. Peoria, Illinois: The Larc Press, 1974. 35p.

17. "Regional Cooperation in Scientific and Technical Information Service." In *A Survey of Automated Activities in the Libraries of Asia and the Far East.* (World Survey Series, V. 5) Peoria, Illinois: The Larc Press, 1974: pp. 11 – 17.

18. "The Application of Information Technology to Close the Information Gap." Paper presented at the First Conference on Asian Library cooperation, Tamsui, Taipei, August 19 – 22, 1974. 12 p.

19. "User and Use Analysis: A Case Study of the Information Utility by Geotechnical Engineers in Asian Countries." *Information Utilities: Proceedings of the 37th Annual Conference of the American Society for Information Science.* Atlanta, Georgia, October 13 – 17, 1974. Edited by Pranas Zunde. Washington, D. C.: 1974, V. II, pp. 133 – 136.

20. With S. W. Massil, Proposal for Library Development at Prince of Songkla University in Southern Thailand. Prepared at the request of the University Development Project Office, Prince of Songkla University. Bangkok: Asian Institute of Technology, 1974. 23p.

21. With S. W. Massil, "Scholarly Publications: Considerations on Bibliographic Control and Dissemination." Scholarly Publishing in Southeast Asia, *Proceedings of the Seminar on Scholarly Publishing in Southeast Asia,* sponsored by the Association of Southeast Asian Institutions

of Higher Learning, University of Malaya, Kuala Lumpur, January 16 – 18, 1975. Edited by Beda Lim. Kuala Lumpur; 1975, pp. 212 – 218.

22. With Jane C. Yang, "International Standard Numbering for Books and Serials and the Standardization of Bibliographic Descriptions." *Journals of Library and Information Science.* V. 1, No. 1 (February 1975): pp. 60 – 66. (In Chinese)

23. "The Experience of a Specialized Information Service in Asia—AGE." Paper presented at the Round Table Conference on Documentation Problems in Developing Countries, Khartoum, Sudan, April 10 – 11, 1975 sponsored by FID/DC and FID National Member in Sudan. Published in *Journal of Library and Information Science.* V. 1, No. 2 (Oct. 1975): pp. 82 – 93.

24. "Recent Important Developments in the Library World." *Bulletin of the Library Association of China.* No. 27 (December 1975): pp. 34 – 36. (In Chinese)

25. "Regional Cooperation for ISDS." *Proceedings of the Third Conference of Southeast Asian Librarians.* Jakarta, Indonesia, December 1 – 5, 1975. Edited by Luwarsih Pringgoadis-urjo and Kardiati Sjahrial. Jakarta; PDIN-LIPI for Ikatan Pustakawan Indonesia (Indonesian Librarians Association), 1977: pp. 159 – 166.

26. The Possibility of Establishing a Regional Centre for the International Serials Data System in Thailand. (SC-76/WS/ 7), Paris: UNESCO, 1976. 43 p.

27. "The Third Conference of Southeast Asian Librarians." *Leads.* V. 18, No. 1 (March 1976): pp. 3 – 4.

28. "Proposal for the Establishment of an ISDS Regional Center for Southeast Asia in Thailand." *Leads.* V. 18, No. 2 (July 1976): pp. 4 – 5.

29. "Cooperative Regional Bibliographic Projects in Southeast Asia." Paper presented at the Library Seminars of the International Association of Oriental Librarians held in conjunction with the 30th International Congress of Human Sciences in Asia and North Africa, Mexico City, August 3 – 8, 1976: p. 17. Published in *UNESCO Bulletin for Libraries.* V. 31. No. 6 (Nov. -Dec. 1977): pp. 344 – 351, 370.

30. With Marjorie Rhoades, "Approaches to Development of Water Resources Scientific Information Systems," *Water Knowledge Transfer: Proceedings of the Second International Conference on Transfer of Water Resources Knowledge.* Colorado State University, June 29-July 1, 1977. Fort Collins, Colorado: Water Resource Publications, 1978, V. 2: pp. 625 – 644.

31. "Sharing Information Resources Through Computer-assisted Systems and Networking." *Resource Sharing of Libraries in Developing Countries. Proceedings of the 1977 IFLA/ UNESCO Pre-Session Seminar for Librarians from Developing Countries.* Antwerp University, August 30 – September 4, 1977. Munchen: K. G. Saur, 1979: pp. 208 – 216. Also published in *Journal of Library and Information Science.* V. 4, No. 1 (April 1978): pp. 14 – 24.

32. "Impacts of International Information Systems on NATIS." Paper presented at Fourth Congress of Southeast Asian Librarians, Bangkok, June 5 – 9, 1978. Published in the *Proceedings of Regional Cooperation for the Development of National Information Services.* Bangkok: Thai Library Association, 1981: pp. 133 – 146.

33. "Online Revolution and Libraries." *Library Planning and Media Technology.* Library Workshop Proceedings, November 28 – 30. 1979. Taipei: Taiwan Normal University Library,

1980: pp. 14 – 17. (In Chinese)

34. "The Current Status of Academic Library Administration in the U. S." Paper presented at the Annual Meeting of Directors of Academic and Research Libraries, Taipei, December 1, 1979: p. 10. (In Chinese)

35. With K. Mulliner and Lian The-Mulliner, "International Information Exchange and Southeast Asia Collections—A View from the U. S." Presented at the 1980 Meeting of the International Association of Orientalist Librarians, Manila, August 17 – 23, 1980: 17 pages. Published in *Journal of Educational Media Science*. V. 18, No. 2 (Winter 1980): pp. 3 – 18.

36. "A Sketch for a Computerized National Library and Information Network." Paper presented at the International Workshop on Chinese Library Automation, Taipei, February 14 – 19, 1981. 11 p.

37. Acquisitions From the Third World, Editor and Compiler, with K. Mulliner, special thematic issue of Library Acquisitions : Practice and Theory. V. 6, No. 2 (1982): pp. 79 – 238.

38. With K. Mulliner, "Library Acquisitions from the Third World; An Introduction." *Library Acquisitions: Practice and Theory*. V. 6, No. 2 (1982): pp. 79 – 85.

39. "Recent Breakthroughs in Library Automation in Taiwan." *Journal of Educational Media Science*. V. 19, No. 2 (Winter 1982): pp. 119 – 136.

40. With K. Mulliner, "International Exchanges of Librarians and the Ohio University Internship Program." Paper presented to the International Relations Round Table of the American Library Association at the ALA Conference in Philadelphia, July 1982. Published in *College & Research Libraries News*. V. 43, No. 10 (November 1982): pp. 345 – 348.

41. "Challenges for the Library and Information Profession," *Bulletin of the Library Association of China*. No. 35 (1983): pp. 235 – 246.

42. "International Library Internships; An Effective Approach to Cooperation." Paper presented to the annual program of the Asian/Pacific American Librarians Association and the Chinese American Librarians Association, in conjunction with the annual American Library Association conference, Los Angeles, June 28 – 29, 1983. Published in *Areas of Cooperation in Library Development in Asian and Pacific Regions*. Athens, Ohio: Chinese-American Librarians Association, 1985: pp. 21 – 27; and, in a revised form, in the *International Library Review*. V. 17, No. 1 (1985): pp. 17 – 25.

43. Areas of Cooperation in Library Development in Asia and Pacific Regions. Papers presented at the 1983 Joint Annual Program of the Asian/Pacific American Librarians Association and Chinese American Librarians Association, June 28 – 29, 1983, Los Angeles, California. Edited with Sally C. Tseng and K. Mulliner. Athens, Ohio: Chinese American Librarians Association, 1985. 63p.

44. With K. Mulliner, E. Hoffmann-Pinther, and Hannah McCauley, "ALICE at One: Candid Reflections on the Adoption, Installation, and Use of the Virginia Tech Library System (VTLS) at Ohio University." Paper presented at the Integrated Online Library Systems Second National Conference, September 13 – 14, 1984, in Atlanta, Georgia. Published in the *Proceedings*. Canfield, Ohio: Genaway & Associates, 1984: pp. 228 – 242.

45. With M. Beckman and Jianyan Huang. "Management of Scientific and Technical

Information Centres: Aspects of Planning a Course Sponsored by IDRC (Canada) and ISTIC (China). " Paper presented at the International Federation for Documentation (FID) Pre-Congress Workshop on Curriculum Development in a Changing World, The Hague, September 3 – 4, 1984. 19 p.

46. Lecture Notes and Suggested Readings on Modern Library Management and Automation. Athens, Ohio, 1985. 87 p.

47. With K. Mulliner, "Educating for International Interdependence: The Role of the Academic Library—Ohio University and Malaysia," at the First Annual Tun Abdul Razak Conference in Malaysia, Athens, Ohio, May 10, 1985. 9p.

48. With K. Mulliner, "Funding the Southeast Asia Collection and Research Resources at Ohio University. " Paper presented at the Annual Meeting of the Association for Asian Studies in Chicago, Illinois, March 21, 1986.

49. "International Exchanges and Internships for Librarians" Paper presented at the LACUNY[①] Institute 86, New York City, April 4, 1986.

50. "Principles and Issues on National Library and Information Policy. " *Papers of the Library Cooperation and Development Seminar*, August 17 – 18, 1986. Taipei: National Central Library, 1987: pp. 5. 1 – 5. 22. Also published in *Journal of Library and Information Science*. V. 13, No. 1 (April 1987): pp. 1 – 16.

51. "Applications of Information Technology in An American Library——The Case of Ohio University Libraries, " published in *First Pacific Conference on New Information Technology for Library and Information Professionals*, June 16 – 18, 1987, Bangkok, Proceedings. Edited by Ching-Chih Chen and David I. Raitt. West Newton, MA: MicroUse Information, 1987: pp. 155 – 164.

52. "Library Automation at Ohio University Library: Past, Present and Future. " In *Collection of Essays Honoring Chiang Wei-Tang on His Ninetieth Birthday*. Taipei: Library Association of China, 1987: pp. 47 – 72.

53. Proceedings of the International Symposium on New Techniques and Applications in Libraries, Xi'an, China, September 8 – 11, 1988. Edited with Zhang Zhiyou. Xi'an: Xi'an Jiaotong University Press, 1988. 576 p.

54. "Trends in Automation in American Academic Libraries: Ohio University's Experience," by Educational Resources Information Center, ED 315 081, ERIC Clearinghouse, May 1989. 20 p. Also published in *Journal of Educational Media & Library Sciences*. V. 27, No. 1 (Autumn 1989): pp. 1 – 23.

55. "Major Milestones in American Library Automation since the 1960s. " *National Central Library News Bulletin*. V. 11, No. 4 (Nov. 1989): pp. 4 – 7. (Speech delivered at the National Central Library in Taipei on June 2, 1989) (In Chinese)

56. "Planning Process and Considerations for a State-Wide Academic Libraries Information System in Ohio. " Second Pacific Conference on New Information Technology for Library and Information Professionals and Educational Media Specialists and Technologists, Singapore, May 29

---

① Library Association of the City University of New York

−31, 1989. Published in *Proceedings*, edited by Ching-chih Chen and David I Raitt. West Newton, MA: MicroUse Information, 1989: 203 − 210. Also published in *Journal of Educational Media & Library Sciences*. V. 27, No. 2 (Winter 1990): pp. 127 − 138.

57. *New Concepts and New Technology in Library Services. Library Lecture Series.* No. 10. Kaohsiung, Taiwan: Sun Yat-Sen University, 1989. 25 p. (In Chinese) Final Report of the INNERTAP Project Review. Consultant Report on the Information Network on New and Renewable Energy Resources and Technologies for Asia and the Pacific, commissioned by the International Development Research Centre. Ottawa, Canada: IDRC, 1990. 33 p.

58. With Anne S. Goss, "Medical Librarianship in China: Recent Developments." *Asian Libraries.* V. 1, No. 1 (March 1991): pp. 80 − 84.

59. "New Visions in Library Automation and Networking——Ohio's Approach to the 1990s." Paper presented at the International Conference on New Frontiers in Library Information Services, May 8 − 12, 1991 Proceedings. 2 vols. Taipei, Taiwan: Central Library, 1992: pp. 361 − 382. A Chinese translation by Bao Ping and Zhang Xiaoyan was published in *Journal of Academic Libraries.* No. 59 (1992): pp. 38 − 45.

60. "The 1991 White House Conference Participant Observations." *ALAO Newsletter.* V. 10, No. 1 (September 1991): pp. 6 − 7.

61. With Judith Sessions and Stacey Kimmel, "OhioLINK: Technology and Teamwork Transforming Ohio Libraries." *Wilson Library Bulletin.* V. 66, No. 10 (June 1992): pp. 43 − 45.

62. With John Evans, "Developing Higher Education Libraries in Papua New Guinea." *Information Development; The International Journal for Librarians, Archivists and Information Specialists.* V. 8, No. 2 (November 1992): pp. 221 − 227.

63. With Gary Hunt, "The Ten Principles for Successful Fundraising." *The Bottom Line.* V. 6, No. 3/4 (Winter 1992/ Spring 1993): pp. 27 − 33.

64. "Advancing Information Technologies: The Role of National Libraries." Presented to the International Conference on National Libraries: Toward the 21st Century, sponsored by the Central Library, Taiwan, April 20 − 24, 1993.

65. "Ohio Academic Libraries Prepare for the 21st Century." Library in the 90's, Selected Papers of the International Symposium on the Latest Development in Technologies of Library Service, September 6 − 10, 1992, Beijing. China. Edited by Sun Chengjian and Jiang Bingxin. Beijing: International Academic Publishers, 1993: pp. 292 − 308.

66. "Managing Information Technology——The Experience of Ohio Academic Libraries," presented to the IX Congress of Southeast Asian Librarians (CONSAL) in Bangkok, May 2 − 7, 1993, and the Seminar on National Academic Library Networking, May 12 − 14, 1993, Chiang Mai, Thailand. Published in *CONSAL IX Papers; Future Dimensions and Library Development.* Bangkok: CONSAL IX Secretariat, 1993: pp. B45 − B62.

67. With Angela Lew, Workshops and Consultation on the Management of Libraries and Information for the Institutes of Education in China, held in Tianjin, Beijing, and Shanghai, July 11 to August 8, 1993. (A World Bank Funded Teacher Training Project) August 15, 1993. 22 p.

68. "Expanding Ties between Ohio and Chinese Libraries." *Ohio Libraries*. V. 6, No. 4 (Fall 1993): pp. 22 – 23.

69. "Managing Information Technology—the Experience of Ohio Academic Libraries." *Chiang Mai University Library Journal*. V. 4 (1994): pp. 20 – 43.

70. With Kent Mulliner, "Southeast Asia Collection Growth in the United States: Ohio University's Experience." In the *Information Challenge*. A Festschrift in Honor of Dr. Donald Wijasuriya. Edited by Ch'ng Kim See. Kuala Lumpur: Knowledge Publishers, 1995: pp. 87 – 103

71. "Networked, Electronic and Virtual Library——Libraries of the 1990s." Paper published in the Proceedings of the International Seminar on Information Technologies and Information Services, October 20 – 24, 1994, Shanghai, People's Republic of China. Beijing: China Social Sciences Publishing House, 1994. V. 2, pp. 167 – 172. Also published in *Journal of Educational Media & Library Sciences*. V. 32, No. 2 (Winter 1995): pp. 119 – 129.

72. "Global Information Access; Libraries as Citizens' Gateway to the World." Paper presented at the Chubu University-Ohio University Conference on Lifelong Learning for the 21st Century: Local and Global Dimensions, October 4 – 6, 1994, Ka-sugai, Japan. The Proceedings of... Kasugai: Chubu University, 1995: pp. 75 – 82.

73. Program CPR/91/420 Basic Education; Administration and Teachers Training. Consultant Report, submitted to United Nations Educational, Scientific and Cultural Organization, June 30, 1995. 34 p.

74. "American Contributions to Modern Library Development in China; A Historic Review." Paper presented at the China——US Conference on Global Information Access; Challenges and Opportunities, held in Beijing, China, August 21 – 23, 1996. 14 p. Also published in *Journal of Information, Communication, and Library Science*. V. 4, No. 4 (Summer 1998): pp. 10 – 20.

75. "Maximizing Information Access and Resource Sharing; The OhioLINK Experience." Paper presented at the 10th International Conference on New Information Technology, March 24 – 26, 1998, Hanoi, Vietnam. Published in its Proceedings, edited by Ching-Chih Chen. West Newton, MA: MicroUse Information, 1998: pp. 149 – 156.

76. "Maximizing Information Access and Resources Sharing; The OhioLINK Approach." Paper presented at the International Conference on New Missions of Academic Libraries in the 21st Century, October 25 – 28, 1998, Beijing, China. Published in its Proceedings. Beijing: Peking University Press, 1998: pp. 283 – 287.

77. "The Ten Principles for Successful Fundraising," coauthored with Gary Hunt, in Sponsoring fur Bibliotheken, edited by Rolf Busch. Berlin: Deutsches Bibliotheksinstiut, 1997: pp. 130 – 141.

78. "Library Cooperation and the Development of a Library Network—The OhioLINK." Paper presented at the Seminar on Library Cooperation, Resource Sharing and the Development of Networks, August 19 – 20, 1999, Bangkok, Thailand, organized by the Rajabhat Institute Bansomdejchaopraya. Published in its Proceedings. Bangkok: Rajabhat Institute Bansomdejchaopraya, 1999: pp. 1 – 27.

79. "The Success of OhioLINK for Information Access and Resources Sharing in a Networked Environment." *Bulletin of Library and Information Science*. No. 30 (August 1999): pp. 1 – 17.

80. "Library Cooperation and Resource Sharing in the Networked Environment." Paper presented in the Seminar on Internet and Library Development, December 4, 1999, Taipei, Taiwan. Published in its Proceedings. Taipei: Library Association of China, 1999: pp. 3 – 44. (In Chinese)

81. "Libraries in the Digital and Networked Knowledge Age of the Twenty-First Century." Paper presented at the Seminar on 21st Century Public Libraries: Vision and Reality, May 1 – 3, 2000, Taipei, Taiwan, organized by the Central Taiwan Office of the Council for Cultural Development of ROC. Published in its Proceedings. Taichung, Taiwan: National Taichung Library, 2000: pp. 43 – 68.

82. "Knowledge Management and the Role of Libraries in the New Century." Published in Prospects of the 21st Century. Taichung, Taiwan: Feng Chia University and Liao Ying-Ming Cultural and Educational Foundation, 2000: pp. 397 – 436.

83. "Does Library have a Role in Knowledge Management." Paper presented at the 12th International Conference on New Information Technology, May 29 – 31, 2001, Beijing, China. Published in its Proceedings, Global Digital Library Development in the New Millennium, edited by Ching-Chih Chen, Beijing: Tsinghua University Press, 2001: pp. 145 – 152.

84. "Strategic Direction of Libraries in Knowledge Management." New Technology of Library and Information Service. No. 93, 2002 Annual: pp. 13 – 17.

85. With Ratana Na-Lamphun, "Focusing on Information and Knowledge Management: Redesigning the Graduate Program of Library and Information Science at Chiang Mai University." *Information Development*. V. 18 No. 1 (March 2002): pp. 47 – 58.

86. "Implementing Knowledge Management, Providing Quality Services, and Facilitating Knowledge Renewal and Creation." Paper presented at the Academic Seminar on Knowledge Management: Opportunities and Challenges for Libraries, May 19 – 22, 2002, Beijing, China, organized by the Documentation and Information Center of the Chinese Academy of Sciences and me National Science and Technology Library. Published in its Proceedings. Beijing: *Chinese Academy of Sciences*. 2002: pp. 90 – 94. Also published in *Newsletter of Library and Information Service*. No. 138 (2002): pp. 2 – 6. (In Chinese)

87. With Peggy Shu-Te Liu, "The Cooperation of Non-profit Organizations Publish and Market Electronic Periodicals: The Case of Bio-One by SPARC and OCLC." *Bulletin of the Library Association of China*. No. 68 (June 2002): pp. 14 – 25. (In Chinese)

88. "Who Should be in Charge of Knowledge Management, Librarians/Libraries or Someone Else." *Journal of Academic Libraries* (大学图书馆学报). V. 20, No. 5 (2002 Special Issue): pp. 79 – 84. Paper presented at the International Conference on Current Situation and Future Trends of Digital Library Development, October 23 – 25, 2002, Beijing, China, in celebration of the centennial of the Peking University Library.

89. "Implementing Knowledge Management, Providing Quality Services, and Promoting Knowledge Renewal," in Proceedings of the Seminar on Knowledge Management: Opportunities

and Challenges for the Library, May 19 – 22, 2002, Beijing. Published by the Documentation and Information Center, Chinese Academy of Sciences, 2002: pp. 90 – 94. (In Chinese)

90. "Libraries in Asia: New Life for Libraries in the Digital Age." *Harvard Asia Pacific Review*. (Fall 2002)

91. "Knowledge Management: The Role of Libraries." *Tianjin Library Journal*. No. 78 (No. 1, 2003): pp. 1 – 5. (In Chinese)

92. With Liren Zheng, "First Decade of the Dr. Shao You Bao Overseas Chinese Documentation and Research Center at Ohio University (1993 – 2003)," published in the Proceeding of the Second International Conference of Institutes & Libraries for Chinese Overseas Studies. "Transnational Networks: Challenges in Research and Documentation of the Chinese Overseas," March 13 – 15, 2003, Hong Kong, organized jointly by the Chinese University of Hong Kong Libraries and Ohio University Libraries. Hong Kong: 2003: 17p.

93. 关于图书馆服务效益评估的若干问题. 大学图书馆学报, 2003 (5): 18 – 22. (In Chinese)

94. "Building a World-class Asian Collection in the Library of Congress for Area Studies, Culture Preservation, Global Understanding, and Knowledge Creation." (Japanese translation on p. 57 – 67. English paper and slides on p. 150 – 169.) Published in the Proceedings of the Symposium "The New Horizon of Library Services Toward the Better Understanding of Asia". November 19, 2003. Kyoto, Japan: National Diet Library, Kansai-kan, 2004. 179 p.

95. "Ching-chih Chen: A Shining Star and Model of Chinese American Library and Information Science Professionals." In Chinese American Librarians Association. *Bridging Cultures: Chinese American Librarians and Their Organization: A Glance at the Thirty Years of CALA, 1973 – 2003*. Edited by Zhijia Shen, Liana Hong Zhou, and Karen T. Wei. 桂林：广西师范大学出版社, 2004: 9 – 25.

96. "Sharing the Treasures of the Asian Collections in the Library of Congress." Paper presented at the Second Shanghai International Library Forum, held at the Shanghai Library, October 12 – 15, 2004. Published in the Proceedings of the Forum. Shanghai: Shanghai Library, 2004.

97. "Historical Resources on Northeast China and Japan in the Library of Congress." Paper presented at the International Conference of the Historical Resources for the Studies of Northeast China and Japan, held at Niigata University in Japan, October 27 – 30, 2004. (In Chinese and Japanese)

98. "Sinological Resources in the Library of Congress," keynote speech at the International Conference on Sinological Resources in the Digital Era, December 7 – 9, 2004, organized by the Central Library (Taiwan) and Center for Sinological Studies, Taipei, Taiwan. 13 pages. Also published in the *Alumni Journal of Taiwan Normal University*. No. 325 (February 2005): pp. 4 – 12. (In Chinese)

99. "Sinological Resources in the Library of Congress." *Culture Communication*. No. 17 (July/August 2005, p. 2) and No. 18 (September/October 2005. p. 3). (In Chinese)

100. "Chinese Resources for Zheng He Studies in the Library of Congress." Paper presented at the Third International Conference of Institutes and Libraries for Chinese Overseas Studies held

in Singapore on August 18 – 21. 2005 under the theme "Maritime Asia and the Chinese Overseas. 1405 – 2005." (I was the co-chair of the conference.)

101. "Building a World-Class Asian Collection in the Digital Age at the Library of Congress," keynote speech at the Symposium on Library Collection in the Digital Age, January 16 – 17, 2006, organized by the National Chung Hsing University Graduate Institute of Library and Information Science and the National Chung Hsing University Library, Taichung, Taiwan. Published in the *Proceedings of the Symposium*. January 2006. 台湾：中兴大学，2006：pp. 11 – 29.

102. Asian Collections in the Digital Age at the Library of Congress, 深图通讯, 2007 (1): 3 – 11.

103. "A History of the East Asian Collections in the Library of Congress: A Bibliographic Guide," in Collecting Asia: East Asian Libraries in North America, 1868 – 2008. Edited by Peter X. Zhou. (Ann Arbor, Michigan: Association for Asian Studies, 2010.) (Asian Past & Present: New Research from AAS, No. 4.) pp. 22 – 31.

104. 美国图书馆自动化五十年主要里程碑, 高校图书馆工作, 2010 (1): 3 – 7.

三、书评 Book Reviews：

1. American Reference Books Annual (1978 – 2008), average of five book reviews per year.
2. Library and Information Science Annual (1998 – 2008), Average of four book reviews per year.

四、期刊编辑 Editorial Responsibilities：

1. Journal of Chinese American Studies (2001 –).
2. 教育资料与图书馆学. 淡江大学教育资料与图书馆学出版社，1980.
3. Journal of Library and Information Science (1975 – 1978).
4. 图书资讯学刊. 台湾大学图书资讯学系，1989.
5. Library Acquisitions: Practice and Theory (1976 – 1984).
6. Network: International Communications in Library Automation (1974 – 1975).
7. Encyclopedia of Overseas Chinese (1993 – 1996).
8. 资讯传播与图书馆学. 世新大学图书资讯学系暨图书馆，1985 – 1999.
9. World Sci – Tech R & D (1996 – 1999).

采访后记

采访李博士是在烟台举办的"中美图书馆员交流项目——山东省图书馆馆长研修班"上，几天交流下来，李老的言谈举止深深感染着我：幽默、睿智，他秉承中华民族文化积淀而成的高贵气质；优雅、淡定，他展现出西方文明滋养的绅士风度。与他的谈话，使人如沐春风。他是著述丰富的图书馆学家，同时也是著名的图书馆活动家。李老已年逾八秩，作为此项目的美方评审员，他辗转中国的多个城市，为促进中美两国图书馆的合作交流不遗余力地奔波，我们在深深感动地同时，也诚挚地说一句：李老，谢谢您！以此向您表达最崇高的敬意！

(原载《山东图书馆学刊》2010年第6期，第1–8页。)

图书、图书馆和图书馆长
——感怀三篇，赠李华伟博士

王汉川

（一）图书

那时候，世界上没有书籍；
只有刻在山崖上的符号和图案。
后来，文字和印刷术的联姻，
有了图书的华诞。
从此，人类文明进入了一个新的纪元；
于是，有了文化的奇异和璀璨。

（二）图书馆

那时候，世界上没有图书馆；
只有零星的书册散落在民间。
后来，众多的图书汇集在一起，
诞生了知识的餐馆。
从此，大众传播进入了一个新的时期；
于是，有了知识的更新和文化的外延。

（三）图书馆长

那时候，我不知道有您；
只有山涧小路上的跋涉和煤油灯下的梦幻。
后来，踏上异国他乡的土地，
我结识了您。
从此，我有了一位新的良师益友；
于是，在博士论文的前言中，
我满怀感激地提到了你的名字。

Hwa-Wei Lee[①]

Mengxiong Liu

On June 22, 1999, the Ohio University News Release announced: "In recognition of his outstanding achievements, Ohio University's Board of Trustees named a new library building the 'Hwa-Wei Lee Annex' and conferred on Dr. Lee the title of Dean of Libraries Emeritus. A permanent office in the Library Annex has been provided to Dr. Lee for his use after retirement."

Dr. Lee's great retirement honor was generated from his lifetime dedication to libraries and his 40-year distinguished career in academic libraries. During his 21-years as the Dean of University Libraries at Ohio University, the University Libraries experienced unprecedented growth and progress under his skillful leadership. The reorganization of the library resulted in more efficient service becoming one of the founding members in OhioLINK, a statewide system pooling materials of all major academic libraries into one unified entity. Library endowments grew to over $8 millions, major renovations were accomplished, a regional annex was constructed, the first digitization project was secured, and library acquisitions exceeded two million volumes. The Library has become one of the top 121 research libraries in the United States and Canada, achieving membership in the highly competitive and prestigious Association of Research Libraries (*Ohio University News Release*, June 22, 1999).

Dr. Lee was also a model of international contribution. Under his administration, an international librarian exchange program was created and developed, and the unique status of depository for four countries was achieved, which allows the Library to receive depository publications from these countries on a continuing basis. He left footprints in five continents as a library consultant and lecturer. "He is a world citizen and a remarkable role model to students and colleagues alike. His career has advanced scholarship and human understanding while setting unparalleled standards of service, loyalty, honor, honesty, and integrity" (Friends of Hwa-Wei Lee Committee, June 22, 1999). His tireless effort in promoting the practice of the boundless modern libraries has made him internationally known (Hong, 1997).

The American Library Association (ALA) also commended Dr. Lee's remarkable contributions to the American, Asian, Chinese and international librarianship. With a resolution, ALA sent a congratulatory note upon the event of his retirement. Dr. Lee served the American Library Association in a variety of capacities, including as a Councilor-at-Large, and the Chair of the Subcommittee on East Asia and Pacific of the International Relations Committee. He also served actively at the Ohio Library Association as a Board Director, was recognized as the Ohio Librarian of the Year in 1987, and was appointed as a delegate to the White House Conference on Library and Information Services in 1991. Dr. Lee was past president of Chinese American Librarians Association, and was the recipient of the CALA Distinguished Services Award in 1984. His valuable contributions also extended to the Asian/Pacific American Librarians Association (APALA). He was the recipient of the APALA Distinguished Services Award in 1983. In addition, Dr. Lee was a much sought after lecturer and consultant in many Asian countries and organized five international conferences. He is the author of three books and more than sixty articles (ALA/IRC East Asia and the Pacific Subcommittee, June 1999). More recently, the Ohio Library Council named him "Hall of Fame Librarian" of 1999. It is the highest honor one can receive as a librarian in Ohio. ("The History and Status of Chinese Americans in Librarianship." *Library Trends*. V. 49, N. 1, 2000.)

(Published in *Library Trends*. V. 49, No. 1, 2000. Also published at the Website of Who's who: http://www.chiamonline.com/People/LP/leehwawei.htm)

[①] From "*The History and Status of Chinese Americans in Librarianship.*" *Library Trends*. V. 49, No. 1, 2000.

(3). 信 函
Letters

Letter from James H. Billington

February 1, 2008

Dear Hwa-Wei,

Thank you for your dedicated service to the Library of Congress and the breadth of institutional and international experience that you brought with you five years ago. Your accomplishments before coming to the Library are well known to me, to your colleagues, and to your international peers, but I shall include a few highlights from your 50 years of librarianship before you arrived in Washington to begin your supreme achievements as Chief of the Library's Asian Division.

After your graduation from National Taiwan Normal University, you earned master's and doctoral degrees in education and library science from the University of Pittsburgh. You began your professional career at the main library of the University of Pittsburgh as a graduate student assistant in 1958, and became a full-time library employee a year later. Your association with other academic libraries in positions of increasing responsibility included Duquesne University; Edinboro University of Pennsylvania; the Asian Institute of Technology in Bangkok, Thailand; Colorado State University; and Ohio University. From 2000 to 2002, you served as a Distinguished Visiting Scholar at OCLC and as a Fulbright Senior Specialist at the University of Chiang Mai in Thailand. Throughout this distinguished career, you authored or co-authored five books and published some 100 professional papers.

During your tenure as Dean of Libraries at Ohio University from 1978 to 1999, the university library achieved membership in the Association of Research Libraries. You received the 1983 Outstanding Administrator Award of Ohio University, the 1987 Ohio Librarian of the Year Award in the State of Ohio, and the 1991 ALA John Ames Humphrey Award for International Librarianship. Upon your retirement as Dean of University Libraries from Ohio University, you received awards for distinguished service from the American Library Association, the Asian/Pacific Librarians Association, the Chinese American Librarians Association, the Library Association of China (Taiwan), OhioLINK, and Ohionet. In recognition of your service to Ohio University, the Dean of Libraries named the first floor of the Vernon R. Alden Library as the Hwa-Wei Lee Center for International Collections. By a resolution of the Board of Trustees of the University, a new library building was named Hwa-Wei Lee Library Annex, and in 1999 the Ohio Library Council inducted you as Ohio Hall of Fame Librarian.

Your international librarianship and professionalism have been exceptional since your arrival at the Library of Congress on February 10, 2003. During your tenure, you worked tirelessly to build our collections and to ensure that our reference service and outreach activities served the nation in the best of possible ways. The reorganization of the division; the establishment of collaborative digitization projects with major national libraries and research institutions in Mainland China, Japan, Korea, and Taiwan; your establishment and support of the Asian Division Friends Society and the Florence Tan Moeson Fund, as well as your recent establishment of the Asian Pacific American Collection Fund, will carry on your good work long after you leave these halls.

On behalf of your colleagues at the Library of Congress, thank you for your generosity, your past and future support of the Asian Division, and your service to the Library, the U. S. Congress, and to the United States.

With my thanks and best wishes for your next adventure.

Sincerely,

James H. Billington
The Librarian of Congress

Dr. Hwa-Wei Lee, Ph. D.
Chief, Asian Division
The Library of Congress
101 Independence Avenue, S. E.
Washington, DC 20540 - 4810

Letter from Carolyn T. Brown

February 6, 2008

Dear Hwa-Wei,

When you came to the Library, you promised me that you would stay for five years. We are all reluctant to see that five years come to an end, but what an astonishing five years you have given to the Asian Division. When you arrived, the Asian Division was a sleepy backwater, and as you leave it is one of the most dynamic divisions of the Library. One of my 3 or 4 greatest successes in my 16 plus years at the Library of Congress was hiring you as chief of the Asian Division, or more accurately, having somehow created the atmosphere and the psychological space that facilitated your wanting to come to lead the Division.

I don't recall the earliest details of the attempt Peter Young and I made to recruit you as acting chief. I do recall that you begged off for health reasons and helped persuade Karl Lo to come, which was a wonderful contribution in itself. When we began searching for a permanent chief, you offered your services in searching for potential candidates. What is most dramatic in my memory was the moment during which I read the email in which you detailed why each potential chief candidate on your list, and there were about 8 of them, had expressed unwillingness to apply for the position. At the very end, with your characteristic modesty, you asked what I might think if you were to submit an application yourself.

When I read that line, I leapt from my chair, dashed to the desk of my special assistant, Sharon Green, and jumping up and down, literally I think, exclaimed, "Hwa-Wei wants to apply! Hwa-Wei wants to apply!" When I could finally contain my exuberance, I wrote you an encouraging reply written with appropriate bureaucratic restraint.

The rest is history, as they say. My expectations of you were high, and you exceeded them beyond my capacity to imagine. I'll enumerate just some of those accomplishments.

You openly gave the Library the benefit of the enormous goodwill you had throughout China and revolutionized our relationship with the library community in that nation. I don't know the details, but the success of the Luce initiatives in Mainland China, the multiple digital projects there and in Taiwan, the broad access to digital resources from Asia, all came about because of your contacts, friendships, and hard work. You initiated the Asian Division's Friends Society, which opened up a network of contacts not previously available to the Library. In the process you turned critics into supporters as well as raising monies for the Division and generating a large number of intellectually substantial events.

You started an Asian American collection, securing a major collection of materials from a Society member and initiating a new area of specialization for the Library. You opened up the Division to support from Japanese constituencies, enlisting among others Toyota as a sponsor for events, and were instrumental in securing an exquisite set of contemporary Japanese prints. You greatly improved multiple dimensions of collections management, including cleaning up the stacks, implementing computerized check-in of serials, inventorying unprocessed collections, and overcoming staff reluctance to move materials to Fort Meade. You also created the Florence Tan Moeson Fund, in one afternoon transforming the donor's original idea of providing a modest gift into one that was substantial enough to fund a major program. You kept your eye on the mission of service, and against the odds and without additional resources, initiated Saturday hours in the reading room.

You reorganized the Division to increase efficiency and effectiveness, even as the budget decreased. You created cross-geographical area teams, which improved the work of the Division and undoubtedly improved staff interactions. You galvanized the staff so that good people who had despaired of making a contribution saw a way to thrive and make the Division strong. Because of your great accomplishments, even in tight budget times you were successful in securing additional staff positions, which you used well.

If I have had a small part in your success, it has only been to explain an arcane bureaucratic system to a newcomer and to remove as many obstacles as I could so that you could be the very best that you are capable of being in this often challenging environment. Your tenure as chief has been a triumph and demonstration of what is possible with a leader of vision and experience, one who long ago discarded the encumbrances of ego and who has led with deep appreciation for the gifts of others, with great humility, and with a rare wisdom.

You have been a gift to the Library and to all who know you.

With warm affection,

Carolyn T. Brown
Director of Scholarly Programs

Letter from Elaine Chao (赵小兰)

February 15, 2008

Dr. Hwa-Wei Lee
Chief of Asian Division
Library of Congress
101 Independence Ave. SE
Thomas Jefferson Building, LJ 150
Washington, DC 20540-4810

Dear Dr. Lee,

Recently I received the news of your retirement as Chief of the Asian Division of the Library of Congress. It seems like just yesterday that we met to celebrate the 75th anniversary of the U.S. Congress's formal authorization of the Asian Collection. What a wonderful event that was!

Your efforts at the Library of Congress have created an invaluable research collection that will continue to help build bridges of understanding between the world's great cultures in America and Asia. It was inspiring to participate in last October's Library of Congress Conference on creating an Asian Pacific American section in the Asian Division. This will ensure the preservation of these many national and international treasures for generations to come.

Your many years of public service are commendable. Best wishes to you and your family for a happy, healthy, and fulfilling retirement.

Sincerely,

Letter from Michael M. Honda

February 15, 2008

Dr. Hwa-Wei Lee
Chief, Asian Division
LJ 150, Library of Congress
101 Independence Avenue, S. E.
Washington, DC 20540-4810

Dear Dr. Lee,

Congratulations on your planned retirement!

After an esteemed five years as the Chief of the Asian Division at the Library of Congress—a bookend to your library profession of fifty years—you indeed deserve to relax and enjoy. But I suspect that you will not slow down, and will continue your many pursuits. As anyone that has met you can attest, the boundless, enthusiastic spirit that drives you will not allow you to stay idle. The countless publications, awards and distinctions throughout your career are a testament to your dedication and hard work.

As Chair of the Congressional Asian Pacific American Caucus, it has been my privilege to have collaborated with you and your dedicated staff at the Asian Division. Our shared pursuit to tell the complete Asian American and Pacific Islander (AAPI) story and dispel the cloak of invisibility and mischaracterization upon the community has given life to a new AAPI Collection at the Library of Congress. This is another milestone of your storied career.

Again, I congratulate and thank you for your nurturing leadership of the Asian Division and the establishment of the AAPI Collection. Best wishes for your retirement—future endeavors. I hope that you will still come to visit with me and expect to see you at various functions as the AAPI Collection develop!

Sincerely.

Michael M. Honda
Chair, Congressional Asian Pacific American Caucus

Speech of Hon. Michael M. Honda of California in the House of Representatives[1]

Thursday, April 10, 2008

Mr. HONDA. Madam Speaker, I rise today to honor the many contributions and achievements of Dr. Hwa-Wei Lee. After an esteemed 5 years as the chief of the Asian Division at the Library of Congress—a bookend to his dedicated 50 years in the library profession, Dr. Lee is retiring. Before joining the Library of Congress in 2003, Dr. Lee had already achieved a distinguished career in the pursuit and preservation of knowledge. He first served at the Main Library of the University of Pittsburgh, where he also completed two master's degrees and a Ph. D. He then advanced his career working at many other libraries, including Duquesne University, Edinboro University of Pennsylvania, Asian Institute of Technology in Bangkok, Thailand, Colorado State University, and Ohio University. Dr. Lee was Dean of Libraries at Ohio University for 21 years. During that time, he was able to transform a relatively unassuming university library into a prestigious member of the Association of Research Libraries, and ranked among the top 70 academic research libraries in North America. Recognizing Dr. Lee's numerous and incredible accomplishments, Ohio University displayed its enormous appreciation of Dr. Lee by not only naming the first floor of its main library the Hwa-Wei Lee Center for International Collections, but also dedicating a new library annex after him.

During his short tenure at the Library of Congress, Dr. Lee focused his energy on completely rejuvenating and reorganizing the Asian Division. He introduced innovative programs designed to improve and expand the division's resources, collections, services, and outreach.

[Page: E578] GPO's PDFAs chair of the Congressional Asian Pacific American Caucus, it has been my privilege to have collaborated with Dr. Lee and his dedicated staff at the Asian Division. Our shared pursuit to tell the complete Asian American and Pacific Islander, AAPI, story and dispel the cloak of invisibility and mischaracterization upon the community has given life to a new AAPI Collection at the Library of Congress. This is another milestone of Dr. Lee's storied career.

Dr. Lee and his lovely wife Mary will soon move to Florida to bask in the sunny rays of retirement. But I suspect that he will not slow down, and will continue his many

pursuits. As anyone who has met Dr. Lee can attest, his boundless, enthusiastic spirit will not allow him to stay idle. In fact, he has already promised to visit the Library frequently and is eager to start his new role as board director of the Asian Division Friends Society.

Madam Speaker, I commend Dr. Hwa-Wei Lee for his dedication and many contributions to the librarian profession and am especially grateful for his nurturing leadership of the Asian Division and of the establishment of the AAPI Collection at the Library of Congress. I wish Dr. Lee and his family all the best for his retirement and their future endeavors.

---

[1] [Page: E577] GPO's PDF

Letter from Deanna Marcum

February 15, 2008

Dear Hwa-Wei,

It is an honor to write this tribute on the occasion of your retirement. You should feel enormously gratified in knowing that you have made a huge difference in this institution, and you have touched the lives of a great number of LC staff, librarians around the world, and international scholars. The phrase "a life well lived" refers specifically to you!

You know better than anyone else how badly you were needed when the Library recruited you to head the Asian Division. Collections were unavailable to the public, bibliographic records were not in the online catalog, staff relations and morale were in disrepair. You had already enjoyed a highly successful career at Ohio University as the University Librarian and, as a consultant, you set OCLC on a path to become highly influential in China. You could have insisted—with complete justification—on enjoying retirement with your family. Instead, your sense of obligation and service led you to accept the job here, and the scholarly and library communities owe you a great deal.

There is almost no comparison of today's Asian Division to the one you inherited. The reorganization has removed the language-based independent units. The staff work harmoniously and productively. The collections are well organized and can be served to the public. You have exponentially raised the public profile of the Asian Division with your seminars and the formation of a Friends group. We have partnerships with countless libraries in all parts of Asia.

At your stage of life, it would have been perfectly understandable if you had been more leisurely. But not Hwa-Wei! You have traveled hundreds of thousands of miles to form partnerships, acquire collections, and create goodwill for the Library of Congress. You have not relied solely on federal dollars, either. You have been a supremely talented fund-raiser and a relationships-builder.

Finally, you have shown that you are not simply looking to others to sustain the Asian Division. When you announced your retirement, you made a substantial financial contribution to your latest campaign—the development of an Asian Pacific American collection. You have set a high standard for those who follow.

Your retirement is bittersweet for me. You certainly deserve some peaceful, more relaxed time with your family and friends, but I shall miss you very much. Your intellect, your passion, and your wisdom have given me great confidence in the capacities and capabilities of the Asian Division. You leave very big shoes to fill.

I send my warmest good wishes to you.

With respect and affection,

Deanna Marcum
Associate Librarian for Library Services

后 记

系统研究和总结20世纪图书馆学家的学术思想与事业贡献，是我们良久的心愿。为此，数年前我已开始启动《周连宽文集》和《杜定友文集》的收集、整理、编辑工作。去年，为庆祝谭祥金、赵燕群两位老师70华诞，我策划、组织出版了《谭祥金赵燕群文集》（上下卷，中山大学出版社出版），深获学界同仁赞许，在图书馆界产生了颇为广泛的积极影响。

李华伟博士是享誉世界的杰出华美图书馆专家和图书馆学家，我之所以能够荣幸地负责编辑出版《李华伟文集》，完全是机缘巧合。

记忆中，我认识李华伟博士大概是在1995年4月中山大学主办"中文文献数据库国际研讨会"时，那时我负责具体会务，与李华伟博士有比较密切的接触，虽然是第一次见面，但是已被李华伟博士超乎寻常的亲和力所感染。其后，在各种国际学术活动中时常有机会与李华伟博士会面，聆听他的教诲，被他的远见卓识和专业精神所感染。在过去的十几年中，我曾邀请李华伟博士数次来中山大学访问讲学。同时，在李华伟博士担任馆长时，我访问过俄亥俄大学，在李华伟博士担任亚洲部主任时访问过美国国会图书馆，还作为李华伟博士主持的美国国会图书馆卢氏基金（Luce Foundation）中文文献采购项目华南地区中心负责人，为美国国会图书馆的中文出版物采访工作过数年，彼此的交往十分密切。但是，这并不意味着我与李华伟博士有着超乎一般图书馆界同仁的学术友谊，因为李华伟博士是一位典型的国际图书馆事业活动家，他对所有人，无论男女老幼，都十分友好，乐善好施，乐于助人，朋友遍及世界各地，而我不过是李华伟博士的众多朋友中的一个普通忘年之友。

2007年11月，在参加南京大学主办的"中美文化交流与图书馆发展国际学术研讨会暨钱存训图书馆开馆典礼"期间，李华伟博士告诉我：他将于2008年从美国国会图书馆正式退休，从此以后不再接受任何长期工作聘任。于是，我邀请李华伟博士在退休以后携夫人到中山大学学术度假数月，如同当年我邀请加州大学圣地亚哥分校（UCSD）东亚图书馆馆长卢国邦（Karl Lo）先生在退休以后来中山大学学术度假一样，没有任何预定的学术度假日程安排，没有时间限制，或参观图书馆，或与学生座谈，或做学术报告，或校园漫步，或珠江夜游，或走亲访友、或故地重游，或游历山川，一切随心所欲。李华伟博士返回美国以后来信答复：夫人身体欠佳，且不太适应大陆的生活，无法一同前来学术度假，但是，他个人可以择日来中山大学访问。

其后，李华伟博士因为积劳成疾，不得不住院手术，来华访问的日程一再延期，直到2009年春才最后确定来华访问的日程。令人惊诧的是，在李华伟博士提供给我的一个多月的来华访问日程中，李华伟博士在广州停留的时间只有几天，其中还包括代表俄亥俄大学图书馆参加在广州暨南大学举行的第四届海外华人研究与文献收藏机构国际会议，其他的日程则是在全国各地访问讲学，从北到南，从东到西，日程十分紧张，完全没有丝毫学术度假的意思。我知道，像我一样向李华伟博士发出邀请的国内同仁非常多，李华伟博士盛情难却，才不得已做出这种安排。我更知道，李华伟博士最大的乐趣就是工作，像离弦的箭一样，李华伟博士不会停下来歇息，任何有关停止工作好好休息的劝说都无济于事。

自2009年起，李华伟博士开始参加中美两国政府共同主持的中美图书馆员专业交流项目，担任该项目的美方评审员，一如既往地频繁穿梭于中美之间，访问讲学、培训中国图书馆员，全然没有半点已经退休的意思。

2010年11月，我赴台北参加"第八次中文文献资源共建共享国际会议"，会议期间再次向李华伟博士提起我2007年在南京大学开会时曾经表达的心愿：邀请李华伟博士来中山大学学术度假，放下一切工作，好好休养一段时间。李华伟博士言：夫人身体欠佳，无法长期离开，难以成行。一日，在同车前往汉学研究中心会场途中，我告知李华伟博士：我负责策划组织的《谭祥金赵燕群文集》即将由中山大学出版社正式出版，上下两卷，超过140万字，届时还将举行首发式，以弘扬前辈的图书馆精神。倘若李华伟博士同意的话，我乐意担当策划编辑出版《李华伟文集》的任务。李华伟博士回应：可以考虑，但需返回美国以后再具体答复。

2010年12月28日下午，《谭祥金赵燕群文集》首发式在中山大学图书馆聚贤厅举行，群贤毕至，羡慕与赞美之声不绝于耳，且有不少学人提议进一步编辑出版其他图书馆学家的文集，以弘扬图书馆之学术与事业。

2011年2月初，谭祥金、赵燕群、吴晞、刘洪辉、杜秦生和我等人在广州增城召开公共图书馆研究院院务委员会会议。在院务会议上，我提议策划编辑出版一套图书馆学人的文集，获得与会者的一致赞同。其后，我们在中山大学图书馆召开了图书馆学人文集的策划会议，商定了编委会的人员构成、编辑原则、编辑方法、入选条件、出版方式、发行办法等主要事宜；并将业已出版的《谭祥金赵燕群文集》列为第一种。会后，我们在往返电子邮件中不断商讨出版这套图书馆学人文集的相关事宜。谭祥金、赵燕群、吴晞建议这套文集采用"图书馆学人系列文集"名称。鉴于我国图书馆学界向来不重视对图书馆学人的研究，图书馆学家的传记著作凤毛麟角，图书馆学家的个人文集或者全集几近空白，现有的选集并不能全面反映图书馆学家的学术成就，而我之所以提议编辑出版这套文集，旨在树立和展示图书馆学家的完整学术形象，因此我建议将这套文集命名为"图书馆学家思想文库"。吴晞十分赞同我提出的"图书馆学家"之说，但是认为"思想文库"有偏废图书馆实践之虞，建议去掉"思想"二字，改为"图书馆学家文库"。吴晞的这项修改建议获得大家的一致赞同，于是《图书馆学家文库》这个丛书名得以正式确立。与此同时，吴晞负责在全国函邀图书馆学专家担任编辑委员会委员，并特邀原文化部副部长、现任中国国家图书馆馆长周和平先生担任《图书馆学家文库》编辑委员会顾问，周和平馆长高度重视这项学术事业，不仅欣然接受邀请，而且亲自为《图书馆学家文库》撰写了总序。至此，有关《图书馆学家文库》的各项前期准备工作均已顺利完成。

在策划《图书馆学家文库》的同时，我一直保持着与李华伟博士的频繁电子邮件联系，商讨设立王肖珠女士纪念奖学金的各项事宜。记得十年前，在俄亥俄大学访问时，我曾询问李华伟博士与原中山大学图书馆馆长、北京图书馆馆长袁同礼先生的关系，李华伟博士告知：袁同礼先生的公子袁清教授是他的妹夫，并言他的姨妈王肖珠女士亦曾担任过岭南大学图书馆馆长（1945－1949），同时嘱托我代为查找相关史料。2005年，我再次出任中山大学资讯管理系主任后，相继设立了沈祖荣沈宝环纪念奖学金、谭祥金赵燕群奖学金等多项图书馆学奖学金。2007年2月，李华伟博士得知我正在致力设立图书馆学奖学金后来信告知：他的姨妈王肖珠女士生前曾留下数万美元，希望捐赠给公益事业，经与王肖珠女士的家人商量，决定在王肖珠女士的母校岭南大学（1952年并入中山大学）设立图书馆学奖学金，以资纪念。由于办理国际捐赠手续比较繁复，颇费周折，设立王肖珠女士纪念奖学金的事情迟迟没有完成。直到今年初，在美国西蒙斯大学陈钦智教授及其担任董事长的全球联接协作有限公司（Global Connection and Collaboration, Inc）的大力支持下，李华伟博士才将5万美元的奖学金本金顺利转至中山大学教育发展基金会，在中山大学正式设立了"王肖珠纪念奖学金"，以奖励品学兼优的图书馆学专业学子。王肖珠女士是李华伟博士从台湾赴美求学的人生与事业导师，该奖学金的设立自然是李华伟博士对姨妈王肖珠女士最好的纪念。今年2月，在王肖珠女士纪念奖学金的设立即将大功告成之际，李华伟博士来信告知：同意我负责编辑出版《李华伟文集》，并提供了详细的个人著述目录。这令我喜出望外，荣幸不已。

按照李华伟博士提供的个人著述目录，我开始着手安排我的博士生查找相关著述的原件，以便编辑整理。2011年3月，中央电视台记者、李华伟传纪的作者杨阳女士寄来了李华伟博士的部分著作；5月，李华伟博士来华访问讲学，在长沙参加国际会议时，谭祥金教授和赵燕群教授专程从广州赴长沙，会见李华伟博士，取回李华伟博士从美国带来的个人著述原件。于是，我们开始电子扫描、格式转换、文本校对、编辑整理和寻找缺失文献等工作。

为了更加生动反映李华伟博士的学术活动，我建议李华伟博士在文集前尽可能收录一些能够反映其职业生涯和学术成就的照片，李华伟博士欣然应允，且耗费了不少精力去整理个人的照片，总计挑选了大约150张颇有意义的照片。这些照片与个人著述相辅相成，交相辉映，可谓珠联璧合。

2011年5月底，李华伟博士返回美国以后曾来电询问《李华伟文集》的计划出版时间，无意间透露他的实际出生年份早于世人所知的年份，今年初已度过80华诞。得知此信息后，我当即决定无论如何要在今年年底以前出版《李华伟文集》，以庆贺李华伟博士80华诞，感谢李华伟博士为中美图书馆交流合作所作出的卓越贡献。于是，我向公共图书馆研究院谭祥金、赵燕群、吴晞等负责人提议：鉴于今年是李华伟博士80华诞，《李华伟文集》的编辑出版工作务必在今年年底以前完成，在举行《李华伟文集》首发式的同时可考虑举办李华伟图书馆学术思想研讨会，以及王肖珠纪念奖学金颁发仪式和李华伟传记首发式等庆祝活动，谭祥金、赵燕群、吴晞等一致认同。于是在编辑《李华伟文集》的同时，公共图书馆研究院开始着手筹备李华伟博士图书馆学术思想研讨会。2011年7月8日，公共图书馆研究院正式发布《李华伟博士图书馆学术思想研讨会征文通知》。征文通知发出后受到海内外图书馆界同仁的热烈反响，美国华美图书馆员协会（CALA）亦来信希望参与举办李华伟博士图书馆学术思想研讨会，以共襄盛举。

在《李华伟文集》首发式和李华伟博士图书馆学术思想研讨会的具体日程确定以后，《李华伟文集》的编辑出版工作便开始进入倒计时。李华伟博士不仅是国际知名的图书馆学家，而且是著名的国际图书馆活动家，其论文和学术报告发表在世界各地，由于时间久远，李华伟博士并没有保留所有的文稿。为此，从2011年7月起，我们开始动用一切关系在世界各地查找稀缺文稿，并加紧进行文集的各项编辑工作。

在查找李华伟博士散见于世界各地的论文与报告中，我们得到了海内外图书馆界同仁的热情帮助和大力支持：美国哈佛大学哈佛学院图书馆高青女士、加州大学欧文分校东亚图书馆馆长张颖博士及其公子张文宇、俄亥俄州立大学图书馆东亚图书馆馆长李国庆博士、美国国会图书馆亚洲部居蜜博士、卢雪乡女士（Judy Lu）、Yuwu Song博士、台湾图书馆学会彭慰秘书长、韵苹女士、政治大学图书资讯与档案学研究所王梅玲教授、台湾师范大学图书馆馆长陈昭珍教授、郭美兰秘书、辅仁大学图书馆馆长林呈潢教授、香港岭南大学图书馆廖柏成、西安交通大学图书馆副馆长邰晶、华东师范大学信息系主任范并思教授、华东师范大学图书馆余海宪馆长、北京大学图书馆肖珑副馆长、《大学图书馆学报》编辑部王波以及泰国、新加坡等地的图书馆和友人，给予了无私的帮助，在此谨致以衷心的感谢！

《李华伟文集》分上下两卷，卷前有"图说李华伟博士"，以图片的方式概述李华伟博士的生活、家庭、事业和学术活动；上卷"学术著作"，收录李华伟博士撰写的博士学位论文、出版的著作和合著著作中独立撰写的章节；下卷"学术论文"，收录李华伟博士发表的学术论文和学术报告文稿，同时附有李华伟著述系年和李华伟研究资料两个附录，以供学人研究参考李华伟博士学术思想。因此，这部《李华伟文集》实际上兼有"李华伟文集"和"李华伟研究文集"双重功能，这将成为今后《图书馆学家文库》编辑出版的基调和特色。

李华伟博士的著述甚丰，编辑整理并非易事，在遵循尊重作者写作习惯且尽可能保持著述原貌的基本原则下，我们对文稿做了如下技术处理：其一，按照主题将全部著述分门别类，同一主题之下的著述按照发表时间的先后顺序排列。其二，李华伟博士以英文著述为主，且时常在不同语言地区的同类学术会议上用英文或中文发表同一论文，为方便英文和中文读者起见，文集同时收录部分同一论文的英文版和中文版（包括他人中文译文）两个版本，在排列时，中文版在前，英文版在后。其三，部分论文或者学术报告有多个修订增补版本，一般收录最完整的版本，如果文字有出入但没有重大修订增补，则收录最早发表的版本。其四、中文著述原件有繁体和简体，一律改为中文简体文字。其五、不改变著述中各级标题的原有顺序编号方式。其六、在文字编辑中，为符合出版规范，不得不按规定修改了一些相关术语。其七、遵照李华伟博士的意见，文集的目录一律采用中英文对照式样，中文题名在前，英文题名在后，同一篇主题的论文有中英文两个版本时则前后接排，不重复翻译题名。

在文集的编辑整理中，由中山大学图书馆、图书馆与资讯科学研究所、资讯管理学院同仁组成的学术团队，做出了至关重要的贡献。我的博士研究生林梦笑、罗惠敏，硕士研究生郭晓敏、李梦霞、晋祎一、郭萌负责李华伟著述的收集、录入、整理和初稿校对工作；林梦笑负责编辑李华伟著述系年和重画文集中的表格、罗惠敏负责重绘文集中的插图；中山大学图书馆司徒峻峰、魏尚文、张琦负责文稿的扫描、整理工作。林梦笑、郭晓敏、罗惠敏负责文集的一校和二校工作；林梦笑、罗惠敏和图书馆与资讯科学研究所副所长潘燕桃博士负责文集的三校和统稿工作。最后，我对书稿进行了全面的编审整理，完成了定稿。文集从收集资料到定稿历时半年，时间紧迫、任务繁重，团队的全体成员始终以饱满的热情全身心地投入各项编辑工作之中，不分昼夜，不顾酷暑，出色地完成了繁重的文集编辑工作。在此谨向团队的各位成员表示衷心的感谢！

《李华伟文集》的出版离不开中山大学出版社的全力支持。社长祁军高度重视《图书馆学家文库》的编辑出版工作，多次参加相关策划会议，并在编辑出版上给予大力支持。王俊辉责任编辑牺牲大量业余时间，夜以继日地全力投入文集的编辑出版工作之中，总编蔡浩然先生不遗余力地编审校对，谭祥金、赵燕群两位老师不辞辛苦地审校文集清样，程杰、蔡筱青等牺牲休息时间全力参与文集清样的校对。没有他们的通力合作和无私奉献，这部《李华伟文集》要在如此紧迫的时间内按时出版是完全不可想象的。在此，谨向中山大学出版社和上述编辑们表示由衷的敬意和感谢！

在出版《李华伟文集》的同时，我们还将重印《谭祥金赵燕群文集》，将这两部文集同时列入《图书馆学家文库》。从明年起，《杜定友文集》、《周连宽文集》、《刘国钧文集》、《谢灼华文集》、《胡述兆文集》、《李德竹文集》、《沈宝环文集》等多位著名图书馆学家的文集将陆续问世。

校雠如扫落叶，随扫随生，无休无止。本书在整理、编辑过程中自然难免有各种瑕疵错漏，敬请读者批评指正。

程焕文　谨记

2011年10月2日

于中山大学康乐园竹帛斋